F
Canada

Fodor's Travel Publications, Inc.
New York•Toronto•London•Sydney•Auckland

ISBN 0–679–02505–7

The introduction by Bob Levin was originally published as "A Sense of Country" in *Maclean's* magazine. Reprinted by permission from *Maclean's.* July 25, 1990.

Fodor's Canada

Editor: Alison Hoffman
Contributors: Bob Blake, Hannah Borgeson, Susan Brown, Silver Don Cameron, Peter Gard, Allan Gould, Arlene Karpan, Robin Karpan, Dorothy Guinan, Caroline Liou, Peter Oliver, Melissa Rivers, David Scott, Ana Watts, Sarah Waxman, Loralee Wenger
Creative Director: Fabrizio La Rocca
Cartographer: David Lindroth
Illustrator: Karl Tanner
Cover Photograph: Peter Guttman

Design: Vignelli Associates

Special Sales

MANUFACTURED IN THE UNITED STATES OF AMERICA
10 9 8 7 6 5 4 3 2 1

Contents

Maps and Plans

Foreword

We wish to express our gratitude to those who helped prepare this guide: the Canadian Consulate General office in New York, particularly Lois Gerber and Barbara Cartwright; the Montréal Convention and Tourism Bureau; the Québec Government Ministry of Tourism, particularly Brian LeCompte, Pauline Roy, and Manon Lefebvre; the Government of Newfoundland and Labrador Department of Development, especially Kay Coxworthy; Dana Ottman of Ontario House in New York; Helen–Jean Newman of the New Brunswick Department of Tourism; the Nova Scotia Department of Tourism, especially Randy Brooks and Lynn McGuinness; also Cathy Quesnelle; Lynda Hanscombe of the PEI Department of Tourism and Parks; Kay Coxworthy at Newfoundland and Labrador Department of Tourism and Culture; the Metropolitan Toronto Convention & Visitors Association; Tourism Vancouver, especially Elvira Quarin; Whistler Resort Association; and the Alberta, Manitoba, and British Columbia Tourism bureaus.

While every care has been taken to ensure the accuracy of the information in this guide, the passage of time will always bring change, and consequently, the publisher cannot accept responsibility for errors that may occur.

All prices and opening times are based on information supplied to us at press time. Hours and admission fees may change, however, and the prudent traveler will avoid inconvenience by calling ahead.

Fodor's wants to hear about your travel experiences, both pleasant and unpleasant. When a hotel or restaurant fails to live up to its billing, let us know and we will investigate the complaint and revise our entries where the facts warrant it. Send your letters to the editors of Fodor's Travel Publications, 201 E. 50th Street, New York, NY 10022.

Highlights '94 and Fodor's Choice

Highlights '94

In 1993 then-prime-minister Brian Mulroney retired, and Kim Cambell was voted in by the Progressive Conservatives, to complete the term. Cambell is the first female prime minister and is expected to run for re-election in 1994.

The 7% **Goods and Services Tax** that went into effect in 1991 imposed on virtually all goods and services, including restaurant meals, fast-food, hotel rooms, car rentals, and admission fees. In some provinces, the nationwide GST tax replaces former provincial taxes, but in others it is levied in addition to provincial taxes. It is refundable however, to tourists from other countries, provided they keep original receipts and apply for the refund. The refund system is complicated, so you may want to obtain information before you travel, by calling 613/991–3346 (outside Canada) or, from within Canada, 800/66–VISIT. You can also write to Revenue Canada, Customs and Excise Visitor's Rebate Program, Ottawa, Canada K1A 1J5, or pick up refund application forms and an explanatory booklet at airports, shops, hotels, and border crossing stations.

Toronto As all of Canada suffered mightily through the recession of the early '90s, Toronto was very hard hit: Several hotels slid into bankruptcy; Air Canada and Canadian Airlines nearly did the same; even the classy, country-wide jewelry chain Birks closed half of its stores. Still, Toronto can hold its head high as a major city in the country that the United Nations recently claimed was the "best place on earth" to live. There's even a plan to spend $750 million in renovating the dreadful Toronto Airport, an improvement that will make the city even more accessible.

Montréal Montréal's first government-run casino is scheduled to open by early 1994 and will be located on Ile Notre-Dame in the Palais de la Civilisation, the site of the French pavilion during Expo '67. The casino, which will cost more than $80 million to set up, will feature 65 blackjack, mini-baccarat, and roulette tables; 1,200 slot machines; and a Keno betting room with a draw every five minutes. The casino will have room for 1,500 gamblers and house a gourmet restaurant, as well.

Québec City Québec City saw little development during the past few years due to the recession, but the few well-invested changes that did occur will grace the city for a long time. In preparation for its 100th birthday celebration in 1993, the Château Frontenac—the city's landmark castle hotel— renovated all guest rooms and built a new wing that included a health spa. The Capitole, a turn-of-the-century theater that reopened its doors in late 1992 after 20 years

in ruin, is more successful than many people had anticipated. Big names, such as the king of the blues B.B. King
and country star Kenny Rogers, packed the spot in 1993,
and more big names are expected for 1994. Other highlights
include the Naturalium (84 rue Dalhousie), a $6 million
natural-science museum in the Vieux-Port that opened in
1993 and houses 100,000 insects, 842 mammals, and 500 fossils.

History buffs may want to visit Grosse Ile before the Canadian government moves ahead with plans to turn it into a
theme park about immigration. The island, situated 48 kilometers downstream form Québec City, served as an immigrant-quarantine station during the 19th century and is the
final resting place for thousands of people (mostly from Ireland) who died there of cholera and typhus. The development plan has sparked the interest of Irish groups that fear
the government will hide the island's tragic history.

What remains on Grosse Ile today—some 40 buildings and
scattered artifacts—needs restoration to survive. Still, the
rolling meadows, mass graves, horse-drawn ambulance,
and abandoned disinfecting house tell the story.

British Columbia The high-speed ferry service **Sealink Express,** carrying
passengers only, continues to effortlessly transport visitors
from downtown Vancouver to downtown Victoria, allowing
visitors to take in both towns without the long trip to and
from the regular car-ferry terminals. Another ferry company, Sea Containers, Ltd., is currently refurbishing its
Princess Marguerite ferry with possible plans to put it to
work on the Vancouver–Prince Rupert route along the Inside Passage. The plans for a new car ferry linking Victoria
with Seattle, Washington, are still in the making.

Local Vancouver sightseeing has been improved, too,
thanks to the **Vancouver Trolleys,** like old-fashioned streetcars, that take you on a guided tour of all the major attractions (Stanley Park, English Bay, Gastown, Robson Street,
Granville Island, the Vancouver Museum, Queen Elizabeth
Park, Chinatown, and Science World) for an all-day unlimited-stop ticket.

Canadian Rockies In the mountainous outback, an ongoing debate continues
regarding trail usage. The **Canadian Parks Service** currently limits mountain biking, for the most part, to fire
roads, while studying the use of bikes on backcountry trails.
Park officials are concerned about encounters between bikers and wildlife (especially bears, who are easily surprised
by swiftly approaching bikes) and about bikers having trouble getting out of the deep backcountry if their bikes break
down.

Manitoba, The prairie provinces are home to a large part of Canada's
Saskatchewan, native population, and increasingly they are sharing their
Alberta culture and history with tourists. The largest and most recent project is **Wanuskewin Heritage Park,** on the outskirts

of Saskatoon. Through displays, cultural presentations, demonstrations, and archaeological digs, the park combines the rich history and prehistory of Northern Plains natives with a look at the lives of today.

Ontario The possibility of a law permitting **casino gambling** has Ontario developers scurrying about looking for likely casino sites to buy. While no decision had been made at press time, general opinion in the province has changed over the past few years to favor such a law, largely because of the success of various lottery programs. The government would likely allow four or five casinos, possibly in Toronto, Sault Ste. Marie, Grand Bend, Ottawa, and Niagara Falls.

Québec Province The ongoing debate about whether or not Québec should secede from the Candian union subsided following the 1992 Canada-wide referendum—but only briefly. The age-old argument inevitably will reappear before the fall of 1994, the deadline for the next provincial election. Once again Quebecers will be asked to choose between federalist Leberals and the nationalist Parti Québécois. On October 26, 1992, Québec and five other provinces voted against the federal government's plan that would have vastly changed Canada's 125-year-old constitution by recognizing Québec as a distinct society and giving more powers to the provincial governments.

Nova Scotia The province's most recently opened national park, **Kekimkujik Seaside Adjunct,** a formerly private preserve, is still wild and remote, though hiking trails make it accessible to the public. To attract convention business, the province has been opening **meeting facilities** in places besides Halifax, which is still the major convention center. Inverary Lodge, in Baddeck, and White Point Beach Lodge, in Liverpool, now offer facilities for groups of 100 to 150.

Prince Edward Island A government announcement of a **causeway** to be built linking New Brunswick and Prince Edward Island has caused mixed reaction on the island. Although improved accessibility may increase tourism revenues and lower the cost of many goods currently shipped to the island, residents also fear disruption of their peaceful, unspoiled lifestyle, which is in itself a tourist draw. No construction date has been set—it may in fact be years away.

New Brunswick A 223-room Sheraton hotel opened in late spring 1992 in **Fredericton,** adding significantly to that city's supply of hotel rooms, although Saint John still offers more beds. About 11 miles west of Fredericton, the **Kings Clear Hotel and Resort** has opened—a new modern hotel, with an interesting history. It is operated by the Malicete Indian Band at Mactaquac, who received government help in building and running the motel as compensation for their voluntary surrender of their traditional net-fishing activity, which was endangering the Atlantic salmon.

The section of the **Trans-Canada Highway** that runs through New Brunswick is being upgraded, with the notable addition of signposts alerting travelers to the existence of special "scenic trails," off-the-beaten-track roads that motorists might otherwise miss.

Newfoundland and Labrador In 1993 the province began gearing up for the celebrations to come in 1997, celebrating John Cabot's landing in North America.

Wilderness Canada Parks Canada is moving toward opening visitor facilities in two new wilderness areas: **Northern Yukon National Park,** which contains one of the world's largest caribou herds, and **Ellesmere Island National Park,** with its extraordinary polar oasis of plant, animal, and bird life.

Fodor's Choice

No two people will agree on what makes a perfect vacation, but it's fun and helpful to know what others think. We hope you'll have a chance to experience some of Fodor's Choices yourself in Canada. For detailed information about each entry, refer to the appropriate chapter.

Toronto

Attractions Harbourfront, downtown Toronto
Ontario Science Centre, northeast Toronto
Royal Ontario Museum, Queen's Park

Shopping Eaton Centre
Kensington Market/Chinatown
Yorkville Avenue/Bloor Street area

Cultural Events Canadian Opera Company at the O'Keefe Centre
National Ballet of Canada at the O'Keefe Centre
Theater at the Royal Alexandra, St. Lawrence Centre, Elgin, and Winter Garden theaters

Restaurants Splendido (*Expensive*)
BamBoo (*Moderate*)
New World (*Moderate*)
Thai Magic (*Moderate*)
Pearl Court (*Inexpensive*)

Hotels Four Seasons Toronto (*Very Expensive*)
Best Western Chestnut Park Hotel (*Expensive*)

Montréal

Attractions Montréal Botanical Garden
Montréal Museum of Fine Arts
La Ronde

Shopping Place Montréal Trust
Rue Faubourg Ste-Catherine
Notre-Dame Ouest for antiques
Marché aux puces (flea market), Vieux-Montréal
Les Promenades de la Cathédrale

Cultural Events L'Opéra de Montréal
L'Orchestre Symphonique de Montréal
Théâtre du Nouveau Monde

Restaurants Les Trois Tilleuls, Montérégie (*Very Expensive*)
Les Mignardises (*Very Expensive*)
Milos (*Very Expensive*)

Hotels Le Quatre Saisons (*Very Expensive*)
Ritz-Carlton (*Very Expensive*)
Hôtel de la Montagne (*Expensive*)
Château Versailles (*Moderate*)

Québec City

Attractions Château Frontenac
Citadelle
Musée de la Civilisation

Shopping Marché du Vieux-Port
La Trois Colombes, Inc.
Quartier Petit-Champlain

Cultural Events Bibliothèque Gabrielle-Roy
Grand Théâtre de Québec
Le Théâtre Capitole

Restaurants À la Table de Serge Bruyère (*Very Expensive*)
Aux Anciens Canadiens (*Expensive*)
L 'Echaudée (*Moderate*)
Chez Temporel (*Inexpensive*)

Hotels Hilton International Québec (*Very Expensive*)
Manoir d'Auteuil (*Expensive*)
L'Auberge du Quartier (*Moderate*)
Hôtel Maison Sainte-Ursule (*Inexpensive*)

Vancouver

Attractions Butchart Gardens, Victoria
Dr. Sun-yat Sen Classical Garden, Stanley Park
Granville Public Market, Granville Island
Vancouver Aquarium

Shopping Fourth Avenue (between Burrard and Balsam streets)
Government Street, Victoria
Market Square, Victoria
Robson Street

Restaurants Les Deux Gros, Whistler *(Expensive)*
Tojo's (*Expensive*)
English Bay Café (*Moderate*)
The Raintree (*Moderate*)
Six Mile House, Victoria *(Inexpensive)*
Phnom Penh (*Inexpensive*)

Hotels Le Chamois, Whistler *(Very Expensive)*
Hotel Grand Pacific, Victoria *(Very Expensive)*
Le Meridien (*Very Expensive*)
Wedgewood Hotel (*Expensive*)
Hotel Georgia (*Moderate*)

Craigmyle Guest House, Victoria (*Inexpensive–Moderate*)
Sylvia Hotel (*Inexpensive*)

British Columbia

Attractions O'Keefe Historic Ranch, Okanagan Valley
Museum of Northern British Columbia, Prince Rupert
Native Heritage Center, Duncan

Great Outdoors Adams River Salmon Run, Okanagan Valley
Inside Passage
Pacific Rim National Park, Vancouver Island

Restaurants Sooke Harbour House, Sooke (*Very Expensive*)
The Aerie, Malahat (*Expensive*)
The Mahle House, Nanaimo (*Moderate*)

Hotels The Aerie, Malahat (*Very Expensive*)
Lake Okanagan Resort, Kelowna (*Very Expensive*)
The Kingfisher Inn, Courtenay (*Moderate*)
Lac le Jeune Resort, Kamloops (*Moderate*)

Canadian Rockies

Sights The drive along the Icefields Parkway
The view from the Jasper Tramway
Lake Louise and Moraine Lake

Sporting Activities Mountaineering around the Columbia Icefields and the
Bugaboos of the British Columbia Rockies
Horse-pack trips in Kananaskis Country
Skiing at Lake Louise, Nakiska, and Panorama
Heli-skiing in the British Columbia Rockies

Restaurants Le Beaujolais, Banff (*Very Expensive*)
Post Hotel, Lake Louise (*Very Expensive*)
One-Twelve, Revelstoke (*Expensive*)
Emerald Lake Lodge, Yoho (*Moderate–Expensive*)
Barbary Coast, Banff (*Inexpensive–Moderate*)

Hotels Chateau Lake Louise (*Very Expensive*)
Emerald Lake Lodge, Yoho (*Expensive*)
Storm Mountain Lodge, Banff (*Moderate–Expensive*)
Kilmorey Lodge, Waterton Lakes (*Moderate*)

Manitoba, Saskatchewan, Alberta

Attractions Alberta Science Centre/Planetarium, Calgary
Devonian Gardens, Calgary
Manitoba Museum of Man and Nature, Winnipeg
Muttart Conservatory, Edmonton
University of Saskatchewan, Saskatoon
Wascana Waterfowl Park Display Ponds, Regina

Shopping Portage Place, Winnipeg
Stephen Avenue Mall, Calgary
Strathdee Shoppes, Regina
West Edmonton Mall

Restaurants Owl's Nest Dining Room, Calgary (*Very Expensive*)
Unheardof Dining Lounge, Edmonton (*Very Expensive*)
Mieka's, Regina (*Expensive*)
Bistro Dansk, Winnipeg (*Moderate*)
Adonis, Saskatoon (*Inexpensive*)
Buzzards Café, Calgary (*Inexpensive*)
Chianti Café, Edmonton (*Inexpensive*)

Hotels Edmonton Hilton (*Very Expensive*)
Westin Hotel, Calgary (*Expensive*)
The Delta, Regina (*Expensive*)
Edmonton House (*Expensive*)
Place Louis Riel, Winnipeg (*Expensive*)
King George, Saskatoon (*Inexpensive*)
Relax Inn South West, Regina (*Inexpensive*)

Province of Ontario

Attractions Old Fort William
Maid of the Mist boats
Sainte Marie Among the Hurons
View of Niagara Falls by helicopter

Restaurants Elora Mill, Elora (*Expensive*)
Inn at the Falls, Bracebridge (*Expensive*)
La Brassine, Goderich (*Moderate*)

Hotels Château Laurier, Ottawa (*Very Expensive*)
Langdon Hall, Cambridge (*Very Expensive*)
Prince of Wales, Niagara-on-the-Lake (*Very Expensive*)
Inn at the Falls, Bracebridge (*Expensive*)
Kettle Creek Inn, Port Stanley (*Moderate-Expensive*)

Province of Québec

Sights Basilica of Ste-Anne de Beaupre
Bonaventure Island, the Gaspé Peninsula

Restaurants L 'Eau à la Bouche, Ste-Adèle (*Very Expensive*)
Chatel Vienna, Ste-Agathe (*Moderate–Expensive*)

Hotels Auberge la Pinsonnière, Cap-à l'Aigle (*Very Expensive*)
Auberge la Maison Otis, Baie-St-Paul (*Expensive–Very Expensive*)
Hostellerie Les Trois Tilleuls, St. Marc sur Richelieu (*Expensive–Very Expensive*)
Manor Hovey, North Hailey (*Very Expensive*)

Hôtel Cap-aux-Pierres, Ile aux Couéres
(*Moderate–Expensive*)

Nova Scotia

Sights The Citadel, Halifax
Fortress Louisbourg, Cape Breton Island
Mabou Harbour, Cape Breton
Peggy's Cove

Restaurants Amherst Shore Country Inn, Amherst (*Expensive*)
Clipper Cay, Halifax (*Expensive*)
Old Man Marias, Halifax (*Moderate*)

Hotels Amherst Shore Country Inn, Lorreville (*Expensive*)

Prince Edward Island

Attractions Annual musical *Anne of Green Gables* at Confederation
Centre of the Arts, Charlottetown
Fort Amherst Port LaJoie National Historic Site, Rocky
Point
Green Gables, Cavendish
Province House, Charlottetown

Restaurants The Griffon Room, Charlottetown (*Moderate–Expensive*)
Claddagh Room Restaurant, Charlottetown
(*Moderate–Expensive*)
Lobster suppers in New Glasgow, New London, and
Hope River (*Moderate*)

Hotels Dalvay-by-the-Sea, Grand Tracadie (*Very Expensive*)
Prince Edward Hotel and Convention Centre,
Charlottetown (*Very Expensive*)
Shaw's Hotel and Cottages, Brackley Beach (*Very
Expensive*)

New Brunswick

Attractions Acadian Village, Grande Anse, near Caraquet
Kings Landing Historical Settlement, Prince William,
near Fredericton

Shopping Craft and antiques shops of St. Andrews and Gagetown
Mulhouse Country Classics, Fredericton

Restaurants La Belle Vie, Saint John (*Expensive*)
Cy's, Moncton (*Moderate*)

Hotels Hotel Beausejour, Moncton (*Expensive*)
Marshlands Inn, Sackville (*Moderate–Expensive*)
Shadow Lawn Country Inn, Saint John
(*Moderate–Expensive*)
Chez Françoise, Shediac (*Inexpensive–Moderate*)

Newfoundland and Labrador

Attractions L 'Anse aux Meadows, northern tip of Newfoundland
Signal Hill, St. John's
Gros Morne Mountain, Gros Morne National Park

Shopping NONIA, St. John's, for crafts

Restaurants The Cellar, Baird's Cove (*Expensive*)
Stone House, Kenna's Hill (*Expensive*)

Hotels Hotel Newfoundland, St. John's (*Expensive*)
Compton House Bed & Breakfast, St. John's (*Moderate*)
Prescott House Bed & Breakfast, St. John's (*Moderate*)

Wilderness Canada

Attractions Klondike Gold Fields, Dawson City
Prince of Wales Northern Heritage Centre, Yellowknife
S. S. *Klondike*, Whitehorse
Virginia Falls, Nahanni National Park

Lodges Westmark Klondike Inn, Whitehorse (*Expensive*)
Belvedere Hotel, Watson Lake (*Moderate*)
Westmark Inn, Dawson City (*Moderate*)

Canada

ARCTIC OCEAN

Arctic Circle

Yukon River

ALASKA
(U.S.)

Porcupine River

Beaufort
Sea

Prince Patrick
Island

Sverdrup Islands

North Magnetic
Pole (c.1980)
+

Mc Clure Strait

Queen Elizabeth Islands

Melville
Island

Bathurst
Island

Viscount Melville
Sound

Banks
Island

Somerset
Island

Prince of
Wales
Island

McClintock Channel

BOOTHIA
PENINSULA

Gulf of Bo

Inuvik

Fort
McPherson

Amundsen
Gulf

Victoria
Island

Dawson

Yukon R.

YUKON

Mackenzie River

Port
Radium

Coppermine

Coppermine R.

Great Bear
Lake

Arctic   Circle

Burwash
Landing

Haines
Junction

Whitehorse
Carcross

CANADIAN

N O R T H W E S T   T E R R I T O R I E

Thelon R.

Juneau

Gulf of
Alaska

Yellowknife

Great Slave
Lake

Dubawnt
Lake

Lake
Nueltin

Hay River

Fort Smith

BRITISH
COLUMBIA

ROCKIES

Athabasca
Lake

Uranium
City

C A N A

Church

Queen
Charlotte
Islands

Prince
Rupert

Peace R.

Peace
River

Fort
McMurray

Reindeer
Lake

Churchill R.

Nelson R.

Prince
George

Dawson
Creek

Fraser R.

Jasper

ALBERTA

Edmonton

La Ronge

Flin Flon

MANITOBA

Saskatchewan R.

Vancouver
Island

Kamloops

Lake Louise

Banff

Calgary

SASKATCHEWAN

Saskatoon

Lake
Winnipeg

Vancouver

Victoria

Columbia R.

Medicine
Hat

Regina

Lake
Manitoba

Portage
la Prairie

Winnipeg

PACIFIC OCEAN

Lethbridge

Moose
Jaw

Kenora

WASHINGTON

Weyburn

Lake of the
Woods

OREGON

MONTANA

NORTH DAKOTA

MINNESOTA

CALIFORNIA

NEVADA

UTAH

IDAHO

WYOMING

SOUTH DAKOTA

U N I T E D   S T A T E S

NEBRASKA

IOWA

ICELAND

GREENLAND
(Denmark)

Denmark Strait

Ellesmere Island

Devon Island

ncaster Sound

Baffin Bay

Baffin Island

Davis Strait

Prince Charles Island

Foxe Basin

Lake Amadjuak

Iqaluit

Lake Harbour

Hudson Strait

Southampton Island

Ivujivik

Coats Island *Mansel Island*

Cape Chidley

Ungava Bay

Labrador Sea

Nain

NEWFOUNDLAND

Battle Harbour

Hudson Bay

D   A

Belcher Islands

Fort Severn

Schefferville

LABRADOR

Goose Bay

Labrador City

Gander

St. John's

Newfoundland

Fort George

QUEBEC

James Bay

Lake Mistassini

Sept-Îles

Anticosti Island

Gulf of St. Lawrence

ST. PIERRE AND MIQUELON
(France)

Moosonee

ONTARIO

GASPÉ PENINSULA

Rimouski

River

PRINCE EDWARD ISLAND

Lake Nipigon

Chicoutimi

Québec City

NEW BRUNSWICK

Sydney

Charlottetown

Cochrane

Ste-Agathe-Des-Monts

Trois-Rivières

Fredericton

NOVA SCOTIA

Thunder Bay

Timmins

Montréal

Saint John

Halifax

Lake Superior

Sudbury

North Bay

Ottawa

St. Lawrence

MAINE

Bay of Fundy

Sault Ste. Marie

Lake Huron

Toronto

Lake Ontario

VT.

N.H.

N

ATLANTIC OCEAN

ISCONSIN

Lake Michigan

MICHIGAN

Niagara Falls

Lake Erie

NEW YORK

MASSACHUSETTS

R.I.

CONN.

ILLINOIS

INDIANA

OHIO

PENNSYLVANIA

N.J.

0   400 miles

0   600 km

World Time Zones

International Date Line

+12 +13 -9 -10 -11 -10 +11 +12

-4 -3 25

-7 -5 -4 -3:30

-8 -6 -5

-6 -4

-4 -5 -4 -3

-5

-4 -3

-3

-3

+11 +12 -11 -10 -9 -8 -7 -6 -5 -4 -3 -2

Numbers below vertical bands relate each zone to Greenwich Mean Time (0 hrs.).
Local times frequently differ from these general indications,
as indicated by light-face numbers on map.

Algiers, **29**	Berlin, **34**	Delhi, **48**	Istanbul, **40**
Anchorage, **3**	Bogotá, **19**	Denver, **8**	Jerusalem, **42**
Athens, **41**	Budapest, **37**	Djakarta, **53**	Johannesburg, **44**
Auckland, **1**	Buenos Aires, **24**	Dublin, **26**	Lima, **20**
Baghdad, **46**	Caracas, **22**	Edmonton, **7**	Lisbon, **28**
Bangkok, **50**	Chicago, **9**	Hong Kong, **56**	London (Greenwich), **27**
Beijing, **54**	Copenhagen, **33**	Honolulu, **2**	Los Angeles, **6**
	Dallas, **10**		Madrid, **38**
			Manila, **57**

Mecca, **47**
Mexico City, **12**
Miami, **18**
Montréal, **15**
Moscow, **45**
Nairobi, **43**
New Orleans, **11**
New York City, **16**

Ottawa, **14**
Paris, **30**
Perth, **58**
Reykjavík, **25**
Rio de Janeiro, **23**
Rome, **39**
Saigon (Ho Chi Minh City), **51**

San Francisco, **5**
Santiago, **21**
Seoul, **59**
Shanghai, **55**
Singapore, **52**
Stockholm, **32**
Sydney, **61**
Tokyo, **60**

Toronto, **13**
Vancouver, **4**
Vienna, **35**
Warsaw, **36**
Washington, D.C., **17**
Yangon, **49**
Zürich, **31**

Introduction

By Bob Levin

Originally from Philadelphia, Pennsylvania, Maclean's Foreign Editor Bob Levin moved to Toronto in October 1985. He traveled from coast to coast for this article on an American's impressions of Canada.

I have not seen any moose. No wolves, no musk-oxen, no cuddly little seals. Even from the cockpit of a small propeller plane, 1,500 feet over the mazelike Mackenzie Delta in the icebound Arctic, I spotted not a single furry polar bear lumbering out of hibernation to complete the picture. "Foxes have been coming right up into the town," advised Ronald Knoller, who runs a general store in the tiny Arctic settlement of Aklavik. "You see them running around, and they've tangled with dog teams." But not when I was there. I did see an impressive elk in Banff National Park, trotting casually by the roadside, but for me Canada's wildlife has consisted mostly of squawking seagulls and mischievous raccoons in my Toronto neighborhood. And maybe that is just as well: It has forced an American, newly arrived, to avoid at least the "moose" half of the hated moose-and-Mounties cliché. While trying to discover the real Canada—especially the one beyond Toronto, which, as non-Torontonians are quick to argue, is not *really* Canada— I have had to focus on its people.

And this is what I have found: most Canadians—regardless of what the media say—are not sitting around worrying about what a Canadian is. Nor do they conform to that other set of stereotypes, the ones Canadians are supposed to hold about themselves. Where are all those pallid, self-doubting people when so many of the ones I have met are colorful, confident, and passionately in love with their land?

All right, I admit it, a few tepid types may reside in Toronto. They certainly show up for baseball games, clapping with the politeness of long-ago tennis fans and mouthing that most insipid of fight songs, "Okay, okay, Blue Jays." In fact, to my mind there is something curiously passionless about the city as a whole, an urban success story boasting everything but a soul. It is kinder, gentler, cleaner, and certainly safer than any U.S. city its size—my visiting American friends invariably find it wonderful and cannot understand its New York–like, love-to-hate-it place in the Canadian national consciousness. My own feelings fall closer to the American view. But "I love Toronto" could never be the city's slogan—no, I *like* Toronto sums it up perfectly.

It has been on trips outside the city, to the more far-flung sectors of this most resolutely regional of nations, that I have found Canada at its more extreme, independent, quirky—even romantic, as un-Canadian a word as that is supposed to be. One snow-swept morning in Pouch Cove, a fishing-village-turned-suburb north of St. John's, Newfoundland, I visited William Noseworthy in his white clapboard house high on Noseworthy's Hill. Blue-eyed and ruddy-cheeked, Noseworthy sat in the kitchen by a wood stove, distractedly smoking a cigarette. He was 66 and had just retired the year before after four decades of fishing, but he still stared out the window at the North Atlantic. "There's something that draws you to it," he said in the rich accent of "the Rock."

His son, 31-year-old Barry, sipping a Labatt's beer, recalled that once, when he was 13, his father caught him whistling in a boat. "He was going to throw me overboard," said Barry. "It's just bad luck." William explained: "You don't whistle on the water. You wouldn't dare. You wouldn't launch your boat on Friday either. They're just superstitions, maybe. But several years ago, someone launched a big fishing trawler on a Friday, and she was lost on a Friday, and all the crew members, too." A minute later, William pulled out a shiny red accordion and played a jig, tapping his foot, but his eyes never left the water.

Newfoundland was also a place to sample Canadian regionalism at its most craggy and entrenched. The province's inshore fishermen claim that their very way of life is endangered by declining cod catches, which they blame on offshore trawling, often by foreigners. And they blame Ottawa for not looking out for their interests—even 40 years after joining Confederation, the old refrain still comes quickly to some residents' lips: "A Newfoundlander first, a Canadian second." But in a Pouch Cove twine store, where four diehard fishermen repaired their cod traps while country music drawled from a tape player, Frank Noseworthy, a slim, mustachioed cousin of Barry, said that he rejected the Newfoundlanders-first sentiment—and would far rather be Canadian than American. "In the States," he said, "them that's got it, gets more; them that don't, gets less. The Canadian government's more generous toward people that don't have."

Noseworthy has met many American tourists and he has not been impressed. "They come in their flashy cars," he said, "putting on airs. They seem to think they're a superior race, but I haven't seen one that's superior to me yet." He poked at the broken twine with his knife. He had one more thing to say, a point of both resentment and pride. "Some of the worst are Newfoundlanders who moved to the States. They forget their roots. They're sort of looking down their noses, instead of appreciating that there are people here trying to maintain their heritage."

Canada has hardly cornered the market on regionalism. A divided United States fought a horrific civil war in the 1860s, and as a northerner who has lived down South, I can attest to the fact that, to some southerners, the old resentments have not gone with the wind. But the United States also has the Melting Pot, the American Dream, the Pledge of Allegiance, the Hollywood-enhanced legends of Davy Crockett and even Ronald Reagan—an ever-enlarging collection of nationalistic symbols, myths, and heroes that bind the country together. Like glue, they may sometimes seem sticky and malodorous, but they do the job.

On the other hand, Canadians, writes Toronto author June Callwood, "have never created a myth that would unify them into nationhood"—except for Québec francophones. The question of Québec nationalism, heating up again over Premier Robert Bourassa's decision last December to prohibit English on outdoor commercial signs, has arisen wherever I have gone in Canada. Much of the sentiment seems to reflect that of Pouch Cove's William Noseworthy, who said, "They're always looking for special treatment—if they want to get out of Canada, let 'em get out."

In Montréal, there is no missing the passion behind the sign law. But in the office of Daniel Latouche, a political scientist and a former adviser to René Lévesque, the separatist Québec premier who died in 1987, I asked whether Québecers had a special affinity for Americans—whether, as Callwood implies, the two share a romantic vision of themselves. "There is a belief here," he replied, "that there are only two kinds of North Americans—Americans and Québecers. Two kinds of people who tried to build what North America is all about. One is much bigger, the other one lost. But both have a dream."

That is the kind of language an American can understand. But it may be a sign of American myopia that few people south of the international border, I suspect, would immediately include Québecers in such a continent-wide club of dreams. In fact, the Québec issue is quite literally foreign to Americans. The closest U.S. equivalent is the current push by Spanish-speakers in some states for official bilingualism; English-speakers have reacted heatedly, and 17 states have now declared English to be their official language. But the Hispanics are mostly recent immigrants, not a cofounding people like Québec francophones—and no American can seriously imagine Florida trying to secede from the union.

In a 37th-floor Montréal office looking out toward the frozen St. Lawrence, I asked commercial lawyer Ronald Montcalm whether there was anything binding the English and French together, any mutual myths or heroes. Montcalm thought about it and smiled. "Our hockey teams—boy, that's Canada's game." I would recall that answer on a plane the next day, when the Edmonton Oilers were on board and a steady stream of young autograph-seekers were interrupting their card game, and center Craig MacTavish talked about how "we're not the biggest country population-wise but we produce the best hockey players." But in Montcalm's office, hockey seemed more than just a sport—it was the great unifier. "At one point," the lawyer said, "Québec ultranationalists were talking about having our own team. The argument against that is,

'Hey, you've got to have Mario Lemieux and Wayne Gretzky on the same team or the Russians will beat us.'"

No Canadian region has left a more indelible impression on me than the North. The frontier is among the most enduring of American symbols, and while the American West was settled long ago, the Canadian North still lies empty and alluring—a distant dreamscape reachable by Boeing 737. Last March, I visited Inuvik, Northwest Territories, a government-built town on the east side of the Mackenzie Delta. It is a place of fur-trimmed parkas and brightly colored houses, with a church shaped like an igloo and a bar called The Zoo.

But, more traditionally, it also has an RCMP detachment, a CBC office, and a Hudson's Bay Co. store. "Twelve hundred miles from anywhere," said Mayor John Hill, "and here's small-town Canada—at least the way the bureaucrats decided it would be." Which raises the question: How can a country whose government knows exactly what a Canadian town should look like—and can create one from scratch 200 kilometers (124 miles) north of the Arctic Circle—have such a famously chronic identity crisis?

For me, Inuvik aroused feelings of ambivalence as sharp as its 30°C (22°F) cold. On the one hand, there is the exhilarating remoteness of the place and the upbeat attitudes of many immigrants to the area— prominent businesspeople who came originally from Scotland, Germany, Greece, even Lebanon. "You've got to have the balls to come and get started in business here," noted Hill, a British transplant. "But once you have, the competitiveness isn't as intense as it would be in, say, Edmonton." On the other hand, there is a local native population with profound problems. I am suspicious of snap impressions. I also know that Americans bear their own shame over their appalling treatment of natives, and I know that, for all the historic wrongs native people have suffered in Canada, they have now organized to elect legislators, fight for land claims, and combat social ills. But in the North, the despairing side of the picture is as obvious as stray beer cans. Inuvik's RCMP Cpl. John de Jong explained that at least 80% of local crimes are alcohol-related. "These are not what you'd call social drinkers," said de Jong. "They drink until the liquor is gone and then they search for more. Then we end up having to look after them one way or the other."

The natives' problems go beyond alcohol—the suicide rate among the Inuit of the Northwest Territories is four times the national average. "There's a lot of grief," confirmed Diane Nelson, a program coordinator with the Canadian Mental Health Association office in Inuvik. "This country is hard to live in, just trying to survive. People get drunk and wander off and die of hypothermia. They fall through the ice. There's a lot of tragedy in their lives." One Métis woman told me that her brother and sister had both died alcohol-related deaths—and that her father and several relatives had sexually abused her from the age of 6 to 17. "It puts you through hell," she said. However, she has managed to get on with her life—she is married and a college graduate.

The social workers and educators in town talked of culture shock—of native people thrust abruptly into the space age and paying the price emotionally; of old amusements like berry-picking and sliding and new ones like watching everpresent videos. In some places the old ways are still evident. One day I traveled the ice road, a slick, winter-only passage on the frozen Mackenzie, more than four feet thick, lined with scrubby bush and spindly black spruce—and speedlimit signs. The Richardson Mountains gleamed in the distance. The buzz of snowmobiles announced the onset of a town. Aklavik, a largely native settlement on the delta's west side, is a motley collection of wood houses, prone to erosion and flooding. Inuvik was designed to replace it, but many residents simply refused to leave. "This was supposed to be a ghost town," recalled Dorothy McLeod, a 59-year-old Métis. "But it's such a good place for hunting and trapping and fishing—you can almost live off the land. In Inuvik, you live out of the stores."

Maybe I was just seizing on hopeful signs; or maybe, like many whites, I tend to romanticize natives and their intense ties to the land. But later, when I thought of Aklavik, I thought also of the Newfoundland fishermen, clinging to a dwindling life in the boats, and of the French nationalists, fighting to preserve their language and culture—and I thought how they would have understood Dorothy McLeod, trying to hold on to the old ways.

Canadians share a collective guilt over the plight of the natives, but they take an often-justified pride in their treatment of other minorities. To an American, Canada's vaunted multiculturalism is, like Québec nationalism, simply a foreign concept. It is also an attractive one, although the gap between theory and practice is sometimes hard to ignore.

What is happening in Vancouver is a case in point. The trouble in Canada's Pacific paradise surrounds home-buyers from Hong Kong, which will become part of mainland China in 1997. The newcomers have cash on hand and have helped to drive up housing prices beyond the range of many Vancouverites, touching off a frenzied real estate boom. Never mind that the overwhelming majority of new British Columbians come not from Hong Kong but from such foreign locales as Alberta and Ontario—public perception has focused on the Asians. "There's always an element of anxiety about change," said Mayor Gordon Campbell. "But with a certain percentage there's clearly an element of racism as well."

Vancouver is undergoing a kind of tolerance test—one that, to some residents, lies at the very core of what it means to be Canadian. "I think Canada is developing some uniqueness," said Saintfield Wong, program coordinator of the Chinese Cultural Centre in Vancouver's Chinatown. "We're more receptive to new ideas—Canada's culture *is* multiculturalism." In his gift shop down the street, however, Harry Con expressed some doubts. The national president of Chinese Freemasons in Canada, Con maintained that multiculturalism keeps Canadians too tied to their old countries. "Everybody sends money home," he said. "Italians, Chinese. Whatever happens over there, people volunteer to help. But if the government here wants to raise taxes, we give them hell. So who loves Canada?"

Dwight Chan plainly does. Chan emigrated from Hong Kong in 1974 and now, at 39, he is a successful Vancouver real estate broker who understands the city's attractions to foreigners—the ocean and mountains, the mild climate, the patently laid-back lifestyle. I asked him, though, whether there is anything to tie newcomers to the country at large; even if current fears dissipate and the latest immigrants end up feeling as welcome as he does, is there, in American terms, such a thing as the Canadian Dream? After a moment's reflection, Chan said, "The Canadian Dream is probably a healthy, stable, and secure way of living, rather than the American Dream of big money. It's to have time to enjoy your life, to play, to travel. This country allows me to do all that, and that feels good to me."

Canada continues to defy easy definition. I have crossed and recrossed time zones, sampled caribou and cod's tongue, and gathered a startling variety of mental images that, like the country itself, may not add up to a coherent whole but certainly make a pretty picture. Canada is *not* the United States—that much is abundantly clear, even if Arctic-dwellers *can* watch Detroit news on television—and its ingrained regionalism is one of its most telling traits. Travel anywhere outside of Ontario, it seems, and over and over people say, as Vancouver's Mayor Campbell did: "We're very proud to be Canadians. But there is a strong sense that the central government does not recognize we're here." Americans say nasty things about Washington, too, but when their government launches an invasion of Grenada, they swiftly rally around.

In general, Canadians also strike me as more outward-looking than Americans. They did not, after all, grow up being told that they already live in the greatest country on earth. "Americans are like TV evangelists," maintained Roger Bill, an Indiana native who is now the Newfoundland-based Atlantic field producer for CBC Radio's *Sunday Morning* show. "They really believe theirs is the best way and everyone else should follow. Canadians aren't nearly so arrogant." They do, however, take a palpable pride in place, with a decided prejudice toward the small, friendly, and relaxed. "I wouldn't live in the States, or in Toronto or Montréal," said Richard Harvey, a high-school principal from Upper Gullies, Newfoundland. "You couldn't pay me enough." I have heard Inuvik people say the same about Yellowknife— and Aklavik people say the same about Inuvik.

I only wish Canadians would say it louder, that they would boast—with the kind of cheerful cockiness I saw at the Calgary Olympics—of a nation vast, varied, scenic, wealthy, safe, fair-minded, and infinitely appealing. I wish they would make an epic movie or two about it, one with endless prairies and dazzling mountains and heroic characters hell-bent on, say, building a railroad clear to the Pacific. I wish they would brag about the CBC and national health insurance, too, and I wish, if they really want to dispel the moose-and-Mounties image, that they would stop making that ubiquitous line of postcards picturing furry seals and polar bears and saying simply, "Canada." But then, I am afraid I sound very much like an American. Only a Canadian can really sum it all up. As Montréal lawyer Montcalm put it, "Funny country, eh?"

1 Essential Information

Before You Go

Government Tourist Offices

In the United States Contact the tourism department of the province or territory you plan to visit: **Tourism British Columbia** (Parliament Buildings, Victoria, BC V8V 1X4, tel. 800/663–6000), **Alberta Tourism** (10155 102 St., Edmonton, AB T5J 4L6, tel. 800/661–8888), **Tourism Saskatchewan** (1919 Saskatchewan Dr., Regina, SK S4P 3V7, tel. 800/667–7191), **Travel Manitoba** (Dept. 20, 155 Carlton St., 7th floor, Winnipeg, MB R3C 3H8, tel. 800/665–0040, ext. 20), **Ontario Travel** (Queen's Park, Toronto, ON M7A 2E5, tel. 800/668–2746), **Tourisme Québec** (C.P. 20 000, Québec City, PQ G1K 7X2, tel. 800/363–7777), **Tourism New Brunswick** (Box 12345, Fredericton, NB E3B 5C3, tel. 800/561–0123), **Nova Scotia Dept. of Tourism and Culture** (Box 130, Halifax, NS B3J 2M7, tel. 800/341–6096), **Prince Edward Island Dept. of Tourism and Parks** (Visitor Services Division, Box 940, Charlottetown, PEI C1A 7M5, tel. 800/565–0267), **Newfoundland and Labrador Dept. of Development (Tourism Branch,** Box 8730, Saint John's, NF A1B 4K2, tel. 800/563–6353), **Tourism Yukon** (Box 2703, Whitehorse, YK Y1A 2C6, tel. 403/667–5340), and **Travel Arctic,** for the Northwest Territories (Box 1320, Yellowknife, NWT X1A 2L9, tel. 800/661–0788).

The U.S. Department of State's **Citizens Emergency Center** issues Consular Information Sheets, which cover crime, security, and health risks as well as embassy locations, entry requirements, currency regulations, and other routine matters. For the latest information, stop in at any passport office, consulate, or embassy; call the interactive hotline (tel. 202/647–5225); or, with your PC's modem, tap into the Bureau of Consular Affairs' computer bulletin board (tel. 202/647–9225).

In the United Kingdom Contact the **Canadian High Commission Department of Tourism,** Canada House, Trafalgar Square, London W1, tel. 071/930–8540; or **Québec Tourism** (59 Pall Mall, London SW1Y 5JH, tel. 071/930–8314), **Ontario Tourism** (21 Knightsbridge, London SW1X 7L7, tel. 071/245–1222), **B.C. House** (1 Regent St., London, SW1Y 4N5, tel. 071/930–6857).

Tours and Packages

Should you buy your travel arrangements to Canada packaged or do it yourself? There are advantages either way. Buying packaged arrangements saves you money, particularly if you can find a program that includes exactly the features you want. You also get a pretty good idea of what your trip will cost from the outset. Generally, you have two options: fully escorted tours and independent packages.

Escorted tours are most often via motorcoach, with a tour director in charge. They're ideal if you don't mind having limited free time and traveling with strangers. Your baggage is handled, your time rigorously scheduled, and most meals planned. Escorted tours are therefore the most hassle-free way to see a destination, as well as generally the least expensive. Independent packages allow plenty of flexibility. They generally include airline travel and hotels, with certain options available, such as sightseeing, car rental, and excursions. Independent packages are usually more expensive than escorted tours, but your time is your own.

Travel agents are your best source of recommendations for both tours and packages. They will have the largest selection, and the cost to you is the same as buying direct. Whatever program you ultimately choose, be sure to find out exactly what is included: taxes, tips, transfers, meals, baggage handling, ground transportation, entertainment, excursions, sports or recreation (and rental equipment if necessary). Ask about the level of hotel used, its location, the size of its rooms, the kind of beds, and its amenities, such as pool, room service, or programs for children, if they're important to you. Find out the operator's cancellation penalties. Nearly everyone charges them, and the only way to avoid them is to buy trip-cancellation insurance (*see* Trip Insurance, *below*). Also ask about the single supplement, a surcharge assessed to solo travelers. Some operators do not make you pay it if you agree to be matched up with a roommate of the same sex, even if one is not found by departure time. Remember that a program that has features you won't use, whether for rental sporting equipment or discounted museum admissions, may not be the most cost-wise choice for you.

Fully Escorted Tours   Escorted tours are usually sold in three categories: deluxe, first-class, and tourist or budget class. The most important differences are the price, of course, and the level of accommodations. Some operators specialize in one category, while others offer a range.

Top operators include **Maupintour** (Box 807, Lawrence, KS 66044, tel. 913/843–1211 or 800/255–4266) and **Tauck Tours** (11 Wilton Rd., Westport, CT 06881, tel. 203/226–6911 or 800/468–2825) in the deluxe category; **Brendan Tours** (15137 Califa St., Van Nuys, CA 91411, tel. 818/985–9696 or 800/421–8446), **Domenico Tours** (751 Broadway, Bayonne, NJ 07002, tel. 201/823–8687 or 800/554–8687), **Gadabout Tours** (700 E. Tahquitz Way, Palm Springs, CA 92262, tel. 619/325–5556 or 800/952–5068), **Globus-Gateway** (95-25 Queens Blvd. Rego Park, NY 11374, tel. 718/268–7000 or 800/221–0090), and **Princess Tours** (2815 Second Ave., Suite 400, Seattle, WA 98121, tel. 206/728–4215 or 800/426–0442) in the first-class category. In the budget category try **Cosmos,** a sister company of Globus-Gateway (*see above*).

Most itineraries are jam-packed with sightseeing, so you see a lot in a short amount of time (usually one place per day). To judge just how fast-paced the tour is, review the itinerary carefully. If you are in a different hotel each night, you will be getting up early each day to head out, travel to your next destination, do some sightseeing, have dinner, and go to bed, then you'll start all over again. If you want some free time, make sure it's mentioned in the tour brochure; if you want to be escorted to every meal, confirm that any tour you consider does that. Also, when comparing programs, be sure to find out if the motorcoach is air-conditioned and has a rest room on board. Make your selection based on price and stops on the itinerary.

Independent Packages   Independent packages are offered by airlines, tour operators who may also do escorted programs, and any number of other companies from large, established firms to small, new entrepreneurs. Contact **Air Canada** (tel. 800/776–3000), **American Airlines Fly AAway Vacations** (tel. 800/321–2121), **Delta Dream Vacations** (tel. 800/872–7786), and **Supercities** (Box 1789, Minneapolis, MN 55440, tel. 800/333–1234).

Their programs come in a wide range of prices based on levels of luxury and options—in addition to hotel and airfare, sightseeing, car rental, transfers, admission to local attractions, and other extras. Note that when pricing different packages, it sometimes pays to purchase the same arrangements separately, as when a rock-bottom promotional airfare is being offered, for example. Again, base your choice on what's available at your budget for the destinations you want to visit.

Special-interest Travel Special-interest programs may be fully escorted or independent. Some require a certain amount of expertise, but most are for the average traveler with an interest and are usually hosted by experts in the subject matter. When the program is escorted, it enjoys the advantages and disadvantages of all escorted programs; because your fellow travelers are apt to be passionate or knowledgeable about the subject, they can prove as enjoyable a part of your travel experience as the destination itself. The price range is wide, but the cost is usually higher—sometimes a lot higher—than for ordinary escorted tours and packages because of the expert guiding and special activities.

Skiing **Air Canada** (*see above*) has skiing programs to both eastern and Rockies resort areas.

Adventure Contact the **American Wilderness Experience** (Box 1486, Boulder, CO 80306, tel. 303/494–2992 or 800/444–0099) and **Tauck Tours** (*see above*), for its several tours to Athabasca Glacier and the Cariboo Mountains.

Whale Watching **Oceanic Society Expeditions** (Fort Mason Center, Blg. E, San Francisco, CA 94123, tel. 415/441–1106 or 800/326–7491) offers a program in July that includes snorkeling with the belugas in the mouth of the Churchill River.

Cruises **Commodore Cruise Line** (800 Douglas Rd., Suite 600, Coral Gables, FL 33134, tel. 305/529–3000 or 800/237–5361) explores coastal Nova Scotia and Prince Edward Island and the St. Lawrence. **Royal Viking Line** (95 Merrick Way, Coral Gables, FL 33134, tel. 305/447–9660 or 800/442–8000) calls at Charlottetown (Prince Edward Island), Halifax (Nova Scotia), St. John (New Brunswick), and Montréal. **Holland America Line** (300 Elliott Ave. W, Seattle, WA 98119, tel. 206/281–3535) and **Princess Cruises** (Box 60010, Los Angeles, CA 90060, tel. 800/421–5522) operate Inside Passage cruises between Vancouver, B.C., and Alaska. **St. Lawrence Cruise Lines** (253 Ontario St., Kingston, ON K7L 2Z4, tel. 800/267–7868) has two replica steamships that cruise the St. Lawrence and Saguenay rivers.

Fall Foliage Contact **Domenico Tours** (*see* Fully Escorted Tours, *above*) and **Parker Tours** (218–14 Northern Blvd., Bayside, NY 11361, tel. 718/428–7800 or 800/833–9600).

When to Go

When to go will depend on your itinerary and your interests. In the maritime provinces of **Nova Scotia, New Brunswick,** and **Prince Edward Island,** the weather is relatively mild, though snow can remain on the ground well into spring and fog is common year-round. In **Newfoundland** and **Labrador** temperatures vary widely; winter days can be about 32 degrees Fahrenheit (0°C) in St. John's—and as low as –50°F (–45°C) in Labrador and on the west coast. **Québec** and **Ontario** have hot, steamy summers and severe winters, with snow lasting from mid-December to mid-March. The whole of eastern Canada enjoys blooming springs and brilliant autumns.

Farther west, in **Manitoba, Saskatchewan,** and **Alberta,** summers are short but sunny, and marked by an occasional heavy shower. In winter, snowfall here is light, but temperatures stay low. Southern **British Columbia** and western **Alberta** have warmer winters and mild summers. Though the weather fluctuates because of the mountain ranges—the Coast Mountains and the eastern chain of the Rockies—the coastal region has the country's mildest winters, with rainfall almost inevitable. Summers here are fairly sunny, but seldom oppressively hot. The best time to visit **northern Canada** is during its short but surprisingly warm summer. The area—which includes the northern parts of the provinces of British Columbia, Alberta, Saskatchewan, Manitoba, Ontario, and Québec, as well as the **Yukon** and **Northwest Territories**—is like Siberia in winter, with devastating cold and dangerous windchill.

Climate The sheer size of Canada—about half the area of the former Soviet Union and larger than China—makes it difficult to generalize. The following are average daily maximum and minimum temperatures for a number of Canada's major cities.

Calgary	**Jan.**	23F	- 5C	**May**	61F	16C	**Sept.**	63F	17C
		2	-17		37	3		39	4
	Feb.	29F	- 2C	**June**	67F	19C	**Oct.**	54F	12C
		8	-13		44	7		30	- 1
	Mar.	34F	1C	**July**	74F	23C	**Nov.**	38F	3C
		14	-10		49	9		17	- 8
	Apr.	49F	9C	**Aug.**	72F	22C	**Dec.**	29F	- 2C
		27	- 3		47	8		8	-13

Edmonton	**Jan.**	14F	-10C	**May**	63F	17C	**Sept.**	62F	17C
		-3	-19		41	5		41	5
	Feb.	22F	- 6C	**June**	69F	21C	**Oct.**	52F	11C
		4	16		48	9		32	0
	Mar.	31F	- 1C	**July**	74F	23C	**Nov.**	32F	0C
		13	-11		53	12		17	- 8
	Apr.	49F	9C	**Aug.**	71F	22C	**Dec.**	21F	6C
		29	- 2		50	10		5	-15

Halifax	**Jan.**	33F	1C	**May**	58F	14C	**Sept.**	67F	19C
		20	- 7		41	5		53	12
	Feb.	33F	1C	**June**	67F	19C	**Oct.**	58F	14C
		19	- 7		50	10		44	7
	Mar.	39F	4C	**July**	73F	23C	**Nov.**	48F	9C
		26	- 3		57	14		36	2
	Apr.	48F	9C	**Aug.**	73F	24C	**Dec.**	37F	3C
		33	1		58	13		25	- 4

Montréal	Jan.	23F	- 5C	May	65F	18C	Sept.	68F	20C
		9	-13		48	9		53	12
	Feb.	25F	- 4C	June	74F	23C	Oct.	57F	14C
		12	-11		58	14		43	6
	Mar.	36F	2C	July	79F	26C	Nov.	42F	6C
		23	- 5		63	17		32	0
	Apr.	52F	11C	Aug.	76F	24C	Dec.	27F	- 3C
		36	2		61	16		16	- 9

Ottawa	Jan.	20F	- 7C	May	65F	18C	Sept.	68F	20C
		4	-16		44	7		49	9
	Feb.	23F	- 5C	June	75F	24C	Oct.	57F	14C
		6	-14		54	12		39	4
	Mar.	34F	1C	July	80F	27C	Nov.	41F	5C
		18	- 8		58	14		29	- 2
	Apr.	51F	11C	Aug.	77F	25C	Dec.	25F	- 4C
		33	1		56	13		12	-11

Québec City	Jan.	20F	- 7C	May	62F	17C	Sept.	66F	19C
		6	-14		43	6		49	9
	Feb.	23F	- 5C	June	72F	22C	Oct.	53F	12C
		8	-13		53	12		39	4
	Mar.	33F	1C	July	78F	26C	Nov.	39F	4C
		19	- 7		58	14		28	- 2
	Apr.	47F	8C	Aug.	75F	24C	Dec.	24F	- 4C
		32	0		56	13		12	-11

Toronto	Jan.	30F	-1C	May	64F	18C	Sept.	71F	22C
		18	-8		47	8		54	12
	Feb.	32F	0C	June	76F	24C	Oct.	60F	16C
		19	-7		57	14		45	7
	Mar.	40F	4C	July	80F	27C	Nov.	46F	8C
		27	-3		62	17		35	2
	Apr.	53F	12C	Aug.	79F	26C	Dec.	34F	1C
		38	3		61	16		23	- 5

Vancouver	Jan.	42F	6C	May	60F	16C	Sept.	65F	18C
		33	1		47	8		52	11
	Feb.	45F	7C	June	65F	18C	Oct.	56F	13C
		36	2		52	11		45	7
	Mar.	48F	9C	July	70F	21C	Nov.	48F	9C
		37	3		55	13		39	4
	Apr.	54F	12C	Aug.	70F	21C	Dec.	43F	6C
		41	5		55	13		35	2

Information Sources For current weather conditions for cities in the United States and abroad, plus the local time and helpful travel tips, call the **Weather Channel Connection** (tel. 900/932–8437; 95¢ per minute) from a touch-tone phone.

Government Holidays

Though banks, schools, and government offices close for national holidays, many stores remain open. As in the United States, the move has been to observe certain holidays on the Monday nearest the actual date, making for a long weekend.

National Holidays National holidays for 1994 are: New Year's Day (January 1), Good Friday (April 1), Easter Monday (April 4), Victoria Day (May 23), Canada Day (July 1), Labor Day (September 5), Thanksgiving (October 10), Remembrance Day (November 11), Christmas (December 25), and Boxing Day (December 26).

Provincial Holidays **Alberta:** Heritage Day (August 1). **British Columbia:** British Columbia Day (August 1). **New Brunswick:** New Brunswick Day (August 1). **Manitoba, Northwest Territories, Ontario, Saskatchewan,** and **Nova Scotia:** Civic Holiday (August 1). **Newfoundland** and **Labrador:** St. Patrick's Day (March 17), St. George's Day (April 26), Discovery Day (June 21), Orangeman's Day (July 12). **Québec:** St. Jean Baptiste Day (June 24). January 2 is also a provincial holiday. **Yukon:** Discovery Day (August 16).

Festivals and Seasonal Events

You're likely to find a festival or special event whenever you travel around Canada, in winter and summer alike. Contact tourist boards to see what's in the offing for the time you'll be visiting, and inquire about any advance tickets you may need. The following are some of the top events.

Alberta **January:** Jasper Winter Festival in Jasper and Marmot Basin features dogsledding, skating, ice sculpting, and other events. **February:** Calgary Winter Festival, with more than 200 events. **April:** Silver Buckle Rodeo at Red Deer attracts cowboys from all over North America. **May:** Edmonton International Children's Festival draws professional musicians, mimes, jugglers, clowns, puppeteers, and singers worldwide; there's also Red Deer Annual Westerner Spring Quarter Horse Show, where horses compete from western Canada and the United States. **June:** Jazz City International Festival in Edmonton features 10 days of jazz concerts, workshops, club dates, and free outdoor events; Ponoka 56th Annual Stampede professional rodeo attracts participants from across the continent. **July:** Canadian Showcase of Ukrainian Culture in Vegreville celebrates with costumes, traditional singing and dancing; Calgary Exhibition and Stampede is one of the most popular Canadian events and includes 10 days of Western showmanship, hot-air balloon races, chuck-wagon races, agricultural shows, crafts exhibits, and Indian dancing; Edmonton's Klondike Days celebrate the town's early frontier community with pancake breakfasts, gambling casinos, gold panning, and raft races. **August:** Fringe Theatre Festival, in Edmonton, is regarded as one of the largest festivals for alternative theater in North America. **September:** Spruce Meadows Masters' Tournament, Calgary, is an international horse-jumping competition at one of North America's leading equestrian centers.

British Columbia **January–February:** The Polar Bear Swim on New Year's Day in Vancouver is said to bring good luck all year. Skiing competitions take place at most alpine ski resorts throughout the province. **March–April:** Pacific Rim Whale Festival celebrates the spring migration of gray whales with guided tours by whale experts and accompanying music and dancing. The Vancouver International Wine Festival is held; Terrific Jazz Party, in Victoria, has 20 top international Dixieland bands.

May: Cloverdale Rodeo in Surrey is rated sixth in the world by the Pro Rodeo Association; Vancouver Children's Festival features free open-air stage performances by more than 20 companies.

June: Canadian International Dragon Boat Festival, in Vancouver, includes entertainment, exotic foods, and the ancient "awakening the dragons" ritual of long, slender boats decorated with huge dragon heads. Whistler Summer Festivals, through September, feature daily street entertainment and a variety of music festivals at the international ski and summer resort.

July: Each year, Harrison Festival of the Arts focuses on different ethnic music, dance, and theater, such as African, Caribbean, and Central American; Vancouver Sea Festival celebrates the city's nautical heritage with the World Championship Bathtub Race, sailing regattas, and windsurfing races.

August: Squamish Days Loggers Sports Festival features loggers from around the world competing in a series of incredible logging feats; the Abbotsford International Airshow is three days of flight performances and a large-aircraft display; Pacific National Exhibition in Vancouver has parades, exhibits, sports, entertainment, and logging contests.

October: The Vancouver International Film Festival is held; Okanagan Wine Festivals occur in the Okanagan-Similkameen area. Cars race through downtown Vancouver in the PGA Indy Car World Series.

December: The Carol Ships, sailboats full of carollers and decorated with colored lights ply the waters of the Vancouver harbor.

Manitoba **February:** Festival du Voyageur, in St. Boniface, Winnipeg, celebrates the history of the region's early fur traders.

March: Royal Manitoba Winter Fair in Brandon.

June: Red River Exhibition, in Winnipeg, features lumberjack contests, body-building shows, and an international band festival.

July: Winnipeg Folk Festival takes place in Birds Hill Park, 24 kilometers (15 miles) northeast of Winnipeg, and features performers singing country, bluegrass, folk, Acadian music, and jazz on 10 stages scattered throughout the park; Threshermen's Reunion, in Austin, features antique tractor races, sheep tying, and threshing contests; Northwest Roundup and Exhibition, in Swan River, includes professional rodeo events, chuck-wagon races, and stage shows.

August: Folklorama is the largest multicultural festival in the world, with more than 40 pavilions throughout Winnipeg; National Ukrainian Festival, in Dauphin, offers costumes, artifacts, exhibits, fiddling contests, dancing, and workshops; Icelandic Festival, in Gimli, gathers the largest Icelandic community outside of Iceland; Pioneer Days, in Steinbach, celebrates the heritage of the Mennonites with demonstrations of threshing and baking, a parade, a horse show, a barbecue, and Mennonite foods.

New Brunswick **June:** Covered Bridge Spud and Spoke Days, in Hartland, features truck-tractor rodeos, beauty pageants, and sporting events.

July: Loyalist Days, in Saint John, celebrates the town's founding with parades, dancing, and sidewalk festivities; the Shediac Lobster Festival takes place in the town that calls itself the Lobster Capital of the World; there's an Irish festival in Chatham; St. Andrews Summer Arts Festival runs throughout July and August.

August: Mirimachi Folk Song Festival, in Newcastle, features fiddling competitions, casinos, beer gardens, and a parade; Foire Brayonne, in Edmundston, is the largest French festival outside of Québec; Festival By the Sea, in Saint John, attracts more than 200 entertainers from across Canada and includes cultural and ethnic performances; Acadian Festival, at Caraquet, celebrates the region's Acadian heritage with folk singing and indigenous food; the Chocolate Festival in St. Stephen includes suppers, displays, and children's events.

Newfoundland and Labrador

June: Opening of rainbow trout and salmon fishing seasons; St. John's Day celebrations in St. John's.

July: Codroy Valley Strawberry Jamboree; Stephenville Festival of the Arts; the Hangashore Folk Festival in Corner Brook; The Exploits Valley Salmon Festival in the Grand Falls area; The Fish, Fun and Folk Festival in Twillingate; the Conception Bay Folk Festival in Carbonear; Signal Hill Tattoo in St. John's through August.

August: The Festival of Flight in Gander; Une Longue Veillée in Cape St. George; The St. John's Regatta, St. John's; The Newfoundland and Labrador Folk Festival in St. John's; The Labrador Straits Bakeapple Folk Festival in southern Labrador.

September: Humber Valley Agricultural Home and Handicraft Exhibition in Deer Lake.

December: First Night is a nonalcoholic New Year's Eve celebration featuring dozens of activities and concerts in St. John's.

Nova Scotia

May: Apple Blossom Festival, in Annapolis Valley, includes dancing, parades, and entertainment.

July: Antigonish Highland Games; Nova Scotia International Tattoo in Halifax has entertainment and competitions; Nova Scotia Bluegrass and Oldtime Music Festival at Ardoise.

August: Mahone Bay Wooden Boat Festival; Nova Scotia Fisheries Exhibition and Fishermen's Reunion in Lunenburg; Lunenburg Folk Harbour Festival; the Nova Scotia Gaelic Mod in St. Anns is a festival of Scottish culture; Scallop Days in Digby.

September: Shearwater International Air Show.

Ontario

February: Ontario Winter Carnival Bon Soo in Sault Ste. Marie. Winterlude-Bal de Neige, Ottawa, encourages ice-sculpting, snowshoe races, ice boating, and other wintertime activities.

April: Maple Syrup Festival in Elmira; Shaw Festival in Niagara-on-the-Lake (through November) presents plays by George Bernard Shaw and his contemporaries.

May: Stratford Festival, in Stratford, features performances of many of Shakespeare's plays through beginning of November; Folk Arts Festival, in St. Catharines; the Canadian Tulip Festival, in Ottawa, heralds the season with 3 million blossoming tulips.

June: Metro International Caravan is an ethnic fair in Toronto; International Festival of Native Arts features dancers, crafts booths, and entertainment in Toronto; Changing of the Guard begins at Ottawa's Parliament Buildings (through August).

July: Canada Day celebrations in Ottawa have entertainment and fireworks; Queen's Plate Thoroughbred horse race takes place in Toronto; Blueberry Festival in Sudbury; Molson INDY race in Toronto; Caribana draws on the riches of Toronto's West Indian community for this Caribbean festival.

August: Glengarry Highland Games, in Maxville, is North America's largest Highland Gathering; Six Nations Native Pageant is an Iroquois celebration and exhibit of the tribe's culture and history in Brantford; Royal Canadian Henley Regatta, in St. Catharines, is the largest rowing regatta in North America; Canadian National Exhibition, in Toronto, features air shows, entertainment, and exhibits.

September: The Canadian Open Golf Championship is in Oakville; Festival of Festivals is an international film festival in Toronto; Niagara Grape and Wine Festival, in St. Catharines, celebrates this fruit.

October: Oktoberfest, in Kitchener–Waterloo, attracts more than half a million enthusiasts to its many beer halls and tents.

November: the Royal Agricultural Winter Fair, in Toronto, is the largest indoor agricultural fair and equestrian competition in the world.

Prince Edward Island
June: Irish Moss Festival in Tignish; Charlottetown Festival Theatre (through September) offers a series of concerts and musicals.

July: Rollo Bay Fiddle Festival; Summerside Lobster Carnival, in Summerside, is a week-long feast of lobster.

August: Highland Games, in Belfast, is a gathering of Scotsmen for games and celebrations; Annual Community Harvest Festival in Kensington; Old Home Week in Charlottetown; Festival Acadien de la Region Evangeline, Wellington Station.

Québec
January: La Fete des Neiges winter carnival in Montréal.

February: Winter Carnival, in Québec City, is an 11-day festival of winter sports competitions, ice-sculpture contests, and parades.

April: Sugaring-off parties throughout the province celebrate the beginning of the maple syrup season.

June: Molson Grand Prix, with some of the world's best drivers, takes place on the Gilles-Villeneuve Race Track, in Montréal; Festival Orford features international artists performing at Orford Park's music center (through August); International Jazz Festival in Québec; International Children's Folklore Festival takes place in Beauport, Québec.

July: Festival International de Jazz de Montréal features more than 1,000 jazz musicians from all over the world for this 10-day series; Québec International Summer Festival offers entertainment in the streets and parks of old Québec City. Juste pour Rire (Just for Laughs) comedy festival features comics from around the world, in French and English; Drummondville World Folklore Festival brings troupes from more than 20 countries to perform in the streets and parks; Matinée Ltd. international will spotlight best women tennis players in Montréal in 1994.

August: Montréal World Film Festival; Hot Air Balloon Festival in Saint-Jean-sur-Richelieu is the biggest gathering of hot air balloons in Canada.

September: Québec International Film Festival in Québec City.

October: Festival of Colors, throughout the province.

Saskatchewan **March:** Winter Festival in Meadow Lake is a three-day festival with a minor hockey tournament, family snowmobile rally, dance, children's events, Jam Can curling, and sled races.
May: International Band and Choral Festival, in Moose Jaw, attracts 7,000 musicians, 100 bands, and 25 choral groups; Vesna Festival, in Saskatoon, is the world's largest Ukrainian cabaret, with traditional Ukrainian food and crafts.
June: Frontier Days Regional Fair and Rodeo, in Swift Current, is a community fair and exhibit with parades, horse show, and rodeo; Mosaic, in Regina, is a festival of cultures from around the world.
July–August: Buffalo Days Exhibition, in Regina, features rides, a grandstand show, dancing, livestock judging, and horse racing; Big Valley Jamboree, in Regina, is a four-day country-music festival; Shakespeare on the Saskatchewan Festival, in Saskatoon, has productions in tents on the banks of the South Saskatchewan River.

Wilderness Canada **February:** The Yukon Sourdough Rendezvous, in Whitehorse, features dog-team races, leg wrestling, log sawing, snowshoe races, local arts and crafts, and talent contests.
June: The Midnight Sun Golf Tournament in Yellowknife tees off at midnight on the first day of summer.
July: Yukon International Festival of Storytelling, Whitehorse, features storytellers from all over the circumpolar North.
August: Dawson City commemorates the Klondike gold strike with the Discovery Days festival, with parades, raft and canoe races, baseball tournaments, and dances.

What to Pack

Clothing How you pack will depend on when you go and what you plan to do. Layering is the best defense against Canada's cold winters; a hat, scarf, and gloves are essential. For summer travel, loose-fitting natural-fiber clothes are best; bring a wool sweater and light jacket. If you're planning to spend time in Canada's larger cities, pack both casual clothes for day touring and more formal wear for evenings out. If your visit includes a stay at a large city hotel, bring a bathing suit in any season to take advantage of the indoor pool.

Miscellaneous If you plan on camping or hiking in the deep woods during the summer, especially in northern Canada, insect repellent is a must, especially in June, which is blackfly season.

Bring an extra pair of eyeglasses or contact lenses. If you have a health problem that may require you to purchase a prescription drug, pack enough to last the duration of the trip, or have your doctor write a prescription using the drug's generic name, since brand names vary from country to country. And don't forget to pack a list of the addresses of offices that supply refunds for lost or stolen traveler's checks.

Luggage Free baggage allowances on an airline depend on the airline,
Regulations the route, and the class of your ticket. In general, on domestic flights and on international flights between the United States and foreign destinations, you are entitled to check two bags—neither exceeding 62 inches, or 158 centimeters (length + width + height), or weighing more than 70 pounds (32 kilograms). A third piece may be brought aboard as a carryon; its

total dimensions are generally limited to less than 45 inches (114 centimeters), so it will fit easily under the seat in front of you or in the overhead compartment. There are variations, so ask in advance. The single rule, a Federal Aviation Administration safety regulation that pertains to carry-on baggage on U.S. airlines, requires only that carryons be properly stowed and allows the airline to limit allowances and tailor them to different aircraft and operational conditions. Charges for excess, oversize, or overweight pieces vary, so inquire before you pack.

Safeguarding Your Luggage Before leaving home, itemize your bags' contents and their worth; this list will help you estimate the extent of your loss if your bags go astray. To minimize that risk, tag them inside and out with your name, address, and phone number. (If you use your home address, cover it so that potential thieves can't see it.) At check-in, make sure that the tag attached by baggage handlers bears the correct three-letter code for your destination. If your bags do not arrive with you, or if you detect damage, do not leave the airport until you've filed a written report with the airline.

Money Matters

American money is readily accepted in much of Canada (especially in communities near the border), and traveler's checks and major U.S. credit cards are accepted in larger cities and resorts.

Traveler's Checks Although you will want plenty of cash when visiting small cities or rural areas, traveler's checks are usually preferable. The most widely recognized are **American Express, Thomas Cook, Visa,** and those issued by major commercial banks such as **Citibank** and **Bank of America.** American Express also issues *Traveler's Cheques for Two,* which can be counter-signed and used by you or your traveling companion. Some checks are free; usually the issuing company or the bank at which you make your purchase charges 1% of the checks' face value as a fee. Be sure to buy a few checks in small denominations to cash toward the end of your trip, when you don't want to be left with more foreign currency than you can spend. Always record the numbers of checks as you spend them, and keep this list separate from the checks.

Currency Exchange Banks and bank-operated exchange booths at airports and railroad stations are usually the best places to change money. Hotels, stores, and privately run exchange firms typically offer less favorable rates.

Before your trip, pay attention to how the dollar is doing vis-à-vis Canadian currency. If the dollar is losing strength, try to pay as many travel bills as possible in advance, especially the big ones. If it is getting stronger, pay for costly items abroad, and use your credit card whenever possible—you'll come out ahead, whether the exchange rate at which your purchase is calculated is the one in effect the day the vendor's bank abroad processes the charge, or the one prevailing on the day the charge company's service center processes it at home.

Getting Money from Home

Cash Machines   Automated-teller machines (ATMs) are proliferating; many are tied to international networks such as **Cirrus** and **Plus.** You can use your bank card at ATMs away from home to withdraw money from an account and get cash advances on a credit-card account (providing your card has been programmed with a personal identification number, or PIN). Check in advance on limits on withdrawals and cash advances within specified periods. Ask whether your bank-card or credit-card PIN number will need to be reprogrammed for use in the area you'll be visiting—a possibility if the number has more than four digits. Remember that on cash advances you are charged interest from the day you get the money from ATMs as well as from tellers. And note that, although transaction fees for ATM withdrawals abroad will probably be higher than fees for withdrawals at home, Cirrus and Plus exchange rates tend to be good.

For specific Cirrus locations in the United States and Canada, call 800/424–7787 and press the area code and first three digits of the number you're calling from (or the calling area where you want an ATM).

American Express   The company's **Express Cash** system lets you withdraw cash
Cardholder   and/or traveler's checks from a worldwide network of 57,000
Services   American Express dispensers and participating bank ATMs. You must *enroll first* (call 800/227–4669 for a form and allow two weeks for processing). Withdrawals are charged not to your card but to a designated bank account. You can withdraw up to $1,000 per seven-day period on the basic card, more if your card is gold or platinum. There is a 2% fee (minimum US$2.50, maximum US$10) for each cash transaction, and a 1% fee for traveler's checks (except for the platinum card), which are available only from American Express dispensers.

At AmEx offices, cardholders can also cash personal checks for up to $1,000 in any seven-day period (21 days abroad); of this $200 can be in cash, more if available, with the balance paid in traveler's checks, for which all but platinum cardholders pay a 1% fee. Higher limits apply to the gold and platinum cards.

Wiring Money   You don't have to be a cardholder to send or receive an **American Express MoneyGram** for up to US$10,000. To send one, go to an American Express MoneyGram agent, pay up to US$1,000 with a credit card and anything over that in cash, and phone a transaction reference number to your intended recipient, who needs only present identification and the reference number to the nearest MoneyGram agent to pick up the cash. There are MoneyGram agents in more than 60 countries (call 800/543–4080 for locations). Fees range from 5% to 10%, depending on the amount and how you pay. You can't use American Express, which is really a convenience card—only Discover, MasterCard, and Visa credit cards.

You can also use **Western Union.** To wire money, take either cash or a check to the nearest office. (Or you can call and use a credit card.) Fees are roughly 5%–10%. Money sent from the United States or Canada will be available for pickup at agent locations in Canada within minutes. (Note that once the money is in the system it can be picked up at *any* location. You don't have to miss your train waiting for it to arrive in City A, because if there's an agent in City B, where you're headed, you can pick it up there, too.) There are approximately 20,000 agents world-wide (call 800/325–6000 for locations).

Canadian Currency

The units of currency in Canada are the Canadian dollar (C$) and the cent, in almost the same denominations as U.S. currency—the $1 bill is no longer used; instead it has been replaced by a $1 coin ($2, $5, $10, $20, 1¢, 5¢, 10¢, 25¢, etc.). The use of $2 paper currency is common here although rare in the United States. At press time (September 1993), the exchange rate was C$1.25 to US$1 and C$2.14 to £1. The Canadian dollar has decreased significantly in value relative to the U.S. dollar in recent months.

What It Will Cost

Throughout this guide, unless otherwise stated, prices are quoted in Canadian dollars.

With some exceptions, most food prices are higher in Canada than in the United States, but lower than in much of Western Europe. The biggest expense of the trip will be accommodations, but a range of choices, from economy to deluxe, is available in metropolitan areas, the country, and in resort areas.

Sample Prices The following prices are for Toronto: Dinner at an Expensive restaurant, without tax, tip, or drinks, will cost $30–$40; Moderate, $20–$30; Inexpensive, under $20. A double room at an Expensive hotel costs $130–$200 or more; Moderate, $90–$130; Inexpensive, $65–$90, with suburban motels being cheaper. (Prices in other cities and regions are often lower.) A soda (pop) costs $1–$1.25; a glass of beer, $3–$6; a sandwich, $3.50–$6; a taxi, as soon as the meter is turned on, $2.20, and $1 for every kilometer; a movie, about $8. (*See* Staying in Canada, GST and Sales Tax, *below*).

Passports and Visas

U.S. Citizens Because of the volume of border traffic between Canada and the United States, entry requirements are fairly simple. Citizens and legal residents of the United States do not need a passport or a visa to enter Canada, but proof of citizenship (a birth certificate, valid passport, or voter registration card) and proof of identity may be requested. U.S. residents entering Canada from a third country must have a valid passport, naturalization certificate, or "green card." For more information, contact the **Canadian Embassy** (501 Pennsylvania Ave. NW, Washington, DC 20001, tel. 202/682–1740).

U.K. Citizens Citizens of the United Kingdom need a valid passport to enter Canada for stays of up to six months; all visitors must have a return ticket out of Canada. Applications for new and renewal passports are available from main post offices as well as at the six passport offices, located in Belfast, Glasgow, Liverpool, London, Newport, and Peterborough. You may apply in person at all passport offices, or by mail to all except the London office. Children under 16 may travel on a parent's passport when accompanying them. All passports are valid for 10 years. Allow a month for processing.

Customs and Duties

On Arrival American and British visitors may bring in the following items duty-free: 200 cigarettes, 50 cigars, and two pounds of tobacco; 1 bottle (1.14 litres or 40 imperial oz.) of liquor, or 24 355 ml. (12 oz.) bottles or cans of beer for personal consumption; gifts up to the value of $40 per gift. A deposit is sometimes required for trailers (refunded upon return). Cats and dogs must have a certificate issued by a licensed veterinarian that clearly identifies the animal and certifies that it has been vaccinated against rabies during the preceding 36 months. Plant material must be declared and inspected.

Returning Home Provided you've been out of the country for at least 48 hours
U.S. Customs and haven't already used the exemption, or any part of it, in the past 30 days, you may bring home US$400 worth of foreign goods duty-free. So can each member of your family, regardless of age; and your exemptions may be pooled, so one of you can bring in more if another brings in less. A flat 10% duty applies to the next US$1,000 of goods; above US$1,400, the rate varies with the merchandise. (If the 48-hour or 30-day limits apply, your duty-free allowance drops to US$25, which may not be pooled.) Please note that these are the *general* rules, applicable to most countries, including Canada.

Travelers 21 or older may bring back 1 liter of alcohol duty-free, provided the beverage laws of the state through which they reenter the United States allow it. In addition, 100 non-Cuban cigars and 200 cigarettes are allowed, regardless of your age. Antiques and works of art more than 100 years old are duty-free.

Gifts valued at less than US$50 may be mailed duty-free to stateside friends and relatives, with a limit of one package per day per addressee (do not send alcohol or tobacco products, nor perfume valued at more than US$5). These gifts do not count as part of your exemption, unless you bring them home with you. Mark the package "Unsolicited Gift" and include the nature of the gift and its retail value.

For a copy of "Know Before You Go," a free brochure detailing what you may and may not bring back to the United States, rates of duty, and other pointers, contact the **U.S. Customs Service** (Box 7407, Washington, DC 20044, tel. 202/927–6724).

U.K. Customs From countries outside the EC such as Canada, you may import duty-free 200 cigarettes, 100 cigarillos, 50 cigars or 250 grams of tobacco; 1 liter of spirits or 2 liters of fortified or sparkling wine; 2 liters of still table wine; 60 millileters of perfume; 250 millileters of toilet water; plus £36 worth of other goods, including gifts and souvenirs.

For further information or a copy of "A Guide for Travellers," which details standard customs procedures as well as what you may bring into the United Kingdom from abroad, contact **HM Customs and Excise** (New King's Beam House, 22 Upper Ground, London SE1 9PJ, tel. 071/620–1313).

Traveling with Cameras, Camcorders, and Laptops

About Film and If your camera is new or if you haven't used it for a while, shoot
Cameras and develop a few rolls of film before leaving home. Pack some

lens tissue and an extra battery for your built-in light meter, and invest in an inexpensive skylight filter, to both protect your lens and provide some definition in hazy shots. Store film in a cool, dry place—never in the car's glove compartment or on the shelf under the rear window.

Films above ISO 400 are more sensitive to damage from airport security X-rays than others; very high-speed films, ISO 1000 and above, are exceedingly vulnerable. To protect your film, don't put it in checked luggage; carry it with you in a plastic bag and ask for a hand inspection. Such requests are honored at American airports, up to the inspector abroad. Don't depend on a lead-lined bag to protect film in checked luggage—the airline may very well turn up the dosage of radiation to see what you've got in there. Airport metal detectors do not harm film, although you'll set off the alarm if you walk through one with a roll in your pocket. Call the Kodak Information Center (tel. 800/242–2424) for details.

About Camcorders Before your trip, put new or long-unused camcorders through their paces, and practice panning and zooming. Invest in a skylight filter to protect the lens, and check the lithium battery that lights up the LCD (liquid crystal display) modes. As for the rechargeable nickel-cadmium batteries that are the camera's power source, take along an extra pair, so while you're using your camcorder you'll have one battery ready and another recharging.

About Videotape Unlike still-camera film, videotape is not damaged by X-rays. However, it may well be harmed by the magnetic field of a walk-through metal detector. Airport security personnel may want you to turn the camcorder on to prove that that's what it is, so make sure the battery is charged when you get to the airport.

About Laptops Security X-rays do not harm hard-disk or floppy-disk storage. Most airlines allow you to use your laptop aloft but request that you turn it off during takeoff and landing so as not to interfere with navigation equipment. Make sure the battery is charged when you arrive at the airport, because you may be asked to turn on the computer at security checkpoints to prove that it is what it appears to be. If you're a heavy computer user, consider traveling with a backup battery. For international travel, register your laptop with U.S. Customs as you leave the country, providing it's manufactured abroad (U.S.-origin items cannot be registered at U.S. Customs); when you do so, you'll get a certificate, good for as long as you own the item, containing your name and address, a description of the laptop, and its serial number, that will quash any questions that may arise on your return. If your laptop is U.S.-made, call the consulate of the country you'll be visiting to find out whether it should be registered with customs in that country upon arrival. Some travelers do this as a matter of course and ask customs officers to sign a document that specifies the total configuration of the system, computer and peripherals, and its value. In addition, before leaving home, find out about repair facilities at your destination.

Language

Canada's two official languages are English and French. Though English is widely spoken, it may be useful to learn a few French phrases if you plan to travel to the province of

Québec or to the French Canadian communities in the maritime provinces (Nova Scotia, New Brunswick, and Prince Edward Island), northern Manitoba, and Ontario. Canadian French, known as Québecois or *joual*, is a colorful language often quite different from that spoken in Paris.

Canada, like the United States, has been settled by successive influxes of immigrants, from the British, Scottish, Irish, and French to the Germans, Scandinavians, Ukrainians, and Chinese. Many of these groups maintain their cultural identity through their native language, and ethnic daily and weekly newspapers are common. Immigration since the 1960s accounts for Asians, Arabs, East Indians, Italians, Hispanics, and Caribbean blacks. The native population of Canada now comprises less than 1% of the population, yet it is possible to hear the languages of Indians and Inuits where these groups reside.

Insurance

For U.S. Residents Most tour operators, travel agents, and insurance agents sell specialized health-and-accident, flight, trip-cancellation, and luggage insurance as well as comprehensive policies with some or all of these features. But before you make any purchase, review your existing health and homeowner policies to find out whether they cover expenses incurred while traveling.

Health-and-Accident Insurance Supplemental health-and-accident insurance for travelers is usually a part of comprehensive policies. Specific policy provisions vary, but they tend to address three general areas, beginning with reimbursement for medical expenses caused by illness or an accident during a trip. Such policies may reimburse anywhere from US$1,000 to US$150,000 worth of medical expenses; dental benefits may also be included. A second common feature is the personal-accident, or death-and-dismemberment, provision, which pays a lump sum to your beneficiaries if you die or to you if you lose one or both limbs or your eyesight. This is similar to the flight insurance described below, although it is not necessarily limited to accidents involving airplanes or even other "common carriers" (buses, trains, and ships) and can be in effect 24 hours a day. The lump sum awarded can range from US$15,000 to US$500,000. A third area generally addressed by these policies is medical assistance (referrals, evacuation, or repatriation and other services). Some policies reimburse travelers for the cost of such services; others may automatically enroll you as a member of a particular medical-assistance company.

Flight Insurance This insurance, often bought as a last-minute impulse at the airport, pays a lump sum to a beneficiary when a plane crashes and the insured dies (and sometimes to a surviving passenger who loses eyesight or a limb); thus it supplements the airlines' own coverage as described in the limits-of-liability paragraphs on your ticket (up to US$75,000 on international flights, US$20,000 on domestic ones—and that is generally subject to litigation). Charging an airline ticket to a major credit card often automatically signs you up for flight insurance; in this case, the coverage may also embrace travel by bus, train, and ship.

Baggage Insurance In the event of loss, damage, or theft on international flights, airlines limit their liability to US$20 per kilogram for checked baggage (roughly about US$640 per 70-pound bag) and

US$400 per passenger for unchecked baggage. On domestic flights, the ceiling is US$1,250 per passenger. Excess-valuation insurance can be bought directly from the airline at check-in but leaves your bags vulnerable on the ground.

Trip Insurance   There are two sides to this coin. **Trip-cancellation-and-inter-ruption insurance** protects you in the event you are unable to undertake or finish your trip. **Default** or **bankruptcy insurance** protects you against a supplier's failure to deliver. Consider the former if your airline ticket, cruise, or package tour does not allow changes or cancellations. The amount of coverage to buy should equal the cost of your trip should you, a traveling companion, or a family member get sick, forcing you to stay home, plus the nondiscounted one-way airline ticket you would need to buy if you had to return home early. Read the fine print carefully; pay attention to sections defining "family member" and "preexisting medical conditions." A characteristic quirk of default policies is that they often do not cover default by travel agencies or default by a tour operator, airline, or cruise line if you bought your tour and the coverage directly from the firm in question. To reduce your need for default insurance, give preference to tours packaged by members of the United States Tour Operators Association (USTOA), which maintains a fund to reimburse clients in the event of member defaults. Even better, pay for travel arrangements with a major credit card, so that you can refuse to pay the bill if services have not been rendered—and let the card company fight your battles.

Comprehensive   Companies supplying comprehensive policies with some or all
Policies   of the above features include **Access America, Inc.,** underwritten by BCS Insurance Company (Box 11188, Richmond, VA 23230, tel. 800/284–8300); **Carefree Travel Insurance,** underwritten by The Hartford (Box 310, 120 Mineola Blvd., Mineola, NY 11501, tel. 516/294–0220 or 800/323–3149); **Tele-Trip** (Mutual of Omaha Plaza, Box 31762, Omaha, NE 68131, tel. 800/228–9792), a subsidiary of Mutual of Omaha; **The Travelers Companies** (1 Tower Sq., Hartford, CT 06183, tel. 203/277–0111 or 800/243–3174); **Travel Guard International,** underwritten by Transamerica Occidental Life Companies (1145 Clark St., Stevens Point, WI 54481, tel. 715/345–0505 or 800/782–5151); and **Wallach and Company, Inc.** (107 W. Federal St., Box 480, Middleburg, VA 22117, tel. 703/687–3166 or 800/237–6615), underwritten by Lloyds, London. These companies may also offer the above types of insurance separately.

U.K. Residents   Most tour operators, travel agents, and insurance agents sell specialized policies covering accident, medical expenses, personal liability, trip cancellation, and loss or theft of personal property. Some policies include coverage for delayed departure and legal expenses, winter sports, accidents, or motoring abroad. You can also purchase an annual travel-insurance policy valid for every trip you make during the year in which it's purchased (usually only trips of less than 90 days). Before you leave, make sure you will be covered if you have a preexisting medical condition or are pregnant; your insurers may not pay for routine or continuing treatment, or may require a note from your doctor certifying your fitness to travel.

For advice by phone or a free booklet, "Holiday Insurance," that sets out what to expect from a holiday-insurance policy and gives price guidelines, contact the **Association of British Insurers** (51 Gresham St., London EC2V 7HQ, tel. 071/600–

3333; 30 Gordon St., Glasgow G1 3PU, tel. 041/226–3905; Scottish Provincial Bldg., Donegall Sq. W, Belfast BT1 6JE, tel. 0232/249176; call for other locations).

Car Rentals

All major car-rental companies are represented in Canada, including **Avis** (tel. 800/331–1212, 800/879–2847 in Canada); **Budget** (tel. 800/527–0700); **Hertz** (tel. 800/654–3001, 800/263-0600 in Canada); **National** (tel. 800/227–7368), affiliated with **Tilden Rent-a-Car** (tel. 514/842–9445). In cities, rates range from about $50 per day for an economy car to $70 for a large car; weekly rates range from $190 to $350. Unlimited mileage rentals are available only in limited areas. This does not include the 7% GST tax.

Requirements Any valid state or national driver's license is acceptable. If you have rented in the United States, be sure to keep the rental contract with you to indicate that use in Canada is authorized by the rental agency.

Extra Charges Picking up the car in one city or country and leaving it in another may entail drop-off charges or one-way service fees, which can be substantial. The cost of a collision or loss-damage waiver (*see below*) can be high, also. Automatic transmissions and air-conditioning are not universally available abroad; ask for them when you book if you want them, and check the cost before you commit yourself to the rental.

Cutting Costs If you know you will want a car for more than a day or two, you can save by planning ahead. Major international companies have programs that discount their standard rates by 15%–30% if you make the reservation before departure (anywhere from two to 14 days), rent for a minimum number of days (typically three or four), and prepay the rental. Ask about these advance-purchase schemes when you call for information. More economical rentals are those that come as part of fly/drive or other packages, even those as bare-bones as the rental plus an airline ticket (*see* Tours and Packages, *above*).

Other sources of savings are the several companies that operate as wholesalers—companies that do not own their own fleets but rent in bulk from those that do and offer advantageous rates to their customers. Rentals through such companies must be arranged and paid for before you leave the United States. Among them is **Auto Europe** (Box 1097, Camden, ME 04843, tel. 207/236–8235, 800/223–5555, in Canada, 800/458–9503). You won't see these wholesalers' deals advertised; they're even better in summer, when business travel is down. Always ask whether the prices are guaranteed in U.S. dollars or foreign currency and if unlimited mileage is available. Find out about any required deposits, cancellation penalties, and drop-off charges, and confirm the cost of the CDW.

One last tip: Remember to fill the tank when you turn in the vehicle, to avoid being charged for refueling at what you'll swear is the most expensive pump in town.

Insurance and Collision Damage Waiver The standard rental contract includes liability coverage (for damage to public property, injury to pedestrians, etc.) and coverage for the car against fire, theft (not included in certain countries), and collision damage with a deductible—most commonly US$2,000–US$3,000, occasionally more. In the case of an accident, you are responsible for the deductible amount unless you've purchased the collision damage waiver (CDW), which costs an average $12 a day, although this varies depending on what you've rented, where, and from whom.

Because this adds up quickly, you may be inclined to say "no thanks"—and that's certainly your option, although the rental agent may not tell you so. Note before you decline that deductibles are occasionally high enough that totaling a car would make you responsible for its full value. Planning ahead will help you make the right decision. By all means, find out if your own insurance covers damage to a rental car while traveling (not simply a car to drive when yours is in for repairs). And check whether charging car rentals to any of your credit cards will get you a CDW at no charge.

Rail Passes

Although **VIA Rail,** Canada's major passenger carrier, has made considerable cuts in its services, it is still possible to travel coast to coast on its trains. The **Canrailpass** allows 12 days of coach-class travel within a 30 day period; sleeping cars are available, but they sell out very early and must be reserved at least a month in advance during the high season. During the high season (June 7–Sept. 30) the pass is US$419.63 for adults age 25–60, US$376.72 for travelers under 25 or over 60. Low season rates (Oct. 1–Dec. 14 and Jan. 6–June 6) are US$282.33 for adults and US$256.58 for youth and seniors. The pass is not valid during the Christmas period (Dec. 15–Jan. 5). The Canrailpass must be purchased prior to arrival in Canada; for more information and reservations, contact VIA Rail (tel. 800/665–0200 in the United States) or Compass Travel (Box 113, Peterborough, PE1 1LE, tel. 0733/51780, in the United Kingdom).

Student and Youth Travel

Travel Agencies The foremost U.S. student travel agency is **Council Travel,** a subsidiary of the nonprofit Council on International Educational Exchange. It specializes in low-cost travel arrangements, is the exclusive U.S. agent for several discount cards, and, with its sister CIEE subsidiary, **Council Charter,** is a source of airfare bargains. The Council Charter brochure and CIEE's twice-yearly *Student Travels* magazine, which details its programs, are available at the Council Travel office at CIEE headquarters (205 E. 42nd Street, New York, NY 10017, tel. 212/661–1450) and at 37 branches in college towns nationwide (free in person, US$1 by mail). The **Educational Travel Center** (ETC, 438 N. Francis St., Madison, WI 53703, tel. 608/256–5551) also offers low-cost rail passes, domestic and international airline tickets (mostly for flights departing from Chicago), and other budgetwise travel arrangements. Other travel agencies catering to students include **Travel Management International** (TMI, 18 Prescott St., Suite 4, Cambridge, MA 02138, tel. 617/661–8187) and **Travel Cuts** (187 College St., Toronto, Ont. M5T 1P7, tel. 416/979–2406).

Discount Cards For discounts on transportation and on museum and attractions admissions, buy the **International Student Identity Card** (ISIC) if you're a bona fide student, or the **International Youth Card** (IYC) if you're under 26. In the United States the ISIC and IYC cards cost US$15 each and include basic travel accident and sickness coverage. Apply to **CIEE** (*see* address *above*, tel. 212/661–1414; the application is in *Student Travels*). In Canada the cards are available for US$15 each from **Travel Cuts** (*see above*). In the United Kingdom they cost £5 and £4 respectively at student unions and student travel companies, including Council Travel's London office (28A Poland St., London W1V 3DB, tel. 071/437–7767).

Hosteling An **International Youth Hostel Federation** (IYHF) membership card is the key to more than 5,300 hostel locations in 59 countries; the sex-segregated, dormitory-style sleeping quarters, including some for families, go for US$7–US$20 a night per person. Membership is available in the United States through **American Youth Hostels** (AYH, 733 15th St. NW, Washington, DC 20005, tel. 202/783–6161), the American link in the worldwide chain, and costs US$25 for adults 18–54, US$10 for those under 18, US$15 for those 55 and over, and US$35 for families. Volume 2 of the two-volume *Guide to Budget Accommodation* lists hostels in Asia and Australasia as well as in Canada and the United States (US$13.95 including postage). IYHF membership is available in Canada through the **Canadian Hostelling Association** (CHA, 1600 James Naismith Dr., Suite 608, Gloucester, Ont. K1B 5N4, tel. 613/748–5638) for $26.75, and in the United Kingdom through the **Youth Hostel Association of England and Wales** (Trevelyan House, 8 St. Stephen's Hill, St. Albans, Herts. AL1 2DY, tel. 0727/55215) for £9.

Traveling with Children

Publications *Family Travel Times,* published 10 times a year by **Travel With**
Newsletter **Your Children** (TWYCH, 45 W. 18th St., 7th Floor Tower, New York, NY 10011, tel. 212/206–0688; annual subscription $55), covers destinations, types of vacations, and modes of travel.

Books *Traveling with Children—And Enjoying It,* by Arlene K. Butler (US$11.95 plus US$3 shipping per book; Globe Pequot Press, Box 833, Old Saybrook, CT 06475, tel. 800/243–0495, in CT, 800/962–0973), helps plan your trip with children, from toddlers to teens. Also from Globe Pequot is *Recommended Family Resorts in the United States, Canada, and the Caribbean,* by Jane Wilford with Janet Tice (US$12.95).

Tour Operators **GrandTravel** (6900 Wisconsin Ave., Suite 706, Chevy Chase, MD 20815, tel. 301/986–0790 or 800/247–7651) offers international and domestic tours for grandparents traveling with their grandchildren. The catalogue, as charmingly written and illustrated as a children's book, positively invites armchair traveling with lap-sitters aboard. **Rascals in Paradise** (650 5th St., Suite 505, San Francisco, CA 94107, tel. 415/978–9800, or 800/872–7225) specializes in programs for families.

Getting There On international flights, the fare for infants under 2 not occu-
Air Fares pying a seat is generally 10% of the accompanying adult's fare; children ages 2–11 usually pay half to two-thirds of the adult fare. On domestic flights, children under 2 not occupying a seat travel free, and older children currently travel on the "lowest applicable" adult fare.

Baggage In general, infants paying 10% of the adult fare are allowed one carry-on bag, not to exceed 70 pounds or 45 inches (length + width + height). The adult baggage allowance applies for children paying half or more of the adult fare. Check with the airline for particulars, especially regarding flights between two foreign destinations, where allowances for infants may be less generous than those above.

Safety Seats The FAA recommends the use of safety seats aloft and details approved models in the free leaflet **"Child/Infant Safety Seats Recommended for Use in Aircraft"** (available from the Federal Aviation Administration, APA–200, 800 Independence Ave. SW, Washington, DC 20591, tel. 202/267–3479). Airline policy varies. U.S. carriers must allow FAA-approved models, but because these seats are strapped into a regular passenger seat, they may require that parents buy a ticket even for an infant under 2 who would otherwise ride free. Foreign carriers may not allow infant seats, may charge the child's rather than the infant's fare for their use, or may require you to hold your baby during takeoff and landing, thus defeating the seat's purpose.

Facilities Aloft Airlines do provide other facilities and services for children, such as children's meals and freestanding bassinets (to those sitting in seats on the bulkhead, where there's enough legroom to accommodate them). Make your request when reserving. The annual February/March issue of *Family Travel Times* gives details of the children's services of dozens of airlines (US$10; *see above*). "Kids and Teens in Flight" (free from the U.S. Department of Transportation, tel. 202/366–2220) offers tips for children flying alone.

Lodging Although most major hotels in Canada welcome children, the policies and programs they offer are usually limited to a free stay for children under a certain age when sharing a room with their parents. For example, the Sheraton Hotels worldwide offer a free stay to children under the age of 17. At Best Westerns, the age limit ranges from 12 to 16, depending on the hotel. Baby-sitting services can often be arranged at the front desk of most hotels. In addition, priority for connecting rooms is often given to families. Inquire about programs and discounts when you make your reservation.

Hints for Travelers with Disabilities

Organizations **Canadian Paraplegic Association National Office** (520 Suther-
In Canada land Dr., Toronto, Ont., M4G 3U9, tel. 416/422–5640) provides information about touring in Canada.

In the United States Several organizations provide travel information for people with disabilities, usually for a membership fee, and some publish newsletters and bulletins. Among them are the **Information Center for Individuals with Disabilities** (Fort Point Pl., in MA, 27–43 Wormwood St., Boston, MA 02210, tel. 617/727–5540 or, in MA, 800/462–5015 between 11 and 4, or leave message; TDD/TTY tel. 617/345–9743); **Mobility International USA** (Box 3551, Eugene, OR 97403, voice and TDD tel. 503/343–1284), the U.S. branch of an international organization based in Britain (*see below*) and present in 30 countries; **MossRehab Hospital Travel Information Service** (1200 W. Tabor Rd., Philadelphia, PA 19141, tel. 215/456–9603, TDD tel. 215/456–9602); the **Society for the Advancement of Travel for the Handicapped** (SATH, 347 5th Ave., Suite 610, New York, NY 10016, tel. 212/447–7284, fax 212/725–8253); the **Travel Industry and Disabled Exchange** (TIDE, 5435 Donna Ave., Tarzana, CA 91356, tel. 818/368–5648); and **Travelin' Talk** (Box 3534, Clarksville, TN 37043, tel. 615/552–6670).

In the United Kingdom Main information sources include the **Royal Association for Disability and Rehabilitation** (RADAR, 25 Mortimer St., London W1N 8AB, tel. 071/637–5400), which publishes travel information for the disabled in Britain, and **Mobility International** (228 Borough High St., London SE1 1JX, tel. 071/403–5688), the headquarters of an international membership organization that serves as a clearinghouse of travel information for people with disabilities.

Travel Agencies and Tour Operators **Directions Unlimited** (720 N. Bedford Rd., Bedford Hills, NY 10507, tel. 914/241–1700), a travel agency, has expertise in tours and cruises for the disabled. **Evergreen Travel Service** (4114 198th St. SW, Suite 13, Lynnwood, WA 98036, tel. 206/776–1184 or 800/435–2288) operates Wings on Wheels Tours for those in wheelchairs, White Cane Tours for the blind, and tours for the deaf and makes group and independent arrangements for travelers with any disability. **Flying Wheels Travel** (143 W. Bridge St., Box 382, Owatonna, MN 55060, tel. 800/535–6790, in MN, 800/722–9351), a tour operator and travel agency, arranges international tours, cruises, and independent travel itineraries for people with mobility disabilities. **Nautilus,** at the same address as TIDE (*see above*), packages tours for the disabled internationally.

Publications In addition to the fact sheets, newsletters, and books mentioned above are several free publications available from the Consumer Information Center (Pueblo, CO 81009): "New Horizons for the Air Traveler with a Disability," a U.S. Department of Transportation booklet describing changes resulting from the 1986 Air Carrier Access Act and those still to come from the 1990 Americans with Disabilities Act (include Department 608Y in the address), and the Airport Operators Council's *Access Travel: Airports* (Dept. 5804), which describes facilities and services for the disabled at more than 500 airports worldwide.

Twin Peaks Press (Box 129, Vancouver, WA 98666, tel. 206/694–2462 or 800/637–2256) publishes the *Directory of Travel Agencies for the Disabled* (US$19.95), listing more than 370 agencies worldwide; *Travel for the Disabled* (US$19.95), listing some 500 access guides and accessible places worldwide; the *Directory of Accessible Van Rentals* (US$9.95) for campers and RV travelers worldwide; and *Wheelchair Vagabond* (US$14.95), a collection of personal travel tips. Add US$2 per book for shipping.

Hints for Older Travelers

Organizations The **American Association of Retired Persons** (AARP, 601 E St. NW, Washington, DC 20049, tel. 202/434–2277) provides independent travelers the Purchase Privilege Program, which offers discounts on hotels, car rentals, and sightseeing, and the AARP Motoring Plan, provided by Amoco, which furnishes domestic trip-routing information and emergency road-service aid for an annual fee of US$39.95 per person or couple (US$59.95 for a premium version). AARP also arranges group tours, cruises, and apartment living through AARP Travel Experience from American Express (400 Pinnacle Way, Suite 450, Norcross, GA 30071, tel. 800/927–0111); these can be booked through travel agents, except for the cruises, which must be booked directly (tel. 800/745–4567). AARP membership is open to those 50 and over; annual dues are US$8 per person or couple.

Two other membership organizations offer discounts on lodgings, car rentals, and other travel products, along with such nontravel perks as magazines and newsletters. The **National Council of Senior Citizens** (1331 F St. NW, Washington, DC 20004, tel. 202/347–8800) is a nonprofit advocacy group with some 5,000 local clubs across the United States; membership costs US$12 per person or couple annually. **Mature Outlook** (6001 N. Clark St., Chicago, IL 60660, tel. 800/336–6330), a Sears Roebuck & Co. subsidiary with 800,000 members, charges US$9.95 for an annual membership.

Note: When using any senior-citizen identification card for reduced hotel rates, mention it when booking, not when checking out. At restaurants, show your card before you're seated; discounts may be limited to certain menus, days, or hours. If you are renting a car, ask about promotional rates that might improve on your senior-citizen discount.

Educational Travel **Elderhostel** (75 Federal St., 3rd floor, Boston, MA 02110, tel. 617/426–7788) is a nonprofit organization that has offered inexpensive study programs for people 60 and older since 1975. Programs take place at more than 1,800 educational institutions in the United States, Canada, and 45 countries; courses cover everything from marine science to Greek myths and cowboy poetry. Participants generally attend lectures in the morning and spend the afternoon sightseeing or on field trips; they live in dorms on the host campuses. Fees for programs in the United States and Canada, which usually last one week, run about US$300, not including transportation.

Tour Operators **Saga International Holidays** (222 Berkeley St., Boston, MA 02116, tel. 800/343–0273), which specializes in group travel for people over 60, offers a selection of variously priced tours and cruises covering five continents. If you want to take your grandchildren, look into **GrandTravel** (*see* Traveling with Children, *above*).

Discounts **VIA Rail Canada** (tel. 800/665–0200) offers those 60 and over a 10% discount on basic transportation for travel any time and with no advance-purchase requirement. This 10% discount can also apply to off-peak reduced fares that have advance-purchase requirements.

Further Reading

Fiction Mordecai Richler is well known as the author of *The Apprenticeship of Duddy Kravitz*, a novel set in Montréal, which was made into a movie. His various collections of essays are also worth exploring. Margaret Atwood, a prolific poet and novelist, is also regarded as a stateswoman of sorts in her native Canada. Her most recent novel, *Cat's Eye*, is set in northern Canada and Toronto. Alice Munro writes about small-town life in Ontario in *The Progress of Love. Northern Lights*, by Howard Norman, focuses on a child's experiences growing up in Manitoba and, later, Toronto. Howard Engel's mystery series features the adventures of Bennie Cooperman, a Toronto-based detective. *The Suicide Murders* is an especially compelling novel from the series. Jack Hodgin's *Spit Delaney's Island* is peopled with loggers, construction workers and other rural Canadians. *Peace Shall Destroy Many* is Rudy Wiebe's account of a Mennonite community in Manitoba. Joy Kogawa's first novel, *Obasan*, tells about the Japanese community of Canada during World War II. *Medicine River* is a collection of short stories by Native American writer Thomas King, who was one of the authors, along with Cheryl Calver and Helen Hoy, of *The Native in Literature*, about the image of Native Americans in literature. For an excellent view of New Brunswick, especially the famed salmon-fishing region called the Miramichi, look for the humorous books *The Americans Are Coming* and *The Last Tasmanian* by local author Herb Curtis.

Nonfiction *Canada North* is by Farley Mowat, as is *Never Cry Wolf*, his humorous account of a naturalist who goes to a remote part of Canada to commune with wolves. Andrew Malcolm gives a cultural and historical overview of the country in *The Canadians*. Stephen Brook's *The Maple Leaf Rag* is a collection of idiosyncratic travel essays. *My Country*, by Pierre Burton, is one of many of Burton's books about Canada worth reading for a personal look at Canada. *Short History of Canada*, by Desmond Morton, is a recent historical account of the country.

Arriving and Departing

From North America by Plane

Flights are either nonstop, direct, or connecting. A **nonstop** flight requires no change of plane and makes no stops. A **direct** flight stops at least once and can involve a change of plane, although the flight number remains the same; if the first leg is late, the second waits. This is not the case with a **connecting** flight, which involves a different plane and a different flight number.

Airports and Airlines You can fly nonstop to Canada from most major U.S. cities; every major U.S. airline has nonstop service. The major international hubs are Montréal, Toronto, and Vancouver, but international flights also fly into Halifax, Calgary, and Edmonton.

Flying Time **To Montréal:** 1½ hours from New York, 2 hours from Chicago, 6 hours from Los Angeles, 6½ hours from London. **To Toronto:** 1½ hours from New York and Chicago, 4½ hours from Los Angeles. **To Calgary:** 5½ hours from New York, 3½ hours from Toronto, 4 hours from Los Angeles. **To Vancouver:** 6½ hours from Montréal, 4 hours from Chicago, 2½ hours from Los Angeles.

Cutting Flight Costs The Sunday travel section of most newspapers is a good source of deals. When booking, particularly through an unfamiliar company, call the Better Business Bureau to find out whether any complaints have been registered against the company, pay with a credit card if you can, and consider trip-cancellation and default insurance (*see* Insurance, *above*).

Promotional Airfares All the less expensive fares, called promotional or discount fares, are round-trip and involve restrictions. The exact nature of the restrictions depends on the airline, the route, and the season and on whether travel is domestic or international, but you must usually buy the ticket—commonly called an APEX (advance purchase excursion) when it's for international travel—in advance (seven, 14, or 21 days are usual). You must also respect certain minimum- and maximum-stay requirements (for instance, over a Saturday night or at least seven and no more than 30, 45, or 90 days), and you must be willing to pay penalties for changes. Airlines generally allow some changes for a fee. But the cheaper the fare, the more likely the ticket is nonrefundable; it would take a death in the family for the airline to give you any of your money back if you had to cancel. The cheapest fares are also subject to availability; because only a certain percentage of the plane's total seats will be sold at that price, they may go quickly.

Consolidators Consolidators or bulk-fare operators—also known as bucket shops—buy blocks of seats on scheduled flights that airlines anticipate they won't be able to sell. They pay wholesale prices, add a markup, and resell the seats to travel agents or directly to the public at prices that still undercut the airline's promotional or discount fares. You pay more than on a charter but ordinarily less than for an APEX ticket, and, even when there is not much of a price difference, the ticket usually comes without the advance-purchase restriction. Moreover, although tickets are marked nonrefundable so you can't turn them in to the airline for a full-fare refund, some consolidators sometimes give you your money back. Carefully read the fine print detailing penalties for changes and cancellations. If you doubt the reliability of a company, call the airline once you've made your booking and confirm that you do, indeed, have a reservation on the flight.

The biggest U.S. consolidator, C.L. Thomson Express, sells only to travel agents. Well-established consolidators selling to the public include **UniTravel** (Box 12485, St. Louis, MO 63132, tel. 314/569–0900 or 800/325–2222); **Council Charter** (205 E. 42nd St., New York, NY 10017, tel. 212/661–0311 or 800/800–8222), a division of the Council on International Educational Exchange and a longtime charter operator now functioning more as a consolidator; and **Travac** (989 6th Ave., New York, NY 10018, tel. 212/563–3303 or 800/872–8800), also a former charterer.

Charter Flights Charters usually have the lowest fares and the most restrictions. Departures are limited and seldom on time, and you can lose all or most of your money if you cancel. (Generally, the closer to departure you cancel, the more you lose, although sometimes you will be charged only a small fee if you supply a substitute passenger.) The charterer, on the other hand, may legally cancel the flight for any reason up to 10 days before departure; within 10 days of departure, the flight may be canceled only if it becomes physically impossible to operate it. The charterer may also revise the itinerary or increase the price after you have bought the ticket, but if the new arrangement constitutes a "major change," you have the right to a refund. Before buying a charter ticket, read the fine print for the company's refund policy and details on major changes. Money for charter flights is usually paid into a bank escrow account, the name of which should be on the contract. If you don't pay by credit card, make your check payable to the escrow account (unless you're dealing with a travel agent, in which case, his or her check should be payable to the escrow account). The Department of Transportation's Consumer Affairs Office (I–25, Washington, DC 20590, tel. 202/366–2220) can answer questions on charters and send you its "Plane Talk: Public Charter Flights" information sheet.

Charter operators may offer flights alone or with ground arrangements that constitute a charter package. Well-established charter operators include **Council Charter** (205 E. 42nd St., New York, NY 10017, tel. 212/661–0311 or 800/800–8222), now largely a consolidator, despite its name, and **Travel Charter** (1120 E. Long Lake Rd., Troy, MI 48098, tel. 313/528–3570 or 800/521–5267), with Midwestern departures. **DER Tours** (Box 1606, Des Plains, IL 60017, tel. 800/782–2424), a charterer and consolidator, sells through travel agents.

Discount Travel Clubs Travel clubs offer their members unsold space on airplanes, cruise ships, and package tours at nearly the last minute and at well below the original cost. Suppliers thus receive some revenue for their "leftovers," and members get a bargain. Membership generally includes a regular bulletin or access to a toll-free telephone hot line giving details of available trips departing anywhere from three or four days to several months in the future. Packages tend to be more common than flights alone, so if airfares are your only interest, read the literature before joining. Reductions on hotels are also available. Clubs include **Discount Travel International** (114 Forrest Ave., Suite 203, Narberth, PA 19072, tel. 215/668–7184; US$45 annually, single or family), **Moment's Notice** (425 Madison Ave., New York, NY 10017, tel. 212/486–0503; US$45 annually, single or family), **Travelers Advantage** (CUC Travel Service, 49 Music Sq. W, Nashville, TN 37203, tel. 800/548–1116; US$49 annually, single or family), and **Worldwide Discount Travel Club** (1674 Meridian Ave., Miami Beach, FL 33139, tel. 305/534–2082; US$50 annually for family, US$40 single).

Enjoying the Flight Fly at night if you're able to sleep on a plane. Because the air aloft is dry, drink plenty of beverages while on board; remember that drinking alcohol contributes to jet lag, as do heavy meals. Sleepers usually prefer window seats to curl up against; restless passengers ask to be on the aisle. Bulkhead seats, in the front row of each cabin, have more legroom, but since there's no seat ahead, trays attach awkwardly to the arms of your seat, and you must stow all possessions overhead. Bulkhead seats are usually reserved for the disabled, the elderly, and people traveling with babies.

Smoking Smoking is now banned on all domestic flights of less than six hours duration in the United States, and on all Canadian flights, including flights to and from Europe and the Far East. The U.S. ban also applies to domestic segments of international flights aboard U.S. and foreign carriers. On U.S. carriers flying to other destinations abroad, a seat in a no-smoking section must be provided for every passenger who requests one, and the section must be enlarged to accommodate such passengers if necessary as long as they have complied with the airline's deadline for check-in and seat assignment. If smoking bothers you, request a seat far from the smoking section.

From the U.S. by Car

Drivers must have proper owner registration and proof of insurance coverage, which is compulsory in Canada. The Canadian Non-Resident Inter-Provincial Motor Vehicle Liability Insurance Card, available from any U.S. insurance company, is accepted as evidence of financial responsibility anywhere in Canada. Minimum insurance requirement in Canada is $200,000, except in Québec where the minimum is $50,000. For more information, contact the Insurance Bureau of Canada (181 University Ave., Toronto, Ontario, M5H 3M7, tel. 416/362–2301). If you are driving a car that is not registered in your name, carry a letter from the owner that authorizes your use of the vehicle. (*See also* Getting around by Car, *below.*) The U.S. Interstate Highway System leads directly into Canada: I–95 from Maine to New Brunswick; I–91 and I–89 from Vermont to Québec; I–87 from New York to Québec; I–81 and a spur off I–90 from New York to Ontario; I–94, I–96, and I–75 from Michigan to Ontario; I–29 from North Dakota to Manitoba; I–15 from Montana to Alberta; and I–5 from Washington state to British Columbia. Most of these connections hook up with the Trans-Canada Highway within a few miles. There are many smaller highway crossings between the two countries as well.

From Alaska, take the Alaska Highway (from Fairbanks), the Klondike Highway (from Skagway), and the Top of the World Highway (to Dawson City).

From the U.S. by Train, Bus, and Ship

By Train **Amtrak** (tel. 800/872–7245) has service from New York to Montréal, New York and Buffalo to Toronto, and Chicago to Toronto. Amtrak's *Montrealer* departs from New York's Pennsylvania Station at 8:25 PM and arrives in Montréal the next day at about 10:45 AM. Sleepers are highly recommended for the overnight trip but must be booked well in advance. The *Montrealer* is the only Amtrak train to Canada that requires reservations.

A second Amtrak train to Montréal leaves New York from Pennsylvania Station in the morning and takes 10½ hours; the trip from New York to Toronto (passing through Buffalo) takes 11 hours and 45 minutes; travel from Chicago to Toronto takes 12 hours. In addition to these direct routes, there are connections from many major cities. On the west coast, Amtrak offers frequent service to Seattle. From there, buses are available to Vancouver and other Canadian destinations. At press time, there is a plan to begin Amtrak service from Seattle to Vancouver.

By Bus **Greyhound** has the most widespread bus service to Canada, but you can get from almost any point in the United States to any point in Canada on its extensive network. One of the longest routes, from New York to Vancouver via Seattle, takes about 3½ days.

By Ship You can take a car ferry between the state of Washington and Vancouver Island or Maine and Nova Scotia (*see* Essential Information in individual chapters). Many Canadian cities are also accessible by water on private yachts and boats. Local marine authorities can advise you about the necessary documentation and procedure.

From the U.K. by Plane

Airlines The major carriers between Great Britain and Canada are **Air Canada** (tel. 081/759–2331 in the London area, or 0800/181313 elsewhere), **British Airways** (tel. 081/897–4000), and **Canadian**

Airlines International (tel. 071/930–3501). Air Canada has the most flights and serves the most cities, with at least one flight a day to Toronto, Vancouver, and Montréal from Heathrow, and considerably more at peak periods. Air Canada also flies to Calgary, Edmonton, Halifax, and St. John's from Heathrow; to Toronto from Birmingham and Manchester; and to Calgary, Halifax, Toronto, and Vancouver from Prestwick (Glasgow). British Airways has as many as 23 flights a week to Canada from Heathrow, serving Montréal, Toronto, and Vancouver. Canadian Airlines International serves Calgary, Edmonton, Ottawa, and Vancouver from London Gatwick, has at least one flight a day to Toronto, and has service from Manchester to Toronto.

Staying in Canada

Getting Around

By Plane **Air Canada** (tel. 800/776–3000) operates in every province. The other major domestic carrier is **Canadian Airlines International** (tel. 800/426–7000). Regularly scheduled flights to every major city and to most smaller cities are available on Air Canada or Canadian Airlines International or the domestic carriers associated with them: **Air Alliance** serves Québec; **Air Atlantic** flies in the Atlantic region; **Air BC** serves British Columbia and Alberta with new extended service out of Portland and Seattle; **Air Nova** serves Atlantic Canada; **Air Ontario** serves the Ontario region; and **First Air** includes a flight from Ottawa to New York. These airlines can be contacted at local numbers within each of the many cities they serve. Check with the territorial tourist agencies for charter companies and with the District Controller of Air Services in the territorial (and provincial) capitals for the locations of air bases that allow private flights and for regulations.

By Train Transcontinental rail service is provided by **VIA Rail Canada** (tel. 800/665–0200). If you're planning on traveling to several major cities in Canada, the train may be your best bet. Routes run across the country as well as within individual provinces, with the exception of the Northwest Territories and the Yukon, Newfoundland and Prince Edward Island.

You can choose either sleeping-car or coach accommodations on most trains. Both classes allow access to dining cars. Sleeping-car passengers can enjoy comfortable parlor cars, drawing rooms, bedrooms, and roomettes. First-class seats, sleeping-car accommodations, and Dayniter seats between Ontario, Québec, and the maritime provinces require reservations. VIA has a new "Silver and Blue" service on its transcontinental trains that provides first-class "cruise" comfort and amenities including exclusive use of their dome car. **Rocky Mountain Railtours** (*see* Compass Travel, *below*) operates spectacular two-day, all daylight rail trips through the Canadian Rockies to the west coast. In the United Kingdom, **Compass Travel** (Box 113, Peterborough, PE1 1LE, tel. 0733/51780) represents both VIA Rail and Rocky Mountain Railtours.

By Bus The bus is an essential form of transportation in Canada, especially if you want to visit out-of-the-way towns that do not have airports or rail lines. Two major bus companies, **Greyhound**

(222 1st Ave. SW, Calgary, Alb. T2P 0A6, tel. 403/265–9111) and **Voyageur** (505 E Boulevard Maisonneuve H2L 1Y4, Montréal, tel. 514/843–4231), offer interprovincial service. In the United Kingdom, contact **Greyhound World Travel Ltd.,** Sussex House, London Road, East Grinstead, West Surrey, RHI9 1LD (tel. 0342/317317).

By Car Canada's highway system is excellent. It includes the Trans-Canada Highway, the longest highway in the world, which runs about 5,000 miles from Victoria, British Columbia, to St. John's, Newfoundland, using ferries to bridge coastal waters at each end. The second-largest Canadian highway, the Yellowhead Highway, follows the old Indian route from the Pacific Coast and over the Rockies to the prairie. North of the population centers, roads become fewer and less developed.

You are required to wear seat belts (and use infant seats) except in the Yukon Territory. Some provinces have a statutory requirement to drive with vehicle headlights on for extended periods after dawn and before sunset. In the Yukon, the law requires headlights on at all times while driving on territory highways.

Speed limits vary from province to province, but they are usually within the 90–100 kph (50–60 mph) range outside the cities. The price of gasoline varies more than the speed limit, from 40¢ to 72¢ a liter. (There are 3.8 liters in a U.S. gallon, 4.5 liters in a Canadian Imperial gallon.) Distances are now always shown in kilometers, and gasoline is always sold in liters. The Imperial gallon is seldom used.

Foreign driver's licenses are valid in Canada. Members of the Automobile Association of America (AAA) can contact the **Canadian Automobile Association** (1775 Courtwood Crescent, Ottawa, Ont. K2C 3J2, tel. 613/226–7631; emergency road service, tel. 800/336–4357). Members of the Automobile Association of Great Britain, the Royal Automobile Club, the Royal Scottish Automobile Club, the Royal Irish Automobile Club and the automobile clubs of the Alliance Internationale de Tourisme (AIT) and Fédération Internationale de l'Automobile (FIA) are entitled to all the services of the CAA on presentation of a membership card.

By Ferry Car ferries provide essential transportation on both the east and west coasts of Canada. **Marine Atlantic** (Box 250, North Sydney, NS B2A 3M3, tel. 902/794–5700 or 800/341–7981) operates ferries between Nova Scotia and Newfoundland; New Brunswick and Prince Edward Island; New Brunswick and Nova Scotia; and also between Portland, Maine, and Nova Scotia. On the west coast, the **British Columbia Ferry Corporation** (1112 Fort St., Victoria, BC V8V 4V2, tel. 604/656–0757) operates 38 ships among 42 ports of call. Other ferries also operate between the state of Washington and British Columbia's Vancouver Island.

Telephones

Phones work as they do in the United States. Drop 25¢ in the slot and dial; pay phones eagerly accept American coins, unlike U.S. phones, which spit out Canadian money. There are no problems dialing direct to the United States; U.S. telephone credit cards are accepted. For directory assistance, dial 1, the area code, and 555–1212. To place calls outside Canada and the United States, dial "0" and ask for the overseas operator.

Mail

Postal Rates In Canada you can buy stamps at the post office or from automatic vending machines in most hotel lobbies, railway stations, airports, bus terminals, many retail outlets, and some newsstands. Within Canada, postcards and letters up to 30 grams cost 46¢; between 30 grams and a kilogram, the cost is $3.75. Letters and postcards to the United States cost 52¢ for up to 30 grams, and $3.40 for up to 250 grams. Prices include GST.

International mail and postcards run 92¢ for up to 30 grams, and $2.10 for up to 100 grams.

Telepost is a fast "next day or sooner" service that combines the CN/CP Telecommunications network with letter-carrier delivery service. Messages may be telephoned to the nearest CN/CP Public Message Centre for delivery anywhere in Canada or the United States. Telepost service is available 24 hours a day, seven days a week, and billing arrangements may be made at the time the message is called in. **Intelpost** allows you to send documents or photographs via satellite to many Canadian, American, and European destinations. This service is available at main postal facilities in Canada, and is paid for in cash.

Visitors may have mail sent to them c/o General Delivery in the town they are visiting, for pickup in person within 15 days, after which it will be returned to the sender.

Tipping

Tips and service charges are not usually added to a bill in Canada. In general, tip 15% of the total bill. This goes for waiters, waitresses, barbers and hairdressers, taxi drivers, etc. Porters and doormen should get about 50¢–$1 a bag ($1 or more in a luxury hotel). For maid service, $1 a day is sufficient ($2 in luxury hotels).

Opening and Closing Times

Stores, shops, and supermarkets are usually open Monday through Saturday from 9 to 6—although in major cities, supermarkets are often open from 7:30 AM until 9 PM. Blue laws are in effect in much of Canada, but a growing number of provinces have stores with limited Sunday hours (usually from noon to 5). Retail stores are generally open on Thursday and Friday evenings, most shopping malls until 9 PM. Most banks in Canada are open Monday through Thursday from 10 to 3, and from 10 to 5 or 6 on Friday. Some banks are open longer hours and are also open on Saturday morning. All banks are closed on national holidays. Drugstores in major cities are often open until 11 PM, and convenience stores are often open 24 hours a day, seven days a week.

GST and Sales Tax

A countrywide goods and services tax of 7% (GST) applies on virtually every transaction in Canada except for the purchase of basic groceries. Nonresidents can get a full GST refund on any purchase taken out of the country and on short-term accommodations (but not on food, drink, tobacco, car or motorhome rentals, or transportation); rebate forms, which must be submitted within 60 days of leaving Canada, may be obtained from certain retailers, duty-free shops, customs officials, or Revenue Canada (Visitor's Rebate Program, Ottawa, Ont. K1A 1J5). Instant rebates are provided by some duty-free shops when leaving Canada, and most provinces do not tax goods that are shipped directly by the vendor to the purchaser's home. You'll need your sales slips.

In addition to the GST, all provinces except Alberta, the Northwest Territories, and the Yukon levy a sales tax from 4% to 12% on most items purchased in shops, on restaurant meals, and sometimes on hotel rooms. Alberta and Ontario charge 5% tax on hotel rooms, for example; British Columbia adds 8%; and New Brunswick, 11%. Nova Scotia, Newfoundland, and Ontario offer a sales-tax rebate system similar to the federal one; call the provincial toll-free information lines for details (*see* Government Tourist Offices, *above*).

Shopping

The current favorable exchange rate can mean savings for Americans, even considering the sales tax and GST.

Antiques On the whole, prices for antiques are lower in Canada than in the United States. Shops along Montréal's rue Sherbrooke Ouest stock everything from ancient maps to fine crystal; Vieux-Montréal and the rue Notre-Dame sell antiques and collectibles ranging from Napoleonic-period furniture to 1950s bric-a-brac. Toronto's offerings are equally eclectic, although priced higher than elsewhere in Canada. (But for comparison's sake, consider that many Toronto antiques dealers send their wares to New York City, where the price is doubled before it goes on the sales floor.) The Yorkville area, with its European collections, caters to interior designers, although the markets at Lansdowne and Harbourfront are livelier and have wider selections. Antiques shopping is a respectable pastime in Vancouver as well, and Victoria offers some of the best buys in antique silver in the shops clustered on Fort Street.

Arts and Crafts Sweaters, silver objects, pottery, and Acadian crafts can be found in abundance in New Brunswick. For pewter, head for Fredericton. For woven items, visit the village of St. Andrews. In Québec, check out the wood carvings. The Mennonite communities of Ontario sell their handmade quilts each May at the Mennonite Relief sale. Prices can run to $2,000 for a large quilt.

Fur You can buy a fur in any big city, but for the best prices, head to Toronto and Montréal, Canada's wholesale fur districts; mink is an especially good buy, and especially in January, when furs go on sale in Canada. Fur garments bought in the United States must be labeled to distinguish farmed from trapped pelts; Canada's trapping business is legal and profitable, and the industry has resisted pressure from the United States to enforce a similar labeling system. If you are concerned about whether the animal was farmed or trapped, you'll have to ask the salesperson.

Native Canadian Art Interest has grown in the highly collectible art and sculpture of the Inuit, usually rendered in soapstone. For the best price and a guarantee of authenticity, purchase Inuit and other native crafts in the province where they originate. Many styles are now attributed to certain tribes and are mass-produced for sale in galleries and shops miles away from their regions of origin. At the very top galleries you can be assured of getting pieces done by individual artists, though the prices will be higher than in the provinces of origin. The Canadian government has registered the symbol of an igloo as a mark of a work's authenticity. Be sure this Canadian government sticker or tag is attached before you make your purchase. Many galleries and shops in the west also carry work done by Native Canadians of the Northwest, who have revived their ancient art. They are known for their highly stylized masks, totem poles, and canoes. Themes and images from nature, such as whales, bears, wolves, and eagles, are prominent in their work. Bright colors and geometric patterns distinguish their woven products: blankets, wall hangings, and clothing.

In and around Calgary you can find ceremonial headdresses, clothing, and tools made by the nomadic Plains tribes. Algonkian and Iroquoian art survives mainly in the museums of eastern Canada and in the gift shops of some of the reservations in Ontario.

Maple Syrup Eastern Canada is famous for its sugar maples. The trees are tapped in early spring, and the sap is collected in buckets to be boiled down into maple syrup. This natural confection is sold all year. Avoid the tourist shops and department stores; for the best prices and information, stop at farm stands and markets in the provinces of Québec, Ontario, and New Brunswick. A small can of syrup costs about \$6–\$9.

National Parks

Banff, the country's first national park, was established in 1885, and since then the national park system has grown to encompass 34 national parks and 112 national historic sites. Because of Canada's eagerness to preserve its environment, new lands are continually being added to this network. Almost every park offers camping—either primitive camping or campsites with various facilities that can accommodate recreational vehicles. Hiking trails weave their way through each of the parks. Among the most popular preserves are Fundy National Park in New Brunswick and several Rocky Mountain parks. Environment Canada (Inquiry Center, Ottawa, Ont. K1A 0H3, tel. 819/997–2800) publishes *Canada's National Parks* and *Canada's National Historic Sites*, with descriptions and other key information.

Participant Sports and Outdoor Activities

Biking Eastern and western Canada offer some of the best bicycling terrain. In the east, bikers favor the Gaspé Peninsula in Québec and the surrounding Atlantic provinces. The terrain varies from very hilly around the Gaspé to flat on Prince Edward Island, and varied in New Brunswick and Nova Scotia. A western tour might include the area around the Rocky Mountains and on through British Columbia. Some cities, such as Vancouver and Ottawa, have bike trails marked throughout town. Write to the provincial tourist boards for road maps (which are more detailed than the maps available at gas stations) and information on local cycling associations.

Boating With so much coastline—on the Atlantic and Pacific, the Great Lakes, major rivers, and thousands of smaller lakes—boating is extremely popular throughout Canada. Boat rentals are widely available, and provincial tourism departments can provide lists of companies.

Camping Canada's 2,000-plus campgrounds range from simple roadside turnoffs with sweeping mountain vistas to fully equipped facilities with groomed sites, trailer hookups, recreational facilities, and vacation village atmosphere. Many of the best sites are in Canada's national and provincial parks, with nominal overnight fees. Commercial campgrounds offer more amenities, such as electrical and water hookups, showers, and even game rooms and grocery stores. They cost more and are—some think—antithetical to the point of camping: getting a little closer to nature. Contact tourist offices for listings.

Canoeing and Kayaking Your degree of expertise and experience will dictate where you will canoe. Beginners will look for waterways in more settled areas; the pros will head north to the streams and rivers that flow into the Arctic Ocean. Provincial tourist offices and the federal Department of Northern Development and Indian Affairs (Ottawa, Ont. K1A OH4, tel. 819/997–0002) can be of assistance, especially in locating an outfitter to suit your needs. You can also contact the **Canadian Recreational Canoeing Association** (5–1029 Hyde Park Rd., London, Ont. N0M 1Z0, tel. 519/473–2109).

Fishing Anglers can find their catch in virtually any region of the country, though restrictions, seasons, license requirements, and bag limits vary from province to province. In addition, a special fishing permit is required to fish in all national parks; it can be obtained at any national park site, for a nominal fee. **Newfoundland** offers cod, mackerel, salmon, and sea trout in the Atlantic and speckled trout and rainbow trout in its other waters. The waters surrounding **Prince Edward Island** have some of the best deep-sea tuna fishing. **Nova Scotia** has some of the most stringent freshwater restrictions in Canada, but the availability of Atlantic salmon, speckled trout, and striped bass makes the effort worthwhile. Salmon, trout, and black bass are abundant in the waters of **New Brunswick,** and although many salmon pools in the streams and rivers are leased to private freeholders, either individuals or clubs, fly fishing is still readily available for visitors. The lakes of **Québec** hold trout, bass, pike, and landlocked salmon, called ouananiche (pronounced *Wah*-nah-nish). Just about every kind of North American freshwater game fish is available in some part of **Ontario. Manitoba** and **Saskatchewan** offer lake trout, brook trout, pike, grayling, walleye, Hudson Bay salmon, and smallmouth bass. They also offer a winter fishing season, but some areas require a guide. **Alberta** is considered a paradise for sportfishers, with its trout in streams; its pike, walleye, and perch in lakes; and its grayling, goldeye, and whitefish in rivers. **British Columbia** is unparalleled for salmon, but only two of the five species may be taken in nontidal waters. **Northwest Territories** offers Arctic char, lake trout, and grayling in the Great Bear and Great Slave lakes.

Golf Every province has something for the duffer, but British Columbia and Ontario dominate the golf scene. Ontario has nearly 400 golf courses. British Columbia also has many golf courses, and Victoria's mild weather makes it especially appealing to golfers. Because public courses are often overcrowded, if you are a member of a golf club, check to see if it has a reciprocal playing arrangement with any of the private clubs in the areas that you will be visiting.

Hiking Miles and miles of trails weave through all of Canada's national and provincial parks. Write to the individual provincial tourist offices (*see* Essential Information in individual chapters) or the Inquiry Center for the National Parks Department (*see* National Parks, *above*).

Horseback Riding This sport is popular out West, especially in places like Banff National Park in Alberta, which has many outfitters that can arrange week-long trips on the park's trails. Contact the park's information center for more details (tel. 403/762–3324) or the Alberta Tourism Department.

Hunting Canada is rich with a variety of game, including deer, black bear, moose, caribou, elk, and wild goose. As with fishing, hunting is governed by federal, provincial, and territorial laws. You will need a hunting license from each province or territory in which you plan to hunt. A federal permit is required for hunting migratory game birds and is available at most Canadian post offices. Weapons of any type are prohibited in many of Canada's provincial parks and reserves and adjacent areas, and no hunting is permitted in Canada's national parks. Guides are required in many places and are available almost everywhere. Provincial tourist offices can provide specific information.

Mountain Climbing Offering mountain climbers a challenge are the summits of Banff and Jasper national parks in Alberta and the provincial park of Mt. Robson and Yoho National Park in British Columbia. Mountain climbing should not be undertaken lightly. Write to the Inquiry Center (*see* National Parks, *above*) for more information about these parks or contact mountaineering organizations listed in individual chapters.

Scuba Diving More than 3,000 shipwrecks lie off the coast of Nova Scotia, making it particularly attractive to divers. The provincial Department of Tourism can provide details on the location of wrecks and where to buy or rent equipment. In Ontario, the Fathom Five National Marine Park has been established at the tip of Georgian Bay's Bruce Peninsula. Here 20 known wrecks can be explored in exceptionally clear waters. A wealth of sea life makes diving in coastal areas of British Columbia particularly attractive. Contact **Dive B.C.** (707 Westminster Ave., Powell River, BC V8A 1C5, tel. 604/485–6267).

Skiing Skiing is probably the most popular winter sport in Canada. For downhill skiing there are slopes in every province, but those in Québec, Alberta, and British Columbia are the best. Alberta and British Columbia also offer heli-skiing trips. For cross-country skiing, almost any provincial or national park will do. (*See* the individual chapters.)

Whale Watching The shores off British Columbia are some of the best places to observe whales, seals, and other natural wildlife. Day-long and sometimes week-long boat trips are offered. In the Pacific Ocean, along Vancouver Island, migrating whales pass on their way to California breeding grounds in the fall and come back in the spring. On the Atlantic coast, the waters around Newfoundland offer excellent whale watching, and giant humpback, right whales, finback and minke whales can be seen in the Bay of Fundy. Boat trips are available from New Brunswick and Nova Scotia.

White-water Rafting There are opportunities for rafting in almost every province, but the white waters of Ontario and British Columbia are especially inviting for thrill seekers. Commercial rafting companies offer a variety of trip packages.

Winter Sports Canadians flourish in winter, as the range of winter sports attests. In addition to the sports already mentioned, at the first drop of a snowflake Canadians will head outside to ice-skate, toboggan, snowmobile, dogsled, snowshoe, and ice-fish.

Spectator Sports

Baseball If you're missing a bit of Americana, don't fret. Baseball has been a favorite in Canada since the major leagues expanded into Montréal in 1969 with the Montréal Expos, and the Toronto Blue Jays formed a World Series–caliber club. The Toronto Blue Jays won the World Series in 1992, the first time a non–U.S. team played in and won the baseball championship. Minor league teams compete in Vancouver, Edmonton, Calgary, Lethbridge, and Medicine Hat.

Curling For a true taste of Canadian sportsmanship you might want to watch a curling match, which is not unlike a shuffleboard game on ice. Two teams of four players each compete by sliding large polished granite stones toward the center of a bullseye, or "house."

Football The Canadian Football League plays the game its own way, allowing three downs, a 110-yard field, and 12 players per side. Teams are located in Toronto, Ottawa, Hamilton, Winnipeg, Regina, Calgary, Edmonton, and Vancouver. The CFL is expanding into the U.S. cities of Sacramento, CA, and San Antonio, TX.

Hockey Officially, Canada's national sport is lacrosse, but ice hockey is the national favorite. It's played by children and professionals alike, with leagues and teams organized everywhere. The National Hockey League teams in Canada include the Vancouver Canucks, Calgary Flames, Winnipeg Jets, Edmonton Oilers, Toronto Maple Leafs, Ottawa Senators, Montréal Canadiens, and Québec Nordiques. The season runs from October to April.

Rodeos and Horse Racing Alberta is rodeo country. Thoroughbred racing during the spring, summer, and fall takes place in Ontario, Manitoba, Saskatchewan, Alberta, and British Columbia.

Dining

The earliest European settlers of Canada—the British and the French—bequeathed a rather bland diet of meat and potatoes. But though there are few really distinct national dishes here, except in Québec, the strong ethnic presence in Canada makes it difficult not to have a good meal. This is especially true in the larger cities, where Greek, Italian, Chinese, Indian, and other immigrants operate restaurants. In addition, each province is well known for various specialties. **Ontario** is famous for its cheeses, while seafood usually heads the menu at restaurants in **British Columbia, Newfoundland, Nova Scotia, New Brunswick,** and **Prince Edward Island.** Fiddleheads, curled young fern fronds picked in the spring, often accompany dishes in the maritime provinces of New Brunswick, Nova Scotia, and Prince Edward Island. Leave your vegetarian tendencies at home when visiting **Alberta** and **Saskatchewan,** where the meals invariably center on thick steaks and roasts. In some areas of Canada, especially in the plains, you may be lucky enough to find some native Indian treats, such as venison, pheasant, and buffalo meat accompanied by fiddlehead ferns in the spring or wild rice. And vestiges of what the European settlers learned from the Indians is evident in the hearty ingredients that make up the French Canadian cuisine, which thrives in **Québec.** To enjoy the best of the province's hearty meat pies and pâtés, head to Québec City; Montréal dining tends to be more classic French than French Canadian.

Lodging

Aside from the quaint hotels of Québec, Canada's range of accommodations more closely resembles that of the United States than Europe. In the cities you'll have a choice of luxury hotels, moderately priced modern properties, and smaller older hotels with perhaps fewer conveniences but a bit more charm. Options in smaller towns and in the country include large full-service resorts; small, privately owned hotels; roadside motels; and bed-and-breakfast establishments. Canada's answer to the small European family-run hotel is the mom-and-pop motel, but even though Canada is as attuned to automobile travel as the United States, you won't find these motels as frequently. Even here you'll need to make reservations at least on the day on which you're planning to pull into town.

Chain Hotels   There are two advantages to staying at a chain hotel. The first is that you'll be assured of standard accommodations, your own bathroom, and a range of services at the front desk. The second is the ease with which you can get information and make or change reservations, since most chains have toll-free booking numbers.

The major hotel chains in Canada include **Best Western International** (tel. 800/528–1234, in the U.K., 081/541–0033), **CP (Canadian Pacific) Hotels & Resorts** (tel. 800/828–7447, in the U.K., 071/798–9866), **Delta Hotels** (tel. 800/877–1133, in the U.K., 071/937–8033), **Four Seasons Hotels** (tel. 800/332–3442, in the U.K., 081/941–7941), **Holiday Inns** (tel. 800/465–4329, in the U.K., 071/722–7755), **Howard Johnson Hotels** (tel. 800/654–2000, in the U.K., 081/688–1640), **Radisson Hotels** (tel. 800/333–3333, in the U.K., 0992/441517), **Ramada** (tel. 800/228–2828, in the U.K., 071/235–5264), **Sheraton** (tel. 800/325–3535, in the U.K., 0800/353535), **Travelodge** (tel. 800/255–3050, in the U.K., 0345/404040), and **Westin Hotels** (tel. 800/228–3000, in the U.K., 071/408–0636).

Room Rates   Expect accommodations to cost more in summer, peak tourist season, than in the off-season. But don't be afraid to ask about special deals and packages when reserving. Big city hotels that cater to business travelers often offer weekend packages, and many city hotels offer rooms at up to 50% off in winter. If you're planning to visit a major city or resort area during the high season, book well in advance. Also be aware of any special events or festivals that may coincide with your visit and block every room for miles around. For resorts and lodges, consider the winter ski-season high as well and plan accordingly (*See* GST and Sales Tax, *above*).

Bed-and-Breakfasts and Country Inns
One way to save on lodging and spend some time with a native Canadian is to stay at a bed-and-breakfast establishment. They are gaining in popularity and are located in both the country and the cities. Every provincial tourist board either has a listing of B&Bs or can refer you to an association that will help you secure reservations. Rates range from $20 to $70 a night and include a Continental or a full breakfast. Because most bed-and-breakfasts are in private homes, you might not have your own bathroom. And some B&B hosts lock up early. Be sure to ask about your host's policies. Room quality varies from home to home as well, so don't be bashful about asking to see a room before making a choice. **Fodor's** guide *Canada's Great Country Inns* lists wonderful places to stay from coast to coast—from unpretentious houses with something special to the elegant Relais & Châteaux (*see below*). You can buy it in most bookstores or ask to have it ordered.

Farm Vacations
Vacations on working farms are one way to enjoy the Canadian countryside. Depending on the size of the farm and the farmer's preferences, you'll be able to observe or even participate in daily activities. These stays include breakfast and some offer other meals and special family rates. For more information about farm vacations, *see* individual chapters.

Dorms and Hostels
There are a few alternatives to camping for those on a budget. Among them are hostels, which are open to young and old, families, and singles (*see* Student and Youth Travel, *above*) and university campuses, which open their dorms to travelers for overnight stays from May through August.

Relais & Châteaux
Canada has 11 members of this prestigious association where rates run from $150 to $450 a night. Many of these small hotels and inns once served as private estates to the Canadian wealthy. One property is set in a wildlife preserve in the Algonquin Park in Ontario; another is in the countryside, just 30 minutes from Montréal. Reservations must be made directly with each property; for a complete list contact **Relais & Châteaux** (tel. 800/743–8033; 800/677–3524 for reservations).

Home Exchange
This is obviously an inexpensive solution to the lodging problem, because house swapping means living rent-free. You find a house, apartment, or other vacation property to exchange for your own by becoming a member of a home-exchange organization, which then sends you its annual directories listing available exchanges and includes your own listing in at least one of them. Arrangements for the actual exchange are made by the two parties to it, not by the organization. Principal clearinghouses include **Intervac U.S./International Home Exchange** (Box 590504, San Francisco, CA 94159, tel. 415/435–3497), the oldest, with thousands of foreign and domestic homes for exchange in its three annual directories; membership is $62, or $72 if you want to receive the directories but remain unlisted. The **Vacation Exchange Club** (Box 650, Key West, FL 33041, tel. 800/638–3841), also with thousands of foreign and domestic listings, publishes four annual directories plus updates; the $50 membership includes your listing in one book. **Loan-a-Home**

(2 Park La., Apt. 6E, Mount Vernon, NY 10552, tel. 914/664–7640) specializes in long-term exchanges; there is no charge to list your home, but the directories cost US$35 or US$45 depending on the number you receive.

Apartment and Villa Rentals If you want a home base that's roomy enough for a family and comes with cooking facilities, a furnished rental may be the solution. It's generally cost-wise, too, although not always—some rentals are luxury properties (economical only when your party is large). Home-exchange directories do list rentals—often second homes owned by prospective house swappers—and there are services that can not only look for a house or apartment for you (even a castle if that's your fancy) but also handle the paperwork. Some send an illustrated catalogue and others send photographs of specific properties, sometimes at a charge; up-front registration fees may apply.

Among the companies is **Rent a Home International** (7200 34th Ave. NW, Seattle, WA 98117, tel. 206/789–9377 or 800/488–7368). **Hideaways International** (15 Goldsmith St., Box 1270, Littleton, MA 01460, tel. 508/486–8955 or 800/843–4433) functions as a travel club. Membership (US$79 yearly per person or family at the same address) includes two annual guides plus quarterly newsletters; rentals are arranged directly between members, not by the club staff.

Provincial Ratings There is no national government rating system for hotels, but many provinces rate their accommodations. For example, in British Columbia and Alberta, a blue Approved Accommodation decal on the window or door of a hotel or motel indicates that it has met provincial hotel association standards for courtesy, comfort, and cleanliness. Ontario's voluntary rating system boasts about 1,000 Ontario properties.

Credit Cards

The following credit card abbreviations are used throughout this guide: AE, American Express; D, Discover; DC, Diners Club; MC, MasterCard; V, Visa. It's a good idea to call ahead to check current credit-card policies.

2 Toronto

By Allan Gould

Author of 18 books, including First Stage—The Making of the Stratford Festival *and* The Big Book of Canadian Humour, *Allan Gould has also written for many Canadian magazines and written and performed political satire and biographical sketches for radio and TV.*

A joke popular in the neighboring province of Québec between the wars went "First prize, one week in Toronto. Second prize, two weeks in Toronto. Third prize, three weeks in Toronto." Toronto was a deadly city, right into the 1950s, at which time its half-million citizens used to rush off to Detroit (a four-hour drive to the southwest) and Buffalo (90 minutes to the south, around Lake Ontario) for a good time. Today, of course, the rushing is in the opposite direction.

Like many cities around the world, Toronto encountered some tough times in 1993: Unemployment is up, upscale restaurants are shutting their doors faster than you can cry waiter!, and the new, brutal 7% federal goods and services tax, alias GST, has shaken businesses and tourism to the core. (In many cases, that 7% is tacked on to the already steep 8% provincial [Ontario] sales tax.) Indeed, a major study taken in Geneva in 1991 rated Toronto as "the most expensive city in the Western Hemisphere, and the 23rd most expensive worldwide." But though Toronto may be expensive for those who live here, it need not be oppressively so for visitors, who can benefit from the city's numerous free events, special hotel packages, and the rebate of much of the GST.

Much of Toronto's excitement is explained by its ethnic diversity. Nearly two-thirds of the 3.2 million people who now live in the metropolitan area were born and raised somewhere else. Half a million Italians live here, as does the largest Chinese community in Canada and the biggest Portuguese colony in North America. What this has meant to Toronto is the rather rapid creation of a vibrant mix of cultures that has echoes of turn-of-the-century New York City—but without the slums, crowding, disease, and tensions.

Still, to give to its burgeoning ethnic population all, or even most, of the credit for Toronto's becoming a cosmopolitan, world-class city in just a few decades would be a kind of reverse racism, and not totally correct, either. Much of the thanks must be given to the so-called dour Scots who set up the banks, built the churches, and created the kind of solid base for a community that would come to such a healthy fruition in the three-plus decades following World War II. Toronto is clearly this country's center of culture, commerce, and communications— "New York run by the Swiss," according to Peter Ustinov.

Toronto has gained the nickname Hollywood North, because literally dozens of major films have been made in this city, especially over the past decade, from *Moonstruck* to *Used People*, and from David Cronenberg's *Dead Ringers* and *Naked Lunch* to such TV series as *Top Cops, Class of '96, Road to Avalon*, and many more. Indeed, it is hard to walk about the city nowadays without tripping over a movie crew and a number of famous people. But since this is Canada—and Toronto—you'll probably all apologize sweetly.

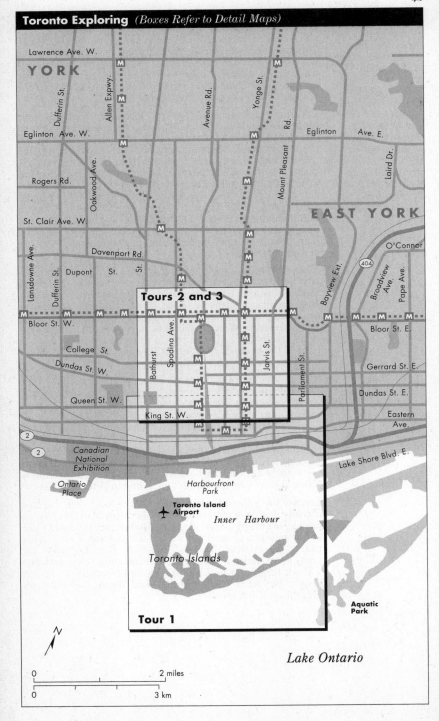

Toronto Exploring *(Boxes Refer to Detail Maps)*

Lawrence Ave. W.

YORK

Dufferin St.

Allen Expwy.

Avenue Rd.

Yonge St.

Rd.

Eglinton Ave. W.

Eglinton Ave. E.

Oakwood Ave.

Laird Dr.

Rogers Rd.

EAST YORK

St. Clair Ave. W.

O'Connor

Lansdowne Ave.

Dufferin St.

Dupont St.

Davenport Rd.

St.

Bayview Ext.

404

Broadview Ave.

Pape Ave.

Tours 2 and 3

Bloor St. W.

Spadina Ave.

Jarvis St.

Bloor St. E.

College St.

Bathurst

Parliament St.

Gerrard St. E.

Dundas St. W.

Dundas St. E.

Queen St. W.

Eastern Ave.

King St. W.

2

2

Canadian National Exhibition

Lake Shore Blvd. E.

Ontario Place

Harbourfront Park

Toronto Island Airport

Inner Harbour

Toronto Islands

Aquatic Park

Tour 1

N

Lake Ontario

| 0 | | 2 miles |

| 0 | | 3 km |

Essential Information

Arriving and Departing by Plane

Airports and Airlines

Flights into Toronto land at the **Lester B. Pearson International Airport,** so named in 1984 to honor Canada's Nobel Peace Prize–winning prime minister of nearly three decades. It's commonly called "the Toronto airport" or "Malton" (after the once-small town where it was built, just northwest of the city), but it's just as often called "impossible," since its terminals are inadequate for the number of travelers who use it. In 1992 more than 21 million passengers passed through the dreadful airport, thus putting it on par with Chicago's O'Hare and New York's JFK. Toronto expects to see close to 28 million passengers annually by the end of the century. As it is, waits for bags are often lengthy—although the free carts are a human touch—and Pearson can be dreadfully overcrowded, both coming and going. Terminal 1, which opened in 1964 to handle 3 million passengers, trafficked more than *10 million* in 1990. The sorely needed Terminal 3 opened in February 1991, after many delays. And, thank heavens, the ugly and uncomfortable Terminal 2 has undergone a $125-million renovation. Additionally, wonder of wonders, an announcement late in 1992 revealed plans for a $750-million massive renovation that will see a jumbo terminal created to replace Terminal 1 and incorporate Terminal 2. Still unresolved, however, is the future for Terminal 3, which primarily handles the ever-tottering-on-bankruptcy Canadian Airlines International.

Toronto is served by **American** (tel. 800/433–7300), **Delta** (tel. 800/843–9378), **Northwest** (tel. 800/225–2525), **United** (tel. 800/241–6522), **USAir** (tel. 800/428–4322), **Air Canada** (tel. 800/422–6232), and **Canadian Airlines International** (tel. 800/387–2737). **Air Ontario,** affiliated with Air Canada (tel. 416/925–2311), flies from the Island Airport to and from Ottawa, Montréal, and London, Ontario. It is a good alternative to Pearson International for those staying downtown and making trips to these other Canadian cities.

Between the Airport and Center City

Although Pearson is not far from the downtown area (about 32 kilometers, or 18 miles), the drive can take well over an hour during Toronto's weekday rush hours (7–9 AM and 3:30–6:30 PM). Taxis and limos to a hotel or attraction near the lake can cost $30 or more. You may negotiate a fare, but the meter *must* be used, and the passenger pays whichever is less. Many airport and downtown hotels offer free buses from each of Toronto's three terminals. Travelers on a budget should consider the express coaches offered by **Grey Coach** (tel. 416/393–7911), which link the airport to three subway stops in the southwest and north-central areas of the city. Buses depart several times each hour, from 8 AM to 11:30 PM. Fares average $6–$7. Even better is the service to and from several downtown hotels, which operates every 30 minutes from 6 AM to midnight daily and costs approximately $11.

Should you be renting a car at the airport, be sure to ask for a street map of the city. Highway 427 runs south, some 5.8 kilometers (3.6 miles) to the lakeshore. Here you pick up the Queen Elizabeth Way (QEW or Queen E) east to the Gardiner Expressway, which runs east into the heart of downtown. If you

take the QEW *west*, you'll find yourself swinging around Lake
Ontario, toward Hamilton, Niagara-on-the-Lake, and Niagara
Falls.

Arriving and Departing by Train, Bus, and Car

By Train **Amtrak** (tel. 800/872–7245) runs a daily train to Toronto from
Chicago (a 12-hour trip), and another from New York City (11
hours). From Union Station you can walk underground to many
hotels—a real boon in inclement weather.

By Bus **Greyhound** (no 800 number; check with local information) and
Grey Coach (tel. 416/393–7911) both have regular bus service
into Toronto from all over the United States. From Detroit, the
trip takes five hours; from Buffalo, two to three hours; from
Chicago and New York City, 11 hours. Buses arrive at 610 Bay
Street, just above Dundas Street.

By Car Drivers should have proper owner registration and proof of
insurance coverage. There is no need for an international
driver's license; any valid one will do. You may be asked several
questions at the border crossing, none of them terribly personal or offensive: your place of birth; your citizenship; your
expected length of stay. Every fourth or fifth car may be
searched, and this can increase the wait at peak visiting times
to 30 minutes. A recent explosion of cross-border shopping
finds thousands of Canadians shuttling across the border every
month to take advantage of lower gas, food, and even appliance
prices, so expect those Detroit–Windsor and Buffalo–Fort Erie
crossings to take even longer, especially on weekends and holidays. It's true, however, that cross-border shopping has de-
creased precipitously along with the collapse of the Canadian
dollar to less than 80¢ (American), but gas is still much cheaper
on the U.S. side.

The wonderfully wide Highway 401—it reaches up to 16 lanes
as it slashes across Metro Toronto from the airport on the west
almost as far as the zoo on the east—is the major link between
Windsor, Ontario (and Detroit), and Montréal, Québec. It's also
known as the Macdonald-Cartier Freeway but is really never
called anything other than "401." There are no tolls, but be
warned: In weekday rush hours the 401 can become dreadfully
crowded, even stop-and-go. Plan your trips to avoid these
times.

Those who are driving from Buffalo, New York, or Niagara
Falls should take the Queen Elizabeth Way, which curves up
along the western shore of Lake Ontario, eventually turns into
the Gardiner Expressway, and flows right into the downtown core.

Yonge Street, which begins at the Lakefront, is called Highway
11 once you get north of Toronto and continues all the way to
the Ontario–Minnesota border, at Rainy River. At 1,896.2 kilometers (1,178.3 miles), it is the longest street in the world (as
noted in the *Guinness Book of World Records*). We trust that
you are duly impressed.

Getting Around

Most of Toronto is laid out on a grid pattern. The key street to
remember is Yonge Street (pronounced "young"), which is the

main north–south artery. Most major cross streets are numbered east and west of Yonge Street. In other words, if you are looking for 180 St. Clair Avenue West, you want a building a few blocks *west* of Yonge Street; 75 Queen Street East is a block or so *east* of Yonge Street.

At press time, the fare for buses, streetcars, and trolleys was $2 in exact change, but 10 adult tickets/tokens cost $13, which lowers the price per journey a bit. All fares will undoubtedly rise at least a nickel or dime during the first week of 1994, since prices did not change in 1993—the first time in a dozen years. Children (2–13) pay only 50¢ in exact change, and may purchase eight tickets for $2.50. Two-fare tickets are available for $3 for adults. Visitors who plan to stay in Toronto for more than a month should consider the **Metropass,** a photo-identity card that costs $67 for adults plus $2.75 extra for the photo (and, yes, probably a few dollars more than that, as of January 1994).

Families should take advantage of the so-called **Day Pass.** It costs $5 and is good for unlimited travel for one person, Monday–Friday after 9:30 AM, and all day Saturday. On Sunday and holidays, it's good for up to six persons (maximum two adults) for unlimited travel. For information on how to take public transit to any street or attraction in the city call 416/393–INFO from 7 AM to 11:30 PM. A very useful **Ride Guide** is published by the Toronto Transit Commission each year. It shows nearly every major place of interest and how to reach it by public transit. These guides are available in most subways and many other places around the city. The subways stop at 2 AM, but the Toronto Transit Commission runs bus service from 1 to 5:30 AM on most major streets, including King, Queen, College, Bloor, Yonge, and as far north as Sheppard, Finch, and Steeles.

By Subway The Toronto Transit Commission runs one of the safest, cleanest, most trustworthy systems of its kind anywhere. There are two major subway lines, with 60 stations along the way: the **Bloor/Danforth Line,** which crosses Toronto about 4.8 kilometers (3 miles) north of the Lakefront, from east to west, and the **Yonge/University/Spadina Line,** which loops north and south, like a giant "U," with the bottom of the "U" at Union Station. Tokens and tickets are sold in each subway station and at hundreds of convenience stores along the many routes of the TTC. Get your transfers just after you pay your fare and enter the subway; you'll find them in machines on your way down to the trains.

By Bus All buses and streetcars accept exact change, tickets, or tokens. Paper transfers are free; pick one up at the time that you pay your fare.

By Taxi The meter begins at $2.20, and includes the first .2 kilometer. Each additional .2 kilometer is 20¢—as is each additional passenger in excess of four. The waiting time "while under engagement" is 20¢ for every 33 seconds—and in one of the horrible traffic jams, this could add up. Still, it's possible to take a cab across downtown Toronto for little more than $5. The largest companies are **Beck** (tel. 416/467–0067), **Co-op** (tel. 416/364–8161), **Diamond** (tel. 416/366–6868), and **Metro** (tel. 416/363–5611). For more information, call the Metro Licensing Commission (tel. 416/392–3000).

By Car Pedestrian crosswalks are sprinkled throughout the city; they are marked clearly by overhead signs and very large painted

Xs. All a pedestrian has to do is stick out a hand, and cars screech to a halt in both directions. Right turns on red lights are nearly always permitted, except where otherwise posted. You must come to a complete stop before making the turn.

Important Addresses and Numbers

Tourist Information The **Metropolitan Toronto Convention & Visitors Association** has its office at Queen's Quay Terminal (207 Queen's Quay W, Suite 509, M5J LA7, tel. 416/203–2500 or 800/363–1990). Booths providing brochures and pamphlets about the city and its attractions, as well as accommodations, are set up in the summer outside the Eaton Centre, on Yonge Street just below Dundas Street, and outside the Royal Ontario Museum.

The **Traveller's Aid Society** is not just for the down-and-out. This is a nonprofit group whose 130 volunteers can recommend restaurants and hotels, and distribute subway maps, tourist publications, and Ontario sales tax rebate forms. *In Union Station, Room B23 on the basement level and also on the Arrivals level; tel. 416/366–7788. Open daily 9 AM–9 PM. In Terminal I at Pearson Airport, Arrivals level, past Customs, near Area B; tel. 416/676–2868. Open daily 9 AM–10 PM. In Terminal II, between International and Domestic Arrivals, tel. 416/676–2869. Open daily 9 AM–10 PM. In Terminal III, Arrivals level, near the International side; tel. 416/612–5890. Open daily 9 AM–10 PM.*

Embassies The **Consulate General of the United States** (360 University Ave., just north of Queen St., M56 1S4, tel. 416/595–1700).

The **Consulate General of Britain** (777 Bay St., at the corner of College St., M56 2G2, tel. 416/593–1267).

For all other consulates—there are dozens of countries represented in Toronto—look up "Consulate Generals" in the white pages of the phone book.

Emergencies Dial 911 for **police** and **ambulance**.

Doctors and Dentists Check the Yellow Pages or ask at your hotel desk. Also, call **Dial-a-Doctor** (tel. 416/492–4713), or the **Dental Emergency Service** (tel. 416/924–8041).

24-hour Pharmacies **Pharma Plus Drugmart** (Church St. and Wellesley Ave., tel. 416/924–7760); **Lucliff Place** (700 Bay and Gerrard, tel. 416/979–2424); **Shoppers Drug Mart** (2500 Hurontario St., Mississauga, tel. 416/277–3665).

Road Emergencies The **CAA** (the Canadian version of AAA) has 24-hour road service (tel. 416/966–3000).

The following gas stations and auto-repair shops are open 24 hours: **Texaco Stations,** at 153 Dundas St. West, behind New City Hall; 333 Davenport, just south of Casa Loma; and 601 Eglington Ave. East, west of the Ontario Science Center. **Cross Town Service Center,** 1467 Bathurst Street, at St. Clair Ave. West, well known and respected for both gas and repairs. **Jim McCormack Esso,** 2901 Sheppard Ave. East, in the Scarborough area, heading toward the Metro Zoo. **Guido's Esso,** 1104 Albion Road, not far from the airport.

Guided Tours

Orientation **Toronto Harbour and Islands Boat Tours** are provided by **Gray Line** (tel. 416/364–2412) on attractive, sleek, Amsterdam-style touring boats, with competent tour guides. The hourly tour visits the Toronto Islands, with lovely views of the Toronto cityscape. Boats leave from the Queen's Quay Terminal daily from early May through mid-October noon–5. Tours leave as late as 7:15 PM during the summer. Other boats depart from the Harbour Castle Westin. At press time, prices are $9.95 adults, $7.95 students and senior citizens, $5.95 children ages 4–14, but rates may increase, so call ahead.

Toronto Tours (tel. 416/869–1372 or 416/868–0400) also provides one-hour boat tours of the Toronto harborfront for similar prices from mid-May through October. It also runs an informative 90-minute tour aboard a restored 1920s trolley car, which goes by both city halls, and through the financial district and the historic St. Lawrence area. **Insight Planners** (tel. 416/868–6565) has been providing creative and reliable tours, particularly to art galleries, since 1974. **Reception Ontario** (tel. 416/636–0082) provides complete tour-planning services, including sightseeing tours, entertainment packages, hotel accommodations, and even guides in various languages. **Happy Day Tours** (tel. 416/593–6220) runs half-day tours of Toronto for about $30 per person, which include admission to Black Creek Pioneer Village and visits to the mansions of Forest Hills, Casa Loma, Chinatown, Queen's Park, Yorkville, and Harbourfront. Book ahead.

Gray Line Sightseeing Bus Tours (tel. 416/351–3311) runs tours during the high season that leave from the Bus Terminal (Bay and Dundas Sts.) and spend 2½ hours visiting such places as Eaton Centre, both city halls, Queen's Park, the University of Toronto, Yorkville, Ontario Place, and Casa Loma—the latter, for a full hour. These charming tours cost about $18 for adults, $12 for children under 12, and run April through November.

Special-interest **Antours** (tel. 416/481–2862) provides several tours of Niagara-on-the-Lake, which include lunch and major performances at the Shaw Festival. **Art Tours of Toronto** (tel. 416/845–4044) offers a series of fall and spring gallery and walking tours. Most tours include lunch, and range from $40 to $50 per person. The **Toronto Stock Exchange** (tel. 416/947–4676) has tours of its exciting new facilities weekdays at 2 PM. The **Bruce Trail Association** (tel. 416/690–4453) arranges day and overnight hikes around Toronto and environs.

Exploring Toronto

Well, now you're in Toronto, and probably in the downtown area. It's rather confusing, isn't it? But once you establish that Lake Ontario runs along the south of the city, and that the fabulous Harbourfront complex is there, as well as the ferry to the lovely Toronto Islands, you are well on your way to orienting yourself.

Imagine the downtown area of Toronto as a large rectangle. The southern boundary is, as you already know, Lake Ontario. The western edge, shooting north to Bloor Street (the northern edge) and beyond, is Spadina Avenue, near the foot of which stands the CN Tower, Harbourfront, and the spectacular new SkyDome Stadium. Just west of the rectangle along the waterfront are the Canadian National Exhibition grounds, site of the enormous annual fair, and Ontario Place, an amusement park built on man-made islands. On the east side of downtown, running from the lakefront north for hundreds of miles (believe it or not), is Yonge Street, which divides the city in half. University Avenue, a major road that parallels Yonge Street, for some reason changes its name to Avenue Road at the corner of Bloor Street, next to the Royal Ontario Museum. A further note: College Street, legitimately named, since many of the University of Toronto's buildings run along it, becomes Carlton Street where it intersects Yonge Street, then heads east.

Highlights for First-time Visitors

Casa Loma, Tour 3: Academia, Culture, Commercialism, Crassness
CN Tower, Tour 1: Waterfront, the Financial District, and the Underground City
Eaton Centre, Tour 2: From Eaton Centre to the City Halls and the Far and Middle East
Harbourfront and Toronto Islands, Tour 1: Waterfront, the Financial District, and the Underground City
Metro Toronto Zoo, *see* What to See and Do with Children
Ontario Science Centre, *see* What to See and Do with Children
Royal Ontario Museum, Tour 3: Academia, Culture, etc.

Tour 1: Waterfront, the Financial District, and the Underground City

Numbers in the margin correspond to points of interest on the Tour 1 map.

Since, as we noted, Toronto has a waterfront as its southernmost border, it seems logical that we begin there. And it shouldn't be too hard to get there, since it's just south of Union Station, which is the terminus of both the University Avenue/Spadina Avenue and Yonge Street subways. Until quite recently, Toronto was notoriously negligent about its waterfront. The Gardiner Expressway, Lakeshore Boulevard, and a network of rusty rail yards stood as hideous barriers to the natural beauty of Lake Ontario.

Just over a decade ago the various levels of government—city, Metro, provincial (Ontario), and federal (Ottawa)—began a struggle to change this unfortunate situation. By that time, most of the area just south of the Gardiner Expressway and Lakeshore Boulevard was overflowing with grain silos, various warehouses, and unattractive (and unsweet-smelling) towers of malt, used by local breweries.

Part of the answer was the building of a very handsome hotel, the Harbour Castle Westin, and an attractive tower of condominiums at the foot of Yonge Street on Harbourfront. The hotel has an exterior, glassed-in elevator that offers guests a view of the waterfront and the Toronto Islands.

Toronto Islands
❶ Just behind the giant Harbour Castle Westin is the debarkation point for ferries to the **Toronto Islands,** surely one of the highlights of any trip to the city—especially from May to Oc-

tober. It takes only eight minutes for the quaint little ferries to chug across the tiny bay. The islands make up one of the world's great parks.

The four thin, curved, tree-lined islands—Centre, Ward's, Algonquin, and Hanlan's Point—have been attracting visitors since 1833, four years before Victoria became queen and just a year before the town of York changed its name to Toronto. And the more than 550 acres of parkland are irresistible, especially during the hot summer months.

The beaches on Ward's tend to be the least crowded. They're also the cleanest, although there have been problems with the cleanliness of Lake Ontario's water over the past decade. Except for the hottest days in August, the Great Lake tends to be uncomfortably chilly, so bring appropriate clothing. You'll be wise to rent a bike for an hour or more and work your way across the interconnected islands.

If you are traveling with children, Centre Island is certainly the one to check out first. A few hundred yards from the ferry docks lies **Centreville,** an amusement park that's supposed to be a turn-of-the-century children's village. The concept works wondrously well: True, the pizza, fries, and hot dogs are barely edible—pack a lunch!—but on the little Main Street there are charming shops, a town hall, a little railroad station, and more than a dozen rides, including a restored 1890s merry-go-round with more than four dozen hand-carved animals. And there's no entrance fee to the modest, 14-acre amusement park, although you'll have to pay a nominal charge for each ride or buy an all-day pass. Perhaps most enjoyable for children is the free **Far Enough Farm,** which is near enough to walk to. It has all kinds of animals to pet and feed, ranging from piglets to geese, cows to birds. *Tel. 416/363–1112. Centreville is open 10:30–8 weekends only Apr. 30–May 15; daily Victoria Day (mid-May)– Labor Day; weekends again Sept. 10–25.*

All transportation on these islands comes to you compliments of your feet: No cars are allowed anywhere. Your nostrils will wonder at the lack of exhaust fumes, while your feet will wonder why you insist on walking all the way along the boardwalk from Centre to Ward's Island (2½ kilometers, or 1½ miles).

Once you've arrived, you'll find **Gibraltar Lighthouse,** built back in 1808, making it the oldest monument in the city that is still standing on its original site. Right next to it is a pond stocked with rainbow trout, and a concession for buying bait and renting rods.

Encircling the islands are sandy beaches, the best ones being those on the southeast tip of Ward's, the southernmost edge of Centre, and the west side of Hanlan's. There are free changing rooms near each of these areas, but no facilities for checking your clothes. Swimming in the various lagoons and channels is prohibited. The winter can be bitter cold on the islands, but snowshoeing and cross-country skiing, with downtown Toronto over your shoulder, will be irresistible to many. In the summer, there are rowboat and canoe rentals, tennis courts, gardens, playgrounds, and a wildlife sanctuary.

The ferries run irregularly during the winter: every half hour or so until 10 or 11 AM, and then every hour or so thereafter. In the summer, the ferries leave three times an hour at the foot of

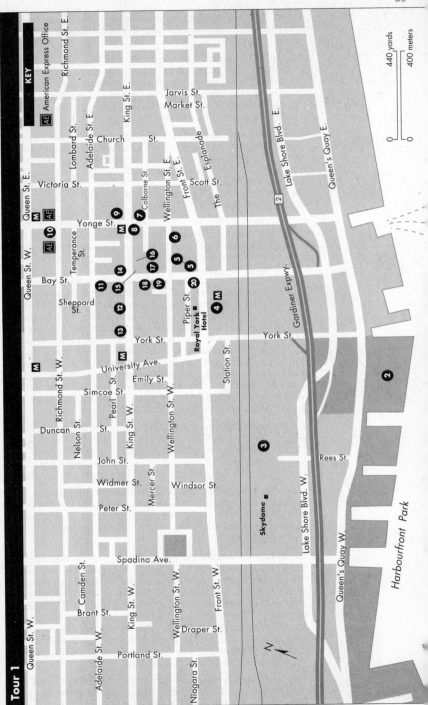

Tour 1

KEY

AE American Express Office

Queen St. E.
Richmond St. E.
Jarvis St.
Market St.
King St. E.
Church St.
Lombard St.
Adelaide St. E.
Victoria St.
Colborne St.
Wellington St. E.
Front St. E.
Scott St.
The Esplanade
Queen St. E.
Queen St. W.
Yonge St.
Temperance St.
Bay St.
Sheppard St.
York St.
Richmond St. W.
University Ave.
Emily St.
Simcoe St.
Pearl St.
Duncan St.
Nelson St.
John St.
Widmer St.
Peter St.
Mercer St.
Windsor St.
King St. W.
Wellington St. W.
Front St. W.
Spadina Ave.
Camden St.
Brant St.
King St. W.
Adelaide St. W.
Portland St.
Niagara St.
Draper St.
Wellington St. W.
Station St.
Piper St.
Royal York Hotel
York St.
Rees St.
Lake Shore Blvd. E.
Lake Shore Blvd. W.
Queen's Quay E.
Queen's Quay W.
Gardiner Expwy.
Skydome
Harbourfront Park
Queen St. W.

440 yards
400 meters

1 The Toronto Islands

The Bay, **10**
BCE Place, **5**
Bank of Commerce building, **16**
Bank of Nova Scotia, **14**
Canada Permanent Trust Building, **11**

CN Tower, **3**
Commerce Court, **17**
Dominion Bank building, **8**
15 Wellington St. W. **6**
First Canadian Place, **12**

Former Toronto Stock Exchange building, **19**
Harbourfront, **2**
"Old" Bank of Commerce Tower, **15**

Royal Bank building, **9**
Royal Bank Plaza, **20**
Toronto-Dominion Centre, **18**

The Toronto Islands, **1**
Toronto Stock Exchange, **13**
Traders Bank, **7**
Union Station, **4**

Bay Street. The cost is $3 adults, $1.25 students and senior citizens, $1 children 2–14, children under 2 free. For a recording giving the schedule and prices, call 416/392–8193; for other information, call 416/392–8186.

Harbourfront

❷

Back at the ferry docks on the mainland, your next move should be to **Harbourfront.** This is a trip that is well worth planning for: Check *Now, eye* magazine, as well as the Thursday edition of the *Toronto Star,* and Saturday's *Globe and Mail* to see what concerts, dances, art shows, and festivals are taking place, and build your visit around them.

Harbourfront is within walking distance of Union Station. Drivers should head for the foot of Bay Street or Spadina Avenue, and park in one of the many lots. For information, call 416/364–5665. There's also a streetcar that swings around from Union Station to Harbourfront, and on to Spadina Avenue.

For many years, as we said, Toronto had good reason to be ashamed of its God-given, man-taken-away waterfront. Today, Harbourfront has become a 100-acre culture and recreation center, drawing more than 3 million visitors each year. Stretching from just west of the Harbour Castle Westin for nearly a mile to Bathurst Street, the complex has become the scene of fabulous entertainment, exquisite buildings, glorious attractions—a true match for San Francisco's Pier 39 and Baltimore's Inner Harbor. Sadly, there have been numerous problems with funding this wonderful concept: All three levels of government—federal, provincial, and local—are fighting over who should pay and what may have to be closed. Still, even if some of Harbourfront's attractions are lost in the bureaucratic flip-flop, this will remain one of Toronto's best tourist spots.

Highlights are many. The **Queen's Quay** (pronounced "key") **Terminal** is a must: The 57-year-old food warehouse was transformed in 1983, at a cost of more than $60 million, into a magnificent eight-story structure with delightful specialty shops, eateries, and the handsome 450-seat Premiere Dance Theatre. The "Traffic Hotline" will even give you current information on "the fastest and easiest route to Queen's Quay," 24 hours a day, seven days a week (tel. 416/363–4411).

Contemporary art exhibits of painting and sculpture, architecture and video, photography and design now take place at the **Power Plant,** just west of Queen's Quay. (The building started in 1927 as a power station for an ice-making plant; you can spot it by the tall red smokestack.)

York Quay Centre has concerts, live theater, readings, even skilled artisans at work in open crafts studios. A shallow pond at the south end is used for canoe lessons in warmer months, and as the largest artificial ice-skating rink in North America in more wintry times. The Nautical Centre nearby has many private firms offering lessons in sailing and canoeing, and vessels for rent.

On **Maple Leaf Quay,** the very popular **Antique Market** takes place every day but Monday. The 70 dealers triple in number each Sunday.

❸

From Harbourfront, it's a short walk to the **CN Tower,** an attraction second only to Eaton Centre.

The CN Tower, the tallest freestanding structure in the world, is found on Front Street, near Spadina Avenue, not far from the waterfront. It's fully 1,815 feet, 5 inches high, and it really is worth a visit, if the weather is clear.

Four elevators zoom up the outside of the $57 million tower. The ride takes but a minute, going at 20 feet a second, a rate of ascent similar to that of a jet-plane takeoff. But each elevator has only one floor-to-ceiling glass wall, preventing vertigo.

The **Skypod,** about two-thirds up the tower, is seven stories high and has two observation decks, a nightclub, and a revolving restaurant. It also has oodles of microwave equipment that is not open to the public but is its true raison d'être.

Level 2 is the **outdoor observation deck,** with an enclosed promenade, and an outdoor balcony for looking straight down at the ground. Level 3 of the Skypod, the **indoor observation deck,** has not only conventional telescopes but also high-powered peritelescopes that almost simulate flight. Also here is a unique Tour Wand System, which provides an audio tour of the City of Toronto. A minitheater shows a presentation on the CN Tower.

The **Space Deck,** which is 33 stories higher, costs $2.50 extra; at an elevation of 1,465 feet, it is the world's highest public observation gallery. But even from the Skypod below, you can often see Lake Simcoe to the north and the mist rising from Niagara Falls to the south. All the decks provide spectacular panoramic views of Toronto, Lake Ontario, and the Toronto Islands. *CN Tower, 301 Front St. W, tel. 416/360–8500. Observation deck: $11.95 adults, $7.95 senior citizens, $5.95 children under 13. Peak visiting hours: 11–4, especially on weekends. Open summers, daily 10 AM–midnight; the rest of the year, opening and closing times vary up to an hour, depending on season; call ahead.*

Tour of the Universe, located at the base of the CN Tower, is a charming one-hour simulated space shuttle journey to Jupiter in the year 2019, with a 64-screen Multivision Wall that briefs you on your upcoming flight, laser "inoculation," an Inter-Planetary Passport souvenir, and a too-brief ride in a flight simulator that provides physical motion to match the spectacular special-effects film. It's very well done and a good attraction to combine with the CN Tower visit. *Tel. 416/360–8500. Admission: $7.95 adults, $6.95 senior citizens, $5.35 children 13–16. Admission to Jupiter and CN Tower: $16.95 adults, $10.50 senior citizens, $8.95 children.*

Financial District

4 One doesn't always recommend visits to a train station, but **Union Station** is special. On the south side of Front Street, between Bay and York streets (and across from the handsome Royal York Hotel), Union Station is a most historic building, though it is of this century. It was designed back in 1907, when trains were still as exciting as space shuttles are today, and it was opened in 1927 by the Prince of Wales. Try to imagine the awe of the immigrants who poured into Toronto between the wars by the tens of thousands, staring up at the towering ceiling of Italian tile or leaning against one of the 22 pillars, each one 40 feet tall and weighing 75 tons. Walk along the lengthy concourse and study the mellow reflection in its walls. Get a sense of the beauty of the light flooding through the high, arched windows at each end of the mammoth hall.

As you come out of Union Station, walk back to Yonge Street and the beautiful **Bank of Montreal** building, at the northwest corner of Front Street. Built around the old bank is one of the two towers of the striking new **BCE Place,** with its exquisite, huge Galleria, completed in mid-1992, which, as one architectural critic wrote, "brings a new level of sophistication to the interior spaces of the city's core." Just steps north is a shabby row of shops, which are among the oldest surviving commercial buildings in the city. Many of the original Georgian facades have been drastically altered, but the one- and two-story buildings give you a sense of the scale of buildings from the 1850s and are the last remnants of the early business community of the then-brand-new city of Toronto.

6 Make a left turn at the first intersection, which is Wellington Street West. **Number 15** is the oldest building on this walk, an elegant stone bank designed in the Greek Revival style.

7 Head back a few steps to Yonge Street and go north again. On the northeast corner of Yonge and Colborne streets, at 67 Yonge Street, is **Traders Bank,** the first "skyscraper" of the city when it went up in 1905–06, complete with an observation deck. The next building to the north, built in 1913, helped make this among the tallest buildings in North America. It is still owned by **Canadian Pacific,** the largest private employer in Canada (planes, trains, hotels, and more).

8 At the southwest corner of King and Yonge streets is the **Dominion Bank building,** erected in 1913 by the same architects who designed the voluptuous Bank of Montreal. It's a classic Chicago-style skyscraper and is well worth a visit inside. Climb the marble and bronze stairway to the opulent banking hall on the second floor, and enjoy the marble floor, marble walls, and the ornate plaster ceiling, which features the coats of arms of the then nine Canadian provinces.

9 On the northeast corner is the original **Royal Bank building,** also put up in 1913. Note the distinctive cornice, the overhanging roof, the decorative pattern of sculpted ox skulls above the ground-floor windows, and the classically detailed leaves at the top of the Corinthian columns.

10 Farther north along Yonge Street, at Richmond Street West, is the original Simpsons department store, now **The Bay.** Built in 1895, it was one of the city's first buildings with a steel-frame construction. There are attractive terra-cotta decorations in the section closest to Yonge Street, which went up in 1908; the part along Richmond Street, near Bay Street, added in 1928, is a fine example of the Art Deco style, popular between the two world wars.

11 Continue a few steps west to Bay Street, a name synonymous with finance and power in Canada, as Wall Street is in the United States. Head south (left), back toward the lakefront. Just south of Adelaide Street, on the west side of Bay Street, is the **Canada Permanent Trust Building** (320 Bay St.). Built in the very year of the stock market crash (and we don't mean the 1987 one), it's a skyscraper in the New York wedding-cake style. Look up at the ornate stone carvings both on the lower stories and on the top, where carved, stylized faces peer down to the street below. Walk through the imposing vaulted entrance, with its polished brass doors, and note that even the elevator doors in the foyer are embossed brass. The spacious banking hall has a vaulted ceiling, marble walls and pillars, and a marble floor with mosaic borders.

12 Turn right (west) along King Street, and on your right is the first of the towering bank buildings that have defined Toronto's skyline over the past two decades. This is **First Canadian Place** (100 King St. W), built in the early 1970s. Its 72 stories were deliberately faced with white marble to contrast with the black of the Toronto-Dominion Centre, to the south, and with the silver of the Commerce Court Tower.

13 Farther along you come to the second phase of the project, opened in 1983, which houses the ultramodern **Toronto Stock Exchange (TSE).** The Exchange Tower (2 First Canadian Pl.) has a Visitor's Center, where visitors can learn about the securities industry through colorful displays, or even join in daily presentations. The attractions are many: a 100-foot public gallery, a 140-seat auditorium, recorded tours, and a mini–slide show of the TSE 300 Composite Index (an echo of the Dow Jones Average). *Tel. 416/947–4670. Admission free. Open weekdays 9:30–4. Public tour daily at 2.*

14 On the northeast corner of King and Bay streets (44 King St. W) is the **Bank of Nova Scotia.** Built between 1949 and 1951, and partially replaced by the recently completed Scotia Tower just to the east, it has sculptural panels inspired by Greek mythology above the large, exterior windows. In the lobby, there are reliefs symbolizing four regions of Canada and a brightly colored gilded plaster ceiling. The original stainless steel-and-glass stairway with marine motifs is attractive, as are the marble counters and floors. The north wall relief depicts some of the industries and enterprises financed by the bank.

15 On the southeast corner of King and Bay streets is the **"Old" Bank of Commerce Tower,** which for a third of a century was the tallest building in the British Commonwealth. Its base has bas-relief carvings, and marvelous animal and floral ornamentation around the vaulted entrance. Because the top is set back, you must look up to see the huge, carved human heads on all four sides of the building.

16 The **Bank of Commerce building** (25 King St. W) was built in the two years following the stock market crash of 1929, but the hard times didn't prevent the creation of a stunning interior of marble floors, limestone walls, and bronze vestibule doors decorated with masks, owls, and animals. In the alcoves on each side of the entrance are murals that trace the history of transportation. The bronze elevator doors are richly decorated, the vaulted banking hall is lit by period chandeliers, and each desk has its own lamp.

17 Just south of the "old tower," at 243 Bay Street, is **Commerce Court,** the bank's 57-story stainless-steel sister. And due west, just across Bay Street, also on the south side of King Street, **18** are the two black towers of the **Toronto-Dominion Centre,** the first International-style skyscrapers built in Toronto, thanks to the "less is more" man, Mies van der Rohe. The two towers went up in the mid-1960s, and they are starkly plain and stripped of ornament. The only decoration consists of geometric repetition, and the only extravagance is the use of rich materials, such as marble counters and leather-covered furniture.

⑲ Immediately south of the T-D Centre towers, at 232 Bay Street, is the **former Toronto Stock Exchange building,** which, for close to half a century, was the financial hub of Toronto. Built in 1937 of polished pink granite and smooth buff limestone, it's a delightful example of Art Deco design. The stainless-steel doors are a wonder, as is the wise and witty stone frieze carved above them. Don't miss the hilarious social commentary up there—the banker with the top hat marching behind the laborer, his hand sneaking into the worker's pocket.

⑳ Walk south another block to the northwest corner of Bay and Front streets: There, in all its golden glory, is the **Royal Bank Plaza,** built only in 1976 but already a classic of its kind. Be sure to go into the 120-foot-high banking hall and admire the lovely hanging sculpture by Jesus Raphael Soto.

Underground City The origins of Toronto's **Underground City**—purportedly the largest pedestrian walkway in the world, and more than four times the size of Montréal's—go back over a generation. One can walk—and shop, eat, and browse—without ever seeing the light of day, from beneath Union Station to the Royal York Hotel, the Toronto-Dominion Centre, First Canadian Place, the Sheraton Centre, the Eaton Centre, and the Atrium. Altogether, it extends through nearly three miles of tunnels and seven subway stops.

Enter the subterranean community from anywhere between Dundas Street on the north and Union Station on the south, and you'll encounter everything from art exhibitions to buskers (the city actually auditions young musicians and licenses the best to perform throughout its subway system and elsewhere) to walkways, fountains, and trees growing as much as two stories high. Because up to 50% of the complex lies underneath Toronto's multibillion-dollar Financial District, you will keep bumping into men and women in business suits, browsing or on lunch breaks.

Tour 2: From Eaton Centre to the City Halls and the Far and Middle East

Numbers in the margin correspond to points of interest on the Tours 2 and 3 map.

From the corners of Yonge and Queen streets, one can begin a tour that will include several of this city's most popular attractions, as well as some of its most interesting neighborhoods. Alas, one of these, Eaton Centre, is closed on Sunday, while others thrive on what is still considered the Lord's Day in the province of Ontario. Still, the following walking/driving tour should make for a very pleasant day in the central and western portions of Toronto's downtown.

Eaton Centre and City Hall ㉑ **Eaton Centre,** a 3-million-square-foot building that extends along the west side of Yonge Street all the way from Queen Street up to Dundas Street (with subway stops at each end), has quickly become the number-one tourist attraction of Toronto. Even people who rank shopping with the flu will still be charmed, even dazzled, for this is a very beautiful environment indeed. From its graceful glass roof, arching 127 feet above the lowest of the mall levels, to Michael Snow's exquisite flock of fiberglass Canada geese floating poetically in the open space of the Galleria, to the glass-enclosed elevators, porthole windows, and nearly two dozen long and graceful escalators, there are plenty of good reasons for visiting Eaton Centre.

Galleria Level 1 contains two food courts; popularly priced fashions; photo, electronics, and record stores; and much "convenience" merchandise. Level 2 is directed to the middle-income shopper, while Level 3, suitably, has the highest elevation, fashion, and prices. **Eaton's,** one of Canada's classic department-store chains, has a nine-floor branch here. At the southern end of Level 3 is a skywalk that connects the Centre to the seven-floor **The Bay** department store across Queen Street.

Dozens of restaurants, from snack to full-service, can be found here. A 17-theater cinema complex—the initial unit of the now worldwide Cineplex chain—is located at the Dundas Street entrance. *Tel. 416/598–2322 for Eaton Centre information. Open weekdays 10–9, Sat. 9:30–6, Sun. 1–5.*

Exit the Eaton Centre at Queen Street and walk just one long block west to Toronto's city halls. Yes, the plural is correct.

㉒ Old City Hall is the very beautiful building at the northeast corner of Queen and Bay streets, sweetly coexisting with the **㉓** futuristic **New City Hall,** just across the street, on the west side. The creator of the old one, which opened in 1899, was none other than E.J. Lennox, who would later design Casa Loma. It was considered one of North America's most impressive municipal halls in its heyday, and since the opening of its younger sister, it has been the site for the provincial courts, county offices, and thousands of low-cost marriages. Do note the hideous gargoyles above the front steps, which were apparently the architect's witty way of mocking certain politicians of the time. The great stained-glass window as you enter is attractive, and the handsome old structure stands in delightful contrast to its daring and unique sibling.

The New City Hall was the result of a massive international competition in 1958. The winning presentation by Finnish architect Viljo Revell was very controversial: two towers of differing height, and curved! But there was and is a logic to it all: An aerial view of the New City Hall shows a circular council chamber sitting like an eye between the two tower "eyelids." Within months of its opening in 1965, the New City Hall became a symbol of a thriving city.

Annual events at the New City Hall include the Spring Flower Show in late March; the Toronto Outdoor Art Exhibition early each July, and the Cavalcade of Lights from late November through Christmas each year, when more than 100,000 sparkling lights are illuminated across both city halls. *Tel. 416/392–7341; TDD 416/392–7354. Underground garage for 2,400 cars. Open weekdays 8:30–4:30. Free 30-minute guided tours. Cafeteria open daily 7:30–4.*

Chinatown and the Museums Just north of the New City Hall begins Toronto's main **Chinatown,** which is the largest in all of North America. There are more than 100,000 Chinese living in the city, which is not bad, considering that just over a century ago there was only one—Sam Ching, who ran a hand laundry on Adelaide Street. Today, Chinatown covers much of the area around Spadina Avenue from Queen Street to College Street, running along Dundas Street nearly as far east as Bay Street.

Tour 2

Tour 3

Tours 2 and 3

KEY

AE American Express Office

0   440 yards
0   400 meters

One of the best times to explore Chinatown is on a Sunday, when, up and down Spadina Avenue and along Dundas Street, Chinese music blasts from storefronts, cash registers ring, abacuses clack, and bakeries, markets, herbalists, and restaurants do their best business of the week. But whatever day you wander, we recommend that you start on Elizabeth Street, just north of the New City Hall, and walk north to Dundas Street, east toward Bay Street, then turn back and walk west to Spadina Avenue. You will be thrilled by the diversity, the excitement, the liveliness—the sheer foreignness of it all.

(24) At the ***Shing Wah Daily News,*** on Hagerman Street near Bay Street (tel. 416/977–3745) you can see some of the 10,000 Chinese characters being typeset and printed, plus samples of **(25)** Blondie and Dagwood speaking Cantonese. **Mon Kuo Trading Co. Ltd.** (120 Elizabeth St.) cultivates tens of thousands of bean sprouts under a sprinkler system in the basement, on their one-week growth to maturity.

On Dundas Street, you'll pass shops selling reasonably priced silk blouses and antique porcelain, silk kimonos for less than half the price elsewhere, lovely sake sets, and women's silk **(26)** suits. Huge Chinese characters hang over the **52nd Division police station,** a large building on the west side of Simcoe Street, just south of Dundas Street. Many of the banks still have abacuses, for those who prefer the 4,000-year-old "hand-held calculators" to modern ones.

(27) Turn south off Dundas Street to the **Ontario College of Art** (100 McCaul St.), one of the major colleges of animation, design, advertising art, tapestry, glassblowing, sculpture, and painting **(28)** in Canada. Directly across the street is **Village by the Grange** (89 McCaul St.), an apartment and shopping complex with more than a hundred shops selling everything from ethnic fast food to serious art. It's a perfect example of wise, careful blending of the commercial and the residential.

(29) Return to Dundas Street and head west to the **Art Gallery of Ontario,** which has been slowly but steadily evolving into one of the better art museums in North America. From extremely modest beginnings in 1900, the AGO is now in the big league in terms of exhibits and support. Recent international exhibits of King Tut, Van Gogh, Turner, Judy Chicago, William Blake, and Picasso will give you an idea of the gallery's importance, image, and profile. The **Henry Moore Sculpture Centre** on the second floor has the largest public collection of Moore's sculpture in the world. Also on the second floor is the **Samuel and Ayala Zacks Wing,** with its fine collection of 20th-century sculpture. The **Canadian Wing** includes major works by such northern lights as Emily Carr, Cornelius Krieghoff, David Milne, and Homer Watson. On the lower level is a "hands-on" room where children are invited to paint, make slides, and otherwise creatively muck about (open Sunday, summers, and holidays).

The Art Gallery of Ontario also has a growing collection of Rembrandt, Hals, Van Dyck, Hogarth, Reynolds, Chardin, Renoir, de Kooning, Rothko, Oldenburg, Picasso, Rodin, Degas, Matisse, and many others. And it also has **The Grange,** a historic house just behind the AGO, a perfect place to browse, either before or after a visit to the art gallery. The recently completed $58-million renovation has made the AGO all the more satisfying, albeit much more expensive. *317 Dundas St.*

W, 3 blocks west of the St. Patrick station of the University subway line, tel. 416/977–0414. Admission: $7.50 adults, $4 senior
citizens and students, children under 12 free with a paying
adult, $15 families (up to 6 members). Open Thurs. and week-
ends 10–5:30; Wed. and Fri. 10–10. Closed Mon. and Tues. except
holidays, when open 10–5:30.

**Spadina and the
Marketplaces**
Toronto's widest street, **Spadina Avenue,** has been pronounced
"Spa-*dye*-nah" for a century and a half, and we are too polite
to point out that it really should be called "Spa-*dee*-na." The
stretch of Spadina from Queen Street to College Street has
never been fashionable, or even worth a visit by most tourists.
Way back, it was just a collection of inexpensive stores, factories that sold to you wholesale if you had connections, ethnic
food and fruit stores, and eateries that gave you your two cents'
worth, usually plain.

And so it remains, with the exception of some often first-class,
if modest-looking, Chinese restaurants sprinkled throughout
the area. Each new wave of immigrants—Jewish, Chinese,
Portuguese, East and West Indian, South American—added
its own flavor to the mix, but Spadina-Kensington's basic bill
of fare is still "bargains galore." Here you'll find gourmet
cheeses at gourmet prices, fresh (no, not fresh-frozen) ocean
fish, fine European kitchenware at half the price of that in
stores in the Yorkville area, yards of remnants piled high in
bins, designer clothes minus the labels, and the occasional
rock-and-roll night spot and interesting greasy spoon.

For any visitor who plans to be in Toronto for more than four
or five days, a few hours exploring the ins and outs of Spadina's
garment district, between College and Queen, could bring
great pleasure—and even greater bargains. Park your car at
the lot just west of Spadina Avenue on St. Andrew's Street (a
long block north of Dundas Street), or take the College or
Queen streetcar to Spadina Avenue. (Also, *see* Shopping,
below.)

㉚ Kensington Market is a delightful side tour off Spadina Avenue.
Here, the bargains are of the more edible kind. All your senses
will be titillated by this old, steamy, smelly, raucous, colorful,
European-style marketplace. Come and explore, especially
during warmer weather, when the goods pour out into the narrow streets: Russian rye breads, barrels of dill pickles, fresh
fish on ice, mountains of cheese, bushels of ripe fruit, and crates
of chickens and rabbits that will have your children both gig-
gling and horrified. Jewish and Eastern European stores sit
side by side with Portuguese, Caribbean, Latin American, and
East Indian stores—with Vietnamese, Japanese, and Chinese
establishments sprinkled throughout. Most shops are open
every day except Sunday, from as early as 6 AM.

Afterward, you can rest in **Bellevue Square** (corner of Denison
Square and Augusta Place), a lovely little park with shady
trees, benches, and a wading pool and playground for children.

Tour 3: Academia, Culture,
Commercialism, Crassness

University Avenue, running from Front Street for about three
miles north to Bloor Street, where it changes its name to Avenue Road and continues north, is one of Toronto's few mistakes.

It's horribly boring, with hospital after office building after insurance company after office building. Yet it is still an interesting start for a healthy walk, because it does have lovely flower beds and fountains in a well-maintained strip along its middle. Still, you may wish to drive this part of the tour.

31 One highlight is **Campbell House** (northwest corner of Queen Street and University Avenue), the stately Georgian mansion of Sir William Campbell, the sixth chief justice of Upper Canada. Built in 1822 and tastefully restored with elegant 18th- and early 19th-century furniture, it is one of Toronto's most charming "living museums." Costumed hostesses will tell you about the social life of the upper class. *Tel. 416/597–0227. Admission: $2.50 adults, $1.25 students and senior citizens. Guided tours available. Open Oct.–mid-May, weekdays 9:30–11:30 and 2:30–4:30; summers, weekdays 9:30–11:30 and 2:30–4:30, weekends noon–4:30.*

32 College Street is the southern boundary of the **University of Toronto.** It goes back to 1827, when King George IV signed a charter for a "King's College in the Town of York, Capital of Upper Canada." The Church of England had control then, but by 1850 the college was proclaimed nondenominational, renamed the University of Toronto, and put under the control of the province. And then, in a spirit of good Christian competition, the Anglicans started Trinity College, the Methodists began Victoria, and the Roman Catholics begat St. Michael's; by the time the Presbyterians founded Knox College, the whole thing was almost out of hand.

But not really: The 17 schools and faculties are now united, and they welcome anyone who can pass the entrance exams and afford the tuition. The architecture is interesting, if uneven. We recommend a walking tour. Enter the campus just behind the Parliament buildings, where Wellesley Street ends. Go under the bridge, past the guardhouse (whose keeper will not let you pass if you are encased in an automobile), and turn right, around King's College Circle.

33 At the top of the circle is **Hart House,** a Gothic-style student center built during the teens of this century by the Masseys— the folks who brought us Massey-Ferguson farm equipment, Massey Hall, Vincent Massey (a governor-general of Canada), and Raymond Massey, the actor. It was once an all-male enclave; today, anyone may visit the Great Hall and the library, both self-conscious imitations of Oxford and Cambridge. Check out the dining hall for its amazing stained-glass windows as well as its food, which is cheap and rather good.

As you continue around King's College Circle, you'll see on
34 your right the Romanesque **University College,** built in 1859.
35 Next is **Knox College,** whose Scottish origins are evident in the bagpipe music that escapes from the building at odd hours. It's been training ministers since 1844, although the building went up only yesterday—1915.

36 You may well wish to tip your hat to the **Medical Sciences Building,** which is no beauty but is where, in 1921, Drs. Banting, Best, and others discovered the insulin that has saved the lives of tens of millions of diabetics around the world.

There is lots more to see and do around the main campus of the
37 University of Toronto. Visit the **Public and Community Rela-**

tions Office (Room 133S, 27 King's College Circle, tel. 416/978–2021), across the field from Hart House, and pick up free maps of the school grounds. Guided one-hour walking tours are held on summer weekdays, setting out from the map room of Hart House at 10:30, 12:30, and 2:30 (tel. 416/978–5000).

Back at College Street and University Avenue, you can see the Victorian structure of the Parliament buildings to the north, with Queen's Park just north of them.

Queen's Park There are a number of meanings to **Queen's Park,** for the native
38 Torontonian as well as the visitor. The term can refer to the charming circular park just a few hundred yards south of the Royal Ontario Museum (on University Avenue, just below Bloor Street). This is a grand place to rest your feet after a long day of shopping or visiting the Royal Ontario Museum. But
39 Queen's Park also refers to the **Ontario Legislative Building,** which is the home of the provincial parliament. The mammoth building was opened back in 1893, a century ago, and is really quite extraordinary, with its rectangular towers, triangular roofs, and circular and oval glass.

40 The **Parliament Buildings** look grotesque to some, with their pink exterior and heavy, almost Romanesque quality. But a close look will show the beautifully complex detail carved in the stone, and on the inside there are huge, lovely halls that echo half a millennium of English architecture. The long hallways are hung with hundreds of oils by Canadian artists, most of which capture scenes of the province's natural beauty. Should you choose to take one of the frequent (and free) tours, you will see the chamber where the 130 elected representatives from across Ontario, called MPPs (Members of Provincial Parliament), meet on a regular basis. There are two heritage rooms— one each for the parliamentary histories of Great Britain and Ontario—filled with old newspapers, periodicals, and pictures. And the lobby holds a fine collection of minerals and rocks of the province. On the lawn in front of the Parliament buildings, facing College Street, are many statues, including one of Queen Victoria and one of Canada's first prime minister, Sir John A. Macdonald. *Tel. 416/965–4028. Guided tours from mid-May to Labor Day, daily on the hour 9–4, weekends every half hour 9–11:30 and 1:30–4; frequent tours the rest of the year; also at 6:45 PM when evening sessions are held. University Ave. subway, College St. stop. There are parking lots in the area and metered parking around Queen's Park Circle.*

41 Just to the north of Queen's Park is the world-class **Royal Ontario Museum.** Once labeled "Canada's single greatest cultural asset" by the Canada Council, the museum floundered throughout much of its existence, which began in 1912 (the same day the *Titanic* sank). It never stopped collecting—always with brilliance—reaching more than 6 million items altogether. But by the 1970s, the monstrous building had leaky roofs, no climate control, and little space to display its glorious treasures. Today, thanks to a major fund-raising effort that brought in $80 million, the museum has the space it needs, and when expansion is completed sometime in the 1990s, the ROM will be the second-largest museum in North America, after New York's Metropolitan Museum of Art.

What makes the ROM unique is the fact that science, art, and archaeology exhibits are all under one roof. The **Dinosaur Col-**

lection will stun children and adults alike. The **Evolution Gallery** has an ongoing audiovisual program on Darwin's theories of evolution. The **Roman Gallery** has the most extensive collection of Roman artifacts in Canada. And the **European Musical Instruments Gallery** has a revolutionary audio system and more than 1,200 instruments dating back to the late 16th century. The **Discovery Gallery** allows children (over age 6) to handle objects from the ROM's collections and to study them, using microscopes, ultraviolet light, and magnifying glasses.

The **Bat Cave,** opened in early 1988, contains 4,000 freeze-dried and artificial bats in a lifelike presentation. Piped-in narration directs visitors on a 15-minute walk through a dimly lit replica of an 8-foot-high limestone tunnel in Jamaica, filled with sounds of dripping water and bat squeaks. In early 1992, the brilliant **Ancient Egypt Gallery** reopened, joined with a brand-new **Nubia Gallery**—the only one in North America. *110 Queens Park, tel. 416/586–5549. Admission: $7 adults; $4 students and senior citizens; children under 4 free; $15 family (up to 6 members). Senior citizens free Tues. (including Gardiner Museum and planetarium shows); all others free Tues. after 4:30. Open daily 10–6 (Tues. and Thurs. until 8). Closed Mon. from Labor Day to mid-May and New Year's Day. Discovery Gallery hours vary; please phone ahead. Take the University subway to the Museum stop; parking is expensive.*

㊷ The **George R. Gardiner Museum of Ceramic Art** has now merged with the ROM, meaning that it costs not a penny more to visit a magnificent $25 million collection of rare European ceramics. The collection features 17th-century English delftware and 18th-century yellow European porcelain. *Across University Ave. from the ROM, Open Tues.–Sun. 10–5.*

㊸ Just south of the ROM is the **McLaughlin Planetarium,** which attracts some 250,000 visitors a year. There are four new 45-minute star shows each year. Open since 1986 is the **Astrocentre,** which has hands-on exhibits, computer terminals designed for both adults and children, and an animated model of the star system. *Tel. 416/586–5736. Admission: $5.50 adults, $3.50 students and senior citizens, $2.75 children 6–18. Senior citizens free on Tues. Open same hours as the ROM, plus evening hours for the star shows. Tel. 416/586–5751 for a taped description of the current night sky.*

㊹ A five-minute walk south of the planetarium will bring you to the **Sigmund Samuel Canadiana Collection** (part of the ROM) of early Canadian furnishings, glassware, silver, and six room settings of 18th- and 19th-century furniture. *14 Queen's Park Crescent W, on the northwest corner of University Ave. and College St. Open Tues.–Sat. 10–5, Sun. 1–5.*

㊺ After so much culture, you may wish to enjoy one of the most dynamic and expensive areas of Toronto—**Bloor and Yorkville.** Some call it Toronto's Rodeo Drive; others call it Toronto's Fifth Avenue. One thing is certain: These blocks are packed with specialty shops, ritzy restaurants, and high-price stores specializing in designer clothes, furs, and jewels.

㊻ The **Colonnade,** on the south side of Bloor Street, a few doors east of University Avenue, has recently undergone a $10 million face-lift. In addition to several levels of luxury residential apartments and private offices, it also has more than two floors of stores selling quality leather goods, perfumes, jewelry, and

European apparel. Take a walk to the upper floor for a fascinating visit to **The Bata Shoe Museum Collection,** the only such exhibition in North America. Some artifacts displayed here are more than 4,000 years old and are from nearly every country in the world. Arranged in three main galleries, the museum features the interactive "Shoe Discovery Centre"; the "Highlights Gallery," boasting famous people's footwear; and the "Feature Gallery," in which North American footwear is displayed. Items such as pressurized sky-diving boots, ironspiked shoes used for crushing chestnuts, and smugglers clogs are just a few of the 4,500 pieces in this collection. *Tel. 416/924–7463. Admission to museum: $3 adults, $1 students, senior citizens, and children, $6 families. Open Tues.–Sun. 11–6.*

A block north of Bloor and Yonge streets is the magnificent **❹ Metropolitan Toronto Library.** Arranged around a tall and wide interior atrium, the library gives a fabulous sense of open space. It was designed by one of Canada's most admired architects, Raymond Moriyama, who also created the Ontario Science Centre. Browsers will appreciate that fully one-third of the more than 1.3 million books—spread across 28 miles of shelves—are open to the public. In the many audio carrels, with headphones, you may listen to any one of more than 10,000 albums. The **Arthur Conan Doyle Room** houses the finest public collection of Holmesiana anywhere, with records, films, photos, books, manuscripts, and letters. *789 Yonge St., just steps north of Bloor St., tel. 416/393–7000. Open May–Sept., Mon.–Thurs. 9–9, Fri. 9–6, Sat. 9–5; Oct.–Apr., Sun. 1:30–5. To get an answer to any question, on any subject, tel. 416/393–7131.*

On the east side of Avenue Road, two blocks north of Bloor **❽** Street, is a don't-miss shopping area—**Hazelton Lanes** (tel. 416/968–8600). Offering everything from Swiss chocolates to Hermès silks and Giorgio Armani's latest fashions, this is a wonderful, magical paean to capitalism. And in 1989 it doubled, in size and glory, with the addition of some 80 new stores.

❾ Casa Loma (1 Austin Terr.; on Spadina Ave., south of St. Clair Ave. W and the St. Clair subway stop) is an honest-to-goodness 20th-century castle, with 98 rooms; two towers; secret panels; long, creepy passageways; and some of the best views of Toronto—all just a short distance from the heart of the city. The medieval-style castle was built shortly before World War I by Sir Henry Pellatt, a soldier and financier who spent more than $3 million to construct his dream. The architect E.J. Lennox, who also designed Toronto's Old City Hall and King Edward Hotel, created a remarkable structure; Toronto's "house on the hill" is a real treat. There are no more guided tours of Casa Loma—you now get automatic tape recordings. That's all for the best, because you can drift through at your own speed while the children rush off to the stables or towers. You'll have walked a good mile by the time you're done, so wear sensible shoes. *Tel. 416/923–1171. Admission: $8 adults, $4.50 senior citizens and children 6–16. Open daily 10–4. Closed Christmas Day and New Year's.*

What to See and Do with Children

Free Attractions The **ferry boat** to the **Toronto Islands** and **Far Enough Farm** (*see* Tour 1, *above*). The **David Dunlap Observatory** in Richmond Hill, just north of Metro Toronto, and the **McLaughlin Plane-**

tarium (*see* Tour 3, *above*). **Harbourfront** nearly always has free events and activities, from painting and sculpting to concerts and plays. **Ontario Place,** just west of Harbourfront, is a waterfront entertainment complex built on three man-made islands that contains something for everyone: the **Cinesphere,** a dome with a six-story movie screen that shows Imax and 70mm films; several shows in pods that float above the water; the *Haida,* a World War II destroyer that's fun to explore; the outdoor **Forum,** where nightly concerts take place; various eateries; and **Children's Village,** with water games, slides, puppet shows, clowns, magicians, and a children's theater. *South of Lakeshore Blvd. across from CNE grounds. Tel. 416/965–7711. Open daily mid-May–mid-Sept. Admission free. Bumper boats, pedal boats, Cinesphere, and concerts have nominal admission fees.*

Modestly Priced Attractions **Apple, strawberry,** and **raspberry picking** are available within a short drive of downtown Toronto. Our favorite place is **Al Ferri's** (15 minutes west of the airport, near the corner of Mississauga Road and Steeles Avenue; tel. 416/455–8202). Please check out Ferri's astonishingly wonderful Macoun apples—like Red Delicious merged with MacIntosh. Glorious! For a free list of places to pick fruits and vegetables in the vicinity of Toronto, call 416/965–7701. The **Art Gallery of Ontario's** hands-on room and Henry Moore sculpture that children love to climb are popular attractions; and the fascinating, historic **Grange** house is another affordable option (*see* Tour 2, *above*). **Casa Loma** (*see* Tour 3, *above*).

More Expensive Attractions The **Ontario Science Centre** has free movies and thrilling space, communications, laser, and electricity exhibits, and an irresistible new exhibit called Challenger. Also, be sure to check out the marvelous permanent exhibit called The Sport Show. *770 Don Mills Rd., about 11 km (7 mi) from downtown. Take the Yonge St. subway from downtown to the Eglinton station and Eglinton E bus to the Don Mills Parkway stop. Tel. 416/696–3127 or 416/429–4100. Admission: $6.25 adults, $5 youths 13–17, $2.25 children 5–12, children under 5 free, $15.75 families (up to 8 members: 2 adults and 6 children). Free after 4 PM Fri. Parking $2. Open Sun.–Thurs. and Sat. 10–6, Fri. 10–9.*

The **Young People's Theatre** (tel. 416/864–9732) often has excellent fare, as do **Roy Thomson Hall** (tel. 416/593–4828) and the **Minkler Auditorium** (tel. 416/491–8877).

The Metro Toronto Zoo was built for animals, not people. The Rouge Valley, just east of Toronto, was an inspired choice of site when it was built in the 1960s, with its varied terrain, from river valley to dense forest, where mammals, birds, reptiles, and fish have been grouped according to where they live in the wild. In most of the regions, you'll find remarkable botanical exhibits in enclosed, climate-controlled pavilions. Don't miss the three-ton banyan tree in the Indo-Malayan Pavilion, the fan-shaped traveler's palm from Madagascar in the African Pavilion, or the perfumed flowers of the jasmine vines in the Eurasian Pavilion. The "round-the-world tour" takes some three hours and is suitable for any kind of weather, because most of the time is spent inside pavilions. It's been estimated that it would take four full days to see everything in the Metro Zoo, so study the map you'll get at the zoo entrance and decide in advance what you wish to see most.

For the younger children, there is the delightful Littlefootland, a special area that allows contact with tame animals, such as rabbits and sheep. In the winter, cross-country skiers follow groomed trails that skirt the animal exhibits. Lessons and rentals are available. There is an electrically powered train that moves silently among the animals without frightening them. It can accommodate wheelchairs (available free inside the main gate), and all pavilions have ramp access. For those on a very tight budget, the zoo is free if you show up the last hour of the day, which is enough time to give you a taste of this very impressive, world-class zoo. *Meadowvale Rd., just north of Highway 401, in Scarborough, a 30-minute drive from downtown. Or take Bus 86A from the Kennedy subway station. Tel. 416/392–5900. Admission: $9 adults, $6 senior citizens and children 12–17, $4 children 5–11. Family rates available. Free parking in winter; parking Mar.–Oct. $4. Open daily except Christmas. Summer, daily 9:30–7; winter, daily 9:30–4:30.*

Off the Beaten Track

Watching the Italian promenade. St. Clair Avenue West, running from Bathurst Street to Dufferin Street and beyond, remains the heart of this city's vibrant Italian community. On many evenings, especially Sunday, the street is filled with thousands of men and women promenading between *gelaterie*, eyeing each other, and generally enjoying their neighbors.

Greektown on a Sunday. The Danforth (Bloor Street east of the Don Valley Parkway) has great Greek restaurants, gift shops, and hundreds of Greek Canadians promenading. Welcome to the Mediterranean!

There's no hotel more romantic than the **Guild Inn** (2010 Guildwood Pkwy., tel. 416/261–3331), and no view of Toronto more wonderful than from **Centre Island at sunset.**

Shopping

Toronto prides itself on having some of the finest shopping in North America; and, indeed, most of the world's name boutiques can be found here. There's also a large artistic and crafts community, with many art galleries, custom jewelers, clothing designers, and artisans selling everything from sophisticated glass sculpture to native art, traditional crafts, antiques, quilts, wood carvings, and pine furniture.

Local food items include wild rice, available in bulk or in gift packages, and maple syrup in jars or cans.

The biggest sale day of the year is Boxing Day, the first business day after Christmas, when nearly everything in the city, including furs, is half-price. In fact, clothing prices tend to drop even further as winter fades. Summer sales start in late June and continue through August.

Bargaining Shoppers can haggle at flea markets, including the Harbourfront Antique Market, and perhaps in the Chinatown and Kensington Market/Spadina Avenue areas.

Refund Information Visitors, including Canadians from other provinces, can receive a refund on the GST and on the 8% Ontario sales tax for purchases over $100 (*see* GST and Sales Tax in Staying in Canada, *above*).

Shopping Districts

The **Yorkville Avenue/Bloor Street area** is where you'll find the big fashion names, fine leather goods, important jewelers, some of the top private art galleries, upscale shoe stores, and discount china and glassware. Streets to explore include Yorkville Avenue, Cumberland Street, and Scollard Street, all running parallel to Bloor Street, and Hazelton Avenue, running north from Yorkville Avenue near Avenue Road. Hazelton Lanes, between Hazelton Avenue and Avenue Road, and the adjacent York Square are among the most chichi shopping areas in Canada, and they are headquarters for café society during the brief annual spell of warm weather.

On **Bloor Street** you'll find such wonderful stores as **Zoe,** with haute couture designs; **The Bay,** a department store with elegant, high-fashion designer clothes for men and women; **Holt Renfrew,** possibly the most stunning store in Toronto, with marble, chrome, glass, and glittering fashions for both sexes; **Eddie Bauer,** selling sturdily made and cleverly designed clothing, equipment, and accessories for all sports; **Harry Rosen** for men; **Georg Jensen;** and shoe shops like **Boutique Quinto** and **David's.** Très expensive, and très good.

The **Eaton Centre** is a very large galleria-style shopping center downtown, on Yonge Street between Queen and Dundas streets. With scores of large and small stores and restaurants, all sheltered from the weather, it's one of the city's major tourist attractions. Generally speaking, the lower levels are lower priced and the higher levels are more expensive.

Queen Street West, starting just west of University Avenue and continuing past Spadina Avenue, creeping ever westward past Bathurst Street, is a trendy area near the Ontario College of Art. Here, you'll find young, hip designers; new and used-book bookstores; vintage clothes; two comic-book stores, including the biggest in North America (**Silver Snail,** No. 367; see also Dragon Lady Comic Shop at No. 200); and the more progressive private galleries.

Harbourfront includes an antiques market that's Canada's biggest on Sunday, when there are about 200 dealers (390 Queen's Quay W, tel. 416/340–8377. Open Tues.–Fri. 11–6, Sat. 10–6, Sun. 8–6). The **Queen's Quay Terminal** is a renovated warehouse that now houses a collection of unique boutiques, craft stalls, patisseries, and so on; it's a great place to buy gifts. There's a free shuttle bus from Union Station, or it's a fairly easy walk. Parking is expensive.

Spadina Avenue, from Wellington Street north to College Street, has plenty of low-price clothing for the whole family, as well as fur and leather factory outlets. **Winner's,** south of King Street, is a good discount outlet for women and children. **Evex Luggage Centre,** 369 Spadina Avenue, south of College, has good discount luggage, handbags, and leather accessories.

Downtown Toronto has a vast underground maze of shopping warrens that burrow in between and underneath the office towers. The tenants of the **Underground City** are mostly the usual assortment of chain stores, and the shopping is rather dull;

also, directions are poorly marked. The network runs roughly from the Royal York Hotel near Union Station north to the Eaton Centre.

Department Stores

The major department stores have branches around the city and flagship stores downtown. They accept major credit cards and have liberal return policies. However, service tends to be very slow and uninformed compared with that of boutiques, and the stores generally lack the cachet of American stores like Bloomingdale's or Macy's. The big names are **Eaton's,** in the Eaton Centre, and **The Bay** (The Hudson's Bay Company), on Yonge Street between Queen and Richmond streets and at Yonge and Bloor streets.

Specialty Shops

Antiques and Galleries Yorkville is the headquarters of the establishment antiques dealers, including **Navarro Gallery** (33 Hazelton Ave., tel. 416/921–0031). There are several other pockets around town, including a strip along Queen Street East, roughly between Sherbourne and George streets.

The Allery (322½ Queen St. W, tel. 416/593–0853) specializes in antique prints and maps. **Art Metropole** (788 King St. W, tel. 416/367–2304) specializes in limited-edition, small-press, or self-published artists' books from around the world. **Ballen-ford Architectural Books** (98 Scollard St., tel. 416/960–0055) has Canada's largest selection of architectural titles and a gallery with usually interesting exhibits of architectural drawings and related work. **Jane Corkin Gallery** (179 John St., north of Queen St., tel. 416/979–1980) specializes in photography. In the same building is **Isaacs Gallery,** owned by Av Isaacs, godfather of many of the established Canadian artists. The more avant-garde galleries include **Cold City** (30 Duncan St.), **YYZ** (1087 Queen St. W), and **Mercer Union** (333 Adelaide St. W). Also check out **Toronto Photographers Workshop** and the other galleries at 80 Spadina Avenue, where you'll usually find at least one opening on a Saturday afternoon. **Prime Canadian Crafts** (229 Queen St. W, tel. 416/593–5750) has an ever-changing array of merchandise. **Quasi Modo** (789 Queen St. W, next door to Dufflet Pastries, tel. 416/366–8370) has a quirky collection of 20th-century furniture and design). You never know what will be on display: vintage bicycles, Noguchi lamps, a corrugated cardboard table by Frank Gehry. **20th Century** (23 Beverley St., just north of Queen St., tel. 416/598–2172) is for serious collectors of 20th-century design, particularly furniture, lamps, jewelry, and decorative arts. Many of the pieces are museum quality, and the owners are extremely erudite.

Books Toronto is rich in bookstores selling new books, used books, best-sellers, and remainders. If you just need a current magazine or a paperback for the plane, there are the ubiquitous chains—Coles, Classic Bookshops, and W. H. Smith. Otherwise, we recommend:

The **Albert Britnell Book Shop** (765 Yonge St., just north of Bloor St., tel. 416/924–3321) has been a Toronto legend since 1893, with a marvelous, British ambience and great browsing.

The **Book Cellar** (1560 Yonge St., above St. Clair Ave., tel. 416/967–5577; 142 Yorkville Ave., near Avenue Rd., tel. 416/925–9955) offers a fine choice of classical records, as well as international political and intellectual journals.

Book City has three locations (501 Bloor St. W, near Honest Ed's, tel. 416/961–4496; Carrot Common, 348 Danforth Ave., near Chester Station, tel. 416/469–9997; and 2350 Bloor St. W., tel. 416/766–9412). It's strong on good remaindered books and has a knowledgeable staff.

Edward's Books and Art, one of the loveliest minichains in the city, now at four locations (356 Queen St. W, near Spadina Ave., tel. 416/593–0126; 2179 Queen St. E, in The Beaches, tel. 416/698–1442; 170 Bloor St. W, in the Park Plaza Hotel, tel. 416/961–2428; and 2200 Yonge St., south of Eglinton Ave., tel. 416/487–5431), advertises huge discounts on best-sellers and remainders in every Saturday's *Globe and Mail.* All are open Sunday.

Longhouse Book Shop (recently relocated to 497 Bloor St. W, just west of Bathurst St., tel. 416/921–9995) stocks only Canadian titles, handsomely shelved or piled high on pine tables: more than 20,000 back titles and new publications.

Bob Miller Book Room (180 Bloor St. W, just northwest of the ROM, tel. 416/922–3557) has the best literature section in the city and a staff that has been with Bob for decades.

Pages Books and Magazines (256 Queen St. W, tel. 416/598–1447) has a wide selection of international and small-press literature; fashion and design books and magazines; and books on film, art, and literary criticism. This is one astoundingly intellectual bookstore!

This Ain't the Rosedale Library (483 Church St., south of Wellesley Ave., tel. 416/929–9912) stocks the largest selection of baseball books in Canada, as well as a good selection of fiction, poetry, photography, design, rock, and jazz books.

Writers & Co. (2005 Yonge Street near Davisville, a few blocks south of Eglinton, tel. 416/481–8432) is arguably Canada's finest literary bookstore, with hard-to-find poets, essayists, and world novelists. If you have been looking for a rare Caribbean poetry collection, a Swedish play in translation, or an Asian novella, this is the store to visit. It's a marvelous place, and they'll be happy to order any book for you.

Clothing **Atomic Age** (350 Queen St. W, tel. 416/977–1296) features the hottest young Toronto designers. (Also in the neighborhood are other stores for the young and zany: **Fab,** at No. 274; **290 Ion,** at No. 290; **B Scene,** at No. 352; **Fashion Crimes,** at No. 395; **Strange,** at No. 319; **Boomer,** for men at No. 309; **Metropolis,** at No. 265; and **I.X.L.,** at No. 198.)

Brown's (1975 Avenue Rd., south of Hwy. 401, tel. 416/489–1975) provides classic clothing for short men and women. There's also a store for men only (545 Queen St. W, tel. 416/368–5937). An offshoot is **Muskat & Brown** (2528 Yonge St., tel. 416/489–4005) for petite women.

Fetoun (97 Scollard St., tel. 416/923–3434) is one of the latest high-fashion emporiums for the nouveau riche. If you go to a lot of charity balls, this is the place to shop.

La Mode de Vija (601 Markham St., in Mirvish Village, tel. 416/534–6711) sells discount designer clothing with names like Anne Klein at good prices.

Sportables (Queen's Quay Terminal, tel. 416/360–6540) offers a good assortment of well-made casual wear in natural fibers.

Vintage Furs (39a Charles St. W, at Bloor and Bay Sts., tel. 416/960–5020) sells secondhand furs for men and women.

Food Markets   **Kensington Market** (northwest of Dundas St. and Spadina Ave.) is an outdoor market with a vibrant ethnic mix. Saturday is the best day to go, preferably by public transit, because parking is difficult.

St. Lawrence Market (Front St. and Jarvis St., tel. 416/392–7219) is best early on Saturday, when, in addition to the permanent indoor market on the south side of Front Street, there's a farmer's market in the building on the north side. The historic south market was once Toronto's city hall, and it fronted the lake before extensive landfill projects were undertaken.

Gift Ideas   **The Back Store** (2111 Yonge St., tel. 416/482–0426) has everything for a friend with an aching spine.

Bragg (446 Queen St., west of Spadina Ave., tel. 416/366–6717) has an amusing assortment of vintage bric-a-brac, china, cards, and jewelry.

Early Learning (387 Queen St. W, tel. 416/598–2135) sells European and Japanese playthings.

Filigree (1210 Yonge St., tel. 415/961–5223) has a good assortment of linens, as well as drawer liners, silver frames, and other Victorian pleasures. In the neighborhood are other gift shops selling fine glass and antiques.

Jewelry   **Secrett Jewel Salon** (150 Bloor St. W, tel. 416/967–7500) is a reputable source of unusual gemstones and fine new and estate jewelry; local gemologists consider it the best in town.

Sports and Fitness

Participant Sports

Contact the Ministry of Tourism and Recreation (Queen's Park, Toronto, Ont. M7A 2R2) for pamphlets on various activities. For information on sports activities in the province, call 800/268–3735 from anywhere in the continental United States and Canada (except the Northwest Territories and the Yukon). In Toronto, contact Ontario Travel (tel. 416/965–4008).

A number of fine **conservation areas** circle Metro Toronto, many less than a half-hour from downtown. Most have large swimming areas, sledding, and cross-country skiing, as well as skating, fishing, and boating. Contact the Metro Conservation Authority (tel. 416/661–6600) and ask for a pamphlet.

Bicycling   There are more than 29 kilometers (18 miles) of street bike routes cutting across the city and dozens more along safer paths through Toronto's many parks. Bikes can be rented on the Toronto Islands. The **Martin Goodman Trail** is a 19-kilometer (12-mile) strip that runs along the waterfront all the way from the Balmy Beach Club in the east end out past the western beaches southwest of High Park. Call the *Toronto Star* (tel. 416/367–2000) for a map.

Metro Parks Department (tel. 416/392–8186) has maps that show bike (and jogging) routes that run through Toronto parkland. **Ontario Cycling** (tel. 416/495–4141) has maps, booklets, and information.

Boating   Grenadier Pond, in High Park, Centre Island, Ontario Place, Harbourfront, and most of the Conservation Areas surrounding Metro Toronto rent canoes, punts, and/or sailboats.

Fishing   One does not have to go very far from downtown Toronto to catch trout, perch, bass, walleye, salmon, muskie, pike, and whitefish. Contact Communication Services, Wildlife Information, Ministry of Natural Resources (Queen's Park, Toronto M7A 1W3, tel. 416/965–4251).

Within Metro Toronto itself, fishing is permitted in the trout pond at Hanlan's Point on Toronto Island, as well as in Grenadier Pond in High Park. And the salmon fishing just off the Scarborough Bluffs, in Toronto's east end, is extraordinary.

There are more than 100 charter boats on Lake Ontario (about $60 for a half-day). Contact **Ontario Travel** (tel. 416/965–4008). Be warned, though: Some fish caught in this province have such high levels of mercury in them that you can take your temperature at the same time that you eat them. It's sad, but water pollution (including acid rain) has taken its toll upon the edibility of many fish in Ontario.

Golf   The season lasts only from April to late October. The top course is **Glen Abbey** (tel. 416/844–1800), where the Canadian Open Championships is held. Cart and greens fees will cost up to $75 on weekends, but this course is a real beauty.

Less challenging courses—and much closer to the heart of the city—include the **Don Valley Golf Course,** just south of Highway 401 (Yonge St., tel. 416/392–2465); the **Flemingdon Park Golf Club** (Don Mills Rd. and Eglinton Ave., tel. 416/429–1740). For other courses, contact Metro Parks (tel. 416/367–8186) or Ontario Travel (tel. 416/965–4008).

Horseback Riding   There are two stables within the city limits. **Central Don Stables,** in Sunnybrook Park (Leslie St. and Eglinton Ave., tel. 416/444–4044), has an indoor arena, an outdoor ring, and about 19 kilometers (nearly 12 miles) of bridle trails through the Don Valley. **Eglinton Equestrian Club** (near Don Mills Rd. and John St., tel. 416/889–6375) has two indoor arenas.

Hotel Health Facilities   Nearly every major hotel in the Metro Toronto area has a decent indoor swimming pool; some even have indoor/outdoor swimming pools. The best include the **Sheraton Centre,** at Queen and Bay streets, and the **Inn on the Park,** at Eglinton Avenue near Leslie Street. Many also have health clubs, with saunas and Nautilus equipment.

Ice Skating   Toronto operates some 30 outdoor artificial rinks and 100 natural-ice rinks—and all are free! Among the most popular are in Nathan Phillips Square, in front of the New City Hall, at Queen and Bay streets; down at Harbourfront, which has Canada's largest outdoor artificial ice rink; College Park, at Yonge and College streets; Grenadier Pond, within High Park, at Bloor and Keele streets; and inside Hazelton Lanes, that classy shopping mall on the edge of Yorkville, on Avenue Road, just above Bloor Street. For details on any city rink, call 416/392–1111.

Jogging The **Martin Goodman Trail** (*see* Bicycling, *above*) is ideal. Also try the boardwalk of The Beaches in the east end, High Park in the west end, the Toronto Islands, or any of Toronto's parks.

Sailing This can be a breeze, especially between April and October. Contact the **Ontario Sailing Association** (tel. 416/495–4240).

Skiing Try Toronto's parks and ravines; High Park; the lakefront
Cross-country along the southern edge of the city; Tommy Thompson Park; Toronto Islands. Check the yellow pages for ski-equipment rentals; there are many places.

Downhill Although there are a few places where one can get a taste of this sport within Metro Toronto, such as **Earl Bales Park,** on Bathurst Street, just south of Sheppard Avenue, and **Centennial Park Ski Hill,** in Etobicoke (tel. 416/394–8754), the *best* alpine hills are a good 30–60 minutes north of the city. These include **Blue Mountain Resorts** (tel. 416/869–3799) in Collingwood, the **Caledon Ski Club** (tel. 416/453–7404) in Caledon, **Glen Eden Ski Area** (tel. 416/878–5011) in Milton, **Hidden Valley** (tel. 705/789–2301) in Huntsville, **Hockley Valley Resort** (tel. 519/942–0754) in Orangeville, **Horseshoe Valley** (tel. 705/835–2790) in Barrie, and **Snow Valley Ski Resort,** just outside Barrie (tel. 416/283–2439). Call 416/963–2992 for daily reports on lifts and surface conditions.

Sleigh Riding and **Black Creek Pioneer Village** (tel. 416/661–6610 or 416/661–
Tobogganing 6600), north of 401 along Highway 400, at Steeles Avenue, is open winter weekends 10–4 for skating, tobogganing, and horse-drawn sleigh rides. The best parks for tobogganing include **High Park,** in the west end, and our favorite, **Winston Churchill Park,** at Spadina and St. Clair avenues, just two blocks from Casa Loma. It is sheer terror.

Tennis The city provides dozens of courts, all free, and many of them floodlighted. Parks with courts open from 7 AM to 11 PM, in season, include the famous High Park in the west end; Stanley Park, on King Street West, three blocks west of Bathurst Street; and Eglinton Park, on Eglinton Avenue West, just east of Avenue Road. Call the **Ontario Tennis Association** (tel. 416/495–4215).

Spectator Sports

Auto Racing For the past several years, the **Molson Indy** (tel. 416/595–5445) has been roaring around the Canadian National Exhibition grounds, including the major thoroughfare of Lakeshore Boulevard, for three days in mid-July. You'll pay more than $85 for a three-day "red" reserved seat, but general admission for the qualification rounds, the practice rounds, and the Indy itself can be as cheap as $10–$20, depending upon the day.

Less than a half-hour drive away is the **Cayuga International Speedway** (tel. 416/765–4461), where international stock-car races are held from May through September.

Baseball The **Toronto Blue Jays,** whose home is the SkyDome, have developed into one of baseball's most dynamic teams. Indeed, their World Series win in 1992 had—and still has—the whole city buzzing. The Jays have the most costly tickets in the major leagues, ranging from rotten $5 seats up to ones that cost $11,

$15, and $19.50, and they usually sell out every single home game, so plan way ahead of your Toronto visit. We hate to give the greedy little capitalists the publicity, but there are nearly always dozens of scalpers hawking tickets just outside the Sky-Dome to that day's game. *A hot tip:* Arrive a bit late, in the second or third inning or so, and they will often unload their tickets at a fraction of what they asked a half hour earlier. *For ticket information, tel. 416/341–1111.*

Canoeing and Rowing The world's largest **canoeing and rowing regatta** is held every July 1, as it has been for more than a century, on Toronto Island's Long Pond. *Canoe Ontario, tel. 416/495–4180.*

Football Although the Canadian Football League has been teetering on the brink of dissolution, the **Toronto Argonauts** have, in recent years, developed into annual contenders. Americans might find the three downs and 110-yard field to be rather quaint, but the game is much like their own. The Argos were bought in 1991 by a consortium that includes Canadian hockey star Wayne Gretzky and Canadian comic actor John Candy, and with new CFL teams practicing in such un-Canadian locations as California and Texas, the long-suffering league hopes to be rejuvenated. *Tel. 416/595–1131 for tickets and information.*

Golf The permanent site of the **Canadian Open** golf championship is Glen Abbey, a course designed by Jack Nicklaus. This tournament is one of golf's Big Five and is always played in late summer. *Less than a 45-min drive west, along the Queen Elizabeth Way (QEW). Tel. 416/844–1800.*

Hockey The **Toronto Maple Leafs** play 40 home games each season (Oct.–Apr.), usually on Wednesday and Saturday nights, in the big, ugly Maple Leaf Gardens. There are always tickets available at each game—at least from scalpers in front of the stadium on Carlton Street, a half-block east of the corner of Yonge and College streets. Call the office (tel. 416/977–1641) at 9 AM sharp on the day of the game you wish to see.

Horse Racing
Harness Racing The **Greenwood** track, built in 1874, is where the best trotters and pacers do their stuff at three annual meetings. *Tel. 416/675–6110. Spring gathering runs Jan.–mid-Mar.; summer meeting, late May–Sept.; the brief winter meeting, the last two weeks in Dec.*

Thoroughbred Racing There are four major racetracks handled by the Ontario Jockey Club (tel. 416/675–6110).

Greenwood Race Track is one of the premier harness tracks in North America and is the home of many of Canada's greatest trotting and pacing events, including the North American Cup. It is located in the city's east end, a 10-minute streetcar ride from downtown, at Woodbine Avenue and Queen Street East, near the lakeshore. *Tel. 416/698–3131. Winter meeting runs late Oct.–early Dec.; spring meeting runs mid-Mar.–late Apr.*

Woodbine Race Track is the showplace of Thoroughbred racing in Canada. *Located 30-min northeast of downtown Toronto, not far from the airport, at Hwy. 27 and Rexdale Blvd., tel. 416/675–6110. Horses run late Apr.–late Oct.*

Mohawk is in the heart of Ontario's Standardbred breeding country, and it features a glass-enclosed, climate-controlled grandstand and other attractive facilities. *A 30-min drive west* *of Toronto, along Hwy. 401, past the town of Milton, tel. 416/854–2255.*

Fort Erie, in the Niagara tourist region, is one of the most picturesque racetracks in the world, with willows, manicured hedges, and flower-bordered infield lakes. It has racing on the dirt as well as on grass, with the year's highlight being the Prince of Wales Stakes, the second jewel in Canada's Triple Crown of Racing. *Tel. 416/871–3200 from Toronto, 716/856–0293 from Buffalo.*

Royal Horse Show This highlight of Canada's equestrian season is part of the Royal Winter Fair each November. *The CNE grounds, Dufferin St., by the waterfront, tel. 416/393–6400.*

Soccer Although Toronto keeps getting and losing and getting a professional soccer team, one can catch this exciting sport, as well as collegiate football, in the very handy **Varsity Stadium.** *Bloor St. W at Bedford, a block west of the Royal Ontario Museum and University Ave, tel. 416/979–2186.*

Dining

Updated by Sara Waxman

Restaurant critic for the Toronto Sun "Cheaper Eats" and "Dining Out" sections, Sara Waxman is the author of three best-selling cookbooks, including Backroads and Country Cooking.

A decade ago visitors to Toronto enjoyed a varied mix of ethnic restaurants, but good food could not be found in the middle ground of gastronomy—between the Italian sandwiches and the Dover sole. Today, Toronto is a city of bistros.

The "bistroization" of Toronto is due in part to a new generation of chefs, the first wave of young people who are just now fanning out across the city, opening neighborhood restaurants that are a little cheaper, slightly less ambitious, and thus more accessible than those of their teachers.

What the bistros serve is another matter. That old tired imitation Continental menu, which Toronto's upper crust dined out on since before the Beatles, is finally dead. We are no longer stuck eating less than perfect imitations of what they do in Paris and Rome. The new bistros are eclectic, as likely to borrow from Bangkok as they are from Los Angeles. Furthermore, their clever mentors have taught the new generation of young chefs to do things that have heretofore been forbidden in kitchens—think for themselves, create dishes based on what dazzles them in the morning market, and use local ingredients and spontaneity of approach.

Highly recommended restaurants in each category are indicated with a star ★.

Category	Cost*
Very Expensive	over $40
Expensive	$30–$40
Moderate	$20–$30
Inexpensive	under $20

*per person without tax, tip, or drinks

Bistros

Expensive
★

Brownes Bistro. In one night, you can count a dozen mink coats. Full-length dark ranch. What does a person who spends $17,000 on a coat want in a restaurant? Apparently she wants an impeccable bistro that avoids the tarted-up Paris look. Everything at Brownes is breathtakingly simple, from the white paper on the tables to the small black and white ceramic tiles. The monochromatic room is colored only by dark wood paneling and one fuchsia azalea at the bar. Lack of pretension is elevated to an art. Brownes's pizza may be the best in Toronto. The *gnocchi* are unexceptional. The bouillabaisse has perfect, sweet little fresh scallops, but a blandness of broth. There are seven main courses, and three of them are lamb. Brownes gives full glory to lamb's heretofore neglected parts, such as lamb shanks (braised till they soften like butter and served in their own heartwarming broth, slightly thickened, with fennel, potatoes, and carrots). A lemon curd and a darkly dense chocolate cake, served with crème fraîche and chocolate sauce, are both very fine. The price of under $70 for two, with wine—a real bargain—makes Brownes the hottest show in town. *4 Woodlawn Ave. E, tel. 416/924–8132. Reservations advised. Dress: casual. AE, MC, V. Closed Sat. and Sun. lunch.*

Moderate
★

BamBoo. Inside a funky little inner courtyard decorated by a bohemian hand—fishnets on the walls, a stand of Muskoka bamboo, fading signs, all bordered by a thatched roof, à la South Pacific—is a relentlessly low-tech club-cum-restaurant that rebukes glitz-crazed Toronto with a smile up its sleeve. More and more ordinary people are going to the BamBoo for one purpose only: to eat food that jumps up joyously on the tongue. You can eat in the club area (240 seats, barnlike but warm) or in the small, funky dining room off to the right. On weekends guests line up for both the food and the live reggae, African, funk, and Latin music, which starts at 10 PM (*see* Nightlife, *below*). Much of the food is spicy. The callalloo, a creamed spinach and coconut soup, is the very weapon that blocked sinuses require. BamBoo's single most popular dish, Thai spicy noodles, comes in three modes—mild, medium, and wow! Mild is a superlative ungreasy wok-fry of rice noodles with peanuts, bean sprouts, chicken, shrimp, tofu, egg, Vietnamese fish sauce, chilies, sugar, garlic, and fresh lime juice. *312 Queen St. W, tel. 416/593–5771. No reservations. Dress: casual. AE, MC, V. Closed Sun.*

Opus. This darkly handsome midtown space is enlivened with clever halogen lighting and furnished with an eye to style, comfort, and big-city taste. Chef Paul Boehmer's inventive cuisine is a sophisticated play on the hearty peasant food we adore. An ever-changing fresh market menu offers appetizers such as Yukon Gold potato soup with marinated beef tenderloin; wild mushroom risotto textured with smoked guinea fowl; roast suckling pig with maple-glazed squash and maple-wheat beer sauce. Main courses include rack of lamb roasted to perfection, slicked with fresh thyme glaze and a pungent black olive confit. Pastas are all homemade and come in appetizer and main-course sizes. Cracked black peppercorn fettuccine with portobello mushrooms and chicken, and the ravioli, plump with shrimp and ginger, in a splendid sauce of Armagnac garlic and chives are not to be missed. Among the three principals here, seven languages are spoken. Fortunately for us, they are also eloquent in the universal language of food. *37 Prince Arthur Ave., tel. 416/921–3105. Reservations advised. Dress: casual. AE, MC, V. Closed lunch.*

Brunch

Moderate **Kensington Kitchen.** Its clientele is the self-consciously unchic
★ University of Toronto people who live in the area and appreciate the ask-nothing ambience. The reigning sensibility belongs
to Said Mukhayesh, who leans heavily toward the healthy, so
his interpretation of Middle East cooking includes whole-
wheat pita; and if there's rice, it's brown. But none of this pre-
vents Mukhayesh from serving wickedly wonderful
spinach-and-cheese ravioli in a dense cream sauce. Ingredients
are fresh and always prepared with affection and care. Where
else do you get velvety *baba ghannoush, lubya* (green beans in
a thick sauce of cinnamon and cardamom), divinely garlicky
fried eggplant, and assertive cream soups? The tabbouleh
(cracked wheat salad with parsley, tomato, and cucumber) is
delicate, and the falafel in pita is a class act. Two people could
lunch splendidly for $20. *124 Harbord St., south of Bloor St., tel.
416/961–3404. Reservations not necessary. Dress: casual.
DC, MC, V.*

Cafés

Inexpensive **L'Express Café.** Just across from the charming Parrot bistro on
Queen Street West is a café that since the fall of 1987 has been
serving good casual food with some dispatch. For under $6,
they take the ordinary (chicken salad, ham and cheese) and
anoint it with goat cheese or roasted red peppers in oil, laid
lovingly between slices of impeccable Italian bread. The pizzas
and savory tarts are enough to justify its existence. (The
former is simple and robust; the latter, a texture of gossamer,
thanks to the 35% cream.) The leek and *chèvre* tart with a touch
of curry is one of the most inventive dishes. *254 Queen St. W,
in walking distance of New City Hall, tel. 416/596–0205. No reservations. Dress: informal. MC, V, for orders over $10. Open for
brunch only on Sun.*

Cajun

Moderate **Southern Accent.** When these cooks blacken something, it
comes out spiced and seared, melting in the middle and with a
sensual surrender ensured by lemony beurre blanc on top. The
appetizers are dazzling—light but tasty daily soups, often
sweet and hot-and-sour. There are crunchy hush puppies
(deep-fried corn fritters), and lovely greens with toasted pe-
cans and citrus-scented vinaigrette. The gumbo, that Cajun
classic based on a dark roux, is a dream from the bayou—highly
flavored pork sausage (called *andouille*) and other meats in a
strong broth based on roux with okra, and topped with a snowy
hill of rice. Jambalaya, the major staple of Louisiana cooking,
is rice-based with andouille, smoked ham, beef, chicken, bacon,
vegetables, and shrimp, in Cajun spices. Southern Accent does
it proud. *595 Markham St., tel. 416/536–3211. Reservations advised. Dress: casual. AE, DC, MC, V. Closed lunch and Mon.
Dec.–Apr.*

Acrobat, **16**
BamBoo, **6**
Brownes Bistro, **21**
Camarra's, **1**
Centro, **20**
Grano, **23**
Kensington
Kitchen, **5**
La Fenice, **10**
Le Bistingo, **7**
L'Express Café, **8**
Marché, **12**
New World, **19**
North 44, **22**
Opus, **17**
Pearl Court, **13**
Renaissance Cafe, **3**
Sante Fe
Bar and Grill, **9**
Southern Accent, **2**
Splendido, **4**
Studio Café, **18**
Thai Magic, **24**
The Vegetarian
Restaurant, **15**
Young Lok, **11**
Young Thailand, **14**

Toronto Dining

KEY

AE American Express Office

Chinese

Moderate
★

New World. There is probably very little that could induce you to penetrate the wilds of Scarborough on a wintry night, but this place can. Again and again and again. Do not miss the New World's *shui kow* soup—a sea of fine stock afloat with freshly made dumplings of chopped shrimp, Chinese mushrooms, and barbecued pork—and the fresh abalone that comes in its shell accompanied by one pristine broccoli floret in a translucent sauce made from beef stock reduced with oyster sauce. It's not on the menu, but the password is "Kam Wong said we could have it." New World is frankly Cantonese. There is a lick and a promise in the direction of Szechuan, but the cook's heart is on the sea. Big, fat, indelicate West Coast oysters come properly (barely) cooked in their own shells, dressed up with black beans, fresh coriander, and chives. Chicken cubes and scallops in phoenix nest are not to be missed. And I have never tasted fish so fresh in hot pots, nor eaten a hot pot crowned with softshell crab and oyster. No reservations are taken for the hot-pot tables, so go early. This place is a treasure. *3600 Victoria Park Ave., tel. 416/498–1818. Reservations advised on weekends. Dress: casual. AE, MC, V.*

Young Lok. Upwardly mobile and still delicious, this is a handsome restaurant in the very attractive Village by the Grange. A nice touch is the outdoor dining offered in summer. The menu is biblical in scope, ranging from tired old Cantonese clichés to the fiery stars of the Szechuan kitchen. The clear soups are great; the panfried pancakes with scallions are a bargain appetizer and wonderful: cheap, greasy, and oniony. The main courses are almost all terrific: Sautéed shrimp with ginger and scallion is crunchy on the outside, sweetly juicy on the inside. Fresh lobster in black bean sauce is a perfect juxtaposition of sweet flesh and salty beans. Vegetarians' hodgepodge, a Young Lok classic, has a variety of crunchy vegetables. Mandarin crispy duck is for all unrepentant grease lovers. Try to make it for dim sum on weekends 11–3. *122 St. Patrick St., at Dundas St., just south of the Art Gallery, tel. 416/593–9819. Reservations advised. Dress: casual. AE, MC, V.*

Inexpensive
★

Pearl Court. In 1991 Pearl Court made a lot of Sinophiles happy: It moved from cramped and dingy quarters to a two-story postmodern dusty-rose and pale-green Chinese heaven. And the quality of the food suffered not a whit. The lobsters in ginger and green onion are still seductive, and the scallops in black bean sauce are fat and fresh. There are also barely cooked, fat, fresh oysters sizzling on a hot iron plate with black pepper and green onion. Or fresh kiwi clams, each one steamed with a half-teaspoon of minced garlic. Garlic is a central theme here. So is fresh coriander. Lemon grass accents the oxtail in a fine citrusy stew pot. Chicken in paper is a platter of little paper packets, each holding a little morsel of pink tender chicken steamed in soy with five-spice powder. Skip the soups, which are bland, and consider the oysters. *663 Gerrard St. E, tel. 416/463–8773. Dress: casual. V.*

French

Expensive–
Moderate
★

Le Bistingo. Certain gifts from chef Claude Bouillet's kitchen are among the finest flavors Toronto can offer: His open ravioli filled with shrimp and scallops are astonishing—toothsome pasta sheets laid over and under with soft, sweet seafood, all bathed in the lightest of *blancs* thinned with fish stock. The house signature appetizer, duck liver sautéed until just pink and soft and napped in a very tart raisin sauce, is fabulous. Among main courses, the fish dishes shine. A perfectly cooked fat red snapper sits on a wondrously astringent bed of stewed endive, surrounded by beurre blanc cleverly thinned with vermouth. Those in the know order a hot dessert with dinner, and are thus seduced by fresh-from-the-oven buttery puff pastry cradling caramelized apples, then bathed in a foam of Calvados sabayon. As if that were not enough, there are sauternes by the glass (or real champagne) to wash it all down. *349 Queen St. W, tel. 416/598–3490. Reservations advised. Dress: casual. AE, MC. V.*

Italian

Expensive **Centro.** Franco Prevedello spent blood, sweat, and $2 million
★ on dreamlike art deco lighting, etched glass, 18-foot ceilings with fat white columns, oxblood leather armchairs, Rosenthal china worth $45 a plate, and the most exciting Italian wine cellar in Toronto. The food can be heavy and overcomplicated— *agnolotti* with too much cream; overcooked poached salmon— but every day it moves closer to inspired Italian country style, with such specialties as poached skate in a mustardy coriander vinaigrette, and a fat, juicy roasted capon breast garnished with fresh pecans and lemon-pepper garlic mayonnaise. *2472 Yonge St., tel. 416/483–2211. Reservations advised. Dress: casual. AE, DC, MC, V. Closed lunch, Sun.*

★ **La Fenice.** This is the most authentic Italian restaurant in Toronto. Luigi Orgera is a ballerina in the kitchen, the Nureyev of the grill. Who else in Toronto has fresh porcini in October? Who else grates heavenly slivers of fresh white truffle on pasta? The antipasto trolley is more Rome than Toronto: mint-scented grilled eggplant; roasted zucchini; tangy salad of shrimps and squid; roasted sweet red peppers anointed in extra-virgin olive oil; and more. His *risotto al mare* is a tiny perfect stew of clams and mussels; the spaghetti is tossed with sweet chunks of sun-dried tomatoes, southern Italy incarnate. In fish, one can expect red and white snapper, yellowtail, and porgy, all as fresh as fish can be in this city. In 1990 La Fenice added a basement pasta bar. It's small and noisy and the chairs are uncomfortable, but for an inexpensive version of the Orgera alchemy, it's worth it. *319 King St. W, near John St., tel. 416/585–2377. Reservations advised. Dress: casual. AE, DC, MC, V. Closed Sat. lunch, Sun.*

★ **Splendido.** Thanks to lighting as fun sculpture, glorious huge painted flowers, and a kitchen full of chefs in painters' hats, all behind a glass wall splashed with colors, Splendido is sophisticated fun. It is Toronto's answer to the Cal/Ital aesthetic: Homemade lamb sausage with silken polenta and a fresh rosemary sauce. Perfectly cooked juicy quails with pasta in tomato sauce. Competent pizzas with the usual new-age toppings. Nice light gnocchi. Rich strong soups with nary a hint of powdered base. The wood-roasted chicken on sourdough bread salad, Italian-style, via Zuni in San Francisco, is wondrously crisp. Rabbit is served in classic Italian style, with creamy porcini fettuccine, kale, and rapini. Avoid the nouvelle items: They sink like stones. Splendido is so fashionable and pretty that the true nature and strength of the food are obscured; it's the ultimate trattoria. *88 Harbord St., tel. 416/929–7788. Reservations advised. Dress: casual but chic. AE, DC, MC, V. Closed lunch.*

Inexpensive **Camarra's.** Pizza heaven, in northwest Toronto. The dough has always been high and soft, with the delightful bite of a leavened dough. And on top are only good ingredients—real Italian plum tomatoes, not the canned tomato sauce of too many Toronto pizzerias. Very casual. *2899 Dufferin St., 1 mi south of Hwy. 401, tel. 416/789–3222. No reservations. Dress: casual. AE, MC, V. Closed Sun. lunch, Tues.*

Mexican

Moderate **Santa Fe Bar & Grill.** You wouldn't be able to find Santa Fe if
★ you didn't know it was here. The only clue to its presence is a big turquoise lizard on the roof. The interior has all the southwestern elements—adobe walls, cowhide tub chairs, wooden chairs painted with a Georgia O'Keeffe palette, southwestern rugs on the walls. The kitchen has troubled itself to stock the staples of casual Mexican cuisine: *chipotles* (smoked jalapeños), *jicamas* (sweet crunchy white tubers), blue corn chips, corn husks, flour tortillas, and black beans. It's fun food. Sip a blue margarita in a huge highball glass with a little pizza or a platter of blue and gold corn chips. The more proper Mexican cooking is done with the right chilies and generosity of spirit. In the evenings Santa Fe transforms into a country hangout, with live music performed on a new, big stage, and lessons offered in the Texas two-step and line dancing. *129 Peter St., tel. 416/345–9345. Reservations advised. Dress: casual. AE, DC, MC, V. Closed Mon. and Tues. lunch and Sun.*

Nouvelle

Expensive **Acrobat.** Eclectically fashioned, this is a witty and well-designed monument to the institutions of dining, drinking, and schmoozing. Inside this utilitarian facade, you'll find wild and wonderful details that defy classification: An aluminum acrobat doing a handstand balances on a ceiling beam, while in the background a waterfall accents the undulating movements of a sculpture made of colored liquor bottles embedded in steel. Look above you at a ceiling with swirling metals illuminated by a complex lighting system. Fashionable patrons perch at the long bar or lounge on sofas and nibble on terrines of silken fois gras with crostini, gorgeous platters of vegetarian spring rolls, and tempura vegetables. Hand-blown aquariums filled with exotic fish separate the dining area from the kitchen where worldly, beautifully presented dishes are prepared. Perfect wild mushroom risotto holds giant sea scallops and white asparagus tips; and barbecued tiger shrimp lurk in a tangle of shimmering linguine, set in a broth laced with matchsticks of fresh ginger and scallions; and rack of lamb is arranged spirally around gnocchi in black-pepper Zinfandel sauce. Desserts are sweet luxuries. *1221 Bay St. (at Bloor), tel. 416/920–2323. Reservations advised. Dress: neat but casual. AE, DC, MC, V. Closed Sun.*

★ **North 44.** Mark McEwan (formerly of Pronto) opened the most visually arresting dining room in Toronto in 1990. North 44, Toronto's longitude, is the restaurant's logo and an oft repeated visual refrain. Everywhere you look there is another design statement. The message is metallic and modern; even the washrooms have the designer touch. One of the five best cooks in Toronto, McEwan specializes in Southwest cuisine with a southeast Asian undertone, all afloat on a sea of beurre blanc and executed with finesse. McEwan dips fresh oysters in cornmeal, fries them crisp on the outside, melting on the inside, and sits them on a chili cream sauce. He pats together corn, potato, and shrimp fragments into a pancake and fries it. Order the huge barely roasted scallops, and you get grilled bok choy and creamed peppers. The fried rock snapper comes with gingered plum tomatoes and a McEwan introduction—french-fried leeks, sophisticated kissin' cousin to onion rings. *2537 Yonge St., tel. 416/487–4897. Reservations advised. Dress: casual. AE, DC, MC, V. Closed Sun. lunch.*

Quick Meals

Moderate **Studio Café.** This is the coffee shop of the Four Seasons Hotel, but it's no ordinary coffee shop. The decor is eye-catchingly chic, with lots of chrome, designer furniture, and designer fabrics. There's art everywhere—paintings by Canadian artists and handmade glass beautifully displayed in illuminated showcases (the glass is for sale). The breakfast menu includes traditional fare as well as a Japanese breakfast of miso soup, grilled salmon, and rice. The lunch and dinner menu offers a wide selection, from pizzas and pastas to halibut burger and "crunchy whole quail," which tastes much better than it sounds. *21 Avenue Rd., just north of Bloor St., tel. 416/964–0411. Reservations advised. Jacket optional. AE, DC, MC, V.*

Inexpensive **Grano.** Franco Prevedello has served as godfather to a winner, helping a young couple, the Martellas, create a basic café—southern Italian style—the prettiest all-day café in Toronto. You order your meal at the bar, and Robert brings it. The soups and antipasti are dreams come true, the soups thick and strong, with fresh thyme and good stock. And some of the antipasti are as good as what you'd get in Bologna: Strips of zucchini are marinated with sweet oregano; a hint of caraway flavors the thin chewy strips of eggplant in oil. Grano's pizzas are so attractive because bread is the secret love at Grano (which means grain). All day the baker toils in the cellar under the café, and all day the breads come upstairs, fragrant and warm: The two most wonderful are the *foccaccia* and the oatmeal buttermilk bread. Avoid the steam-table stuff. *2035 Yonge St., below Eglinton Ave., tel. 416/440–1986. Dress: casual. AE, DC, MC, V. Closed Sun.*

Marché. Designed to be a microcosm of a European marketplace, this eatery is actually a study in organization and creativity. The constantly changing decor consists of an 18,000-square-foot vista of baskets of fruits, nuts, and vegetables; mountains of meats and fish on ice; and freshly made pasta. Take a big whiff of the air—perfumed with bread and pastries baking; chicken and game birds broiling; seafood and fish steaming and pan-frying; lamb and steaks grilling; and aromatic sauces simmering with tomatoes, peppers, garlic, and herbs. An immense and affordable wine list is offered, too. The dining rooms are as diverse as the selections: La Poterie is an artisans cottage, La Brasserie du Nord typifies a Parisian tavern, La Petite Auberge looks like a French country inn, and L'Orangerie is a gazebo under spreading tree branches. To experience Marché, you must first pick up a shopping cart and a tray and stroll through the marketplace, choosing as much or as little as you wish. Everything is prepared before your eyes, 365 days a year, 7:30 AM—2 AM. As you walk through you'll notice the mixed clientele: Black leather jackets rub shoulders with black-tie socialites, and young parents with children share dining rooms with execs with briefcases. *BCE Place, Yonge and Wellington Sts, tel. 416/366–8986. No reservations. Dress: casual. AE, DC, MC, V.*

Thai

Moderate   **Thai Magic.** Consistency and competence are the bywords
★   here; the food is neither greasy nor too sweet. But chiliphobes, beware: The divine Thai Magic mussels, steamed with curry sauce and unctuous coconut cream, are mouthburners, as is the otherwise lovely chicken coconut soup, Thailand's national soup, which is an amalgam of smooth (coconut) and sharp (kha, a gingerlike root). Barbecued foods, a piece of Thai magic served with a sweet/spicy peanut sauce, are short on chilies and long on charm. Even the satay is very good, as far as satay goes (which is not very far, considering the relative banality of meat on a stick). *1118 Yonge St., tel. 416/968–7366. Reservations advised on weekends. Dress: casual. AE, MC, V. Closed Sun.*

Inexpensive   **Young Thailand.** This modest-looking restaurant in a slightly offbeat location is worth searching out. The dining room is open and airy, its plainness tempered with a few decorative touches to suggest Thai connections. Chef and owner Wandee Young, well known from her days at the Bamboo, here displays her skills at combining the herbs and flavors that are characteristically Thai. The food is fresh and varied and includes the popular *phad thai,* a noodle dish with shrimp, slivers of chicken, egg, bean sprouts, and a squeeze of lime. The delightful green mango salad has shrimp, chicken, and red onion. Some of the dishes have a sweetness reminiscent of Cantonese food, and some can be searing, most notably the *tom yum goong* soup, which includes a few tiger shrimp, lemon grass, lime juice, mushrooms, and some vicious red chilies. *111 Gerrard St. E, tel. 416/599–9099. Reservations recommended. Dress: informal. DC, MC, V. Closed lunch Sat. and Sun.*

Vegetarian

Inexpensive   **Renaissance Cafe.** A modest restaurant with a limited but cosmopolitan menu—the likes of ratatouille and curries. The daily buffet lunches are pleasant. *509 Bloor St. W, near Bathurst St.; tel. 416/968–6639. Dress: casual. Reservations advised. AE, DC, MC, V.*
The Vegetarian Restaurant. For the uninitiated, there are lovely soups and salads; for the adventuresome, soyburgers and tofu bourguignon. It's in a cheerfully renovated Victorian house, with cafeteria-style service. *4 Dundonald St., just east of Yonge St., tel. 416/961–9522. Dress: casual. No reservations. DC, MC, V. Closed Sun. lunch.*

Lodging

Places to stay in this cosmopolitan city range, as one might expect, from luxurious hotels to budget motels to a handful of bed-and-breakfasts. Prices are cut nearly in half over weekends and during special times of the year (many Toronto hotels drop their rates a full 50% in January and February). Due, in part, to the economy, major hotels such as the Sutton Place and the Chestnut Park are in bankruptcy (but still operating), and others are suffering. Wherever you stay in Toronto, you should be able to bargain for a lower-than-standard rate. You can insist on corporate prices or demand special deals, and you should nearly always get your request granted, as long as rooms are available.

Accommodation Toronto (tel. 416/596–7117), a service of the Hotel Association of Toronto, is an excellent source for finding the room and price you want. Don't forget to ask about family deals and special packages. You might also try the **Metropolitan Bed & Breakfast** registry service (615 Mt. Pleasant Rd., Suite 269, Toronto M4S 3C5, tel. 416/964–2566, fax 416/537–0233).

Highly recommended properties in each category are indicated by a star ★.

Category	Cost*
Very Expensive	over $175
Expensive	$125–$175
Moderate	$70–$125
Inexpensive	under $70

All prices are for a standard double room, excluding optional service charge.

Very Expensive

★ **Four Seasons Toronto.** It's hard to imagine a lovelier or more exclusive hotel than the Four Seasons, which is usually rated among the top two dozen hotels in the world and one of the top three in North America. The location is ideal: on the edge of Yorkville, a few meters from the Royal Ontario Museum. The 380 units are tastefully appointed. Maids come twice a day, and there are comfortable bathrobes, oversize towels, fresh flowers, and a fine indoor/outdoor pool. Even the special family rates, however, will not drop the cost much below $200 a night. Yet during such slow months as January through March, sometimes into April, rooms on weekends have been offered for less than $150 per night (per person), and there is reason to believe that this tradition will continue in 1994. Its restaurants include the Studio Café, the Lobby Bar, La Serre, for dinner only, and the formal dining room, Truffles. *21 Avenue Rd., M5R 2G1, a block north of Bloor St., tel. 416/964–0411 or 800/332–3442. AE, DC, MC, V.*

Harbour Castle Westin. This was a Hilton International hotel until 1987, when Westin and Hilton suddenly switched owner-

ship of their major downtown Toronto hotels. A favorite with conventioneers, it's located just steps from Harbourfront and the Toronto Islands ferry. It's a bit inconvenient to the city's amenities except for those directly on the lakeshore, but it enjoys the best views of any hotel in the city. There's a shuttle bus service to downtown business and shopping, and the swimming pool, squash courts, and health club are among the best in town. Its 900 rooms are well appointed and tastefully modern, and the frequent family and weekend rates help bring its regular price down by as much as a third. Its Regatta restaurant is open all day, and the revolving Lighthouse restaurant, atop the 37th floor, is open for lunch and dinner. And what a view! *1 Harbour Sq., M5J 1A6, tel. 416/869–1600 or 800/228–3000. AE, DC, MC, V.*

Park Plaza Hotel. It may lack a pool, but it has one of the best locations in the city: a short distance from the Royal Ontario Museum, Queen's Park, and the Yorkville shopping area. The 350 units are well appointed in a plush, old-fashioned way, and they seem to coast by on their old-shoe familiarity to regular Toronto visitors who have been staying in them since the days when there was much less choice. The Roof Restaurant was once described by novelist Mordecai Richler as "the only civilized place in Toronto," and the Prince Arthur Room is open for good (business) breakfasts and lunch. Additions now include a 550-seat ballroom, a business center, a palm court, and a restaurant in the lobby, all designed by Zeidler Roberts Partnership, the same architects who were responsible for the Eaton Centre and Ontario Place. Through 1993, double rooms on weekends cost as little as $109, including breakfast and parking. *4 Avenue Rd., M5R 2E8, at the corner of Bloor St. W, tel. 416/924–5471 or 800/268–4927. AE, DC, MC, V.*

Expensive

★ **Best Western Chestnut Park Hotel.** One of the newest—and biggest—additions to Toronto's hotel scene, this handsome 16-floor hotel with glass-enclosed atrium lobby could hardly be more convenient: just steps behind City Hall and a few short blocks from Eaton Centre. The 522 guest rooms, which include 21 for the disabled, are all well decorated, with finely crafted furniture and desks; many have queen- and king-size beds. Recreational facilities include a large heated indoor pool, sauna, Jacuzzi, health club and gymnasium, and a children's creative center. Its restaurant, The Tapestry, is open for all meals. In addition, the Chestnut Park is now connected by a walkway from the mezzanine level to a Museum of Textiles, where some 15,000 textiles from around the world are displayed—the only museum of its kind in Canada. *108 Chestnut St., M5G 1R3, just north of Nathan Phillips Sq., tel. 416/977–5000. AE, DC, MC, V.*

Novotel Toronto Centre. This moderately priced hotel—part of a popular French chain—opened in December 1987. There are 266 modest, modern rooms on nine floors in the heart of downtown, within walking distance of Harbourfront and the CN Tower. Facilities include an indoor pool, whirlpool, exercise room, and sauna, and its Café Nicole is open all day. *45 The Esplanade, M5E 1W2, tel. 416/367–8900 or 800/221–4542. AE, DC, MC, V.*

Sheraton Centre. This 1,430-room conventioneer's tower is across from the New City Hall, just a block from Eaton Centre. The below-ground level is part of Toronto's labyrinth of shop-lined corridors, and there are more shops on the ground and second floors. The restaurants' reach seems to exceed their grasp, but the Long Bar, overlooking Nathan Phillips Square, is a great place to meet friends for a drink. There's a nonsmoking floor and various special rates and packages. Facilities include a huge indoor/outdoor pool, hot tub, sauna, and workout room. As of 1992, $47 million had been spent on marvelous renovations, with completely refurbished guest rooms and bathrooms, six new floors in the exclusive Sheraton Towers, and 15 new, automated check-in and cashier stations. *123 Queen St. W, M5H 2M9, tel. 416/361–1000 or 800/325–3535. AE, DC, MC, V.*

Toronto Hilton International. This hotel, in the financial district, recently switched ownership with the Westin. The 600 rooms are newly renovated, and its nearness to New City Hall, major businesses, and more makes it a convenient base for most visitors. The indoor/outdoor pool is modest, but the view of the city from the glass-enclosed elevators is a thrill. It has the Garden Court lobby restaurant and Trader Vic's, which is open for lunch and dinner. *145 Richmond St. W and University Ave., M5H 3M6, tel. 416/869–3456. AE, DC, MC, V.*

Inexpensive

Hotel Ibis. This recent hotel belongs to one of Europe's leading chains. It is located just a few blocks from the New City Hall and Eaton Centre. As it proudly declares, "No bellhops, door-men, or concierges. No gushing fountains. And no room service with fancy silver trays." What it does have are 294 comfortable rooms with bare necessities (as well as 10 others specially designed and equipped for the disabled). There's no pool, but a lounge called The Bar and a restaurant called Le Restaurant take care of your generic needs. *240 Jarvis St., M5B 2B8, tel. 416/593–9400. AE, DC, MC, V.*

Journey's End Hotels. This is a rapidly growing chain that offers three convenient Toronto locations. The airport hotel costs about $100 for up to four people, with 10% off for corporate travelers and senior citizens; the two downtown locations charge only about $60 on weekend nights. These latter-mentioned lodgings are an easy walk from many of the sights. Don't expect original antiques here, but all rooms are spotlessly clean and quite pleasant, and some locations have restaurants. No pools or saunas or convention rooms, but the prices are so low, how can you complain? *262 Carlingview Dr., M9W 5G1, near Hwy. 427 (airport), 258 suites; 280 Bloor St. W. M5S 1V8, a few blocks west of Avenue/University, 214 rooms; 111 Lombard St., M5C 2T9, near Queen and Jarvis, 196 rooms; tel. 800/668–4200; in Toronto, 416/624–8200. AE, DC, MC, V.*

Toronto Bed & Breakfast. More than two dozen private homes are affiliated with this service, most of them scattered across Metro Toronto. Rooms cost as little as $50 a night and include breakfast. *Tel. 416/961–3676.*

The Arts and Nightlife

The Arts

Toronto is the capital of the lively arts in Canada. True, Winnipeg has a very fine ballet, and Montréal's orchestra is superb. But in nearly every aspect of music, opera, dance, and theater, Toronto is truly the New York City of the North.

The best places to get information on cultural happenings are in the Thursday editions of the *Toronto Star*; the Saturday *Globe and Mail*, the free weeklies *Now* and *eye*, and *Toronto Life*. For half-price tickets on the day of a performance, don't forget the **Five Star Tickets booth,** located in the Royal Ontario Museum lobby during the winter and, at other times, at the corner of Yonge and Dundas streets, outside the Eaton Centre. The museum booth is open daily 10–7, the Yonge and Dundas booth is open—in good weather—Monday–Saturday noon– 7:30, and Sunday 11–3. Tickets are sold for cash only, all sales are final, and a small service charge is added to the price of each ticket. The booth outside the Eaton Centre also gives out piles of superb brochures and pamphlets on the city.

Concert Halls and Theaters The **Roy Thomson Hall** (just below the CN Tower) has become since 1982 the most important concert hall in Toronto. It is the home today of the Toronto Symphony and the Toronto Mendelssohn Choir, one of the world's finest choral groups. It also hosts orchestras from around the world and popular entertainers from Liza Minnelli to Anne Murray. *60 Simcoe St., at the corner of King Street W, a block west of University Ave., tel. 416/593–4828. Tickets $20–$60 (best rows H and J in the orchestra and row L upstairs). Rush seats are sold the day of a performance, two hours before show time. Tours of the stunning structure take place Mon.–Sat. 12:30 PM (cost: $3, but do call; it is subject to cancellation. Tel. 416/593–4822, ext. 363. On Wed. at 12:30 you can tour the impressive organ for $5).*

Massey Hall has always been cramped and dingy, but its near-perfect acoustics and its handsome, U-shape tiers sloping down to the stage have made it a happy place to hear the Toronto Symphony, or almost anyone else in the world of music, for almost a century. The nearly 2,800 seats are not terribly comfortable, but it remains a venerable place to catch the greats and near-greats. *178 Victoria St. at Shuster, a few feet east of the Eaton Centre, tel. 416/593–4828. Best seats are rows G–M, center, and in the balcony, rows 32–50.*

The **O'Keefe Centre** has become the home of the Canadian Opera Company and the National Ballet of Canada. It is also home to visiting comedians, pre-Broadway musicals, rock stars, and almost anyone else who can fill it. When it was built in 1960, its 3,167 seats made it the largest concert hall on the continent. *1 Front St. E, a block east of Union Station, tel. 416/872–2262. Tickets $20–$50. Try for seats close to A47–48; avoid the very front rows, such as AA, BB, etc.*

About 50 yards east of the O'Keefe is the **St. Lawrence Centre for the Arts.** Since 1970, it has been presenting everything from live theater to string quartets and forums on city issues. The main hall, the luxuriously appointed **Bluma Appel Theatre,** hosts the often brilliant productions of the **Canadian Stage**

Company and **Theater Plus.** Classical and contemporary plays are often on a level with the best of Broadway and London's West End. *Front St. at the corner of Scott St., tel. 416/366–7723. Tickets $20–$45. Try for rows E–N, seats 1–10.*

The other important theater in the city is the **Royal Alexandra,** which has been the place to be seen in Toronto since its opening in 1907. The plush red seats, gold brocade, and baroque swirls and curlicues all make theatergoing a refined experience. It's astonishing to recall that all this magnificence was about to be torn down in the 1960s, but was rescued by none other than "Honest Ed" Mirvish of discount-store fame. He not only restored the theater to its former glory but also made it profitable. *260 King St. W, tel. 416/872–3333. Tickets $35–$75 (more for major musicals). Student tickets as low as $15. Avoid rows A and B; try for rows C–L center. For musicals, try the first rows of the first balcony.*

Classical Concerts   **The Toronto Symphony,** now over 65 years old, is not about to retire. Since 1922, with conductors of the quality of Seiji Ozawa, Walter Susskind, Sir Thomas Beecham, and Andrew Davis, it has achieved world acclaim. Its music director is Maestro Gunther Herbig. When the TS is home, it presents about three concerts weekly from September to May in Roy Thomson Hall (*see above*) and a miniseason each summer at Ontario Place. Tickets $16–$35.

The **Toronto Mendelssohn Choir** often guests with the Toronto Symphony. This 180-singer group, going since 1894, has been applauded worldwide, and its *Messiah* is handeled well every Christmas (no, we couldn't resist that). *For program information, tel. 416/598–0422; for tickets, Roy Thomson Hall.*

Opera   Since its founding in 1950, the **Canadian Opera Company** has grown into the largest producer of opera in Canada. Each year, at Toronto's O'Keefe Centre, more than 150,000 people attend the season of seven operas, with such world-class performers as Joan Sutherland, Grace Bumbry, Martina Arroyo, Marilyn Horne, and Canada's own Louis Quilico and Maureen Forrester. The COC also performs mini-operas in a tent during the summer, at Harbourfront. *Tel. 416/363–8231 or 416/393–7469.*

Dance   **National Ballet of Canada** made its official debut in 1951. In less than four decades, the company has done some extraordinary things, with such principal dancers as Karen Kain, Frank Augustyn, Kevin Pugh, and Owen Montague all wowing the Russians at the Moscow competitions. *Performances Nov., Feb., and May at the O'Keefe Centre (see above); in summer at Ontario Pl. Office, tel. 416/362–1041, 416/872–1111, or 416/872–2277. Tickets $15–$55.*

Toronto Dance Theatre, its roots in the Martha Graham tradition, tours Canada and has played major festivals in England, Europe, and the United States. *Most performances are in the Premiere Dance Theatre, at Harbourfront, 235 Queen's Quay W, tel. 416/869–8444.*

Theater   There are more than four dozen performing spaces in Toronto; we will mention only a handful of the most prominent.

The **Young People's Theatre,** the only theater center in the country devoted solely to children, does not condescend or compromise its dramatic integrity. *165 Front St. E, near Sherbourne, tel. 416/864–9732.*

The **Elgin** and **Winter Garden Theaters** are two recently renovated old vaudeville places, stacked upon each other. (The
Elgin, downstairs, has about 1,500 seats; the Winter Garden is
some 500 seats smaller; both are stunningly attractive.) *189
Yonge St., just north of Queen, tel. 416/872–5555.*

Second City, just east of the heart of downtown, has been providing some of the best comedy in North America since its
owner Andrew Alexander bought the rights to the name for
one dollar. Among those who have cut their teeth on the
Toronto stage are the late Gilda Radner, Dan Aykroyd, Martin
Short, Andrea Martin, Catherine O'Hara, and John Candy.
Shows can be seen alone or in a dinner-theater package. *Old
Firehall Theatre, 110 Lombard St., corner of Jarvis St., tel.
416/863–1111.*

When planning your trip to Toronto, consider contacting the
North York Performing Arts Centre (5040 Yonge St., tel.
416/733–9388)—situated less than a half-hour's drive north of
the waterfront—to see the wildly acclaimed Hal Prince production of the classic American musical **Show Boat;** the for-
ever-running **Phantom of the Opera** at the stunning **Pantages
Theatre** downtown; and **Miss Saigon,** which should run a long
time at the new **Prince of Wales Theatre,** next to the Royal Alex.
Expect good seats to run close to $100 each, but these Broad-
way-quality productions are worth paying for.

Next to Second City, **Yuk-Yuk's Komedy Kabaret** has always
been the major place for comedy in Toronto. This is where the
zany comedian Howie Mandel and the inspired impressionist
Jim Carrey got their starts, and where such comic luminaries
as George Carlin, Rodney Dangerfield, Robin Williams, and
Mort Sahl have presented their best routines. *1280 Bay St., just
above Bloor St., 2335 Yonge St., just above Eglinton Ave. and
5165 Dixie, just above Eglinton, tel. 416/967–6425. Cover charge:
$7 and up. Yonge St. location closed Sun.*

Mysteriously Yours ... should be of special interest to murder-
mystery buffs. On Thursday, Friday, and Saturday evenings, a
"despicable crime" is perpetrated at the Royal York Hotel. The
mystery begins to unravel during dinner (cocktails at 6:30) and
is solved after dinner, by 10. The complete dinner and mystery
costs $50–$60 per person, including tax and tip. Call Brian
Caws at 416/486–7469 or 800/NOT–DEAD.

Film Every September since 1976, Toronto has been holding a
world-class film festival, called—with no great modesty—**The
Festival of Festivals** (tel. 416/967–7371). Whether retrospec-
tives of the films of Marguerite Duras, Jean-Luc Godard, and
Max Ophuls, or tributes to the careers of Martin Scorsese,
Robert Duvall, and John Schlesinger, this is the time for lovers
of film.

Toronto is one of the film capitals of the world, and you can
often catch a movie here that is not showing anywhere else—or
even available on video.

Carlton Cinemas, part of the Cineplex chain, shows rare, important films from around the world in nearly a dozen screen-
ing rooms. *20 Carlton St., just steps east of the College St.
subway, tel. 416/296–FILM.*

Nightlife

Jazz Clubs **Bermuda Onion Restaurant and Jazz Club,** just southeast of the hot corner of Bloor and University, provides endless neon, aluminum tables, and some of the best jazz in Toronto. There's even a Sunday jazz brunch! *131 Bloor St. W, tel. 416/925–1470.*

A few blocks east of Eaton Centre is **George's Spaghetti House** (290 Dundas St. E, corner of Sherbourne St., tel. 416/923– 9887), the oldest jazz club in the city. The music starts at 8:30 PM, with the world-famous Moe Koffman (of "Swinging Shepherd Blues" fame) performing one week each month. (For Moe, and on weekends, you'll need reservations.) George's has a modest cover charge and a decent Italian menu. *Closed Sun.*

Chick 'n Deli has long been one of the great jazz places in Toronto. A casual atmosphere prevails, and the lack of dress code helps with the neighborhood-bar ambience. There's a dance floor and dark wood everywhere, giving it a publike feel. It's also famous for wings and live music; the former half-price, Mon.–Tues. until 9, the latter playing at 9 PM most nights, and 7:30 on Sunday. Check out the occasional jazz shows, and Sunday brunch—all you can eat for less than $10. *744 Mount Pleasant Rd., near Eglinton Ave., tel. 416/489–3363 or 489–7931.*

Top O' The Senator, this city's first club exclusively for jazz, has the atmosphere of a between-the-wars lounge. With its long wooden bar and towering dark-blue ceilings, this is one fabulous place. *249 Victoria St., tel. 416/364–7517.*

Rock and Most major international recording companies have offices in
Popular Music Toronto, so the city is a regular stop for top musical performers of today, whether Frank Sinatra, Billy Joel, Whitney Houston, Sting, Michael Jackson, or Bruce Springsteen. Tickets ($15– $40) can usually be booked through **Ticketmaster** (tel. 416/872– 1111).

Major venues include the **SkyDome,** on Front Street, tel. 416/963–3513; **Maple Leaf Gardens,** 60 Carlton Street, a block east of Yonge Street and the College Street subway stop, tel. 416/977–1641; the **O'Keefe Centre,** Yonge and Front streets, tel. BASS, 416/872–2262; and **Exhibition Stadium,** at the CNE grounds, tel. 416/393–6000. **Ontario Place** (tel. 416/965–7711) has pop, rock, and jazz concerts all summer at a nominal cost. We say "nominal" because you may pay around $10 to see/hear a fabulous singer or group (or orchestra or ballet corps) that would cost you $25–$50 elsewhere. This is one of the loveliest and least expensive places for concerts in all of Toronto.

Kingswood Music Theatre, next to Canada's Wonderland, also has important rock and pop concerts during the warmer months. *Hwy. 400, 10 min north of Hwy. 401, tel. 416/832–8131. Admission usually less than $10 above the cost of Canada's Wonderland.*

Since May 1989, **Superstars Niteclub** has been packing 1,700 people nightly into its giant room. Monday through Wednesday, it has professional acts, on the line of The Fixx, Jerry Seinfeld, and the late Sam Kineson, with prices ranging $10–$25. Thursday to Saturday is for dancing, with a cover of about $9. Hamburgers, chicken fingers, etc., provide the fuel. Laws banning liquor from being served on Sunday have freed the owners to use the place for children's and teen's concerts, featuring rap groups. *6487 Dixie Rd., 1 mi north of Hwy. 401, tel. 416/670–2211. Open Mon.–Sat. 7 PM–2 AM.*

A major showcase for more daring arts in Toronto has long been **The Rivoli,** along the Queen Street "mall." A place for new, local artists not yet established enough to have their own gallery showings, the back room functions as a club, with theater happenings, "new music" (progressive rock and jazz), comedy troupes with very funny improvisations twice a month, and more. *332 Queen St. W, just west of University Ave., tel. 416/597–0794. No dress code. Cover charge: $5–$10. Closed Sun.*

Rhythm and Blues The undisputed champion of R&B in Toronto is **Club Bluenote,** a few blocks north of the Yorkville area. It's unique, with many world-class musicians and singers frequenting it, and occasionally getting up and doing their stuff. The club has a small dance floor and attracts a 25–50 year-old upper-class clientele. And this is no hit bar; people come here to listen to music in a serious way. When Whitney Houston, Sugar Ray Leonard, et al., are in town, this is where they go. *128 Pears Ave., tel. 416/924–8244. Usually closed Sun. Cover charge: $8–$10.*

Right next door is **Network,** an entertainment lounge specializing in name acts of the quality of The Stylistics, Junior Walker, and Goodman and Brown. It's a supper club and show, with the cover and buffet combined at a reasonable $20 or so. The only dress code is "No Jeans," and there is a dance floor. The clientele is urban professionals in their early thirties; the decor is modern—brass, black, polished oak. *138 Pears Ave., near Davenport Rd., tel. 416/924–1768.*

Albert's Hall has been called one of the top 25 bars in all of North America, in spite of its shabby decor. It features top blues bands. The crowd is older and more laid-back than downstairs, in the Brunswick, but it's still noisy and friendly—and loud. *481 Bloor St. W, near Spadina Ave., tel. 416/964–2242. Cover charge on weekends; closed Sun.*

Dancing DJs play '60s music (downstairs) and '90s music (upstairs) in a four-story century-old funhouse named **Big Bop.** Thursday night is Ladies' Night, with no cover for women. In rebellion against the New York School of Glitzy, there is no chrome or mirrors—just a deliberate effort to be campy, vibrant, and unpretentious. The clientele is 18–25. It's a true meat market, but it doesn't pretend to be otherwise. Capacity is 800, and jeans are de rigueur. Many international stars walk in, but the owner insists that it's no big deal. (No big deal? Jack Nicholson. William Hurt. Matt Dillon!) *651 Queen St. W, tel. 416/366–6699. Open weekends to 3 AM.*

In the heart of Yorkville is **The Copa,** which has to be seen to be believed. The former warehouse is gigantic, with a capacity of 1,100! The crowd is in the 20–25 range and on the prowl. There's a zillion-dollar light show, with lasers and video screens. Tina Turner played for its grand opening; B.B. King and Ray Parker, Jr., have also performed here. The music is Top-40; on Sunday nights, it gets funkier. *21 Scollard St., entrance off Yorkville Ave., tel. 416/922–6500. Cover charge: $10.*

Heartbreak Hotel is all concrete and steel, and was known as the **Boom Boom Room,** one of Toronto's best rock-and-roll dance places, until the late 1980s. Here you can hear and dance to heavy metal or more trendy beats, with the worst sexism showing in the prices: "Guys, $5, Girls, $3." Ages range from 19 to 30, so beware. *650¹/₂ Queen St. W, 2 blocks west of Bathurst, tel. 416/368–6468. Open Wed.–Sat., 9 PM–2 AM.*

A bar/club called **StiLife** recently opened downtown and is very popular. It caters to an older (25–35) crowd and to rapidly aging 40-year-olds. The decor is metallic and modular, with all the furnishings custom-made. The art is aided by sophisticated lighting. No jeans or sneakers. A DJ provides dance music, and the clientele is Yorkville-ish, with many clothing designers, other restaurant owners, etc. Check out the bathrooms—you'll find out why. *217 Richmond St. W, tel. 416/593–6116. Closed Sun. Cover charge: $6–$15.*

Rockit has been described as "the mainstream dance crowd's terrestrial equivalent to rock-and-roll heaven." The pizza is dynamite, the wood-and-brass bar is gorgeous, and upstairs are the college kids in uniform (cool ties and designer jeans), dancing away to the Big Hits. *120 Church St., just east of Yonge Street, tel. 416/947–9555.*

Lounges Up on the 51st floor of the ManuLife Centre, **The Aquarius Lounge** is the highest piano lounge in the city. The busy time in the summer is Thursday–Saturday after 8:30 PM, but there's a high turnover, so the wait is never too long. In the winter, the lines begin as early as 8 PM. Its romantic atmosphere makes this a marvelous place for a date. No shorts, but jeans are allowed. *55 Bloor St. W, at Bay St., tel. 416/967–5225.*

In the Brownstone Hotel is **Notes,** an intimate bar/restaurant with a grand piano and a grand bar around it. It's done up in pink and beige tones, with black-lacquer furniture and antiques. You'll find no windows here, and the lighting is dim, but it's a good, quiet place to get to know someone. Dinner for two runs about $40–$50, including wine (their fresh sole is fine). A fine pianist entertains Tuesday–Saturday. *15 Charles St. E, tel. 416/924–7381.*

In the classy Four Seasons Hotel is **La Serre,** which looks like a library in a mansion: plush and green, with lots of brass and dark wood. It has a stand-up piano bar and a pianist worth standing for. Drinks, coffees, and teas are all expensive, but what can you expect in one of the costliest hotels in the country? Weekdays attract a business crowd, weekends bring out the couples. *Avenue Rd. and Yorkville Ave., tel. 416/964–0411.*

The **Park Plaza Roof Lounge** has been used as a setting in the writings of such Canadian literary luminaries as Margaret Atwood and Mordecai Richler. The decor used to be plush, in an older European style, with chandelier, marble tables, and waiters in red jackets. It remains an important hangout for the upper-middle class, businesspeople, professional, and, *bien sur,* literary types. It was renovated in 1990, but it's still gorgeous and tasteful. *In the Park Plaza Hotel, Avenue Rd. and Bloor St., tel. 416/924–5471.*

3 Montréal

By Patricia Lowe

Updated by
Dorothy Guinan

"Plus ça change, plus c'est la mème chose," like other travel clichés, no longer applies to Montréal, which marked its 350th anniversary in 1992. For years, as Québec's largest city and the world's third-largest French-speaking metropolis, Montréal clung to an international reputation attained in the heyday of former Mayor Jean Drapeau, who brought his beloved hometown the 1967 World's Fair (Expo '67), the Métro subway, its Underground City, and the 1976 Summer Olympics. During his nearly three decades in power, Drapeau's entrepreneurial spirit added pizzazz to this transportation and financial capital at the gateway to the St. Lawrence Seaway.

But with the arrival of a nationalist provincial government in 1976, the mayor and Montréal were forced to rest on their laurels as the province agonized over its place in Canada. Separation from the rest of the country was seriously considered. The provincial government passed Bill 101, a controversial language act (still in force) making French the official language of business and public communication. For the city it was a wrenching ideological change; the only difference that visitors saw was that English or bilingual billboards and public signs were replaced by French ones.

Nearly 60% of the province's population opted in 1980 to remain in the federal family, but a decade later, French-speaking Québeckers' (Québécois') old animosities regarding English Canada were rekindled when Prime Minister Mulroney attempted to unite all 10 provinces through a constitutional agreement called the Meech Lake accord. However, the legislatures of two provinces did not ratify the accord. In 1992, Mulroney came up with a more elaborate plan, this time allowing the Canadian people to decide in a referendum. On October 26, six provinces rejected a deal that would have radically changed the country's 125-year-old Constitution. Today, the problem remains unresolved.

The melding of old and new architecture that characterizes this city is no more apparent than in the flamboyant office tower of La Maison des Coopérants. Even though the design of this 35-story pink glass structure imitates the Gothic-style Christ Church Cathedral it overshadows, it was not what the earnest French missionaries who founded Montréal envisioned. What today is a metropolis of 3.1 million—some 15% of English mother tongue—began as 54 dedicated souls from France who landed on Montréal island in 1642 to convert the Indians to Christianity.

For nearly 200 years city life was confined to a 95-acre walled community, today's Vieux-Montréal and a protected historic site. Ville-Marie became a fur-trading center, the chief embarkation point for the voyageurs setting off on discovery and trapping expeditions. This business quickly usurped religion as the settlement's raison d'être, along with its role as a major port at the confluence of the St. Lawrence and Ottawa rivers.

The Old Montréal of the French regime lasted until 1759, when during one of the battles of the Seven Years' War, British troops easily forced the poorly fortified and demoralized city to surrender. The Treaty of Paris ended the war in 1763, and Québec became one of Great Britain's most valuable colonies. British and Scottish settlers poured in to take advantage of Montréal's geography and economic potential. When it was incorporated

Montréal Exploring *(Boxes Refer to Detail Maps)*

Tour 3

Tour 2

rue Villeneuve

av. Christophe-Colomb

av. du Mont-Royal

rue Marie-Anne

de Marie-Anne

avenue Laval

av. Duluth

blvd St-Laurent

St-Urbain

av. des Pins

r. Jeanne-Mance

r. Prince Arthur

Milton

rue Sherbrooke

rue Ontario

rue Aylmer

côte du Beaver Hall

University

r. de Bleury

av. Viger

rue Ste-Catherine

blvd. René-Lévesque

r. de la Gauchetière

rue St-Antoine

rue Notre-Dame

rue Peel

rue Mill

autoroute Bonaventure

avenue Pierre-Dupuy

rue St-Denis

rue Rachel

rue Roy

rue Fabre

rue de Lanaudière

avenue du Parc Lafontaine

avenue Calixa-Lavallée

avenue Papineau

avenue de Lorimier

Parthenais

Panet

rue Chapleau

rue d'Iberville

Parc Lafontaine

rue Amherst

blvd. de Maisonneuve

rue Sherbrooke

rue Hochelaga

rue de Rouen

rue Hogan

rue Bercy

rue Ontario

rue Davidson

rue Moreau

rue Ste-Catherine

rue Notre-Dame

Olympic Park

Tour 1

Pont Jacques-Cartier

Île Ste-Hélène

Pont de la Concorde

Île Notre-Dame

Fleuve Saint-Laurent

Pont Victoria

N

0   1/2 mile

0   500 meters

as a city in 1832, it was a leading colonial capital of business, finance, and transportation.

Montréal is still Canada's transport hub: It is home to the national railway and airline, the largest private rail company (Canadian Pacific), the International Air Transport Association (IATA), and the United Nations' International Civil Aviation Organization (ICAO) on Sherbrooke.

Solidly established by the late 19th century, downtown today still reminds visitors of its grand old days, particularly along rue Sherbrooke, the lifeline of chic Montréal. The busy flower-lined stretch between rues Guy and University takes in the de la Montagne–Crescent–Bishop–Mackay sector, where sophisticated restaurants, cafés, and bars share canopied facades with haute-couture salons, antiques shops, and art galleries.

Rue Peel, between rue Sherbrooke and Place du Canada, rolls through the Montréal most tourists visit. The recently renovated Dominion Square Building is the art deco home of tourism offices and information bureaus. Bus tours, taxi guides, and *calèches* (horse-drawn carriages) all depart from some point around this public park.

To the east, rue St-Denis and the surrounding Latin Quarter attract Francophiles; a more ethnic flavor characterizes the Chinese, Greek, Portuguese, and other districts around Prince Arthur's pedestrian mall, boulevard St-Laurent, and avenue du Parc.

A bohemian atmosphere pervades rue Prince Arthur, blocked off to traffic between boulevard St-Laurent and Carré St-Louis. What the mall's many restaurants sometimes lack in quality they make up for in ethnic diversity—Chinese, Greek, Italian, Polish, Québecois, and Vietnamese—and price, especially at establishments where you supply the liquor (BYO). Some 12,000 Portuguese residents live in the area's St-Louis district, and their bright pastel houses and lush front gardens have contributed to the neighborhood's renaissance.

Early in this century, rue St-Denis cut through a bourgeois neighborhood of large, comfortable residences. After a period of decline, it revived in the early 1970s, and then boomed, largely as a result of the 1979 opening of Université du Québec's Montréal campus and the launch of the International Jazz Festival in the summer of 1980. Rows of French and ethnic restaurants, charming bistros, even hangouts for chess masters cater to Franco- and Anglo-academics, and stylish intellectuals prowl the Québec designer boutiques, antiques shops, and art galleries.

Activity reaches its peak during the 10 days in late June and early July, when some 500,000 jazz buffs descend upon the city to hear music giants such as Pat Metheny and Montréal-born Oscar Peterson. Theaters hosting the 1,000 or so performers range from sidewalk stages to Place des Arts, the main performing arts center in downtown Montréal.

The popularity of the jazz festival is rivaled only by August's World Film Festival, also featured near this area at Place des Arts and Cinéma Le Parisien on rue Ste-Catherine, among other venues.

Place des Arts and the adjacent Complexe Desjardins constitute another intriguing hive of activity. Now joined by the new home of the Musée d'Art Contemporain, which opened in 1992, Place des Arts is really three separate halls built around a sweeping plaza overlooking rue Ste-Catherine.

One often-overlooked sector of the city requires a Métro ride but is worth the fare for a varied tour of Olympic and de Maisonneuve parks, the Château Dufresne Decorative Arts Museum, the Botanical Garden, and the Biodome—all located at or near the corner of boulevard Pie-IX (Métro station of the same name) and rue Sherbrooke Est.

This triangle in the east end is distinguished by the flying-saucer design of the Olympic Stadium, completed by the world's "tallest inclined tower." The stadium's latest attraction is the funicular cable car that speeds sightseers to its observation deck for a spectacular view of the island of Montréal.

Essential Information

Arriving and Departing by Plane

Airports Montréal is served by two airports: **Dorval International,** 22½ kilometers (14 miles) west of the city, handles domestic and most U.S. flights; **Mirabel International,** 54½ kilometers (34 miles) northwest of the city, is a hub for the rest of the international trade.

Airlines From the United States: **Air Canada** (tel. 514/393–3333 or 800/361–8620) has nonstop service from New York, Miami, and Tampa; nonstop from Boston via Air Canada's connector airline, **Air Alliance;** direct service is available from Los Angeles and San Francisco. **American Airlines** (tel. 800/433–7300) has nonstop service from Chicago with connections from the rest of the United States. **British Airways** (tel. 514/287–9133; in Québec province, 800/668–1059) has nonstop service from Detroit to Montréal. **Canadian Airlines International,** formerly CP Air (tel. 514/847–2211; in Canada, 800/363–7530; in U.S., 800/426–7000), has a nonstop charter from Fort Lauderdale and direct or connecting service from Hawaii and Los Angeles. **Delta Air Lines** (tel. 514/337–5520, in Québec Province, 800/361–1970; in U.S., 800/221–1212) has nonstops from Boston, Hartford, Connecticut, and Miami and connecting service from most major U.S. cities. **USAir** (tel. 800/428–4322) has nonstop service from Buffalo and Syracuse, New York, and from Pittsburgh.

Flying Time From New York, 1½ hours; from Chicago, two hours; from Los Angeles, 6½ hours (with a connection).

Between the Airports and Center City Dorval Airport is about a 20- to 30-minute drive from downtown Montréal, and Mirabel International is about a 45-minute drive away.

By Taxi A taxi from Dorval to downtown will cost $25. The taxi rates from Mirabel to the center of Montréal are $56, and you can count on about the same cost for a taxi between the two airports. All taxi companies in Montréal must charge the same rates by law. It is best to have Canadian money with you, because the exchange rate for U.S. dollars is at the driver's discretion.

By Bus   **Aéroplus** (tel. 514/476–1100) provides a much cheaper alternative into town from Mirabel. For $14 an Aéroplus van will take you into the city, with stops at Le Reine Elizabeth (Queen Elizabeth)—next to Gare Centrale—and the Voyageur bus station. It runs every hour from 4 AM until noon and 8 PM until 2 AM, and every half hour between 12:30 and 7:30. Bus service between Mirabel and Dorval is also available for $12, every hour from 9:20 AM until 11:20 AM and 8:20 PM until 11:20 PM. Between 11:40 AM and 8 PM the bus runs every 20 minutes.

Grayline (tel. 514/934–1222) offers bus transportation between Dorval and downtown Montréal for $9. On weekdays it runs every 20 minutes between 7:30 AM and 12:30 AM; on weekends every half hour between 7:30 AM and 12:30 AM.

Arriving and Departing by Train, Bus, and Car

By Train   The Gare Centrale (Central Station), on rue de la Gauchetière between rues University and Mansfield (behind La Reine Elizabeth—Queen Elizabeth Hotel—on boulevard René-Lévesque Ouest), is the rail terminus for all trains from the United States and from other Canadian provinces. It is connected by underground passageway to the Métro's Bonaventure stop (schedule information, tel. 514/871–1331).

Amtrak (tel. 800/USA–RAIL) offers the all-reserved overnight *Montrealer,* which gives travelers in the Northeast the option of day or night transportation. It has a dining car with snacks and full dinners. Sleepers are available and advised because the reclining seat-footrest combination is not conducive to a good night's sleep. Make sleeper reservations well in advance, since they book early. The unreserved *Adirondack* departs New York's Penn Station every morning and takes 10½ hours to reach Montréal. It has a snack car but no dinner service or sleepers. A round-trip ticket on either train is cheaper than two one-way fares, except during major holidays.

VIA Rail (tel. 514/871–1331; in Québec province, 800/361–5390; in the United States, 800/561–3949) connects Montréal by train with all the major cities of Canada, including Québec City, Halifax, Ottawa, Toronto, Winnipeg, Edmonton, and Vancouver.

By Bus   **Greyhound** has coast-to-coast service and serves Montréal with buses arriving from and departing for various cities in North America. **Voyageur** and **Voyageur-Colonial** service destinations primarily within Québec and Ontario. **Vermont Transit** (tel. 514/842–2281) also serves Montréal, by way of Boston, New York, and other points in New England. Both lines use the city's downtown bus terminal, Terminus Voyageur (tel. 514/842–2281), which connects with the Berri-UQAM Métro station in downtown.

By Car   Travelers can reach Montréal by a number of highways. It is accessible from the rest of Canada via Trans-Canada Highway 401, which connects from the east and west via Highways 20 and 40. The New York State Thruway (I–87) becomes Highway 15 at the Canadian border, and then it's 47 kilometers (30 miles) to the outskirts of Montréal. U.S. I–89 becomes two-lane Route 133 at the border, which is Highway 10 at St-Jean. From I–91 from Boston, you must take Highways 55 and 10 to reach Montréal. At the border you clear Canadian Customs, so be prepared with proof of citizenship and your vehicle's ownership papers. On holidays and during the peak summer season, expect waits of a half hour or more at the major crossings.

Once you're in Québec, the road signs will be in French, but they're designed so you shouldn't have much trouble understanding them. The speed limit is posted in kilometers; on highways the limit is 100 kph (about 62 mph). There are extremely heavy penalties for driving while intoxicated, and drivers and front-seat passengers must wear over-the-shoulder seat belts. Gasoline is sold in liters (3.75 liters equal 1 U.S. gallon), and lead-free is called *sans plomb*. If you're traveling in the depths of winter, remember that your car may not start on extra-cold mornings unless it has been kept in a heated garage. All Montréal parking signs are in French, so brush up on your *gauche* (left) and *droit* (right).

You should be aware that Montréal police have a diligent towaway and fine system for cars double-parked or stopped in no-stopping zones in downtown Montréal during rush hours and business hours. The penalty will cost between $30 and $40. If your car is towed away while illegally parked, it will cost an additional $35 to retrieve it. New York State, Maine, and Ontario residents should drive with extra care in Québec: Traffic violations in the province (and vice versa) are entered on their driving records.

Getting Around

By Métro and Bus You should be armed with a few maps to see Montréal, but you won't need a car; public transit will do quite well, thank you. The Métro is clean, quiet (it runs on rubber wheels), and relatively safe, and it's heated in winter and cooled in summer. Métro hours are from 5:30 AM to 12:30 AM Sunday through Friday, and 5:30 AM to 1 AM on Saturday. The Blue Line runs daily from 5:30 AM to 11 PM. Trains run as often as every three minutes on the most crowded lines. It's also connected to the 15 kilometers (9.3 miles) of the Underground City, so you may not need to go outside during bad weather. Each of the 65 Métro stops has been individually designed and decorated; Berri-UQAM has stained glass, and at Place d'Armes a small collection of archaeological artifacts is exhibited. The recently opened stations between Snowdon and Jean-Talon on the Blue Line are worth a visit, particularly Outremont, with its glass-block design. Each station connects with one or more bus routes, which cover the rest of the island. The STCUM (Société de Transport de la Communauté Urbaine de Montréal) administers both the Métro and the buses, so the same tickets and transfers are valid on either service. You should be able to go within a few blocks of anywhere in the city on one fare. At press time (spring 1993) rates are: $1.75; six tickets, $6; monthly pass, $43.

Free maps may be obtained at Métro ticket booths. Try to get the *Carte Réseau* (system map); it's the most complete. Transfers from Métro to buses are available from the dispenser just beyond the ticket booth inside the station. Bus-to-bus and bus-to-Métro transfers may be obtained from the bus driver. Information on reaching your destination can be had by dialing 514/AUTOBUS (288–6287).

By Taxi Taxis in Montréal all run on the same rate: $2.25 minimum and $1 a kilometer (at press time). They're usually prompt and re-

Montréal Metro

liable, although they may be hard to find on rainy nights after the Métro has closed. Each carries on its roof a white or orange plastic sign that is lit when available and off when occupied.

Important Addresses and Numbers

Tourist Information **Greater Montreal Convention and Tourism Bureau,** 1555 rue Peel, Suite 600, Montréal, Québec H3A 1X6 (tel. 514/844–5400 or 800/363–7777) or **Tourisme-Québec** (tel. 514/873–2015).

Stop by the new downtown headquarters for Info-Touriste, the new home of Tourisme-Québec (tel. 514/873–2015 or 800/363–7777), on the north side of Square Dorchester. It's run by the Greater Montreal Convention and Tourism Bureau, and is open daily, June 10–Labor Day, 8:30 AM–7:30 PM; Labor Day–June 9, 9–6. Info-Touriste also operates a smaller tourist information center at 174 rue Notre-Dame Est (tel. 514/873–2015) in Vieux-Montréal, at the corner of Place Jacques-Cartier, and is open Labor Day–mid-May, daily 9–1 and 2–5; mid-May–Labor Day, daily 9–7.

Consulates **United States** (1155 St-Alexandre, Métro Place des Arts, tel. 514/398–9695).

United Kingdom (1155 rue University, Métro McGill, tel. 514/866–5863).

Emergencies Dialing 911 will put you through to the **police, fire,** and **ambulance.**

Doctors and
Dentists The U.S. Consulate cannot recommend specific doctors and dentists but does provide a list of various specialists in the Montréal area. Call in advance (tel. 514/398–9695) to make sure the consulate is open.

Dental clinic (tel. 514/342–4444) open 24 hours, Sun. emergency appointments only; **Montréal General Hospital** (tel. 514/937–6011); the **Québec Poison Control Centre** (800/463–5060); **Touring Club de Montréal-AAA, CAA, RAC** (514/861–7111).

Late-night
Pharmacies Many pharmacies are open weeknights until 11 PM, weekends until 10, including: **Jean Coutu** (1370 Mt. Royal, tel. 514/527–8827; 1836 Ste-Catherine O, tel. 514/933–4221).

Travel Agencies **American Express** (1141 boul. de Maisonneuve O, tel. 514/284–3300). **Thomas Cook** (1155 rue University, Suite 314, tel. 514/398–0555).

Opening and Closing Times

Banks are open weekdays from 10 to 4, with some banks open until 5 on weekdays and on Saturday morning. Many Montréal banks also have 24-hour banking-machine services.

A new law that passed in December 1992 allows shops to stay open weekdays 9–9 and weekends 9–5. However, many merchants close Monday–Wednesday evenings and on Sunday. You'll find many specialty service shops closed on Monday, particularly in predominantly French neighborhoods. Stores in designated tourist zones, such as Vieux-Montréal, remain open on Sunday.

Guided Tours

Orientation **Gray Line** (tel. 514/934–1222) has eight different tours of Montréal in the summer, and one tour during the winter, including Île Ste-Hélène and the Laurentians. It offers pickup service at the major hotels, or you may board the buses at Info-Touriste (1001 Square Dorchester).

Amphi Tour Ltée (tel. 514/386–1298) offers a unique tour of Vieux-Montréal (Old Montréal) and the Vieux-Port (Old Port) on both land and water in an amphibious bus. The one-hour tours run from May 1 to October 31.

Boat Tours **Montreal Harbour Cruises** (tel. 514/842–3871) offers two-hour and day-long harbor cruises daily, between May 1 and mid-October. Vessels have room for up to 400 passengers, and evening dinner cruises are available. Boats leave several times a day from the Clock Tower Pier at the foot of rue Berri in the Vieux-Port next to Vieux-Montréal (Métro Champs-de-Mars).

Calèche Rides Open horse-drawn carriages—fleece-lined in winter—leave from rue Notre-Dame between rue Bonsecours and rue Gosford, Square Dorchester, Place d'Armes and rue de la Commune. An hour-long ride is about $45 (tel. 514/653–0751).

Exploring Montréal

By Andrew Coe

Updated by Dorothy Guinan

When you explore Montréal, there will be very little to remind you that it's an island. It lies in the St. Lawrence River roughly equidistant (256 kilometers, or 160 miles) from Lake Ontario and the point where the river widens into a bay. For its entire length, the St. Lawrence is flanked by flat, rich bottomland for 48 kilometers (30 miles) or more on each side. The only rise in the landscape is the 233-meter (764-foot) Mont Royal, which gave Montréal its name. The island itself is 51 kilometers (32 miles) long and 14 kilometers (9 miles) wide and is bounded on the north by the narrow Rivière des Prairies and on the south by the St. Lawrence. Aside from Mont Royal, the island is relatively flat, and because the majority of attractions are clustered around this hill, most tourists don't visit the rest of the island.

Head to the Mont Royal Belvedere (lookout) for a panoramic view of the city. You can drive most of the way, park, and walk 1/2 kilometer (1/4 mile) or hike all the way up from avenues Côte-des-Neiges or Côte des Pins. If you look directly out—southeast—from the belvedere, at the foot of the hill will be the McGill University campus and, surrounding it, the skyscrapers of downtown Montréal. Just beyond, along the banks of the St. Lawrence, are the stone houses of Vieux-Montréal. Hugging the opposite banks are the Îles Ste-Hélène and Notre-Dame (St. Helen's and Notre-Dame islands), sites of La Ronde amusement park, the Biosphere, the Palais de la Civilisation exhibition center, acres of parkland, and the Lac de l'Île Notre-Dame public beach.

There are a host of attractions that you can see on all-day and half-day trips. The most popular are the amusement park complex on Île St-Hélène and the Olympic Stadium and its neighbor, the Botanical Garden. The 500 forested acres of Parc du Mont-Royal are busy with joggers, strollers, and skaters all year. Beyond the city limits are the Eastern Townships and the Laurentians for day trips or weekends in the country.

Montréal is easy to explore. Street signs, subways, and bus lines are clearly marked. The city is divided by a grid of streets roughly aligned east–west and north–south. (This grid is tilted about 40 degrees off—to the left of—true north, so west is actually southwest and so on.) North–south street numbers begin at the Fleuve St-Laurent (St. Lawrence River) and increase as you head north. East–west street numbers begin at boulevard St-Laurent, which divides Montréal into east and west halves. The city is not so large that seasoned walkers can't see all the districts around the base of Mont Royal on foot.

Highlights for First-time Visitors

Botanical Garden/Olympic Park complex (*see* Parks and Gardens, *below*)
Historic Montréal, Tour 1: Vieux-Montréal
Mont Royal (*see* Parks and Gardens, *below*)
Rue St-Denis, Tour 3: St-Denis, Prince Arthur, and North
Rue Sherbrooke Ouest, Tour 2: Downtown Montréal

Tour 1: Vieux-Montréal (Old Montréal)

Numbers in the margin correspond to points of interest on the Tour 1: Vieux-Montréal map.

The Fleuve St-Laurent was the highway on which the first settlers arrived in 1642. Just past the island of Montréal are the Lachine Rapids, a series of violent falls over which the French colonists' boats could not safely travel. It was natural for them to build their houses just above the rapids, near the site of an old Iroquois settlement on the bank of the river nearest Mont Royal. In the mid-17th century Montréal consisted of a handful of wood houses clustered around a pair of stone buildings, the whole flimsily fortified by a wood stockade. For the next three centuries this district—bounded by rues McGill and Berri on the east and west, rue St-Antoine on the north, and the river to the south—was the financial and political heart of the city. Government buildings, the largest church, the stock exchange, the main market, and the port were there. The narrow but relatively straight streets were cobblestone and lined with solid, occasionally elegant houses, office buildings, and warehouses—also made of stone. Exiting the city meant using one of four gates through the thick stone wall that protected against Indians and marauding European powers. Montréal quickly grew past the bounds of its fortifications, however, and by World War I the center of the city had moved toward Mont Royal. The new heart of Montréal became Dominion Square (now Square Dorchester). For the next two decades Vieux-Montréal, as it became known, was gradually abandoned, the warehouses and offices emptied. In 1962 the city began studying ways to revitalize Vieux-Montréal, and a decade of renovations and restorations began.

Today, Vieux-Montréal is a center of cultural life and municipal government, if not of commerce and politics. Most of the summer activities revolve around Place Jacques-Cartier, which becomes a pedestrian mall with street performers and outdoor cafés spilling out of restaurants. This lovely square is a good place to view the fireworks festival, and it's adjacent to the Vieux-Port exhibition grounds and the docks for the harbor cruises. Classical music concerts are staged all year long at the Notre-Dame Basilica, which possesses one of the finest organs in North America, and plays are staged in English by the Centaur Theatre in the old stock-exchange building. This district has six museums devoted to history, religion, and decorative and fine arts.

To begin your tour of Vieux-Montréal, take the Métro to the Place d'Armes station, beneath the Palais des Congrès convention center, and walk 1½ blocks south on rue St-Urbain to **Place d'Armes.** In the 1600s, Place d'Armes was the site of battles with the Iroquois and later became the center of Montréal's "Upper Town." In the middle of the square is a statue of Paul de Chomedey, Sieur de Maisonneuve, the founder of Montréal. In 1644 he was wounded here in a battle with 200 Indians. Historians recently uncovered a network of tunnels beneath the square; they connected the various buildings, and one tunnel ran down to the river. These precursors of the Underground City protected the colonists from the extremes of winter weather and provided an escape route should the city be over-

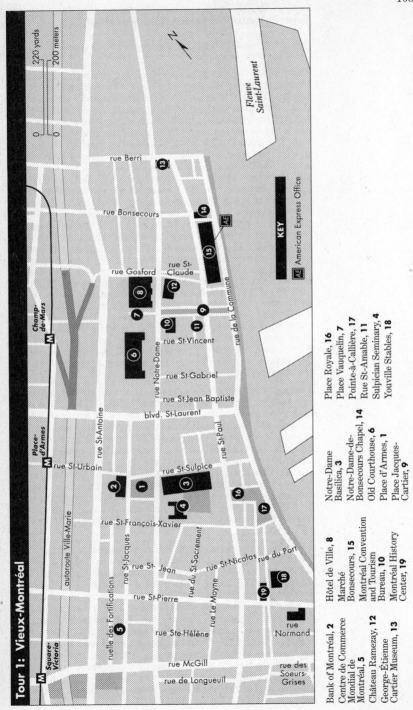

Tour 1: Vieux-Montréal

Bank of Montréal, **2**

Centre de Commerce Mondial de Montréal, **5**

Château Ramezay, **12**

George-Étienne Cartier Museum, **13**

Hôtel de Ville, **8**

Marché Bonsecours, **15**

Montréal Convention and Tourism Bureau, **10**

Montréal History Center, **19**

Notre-Dame Basilica, **3**

Notre-Dame-de-Bonsecours Chapel, **14**

Old Courthouse, **6**

Place d'Armes, **1**

Place Jacques-Cartier, **9**

Place Royale, **16**

Place Vauquelin, **7**

Pointe-à-Callière, **17**

Rue St-Amable, **11**

Sulpician Seminary, **4**

Youville Stables, **18**

KEY

AE American Express Office

run. Unfortunately, the tunnels are too small and dangerous to visit. Calèches are available at the south end of the square.

2 The north side of the square is dominated by the **Bank of Montréal,** an impressive building with Corinthian columns (remodeled by renowned architects McKim, Mead & White in 1905) that houses a small, interesting numismatics museum. *129 rue St-Jacques. Admission free. Open weekdays 9–5.*

The office building to the west of the square is the site of the old Café Dillon, a famous gourmet restaurant frequented by members of the fur traders' Beaver Club (*see* Dining, *below*). Two extremely important edifices form the south end of Place d'Armes: the Sulpician Seminary, the oldest building in Montréal, and the imposing Notre-Dame Basilica.

The first church called Notre-Dame was a bark-covered structure built within the fort in 1642, the year the first settlers arrived. Three times it was torn down and rebuilt, each time in a different spot, each time larger and more ornate. The enor-
3 mous (3,800-seat) neo-Gothic **Notre-Dame Basilica,** which opened in 1829, is the most recent. The twin towers, named Temperance and Perseverance, are 227 meters (69 feet) high, and the western one holds one of North America's largest bells, the 12-ton Gros Bourdon. The interior of the church was designed in medieval style by Victor Bourgeau, with stained-glass windows, a stunning blue vault ceiling with gold stars, and pine and walnut wood carving in traditional Québec style. The church has many unique features: It is rectangular rather than cruciform in shape; it faces south rather than east; the floor slopes down 4 meters (1¼ feet) from back to front; and it has twin rows of balconies on each side. The Casavants, a Québec family, built the 5,722-pipe organ, one of the largest on the continent. Notre-Dame has particularly excellent acoustics and is often the site of Montréal Symphony (tel. 514/842–9951) concerts, notably, Handel's *Messiah* during the week before Christmas and the Mozart Plus Festival in July. Behind the main altar is the Sacré-Coeur Chapel, which was destroyed by fire in 1978 and rebuilt in five different styles. Also in the back of the church is a small museum of religious paintings and historical objects. *116 rue Notre-Dame O. Basilica: tel. 514/849–1070. Open Labor Day–June 24, daily 7–6; June 25–Labor Day, daily 7 AM–8 PM. Guided tours daily (except Sun. morning) May–June 24, 9–4; June 24–Labor Day, 8:30–4:30; Labor Day–mid-Oct., 9–4. Museum: tel. 514/842–2925. Admission: $1 adults, 50¢ children. Open weekends 9:30–5.*

4 The low, more retiring stone building behind a wall to the west of the basilica is the **Sulpician Seminary.** This is Montréal's oldest building, built in 1685, and is still a residence for the Sulpician order (unfortunately, it's closed to the public). For almost two centuries, until 1854, the Sulpicians were *the* political power in the city, because they owned the property rights to the island of Montréal. They were also instrumental in recruiting and equipping colonists for New France. The building itself is considered the finest, most elegant example of rustic 17th-century Québec architecture. The clock on the roof over the main doorway is the oldest (pre-1701) public timepiece in North America. Behind the seminary building is a small garden, another Montréal first.

The street that runs alongside the basilica, **rue St-Sulpice,** was the first street in Montréal. On the eastern side of the street there's a plaque marking where the Hôtel-Dieu, the city's first hospital, was built in 1644. Now cross rue St-Sulpice—the Art Deco **Aldred Building** sits on the far left corner—and take rue Notre-Dame Est. One block farther, just past boulevard St-Laurent, on the left, rises the black-glass-sheathed **Palais de Justice** (1971), which houses the higher courts for both the city and the province. (Québec's legal system is based on the Napoleonic Code for civil cases and on British common law for criminal cases.)

5 A few blocks northwest on rue St-Jacques and rue St-Pierre is the site of the new **Centre de Commerce Mondial de Montréal** (World Trade Centre of Montréal), an ambitious block-long complex that combines old and new. It's home to the new Inter-Continental Hotel in Montréal, a retail mall, and office space. Developers of this innovative complex have gambled that they can attract businesses back from downtown to rue St-Jacques, which, when it was known as St. James Street, was the financial center of Canada.

6 In the direction of rue Notre-Dame, the large domed building at 155 rue Notre-Dame Est is the classic revival–style **Old Courthouse** (1857), now municipal offices. Across the street, at 160 rue Notre-Dame Est, is the **Maison de la Sauvegarde** (1811), one of the oldest houses in the city and now home to the European sausage restaurant, Chez Better (*see* Dining, *below*).

7 The Old Courthouse abuts the small **Place Vauquelin,** named after the 18th-century naval hero who is memorialized by a statue in its center. North of this square is **Champs-de-Mars,** the former site of a colonial military parade ground, for years a parking lot, and since a year of landscaping, completely transformed into a public park more in keeping with its origins. The ornate building on the east side of Place Vauquelin is the Second Empire–style **Hôtel de Ville** (City Hall, 1878). On July 24, **8** 1967, French President Charles de Gaulle stood on the central balcony of the hotel and made his famous *"Vive le Québec libre"* speech.

9 You are in a perfect spot to explore **Place Jacques-Cartier,** the heart of Vieux-Montréal. This two-block-long square opened in 1804 as a municipal market, and every summer it is transformed into a flower market. The 1809 monument at the top of the place celebrates Lord Nelson's victory at Trafalgar. At the western corner of rue Notre-Dame is a small building (1811), site of the old Silver Dollar Saloon, so named because there were 350 silver dollars nailed to the floor. Today it's the home **10** of the **Greater Montreal Convention and Tourism Bureau** (*see* Important Addresses and Numbers, *above*). Both sides of the place are lined with two- and three-story stone buildings that were originally homes or hotels.

Time Out **Le St-Amable** (188 rue St-Amable, tel. 514/866–3471) features a Businessmen's Lunch weekdays from noon to 3 PM, but you don't have to be an executive or even be dressed like one to sample such classics as fresh poached salmon or grilled New Zealand lamb chops.

11 In the summer, the one-block **rue St-Amable** becomes a marketplace for local jewelers, artists, and craftspeople. From the bottom of Place Jacques-Cartier you can stroll out into the **Port of Montreal Exhibition Ground,** where from Winter Carnival through summer there is always something going on. At the foot of boulevard St-Laurent and rue de la Commune are the port's major exhibitions: **Images du Futur, IMAX Super Cinema,** and **Expotec.**

Retrace your steps to the north end of Place Jacques-Cartier, then continue east on rue Notre-Dame. At the corner of rue **⑫** St-Claude on the right is **Château Ramezay** (1705), built as the residence of the 11th governor of Montréal, Claude de Ramezay. In 1775–76 it was the headquarters for American troops seeking to conquer Canada. Benjamin Franklin stayed here during that winter occupation. One of the most elegant colonial buildings still standing in Montréal, the château is now a museum, and it has been restored to the style of Governor de Ramezay's day. The ground floor is furnished like a gentleman's residence of New France, with dining room, bedroom, and office. *280 rue Notre-Dame E, tel. 514/861–3708. Admission: $5 adults, $3 students, $2 senior citizens, $10 families. Wheelchair visitors are advised to reserve 1 day in advance. Open Tues.–Sun. 10–4:30.*

At the end of rue St. Paul are two houses built by Sir George-Étienne Cartier, a 19th-century Canadian statesman. They re**⑬** cently have been opened as the **George-Étienne Cartier Museum.** Downstairs displays focus on the political career of this Québec-born Father of Canadian Confederation. Upstairs rooms are furnished as they would have been in the 1850s and 1860s when the Cartiers lived here. *458 rue Notre-Dame E, tel. 514/283–2282. Admission free. Open in summer, daily 9–5; rest of the year, Wed.–Sun. 10–noon and 1–5.*

One block back on rue St. Paul is rue Bonsecours, one of the oldest streets in the city. At the end of rue Bonsecours is the **⑭** small but beautiful **Notre-Dame-de-Bonsecours Chapel.** Marguerite de Bourgeoys, who was canonized in 1983, helped found Montréal and dedicated this chapel to the Virgin Mary in 1657. It became known as a sailor's church, and small wood models of sailing ships are suspended from the ceiling just above the congregation. In the basement there is a small, strange museum honoring the saint that includes a story of her life modeled by little dolls in a series of dioramas. A gift shop sells Marguerite de Bourgeoys souvenirs. From the museum you can climb to the rather precarious bell tower (beware of the slippery metal steps in winter) for a fine view of Vieux-Montréal and the port. *400 rue St-Paul E, tel. 514/845–9991. Admission: $2 adults, $1 students, 50¢ children. Chapel and museum open May–Oct., 9–4:30; Nov.–Apr., 10:30–2:30. Closed Mon.*

At the corner of St-Paul and Bonsecours is the historic **Maison du Calvet,** now a charming café. Double back and head west on rue St-Paul. The long, large, domed building to the left is the **⑮** **Marché Bonsecours** (1845), for many years Montréal's main produce, meat, and fish market and now municipal offices. The market has been transformed into a permanent cultural center with temporary exhibits on Montréal.

Rue St-Paul is the most fashionable street in Vieux-Montréal. For almost 20 blocks it is lined with fine restaurants, shops, and even a few nightclubs. Québecois handcrafts are a specialty here, with shops at 88, 136, and 272 rue St-Paul Est. **L'Air du**

Temps, at 191 rue St-Paul Ouest, is one of the city's top jazz clubs. Nightly shows usually feature local talent, with occasional international name bands. Take rue St-Paul eight short blocks west of Place Jacques-Cartier, and you will come to

16 **Place Royale,** the site of the first permanent settlement in Montréal.

17 Behind the Old Customs House you will find **Pointe-à-Callière,** a small park that commemorates the settlers' first landing. A small stream used to flow into the St. Lawrence here, and it was on the point of land between the two waters that the colonists landed their four boats at its mouth on May 17, 1642. After they built the stockade and the first buildings at this site, the settlement was almost washed away the next Christmas by a flood. When it was spared, de Maisonneuve placed a cross on top of Mont Royal as thanks to God. A 1½-block walk down rue

18 William takes you to the **Youville Stables** on the left. These low stone buildings enclosing a garden were originally built as warehouses in 1825 (they never were stables). A group of businesspeople renovated them in 1968, and the buildings now house offices, shops, and restaurants.

19 Across rue William from the stables is the **Montréal History Centre.** Visitors to this high-tech museum are led through a series of audiovisual environments depicting the life and history of Montréal. *335 Place d'Youville, tel. 514/872–3207. Admission: $4.25 adults, $2.75 senior citizens and students 6–17, children under 6 free (Jan. 5–Apr.); $4.50 adults, $3 senior citizens and students 6–17, children under 6 free (May–Dec.). Open Jan. 5–May 2, Tues.–Sun. 10–5; May 3–July 4, daily 9–5; July 5–Sept. 6, daily 10–6; Sept. 7–Dec. 12, Tues.–Sun. 10–5.*

Tour 2: Downtown

Numbers in the margin correspond to points of interest on the Tour 2: Downtown Montréal map.

Downtown is a sprawling 30-by 8-block area bounded by avenue Atwater and boulevard St-Laurent on the west and east, respectively, avenue des Pins on the north, and rue St-Antoine on the south.

After 1700, Vieux-Montréal wasn't big enough for the rapidly expanding city. In 1701 the French administration signed a peace treaty with the Iroquois, and the colonists began to feel safe about building outside Montréal's fortifications. The city inched northward, toward Mont Royal, particularly after the English conquest in 1760. By the end of the 19th century, rue Ste-Catherine was the main commercial thoroughfare, and the city's elite built mansions on the slope of the mountain. Since 1960 city planners have made a concerted effort to move the focus eastward. With the opening of Place des Arts (1963) and the Complexe Desjardins (1976), the city center shifted in that direction. It hasn't landed on any one corner yet, although some Montréalers will tell you it's at the intersection of avenue McGill College and rue Ste-Catherine.

A major development of the past 30 years is the inauguration of the **Underground City,** an enormous network of passages linking various shopping and office complexes. These have served to keep the retail trade in the downtown area, as well as to make shoppers and workers immune to the hardships of the Canadian winter.

Our tour of downtown—unless you are hale of limb you may not be able to do all of it in a day—begins at the McGill Métro station. The corner of rue University and boulevard de Maisonneuve has recently been the center of intensive development. Two huge office buildings, **2020 University** and **Galleries 2001,** with malls at street and basement levels, rise from the north side of the intersection. The southwest corner, indeed the entire block, is taken up by **Eaton** (*see* Shopping, *below*), one of the Big Three department stores in the city. Aside from many floors of mid-priced clothing and other merchandise, the real attraction of Eaton is the ninth-floor art deco dining room.

Time Out   **Eaton le 9e** was modeled after the dining room of the luxury liner *Île-de-France,* Lady Eaton's favorite cruise ship. Elegant marble columns hold up the ceiling, and the walls are decorated with two art deco murals featuring willowy ladies at leisure. The patrons are usually shoppers, of course, dining on pasta, fish, and meat dishes. The service is practical and fast; the decor's the thing. *677 rue Ste-Catherine O, tel. 514/284–8421. AE, MC, V. Open Mon.–Wed. 11:30–3, Thurs. and Fri. 11:30–3 and 4:30–7, Sat. 11:30–3. Closed Sun.*

Eaton is connected to the **Eaton Centre** shopping complex via passageways; it is connected as well to the McGill Métro and Les Promenades de la Cathédrale and La Baie (The Bay) eastward and Place Montréal Trust westward.

㉑ Across rue University from Eaton stands **Christ Church Cathedral** (1859), the main church of the Anglican Diocese of Montréal. In early 1988 this building was a sight. Plagued by years of high maintenance costs and declining membership, the church fathers leased their land and air rights to a consortium of developers for 99 years. All the land beneath and surrounding the cathedral was removed, and the structure was supported solely by a number of huge steel stilts. The glass 34-story office tower behind the cathedral, **La Maison des Coopérants,** and Les Promenades de la Cathédrale retail complex beneath it, are the products of that agreement.

㉒ **Place Ville-Marie** is an office, retail, and mall complex that signaled a new era for Montréal when it opened in 1962. It was the first link in the huge chain of the Underground City, which meant that people could have access to all the services of the city without setting foot outside. It was also the first step Montréal took to claiming its place as an international city. The labyrinth that is the Underground City now includes six hotels, thousands of offices, 30 movie theaters, more than 1,000 boutiques, hundreds of restaurants, and almost 15 kilometers (9.3 miles) of passageways.

㉓ From Place Ville-Marie head south via the passageways toward **Le Reine Elizabeth (Queen Elizabeth)** hotel. You can reach the **Gare Centrale (Central Railway Station)** just behind the hotel. Trains from the United States and the rest of Canada arrive here. Then follow the signs marked "Métro/Place
㉔ Bonaventure" to **Place Bonaventure,** the largest commercial building in Canada. On the lower floors there are shops and restaurants, then come exposition halls and offices, and finally

Tour 2: Downtown Montréal

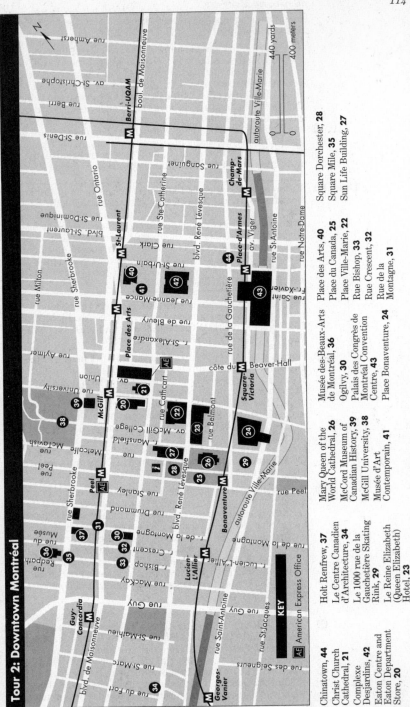

Chinatown, **44**
Christ Church
Cathedral, **21**
Complexe
Desjardins, **42**
Eaton Centre and
Eaton Department
Store, **20**

Holt Renfrew, **37**
Le Centre Canadien
d'Architecture, **34**
Le 1000 rue de la
Gauchetière Skating
Rink, **29**
Le Reine Elizabeth
(Queen Elizabeth)
Hotel, **23**

Mary Queen of the
World Cathedral, **26**
McCord Museum of
Canadian History, **39**
McGill University, **38**
Musée d'Art
Contemporain, **41**

Musée des-Beaux-Arts
de Montréal, **36**
Ogilvy, **30**
Palais des Congrès de
Montréal Convention
Centre, **43**
Place Bonaventure, **24**

Place des Arts, **40**
Place du Canada, **25**
Place Ville-Marie, **22**
Rue Bishop, **33**
Rue Crescent, **32**
Rue de la
Montagne, **31**

Square Dorchester, **28**
Square Mile, **35**
Sun Life Building, **27**

KEY

AE American Express Office

the whole thing is topped by the Bonaventure Hilton International (*see* Lodging, *below*) and 2½ acres of gardens. From here take the route marked "Place du Canada," which will bring you to the mall in the base of the **Le Château Champlain.** This building is known as the Cheesegrater because of its rows and rows of half-moon-shape windows (*see* Lodging, *below*). Our exploration of this leg of the Underground City will end at **Windsor Station** (follow the signs). This was the second railway station built in Montréal by the Canadian Pacific Railway Company. Windsor Station was designed in 1889 by George Price, a New York architect, with a massive rustic stone exterior holding up an amazing steel-and-glass roof over an arcade.

It's time for a bit of fresh air now, so exit at the north end of Windsor Station and cross the street to the park known as **㉕ Place du Canada.** In the center of the park there is a statue to Sir John A. MacDonald, Canada's first prime minister. Then **㉖** cross the park and rue de la Cathédrale to the **Mary Queen of the World Cathedral** (1894), which you enter on boulevard René-Lévesque. This church is modeled after St. Peter's Basilica in Rome. Victor Bourgeau, the same architect who did the interior of Notre-Dame in Vieux-Montréal, thought the idea of the cathedral's design terrible but completed it after the original architect proved incompetent. Inside there is even a canopy over the altar that is a miniature copy of Bernini's *baldacchino* in St. Peter's. The massive gray granite edifice across boule- **㉗** vard René-Lévesque from the cathedral is the **Sun Life Building** (1914), at one time the largest building in the British Commonwealth. During World War II much of England's financial reserves and national treasures were stored in Sun Life's vaults. The park that faces the Sun Life building just north of **㉘** boulevard René-Lévesque is **Square Dorchester,** for many years the heart of Montréal. Until 1870 a Catholic burial ground occupied this block (and there are still bodies buried beneath the grass), but with the rapid development of the area, the city fathers decided to turn it into a park. The statuary of Square Dorchester includes a monument to the Boer War in the center and a statue of the Scottish poet Robert Burns near rue Peel.

In the large skyscraper just south of Square Dorchester is an **㉙** indoor skating rink, **Le 1000 rue de la Gauchetière,** that is open year-round. Located in the 1000 rue de la Gauchetière office tower, the $5 million rink is bathed in natural light and surrounded by a host of amenities, such as cafés, a food court, and a winter garden. It's open to all levels of skaters, and skate rentals and lockers are available. There are also a regular program of ice shows, Saturday-night skating to rock music, and skating lessons. *1000 rue de la Gauchetière, tel. 514/499–2001.*

A block north of Square Dorchester is rue Ste-Catherine, the main retail shopping street of Montréal. Three blocks west, at 1307 rue Ste-Catherine Ouest and rue de la Montagne, is **㉚ Ogilvy,** the last of the Big Three department stores. The store has been divided into individual name boutiques that sell generally pricier lines than does La Baie or Eaton. Most days at noon a bagpiper plays Scottish airs as he circumnavigates the **㉛ ㉜** ground floor. **Rue de la Montagne,** and **rues Crescent** and **㉝ Bishop,** the two streets just west of it, constitute the heart of Montréal's downtown nightlife and restaurant scene. This area once formed the playing fields of the Montréal Lacrosse and

Cricket Grounds, and later it became an exclusive suburb lined with millionaires' row houses. Since then these three streets between rues Sherbrooke and Ste-Catherine have become fertile ground for trendy bars, restaurants, and shops ensconced in those old row houses.

While you're in the vicinity, take in one of downtown's newest **(34)** attractions, **Le Centre Canadien d'Architecture (Canadian Centre for Architecture),** just four blocks west at rue St-Marc on rue Baile. The lifelong dream of its founding director, Phyllis Lambert (of the Bronfman fortune), the CCA opened in May 1989 and houses one of the world's premier architectural collections. *1920 rue Baile, tel. 514/939–7000. Admission free to children under 12 and Thurs. eve. to adults; otherwise, $5 adults, $3 senior citizens and students. Open Wed. and Fri. 11–6, Thurs. 11–8, weekends 11–5. Group rates available. Reservations required.*

Now that you're in the mood for historic pursuits, backtrack to rues Ste-Catherine and Bishop. By walking two blocks north on rue Bishop to rue Sherbrooke, you enter a very different environment: the exclusive neighborhood known as the **(35)** **Square Mile.**

Directly across the street from the end of rue Bishop is the **(36)** **Musée des Beaux-Arts de Montréal (Montreal Museum of Fine Arts),** the oldest established museum in Canada (1860). The present building was completed in 1912 and holds a large collection of European and North American fine and decorative art; ancient treasures from Europe, the Near East, Asia, Africa, and America; art from Québec and Canada; and Indian and Eskimo artifacts. From June through October there is usually one world-class exhibition, such as the inventions of Leonardo da Vinci or the works of Marc Chagall.

The Museum of Fine Arts has undergone a major expansion, with a new wing opened in 1991. The museum has a gift shop, an art-book store, a restaurant and cafeteria, and a gallery from which you can buy or rent original paintings by local artists. *1379 rue Sherbrooke O, tel. 514/285–1600. Admission: permanent collection, $4.75 adults, $3 students, $1 children 12 and under and senior citizens; visiting exhibitions, $9.50 adults, $4.75 students and senior citizens, $2 children 12 and under; audio guides, $4. Open Tues., Thurs., Fri., and Sun. 11–6; Wed. and Sat. 11–9.*

Walking east on rue Sherbrooke brings you to the small and **(37)** exclusive **Holt Renfrew** department store, perhaps the city's fanciest, at the corner of boulevard de la Montagne (*see* Shopping, *below*). A few blocks farther east along rue Drummond stands the **Ritz-Carlton,** the grande dame of Montréal hotels. It was built in 1912 so the local millionaires' European friends would have a suitable place to stay. Take a peek in the elegant Café de Paris restaurant. It's Montréal's biggest power dining spot, and you just might see the prime minister dining there. (For more on the Ritz-Carlton and its restaurants, *see* Lodging and Dining sections, *below.*) The Ritz-Carlton's only real competition in town is the modern and elegant **Hôtel Quatre Saisons (Four Seasons),** two blocks west at rues Sherbrooke and Peel. Just beyond this hotel on the other side of the street **(38)** begins the grassy **McGill University** campus. James McGill, a wealthy Scottish fur trader, bequeathed the money and the

land for this institution, which opened in 1828 and is perhaps
the finest English-language school of higher education in the
nation. The student body numbers 15,000, and the university
is best known for its medical and engineering schools.

39 Just across rue Sherbrooke from the campus is the **McCord
Museum of Canadian History,** which has reopened after undergoing expansion and renovation work for two years. The quality and extent of the McCord collections, which date primarily
from the 18th century, make it one of the best history museums
in Canada. The collections document the environment of Canadian native peoples and feature costumes and textiles, decorative arts, paintings, prints and drawings, and the
700,000-print-and-negative Notman Photographic Archives,
which highlights 19th-century life in Montréal. The McCord is
the only museum in Canada with a permanent costume gallery.
There are guided tours (call for times), a reading room and
documentation center, a gift shop and bookstore, and a tearoom. *690 rue Sherbrooke O, tel. 514/398–7100. Admission: $5
adults, $3 senior citizens, $2 students, $8 families, $3 per person
in groups, children under 12 free. Open Tues., Wed., and Fri.
10–6; Thurs. 10–9; Sat. and Sun. 10–5. Closed Mon., except on
statutory holidays.*

Turn right on rue University and walk a block to the McGill
Métro station. Take the train one stop in the direction of
Honoré-Beaugrand to the Place des Arts station.

Montréal's Métro opened in 1966 with well-designed stations—
many decorated with works of art—and modern trains running
on quiet pneumatic wheels. Today there are 65 stations on four
lines with 65 kilometers (40 miles) of track. The 759 train cars
carry more than 700,000 passengers a day. When you exit at
40 **Place des Arts,** follow the signs to the theater complex of the
same name. From here you can walk the five blocks to Vieux-
Montréal totally underground. Place des Arts, which opened
in 1963, is reminiscent of New York's Lincoln Center in that it
is a government-subsidized complex of three very modern
theaters. The largest, Salle Wilfrid Pelletier, is the home of the
Orchestre Symphonique de Montréal (Montreal Symphony
Orchestra), which has won international raves under the baton
of Charles Dutoit. The Orchestre Métropolitain de Montréal,
Grands Ballets Canadiens, and the Opéra du Québec also stage
productions here.

41 The complex also houses the **Musée d'Art Contemporain,** the
city's modern art museum, which moved here from Cité du
Havre in 1991. The museum's large permanent collection represents works by Québecois, Canadian, and international artists in every medium. The museum often features weekend
programs, with many child-oriented activities, and almost all
are free. There are guided tours, though hours vary and groups
of more than 15 are asked to make a reservation. *185 rue Ste-
Catherine O, tel. 514/847–6226. Admission: $4.75 adults, $3.75
senior citizens, $2.75 students, children under 12 free. Wed.
evenings free. Open Tues.–Sun. 11–6 and Wed. until 9.*

42 While still in Place des Arts, follow the signs to the **Complexe
Desjardins.** Built in 1976, this is another office building, hotel,
and mall development along the lines of Place Ville-Marie. The
luxurious Meridien Hotel (*see* Lodging, *below*) rises from its
northwest corner. The large galleria space is the scene of all

types of performances, from lectures on Japanese massage techniques to pop music, as well as avid shopping in the dozens of stores. The next development south is the **Complexe Guy-Favreau,** a huge federal office building named after the Canadian Minister of Justice in the early '60s. If you continue in a straight line, you will hit the **Palais des Congrès de Montréal Convention Centre** above the Place d'Armes Métro stop. But if you take a left out of Guy-Favreau onto rue de la Gauchetière, you will be in **Chinatown,** a relief after all that artificially enclosed retail space.

The Chinese first came to Montréal in large numbers after 1880, following the construction of the transcontinental railroad. They settled in an 18-block area between boulevard René-Lévesque and avenue Viger to the north and south, and near rues Hôtel de Ville and Bleury on the east and west, an area that became known as Chinatown, where there are many restaurants, food stores, and gift shops.

Tour 3: St-Denis, Prince Arthur, and North

Numbers in the margin correspond to points of interest on the Tour 3: St-Denis, Prince Arthur, and North map.

After a long day of fulfilling your touristic obligations at the historical sites and museums of downtown and Vieux-Montréal, it's good to relax and indulge in some primal pleasures, such as eating, shopping, and nightlife. For these and other diversions, head to the neighborhoods east and north of downtown. Our tour begins in the Latin Quarter, the main student district, then wends its way north.

The southern section of this area, around the base of rue St-Denis, was one of the city's first residential neighborhoods, built in the 19th century as the city burst the bounds of Vieux-Montréal. Then known as Faubourg St-Laurent, it was the home of many wealthy families. The lands to the north of present-day rue Sherbrooke were mostly farms and limestone quarries.

Our tour begins at the **Berri-UQAM** Métro stop, perhaps the most important in the whole city, because three lines intersect here. This area, particularly along **rue St-Denis** on each side of boulevard de Maisonneuve, is known as the **Latin Quarter** and is the site of the **Université du Québec à Montréal** and a number of other educational institutions. Rue St-Denis is lined with cafés, bistros, and restaurants that attract the academic crowd. On rue Ste-Catherine there are a number of low-rent nightclubs popular with avant-garde rock-and-roll types. Just west of rue St-Denis you find the **Cinémathèque Québecoise,** a museum and repertory movie house. For $3 you can visit the permanent exhibition on the history of filmmaking equipment and see two movies. The museum also houses one of the largest cinematic reference libraries in the world. *335 boul. de Maisonneuve O, tel. 514/842–9763. Admission free; movies $3. Library, museum, and theater open June–Aug., weekdays 12:30–4:30; Sept.–May, Mon. and Fri. 12:30–5, Tues.–Thurs 12:30–8:30.*

Around the corner and half a block north on rue St-Denis stands the 2,500-seat **Théâtre St-Denis,** the second-largest auditorium in Montréal (after Salle Wilfrid Pelletier in Place des Arts). Sarah Bernhardt and numerous other famous actors

Tour 3: St-Denis, Prince Arthur, and North

have graced its stage. It currently is the main site for the summertime concerts of the Montréal International Jazz Festival. On the next block north you see the Beaux Arts **Bibliothèque Nationale du Québec** (1915), a library that houses Québec's official archives (1700 rue St-Denis; open Tues.–Sat. 9–5). If you have a lot of money and some hours set aside for dining, try **Les Mignardises** at 2035–37 rue St-Denis just south of rue Sherbrooke (*see* Dining, *below*).

Continue north on rue St-Denis past rue Sherbrooke. On the right, above the Sherbrooke Métro station, is the **Hôtel de l'Institut,** the hands-on training academy of the government **47** *hôtelier* school. To the left is the small **Square St-Louis,** once considered among the most beautiful in Montréal. Unfortunately, now it is a haven for neighborhood panhandlers and the growing numbers of homeless in the city; as a result, the ambience has changed. In its heyday, this was the focal point of the community, and the surrounding neighborhood takes its name from the once grand square. Originally a reservoir, these blocks became a park in 1879 and attracted upper-middle-class families and artists to the area. French Canadian poets were among the most famous creative people to occupy the houses back then, and the neighborhood is the home today for Montréal painters, filmmakers, musicians, and writers. On the wall of 336 Square St-Louis you can see—and read, if your French is good—a long poem by Michel Bujold.

48 **Rue Prince Arthur** begins at the western end of Square St-Louis. In the '60s the young people who moved to the neighborhood transformed the next few blocks into a small hippie bazaar of clothing, leather, and smoke shops. It remains a center of youth culture, although it's much tamer and more commercial. In 1981 the city turned the blocks between avenue Laval and boulevard St-Laurent into a pedestrian mall. Hippie shops live on today as inexpensive Greek, Vietnamese, Italian, Polish, and Chinese restaurants and boîtes of the singles-bar variety.

49 When you reach **boulevard St-Laurent,** take a left and stroll south on the street that cuts through Montréal life in a number of ways. First, this is the east–west dividing street; like the Greenwich meridian, boulevard St-Laurent is where all the numbers begin. The street is also lined with shops and restaurants that represent the incredible ethnic diversity of Montréal. Until the late 19th century this was a neighborhood first of farms and then of middle-class Anglophone residences. It was on boulevard St-Laurent in 1892 that the first electric tramway was installed that could climb the slope to Plâteau Mont-Royal. Working-class families, who couldn't afford a horse and buggy to pull them up the hill, began to move in. In the 1880s the first of many waves of Russian-Jewish immigrants escaping the pogroms arrived and settled here. Boulevard St-Laurent became known as The Main, as in "main street," and Yiddish was the primary language spoken along some stretches. The Russian Jews were followed by Greeks, Eastern Europeans, Portuguese, and, most recently, Latin Americans.

50 Just north of rue Sherbrooke is the new **International Museum of Humor.** An offshoot of the highly successful Just for Laughs comedy festival, the multimedia museum celebrates humor in all its forms—from advertising and political cartoons to film and television. Visitors to the museum are first handed head-phones and introduced to the "scientific" theory of humor; they are then guided through temporary exhibitions, which change annually. There is also Le Panthéon de l'Humour (The Humor Hall of Fame), which honors comics who have made their mark in the world of comedy. The museum supports new talent with a cabaret open to stand-up comics. Located in the former Ekers Brewery, the museum is home to a production center for the École Nationale de l'Humour, a school that trains budding comics. There's a restaurant, as well as a boutique that sells anything related to the world of humor. Call for schedule and admission information since both vary. *2111 boul. St-Laurent, tel. 514/845–4000.*

Leaving the museum, turn right. The next 10 blocks are filled with delis, junk stores, restaurants, luncheonettes, and cloth-ing stores, as well as fashionable boutiques, bistros, cafés, bars, nightclubs, bookstores, and galleries exhibiting the work of the latest wave of "immigrants" to the area—gentrifiers and art-ists. The block between rues Roy and Napoléon is particularly rich in delights. Just east at 76 rue Roy is **Waldman's Fish Mar-ket,** reputed to be the largest wholesale/retail fish market in North America. **Warshaw's Supermarket** at 3863 boulevard St-Laurent is a huge Eastern European–style emporium that sells all sorts of delicacies.

🟤51 A few doors up the street from Warshaw's—at No. 3895—is **Schwartz's Delicatessen.** Among the many contenders for the "smoked-meat king" title in Montréal, Schwartz's is most fre-quently at the top. Smoked meat is just about all it serves, but the meat comes in lean, medium, or fatty cuts. The waiters give you your food and take your money, and that's that.

A block north is **Moishe's** (*see* Dining, *below*), home of the best, but priciest, steaks in Montréal as well as the noisiest atmos-
🟤52 phere. The next corner is **rue Duluth,** where merchants are seeking to re-create rue Prince Arthur. If you take a walk to the right all the way to rue St-Denis, you will find Greek and Vietnamese restaurants and boutiques and art galleries on either side of the street. A left turn on rue Duluth and a three-
🟤53 block walk brings you to **Parc Jeanne-Mance,** a flat, open field that's a perfect spot for a picnic of delicacies purchased on The Main. The park segues into the 2 wooded, hilly square kilome-ters (494 acres) of **Parc Mont-Royal.**

🟤54 **Avenue du Parc** forms the western border of Parc Jeanne-Mance. To get there either cut through the park or take a left on avenue du Mont-Royal at the north end. No. 93 avenue du Mont-Royal Ouest is the home of **Beauty's,** a restaurant spe-cializing in bagels, lox, pancakes, and omelets. Expect a line weekend mornings. Turn right and head north to **avenue Laurier.** All along this avenue, from Côte Ste-Catherine to boulevard St-Laurent, are some of the fanciest fur stores, bou-tiques, pastry shops, and jewelers in the city. For a quick choco-late eclair bracer or two, go to **Lenôtre Paris,** at 1050 avenue Laurier O, a branch of the Parisian shop of the same name.

Time Out **La Petite Ardoise** is a casual, slightly arty café that serves soups, quiches, sandwiches, and more-expensive daily specials. The onion soup is lovingly overdosed with cheese, bread, and onions. Whether it's breakfast, lunch, or dinner, the best accompaniment for your meal is a big, steamy bowl of creamy café au lait. This café is a perfect place to take a breather from shopping. *222 av. Laurier O, tel. 514/495–4961. AE, MC, V. Open 8 AM–midnight, later on weekends.*

The next three blocks of avenue du Parc form the heart of the Greek district. Try **Symposium,** at No. 5334, or the neighboring **Milos** at 5357 avenue du Parc (*see* Dining, *below*) for some of the best Greek appetizers, grilled seafood, and atmosphere you'll find in this hemisphere.

55 **Avenue Fairmount,** a block north of avenue Laurier, is the site of two small but internationally known culinary landmarks. The **Fairmount Bagel Factory,** at 74 avenue Fairmount Ouest, claims to make the best bagels in the world.

56 Half a block east, on the corner of avenue Fairmount and rue Clark, stands the famous **Wilensky's Light Lunch** (*see* Dining, *below*). Moviegoers will recognize this Montréal institution from *The Apprenticeship of Duddy Kravitz,* based on the Mordecai Richler novel of the same name. Lunch is all that's served here, and it certainly is light on the wallet. A couple of dollars will get you a hot dog or a bologna, salami, and mustard pretzel-roll sandwich with a strawberry soda. Books are available for perusing. The atmosphere is free.

Parks and Gardens

Numbers in the margin correspond to points of interest on the Olympic Park and Botanical Garden map.

Of Montréal's three major parks, **Lafontaine** is the smallest (the other two are Parc Mont-Royal and Île Ste-Hélène). Parc Lafontaine, founded in 1867, is divided into eastern and western halves. The eastern half is French style; the paths, gardens, and lawns are laid out in rigid geometric shapes. There are two public swimming pools on the north end, along rue Rachel. In the winter the park is open for ice skating. The western half is designed on the English system, in which the meandering paths and irregularly shaped ponds follow the natural contours of the topography. Pedal boats can be rented for a paddle around one of two man-made lakes. Its band shell is the site of many free outdoor summertime concerts, performances by dance and theater groups, and film screenings. Take the Métro to the Sherbrooke station and walk eight blocks east along rue Cherrier until avenue Parc Lafontaine. *3933 ave. Parc Lafontaine, tel. 514/872–6211. Open 9 AM–10 PM.*

The giant, mollusk-shape **Olympic Stadium** and the tilted tower that supports the roof are probably the preeminent symbols of modern Montréal. Planning for the Olympic Stadium complex began in 1972, and construction in the old Parc Maisonneuve started soon afterward. The Olympics took place in 1976, but the construction of the stadium's roof and tower was not completed until 1989. Many Montréalers were proud of what they had—at least until the summer of 1991, when a 55-ton concrete beam in the stadium came crashing to the ground. The stadium was forced to close for several months, forcing the Montréal Expos major-league baseball team to play its home games on the road. The stadium's retractable roof has never worked properly, and Montréal homeowners and cigarette smokers are still paying the bill for the $1 billion–plus stadium.

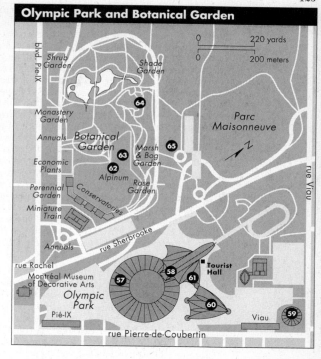

57 58 59 Disgruntled Montréalers have nicknamed the Olympic Stadium the Big Owe and the Big Uh-Oh! The Olympic Park includes the 70,000-seat **Olympic Stadium,** the **Olympic Tower,** six swimming pools, the **Aréna Maurice-Richard,** and the Olympic Village. Daily guided tours (tel. 514/252–8687) of the entire complex leave from Tourist Hall at 11 AM, 12:40 PM, 2 PM, and 3:40 PM; two are in English, two are in French. Perhaps the most popular visitor activity is a ride up to the tilted tower's observatory on the Funicular, the exterior cable car. The two-level cable car holds 90 people and takes two minutes to climb the 270 meters (890 feet) to the observatory, from which you can see up to 80 kilometers (50 miles) on clear days.

60 The **Biodôme,** in the former Olympic Park Velodrome, opened in June of 1992. This natural sciences museum combines four ecosystems—the boreal forest, tropical forest, polar world, and St. Lawrence River—under one climate-controlled dome. Visitors follow protected pathways through each environment, observing indigenous flora and fauna of each of the ecosystems. Animals from the former zoo at Angrignon Park and the now closed aquarium on Île Ste-Hélène have been incorporated into this new center. *Tel. 514/872–3034 for information on rates and hours.*

61 If you've brought your swimsuit and towels, take a dip at the **Aquatic Center** (tel. 514/252–4622 for hours). There are also a cafeteria and a souvenir shop on the grounds. You can reach the **Olympic Park** via the Pie-IX or Viau Métro stations (the latter is nearer the stadium entrance).

Continuing your back-to-nature experience, cross rue Sherbrooke to the north of the Olympic Park (or take the free shut-
62 tle bus) to reach the **Botanical Garden** (closest Métro stop is
Pie-IX). Founded in 1931, this garden is said to be one of the
largest in the world. During the summer you can visit the 73
hectares (181 acres) of outdoor gardens—a favorite is the poi-
sonous-plants garden; the 10 exhibition greenhouses are open
year-round. There are more than 26,000 species of plants here.
63 When the 5-acre **Montréal-Shanghai "Dream Lake" Garden**
opened here in June 1991, it became the site of the largest Chinese garden outside Asia. The authentic Ming-style garden has
seven elegant pavilions, including a large exhibition hall featuring periodic shows and a 30-foot rockery around a central
reflecting pool. There is also an impressive collection of pen-
64 jings or Chinese bonsais (miniature trees). A **Japanese Garden**
and its pavilion, where guests may join a formal tea ceremony,
65 are next to the "Dream Lake." The **Insectarium,** a bug-shaped
building, houses more than 250,000 insect specimens collected
by Montréal entomologist Georges Brossard. *4101 rue Sherbrooke E, tel. 514/872–1400. Admission to the greenhouses and
the Insectarium May–Oct.: $7 adults, $3.50 children 6–17, $5
senior citizens; Nov.–Apr.: $5 adults, $2.50 children 6–17, $3.50
senior citizens.*

Île Ste-Hélène (along with Île Notre-Dame, the former site of
the Expo '67 World's Fair), opposite Vieux-Montréal in the middle of the St. Lawrence River, draws big crowds, particularly
during the warm months. You can reach it via either the Victoria or Jacques-Cartier bridges, via the Métro to the Île Ste-
Hélène station, or by city bus (summer only) from downtown.
Île Ste-Hélène is a wooded, rolling park perfect for picnicking
in the summer and cross-country skiing and ice skating during
the snow season. The former 1967 World's Fair site on the island has been upgraded. Buckminster Fuller's biosphere (the
world's largest geodesic dome when the famous architect and
engineer built it for Expo '67, but since ravaged by fire) is
scheduled to reopen in 1995 as a permanent water and environment interpretation center.

La Ronde was created as part of the Expo celebration. This
world-class amusement park boasts a huge new roller coaster
(the second-highest in the world), water slides with incredible
drops, an international circus, Ferris wheels, boat rides, and
rides, rides, rides. The **Aqua Park** shares the island with La
Ronde and has 20 of its own thrilling slides and pools. Admission includes amusement park as well as the water slides, and
is good all day. Both parks have the same schedule. There are
also haunted houses, musical cabarets, Wild West shows, restaurants, snack bars, and the obligatory monorail and cable-
car rides. La Ronde is also the site of the annual Benson &
Hedges International Fireworks Competition, on Saturday or
Sunday nights during June and July. A ticket, which includes
a reserved seat for the show and an amusement park pass,
costs $22.75. *Île Ste-Hélène, tel. 514/872–6222 or 800/361–7178
for La Ronde; 514/790–1245 or 800/361–4595 for fireworks.
Admission: $19.25 adults, $9.50 children, $44.50 families. Open
May and early June, weekends only; mid-June–Aug., Sun.–
Thurs. 11 AM–midnight, Fri.–Sat. 11 AM–1 AM.*

A stroll back along the north side of the island brings you to
the **Old Fort** just under the Jacques-Cartier Bridge. This

former British arsenal has been turned into the **David M. Stewart Museum** and a dinner theater called **Le Festin du Gouverneur.** The latter is a re-creation of a 17th-century banquet, complete with balladeers and comedy skits. In the military museum are displays of old firearms, maps, scientific instruments, uniforms, and documents of colonial times. During the summer the parade ground is the scene of mock battles—cannons and all—by the Compagnie Franche de la Marine and bagpipe concerts by the 78th Fraser Highlanders. *Tel. 514/861–6701. Admission: $3 adults, $2 children and senior citizens. Open summer, 10–6, closed Tues.; winter, 10–5, closed Tues.*

In mid-June, **Île Notre-Dame** is the site of the Molson Grand Prix du Canada, a top Formula I international circuit auto race at the Gilles Villeneuve Race Track.

Île Notre-Dame is also site of the city's only natural beach on **Lac de l'Île Notre-Dame.** Opened in the summer of 1990, it was an immediate success and is now packed on every hot, sunny day. Just a Métro stop away (Île Ste-Hélène Métro) from downtown, the beach is an oasis, with clear lake water filtered by a treatment system that relies on aquatic plants, and an inviting stretch of lawn and trees rimmed with sand. Lifeguards are on duty; there is a shop that rents swimming and boating accessories, and there are picnic areas and a restaurant on the premises. There is also a moderate admission fee.

The **Parc Mont-Royal,** the finest in the city, is not easy to overlook. These 494 acres of forest and paths at the heart of the city were designed by Frederick Law Olmsted, the celebrated architect of New York's Central Park. He believed that communion with nature could cure body and soul. The park is designed following the natural topography and accentuating its features, as in the English mode. You can go skating on Beaver Lake in the winter, visit one of the two lookouts and scan the horizon, or study the park interpretation center in the chalet at the Mont Royal belvedere. Horse-drawn transport is popular year-round: sleigh rides in winter and calèche rides in summer. On the eastern side of the hill stands the 30-meter (100-foot) steel cross that is the symbol of the city.

Shrines

St. Joseph's Oratory, on the northwest side of Mont Royal, is a Catholic shrine on a par with Lourdes or Fatima. Take the blue Métro line to the Côte-des-Neiges station, then walk three blocks uphill on the chemin de la Côte-des-Neiges. You can't miss the enormous church up on the hillside. Brother André, a member of the Society of the Brothers of the Holy Cross, constructed a small chapel to St. Joseph, Canada's patron saint, in 1904. Brother André was credited with a number of miracles and was beatified in 1982. His chapel became a pilgrimage site, the only one to St. Joseph in the world (St. Joseph is the patron saint of healing). The dome is among the world's largest, and while the interior is of little aesthetic interest, there is a small museum dedicated to the life of the Holy Family and containing many displays, including thousands of crutches discarded by the formerly crippled faithful. From early December through February the museum features a display of crèches (nativity scenes) from all over the world. Carillon, choral, and organ concerts are held weekly at the oratory during the summer, and you can still visit Brother André's original chapel and tomb at the side of the massive basilica. *3800 chemin Queen Mary, tel. 514/733–8211. Open daily 6 AM–9:30 PM; June–Aug. 6 AM—10 PM.*

Montréal for Free

The Saidye Bronfman Centre hands-on fine arts school has open-house activities, gallery exhibitions, and public affairs lectures (*see* Off the Beaten Track, *below*).

Classical and pop concerts, dance performances, and theater are held at **Parc de Lafontaine,** rue Rachel.

Picnic in **Parc Mont-Royal,** sail miniature boats in its Beaver Lake during the summer, and skate on it during the winter (*see* Parks and Gardens, *above*).

Bicycle along Montréal's waterfront to the Lachine Canal, atop its mountain, or through the Vieux-Port (*see* Participant Sports, *below*).

Le Centre Canadien d'Architecture is free on Thursday evenings (*see* Tour 2, *above*).

What to See and Do with Children

Biodôme de Montréal at Olympic Park (*see* Parks and Gardens, *above).*

At the Old Fort on Île Ste-Hélène, now the site of the **David M. Stewart Museum,** mock battles, military drills, military-history exhibitions, and bagpipe concerts take place all summer long (*see* Parks and Gardens, *above*).

Dow Planetarium. The heavens are reproduced with the aid of a giant Zeiss projector on the inside of the planetarium's vaulted dome. *1000 rue St-Jacques, tel. 514/872–4530. Admission: $4 adults, $2.50 children and senior citizens; this may vary. Open Tues.–Sun. 12:30–8:30.*

Images du Futur offers futuristic, interactive exhibitions. *Vieux-Port at boul. St-Laurent and rue de la Commune, tel. 514/849–1612. Open mid-May–mid-Sept., daily 10 AM–11 PM.*

IMAX Super Cinema offers films on a seven-story-tall screen. Next to Images du Futur is **Expotec,** a hands-on scientific exhibition. *Vieux-Port, Shed No. 7, tel. 514/496–IMAX for information, 514/790–1245 for tickets. Admission: $11.50 adults, $9.50 students and senior citizens, $7 children, but prices vary. Open daily 10–10.*

The Botanical Garden's Insectarium (*see* Parks and Gardens, *above*).

La Ronde's Amusement Park (*see* Parks and Gardens, *above*).

Olympic Tower. Zoom up the "tallest-inclined-tower-in-the-world" on the funicular for a 50-mile panorama of Montréal and its environs (*see* Parks and Gardens, *above*).

Indoor skating year-round at the **Le 1000 rue de la Gauchetière** (*see* Tour 2, *above*).

Off the Beaten Track

Just two blocks west of Victoria and the Métro Côte-Ste-Catherine station is the **Saidye Bronfman Centre.** This multidisciplinary institution has long been recognized as a focus of cultural activity for the Jewish community in particular and for Montréal as a whole. The center was a gift from the children of Saidye Bronfman in honor of their mother's lifelong commitment to the arts. In fact, the Mies van der Rohe–inspired building was originally designed by Mrs. Bronfman's daughter, Montréal architect Phyllis Lambert. Accessible by car, just one block east of the Décarie Expressway and about four blocks north of chemin Queen Mary, the center is well worth the trip.

Many of its activities, such as gallery exhibits, lectures on public and Jewish affairs, performances, and concerts, are offered free to the public. The center, open year-round, is home to the Yiddish Theatre Group, one of the few Yiddish companies performing today in North America. The theater also presents English works, often by local playwrights. Many an artist has passed through the doors of the center's School of Fine Arts. *5170 Côte Ste-Catherine, tel. 514/739–2301; box office 514/739–7944. Admission to gallery free; theater tickets vary. Open Mon.–Thurs. 9–9, Fri. 9–3, Sun. 10–5. Closed Fri. after 3, Sat., and Jewish holidays.*

Accessible by metro and bus is **Maison Saint-Gabriel,** which dates back to 1668, when it served as a boarding school for Les Filles du Roy—the young women, many of them orphans, who were brought over to New France to marry the predominantly male settlers. Here Montréal's first teacher (and Canada's first female saint), Marguerite Bourgeoys, patiently trained the "King's wards" to take on their duties as wives and mothers. The house was renovated in 1960. A typical "habitant" farmhouse, it displays furnishings and household objects from the 17th, 18th, and 19th centuries, as well as a kitchen much like the one Les Filles would have learned to bake in before setting off for their new homes. You can see the exhibits by guided tour only mid-April to mid-December. It is advisable to call beforehand. *2146 Place Dublin (Square-Victoria Métro, then transfer to Bus 61), tel. 514/935–8136. Admission: $3 adults, $2 students 8–16 and senior citizens. Tours Tues.–Sat., 1:30 and 3; Sun. 1:30, 2:30, and 3:30.*

Shopping

By Patricia Lowe

Updated by Dorothy Guinan

Montréalers *magasinent* (go shopping) with a vengeance, so it's no surprise that the city has 160 multifaceted retail areas encompassing some 6,200 stores. Between 1990 and 1992, some 800 new boutiques and retail outlets were added to this rough estimate.

Visitors usually reserve at least one day to hunt for either exclusive fashions along rue Sherbrooke or bargains at the Vieux-Montréal flea market. But there are specific items that the wise shopper seeks out in Montréal.

Montréal is one of the fur capitals of the world. Close to 85% of Canada's fur manufacturers are based in the city, as are many of their retail outlets: **Alexandor** (2025 rue de la Montagne), **Shuchat** (402 de Maisonneuve O), **Grosvenor** (400 boulevard de Maisonneuve O), **McComber** (440 boulevard de Maisonneuve O), and **Birger Christensen at Holt Renfrew** (1300 rue Sherbrooke O) are a few of the better showrooms.

Fine English bone china, crystal, and woolens are more readily available and cheaper in metropolitan stores than in their U.S. equivalents, thanks to Canada's tariff status as a Commonwealth country. There are three **Jaeger** boutiques (Ogilvy downtown, Centre Rockland in the town of Mount Royal, and Centre Fairview in the West Island) selling traditional woolen sweaters, along with $700 pure-wool suits. Collectors of china and crystal will find reasonable prices at **Caplan Duval** (Côte-St-Luc's Cavendish Mall and Montréal's Plaza Côte-des-Neiges), which offers an overwhelming variety of patterns.

Today, only dedicated connoisseurs can uncover real treasures in traditional pine Canadiana, but scouting around for Québec *antiquités* and art can be fun and rewarding, especially along increasingly gentrified rue Notre-Dame Ouest.

The Montréal area has six major retail districts: the city center (or downtown), Vieux-Montréal, rue Notre-Dame Ouest, the Plâteau Mont-Royal–St-Denis area, the upper St-Laurent–Laurier Ouest areas of Outremont, and the city of Westmount.

Just about all stores, with the exception of some bargain outlets and a few selective art and antiques galleries, accept major credit cards. Buy your Canadian money at a bank or exchange bureau beforehand to take advantage of the latest rates on the dollar. Most purchases are subject to a federal goods and services tax of 7% as well as a provincial tax of 8%.

If you think you might be buying fur, it is wise to check with your country's customs officials before leaving to find out which animals are considered endangered and cannot be imported. Do the same if you think you might be buying Eskimo carvings, many of which are made of whalebone and ivory and cannot be brought into the United States.

(For general opening times, *see* Opening and Closing Times in Essential Information, *above*.)

City Center

Central downtown is Montréal's largest retail district. It takes in rue Sherbrooke, boulevard de Maisonneuve, rue Ste-Catherine, and the side streets between them. Because of the proximity and variety of shops, it's the best shopping bet for visitors in town overnight or over a weekend.

Faubourg Several new or soon-to-open complexes have added glamour to **Ste-Catherine** the city-center shopping scene. A good place to start is the **Faubourg Ste-Catherine,** Montréal's answer to Boston's Quincy Market. At the corner of rues Ste-Catherine Ouest and Guy, it is a vast bazaar housed in a former parking and auto-body garage abutting the Grey Nuns' convent grounds. Three levels of clothing and crafts boutiques, as well as food counters selling fruits and vegetables, pastry, baked goods, and meats, surround the central atrium of tiered fountains and islands of café tables and chairs where food-fair kiosks sell snacks such as egg rolls, pizza, souvlaki, and sushi. This is the place to pick up Québec maple syrup and maple candy, at the pine-decorated boutique at street level, or a fine French wine, about $30, at the government-run **Société d'Alcools du Québec.** Prices at most stores are generally reasonable here, especially if you're sampling the varied ethnic cuisine at any of the snack counters.

Les Cours Mont-Royal Continuing east on Ste-Catherine, the *très élégant* **Les Cours Mont-Royal** dominates the east side of rue Peel between this main shopping thoroughfare and boulevard de Maisonneuve. This mall caters to expensive tastes, but even bargain hunters find it an intriguing spot for window shopping.

Place Montréal Trust Just two blocks away, **Place Montréal Trust** at McGill College is the lively entrance to an imposing glass office tower. Shoppers, fooled by the aqua and pastel decor, may think they have stumbled into a California mall. Prices at the 110 outlets range from hundreds (for designs by **Alfred Sung,** haute couture at **Gigi** or **Rodier,** or men's high fashion at **Bally**) to mere dollars (for sensible cotton boys' T-shirts, or beef-and-kidney pies or minced tarts at the British dry goods and food store **Marks & Spencer**). These imported goodies share the floor space with moderately ticketed ladies' suits, menswear, lingerie, and children's clothing. Marks & Spencer is a far cry from neighboring **Abercrombie and Fitch,** which stocks the offbeat and the outrageous, such as a fold-up, miniature billiards table or a $5,995 toy sports car.

Les Cours Mont-Royal and this complex have competition from the **Centre Eaton** and **Les Promenades de la Cathédrale.** All four of these centers are linked to the Underground City retail network. Always a favorite with visitors, the nearly 15-kilometer (9-mile) "city below" draws large crowds to its shop-lined corridors honeycombing between Les Promenades de la Cathédrale, Place Ville-Marie, Place Bonaventure, and Complexe Desjardins.

Les Promenades de la Cathédrale Nestled between Eaton and La Baie department stores, this underground retail complex is already proving popular with Montréalers. Its unusual location makes it a sightseeing adventure as well: It's connected to the McGill Métro and located directly beneath the stately and historic Christ Church Cathedral. A highlight (some say a travesty) of the retail mall's design is the replication of architectural details found in the cathedral above. Among its 150 boutiques and chain stores, Les Promenades boasts Canada's largest "Linen Chest" outlet, with hundreds of bedspreads and duvets draped over revolving racks plus aisles of china, crystal, linen, and silver.

Place Ville-Marie Weatherproof shopping began in 1962 beneath the 42-story cruciform towers of Place Ville-Marie on boulevard René-Lévesque (formerly Dorchester Boulevard) at rue University. A recent renovation has opened Place Ville-Marie up to the light, creating a more cheerful ambience as well as adding stores.

Stylish women head to Place Ville-Marie's 100-plus retail outlets for the clothes: haute couture at **Tristan, Iseut, JC Creations, Cactus,** and **Danier.** Traditionalists will love **Aquascutum.** More affordable clothes shops include **Dalmy's, Marie Claire, Reitman's,** and, for shoes, **Mayfair, Brown's, François Villon,** and **French.**

Place Bonaventure From here it's an easy underground trip through Gare Centrale (the train station) to Place Bonaventure's mall beneath one of Canada's largest commercial buildings. It houses some

120 stores, ranging from the trendy (**Au Coton** and **Bikini Village**) to the exclusive (**Armand Boudrias** boutique). There are also a number of fun shops: **Aldo** for trendy leather wear; and **Ici-Bas** for outrageous hose.

Complexe Desjardins Still in the downtown area but a bit farther east on boulevard René-Lévesque is Complexe Desjardins. It's a fast ride via the Métro at Bonaventure station; just get off at Place des Arts and follow the tunnels to Desjardins' multitiered atrium mall. Filled with splashing fountains and exotic plants, Desjardins exudes a Mediterranean joie de vivre, even when it's below freezing outside. Roughly 80 stores include budget outlets like **Le Château** for fashion as well as the exclusive **Redeor,** where wool and jersey-knit ensembles start at about $150.

Department Stores **Eaton** is the city's leading department store and part of Canada's largest chain. Founded in Toronto by Timothy Eaton, the first Montréal outlet appeared in 1925. It now sells everything—from the art decorating the top-floor restaurant entrance to zucchini loaves in the basement bakery. The main restaurant is an unusual art deco replica of the dining room aboard the old *Île-de-France* ocean liner, once Lady Eaton's favorite cruise ship.

The nearby sandstone building housing **La Baie** opened in 1891, although the original Henry Morgan Company that founded it moved to Montréal in 1843. Morgan's was purchased in 1960 by the Hudson Bay Company, which was founded in 1670 by famous Montréal voyageurs and trappers Radisson and Grosseilliers. La Baie is known for its Hudson Bay red-, green-, and white-striped blankets and duffel coats. It also sells the typical department store fare.

Exclusive **Holt Renfrew**, at 1300 rue Sherbrooke Ouest, is known for its furs. The city's oldest store, it was established in 1837 as Henderson, Holt and Renfrew Furriers and made its name supplying coats to four generations of British royalty. When Queen Elizabeth II married Prince Phillip in 1947, Holt's created a priceless Labrador mink as a wedding gift. Holt's carries the exclusive and pricey line of furs by Denmark's Birger Christensen, as well as the haute-couture and prêt-à-porter collections of Yves St-Laurent.

Around the corner and two blocks down rue de la Montagne, at **Ogilvy** (1307 rue Ste-Catherine O), a kilted piper regales shoppers every day at noon. An institution with Montréalers since 1865, the once-homey department store has undergone a miraculous face-lift. Fortunately, it has preserved its delicate pink glass chandeliers and still stocks traditional apparel—Aquascutum, Jaeger, tweeds for men, and smocked dresses for little girls.

This area—bounded by rues Sherbrooke and Ste-Catherine, and rues de la Montagne and Crescent—also boasts antiques and art galleries as well as designer salons. Rue Sherbrooke is lined with an array of art and antiques galleries as well as tony clothing stores. Rue Crescent is a tempting blend of antiques, fashions, and jewelry boutiques displayed beneath colorful awnings.

Vieux-Montréal

The second major shopping district, historic Vieux-Montréal, can be a tourist trap, but a shopping spree there can be a lot less expensive and more relaxing than shopping downtown. Both rues Notre-Dame and St-Jacques, from rue McGill to Place Jacques-Cartier, are lined with low to moderately priced fashion boutiques, garish souvenir shops slung with thousands of Montréal T-shirts, and shoe stores.

Along the edge of Vieux-Montréal is Montréal's rejuvenated waterfront, the Vieux-Port, which hosts a sprawling flea market, the **Marché aux Puces,** on Quai King Edward (King Edward Pier). Dealers and pickers search for secondhand steals and antique treasures as they prowl through the huge hangar that is open Wednesday through Sunday from spring through early fall.

Notre-Dame Ouest

The place for antiquing is the city's third shopping sector, beginning at rue Guy and continuing west to avenue Atwater (a five-minute walk south from the Lionel-Groulx Métro station). Once a shabby strip of run-down secondhand stores, this area has blossomed beyond its former nickname of Attic Row. It now has the highest concentration of antiques, collectibles, and curiosity shops in Montréal. Collectors can find Canadian pine furniture—armoires, cabinets, spinning wheels, rocking chairs—for reasonable prices here. Consider a Sunday tour, beginning with brunch at **Salon de Thé Ambiance,** a charming restaurant that also sells antiques (No. 1874).

Plateau Mont-Royal and St-Denis

Popular with students, academics, and journalists, this easterly neighborhood embraces boulevard St-Laurent, the longtime student ghetto surrounding the Prince Arthur mall, St-Denis and its Latin Quarter near the Université du Québec à Montréal campus, and the Plateau district. Plateau Mont-Royal and St-Denis attract a trendier, more avant-garde crowd than the determined antiquers along Notre-Dame.

Boulevard St-Laurent—dubbed "The Main" because it divides the island of Montréal into east and west—has always been a lively commercial artery. It was first developed by Jewish merchants who set up shop here in the early 1900s. Cutting a broad swath across the island's center, this long boulevard has an international flavor, with its mélange of stores run by Chinese, Greek, Latin American, Portuguese, Slav, and Vietnamese immigrants. Lower boulevard St-Laurent is lined with discount clothing and bric-a-brac stores, secondhand shops, electronics outlets, and groceries selling kosher meats, Hungarian pastries, Peking duck, and natural foods.

While boulevard St-Laurent's personality is multiethnic, rue St-Denis's is distinctly French. (Both are lengthy arteries, so make use of Bus 55 for boulevard St-Laurent, Bus 31 and 30 along rue St-Denis.) More academic in makeup, the boulevard has awnings that shelter bookstores (mostly French), art galleries, antiques stores, and a range of boutiques.

Upper St-Laurent and Laurier Ouest

Upper boulevard St-Laurent (for our purposes, roughly from avenue du Mont-Royal north to rue St-Viateur), intersecting with avenue Laurier Ouest and climbing the mountain to rue Bernard, has blossomed into one of Montréal's chicest *quartiers* in recent years. It's not entirely surprising, given that much of this area lies within or adjacent to Outremont, traditionally the enclave for wealthy Francophone Montréalers, with restaurants, boutiques, nightclubs, and bistros catering to the upscale visitor. In addition, the influx of a new generation of multiethnic professionals, artists, and entrepreneurs is making its mark on the area. It now rivals St-Denis, downtown and Laurier Ouest as a cultural hot spot, and it is reminiscent of New York City's SoHo.

Avenue Laurier Ouest, from boulevard St-Laurent to chemin de la Côte-Ste-Catherine, is roughly an eight-block stretch; you'll crisscross it many times as you explore its Québec-style shops, which carry everything from crafts and clothing to books and paintings.

Square Westmount and Avenue Greene

Visitors with time to shop or friends in the elegant residential neighborhood of Westmount, a separate municipality in the middle of the island of Montréal, should explore Square Westmount and adjacent avenue Greene. Next door to downtown, these malls are on the Angrignon Métro line, easily accessible via the Atwater station, which has an exit at Square Westmount. Just follow the tunnel to this mall's 90 or so exclusive shops.

The square's plaza opens onto avenue Greene's two-block shopping area, which is lined with trees and flowers. Its red-brick row houses and even the renovated old post office are home to a wealth of boutiques and shops.

Sports and Fitness

The range of sporting activities available in Montréal is testament to Montréalers' love of the outdoors. With world-class skiing in the Laurentians less than an hour away and dozens of skating rinks within the city limits, they revel in winter. When the last snowflake has melted, they store away skis, poles, and skates and dust off their bikes, tennis rackets, and fishing poles. And year-round they watch the pros at hockey matches, baseball games, car races, and tennis tournaments.

Participant Sports

Bicycling The island of Montréal—except for Mont Royal itself—is quite flat, and there are more than 20 cycling paths around the metropolitan area. Among the most popular are those on Île Ste-Hélène, along the Lachine Canal, and in Angrignon and Vieux-Port parks. You can rent 10-speed bicycles at **Cyclo-Touriste** at the Centre Info-Touriste (1001 Dorchester Sq., tel. 514/393–1528).

Parks Canada conducts guided cycling tours along the historic **Lachine Canal** (1825) every summer weekend. For more details, call 514/283–6054 or 514/637–7433.

Golf For a complete listing of the many golf courses in the Montréal area, call **Tourisme-Québec** at 514/873–2015.

Hunting and Fishing Québec's rich waters are filled with fish, but before you begin the chase, you need to purchase a license from the Ministère des Loisirs, de la Chasse et de la Pêche or from an authorized agent. The lakes and rivers around Montréal teem with fish, and a number of guides offer day trips. For complete information, call **Tourisme-Québec** (tel. 514/873–2015).

Ice Skating There are at least 195 outdoor and 21 indoor rinks in the city. You'll probably find one in the nearest park. Call parks and recreation (tel. 514/872–6211).

Jogging Montréal became a runner's city following the 1976 Olympics. There are paths in most city parks, but for running with a panoramic view, head to the dirt track in **Parc du Mont-Royal** (take rue Peel, then the steps up to the track).

Rafting Montréal is the only city in the world where you can step off a downtown dock and minutes later be crashing through Class V white water in a sturdy aluminum jet boat. The Lachine Rapids, just south of Vieux-Montréal, were responsible for the founding of Montréal. The roiling waves were too treacherous for the first settlers to maneuver, so they founded Ville-Marie, the forerunner of Vieux-Montréal. Modern voyageurs suit up for the 45-minute jet-boat trip in multiple layers of wool and rain gear, but it's nearly impossible to stay dry—or to have a bad time. *Lachine Rapids Tours Ltd., 105 rue de la Commune, Vieux-Montréal, tel. 514/284–9607. 5 trips daily, departing from Quai Victoria May–Sept., 10, noon, 2, 4, and 6. Trips are narrated in French and English and reservations are necessary. Rates: $45 adults, $40 senior citizens, $35 children 13–18, $25 children 6–12. Special group and family rates are available.*

Skiing
Downhill For the big slopes you'll have to go northwest to the Laurentians or south to the Eastern Townships, an hour or two away by car. There is a small slope in Parc du Mont-Royal. Pick up the Ski-Québec brochure at one of the Tourisme-Québec offices.

Cross-country Trails crisscross most of the city's parks, including Notre-Dame and Île Ste-Hélène, Angrignon, Maisonneuve, and Mont-Royal.

Squash You can reserve court time for this fast-paced racquet sport at **Nautilus Centre St-Laurent Côte-de-Liesse Racquet Club** (8305 chemin Côte-de-Liesse, tel. 514/739–3654).

Swimming There is a large indoor pool at the **Olympic Park** (Métro Viau, tel. 514/252–4622) and another at the **Centre Sportif et des Loisirs Claude-Robillard** (1000 av. Emile Journault, tel. 514/872–6900). The outdoor pool on Île Ste-Hélène is an extremely popular (and crowded) summer gathering place, open June–Labor Day. The new city-run beach at Île Notre-Dame is the only natural swimming hole in Montréal (tel. 514/872–6211).

Tennis There are public courts in the Jeanne-Mance, Kent, LaFontaine, and Somerled parks. For details, call Montreal Sports and Recreation (tel. 514/872–6211).

Windsurfing and Sailing Sailboards and small sailboats can be rented at **L'École de Voile de Lachine** (2105 boul. St-Joseph, Lachine, tel. 514/634–4326) and the **Société de l'Île Notre-Dame** (Île Notre-Dame, tel. 514/872–6093).

Spectator Sports

Baseball The National League **Montreal Expos** play at the Olympic Stadium from April through September. For information and reservations, call 514/253–3434 or 800/463–9767.

Cycling **Le Tour de l'Île de Montréal** has made the *Guinness Book of World Records* for attracting the greatest number of participants. More than 30,000 amateur cyclists participate in "North America's most important amateur cycling event" each June, wending their way 70 kilometers (38 miles) through the streets and parks of Montréal (514/847–8687).

Grand Prix The annual **Molson Grand Prix du Canada,** which draws top Formula 1 racers from around the world, takes place every June at the Gilles Villeneuve Race Track on Île Notre-Dame (tel. 514/392–0000 for tickets, tel. 514/392–4731 for information).

Hockey The **Montréal Canadiens,** winners of 23 Stanley Cups, meet National Hockey League rivals at the Forum (2313 rue Ste-Catherine O, tel. 514/932–2582) from October to April.

Dining

The promise of a good meal is easily satisfied in Montréal. Les Montréalais don't "eat out"; they "dine." And they are passionate about dining. The city has more than 7,000 restaurants of every price representing more than 35 ethnic groups. It has culinary institutions like Les Mignardises, Le Paris, and the Beaver Club, which emphasize classic cuisine and tradition. Delicatessens such as Briskets, Schwartz's, and Wilensky's are mainstays for budget dining. In between there are ethnic eateries featuring the foods of China, Greece, India, Morocco, and Italy. Then there are the ubiquitous inexpensive fast-food outlets and coffee shops. But above all, Montréal is distinguished by the European ambience of its restaurants. Catch a glimpse of the eateries' terraces from midday to 2 PM for a look at the hours that Montréal diners take most seriously. Each of the city's well-known bistros is more Parisian than the last. The challenge to dining in Montréal is choosing from among the thousands of restaurants and the varieties of inexpensive fast-food outlets and coffee shops.

Many expensive French and Continental restaurants offer two options, which can be a blessing or a burden to your wallet. Either choice guarantees you a great meal. Instead of ordering à la carte—you select each dish—you can opt for the table d'hôte or the *menu de dégustation.* The table d'hôte is a complete two- to four-course meal chosen by the chef. It is less expensive than a complete meal ordered à la carte and often offers interesting special dishes. It also may take less time to prepare. If you want to splurge with your time and money, indulge yourself with the *menu de dégustation,* a five- to seven-course dinner executed by the chef. It usually includes, in this order, salad, soup, a fish dish, sherbet, a meat dish, dessert, and coffee or tea. At the city's finest restaurants, this menu for two and a good bottle of wine can cost $170 and last three or four hours. But it's worth every cent and every second.

Montréal restaurants are refreshingly relaxed. Although many of the hotel restaurants require a jacket and tie, neatness (no torn T-shirts and scruffy jeans) is appreciated in most of the other restaurants. Lunch hour is generally from noon to 2:30 and dinner from 6 to 11 or midnight. (Montréalers like to dine late, particularly on summer weekends.) Some restaurants are closed on Sunday or Monday. Because there is no consistent annual closing among Montréal eateries—some will take time off in August, while others will close around Christmas and January—call ahead to avoid disappointment.

Highly recommended restaurants in each price category are indicated by a star ★.

Category	Cost*
Very Expensive	over $30
Expensive	$20–$30
Moderate	$10–$20
Inexpensive	$5–$10

per person without tax (combined GST of 7% and provincial tax of 4% on all meals), service, or drinks

Chinese

Moderate– Expensive **Zen.** At press time this mod establishment in the basement of Le Quatre Saisons (*see below*) was offering a $19 fixed-price menu that should not be missed. Called the Zen Experience, the meal is a kind of all-you-can-eat extravaganza, except that instead of helping yourself to a buffet of precooked dishes, you are presented with a menu of 41 items and asked to select one at a time until you can't possibly eat anymore. The food is delicate Chinese with some Thai, Malaysian, and Indonesian dishes mixed in for variety. Try the fillet of chicken with crispy spinach, eggplant croquettes with sweet-and-sour sauce, and Mother Ma's shredded zucchini with spicy garlic sauce. This is very fine Chinese cuisine for which the restaurant normally charges three times the price. Check to make sure the Zen Experience is still being offered. *Le Quatre Saisons, 1050 Sherbrooke St. W, tel. 514/499–0801. Reservations advised. Dress: casual but neat. AE, DC, MC, V.*

Moderate **Cathay Restaurant.** Hong Kong investors, fearful of their city's future, are pouring money into Montréal's and other China-towns in North America. Among other businesses, they're opening slick, Hong Kong–style restaurants and competing with the older Chinese eateries. The consumer wins in these restaurant wars. The 15-year-old Cathay was remodeled and expanded in 1985, and is now the most popular and largest dim sum restaurant in the city. The two floors are both huge rooms with institutional dropped ceilings and the usual red and gold Chinese stage decorations. From 11 AM to 2:30 PM, waitresses emerge from the kitchen pushing carts laden with steaming beef dumplings in bamboo steamers, spicy cuttlefish, shrimp

Montréal Dining

KEY

AE American Express Office

rice noodles, bean-curd rolls, and on and on. *73 rue de la Gauchetière O, Chinatown, tel. 514/866–3131. Reservations accepted. Dress: casual. AE, MC, V.*

Inexpensive **Tai Kim Lung.** This small restaurant along the Chinatown pedestrian mall serves one of the better deals in the area: a Cantonese selection of wonton soup, one egg roll, diced chicken with cashews, fried rice and crisp vegetables, tea, and an almond cookie will come in under $5. The table d'hôte offerings here are always wholesome and filling, though sometimes bland, for example the beef with broccoli. There are four or five selections each of either spicy Szechuan dishes, such as hot General Tao chicken, or milder Cantonese offerings like the fillet of *Doré* (walleyed pike) in a garlic sauce. There is also an extensive, more complicated (and in many cases, more expensive) menu to choose from. The decor—muted, toasted wheat-colored walls, mirrors, and soft lighting—is restful, even during the noontime rush. To keep the meal authentic, some regulars order Great Wall Chinese wine, but the bar also carries French wine as well as a decent house label that may be had by the glass. *74 rue de la a Gauchetière O (Place d'Armes Métro), tel. 514/861–7556. Reservations not required. Dress: casual. AE, MC, V. Closed Sun. lunch.*

Continental

Inexpensive **La Charade.** A short walk east from City Hall on rue Notre-Dame Est, this storefront restaurant is a gathering place for civil servants and some of the more budget-minded city councillors. The restaurant is cozy, and the food, although not gourmet fare, is plentiful and varied, served up by a pleasant staff. The menu features Italian and French dishes, with a sprinkling of other choices like paella with a tangy tomato sauce, and chicken or shrimp brochettes. The accent is definitely on pasta, offering five or six different linguine selections, for example, and there are a hearty veal Parmesan, one of the tastier dishes, and *coq au vin*, a hefty portion of chicken stewed in a thick wine sauce with onions and mushrooms. Lighter eaters may sample seafood stews of *moules* (mussels) and shrimp or a Caesar or shrimp salad. The table d'hôte offers a choice of meals with soup, a main course, and coffee, many of which come to less than $15 (excluding taxes). Of course, ordering up a carafe of house wine or a bottle of imported beer adds to the bill. *358 rue Notre-Dame E (Champ-de-Mars Métro), tel. 514/861–8756. Reservations not required. Dress: casual. MC, V.*

Delicatessens

Inexpensive **Bens.** On the menu of this large, efficient deli, all the items with "Bens" in the name are red or are covered in red: "Bens Cheesecake" is smothered in strawberries; "Bens Ice Cold Drink" is the color of electric cherry juice; and the specialty, the "Big Ben Sandwich," is two slices of rye bread enclosing a seductive, pink pile of juicy smoked meat (Montréal's version of corned beef). According to Bens lore, the founder, Ben Kravitz, brought the first smoked-meat sandwich to Montréal in 1908. The rest, as they say, is history. A number of the walls are devoted to photos of celebrities who have visited Bens. The decor is strictly '50s, with yellow and green walls and vaguely art deco, institutional furniture. The waiters are often wisecracking characters but are nonetheless incredibly efficient. Beer, wine, and cocktails are served. *990 boul. de Maisonneuve O, downtown, tel. 514/844–1000. No reservations. Dress: casual. MC, V.*

Wilensky's Light Lunch. Since 1932 the Wilensky family has served up its special: Italian-American salami on a Jewish roll, generously slathered with mustard. Served hot, it's a meal in itself. You can also get hot dogs or a grilled sandwich, which comes with a marinated pickle and an old-fashioned sparkling beverage. The regulars at the counter are among the most colorful in Montréal. A visit here is a must. This neighborhood haunt was the setting for the film *The Apprenticeship of Duddy Kravitz*, from the novel by Mordecai Richler. The service, which is not very friendly, does not prompt one to linger, but the prices make up for it. *34 Fairmount O, tel. 514/271–0247. No reservations. Dress: informal. No credit cards. No liquor license. Closed weekends.*

French

Very Expensive **The Beaver Club.** Early fur traders started the Beaver Club in a shack during Montréal's colonial days. In the 19th century it became a social club for the city's business and political elite. It still has the august atmosphere of a men's club devoted to those who trap: Pelts of bear, buffalo, and beaver still line the walls with members' engraved copper plates. The Beaver Club is a gourmet French restaurant open to anyone with a reservation who arrives in the proper attire. Master chef John Cordeaux has a large and devoted following. The luncheon table d'hôte includes such dishes as terrine of duckling with pistachios and onion, and cranberry compote. For more mundane tastes, the restaurant also specializes in meaty dishes like roast prime rib of beef au jus. The Beaver Club always offers one or two low-fat, low-salt, low-calorie plates. The waiters are veteran (Charles, the maître d', has worked here for more than 20 years), and the service is as excellent as the food. *La Reine Elizabeth, 900 boul. René-Lévesque O, downtown, tel. 514/861–3511. Reservations required. Jacket and tie required. AE, D, DC, MC, V.*

Le Lutetia. This magnificent restaurant is worth a little detour, if only for the piano bar happy hour. The plethora of styles—rococo, renaissance, empire, fin de siècle, and baroque—is a spectacle in itself. This outrageously romantic restaurant is the perfect choice for a tête-à-tête by candlelight. The French cuisine, sometimes nouvelle, sometimes classic, is always served under a silver cover. Behind their glass partition, the cooks busy themselves and give the clientele an appetizing show, even at the busiest moments. The *menu gastronomique* changes each week according to the market and the seasons. The menu changes frequently as well, with creative dishes like shrimp with fennel in puff pastry, ballotine of pheasant in a brioche dough, noisettes of veal *périgourdine* (with truffles), or medallions of beef with coarse mustard, all preceding the cheese or the dessert cart. There is a very good wine list and champagne. *1430 rue de la Montagne, tel. 514/288–5656. Reservations advised. Dress: neat but casual. Terrace on the roof in summer. AE, D, DC, MC, V.*

★ **Les Halles.** Definitely French, this restaurant took its name from the celebrated Parisian market. Its old-France character, enhanced by mirrors and typical bistro inscriptions, will give you the feeling of having gone from busy rue Crescent to even busier rue Montorgueil. However, dependable cuisine and tradition make Les Halles very efficient. The fussy waiters, with their white aprons and towels on their arms, seem to come straight out of a '40s French film. The wine cellar is exceptional and contains about 250 different bottles, with prices ranging from $20 to $540 a bottle. The menu shows a lot of imagination without ignoring the classics: Grapefruit Marie-Louise with scallops and lobster, poêlée d'escargots, or duck with pears sit comfortably beside the chef's ventures into nouvelle cuisine, such as his lobster with ginger and coconut. The desserts are classic, delicious, and remarkably fresh. The Paris-Brest, a puff pastry with praline cream inside, is one of the best in town. *1450 rue Crescent, tel. 514/844–2328. Reservations advised. Dress: neat but casual. AE, DC, MC, V. Closed Sun.–Mon. lunch and some holidays.*

★ **Les Mignardises.** Chef Jean-Pierre Monnet used to run the kitchen at Les Halles. Now that he has his own place, his talents are given free range. Les Mignardises is considered the finest and certainly the most expensive restaurant in town. You enter via the bar and climb up one flight to the simple, elegant dining room decorated with copper pans hanging from the exposed-brick walls. The dining area holds only about 20 tables, so reservations are a must. If your wallet is full, you can choose the six-course *menu de dégustation* ($68.50). But if you're on a budget, it's still possible to enjoy a full meal. The three-course table d'hôte lunch menu allows you to sample delicious dishes like fish salad on gazpacho or marinated duck breast with vinegar sauce. In the evening, the chef's creations include *panaché de poisson* (salmon and lotte served with a tangy lime sauce) and *noisette de faux filet* (tender beef medallions in sherry wine). The presentation always takes a back seat to the taste. As you would expect, the wine list is large and pricey. The waiters and waitresses are prompt, knowledgeable, and friendly. *2035–37 rue St-Denis, near Berri and Sherbrooke métros, tel. 514/842–1151. Reservations required. Dress: casual, but no jeans or T-shirts. AE, DC, MC, V.*

Expensive **Auberge le Vieux St-Gabriel.** Established in a big stone house in 1754, this restaurant claims to be housed in the oldest inn in North America. The interior is lined with rough stone walls, and enormous old beams hold up the ceilings. The fare is hearty yet unadventurous French, with a bit of local Québecois flavor: You may want to start off with the maple smoke salmon, followed by sautéed shrimp on a bed of buttered leeks, although the rack of lamb seasoned with fresh thyme is the chef's specialty. For the brave diner, the Unforgettable 1754 is an old-fashioned Québecois experience: a steaming bowl of pea soup à la Canadienne for starters, then torié (meat pie), baked beans, pigs knuckles, and homemade ketchup. The restaurant seats close to 500 people, but you'd never guess it because there are so many separate dining rooms. *426 rue St-Gabriel, Vieux-Montréal, tel. 514/878–3561. Reservations advised. Dress: neat but casual. AE, DC, MC, V. Closed Sat. lunch.*

Le Café de Paris. This restaurant, a study in atmosphere, has patrons seated at large, well-spaced tables in a room ablaze with flowers and with light streaming through the French windows. Renovated in 1991, the Ritz garden, with its picturesque duck pond, is open for summer dining alfresco. Inside or outside the waiters provide perfect, unobtrusive service. The menu opens with a selection of fresh caviar flown in from Petrossian's in New York City. You can choose from classics such as calf sweetbreads with a slightly bitter endive sauce or the flambéed fillet of buffalo with green peppercorns. At meal's end the waiter will trundle over the dessert cart; the crème brûlée with raisins is a favorite. The wine list includes everything from reasonably priced bottles to extremely expensive vintages. The table to the right rear of the dining room as you enter is where the prime minister dines when in town. If the prime minister is not there, you are likely to see other national political and financial figures supping or schmoozing among the tables. *Hôtel Ritz-Carlton, 1228 rue Sherbrooke O, tel. 514/842–4212. Reservations required. Jacket required at lunch and dinner. AE, D, DC, MC, V.*

Le Cercle. Le Quatre Saisons' management claims to have invented Montréal's version of power dining here. (The competition with the Ritz-Carlton continues.) Le Cercle certainly has the power look. The choicest seats are on a raised circular platform, encircled by a white Hellenistic colonnade. In these impressive surroundings Québec's political and business leaders dine on first-class nouvelle cuisine. Many must suffer from high blood pressure, because the menu features "alternative cuisine" dishes with reduced salt, cholesterol, and calories. The grilled lamb chops with mint dressing are not on this list. If you are on a budget, stop in for lunch and have the onion soup with a ham and cheese sandwich on French bread. Power breakfasts start at 6:30 AM. The standard of service here, as in the rest of the hotel, is high. The wine list is expensive and excellent, of course. *Le Quatre Saisons, 1050 rue Sherbrooke O, tel. 514/284–1110. Reservations advised. AE, DC, MC, V.*

Moderate–Expensive
★

L'Express. The crowd is elbow to elbow, and the animated atmosphere is reminiscent of a Paris train station at this earnest establishment. L'Express has earned the title "best bistro in town." It is also the best stocked. Popular media figures come here to be seen, a task made easier by the mirrored walls. The atmosphere is smoky, and the noise level at its peak on weekend evenings. The cuisine is always impeccable, the service is fast, and the prices are very good. L'Express has one of the best and most original wine cellars in town. Wine and champagne are available by the glass as well as by the bottle. The steak tartare with french fries, the salmon with sorrel, the calves' liver with tarragon, the first course of chicken livers with pistachios, or even the modest smoked salmon are all marvelous year-round. There are specials of the day to give the many regulars a change of pace. Jars of gherkins and fresh *baguettes*, cheeses aged to perfection, and quality eaux-de-vie make the pleasure last longer. *3927 rue St-Denis, tel. 514/845–5333. Reservations required. Dress: neat but casual. AE, DC, MC, V.*

Greek

Very Expensive
★

Milos. Nets, ropes, floats, and lanterns—the usual cliché symbols of the sea—hang from Milos's walls and ceilings. The real display, however, is in the refrigerated cases and on the beds of ice in the back by the kitchen: fresh fish from all over the world; octopus, squid, and shrimp; crabs, oysters, and sea urchins; lamb chops, steaks, and chicken; and vegetables, cheese, and olives. The seafood is flown in from wholesalers in Nova

Scotia, New York, Florida, and Athens. A meal can start out with chewy, tender, and hot octopus, or, if you're adventurous, you might try the cool and creamy roe scooped from raw sea urchins. The main dish at Milos is usually fish—pick whatever looks freshest—grilled over charcoal and seasoned with parsley, capers, and lemon juice. It's done to a turn and is achingly delicious. The fish are priced by the pound, and you can order one large fish to serve two or more. The bountiful Greek salad (enough for two) is a perfect side dish or can be a meal itself. For dessert you might try the traditional baklava, or for something lighter, the fresh fruit plate. The waiters are professional but not always knowledgeable about the array of exotic seafood available. Milos is a healthy walk from Métro Laurier. You can also take Bus 51 from the same Métro stop and ask the driver to let you off at avenue du Parc; Milos is halfway up the block to the right. *5357 av. du Parc, tel. 514/272–3522. Reservations required. Dress: casual. AE, MC, V.*

Indian

Moderate–Expensive **Le Taj.** One of the rare Indian restaurants in town in which the decor and the music are appropriate. The cuisine of the north of India is honored here, less spicy and more refined than that of the south. The tandoori ovens seal in the flavors of the grilled meat and fish, the *nan* bread comes piping hot to the table, and behind a glass partition the cook retrieves the skewers with his bare hands from the hot coals just like an experienced fakir. There are a few vegetarian specialties on the menu; for example, the *taj-thali*, consisting of lentils, chili *pakoras, basmati* rice, and *saag panir*—spicy white cheese with spinach. The tandoori quail and the nan stuffed with meat go well together, as does a whole series of dry curries, from lamb to chicken and beef with aromatic rice. A nine-course buffet is served daily at lunch for under $10. The desserts, coconut ice cream, or mangoes (canned) are sometimes decorated with pure silver leaves if the patron so desires. Other cultures, other mores! The tea scented with cloves is delicious; it cleans the palate, warms in winter, and cools in summer. *2077 rue Stanley, tel. 514/845–9015. Weekend reservations advised. Dress: neat but casual. AE, MC, V.*

Italian

Expensive **Bocca d'Oro.** This Italian restaurant next to Métro Guy has a huge menu offering a wide variety of appetizers, pastas, veal, and vegetarian dishes. One pasta specialty is *tritico di pasta,* which is one helping each of spinach ravioli with salmon and caviar, shell-fish marinara, and spaghetti primavera. A good choice from the dozen or so veal dishes is scaloppine *zingara* (with tomatoes, mushrooms, pickles, and olives). Calorie counters can eat guilt-free the *tajiolini misteriosi,* a pasta, avocado, and shrimp dish in white wine. With the dessert and coffee, the waiters bring out a big bowl of walnuts for you to crack at your table (nutcrackers provided). The two floors of dining rooms are decorated with brass rails, wood paneling, and paintings, and Italian pop songs play in the background. The staff is extremely friendly and professional; if you're in a hurry, they'll serve your meal in record time. *1448 rue St-Mathieu, downtown, tel. 514/933–8414. Reservations advised. Dress: neat but casual. AE, DC, MC, V. Closed Sun.*

Moderate **Pizzaiole.** The wood-fired oven pizzas have had no respite since they started to appear in Montréal in the beginning of the 1980s. Pizzaiole, the pioneer in the field, is still by far the best. The two branches have somewhat adopted the same fresh decor emphasizing the brick oven, but the clientele and the ambience of the rue Crescent location are a bit younger. In both places, there are about 20 possible combinations, without counting the toppings and extras that personalize a pizza in no time at all. Whether you choose a simple tomato-cheese or a ratatouille on a whole-wheat crust, you'll find that all the pizzas are made to order and brought immediately to the table. The calzone, a turnover filled with a variety of meats and cheeses, is worth the trip. Try the thirst-quenching Québec-brewed Boréale beer on tap, or the local St. Ambroise bottled beer. *Two locations: 1446-A rue Crescent, tel. 514/845–4158; 5100 rue Hutchison, tel. 514/274–9349. AE, DC, MC, V.*

Japanese

Expensive– **Katsura.** This cool, elegant Japanese restaurant introduced
Very Expensive sushi to Montréal and is the haunt of businesspeople who equate raw food with power. If you're with a group or just want privacy, you can reserve a tatami room closed off from the rest of the restaurant by rice-paper screens. The sushi chefs create an assortment of raw seafood delicacies, as well as their own delicious invention, the Canada roll (smoked salmon and salmon caviar) at the sushi bar at the rear. Sushi connoisseurs may find some offerings less than top quality. The service is excellent, but if you sample all the sushi, the tab can be exorbitant. *2170 rue de la Montagne, downtown between Peel and Guy métros, tel. 514/849–1172. Reservations required, but you might get a seat at the sushi bar without them. Dress: neat but casual. AE, DC, MC, V. Closed weekend lunch.*

Lebanese

Inexpensive **Basha.** The neon lights along gaudy rue Ste-Catherine and the ebb and flow of the crowd make this fast-food restaurant an entertaining spot for a quick evening bite. Bistro chairs and bare tables make up the utilitarian decor, and diners pick up plastic trays and choose their kebabs and falafels from the cafeteria-style counter. The menu, with prices as low as $2 and $3, includes beef and lamb shish-kebab sandwiches and platters, chicken brochettes, a daily falafel special, and a "Basha" grill platter. Open until 3 AM on weekends and until midnight during the week, this is one of the city's night-owl meccas; Montréalers stop by after a late movie for sticky, sweet Arab pastries and coffee. *930 rue Ste-Catherine O, level 2 (McGill or Peel Métro), tel. 514/866–4272. There is another downtown location at 2140 rue Guy, tel. 514/932–6682. Reservations not necessary. Dress: casual. No credit cards.*

Sausages

Inexpensive **Chez Better.** The rustic fieldstone walls of historic Maison Sauvegarde create a fitting ambience for this North American branch of a popular European sausage house. Although the atmosphere—exposed stone walls, casement windows, dimmed lighting—is upscale, the limited nature of the menu keeps prices down, to only $3.25 (excluding taxes) in the case of the "Better Special," a satisfying sandwich of one mild sausage on freshly baked bread. It's a convenient refueling stop for visitors touring Vieux-Montréal, only a few steps from Place Jacques-Cartier and the Info-Touriste center on rue Notre-Dame Est. This Notre-Dame restaurant is the most elegant of the five "Betters," although all serve the same wide variety of sausages, imported beers, and rich desserts. Service is politely efficient and the noontime crowd lively; dining is more subdued in the evenings. *160 rue Notre-Dame E (Champ-de-Mars Métro), 5400 chemin Côte-des-Neiges, 1310 boul. de Maisonneuve, 4382 boul. St-Laurent, and 1430 rue Stanley; tel. 514/861–2617. Reservations not necessary. Dress: casual. AE, MC, V.*

Seafood

Expensive **Chez Delmo.** This stretch of rue Notre-Dame is halfway be-
★ tween the courts and the stock exchange, and at lunchtime Chez Delmo is filled with professionals gobbling oysters and fish. The first room as you enter is lined with two long, dark, wood bars, which are preferred by those wishing a fast lunch. Above one is a mural depicting a medieval feast. The back room is a more sedate and cheerful dining room. In either room the dining is excellent and the seafood fresh. A good first course, or perhaps a light lunch, is the seafood salad, a delicious mix of shrimp, lobster, crab, and artichoke hearts on a bed of Boston lettuce, sprinkled with a scalliony vinaigrette. The poached salmon with hollandaise is a nice slab of perfectly cooked fish with potatoes and broccoli. The lobsters and oysters are priced according to market rates. Chez Delmo was founded at the same address in 1910. The service is efficient and low-key. *211–215 rue Notre-Dame O, Vieux-Montréal, tel. 514/849–4061. Dinner reservations advised. Dress: neat but casual. AE, DC, MC, V. Closed Sun., two weeks in mid-summer, and Christmas week.*

Steaks

Expensive **Moishe's.** A paradise for carnivores, Moishe's is the last place
★ to receive dietetic advice. The meat portions are as large as a pound, which will no doubt send your cholesterol level way up. Rib steak, T-bone, and filet Mignon are all grilled on wood and presented with dill-scented pickles, cole slaw, and french fries or baked potato. The meat, imported from the western United States, is juicy and tender, marbled and delectable, and aged 21 days in the restaurant's cold chambers. Moishe's grouchy service, its white aluminum-siding exterior and dark interior (reminiscent of an all-male private club), and its tasteless desserts don't seem to frighten away the real meat eaters. For those with a smaller appetite, the portions can be shared, but it will cost you an additional $4 and the waiter's reproachful look. *3961 boul. St-Laurent, tel. 514/845–3509. Reservations required for parties of 3 or more. Dress: casual. AE, DC, MC, V.*

Inexpensive **Le Tramway.** The cheery, fire-engine-red facade of this steak and burger restaurant draws diners off rue Ste-Catherine, especially in winter, when the lanterns inside glow a warm welcome. Once you're aboard, the Tramway is a trip back some 50 years to a time when streetcars, not the Métro, ferried people around downtown Montréal. Interior decorations are refashioned memorabilia: old lamp fixtures, former fare boxes that now hold plants, and overhead racks now used as shelves above the shiny, red banquettes. A reasonably priced menu concentrates on juicy hamburgers, although there is a "jumbo" smoked-meat sandwich with dill pickle and fries and a great thick Polish sausage garnished with sauerkraut and salad, all under $10. There are a few, more expensive selections, such as the charbroiled, prime-rib steak and filet Mignon, so this streetcar is a desirable choice for family diners with varying tastes and appetites. *1122 rue Ste-Catherine O, tel. 514/875–6300. No reservations. Dress: informal. AE, DC, MC, V.*

Tearooms

Inexpensive–Moderate **La Chartreuse.** This tiny tearoom, in the Viennese tradition, has big surprises in store. Although it's best known for its scrumptious desserts, the tearoom serves quiches, salads, and soups as well. On the counter are exhibited heavy and filling cakes, sparsely decorated but mouth-watering—*rigo iancsi*, a Hungarian cake smothered in chocolate sauce, and the gâteau autrichien au café, a cake with nuts and whipped cream make your time at La Chartreuse well spent. One moment on the lips, forever on the hips! The espresso and cappuccino complement the desserts, and the coffee is served with liqueurs, chocolate, cinnamon, or cream (whipped or not). Mozart is played discreetly in the background. *3439 rue St-Denis, tel. 514/842–0793. No reservations. Dress: casual. No credit cards. Closed Mon.*

Restaurants near Montréal

Very Expensive **★ La Sucrerie de la Montagne.** On the road to Rigaud in the direction of Ottawa, maple syrup flows from carafes year-round and seasons the plates of pork and beans, *tourtière*, maple-glazed ham, omelet soufflés, and crepes cooked over wood fires at this old-fashioned sugar hut. Even the bread is baked on the premises in the old brick ovens fired with maple wood. Everything in this young maple grove is intended to re-create the atmosphere of the sugar season: from the sap flowing in the snow (in season) to the workhorses to men collecting the sap bucket by bucket. Pierre Faucher, the owner of this immense sugar cabin, who looks more like a lumberjack than a restaurateur, greets the Sunday passersby as well as the buses overflowing with Japanese tourists in the middle of July. An old-fashioned general store sells Québec handcrafts and maple syrup. During the sugaring season (March–mid-April) a complete meal costs $28 adults, $14 children 8–12, $8 children 3–7; off-season it costs $30 for lunch and $40 for dinner for adults. Ask about reduced rates for children. *300 rang St-Georges, Rigaud (Rte. 40, exit 17), tel. 514/451–5204. Reservations required. Dress: informal. AE, MC, V.*

★ Les Trois Tilleuls. In Saint Marc sur Richelieu, 20 minutes southeast of town, you can lunch or dine on delectable food right on the Rivière Richelieu. This romantic small inn, one of the Relais et Chateau chain, has a terrace on the river and a large, airy dining room. Chef Roger Robin is generous with his recipes, too. You can even stay overnight in one of the two dozen rooms or in the palatial royal suite if you really want to splurge. *290 rue Richelieu, Saint Marc sur Richelieu, tel. 514/584–2231, fax 514/584–3146. Reservations required. Dress: neat but casual. AE, DC, MC, V.*

Expensive **Le Mitoyen**. North of the city, in the small village of Ste-Dorothée (today part of the city of Laval), is this great French restaurant that leans resolutely in favor of nouvelle cuisine. People come mainly from Montréal to taste the inventions of the self-taught chef. The meticulously decorated old house with the red roof is a haven for gourmands. Although it changes along with the seasons, the menu will always include delicious creations such as galette of smoked salmon, sweetbreads ragout with artichoke hearts, guinea hen with sherry wine vinegar, and quail with juniper berries in puff pastry. All are heavenly. For dessert, the maple nougat glacé or the poached pears in red wine and pepper end the meal elegantly. *652 Place Publique Ste-Dorothée, Laval (Rte. 13 N), tel. 514/689–2977. Reservations required. Dress: neat but casual. AE, MC, V. Closed Mon. and lunch daily (except on Sun.)*

Lodging

On the island of Montréal alone there are 29,000 rooms available in every type of accommodation, from world-class luxury hotels to youth hostels, from student dormitories to budget executive motels. Keep in mind that during peak season (May–August) it may be difficult to find a bed without reserving, and most, but not all, hotels raise their prices. Prices often drop from mid-November to early April. Throughout the year a number of the better hotels have two-night, three-day, double-occupancy packages that offer substantial discounts.

If you arrive in Montréal without a hotel reservation, the tourism information booths at either airport can provide you with a list of hotels and room availability. You must, however, make the reservation yourself. There are no information booths at the Voyageur bus terminal, but the Gare Centrale is directly behind Le Reine Elizabeth hotel.

The following list is composed of recommended lodgings in Montréal for various budgets. The rates quoted are for a standard double room in May 1993; off-season rates are almost always lower.

Highly recommended hotels in each price category are indicated by a star ★.

Category	Cost*
Very Expensive	over $160
Expensive	$120–$160
Moderate	$85–$120
Inexpensive	under $85

All prices are for a standard double room, excluding an optional service charge.

Downtown

Very Expensive **Bonaventure Hilton International**. This 393-room Hilton—situated atop a Métro station, the Place Bonaventure exhibition center, and a mall crowded with shops and restaurants—

sits 17 floors above the street. From the outside the massive building is uninviting, but the kind staff inside warms things up. When you exit the elevator, you find yourself in a spacious reception area flanked by an outdoor swimming pool (heated year-round) and 2½ acres of gardens, complete with ducks. Also on this floor is a complex of three restaurants and a nightclub that features well-known international entertainers. Le Castillon is the flagship restaurant, known for its three-course, 55-minute businessman's lunch. On Sunday, there's a special theme menu. All rooms have fully stocked minibars and black-and-white TVs in the bathrooms. The furnishings are a bit dowdy, but comfortable. The Bonaventure has excellent access to the Métro station of the same name beneath it and to all the shops at Place Ville-Marie through the Underground City. *1 Place Bonaventure, H5A 1E4, tel. 514/878–2332 or 800/445–8667. 393 rooms. Facilities: 3 restaurants, nightclub, health club with sauna, outdoor pool, rooftop garden, gift shop (hotel is located in a building with a shopping mall), and 24-hr room service. AE, D, DC, MC, V.*

Hôtel du Parc. Half a block away from the acres of greenery in Parc du Mont-Royal is this perfectly located hotel, which caters mostly to a corporate clientele. Rooms are large, and the decor is modern and well maintained. From the lobby you can descend to a shopping mall with many stores and movie theaters. The nightlife of rue Prince Arthur is six blocks away. *3625 av. du Parc, H2X 3P8, tel. 514/288–6666, in Canada, 800/363–0735; in U.S., 800/448–8355. 358 rooms, 20 suites. Facilities: restaurant, café-bar; health club, squash courts, 2 swimming pools, tennis court, nonsmoking floors, and gift shop. AE, D, DC, MC, V.*

Hotel Inter-Continental Montréal. This first Inter-Continental property in Montréal, built in 1991, brings hotel luxury to Vieux-Montréal for the first time in decades. The 24-story hotel is linked to the World Trade Centre, the block-long retail and office development that combines old and new in the former financial heart of the city, close to Vieux-Montréal attractions and the Palais des Congrès convention center. Le Continent, the elegant restaurant located in the main lobby, serves international cuisine, and there are also two bars, including Chez Plume, at ground level. The rooms are done in soft pastel colors, and match the Victorian flavor of the banquet center in the Nordheimer Building next door. The interior of the hotel makes rich use of granite and wood paneling. Other facilities include minibars and refrigerators in rooms, 12 meeting rooms, twice-daily maid service, complimentary shoe shine, a daily newspaper, and a ballroom once frequented by actress Sarah Bernhardt. *360 rue St-Antoine O, H2Y 3X4, tel. 514/987–9900, in U.S., 800/327–0200; in Canada, 800/361–3600. 335 rooms, 22 suites. Facilities: restaurant, health club with sauna, indoor pool, cable TV, and 24-hour room service. AE, DC, MC, V.*

Hôtel Vogue. One of Montréal's newest and most elegant hotels, the Vogue opened in late 1990, happily surprising everyone who remembered this building as a drab office tower. Now beautifully transformed, with tall windows and a facade of polished rose granite and deep aqua trim, this hotel is chic, sophisticated, and in the heart of downtown, right across rue de la Montagne from Ogilvy department store. The lobby's focal point, the L'Opéra Bar, boasts an expansive bay window. Room furnishings are decorated in striped silk, and double, queen- and king-size beds are draped with satiny duvets. Fax machines and multiline telephones in rooms appeal to business

Montréal Lodging

148

travelers. Bathrooms come with Jacuzzis, televisions, and phones. The Société Café on the lobby level is already a favorite among downtowners. *1425 rue de la Montagne, H3G 1Z3, tel. 514/285–5555 or 800/465–6654. 148 rooms, 6 suites. Facilities: restaurant, bar, and exercise room. AE, D, DC, MC, V.*

Le Centre Sheraton. In a huge 37-story complex well placed between the downtown business district and the restaurant streets of Crescent and Bishop, this Sheraton offers a wide variety of services to both the business and tourist crowds. It's also a favorite with international entertainment celebrities. There are two restaurants, two bars, an indoor pool, a health club, and indoor parking. The elite, five-story Towers section is geared toward business travelers. The Sheraton caters to conventions, so expect to encounter such groups when you stay here. Though the decor is beige and unremarkable (once inside you could be in any large, modern hotel in any North American metropolis), the location's the thing. *1201 boul. René-Lévesque O, H3B 2L7, tel. 514/878–2000 or 800/325–3535. 824 rooms, 40 suites. Facilities: 2 restaurants, 2 bars, health club with whirlpool and sauna, indoor pool, unisex beauty parlor, and gift shop. AE, D, DC, MC, V.*

Le Meridien. This Air France property rises 12 stories from the center of the Complexe Desjardins, a boutique-rich mall in the center of the plushest stretch of the Underground City. The hotel caters to businesspeople and tourists who want ultramodern European style and convenience. Le Meridien is designed on a plan of circles of privilege within these already-exclusive surroundings. For instance, within Le Café Fleuri French restaurant there's a chicer, pricier enclave called Le Club. There are non-smoking floors and an indoor pool, sauna, and whirlpool facility. And if the atmosphere ever seems too confining, you can always burst out the door and go to Chinatown, a five-minute walk away. *4 Complexe Desjardins, C.P. 130, H5B 1E5, tel. 514/285–1450 or 800/543–4300. 572 rooms, 28 suites. Facilities: 3 restaurants, business center, piano bar, indoor pool, sauna, whirlpool, YMCA and YWCA nearby, and baby-sitting services located in complex with shops and boutiques. AE, D, DC, MC, V.*

★ **Le Quatre Saisons.** Service and hospitality make this establishment stand out among Montréal's best hotels. The shiny brass entrance opens onto a small lobby with a usually busy concierge desk and a discreet reception counter. The clientele here is primarily corporate, and the large rooms are decorated to serve that market: floral chintzes, plush carpeting, and English traditional furnishings. Even the least expensive room has a bathroom telephone, minibar, hair dryer, and safe. For stress control, the hotel has a well-equipped health club, a heated outdoor swimming pool with a swimming tunnel connecting it to the building, a whirlpool, and two saunas. Two of the city's best restaurants are located here–Le Cercle and Zen. *1050 rue Sherbrooke O., H3A 2R6, tel. 514/284–1110 or 800/332–3442. 300 rooms, including 29 suites. Facilities: 2 restaurants, lounge, health club, heated outdoor pool, and 24-hour room service.*

★ **Le Reine Elizabeth.** If the Ritz-Carlton is a stately old cruise ship, then the Queen Elizabeth, also called Le Reine Elizabeth, is a battleship. Massive and gray, this Canadian Pacific hotel sits on top of the Gare Centrale train station in the very heart of the city, beside Mary Queen of the World Catholic Cathedral and across the street from Place Ville-Marie. The lobby is a bit too much like a railway station—hordes march this way and that—to be attractive and personal, but upstairs the rooms are modern, spacious, and spotless, especially in the more expensive Entrée Gold section. All the latest gadgets and other trappings of luxury are present. The hotel is home to the Beaver Club (*see* Dining, *above*), a flagship restaurant that is considered an institution. There's a cheaper restaurant, too, as well as four lounges. Conventions are a specialty here. *900 boul. René-Lévesque O, H3B 4A5, tel. 514/861–3511 or 800/441–1414. 929 rooms, 81 suites. Facilities: 4 restaurants, 2 bars-lounges, beauty salon, boutiques, and gift shops. AE, D, DC, MC, V.*

★ **Ritz-Carlton.** This property floats like a stately old luxury liner along rue Sherbrooke. It was opened in 1912 by a consortium of local investors who wanted a hotel in which their rich European friends could stay and indulge their champagne-and-caviar tastes. Since then many earthshaking events have occurred here, including the marriage of Elizabeth Taylor and Richard Burton. Power breakfasts, lunches, and dinners are the rule at the elegant Café de Paris, and the prime minister and others in the national government are frequently sighted eating here. A less heady atmosphere prevails at the Ritz-Carlton's two other excellent restaurants. Guest rooms are a successful blend of Edwardian style—some suites have working fireplaces—with such modern accessories as electronic safes. Careful and personal attention are hallmarks of the Ritz-Carlton's service. Even if you're not a guest, stop by the Ritz's Hotel Courtyard during the summer for afternoon tea and to see the duck pond, a Ritz tradition since 1912. *1228 rue Sherbrooke O, H3G 1H6, tel. 514/842–4212 or 800/223–6800. 201 rooms, 39 suites. Facilities: restaurant, bar, piano bar, gift shop, barber shop, and 24-hour room service. AE, DC, MC, V.*

Expensive **Delta Montréal.** The French-style Delta is making a bid to break into the ranks of Montréal's world-class hotels. Many of the spacious guest rooms have balconies and excellent views of the city. The Le Bouquet restaurant and the piano lounge are designed like 19th-century Parisian establishments, with dark wood paneling and brass chandeliers. The cuisine is Continental and not above trendy touches like grilling over mesquite. The Delta has the most complete exercise and pool facility in Montréal. There are indoor and outdoor pools, two international squash courts, an exercise room, a sauna, and a whirlpool. The innovative Children's Creative Centre lets your children play (under supervision) while you gallivant around town. *475 av. President-Kennedy, H3A 2T4, tel. 514/286–1986 or 800/268–1133. 443 rooms, 10 suites. Facilities: restaurant; jazz bar (which also serves lunch weekdays); indoor and outdoor pools; health club with whirlpool, sauna, squash courts, aerobics classes; children's center; gift shop; and pinball and video-game rooms. AE, DC, MC, V.*

Holiday Inn Crowne Plaza. The flagship of the Holiday Inn chain's downtown Montréal hotels, the Crowne Plaza could just as well have been plopped down in Las Vegas or Atlanta. On the other hand, one doesn't stay in Holiday Inns for originality of design. This hotel *does* sparkle: It was recently renovated from top to bottom and has the largest indoor pool of the city's hotels, in addition to a health club, café-restaurant, and two bars. It has two suites, a penthouse, and two business floors. Popular for conventions, this hotel is near Métro McGill, rue

Sherbrooke shopping, and downtown. *420 rue Sherbrooke O, H3A 1B4, tel. 514/842–6111 or 800/465–4329. 478 rooms, 6 suites. Facilities: café-restaurant, 2 bars, indoor pool, health club with sauna and whirlpool, unisex beauty parlor, and gift shop. AE, D, DC, MC, V.*

★ **Hôtel de la Montagne.** Upon entering the reception area you'll be greeted by a naked, butterfly-winged nymph who rises out of a fountain. An enormous crystal chandelier hangs from the ceiling and tinkles to the beat of disco music played a little too loudly. The decor resembles Versailles rebuilt with a dash of art nouveau and is reminiscent of a mid-'70s discothèque. The rooms are tamer, large, and comfortable. As for the food, it's excellent, especially in the main restaurant—Le Lutetia—known as one of the best and most innovative gourmet eateries in Montréal (*see* Dining, *above*). Tea and cocktails are served in the two lobby bars on each side of the hall, and a tunnel connects the hotel to Thursday's/Les Beaux Jeudis, a popular singles bar, restaurant, and dance club all rolled into one. Clientele is a truly bilingual mixture of French-speaking Montréalers stopping by for a drink and Torontonians in town on business. If you're staying elsewhere, the reception area is at least worth a visit. *1430 rue de la Montagne, H3G 1Z5, tel. 514/288–5656 or 800/361–6262. 135 rooms. Facilities: 2 restaurants, disco-bar, and outdoor pool. AE, D, DC, MC, V.*

La Citadelle. There's a small pack of hotels on rue Sherbrooke, all of them convenient to Place des Arts, shopping, and the financial district; La Citadelle, a Clarion Hotel property, is one of them. This relatively small business hotel offers both four-star elegance in a low-key atmosphere and service, along with all the features of its better-known brethren: minibars, in-room movies, a small health club with an indoor pool, etc. There's also a passable French restaurant, C'est La Vie. *410 rue Sherbrooke O, H3A 1B3, tel. 514/844–8851 or 800/465–6654. 180 rooms. Facilities: restaurant, lounge, health club with Nautilus, sauna, and steam room, indoor pool, gift shop. AE, DC, MC, V.*

Le Château Champlain. In the heart of downtown Montréal, at the southern end of Place du Canada, is this 36-floor skyscraper with distinctive half moon–shape windows. The decor inside is formal, with only 20 rooms per floor. A number of floors are reserved for nonsmokers. Underground passageways connect the Champlain with the Bonaventure Métro station, the Bonaventure Hilton International, and Place Ville-Marie. *1 Place du Canada, H3B 4C9, tel. 514/878–9000 or 800/268–9411. 510 rooms, 46 suites. Facilities: 3 restaurants, lounge, health club with sauna and whirlpool, large indoor pool, and gift shops. AE, DC, MC, V.*

Le Shangrila Best Western. If you're a frequent traveler to Montréal, you may want to try something different: an Oriental-style hotel. The hotel's decor from reception to restaurant to rooms is modern, with an amalgam of Korean, Chinese, Japanese, and Indian motifs and artwork. In addition to special corporate-class extras, such as a lounge for buffet breakfasts and snacks, there are also pluses for the fitness fanatic: more than 10 health rooms—private rooms with exercise facilities. For your hunger pangs, there's a large Szechuan-style restaurant, Dynastie de Ming, on the lobby level. During the week the clientele is corporate; on weekends most of the guests are tourists from the United States and Ontario. Le Shangrila is situated across the street from Le Quatre Saisons on rue Sherbrooke, one block from Métro Peel. *3407 rue Peel, H3A 1W7, tel. 514/288–4141 or 800/361–7791. 146 rooms, 17 suites. Facilities: café, restaurant, bar, business lounge, gift shop, and salon. AE, D, DC, MC, V.*

Moderate **Château Versailles.** The excellently situated, small, charming
★ hotel occupies a row of four converted mansions on rue Sherbrooke Ouest. The owners have decorated it with many antique paintings, tapestries, and furnishings; some rooms have ornate moldings and plaster decorations on the walls and ceilings. Each room also has a full bath, TV, and air-conditioning. The reception area is designed to look like a European pension. Across the street, at 1808 rue Sherbrooke, the Villeneuve family has added a former apartment hotel as an annex to the original town houses. Called La Tour Versailles, it offers 107 larger, more Spartan rooms—at the same reasonable price—and a restaurant run by Christien Lévêque, former chef at the Ritz. It's aptly called the Champs-Élysées. The staff is extremely helpful and friendly. The Versailles is unassuming, not too expensive, and classy. *1659 rue Sherbrooke O (near Métro Guy-Concordia), H3H 1E3, tel. 514/933–3611 or 800/361–3664. 70 rooms in Château, 105 rooms, 2 suites in La Tour. Facilities: breakfast room in the Château, restaurant in La Tour. AE, DC, MC, V.*

★ **Hôtel Radisson des Gouverneurs de Montréal.** Abutting the stock exchange, this property rises above a stunning three-story atrium-reception area and is especially attractive to the convention crowds. It's centrally located and is nearby the Place Bonaventure, the western fringe of Vieux-Montréal, and the Métro Square Victoria (accessible via an underground passage). Amenities include the usual health club and pool facilities, a more exclusive floor for higher-paying guests, and a shopping arcade on the underground level. Most outstanding, however, are the restaurants. The Tour de Ville on the top floor is the city's only revolving restaurant, and its bar has live jazz nightly. Chez Antoine, an art nouveau–style bistro, serves gourmet salads and sandwiches. *777 rue University, H3C 3Z7, tel. 514/879–1370 or 800/361–8155. 692 rooms, 23 suites. Facilities: 2 restaurants, bar, health club with spa and steam room, indoor pool, and gift shop. AE, DC, MC, V.*

Howard Johnson Hôtel Plaza. This medium-size, medium-price hotel, next to the McGill campus, caters to the business trade and families. Exercise machines and a spa with sauna have been added, and the lobby was redone. The decor of the restaurant is Italianate, with lots of brass and marble and with bay windows overlooking the street. There's also a terrace for summer dining outdoors. The Hôtel Plaza is handy to downtown business and shopping areas. *475 rue Sherbrooke O, H3A 2L9, tel. 514/842–3961 or 800/446–4656. 200 rooms. Facilities: restaurant and café. AE, DC, MC, V.*

Le Nouvel Hôtel. is what hotel managers like to call a "new concept"—in its four towers it has studios and 2½-room apartments. It's not very classy, but it's all relatively new, brightly colored, and functional. Le Nouvel Hôtel is near the restaurant district, five or six blocks from the heart of downtown and two blocks from the Guy-Concordia Métro station. *1740 boul. René-Lévesque O, H3H 1R3, tel. 514/931–8841 or 800/363–6063. 126 rooms, 60 2½-room units. Facilities: restaurant, bar, gift shop, and outdoor pool. AE, DC, MC, V.*

Lord Berri. Next to the Université du Québec à Montréal, the Lord Berri is a new, moderately priced hotel convenient to the restaurants and nightlife of rue St-Denis. It offers some of the services of its more expensive competition: minibars, in-room movies, and nonsmoking floors. The Il Cavaliere restaurant serves Italian food and is popular with a local clientele. The Berri-UQAM Métro stop is a block away. *1199 rue Berri, H2L 4C6, tel. 514/845–9236 or 800/363–0363. 154 rooms. Facilities: restaurant and gift shop. AE, DC, MC, V.*

Inexpensive **Le Royal Roussillon.** This hotel is adjacent to the Terminus Voyageur bus station (buses park directly beneath one wing of the hotel), and some of the bus station aura seems to rub off on the Roussillon; it's a little dingy. But if you're stumbling after a long bus ride and want somewhere to stay, *now,* the Rousillon's rooms are large and clean, the service is friendly, and the price is right. It's also handy to the Berri-UQAM Métro station. *1600 rue St-Hubert, H2L 3Z3, tel. 514/849–3214. 147 rooms. Facilities: restaurant. AE, DC, MC, V.*

YMCA. This clean Y is downtown, next to Peel Métro station. Book at least two days in advance. Women should book seven days ahead because there are fewer rooms with showers for them. Anyone staying summer weekends must book a week ahead, as well. *1450 rue Stanley, H3A 2W6, tel. 514/849–8393. 331 rooms, 429 beds. AE, MC, V.*

YWCA. Very close to dozens of restaurants, the Y is right downtown, one block from rue Ste-Catherine. Although men can eat at the café, the overnight facilities and health club are for women only. If you want a room with any amenities you must book in advance. *1355 boul. René-Lévesque, H3G 1P3, tel. 514/866–9941. 107 rooms, some with sink and bath. Facilities: café, gym, pool, sauna, whirlpool, weight room, fitness classes. MC, V.*

McGill University Area

Inexpensive **Auberge de Jeunesse Internationale de Montréal.** The youth hostel near the McGill campus in the student ghetto charges $15 for members, $16 for non-Canadian nonmembers, and $17 for Canadian nonmembers, per night per person. Reserve early during the summer tourist season. *3541 rue Aylmer, H2X 2B9, tel. 514/843–3317. 112 beds. Facilities: rooms for 4–12 people (same sex); a few rooms available for couples and families. MC, V.*

McGill Student Apartments. From mid-May to mid-August, when McGill is on summer recess, you can stay in its dorms on the grassy, quiet campus in the heart of the city. Nightly rates: $26.50 students; $36.50 nonstudents (single rooms only). *3935 rue University, H3A 2B4, tel. 514/398–6367. 1,000 rooms. Facilities: campus swimming pool and health facilities (visitors must pay to use them).*

Université de Montréal Area

Inexpensive **Université de Montréal Residence.** The university's student housing accepts visitors from May 9 to August 22. It's on the other side of Mont Royal, a long walk from downtown and Vieux-Montréal, but there's the new Université de Montréal Métro stop right next to the campus. Nightly rates: $21 students per night, $90 students per week, $31 nonstudents per night. *2350 boul. Édouard-Montpetit, H3C 3J7, tel. 514/343–6531. 1,171 rooms. Facilities: campus sports center with pool and gym (visitors must pay to use it). AE, MC, V.*

Bed-and-Breakfasts

Bed and Breakfast à Montréal. Most of the more than 50 homes are downtown or in the elegant neighborhoods of Westmount and Outremont. Some of them can be quite ritzy. Others are less expensive, but all provide breakfast and a wealth of information about the city. *Contact: Marian Kahn, Box 575, Snowdon Station, Montréal H3X 3T8, tel. 514/738–9410. Single $35–$55, double $55–$105. AE, MC, V accepted for deposits only; the balance must be paid with cash or traveler's checks.*

Downtown B & B Network. This organization will put you in touch with 75 homes and apartments, mostly around the downtown core and along rue Sherbrooke, that have one or more rooms available for visitors. These homes generally are clean, lovingly kept up, and filled with antiques. Even during the height of the tourist season, this organization has rooms open. *Contact: Bob Finkelstein, 3458 av. Laval (at rue Sherbrooke), Montréal H2X 3C8, tel. 514/289–9749. Single $25–$40, double $35–$55. AE, MC, V.*

The Arts and Nightlife

The entertainment section of the *Gazette*, the English-language daily paper, is a good place to find out about upcoming events in Montréal. The Friday weekend guide has an especially good list of all events at the city's concert halls, theaters, clubs, dance spaces, and movie houses.

For tickets to major pop and rock concerts, shows, festivals, and hockey and baseball games, go to the individual box offices or call Admission (tel. 514/790–1245). Ticketron outlets are located in La Baie department store and in all Provigo supermarkets. Place des Arts tickets may be purchased at its box office underneath the Salle Wilfrid-Pelletier, next to the Métro station.

The Arts

Music The **Orchestre Symphonique de Montréal** has gained world renown under the baton of Charles Dutoit. When not on tour its regular venue is the Salle Wilfrid-Pelletier at the Place des Arts. The orchestra also gives Christmas and summer concerts in the Notre-Dame Basilica and pop concerts at the Arena Maurice Richard in the Olympic Park. For tickets and program information, call 514/842–9951. Also check the *Gazette* listings for its free summertime concerts in Montréal's city parks. Montréal's other orchestra, the **Orchestre Métropolitain de Montréal** (tel. 514/598–0870), also stars at Place des Arts most weeks during the October–May season. McGill University, at Pollack Concert Hall (tel. 514/398–4547) and Redpath Hall (tel. 514/398–8993), is also the site of many classical concerts. The most notable are given by the **McGill Chamber Orchestra,** which also occasionally plays at Place des Arts with guest artists. **L'Opéra de Montréal,** founded in 1980, stages four productions a year at Place des Arts (tel. 514/985–2222).

The 20,000-seat **Montréal Forum** (tel. 514/932–6131) and the much larger Olympic Stadium are where rock and pop concerts are staged. More intimate concert halls include the **Théâtre St-Denis** (1594 rue St-Denis, tel. 514/849–4211) and the **Spectrum** (318 rue Ste-Catherine O, tel. 514/861–5851).

Theater   French-speaking theater lovers will find a wealth of dramatic productions. There are at least 10 major companies in town, some of which have an international reputation. Best bets are productions at **Théâtre d'Aujourd'hui** (3900 rue St. Denis, tel. 514/282–3900), **Théâtre du Nouveau Monde** (84 rue Ste-Catherine O, tel. 514/861–0563), and **Théâtre du Rideau Vert** (4664 rue St-Denis, tel. 514/844–1793). Anglophones have less to choose from, unless they want to chance the language barrier. **Centaur Theatre,** the best-known English theatrical company, stages productions in the Beaux Arts–style former stock exchange building at 453 rue St-François-Xavier in Vieux-Montréal (tel. 514/288–3161). English-language plays can also be seen at the **Saidye Bronfman Centre** at 5170 chemin de la Côte Ste-Catherine (tel. 514/739–7944). Michel Tremblay is Montréal's premier playwright, and all of his plays are worth seeing, even if in the English translation. Touring companies of Broadway productions can often be seen at the completely renovated and expanded **Théâtre St-Denis** on rue St-Denis (tel. 514/849–4211), as well as at Place des Arts (tel. 514/842–2112)—especially during the summer months.

Dance   Traditional and contemporary dance companies thrive in Montréal, though many take to the road or are on hiatus in the summer. Among the best known are **Ballets Classiques de Montréal** (tel. 514/866–1771); **Les Grands Ballets Canadiens,** the leading Québec company (tel. 514/849–8681); **O Vertigo Danse** (tel. 514/251–9177); **Montréal Danse** (tel. 514/845–2031); **LaLaLa Human Steps** (tel. 514/288–8266); **Les Ballets Jazz de Montréal** (tel. 514/982–6771); **Margie Gillis Fondation de Danse** (tel. 514/845–3115); and **Tangente** (tel. 514/525-5584)—a nucleus for many of the more avant-garde dance troupes. When not on tour, many of these artists can be seen at Place des Arts or at any of the Maisons de la Culture (tel. 514/872–6211) performance spaces around town. Montréal's dancers have a brand-new downtown performance and rehearsal space, the Agora Dance Theatre, affiliated with the Université de Montréal dance faculty (840 rue Chérrier E, tel. 514/525–1500). Check newspaper listings for details. Every other September (that is, in the odd-numbered years, such as 1993), the **Festival International de Nouvelle Danse** brings "new" dance to various venues around town. Tickets for this event always sell quickly.

Nightlife

Bars and Clubs   Elegant dinner-theater productions have revitalized Montréal's English theater. Prices range from about $12 for the show alone to more than $50 for the show and dinner (not including drinks—which can run up to about $6.50 each—tips, or tax). **La Diligence** (tel. 514/731–7771) has two dinner theaters and a solid reputation for presenting polished performances of popular productions—usually Broadway hits, as well as light musical comedies and plays in English. **The Csarda Restaurant** (3479 boul. St-Laurent) features Hungarian music Thursday through Sunday nights (tel. 514/843–7519). **Le Festin du Gouverneur,** at the old fort on Île Ste-Hélène (tel. 514/879–

1141), offers a unique dinner-theater experience. Light operatic airs, beautifully rendered as a merry 17th-century frolic in the military barracks mess hall, are served up with copious amounts of food and drinks. Great for group outings. **The Foolhouse Theater Company** (tel. 514/369–3330) stages musical comedies, such as its local hit *Let's Go to the Ritz*, at various venues around town. Call for its latest show times and places.

Classical   For classical music, drop by the Bar de Vieux Montréal (tel. 514/499–9403), at 408 rue St. Francois-Xavier.

Jazz   Montréal has a very active local jazz scene. The best-known club is Vieux-Montréal's **L'Air du Temps** (191 rue St-Paul O, tel. 514/842–2003). This small, smoky club presents 90% local talent and 10% international acts from 5 PM on into the night. There's a cover charge Thursday through Saturday. Downtown, duck into **Biddle's** (tel. 514/842–8656), at 2060 rue Aylmer, where bassist Charles Biddle holds forth most evenings when he's not appearing at a local hotel. Bernard Primeau's Trio are weekend regulars. This upscale club is also a restaurant that serves ribs and chicken. There's a cover charge for the big acts. You also might try **Le Grand Café** (tel. 514/849–6955), at 1720 rue St-Denis. **Le Bijou** (tel. 514/288–5508), at 300 rue Lemoyne, is another sure bet.

Rock   Rock clubs seem to spring up, flourish, then fizzle out overnight. **Club Soda** (tel. 514/270–7848), at 5240 avenue du Parc, the granddaddy of them all, sports a neon martini glass complete with neon effervescence outside. Inside it's a small hall with a stage, three bars, and room for about 400 people. International rock acts play here, as does local talent. It's also a venue for the comedy and jazz festivals. Open seven nights from 8 PM to 3 AM; admission ranges from nothing up to $20, depending. **Foufounes Électriques** (tel. 514/845–5484)—which translates as "electric buttocks"—at 97 rue Ste-Catherine Est in the Latin Quarter is the downscale, more avant-garde competitor of Club Soda. Foufounes is the center for the local band scene and also attracts up-and-coming acts from the United States. There's a "quiet" section for conversation and a "loud" section for music and dancing. Open weekdays 1 PM–3 AM, weekends 7 PM–3 AM; admission varies. Other clubs include **Déjà Vu** (1224 rue Bishop, tel. 514/866–0512), **Station 10** (2071 rue Ste-Catherine O, tel. 514/934–0484), and **Back Street Rock Bar** (382 rue Mayor, tel. 514/987–7671).

Discos   Montréalers are as into discos as you could imagine. The newest and the glitziest is **Metropolis** (tel. 514/288–2020), at 59 rue Ste-Catherine Est. The crowd is young, primarily French-speaking, and clad in black. It's open on weekends only, and costs $5 on Friday, $8 on Saturday. If a band is appearing, the admission fee is more. The more popular discothèques are **Hard Rock Café** (1458 rue Crescent, tel. 514/987–1420) and the **Crocodile** (636 rue Cathcart, tel. 514/866–4979).

4 Québec City

By Alice H. Oshins

Updated by Dorothy
Guinan

An excursion to French-speaking Canada is incomplete without a visit to Québec City, located in one of the most beautiful natural settings in North America. The Vieille Ville (Old City) measures 7 square miles (11 square kilometers) and is a lot of ground to cover. This well-preserved part of town is a small and dense place, steeped in four centuries of history and French tradition. Once you begin to explore firsthand the 17th- and 18th-century buildings, the ramparts that once protected the city, and the numerous parks and monuments, you will soon realize how much there is to see.

The oldest municipality in Québec province, Québec City was the first settlement of French explorers, fur trappers, and missionaries in the 17th century, who came here to establish the colony of New France. Today it still resembles a French provincial town in many ways, with its family-oriented residents with strong ties to their past. More than 95% of its metropolitan population of 650,000 are French-speaking. Québec City is also a fortified city, the only one in North America, an attribute that led UNESCO to declare it a world heritage treasure.

Québec City is huddled on a cliff above the St. Lawrence River, at a point where the body of water narrows; this strategic location forged its historic destiny as a military stronghold. When Winston Churchill visited Québec City in the early 1940s, he named it "Gibraltar of North America" because of its position at the gateway to the continent. The city's military prominence paved the way for its leading political role, first as the French colony's administrative center and eventually as the capital of Québec province.

In 1535, French explorer Jacques Cartier first came upon what the Algonquin Indians called "Kebec," meaning "where the river narrows." New France, however, was not actually founded in the area of what is now Québec City until 1608, when another French explorer, Samuel de Champlain, recognized the military advantages of the location and set up a fort. Along the banks of the St. Lawrence, on the spot now called Place Royale, this fort developed into an economic center for fur trade and shipbuilding. Twelve years later, de Champlain realized the French colony's vulnerability to attacks from above and expanded its boundaries to the top of the cliff, where he built the fort Château St-Louis on the site of the present-day Château Frontenac.

During the early days of New France, the French and British fought for control of the area. In 1690, when an expedition led by Admiral Sir William Phipps arrived from England, Comte de Frontenac, New France's most illustrious governor, issued his famous statement, "Tell your lord that I will reply with the mouth of my cannons."

England was determined to conquer New France. The French constructed walls and other military structures and had the advantage of the defensive position on top of the cliff, but they still had to contend with Britain's naval supremacy. On September 13, 1759, the British army, led by General James Wolfe, scaled the colony's cliff and took the French troops led by Général Louis-Joseph Montcalm by surprise. The British defeated the French in a 20-minute battle on the Plains of Abraham, and New France came under English rule.

Metropolitan Québec City Exploring *(Box Refers to Detail Map)*

SAINT-EMILE

blvd. Jean-Talon ouest

80e rue est

80e rue ouest

369

369

boulevard St-Joseph

CHARLESBOUR

358

boulevard des Gradins

autoroute Laurentienne

73

av. Chauveau

boulevard St-Jacques

R. du Berger

40

371

boulevard de l'Ormière

R. St. Charles

autoroute de la Capitale

autoroute du Vallon

blvd. Pierre-Bertrand

VANIER

358

N

138

av. St-Sac.

autoroute Henry IV

boulevard Wilfrid-Hamel

R. Lorette

40

autoroute Charest

du Versant-Nord

boulevard

SAINTE-FOY

Ste-Foy

chemin des Quatre-Bourgeois

175

autoroute Duplessis

chemin

route de

chemin de l'Église

autoroute Henry IV

Hochelaga

rue Lapointe

SILLER

Shopping
Centres

0 ____ 1 mile

0 ____ 1 km

540

GIFFARD

BEAUPORT

rue Seigneurial

avenue Royale

avenue Bourg-Royal

320

TO
ÎLE D'ORLEANS,
COTE DE BEAUPRÉ

avenue

chemin Royal

blvd. d Ste-Anne

blvd. Henri-Bourassa

blvd. d Estimauville

Baie de Beauport

440

1re Avenue

av. du Colisée

avenue Lamontagne

chemin de la Canardière

autoroute Dufferin-Montmorency

360

QUEBEC *Estuaire de la*
Rivière St-Charles

Rivière St-Charles

3e Avenue

Tours 1 & 2
LOWER
TOWN

LEVIS

UPPER
TOWN

autoroute Charest

440

chemin Ste-Foy

Grande Allée

Tour 3

boulevard Réné Levesque

175

chemin St-Louis

132

Champlain

blvd.

Fleuve Saint-Laurent

Louis

**ST-DAVID-
DE-L'AUBERIVIERE**

20

The British brought their mastery of trade to the region. In the 18th century, Québec City's economy prospered because of the success of the fishing, fur trading, shipbuilding, and timber industries. In order to further protect the city from invasion, the British continued to expand upon the fortifications left by the French. Defensive structures that were built included a wall encircling the city and a star-shaped citadel, both of which still enhance the city's urban landscape. The city remained under British rule until 1867, when the Act of Confederation united several Canadian provinces (Québec, Ontario, New Brunswick, and Nova Scotia) and designated Québec City the capital of the province of Québec.

During the mid-19th century, the economic center of eastern Canada shifted west from Québec City to Montréal and Toronto. Today government is Québec City's main business: About 30,000 civil-service employees work and live in the area. Office complexes continue to appear outside the older portion of town; modern malls, convention centers, and imposing hotels now cater to an established business clientele.

Despite the period of British rule, Québec City has remained a center of French Canadian culture. It is home to Université Laval (Laval University), a large Catholic institution that grew out of Séminaire de Québec (Québec Seminary), founded in 1663 by French bishop François de Montmorency Laval; today Laval has a sprawling campus in the suburb of Sainte-Foy. Québec City also has several theaters, including the Grand Théâtre de Québec, where local artists perform plays that deal directly with French Canadian culture. The Québec government has completely restored many of the centuries-old buildings of Place Royale, one of the oldest districts on the continent. The city's ancient stone churches and homes, as well as its cultural institutions, such as Musée de Québec and Musée de la Civilisation, are firmly rooted in French Canadian society.

Québec City is a wonderful place in which to wander on foot. Its natural beauty is world renowned. You're bound to enjoy the view from Parc Montmorency (Montmorency Park), where the Laurentian Mountains jut majestically over the St. Lawrence River. Even more impressive vistas may be gazed upon if you walk along the walls or climb to the city's highest point, Cap Diamant (Cape Diamond). Several blissful days may be spent investigating the narrow cobblestone streets of the historic Old City, browsing for local arts and crafts in the boutiques of quartier Petit-Champlain, or strolling the Terrasse Dufferin promenade along the river. When you've worked up an appetite, you can stop to indulge in one of the many reliable cafés and restaurants, with a choice of French, Québecois, and international fare. If you've had enough of the past, another vibrant, modern part of town beckons beyond the city gates. And if you're tired of walking you can always board a calèche (horse-drawn carriage) near the city gates or hop on the ferry across the St. Lawrence River to Lévis for a thrilling view of the Québec City skyline. What follows will help you uncover some of the secrets of this exuberant, romantic place.

Arriving and Departing

By Plane

Airports/Airlines Québec City has one airport, **Québec City International Airport,** located in the suburb of Sainte-Foy, approximately 19 kilometers (12 miles) from downtown. Few U.S. airlines fly directly to Québec City. You usually have to stop in Montréal or Toronto and take one of the regional and commuter airlines, such as Air Canada's **Air Alliance** (tel. 418/692–0770) or **Canadian Airlines International** (tel. 418/692–1031). Air Alliance offers a direct flight between Newark, New Jersey, and Québec City six days a week.

Between the Airport and Québec City The ride from the airport into town should be no longer than 30 minutes. Most hotels do not have an airport shuttle, but they will make a reservation for you with a bus company. If you're not in a rush, a shuttle bus offered by Maple Leaf Tours (*see below*) is convenient and only half the price of a taxi.

By Bus **Maple Leaf Tours** (240 3ième rue, tel. 418/649–9226) has a shuttle bus that runs from the airport to hotels and costs under $10 one way. The shuttle makes seven trips to and from the airport every day except on weekends, when it makes five round-trips. A schedule is posted at the airport. Stops include the major hotels in town, and any other hotel upon request. Reservations are necessary.

By Taxi Taxis are always available immediately outside the airport exit near the baggage claim area. Some local taxi companies are **Taxi Québec** (975 8ième av., tel. 418/522–2001) and **Taxi Coop de Québec** (496 2ième av., tel. 418/525–5191), the largest company in the city. A ride into the city will cost approximately $25.

By Limousine Private limo service is expensive, starting at $50 for the ride from the airport into Québec City. Try **Service de Limousines** (30 chemin de la Cornière, Lac Beauport, tel. 418/849–7473). Some of the local tour companies offer car service to the airport or act as a referral service. **Maple Leaf Tours** (240 3ième rue, tel. 418/649–9226) has a private car service for about $58.

By Car If you're driving from the airport, take Route 540 (Autoroute Duplessis) to Route 175 (boul. Laurier), which becomes Grande Allée and leads right to the Old City. The ride is about 30 minutes and may be only slightly longer (45 minutes or so) during rush hours (7:30 AM–8:30 AM into town, and 4 PM–5:30 PM leaving town).

By Car, Train, and Bus

By Car Montréal and Québec City are connected by Autoroute 20 on the south shore of the St. Lawrence River and by Autoroute 40 on the north shore. On both highways, the ride between the two cities is about 240 kilometers (150 miles) and takes approximately three hours. U.S. I–87 in New York, U.S. I–89 in Vermont, and U.S. I–91 in New Hampshire connect with Autoroute 20. Highway 401 from Toronto also connects with Autoroute 20.

Driving northeast from Montréal on Autoroute 20, follow signs for Pont Pierre-Laporte (Pierre-Laporte Bridge) as you approach Québec City. After you've crossed the bridge, turn right onto boulevard Laurier (Route 175), which becomes the Grande Allée leading into Québec City.

It is necessary to have a car only if you are planning to visit outlying areas. The narrow streets of the Old City leave few two-hour metered parking spaces available. However, there are several parking garages at central locations in town, with rates running approximately $10 a day. Main garages are located at City Hall, Place d'Youville, Complex G, Place Québec, Château Frontenac, Québec Seminary, rue St-Paul, and the Old Port.

Rental Cars *See* Car Rentals in Chapter 1.

By Train **VIA Rail,** Canada's passenger rail service, travels from Montréal to Québec City four times daily on weekdays, and three times a day on weekends. The trip follows the south shore of the St. Lawrence River, and takes less than three hours. The train makes a stop in Sainte-Foy and has first-class service available. Tickets must be purchased in advance at any VIA Rail office or travel agent. The basic one-way rate is about $45. At certain periods throughout the year, that price is reduced to $29. Reservations must be made at least five days in advance. The discount is not offered on Friday, Sunday, or holidays. First-class service costs about $72 each way. *Tel. 418/692–3940; in Québec City and in Sainte-Foy, 800/361–5390; in Québec province, tel. 800/361–5390.*

The train arrives in Québec City at the 19th-century **Gare du Palais** (450 rue de la Gare du Palais, tel. 418/524–6452), in the heart of the Old City. Take a taxi to your hotel or walk, depending on how much luggage you have and where your hotel is located.

By Bus **Voyageur Inc.** provides regular service from Montréal to Québec City daily, departing hourly 6 AM–9 PM, and another bus at 11 PM. On Friday, Saturday, and Sunday there is an additional departure at 1 AM. The cost of the three-hour ride is $36 one way. A round-trip costs $51, if you return within 10 days and do not travel on Friday. Senior citizens travel for $25 each way. You can only purchase tickets at the terminal; tickets are not sold on the bus.

Bus Terminals **Montréal:** Voyageur Terminal (505 boul. de Maisonneuve E, tel. 514/842–2281).

Québec: Downtown Terminal (225 boul. Charest E, tel. 418/524–4692); Sainte-Foy Terminal (2700 boul. Laurier, tel. 418/651–7015).

Staying in Québec City

Getting Around

Walking is the best way to explore Québec City. The Old City measures 7 square miles (11 square kilometers), and most historic sites, hotels, and restaurants are located within the walls or a short distance outside. City maps are available at tourist information offices.

By Bus The public transportation system in Québec City is dependable, and buses run frequently. You can get to anywhere in

Québec City and the outlying areas, although you may be required to transfer. The city's transit system, **Commission de Transport de la Communauté Urbaine de Québec (CTCUQ)** (tel. 418/627–2511) runs buses approximately every 15 or 20 minutes that stop at major points around town. The cost is $1.80 for adults, $1.25 for children; you'll need exact change. All buses stop in Lower Town at Place Jacques-Cartier or outside St-Jean Gate at Place d'Youville in Upper Town. Transportation maps are available at tourist information offices.

By Taxi Taxis are stationed in front of major hotels, including the Château Frontenac, Hilton International, Loews Le Concorde, and Hôtel des Gouverneurs, as well as in front of Hôtel de Ville (City Hall) along rue des Jardins and Place d'Youville outside St-Jean Gate. For radio-dispatched cars, try **Taxi Coop de Québec** (tel. 418/525–5191) and **Taxi Québec** (tel.418/522–2001). Passengers are charged an initial $2.25, plus $1 for each kilometer.

By Limousine **Service de Limousines de la Capitale** (1400 av. St-Jean-Baptiste, Suite 140, tel. 418/872–2664) and **Service de Limousines Québec** (30 chemin de la Cornière, Lac Beauport, tel. 418/849–7473) have 24-hour service.

Important Addresses and Numbers

Tourist Information **Québec City Region Tourism and Convention Bureau** has two tourist information centers:

Québec City: 60 rue d'Auteuil, tel. 418/692–2471. Open June–August, daily 8:30 AM–8 PM; September–mid-October, daily 8:30–5:30; mid-October–mid-April, weekdays 9–5; mid-April–May, weekdays 8:30–5:30.

Sainte-Foy: 3005 boul. Laurier (near the Québec and Pierre-Laporte bridges), tel. 418/651–2882. Open June–August, daily 8:30 AM–8 PM; September–mid-October, daily 8:30–6; mid-October–mid-April, daily 9–5; mid-April–May, daily 8:30–6.

Québec Government Tourism Department: 12 rue Ste-Anne (Place d'Armes), tel. 418/643–2280 or 800/363–7777. Open 9–5; summer open 8:30–7:30.

U.S. Consulate The consulate (2 Place Terrasse Dufferin, tel. 418/692–2095) faces the Governors Park near the Château Frontenac.

Emergencies **Police** and **fire,** tel. 418/691–6911; **provincial police,** tel. 418/623–6262.

Medical Care **Hôtel-Dieu Hospital** (11 côte du Palais, tel. 418/691–5042) is the main hospital inside the Old City; **Jeffrey Hale Hospital** (1250 chemin Sainte-Foy, tel. 418/683–4471) is opposite St. Sacrament Church.

24-hour Medical Service (tel. 418/687–9915).

Distress Center (tel. 418/683–2153).

24-hour Poison Center (tel. 418/656–8090).

Dental Service 1175 rue Lavigerie, Room 100, Sainte-Foy, tel. 418/653–5412; weekends, tel. 418/656–6060. Open Monday and Tuesday 8–8, Wednesday and Thursday 8–5, Friday 8–4.

Pharmacy **Pharmacie Brunet** (Les Galeries Charlesbourg, 4266 1ière av., north of Québec City in Charlesbourg, tel. 418/623–1571) is open Monday–Saturday 8 AM–midnight, Sunday 10 AM–midnight.

Road Conditions Tel. 418/643–6830.

Weather Tel. 418/877–8787.

English-language **La Maison Anglaise** (Place de la Cité, Sainte-Foy, tel. 418/654–
Bookstore 9523).

Travel Agencies **Inter-Voyage** (1095 rue Scott, tel. 418/524–1414) is located on
the first floor of the Édifice Bon Pasteur (Bon Pasteur Building), on the corner of rue St-Amable and rue Scott, near the Parliament. It's open Monday–Wednesday 8:30–5:30, Thursday and Friday 8:30–8.

Opening and Closing Times

Most banks are open Monday through Wednesday 10–3 and close later on Thursday and Friday. **Bank of Montreal** (Place Laurier, 2700 boul. Laurier, Sainte-Foy, tel. 418/525–3786) is open on Saturday 10–3. For currency exchange, **Banque d'Amérique** (24 côte de la Fabrique, tel. 418/694–1937) is open late June–August, weekdays 9–6, weekends 9–5; Sept.–late June, weekdays 9–5, weekends 10–4.

Museum hours are typically 10–5, with longer evening hours during summer months. Most are closed on Monday.

Shopping hours are Monday through Wednesday 9:30–5:30, Thursday and Friday 9:30–9, and Saturday 9:30–5. Stores tend to stay open later during summer months.

During the winter, many attractions and shops change their hours; visitors are advised to call ahead.

Guided Tours

Orientation Tours The three major touring companies—Gray Line, Maple Leaf,
By Bus and Visite Touristique de Québec—offer similar full- and half-day guided bus tours in English. Tours cover such sights as Québec City, Montmorency Falls, and Sainte-Anne-de-Beaupré; combination city and harbor cruise tours are also available. Québec City tours operate year-round; other excursions to outlying areas may operate only in the summer.

Tickets for **Gray Line** (720 rue des Rocailles; departure from Château Frontenac terrace, tel. 418/622–7420) bus tours can be purchased at most major hotels or at the kiosk at Terrasse Dufferin at Place d'Armes. Tours run mid-May–mid-October and cost adults $23–$45, children 4–12 half-price.

Maple Leaf Sightseeing Tours (240 3ième rue, tel. 418/649–9226) offers guided tours in a minibus. Call for a reservation, and the company will pick you up at your hotel. Prices are $20–$60, with reduced rates for children.

Visite Touristique de Québec (C.P. 246, Québec, tel. 418/653–9722) gives tours in a panoramic bus, and charges $20–$44, with reduced rates for children.

Smaller companies offering tours include **La Tournée du Québec Inc.** (tel. 418/831–1385), **Fleur de Lys** (418/831–0188), and **Group Voyages Québec Inc.** (tel. 418/525–4585).

By Ferry The Québec-Lévis ferry offers a 15-minute crossing of the St. Lawrence River to the town of Lévis. The first ferry leaves daily at 6:30 AM from the pier at rue Dalhousie, across from Place Royale. Crossings run every half hour from 7:30 AM until 11 AM and noon until 6:30 PM, then hourly until 2:30 AM, with a final crossing at 3:45 AM. *Tel. 418/644–3704. Cost: $1.50 adults, $1 children 5–11 and senior citizens.*

By Horse-drawn Carriage Hire a calèche (horse-drawn carriage) on rue d'Auteuil between the St-Louis and Kent gates from **André Beaurivage** (tel. 418/687–9797). The cost is about $50 without tax or tip, for a 45-minute tour of the Old City. Some drivers talk about Québec's history and others don't. So if you want a storyteller, ask in advance.

Special-interest Tours
Boat Trips **Beau Temps, Mauvais Temps** (991 rte. Prévost, Île d'Orléans, tel. 418/828–2275) offers two river cruises that stop to tour neighboring islands. Boats depart from piers at Saint-Laurent on Île d'Orléans, and Pier 19 at Vieux-Port, in Québec. The boat trip to Île-aux-Grues costs $80 for adults, with reduced rates for children. The boat trip to Grosse-Île costs $72 for adults; children under 12 are not accepted. Both trips include a light lunch.

Croisières AML Inc. (Pier Chouinard, 10 rue Dalhousie, across the street from the funicular, tel. 418/692–1159) runs cruises on the St. Lawrence River aboard the MV *Louis-Jolliet*. One- to three-hour cruises from May through mid-October cost $13–$24 for adults, $7–$12 for children 5 and over, $12–$22 for senior citizens.

Île d'Orléans **Beau Temps, Mauvais Temps** (991 rte. Prévost, Île d'Orléans, 418/828–2275) has guided tours of Île d'Orléans by bus, walking tours of the island's historic manors and churches, and trips to a maple-sugar hut.

Walking Tours **Baillairgé Cultural Tours, Inc.** (2216 chemin du Foulon, Sillery, tel. 418/658–4799) has a 2½-hour walking tour, "Québec on Foot," from late June through September at 9:30 AM and 2 PM daily. The tour begins at the Musée du Fort and includes sights in both the Upper and Lower towns. The cost is about $13 adults, children under 12 free.

Exploring Québec City

Québec City's split-level landscape is notable for having one part on the cape (Upper Town) and the other along the shores of the St. Lawrence (Lower Town). If you look out from the Terrasse Dufferin boardwalk in Upper Town, you will see the rooftops of Lower Town buildings directly below. Separating these two sections of the city is steep and precipitous rock, against which were built the city's more than 25 *escaliers* (staircases). Today you can also take the *funiculaire* (funicular), a cable car that climbs and descends the cliff between Terrasse Dufferin and the Maison Jolliet in Lower Town.

With the exception of some of the outlying suburbs, most of Québec City's historic area will interest tourists. The first two tours offered here remain primarily in the oldest sections of town, while the third tour strays off the beaten path to provide a glimpse of the modern part of the city.

Tour 1: Upper Town

*Numbers in the margin correspond to points of interest on the
Tours 1 and 2: Upper and Lower Towns map.*

This tour takes you to the most prominent buildings of its earliest inhabitants, who came from Europe in the 17th century
to set up political, educational, and religious institutions.
Upper Town became the political capital of the colony of New
France and, later, of British North America. It was also the
place where the religious orders first set down their roots: The
Jesuits founded the first school for priests in 1635; the Ursuline
nuns, a school for girls in 1639; and the Augustine nuns, the
first hospital in 1639. Historic buildings, with thick stone walls,
large wood doors, glimmering copper roofs, and majestic
steeples, compose the heart of the city.

Begin this tour where rue St-Louis meets rue du Fort at Upper
❶ Town's most central location, **Place d'Armes.** For centuries, this
square seated on a cliff has been a meeting place for parades
and military events. It is bordered by government buildings;
at its west side, the majestic **Ancien Palais de Justice** (Old
Courthouse), a Renaissance building from 1887, replaced the
original 1650 courthouse, which was smaller and situated farther from the square. The present courthouse stands on land
that was occupied by a church and convent of the Recollet missionaries (Franciscan monks), who in 1615 were the first order
of priests to arrive in New France. The Gothic fountain at the
center of Place d'Armes pays tribute to their arrival.

The colony's former treasury building, **Maison Maillou,** at the
south end at 17 rue St-Louis, possesses architectural traits
typical of New France: a sharply slanted roof, dormer windows,
concrete chimneys, shutters with iron hinges, and limestone
walls. Built between 1736 and 1753, it marks the end of rue du
Trésor, the road colonists took on their way to pay rent to the
king's officials. Maison Maillou is not open to tourists and is
now used as the location for the Québec City Chamber of Commerce offices.

You are now within a few steps east of Québec City's most cele-
❷ brated landmark, **Château Frontenac** (1 rue des Carrières, tel.
418/692–3861), once the administrative and military headquarters of New France. The imposing green-turreted castle with
its slanting copper roof owes its name to the Comte de Frontenac, governor of the French colony between 1672 and 1698.
Looking at the magnificence of the château, you can see why
Frontenac said, "For me, there is no site more beautiful nor
more grandiose than that of Québec City."

Samuel de Champlain, who founded Québec City in 1608, was
responsible for Château St-Louis, the first structure to appear
on the site of the Frontenac; it was built between 1620 and 1624
as a residence for colonial governors. In 1784, Château Haldimand was constructed here, but it was demolished in 1892 to
make way for Château Frontenac. The latter was built as a
hotel in 1893, and it was considered to be remarkably luxurious
at that time: Guest rooms contained fireplaces, private bathrooms, and marble fixtures, and a special commissioner traveled to England and France in search of antiques for the
establishment. The hotel was designed by New York architect
Bruce Price, who also worked on Québec City's **Gare du Palais**

(Rail Station) and other Canadian landmarks, such as Montréal's Windsor Station. The Frontenac was completed in 1925 with the addition of a 20-story central tower. Owned by Canadian Pacific Hotels, it has accumulated a star-studded guest roster, including Queen Elizabeth, Madame Chiang Kai-shek, Ronald Reagan, and François Mitterrand, as well as Franklin Roosevelt and Winston Churchill, who convened here in 1943 and 1944 for two wartime conferences. As you head to the boardwalk behind the Frontenac, notice the glorious bronze statue of Samuel de Champlain, situated where he built his residence. The statue's steps are made of des Vosges granite, and the pedestal consists of Château-Landon stone, the same material used for the Arc de Triomphe in Paris.

❸ Walk south along the boardwalk called the **Terrasse Dufferin** for a panoramic view of the St. Lawrence River, the town of Lévis on the opposite shore, Île d'Orléans, and the Laurentian Mountains. The wide boardwalk, with an intricate wrought-iron guardrail, was named after Lord Dufferin, who was governor of Canada between 1872 and 1878 and who had this walkway constructed in 1878. At its western tip begins the **Promenade des Gouverneurs,** which skirts along the cliff and leads up to Québec's highest point, Cap Diamant (Cape Diamond), and also to the Citadel.

❹ As you pass to the southern side of the Frontenac, you will come to a small park called **Jardin des Gouverneurs** (Governors' Park), which is bordered by three streets of old manors. During the French regime, the public area served as a garden for the governors who resided in Château St-Louis. The park's Wolfe-Montcalm Monument, a 50-foot obelisk, is unique in that it pays tribute to both a winning (English) and a losing (French) general. The monument recalls the 1759 battle on the Plains of Abraham, which ended French rule of New France. British General James Wolfe lived only long enough to hear of his victory; French Général Louis-Joseph Montcalm died shortly after Wolfe with the knowledge that the city was lost. *Admission free. Open daily.*

On the southeast corner of the park is the **U.S. Consulate** (2 Place Terrasse Dufferin). On the south side of the park is **avenue Ste-Geneviève,** lined with well-preserved Victorian homes dating from 1850 to 1900 that have been converted to quaint old-fashioned inns.

❺ Once you've stopped admiring the view from the park, make your way to the north side and follow rue Mont Carmel until you come to another small park landscaped with footpaths and flower beds, **Cavalier du Moulin.** The former stone windmill, which became part of the French fortifications, was considered during the 17th century to be located on the outskirts of town because most of the city was situated below the cliff. The windmill was strategically placed so that its cannons could destroy the Cap-Diamant Redoubt (situated near Promenade des Gouverneurs) and the St-Louis Bastion (near St-Louis Gate) in the event that New France was captured by the British. *Admission free. Open May–Nov., daily 7 AM–9 PM.*

❻ Retrace your steps down rue Mont Carmel, turn left on rue Haldimand and left again on rue St-Louis; then make a right on rue du Parloir until it intersects with a tiny street called rue Donnacona. At 12 rue Donnacona, you'll find the **Couvent des**

Tours 1 and 2: Upper and Lower Towns

Havre de Québec

rue Abraham Martin

rue Lacroix

rue St-Paul

côte Dinan

rue des Remparts

12

rue Charlevoix

rue Hamel

28 r. des Remparts

rue St-Flavien

r. du Garneau

uuveau

rue Ferland

rue St-André

rue St-Paul

r. de la Fabrique

Jardins

rue Ste-Famille

rue Hébert

r. Laval

rue de l'Université

Bassin Louise

rue Abraham Martin

rue Dalhousie

Lock

r. de Quercy

11

13

rue Ste-Anne

10

Trésor

rue du Fort

Tourist
Office

Parc
Montmorency

27 rue St-André

r. du Sault-au-Matelot

rue St-Pierre

rue St-Jacques

rue St-Paul

rue Prince-de-Galles

26

VIEUX-PORT

1

Escalier
Casse-Cou

15

14

Funiculaire

Porte
Prescott

2

côte de

rue St-Antoine

rue Dalhousie

25

urin

rue du

Petit Champlain sous le Fort

côte de

r. Notre-Dame r. du Porche

rue St-André

la Montagne

24

16

21

rue du
Marché
Champlain

20

19

rue Champlain

18

22

QUARTIER
PETIT-
CHAMPLAIN

23

Promenade de la Pointe-à-Carcy

Fleuve Saint-Laurent

N

0   440 yds.

0   400 meters

TO LÉVIS

Ursulines (Ursuline Convent), the site of North America's oldest teaching institution for girls, which is still a private school. Founded in 1639 by two French nuns, the convent has many of its original walls still intact.

Within the convent walls, the **Musée des Ursulines** (Ursuline Museum) is housed in the former residence of one of the founders, Madame de la Peltrie. The museum offers an informative perspective on 120 years of the Ursulines' life under the French regime, from 1639 to 1759. Exhibits tell of the early days of New France. For instance, you'll discover that because the Ursulines were without heat in winter, their heavy clothing sometimes weighed as much as 20 pounds. You'll also see why it took an Ursuline nun nine years of training to attain the level of a professional embroiderer; the museum contains magnificent pieces of ornate embroidery, such as altar frontals having gold and silver threads intertwined with precious jewels. *12 rue Donnacona, tel. 418/694–0694. Admission: $3 adults, $1 students and senior citizens, $4.25 families. Open Jan.–Nov., Tues.–Sat. 9:30–noon and 1:30–5:15, Sun. 12:30–5:30.*

At the same address is the **Chapelle des Ursulines** (Ursuline Chapel), where French Général Montcalm was buried after he died in the 1759 battle. The chapel's exterior was rebuilt in 1902, but the interior contains the original chapel, which is the work of sculptor Pierre-Noël Levasseur, accomplished between 1726 and 1736. The votive lamp here was lit in 1717 and has never been extinguished. *12 rue Donnacona. Admission free. Open May–Oct., same hours as Ursuline Museum.*

Next to the museum at the **Centre Marie-de-l'Incarnation** are a bookstore and an exhibit on the life of the Ursulines' first superior, who came from France and cofounded the convent. *10 rue Donnacona, tel. 418/692–1569. Admission free. Open Feb.–Nov., Tues.–Sat. 10–11:30 and 2–4:30, Sun. 2–4:30; closed Dec. and Jan.*

Time Out   The neon-lit **Café Taste-Vin,** on the corner of rue des Jardins and rue St-Louis, shares a kitchen with the gourmet restaurant next door. The two eateries also share chefs when it comes to salads, pastries, and desserts, making the café an ideal stop for the weary tourist. *32 rue St-Louis, tel. 418/692–4191. AE, DC, MC, V. Open mid-Feb.–Nov., daily 7:30 AM–11 PM.*

❼ From rue Donnacona, walk north to rue des Jardins. Within a few yards you'll see the **Holy Trinity Anglican Cathedral.** This stone church dates to 1804 and is the first Anglican cathedral outside the British Isles. Its simple and dignified facade is reminiscent of London's St. Martin-in-the-Fields. The cathedral's land was originally given to the Recollet fathers (Franciscan monks from France) in 1681 by the king of France for a church and monastery. When Québec came under British rule, the Recollets made the church available to the Anglicans for services. Later, King George III of England ordered construction of the present cathedral, the requirement being that an area be set aside for members of the royal family. A portion of the north balcony still remains exclusively for the use of the reigning sovereign or her representative. The church houses precious objects donated by George III. The oak benches were imported from the Royal Forest at Windsor. The cathedral's impressive rear organ has more than 2,500 pipes. *31 rue des*

*Jardins, tel. 418/692–2193. Admission free. Open June–Aug.,
daily 9–9; Sept.–mid-Oct., weekdays 9–3.*

The building on the corner of rue des Jardins and rue Ste-Anne
is one of Québec City's finest art deco structures. Geometric
patterns of stone and wrought iron decorate the interior of the
⑧ Hôtel Clarendon (57 rue Ste-Anne, tel. 418/692–2480). Although the Clarendon dates back to 1866, it was reconstructed
with its current art deco decor in 1930.

More art deco design can be found next door at 65 rue Ste-
⑨ Anne, the 15-story **Édifice Price** (Price Building). The city's
first skyscraper was built in 1929 and served as the headquarters of the Price Brothers Company, the lumber company
founded in Canada by Sir William Price. Today it is owned by
the provincial government and houses the offices of Québec
City's mayor. Don't miss the interior: Exquisite copper plaques
depict scenes of the company's early pulp and paper activities,
while the two artfully carved maple-wood elevators are '30s
classics.

Head back on rue Ste-Anne past the Holy Trinity Anglican Cathedral and continue straight on this street until it becomes a
narrow, cobblestone thoroughfare lined with boutiques and
restaurants. During the summer, the activity here starts buzzing early in the morning and continues until late at night.
Stores stay open, artists paint, and street musicians perform
as long as there is an audience, even if it's one o'clock in the
morning.

⑩ Turn left into a narrow alley called **rue du Trésor**, where hundreds of colorful prints, paintings, and other artworks are on
display. You won't necessarily find masterpieces here, but this
walkway is a good stop for a souvenir sketch or two. During
the French regime people came to this street to pay rent to the
crown; the royal treasury stood at the end of the street, at Maison Maillou.

At the bottom of rue du Trésor, turn left on rue Buade. When
you reach the corner of côte de la Fabrique, you'll see the
⑪ Basilique Notre-Dame-de-Québec (Our Lady of Québec Basilica), with the oldest parish in North America, dating to 1647.
The basilica has been rebuilt on three separate occasions: in
the early 1700s, when François de Montmorency Laval was the
first bishop; in 1759, after cannons at Lévis aimed fire at it
during the siege of Québec, and in 1922, after a fire. This basilica has a somber ambience despite its ornate interior, which
includes a canopy dais over the episcopal throne, a ceiling of
clouds decorated with gold leaf, richly colored stained-glass
windows, and a chancel lamp that was a gift of Louis XIV. Perhaps the solemn mood here may be attributed to the basilica's
large and famous crypt, which was Québec City's first cemetery; more than 900 people are interred here, including 20 bish-
ops and four governors of New France. The founder of Québec
City, Samuel de Champlain, is believed to be buried somewhere
near the basilica. Archaeologists have been searching for his
tomb for more than 40 years. *16 rue Buade, tel. 418/692–2533.
Admission free. Open daily 9–noon and 12:30–5.*

The basilica marks the beginning of Québec City's Latin Quarter, which extends to the streets northwest of Québec Seminary (rue Buade, rue des Remparts, côte de la Fabrique, and
côte du Palais) as far as rue St-Jean. This district was deemed

the Latin Quarter because Latin was once a required language course at the seminary and was spoken among the students. Although Latin is no longer compulsory and Québec Seminary–Laval University has moved out to a larger campus in Sainte-Foy, students still cling to this neighborhood.

Head down côte de la Fabrique and turn right when it meets rue Collins. The cluster of old stone buildings sequestered at **⑫** the end of the street is the **Monastère des Augustines de l'Hôtel-Dieu de Québec** (Augustine Monastery). Augustine nuns arrived from Dieppe, France, in 1639 with a mission to care for the sick in the new colony, and they established the first hospital north of Mexico, the **Hôtel-Dieu Hospital,** which is the large building west of the monastery. The **Musée des Augustines** (Augustine Museum) is housed in hospital-like quarters with large sterile corridors leading into a ward that features a small exhibit of antique medical instruments used by the Augustines, such as an 1850 microscope and a pill-making device from the 17th century.

Upon request, the Augustines also offer guided tours of the chapel (1800) and the cellars used by the nuns as a hiding place beginning in 1659, during bombardments from the British. *32 rue Charlevoix, tel. 418/692–2492. Admission free. Open Tues.–Sat. 9:30–11:30 and 1:30–5, Sun. 1:30–5.*

Time Out   For a crusty white or whole-wheat croissant, try **Croissant Plus** (50 rue Garneau, tel. 418/692–4215).

Retrace your steps on Collins Street and côte de la Fabrique. When you reach rue Ste-Famille on the left, you will find the **⑬** wrought-iron entrance gates of the **Séminaire de Québec** (Québec Seminary). Behind these gates lies a tranquil courtyard surrounded by austere stone buildings with rising steeples; these structures have housed classrooms and student residences since 1663. The seminary was founded by François de Montmorency Laval, the first bishop of New France, to train priests of the new colony. In 1852 the seminary became Université Laval (Laval University), the first Catholic university in North America. The university eventually outgrew these cramped quarters; in 1946, Laval moved to a larger, modern campus in the suburb of Sainte-Foy. The Musée du Séminaire (*see below*) offers guided tours of the seminary during the summer. *1 côte de la Fabrique.*

Head north across the courtyard to the **Musée du Séminaire** (Seminary Museum). Housed in a former student residence, the museum focuses on the three centuries of the seminary's existence, until 1940. It emphasizes European secular and religious works of art; there are more than 400 landscape and still-life paintings dating as far back as the 15th century. The museum also houses a showcase of scientific instruments that were acquired through the centuries for the purposes of research and teaching. A former chapel has been renovated and now holds an exhibit of elegant religious and secular antique silver. The museum also has a rare collection of Canadian money that was used in colonial times. *9 rue de l'Université, tel. 418/692–2843. Admission: $3 adults, $1.50 students, $1 children under 16, $2 senior citizens, $6 families; Tues. free. Open June–Sept., Tues.–Sun. 10–5:30; Oct.–May, Tues.–Sun. 10–5; closed Mon. year-round.*

Then visit the Québec Seminary's **Chapelle Extérieure** (Outer Chapel), at the seminary's west entrance. The small Roman-style chapel was built in 1888, after the fire destroyed the first chapel, built in 1750. In 1950 a memorial crypt of Laval was added here. The chapel is open in the summer only, and follows the same schedule as the museum (*see above*).

⑭ Now exit the seminary from the east at rue de l'Université and head south to côte de la Montagne, where **Parc Montmorency** (Montmorency Park) straddles the hill between Upper Town and Lower Town. This park marks the spot where Canada's first wheat was grown in 1618 and where the nation's first legislation was passed in 1694. A monument stands in tribute to Louis Herbert, a former apothecary and the first Canadian farmer, who cleared and tilled this area's land.

In 1688, Monseigneur de Saint-Vallier, the second bishop of New France, had his residence, the first episcopal palace, built here. In 1792 the palace's chapel became the seat of the first parliament of Lower Canada. The chapel was demolished in 1833, and a new legislative building was constructed that served as Québec's parliament until 1883, when it was destroyed by fire. A park monument commemorates Georges-Étienne Cartier, a French Canadian political leader and a father of the 1867 Confederation.

⑮ Take the **Escalier Frontenac** (Frontenac Stairway) up to the north end of the Terrasse Dufferin. You may be out of breath, but the climb is worth it for the 30-minute recap on the six sieges of Québec City at the **Musée du Fort** (Fort Museum). This museum's sole exhibit is a sound-and-light show with a model of 18th-century Québec that reenacts the region's most important battles, including the Battle of the Plains of Abraham and the 1775 attack by American generals Arnold and Montgomery. *10 rue Ste-Anne, tel. 418/692–2175. Admission: $5.50 adults, $3.75 students and senior citizens. Open Jan. and Nov., weekdays 11–3, Sat. 10–5, Sun. noon–5; early Feb.–mid-Feb., Apr.–June, and Sept.–Oct., weekdays 10–12:30 and 2–5, weekends 10–5; mid-Feb.–Mar., weekdays 11–12:30 and 2–4, Sat. 10–5, Sun. noon–5; July–Aug., daily 10–6.*

As you exit from the museum, head southeast to the funicular booth along Terrasse Dufferin. Ride the funicular ($1.10) to Lower Town to begin Tour 2.

Tour 2: Lower Town

New France began to flourish in the streets of Lower Town along the banks of the St. Lawrence River. These streets became the colony's economic crossroads, where furs were traded, ships came in, and merchants established their residences.

Despite the status of Lower Town as the oldest neighborhood in North America, its narrow and time-worn thoroughfares have a new and polished look. In the '60s, after a century of decay as the commercial boom moved west and left Lower Town an abandoned district, the Québec government committed millions of dollars to restore the area to the way it had been during the days of New France. Today modern boutiques, restaurants, galleries, and shops catering to tourists occupy the former warehouses and residences.

Begin this tour on the northern tip of rue du Petit-Champlain
16 at **Maison Louis-Jolliet** (16 rue du Petit-Champlain, tel.
418/692–1132), which houses the lower station of the funicular
and a souvenir shop. Built in 1683, this home was used by the
first settlers of New France as a base for further westward
explorations. It was in 1672, however, that Louis Jolliet—the
first Canadian born in Québec to make history—discovered the
Mississippi River. A monument commemorating this discovery
stands in the park next to the house. At the north side of the
house is **Escalier Casse-Cou** (Breakneck Steps), the city's first
iron stairway. Its steepness is ample evidence of how it got its
name. Its ambitious 1893 design was by Charles Baillairgé, a
city architect and engineer, and it was built on the site of the
original 17th-century stairway that linked Upper Town and
Lower Town during the French regime. Today tourist
shops, quaint boutiques, and restaurants are situated at various levels.

17 Heading south on **rue du Petit-Champlain,** the city's oldest
street, you'll notice the cliff on the right that borders this narrow thoroughfare, with Upper Town situated on the heights
above. Rue du Petit-Champlain retains its size from when it
was the main street of a harbor village, replete with trading
posts and the homes of rich merchants. In 1977 artists, craftsmen, and private investors decided to initiate a revival of the
street; today it consists of pleasant boutiques and cafés. The
best buys here are found in the ceramics, wood carvings, and
jewelry done by local artists. Natural-fiber weaving, Inuit
carvings, hand-painted silks, and enameled copper crafts are
some of the local specialties for sale.

At the point where rue du Petit-Champlain intersects with
boulevard Champlain, make a U-turn to head back north. One
block farther, at the corner of rue du Marché-Champlain, you'll
18 find **Maison Chevalier,** an annex of the ethnographic Civilization Museum. This old stone house was built in 1752 for
shipowner Jean-Baptiste Chevalier. It was restored in 1959,
adding two 17th-century buildings to the original structure.
Inside you will find the original wood beams and stone fireplaces, and an exhibit of 18th-century furniture. *60 rue du Marché-Champlain, tel. 418/643–9689. Admission free. Open
mid-May–late June, Tues.–Sun. 10–5; late June–early Sept.,
daily 10–5; early Sept.–mid-Oct., Tues.–Sun. 10–5.*

East of Maison Chevalier, take rue Notre-Dame, which leads
19 directly to **Place Royale,** formerly the heart of New France.
This cobblestone square is encircled by buildings with steep
Normandy-style roofs, dormer windows, and several chimneys. These were once the homes of wealthy merchants. Until
1686 the area was called Place du Marché, but its name was
changed when a bust of Louis XIV, "*le Roi Soleil*" (the Sun
King), was erected at its center.

During the late 1600s and early 1700s, when Place Royale was
continually under threat of attacks from the British, the colonists progressively moved to higher and safer quarters atop
the cliff in Upper Town. Yet after the French colony fell to British rule in 1759, Place Royale flourished again with shipbuilding, logging, fishing, and fur trading.

The small stone church at the south side of the Place Royale is
20 the **Église Notre-Dame-des-Victoires** (Our Lady of Victory

Church), the oldest church in Québec, dating to 1688. It was built on the site of Samuel de Champlain's first residence, which also served as a fort and trading post. However, the church had to be completely restored on two occasions: after a fire in 1759 and more recently in 1969. It got its name from two French victories against the British: one in 1690 against Admiral William Phipps and another in 1711 against Sir Hovendon Walker. The interior contains copies of such European masters as Van Dyck, Rubens, and Boyermans; its altar resembles the shape of a fort. A scale model suspended from the ceiling represents *Le Brezé*, the boat that transported French soldiers to New France in 1664. The side chapel is dedicated to Sainte-Geneviève, the guardian saint of Paris. From May until October, mass is offered on Sunday mornings at 8:30, 9:45, 11, and noon. During the winter months, Sunday mass is at 9:30, 11, and noon. *Place Royale, tel. 418/692–1650. Admission free. Open mid-May–Sept., daily 9–4:30, except during mass, marriages, and funerals; Oct.–mid-May, Tues.–Sat. 8:30–noon.*

㉑ Turn to the northwest corner of the square to the cool, dark, and musty cellars of the **Maison des Vins,** a former warehouse dating to 1689; here the Québec Société des Alcools sells more than 1,000 kinds of rare and vintage wines, which range in price from $10 to $1,000. *1 Place Royale, tel. 418/643–1214. Admission free. Open Tues.–Wed. 9:30–5:30, Thurs.–Fri. 9:30–9, Sat. 9:30–5. Closed Sun. and Mon.*

㉒ On the east side of Place Royale, take rue de la Place, which leads to an open square, **Place de Paris,** a newcomer to these historic quarters. Looming at its center is a black-and-white geometric sculpture, *Dialogue avec l'Histoire* (Dialogue with History), a gift from France positioned on the site where the first French settlers landed. Paris Mayor Jacques Chirac inaugurated the square in August 1987 with Québec City's Mayor Jean Pelletier. Its French counterpart is the Place du Québec, inaugurated in 1984 at St-Germain-des-Prés in Paris.

㉓ At this point of the tour you may conveniently catch the 15-minute **Lévis-Québec ferry** on the opposite shore of the St. Lawrence River. The boat docks a block south on rue Dalhousie; we recommend that you take the ferry for the opportunity of an unprecedented view of Québec City's skyline, with the Château Frontenac and the Québec Seminary high above the cliff. The view is even more impressive at night. *The first ferry leaves at 6:30 AM. Crossings run every half hour 7:30 AM–11 and noon–6:30 PM, then hourly until 2:30 AM. Final crossing at 3:45 AM. Cost: $1.50 adults, $1 children and senior citizens.*

Time Out **Café Loft,** located in a converted garage on rue Dalhousie between Place de Paris and the Civilization Museum, offers delectable desserts, such as a pyramid-shape chocolate cake. Grab an inviting *baguette* sandwich and equally scrumptious quiches and salads. *49 rue Dalhousie, tel. 418/692–4864. AE, MC, V. Open Mon.–Thurs. 11 AM–midnight, Fri. 11 AM–1 AM, Sat. 9 AM–1 AM, Sun. 9 AM–midnight.*

㉔ Next door to the Café Loft you will notice the new diorama, **Explore.** This 30-minute sound-and-light show works on the same principle as the one at the Musée du Fort (*see* Tour 1), except that it uses more modern diorama technology. The show tells the story of Québec and the age of exploration, opening with the native Indians and leading up to Cartier's entrance into the St. Lawrence River. *63 rue Dalhousie, tel.418/692–2063. Admission: $5.50 adults, $3.75 children and senior citizens. Open Jan. and Nov., weekdays 11–3, Sat. 10–5, Sun. noon–5; early Feb. 3–mid-Feb., Apr.–June, and Sept.–Oct., weekdays 10–12:30 and 2–5, weekends 10–5; mid-Feb.–Mar., weekdays 11–12:30 and 2–4, Sat. 10–5, Sun. noon–5; July–Aug., daily 10–6.*

㉕ Continue north on the rue Dalhousie until you come to the **Musée de la Civilisation** (Civilization Museum). Wedged into the foot of the cliff, this spacious museum, with its striking limestone and glass facade, has been artfully designed to blend into the city landscape. Architect Moshe Safdie skillfully incorporated three historic buildings into the museum's modern structure: the house Estèbe, the site of the First Bank of Québec, and the Maison Pagé-Quercy. Many of the materials that were used to construct the newer portions of the museum are native to Québec province. The building's campanile echoes the shape of church steeples throughout the city.

The museum, which opened officially in 1988, houses innovative, entertaining, and sometimes playful exhibits devoted to aspects of Québec's culture and civilization. Several of the shows, with their imaginative use of artwork, video screens, computers, and sound, will appeal to both adults and children. Also featured are several temporary shows a year; an excellent permanent exhibition, "Memoires" ("Memories"), considers both Québec's history and French Canadian society today. In addition, there are dance, music, and theater performances and a good boutique for high-quality souvenirs. Guides are available in the exhibition rooms. *85 rue Dalhousie, tel. 418/643–2158. Admission: $4.75 adults, $3.75 senior citizens, $2.75 students; children under 16 free; Tues. free. Open late June–early Sept., Thurs.–Tues. 10–7, Wed. 10–9; early Sept.–late June, Tues., Thurs.–Sun. 10–5, Wed. 10–9; closed Mon.*

㉖ From rue Dalhousie, head east toward the river to the **Vieux-Port de Québec** (Old Port of Québec). The breezes here from the St. Lawrence provide a cool reprieve on a hot summer's day. The old harbor dates to the 17th century, when ships first arrived from Europe bringing supplies and settlers to the new colony. At one time this port was among the busiest on the continent: Between 1797 and 1897, Québec shipyards turned out more than 2,500 ships, many of which passed the 1,000-ton mark. Yet Québec City's port saw a rapid decline after steel replaced wood and the channel to Montréal was deepened to allow larger boats to reach a good port upstream. In 1984, the 72-acre port was restored with a $100 million grant from the federal government; today it encompasses several parks and the **Agora,** the city's largest open-air theater. You can stroll along the riverside promenade, where merchant and cruise ships are docked. At its northern end, where the St. Charles meets the St. Lawrence, a lock protects the marina in the Louise basin from the generous tides of the St. Lawrence. Because Québec City is close to the Atlantic Ocean, it is susceptible to tides, which can range from 9 to 16 feet. At the northwest area of the port, an exhibition center, **Port de Québec in the 19th Century,** presents the history of the port in relation to the lumber trade and shipbuilding. *100 rue St-André, tel. 418/648–3300.*

The port's northwestern tip features the **Marché du Vieux-Port** (Farmer's Market), where farmers come from the countryside to sell their fresh produce. *Admission free. Open May–Oct., daily 8–8.*

㉗ You are now in the ideal spot to explore Québec City's **antiques district.** One block south from rue St-André, antiques boutiques cluster along rue St-Pierre and rue St-Paul (*see* Shopping, *below*). Rue St-Paul was formerly part of a business district where warehouses, stores, and businesses once abounded. After World War I, when shipping and commercial activities plummeted, the street consisted mainly of empty warehouses and offices. In 1964, the low rent and commercial nature of the area attracted several antiques dealers, who set up shops along rue St-Paul. Today numerous cafés, restaurants, and art galleries have turned this area into one of the town's more fashionable sections.

Walk west along rue St-Paul and turn left onto a steep brick incline called côte Dambourges; when you reach côte de la Cantonerie, take the stairs back on the cliff to rue des Remparts. Continue approximately a block west along rue des Remparts until you come to the last building in a row of purple houses.

㉘ **Maison Montcalm** was the home of French Général Louis-Joseph Montcalm from 1758 until the capitulation of New France. A plaque dedicated to the general is situated on the right side of the house.

Continue west on rue des Remparts and turn left on rue de l'Arsenal, which brings you to the **Parc de l'Artillerie** (Artillery **㉙** Park). This National Historic Park is a complex of 20 military, industrial, and civilian buildings, so situated to guard the St. Charles River and the Old Port. Its earliest buildings served as headquarters for the French garrison and were taken over in 1759 by the British Royal Artillery soldiers. The defense complex was used as a fortress, barracks, and cartridge factory during the American siege of Québec in 1775 and 1776. The area was converted to an industrial complex providing ammunition for the Canadian army from 1879 until 1964, when it became a historic park. *2 rue d'Auteil, tel. 418/648–4205. Admission: $3 adults, $1.50 children 6–16, senior citizens and children under 6 free, $6.25 families. Open late June–early Sept.*

One of the three buildings you may visit is a former **powder house,** which in 1903 became a shell foundry. The building houses a detailed model of Québec City in 1808, rendered by two surveyors in the office of the Royal Engineers Corps, Jean-Baptiste Duberger of Québec and John By of England. The wood model was intended to show British officials (it was sent to England in 1813) the strategic importance of Québec so that more money would be provided to expand the city's fortifications. The model, which details the city's houses, buildings, streets, and military structures, offers the most accurate picture of Québec during the early 19th century. *Open early Sept.–early May, daily 1–5; early May–early Sept., daily 10–5.*

The **Dauphine Redoubt** (*dauphine* in French means "heir apparent") was named after the son of Louis XIV and was constructed from 1712 to 1748. It served as a barracks for the French garrison until 1760, when it became an officers' mess for the Royal Artillery Regiment. When the British called their soldiers back to England in 1871, it became a residence for the Canadian Arsenal superintendent. *Open late June–early Sept., daily 10–5.*

The **Officers' Quarters** building, a dwelling for Royal Artillery officers until 1871 when the British army departed, is now a museum for children, with shows on military life during the British regime. *Open late June–early Sept., daily 10–5.*

Tour 3: Outside the City Walls

Numbers in the margin correspond to points of interest on the Tour 3: Outside the City Walls map.

In the 20th century, Québec City grew into a modern metropolis outside the city walls and its historic confines. In this tour, you will see a glimpse of modern-day Québec City and explore neighborhoods typically left off the tourist track.

30 Start close to St-Louis Gate at **Parc de l'Esplanade** (Esplanade Park), the site of a former military drill and parade ground. In the 19th century, this area was a clear and uncluttered space surrounded by a picket fence and poplar trees. Today you'll find the completely renovated **Poudrière de l'Esplanade** (Powder Magazine), which the British constructed in 1820; it houses a model depicting the evolution of the wall surrounding the Old City. *100 rue St-Louis, tel. 418/648–7016. Admission free. Open Apr.–Oct., daily 10–5, Nov.–Feb. reservations only.*

Esplanade Park is also the starting point to walk the city's 4.6 kilometers (3 miles) of walls; in the summer, guided tours begin here. The French began building ramparts along the city's natural cliff as early as 1690 to protect themselves from British invaders. But by 1759, when the British gained control of New France, the walls were still incomplete; the British took a century to finish them.

31 From the Powder Magazine, head south on côte de la Citadelle, which leads directly to the **Citadelle** (Citadel). Built at the city's highest point, the Citadel is the largest fortified base in North America still occupied by troops. The 25-building fortress was intended to protect the port, prevent the enemy from taking up a position on the Plains of Abraham, and provide a last refuge in case of an attack. The French had constructed previous structures on this site based on plans of Québec engineer Gaspard Chaussegros de Léry, who came to the region in 1716.

Having inherited incomplete fortifications, the British sought to complete the Citadel to protect themselves against retaliations from the French. As fate would have it, by the time the Citadel was completed in 1832, the invasions and attacks against Québec City had ended.

Since 1920 the Citadel has served as a base for the Royal 22nd Regiment. A collection of firearms, uniforms, and decorations from the 17th century is housed in the **Royal 22nd Regiment Museum,** located in the former powder house, built in 1750. If weather permits, you may witness the Changing of the Guard, an elaborate ceremony in which the troops parade before the Citadel in the customary red coats and black fur hats. *1 côte de la Citadelle, tel. 418/648–3563. Guided tours only. Admission: $4 adults, $2 students; disabled persons free. Open mid-Mar.–Apr., daily 10–3; May–June, daily 9–4; July–early Sept., daily 10–6; early Sept.–Oct., daily 9–4; Nov.–early Feb. and mid-Feb.–mid-March, groups only and reservations necessary; early Feb.– mid-Feb., daily 10–2. Changing of the Guard: mid-June–Labor*

Tour 3: Outside the City Walls

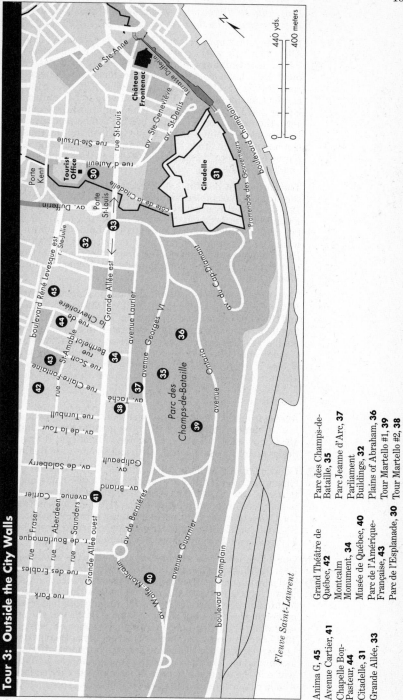

Anima G, **45**
Avenue Cartier, **41**
Chapelle Bon-
Pasteur, **44**
Citadelle, **31**
Grande Allée, **33**

Grand Théâtre de
Québec, **42**
Montcalm
Monument, **34**
Musée de Québec, **40**
Parc de l'Amérique-
Française, **43**
Parc de l'Esplanade, **30**

Parc des Champs-de-
Bataille, **35**
Parc Jeanne d'Arc, **37**
Parliament
Buildings, **32**
Plains of Abraham, **36**
Tour Martello #1, **39**
Tour Martello #2, **38**

Day, daily 10. Tattoo: July–Aug., Tues., Thurs., Sat., and Sun. 7 PM (for visitors on the 6 PM tour only).

Retrace your steps back down côte de la Citadelle to Grande Allée. Continue west until you come to the Renaissance-style **③② Parliament Buildings,** which mark the area known as **Parliament Hill,** headquarters of the provincial government. The constitution of 1791 designated Québec City the capital of Lower Canada until the 1840 Act of Union that united both Upper and Lower Canada and made Montréal the capital. In 1867, the Act of Confederation, uniting Québec, Ontario, New Brunswick, and Nova Scotia, made Québec City the capital of Québec province. Today the government is the biggest employer in Québec City, with about 30,000 civil servants working and living in the area.

The Parliament Buildings, erected between 1877 and 1884, are the seat of **L'Assemblée Nationale** (the National Assembly) of 125 provincial representatives. Québec architect Eugène-Étienne Taché designed the classic and stately buildings in the late 17th-century Renaissance style of Louis XIV, with four wings set in a square around an interior court. In front of the Parliament, statues pay tribute to important figures of Québec history: Cartier, de Champlain, de Frontenac, Wolfe, and Montcalm.

The Parliament offers a 30-minute tour (in English or French) of the President's Gallery, the National Assembly Chamber, and the Legislative Council Chamber. The chamber of the 125-member National Assembly is decorated in green, white, and gold, colors that correspond to the House of Commons in both London and Ottawa. *Corner of av. Dufferin and Grande Allée E, door 3, tel. 418/643-7239. Admission free. Guided tours Jan.–May and Sept.–Nov., weekdays 9–4:30; late June–Aug., daily 9–5. Closed Dec. and early June–late June. Reservations necessary.*

Across from the Parliament on the south side of Grande Allée is the **Manège Militaire,** a turreted granite armory built in 1888, four years after the Parliament Buildings. It was also designed by Taché. It is still a drill hall for the 22nd Regiment.

③③ Continue along **Grande Allée,** Québec City's version of the Champs-Élysées, with its array of trendy cafés, clubs, and restaurants. One of the oldest streets, Grande Allée was the route people took from outlying areas to sell their furs in Québec City. The street actually has four names: in the old city, it is rue St-Louis; outside the walls, Grande Allée; farther west, chemin St-Louis; and farther still, boulevard Laurier.

One block after the armory, on your left (the south side of Grande Allée) you'll come to Place Montcalm. If you turn left, **③④** you'll be facing the **Montcalm Monument.** France and Canada joined together to erect this monument honoring Louis-Joseph Montcalm, who claimed his fame by winning four major battles in North America—but his most famous battle was the one he lost, when the British conquered New France on September 13, 1759. Montcalm was north of Québec City at Beauport when he learned that the British attack was imminent. He quickly assembled his troops to meet the enemy and was wounded in battle in the leg and stomach. Montcalm was carried into the walled city, where he died the next morning.

③⑤ Continue south on Place Montcalm to one of North America's largest and most scenic parks, **Parc des Champs-de-Bataille** (Battlefields Park). This 250-acre area of gently rolling slopes offers unparalleled views of the St. Lawrence River. West of ③⑥ the citadel are the **Plains of Abraham,** the site of the famous 1759 battle that decided the fate of New France. The Plains of Abraham were named after the river pilot Abraham Martin, who arrived in 1620 and owned several acres here. *A free shuttle bus circles the Plains of Abraham, with 11 stops. Also, an hour-long free, guided bus tour of the Plains of Abraham is offered, leaving from the Battlefield Park Interpretation Center (Pavil-lon Baillargé, Musée de Québec, tel. 418/648–4071) mid-June–Aug. Telephone for departure times.*

Take avenue Laurier, which runs parallel to Battlefields Park, a block west until you come to a neatly tended garden called ③⑦ **Parc Jeanne d'Arc** (Joan of Arc Park); it is abundant with col-orful flowers and is centered on an equestrian statue of Jeanne d'Arc. A symbol of courage, this statue stands in tribute to the heroes of 1759 near the place where New France was lost to the British. The park also commemorates the Canadian na-tional anthem *Oh Canada;* it was played here for the first time on June 24, 1880.

If you continue west on avenue Laurier, you'll see a stone oval ③⑧ defense tower, **Tour Martello #2** (Martello Tower), on the north corner of avenue Taché and avenue Laurier. This is the second of four Martello towers built in the early 19th century around Québec City to slow the enemy's approach to the city. At the ③⑨ left, toward the south end of the park, stands **Tour Martello #1,** which was built between 1802 and 1810.

Of the 16 Martello towers in all of Canada, four were built in Québec City because the British government feared an inva-sion after the American Revolution. Tour #3 was located near Jeffery Hale Hospital in order to guard westward entry to the city, but it was demolished in 1904. Tour #4 is located on rue Lavigueur overlooking rivière St-Charles (St. Charles River). Towers 1 and 2 are open to the public.

Continue a block west on rue de Bernières and then follow ave-nue George V along the outskirts of Battlefields Park until it intersects with avenue Wolfe-Montcalm. You'll come to the tall **Wolfe Monument,** which marks the place where the British general died. Wolfe landed his troops less than 2 miles (about 3 kilometers) from the city's walls; the 4,500 English soldiers scaled the cliff and opened fire on the Plains of Abraham. Wolfe was mortally wounded in battle and was carried behind the lines to this spot.

Turn left on avenue Wolfe-Montcalm for a leisurely stroll ④⓪ through the **Musée de Québec** (Québec Museum). This neoclas-sical beaux-arts showcase houses the finest collection of Québec art. With one of the largest acquisition budgets of Can-ada's museums, it possesses more than 18,000 traditional and contemporary pieces. The portraits done by artists well known in the area, such as Ozias Leduc (1864–1955) and Horatio Walker (1858–1938), are particularly notable; some locals find paintings of their relatives on the walls here. The museum's very formal and dignified building in Battlefields Park was designed by Wilfrid Lacroix and erected in 1933 to commemo-rate the tricentennial anniversary of the founding of Québec.

The museum recently received $22.4 million from the provincial government to renovate the original building, incorporating the space of a nearby, abandoned prison dating to 1867. A hallway of cells, with the iron bars and courtyard still intact, has been preserved as part of a permanent exhibition portraying the prison's history. *1 av. Wolfe-Montcalm, tel. 418/643–2150. Admission: $4.75 adults, $3.75 students and senior citizens, children under 16 free. Open mid-June–mid-Sept., Thurs.–Tues. 10–6, Wed. 10–10; mid-Sept.–mid-June, Tues., Thurs.–Sun. 10–6, Wed. 10–10; closed Mon.*

From the museum head north on avenue Wolfe-Montcalm, turning right on Grande Allée and walking a block until you reach avenue Cartier. At 115 Grande Allée Ouest is the **Krieghoff House.** This typical Québec home with its bell-shape roof and dormer windows is closed to tourists, but it's worth noting for its former owner, Cornelius Krieghoff, who lived there from 1858 to 1860. One of Canada's most famous landscape painters, Krieghoff was among the first to depict Québec scenery. Born in Amsterdam in 1815, he served in the American army, married a French Canadian in 1839, and settled in Québec in 1852.

❹ Head north on **avenue Cartier** to indulge in the pleasures offered by the many good restaurants, clubs, and cafés lining the block. On the east side, stroll through the food mall, **Alimentation Petit-Cartier** (1191 avenue Cartier, tel. 418/524–3682). Here you'll find a supermarket and shops that sell French delicacies—cheeses, pastries, breads, and candies. Some of the better stores are **Boulangerie La Mère-Michele,** for breads and pastries such as petit fours, and **Le Vrac du Quartier,** where you can buy just about anything from spices to cookies in amounts you measure yourself. The mall also houses three restaurants: Café Rousseau, Le Piazetta, and Le Graffiti (*see* Dining, *below*).

Time Out   On the east side of avenue Cartier is **Café Krieghoff,** named after the 19th-century painter who lived nearby. Grab a newspaper, play a game of chess, drink some of the best coffee in town, and complement it with a quiche, a croissant, or a dessert. *1089 av. Cartier, tel. 418/522–3711. MC, V. Open Sun.–Wed. 7 AM–midnight, Thurs.–Sat. 7 AM–1 AM.*

---

❹ If you continue north along avenue Cartier, the first major intersection is boulevard St-Cyrille Est. Turn right and walk two blocks to the concrete modern building of the **Grand Théâtre de Québec,** a center for the city's performing arts and home of the music school, La Conservatoire de Musique de Québec. Opened in 1971, the theater incorporates two main halls, both named after 19th-century Canadian poets. The "Grande Salle" of Louis-Frechette, named after the first Québec poet and writer to be honored by the French Academy, holds 1,800 seats and is used for concerts, opera, and theater. The "Petite Salle" of Octave-Crémazie, used for experimental theater and variety shows, derives its name from the poet who stirred the rise of Québec nationalism in the mid-19th century.

As the complex was being constructed, Montréal architect Victor Prus commissioned Jordi Bonet, a Québec sculptor, to work simultaneously on a three-wall mural. The themes depicted in the three sections are death, life, and liberty. Bonet wrote "La Liberté" on one wall to symbolize the Québecois' struggle for freedom and cultural distinction. The theater has a full repertoire in the winter, but no shows in the summer. *269 boul. St-Cyrille E, tel. 418/646–0609. Guided tours offered daily 9–5. Reservations necessary.*

❹❸ High-waving flags east of the Grand Théâtre are displayed in the **Parc de l'Amérique-Française,** dedicated to places in North America with a French-speaking population. Québec's own Fleur de Lys leads the way. The colors of blue and white, an emblem of Sun King Louis XIV, constitute a reminder of Québec's French origins, culture, and language. Inaugurated in 1985 by Québec Prime Minister Réne Lévesque, the park also has flags from Acadia, British Columbia, Louisiana, Manitoba, Saskatchewan, and Ontario.

❹❹ Take rue Claire-Fontaine a block south, turn left on rue St-Amable, and then left again on rue de la Chevrotière. On the west side of the street you'll see the **Chapelle Bon-Pasteur** (Bon-Pasteur Chapel), which is surrounded by modern office complexes. This slender church with a steep sloping roof was designed by Charles Baillargé in 1868. Its ornate interior in a baroque style has carved wood designs painted elaborately in gold leaf. The chapel houses 32 religious paintings done by the Sisters of the community from 1868 to 1910. Classical concerts are performed here between October and June. *1080 rue de la Chevrotière, tel. 418/641–1069 or 418/648–9710. Admission free. Open May–Sept., Tues.–Sun. 1–4; Oct.–Apr., by reservation only; musical artists' Mass Sun. at 10:45.*

❹❺ Across rue de la Chevrotière is the entrance of a large, gray concrete modern office tower called **Anima G** (Complex G), Québec's tallest office building. The structure, 31 stories high, has by far the best view of the city and the environs. An express elevator ascends to the observation gallery on top. *1037 rue de la Chevrotière, tel. 418/644–9841. Admission free. Open Mon.–Fri. 10–4, weekends and holidays 1–5; observation gallery may close later during summer. Closed mid-Dec.–mid-Jan.*

What to See and Do with Children

Aquarium du Québec (Québec Aquarium). The aquarium, situated above the St. Lawrence River, houses more than 300 species of marine life, including reptiles, exotic fish, and seals from the lower St. Lawrence River. A wooded picnic area makes this spot ideal for a family outing. The Québec City transit system, Commission de Transport de la Communauté Urbaine de Québec (CTCUQ) (tel. 418/659–5264), runs buses here. *1675 av. du Parc, Sainte-Foy, tel. 418/659–5266. Admission: (Apr.–Oct.) $5.25 adults, $1.25 children under 14, $4.50 senior citizens, $10 families; (Nov.–Mar.) $5 adults, $1 children under 14, $4.25 senior citizens, $10 families. Open daily 9–5.*

Jardin Zoologique du Québec (Québec Zoological Gardens). Children usually enjoy going to zoos, but this one is especially scenic because of the DuBerger River, which traverses the grounds. About 250 animal species reside here, including bears, wildcats, primates, and birds of prey. Children will enjoy the farm and the horse-drawn carriage rides. The zoo is situated 11 kilometers (7 miles) west of Québec City on Route 73. Québec Urban Community Transit (tel. 418/627–2511) operates buses here. *8191 av. du Zoo, Charlesbourg, tel. 418/622–0312. Admission: (June–Sept.) $7.50 adults, $1.50 children* *under 14, $5.50 senior citizens, $15 families; (Oct.–May) free weekdays, on weekends $4.75 adults, $1.50 children under 14, $3.50 senior citizens, $9 families. Open June–Sept., daily 9:30–6; Oct.–May, daily 9:30–5.*

Parc Cartier-Brébeuf. Stretched along the north bank of the St. Charles River, this national historic park commemorates the area where French explorer Jacques Cartier spent his first winter in Canada (1535–36); it also pays tribute to Father Jean de Brébeuf, founder of the Jesuit Order in New France. A replica of the *Grande Hermine*, the ship Cartier used on his second expedition to America, is stationed here. Playgrounds and 9 kilometers (5 1/2 miles) of walking paths are available. *175 rue de l'Espinay, tel. 418/648–4038. Admission free. Open early Apr.–late Apr., early Sept.–late Oct., and late Jan.–Mar., Tues.–Fri. 10–noon and 1–4, Sat.–Mon. 1–4; early May–early Sept., daily 10–5; late Oct.–late Nov., Mon. 1–5, Tues.–Fri. 10–noon and 1–4. Reservations necessary late Apr.–early May and late Nov. 27–late Jan.*

Parc de l'Artillerie (Artillery Park). This 20-building complex near St-Jean Gate has for centuries played an important part in the city's defense structures. The Officers' Quarters, barracks for Royal Artillery officers until 1871, has a special program for children designed to show how the military lived when Québec was a British colony, from 1759 to 1867. Children's toys and educational games are also available. *2 rue d'Auteil, tel. 418/648–4205. Admission: $3 adults, $1.50 children 6–16, $6 families, senior citizens and children under 6 free. Open late June–early Sept.*

Parc du Porche. This playground has ladders and swings in a historic setting just outside Place Royale (between rue du Porche and rue de l'Union). *Admission free. Open daily.*

Shopping

Shopping is European-style along the fashionable streets of Québec City. The boutiques and specialty shops clustered along narrow streets (such as rue du Petit-Champlain, or rue Buade and rue St-Jean in the Latin Quarter) are located within one of the most striking historic settings on the continent.

Prices in Québec City tend to be on a par for the most part with those in Montréal and other North American cities, so you won't have much luck hunting bargains. When sales occur, they are usually listed in the French daily newspaper, *Le Soleil.*

Stores are generally open Monday through Wednesday 9:30–5:30, Thursday and Friday until 9, and Saturday until 5. During the summer, shops may be open seven days a week, and most have later evening hours.

Shopping Centers

The mall situated closest to the Old City is **Place Québec** (5 Place Québec, tel. 418/529–0551), near the National Assembly. This multilevel shopping complex and convention center with 40 stores is connected to the Hilton International. **Alimentation Petit-Cartier** (1191 av. Cartier, tel. 418/524–3682), located off Grande Allée and a 15-minute walk from St-Louis Gate, is a food mall for gourmets, with everything from utensils to petits fours.

Other shopping centers are approximately a 15-minute drive west along Grande Allée. **Place Sainte-Foy** (2450 boul. Laurier, Sainte-Foy, tel. 418/653–4184) has 120 specialty stores. Next door is **Place Belle Coeur** (2600 boul. Laurier, Sainte-Foy, tel. 418/657–6920), with 34 boutiques. Directly behind this mall you'll find the new **Place de la Cité** (2635 boul. Hochelaga, Sainte-Foy, tel. 418/657–6920), with 40 shops. And finally there is the massive **Place Laurier** (2700 boul. Laurier, Sainte-Foy, tel. 418/653–9318), with more than 350 stores.

Quartier Petit-Champlain (tel. 418/692–2613) in Lower Town is a pedestrian mall with some 40 boutiques, local businesses, and restaurants. This popular district is the best area to find native Québec arts and crafts, such as wood sculptures, weaving, ceramics, and jewelry. Recommended stores in the area are **Poten-Ciel** (27 rue du Petit-Champlain, tel. 418/692–1743) for ceramics and **Pauline Pelletier** (38 rue du Petit-Champlain, tel. 418/692–4871) for porcelain.

Department Stores

Large department stores can be found in the malls of the suburb of Sainte-Foy, but some have outlets inside Québec City's walls.

Holt Renfrew & Co., Ltd. (Place Sainte-Foy, Sainte-Foy, tel. 418/656–6783), one of the city's more exclusive stores, carries furs, perfume, and tailored designer collections for men and women.

La Baie (Place Laurier, Sainte-Foy, tel. 418/627–5959) is Québec's version of the Canadian Hudson's Bay Company conglomerate, founded in 1670 by Montréal trappers Pierre Radisson and Medard de Groseillers; the company established the first network of stores in the Canadian frontier. Today, La Baie carries both men's and women's clothing and household wares.

Simons (20 côte de la Fabrique, tel. 418/692–3630), one of Québec City's oldest family stores, used to be the city's only source for fine British woolens and tweeds, and now the store has added a large selection of designer clothing, linens, and other household items.

Food and Flea Markets

Marché du Vieux-Port enables farmers from the Québec countryside to sell their fresh produce in the Old Port near rue St-André, from May through October, 8 AM–8 PM.

Rue du Trésor offers a flea market near the Place d'Armes that features sketches, paintings, and etchings by local artists. Fine portraits of the Québec City landscape and region are plentiful. Good, inexpensive souvenirs also may be purchased here (*see* Tour 1, *above*).

Specialty Stores

Antiques Québec City's antiques district is located in the area of rue St-Paul and rue St-Pierre, across from the Old Port. French Canadian, Victorian, and art deco furniture, along with clocks, silverware, and porcelain, are some of the rare collectibles that can be found here. Authentic Québec pine furniture, characterized by simple forms and lines, is becoming increasingly rare and costly.

L'Héritage Antiquités (109 rue St-Paul, tel. 418/692–1681) specializes in precious Québecois furniture from the 18th century. **Antiquités Zaor** (112 rue St-Paul, tel. 418/692–0581), the oldest store on rue St-Paul, is still the best place in the area to find excellent English, French, and Canadian antiques. The floor upstairs houses a fine collection of Québec wood furniture.

Art **Aux Multiples Collections** (69 rue Ste-Anne, tel. 418/692–1230) and **Galerie Brousseau et Brousseau** (Château Frontenac, 1 rue des Carrières, tel. 418/694–1828) feature a good selection of Inuit art done by Canada's native people, as well as antique furniture and accessories such as sculpted wood ducks.

Galerie Madeleine Lacerte (1 côte Dinan, tel. 418/692–1566), situated in Lower Town, features contemporary art and sculpture for sale.

Books English-language books are difficult to find in Québec. One of the city's first bookstores, **Librarie Garneau** (24 côte de la Fabrique, tel. 418/692–4262), is centrally located near City Hall and carries mostly volumes in French. Other popular bookstores in the city include **La Maison Anglaise** (Place de la Cité, Sainte-Foy, tel. 418/654–9523), with the best selection of English-language titles in the area, and **Classic Bookshop** (Place Laurier, boul. Laurier, tel. 418/653–8683).

Clothing **François and Hélène Cote** (20 Cul de Sac, tel. 418/692–3395) is a chic boutique with fashions for men and women.

La Maison Darlington (7 rue Buade, tel. 418/692–2268) carries well-made woolens, dresses, and suits for women by fine names in couture.

Louis Laflamme (Place Québec, tel. 418/523–6633) has a large selection of stylish men's clothes.

Crafts **Les Trois Colombes Inc.** (46 rue St-Louis, tel. 418/694–1114) offers only items made by hand. You will find two floors filled with such goods as clothing made from hand-spun fabric, Indian and Inuit carvings, jewelry, pottery, and paintings.

Fur Fur trade has been an important industry for centuries in the area. Québec City is a good place to purchase high-quality furs at fairly reasonable prices. Since 1894, one of the best furriers in town has been **Jos Robitaille** (Place Sainte-Foy, Sainte-Foy, tel. 418/650–6185). The department store **J.B. Laliberté** (Mail Centre-Ville, tel. 418/525–4841) also carries furs.

Gifts **Collection Lazuli** (774 rue St-Jean, tel. 418/525–6528) features a tasteful selection of unusual art objects, gifts, and jewelry from around the world.

Jewelry **Bijouterie Louis Perrier** (48 rue du Petit-Champlain, tel. 418/692–4633) has Québec-made gold and silver jewelry. Exclusive jewelry can also be found at **Zimmermann** (46 côte de la Fabrique, tel. 418/692–2672).

Sports and Fitness

Two parks are central to Québec City: the 250-acre Battlefields Park, with its panoramic views of the St. Lawrence River, and Cartier-Brébeuf Park, which runs along the St. Charles River.

Both are favorite spots for outdoor sports such as jogging, biking, and cross-country skiing. Scenic rivers and mountains close by (no more than 30 minutes by car) make this city ideal for the sporting life. For information about sports and fitness, contact **Québec City Region and Convention Bureau** (60 rue d'Auteuil, Québec G1R 4C4, tel. 418/692–2471) or **Québec City Bureau of Parks and Recreation** (65 rue Ste-Anne, 5th floor, Québec, G1R 4S9, tel. 418/691–6278).

Participant Sports

Bicycling Short bike paths with rolling hills are found in Battlefields Park, located at the south side of the city. The best bet for a longer ride over flat terrain is the path north of the city skirting the St. Charles River; this route can be reached from Third Avenue near the Marie de l'Incarnation Bridge. Paths along the côte de Beaupré, beginning at the union of the St. Charles and St. Lawrence rivers, are especially scenic. They begin northeast of the city at rue de la Verandrye and boulevard Montmorency and continue 10 kilometers (6 miles) along the coast to Montmorency Falls.

Bicycles can be rented at **Location Petit Champlain** (94 rue du Petit-Champlain, tel. 418/692–2817).

Boating Lakes around the Québec City area have facilities for boating and canoeing. Take Route 73 north of the city to Saint-Dunstan de Lac Beauport, then take Exit 157, boulevard du Lac, to **Lac Beauport** (tel. 418/849–2821), one of the best nearby resorts. Boats and boards can be rented at **Campex** (8 chemin de l'Orrée, Lac Beauport, tel. 418/849–2236) for canoeing, kayaking, and windsurfing. You can also rent boats in **Lac St-Joseph**, 40 kilometers (25 miles) northwest of Québec City, at **La Vigie** (tel. 418/875–2727).

Fishing Permits are needed for hunting and fishing in Québec. They are available from the **Ministry of Recreation, Hunting, and Fishing** (Place de la Capitale, 150 boul. Réné Levesque E, tel. 418/643–3127). The ministry also publishes a pamphlet on fishing regulations that is available at tourist information offices.

Réserve Faunique des Laurentides (tel. 418/848–2422) is a wildlife reserve with good lakes for fishing approximately 48 kilometers (30 miles) north of Québec City via Route 73.

Golf The Québec City region has 18 golf courses, and several are open to the public. Reservations during summer months are essential. **Club de Golf de Cap Rouge** (4600 rue St-Felix, tel. 418/653–9381) in Cap Rouge, with 18 holes, is one of the closest courses to Québec City. **Club de Golf de Beauport** (3233 rue Clemenceau, tel. 418/663–1578), a nine-hole course, is 20 minutes by car via Route 73 N. **Parc du Mont Sainte-Anne** (Rte. 360, C.P. 653 Beaupré, tel. 418/827–3778), a half-hour drive north of Québec, has one of the best 18-hole courses in the region.

Health and Fitness Clubs One of the city's most popular health clubs is **Club Entrain** (Place Belle Cour, 2600 boul. Laurier, tel. 418/658–7771). Facilities include a weight room with Nautilus; a sauna; a whirlpool; aerobics classes; and racquetball and squash courts.

Nonguests at **Hôtel des Gouverneurs** (690 boul. Réné Levesque E, tel. 418/647–1717) can use the health club facilities, which include weights, a sauna, a whirlpool, and an outdoor heated pool, for a $5 fee.

Hilton International Québec (3 Place Québec, tel. 418/647–2411) has a smaller health club with weights, a sauna, and an outdoor pool available to nonguests for a $10 fee.

Pool facilities cost $2.50 at the **YMCA** (855 av. Holland, tel. 418/683–2155).

Hiking/Jogging The Parc Cartier-Brébeuf, north of the Old City along the banks of the St. Charles River, has about 13 kilometers (8 miles) of hiking trails. For more mountainous terrain, head 19 kilometers (12 miles) north via Route 73 to Lac Beauport. **Villages des Sports** (1860 boul. Valcartier, Val Cartier, tel. 418/844–3725), a man-made sports complex 24 kilometers (15 miles) from downtown on Route 371, has 16 kilometers (10 miles) of trails. For jogging, Battlefields Park and Parc Cartier-Brébeuf are the most popular places in the area.

Horseback Riding **Jacques Cartier Excursions** (978 av. Jacques Cartier N, Tewkesbury, tel. 418/848–7238), also known for rafting, offers summer and winter horseback riding. An excursion includes an hour of instruction and three hours of riding, and costs $49 on weekends, $39 weekdays.

Rafting Jacques Cartier River, about 48 kilometers (30 miles) northwest of Québec City, provides good rafting; the waterway flows south from Laurentian Park 56 kilometers (35 miles) from Québec City into the St. Lawrence River.
Jacques Cartier Excursions (978 av. Jacques Cartier N, Tewkesbury, G0A 4P0, tel. 418/848–7238) offers rafting trips on the Jacques Cartier River. Tours originate from Tewkesbury, a half-hour drive from Québec City, from May through September. A half-day tour costs $54 on weekends, $44 on weekdays. A full day costs $69 on weekends, $55 on weekdays. In the winter, snow-rafting excursions are available, and include a 2¹/₂-hour sleigh ride and all-day mountain sliding in river rafts. The total cost is $41.
Nouveau Monde, Expeditions en Rivière (C.P. 100, chemin de la Rivière Rouge, Calumet, J0V 1B0, tel. 800/361–5033) has excursions on the Jacques Cartier River from mid-May through September. A half day on weekdays costs $55, on weekends $63. A second trip down the river costs $24. Reserve one month in advance for weekends, two weeks in advance for weekdays.

Skating The ice-skating season runs December through March. There is a 3.8-kilometer (2.4-mile) stretch for skating along the St. Charles River, between the Samson and Marie de l'Incarnation bridges, January through March, depending on the ice. Rentals and changing rooms are nearby. *Skating hours: weekdays noon–10, weekends 10–10.*

Place d'Youville, just outside St-Jean Gate, has an outdoor skating rink open from November to April. Nighttime skating can be done at **Villages des Sports** (1860 boul. Valcartier, Val Cartier, tel. 418/844–3725).

Skiing Numerous trails exist for cross-country skiing enthusiasts.
Cross-country Battlefields Park on Québec City's south side, which you can access on Place Montcalm, has scenic marked trails. For information, call **Québec City Bureau of Parks and Recreation** (tel. 418/691–6017). Lac Beauport, 19 kilometers (12 miles) north of the city, has more than 20 marked trails (250 kilometers; 155

miles). Contact **Les Sentiers du Moulin** (99 chemin du Moulin, tel. 418/849–2778). **Parc du Mont Sainte-Anne** (Rte. 360, C.P. 400 Beaupré, G0A 1E0, tel. 418/827–4561), which is 40 kilometers (25 miles) northeast of Québec City, has 235 kilometers (141 miles) of cross-country trails. Contact **Rang Saint-Julien** (tel. 418/827–4561, ext. 408) for more information.

Downhill Four alpine ski resorts, all with night skiing, are located within a 30-minute drive of Québec City. **Parc du Mont Sainte-Anne** (Rte. 360, C.P. 400 Beaupré, G0A 1E0, tel. 418/827–4561) is the largest resort in eastern Canada, with 50 downhill trails, 11 lifts, and a gondola. **Stoneham** (1420 av. Hibou, Stoneham, Québec, G0A 4P0, tel. 418/848–2411) is known for its long, easy slopes with 25 downhill runs and 10 lifts. Two smaller alpine centers can be found at Lac Beauport: 14 trails at **Mont St-Castin** (82 chemin le Tour du Lac, Box 1129, Lac Beauport, Québec G0A 2C0, tel. 418/849–6776) and 24 trails at **Le Relais** (1084 boul. du Lac, Box 280, Lac Beauport, Québec G0A 2C0, tel. 418/849–1851). Upon request, most major hotels arrange skibus service for guests for a fee.

A municipal bus service, **Skibus** (tel. 418/627–2511), is offered on Saturday and Sunday. It leaves from Place Laurier (2700 boul. Laurier, Sainte-Foy) at 8 AM for Stoneham and Mont Sainte-Anne and returns once a day at 5:05. The cost each way is $3.50 for Stoneham and $4 for Mont Sainte-Anne.

Visite Touristique de Québec (tel. 418/653–9722) offers a bus service to Mont Sainte-Anne and Stoneham. For Mont Sainte-Anne, it leaves from major hotels in Québec and Sainte-Foy daily between 7:30 AM and 8:30 AM and returns at 4:30 PM. For Stoneham, it leaves from major hotels daily between 7:45 AM and 8:45 AM, and returns at 4:30 PM. It costs $8 each way. Telephone for reservations.

A brochure about ski centers in Québec is available at Québec Tourism and Convention Bureaus or by telephoning 800/363–7777.

Tennis At **Montcalm Tennis Club** (901 boul. Champlain, Sillery, tel. 418/687–1250), south of Québec City in Sillery, four indoor and seven outdoor courts are open daily from 8 AM to 10 PM. Twelve indoor courts are also available at **Tennisport** (6280 boul. Hammel, Ancienne Lorette, tel. 418/872–0111).

Spectator Sports

Tickets for sporting events can be purchased at **Colisée de Québec** (Québec Coliseum; 2205 av. du Colisée, tel. 418/523–3333 or 800/463–3333) or through Billetech, whose main outlet is at the **Grand Théâtre de Québec** (269 boul. St-Cyrille E, tel. 418/643–8131). Other outlets are situated at Bibliothèque Gabrielle-Roy, Palais Montcalm, La Baie department store (Place Laurier, Sainte-Foy, tel. 418/627–5959), and Provigo supermarkets. The outlet hours vary depending on the location.

Harness Racing Horse racing is on view at the racetrack **Hippodrome de Québec.** *C.P. 2053, Parc de l'Exposition, tel. 418/524–5283. Admission: $2.50 adults, $1.50 children under 10 and senior citizens.*

Hockey A National Hockey League team, the Québec Nordiques, plays at the **Colisée de Québec** (Québec Coliseum). *2205 av. du Colisée,*

Parc de l'Exposition, tel. 418/523–3333 or 800/463–3333. Open Oct.–Mar.

Dining

Québec City reveals its French heritage most obviously in its cuisine. You'll discover a French touch in the city's numerous cafés and brasseries and in the artful presentation of dishes at local restaurants. Most dining establishments usually have a selection of dishes à la carte, but you'll usually find more creative specialties by opting for the table d'hôte, a two- to four-course meal chosen daily by the chef. At dinner, many restaurants will offer a *menu de dégustation,* a five- to seven-course dinner of the chef's finest creations.

Although most visitors will find a gourmet meal in their price range, budget-conscious diners may want to try out the more expensive establishments during lunchtime. Lunch usually costs about 30% less than dinner, and many of the same dishes are available. Lunch is usually served 11:30 AM through 2:30 PM; dinner, 6:30 until about 11 PM. You should tip about 15% of the bill.

Québec City is the best place in the province to sample French Canadian cuisine, composed of robust, uncomplicated dishes that make use of the region's bounty of foods, including fowl and wild game (caribou, quail, venison), maple syrup, and various berries and nuts. Because Québec has a cold climate for a good portion of the year, it has a traditionally heavy cuisine, with such specialties as *cretons* (pâtés), *tourtière* (meat pie), and *tarte au sucre* (maple-syrup pie).

Highly recommended restaurants in each price category are indicated by a star ★.

Category	Cost*
Very Expensive	over $30
Expensive	$20–$30
Moderate	$10–$20
Inexpensive	under $10

*per person, excluding drinks, service, 7% federal sales tax, and 4% provincial sales tax

Very Expensive

★ **A la Table de Serge Bruyère.** This restaurant has put Québec on the map of great gastronomic cities. The city's most famous culinary institution serves classic French cuisine presented with plenty of crystal, silver, and fresh flowers and with relentless attention to detail. Only one sitting is offered each night. Chef Serge Bruyère came to Québec City from Lyons, France, and worked at various restaurants until he opened his own in 1980. The *menu gourmand* is a five-course meal for $47. The extensive wine list starts at $26 and goes up to $800. Wine is also available by the glass. Specialties include scampi in puff pastry with fresh tomatoes, scallop stew with watercress, and duckling supreme with blueberry sauce. In 1984, Bruyère expanded inside the restaurant's old 1843 Livernois building and created a minimall with a European-style tearoom, a contemporary piano bar, and a food store—all serving gourmet treats from his celebrated kitchen. If A la Table de Serge Bruyère is out of your price range, **A la Petite Table** in the food mall is less formal and less expensive, with such dishes as seafood terrine and pork with estragon sauce. *1200 rue St-Jean, tel. 418/694–0618. Reservations required. Jacket required. AE, MC, V. No lunch weekends.*

Café de la Paix. An evening spent at this local favorite takes you back to a dining experience in Paris circa 1930. The tables could not get closer nor the lights dimmer amid the art deco extravagance of lamps in Venetian glass, wood sculpted in geometric patterns, and stained-glass windows. The food is on a par with other fine restaurants in the city, but there are hints that the chefs are relying on their reputations (the restaurant dates back from 1952). The table d'hôte includes such tasty dishes as pheasant with peaches. Salmon comes with four sauces: raspberry vinegar, hollandaise, tarragon, or mustard. The meat entrées, including filet Mignon and leg of lamb, are also recommended. You choose your dessert from a cart; try the fresh fruit and the chocolate truffle cake. The service is prompt and attentive. Private dining rooms are available on the second floor. *44 rue des Jardins, tel. 418/692–1430. Reservations advised. Dress: neat but casual. AE, DC, MC, V. No lunch Sun. in winter.*

Le Marie Clarisse. Wood-beam ceilings, stone walls, sea-blue decor, and a lit fireplace make this dining spot one of the coziest in town. Housed in an ancient building on the bottom of the Breakneck Steps near Place Royale, Le Marie Clarisse is well known for its unique seafood dishes, such as halibut with nuts and honey and scallops with port and paprika. Occasionally, the menu includes a good game dish such as caribou with curry. The *menu du jour* has about seven entrées to choose from; dinner includes soup, salad, dessert, and coffee. Wines are served from the restaurant's cellar. *12 rue du Petit-Champlain, tel. 418/692–0857. Reservations required. Dress: neat but casual. AE, DC, MC, V. Closed lunch Sat. and all day Sun.*

★ **Le Saint-Amour.** This restaurant has all the makings of a true haute-cuisine establishment without having a pretentious atmosphere. A light and airy atrium, with a retractable roof used for outdoor dining in summer, creates a relaxed dining ambience. Chef Jean-Luc Boulay continues to educate himself by taking various courses in France; his studies pay off in the creation of such specialties as stuffed quails in port sauce and salmon with light chive mousse. Sauces here are light, with no flour or butter. The *menu de dégustation* has nine courses, and the *menu gastronomique* has seven courses. If you plan to order one of these two menus, it's a good idea to mention this when making your reservation. Wines can be ordered by the glass to complement courses. The chef's true expertise shines when it comes to his diverse dessert menu. Try the nougat ice cream with fresh figs or the three-chocolate cake. Better yet, order the Saint-Amour assortment of desserts. *48 rue Ste-Ursule, tel. 418/694–0667. Reservations advised. Dress: neat but casual. AE, DC, MC, V.*

Dining

Lodging

Québec City Dining and Lodging

Expensive

★ **Aux Anciens Canadiens.** This establishment is named after a book by Philippe-Aubert de Gaspé, who once resided here. The place is worth trying for the experience of tasting authentic French Canadian cooking. The house dates back to 1675 and has four dining rooms with different themes. The *vaisselier* (dish room) is bright and cheerful, with colorful antique dishes, a fireplace, and an antique stove. Another room displays guns from the French regime. The hearty specialties include duck in maple glaze and lamb with blueberry wine sauce. The restaurant also serves the best caribou drink in town. (Caribou is a local beverage made with sweet red wine and whiskey, and is known for its kick.) *34 rue St-Louis, tel. 418/692–1627. Reservations advised. Dress: casual. AE, MC, V.*

L'Astral. This circular restaurant on the 29th floor of the Hôtel Loews Le Concorde revolves high above Battlefields Park and the Old City. The food, while showing signs of improvement, is not the best in town, but the views are excellent. The modern and uninspired decor does not detract from the view, either; there's no room for anything besides the dining tables next to large windows and the vast buffet of salads, meat, and poultry dishes. Sunday brunch offers more than 45 items for $22.95 for adults; children under 12, $10. *1225 Place Montcalm, tel.418/647–2222. Reservations advised. Dress: neat but casual. AE, DC, MC, V.*

Le Graffiti. A good alternative to Old City dining, this restaurant, housed in a modern gourmet food mall, serves the cuisine of Provence. It's a romantic setting, with dark mahogany-paneled walls and large bay windows that look out onto the passersby along avenue Cartier. The distinctive menu typically includes a choice of chicken, beef, and seafood dishes such as scampi spiced with basil and red pepper, and chicken liver mousse with pistachios. The reasonably priced table d'hôte comes with soup, appetizer, entrée, dessert, and coffee. Desserts are made fresh each day. *1191 av. Cartier, tel. 418/529–4949. Reservations advised. Dress: neat but casual. AE, DC, MC, V.*

★ **Gambrinus.** This comfortable restaurant offers excellent Continental cuisine in two elegant, mahogany-paneled, plant-filled dining rooms with windows facing the street. The reliable menu features a range of meat, fish, and pasta entrées, with such specialties as pheasant supreme with fruit, seafood in puff pastry with saffron, and rack of lamb with basil. The table d'hôte is a good bet and provides generous portions and delectable desserts. Service here is unrushed and thoroughly professional. Gambrinus is conveniently located near rue du Trésor and the Château Frontenac. *15 rue du Fort, tel. 418/692–5144. Reservations advised. Dress: neat but casual. AE, DC, MC, V. No lunch weekends.*

★ **Le Paris Brest.** This busy restaurant on Grande Allée serves a gregarious crowd attracted to its tastefully presented French dishes. Its angular halogen lighting and soft yellow walls adds a fresh, modern touch to this historic building. Traditional fare such as *escargots au Pernod* (snails with Pernod) and steak tartare are offered with special touches such as a tomato carved in the shape of a rose. Popular dishes served here include lamb with herbs from Provence and beef Wellington. A la carte and main-course dishes are accompanied by a generous side platter of vegetables. Wine prices range from $22 to $250. *590 Grande Allée E, tel. 418/529–2243. Reservations advised. Dress: neat but casual. AE, DC, MC, V.*

Restaurant au Parmesan. This restaurant has a wide variety of Italian cuisine that's reasonably priced and served by a friendly staff. But if it's intimacy you're after, this is not the place to be. The atmosphere is boisterous and jovial, and tables are close together. Thousands of bottles with unusual shapes line the walls, and an accordion player will serenade you over typical dishes such as *gnocchi* (potato dumplings) with tomato sauce and tortellini with cream sauce. *38 rue St-Louis, tel. 418/692–0341. Reservations advised. Dress: casual. AE, DC, MC, V.*

Moderate

Chalet Suisse. This large chalet close to Place d'Armes serves Swiss cuisine. Fondues are a mainstay, and there are 25 different ones to choose from, with the Gruyère and the chocolate fondues being two of the tastiest house specialties. Another popular dish is *raclette*, a Swiss dish with melted cheese, served with bread and potatoes as well as diverse flavorings such as onions, pickles, and ham. The spacious chalet looms three stories high with clichéd murals of alpine scenes. In the summer, there are umbrella-shaded café tables outside. *32 rue Ste-Anne, tel. 418/694–1320. Reservations accepted. Dress: informal. AE, DC, MC, V.*

L'Apsara. Near St-Louis Gate, this restaurant serves innovative dishes from Vietnam, Thailand, and Cambodia. The Cambodian family that owns the restaurant excels at using both subtle and tangy spices to create unique flavors that are ideal for those seeking a reprieve from French fare. The decor combines Western and Eastern motifs, with flowered wallpaper, Oriental art, and small fountains. Good starters are *fleur de pailin* (a rice paste roll filled with fresh vegetables, meat, and shrimp) or *mou sati* (pork kebabs with peanut sauce and coconut milk). The assorted miniature Cambodian pastries are delicious with tea served from a little elephant container. *71 rue d'Auteuil, tel. 418/694–0232. Reservations accepted. Dress: casual. AE, MC, V.*

Le Café de la Terrasse. This restaurant, housed in the landmark Château Frontenac, does not share the hotel's opulence, but it does offer a view along Terrasse Dufferin and the St. Lawrence River. You can try the businessman's breakfast buffet of fruits, omelets, and croissants and an à la carte lunch menu of salads and sandwiches. Standard but dependable Continental dishes are served during the lunch and dinner buffets. *Château Frontenac, 1 rue Carrières, tel. 418/692–3861. Reservations accepted. Dress: neat but casual. AE, DC, MC, V.*

★ **L'Echaudée** (Whitewash). This chic black-and-white bistro attracts a mix of business and tourist clientele because of its location between the financial and antiques districts in Lower Town. The modern decor features a stark dining area with a mirrored wall and a stainless-steel bar where you dine atop high stools. Lunch offerings include *cuisse de canard confit* (duck confit) with french fries and fresh seafood salad. The three-course brunch for Sunday antiques shoppers includes giant croissants and a tantalizing array of desserts. *73 Sault-au-Matelot, tel. 418/692–1299. Weekend reservations advised.*

Dress: casual. AE, DC, MC, V. Closed Sun. and Mon. nights Sept.–May.

Inexpensive

Casse-Crêpe Breton. Crêpes in generous proportions are served in this small, square, diner-style restaurant on rue St-Jean. From a menu of 15 ingredients, pick your own chocolate or fruit combinations, or design a larger meal with cheese, ham, and vegetables. The tables surround three round hot plates at which you watch your creations being made. Crêpes made with two to five ingredients cost under $5. *1136 rue St-Jean. tel. 418/692–0438. No reservations. Dress: casual. No credit cards. Open 7:30 AM–midnight.*

★ **Chez Temporel.** Tucked behind rue St-Jean and côte de la Fabrique, this homey café is an experience *très français.* The aroma of fresh coffee fills the air. The rustic decor incorporates wooden tables, chairs, and benches, while a tiny staircase winds to an upper level. Croissants are made in-house; the staff will fill them with Gruyère and ham or anything else you want. Try the equally delicious croque-monsieur and quiche Lorraine. *25 rue Couillard, tel. 418/694–1813. No reservations. Dress: casual. No credit cards. Open 7 AM–1 AM.*

Le Cochon Dingue. Across the street from the ferry in Lower Town is this cheerful café (whose name translsates to "The Crazy Pig"), with sidewalk tables and indoor dining rooms, which artfully blend the chic and the antique. Black-and-white checkerboard floors contrast with ancient stone walls that are typical of the oldest sections of town. Café fare includes dependably tasty homemade quiches, thick soups, and such desserts as fresh raspberry tarte and maple-sugar pie. *46 boul. Champlain, tel. 418/692–2013. Reservations accepted. Dress: informal. AE, MC, V. Open weekdays 7 AM–11 PM, weekends 7 AM–midnight.*

Mille Feuille. In the heart of the Latin Quarter is this vegetarian restaurant situated in a well-preserved, historic building that dates to 1782. The daily menu offers three or four creative dishes, such as cabbage leaves stuffed with brown rice and vegetables, topped with rich tomato sauce and fresh Parmesan cheese, and Greek-style pizza with black olives. All dishes are served with soup and salad. On Saturday and Sunday a "health brunch" is served from 9 AM to 3 PM, and costs about $6. *32 rue Sainte-Angèle, tel. 418/692–2147. Reservations accepted. Dress: informal. MC, V.*

Pizzeria d'Youville. This restaurant located in the lively Latin Quarter has a pizza for everyone, with more than 25 combinations. Tasty pies are cooked in a wood oven and then heated by fire at your table. You can go beyond tomato sauce and cheese here and try the Hawaiian pizza, with ham, cheese, and pineapple, or L'Amalfitana, which combines tomato sauce, cheese, shrimp, and garlic. Meat dishes, pasta, and salads are also on offer. *1014 rue St-Jean, tel. 418/694–0299. Reservations accepted. Dress: informal. AE, DC, MC, V.*

Lodging

With more than 35 hotels within its walls, Québec City has a range of lodging options. Landmark hotels stand as prominent as the city's most historic sites; modern high rises outside the ramparts offer spectacular views of the Old City. Also, visitors can immerse themselves in the city's historic charm by staying in one of the many old-fashioned inns where no two rooms are alike.

Whichever kind of accommodations you choose, during peak season, from May through September, be sure to make a reservation. If you are planning to visit during the summer or at the time of the Winter Carnival in February, you may have trouble finding a room without one. During busy times, hotel rates are usually 30% above prices at other times of the year. From November through April, many of the city's lodging places offer discount weekend packages and other promotions.

Highly recommended properties in each price category are indicated by a star ★.

Category	Cost*
Very Expensive	over $140
Expensive	$85–$140
Moderate	$50–$85
Inexpensive	under $50

All prices are for a standard double room, excluding 7% federal sales tax, 4% provincial sales tax, and an optional service charge.

Very Expensive

Château Bonne Entente. If you have a car, you may want to stay at this sprawling resort located 10 minutes from the airport and 20 minutes from the walled city. The hotel is more commonly called "The Other Château," the country cousin of the urban Frontenac. It was a private mansion until 1940, when it became a hotel; a $7 million renovation several years ago has helped this establishment to become a popular spot for the well-heeled. In the newer section, rooms are decorated in contemporary style with fine wood, plush carpeting, and all the modern amenities. The other rooms are furnished with antiques, and a rustic atmosphere prevails. The property encompasses 11 acres of land with a main complex as well as separate cottage rooms in back. *3400 chemin Ste-Foy, Sainte-Foy G1X 1S6, tel. 418/653–5221 or 800/463–4390. 168 rooms. Facilities: bar, 2 restaurants, outdoor pool, tennis court, trout fishing in back pond, full day care. AE, DC, MC, V.*

★ **Château Frontenac.** Towering above the St. Lawrence River, the Château Frontenac is indisputably Québec City's most renowned landmark. Although the Frontenac can no longer claim to be the city's top-rated hotel, the mystique of staying at "the château" endures. Its public rooms, from the intimate piano bar to its 700-seat ballroom, which is reminiscent of the Versailles Hall of Mirrors, have all the opulence of years gone by, and almost all the guest rooms offer excellent views. You must make a reservation in advance, as the average booking rate is 80% a year. A five-year, $60 million renovation was completed in 1993, in time for the hotel's 100th birthday. A new wing of rooms was added, as was a long-awaited health spa. The Frontenac has one of the finer restaurants in town, Le Champlain, where classic French cuisine is served by waiters dressed in traditional French costumes. The ground floor has several luxury shops and a restaurant, Le Café de la Terrasse (*see* Dining, *above*). *1 rue des Carrières, G1R 4P5, tel. 418/692–3861 or 800/268–9420. 610 rooms. Facilities: 3 restaurants, 2 bars, health spa, indoor pool. AE, DC, MC, V.*

★ **Hilton International Québec.** Just outside St-Jean Gate, the Hilton rises from the shadow of Parliament Hill as the city's finest luxury hotel. It has such spacious facilities and efficient services that it could easily cater exclusively to the convention crowd. Instead, it has adapted its renowned comfort and dependable service to tourists. The sprawling atrium lobby is flanked with a bar and an open-air restaurant, and it offers the added convenience of being connected with the mall, Place Québec, which offers 65 shops and boutiques. Ultramodern rooms with pine furniture feature tall windows so that rooms on upper floors give fine views of the Old City. *3 Place Québec, G1K 7M9, tel. 418/647–2411 or 800/445–8667. 565 rooms, 36 suites. Facilities: outdoor pool, health club, sauna, whirlpool, 2 restaurants, piano bar. AE, DC, MC, V.*

Hôtel Radisson Gouverneurs Québec. Opposite the Parliament Buildings, this large, full-service establishment is part of a Québec chain with 12 hotels in the province. Formerly called Auberge des Gouverneurs when it opened in 1975, the hotel has upgraded its light and spacious rooms by furnishing them with luminous pastel decor, wood furniture, and marble bathrooms. VIP floors were designed to lure the business traveler, but there is also plenty of room for tourists. Although it is part of a tall office complex, the hotel occupies only the first six floors, so views of the Old City are limited. The hotel boasts a year-round outdoor swimming pool, perfect for use even when the weather is frigid. *690 boul. Réné Levesque E, G1R 5A8, tel. 418/647–1717 or 800/333–3333. 377 rooms with private bath. Facilities: health club, heated outdoor pool, sauna, whirlpool, piano bar, restaurant. AE, DC, MC, V.*

★ **Hôtel Loews Le Concorde.** When Le Concorde was built in 1974, the shockingly tall concrete structure went up with controversy because it was taking the place of 19th-century Victorian homes. Yet of all the modern hotels outside the city gates, tourists will probably find that Le Concorde occupies one of the most convenient locations for city touring and nightlife. Inside the hotel there's almost as much going on as at the cafés and restaurants along the nearby Grande Allée; Le Concorde offers the revolving restaurant L'Astral, a sidewalk café, a bar, and a disco. Rooms have good views of Battlefields Park, and nearly all have been redone in modern decor combined with traditional furnishings. Amenities for business travelers have expanded; one of the new VIP floors is reserved for female executives. *1225 Place Montcalm, G1R 4W6, tel. 418/647–2222 or 800/463–5256; in the U.S., tel. 800/223–0888. 424 rooms. Facilities: heated outdoor pool, sauna, whirlpool, health club, bar,* *disco, 2 restaurants (L'Astral on the 28th floor and a sidewalk café). AE, DC, MC, V.*

Expensive

Le Château de Pierre. Built in 1853 and converted from a private residence in 1960, this tidy Victorian manor on a picturesque street has kept its English origins alive. The high-ceilinged halls have ornate chandeliers. The rooms are imaginatively decorated with floral themes, and each usually has some special added feature—a balcony, fireplace, or vanity room—to lend some extra charm. Rooms in the front face imposing old stone buildings across the way that date from the English regime. *17 av. Ste-Geneviève, G1R 4A8, tel. 418/694–0429. 15 rooms with private bath and air-conditioning. MC, V.*

L'Hôtel du Théâtre. There's much history that accompanies this hotel, located in the Capitole Building just outside the St-Jean Gate. In 1903 this property opened as an avant-garde theater, then in the 1920s—the era of silent films—it became a movie house, and some 12 years ago the doors closed in ruin. However, in 1992 the hotel came back to life, following a $15 million restoration, which transformed this historic building into an exclusive 40-room lodging, Italian bistro, and an elaborate 1920s cabaret-style dinner theater (*see* Arts and Nightlife, *below*). A glitzy show-biz theme is prevalent throughout the hotel, with stars on carpets, doors, and keys. Rooms are small and simple, highlighted with a few rich details. Ceilings are painted within sculpted moldings with a blue-and-white sky motif; beds are adorned with white down-filled comforters, and plush terry-cloth bathrobes await guests in every room. *972 rue St-Jean, G1R 1R5, tel. 418/694–4040. 40 rooms. Facilities: restaurant, theater. AE, MC, V.*

L'Hôtel du Vieux Québec. Located in the heart of the Latin Quarter on rue St-Jean, this hotel has a brick exterior that gets lost amid the more striking historic structures around it. The establishment was once an apartment building and has the long-term visitor in mind. The interior design is simple, featuring sparsely decorated but comfortable rooms decorated in pastel colors. The hotel recently added five fresh, new rooms on the main floor, overlooking Québec's busy main street. Many rooms have a full kitchenette with a stove, cabinets, a sink, and a refrigerator; all have cable TV. Dishes and cooking utensils can be rented for $10. *1190 rue St-Jean, G1R 1S6, tel. 418/692–1850. 39 units with private bath. AE, MC, V.*

★ **Manoir d'Auteuil.** Originally a private home, this lodging is one of the more lavish manors in town, artfully revamped at great expense. An ornate sculpted iron banister wraps around four floors; guest rooms feature detailed trimmings in mahogany and marble and blend modern design with the art deco structure. Each room differs in shape and design; one room was formerly the residence's chapel, while another has become a duplex with a luxurious marble bathroom on the second floor. Some rooms look out onto the wall between the St-Louis and St-Jean gates. Unrenovated rooms are cheaper. At press time, Manoir d'Auteuil had just changed ownership; the new owners are hoping to finish the renovations. *49 rue d'Auteuil, G1R 4C2, tel. 418/694–1173. 16 rooms with private bath. AE, MC, V.*

Manoir Sainte-Geneviève. This quaint and elaborately decorated hotel dating from 1880 stands near the Château Frontenac, on the southwest corner of the Jardin des Governeurs. A plush Victorian ambience is created with fanciful wallpaper and rooms decorated with precious stately English manor furnishings, such as marble lamps, large wooden bedposts, and velvet upholstery; you'll feel as if you are staying in a secluded country inn. A hidden porch facing the Citadel is perfect for relaxing and soaking in the atmosphere of Upper Town. Service here is personal and genteel. One suite on the ground floor has a private entrance. *13 av. Ste-Geneviève, G1R 4A7, tel. 418/694–1666. 11 rooms with private bath; 7 rooms have air-conditioning, color TV. No credit cards.*

Moderate

Château de la Terrasse. Although this four-story inn may not have the same charm as others in the city, it does have something that the others are lacking: This is the sole inn within the area that has a view of the St. Lawrence River. However, only half of the rooms face the river; others in the rear look out onto the backs of buildings. While the interior hints at having once possessed a refined and elegant decor, by its high ceilings and stained glass lining the large bay windows, the furnishings these days are plain and unremarkable. *6 Place Terrasse Dufferin, G1R 4N5, tel. 418/694–9472. 18 rooms with private bath. V.*

Hôtel Château Laurier. This medium-size hotel closely resembles a dormitory, which may explain why it attracts a youthful clientele. In addition to its unelaborate decor, the hotel is located at one of the liveliest intersections in town, and its front doors open up to the nightlife on Grande Allée. In the lobby, couches are clustered around a central television. Guest rooms are spacious, but some of the no-frills furnishings appear worn. Rooms either look onto Parliament Hill or face Grande Allée, the latter being the noisiest at night. *695 Grande Allée E, G1R 2K4, tel. 418/522–8108. 55 rooms with private bath. Free parking. AE, DC, MC, V.*

★ **L'Auberge du Quartier.** This small, amiable inn, situated in a house dating from 1852, will please those seeking moderately priced lodging with a personal touch. Proprietors Lise Provost and Pierre Couture are highly attentive to their guests' needs. The cheerful rooms, without phones or televisions, are modestly furnished but well maintained; two of them have fireplaces. Rooms 5 and 8 are recommended for couples. A suite of rooms on the third floor can accommodate a family at a reasonable cost. This is one of the few inns in the area that offers a tasty Continental breakfast of warm croissants, homemade banana bread and preserves, strong coffee, and fresh fruits. A 20-minute walk west from the Old City, L'Auberge du Quartier is convenient to avenue Cartier and Grande Allée nightlife; joggers can use Battlefields Park across the street. *170 Grande Allée O, G1R 2G9, tel. 418/525–9726. 13 rooms, 11 with private bath. Free parking. AE, MC, V.*

L'Auberge Saint-Louis. This hotel is perfect for the traveler with convenience in mind; its central location on the main street of the city can't be beat. The inn features small rooms, tall staircases, and a lobby resembling a European pension. Guest rooms contain comfortable but bare-bones furniture. The ultrabudget room on the fourth floor is just big enough for a bed. The service here is friendly and hospitable. Most guest rooms share floor bathrooms or have a semibathroom. *48 rue St-*

Louis, G1R 3Z3, tel. 418/692–2424. 22 rooms, 8 with private bath. MC, V.

Inexpensive

★ **Hôtel Maison Sainte-Ursule.** Situated on a tiny street west of the Ursuline Convent, this well-kept hotel is a boon for the sophisticated yet economical traveler, offering both historic charm and reasonable prices. The building, constructed in 1780, is typical of the architecture of New France, with dormer windows, small doors, and a slanting roof. Immaculate accommodations contain the old-fashioned basics, with sturdy and simple wood furniture; some rooms even have the original pint-size doors. Seven rooms are located in an annex in a private rear courtyard that becomes a garden in the summer. The amiable staff is eager to see that guests are comfortable. *40 rue Ste-Ursule, G1R 4E2, tel. 418/694–9794. 15 rooms, 12 with private bath. MC, V.*

Manoir des Remparts. There's nothing fancy about this hotel, which is on a residential street bordering the north side of Québec City's natural cliff. But this manor offers just enough to attract the budget-conscious traveler: spacious and clean rooms with back-to-basics old-time furnishings. The halls are well lighted and considered large for a residence in the Old City. Guest rooms have private bath or share a bath on the floor but don't have telephones or televisions. *3¹/2 rue des Remparts, G1R 3R4, tel. 418/692–2056. AE, MC, V.*

Bed-and-Breakfasts

Québec City has a large number of bed-and-breakfast and hostel accommodations. To guarantee a room during peak season, be sure to reserve in advance. **Québec City Tourist Information** (60 rue d'Auteuil, G1R 4C4, tel. 418/692–2471) has B&B listings. **Bed and Breakfast–Bonjour Québec** (3765 boul. Monaco, G1P 3J3, tel. 418/527–1465) has several B&Bs to choose from. Reserve in advance in the summer. Prices range from $35 for a single room to $60 for a double. Apartments are available for $85–$95.

The Arts and Nightlife

For a place its size, Québec City boasts a wide variety of cultural events, from the reputable Québec Symphony Orchestra to several small theater companies. The arts scene changes significantly depending on the season. From September to May, a steady repertoire of concerts, plays, and performances is presented in theaters and halls around town. In summer, indoor theaters close to make room for several outdoor stages.

For arts and entertainment listings in English, consult the *Québec Chronicle-Telegraph,* published on Wednesday. Each day in the French-language daily newspaper, *Le Soleil,* listings appear on a page called "Où Aller à Québec" ("Where to Go in Québec"). *Voilà Québec* and *Hospitalité Québec* are bilingual quarterly entertainment guides distributed free in tourist information areas.

Tickets for most shows can be purchased through **Billetech,** whose main outlet is the Grand Théâtre de Québec (269 boul.

St-Cyrille E, tel. 418/643–8131). Other outlets are located at Bibliothèque Gabrielle-Roy, Colisée, Implanthéâtre, Palais Montcalm, Salle Albert-Rousseau, La Baie department store (Place Laurier, tel. 418/627–5959), and Provigo supermarkets. Outlet hours vary, depending on the location.

The Arts

Dance **Grand Théâtre de Québec** (269 boul. St-Cyrille E, tel. 418/643–8131) presents a dance series with both Canadian and international companies. Dancers also appear at Bibliothèque Gabrielle-Roy, Salle Albert-Rousseau, and the Palais Montcalm (*see* Theater, *below,* for more information).

Film Most theaters present French films and American films dubbed into French. Two popular theaters are **Cinéma de Paris** (966 rue St-Jean, tel. 418/694–0891) and **Cinéma Place Charest** (500 rue du Pont, tel. 418/529–9745). **Cinémas Sainte-Foy** (Place Sainte-Foy, Sainte-Foy, tel. 418/656–0592) almost always features films in English.

Music **L'Orchestre Symphonique de Québec** (Québec Symphony Orchestra) is Canada's oldest. It performs at Louis-Frechette Hall in the **Grand Théâtre de Québec** (269 boul. St-Cyrille E, tel. 418/643–8131).

Bibliothèque Gabrielle-Roy (350 rue St-Joseph E, tel. 418/529–0924). Classical concerts are offered at the Auditorium Joseph Lavergne. Tickets must be purchased in advance at the library.

Colisée de Québec (2205 av. du Colisée, Parc de l'Exposition, tel. 418/691–7211). Popular music concerts are often booked here.

Theater All theater productions are in French. The following theaters schedule shows from September through April:

Grand Théâtre de Québec (269 boul. St-Cyrille E, tel. 418/643–8131). Classic and contemporary plays are staged by the leading local theater company, le Théâtre du Trident (tel. 418/643–5873).

Palais Montcalm (995 Place d'Youville, tel. 418/670–9011). This municipal theater outside St-Jean Gate features a broad range of productions.

Salle Albert-Rousseau (2410 chemin Ste-Foy, Sainte-Foy, tel. 418/659–6710). A diverse repertoire, from classical to comedy, is offered here.

Théâtre Capitole (972 rue St-Jean, tel. 418/694–4444). This recently restored turn-of-the-century cabaret-style theater offers a diverse repertoire of classical and pop music, plays, and comedy shows.

Théâtre de la Bordée (1143 rue St-Jean, tel. 418/694–9631). This local company presents small-scale productions.

Théâtre Périscope (2 rue Crémazie E, tel. 418/529–2183). This multipurpose, experimental theater offers about 200 presentations a year, including performances for children.

Summer Theater **Agora** (120 rue Dalhousie; for tickets and information, contact Billetech, tel. 418/643–8131). The largest open-air amphitheater in the Old Port, between the river and the customs building, features variety shows, plays, and classical and contemporary music concerts.

Place d'Youville (tel. 418/670–9011). During the summer, open-air concerts are presented here, just outside St-Jean Gate. Recent renovations have made this spot quite enjoyable.

Théâtre du Bois du Coulonge (office: 81 rue St-Pierre, tel. 418/692–3064). One of the most delightful theater settings in town is situated in Battlefields Park (1215 chemin St-Louis, Sillery), near the Québec Museum.

Nightlife

Nightlife in Québec City is centered on the clubs and cafés of rue St-Jean, avenue Cartier, and Grande Allée. In the winter, evening activity is livelier toward the end of the week, beginning on Wednesday. But as the warmer temperatures set in, the café-terrace crowd emerges, and bars stay open seven days a week. Most bars and clubs stay open until 3 AM.

Bars and Lounges **Le Central** (1200 rue St-Jean, tel. 418/694–0618). At this stylish piano bar at Serge Bruyère's restaurant complex, you can order from the restaurant's sophisticated haute-cuisine menu.
Le Pub Saint-Alexandre (1087 rue St-Jean, tel. 418/694–0015). This popular English-style pub, formerly a men-only tavern, is a good place to look for your favorite brand of beer. There are approximately 135 different kinds.
Vogue and **Sherlock Holmes** (1170 d'Artigny, tel. 418/529–9973). You'll find mainly Yuppies at these two bars stacked one on top of the other. Sherlock Holmes is a pub-restaurant downstairs; for dancing, try Vogue upstairs.

Disco **Chez Dagobert** (600 Grande Allée E, tel. 418/522–0393). You'll find a little bit of everything—live rock bands to loud disco—at this large and popular club.
Le Dancing (1225 Place Montcalm, tel. 414/647–2222). Music videos and a loud stereo blare from this night spot on the lower level of the Hôtel Loews Le Concorde.
Merlin (1179 av. Cartier, tel. 418/529–9567). This one-room disco is packed nightly. It's a favorite Québecois hangout.

Folk, Jazz, and **Chez Son Père** (24 St-Stanislas, tel. 418/692–5308). French Ca-
Blues nadian folk songs fill this smoke-filled pub on the second floor of an old building in the Latin Quarter. Singers perform every Wednesday through Friday night.
Le d'Auteuil (35 rue d'Auteuil, tel. 418/692–2263). Rhythm and blues, jazz, and blues emanate from this converted church across from Kent Gate.
L'Emprise at Hôtel Clarendon (57 rue Ste-Anne, tel. 418/692–2480). The first jazz bar in Québec City is the preferred spot for enthusiasts. The art deco decor sets the mood for the Jazz Age rhythms.

Excursion 1: Côte de Beaupré

As legend tells it, when explorer Jacques Cartier first gained sight of the north shore of the St. Lawrence River in 1535, he exclaimed, *"Quel beau pré!"* ("What a lovely meadow!"), because the area was the first inviting piece of land he had spotted since leaving France. Today this fertile meadow, first settled by French farmers, is known as Côte de Beaupré (Beaupré Coast), stretching 40 kilometers (25 miles) from Québec City to the famous pilgrimage site of Sainte-Anne-de-Beaupré. The impressive Montmorency Falls are located midway between these two points.

Tourist Information

Beaupré Coast Interpretation Center, housed in the old mill Petit-Pré, built in 1695, features displays on the history and development of the region. *7007 av. Royale, Château-Richer, tel. 418/824–3677. Admission: $1. Open June–Labor Day, daily 9–noon and 1–5.*

Beau Temps, Mauvais Temps, offers guided bus tours and walking tours of the Côte de Beaupré. *991 rte. Prévost, Île d'Orléans, tel. 418/828–2275.*

The offices of the **Québec City Region Tourism and Convention Bureau** (418/692–2471) can provide information on tours of the Côte de Beaupré (*see* Staying in Québec City, *above*).

Guided Tours

Québec City touring companies, such as **Gray Line** (tel. 418/622–7420) and **Maple Leaf Sightseeing Tours** (tel. 418/649–9226), offer day excursions along the Côte de Beaupré, with stops at Montmorency Falls and the Sainte-Anne-de-Beaupré Basilica.

Arriving and Departing

By Car To reach Montmorency Falls, take Route 440 (Dufferin-Montmorency Autoroute) northeast from Québec City. Approximately 9.6 kilometers (6 miles) east of the city is the exit for Montmorency Falls. To drive directly to Sainte-Anne-de-Beaupré, continue northeast on Route 440 for approximately 29 kilometers (18 miles) and exit at Sainte-Anne-de-Beaupré.

An alternative way to reach Sainte-Anne-de-Beaupré is to take Route 360 or avenue Royale. Take Route 440 from Québec City, turn left at d'Estimauville, and right on boulevard des Chutes until it intersects with Route 360. Also called "le chemin du Roi" (the King's Road), this panoramic route is one of the oldest in North America, winding 30 kilometers (18.8 miles) along the steep ridge of the Côte de Beaupré. The road borders 17th- and 18th-century farmhouses, historic churches, and Normandy-style homes with half-buried root cellars. Route 360 goes past the Sainte-Anne-de-Beaupré Basilica.

Montmorency Falls

Begin this excursion with a visit to **Montmorency Falls.** The Montmorency River, named after Charles de Montmorency, who was a governor of New France, cascades over a coastal cliff and offers one of the most beautiful sights in the province. The falls, which are actually 50% higher than the wider Niagara Falls, measure 83 meters (274 feet) in height. During very cold weather conditions, the falls' heavy spray freezes and forms a giant loaf-shape ice cone known to Québecois as the Pain du Sucre (Sugarloaf); this phenomenon attracts sledders and sliders from Québec City. In the warmer months, a park in the river's gorge leads to an observation terrace that is continuously sprayed by a fine drizzle from water pounding onto the cliff rocks. The top of the falls can be observed from avenue Royale. *Admission free. Open daily.*

Time Out **Restaurant Baker** (8790 av. Royale, Château-Richer, tel. 418/824–4478), on the way to Sainte-Anne-de Beaupré on Route 360, is a good, old-fashioned rustic restaurant that serves such hearty traditional French Canadian dishes as meat pie, pea soup, pâtés, and maple-sugar pie.

Basilique Sainte-Anne-de-Beaupré

The monumental and inspiring **Basilique Sainte-Anne-de-Beaupré** (Sainte-Anne-de-Beaupré Basilica) is located in a small town with the same name. The basilica has become a popular attraction as well as an important shrine: More than half a million people visit the site each year.

The French brought their devotion to Saint Anne with them when they sailed across the Atlantic to New France. In 1650, Breton sailors caught in a storm vowed to erect a chapel in honor of this patron saint at the exact spot where they would land. The present-day neo-Roman basilica constructed in 1923 was the fifth to be built on the site where the sailors first touched ground.

According to local legend, Saint Anne was responsible over the years for saving voyagers from shipwrecks in the harsh waters of the St. Lawrence. Tributes to her miraculous powers can be seen in the shrine's various mosaics, murals, altars, and church ceilings. A bas-relief at the entrance depicts Saint Anne welcoming her pilgrims, and ceiling mosaics represent details from her life. Numerous crutches and braces posted on the back pillars have been left by those who have felt the healing powers of Saint Anne.

The basilica, which is in the shape of a Latin cross, has two granite steeples jutting from its gigantic structure. Its interior has 22 chapels and 18 altars, as well as round arches and numerous ornaments in the Romanesque style. The 214 stained-glass windows by Frenchmen Auguste Labouret and Pierre Chaudière, finished in 1949, tell a story of salvation through personages who were believed to be instruments of God over the centuries. Other features of the shrine include intricately carved wood pews decorated with various animals and several smaller altars (behind the main altar) that are dedicated to different saints.

The original wood chapel built in the village of Sainte-Anne-de-Beaupré in the 17th century was situated too close to the St. Lawrence and was swept away by flooding of the river. In 1676, the chapel was replaced by a stone church that was visited by pilgrims for more than a century, but this structure was also demolished in 1872. The first basilica, which replaced the stone church, was destroyed by a fire in 1922. The following year architects Maxime Rosin from Paris and Louis-N. Audet from Québec province designed the basilica that now stands. *10,018 av. Royale, Sainte-Anne-de-Beaupré, tel. 418/827–3781. Admission free. Open year-round. Reception booth open mid-May–mid-July, 8:30–5:30; mid-July–late July, 8:30–7; Aug.–mid-Oct., 8:30–5:30. Tours daily in summer at 1 PM start at the information booth at the southwest corner of the courtyard outside the basilica. Guided tours during the off-season (mid-Oct.–mid-May) can be arranged by phoning in advance.*

Across the street from the basilica on avenue Royale is the **Commemorative Chapel,** designed by Claude Bailiff and built in 1878. The memorial chapel was constructed on the location of the transept of a stone church built in 1676 and contains the old building's foundations. Among the remnants housed here are the old church's bell, dating from 1696; an early 18th-century altar designed by Vezina; a crucifix sculpted by François-Noël Levaseur in 1775; and a pulpit designed by François Baillargé in 1807.

Excursion 2: Ile d'Orléans

Île d'Orléans, an island slightly downstream in a northeasterly direction from Québec City, exemplifies the historic charm of rural Québec province with its quiet, traditional life-style. A drive around the island will take you past stone churches that are among the oldest in the region and centuries-old houses amid acres of lush orchards and cultivated farmland. Horse-drawn carriages are still a means of transport. Île d'Orléans is also an important marketplace that provides fresh produce daily for Québec City; roadside stands on the island sell a variety of local products, such as crocheted blankets, woven articles, maple syrup, homemade bread and jams, and fruits and vegetables.

The island was discovered at about the same time as Québec City in 1535. Explorer Jacques Cartier noticed an abundance of vines on the island and called it the "Island of Bacchus," after the Greek god of wine. In 1536, Cartier renamed the island in honor of the duke of Orléans, son of the king of France, François I. Long considered part of the domain of Côte de Beaupré, the island was not given its seignorial autonomy until 1636, when it was bought by La Compagne des Cents Associés, a group formed by Louis XIII to promote settlement in New France.

The island, about 9 kilometers (5 miles) wide and 34 kilometers (21 miles) long, is now composed of six small villages. These villages have sought over the years to remain relatively private residential and agricultural communities; the island's bridge to the mainland was built only in 1935.

Important Addresses and Numbers

Tourist Information
Beau Temps, Mauvais Temps has a tourist office located in Saint-Pierre (991 rte. Prévost, tel. 418/828–2275). *Open Feb.–May, weekdays 8:30–4; June–Sept., daily 8:30 AM–8 PM; Oct.–Jan., will respond to messages left on answering machine.*

The island's Chamber of Commerce operates a tourist information kiosk situated at the west corner of côte du Pont and chemin Royal. *490 côte du Pont, Saint-Pierre, tel. 418/828–9411. Open mid-May–Oct., daily 8:30–6; Nov.–mid-May, Mon.–Fri. 8:30–12:30 and 1:30–4:30.*

Medical Clinic
Centre Médical (1015 rte. Prévost, Saint-Pierre, tel. 418/828–2213) is the only medical clinic on the island.

Guided Tours

Beau Temps, Mauvais Temps (991 rte. Prévost, Saint-Pierre, Île d'Orléans, tel. 418/828–2275) offers guided tours of three villages: Sainte-Pétronille, Saint-Pierre and Saint-Francois. River excursions that depart from Saint-Laurent are also available from mid-May–mid-September. The company is also a referral service for lodging.

Beau Temps, Mauvais Temps also sells dinner-theater packages, which include a meal at one of the island's restaurants, followed by a play at one of three theaters on Île d'Orléans and the Côte de Beaupré. *mid-May–Labor Day. Cost: Wed. and Thurs. $40–$55, Fri.–Sun. $42–$57.*

The Québec City touring companies, including **Maple Leaf Sightseeing Tours** (tel. 418/649–9226), **Gray Line** (tel. 418/622–7420), and **Visite Touristiques de Québec** (tel. 418/653–9722) offer full- and half-day bus tours of the western tip of the island, combined with sightseeing along the Côte de Beaupré.

Any of the offices of the **Québec City Region Tourism and Convention Bureau** can also provide information on tours and accommodations on the island (*see* Staying in Québec City, *above*).

Arriving and Departing

By Car Île d'Orléans has no public transportation; cars are the only way to get to and around the island, unless you take a guided tour (*see* Guided Tours, *above*). Parking on the island is never a problem; you can always stop and explore the villages on foot. The main road, chemin Royal (Route 368), extends 67 kilometers (40 miles) through the island's six villages; street numbers along chemin Royal begin at No. 1 for each municipality.

From Québec City, take Route 440 (Dufferin-Montmorency Autoroute) northeast. After a drive of approximately 10 kilometers (7 miles) take the bridge, Pont de l'Île d'Orléans, to reach the island. Before you get to the island's only traffic light, turn right heading west on chemin Royal to begin the exploring tour, *below.*

Exploring Île d'Orléans

Numbers in the margin correspond to points of interest on the Île d'Orléans map.

Start your tour heading west on chemin Royal to **Sainte-Pétronille,** the first village to be settled on the island. Founded in 1648, the community was chosen in 1759 by British General James Wolfe for his headquarters. With 40,000 soldiers and a hundred ships, the English bombarded French-occupied Québec City and Côte de Beaupré.

During the late-19th century, the English population of Québec developed Sainte-Pétronille into a resort village. This section is considered by many to be the island's most beautiful area, not only because of the spectacular views it offers of Montmorency Falls and Québec City but also for the stylish English villas and exquisitely tended gardens that can be seen from the roadside.

On the left at 20 chemin Royal is the **Plante family farm,** where you can stop to pick apples (in season) or buy some of the island's fresh fruits and vegetables.

① Farther along on the right is the **Maison Gourdeau de Beaulieu House** (137 chemin Royal), the island's first home, built in 1648 for Jacques Gourdeau de Beaulieu, who was the first seigneur of Sainte-Pétronille. Today this white building with blue shutters is still owned by his descendants. Over the years, the house has been remodeled and it now incorporates both French and Québecois styles. Its thick walls and dormer windows are characteristic of Breton architecture, but its sloping bell-shape roof, designed to protect buildings from large amounts of snow, is typically Québecois.

After you descend an incline, turn right beside the river on the **②** tiny street called **rue Horatio-Walker,** named after the 19th-century painter known for his landscapes of the island. Walker lived on this street from 1904 until his death in 1938. Around the corner are his home and studio, where exhibits of his paintings are held during the summer. *Open only upon reservation with Beau Temps, Mauvais Temps (tel. 418/828–2275).*

Rue Horatio-Walker was also the place where people crossed the St. Lawrence by an ice path in the winter to go from the island to the mainland before the bridge was built in 1935.

Farther along chemin Royal, at the border of Sainte-Pétronille and Saint-Laurent, look for a large boulder situated in the middle of nowhere. The **roche à Maranda,** named after the owner of the property where the rock was discovered in the 19th century, is one of the oldest rock formations in the world. When the glaciers melted in 9000 BC, the land at the foot of the Laurentian mountains (today the Côte de Beaupré) was flooded and formed the Sea of Champlain. As the waters receded, the island detached itself from the land, and such rocks as this one rolled down with glacial water from the Laurentians, onto lower land.

As you approach the village of Saint-Laurent, you'll find the **③** **studio of blacksmith Guy Bel** (2200 chemin Royal, tel. 418/828–9300), a talented and well-known local craftsman who has done the ironwork restoration for Québec City. He was born in Lyons, France, and studied there at the École des Beaux Arts. In the summer, you can watch him hard at work; his stylish candlesticks, mantels, and other ironworks are for sale.

Saint-Laurent, founded in 1679, is one of the island's maritime villages. Until as late as 1935, residents here used boats as their main means of transportation. Next to the village's marina **④** stands the tall, inspiring **Saint-Laurent Church.** Built in 1860, it was erected on the site of an 18th-century church that, because of its poor construction, had to be torn down. One of the church's procession chapels is a miniature stone replica of the church; the other wood chapel houses a gallery where artists display their work in the summer. *1532 chemin Royal. Admission free. Open daily in summer only.*

Île d'Orléans is known for its superb fruits, and you won't find better strawberries anywhere else in the province. There are about two dozen spots where you can pick your own. One of the **⑤** larger fields, **Domaine de l'Auto-Cueillette** (211 chemin Royal), is located in Saint-Laurent. You can buy an empty basket here

Île d'Orléans

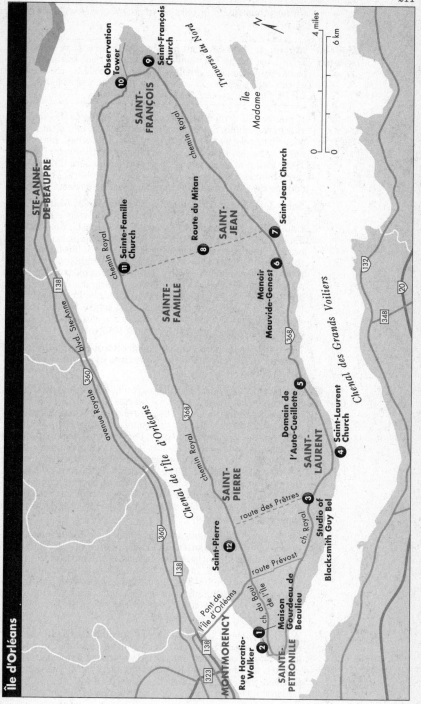

STE-ANNE-
DE-BEAUPRÉ

MONTMORENCY

SAINTE-
PÉTRONILLE

Rue Horatio-
Walker

Maison
Gourdeau de
Beaulieu

Pont de
l'île d'Orléans

ch. du Bout
de l'île

Studio of
Blacksmith Guy Bel

route Prévost

route des Prêtres

Saint-Pierre

SAINT-
PIERRE

SAINT-
LAURENT

Saint-Laurent
Church

Domain de
l'Auto-Cueillette

ch. Royal

avenue Royale

chemin Royal

Chenal de l'île d'Orléans

SAINTE-
FAMILLE

Sainte-Famille
Church

chemin Royal

Route du Mitan

SAINT-
JEAN

Manoir
Mauvide-Genest

Saint-Jean Church

Chenal des Grands Voiliers

SAINT-
FRANÇOIS

Observation
Tower

Saint-François
Church

Traverse du Nord

Île
Madame

blvd Ste-Anne

1
2
3
4
5
6
7
8
9
10
11
12

138
323
360
368
132
348
20

N

0   4 miles
0   6 km

for less than 50¢; a full basket of strawberries will cost about $5.

Time Out **Moulin de Saint-Laurent** is an early 18th-century stone mill. Dine here in the herb-and-flower garden out back. Scrumptious snacks, such as quiches, bagels, and salads, are available at the café-terrace. *754 chemin Royal, tel. 418/829–3888. AE, MC, V. Open May–Oct. for lunch and dinner.*

If you continue on chemin Royal, you'll come to the southern side of the island, **Saint-Jean,** a village whose inhabitants were once river pilots and navigators. Most of its small, homogeneous row homes were built close to the river between 1840 and 1860. Being at sea most of the time, the sailors did not need large homes and plots of land as did the farmers. The island's sudden drop in elevation is most noticeable in Saint-Jean.

❻ Saint-Jean's beautiful Normandy-style manor, **Manoir Mauvide-Genest,** was built in 1734 for Jean Mauvide—surgeon to Louis XV—and his wife, Marie-Anne Genest. Most notable about this house, which still has its original thick walls, ceiling beams, and fireplaces, is the degree to which it has held up over the years, in spite of being targeted by English guns during the 1759 siege of Québec City. The home is a pleasure to roam; all rooms are furnished with original antiques from the 18th and 19th centuries. It also offers an exhibit on French architecture and a downstairs restaurant that serves French cuisine. *1451 chemin Royal, tel. 418/829–2630. Open late June 24–Aug., daily 10–5; Sept.–mid-Oct., weekends 10–5.*

North of the manor stands **Théâtre Paul-Hébert,** an indoor summer theater founded five years ago by an actor who lives on the island.

❼ At the opposite end of the village, you'll see **Saint-Jean Church,** a massive granite structure with large red doors and a towering steeple built in 1749. The church bears a remarkable resemblance to a ship; it is big and round and appears to be sitting right on the St. Lawrence River. Paintings of the patron saints of seamen line the interior walls. The church's cemetery is also intriguing, especially if you can read French. Back in the 18th century, piloting the St. Lawrence was a dangerous profession; the boats could not easily handle the rough currents. The cemetery tombstones recall the tragedies of lost life in these harsh waters. *2001 chemin Royal, tel. 418/829–3182. Admission free. Open daily in the summer.*

As you leave Saint-Jean, chemin Royal mounts the incline and **❽** crosses **route du Mitan.** In old French, *mitan* means "halfway." This road, dividing the island in half, is the most direct route from north to south. It is also the most beautiful on the island, with acres of tended farmland, apple orchards, and maple groves. If you're running out of time and want to end the tour here, take route du Mitan, which brings you to Saint-Pierre and the bridge to the mainland.

When you come to 17th-century farmhouses separated by sprawling open fields, you know you've reached the island's least-toured and most rustic village, **Saint-François.** At the eastern tip of the island, this community is the one situated farthest from the St. Lawrence River and was originally settled mainly by farmers. Saint-François is also the perfect place to visit one of the island's *cabanes à sucre* (maple-sugaring huts) found along chemin Royal. Stop at a hut for a tasting tour; sap is gathered from the maple groves and boiled until it turns to a syrup. When it is poured on ice, it tastes like a delicious toffee. The maple season is late March through April.

9 Straight on chemin Royal is **Saint-François Church,** built in 1734 and one of eight provincial churches dating from the French regime. At the time the English seized Québec in 1759, General Wolfe knew Saint-François to be among the better strategic points along the St. Lawrence. Consequently, he stationed the British troops here and used the church as a military hospital. In May 1988, a fatal car crash set the church on fire. Although it is in the process of being rebuilt, most of the interior treasures were lost.

10 About a mile down the road is a picnic area with a wood **observation tower** situated for perfect viewing of the majestic St. Lawrence at its widest point, 10 times as wide as it is near Québec City. During the spring and autumn months, you can observe wild Canada geese here.

Heading north on chemin Royal, you'll come to one of the island's earliest villages, Sainte-Famille, which was founded in 1661. The scenery is exquisite here; there are abundant apple orchards and strawberry fields with a view of Côte de Beaupré and Mont Sainte-Anne in the distance. But the village also has plenty of man-made historic charm; it has the area's highest concentration of stone houses dating from the French regime.

11 Take a quick look at **Sainte-Famille Church,** which was constructed in 1749, later than some of the others on the island. This impressive structure is the only church in the province to have three bell towers at the front. Its ceiling was redone in the mid-19th century with elaborate designs in wood and gold. The church also holds a famous painting, *L'Enfant Jésus Voyant la Croix,* done in 1670 by Frère Luc (Father Luc), who was sent from France to decorate churches in the area. *3915 chemin Royal. Admission free. Open daily in summer.*

12 The next village situated on the north side of the island, **Saint-Pierre,** was established a bit later than Sainte-Famille, in 1679. Its church, though, is older—dating back to 1717—and is officially the oldest on the island. **Saint-Pierre Church** is no longer open for worship, but it was restored during the 1960s and is open to tourists. Many of its original components are still intact, such as benches with compartments below, where hot bricks and stones were placed to keep people warm during winter services. *1243 chemin Royal. Admission free. Open daily in summer.*

Because Saint-Pierre is situated on a plateau with the island's most fertile land, the village has long been the center of traditional farming industries. The best products grown here are potatoes, asparagus, and corn, and the many dairy farms have given the village a renowned reputation for butter and other dairy products. At 2370 chemin Royal is the former home of Felix Leclerc, one of the many artists who have made the island their home. Leclerc, the father of Québecois folk singing, lived here until he died in August 1988.

If you continue west on chemin Royal, just up ahead are the bridge back to the mainland and Route 440.

Dining and Lodging

For price categories, *see* Québec City Dining and Lodging, *above*.

Dining   **La Goéliche.** This rustic inn has a romantic dining room with
Expensive windows overlooking the St. Lawrence River and a view of
Québec City, but the main reason to dine here is the good food.
The first rule of the kitchen is that only the freshest ingredients
from the island's farms can be used. The menu is classic French
and depends upon the fruits and vegetables in season. Lunch
is a moderately priced à la carte selection of salads, quiches,
and omelets. The evening's menu is more expensive and features such specialties as quail with red vermouth and chicken
with pistachio mousseline. The desserts, such as maple syrup
mousse with strawberry syrup, have a regional flavor. *22 chemin du Quai, Sainte-Pétronille, tel. 418/828–2248. Reservations
advised. Dress: neat but casual. MC, V.*

L'Atre. After you park your car, you'll take a horse-drawn carriage to a 17th-century Normandy-style house furnished with
Québecois pine antiques. True to the establishment's name,
which means "hearth," all the traditional dishes are cooked and
served from a fireplace. The menu emphasizes hearty fare,
such as beef Bourguignon and *tourtière* (meat pie), with maple-
sugar pie for dessert. La Grande Fête (The Big Feast) is a nine-
course dinner that costs about $60. Half way through the meal,
guests visit the attic for a nip of maple syrup liqueur. *4403 chemin Royal, Sainte-Famille, tel. 418/829–2474. Reservations required. Dress: neat but casual. AE, MC, V. Open
mid-May–mid-Oct., and occasionally in winter; call ahead.*

Lodging   **Auberge le Chaumonot.** This medium-size hotel in rural Saint-
Moderate François is right near the St. Lawrence River's widest point.
The inn's large bay windows capitalize on the view of the river
and neighboring islands, but the decor is uninspired, with simple wood furniture of the island. The service here is efficient
and friendly. The restaurant serves Continental cuisine, with
table d'hôte and à la carte menus. *425 chemin Royal, Saint-
François, G0A 3S0, tel. 418/829–2735. 8 rooms with private bath
and air-conditioning. Facilities: outdoor swimming pool, restaurant. AE, MC, V. Closed Oct.–Apr.*

La Goéliche. This 1890 Victorian country inn stands just steps
away from the St. Lawrence River in the village of Sainte-
Pétronille. Québecois antiques decorate light and spacious
rooms with their original wood floors. Rooms are on the second
and third floors, and half of them look out across the river to
Québec City. The rooms have no television, but they do have
phones. *22 chemin du Quai, Sainte-Pétronille, G0A 4C0, tel.
418/828–2248. 25 rooms, 18 with private bath. Facilities: 2 restaurants. MC, V.*

You can get to know the island by staying at one of its 30 bed-
and-breakfasts. Reservations are necessary. The price for a
room, double occupancy, runs about $40–$85. **Beau Temps,
Mauvais Temps** (tel. 418/828–2275) is a referral service for
these accommodations.

5 Vancouver

Updated by Loralee Wenger

Vancouver is a young city, even by North American standards. While three to four hundred years of settlement may make cities like Québec and Halifax historically interesting to travelers, Vancouver's youthful vigor attracts visitors to its powerful elements that have not yet been ground down by time. Vancouver is just over a hundred years old; it was not yet a town in 1870, when British Columbia became part of the Canadian confederation. The city's history, such as it is, remains visible to the naked eye: Eras are stacked east to west along the waterfront like some century-old archaeological dig—from cobbled, late-Victorian Gastown to shiny postmodern glass cathedrals of commerce grazing the sunset.

The Chinese were among the first to recognize the possibilities of Vancouver's setting. They came to British Columbia during the 1850s seeking the gold that inspired them to name the province *Gum-shan,* or Gold Mountain. They built the Canadian Pacific Railway that gave Vancouver's original townsite a purpose—one beyond the natural splendor that Royal Navy Capt. George Vancouver admired during his lunchtime cruise around its harbor on June 13, 1792. The transcontinental railway, along with its Great White Fleet of clipper ships, gave Vancouver a full week's edge over the California ports in shipping tea and silk to New York at the dawn of the 20th century.

Vancouver's natural charms are less scattered than in other cities. On clear days, the mountains appear close enough to touch. Two 1,000-acre wilderness parks lie within the city limits. The salt water of the Pacific and fresh water direct from the Rocky Mountain Trench form the city's northern and southern boundaries.

Bring a healthy sense of reverence when you visit: Vancouver is a spiritual place. For its original inhabitants, the Coast Salish peoples, it was the sacred spot where the mythical Thunderbird and Killer Whale flung wind and rain all about the heavens during their epic battles—how else to explain the coast's occasional climatic fits of temper? Devotees of a later religious tradition might worship in the sepulchre of Stanley Park or in the polished, incense-filled quiet of St. James Anglican Church, designed by English architect Sir Adrian Gilbert Scott and perhaps Vancouver's finest building.

Vancouver has a level of nightlife possible only in a place where the finer things in life have never been driven out to the suburbs and where sidewalks have never rolled up at 5 PM. There is no shortage of excellent hotels and restaurants here either. But you can find good theater, accommodations, and dining almost anywhere these days. Vancouver's *real* culture consists of its tall fir trees practically downtown and its towering rock spires close by, the ocean at your doorstep, and people from every corner of the earth all around you.

Essential Information

Arriving and Departing by Plane

Airport and Airlines
International Airports

Vancouver International Airport is on an island about 14 kilometers (9 miles) south of downtown. The main terminal building has three levels: departures, international arrivals, and domestic arrivals; a small south terminal building services flights to secondary destinations within the province. **American Airlines** (tel. 800/433–7300), **Continental** (tel. 800/525–0280), **Delta** (tel. 604/221–1212), **Horizon Air** (800/547–9308), and **United** (tel. 800/241–6522) fly into the airport. The two major domestic airlines are **Air Canada** (tel. 604/688–5515) and **Canadian Airlines** (tel. 604/279–6611).

Other Facilities **Air BC** (tel. 604/688-5515) offers 30-minute harbor-to-harbor service (downtown Vancouver to downtown Victoria) several times a day. Planes leave from near the Bayshore Hotel. **Helijet Airways** (tel. 604/273–1414) has helicopter service from downtown Vancouver to downtown Victoria and Whistler. The heliport is near Vancouver's Pan Pacific Hotel.

Between the Airport and Downtown The drive from the airport to downtown is 20–45 minutes, depending on the time of day. Airport hotels offer free shuttle service to and from the airport.

By Bus The **Airport Express** (tel. 604/261–2299) bus leaves the domestic arrivals level of the terminal building every 15 minutes in summer and every 30 minutes in winter, stopping at major downtown hotels and the bus depot. It operates from 5:30 AM until 12:30 AM. The fare is $8.25 one-way and $14 round-trip.

By Taxi Taxi stands are in front of the terminal building on domestic and international arrivals levels. Taxi fare to downtown is about $24. Area cab companies are **Yellow** (tel. 604/681–3311) and **Black Top** (tel. 604/681–2181).

By Limousine Limousine service from **Airlimo** (tel. 604/273–1331) costs about the same as a taxi to downtown: The current rate is about $28.

Arriving and Departing

By Car From the south, I–5 from Seattle becomes **Highway 99** at the U.S.–Canada border. Vancouver is a three-hour drive from Seattle. Avoid border crossings during peak times: holidays and weekends.

Highway 1, the **Trans-Canada Highway,** enters Vancouver from the east. If you enter the city after rush hour (8:30 AM), you should not have a problem with traffic.

By Ferry **BC Ferries** operates two major ferry terminals outside Vancouver. From Tsawwassen to the south (an hour's drive from downtown), ferries sail to Victoria and Nanaimo on Vancouver Island and through the Gulf Islands (the small islands between the mainland and Vancouver Island). From Horseshoe Bay (30 minutes north from downtown), ferries sail a short distance up the coast and to Nanaimo on Vancouver Island. Call (tel. 604/685–1021) for departure and arrival times.

Sealink Express (tel. 604/687–6925) takes passengers by high-speed catamaran from downtown Vancouver to downtown Victoria in 2 1/2 hours. The two boats each seat 302 people and have such airplane-type amenities as movies, work tables, and headphones for music; there are also fax machines, telephones, two snack bars, a children's playroom, and a newsstand on board. Tickets cost $32.95 one-way, $59.95 round-trip.

By Train The Pacific Central Station (1150 Station St.) is the hub for rail, bus, and SkyTrain service. The **VIA Rail** (tel. 800/561–8630) station is at Main Street and Terminal Avenue. VIA provides service through the Rockies to Banff. Passenger trains leave

Vancouver Exploring *(Boxes Refer to Detail Maps)*

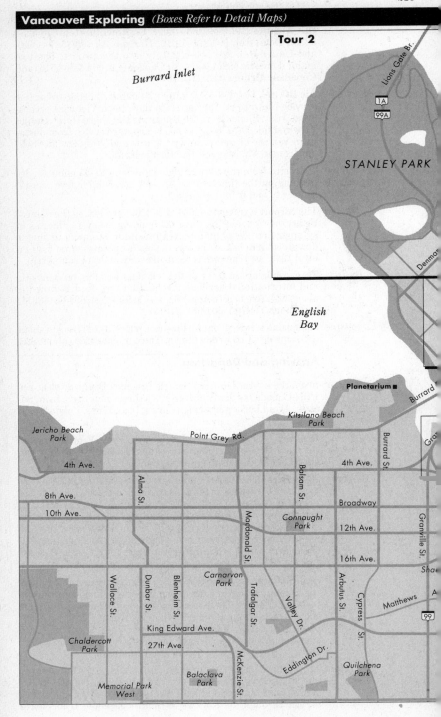

Burrard Inlet

Tour 2

Lions Gate Br.

1A
99A

STANLEY PARK

Denman

English Bay

Planetarium ■

Burrard

Kitsilano Beach Park

Jericho Beach Park

Point Grey Rd.

4th Ave.

Gran

Burrard St.

4th Ave.

Alma St.

8th Ave.

Broadway

10th Ave.

Balsam St.

Connaught Park

12th Ave.

Granville St.

Macdonald St.

16th Ave.

Sha

Carnarvon Park

Wallace St.

Dunbar St.

Blenheim St.

Trafalgar St.

Arbutus St.

Cypress St.

Matthews

A

Valley Dr.

99

King Edward Ave.

Chaldercott Park

27th Ave.

McKenzie St.

Eddington Dr.

Quilchena Park

Balaclava Park

Memorial Park West

NORTH VANCOUVER

Burrard Inlet

N

0   1 mile
0   1 km

Pender St.

Georgia St.

Robson St.

...ro St.

Hastings St.

Dunsmuir St.

Cordova St.

Powell St.

Hastings St.

7A

Burrard St.

Howe St.

Seymour St.

Powell St.

Davie St.

Richards St.

...cific St.

B.C. Place
Stadium ■

Strathcona
Park

Tour 1

Clark

Victoria

Terminal Ave.

Cambie Br.

False Creek

2nd Ave.

Quebec St.

Tour 3

Broadway

12th Ave.

7

Cedar
Cottage
Park

Commercial

Oak St.

Heather St.

16th Ave.

Clarke
Park

Windsor St.

Knight St.

Cambie St.

Manitoba St.

Main St.

Fraser St.

28th Ave.

King Edward

1A

99A

Victoria Dr.

33rd Ave.

Queen Elizabeth
Park

the **BC Rail** (tel. 604/631–3500) station in North Vancouver for Whistler and the interior of British Columbia. There is no Amtrak service from Seattle.

By Bus **Greyhound** (tel. 604/662–3222) is the biggest bus line servicing Vancouver. The Pacific Central Station (1150 Station St.) is the depot. **Quick Shuttle** (tel. 604/526–2836) bus service runs between Vancouver and Seattle six times a day.

Getting Around

By Car Although no freeways cross Vancouver, rush-hour traffic is not yet horrendous. The worst rush-hour bottlenecks are the North Shore bridges, the George Massey Tunnel on Highway 99 south of Vancouver, and Highway 1 through Coquitlam and Surrey.

By Subway Vancouver has a one-line, 25-kilometer (15-mile) rapid transit system called **SkyTrain,** which travels underground downtown and is elevated for the rest of its route to New Westminster and Surrey. Trains leave about every five minutes. Tickets must be carried with you as proof of payment, and are sold at each station from machines; correct change is not necessary. You may use transfers from SkyTrain to SeaBus and BC Transit buses (*see below*) and vice versa.

By Bus Exact change is needed to ride the buses: $1.50 adults, 75¢ for senior citizens and children 5–13. Books of 25 tickets are sold at convenience stores and newsstands; look for a red, white, and blue "Fare Dealer" sign. Day passes, good for unlimited travel after 9:30 AM, cost $4.50 for adults. They are available from fare dealers and any SeaBus or SkyTrain station. Transfers are valid for 90 minutes and allow travel in both directions.

By Taxi It is difficult to hail a cab in Vancouver; unless you're near a hotel, you'd have better luck calling a taxi service. Try **Yellow** (tel. 604/681–3311) or **Black Top** (tel. 604/681–2181).

By SeaBus The **SeaBus** is a 400-passenger commuter ferry that crosses Burrard Inlet from the foot of Lonsdale (North Vancouver) to downtown. The ride takes 13 minutes and costs the same as the transit bus. With a transfer, connection can be made with any BC Transit bus or SkyTrain.

Important Addresses and Numbers

Tourist Information **Vancouver Travel Infocentre** (200 Burrard St., tel. 604/683–2000) provides maps and information about the city and is open in summer, daily 8–6; in winter, Monday–Saturday 9–5. A kiosk in Pacific Centre Mall is open daily in summer, Monday–Saturday 9:30–5, Sunday noon–5; in winter, Monday–Saturday 9–5. Eaton's department store downtown also has a tourist information counter that is open all year.

Embassies There are no embassies in Vancouver, only consulates and trade commissions: **United States** (1075 W. Pender St., tel. 604/685–4311) and **United Kingdom** (800–1111 Melville St., tel. 604/683–4421). For a complete listing, see the Yellow Pages.

Emergencies Call 911 for **police, fire department,** and **ambulance.**

Hospitals and Clinics **St. Paul's Hospital** (1081 Burrard St., tel. 604/682–2344), a downtown hospital, has an emergency ward. **Medicentre** (1055

Dunsmuir St., lower level, tel. 604/683–8138), a drop-in clinic on the lower level of the Bentall Centre, is open weekdays.

Dentist The counterpart to Medicentre is **Dentacentre** (1055 Dunsmuir St., lower level, tel. 604/669–6700), which is next door and is also open weekdays.

Late-night **Shopper's Drug Mart** (1125 Davie St., tel. 604/685–6445) is open
Pharmacy until midnight every night except Sunday, when it closes at 9.

Road Emergencies **BCAA** (tel. 604/293–2222) has 24-hour emergency road service for members of AAA or CAA.

Travel Agencies **American Express Travel Service** (1040 W. Georgia St., tel. 604/669–2813), **Hagen's Travel** (210–850 W. Hastings St., tel. 604/684–2448), and **P. Lawson Travel** (409 Granville St., tel. 604/682–4272).

Opening and Closing Times

Banks traditionally are open Monday–Thursday 10–3 and Friday 10–6, but many banks have extended hours and are open on Saturday, particularly outside of downtown.

Museums are generally open 10–5, including Saturday and Sunday. Most are open one evening a week as well.

Department store hours are Monday–Wednesday and Saturday 9:30–6, Thursday and Friday 9:30–9, and Sunday noon–5. Many smaller stores are also open Sunday. Robson Street and Chinatown are particularly good for Sunday shopping.

Guided Tours

Orientation **Gray Line** (tel. 604/879-3363), the largest tour operator, offers the 3½-hour Grand City bus tour year-round. Departing from the Hotel Vancouver, the tour includes Stanley Park, Chinatown, Gastown, English Bay, and Queen Elizabeth Park and costs about $31. **Westcoast City and Nature Sightseeing** (tel. 604/451-5581) accommodates up to 24 people in vans that run a 3½-hour City Highlights Tour for $27 (pickup available from any downtown location). A short city tour (2½ hours) is offered by **Vance Tours** (tel. 604/941-5660) in minibuses and costs $29.

The **Vancouver Trolley Company** (tel. 604/451-5581) runs turn-of-the-century–style trolleys through Vancouver from April to October on a 1½-hour narrated tour of Stanley Park, Gastown, English Bay, the Vancouver Museum, Granville Island, Queen Elizabeth Park, Science World, and Chinatown, among other sights. A day pass allows you to complete one full circuit, getting off and on as often as you like. Start the trip at any of the sights and buy a ticket on board. It's a perfect way to deal with a rainy day in Vancouver. Adult fare is $15, children's $7.

North Shore tours usually include any or several of the following: a gondola ride up Grouse Mountain, a walk across the Capilano Suspension Bridge, a stop at a salmon hatchery, the Lonsdale Quay Market, and a ride back to town on the SeaBus. Half-day tours cost about $35 and are offered by **Landsea Tours** (tel. 604/255–7272), **Harbour Ferries** (tel. 604/687–9558), **Gray Line** (tel. 604/879-3363), and **Pacific Coach Lines** (tel. 604/662–7575).

Air Tours Tour the mountains and fjords of the North Shore by helicopter for $165 per person (minimum of three people) for 45 minutes: **Vancouver Helicopters** (tel. 604/270–1484) flies from the Harbour Heliport downtown. Or see Vancouver from the air for $60 for 20 minutes: **Harbour Air**'s (tel. 604/688–1277) seaplanes leave from beside the Bayshore Hotel.

Boat Tours The Royal Hudson, Canada's only functioning steam train, heads along the mountainous coast up Howe Sound to the logging town of Squamish. After a break to explore, you sail back to Vancouver via the MV *Britannia*. This highly recommended excursion costs about $45, takes 6½ hours, and is organized by **Harbour Ferries** (tel. 604/687–9558). Reservations are necessary.

The SS *Beaver* (tel. 604/682–7284), a replica of a Hudson Bay fur-trading vessel that ran aground here in 1888, offers two trips. One is the Harbour Sunset Dinner Cruise, a four-hour trip with a barbecue dinner; the other is a four-hour daytime trip up Indian Arm with salmon for lunch. Each is about $50 and reservations are necessary for both.

Harbour Ferries (tel. 604/687–9558) takes a 1½-hour tour of Burrard Inlet in a paddlewheeler, and costs about $20.

Fraser River Connection (tel. 604/525–4465) will take you on a four-hour tour of a fascinating working river—past log booms, tugs, and houseboats. Ride from New Westminster to Fort Langley, aboard a convincing replica of an 1800s-era paddlewheeler, for about $25.

Personal Guides **Early Motion Tours** (tel. 604/687–5088) covers Vancouver in a Model-A Ford convertible that comfortably seats about four people. For about $60, up to four people can take an hour-long trip around downtown, Chinatown, and Stanley Park.

AAA Horse & Carriage (tel. 604/681–5115) has a 50-minute tour of Stanley Park, along the waterfront, and through a cedar forest and a rose garden for about $10.

Exploring Vancouver

The heart of Vancouver—which includes the downtown area, Stanley Park, and the West End high-rise residential neighborhood—sits on a peninsula bordered by English Bay and the Pacific Ocean to the west; by False Creek, an inlet on which you will find Granville Island, to the south; and to the north by Burrard Inlet, the working port of the city, past which loom the North Shore mountains. The oldest part of the city—Gastown and Chinatown—lies at the edge of Burrard Inlet, around Main Street, which runs north–south and is roughly the dividing line between the east side and the west side. All the avenues, which are numbered, have east and west designations.

Highlights for First-time Visitors

Chinatown, Tour 1: Downtown Vancouver
English Bay, Tour 2: Stanley Park
Granville Island, Tour 3: Granville Island
Stanley Park, Tour 2: Stanley Park

Tour 1: Downtown Vancouver

Numbers in the margin correspond to points of interest on the Tour 1: Downtown Vancouver map.

❶ You can logically begin your downtown tour in either of two ways. If you're in for a day of shopping, amble down **Robson Street** (*see* Shopping, *below*), where you'll find any item from souvenirs to high fashions, from espresso to sushi.

❷ If you opt otherwise, start at **Robson Square,** built in 1975 and designed by architect Arthur Erickson to be the gathering place of downtown Vancouver. The complex, which functions from the outside as a park, encompasses the Vancouver Art Gallery and government offices and law courts that have been built under landscaped walkways, a block-long glass canopy, and a waterfall that helps mask traffic noise. An ice-skating rink and restaurants occupy the below-street level.

❸ The **Vancouver Art Gallery** that heads the square was a neoclassical-style 1912 courthouse until Erickson converted it in 1980. Notice some details: lions that guard the majestic front steps and the use of columns and domes—features borrowed from ancient Roman architecture. In back of the old courthouse, a more modest staircase now serves as a speakers' corner. *750 Hornby St., tel. 604/682–5621. Admission: $4.50 adults, $2.50 students and senior citizens; free Thurs. eve. Open Mon.– Wed., and Sat. 10–5; Thurs. 10–9; Sun. noon–5.*

❹ Directly across Hornby Street is the **Hotel Vancouver** (1939), one of the last of the railway-built hotels. (The last one built was the Chateau Whistler, in 1989.) Reminiscent of a medieval French castle, this château style has been incorporated into hotels throughout almost every major Canadian city. With the onset of the depression, construction was halted here, and the hotel was finished only in time for the visit of King George VI in 1939. It has been renovated twice: During the 1960s it was unfortunately modernized, but the more recent refurbishment is more in keeping with the spirit of what is the most recognizable roof on Vancouver's skyline. The exterior of the building has carvings of malevolent gargoyles at the corners, an ornate chimney, Indian chiefs on the Hornby Street side, and an assortment of grotesque mythological figures.

❺ **Christ Church Cathedral** (1895), across the street from the Hotel Vancouver, is the oldest church in Vancouver. The tiny church was built in a Gothic style with buttresses and pointed arched windows and looks like the parish church of an English village. By contrast, the cathedral's rough-hewn interior is that of a frontier town, with Douglas-fir beams and carpenter woodwork that offers excellent acoustics for the frequent vespers, carol services, and Gregorian chants presented here. *690 Burrard St., tel. 604/682–3848.*

❻ **Cathedral Place,** on the corner of Hornby and Georgia streets, is a spectacular office tower adjacent to Christ Church Cathedral. Three large sculptures of nurses at the corners of the building are replicas of the statues that graced the art deco Georgia Medical-Dental Building, the site's previous structure.

A restored terra-cotta arch—formerly the front entrance to the medical building—and frieze panels showing scenes of in-

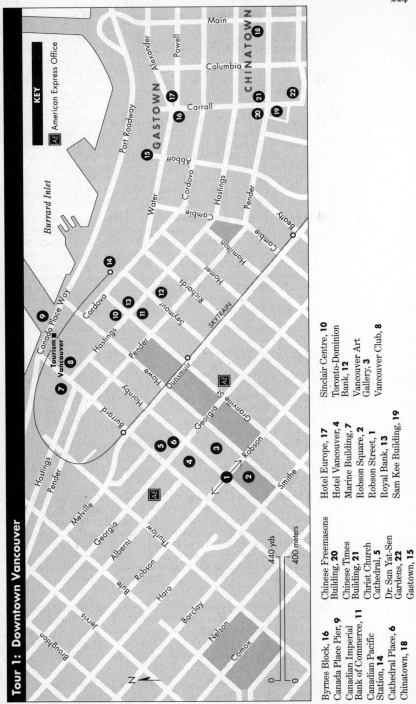

Tour 1: Downtown Vancouver

KEY

AE American Express Office

Byrnes Block, **16**
Canada Place Pier, **9**
Canadian Imperial Bank of Commerce, **11**
Canadian Pacific Station, **14**
Cathedral Place, **6**
Chinatown, **18**

Chinese Freemasons Building, **20**
Chinese Times Building, **21**
Christ Church Cathedral, **5**
Dr. Sun Yat-Sen Gardens, **22**
Gastown, **15**

Hotel Europe, **17**
Hotel Vancouver, **4**
Marine Building, **7**
Robson Square, **2**
Robson Street, **1**
Royal Bank, **13**
Sam Kee Building, **19**

Sinclair Centre, **10**
Toronto-Dominion Bank, **12**
Vancouver Art Gallery, **3**
Vancouver Club, **8**

dividuals administering care now grace the **Canadian Craft Museum,** across the courtyard. Originally founded in 1980, but opened on this site in 1992, the Craft Museum is the first national cultural facility dedicated to craft—historical and contemporary, functional and decorative. Craft embodies the human need for artistic expression in everyday life, and examples here range from elegantly carved utensils with decorative handles to colorful hand-spun and hand-woven garments. The three-level museum offers exhibits, workshops, and the Gallery Shop, which specializes in, of course, Canadian crafts. The restful courtyard is a quiet place to take a break. *639 Hornby St., tel 604/687–8266. Admission: $2.50 adults, $1.50 senior citizens and students, children under 12 free. Open Mon.–Sat. 9:30–5:30, Sun. and holidays noon–5.*

Cathedral Place also is the site of the **Sri Lankan Gem Museum,** which opened in 1993. The museum features a floor of 900 polished agates set in aggregate, and some $5 million worth of gemstones, including moonstones, rubies, lapis, diamonds, garnets, jade, and emeralds. Many of the gems are from Sri Lanka. *150 925 W. Georgia St., tel. 604/662–7708. Admission: $5 (proceeds go to the Vancouver Symphony Orchestra). Open Mon.–Sat. 10:30–5:30.*

⑦ The **Marine Building** (1931), at the foot of Burrard Street, is Canada's best example of Art Deco style. Terra-cotta bas reliefs depict the history of transportation: Airships, biplanes, steamships, locomotives, and submarines are figured. These motifs were once considered radical and modernistic adornments, because most buildings were still using classical or Gothic ornamentation. From the east, the Marine Building is reflected in bronze by 999 West Hastings, and in silver from the southeast by the Canadian Imperial Bank of Commerce. Stand on the corner of Hastings and Hornby streets for the best view of the Marine Building.

A nice walk is along Hastings Street—the old financial district. Until the 1966–1972 period, when the first of the bank towers and underground malls on West Georgia Street were developed, this was Canada's westernmost business terminus. The temple-style banks, businessmen's clubs, and investment houses survive as evidence of the city's sophisticated architec-
⑧ tural advances prior to World War I. The **Vancouver Club,** built between 1912 and 1914, was a gathering place for the city's elite. Its architectural design is reminiscent of private clubs in England that were inspired by Italian Renaissance palaces. The Vancouver Club is still the private haunt of some of the city's businessmen. *915 W. Hastings St., tel. 604/685–9321.*

⑨ The foot of Howe Street, north of Hastings, is **Canada Place Pier.** Originally built on an old cargo pier to be the off-site Canadian pavilion in Expo '86, Canada Place was later converted into Vancouver's Trade and Convention Center. It is dominated at the shore end by the luxurious Pan Pacific Hotel (*see* Lodging, *below*), with its spectacular three-story lobby and waterfall. The convention space is covered by a fabric roof shaped like 10 sails, which has become a landmark of Vancouver's skyline. Below is a cruise ship facility, and at the north end are an Imax theater, a restaurant, and an outdoor performance space. A promenade runs along the pier's west side with views of the Burrard Inlet harbor and Stanley Park. *999 Canada Pl., tel. 604/688–8687.*

Time Out Across the street and accessible via an enclosed walkway is the luxurious **Waterfront Centre Hotel,** a 23-story glass structure that opened in 1992. The lobby, lounge, and restaurant offer stunning views of Burrard Inlet; at night, the casual Herons Lounge with a fireplace features relaxing piano music. Weather permitting, you can enjoy the view even more from the patio outside Herons Restaurant, where the menu offers local and regional Pacific Rim specialties. *900 Canada Place Way, tel. 604/691-1991.*

Just next door to the Waterfront Centre Hotel is the **Tourism Vancouver Infocentre** (200 Burrard St., tel. 604/682–2222), with brochures and personnel to answer questions, as well as an attractive Northwest Coast native art collection.

🔟 Walk back up to Hastings and Howe streets to the **Sinclair Centre.** Vancouver's outstanding architect, Richard Henriquez, has knitted four government office buildings (built 1905–1939) into an office-retail complex. The two Hastings Street buildings—the 1905 post office with the elegant clock tower and the 1913 Winch Building—are linked with the Post Office Extension and Customs Examining Warehouse to the north. Painstaking and very costly restoration involved finding master masons—the original terrazzo suppliers in Europe—and uncovering and refurbishing the pressed-metal ceilings.

Walking a bit farther up Hastings, at Granville Street, will reveal one of Vancouver's oldest and most impressive charter ⓫ banks, the former **Canadian Imperial Bank of Commerce** head-quarters (1906–1908); the columns, arches, and details are of ⓬ typically Roman influence. The **Toronto–Dominion Bank,** one block east, is of the same style but was built in 1920.

Backtrack directly across from the CIBC on Hastings Street ⓭ to the more Gothic **Royal Bank.** It was intended to be half of a symmetrical building that was never completed, due to the depression. Striking, though, is the magnificent hall, ecclesiastical in style, reminiscent of a European cathedral.

⓮ At the foot of Seymour Street is the **Canadian Pacific Station,** the third and most pretentious of three Canadian Pacific Railway passenger terminals. Constructed in 1912–1914, this terminal replaced the other two as the western terminus for Canada's transcontinental railway. After Canada's railways merged, the station became obsolete until a 1978 renovation turned it into an office-retail complex and SeaBus terminal. Murals in the waiting rooms show passengers what kind of scenery to expect on their journeys across Canada.

From Seymour Street, pick up Water Street, on your way to ⓯ **Gastown.** Named after the original townsite saloon keeper, "Gassy" Jack Deighton, Gastown is where Vancouver originated. Deighton arrived at Burrard Inlet in 1867 with his Indian wife, a barrel of whiskey, and few amenities. A statue of Gassy Jack stands on the north side of Maple Tree Square, the intersection of five streets, where he built his first saloon.

When the transcontinental train arrived in 1887, Gastown became the transfer point for trade with the Orient and was soon crowded with hotels and warehouses. The Klondike gold rush encouraged further development until 1912, when the "Golden Years" ended. The 1930s–1950s saw hotels being converted into rooming houses and the warehouse district shifting elsewhere. The area gradually became unattended and run-down. However, both Gastown and Chinatown were declared historic areas and have been revitalized.

16 The **Byrnes Block** building was constructed on the corner of Water and Carrall streets (the site of Gassy Jack's second saloon) after the 1886 Great Fire. The date is just visible at the top of the building above the door where it says "Herman Block," which was its name for a short time. The extravagantly detailed Alhambra Hotel that was situated here was luxury class for the time, at a cost of a dollar a night.

Tucked behind 2 Water Street are **Blood Alley** and **Gaoler's Mews.** Once the site of the city's first civic buildings—the constable's cabin and courthouse, and a two-cell log jail—today the cobblestone street with antique streetlighting is the home of architectural offices.

17 The **Hotel Europe** (1908–1909), a flatiron building at Powell and Alexander streets, was billed as the best hotel in the city and was Vancouver's first reinforced concrete structure. Designed as a functional commercial building, the hotel lacks ornamentation and fine detail, a style unusually utilitarian for the time.

18 From Maple Tree Square, walk three blocks up Carrall Street to Pender Street, where **Chinatown** begins. There was already a sizable Chinese community in British Columbia because of the 1858 Cariboo gold rush in central British Columbia, but the biggest influx from China occurred in the 1880s, during construction of the Canadian Pacific Railway, when 15,000 laborers were imported. The Chinese were among the first inhabitants of Vancouver, and some of the oldest buildings in the city are in Chinatown.

Even while doing the hazardous work of blasting the railbed through the Rocky Mountains, the Chinese were discriminated against. The Anti-Asiatic Riots of 1907 stopped growth in Chinatown for 50 years, and immigration from China was discouraged by more and more restrictive policies, climaxing in a $500 head tax during the 1920s.

In the 1960s the city council was planning bulldozer urban renewal for Strathcona, the residential part of Chinatown, and freeway connections through the most historic blocks of Chinatown were charted. Fortunately, the plans were halted, and today Chinatown is an expanding, vital district fueled by investment from Vancouver's most notable newcomers—immigrants from Hong Kong. It is best to view the buildings in Chinatown from the south side of Pender Street, where the Chinese Cultural Center stands. From here you'll get a view of important details that adorn the upper stories. The style of architecture in Vancouver's Chinatown is patterned on that of Canton and won't be seen in any other Canadian cities.

19 The corner of Carrall and East Pender streets, now the western boundary of Chinatown, is one of the neighborhood's most historic spots. Standing at 8 West Pender Street is the **Sam Kee Building,** recognized by *Ripley's Believe It or Not!* as the narrowest building in the world, at just 6 feet wide. The 1913 structure still exists, with its bay windows overhanging the street and a basement that burrows under the sidewalk.

20 The **Chinese Freemasons Building** (1901) at 1 West Pender Street has two completely different styles of facades: The side facing Chinatown displays a fine example of Cantonese-imported recessed balconies; on the Carrall Street side, the standard Victorian style common throughout the British Empire is displayed. It was in this building that Dr. Sun Yat-sen hid for months from the agents of the Manchu dynasty while he raised funds for its overthrow, which he accomplished in 1911.

21 Directly across Carrall Street is the **Chinese Times Building**, constructed in 1902. Inside, there is a hidden mezzanine floor from which police officers could hear the clicking sounds of clandestine mah-jongg games played after sunset. Attempts by vice squads to enforce restrictive policies against the Chinese gamblers proved fruitless, because police were unable to find the players, who were hidden on the secret floor.

22 Planning for the **Chinese Cultural Center** and **Dr. Sun Yat-sen Gardens** (1980–1987) began during the late 1960s; the first phase was designed by James Cheng, a former associate of Arthur Erickson. The cultural center has exhibition space, classrooms, and meeting rooms. The Dr. Sun Yat-sen Gardens, located behind the cultural center, were built by 52 artisans from Suzhou, the Garden City of the People's Republic. The gardens incorporate design elements and traditional materials from several of that city's centuries-old private gardens and are the first living classical Chinese gardens built outside China. As you walk through the gardens, remember that no power tools, screws, or nails were used in the construction. Free guided tours are offered throughout the day; telephone for times. *Dr. Sun Yat-sen Gardens. 578 Carrall St., tel. 604/689–7133. Admission: $3.50 adults, $2.50 senior citizens and students, $7 families. Open May–Sept., daily 10–8; Oct.–Apr., daily 10–4:30.*

Tour 2: Stanley Park

Numbers in the margin correspond to points of interest on the Tour 2: Stanley Park map.

A 1,000-acre wilderness park just blocks from the downtown section of a major city is a rarity but is one of Vancouver's major attractions. In the 1860s, due to a threat of American invasion, the area that is now Stanley Park was designated a military reserve (though it was never needed). When the city of Vancouver was incorporated in 1886, the council's first act was to request that the land be set aside for a park. In 1888 permission was granted and the grounds were named Stanley Park after Lord Stanley, then governor general of Canada (the same person after whom hockey's Stanley Cup is named).

An afternoon in Stanley Park gives you a capsule tour of Vancouver that includes beaches, the ocean, the harbor, Douglas fir and cedar forests, and a good look at the North Shore mountains. The park sits on a peninsula, and along the shore is a pathway 9 kilometers (5 1/2 miles) long called the seawall. You can walk or bicycle all the way around or follow the shorter route suggested below.

Bicycles are for rent at the foot of Georgia Street near the park entrance. Cyclists must ride in a counterclockwise direction and stay on their side of the path. A good place for pedestrians

Tour 2: Stanley Park

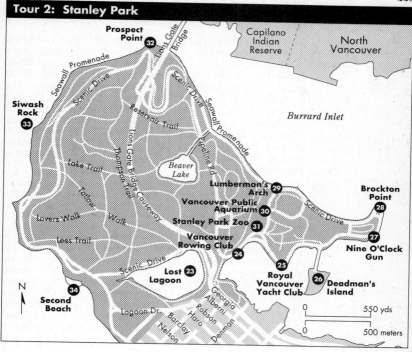

23 to start is at the foot of Alberni Street beside **Lost Lagoon.** Go through the underpass and veer right to the seawall.

24 The old wood structure that you pass is the **Vancouver Rowing Club,** a private athletic club (established 1903); a bit farther **25** along is the **Royal Vancouver Yacht Club.**

26 About ½ kilometer (⅓ mile) away is the causeway to **Deadman's Island,** a former burial ground for the local Salish Indians and the early settlers. It is now a small naval training base called the HMCS *Discovery* that is not open to the public.

27 Just ahead is the **Nine O'Clock Gun,** a cannonlike apparatus that sits by the water's edge. Originally used to alert fishermen to a curfew ending weekend fishing, now it automatically signals every night at 9.

28 Farther along is **Brockton Point** and its small but functional lighthouse and foghorn. The **totem poles,** which are situated more inland, make a popular photo spot for tourists. Totem poles were not carved in the Vancouver area; they were brought to the park from the north coast of British Columbia and were carved by the Kwakiutl and Haida peoples late in the last century. These cedar poles with carved animals, fish, birds, or mythological creatures were like family coats-of-arms or crests.

29 At kilometer 3 (mile 2) is **Lumberman's Arch,** a huge log archway dedicated to the workers in Vancouver's first industry. Beside the arch is an asphalt path that leads back to Lost Lagoon, for those who want a shorter walk. (It's about a third of the

③⓪ distance.) This path also leads to the **Vancouver Public Aquarium.**

Also part of this attraction is the humid Amazon rain-forest gallery, through which you can walk, with its piranhas, giant cockroaches, alligators, tropical birds, and jungle vegetation. Other displays show the underwater life of coastal British Columbia, the Canadian arctic, and other areas of the world. The Clamshell Gift Shop next to the aquarium is one of the best spots in town for high-quality souvenirs and gifts, most with an emphasis on natural history. *Aquarium, tel. 604/682–1118. Admission: $8.50 adults, $7.25 senior citizens and youths, $5.25 children 5–12. Open daily in summer 9:30–8; daily in winter 10–5:30. Clamshell open July–Labor Day, daily 9:30–8; rest of year, daily 10–5:30.*

③① Next to the aquarium is the **Stanley Park Zoo,** a friendly place, easily seen in an hour or two. Except for the polar bears, most of the animals are small—monkeys, seals, exotic birds, penguins, and playful otters.

About 1 kilometer (³/₄ mile) farther is the **Lions Gate Bridge—** the halfway point of the seawall. On the other side of the bridge
③② is **Prospect Point,** where you can see cormorants in their seaweed nests on the ledges along the cliffs. The large black diving birds are recognized by their long necks and beaks; when not nesting, they often perch atop floating logs or boulders. Another remarkable bird found along the shore in the park is the beautiful great blue heron, which reaches up to 4 feet tall and has a wing span of 6 feet. The heron preys on passing fish in the waters here; the oldest heron rookery in British Columbia is in the trees around the zoo.

Continuing around the seawall you will come to the **English Bay** side and the beginning of sandy beaches. The imposing
③③ rock just offshore is **Siwash Rock.** Legend tells of a young Indian who, about to become a father, bathed persistently to wash his sins away so that his son could be born pure; for his devotion he was blessed by the gods and immortalized in the shape of Siwash Rock. Two small rocks, said to be his wife and child, are just up on the cliff above the site.

Time Out   Along the seawall is one of Vancouver's best restaurants, the **Teahouse at Ferguson Point.** Set on the great lawn among Douglas fir and cedar trees, the restaurant is the perfect stopover for a summer weekend lunch or brunch. If you want just a snack, a park concession stand is also at Ferguson Point.

The next attraction along the seawall is the large saltwater pool
③④ at **Second Beach.** In the summer it is a children's pool with lifeguards, but during winter the pool is drained and skateboarders perform stunts. At the pool you can take a shortcut back to Lost Lagoon. To take the shortcut, walk along the perpendicular road behind the pool, which cuts into the park. The wood footbridge that's ahead will lead you to a path along the south side of the lagoon and to your starting point at the foot of Alberni or Georgia street.

If you continue along the seawall, it will emerge out of the park into a high-rise residential neighborhood, the **West End.** You can walk back to Alberni Street along Denman Street, where there are plenty of places to stop for coffee, ice cream, or a drink.

Tour 3: Granville Island

Numbers in the margin correspond to points of interest on the Tour 3: Granville Island map.

Granville Island was just a sandbar until World War I, when the federal government dredged False Creek for access to the sawmills that lined the shore. The sludge from the creek was heaped up onto a sandbar to create Granville Island so that it could house the much-needed industrial- and logging-equipment plants for British Columbia. By the late 1960s, however, many of the businesses that had once flourished on Granville Island had deteriorated. Buildings were rotted, rat-infested, and dangerous. In 1971, the federal government bought up leases from businesses that wanted to leave, and offered an imaginative plan to refurbish the island. A public market was introduced, and marine activities and artisans' studios were supported. The opposite shore of False Creek was the site of the 1986 World's Fair and is now part of the largest urban redevelopment plan in North America.

The small island has no residents except for a small houseboat community. Most of the previously used industrial buildings and tin sheds have been retained but are painted in upbeat reds, yellows, and blues. Through a committee of community representatives, the government regulates the types of businesses that settle on Granville Island; most of the businesses permitted here involve food, crafts, marine activities, and the arts.

Access on foot to Granville Island starts with a 15-minute walk from downtown Vancouver to the south end of Thurlow Street. From a dock behind the Vancouver Aquatic Center, the Granville Island ferry leaves every six minutes for the short trip across False Creek to the Granville Island Public Market. These pudgy boats are a great way to see the sights on False Creek, but for a longer ferry ride, go to the Maritime Museum (1905 Ogden St., tel. 604/737–2211), where visitors can board the wheelhouse of a tugboat and chart the coastal waters of British Columbia. For more information, call Granville Island Ferries (tel. 604/684–7781).

Another way to reach the island is to take a 20-minute ride on a BC Transit (tel. 604/261–5100) bus. Take a UBC, Granville, Arbutus, Cambie, or Oak bus from downtown to Granville and Broadway, and transfer to the Granville Island bus No. 51. Parking is limited, but if you must take a car, go early in the week and early in the day to avoid crowds. Parking is free for one to three hours; an alternative is to pay for parking in the garages on the island if you can find a space.

㉟ The ferry to Granville Island will drop you off at the **Granville Island Public Market,** where food stalls are enclosed in the 50,000-square-foot building. Since the government allows no chain stores, each outlet is unique, and most are of good quality. You probably won't be able to leave the market without a snack, espresso, or fixings for a lunch out on the wharf. Don't miss the charcoal-grilled oysters from **Sea-kist,** fish chowder or bouillabaisse from the **Stock Market,** fresh fudge at **Olde World Fudge,**

or smoked salmon from the **Salmon Shop.** Year-round you'll see mounds of raspberries, strawberries, blueberries, and even more exotic fruits like persimmons and lychees. On the water side of the market is lots of outdoor seating. *Public Market, tel. 604/666–6477. Open June–Aug., daily 9–6; closed Mon. Sept.–May except holidays.*

36 The **Granville Island Information Centre,** kitty-corner to the market, is a good place to get oriented to the island. Maps are available, and a slide show depicts the evolution of Granville Island. Ask here about special-events days; perhaps there's a boat show, outdoor concert, dance performance, or some other happening. *1592 Johnston St., tel. 604/666–5784. Open daily 9–6.*

Continue walking south on Johnston Street, along a clockwise loop of the island. Next is **Ocean Cement,** one of the last of the island's former industries; its lease does not expire until the year 2004.

37 Next door is the **Emily Carr College of Art and Design.** Just inside the front door, to your right, is the **Charles H. Scott Gallery,** which hosts contemporary multimedia exhibits. *1399 Johnston St., tel. 604/687–2345. Admission free. Open daily 11–5, Thurs. 11–8.*

Past the art school, on the left, is one of the only **houseboat communities** in Vancouver; others have been banned by the city because of problems with sewage and property taxes. The owners of this community appealed the ban and won special status. Take the boardwalk that starts at the houseboats and continues partway around the island.

As you circle around to Cartwright Street, stop in **Kakali** at number 1249, where you can watch the process of making fine handmade paper from all sorts of materials like blue jeans, herbs, and sequins. Another unusual artisan on the island is the **glassblower** at 1440 Old Bridge Street, around the corner.

The next two attractions will make any child's visit to Granville Island a thrill. First, on Cartwright Street, is the children's **38** **water park,** with a wading pool, sprinklers, and a fire hydrant made for children to shower one another. A bit farther down, **39** beside Isadora's restaurant, is the **Kids Only Market,** with two floors of small shops selling toys, arts-and-crafts materials, dolls, records and tapes, chemistry sets, and other sorts of kid stuff. *Water park. 1318 Cartwright St., tel. 604/665–3425. Admission free. Open June–Aug., daily 10–6. Kids Only Market. 1496 Cartwright St., tel. 604/689–8447. Open daily 10–6.*

40 At the **Granville Island Brewery,** next door, you can take a half-hour tour every afternoon; at the end of the tour, sample the Granville Island lager that is produced here and sold locally in most restaurants. *Tel. 604/688–9927. Admission free. Tours daily at 1 and 3.*

Cross Anderson Street and walk down Duranleau Street. On your left, the scuba-diving pool in **Adrenalin Sports** marks the **41** start of the **Maritime Market,** a string of businesses all geared to the sea. The first walkway to the left, Maritime Mews, leads to marinas and dry docks. There are dozens of outfits in the Maritime Market that charter boats (with or without skippers) or run cruise-and-learn trips.

Another way to take to the water is by kayak. Take a lesson or rent a kayak from **Ecomarine Ocean Kayak Center** (1668 Duranleau St., tel. 604/689–7575). Owner John Dowd is considered *the* expert on Pacific Northwest ocean kayaking.

Time Out **Bridges** (1696 Duranleau St., tel. 604/687–4400), in the bright yellow building across from the market, is a good spot to have lunch, especially on a warm summer's day. Eat on the spacious deck that looks out on the sailboats, fishing boats, and other water activities.

42 The last place to explore on Granville Island is the blue building next to Ecomarine on Duranleau Street, the **Net Loft.** The loft is a collection of small, high-quality stores—good places to find a gift to take home: a bookstore, crafts store/gallery, kitchenware shop, postcard shop, custom-made hat shop, handmade paper store, British Columbian native Indian gallery, do-it-yourself jewelry store, and more reside here.

43 Behind Blackberry Books, in the Net Loft complex, is the **Bill Reid's studio,** belonging to British Columbia's most respected Haida Indian carver. His *The Raven and the First Men,* which took five carvers more than three years to complete, is in the Museum of Anthropology (*see* Other Museums, *below*); Reid's Pacific Northwest Coast Indian artworks are world renowned. Although you can't visit the studio, there are large windows through which you can look.

Since you have come full circle, you can either take the ferry back to downtown Vancouver or stay for dinner and catch a play at the **Arts Club** (tel. 604/687–1644) or the **Waterfront Theater** (tel. 604/685–6217).

Other Museums

The **Maritime Museum** traces the history of marine activities on the west coast. Permanent exhibits depict the port of Vancouver, the fishing industry, and early explorers; the model ships on display are a delight. Traveling exhibits vary but always have a maritime theme. Guided tours are led through the double-masted schooner *St. Roch*, the first ship to sail in both directions through the treacherous Northwest Passage. A changing variety of restored heritage boats from different cultures are moored behind the museum, and a huge Kwakiutl totem pole stands out front. *North foot of Cypress St., tel. 604/737–2211. Admission: $5 adults, $2.50 children, students, and senior citizens, $8 families. Open daily 10–5, closed Mon. in winter. Access available by the Granville Island Ferries.*

The **Museum of Anthropology**, focusing on the arts of the Pacific Northwest Indians, is Vancouver's most spectacular museum. It's situated on the campus of the University of British Columbia and housed in an award-winning glass-and-concrete structure designed by Arthur Erickson. In the Great Hall are large and dramatic totem poles, ceremonial archways, and dugout canoes—all adorned with carvings of frogs, eagles, ravens, bears, and salmon. Also showcased are exquisite carvings of gold, silver, and argillite (a black stone found in the Queen Charlotte Islands), as well as masks, tools, and costumes from many other cultures. Also in the museum is a ceramics wing, which houses about 600 pieces from 15th- to 19th-century Europe. *6393 N.W. Marine Dr., tel. 604/822–3825. Admission: $5 adults, $2.50 students 6–18 and senior citizens; free Tues. evenings. Open Tues. 11–9, Wed.–Sun. 11–5.*

Science World is in a gigantic shiny dome that was built for Expo 86 for an Omnimax Theater—the world's largest dome screen. The hands-on museum encourages visitors to touch and participate in the theme exhibits. A special gallery, the Search Gallery, is aimed at younger children, as are the fun-filled demonstrations given in Center Stage. *1455 Quebec St., tel. 604/687–7832. Admission to Science World: $7 adults, $4.50 senior citizens and children. Admission to Omnimax is the same; for admission to both you get a discount. Open weekdays 10–5, Sat. 10–9.*

Vancouver Museum displays permanent exhibits that focus on the city's early history and native art and culture. Life-size replicas of an 1897 Canadian Pacific Railway passenger car, a trading post, and a Victorian parlor, as well as a real dugout canoe are highlights. Also on the site are the Planetarium and Observatory (*see* Off the Beaten Track, *below*). *1100 Chestnut St., tel. 604/736–7736. Admission: $5 adults, $2.50 senior citizens and children. Open Tues.–Sun. 10–5 in winter; daily 10–5 in summer.*

Other Parks and Gardens

Nitobe Garden is a small (2.4-acre) garden that is considered the most authentic Japanese garden outside Japan. The circular path around the park symbolizes the cycle of life and provides a tranquil view from every direction. In April and May cherry blossoms are the highlight, and in June the irises are magnificent. *1903 West Mall, Univ. of B.C., tel. 604/822–4208. Admission: $2 adults, $1.25 senior citizens and students, free Wed. and every day Oct. 11–Mar. 17. Open daily 10–dusk in summer; Mon.–Fri. in winter; phone for specific closing times.*

Pacific Spirit Park (W. 16th Ave., tel. 604/224–5739) is a 1,000-acre park that is bigger and more rugged than Stanley Park. Pacific Spirit's only amenities are 61 kilometers (30 miles) of trails, a few washrooms, and a couple of signboard maps. Go for a wonderful walk in the west coast woods—it's hard to believe that you are only 15 minutes from downtown Vancouver.

Queen Elizabeth Park has lavish gardens and lots of grassy picnicking spots. Illuminated fountains; the botanical Bloedel Conservatory, with tropical and desert zones and 20 species of free-flying tropical birds; and other facilities including 20 tennis courts, lawn bowling, pitch and putt, and a restaurant are on the grounds. *Cambie St. and 25th Ave., tel. 604/872–5513. Admission to conservatory: $2.85 adults, $1.40 senior citizens and students, $5.70 families. Open May–Sept., weekdays 9–8, weekends 10–9; Oct.–Apr., daily 10–5.*

Van Dusen Botanical Garden was a 55-acre golf course but is now the grounds of one of the largest collections of ornamental plants in Canada. Native and exotic plant displays include the shrubbery maze and the rhododendrons in May and June. For a bite to eat, stop into Sprinklers Restaurant (tel. 604/261–0011), on the grounds. *5251 Oak St. at 37th Ave., tel. 604/266–7194. Admission: $4.50 adults, $2.25 senior citizens and children 13–18, $9 families; half-price off-season. Garden open 10–dusk.*

Vancouver for Free

Among the public galleries and museums that offer free admission on certain days are: The **Vancouver Art Gallery** (750 Hornby St., tel. 604/682–5621) is free on Thursday evenings; the **Museum of Anthropology** (6393 N.W. Marine Dr., tel. 604/822–3825) is free Tuesday evenings; the **Vancouver Museum** (1100 Chestnut St., tel. 604/736–7736) is free on the first Thursday evening of every month (it is also free every Tuesday for senior citizens).

The **University of British Columbia Botanical Garden** and **Nitobe Garden** (tel. 604/822–4208), a well-established Japanese garden also at UBC, are free on Wednesday and all winter.

What to See and Do with Children

Take your pint-size chef out to Sunday brunch at **Griffin's** (900 W. Georgia St., tel. 604/684–3131), the bistro-style restaurant in the Hotel Vancouver, where the little ones don small-person-size aprons and make their own pancakes and churn ice cream.

Stanley Park Zoo (*see* Tour 2: Stanley Park, *above*).

The **miniature steam train** in Stanley Park, just five minutes northwest of the aquarium, is a big hit with children as it chugs through the forest.

Splashdown Park (Hwy. 17, just before the Tsawwassen Ferry causeway, tel. 604/943–2251), 38 kilometers (24 miles) outside

Vancouver, is a giant waterslide park with 11 slides (for toddlers to adults), heated water, picnic tables, and minigolf.

Richmond Nature Park (No. 5 Rd. exit from Hwy. 99, tel. 604/273–7015), with its displays and games in the Nature House, is geared toward children. Guides answer questions and give tours. Since the park sits on a natural bog, rubber boots are recommended if it's been wet, but a boardwalk around the duck pond makes some of the park accessible to strollers and wheelchairs.

Maplewood Farms (405 Seymour River Pl., tel. 604/929–5610), a 20-minute drive from downtown Vancouver, is set up like a small farm, with all the barnyard animals for children to see and pet. Cows are milked every day at 1:15.

Kids Only Market (*see* Tour 3: Granville Island, *above*).

The Planetarium (1100 Chestnut St., tel. 604/736–3656), on the same site as the Vancouver Museum in Vanier Park, has astronomy shows each afternoon and evening, and laser rock music shows later in the night.

Science World (*see* Other Museums, *above*).

Vancouver Aquarium (*see* Tour 2: Stanley Park, *above*).

Off the Beaten Track

On the North Shore you can get a taste of the mountains and test your mettle at the **Lynn Canyon Suspension Bridge** (Lynn Headwaters Regional Park, North Vancouver, tel. 604/987–5922), which hangs 240 feet above Lynn Creek. Also on the North Shore is the **Capilano Fish Hatchery** in the Regional Park (4500 Capilano Park Rd., tel. 604/666–1790), with exhibits about salmon.

If the sky is clear, the telescope at the **Gordon Southam Observatory** (1100 Chestnut St., in Vanier Park, tel. 604/738–2855) will be focused on whatever stars or planets are worth watching that night. While you're there, visit the planetarium on the site. Open Friday, Saturday, Sunday, and holiday evenings.

The **Beatles Museum** (456 Seymour St., tel. 604/685–8841) exhibits memorabilia from the early years of the Fab Four. Admission is $3, and the museum is open daily 10–6, Sunday noon–6.

Shopping

Unlike many cities where suburban malls have taken over, Vancouver has a downtown area that is still lined with individual boutiques and specialty shops. Stores are usually open daily and on Thursday and Friday nights, and Sundays noon to 5.

Shopping Districts

The immense **Pacific Center Mall,** in the heart of downtown, connects Eaton's and The Bay department stores, which stand at opposite corners of Georgia and Granville streets. Pacific Center is on two levels and is mostly underground.

A new commercial center has developed around **Sinclair Center** (*see* Tour 1, *above*), which caters to sophisticated and upscale tastes.

On the opposite side of Pacific Center is **Robson Street,** stretching from Burrard to Bute streets, and chockablock with small stores and cafés. Vancouver's liveliest street is not only for the fashion conscious, it also provides many excellent corners for people watching.

Two other shopping districts, one on **West 41st Avenue** between West Boulevard and Larch Street in Kerrisdale and the other on **West 10th** from Discovery Street west, are both in upscale neighborhoods and have high-quality shops and restaurants.

Fourth Avenue, from Burrard to Balsam streets, offers an eclectic mix of stores (from sophisticated women's clothing to surfboards and Jams).

In addition to the Pacific Center Mall, **Oakridge Shopping Center** at Cambie Street and 41st Avenue has chic, expensive stores that are fun to browse.

Ethnic Districts **Chinatown** (*see* Tour 1, *above*)—centered on Pender and Main streets—is an exciting and animated place for restaurants, exotic foodstuffs, and distinctive architecture.

Commercial Drive (around East 1st Avenue) is the heart of the Italian community, here called **Little Italy.** You can sip cappuccino in coffee bars where you may be the only one speaking English, or buy sun-dried tomatoes, real Parmesan, or an espresso machine.

The **East Indian shopping district** is on Main Street around 50th Avenue. Curry houses, sweet shops, grocery stores, and sari shops abound.

A small **Japantown** on Powell Street at Dunlevy Street is made up of grocery stores, fish stores, and a few restaurants.

Department Stores

The biggest department stores in Vancouver, **Eaton's, Holt Renfew,** and **The Bay,** are Canadian owned and located downtown and at most malls.

Flea Markets

A huge flea market (703 Terminal Ave., tel. 604/685–0666), with more than 300 stalls, is held Saturday, Sunday, and holidays from 8 to 4. It is easily accessible from downtown via SkyTrain, if you exit at the Main Street station.

Auctions

On Wednesday at noon and 7 PM, auctions are held at **Love's** (1635 W. Broadway, tel. 604/733–1157). **Maynard's** (415 W. 2nd Ave., tel. 604/876–6787) has home furnishings auctions on Wednesday at 7 PM. Phone for times of art and antiques auctions.

Specialty Stores

Antiques A stretch of antiques stores runs along Main Street from 19th to 35th avenues. On 10th Avenue near Alma are a few antiques stores that specialize in Canadiana, including **Folkart Interiors** (3715 W. 10th Ave.) and **Old Country Antique Co.** (3720 W. 10th Ave.). Also try **Canada West** (3607 W. Broadway). For very refined antiques, see **Artemis** (321 Water St.) in Gastown. For Oriental rugs, go to Granville Street between 7th and 14th avenues.

Art Galleries There are many private galleries throughout Vancouver. The best of them are **Buschlen-Mowatt** (1445 W. Georgia St., tel. 604/682–1234), **Diane Farris** (1565 W. 7th Ave., tel. 604/737–2629), **Equinox** (2321 Granville St., tel. 604/736–2405), and the **Heffel Gallery** (2247 Granville St., tel. 604/732–6505). Call all galleries before visiting to make sure they are open.

Books The best general bookstores are **Duthie's,** located downtown (919 Robson St.) and near the university (4444 W. 10th Ave.), and **Blackberry Books** (1663 Duranleau St.) on Granville Island.

Specialty bookstores include **The Travel Bug** (2667 W. Broadway) and **World Wide Books and Maps** (736 Granville St., downstairs) for travel books, **Vancouver Kidsbooks** (3083 W. Broadway), **Sportsbooks Plus** (230 W. Broadway), and **Pink Peppercorn** (2686 W. Broadway) for cookbooks, and **William McCarley** (213 Carrall St.) for design and architecture.

Most of the secondhand and antiquarian dealers, such as **William Hoffer** (60 Powell St.) and **Colophon Books** (407 W. Cordova St., upstairs), are in the Gastown area. A block or two away are **McLeod's** (455 W. Pender St. and around the corner at 432 Richards St.), **Ainsworth's** (321 W. Pender St.), and **Bond's** (319 W. Hastings St.). **Lawrence Books** (3591 W. 41st Ave.) is out of the way but is probably the best used-books bookstore in town.

Children's Stores An unusual children's store worth checking out is **The Imagination Market** (528 Powell St.), an oddball warehouse-type store selling recycled industrial goods for arts-and-crafts materials: barrels of metallic plastic, feathers, fluorescent-colored paper, buttons, bits of Plexiglas, and other materials by the bagful.

Clothing Several high-quality men's clothing stores are in the business
Men district: **Edward Chapman** (833 W. Pender St.) has conservative looks; **E.A. Lee** (466 Howe St.) is stylish; **Leone** (757 W. Hastings St.) is ultrachic.

A few blocks away, at Pacific Center, are **Harry Rosen, Eddie Bauer,** and **Holt Renfrew.** If your tastes are traditional, don't miss **George Straith** (900 W. Georgia St.) in the Hotel Vancouver.

On Robson Street, a more trendy shopping area, are **Boy's Co.** (No. 1080) and **Club Monaco** (No. 1153), for casual wear.

Outside downtown Vancouver there are two men's boutiques selling Italian imports: **Mondo Uomo** (2709 Granville St.) and **Boboli** (2776 Granville St.).

In Kerrisdale, three excellent men's clothing stores are **Finn's** (2159 W. 41st Ave.), **Hill's** (2125 W. 41st Ave.), and, across the street, **S. Lampman** (2126 W. 41st Ave.).

Women For women's fashions, visit **E.A. Lee** (466 Howe St.), **Wear Else?** (789 W. Pender St.), **Leone** (757 W. Hastings St.), and the more conservative **Chapy's** (833 W. Pender St.), all in the business district.

On Robson Street, look for **Margareta** (No. 948), **Alfred Sung** (No. 1143), **Club Monaco** (No. 1153), and a lingerie shop, **La Vie en Rose** (No. 1001). The two blocks between Burrard and Bute have six shoe stores.

Two expensive and very stylish import stores in South Granville are **Boboli** (2776 Granville St.) and **Bacci** (2788 Granville St.). Nearby, one of the largest and best shoe stores in town is **Freedman Shoes** (2867 Granville St.).

On the west side **Enda B.** (4346 W. 10th Ave.) and **Wear Else?** (2360 W. 4th Ave.) are the largest and best stores for high-quality fashions, but there's also **Bali Bali** for the more exotic (4462 W. 10th Ave.) and **Zig Zag** (4424 W. 10th Ave.) for fashion accessories.

Gifts Want something special to take home from British Columbia? The best places for good-quality souvenirs are the **Vancouver Art Gallery** (750 Hornby St.) and the **Clamshell Gift Shop** at the aquarium in Stanley Park. The **Salmon Shop** in the Granville Island Public Market will wrap smoked salmon for travel. In Gastown, Haida and Salish Indian art is available at **Images for a Canadian Heritage** (164 Water St.). Near Granville Island is **Leona Lattimer** (1590 W. 2nd Ave.), where the inside of her shop is built like an Indian longhouse and is full of Indian arts and crafts ranging from cheap to priceless.

Sports and the Outdoors

Participant Sports

Biking **Stanley Park** (*see* Tour 2 in Exploring Vancouver, *above*) is the most popular spot for family cycling. Rentals are available here from **Bayshore Bicycles** (745 Denman St., tel. 604/688–2453) or around the corner at **Stanley Park Rentals** (676 Chilco St., tel. 604/681–5581).

Another biking route is along the north or south shores of **False Creek.** Rent bikes at **Robson Cycles** (1840 Fir St., tel. 604/731–5552), near Granville Island.

Fishing You can fish for salmon all year in coastal British Columbia. **Sewell's Marina Horseshoe Bay** (6695 Nelson St., Horseshoe Bay, tel. 604/921–3474) organizes a daily four-hour trip on Howe Sound or has hourly rates on U-drives. **Bayshore Yacht Charters** (1601 W. Georgia St., tel. 604/691–6936) has a daily five-hour fishing trip; boats are moored five minutes from downtown Vancouver. **Island Charters** (Duranleau St., Granville Island, tel. 604/688–6625) arranges charters or boat shares and supplies all gear.

Golf Lower Mainland golf courses are open all year. **Fraserview Golf Course** (tel. 604/327–3717), a spacious course with fairways well defined by hills and mature conifers and deciduous trees, is the busiest course in the country. Fraserview is also the most central, about 20 minutes from downtown. **Seymour Golf and Country Club** (tel. 604/929–5491), on the south side of Mt. Seymour, on the North Shore, is a semiprivate club that is open to the public on Monday and Friday. One of the finest public courses in the country is **Peace Portal** (tel. 604/538–4818), near White Rock, a 45-minute drive from downtown.

Health and Fitness Clubs Both the **YMCA** (955 Burrard St., tel. 604/681–0221) and the **YWCA** (580 Burrard St., tel. 604/683–2531) downtown have drop-in rates that let you participate in all activities for the day. Both have pools, weight rooms, and fitness classes; the YMCA has racquetball, squash, and handball courts. Two other recommended clubs are **Chancery Squash Club** (202–865 Hornby St., tel. 604/682–3752) and **Tower Courts Racquet and Fitness Club** (1055 Dunsmuir St., lower level, tel. 604/689–4424), both with racquetball courts, weight rooms, and aerobics.

Hiking **Pacific Spirit Park** is a 1,000-acre wilderness park with 48 kilometers (30 miles) of hiking trails (*see* Other Parks and Gardens in Exploring Vancouver, *above*).

The **Capilano Regional Park** (*see* Off the Beaten Track, in Exploring Vancouver, *above*), on the North Shore, provides a scenic hike.

Jogging The seawall around **Stanley Park** (*see* Tour 2 in Exploring Vancouver, *above*) is 9 kilometers (5½ miles) and gives an excellent minitour of the city. A shorter run of 4 kilometers (2½ miles) in the park is around **Lost Lagoon.**

Skiing
Cross-country The best cross-country skiing is at **Cypress Bowl Ski Area** (tel. 604/926–6007).

Downhill Vancouver is two hours away from **Whistler/Blackcomb** (Whistler Resort Association, tel. 604/685–3650; snow report, tel. 604/687–7507), one of the top ski spots in North America.

There are three ski areas on the North Shore mountains, close to Vancouver, with night skiing. The snow is not as good as at Whistler, and the runs are generally used by novice, junior, and family skiers or those who want a quick ski after work. **Cypress Bowl** (tel. 604/926–5612; snow report, tel. 604/926–6007) has the most and the longest runs; **Grouse Mountain** (tel. 604/984–0661; snow report, tel. 604/986–6262) has extensive night skiing, restaurants, and bars; and **Mt. Seymour** (tel. 604/986–2261; snow report, tel. 604/986–3444) is the highest in the area, so the snow is a little better.

Water Sports
Kayaking Rent a kayak from **Ecomarine Ocean Kayak Center** (tel. 604/689–7575) on Granville Island (*see* Tour 3 in Exploring Vancouver, *above*).

Rafting The Thompson, the Chilliwack, and the Fraser are the principal rafting rivers in southwestern British Columbia. The Fraser River has whirlpools and big waves, but for frothing white water, try the Thompson and Chilliwack rivers. Trips range from three hours to several days. Some well-qualified outfitters that lead trips are **Kumsheen** (Lytton, tel. 604/455–2296; in British Columbia, 800/482–2269), **Hyak Wilderness Adventures** (Vancouver, tel. 604/734–8622), and **Canadian River Expeditions** (Vancouver, tel. 604/738–4449).

Sailing Several charter companies offer a cruise-and-learn vacation, usually to the Gulf Islands. The five-day trip is a crash course teaching the ins and outs of sailing. **Sea Wing Sailing Group, Ltd.** (Granville Island, tel. 604/669–0840) and **Pacific Quest** (Granville Island, tel. 604/682–2205) offer this package.

Windsurfing Boards can be rented at **Windsure Windsurfing School** (Jericho Beach, tel. 604/224–0615) and **Windmaster** (English Bay Beach, tel. 604/685–7245).

Spectator Sports

The **Vancouver Canucks** (tel. 604/254–5141) of the National Hockey League play in the Coliseum October–April. The **Canadians** (tel. 604/872–5232) play baseball in an old-time outdoor stadium in the Pacific Coast League. Their season runs April–September. The **B.C. Lions** (tel. 604/585–3323) football team scrimmages at the B.C. Place Stadium downtown June–November. Tickets are available from Ticketmaster (tel. 604/280–4444).

Beaches

An almost continuous string of beaches runs from Stanley Park to the University of British Columbia. Children and hardy swimmers can take the cool water, but most others prefer to sunbathe; these beaches are sandy, with grassy areas running alongside. Note that liquor is prohibited in parks and on beaches. For information on beaches, call the **Parks Department of the City of Vancouver** (tel. 604/681–1141).

Kitsilano Beach. Kits Beach, with a lifeguard, is the busiest of them all—transistor radios, volleyball games, and sleek young people are ever present. The part of the beach nearest the Maritime Museum is the quietest. Facilities include a playground, tennis courts, heated saltwater pool (good for serious swimmers to toddlers), concession stands, and many nearby restaurants and cafés.

Point Grey Beaches. Jericho, Locarno, and Spanish Banks begin at the end of Point Grey Road. This string of beaches has a huge expanse of sand, especially in the summer and at low tide. The shallow water here is warmed slightly by the sun and the sand and so is best for swimming. Farther out, toward Spanish Banks, you'll find the beach becomes less crowded, but the last concession stand and washrooms are at Locarno. If you keep walking along the beach just past Point Grey, you'll hit Wreck Beach, Vancouver's nude beach. It is also accessible from Marine Drive at the university, but there is a fairly steep climb from the beach to the road.

West End Beaches. Second Beach and Third Beach, along Beach Drive in Stanley Park, are large family beaches. Second Beach has a guarded saltwater pool. Both have concession stands and washrooms. Farther along Beach Drive, at the foot of Jervis Street, is Sunset Beach, a surprisingly quiet beach, considering the location. A lifeguard is on duty, but there are no facilities.

Dining

Among other allures, experiencing Vancouver's diverse gastronomical pleasures makes a visit to the city worthwhile. Restaurants appear throughout Vancouver—from the bustling downtown area to trendy beachside neighborhoods—making the diversity of the establishments' surroundings as enticing as the succulent cuisine they serve. A new wave of Chinese immigration and Japanese tourism has brought a proliferation of upscale Chinese and Japanese restaurants, offering dishes that would be at home in their own leading cities. Restaurants featuring Pacific Northwest fare—including homegrown regional favorites such as salmon and oysters, accompanied by British Columbia and Washington State wines—have become some of the city's leading attractions.

Highly recommended restaurants in each price category are indicated by a star ★.

Category	*Cost
Very Expensive	over $40
Expensive	$30—$40
Moderate	$20—$30
Inexpensive	under $20

per person, including appetizer, entrée and dessert; excluding drinks, service, and sales tax

American **Isadora's.** Not only does Isadora's offer good coffee, a menu that ranges from samosas to lox and bagels, and children's specials, but there is also an inside play area packed with toys. Rest rooms with changing tables accommodate families. In the summer, the restaurant opens onto Granville Island's waterpark, so kids can entertain themselves. Service can be slow, but Isadora's staff is friendly. *1540 Old Bridge St., Granville Island, tel. 604/681–8816. Reservations required for 6 or more. Dress: casual. MC, V. Closed dinner Mon. Sept.–May. Inexpensive.*

Nazarre BBQ Chicken. The best barbecued chicken in several hundred miles comes from this funky storefront on Commercial Drive. Owner Gerry Moutal massages his chickens for tenderness before he puts them on the rotisserie and bastes them in a mixture of rum and spices. Chicken comes with roasted potatoes and a choice of mild, hot, extra hot, or hot garlic sauce. You can eat in, at one of four rickety tables, or take out. *1408 Commercial Dr., tel. 604/251–1844. No reservations. Dress: casual. No credit cards. Inexpensive.*

Cambodian/ **Phnom Penh Restaurant.** A block away from the bustle of Kee-
Vietnamese fer Street, the Phnom Penh is part of a small cluster of South-
★ east Asian shops on the fringes of Chinatown. Simple, pleasant decor abounds: arborite tables, potted plants, and framed views of Ankor Wat on the walls. The hospitable staff serves unusually robust Vietnamese fare, including crisp, peppery garlic prawns fried in the shell and slices of beef crusted with ground salt and pepper mixed in the warm beef salad. The decor in the new Broadway location is fancier and the food is every bit as good as at East Georgia Street. *244 E. Georgia St.,*

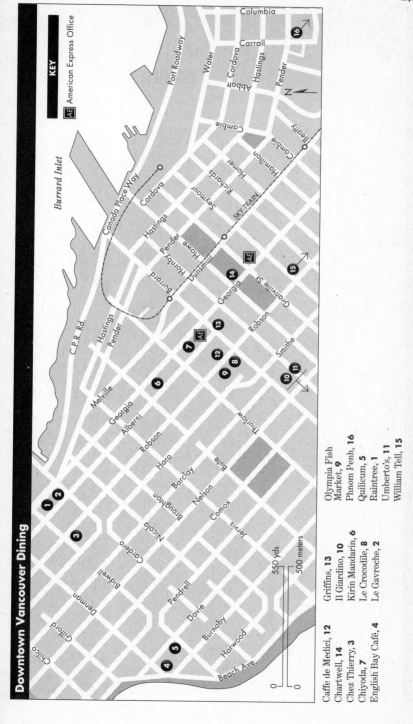

Downtown Vancouver Dining

Caffe de Medici, **12**
Chartwell, **14**
Chez Thierry, **3**
Chiyoda, **7**
English Bay Café, **4**

Griffins, **13**
Il Giardino, **10**
Kirin Mandarin, **6**
Le Crocodile, **8**
Le Gavroche, **2**

Olympia Fish
Market, **9**
Phnom Penh, **16**
Quilicum, **5**
Raintree, **1**
Umberto's, **11**
William Tell, **15**

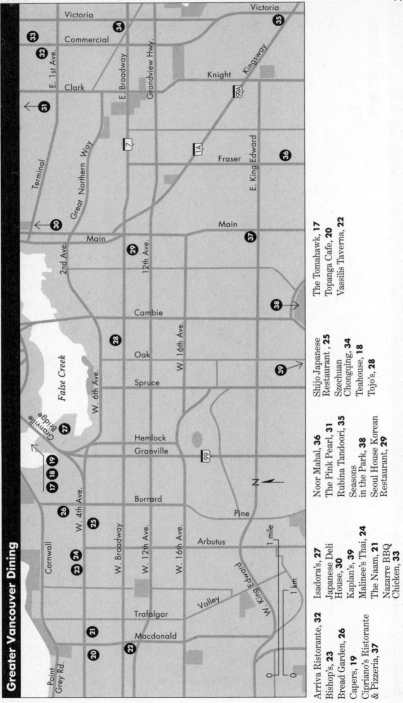

Greater Vancouver Dining

244

Victoria
Commercial
E. 1st Ave.
Clark
Terminal
Great Northern Way
2nd Ave.
Main
12th Ave.
Cambie
Oak
W. 16th Ave.
Spruce
False Creek
W. 6th Ave.
Granville Bridge
Hemlock
Granville
Burrard
Pine
Arbutus
Cornwall
W. 4th Ave.
W. Broadway
W. 12th Ave.
W. 16th Ave.
Trafalgar
Macdonald
Point Grey Rd.
Valley
W. King Edward

Victoria
E. Broadway
Grandview Hwy.
Knight
Kingsway
Fraser
E. King Edward
Main

N

1 mile
1 km
0
0

Arriva Ristorante, 32
Bishop's, 23
Bread Garden, 26
Capers, 19
Cipriano's Ristorante & Pizzeria, 37

Isadora's, 27
Japanese Deli House, 30
Kaplan's, 39
Malinee's Thai, 24
The Naam, 21
Nazarre BBQ Chicken, 33

Noor Mahal, 36
The Pink Pearl, 31
Rubina Tandoori, 35
Seasons in the Park, 38
Seoul House Korean Restaurant, 29

Shijo Japanese Restaurant, 25
Szechuan Chongqing, 34
Teahouse, 18
Tojo's, 28

The Tomahawk, 17
Topanga Cafe, 20
Vassilis Taverna, 22

tel. 604/682–5777; 955 W. Broadway, tel. 604/734–8898. No reservations for lunch; reservations for 5 or more only for dinner. Dress: casual. DC, MC. Closed Tues. Inexpensive.

Chinese ★ **Kirin Mandarin Restaurant.** Kirin, located two blocks from most of the major downtown hotels, presents attentively served Chinese food in posh, elegant surroundings. Live fish in tanks set into the slate green walls remind one of an aquarium displayed in a lavishly decorated home. Drawn from a smattering of northern Chinese cuisines, dishes include Shanghai-style smoked eel, Peking duck, and Szechuan hot-and-spicy scallops. *1166 Alberni St., tel. 604/682–8833. Reservations advised. Dress: neat but casual. AE, DC, MC, V. Moderate.*

★ **The Pink Pearl.** In the world of Cantonese restaurants, biggest may very well be best: This 650-seat restaurant certainly wins the prize in this city. The huge, noisy room features tanks of live seafood—crab, shrimp, geoduck, oysters, abalone, rock cod, lobsters, and scallops. Menu highlights include clams in black bean sauce, crab sautéed with five spices (a spicy dish sometimes translated as crab with peppery salt), and Pink Pearl's version of crispy-skinned chicken. Arrive early for dim sum on the weekend if you don't want to be caught in the lineup. *1132 E. Hastings St., tel.604/253–4316. Reservations advised. Dress: casual. AE, DC, MC, V. Moderate.*

Szechuan Chongqing. Although fancier Szechuan restaurants can be found, the continued popularity of this unpretentious, white-tablecloth restaurant in a revamped fried-chicken franchise speaks for itself. Try the Szechuan-style fried green beans, steamed and tossed with spiced ground pork, or the Chongqing chicken—a boneless chicken served on a bed of spinach cooked in dry heat until crisp, giving it the texture of dried seaweed and a salty, rich, and nutty taste. *2495 Victoria Dr., tel. 604/254–7434. Reservations advised. Dress: casual. AE, MC, V. Inexpensive.*

Continental ★ **Chartwell.** Named after Sir Winston Churchill's country home (a painting of which hangs over the green marble fireplace), the flagship dining room at the Four Seasons Hotel (*see* Lodging, *below*) looks like an upper-class British men's club. Floor-to-ceiling dark wood paneling, deep leather chairs to sink back in and sip claret, plus a quiet setting make this the city's top spot for a power lunch. The chefs cook robust, inventive Continental food with lighter offerings and a variety of low-calorie, low-fat entrées. A salad of smoked loin of wild boar comes sprinkled with hazelnuts; Wiener schnitzel with roast potatoes is a favorite. Conclude the meal with port and Stilton. *791 W. Georgia St., tel. 604/844–6715. Reservations advised. Jacket suggested. AE, DC, MC, V. Closed weekends for lunch. Expensive.*

Seasons in the Park. Seasons has a commanding view over the park gardens to the city lights and the mountains beyond. A comfortable room with lots of light wood, white tablecloths, and deep-pile carpeting, this restaurant in Queen Elizabeth Park serves a conservative Continental menu with standards such as grilled salmon with fresh mint and roast duck with Bing cherry sauce. *Queen Elizabeth Park, tel. 604/874–8008. Reservations advised. Dress: neat but casual. AE, MC, V. Closed Christmas Day. Expensive.*

★ **The Teahouse Restaurant at Ferguson Point.** The best of the Stanley Park restaurants is perfectly poised for watching sunsets over the water, especially from its newer wing, a glassed-in room that conveys a conservatorylike ambience. Although the teahouse has a less innovative menu than its sister restaurant—Seasons in the Park—certain specialties such as the cream of carrot soup, duck in cassis, and the perfectly grilled fish don't need any meddling. For dessert, there's baked Alaska—a natural for this restaurant. *Ferguson Point in Stanley Park, tel. 604/669–3281. Reservations required. Dress: neat but casual. AE, MC, V. Closed Christmas Day. Expensive.*

The William Tell. Silver underliners, embossed linen napkins, and a silver flower vase on each table set the tone of Swiss luxury. The William Tell's well-established reputation for excellent Continental food continues at its quarters on the main floor of the Georgian Court Hotel, located 10 minutes from the central business district. Chef Pierre Dubrelle, a member of the gold medal–winning Canadian team at the 1988 Culinary Olympics, offers locally raised pheasant with glazed grapes and red wine sauce, sautéed veal sweetbreads with red onion marmalade and marsala sauce, and the Swiss specialty *Buendnerfleisch* (paper-thin slices of air-dried beef). Professional and discreet service contributes to the restaurant's excellence. *765 Beatty St., tel. 604/688–3504. Reservations advised. Jacket required at dinner. AE, DC, MC, V. Expensive.*

★ **English Bay Café.** Downstairs, the English Bay Café is a noisy bistro serving eggs Benedict, pasta, and fish specialties such as snapper or clam-and-sausage pasta. Upstairs, in the more serious dining room, you'll find the chef's fondness for venison and racks of lamb. Regardless of the level, however, when you look out the windows, it's all the same: With English Bay just two lanes of traffic away, you're guaranteed a glorious view of the sunset. Both bars are substantial; the bistro offers a large choice of imported beers. Valet parking is available and well worth the money. *1795 Beach Ave., tel. 604/669–2225. Reservations required. Dress: casual downstairs; neat but casual upstairs. AE, DC, MC, V. Moderate.*

Deli/Bakery **The Bread Garden Bakery, Café & Espresso Bar.** What began as a croissant bakery has taken over two neighboring stores and is now the ultimate Kitsilano 24-hour hangout. Salads, smoked salmon pizzas, quiches, elaborate cakes and pies, giant muffins, and cappuccino bring a steady stream of the young and fashionable. The Bread Garden To Go, next door, serves over-the-counter, but you may still be subjected to an irritatingly long wait in line; things just don't happen fast here. *1880 W. 1st Ave., tel. 604/ 738–6684; 812 Bute St., tel. 604/688–3213. No reservations. Dress: casual. MC, V. Inexpensive.*

★ **Kaplan's Deli, Restaurant and Bakery.** Tucked into a minimall on Oak Street (the road that leads to the Tsawwassen ferries and Seattle), Kaplan's is the traveler's last chance for authentic Jewish deli food before leaving town. Eat in at booths, or take your chopped liver, chopped herring, lox, and homemade corned beef with you. The bakery makes justly famous cinnamon buns. *5775 Oak St., tel. 604/263–2625. No reservations. Dress: casual. MC, V. Closed Jewish holidays. Inexpensive.*

East Indian **Rubina Tandoori.** If one must single out the best East Indian
★ food in the city, then Rubina Tandoori, 20 minutes from downtown, ranks as a top contender. The large menu spans most of the subcontinent's cuisines, and the especially popular *chevda* (East Indian salty snack) gets shipped to fans all over North

America. Maître d' Shaffeen Jamal has a phenomenal memory for faces. Nonsmokers get the smaller, funkier back room with the paintings of coupling gods and goddesses; smokers get the big, upholstered banquettes in the new room. *1962 Kingsway, tel. 604/874–3621. Reservations advised on weekends. Dress: casual. MC, V. Closed lunch and Sun. Moderate.*

Noor Mahal. The only Lower Mainland restaurant that specializes in South Indian food, the Noor Mahal provides good-size portions at a reasonable price in authentic surroundings. The pink walls help to create the light and airy decor. Try a *dosa*—a lacy pancake made from bean, rice, and semolina flour, stuffed with curried potatoes, shrimp, or chicken—for lunch. Owners Susan and Paul Singh double as staff, so service can be slow and harried during busy periods. *4354 Fraser St., tel. 604/873–9263. Reservations advised on weekends. Dress: casual. AE, MC, V. Closed lunch. Inexpensive.*

French **Le Gavroche.** Time has stood still in this charming turn-of-the-
★ century house, where a woman dining with a man will be offered a menu without prices. Featuring classic French cooking, lightened—but by no means reduced—to nouvelle cuisine, Le Gavroche's menu also includes simple listings such as smoked salmon with blinis and sour cream. Other options may be as complex as smoked pheasant breast on a puree of celeriac, shallots, and wine with a light truffle sauce. The excellent wine list stresses Bordeaux. No reservations are necessary after 9:30, when the late-dessert menu is offered. Tables by the front window promise mountains-and-water views. *1616 Alberni St., tel. 604/685–3924. Reservations advised on weekends. Jacket and tie advised. AE, MC, V. Closed lunch, Sun., and holidays. Expensive.*

Chez Thierry. This cozy bistro on the Stanley Park end of Robson Street adds pizzazz to a celebration: Owner Thierry Damilano stylishly slashes open champagne bottles with a sword on request. The country-style French cooking emphasizes seafood. Try watercress and smoked salmon salad; fresh tuna grilled with artichokes, garlic, and tomatoes; and apple tarte Tatin for dessert. During the week the intimate dining room promises a relaxing meal; on the weekend, however, with every one of the 16 tables jammed, the restaurant gets noisy. *1674 Robson St., tel. 604/688–0919. Reservations required on weekends. Dress: casual. AE, DC, MC, V. Closed lunch and Dec. 24–26. Moderate.*

★ **Le Crocodile.** Why do people want to sit packed tighter than sardines in this tiny bistro? Because chef Michael Jacob serves extremely well cooked, simple food at very moderate prices. His Alsatian background shines with the caramelly, sweet onion tart. Anything that involves innards is superb, and even old standards such as duck à l'orange are worth ordering here. The one flaw? A small, overpriced wine list. *909 Burrard St., tel. 604/669–4298. Reservations required. Dress casual. AE, DC, MC, V. Closed Sat. lunch and Sun. Moderate.*

Greek **Vassilis Taverna.** The menu in this family-run restaurant, located in the heart of the city's small Greek community, is almost as conventional as the decor: checked tablecloths and mandatory paintings of white fishing villages and the blue Aegean Sea. At Vassilis, though, even standards become memorable due to the flawless preparation. The house specialty is a deceptively simple *kotopoulo* (a half-chicken, pounded flat, herbed, and charbroiled); the lamb fricassee with artichoke hearts and broad beans in an egg-lemon sauce is more complicated, though not necessarily better. Save room for a *navarino*, a creamy custard square topped with whipped cream and ground nuts. *2884 W. Broadway, tel. 604/733–3231. Reservations advised on weekends. Dress: casual. AE, DC, MC, V. Closed Mon. and lunch Sat. and Sun. Moderate.*

Health Food **Capers.** Hidden in the back of the most lavishly handsome
★ health food store in the Lower Mainland, Capers (open for breakfast, lunch, and dinner) drips with earth-mother chic: wood tables, potted plants, and heady smells from the store's bakery. Breakfast starts weekdays at 7:30, weekends at 8. Eggs and bacon? Sure, but Capers serves free-range eggs, as well as bacon without additives. Feather-light blueberry pancakes crammed with berries star here. The view of the water compensates for service that can be slow and forgetful. *2496 Marine Dr., W. Vancouver, tel. 604/925–3316. No reservations. Dress: casual. MC, V. Closed dinner Sun. Inexpensive.*

The Naam Restaurant. Vancouver's oldest alternative restaurant is now open 24 hours, so those needing to satisfy a late-night tofu-burger craving, rest easy. The Naam has left its caffeine- and alcohol-free days behind and now serves wine, beer, cappuccino, and wicked chocolate desserts, along with the vegetarian stir-fries. Wood tables and kitchen chairs make for a homey atmosphere. On warm summer evenings, the outdoor courtyard at the back of the restaurant welcomes diners. *2724 W. 4th Ave., tel. 604/738–7151. Reservations required for 6 or more. Dress: casual. MC, V. Inexpensive.*

Italian **Caffe de Medici.** It takes shifting gears as you leave the stark
★ concrete walls of the Robson Galleria behind and step into this elegant restaurant with its ornate molded ceilings, rich green velvet curtains and chair coverings, and portraits of the de Medici family. But after a little wine, an evening's exposure to courtly waiters, and a superb meal, you may begin to wish the outside world conformed more closely to this peaceful environment. Although an enticing antipasto table sits in the center of the room, consider the *Bresaola* (air-dried beef marinated in olive oil, lemon, and pepper) as a worthwhile appetizer. Try the rack of lamb in a mint, mustard, and Martini & Rossi sauce. Any of the pastas is a safe bet. *1025 Robson St., tel. 604/669–9322. Reservations advised. Jacket advised. AE, DC, MC, V. Closed lunch Sat. and Sun. Expensive.*

Il Giardino di Umberto, Umberto's. First came Umberto's, a Florentine restaurant serving classic northern Italian food, installed in a century-old Vancouver home at the foot of Hornby Street. Then, next door, Umberto Menghi built Il Giardino, a sunny, light-splashed restaurant styled after a Tuscan house. This restaurant features braided breast of pheasant with polenta and reindeer fillet with crushed peppercorn sauce. Il Giardino attracts a regular young, moneyed crowd, while Umberto's is more quiet and sedate. Fish is treated either Italian style—rainbow trout grilled and served with sun-dried tomatoes, black olives, and pine-nuts—or with a taste of the Far East, as in yellow-fin tuna grilled with wasabi butter. *Il Giardino, 1382 Hornby St., tel. 604/669–2422. Umberto's, 1380 Hornby St., tel. 604/687–6316. Reservations advised. Dress: neat but casual. AE, DC, MC, V. Umberto's closed lunch and Sun., Mon. Il Giardino closed lunch Sat. and Sun. Expensive.*

Arriva Ristorante. Commercial Drive Italian restaurants, like Chinese restaurants in Chinatown, are best looked at with a skeptical eye. The best of the breed are elsewhere, and what's left is often found cranking out North Americanized travesties of the home country's food. Arriva is one Little Italy restaurant that's worth the drive, and it's a welcome find if you've spent the day shopping in Italian groceries. There's a version of spaghetti and meatballs on the menu, ziti with spicy squid sauce, and a fusili with wild game—"Bambi and Bugs Bunny," as the waiters have affectionately coined it. The antipasto plate includes a heaping order of octopus, shrimp, roasted red peppers, cheese, sausage, and fat lima beans in an herby marinade. Don't miss the orange sherbet served in a hollowed-out orange for dessert. *1537 Commercial Dr., tel. 604/251–1177. Reservations advised. Dress: casual. AE, DC, MC, V. Closed lunch Sat. and Sun. Moderate.*

Griffin's. Sunday brunch here was rated as top entertainment in 1992 by the daily newspaper, *The Province.* The ambience is fun, energetic, and kid-oriented: Kids in aprons (provided by the restaurant) whip up their own pancakes and take turns churning ice cream for dessert. The rest of the week the emphasis is on the adult crowd. This brasserie uniquely blends the charm of old Italy with the flair of sophisticated design and fresh, regional ingredients. Squash-yellow walls, bold black-and-white tiles, and splashy food art by Mary Frances Tuck enhance Griffin's liveliness. The hotel's gargoyles are repeated in stenciling on the walls and in the red, yellow, and green carpet. The brasserie features an open kichen that prepares inspirational cuisine, including buffet selections such as convict bread, a round loaf stuffed with soft, fresh goat cheese, olives, tomatoes, and peppers in olive oil; smoked salmon; chicken pasta al pesto; and baked Pacific black cod with herbed crumbs. There's a pizza buffet on Saturday. *900 W. Georgia St., tel. 604/684–3131. Reservations advised. Dress: casual but neat. AE, DC, MC, V. Moderate*

Cipriano's Ristorante & Pizzeria. Formerly a Greek pizza parlor, Cipriano's has been transformed into an Italian restaurant, with green-white-and-red walls representing the Italian flag, Mama-mia!—inexpensive and hearty Italian food is the mainstay here, including good pizza, even better pasta, and the "Pappa" lasagna. *3995 Main St., tel. 604/879–0020. Reservations accepted. Dress: casual. V. Closed lunch and Mon. Inexpensive.*

Japanese
★

Tojo's. Hidekazu Tojo is a sushi-making legend here. His handsome blond-wood tatami rooms, on the second floor of a new green-glass tower in the hospital district on West Broadway, provide proper ambience for intimate dining, but Tojo's 10-seat sushi bar stands as the centerpiece. With Tojo presiding, it is a convivial place for dinner and offers a ringside seat for watching the creation of edible art. Although tempura and teriyaki dinners will satisfy, the seasonal menu is more exciting. In October, ask for *dobbin mushi,* a soup made from pine mushrooms that's served in a teapot. In spring, try sushi made from scallops and pink cherry blossoms. *777 W. Broadway, No. 202, tel. 604/872–8050. Reservations advised on weekends. Dress: neat but casual. AE, DC, MC, V. Closed lunch and Sun.; Dec. 24–26. Expensive.*

Chiyoda. The robata bar curves like an oversize sushi bar through Chiyoda's main room: On one side are the customers and an array of flat baskets full of the day's offerings; on the other side are the robata chefs and grills. There are 35 choices of things to grill, from squid, snapper, and oysters to eggplant, mushrooms, onions, and potatoes. The finished dishes, dressed with sake, soy, or *ponzu* sauce, are dramatically passed over on the end of a long wooden paddle. If Japanese food means only sushi and tempura to you, check this out. *1050 Alberni St., tel. 604/688–5050. Reservations accepted. Dress: casual. AE, MC, V. Closed lunch Sat. and Sun.; closed Sun. off-season. Moderate.*

Shijo Japanese Restaurant. Shijo has an excellent and very large sushi bar, a smaller robata bar, tatami rooms, and a row of tables overlooking bustling Fourth Avenue. The epitome of modern urban Japanese chic is conveyed through the jazz music, handsome lamps with a patinated bronze finish, and lots of black wood. Count on creatively prepared sushi, eggplant *dengaku* topped with light and dark miso paste and broiled, and shiitake *foil yaki* (fresh shiitake mushrooms cooked in foil with *ponzu* sauce). *1926 W. 4th Ave., tel. 604/732–4676. Reservations advised. Dress: casual. AE, MC, V. Closed lunch, Sat. and Sun. Moderate.*

Japanese Deli House. The least expensive sushi in town is served in this high-ceilinged room on the main floor of a turn-of-the-century building on Powell Street, once the heart of Vancouver's Japantown. Along with the standard sushi-bar menu, Japanese Deli House makes a pungent but tender, hot ginger squid appetizer from baby squid caught off the Thai coast, and a geoduck appetizer in mayonnaise worth wandering off the beaten path for. The food is especially fresh and good if you can make it an early lunch: Nigiri sushi and sushi rolls are made at 11 AM for the 11:30 opening. *381 Powell St., tel. 604/681–6484. No reservations. Dress: casual. No credit cards. Closed lunch Mon. Inexpensive.*

Korean **Seoul House Korean Restaurant.** The shining star in a desperately ugly section of East Broadway, Seoul House is a bright restaurant, decorated in Japanese style, that serves a full menu of Japanese and Korean food. The best bet is the Korean barbecue, which you cook at your table. A barbecue dinner of marinated beef, pork, chicken, or fish comes complete with a half dozen side dishes—*kim chee* (Korea's national pickle), salads, stir-fried rice, and pickled vegetables—as well as soup and rice. Service can be chaotic in this very popular restaurant. *36 E. Broadway, tel. 604/874–4131. Reservations advised. Dress: casual. MC, V. Closed lunch Sun. Inexpensive.*

Mexican **Topanga Cafe.** Arrive before 6:30 or after 8 PM to avoid waiting in line for this 40-seat Kitsilano classic. The California-Mexican food hasn't changed much in the 15 years the Topanga has been dishing up fresh salsa and homemade tortilla chips. Quantities are still huge and prices are low. Kids can color blank menu covers while waiting for food; a hundred or more of the clientele's best efforts are framed and on the walls. *2904 4th Ave., tel. 604/ 733–3713. No reservations. Dress: casual. MC, V. Closed Sun. Inexpensive.*

Nouvelle **Bishop's.** John Bishop established Vancouver's most influen-
★ tial restaurant in 1987 by serving West Coast Continental cuisine with an emphasis on British Columbia seafood. Penne with grilled eggplant, roasted peppers, and basil pasta cohabit the menu with medallions of venison, rack of lamb, and beef tenderloin. The small white rooms—their only ornament some splashy, expressionist paintings—are favored by Pierre Trudeau and by Robert De Niro when he's on location in Vancouver. *2183 W. 4th Ave., tel. 604/738–2025. Reservations re-*

quired. Dress: casual. AE, DC, MC, V. Closed 1st week in Jan., lunch Sat. and Sun. Expensive.

Pacific Northwest **Quilicum.** Only a few blocks from English Bay, this downstairs "longhouse" serves the original Northwest Coast cuisine: bannock bread, baked sweet potato with hazelnuts, alder-grilled salmon, and soapberries for dessert. Try the authentic but odd dish—oolichan grease—that's prepared from candlefish. Native music is piped in, and Northwest Coast masks (for sale) peer out from the walls. *1724 Davie St., tel. 604/681–7044. Reservations advised. Dress: casual. AE, MC, V. Closed lunch Sat.– Tues. Moderate.*

★ **The Raintree.** This cool, spacious restaurant offers a local menu and wine list, which features vintages from British Columbia, Washington, and Oregon. Raintree bakes its own bread, makes luxurious soups, and offers old favorites such as a slab of apple pie for dessert. With main courses, which change daily depending on market availability, the kitchen, focusing on healthy choices, teeters between willfully eccentric and exceedingly simple. Specials could include Queen Charlotte abalone and side-stripe shrimps, stir-fried with scallions and spinach in chamomile essence; and grilled lamb chops with a mint and pear puree. Leon's Bar and Grill, on the ground floor, stocks local beers and a respectable number of single-malt scotches. The pub-food menu includes organic-beef burgers and vegetarian chili. The $14 fixed-price Sunday brunch features ricotta and apple-stuffed French toast, sockeye salmon hash, and apricot-hazelnut pancakes, plus several other courses. *1630 Alberni St., tel. 604/688–5570. Reservations advised on weekends. Dress: casual. AE, DC, MC, V. Closed lunch Sat. and Dec. 24–26. Moderate.*

The Tomahawk. North Vancouver was mostly trees 66 years ago, when the Tomahawk first opened. Over the years, the original hamburger stand grew and mutated into part Northwest Coast Indian kitsch museum, part gift shop, and part restaurant. Renowned for its Yukon breakfast—five slices of back bacon, two eggs, hash browns, and toast—the Tomahawk also serves gigantic muffins, excellent French toast, and pancakes. The menu switches to oysters, trout, and burgers named after Indian chiefs for lunch and dinner. *1550 Philip Ave., tel. 604/988– 2612. No reservations. Dress: casual. AE, MC, V. Inexpensive.*

Seafood **Olympia Fish Market and Oyster Co. Ltd.** Some of the city's best fish-and-chips are fried in this tiny shop located behind a fish store in the middle of the Robson Street shopping district. The choice is halibut, cod, prawns, calamari, and whatever's on special in the store, served with genuine—never frozen— french fries. *1094 Robson St., tel. 604/685–0716. No reservations. Dress: casual. DC, V. Inexpensive.*

Thai **Malinee's Thai.** The city's most consistently interesting Thai
★ food can be found in this typically Southeast Asian–style room, tapestries adorning the walls. The owners, two Canadians who lived several years in Thailand, can give you detailed descriptions of every dish on the menu. Steamed fish with ginger, pickled plums, and red chili sauce is on the regular menu; a steamed whole red snapper marinated in oyster sauce, ginger, cilantro, red pepper, and lime juice is a special worth ordering when available. *2153 W. 4th Ave., tel. 604/737–0097. Reservations advised. Dress: casual. AE, DC, MC, V. Closed lunch. Moderate.*

Lodging

Lodging has become a major business for Vancouver, a fairly young city that hosts a lot of Asian businesspeople who are used to an above-average level of service. Although by some standards pricey, properties here are highly competitive, and you can expect the service to reflect this trend.

Highly recommended lodgings in each price category are indicated by a star ★.

Category	Cost*
Very Expensive	over $180
Expensive	$140–$180
Moderate	$90–$139
Inexpensive	under $90

All prices are for a standard double room for two, excluding 10% provincial accommodation tax, 15% service charge, and 7% GST.

Very Expensive **Four Seasons.** This 28-story hotel is adjacent to the Vancouver Stock Exchange and is attached to the Pacific Centre shopping mall. Standard rooms are not large; corner deluxe or deluxe Four Seasons rooms are recommended. Expect tasteful and stylish decor in the rooms and hallways, providing a calm mood despite the bustling hotel. A huge sun deck and indoor-outdoor pool are part of the complete health club facilities. Service is outstanding, and the Four Seasons has all the amenities. The formal dining room, Chartwell (*see* Dining, *above*), is one of the best in the city. *791 W. Georgia St., V6C 2T4, tel. 604/689–9333; in Canada, 800/268–6282; in the U.S., 800/332–3442; fax 604/844–6744. 317 rooms, 68 suites. Facilities: restaurant, café, bars, indoor-outdoor pool, sun deck, weight room, aerobics classes, sauna, Jacuzzi, ping-pong. AE, DC, MC, V.*

★ **Le Meridien.** This property feels more like an exclusive guest house than a large hotel: Its lobby has sumptuously thick carpets, enormous displays of flowers, and a newsstand situated discreetly down the hall. The rooms are even better, furnished with rich, dark woods reminiscent of 19th-century France. Bathrobes, slippers, and umbrellas in the room attest to the attention to detail here. Despite the size of this hotel, the Le Meridien in Vancouver has achieved and maintained a level of intimacy and exclusivity. The **Café Fleuri** serves one of the best Sunday brunches in town (plus a chocolate buffet on Thursday, Friday, and Saturday evenings), and **Le Club,** a fine French restaurant, is a special-occasion place. Lots of leather, dark wood, wingback chairs, and a fireplace give the **Gerard** bar the feel of a refined gentlemen's club. *845 Burrard St., V6Z 2K6, tel. 604/682–5511, fax 604/682–5513. 350 doubles, 47 suites. Facilities: restaurant, café, bar, business center, health club with pool, Jacuzzi, sauna, steam room, tanning bed, masseuse, salon, weights, exercise equipment, adjoining apartment hotel. AE, DC, MC, V.*

★ **Pan Pacific.** Canada Place sits on a pier right by the financial district and houses the luxurious Pan Pacific Hotel (built in 1986 for the Expo), the Vancouver Trade and Convention Centre, and a cruise-ship terminal. The lobby has a dramatic three-

Vancouver Lodging

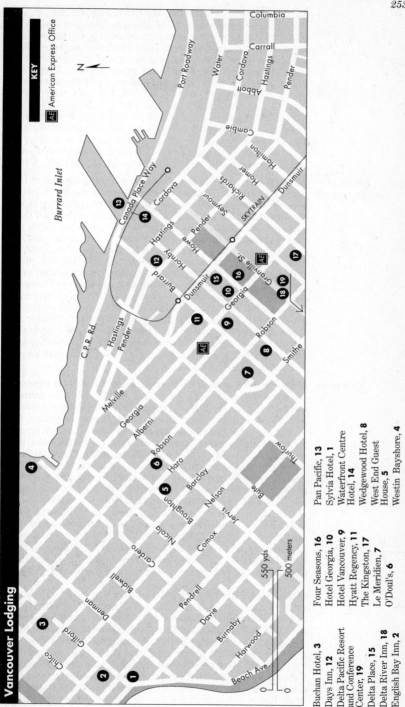

KEY

AE American Express Office

N

Burrard Inlet

Buchan Hotel, **3**
Days Inn, **12**
Delta Pacific Resort
  and Conference
  Center, **19**
Delta Place, **15**
Delta River Inn, **18**
English Bay Inn, **2**

Four Seasons, **16**
Hotel Georgia, **10**
Hotel Vancouver, **9**
Hyatt Regency, **11**
The Kingston, **17**
Le Meridien, **7**
O'Doul's, **6**

Pan Pacific, **13**
Sylvia Hotel, **1**
Waterfront Centre
  Hotel, **14**
Wedgewood Hotel, **8**
West End Guest
  House, **5**
Westin Bayshore, **4**

story atrium with a waterfall, and the lounge, restaurant, and café all have huge expanses of glass, so that you are rarely without a harbor view or mountain backdrop. Earthtones and Japanese detail give the rooms an understated elegance. Make sure you get a room that looks out on the water. The health club has a $15 fee that's well worth the price. The Pan Pacific is a grand, luxurious, busy hotel, but it is not a pick for an intimate weekend getaway. *300–999 Canada Pl., V6C 3B5, tel. 604/662–8211; in Canada, 800/663–1515; in the U.S., 800/937–1515; fax 604/685–8690. 468 doubles, 40 suites. Facilities: 3 restaurants, bar, health club with indoor track, sauna, steam room, state-of-the-art aerobics equipment, weights, massage and Shiatsu, sports lounge with wide-screen TV, squash, racquetball, and paddle-tennis courts, heated outdoor pool. AE, DC, MC, V.*

**Expensive–
Very Expensive** **Westin Bayshore.** This hotel is the closest thing to a resort that you'll find in the downtown area. Because the Bayshore is perched right on the best part of the harbor, because it is a five-minute walk from Stanley Park, because of the truly fabulous view, and because of its huge outdoor pool, sun deck, and grassy areas, it is the perfect place to stay during the summer, especially for a family. The tower is the newer section, so rooms there are better furnished and larger and offer the best views of the water. The café is okay, and Trader Vic's, the hotel's dining room, is a pleasant, Polynesian-style experience. There are also several neighborhood restaurants. *1601 W. Georgia St., V6G 2V4, tel. 604/682–3377 or 800/228–3000; fax 604/691–6959. 481 doubles, 38 suites, 2 floors for the disabled. Facilities: restaurant, café, bars, free shuttle service downtown, bicycle rentals, marina with fishing and sailing charters, health club with indoor and outdoor pools, Jacuzzi, sun deck, masseur, sauna, pool table. AE, DC, MC, V.*

Expensive **Delta Pacific Resort & Conference Center.** It's not a view or a shoreline that makes this place (five minutes from the airport) a resort, it's the facilities on the 12-acre site: three swimming pools (one indoor), four all-year tennis courts with a pro (matching list for partners), an outdoor fitness circuit, squash courts, aqua-exercise classes, outdoor volleyball nets, golf practice nets, a play center for children, summer camps for 5- to 12-year-olds, and a playground. In spite of the hotel's enormity, the atmosphere is casual and friendly. There are two guest-room towers and a few low-rise buildings for convention facilities. The resort was renovated in 1991–92, so guest rooms are modern with contemporary decor and pleasant color schemes. The Japanese restaurant is expensive and not the best value. *10251 St. Edwards Dr., V6X 2M9, tel. 604/278–9611; in Canada, 800/268–1133; in the U.S., 800/877–1133; fax 604/276–1122. 460 doubles, 4 suites. Facilities: restaurant, café, bar, shuttle to airport and shopping center, meeting rooms. AE, DC, MC, V.*

Delta Place. This 18-story hotel was built in 1985 by the luxurious Hong Kong Mandarin chain but was sold to Delta Hotels in 1987. Although the rates went down, the surroundings did not change: The lobby is still restrained and tasteful—one has to look for the registration desk. A slight Oriental theme is given to the deluxe furnishings, and dark, rich mahogany is everywhere. Most rooms have small balconies, and the studio suites are recommended since they are much roomier and only slightly more expensive than a standard room. Continental breakfast is included with your stay. The business center has secretarial services, work stations, cellular phones for rent, and small meeting rooms. The restaurant and bar are adequate and the location is perfect; the business and shopping district is a five-minute walk away. *645 Howe St., V6C 2Y9, tel. 604/687–1122; in Canada, 800/268–1133; in the U.S., 800/877–1133; fax 604/643–7267. 181 doubles, 16 suites. Facilities: restaurant, bar, squash and racquetball courts, lap pool, weight room. AE, DC, MC, V.*

Delta River Inn. This hotel, on the edge of the Fraser River, is two minutes from the airport. Rooms on the south side get the best view. Although renovations began in 1990, the River Inn still has a way to go to compete with others in the price range: The rooms here just don't have the style and pizzazz of the others. The hotel's draw lies in its proximity to the airport and its attachment to the marina, which organizes fishing charters so there are things for guests to do here. Food does not seem to be a priority with Delta. *3500 Cessena Dr., V7B 1C7, tel. 604/278–1241; in Canada, 800/268–1133; in the U.S., 800/277–1133; fax 604/276–1975. 410 doubles, 6 suites. Facilities: jogging route, outdoor pool, free shuttle to airport, shopping center, and extensive health club at the nearby Delta Pacific Resort. AE, DC, MC, V.*

★ **Hotel Vancouver.** The Hotel Vancouver, which opened in 1939 by the Canadian National Railway, is one of the grand old ladies of the chateau-style hotels that appear across Canada. Its copper roof dominates the city's skyline, and the hotel itself commands a regal position in the center of town across from the art gallery and Cathedral Place. Even the standard guest rooms lend an air of prestige with mahogany furniture, TVs in armoires, attractive linens, and the original, deep bathtubs. The whole design is by far more classic than what you'll find at the Hyatt Regency or the Four Seasons. The hotel's two floors of Entrée Gold feature extra services and amenities, including complimentary breakfast in a private, luxurious lounge. Entrée Gold suites are spacious with French doors, graceful wing-back chairs, and fine mahogany furniture. The style and elegance of the Hotel Vancouver especially leave their mark on these floors. The hotel features the Roof Restaurant, which offers spectacular views with fine dining and dancing to live entertainment nightly. Reservations for Griffin's, the hotel's bistro-style restaurant—one of the most popular eateries in the city—are a must; there's a pizza buffet Saturday and a Tex-Mex Sunday brunch where children get into the act, making pancakes and churning ice cream. *900 W. Georgia St., V6C 2W6, tel. 604/684–3131 or 800/441–1414; fax 604/662–1937. 466 doubles, 42 suites, rooms for guests with disabilities. Facilities: 2 restaurants, 2 bars, two-line telephones, health club with lap pool, exercise machines, tanning bed, sun deck. AE, CB, DC, MC, V.*

Hyatt Regency. The 34-story hotel, which opened in 1973, completed an $11 million renovation in 1992. The Hyatt's standard rooms are the largest in the city and have been decorated in deep, dramatic colors and dark wood. Ask for a corner room with a balcony on the north or west side. The lobby, with its four-story atrium, however, can't escape the feel of a large convention hotel. For a small fee, the Regency Club gives you the exclusivity of three floors accessed by keyed elevators, your own concierge, a private lounge with a stereo and large TV, complimentary breakfast, 5 PM hors d'oeuvres, and evening pastries. Robes and special toiletries are also in the Regency

Club rooms. For a hotel restaurant, Fish & Co. is unusual in that the room is casual, the atmosphere fun, and the food good. The Gallery Lounge is one of the most pleasant in town. Health club facilities include outdoor heated pool, saunas, exercise machine, and access to a nearby fitness center with racquetball and squash courts. *655 Burrard St., V6C 2R7, tel. 604/687–6543 or 800/233–1234, fax 604/689–3707. 612 doubles, 34 suites. Facilities: restaurant, café, 2 bars, health club. AE, DC, MC, V.*

O'Doul's. This conveniently situated hotel on a lively street, with loads of shops and restaurants, is only a five-minute walk from either the heart of downtown or Stanley Park. It's a great location if you're traveling with teenagers who want time on their own. Among mid-range hotels, this is one of the more thoughtful: Public areas are very well maintained, and to insure extra security guests must use their room keys to operate the elevators. The rooms aren't what you'd expect, either: The decor is modern, with pastel color schemes. Deluxe rooms (with king-size beds) face Robson Street and are worth the price, especially off-season, when rates plummet. *1300 Robson St., V6E 1C5, tel. 604/684–8461 or 800/663–5491, fax 604/684–8326. 119 doubles, 11 suites. Facilities: 3 telephones in every room, pool, Jacuzzi, steam rooms, exercise machines. AE, DC, MC, V.*

Waterfront Centre Hotel. This dramatically elegant, 23-story glass hotel opened in 1991 across from Canada Place, the Convention Centre, and the cruise-ship terminal—all of which can be reached from the hotel by an enclosed walkway. Views from the caramel-colored lobby and many of the guest rooms are of Burrard Inlet; other guest rooms look out onto the mountains. The Entrée Gold floor has a lounge, terrace, and includes a concierge, board room, shoe-shine service, deluxe breakfast, cocktail-hour canapes, and honor bar. All guest rooms are attractively furnished with contemporary artwork, minibars, and armoires concealing the TV. A pleasant place for guests to enjoy a drink is Herons Lounge, off of the lobby area. But as the evening progresses, the activity usually moves into Herons Restaurant, where a Mediterranean ambience prevails and guests can watch their meals being prepared in the open kitchen and rotisserie. Sundays here are high spirited, as live Gospel singers entertain and inspire during a lavish brunch that includes imaginative dishes and decadent desserts. The property's health club includes a whirlpool, enclosed walkway to an outdoor heated pool, a variety of exercise equipment, a steam room, and massage services. *900 Canada Place Way, V6C 3L5, tel. 604/691–1991 or 800/441–1414; fax 604/691–1999. 460 doubles, 29 suites. Facilities: restaurants, health club, whirlpool, heated outdoor pool, steam room. AE, CB, DC, MC, V.*

★ **Wedgewood Hotel.** This hotel upholds its reputation for being a small, elegant property run by an owner who fervently cares about her guests. The intimate lobby is decorated in fine detail with polished brass, beveled glass, a fireplace, and tasteful artwork. All the extra touches are here, too: nightly turndown service, afternoon ice delivery, dark-out drapes, flowers growing on the balcony, terry-cloth robes, and morning newspaper. No tour groups or conventions stop here; the Wedgewood's clients are almost exclusively corporate, except on weekends, when the place turns into a couple's retreat. Health facilities are next door at the excellent Chancery Squash Club. The lounge and restaurant couldn't be better. It's a treasure. *845*

Hornby St., V6Z 1V1, tel. 604/689–7777 or 800/663–0666, fax 604/688–3074. 60 doubles, 33 suites. Facilities: 2 restaurants, bar; use of the adjacent Chancery Squash Club with 7 squash courts, weight room, aerobics, sauna, and whirlpool. AE, DC, MC, V.

Moderate **Days Inn.** For the businessperson looking for a bargain, this location is tops. The six-story hotel, which opened as the Abbotsford in 1920, is the only moderately priced hotel in the business core. Recent renovations of the guest rooms and the lobby have made this accommodation even more agreeable. Although it's a basic hotel, rooms are bright, clean, and functional; standard units are very large, but there is no room service and few amenities. Suites 310, 410, 510, and 610 have a harbor view. The bar, the **Bombay Bicycle Club,** is a favorite with businesspeople. *921 W. Pender St., V6C 1M2, tel. 604/681–4335, fax 604/681–7808. 74 doubles, 11 suites. Facilities: restaurant, 2 bars, free overnight parking. AE, DC, MC, V.*

★ **English Bay Inn.** The newly renovated 1930s Tudor house in which this inn sits is one block from the ocean and Stanley Park in a quiet residential part of the West End. The five small guest rooms—each with private bath—have wonderful sleigh beds with matching armoires, Ralph Lauren linen, and alabaster lighting fixtures. The common areas are generous and elegantly furnished: The sophisticated but cozy parlor has wingback chairs, a fireplace, and French doors opening onto the back of the inn. A small, sunny English country garden graces the back of the inn. Breakfast is served in a rather formal dining room furnished with a Gothic dining room suite, a fireplace, and an 18th-century grandfather clock. *1968 Comox St., V6G 1R4, tel. 604/683–8002. 5 rooms. Facilities: off-street parking. AE, MC, V.*

★ **Hotel Georgia.** This handsome 12-story hotel, built in 1927, has such Old World features as a dark-wood-paneled lobby, ornate brass elevators, and a subdued, genteel atmosphere. Although it's lacking in extra amenities, the Georgia is a reliable and satisfactory deal. Rooms are small but well furnished, with nothing worn around the edges. Executive rooms have an almost separate seating area; rooms facing the art gallery have the best views. From this hotel (situated across from the Four Seasons) it's a five-minute walk to the business district. *801 W. Georgia St., V6C 1P7, tel. 604/682–5566 or 800/663–1111, fax 604/682–8192. 310 doubles, 4 suites. Facilities: restaurant, 3 bars. AE, DC, MC, V.*

★ **West End Guest House.** Judge this lovely Victorian house, built in 1906, by its gracious front parlor, cozy fireplace, and early 1900s furniture rather than by its bright pink exterior. Most of the small but extraordinarily handsome rooms have high brass beds, antiques, gorgeous linens, and dozens of old framed pictures of Vancouver. However, avoid the basement rooms. All units have phones, TVs, modern bathrooms, and newly papered walls. There's a veranda for people watching, and a back deck for sunbathing. A full breakfast is included and can be served in bed. The inn's genial host, Evan Penner, has learned that it is the little things that make the difference, including a predinner glass of sherry, duvets and feather mattress-pads, terry bathrobes, hand-knit slippers, turn-down service, and a goodnight tart. The inn is in a residential neighborhood that is a 15-minute walk from downtown and Stanley Park and two minutes from Robson Street. This is a nonsmoking establishment. *1362 Haro St., V6E 1G2, tel. 604/681–2889, fax 604/688–8812. 7 rooms. Facilities: off-street parking. AE, MC, V.*

Inexpensive **Buchan Hotel.** This three-story 1930s building is conveniently
★ set in a tree-lined residential street a block from Stanley Park,
a block from shops and restaurants on Denman Street, and a
15-minute walk from the liveliest part of Robson Street. The
hallways appear a bit institutional, but the rooms are bright
and clean. Furnishings, in good condition, consist of a color TV
and a wood-grained arborite desk and chest of drawers. The
rooms are small and the bathrooms tiny. None of the rooms
have phones and you have to park on the street, but with this
location you probably won't use your car much. Rooms on the
east side are brightest and overlook a park; front corner rooms
are the biggest. A popular restaurant with an eclectic menu is
in the basement and is open for dinner. *1906 Haro St., V6G 1H7,
tel. 604/685–5354 or 800/668–6654, fax 604/685–5367. 60 rooms,
30 with private bath. Facilities: TV lounge, laundry room. AE,
DC, MC, V.*

The Kingston. The Kingston is a small budget hotel in a location
convenient for shopping. It is an old-style, four-story hotel,
with no elevator—the type of establishment you'd find in
Europe. The Spartan rooms are small and immaculate and
share a bathroom down the hall. All rooms have phones but no
TVs. Rooms on the south side are brighter. Continental breakfast is included. *757 Richards St., V6B 3A6, tel. 604/684–9024,
fax 604/684–9917. 60 rooms, 7 with bath. Facilities: sauna, coin-
op laundry, TV lounge, free nighttime parking. AE, MC, V.*

★ **Sylvia Hotel.** Perhaps the Sylvia Hotel is the best bargain in
Vancouver, but don't count on staying here June–August unless
you've booked six months ahead. What makes this hotel so
popular are its low rates and near-perfect location: about 25
feet from the beach, 200 feet from Stanley Park, and a 20-
minute walk from downtown. Vancouverites are particularly
fond of the eight-story ivy-covered brick building—it was once
the tallest building in the West End and the first to open a
cocktail bar in the city, in 1954. It's part of the local history and
was declared a protected heritage building in the 1970s. Rooms
are unadorned and have basic plain furnishings that have probably been around for more than 20 years—not much to look at,
but the view and price make it worthwhile. Suites are huge, and
all have kitchens, making this a perfect family accommodation.
There is little difference between the old and new wings. *1154
Gilford St., V6G 2P6, tel. 604/681–9321. 97 doubles, 18 suites. Facilities: restaurant, lounge, parking. AE, DC, MC, V.*

The Arts and Nightlife

For information on events, look in the entertainment section of
the *Vancouver Sun;* also, Thursday's paper has complete listings in the **"What's On"** column, and there's the **Arts Hotline**
(tel. 604/684–ARTS). For tickets to major events, book through
Ticketmaster (tel. 604/280–3311).

The Arts

Theater The **Vancouver Playhouse** (Hamilton St., tel. 604/872–6622) is
the most established venue in Vancouver. The **Arts Club Theatre** (tel. 604/687–1644), with two stages on Granville Island

(1585 Johnston St.) and performances all year, is the most active. Both feature mainstream theatrical shows. **Carousel Theater** (tel. 604/669–3410), which performs off-off Broadway shows at the Waterfront Theatre (1405 Anderson St.) on Granville Island, and **Touchstone** (tel. 604/687–8737), at the Firehall Theater (280 E. Cordova St.), are smaller but lively companies. The **Back Alley Theatre** (751 Thurlow St., tel. 604/688–7013) hosts **Theatresports,** a hilarious improv event. The **Vancouver East Cultural Centre** (1895 Venables St., tel. 604/254–9578) is a multipurpose performance space that always hosts high-caliber shows.

Music   The **Vancouver Symphony Orchestra** (tel. 604/684–9100) and the **CBC Orchestra** (tel. 604/662–6000) play at the restored **Orpheum Theatre** (601 Smithe St.). Choral groups like the **Bach Choir** (tel. 604/921–8012), the **Cantata Singers** (no tel.), and the **Vancouver Chamber Choir** (tel. 604/738–6822) play a major role in Vancouver's classical music scene. The **Early Music Society** (tel. 604/732–1610) performs medieval, renaissance, and baroque music throughout the year and hosts the Vancouver Early Music Summer Festival, one of the most important early music festivals in North America. Concerts by the **Friends of Chamber Music** (no tel.) and the **Vancouver Recital Society** (tel. 604/736–6034) are always of excellent quality.

Vancouver Opera (tel. 604/682–2871) stages four productions a year, usually in October, January, March, and May, at the **Queen Elizabeth Theatre** (600 Hamilton St.). Productions are high caliber with both local and imported talent.

Dance   Watch for **Ballet BC's Dance Alive!** series, presenting visiting or local ballet companies (from the Kirov to Ballet BC). Most performances by these companies can be seen at the Orpheum or the Queen Elizabeth Theatre (*see above*). Local modern dance companies worth seeing are **Karen Jamison, Judith Marcuse,** and **JumpStart.**

Film   Two theaters have distinguished themselves by avoiding the regular movie fare: **Ridge Theatre** (3131 Arbutus St., tel. 604/738–6311), which generally plays foreign films and rerun double-bills, and **Pacific Cinématèque Pacifique** (1131 Howe St., tel. 604/688–3456), which goes for even more esoteric foreign and art films. The **Vancouver International Film Festival** (tel. 604/685–0260) is held in September and October in several theaters around town.

Nightlife

Bars and Lounges   The **Gérard Lounge** (845 Burrard St., tel. 604/682–5511) at Le Meridien Hotel is probably the nicest in the city because of its fireplaces, wingback chairs, dark wood, and leather. For spectacular views, head up to the **Roof Lounge** (900 W. Georgia St., tel. 604/684–3131), in the Hotel Vancouver, where a pianist plays nightly. The **Bacchus Lounge** (845 Hornby St., tel. 604/689–7777) in the Wedgewood Hotel is stylish and sophisticated. The **Gallery Lounge** (655 Burrard St., tel. 604/687–6543) in the Hyatt is a genteel bar, with lots of windows letting in the sun and giving views of the action on the bustling street. The **Garden Lounge** (791 W. Georgia St., tel. 604/689–9333) in the Four Seasons is bright and airy with greenery and a waterfall, plus big soft chairs you won't want to get out of. For a more lively atmosphere, try **Joe Fortes** (777 Thurlow St., 604/669–

1940), or **Night Court** (801 W. Georgia St., tel. 604/682–5566) in the Georgia Hotel.

The **English Bay Café** (1795 Beach Ave., tel. 604/669–2225) is the place to go to catch the sunset over English Bay. **La Bodega** (1277 Howe St., tel. 604/684–8815), beneath the Château Madrid, is a popular Spanish tapas bar.

Two bars on Granville Island catering to the after-work crowd are **Bridges** (tel. 604/687–4400), near the Public Market, and the upscale **Pelican Bay** (tel. 604/683–7373), in the Granville Island Hotel, at the other end of the island. The **Backstage Lounge** (1585 Johnston St., tel. 604/687–1354), behind the main stage at the Arts Club Theatre, features one of the largest selections of scotches in town, and is the hangout for local and touring musicians and actors.

Music While discos come and go, lines still form every weekend at
Discos **Richard's on Richards** (1036 Richards St., tel. 604/687–6794) for live and taped Top-40 music.

Jazz A jazz and blues hotline (tel. 604/682–0706) gives you current information on concerts and clubs. **Carnegie's** (1619 W. Broadway, tel. 604/733–4141), and the **Alma Street Café** (2505 Alma St., tel. 604/222–2244), both restaurants, are traditional venues with good mainstream jazz. The **Glass Slipper** (185 E. 11th Ave., tel. 604/877–0066) has mainstream to contemporary jazz with a more underground atmosphere.

Rock The **Town Pump** (66 Water St., tel. 604/683–6695) is the main venue for local and touring rock bands. The **Soft Rock Café** (1925 W. 4th Ave., tel. 604/736–8480) is decidedly more upscale. There's live music with dinner. The **86th Street Music Hall** (750 Pacific Blvd., tel. 604/683–8687) serves up big-name bands. The **Commodore Ballroom** (870 Granville St., tel. 604/681–7838), a Vancouver institution, has been restored to its original, art deco style and offers live music ranging from B.B. King to zydeco bands.

Casinos A few casinos have been licensed recently in Vancouver, and proceeds go to local charities and arts groups. No alcohol is served. Downtown there are the **Royal Diamond Casino** (535 Davie St., tel. 604/685–2340) and the **Great Canadian Casino** (2477 Heather St., tel. 604/872–5543) in the Holiday Inn.

Comedy **Yuk Yuks** (750 Pacific Blvd., tel. 604/687–5233) is good for a few laughs. **Punchlines Comedy Theatre** (15 Water St., tel. 604/684–3015), another fun place, is in Gastown.

Excursion to Victoria

Important Addresses and Numbers

Tourist **Tourism Victoria** (812 Wharf St., Victoria V8W 1T3, tel.
Information 604/382–2127 or 800/663–3883).

Emergencies Dial **911** in Victoria.

Hospitals **Victoria General Hospital** (35 Helmcken St., tel. 604/727–4181).

Late-night All-night pharmacies are unknown in British Columbia, even
Pharmacies in the largest cities, although some pharmacies do offer after-hours emergency numbers. Generally, emergency prescriptions can be filled through major hospitals. **McGill and Orme**

Pharmacies (649 Fort St., tel. 604/384–1195) could provide assistance.

Arriving and Departing by Plane

Airports and Airlines
Victoria International Airport serves Victoria. **Air Canada** (tel. 604/360–9074; in the U.S., 800/458–5811) and **Canadian Airlines International** (tel. 604/382–6111; in the U.S., 800/426–7000) are the two dominant carriers. **Air B.C.** (tel. 604/360–9074; in the U.S., 800/663–0522) provides both airport-to-airport and harbor-to-harbor service from Vancouver to Victoria at least hourly. Both flights take about 35 minutes. **Air B.C.** is the major regional line and runs daily flights between Seattle and Victoria. **Helijet Airways** (tel. 604/382–6222) helicopter service is available from downtown Vancouver to downtown Victoria.

Arriving and Departing by Car, Bus, and Boat

By Car The TransCanada Highway, Route 1, runs south from Nanaimo to Victoria. Route 14 connects Sooke to Port Renfrew, on the West Coast of Vancouver Island, with Victoria.

By Bus **Greyhound** (tel. 604/388–5348; in Seattle, 206/624–3456) connects destinations throughout British Columbia with cities and towns throughout the Pacific North Coast.

By Boat **BC Ferries** (tel. 604/656–0757) travel year-round from Tsawwassen, just south of Vancouver, to Swartz Bay, a 30-minute trip by car or bus from Victoria.

Sealink Express (tel. 604/687–6925) offers high-speed (2 1/2-hour) catamaran service between downtown Vancouver and downtown Victoria. One-way fares for adults are $32.95, and round-trip is $59.95.

There is year-round passenger service (closed Christmas) between Victoria and Seattle via the *Victoria Clipper* (tel. 800/888–2535).

Washington State Ferries (tel. in Victoria, 604/656–1551; in Seattle, 206/464–6400) cross daily, year-round, between Sidney, just north of Victoria, and Anacortes, WA. **Black Ball Transport** (tel. in Victoria, 604/386–2202; in Seattle, 206/622–2222) operates between Victoria and Port Angeles, WA.

Getting Around

For the most part, Victoria is a walker's city; most of its main attractions are downtown or are a few blocks from the core. Attractions on the outskirts of downtown can easily be reached by bus or a short cab ride (though taxis can be alarmingly expensive). In the summer you have the added option of horse-drawn carriage, bicycle, boat, or double-decker bus tours.

By Bus The **BC Transit System** (tel. 604/382–6161) runs a fairly extensive service throughout Victoria and the surrounding areas, with an all-day pass that costs $4 for adults, $3 for students and senior citizens. Passes are sold at many outlets in downtown Victoria, including Eaton Centre and Harbour Square Ticket Centre.

Guided Tours

Tally-ho Horsedrawn Tours (tel. 604/479–1113) offers visitors
a get- acquainted session with downtown Victoria that includes
Beacon Hill Park.

Exploring Victoria

*Numbers in the margin correspond to points of interest on the
Downtown Victoria map.*

Victoria, originally Fort Victoria, was the first European settlement on Vancouver Island and is the oldest city on Canada's
west coast. It was chosen in 1842 by James Douglas to be the
Hudson's Bay Company's most western outpost, and it became
the capital of British Columbia in 1868. Today it's a compact
seaside town laced with tea shops and gardens. Though it's
quite touristy during the high summer season, it's also at its
prettiest, with flowers hanging from turn-of-the-century building posts and strollers feasting on the beauty of Victoria's natural harbor.

❶ A logical place to begin this tour is at the **Visitors Information
Centre,** located on the waterfront. *812 Wharf St., tel. 604/382–
2127. Open July, Aug., daily 9–9; May, June, Sept., Oct., daily
9–7; Nov.–Apr., daily 9–5.*

❷ Just across the way is the **Empress Hotel,** which originally
opened in 1908, and is a symbol both of the city and of the Canadian Pacific Railway. Designed by Francis Rattenbury,
whose works dot Victoria, the property is another of the great
châteaux built by Canadian Pacific, the still-current owners
who also built the Château Frontenac in Québec City, Château
Laurier in Ottawa, and Château Lake Louise in Alberta. The
$45 million face-lift was a hot topic of discussion in traditional
Victoria, though not all of the comments have been positive:
For contrast, take a pleasant stroll through the modern, elegantly designed Victoria Conference Centre at the south end
of the Empress. Criticism aside, the ingredients that made the
488-room hotel a tourist attraction in the past are still alive.
Stop in for high tea—served at hour-and-a-half intervals during the afternoon. *721 Government St., tel. 604/384–8111. Proper
dress required; no jeans, shorts, or T-shirts.*

Around the corner from the Empress is **Miniature World,** on
Humboldt Street, where small replicas of people, trains, and
historic events are displayed. The exhibit seems at times like
a mix of fact and fiction, with the models laid out so delicately.
*649 Humboldt St., tel. 604/385–9731. Admission: $6.50 adults,
$5.50 children 12–17, $4.50 children 4–11, disabled persons with
escort free. Open mid-June–mid-Sept., daily 8:30–10 PM; mid-
Sept.–mid-June, daily 9–5.*

A short walk around the harbor leads you to the old CPR
Steamship Terminal, also designed by Rattenbury and com-
❸ pleted in 1924. Today it is the **Royal London Wax Museum,**
housing more than 200 wax figures, including replicas of Queen
Victoria, Elvis, and Marilyn Monroe. *470 Belleville St., tel.
604/388–4461. Admission: $6.50 adults, $5.50 students and senior citizens, $3.50 children 5–12. Open May–Aug., daily 9–9;
Sept.–Apr., daily 9–5.*

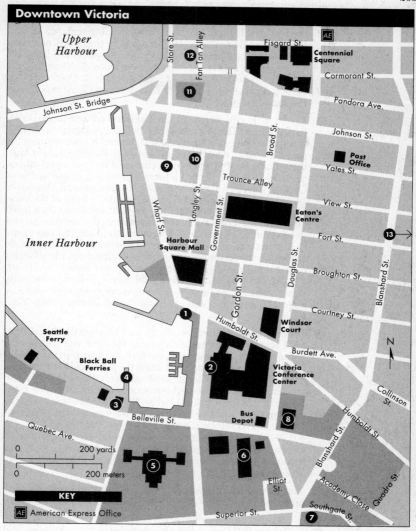

Downtown Victoria

Upper Harbour

Inner Harbour

Johnson St. Bridge

Seattle Ferry

Black Ball Ferries

Quebec Ave.

Belleville St.

Store St.

Fan Tan Alley

Fisgard St.

Centennial Square

Cormorant St.

Pandora Ave.

Johnson St.

Post Office

Yates St.

Trounce Alley

View St.

Eaton's Centre

Fort St.

Broughton St.

Courtney St.

Windsor Court

Burdett Ave.

Victoria Conference Center

Collinson St.

Humboldt St.

Bus Depot

Elliot St.

Superior St.

Southgate St.

Academy Close

Quadra St.

Blanshard St.

Broad St.

Douglas St.

Gordon St.

Government St.

Langley St.

Wharf St.

Harbour Square Mall

Humboldt St.

N

0 200 yards
0 200 meters

KEY

AE American Express Office

Bastion Square, **9**
Beacon Hill Park, **7**
Chinatown, **12**
Craigdarroch Castle, **13**
Crystal Gardens, **8**

Empress Hotel, **2**
Legislative/ Parliament Buildings, **5**
Maritime Museum, **10**
Market Square, **11**
Pacific Undersea Garden, **4**

Royal British Columbia Museum, **6**
Royal London Wax Museum, **3**
Visitors Information Centre, **1**

4 Next to the wax museum is the **Pacific Undersea Gardens,** where more than 5,000 marine specimens are on display in their natural habitat. You also get performing scuba divers and a giant Pacific octopus. Unfortunately, there are no washrooms, and the site is not wheelchair accessible. *490 Belleville St., tel. 604/382–5717. Admission: $6 adults, $5.50 senior citizens, $4.50 children 12–17, $2.75 children 5–11. Open Oct.–end of May, daily 10–5; summer, daily 9–9; closed Christmas. Shows run about every 45 minutes.*

5 Across Belleville Street is the **Legislative Parliament Buildings** complex. The stone-exterior building, completed in 1897, dominates the inner harbor and is flanked by two statues: Sir James Douglas, who chose the location of Victoria, and Sir Matthew Baille Begbie, the man in charge of law and order during the gold-rush era. Atop the central dome is a gilded statue of Captain George Vancouver, who first sailed around Vancouver Island; a statue of Queen Victoria stands in front of the complex; and outlining the building at night are more than 3,000 lights. Another of Rattenbury's creations, the complex gives a good example of the rigid symmetry and European elegance that characterize much of the city's architecture. The public can watch the assembly, when it's in session, from the galleries overlooking the Legislative Chamber. *501 Belleville St., tel. 604/387–3046. Admission free. Tours run several times daily and are conducted in at least 4 languages in summer and 3 in winter. Open Sept.–June, weekdays 8:30–5; summer, daily 8:30–5:30.*

6 Follow Belleville Street one block east to reach the **Royal British Columbia Museum.** Adults and children can wander for hours through the centuries, back 12,000 years. In the prehistoric exhibit, you can actually smell the pines and hear the calls of mammoths and other ancient wildlife. Other exhibits allow you to explore a turn-of-the-century town, with trains rumbling past; in the Kwakiutl Indian Bighouse, the smell of cedar envelops you, while piped-in potlatch songs tell the origins of the genuine ceremonial house before you. *675 Belleville St., tel. 604/387–3014. Admission: Free Mon., Oct.–Apr.; otherwise $5 adults, $3 students and senior citizens, $2 children 6–18 and disabled persons. Open Oct.–Apr., daily 10–5:30; May–Sept., daily 9:30–7; closed Christmas.*

The **Newcombe Theatre** behind the museum presents slide talks and films. *Tel. 604/387–5822. Admission by donation.*

A walk east on Belleville Street to Douglas Street will lead you

7 to **Beacon Hill Park,** a favorite place for joggers, walkers, and cyclists. The park's southern lawns offer one of the best views of the Olympic Mountains and the Strait of Juan de Fuca. There are also lakes, walking paths, abundant flowers, a wading pool, petting zoo, and an outdoor amphitheater for Sunday-afternoon concerts.

From the park, go north on Douglas Street and stop off at the

8 **Crystal Gardens.** Opened in 1925 as the largest swimming pool in the British Empire, this glass-roof building—now owned by the provincial government—is home to flamingos, macaws, 75 varieties of other birds, hundreds of blooming flowers, penguins, and monkeys. At street level there are several boutiques and Rattenbury's Restaurant, one of Victoria's well-frequented establishments. *713 Douglas St., tel. 604/381–1213.*

Admission: $3 adults, $2 children 6–16 and senior citizens. Open Oct.–Apr., daily 10–5:30; summer, daily 9–9.

9 From Crystal Gardens continue on Douglas Street going north to View Street, west to **Bastion Square,** with its gas lamps, restaurants, cobblestone streets, and small shops. This is the spot James Douglas chose as the original Fort Victoria in 1843 and the original Hudson's Bay Company trading post. Today fashion boutiques and restaurants occupy the old buildings. At the Wharf Street end of the square are some benches where you can rest your feet and catch a great view of the harbor. While you're here, you may want to stop in at what was Victoria's **10** original courthouse but is now the **Maritime Museum of British Columbia.** Dugout canoes, model ships, Royal Navy charts, photographs, uniforms, and ship's bells chronicle Victoria's seafaring history. A seldom-used 100-year-old cage lift, believed to be the oldest in North America, ascends to the third floor. In 1995, however, a new museum is scheduled to open and replace this facility. *28 Bastion Sq., tel. 604/385–4222. Admission: $5 adults, $3 children 12–17, $2 children 6–11. Open Oct. 1–May 31, daily 9:30–4:30; June 1–Sept. 30, daily 9–6. Closed Christmas and New Year's Day.*

11 West of Government Street, between Pandora Avenue and Johnson Street, is **Market Square,** offering a variety of specialty shops and boutiques and considered one of the most picturesque shopping districts in the city. At the turn of the century this area—once part of Chinatown—provided everything a visitor desired: food, lodging, entertainment. Today the square has been restored to its original, pre-1900s character.

12 Just around the corner from Market Square is Fisgard Street, the heart of one of the oldest **Chinatowns** in Canada. It was the Chinese who were responsible for building much of the Canadian Pacific Railway in the 19th century, and their influences still mark the region. If you enter Chinatown from Government Street, you'll walk under the elaborate **Gate of Harmonious Interest,** made from Taiwanese ceramic tiles and decorative panels. Along the street, merchants display fragile paper lanterns, embroidered silks, imported fruits, and vegetables. **Fan Tan Alley,** situated just off Fisgard Street, holds claim not only to being the narrowest street in Canada but also to having been the gambling and opium center of Chinatown, where mahjongg, fantan, and dominoes games were played.

13 A 15-minute walk or a short drive east on Fort Street will take you to Joan Crescent, where **Craigdarroch Castle** stands. This lavish mansion was built as the home of British Columbia's first millionaire, Robert Dunsmuir, who oversaw coal mining for the Hudson's Bay Company. (He died before the castle's completion in about 1890.) Recently converted into a museum depicting turn-of-the-century life-style, the castle is strikingly authentic, with elaborately framed landscape paintings, stained-glass windows, carved woodwork—precut in Chicago for Dunsmuir and sent by rail—and rooms for billiards and smoking. The location offers a wonderful view of downtown Victoria from the fifth-floor tower; guided tours are given. *1050 Joan Crescent, Victoria, tel. 604/592–5323. Admission: $5.50 adults, $4.50 students, children under 12 by donation. Open mid-June–Aug., daily 9–7:30; Sept.–mid-June, daily 10–5.*

What to See and Do with Children

Anne Hathaway's Cottage, tucked away in a unique Englishvillage complex, is a full-size replica of the original thatched home in Stratford-Upon-Avon, England. The building and the 16th-century antiques inside are typical of Shakespeare's era. The Olde England Inn, on the grounds, is a pleasant spot for tea or a traditional English-style meal. You can also stay ($68–$184; AE, DC, MC, V) in one of the 50 antiques-furnished rooms, some complete with four-poster beds. *429 Lampson St., Victoria, V9A 5Y9, tel. 604/388–4353. Admission: $5.75 adults, $3.50 senior citizens and children 8–17, children under 8 free. Open June–Sept., daily 9–9; rest of year, daily 10–4. Guided tours leave from the inn during the winter and directly from the cottage in summer. From downtown Victoria, take the Munro bus to the door.*

Pacific Undersea Gardens (*see* Exploring Victoria, *above*).

Swan Lake Christmas Hill Nature Sanctuary. This 23-acre lake, set within 110 acres of open fields and wetlands out Blanshard Street, is 10 minutes from downtown. From the 1½-mile chip trail and floating boardwalk, birders can spot a variety of waterfowl in winter and nesting birds in the tall grasses. Children will enjoy the displays and games in the nature house. *3873 Swan Lake Rd. (take the No. 70/No. 75 bus), tel. 604/479–0211. Admission free. Open year-round; nature House open Mon.–Fri. 8:30–4; weekends and holidays 12–4.*

Off The Beaten Track

Butchart Gardens, situated on the 130-acre Butchart estate about 21 kilometers (13 miles) north of downtown Victoria, offers more than 700 varieties of flowers and includes Italian, Japanese, and English rose gardens. During the summer, many of the exhibits are illuminated at night. Once a limestone quarry, the grounds were transformed in 1904 when Canadian cement pioneer Robert Butchart began building bridges and walkways and planting shrubs and flowers on the 50-acre (20-hectare) site. The grounds are lighted with beautiful displays during the Christmas season. Also on the premises are a gift shop, teahouse, and restaurants. *800 Benvenuto Ave., Victoria, tel. 604/652–5256. Admission: $9.50 adults, $5 children 12–17, $1 children under 12 excluding GST.*

Shopping

Shopping in Victoria is easy: Virtually everything can be found in the downtown area, beginning at the Empress and walking north along Government Street. In succession you'll hit **Roger's Chocolates** (tel. 604/384–7021), for fine chocolates; **George Straith Ltd.** (tel. 604/384–6912), for woolens; **Edinburgh Tartan Shop** (tel. 604/388–9312), for traditional Scottish clothing and accessories; **Gallery of the Arctic** (tel. 604/382–9012), for good-quality Inuit art; **Munro's Books** (tel. 604/382–2464), for the best selection of Victoriana in the city; and **Old Morris Tobacconist, Ltd.** (tel. 604/382–4811), for unusual pipe tobacco blends.

On the block of Douglas Street behind the Empress are shops like the exclusive **G. Gagliano of Florence,** with beautiful Italian leather goods; **LeJame Fashions,** with clothing designed and manufactured in Victoria, and the **Stephen Lowe Art Gallery.** Handy, also, is the **Currency Exchange,** which is open daily. The **Eaton Centre** at Government and Fort streets is both a department store and a series of small boutiques, with a total of 140 shops and restaurants. Market Square, between Johnson and Pandora, has three stories of specialty shops.

At last count, Victoria had 60-plus **antiques shops** specializing in coins, stamps, estate jewelry, rare books, crystal, china, furniture, or paintings and other works of art. A short walk on Fort Street going away from the harbor will take you to **Antique Row** between Blanshard and Cook streets. **Waller Antiques** (tel. 604/388–6116) and **Newberry Antiques** (tel. 604/388–7732) offer a wide selection of furniture and collectibles. You will also find antiques on the west side of Government Street near the **Old Town.**

A 10-minute drive (or the No. 1/No. 2 bus) from downtown out Fort Street to Oak Bay Avenue will take you to one of the few residential shopping areas that is not a mall. The **Oak Bay Village** is great for browsing, buying, or an afternoon *cuppa'*. Start at the corner of Oak Bay and Foul Bay and work your way east toward the water.

Sports and Outdoor Activities

Golf Though **Victoria Golf Club** (1110 Beach Dr., Victoria, tel. 604/598–4321) is private, it's open to other private-club members. This windy course is the oldest (built in 1893) in British Columbia and offers a spectacular view of the Strait of Juan de Fuca. **Uplands Golf Club** (3300 Cadboro Bay Rd., Victoria, tel. 604/592–1818) is a flat, semiprivate course (it becomes public after 2). **Cedar Hill Municipal** (1400 Derby Rd., Victoria, tel. 604/595–3103) is a public course with up-and-down terrain. **Royal Oak Golf Club** (4680 Elk Lake Dr., Victoria, tel. 604/658–1433) is the newest nine-hole course in the area. **Gorge Vale Golf Club** (1005 Craigflower Rd., Victoria, tel. 604/386–3401) is a semiprivate course but is open to the public. It has punitive traps and a deep gorge that eats up golf balls. **Glen Meadows Golf and Country Club** (1050 McTavish Rd., Sidney, tel. 604/656–3921), situated near the ferry terminal, is a semiprivate course that's open to the public at select times.

Dining and Lodging

Dining For prices *see* Dining chart for Vancouver, *above.*

Chez Daniel. One of Victoria's old standbys, Chez Daniel offers dishes that are rich, though the nouvelle influence has found its way into a few of the offerings. The interior, following a burgundy color scheme, seems to match the traditional rich, caloric cuisine. The wine list is varied, and the menu has a wide selection of basic dishes: rabbit, salmon, duck, steak. This is a restaurant where you linger for the evening in the romantic atmosphere. *2524 Estevan Ave., tel. 604/592–7424. Reservations advised. Jacket advised. AE, MC, V. Closed lunch and Sun.–Mon. Expensive.*

Chez Pierre. Established in 1973, this is the oldest French restaurant in Victoria, and the downtown location, combined with an intimate, rustic decor, creates a pleasant ambience. House specialties include *canard à l'orange* (duckling in orange sauce), rack of lamb, and British Columbia salmon. Although a tourist destination, this restaurant has managed to maintain its high quality over the years. *512 Yates, tel. 604/388–7711. Reservations advised. Dress: casual but neat. AE, MC, V. Closed lunch and Sun.–Mon. Moderate–Expensive.*

Swan's Café. Here's a good choice for a casual meal with Mediterranean and pan-Pacific flair. Inside the historic building in which the café is housed are lavish bouquets of fresh flowers and original artwork collected by owner Michael Williams. Creatively prepared salads and succulent stir-fries are recommended. The brew pub on the premises sometimes features live music and is the busiest pub in the city. *506 Pandora Ave., tel. 604/361–3310. Reservations accepted. Dress: casual. MC, V. Moderate–Expensive.*

Camilles. This restaurant is romantic, intimate, and one of the few West Coast–cuisine restaurants in Victoria. House specialties such as chicken Napoli, papaya brochettes (prawns wrapped around chunks of papaya in a lime and jalapeño marinade), phyllo-wrapped salmon (fresh fillet of salmon in phyllo pastry) are all served in generous portions. Camilles also has an extensive wine cellar, uncommon in Victoria. *45 Bastion Sq., tel. 604/381–3433. Reservations advised. Dress: casual but neat. MC, V. Closed lunch and Sun.–Mon. Moderate.*

French Connection. Located in one of Victoria's Heritage homes, built in 1884, the restaurant has maintained the character of the time. From the outside, ornate details indicate the French tradition that you will find in the service and on the menu. The food is prepared with care, with an emphasis on the sauces. *512 Simcoe St., tel. 604/385–7014. Reservations required. Dress: casual. AE, MC, V. Closed Sat.–Mon. lunch and Sun. Moderate.*

★ **La Ville d'Is.** This historic brick building houses one of the best seafood restaurants in Victoria. Both the quality and price are right. Run by Michel Duteau, a Brittany native, the restaurant is cozy and friendly, with an outside café open May–October. An extensive, imaginative wine list features bottles from the Loire Valley that go well with the seafood, rabbit, lamb, and beef tenderloin specials. Try the *perche de la Nouvelle Zélande* (orange roughie in muscadet with herbs) or lobster soufflé for a unique taste. *26 Bastion Sq., tel. 604/388–9414. Reservations advised. Dress: casual but neat. AE, MC, V. Closed Sun. and Jan. Moderate.*

★ **Pagliacci's.** If you want Italian food, Pagliacci's is a must. Featured are dozens of pasta dishes, quiches, veal, and chicken in marsala sauce with fettuccine. The pastas are freshly made inhouse. The orange-color walls are covered with photos of Hollywood stars, so there's always something to look at here. *1011 Broad St., tel. 604/386–1662. No reservations. Dress: casual. MC, V. Moderate.*

Blethering Place. Next to a teddy bear shop in Oak Bay is this clubby, neighborhood restaurant populated by dignified ladies sipping afternoon tea and blethering over crumpets, tarts, and scones. The menu points out that "blethering" is Scottish for "voluble, senseless talking." Later, neighborhood families stroll in for a dinner of steak-and-kidney pie, East Indian curries, and wonderfully rich desserts. Wines from British Columbia are featured. *2250 Oak Ave., tel. 604/598–1413. Reservations* advised. *Dress: casual but neat. AE, MC, V. Inexpensive–Moderate.*

Don Mee's. A large neon sign signals guests to Don Mee, a traditional Chinese restaurant. The long, red staircase leads to an expansive, comfortable restaurant for entrées such as sweet-and-sour chicken, almond duck, and bean curd with broccoli. *538 Fisgard St., tel. 604/383–1032. Reservations accepted. Dress: casual. MC, V. Inexpensive–Moderate.*

Le Petite Saigon. This is a small, intimate café-style restaurant, offering a quiet dining experience with beautifully presented meals and a fare that is primarily Vietnamese, with a touch of French. The crab, asparagus, and egg swirl soup is a specialty of the house, and combination meals are cheap and tasty. *1010 Langley St., tel. 604/386–1412. Dress: casual. AE, MC, V. Closed Sat. lunch and Sun. Inexpensive–Moderate.*

Cafe Mexico. Hearty portions of Mexican food, such as *pollo chipolte* (grilled chicken with melted cheddar and spicy sauce, on a bed of rice) are served inside this spacious, redbrick dining establishment, situated just off the waterfront. Bullfight ads and cactus plants decorate the restaurant and reinforce its character and Mexican theme. *1425 Store St., tel. 604/386–5454. Reservations accepted. Dress: casual. AE, MC, V. Inexpensive.*

Periklis. Standard Greek cuisine is offered in this warm, taverna-style restaurant, but there are also steaks and ribs on the menu. On the weekends you can enjoy Greek and belly dancing, but be prepared for the hordes of people who come for the entertainment. *531 Yates St., tel. 604/386–3313. Reservations accepted. Dress: casual. Closed weekend lunch; during summer, open Sat. lunch. AE, MC, V. Inexpensive.*

★ **Six-Mile-House.** This 1855 carriage house is a Victoria landmark. The brass, carved oak moldings and stained glass set a festive mood for the evening. The menu is constantly changing but always features seafood selections and burgers. Try the cider or one of the many international beers offered. *494 Island Hwy., tel. 604/478–3121. Reservations accepted. Dress: casual. MC, V. Inexpensive.*

Lodging

Category	Cost*
Very Expensive	over $180
Expensive	$110–$179
Moderate	$70–$109
Inexpensive	under $70

*All prices are for a standard double room for two, excluding 10% provincial accommodation tax, service charge, and 7% GST.

★ **The Empress Hotel.** This is Victoria's dowager queen with a face-lift. First opened in 1908, the hotel underwent a $45 million dollar renovation in 1989 that enhanced its Edwardian charm, updated existing guest rooms, and added some 45 new ones. Stained glass, carved archways, and hardwood floors are used effectively. The Empress dominates the inner-harbor area and is the city's primary meeting place for politicians, locals, and tourists. From the Lobby Lounge, guests can have a splendid view of the harbor. Afternoon tea has been a tradition here since 1908, but it's so popular today, reservations are a must. The Bengal Lounge is full of colonial charm from British India, including a stuffed Bengal tiger, overhead fans, and mosquito netting. *721 Government St., V8W 1W5, in Canada, tel. 604/384–8111 or 800/268–9411; in the U.S., 800/828–7447; fax 604/381–4334. 481 rooms. Facilities: 2 restaurants, café, 2 lounges, conference center, indoor pool, sauna, health club, in-room movies, cable TV, Christmas discount, family discount. AE, DC, MC, V. Very Expensive.*

★ **Abigail's.** A Tudor country inn with gardens and crystal chandeliers, Abigail's is not only lovely but also conveniently located four blocks east of downtown. All guest rooms are prettily detailed with a contemporary color schemes. Down comforters, together with Jacuzzis and fireplaces in some, add to the pampering atmosphere. There's a sense of elegant informality about the hotel, noticed especially in the guest library and sitting room, where you'll want to spend an hour or so relaxing in the evening. Breakfast, included in the room rate, is served from 8 to 9:30 in the downstairs dining room. *906 McClure St., V8V 3E7, tel. 604/388–5363; fax 604/361–1905. 16 rooms. MC. Expensive.*

★ **The Beaconsfield Inn.** Built in 1875 and restored in 1984, the Beaconsfield has retained its Old World charm. Dark mahogany wood appears throughout the house; down comforters and some canopy beds and claw-foot tubs adorn the rooms, reinforcing the Edwardian style of this residentially situated inn. Some of the rooms have fireplaces and Jacuzzis. An added plus is the guest library and conservatory/sun room. Full breakfast, with homemade muffins, and a cocktail hour (6–7 PM), with sherry, cheese, and fruit, are included in the room rates. *998 Humboldt St., V8V 2Z8, tel. 604/384–4044; fax 604/361–1908. 12 rooms. Facilities: library, Jacuzzi. MC. Expensive.*

The Bedford Hotel. This European-style hotel, located in the heart of downtown, is reminiscent of San Francisco's small hotels, with personalized service and strict attention to details. In keeping with the theme, rooms follow an earthen color scheme, and many have goose-down comforters, fireplaces, and Jacuzzis. Meeting rooms and small conference facilities are available also, making this a good businessperson's lodging. An extensive breakfast is included in the room rate. *1140 Government St., V8W 1Y2, tel. 604/384–6835 or 800/665–6500; fax 604/386–8930. 40 rooms. Facilities: restaurant, pub. AE, MC, V. Expensive.*

Chateau Victoria. This 19-story hotel, situated across from Victoria's new Conference Centre, near the inner harbor and the Royal British Columbia Museum, promises wonderful views from its upper rooms and its rooftop restaurant. Following a Victorian motif, the rooms are warm and spacious, some with balconies or sitting areas and kitchenettes. *740 Burdett Ave., V8W 1B2, tel. 604/382–4221 or 800/663–5891; fax 604/380–1950. 178 rooms. Facilities: restaurants, lounge, indoor pool, whirlpool, meeting rooms, courtesy vans to ferry, access to health club. AE, MC. Expensive.*

Dashwood Manor. If you want a quiet place with a great view, this is it. Located on the waterfront next to Beacon Hill Park, this Heritage Tudor mansion, built in 1912 on property once owned by Governor Sir James Douglas, offers panoramic views of the Strait of Juan de Fuca and the Olympic Mountains. This B&B lacks some of the charm that many offer because the parlor and dining rooms have been made into guest quarters. The only place for guests to congregate is in the tiny office, where sherry or wine is offered in the afternoon. Three guest rooms have fireplaces, and all rooms come with a fully stocked frig; and breakfast is "make your own." *1 Cook St., V8V 3W6, tel. 604/385–5517. 14 rooms. AE, MC. Expensive.*

Mulberry Manor. This Tudor mansion is a special place for a number of reasons: It is the last building to have been designed by Victoria architect Simon McClure; the grounds were designed and, until recently, maintained by a gardener at the world-famous Butchart Gardens; the manor has been restored and decorated to magazine-cover perfection with antiques, sumptuous linens, and tiled baths. Hosts Susan and Tony Temple are charming and provide gourmet breakfasts with home-made jams and great coffee. *611 Foul Bay Rd., V8S 1H2, tel. 604/370–1918. 2 rooms, 2 suites. MC, V. Expensive.*

★ **Holland House Inn.** Two blocks from the inner harbor, legislative buildings, and ferry terminals, this nonsmoking hotel has a sense of casual elegance. Some of the individually designed rooms have original fine art created by the owner, and some have four-poster beds and fireplaces. All rooms have private baths, and all but two have their own balconies. A gourmet breakfast is served and included in room rates. You'll recognize the house by the picket fence around it. *595 Michigan St., V8V 1S7, tel. and fax 604/384–6644. 10 rooms. Facilities: lounge. AE, DC, MC, V. Expensive.*

★ **Hotel Grand Pacific.** This is one of Victoria's newest and finest hotels, with a lot of mahogany woodwork and an elegant ambience. Overlooking the harbor, and adjacent to the legislative buildings, the hotel accommodates business and vacationing people looking for comfort, convenience, and great scenery; all rooms have terraces, with views of either the harbor or the Olympic Mountains. The health club is elaborate, equipped with Nautilus, racquetball court, and sauna. *450 Québec St., V8V 1W5, tel. 604/386–0450 or 800/663–7550; fax 604/383–7603. 149 rooms. Facilities: restaurant, lounge, sauna, whirlpool, fitness center, convention facilities, underground parking, indoor pool. AE, D, DC, MC, V. Expensive.*

Ocean Pointe Resort. Set across the "blue bridge" from downtown Victoria, the resort, with a northern European ambience, opened in the summer of 1992 on the site of an old shingle mill and an area once claimed by the Songhees natives. Public rooms and half of the guest rooms offer romantic evening views of downtown Victoria and the parliament buildings, bedecked with some 3,000 twinkling lights. Guest rooms are spacious and some feature floor-to-ceiling windows and small balconies.The property offers a rich cache of amenities, including hydrotherapy, micronized marine algae body wrap, massages, aerobics, and beauty treatments in the spa. There are salads and sandwiches in the Boardwalk Café; steaks and seafood in the Boardwalk Brasserie; and Pacific Northwest and Continental entrées, along with low-calorie, low-fat spa cuisine in the Victorian Restaurant. *45 Songhees Rd., Victoria V9A 6T3, tel. 604/360–2999 or 800/667–4677; fax 604/360–1041. 213 rooms, 37 housekeeping suites w/kitchens. Facilities: 3 restaurants, lounge, 3 tennis courts, whirlpool, sauna, exercise room, indoor pool, squash and racquetball court, beauty parlor, supervised playroom. Reservations advised in restaurant. MC, V. Expensive.*

Victoria Regent Hotel. Originally built as an apartment, this is now a posh, condo-living hotel that offers views of the harbor or city. The outside is plain, with a glass facade, but the interior is sumptuously decorated with warm earth tones and modern furnishings; each apartment has a living room, dining room, deck, kitchen, and one or two bedrooms with bath. *1234 Wharf St., V8W 3H9, tel. 604/386–2211 or 800/663–7472; fax 604/386–2622. 47 rooms, including 32 suites. Facilities: restaurant, free parking, laundromat. AE, D, DC, MC, V. Expensive.*

Oak Bay Beach Hotel. This Tudor-style hotel in Oak Bay, on the southwest side of the Saanich Peninsula, is well removed from the bustle of downtown. There's a wonderful atmosphere here, though; the hotel, situated oceanside, overlooks the Haro Strait and catches the setting sun. The interior decor is as dreamy as the grounds, with antiques and flower prints decorating the rooms. The restaurant, Tudor Room by the Sea, is average, but the bar with its cozy fireplace is truly romantic. *1175 Beach Dr., V8S 2N2, tel. and fax 604/598–4556. 51 rooms. Facilities: restaurant, pub, yacht for cruises, access to health club. AE, DC, MC, V. Moderate–Very Expensive.*

Admiral Motel. Located on the Victoria harbor and along the tourist strip, this motel is right where the action is, although it is relatively quiet in the evening. If you're looking for a basic, clean lodging, the Admiral is just that. The amicable owners take good care of the newly refurbished rooms, and small pets are permitted. *257 Belleville St., V8V 1X1, tel. 604/388–6267. 29 rooms, 23 with kitchens. Facilities: cable TV, free parking, laundry. AE, D, MC, V. Inexpensive–Moderate.*

★ **Craigmyle Guest House.** At this typical English-style bed-and-breakfast you'll find a casual, homey feeling without expensive designer touches. In the shade of Craigdarroch Castle, about 2 kilometers (1 mile) from the downtown core, this lodge, built in 1913, has a special view of the castle. The rooms are small and simple, but most units have a private bath. The main lounge features high ceilings and a huge fireplace. A hearty English-style breakfast, with homemade preserves, porridge, and eggs is served. Hosts are very friendly and chatty. *1037 Craigdarroch Rd., V8S 2A5, tel. 604/595–5411, fax 604/370–5276. 19 rooms, 15 with private bath. MC, V. Inexpensive–Moderate.*

The Arts and Nightlife

The Arts The **Art Gallery of Greater Victoria** is considered one of Can-
Galleries ada's finest art museums and is home both to large collections of Chinese and Japanese ceramics and other art and to the only authentic Shinto shrine in North America. The gallery hosts about 40 different temporary exhibitions yearly. *1040 Moss St., Victoria, tel. 604/384–4101. Admission: $3 adults, $1.50 students and senior citizens, children under 12 free; free Thurs. after 5, though donations are accepted. Open Mon.–Wed. and Fri.–Sat. 10–5, Thurs. 10–9, Sun. 1–5.*

The **Emily Carr Gallery** (under the auspices of the Greater Victoria Gallery) presents the art of and films about this renowned artist, who was a contemporary of the Group of Seven. *1107 Wharf St., Victoria, tel. 604/384–3130.*

Among the numerous commercial galleries, the **Fran Willis North Park Gallery** (200–1619 Store St., tel. 604/381–3422) is a good bet. In a gorgeously restored warehouse near the waterfront, it shows contemporary paintings and sculpture by local artists; music is performed from time to time. For a further look at what's going on in Victoria's art scene, try the **Winchester Galleries** (tel. 604/595–2777), the **Nunavut Gallery** (tel. 604/598–1344), and the **Barton Leir Gallery** (tel. 604/383–6477).

Music   The **Victoria Symphony** has a winter schedule and a summer season, playing in the recently refurbished **Royal Theatre** (805 Broughton St., Victoria, tel. 604/361–0820) and at the **University Centre Auditorium** (Finnerty Rd., Victoria, tel. 604/721–8480). The **Pacific Opera Victoria** performs three productions a year in the 800-seat **McPherson Playhouse** (3 Centennial Sq., tel. 604/386–6121), adjoining the Victoria City Hall. The **Victoria International Music Festival** (tel. 604/736–2119) features internationally acclaimed musicians, dancers, and singers each summer from the first week in July through late August.

The **Victoria Jazz Society** (tel. 604/388–4423) organizes an annual **JazzFest International** in late June, which in the past has featured jazz, blues, and world-beat artists such as Dizzy Gillespie, Frank Morgan, Ellis Marsalis, and Aster Aweke.

For listings of clubs and restaurants featuring jazz during the year, call **Jazz Hotline** (604/658–5255).

Theater   Live theater can be seen at the **Belfry Theatre** (1291 Gladstone Ave., Victoria, tel. 604/385–6815), **Phoenix Theatre** (Finnerty Rd., tel. 604/721–8000) at the University of Victoria, **Victoria Theatre Guild** (805 Langham Ct., tel. 604/384–2142), and **McPherson Playhouse** (3 Centennial Sq., tel. 604/386–6121).

Nightlife   After 8 PM, **Tudor House Hotel Pub** (533 Admirals Rd., tel. 604/389–9943) becomes a pub attracting the younger set. There's a dance floor and large screen for disco and video entertainment nightly.

Harpo's (15 Bastion Sq., tel. 604/385–5333) features live rock, blues, and jazz, with visits from internationally recognized bands.

Excursion to Whistler

Important Addresses and Numbers

Tourist Information   Contact the **Whistler Resort Association** (4010 Whistler Way, Whistler V0N 1B4; in Whistler, tel. 604/932–3928; reservations, tel. 604/932–4222; in the U.S. and Canada, tel. 800/944–7853). In Whistler Village an information booth at the front door of the Conference Center is open 8:30–8.

A provincial government **Travel Infocentre** (tel. 604/932–5528) is on the main highway, about 1 1/2 kilometers (a mile) south of Whistler.

Emergencies   Dial 0 for **police, ambulance,** or **poison control.**

Arriving and Departing by Car

By Car   Arriving time from Seattle to Vancouver is about three hours. Whistler is 1 1/2 to two hours north of Vancouver via Route 99, the Sea-to-Sky Highway.

Getting Around

By Bus **Maverick Coach Lines** (tel. 604/932–5031) has buses leaving every couple of hours from the bus depot in downtown Vancouver. The bus stops at Whistler Village and the fare is under $14 one way. During ski season, the last bus leaves Whistler at 10 PM.

Perimiter Bus Transportation (tel. 604/266–5386) has daily service, November–April and June–September from Vancouver Airport to Whistler. Reservations are necessary 24 hours in advance; the ticket booth is on the arrivals level of the airport.

By Train **BC Rail** (tel. 604/932–2134) travels north from Vancouver to Whistler along a beautiful route. The Vancouver Bus Terminal and the North Vancouver Station are connected by bus shuttle.

Exploring Whistler

If you think of skiing when you hear mention of **Whistler,** British Columbia, you're thinking on track. Whistler and Blackcomb mountains, part of the Whistler Resort Association, are the two biggest ski mountains in North America; there's summer glacier skiing, the longest vertical drop in North America, and the most advanced lifts in the world. At the base of the mountains is Whistler Village—a small community of lodgings, restaurants, pubs, gift shops, and boutiques. With more than 60 hotels, most of which are arranged within a five-minute walk between the mountains, the site is frenzied with activity. Culinary options within the village range from burgers to French, Japanese to deli cuisine; and nightly entertainment runs the gamut from sophisticated piano bars to casual pubs.

In the winter, the village buzzes with skiers taking to the slopes in vibrantly colored attire, but as the scenery changes from winter's snow-white to summer's lush-green landscapes, the mood of Whistler changes, too. Things seem to slow down a bit, and the resort sheds some of its competitive edge and welcomes a more relaxed, slower-paced environment. Even the local golf tournaments and the triathlon are interspersed with Mozart and bluegrass festivals.

Adjacent to the area is the 78,000-acre (31,579-hectare) **Garibaldi Provincial Park,** with dense mountainous forests splashed with hospitable lakes and streams. But even if you don't want to roam much farther than the village, there are five lakes for canoeing, fishing, swimming, and windsurfing, and many nearby hiking and mountain-bike trails.

No matter what the season, though, Whistler Village is very accessible to the pedestrian. Anywhere you want to go within the resort is at most five minutes away, and parking lots are just outside the village. The bases of Whistler and Blackcomb mountains are also just at the edge; in fact, you can ski right into the lower level of the Chateau Whistler Hotel, and all 2,700 of the village's hotel rooms are less than 1,000 feet from the lifts.

If you are interested in a tour of the area, **Alpine Adventure Tours** (tel. 604/932–2705) has a Whistler history tour of the valley and a Squamish day trip.

Scenic Drives

Completion of a new highway opened the **Coast Mountain Circle,** linking Vancouver to Cariboo Country. This 702-kilometer (435-mile) route takes in spectacular Howe Sound, the deepwater port of Squamish, Whistler Resort, and Pemberton Valley before heading back to Vancouver through scenic Fraser Canyon and Harrison Hot Springs. The loop makes a comfortable two- to three-day journey. For more information contact the **Tourism Association of Southwestern B.C.** (304–828 W. 8th Ave., Vancouver V52 1E2, tel. 604/876–3088 or 800/667–3306).

Sports and the Outdoors

Canoeing and Kayaking You'll see lots of canoes and kayaks at the many lakes and rivers near **Whistler.** If you want to get in on the fun, rentals are available at both **Lakeside Park** and **Wayside Park.** Another spot that's perfect for canoeing is the **River of Golden Dreams,** either from Meadow Park to Green Lake or upstream to Twin Bridges. Kayakers looking for a thrill may want to try **Green River** from Green Lake to Pemberton. Call **Whistler Outdoor Experience** (tel. 604/932–3389) or **Sea to Sky Kayaking** (tel. 604/8989–5498) for equipment or guided trips.

Fishing **Whistler Backcountry Adventures** (tel. 604/938–1410) or **Whistler Fishing Guides** (tel. 604/932–4267) will take care of anything you need—equipment, guides, and transportation. All five of the lakes around Whistler are stocked with trout, but the area around **Dream River Park** is one of the most popular fishing spots. Slightly farther afield, try **Cheakamus Lake, Daisy Lake,** and **Callaghan Lake.**

Golf Arnold Palmer designed the par-72 championship **Whistler Golf Course** (tel. 604/932–4544), which is said to be a "good four-iron shot from the village." The course is very scenic, fairly flat, and challenging for the experienced, but pleasant for beginners. The relatively new **Predator Ridge Golf Resort** (360 Commonage Rd., Vernon, tel. 604/542–3436) is a very challenging public course. The area's newest offering, the **Robert Trent Jones Jr. Golf Course** (4599 Chateau Blvd., tel. 604/938–8000), is equally scenic, nestled at the foot of the mountain on the opposite side of Whistler Village.

Skiing
Downhill Whistler Resort has more than 200 runs along with hotels and restaurants, and, like Whistler, is in the process of rapidly expanding. The vertical drops and elevation at **Blackcomb** and **Whistler** mountains are, perhaps, the most impressive features to skiers. Blackcomb has a 5,280-foot vertical drop (North America's longest); Whistler has a 5,020-foot drop. The top elevation is 7,494 feet on Blackcomb and 7,160 on Whistler. These mountains also have the most advanced ski-lift technology, with lift capacity on Blackcomb being 26,350 skiers per hour; on Whistler, 22,295 per hour. Blackcomb and Whistler have more than 100 marked trails each and receive an average of 450 inches of snow per year; Blackcomb is open June–August for summer glacier skiing. **Whistler Ski School** (tel. 604/932–3434) and **Blackcomb Ski School** (tel. 604/932–3141) offer lessons to skiers of all levels.

Heli- and Snowcat Skiing In Whistler, **Mountain Heli-Sports** (tel. 604/932–2070 or 604/932–3512), **Tyax Heli-Skiing** (tel. 604/932–7007), and **Whis-**

tler Heli-Skiing (tel. 604/932–4105) have day trips with up to four glacier runs, or 12,000 vertical feet of skiing for experienced skiers; the cost is about $300.

Dining

For prices *see* Dining chart for Vancouver, *above.*

Lodging

All lodgings can be booked through the Whistler Resort Association (tel. 604/932–4222 or 800/944–7853).

For prices *see* Lodging chart for Victoria, *above.*

Dining **Il Caminetto Di Umberto; Trattoria di Umberto; Settebello's.** Umberto Menghi is Vancouver's best-known restaurateur because of his fabulously successful Italian restaurants. Now there are three in Whistler. Il Caminetto and the Trattoria are in the village, and Settebello's is in Whistler Creek, about 3 kilometers (about 2 miles) south. Umberto offers home-style Italian cooking and specializes in pasta dishes like crab-stuffed cannelloni or a four-cheese lasagna that mix well with the relaxed atmosphere. The Trattoria has a Tuscan-style rotisserie, featuring a pasta dish served with a tray of chopped tomatoes, hot pepper, basil, olive oil, anchovies, and Parmesan so that you can mix it as spicy and flavorful as you like. Settebello's specialty is lean grilled beef and chicken, and Il Caminetto, perhaps the best restaurant in the Whistler area, is known for its veal, osso buco, and zabaglione. *Il Caminetto: 4242 Village Stroll, tel. 604/932–4442; Trattoria: Mountainside Lodge, tel. 604/932–5858; Settebello's: Whistler Creek Lodge, tel. 604/932–3000. Reservations advised for dinner. Dress: neat but casual. AE, DC, MC, V. Expensive.*

★ **Les Deux Gros.** The name means "the two fat guys," which may explain the restaurant's motto, "Never trust a skinny chef." Portions of the country French cuisine are generous indeed. The spinach-and-warm-duck salad, steak tartare, juicy rack of lamb, and salmon Wellington are all superbly crafted and presented, and the service is friendly but unobtrusive. Located just southwest of the village, this is the spot for that special romantic dinner; request one of the prime tables by the massive stone fireplace. *1200 Alta Lake Rd., tel. 604/932–4611. Dinner only. Reservations advised. Dress: neat but casual. AE, DC, MC, V. Expensive.*

The Wildflower Cafe. Although this is the main dining room of the Chateau Whistler, it's an informal, comfortable restaurant. Huge picture windows overlook the ski slopes and let in the bright sun reflected off the snow. The rustic effect of the Chateau Whistler lobby continues in the Wildflower—more than 100 antique wood birdhouses decorate the room, and chairs and tables have that farmhouse look. Although there is an à la carte menu that focuses on Pacific Northwest cuisine, the restaurant features terrific breakfast, lunch, and dinner buffets that may include fresh crepes and omelets, sweet potato–and–parsnip soup, barbecued salmon, smoked halibut, artichoke-and-mushroom salad, pepper salad, seafood pâté, pasta in a spicy tomato sauce, and cold meats. *Chateau Whistler Hotel, tel. 604/938–8000. Reservations advised for dinner. Dress: neat but casual. AE, DC, MC, V. Expensive.*

Lodging
★

Le Chamois. Sharing the prime ski-in, ski-out location at the base of the Blackcomb runs is this elegant, new luxury hotel. Of the 50 spacious guest rooms with convenience kitchens, the most popular are the studios with Jacuzzi tubs set in the living room in front of bay windows overlooking the slopes and lifts. Guests can keep an eye on the action also from the glass elevators and the heated outdoor pool. *4557 Blackcomb Way, tel. 604/932–8700; in the U.S. and Canada, 800/777–0185; fax 604/938–1888. 50 suites and studios, rooms for the disabled. Facilities: 2 restaurants, outdoor heated pool, Jacuzzi, fitness room, laundry room, complimentary valet ski locker, parking, shuttle to village. AE, DC, MC, V. Very Expensive.*

Chateau Whistler. Whistler's most extravagant hotel is a large and friendly looking fortress, just outside the village. It was built and run by Canadian Pacific Railway. It is the same style as the Banff Springs Hotel and the Jasper Park Lodge; the marvelous lobby is filled with rustic Canadiana, handmade Mennonite rugs, enormous fireplaces, and enticing overstuffed sofas. Floor-to-ceiling windows in the lounge, the health club, and the Wildflower Cafe overlook the base of Blackcomb Mountain. It's possible to schuss from there right into the basement of the hotel. The standard rooms are called premier and are fairly small, but the suites are fit for royalty, with specially commissioned quilts and artwork, and are complemented by antique furnishings. Both the Wildflower Cafe (*see* Dining, *above*) and La Fiesta, a tapas bar, are very good choices for a meal. Look for summer rates that drop by 50%. *4599 Chateau Blvd., Box 100, V0N 1B0, tel. 604/938–8000; in the U.S., 800/828–7447; in Canada, 800/528–0444; fax 604/938–2020. 303 doubles, 40 suites, rooms for the disabled. Facilities: 2 restaurants, bar, indoor-outdoor pool, indoor and outdoor Jacuzzis, morning stretch classes for skiers, 3 covered tennis courts, golf course. AE, DC, MC, V. Expensive.*

Pension Edelweiss. The Edelweiss is one of seven charming and very European bed-and-breakfasts around Whistler, and it's within walking distance of Whistler Village. Rooms have balconies and fireplaces and that crisp, northern European spic-and-span feel, in keeping with the Bavarian chalet style of the house. Each morning a different breakfast (included in room rate) is served: Scandinavian, American, French, German. *7162 Nancy Greene Way, Box 850, tel. 604/932–3641, fax 604/932–3776. 8 rooms, all with private bath. Facilities: sauna, Jacuzzi, transportation to lifts. MC, V. Inexpensive–Moderate.*

6 British Columbia

By Ray Chatelin

*Updated by
Melissa Rivers*

Canada's third-largest province (only [...]
bigger), British Columbia occupies [...]
total surface area, stretching from the [...]
vinces of Alberta, Saskatchewan, ar [...]
U.S. border to the Yukon and North[...]
more than 360,000 square miles, making it larg[...]
American state except Alaska.

But size alone doesn't account for British Columbia's po[...]
ity as a vacation destination. Even easterners, content in [...]
fact that Ontario and Québec form the industrial heartland oi
Canada, admit that British Columbia is the most spectacular
part of the nation, with salmon-rich waters, abundant coastal
scenery, and stretches of snow-capped peaks.

The region's natural splendor has ironically become the source
of one of its more serious conflicts. For more than a century,
logging companies have depended on the abundant supply of
British Columbia wood, and whole towns are still centered on
the industry. But environmentalists and many residents see
the industry as a threat to the natural surroundings. Com-
promises have been achieved in recent years, but the issue is
far from resolved.

The province used to be very British and predictable, reflecting its colonial heritage, but no longer. Vancouver, for
example, has become an international city whose relaxed life-
style is spiced by a rich and varied cultural scene embracing
large Japanese, Chinese, Italian, and Greek communities.
Even Victoria, which clings with restrained passion to British
traditions and life-styles, has undergone an international meta-
morphosis in recent years.

No matter how modern the province, evidence remains of the
earliest settlers, Pacific Coast natives (Haida Gwaii, Kwakiutl,
Nootka, Salish, and others), who occupied the land for more
than 12,000 years before the first Europeans arrived en masse
in the late 19th century.

But material proof of their heritage may not be enough for
today's native residents, who often face social barriers that
have kept them from the mainstream of the province's rich
economy. Although some have gained university educations
and have fashioned careers, many are just now beginning to
make demands on the nonnative population. In dispute are
thousands of square miles of land claimed as aboriginal territory, some of which is located within major cities such as Vancouver, Prince George, and Prince Rupert.

Although the issue of ownership remains inconclusive, testimony of British Columbia's roots is apparent throughout the
province, from small-town boutiques to big-city dining establishments. Native arts, such as wood-carved objects and silver-
etched pendants, fetch top dollar from visitors and residents
alike, and native Canadian restaurants prepare authentic culinary delights from traditional recipes.

Essential Information

Important Addresses and Numbers

Tourist Information For information concerning the province contact the **Ministry of Tourism and Provincial Secretary** (Parliament Buildings, Victoria V8V 1X4, tel. 604/387–1642 or 800/663–6000). More than 140 communities in the province have **Travel Infocentres.**

The principal regional tourist offices are: **Tourism Association of Southwestern B.C.** (304–828 W. 8th Ave., Vancouver V5Z 1E2, tel. 604/876–3088; in the U.S., 800/667–3306, fax 604/876–8916); **Tourism Association of Vancouver Island** (302–45 Bastion Sq., Victoria V8W 1J1, tel. 604/382–3551, fax 604/382–3532); **Okanagan–Similkameen Tourist Association** (104–515 Hwy. 97 S, Kelowna V1Z 3J2, tel. 604/769–5959, fax 604/861–7493); **High Country Tourist Association** (403–186 Victoria St., Box 962, Kamloops V2C 6H1, tel. 604/372–7770, fax 604/828–4656); **North By Northwest Tourism** (3840 Alfred Ave., Box 1030, Smithers V0J 2N0, tel. 604/847–5227, fax 604/847–7585); **Rocky Mountain Visitors Association** (495 Wallinger Ave., Box 10, Kimberley V1A 2Y5, tel. 604/427–4838, fax 604/427–3344); **Prince Rupert Convention and Visitors Bureau** (100 McBride St., Box 669 CMG, Prince Rupert V8J 3S1, tel. 604/624–5637); **Kootenay Country Tourist Association** (610 Railway St., Nelson V1L 1H4, tel. 604/352–6033, fax 604/352–1656); **Cariboo Chilcotin Coast Tourist Association** (190 Yorston St., Box 4900, Williams Lake V2G 2V8, tel. 604/392–2226 or 800/663–5885, fax 604/392–2838); **Peace River Alaska Highway Tourist Association** (106319–100th St., Box 6850, Fort St. John V1J 4J3, tel. 604/785–2544, fax 604/785–4424).

Emergencies Dial **911** in Vancouver and Victoria; dial **0** elsewhere in the province for **police, ambulance,** or **poison control.**

Hospitals British Columbia has hospitals in virtually every town, including: in Prince George, **Prince George Regional Hospital** (2000 15th Ave., tel. 604/565–2000 or for emergencies, 604/565–2444); in Chilliwack, **Chilliwack General Hospital** (45600 Menholm, tel. 604/795–4141); in Kamloops, **Royal Inland Hospital** (311 Columbia St., tel. 604/374–5111); in Kelowna, **Kelowna General Hospital** (2268 Pandosy St., tel. 604/862–4000).

Late-night Pharmacies All-night pharmacies are unknown in British Columbia, even in the largest cities, although some pharmacies do offer after-hours emergency numbers. Generally, emergency prescriptions can be filled through major hospitals. The following is a list of some pharmacies that could provide assistance: in Prince George, **Hart Drugs** (3789 W. Austin Rd., tel. 604/962–9666); in Kamloops, **Kipp-Mallery I.D.A. Pharmacy** (273 Victoria St., tel. 604/372–2531); in Hope, **Pharmasave Drugs** (240 Wallace St., tel. 604/869–2486).

Arriving and Departing by Plane

Airports and Airlines British Columbia is served by **Victoria International Airport** and **Vancouver International Airport.** Domestic airports are in most cities. **Air Canada** (tel. in Vancouver, 604/688–5515; in the U.S., 800/776–3000) and **Canadian Airlines International** (tel. in Vancouver, 604/279–6611; in the U.S., 800/426–7000) are the two dominant carriers. **Air B.C.** (tel. in Vancouver, 604/688–5515; in Victoria, 604/360–9074; in the U.S., 800/776–3000) is the major regional line and runs daily flights between Seattle and Victoria.

Arriving and Departing by Car, Bus, and Boat

By Car Driving time from Seattle to Vancouver is about 2¹/₂ hours. From other Canadian regions, there are three main routes leading into British Columbia: through Sparwood, in the south, take Highway 3; from Jasper and Banff, in the central region, travel on Route 1 (Trans-Canada) or Highway 5; and through Dawson Creek, in the north, follow Highways 2 and 97.

By Bus **Greyhound** (tel. in Vancouver, 604/662–3222; in Seattle, 206/624–3456) connects destinations throughout British Columbia with cities and towns throughout the Pacific North Coast.

By Boat There is year-round passenger service (closed Christmas) between Victoria and Seattle via the *Victoria Clipper* (tel. 800/888–2535).

Washington State Ferries (tel. in Victoria, 604/656–1531; in Seattle, 206/464–6400) cross daily, year-round, between Sidney, just north of Victoria, and Anacortes, WA. **Black Ball Transport** (tel. in Victoria, 604/386–2202; in Seattle, 206/622–2222) operates between Victoria and Port Angeles, WA.

Getting Around

By Air **Trans Provincial Airlines** (tel. in Prince Rupert, 604/627–1341;
Queen Charlotte in Sandspit, 604/637–5355) runs scheduled floatplanes between
Islands Sandspit, Masset, Queen Charlotte City, and Prince Rupert daily except Christmas, December 26, and New Year's Day.

Air B.C. provides both airport-to-airport and harbor-to-harbor service from Vancouver to Victoria at least hourly. Both flights take about 35 minutes.

Vancouver Island **Helijet Airways** (tel. 604/273–1414 or 604/382–6222) helicopter service is available from downtown Vancouver to downtown Victoria.

By Car Major roads in British Columbia, and most secondary roads, are paved and well engineered. Mountain driving is slower but more scenic. There are no roads on the mainland coast once you leave the populated areas of the southwest corner near Vancouver.

Car Rentals Most major agencies, including **Avis, Budget,** and **Hertz,** service cities throughout the province (*see* Renting and Leasing Cars in Chapter 1).

By Bus **Greyhound Lines of Canada** (tel. 604/662–3222 or 604/388–5248) serves the area with hundreds of stops in the province.

North of **Farwest Bus Lines** (tel. 604/624–6400) serves Prince Rupert,
Vancouver Island Terrace, Kitimat, Stewart, and Smithers.

Vancouver Island **Pacific Coach Lines** (tel. 800/661–1725) operates daily connecting service between Victoria and Vancouver via B.C. Ferries. **Island Coach Lines** (tel. 604/385–4411) serves the Vancouver Island area. **Maverick Coach Lines** (tel. 604/255–1171) services Nanaimo from Vancouver, via B.C. Ferries (*see below*).

By Ferry   **B.C. Ferries** (tel. in Vancouver, 604/685–1021; in Victoria, 604/656–0757; in Nanaimo, 604/753–6626) has an efficient cross-strait ferry service from Tsawwassen and Horseshoe Bay (both just outside of Vancouver) to Vancouver Island (Victoria and Nanaimo), and the Gulf Islands. Ferries usually depart on the hour 7 AM–9 PM and can carry about 360 cars and 1,500 passengers. Ferries also run from Powell River, Campbell River, Comox, and Port McNeill to the Gulf Islands; from Port Hardy to Prince Rupert; and from Prince Rupert to the Queen Charlotte Islands, although schedules vary greatly. When traveling with a car during summer months, expect a long line and delays. For schedule information call the numbers above for a 24-hour recorded message.

Royal Sealink Express (tel. 604/687–6925) is a new passenger service (no cars) that takes people by high-speed catamaran between downtown Victoria and downtown Vancouver in 2½ hours.

By Train   **BC Rail** (in Vancouver, tel. 604/984–5246 or 604/631–3500; in Prince George, tel. 604/564–9080) travels from Vancouver to Prince George, a 747-kilometer (463-mile route) including daily service to Whistler. **Via Rail** (tel. 800/561–8630 in B.C.) offers service between Prince Rupert and Prince George.

Vancouver Island   **Esquimalt & Nanaimo Rail Liner** (450 Pandora Ave., Victoria V8W 3L5, tel. 604/383–4324; in B.C., 800/561–8630), operated by Via Rail, travels from Victoria to Courtenay and returns. It leaves Victoria's Pandora Avenue Station daily at 8:15 AM, arrives in Courtenay by 12:50 PM, and departs 25 minutes later for a 5:45 PM return.

Guided Tours

Orientation   The following operators offer tours throughout the province: **Classic Holidays Tour & Travel** (102–75 W. Broadway, Vancouver V5Y 1P1, tel. 604/875–6377); **Klineburger Worldwide Travel** (3627 1st Ave. S, Seattle, WA 98134, tel. 206/343–9699); and **Sea to Sky** (1928 Nelson Ave., W. Vancouver V7V 2P4, tel. 604/984–2224).

Special-interest   A few Vancouver Island–based companies that conduct whale-
Nature Tours   watching tours are: **Subtidal Adventures** (Box 253, Ucluelet V0R 3A0, tel. 604/726–7336), **Inter-Island Excursions** (Box 393, Tofino V0R 2Z0, tel. 604/725–3163), **Jamie's Whale Station** (Box 590, Tofino V0R 2Z0, tel. 604/725–3919), **Tofino Sea-Kayaking Company** (Box 620, Tofino, VOR 2Z0, tel. 604/725–4222), and, near Port Hardy, **Stubbs Island Charters** (Box 7, Telegraph Cove V0N 3J0, tel. 604/928–3185).

Ecosummer Expeditions (1516 Duranleau St., Vancouver V6H 3S4, tel. 604/669–7741) runs ecological tours of the Queen Charlotte Islands.

Exploring British Columbia

When traveling by car, keep in mind that more than three-quarters of British Columbia is mountainous terrain. Trips that appear relatively short may take longer, especially in the northern regions and along the coast, where roads are often narrow and winding. In certain areas—most of the uninhabited west coast of Vancouver Island, for example—roads do not exist.

Within British Columbia, there is a vast range of climates, largely a result of the province's size, its mountainous topography, and its border on the Pacific. Vancouver Island, surrounded by Pacific waters, experiences relatively mild winters and summers (usually above 32 degrees winter, below 80 degrees summer), although it rains a lot in the winter. Likewise, the northern coast around Prince Rupert and the Queen Charlotte Islands has wet winter months and few extremes in temperature. But as you move inland, and especially toward the Peace River region in the north, the climate becomes much colder. In the southern interior, the Okanagan Valley has an arid climate, with temperatures dropping below the freezing level in winter and sometimes reaching 90 degrees during the summer.

Highlights for First-time Visitors

Kilby General Store Museum, Tour 3: Okanagan Valley and Environs
Mintner Gardens, Tour 3: Okanagan Valley and Environs
Naikoon Provincial Park, Tour 2: North of Vancouver Island
O'Keefe Historic Ranch, Tour 3: Okanagan Valley and Environs
Pacific Rim National Park, Tour 1: Vancouver Island

Tour 1: Vancouver Island

Vancouver Island, the largest island on the west coast, stretches 450 kilometers (280 miles) from Victoria in the south to Cape Scott, although 97% of the population live between Victoria and Campbell River (halfway up the island); 50% of them live in Victoria itself. Geographically, the differences between the east and west are impressive. The western side is wild, often inhospitable, with just a handful of small settlements. Virtually all of the island's human habitation is on the eastern coast, where the weather is gentler and the topography is low-lying.

The cultural heritage of the island is from the Kwakiutl, Nootka, and Coastal Salish native groups. Native art and cultural centers flourish throughout the region, especially in the lower section of the island. These centers enable visitors to catch a glimpse of contemporary native culture.

Mining, logging, and tourism are the important island industries. But environmental issues, such as logging practices by British Columbia's lumber companies, are becoming important to islanders—both native and nonnative. Residents are working to reach a happy coexistence with the island's wilderness and its economy, which is dependent on industrial development and tourism.

Numbers in the margin correspond to points of interest on the Vancouver Island map.

❶ Beginning your driving tour from Victoria (*see* Chapter 5), take Highway 14 west to **Sooke** (26 miles, or 42 kilometers, west of Victoria), a logging, fishing, and farming community. **East Sooke Park,** on the east side of the harbor, offers 3,500 acres of beaches, hiking trails, and meadows with wildflowers. You can also visit the **Sooke Region Museum and Travel Infocentre,** with Salish and Nootka crafts, artifacts from 19th-century Sooke, barbecued salmon, and strawberry shortcake on the front lawn during the summer, and plenty of information about the region. *2070 Phillips Rd., Box 774, V0S 1N0, tel. 604/642–6351. Admission free; donations accepted. Open summer, daily 9–6; winter, Tues.–Sun. and holiday Mon., 9–5; closed Christmas and Boxing Day (Dec. 26).*

Time Out **Seventeen Mile House** (5121 Sooke Rd., Sooke, tel. 604/642–5942) is on the road to Sooke from Victoria. Stop here for English pub fare, a beer, or fresh local seafood. Built as a hotel, the house is an education in turn-of-the-century island architecture, as well.

The adventurous can continue on Highway 14 west and pick up the logging road from Port Renfrew back to the east coast, although conditions on the gravel road may be hazardous, especially on weekdays with the trucks rolling by. The more reliable route backtracks to Victoria, then follows the Trans-Canada Highway up the eastern coast toward Nanaimo, the mid-island B.C. Ferries terminal point. On your way you'll **❷** pass through the town of **Duncan** (about 60 kilometers, or 37 miles, north of Victoria), nicknamed City of Totems for the many totem poles that dot the small community. The two carvings behind the City Hall are worth a short trip off the main road. Duncan is also home to the **Native Heritage Centre.** Covering 13 acres of land on the banks of the Cowichan River, the center features a native big house, fantastic theater and interpretive dance presentations, an arts-and-crafts gallery that focuses on carvings and weaving traditions, and picnic meals of smoked salmon next to the river. *200 Cowichan Way, Duncan, tel. 604/746–8119. Admission: $6 adults, $5.50 senior citizens and students, $2 children 6–12, children under 5 free. Open May–Sept., daily 9:30–5:30; Oct.–Apr., 10–4:30.*

Also in Duncan is the **B.C. Forest Museum.** More a park than a museum, the attraction spans more than 40 hectares (100 acres), combining indoor and outdoor exhibits that focus on the history of forestry in British Columbia. You ride an original steam locomotive around the property and over an old wood trestle bridge. The exhibit feature logging and milling equipment. *RR 4 Trans-Canada Hwy., tel. 604/746–1251. Admission: $5 adults, $4 senior citizens and children 13–18, $2.50 children 6–12. Open May–late Sept., daily 9:30–6. For off-season visits, call for an appointment.*

❸ Just north of Duncan, the small town of **Chemainus** has become known recently for the bold epic murals that decorate its landscape. Once dependent on the lumber industry, the town began

Vancouver Island

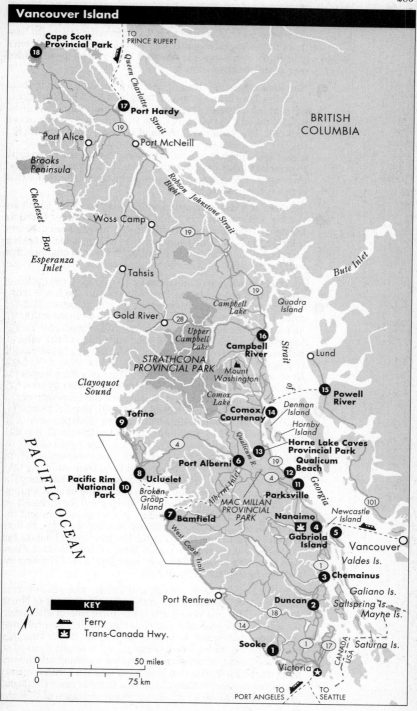

BRITISH COLUMBIA

TO PRINCE RUPERT

Queen Charlotte Strait

18 Cape Scott Provincial Park

17 Port Hardy

Port Alice

Port McNeill

Brooks Peninsula

Robson Johnstone Strait

Cheeseset Bay

Woss Camp

(19)

Esperanza Inlet

Tahsis

Bute Inlet

Campbell Lake

Quadra Island

Gold River (28)

Upper Campbell Lake

STRATHCONA PROVINCIAL PARK

16 Campbell River

▲ Mount Washington

Lund

Clayoquot Sound

Strait

of

15 Powell River

Comox Lake

Denman Island

9 Tofino

14 Comox/ Courtenay

Hornby Island

Qualicum R.

Horne Lake Caves Provincial Park

(4)

13

PACIFIC OCEAN

8 Ucluelet

Port Alberni **6**

(19)

12 **Qualicum Beach**

Pacific Rim National Park **10**

Broken Group Island

(4)

11 **Parksville**

Georgia

(101)

Alberni Inlet

MAC MILLAN PROVINCIAL PARK

7 Bamfield

Nanaimo

4

Newcastle Island

5

West Coast Trail

Gabriola Island

Vancouver

Valdes Is.

3 **Chemainus**

Port Renfrew

(1)

2 **Duncan**

Galiano Is.

Saltspring Is.

Mayhe Is.

KEY

⛴ Ferry

⛟ Trans-Canada Hwy.

1 **Sooke**

(14)

(18)

(1)

(17)

Saturna Is.

CANADA USA

0 ___ 50 miles

0 ___ 75 km

Victoria ★

TO PORT ANGELES

TO SEATTLE

to revitalize in the early 1980s when its mill closed down. Since then, more than 25 murals depicting local historical events have been painted around town by international artists. Restaurants, shops, cafés, and coffee bars have added to the town's growth. Footsteps on the sidewalk lead you on a self-guided tour of the murals.

4 **Nanaimo,** across the strait of Georgia from Vancouver, is about an hour's drive from Victoria. Throughout the Nanaimo region, petroglyphs (rock carvings) representing humans, birds, wolves, lizards, sea monsters, and supernatural creatures can be found. The **Nanaimo Centennial Museum** (100 Cameron St., tel. 604/753–1821) will give you information about local carvings. Eight kilometers (5 miles) south of town is the **Petroglyph Provincial Park,** where designs estimated to have been carved thousands of years ago can be seen along the marked trails that begin at the parking lot.

5 Nanaimo is a convenient departure point for other island activities. A 20-minute ferry ride leaves from town for **Gabriola Island,** a rustic, rural island with lodging; and a 10-minute ferry takes you to **Newcastle Island,** where you can picnic, ride your bicycle, walk on trails leading past old mines and quarries, and wait for glimpses of deer, rabbits, and eagles.

6 As you continue north on Highway 19, you have the option of taking Highway 4 west to Port Alberni and the lower west-coast towns. **Port Alberni** is about an 80-kilometer (49-mile) drive from Nanaimo and is mainly a pulp-and-saw-mill town and a stopover for those on the way to Ucluelet and Tofino, though fishermen will want to take advantage of the salmon-rich waters. While you're there, consider taking a breathtaking trip down the Alberni Inlet to Barkley Sound aboard the *Lady Rose*, a Scottish ship, built in 1937. The *Lady Rose* leaves the Argyle Street dock Tuesday, Thursday, and Saturday (and Friday and Sunday in July and August) for the four-hour cruise
7 to **Bamfield,** a remote village of about 200. Bamfield's seaside boardwalk affords an uninterrupted view of ships heading up the inlet to Port Alberni. Oddly, for a place this small, it is well equipped to handle overnight visitors. The west coast is invaded every summer by fishermen, kayakers, scuba divers, and hikers. Bamfield is also a good base from which to take boating trips to the Broken Group Islands and hikes along the West Coast Trail (*see below*). From early June to mid-September the *Lady Rose* and *Francis Barkley* sail for Ucluelet on Monday, Wednesday, and Friday. It's a unique trip and deserves all the accolades it receives. Most of the trips, to both Bamfield and Ucluelet, stop at the Broken Group Islands, but call ahead to make sure. *Argyle St. dock, tel. 604/723–8313. Bamfield fare: $32; Broken Group Islands fare: $34; Ucluelet fare: $36. Sailings depart daily at 8 AM.*

8 North of Bamfield are Ucluelet and Tofino—the whale-watching capitals of Canada, if not of the whole west coast of North America. The two towns are quite different in character, though both are relaxed in the winter and swell to several times their sizes in summer. **Ucluelet,** which in the native language means "people with a safe landing place," is totally focused on the sea. Fishing, water tours, and whale watching are the primary activities. Whale watching is big business, with a variety of charter companies that take tourist boats to greet the 20,000 gray whales that pass within a very short distance of Ucluelet on their migration to the Bering Sea every March–May. Sometimes the migrating whales can even be seen from the Ucluelet shore.

9 **Tofino,** on the other hand, is more commercial, with beachfront resorts, motels, and several unique bed-and-breakfast establishments. But the surrounding area remains natural. You can walk along the beach discovering caves on the way, cruise around the ancient forests of Meares Island, or take an hour-long water taxi to the hot springs north of town.

Ucluelet and Tofino bookend the Long Beach section of the
10 **Pacific Rim National Park** (Box 280, Ucluelet, V0R 3A0, tel. 604/726–7721), the first national marine park in Canada. The park itself comprises three separate areas—Long Beach, the Broken Group Islands, and the West Coast Trail. Each accommodates a specific interest.

The unit of **Long Beach** gets its name from an 11-kilometer (7-mile) strip of hard-packed white sand strewn with twisted driftwood, shells, and the occasional Japanese glass fishing float. The beach is a favorite spot during the summer, and you often have to fight heavy traffic along the twisting 85 kilometers (53 miles) of Highway 4 from Port Alberni.

The 100 islands of the **Broken Group Islands** can be reached only by boat. Many boating tours are available from Ucluelet, which rests at the southern end of Long Beach, and from Bamfield and Port Alberni. The 100 islands are alive with sea lions, seals, and whales. The sheltered lagoons of Gibraltar, Jacques, and Hand islands offer protection and good boating conditions, but go with a guide.

The third element of the park is the **West Coast Trail** (*see* Hiking, *below*), which stretches along the coast from Bamfield to Port Renfrew. After the SS *Valencia* ran aground in 1906, killing all the crew and passengers, the Canadian government constructed the lifesaving trail to help future victims of shipwrecks reach safe ground. The trail remains, with demanding bogs, steep slopes and gullies, cliffs (with ladders), slippery boardwalks, and insects. Although it presents many obstacles for hikers, the rewards are the panoramic views of the sea, dense rain forest, sandstone cliffs with waterfalls, and wildlife that includes gray whales and seals.

Heading back to the east coast from Port Alberni, stop off at **Cathedral Grove,** located in MacMillan Provincial Park on Highway 4. Walking trails lead you past Douglas fir trees and western red cedars, some about 800 years old. Their remarkable height creates a spiritual effect, as though you were gazing at a cathedral ceiling. Another stop along the way is **Butterfly World** (Alberni Hwy., Box 36, Coombs, V0R 1MO, tel. 604/248–7026), an enclosed tropical garden housing a massive collection of exotic, free-flying tropical butterflies.

11 At the junction of Highways 4 and 19 is **Parksville**—one of the east island's primary resort areas with lodges and waterfront motels catering to families, campers, and boaters. In **Rathtrevor Provincial Park,** 1½ kilometers (about 1 mile) south of Parksville, high tide brings ashore the warmest ocean water in British Columbia. Swimmers should time their visits accordingly.

⑫ Just 12 kilometers (7 miles) north of Parksville is **Qualicum Beach,** known largely for its salmon fishing and opportunities for beachcombing along the long, sandy beaches. The nonprofit **Old School House Gallery and Art Centre** (122 Fern Rd. W, tel. 604/752–6133), with nine working studios, shows and sells the work of local artists and artisans.

Continue north, then head west off the highway and follow signs for about 15 kilometers (9 miles) to Horne Lake and the

⑬ **Horne Lake Caves Provincial Park.** Three of the six caves are open at all times. If you decide to venture in, bring along a flashlight, warm clothes, and a hard hat, and be prepared to bend and even crawl. Riverbend Cave, spanning 383 meters (1,259 feet), requires ladders and ropes in some parts, and can only be explored with a guided tour. Spelunking lessons and tours are offered for all levels, from beginner to advanced. *Tel. 604/248–3931. Fees for tours vary depending on ability level. Reservations suggested for tours.*

Between the Horne Lakes turnoff and the twin cities of Comox and Courtenay is tiny Buckley Bay, where ferries leave for **Denman Island,** with connecting service to **Hornby Island.** Denman offers old-growth forests and long sandy beaches, while Hornby's spectacular beaches have earned it the nickname the Undiscovered Hawaii of British Columbia. Many artists have settled on the islands, establishing studios for pottery, jewelry, wood carving, and sculpture.

⑭ **Comox** and **Courtenay** are near **Strathcona Provincial Park** and are commonly used as a base for anyone skiing Mt. Washington in the winter. Strathcona, the largest provincial park on Vancouver Island, encompasses **Mt. Golden Hinde,** at 2,200 meters (7,218 feet) the island's highest mountain; and **Della Falls,** Canada's highest waterfall, reaching 440 meters (1,443 feet). The park's multitude of lakes and 161 campsites attract summer canoers, fishermen, and wilderness campers, and the **Strathcona Park Lodge and Outdoor Information Center,** well known for its wilderness-skills programs, provides information on the park's facilities. *Information Center, Hwy. 28, on Upper Campbell Lake, about 45 km (28 mi) west of Hwy. 19, Box 2160, Campbell River, V9W 5C9, tel. 604/286–3122.*

⑮ From Comox, you can take a 75-minute ferry east across the Strait of Georgia to **Powell River,** a city established around the MacMillan pulp-and-paper mill, which opened in 1912. Renowned as a year-round salmon-fishing destination, the mainland's Sunshine Coast town has 30 regional lakes that offer exceptional trout fishing, as well. For information contact **Powell River Travel Info Center** (6807 Wharf St., tel. 604/485–4051).

⑯ **Campbell River** is ringed by shopping centers that make it look like a free-zoned mess. But people don't come here for the aesthetics, they come for the fish; some of the biggest salmon ever caught on a line have been landed just off the coast at Campbell River. At the mouth of the town's namesake, you can try for membership in Campbell River's Tyee Club, which would allow you to fish in a specific area, and possibly land a giant chinook. Requirements for membership in the club include registering and landing a tyee (a spring salmon weighing 30 pounds or more). Coho salmon and cutthroat trout are also plentiful in the river. *Travel Information Center, 1235 Island Hwy., Box 400,*

*Campbell River, V9W 5B6, tel. 604/287–4636. Open late June–
Labor Day, daily 8–6; rest of year, Mon.–Fri. 9–5.*

Pods of resident Orcas live nearby year-round in Johnstone
Strait; and in Robson Bight they like using the beaches to rub
against. Because of their presence, Robson Bight has been
made into an ecological preserve: Whales must not be dis-
turbed by human observers there. Some of the island's best
whale-watching tours, however, are conducted nearby, out of
Telegraph Cove, a village built on pilings over water.

17 Farther north is **Port Hardy,** the departure and arrival point
for B.C. Ferries going through the Inside Passage to and from
Prince Rupert, the coastal port serving the Queen Charlotte
Islands. During the summer the town can be crowded, so book
your accommodations well in advance.

If you choose to continue to the northernmost point on Vancouver Island, drive about 60 kilometers (about 37 miles) on log-
18 ging roads to reach **Cape Scott Provincial Park,** a wilderness
camping region designed for well-equipped and experienced
hikers. At Sand Neck, a strip of land that joins the cape to the
mainland of the island, you can see both the eastern and western shores at once.

Tour 2: North of Vancouver Island

*Numbers in the margin correspond to points of interest on the
British Columbia map.*

19 Cruising the 274-nautical-mile **Inside Passage,** between Port
Hardy on northern Vancouver Island and Prince Rupert, is a
sail through a sheltered marine highway that follows a series
of natural channels behind protective islands along the green-
and-blue shaded British Columbia coast. The undisturbed
landscape of rising mountains and humpbacked islands has a
prehistoric look that leaves an indelible impression.

After a short segment in the open ocean, the 410-foot MV
Queen of the North ducks in behind Calvert Island into Fitz
Hugh Sound. From there, its route is protected from ocean
swells all the way through Finlayson and Grenville channels,
which are flanked by high, densely wooded mountains that rise
steeply, in places, from narrow gorges. The *Queen of the North*
carries up to 800 passengers and 157 vehicles, and takes close
to an entire day to make the Port Hardy to Prince Rupert trip.
The ship has plenty of deck space plus lounge areas, a self-
serve cafeteria, and a satisfactory restaurant that offers a plentiful buffet. Day-use cabins are available for an additional fee.
Children can play in the Captain Kids Room. *British Columbia
Ferry Corporation, 1112 Fort St., Victoria V8V 4V2, tel. 604/386–
3431. Cost varies according to cabin, vehicle, and time of season.
Reservations required for the cruise and advised for hotel accommodations at ports of call. Oct. 1–Apr. 30 sailings are once
weekly; May 1–May 31 sailings twice-weekly; June 1–Sept. 30
sailings daily, departing on alternate days from Port Hardy and
Prince Rupert; departure time 7:30 AM, arrival time 10:30 PM.
Schedule and fares subject to change.*

An alternative to the ferry cruise along the Inside Passage is
one of the more expensive luxury-liner cruises that sail along
the B.C. coast (*see* Chapter 1) from Vancouver to Alaska.

British Columbia

ALASKA
(USA)

Takla
Lake

Hazelton
24

(37)

Babine
Lake

Terrace
22

Skeena River

(37)

25
**Lakes
District**

(16)

Stua
Lak

**Prince
Rupert**
20

(16)

23 *Kitimat*

*Douglas
Channel*

Ootsa Lake

Eutsuk Lake

*TWEEDSMUIR
PARK*

NAIKOON
PROVINCIAL
PARK

Hecate Strait

Grenville Channel

(16) ○ Tlell
*Graham
Island*
○ Skidegate

**21 Queen
Charlotte
Islands**

*Moresby
Island*

Finlayson Channel

(20)

**Inside
Passage**
19

Fitz Hugh Sound

Queen Charlotte

COAST

MOU

Strait

Cape Scott

(19)
○ **Port
Hardy**

Vancouver Island
1 — 18

(19)

Camp
F

(28)

Co

STRATHCO
PARK

PACIFIC OCEAN

Tofino ○

N

KEY
— Rail Lines
⛴ Ferry
🚻 Trans-Canada Hwy.

0   100 miles

0   140 km

⑳ **Prince Rupert,** the final stop on the B.C. Ferries route through the Inside Passage, is about 750 air kilometers (465 miles) northwest of Vancouver, though it takes more than 20 hours to drive the mountainous 1,500 kilometers (936 miles). Prince Rupert has a mild but wet climate, so take rain gear.

The town lives off fishing, fish processing, logging, saw-and pulp-mill operations, and deep-sea shipping. A gondola ride to the top of Mt. Hays, located just outside the downtown area, offers magnificent views on a clear day of the industrial harbor, the Queen Charlotte Islands, and the mountains of Alaska. You can ski Mt. Hays during the winter and picnic in the summer. Prince Rupert is also a place where British Columbia's cultural heritage is quite evident. The **Museum of Northern British Columbia** has one of the finest collections throughout the province of coastal native art, some artifacts dating back 10,000 years. Native artisans carve totem poles in the carving shed and, during the summer, the museum runs a 2½-hour boat tour of the harbor and Metlakatla native village. *1st Ave. and McBride St., Prince Rupert, tel. 604/624–3207. Admission: free; donations accepted. Open Sept–May, Mon.–Sat. 10–5; June–Aug., Mon–Sat. 9–9, Sun. 9–5.*

From Prince Rupert you can continue on to explore either the Alaskan Panhandle, the Queen Charlotte Islands, or interior British Columbia. If you wish to proceed north through the Alaskan waterways to Skagway, board the **Alaska Marine Highway System ferry** (tel. in Prince Rupert, 604/627–1744 or 800/642–0066), which docks alongside the *Queen of the North* in Prince Rupert. Alaska ferries travel this route four times a week in the summer, twice a week otherwise.

㉑ The popular vacation destination, the **Queen Charlotte Islands,** or misty islands, though once the remote preserve of the Haida Gwaii natives, is now easily accessible by ferry. Today the Haida Gwaii make up only one sixth of the population, but they continue to infuse the island with a sense of the Haida Gwaii past and contribute to the logging and fishing industries, and to tourism, as well. Haida Gwaii elders lead tours—an essential service if you want to reach the isolated, abandoned villages. Though the region has become a popular tourist destination, limited accommodations make it necessary to reserve guest rooms well in advance.

The *Queen of Prince Rupert* (tel. in Prince Rupert, 604/624–9627) sails four to five times a week between June and September, and can easily accommodate recreational vehicles. Crossing the Hecate Strait from Prince Rupert to Skidegate, near Queen Charlotte on Graham Island, takes about six hours. Schedules vary, so call ahead—a good idea anyway because the boat fills up quickly. The **MV *Kwuna,*** a B.C. Ferries ship, connects Skidegate Landing to Alliford Bay on Moresby Island, with 12 20-minute sailings daily. Access to smaller islands off Graham Island (the northernmost and largest of the group of 150) and Moresby Island is by boat or air, but plans should be made in advance through a travel agent.

In the Queen Charlottes, there are 150 kilometers (93 miles) of paved road, most of it on Graham Island, connecting Queen Charlotte in the south to Masset in the north. Some of the other islands are laced with gravel roads, most of which can be accessed with any sturdy car or RV. The rugged, rocky west coast of the archipelago faces the ocean; the east coast has many broad sandy beaches. Throughout, the mountains and shores are often shrouded in fog and rain-laden clouds, adding to the mysteriousness of the islands.

Naikoon Provincial Park (tel. 604/557–4390), in the northeast corner of Graham, preserves a large section of the unique wilderness found here, where low-lying swamps, pine and cedar forests, lakes, beaches, trails, and wildlife combine to create an intriguing environment. Take the 5-kilometer (3-mile) walk from the Tlell Picnic Site to the beach, and on to the bow section of the old wooden shipwreck of the *Pezuta*, a 1928 log-hauling vessel. On the southern end of Graham Island, the **Queen Charlotte Islands Museum** has a small but impressive display of Haida Gwaii totem poles, masks, and carvings of both silver and argillite (a hard black slate). There is also a natural-history exhibit, which gives interesting background on the wildlife of the islands. *Box 1373, Skidegate V0T 1S1, tel. 604/559–4643. Admission: $2.25 adults, children 13 and under free. Open Apr.– late Oct., weekdays 9–5, weekends 1–5; winter, Wed.–Sun. 1–5.*

If you have time on Graham Island, drive up to Old Masset on the northern coast, site of the **Ed Jones Haida Museum.** Exhibits here include totems and artifacts. Nearby, artists sell their work from their homes. South of Graham, in and around South Moresby National Park Reserve, lie most of the better-known abandoned Haida Gwaii villages, which are accessible by water. Visiting some of the villages requires at least several days, and lots of planning for the wilderness. You (or your tour) need to contact the Skidegate Band Council and the Canadian Parks Services before you go.

For more information on the Queen Charlotte Islands, contact the **Queen Charlotte Islands Travel Information Center** (Box 337, Queen Charlotte V0T 1S0, tel. 604/559–4742).

To see interior British Columbia, take Highway 16 east from Prince Rupert. En route you'll pass through or near such communities as **Terrace,** with a hot-springs complex at the Mt. Layton Resort, skiing at Shames Mountain, and excellent fishing in the Skeena River; and **Kitimat** (on Highway 37, south of Terrace), at the head of the Douglas Channel, where the fishing is superb. At **Hazelton,** a town rich in the culture of the Gitksan and Wet'suwet'en peoples you must visit **'Ksan,** just outside town, a re-created Gitksan village. The brightly painted community of six longhouses is a replica of the one that stood on the same site when the first explorers arrived in the last century. The **National Exhibition Centre and Museum** displays works and artifacts from the Upper Skeena River region. A workshop, often used by 'Ksan artists, is open to the public, and three other longhouses can be visited on a 45-minute tour: One features contemporary masks and robes, another has song-and-dance dramas in the summer. A gift shop and museum are on the grounds. *Box 333, Hazelton, V0J 1Y0, tel. 604/842–5723. Admission: $5 adults, $3.50 senior citizens, $3 students, $2 children 5–12. Open May–mid-Oct., daily 9–6; mid-Oct.–Apr., weekdays 9–5. Tours given May–mid-Oct., on the hour.*

North of Highway 16 you pass by the serene **Lakes District,** which is popular for camping, fishing, and water sports, before coming to **Prince George** (Tourism Prince George, 1198 Victoria St., V2L 2L2, tel. 604/562–3700), British Columbia's third-largest city. This provincial hub contains a regional historic museum (tel. 604/562–1612), a railroad museum (tel. 604/563–7351; open May–Labor Day), and the Prince George Native Art Gallery (tel. 604/562–7385). From Prince George you can turn south on Highway 97 for Kamloops and the Okanagan Valley (*see* Scenic Drives, *below*), or you can continue on Highway 16, then on 5 for a longer (some say even more spectacular) route to the same place.

Tour 3: Okanagan Valley and Environs, Including Rainbow and High Country

The Okanagan Valley is part of a highland plateau between the Cascade range of mountains on the west and the Monashee mountains on the east. Though small in size (only 3% of the province's total land mass), the area contains the interior's largest concentration of people. Dominating the valley is Okanagan Lake, a vacation hot-spot for tourists from the west coast and Alberta. In summer months it can be difficult to find rooms. The largest towns along the lake are Vernon at the north end, Kelowna in the middle, and Penticton at the south. Between, and along the lake, are the recreational and resort communities of **Summerland, Peachland, Westbank,** and **Oyama,** which are popular tourist destinations and have camping facilities, motels, and cabins. Favorite local lore tells of the legendary Ogopogo, a snakelike creature that inhabits the lake between Peachland and Summerland.

The valley is the fruit-growing capital of Canada, producing apricots, cherries, pears, plums, apples, and peaches. A visit to the region from mid-April through early June promises to jolt your senses with the brightness and fragrance of the spring blossoms.

27 We arrive in the valley by way of **Kamloops** (which is officially a part of High Country, not Okanagan), a convenient passageway from Fraser Canyon and Thompson Valley, and a stop on the Canadian Pacific Railroad. The town is 50 minutes northeast of Vancouver by air and 425 kilometers (260 miles) by road and is surrounded by 500 lakes, which provide an abundance of trout, Dolly Varden, and kokanee. During late September and October, however, attention turns to the sockeye salmon, when thousands of these fish—intent on breeding—return home to their birth waters in Adams River (only 65 kilometers, or 40 miles, east of Kamloops off the Trans-Canada Highway).

Once every four year—the last time was 1990—the sockeye run reaches a massive scale, as more than a million salmon pack the waters and up to 500,000 visitors come to observe. The **Roderick Haig-Brown Conservation Area,** which protects the 11-kilometer (7-mile) stretch of Adams River, is the best place to watch.

Wildlife enthusiasts will also enjoy the **Kamloops Wildlife Park** (Box 698, Kamloops, V2C 5L7, tel. 604/573–3242), a 55-acre compound housing 71 species in fairly natural habitats. Canyon hiking trails, a miniature railway, and adjacent waterslides provide something for everyone in the family.

Vernon, Kelowna, and Penticton, running south along Highway 97, like to believe each has a distinct personality, but local rivalries aside, the towns are actually one large unit. Okanagan Lake is their glue, offering recreation, lodging, and restaurants.

28 Of the three, **Vernon** is the least dependent on tourism, organized instead around forestry and agriculture. The city borders on two other lakes besides Okanagan, the most enticing of which is Kalamalka Lake. The **Kalamalka Lake Provincial Park** has warm waters, and some of the most scenic viewpoints and hiking trails in the region. Twelve kilometers (7.5 miles) north of Vernon, the **O'Keefe Historic Ranch** gives visitors a window on cattle-ranch life at the turn of the century. The O'Keefe house is a late 19th-century Victorian mansion opulently furnished with original antiques. On the grounds, which now are 50 acres (20 hectares), there are a Chinese cooks' house, St. Ann's Church, a blacksmith shop, a reconstructed general store, and a display of the old Shuswap and Okanagan Railroad. Also featured are a contemporary restaurant and gift shop. *9830 Hwy. 97, 12 km (8 mi) north of Vernon, tel. 604/542–7868. Admission: $4.50 adults, $3.50 senior citizens and children 13–18, $2.50 children 6–12; family and group rates available. Open mid-May–mid-Oct., daily 9–5.*

29 **Kelowna,** the largest city in the Okanagan, is home to **Father Pandosy's Mission,** the first nonnative settlement in the region, founded in 1859. *3685 Benvouline Rd., tel. 604/860–8369. Admission free. Open daily 9–5.*

The city also offers the area's only tour of a **fruit orchard;** a covered wagon, pulled by a tractor, takes you on the hour-long narrated excursion. *2750 KLO Rd., East Kelowna, tel. 604/769–4719. Admission: $6.50 adults, $5.50 senior citizens, accompanied children free. Open July 1–early Sept., weekdays 10–4, weekends 10–12.*

Kelowna is the geographic center of the valley's wine industry, with **Calona Wines Ltd.** (1125 Richter St., tel. 604/762–3332), British Columbia's oldest and biggest winemaker. Also around Kelowna are smaller but more intimate wineries, including **Gray Monk Cellars** (1051 Camp Rd., 8 km, or 5 mi, west of Winfield, off Hwy. 97, tel. 604/766–3168), and **Cedarcreek Estate Winery** (5445 Lakeshore Rd., 12 km, or 7.5 mi, south of Kelowna, off Hwy. 97 on the corner of Pandosy and Lakeshore Rds., tel. 604/764–8866).

30 **Penticton** is the most tourist-oriented of the three. While its winter population is about 25,000, its population in summer nears 130,000. An 11-kilometer (5-mile) drive south on Highway 97 takes you to the **Okanagan Game Farm** (tel. 604/497–5405), with more than 650 species of wild animals from around the world. Farther south, off Highway 3 and along the U.S. border, **Cathedral Provincial Park** (tel. 604/494–0321) features 82,000 acres (33,198 hectares) of lakes and rolling meadows, teeming with mule deer, mountain goats, and California bighorn sheep. To reach the main part of the park, either take the steep, eight-hour hike, or arrange (and pay in advance) for the Cathedral Lake Resort (in the park, tel. 604/499–5848) to transport you by four-wheel drive. There are 16 campsites in the park.

Winding farther south, Highway 3 connects with the Trans-Canada Highway (Highway 1), which parallels the Fraser River through the region known as **Rainbow Country.** A glimpse through the mists above roiling **Hell's Gate,** off Highway 1 in Fraser Canyon, hints at how the region got its name. An airtram carries visitors across the foaming canyon, above the fishway, where millions of sockeye salmon fight their way upriver to spawning grounds each September. In addition to interpretive displays on the life cycle of the salmon, you'll find a fudge factory, gift shop, and restaurant at the lower airtram terminal. *Box 129, Hope, tel. 604/867–9277. Admission: $8 adults, $7 senior citizens, $4 children. Open mid-Apr.–mid-June and mid-Sept.–mid-Oct,, Mon.–Thurs. 9–5 and Fri.–Sun. 9–7; mid-June–early Sept., daily 9–7.*

Continue southwest on Highway 1 to the well-signed **Mintner Gardens** at Exit 135 in Rosedale. This 27-acre compound contains 11 beautifully presented theme gardens—Chinese, rose, English, fern, fragrance, and more—along with aviaries and ponds. There are even farmyard animals, playgrounds, and a giant evergreen maze to entertain the kids. *52892 Bunker Rd., Rosedale, tel. 604/794–7191. Admission: $7.50 adults, $6.50 senior citizens, $3.50 children 6–12, children under 6 free. Open Apr.–Oct., daily 9–dusk.*

It's hard to miss the **Trans-Canada Waterslides,** just across the highway. This tremendously popular waterpark features slides with names such as Kamikaze, Cannonball, Super Heroes, and Flash Flood, along with wave and soaking pools, snack bars, and sunbathing areas to provide plenty of warm-weather fun. *Bridal Falls Rd., Rosedale, tel. 604/794–7455. Admission: $10.75 adults, $7.50 children, children under 3 free. Open mid-May– mid-June, weekends 10–8, mid-June–mid- Aug., daily 10–9.*

31 The same exit also leads to **Harrison Hot Springs,** a small resort community at the southern tip of picturesque Harrison Lake. Vacationers flock here to relax and rejuvenate in this almost pristine natural setting. Mountains surround the (64-kilometer, or 40-mile) lake that is ringed by pretty beaches and provides a broad range of outdoor activities to enjoy, in addition to the hot springs. Located across from the beach in the large building to the left of the Harrison Hot Springs Hotel is a spring-fed public pool. *100 Esplanade, Harrison Hot Springs, tel. 604/796–2244. Admission: $5 adults, $3.50 senior citizens and children, children under 5 free; unlimited-entry day passes $7 adults, $5 children. Open Sun.–Thurs. 8 AM–9 PM, Fri.– Sat. 8–10.*

A tour of the **Kilby General Store Museum,** a heritage attraction in nearby Harrison Mills, takes you back in time to British Columbia as it was in the 1920s. Visitors tour the general store and hotel of T. Kilby, a pioneer of the area, and chat with the shopkeeper, sniff whatever is simmering on the wood-burning stove, and tramp through the orchards, stockroom, fueling station, barn, and dairy house on the grounds. This is a fine slice of living history. *215 Kilby Rd. (1.6 km [1 mi] off Hwy. 7 on north shore of Frazer River; follow signs), Harrison Mills, tel. 604/796–9576. Admission: $4.50 adults, $4 senior citizens, $2.50 children, children under 5 free. Open May–June and Labor Day–mid-Oct., Thurs.–Mon. 10–4; July–Aug., daily 10–5, and mid-Oct.–Nov. 1, daily 10–4.*

Scenic Drives

The **Gold Rush Trail** is a 640-kilometer (400-mile) route along which the frontiersmen traveled in search of gold in the 19th and early 20th centuries. The interior British Columbia trail begins just below Prince George in the north, and extends to Lillooet in the south, but juts off at points in between. Following the route you can travel through Quesnel, Williams Lake, Wells, Barkerville, along the Fraser Canyon, and Cache Creek. Most towns and communities through which the trail passes have re-created villages, history museums, or historic sites that help to tell the story of the gold-rush era. For more information contact the **Cariboo Chilcotin Coast Tourist Association** (Box 4900, Williams Lake V2G 2V8, tel. 604/392–2226; in U.S. 800/663–5885, fax 604/392–2838).

Completion of a new highway opened the **Coast Mountain Circle,** linking Vancouver to Cariboo Country. This 702-kilometer (435-mile) route takes in spectacular Howe Sound, the deepwater port of Squamish, Whistler Resort, and Pemberton Valley before heading back to Vancouver through scenic Fraser Canyon and Harrison Hot Springs. The loop makes a comfortable two- to three-day journey. For more information contact the **Tourism Association of Southwestern B.C.** (304–828 W. 8th Ave., Vancouver V5Z 1E2, tel. 604/876–3088 or 800/667–3306).

Shopping

Okanagan Valley The **Peter Flanagan Okanagan Pottery Studio** (tel. 604/767–2010), located on Highway 97 in Peachland, sells handcrafted ceramics.

Geert Maas Sculpture Gardens, Gallery, and Studio. World-class sculptor Geert Maas exhibits his art in an indoor gallery and a one-acre garden, in the hills above Kelowna. Maas, who works in bronze, stoneware, and mixed media, creates distinctive abstract figures with a round and fluid quality. He also sells medallions, original paintings, and etchings. *R.R. 1250 Reynolds Rd., Kelowna, V1Y 7P9, tel. 604/860–7012. Admission free. Open year-round; call for exact hours.*

Prince Rupert Native art and other local crafts are available at **Studio 9** (516 3rd Ave. W, tel. 604/624–2366).

Queen Charlotte Islands The Haida Gwaii carve valuable figurines from the hard, black slate called argillite. The specific variety used by the Haidas is found only on the islands. Their works can be found at the **Adams Family House of Silver** (tel. 604/626–3215), in Old Masset, behind the Ed Jones Haida Museum, and at **Joy's Island Jewellers** (tel. 604/559–4742) in Queen Charlotte. Other island specialties are silk-screen prints and silver jewelry.

Vancouver Island Duncan is the home of Cowichan wool sweaters, handknitted by the Cowichan people. A large selection is available from **Hills Indian Crafts** (tel. 604/746–6731) and **Big Foot Trading Post** (tel. 604/748–1153), both on the main highway, about 1½ kilometers (1 mile) south of Duncan. Also check out **Modeste Wool Carding** (2615 Modeste Rd., Duncan, tel. 604/748–8983), about a half mile off the highway in nearby Koksilah.

Sports and Outdoor Activities

Canoeing and Kayaking Canoeing and kayaking are favorite ways to explore the miles of extended, interconnected waterways and the breathtaking coastline of British Columbia. The **Inside Passage, Queen Charlotte Strait, Georgia Strait,** and the other island-dotted straits and sounds that border the mainland provide fairly protected sea-going from Washington State to the Alaskan border, with numerous marine parks to explore along the way. Another particular favorite among paddlers is the **Powell Forest Canoe Route,** an 80-kilometer (50-mile) circuit of 12 lakes connected by streams, rivers, and well-maintained portage trails.

For rentals on Vancouver Island, contact **Tofino Sea-Kayaking Company** (Box 620, Tofino, tel. 604/725–4222) and **Stubbs Island Charters** (Box 7, Telegraph Cove, tel. 604/928–3185). On the mainland, try **Clipper Canoes** (1717 Salton Rd., Box 115, Abbotsford, tel. 604/853–9320) or **Lavington Rental** (5562 Hwy. 6, Vernon, tel. 604/542–4788).

Fishing Miles of coastline and thousands of lakes, rivers, and streams bring more than 750,000 fishermen to British Columbia each year. The waters of the province hold 74 species of fish (25 of them sport fish), including Chinook salmon and rainbow trout. An annual freshwater-fishing license is about $19 for Canadians, $17 for B.C. residents. For a nonresident or non-Canadian, it's $10–$15 for six days, and $27 annually. A saltwater-fishing license for one day costs $3.75 for Canadian residents and non-Canadians, and is available at virtually every fishing lodge and sporting-goods outlet along the coast. Annual licenses are about $11 for non-B.C. Canadians and $38 for non-Canadians.

For updated fishing information and regulations, contact the **B.C. Fish Branch** (Ministry of Environment, 810 Blanshard St., Victoria V8V 1X5, tel. 604/387–4573). For a guide to saltwater fishing, contact the **Department of Fisheries and Oceans** (Recreational Fisheries Div., Station 415, 555 W. Hastings St., Vancouver V6B 5G3, tel. 604/666–3271).

Golf There are more than 200 golf courses in British Columbia, and the figure is growing. The province is now an Official Golf Destination of the PGA Tour in Canada and of the American PGA tour. Greens fees are about $20–$40. The topography in British Columbia tends to be mountainous, and many courses have fine views as well as treacherous approaches to greens.

Okanagan Valley and Environs The Okanagan has a central tee-time booking service for out-of-town golfers that lists all of the Okanagan/Interior British Columbia courses below. *Box 342, Westbank V0H 2A0, tel. 604/768–7500, call collect. Open May 15–Oct. 15, Mon.–Fri. 9–5; leave message if no one is there.*

Gallaghers Canyon Golf Resort (4320 McCulloch Rd., Kelowna, tel. 604/861–4240) is one of the most challenging courses in British Columbia, with long, rolling, and twisting fairways. **Kelowna Golf and Country Club** (1297 Glenmore Dr., Kelowna, tel. 604/763–2736) is a private club that favors straight drivers; visitors are welcome but advised to avoid weekends. **Osoyoos Golf and Country Club** (20th Ave., Osoyoos, tel. 604/495–7003) provides a green setting in the dry, parched hills; only two of the 12 par-fours on the course are under 350 yards. Visitors are welcome. **Penticton Golf and Country Club** (799 Eckhardt Ave. W, Penticton, tel. 604/492–8727) has 10 acres of water hazards, challenging traps, and bunkers; it is a semi-private club that welcomes visitors. **Rivershore Golf Club** (off Old Shuswap Rd., Kamloops, tel. 604/573–4622) is a Robert Trent Jones–designed course and is one of British Columbia's longest, at 7,007 yards. Visitors are welcome. **Salmon Arm Golf Course** (3400 Hwy. 97B, Salmon Arm, tel. 604/832–4727) welcomes visitors to its hilly terrain. **Shadow Ridge Golf Club** (3770 Bullman Rd., Kelowna, tel. 604/765–7777) is a relatively new course, set in a valley and surrounded by orchards. **Summerland Golf and Country Club** (2405 Mountain Rd., Summerland, tel. 604/494–9554) is slightly off the beaten track but has two distinctly different nines with the front nine clear and the back nine cut through a pine forest. **Twin Lakes Golf and Country Resort** (Hwy. 3A, Kaleden, tel. 604/497–5359) has an on-site RV park.

Vancouver Island   Golf is also very popular on Vancouver Island, so there are many good courses to choose from, including: the **Glen Meadows Golf Club** (1050 McTavish Rd., Sidney, tel. 604/656–3136) on the Saanich Peninsula; the **Morningstar Golf Course** (525 Lowery St., Parksville, tel. 604/248–8161) not far from Nanaimo; and the **Long Beach Golf Course** (Pacific Rim Hwy., Tofino, tel. 604/725–3332) on the west side of the island.

Hiking   One of the most challenging hikes in British Columbia is along the **West Coast Trail** (*see* Exploring, Tour 1) in Pacific Rim National Park (tel. 604/726–4212), on Vancouver Island. The demanding 77-kilometer (47-mile) trail is for experienced hikers and follows part of the coast dubbed the "Graveyard of the Pacific," so-called because of the large number of shipwrecks that have occurred there. It can be traveled only on foot, takes an average of six days to complete, and is open from mid-May to late September. A permit is necessary to hike this trail; reservations are available from March through September.

In the Okanagan Valley, hikers will enjoy exploring the railbeds, trestles, tunnels, and abandoned stations of the **Kettle Valley Railway** network, stretching along Lake Okanagan between Penticton and Kelowna. The going is mild; just remember to make enough noise to let the rattlesnakes and bears know you're coming. The Chambers of Commerce for Kelowna (tel. 604/861–1515) and Penticton (tel. 604/492–4103) can provide maps and information.

Virtually all of British Columbia's provincial parks have fine hiking trail networks. The **Ministry of Parks** (1610 Mt. Seymour Rd., N. Vancouver V7G 1L3, tel. 604/929–1291) offers detailed information on those in the area you plan to visit.

Heli-hiking   Heli-hiking is very popular in this province; helicopters deliver hikers to untouched high alpine meadows and verdant mountain tops that have remained virtually untouched because of their inaccessibility. **Alpine Rafting Company** (Box 1409, Golden V0A 1H0, tel. 604/344–5016), **Fraser River Raft Expeditions Ltd.** (Box 10, Yale V0K 2S0, tel. 604/863–2336), **Highland Helicopter** (1685 Tranmer, Agassiz V0M 1K0, tel. 604/796–9610), and **Mount Robson Adventure Holidays** (Box 687, Valemount V0E 2Z0, tel. 604/566–4386) can provide further information.

Rafting With beautiful rivers such as Adams, Clearwater, Fraser, Illecillewaet, and Thompson interlacing the High Country, Okanagan Valley, and Fraser Canyon, there is a diverse range of
rafting trips from which to choose. Operators such as **Clearwater Expeditions** (613 Bissette Rd., Kamloops V2B 6L3, tel.
604/579–8360), **Fraser River Raft Expeditions Ltd.** (Box 10, Yale
V0K 2S0, tel. 604/863–2336), **Hyak Rafting** (1975 Maple St.,
Vancouver V6J 3S9, tel. 604/734–8622), and **Alpine Rafting
Company** (Box 1409, Golden V0A 1H0, tel. 604/344–5016) provide options from lazy, half-day floats to exhilarating white-
water journeys of up to a week.

Skiing British Columbia has hundreds of kilometers of groomed
Cross-country cross-country (Nordic) ski trails in the provincial parks and
more than 40 cross-country resorts. Most downhill destinations have carved out Nordic routes along the valleys, and
there are literally thousands more trails in unmanaged areas
of British Columbia.

For cross-country enthusiasts, two of the finest in the province
are **Lac le Jeune** (Box 3215, Kamloops V2C 6B8, tel. 604/732–
2722), 30 kilometers (18 miles) southwest of Kamloops, and
Manning Park Resort (Manning Park V0X 1R0, tel. 604/840–
8822) en route to the Okanagan, about 200 kilometers (124
miles) east of Vancouver. Manning Park also has downhill facilities, which are just as popular as the nordic program. On
Vancouver Island, **Mt. Washington** and **Mt. Cain Alpine Park**
(*see below*) have nordic facilities, as do **Apex Alpine** and **Silver
Star Mountain Resort** (*see below*) in the Okanagan Valley.

Downhill With more than half the province situated higher than 4,200
feet above sea level, new downhill courses are constantly opening. At the moment, more than 40 major resorts have downhill
facilities.

On Vancouver Island, **Mt. Washington Ski Resort Ltd.** (Box
3069, Courtenay V9N 5N3, tel. 604/338–1386), with more than
40 runs and an elevation of 5,200 feet, is the largest ski area on
Vancouver Island, and the third-largest in terms of visitors, in
the province. Located in the Comox Valley, it's a modern, well-
organized mountain with snowpack averaging 472 inches a
year. It also has 30 kilometers (19 miles) of double trackset
Nordic trails. Other island ski areas are **Forbidden Plateau**
(2050 Cliffe Ave., Courtenay V9N 2L3, tel. 604/334–4744), located near Mt. Washington, with 15 runs and a fall of 1,150 feet;
and **Mt. Cain** (Box 1225, Port McNeill V0N 2R0, tel. 604/956–
3849), on the northern part of the island near the community
of Sayward off Highway 19, with 16 runs and a fall of 1,500 feet.

The Okanagan Valley region, four hours east by car from Vancouver, or one hour by air, offers some of the best ski bargains
in the province. **Big White Ski Resort** (Box 2039, Station R,
Kelowna V1X 4K5, tel. 604/765–3101) is the highest ski area in
British Columbia, though Whistler has a longer free fall. The
resort has more than 45 runs along with hotels, restaurants,
and, like Whistler, is in the process of rapidly expanding. **Silver
Star Mountain Resort** (Box 2, Silver Star Mountain V0E 1G0,
tel. 604/542–0224), with more than 61 runs, offers well-lighted
night skiing. The complete village at the base of the mountain
has enough hotels to accommodate 725 people. **Apex Alpine**
(Box 1060, Penticton V2A 7N7, tel. 604/493–3200) has 45 runs
and is the largest ski resort in South Okanagan. On-mountain

condominiums—many for rent—can accommodate a total of 350.

Kootenay Country (*see* Canadian Rockies, Chapter 7), a southeastern section of British Columbia that includes the Rockies, Purcells, Selkirks, and Monashees, features two major resorts: **Whitewater** (Box 60, Nelson V1L 5P7, tel. 604/354–4944), with more than 20 runs and a lot of powder skiing; and **Red Mountain Resorts** (Box 670, Rossland V0G 1Y0, tel. 604/362–7384), which spans two mountains and three mountain faces, and has 30 marked runs.

The resorts in the High Country reflect British Columbia's most diverse topographical area. At 3,100 feet of vertical drop, **Tod Mountain** (Box 869, Kamloops V2C 5M8, tel. 604/578–7222) has 47 runs. On-mountain accommodations are limited to private condominium rentals and a bed-and-breakfast that accommodates up to 32 people. **Mt. Mackenzie** (Box 1000, Revelstoke V0E 2S0, tel. 604/837–5268) has 20 runs and offers deep-powder skiing. Revelstoke, located 5 kilometers (3 miles) from the base, has a wide selection of lodging.

Heli- and Snowcat Skiing — Heli-skiing operators are often located at well-established resorts, taking clients into otherwise inaccessible deep-powder regions of the mountains. Others operate as independents and offer accommodations, dining, and recreational facilities in their deluxe lodges. Some companies offer Snowcat skiing, in which an enclosed all-terrain vehicle takes you into the wilderness areas.

In Kootenay Country, try **Kootenay Helicopter Skiing** (Box 717, Nakusp V0G 1R0, tel. 604/265–3121; in B.C., Alberta, and the U.S., 800/663–0100). With accommodations at Kuskanax-Lodge, they run seven-day packages to and from Kelowna, Spokane, WA, and Castlegar. **Selkirk Wilderness Skiing** (1 Meadow Creek Rd., Meadow Creek V0G 1N0, tel. 604/366–4424) offers six-day packages (including remote lodging) to and from Nelson.

In the High Country, **Cat Powder Skiing** (Box 1479, Revelstoke V0E 2S0, tel. 604/837–9489) organizes two-, three-, and five-day, all-inclusive packages that run into the Selkirks and on the upper slopes of Mt. MacKenzie in Revelstoke.

Dining and Lodging

Dining

Throughout British Columbia you'll find a variety of cuisines, from Vancouver Island's seafood places to interior British Columbia's wild game–oriented menus. Prices vary from location to location, but ratings reflect the categories listed on the dining chart.

Category	Cost*
Very Expensive	over $35
Expensive	$25–$35

Moderate	$15–$25
Inexpensive	under $15

per person, excluding drinks, service, and 7% GST, in Canadian dollars

Highly recommended restaurants in each price category are indicated by a star ★.

Lodging

The lodging possibilities across the region are as diverse as the restaurant menus. Accommodations range from bed-and-breakfast inns and rustic cabins to deluxe chain hotels. In the cities, especially, there is an abundance of accommodations, but once you get off the beaten track, guest rooms are often a rare commodity and may require advance booking.

Category	Cost*
Very Expensive	over $125
Expensive	$90–$125
Moderate	$50–$90
Inexpensive	under $50

All prices are for a standard double room, excluding 7% GST. Prices are in Canadian dollars.

Highly recommended lodgings in each price category are indicated by a star ★.

Vancouver Island

Campbell River
Dining
★

Royal Coachman Inn. This is another of those informal, blackboard-menu restaurants that dot the landscape of the island. The menu is surprisingly daring for what is essentially a high-end pub, and the inn draws crowds nightly, especially on Tuesday and Saturday (prime rib nights). The menu, however, changes daily, so if ribs aren't your favorite, try one of the other specials. Come early for both lunch and dinner to beat the crowds. *84 Dogwood St., tel. 604/286–0231. No reservations. Dress: casual. AE, MC, V. Inexpensive–Moderate.*

Dining and Lodging

Tsa-Kwa-Luten Lodge. This resort, operated by members of the Kwakiutl tribe, offers authentic Pacific Coast native food and cultural activities. It is located on a high bluff amid 1,100 acres of forest on Quadra Island, a 10-minute ferry ride from Campbell River. Each room in the main lodge has a sea view from a deck or patio; many have a fireplace and loft. There are also four beachfront cabins with fireplace, whirlpool tub, kitchen facilities, and private veranda. Guests are invited to take part in traditional dances in the resort's lounge, which resembles a longhouse, and to visit nearby petroglyphs to make rubbings. *Box 460, Quathiaski Cove, VOP 1NO, tel. 604/285–2042 or 800/665–7745, fax 604/285–2532. 26 rooms, 4 cabins. Facilities: restaurant, lounge, fitness room, sauna, Jacuzzi,* *mountain bikes, guided salmon fishing. AE, DC, MC, V. Very Expensive.*

★ **April Point Lodge and Fishing Resort.** Operated for almost 50 years by the friendly Peterson family, it comes as no surprise that April Point Lodge has developed a tremendous reputation and whopping amount of repeat business among vacationers. Spread across a point of Quadra Island, and stretching into Discovery Passage across from Campbell River, the 1944 cedar lodge is surrounded by refurbished fishermen's cabins and guest houses that have been added over the years. For the most part, the accommodations are tidy and comfortable rather than fancy; most have kitchen facilities, fireplaces, and sun decks, and a few are equipped with Jacuzzi baths and hot tubs. Kwaki-utl and Haida Gwaii art adorn the comfortable lounge and dining room where fine regional cuisine is featured. Special native feasts on the beach on warm summer nights are especially memorable, with spitted salmon roasted over an open fire; fresh steamed scallops, prawns, and clams; and one of the wines from the extensive cellar. *1000 April Point Rd., Box 1, V9W 4Z9, tel. 604/285–2222; fax 604/285–2411. 33 units. Facilities: restaurant, lounge, gift shop, universal gym, pool, nature trails, bikes marina, sea plane dock, salmon charters and nature tours available. AE, D, DC, MC, V. Some units closed Oct.–Apr. Expensive.*

Comox/Courtenay
Dining
★

The Old House Restaurant. This split-character restaurant offers both formal and casual dining, in a restored 1938 home with large cedar beams and a stone fireplace. Upstairs, among linen and fresh flowers, you select from an innovative Continental menu, with a delightful pepper steak leading as the house specialty. Downstairs, where it is decidedly more informal, you can get sandwiches, pastas, and salads. *1760 Riverside La., Courtenay, tel. 604/338–5406. Reservations advised upstairs; no reservations downstairs. Dress: casual but neat upstairs; casual downstairs. AE, DC, MC, V. Moderate.*

Lodging

The Greystone Manor. This nonsmoking bed-and-breakfast, set in a 70-year-old house with period furnishings, looks right out on Comox Harbor, where a playful colony of seals is often visible from the house. The antiques, wood stove, and wood paneling add to the hospitable, cozy feel of this inn. Breakfast, which includes fresh fruit, muffins, fruit pancakes, or quiche, is enough to keep you filled most of the day. *4014 Haas Rd., Courtenay V9N 8H9, tel. 604/338–1422. 4 rooms share 2 baths. Facilities: garden, walking trails. MC. Moderate.*

★ **The Kingfisher.** This hotel, situated among trees and overlooking the Strait of Georgia, is located five minutes south of Courtenay, but still it has some nice touches. The inn's solid furnishings, clean white-stucco walls, bright lobby with lots of greenery, and rooms with mountain and ocean views offer a nice change from the majority of plain accommodations lining the main drag. *Site 672, RR 6, Courtenay V9N 8H9, tel. 604/338–1323. 30 units. Facilities: restaurant, lounge, 2 tennis courts, outdoor pool, sauna, whirlpool. AE, D, DC, MC, V. Moderate.*

Malahat
Dining and Lodging
★

The Aerie. The million-dollar view of Finlayson Arm and the Gulf Islands persuaded Austrians Leo and Maria Schuster to build their small, luxury resort. In this Mediterranean-style villa, some rooms have a patio; others have whirlpool tubs tucked into window nooks to take advantage of the scenery. The dining room is open to the public for stunning dinner views and outstanding cuisine. The maple-smoked salmon, pheasant consommé, medallions of venison in morel sauce, and crème brûlée with fruit sorbet are more than worth the short drive from Victoria. *600 Ebedora Ln., V0R 2L0, tel. 604/743–7115 or 604/743–4055; fax 604/743–4766. 8 rooms, 5 suites. Facilities: restaurant, indoor and outdoor Jacuzzis, sauna, exercise room, library, helipad, nature trails. Reservations advised for restaurant. AE, MC, V. Expensive–Very Expensive.*

Nanaimo
Dining
★ **The Mahle House.** This casually elegant place serves innovative Northwest cuisine, such as braised rabbit with Dijon mustard and red wine sauce. Twelve items adorn the regular menu, including a succulent carrot and ginger soup, and a catch of the day. Care to detail, an intimate setting, and a new addition to the three country-style rooms make this one of the finest dining experiences in the region. *Cedar and Heemer Rds., tel. 604/722–3621. Reservations advised. Dress: casual but neat. MC, V. Closed lunch and Mon.–Tues. Moderate.*

★ **The Grotto.** A perennial favorite, The Grotto is a Nanaimo institution that specializes in a variety of seafood. The restaurant is set against a waterfront background, and dining here is relaxed and casual. Try the spare ribs, gourmet pizzas, or the seafood platter—zum-zum—that's big enough for two. *1511 Stewart Ave., tel. 604/753–3303. Reservations accepted. Dress: casual. AE, MC, V. Closed lunch and Sun. Inexpensive–Moderate.*

Dining and Lodging
★ **Yellow Point Lodge.** Yellow Point is a spit of land south of Nanaimo, east of Ladysmith, that has a series of luxurious rustic lodges of which this is the finest example. Rebuilt in 1986 after a fire destroyed the original, the lodge lost almost nothing in ambience and gained a great deal: Nine larger rooms have better facilities (all have private baths and are available year-round). Situated on a rocky knoll overlooking the Stuart Channel are beach cabins, field cabins, a range of different-size cottages, and beach barracks (closed mid-October to mid-April) for the hardy (the summer-use cabins, cottages, and barracks have no running water and share a central bathhouse). Beach cabins can be private and include tree-trunk beds and wood-burning stoves; beach barracks are not as sound, and noises carry from unit to unit, but the location along the shore makes them popular. One hundred eighty acres of land allows for strolling and exploring. Three full meals and snacks are included in the tariff. *Yellow Point Rd., RR 3, Ladysmith V0R 2E0, tel. 604/245–7422. 50 rooms. Facilities: restaurant (for guests only), 2 tennis courts, seawater pool, hot tub, sauna, canoes, mountain bikes. MC, V. Inexpensive–Expensive.*

Dorchester Hotel. Upbeat Mediterranean tones of champagne, ochre, and teal replace the old drab blue exterior of the Dorchester. Once the Nanaimo Opera House, this elegant hotel overlooking the harbor has a distinctive character, with gold knockers on each of the doors, winding hallways, and a spacious library. The rooms are small but exceptionally comfortable, and most have views of the harbor. *70 Church St., V9R 5H4, tel. 604/754–6835; fax 604/754–2638. 70 rooms. Facilities: restaurant, meeting rooms, fitness room, lounge, library, rooftop patio. AE, DC, MC, V. Moderate.*

Dining and Lodging **La Coast Bastion Inn.** This hotel is conveniently located downtown near the ferry terminal, train, and bus stations. All rooms with balconies have views of the old Hudson's Bay fort and the ocean and are modernly furnished. The three eating/entertainment establishments located within the hotel make this a self-sufficient accommodation. *11 Bastion St., V9R 2Z9, tel. 604/753–6601, or 800/663–1144 in the U.S. 179 rooms. Facilities: restaurant, lounge, Irish deli/pub, gift shop, boutique, convention rooms, sauna, hot tub, gym. AE, DC, MC, V. Expensive–Very Expensive.*

Parksville
Dining and Lodging

Beach Acres Resort Hotel. For a family vacation, this collection of cottages set in the woods facing the Georgia Strait is both charming and practical. Each unit has one or two bedrooms, living room, kitchen, fireplace, and storage areas. *1015 E. Island Hwy., V9P 2E4, tel. 604/248–3424; fax 604/248–6145. 60 cottages. Facilities: restaurant, indoor pool, sauna, whirlpool, playground, 3 tennis courts, health club. AE, DC, MC, V. 1-week minimum July–Aug. Very Expensive.*

The Roadhouse Inn. This Swiss chalet, set on three acres, is central to four of the region's golf courses. There are only a limited number of rooms, but all are comfortable. *1223 Smithers Rd., V9P 2C1, tel. 604/248–2912. 6 rooms. Facilities: restaurant. MC, V. Inexpensive–Moderate.*

Port Hardy
Dining and Lodging

Glen Lyon Inn. All of the rooms have a full ocean view of Hardy Bay and, like most area motels, have clean, modern amenities. Eagles are often on the premises, eyeing the water for fish to prey on. It's a short ride from the inn to the ferry terminal. *6345 Hardy Bay Rd., Box 103, V0N 2P0, tel. 604/949–7115; fax 604/949–7415. 29 rooms. Facilities: restaurant, lounge, nearby marina, boat launch. AE, DC, MC, V. Moderate.*

Sidney
Lodging
★

Borthwick Country Manor. Flower boxes and awnings adorn the windows of this Tudor home, built in 1979 on Vancouver Island's Saanich Peninsula. It is ideally located in the quiet countryside within minutes of Victoria, Butchart Gardens, the airport, and Washington and British Columbia ferries. Owners Joyce and Watson Borthwick's interest in collecting and refinishing antiques is evident throughout the house, from the elaborately carved 17th-century mahogany table and Victorian balloon-back chairs and sideboard in the dining room, to a Canadian bedstead and early American dresser, both of mahogany, in the largest guest room. French doors lead to the backyard, with gardens to admire and a hot tub to enjoy. *9750 Ardmore Dr.,RR 2,, V8L 3S1, tel. 604/656–9498; fax 604/474–7250. 5 rooms. Facilities: hot tub, fishing charters available. MC, V. Closed Dec. Moderate–Expensive.*

Sooke
Dining and Lodging
★

Ocean Wilderness. This large 1940s log cabin sits on five forested, beachfront acres, 13 kilometer (8 miles) west of Sooke. Owner Bill Paine, a retired sea captain, and his wife, Marion, added seven guest rooms in a rough cedar addition in 1990. The pair of auction buffs has furnished their home with a fine collection of Victorian antiques. Romantic canopies and ruffled linens on high beds dominate the spacious guest rooms, which have sitting areas with views of either the Strait of Juan de Fuca or the gardens in the back. Just outside, stepping stones lead to a hot tub housed in a Japanese-style gazebo near awinding path that descends to the beach cove. *109 W. Coast Rd., RR 2,V0S 1N0, tel. and fax 604/646–2116. 7 rooms. Facilities: private decks or patios, hot tub, hiking trails, meal service available. MC, V. Moderate–Expensive.*

★ **Sooke Harbour House.** This original 1931 clapboard farmhouse turned inn presents three suites, a 10-room addition, and a dining room—all of which exude elegance. One of the finest restaurants in British Columbia, it is well worth the trip to Sooke, from Victoria. The fish is just-caught fresh, and the herbs, picked from some 200 varieties, are grown on the property. Four chefs sharing the kitchen guarantees an abundance of creative dishes. On a nice summer evening you may want to sit on the terrace, where you can catch a glimpse of the sea mammals that play by the spit of land in front of the restaurant. Equally exquisite are the romantic guest rooms, with natural wood and white finishes adding to each unit's unique theme. Rooms range from the Herb Garden Room—decorated in shades of mint, with French doors opening onto a private patio—to the Longhouse Room, complete with Native American furnishings. All units, with fireplaces and either ocean or mountain views, come with fresh flowers, a decanter of port, and wet bars that include herbal teas and cookies. Breakfast and lunch are included in your room rate, but you must make a reservation for your meals. Likewise, reservations for nonguests for dinner are essential. Hosts Fredrica and Sinclair Philip have been paying attention to details here since 1979. *1528 Whiffen Spit Rd., RR 4, V0S 1N0, tel. 604/642–3421; fax 604/642–6988. 13 rooms. Facilities: restaurant. Closed lunch except for hotel guests. Dress: casual but neat. AE, MC, V. Very Expensive.*

Ucluelet/Tofino **Whale's Tale.** This is a no-frills, dark but warmly decorated
Dining down-to-earth place where cooking and the rustic decor go hand-in-hand. The view isn't much, but the cedar-shingle building, set on pilings, shakes with a good gust of wind. The menu is highlighted by prime rib and a variety of local seafood. *1861 Peninsula Rd., Ucluelet, tel. 604/726–4621. Dress: casual. MC, V. Closed lunch and Nov.–Jan. Moderate.*

★ **The Wickaninnish Restaurant.** Before the Canadian government acquired this wonderful wood building for its interpretive center, it was a unique inn. It is still a restaurant, with an ambience—the beach setting, combined with the building's glass exterior and stone-and-beam interior, accented by a stone fireplace—that cannot be matched anywhere else in the area. Seafood is the primary choice here—especially the West Coast chowder—but if you take the chicken-and-prawn stir-fry, you won't be disappointed. *On Long Beach, 16 km (11 mi) north of Ucluelet, tel. 604/726–7706. Reservations advised for 7 or more. Dress: casual. AE, MC, V. Closed mid-Oct.–mid-Feb. Moderate.*

Lodging **Chesterman's Beach Bed and Breakfast.** This is one of several
★ small, romantic bed-and-breakfasts located on the beach, but the front yard—which is the rolling ocean surf—makes this one unique. You can while away the hours just walking the beach, searching the tidal pools, or—from March to October—watching whales migrating by the front door. The self-contained suite in the main house and the separate Lookout Suite are romantic, cozy, and unique; both have comfortable beds and a view of the beach. The self-sufficient one-bedroom garden cottage offers no ocean view but accommodates up to four; it's a good option for a family vacation. Owner Joan Dublanko makes hot muffins every morning. *1345 Chesterman's Beach Rd., Tofino V0R 2Z0, tel. 604/725–3726. 3 suites. Facilities: bikes, surfboards, beach. MC, V. Expensive–Very Expensive.*

Canadian Princess Fishing Resort. If old ships are to your liking, book a berth on this converted survey ship which has 30 comfortable, but hardly opulent, staterooms. Each offers one to four berths, and all share washrooms; for something a bit more spacious, request the captain's cabin. Roomier than the ship cabins and complete with more contemporary furnishings are the resort's deluxe shoreside rooms. Promising an unusual experience, this Spartan resort provides the bare necessities—mostly to the many fishermen who flock here during the summer. *The Boat Basin, Box 939, Ucluelet V0R 3A0, tel. 604/726-7771 or 800/663-7090; fax 604/726-7121. 76 sleeping units. Facilities: 10 charter boats. AE, MC, V. Moderate–Expensive.*

Pacific Sands Beach Resort. Just a mile north of Pacific Rim National Park is this rustic resort with motel suites and individual two-bedroom cottages. The motel rooms are basic with modern furnishings, but fireplaces make them seem cozier. Some of the rooms in the new, three-story addition have Jacuzzi tubs. Pacific Sands is close to Long Beach golf course and is on the ocean. *1421 Pacific Rim Hwy., Box 237, Tofino V0R 2Z0, tel. 604/725-3322; fax 604/725-3155. 66 rooms. AE, MC, V. Moderate–Expensive.*

North of Vancouver Island

Prince Rupert
Dining

Smile's Seafood Café. If you don't mind walking among the fish-processing plants by the railway, you'll find this place a real change of pace. It has been a mainstay of Prince Rupert since 1935 and has succeeded because it provides small-town friendly service along with its seafood menu. Favorites include the halibut cheeks and the fisherman's platter. *113 George Hills Way, tel. 604/624-3072. No reservations. Dress: casual. MC, V. Moderate.*

Lodging

Highliner Inn. This modern high rise near the waterfront is conveniently situated and relatively well priced. It's in the heart of the downtown shopping district and is only one block from the airline terminal building. Ask for a room with a private balcony and view of the harbor. *815 1st Ave. W, V8J 1B3, tel. 604/624-9060; fax 604/627-7759. 96 rooms. Facilities: restaurant, lounge, convention rooms, beauty salon, laundromat. AE, DC, MC, V. Moderate.*

Dining and Lodging
★

Crest Motor Hotel. It may surprise you to find a four-diamond AAA hotel in this small community, but this warm, modern hotel is probably the finest in the north. It's one block away from the two shopping centers but is situated on a bluff overlooking the harbor. The pleasantly decorated restaurant has brass rails, beam ceilings, and a waterfront view, and specializes in seafood; particularly outstanding are the salmon dishes. *222 1st Ave. W, V8J 3P6, tel. 604/624-6771; in Canada, 800/663-8150; fax 604/627-7666. 103 rooms. Facilities: restaurant, lounge, coffee shop. Reservations required for restaurant. Dress: casual but neat. AE, D, DC, MC, V. Moderate–Expensive.*

Queen Charlotte Islands
Lodging

Alaska View Lodge. On a clear day, you can step onto your porch at this bed-and-breakfast and see the mountains of Alaska in the distance. The lodge is bordered by a long stretch of sandy beach on one side and by woods on the other. Eliane and Charly Feller, both European by origin, offer simple beach-house rooms with few of the amenities you're likely to find in a Hilton; but the private balconies more than compensate. For an additional cost, Eliane makes a three-course dinner, using classical recipes based on Queen Charlotte fare, such as home-smoked salmon, scallops, and Dungeness crab. *Tow Hill Rd., Box 227, Masset V0T 1M0, tel. 604/626–3333. 4 rooms. No credit cards. Moderate.*

Spruce Point Lodge. This cedar-sided building, encircled by a balcony, attracts families and couples because of its inexpensive rates and down-home feel. Like most Queen Charlotte accommodations, this one is more rustic than luxurious and features locally made pine furnishings that go with the northern-woods motif. For the money you get a Continental breakfast and an occasional seafood barbecue, with a menu that depends on the daily catch. Kayakers and hikers on a budget should ask about the bunk rooms, usually available at a low nightly rate. *609 6th Ave., Queen Charlotte V0T 1S0, tel. 604/559–8234. 7 rooms. MC, V. Inexpensive.*

Dining and Lodging

Tlell River House. The smell of fresh-cut wood welcomes you into this new, secluded lodge overlooking the Tlell River. From the property in the middle of the woods, it's only a few hundred feet to the beach (and the shipwreck of the *Pezuta*). The rooms feature all-wood paneling, floral curtains, and thick down comforters; many have views of the river. The restaurant serves excellent seafood and a variety of deliciously rich cheesecakes. *Beitush Rd., just south of the Tlell River Bridge on Hwy. 16, Box 56, Tlell V0T 1Y0, tel. 604/557–4211, fax 604/557–4622. 10 rooms. Facilities: restaurant, lounge, meeting room, laundromat, boat rentals, guided fishing trips. MC, V. Moderate.*

Okanagan Valley and Environs
Including Rainbow and High Country

Harrison Hot Springs Dining
★

The Black Forest. Ask the locals where to dine and they'll send you here, a charming Bavarian dining room on Harrison Village Esplanade, overlooking the lake. It comes as no surprise that the specialties here are German standards, from schnitzels to Black Forest cake, with a few Continental dishes (mainly steaks and seafood) thrown in for good measure. Hearty German beer and an array of wines round out the selection. *180 Esplanade, tel. 604/796–9343. Reservations advised. Dress: casual but neat. MC, V. Closed lunch. Moderate–Expensive.*

Dining and Lodging
★

Harrison Hot Springs Hotel. Ever since fur traders and gold miners discovered the soothing hot springs in the late 1800s, Harrison has been a favored stopover spot. The St. Alice Hotel, built in 1896 to accommodate these weary travelers, was destroyed by fire, and from its ashes rose the Harrison Hot Springs Hotel in the 1920s. The property has continued to grow over the decades, and, for the most part, you can tell from the decor when sections were built. The most reasonably priced rooms located in the original building and west tower are dated, with worn furnishings, fixtures, and carpets; those in the new east tower (added in 1989) are much more modern and plush, with a heftier price tag. The long list of amenities and scenic lakeside location give the hotel a resort feel; plans to add a PGA-rated 18-hole golf course are underway. Bring a robe to make the trip from your room to the indoor hot spring-fed pools or heated outdoor pool. *100 Esplanade, Harrison Hot Springs V0M 1K0, tel. 604/796–2244; in the Pacific Northwest, 800/663–2266; fax 604/796–9374. 290 rooms, 12 cottages. Facilities: 2 restaurants, lounge, 2 indoor pools, 1 outdoor pool, saunas, 3 tennis courts, 9-hole executive golf course, games room, gift shops,* beauty salon, health club, complimentary afternoon tea, bike rentals, hiking trails. Reservations advised for restaurant. Dress: neat. AE, DC, MC, V. Moderate–Very Expensive.

Kamloops
Dining and Lodging
★

Lac le Jeune Resort. This is the property that locals use when they want to combine the outdoors and sophisticated, modern surroundings. With 160 kilometers (99 miles) of cross-country skiing, a lake stocked with trout, and a restaurant that serves robust helpings, this is a good choice for an accommodation. The rustic, self-sufficient cabins are perfect for families because of their ample size and amenities, and pets are permitted. There are also comfortable, spacious rooms in the main lodge, with no phones or televisions to distract from the beauty of the setting. *Off Coquihala Hwy., 29 km (18 mi) southwest of Kamloops, Box 3215, Kamloops V2C 6B8, tel. 604/372–2722 or 800/561–5253, fax 604/372–8755. 28 rooms, 4-plex chalet, 6 cabins. Facilities: restaurant, lounge, meeting room, gift shop, theater, games room, indoor whirlpool, sauna, boat and ski rentals. AE, D, DC, MC, V. Moderate–Expensive.*

Kelowna
Dining

Papillon. This contemporarily furnished restaurant features a Continental menu that offers pasta, seafood, and steak. While seafood is not necessarily the specialty here, the prawns and scallops Caribbean is superb and highly recommended. The wine list includes a wide selection of imported and local wines that work nicely with the meals. *375 Leon Ave., tel. 604/763–3833. Reservations advised. Dress: neat but casual. AE, MC, V. Closed weekend lunch. Moderate–Expensive.*

Dining and Lodging

Hotel Eldorado. In 1989, the owners bought the old Eldorado Arms, built in 1926, and floated it by barge to its present location. Shortly thereafter, the old property burned down, but a new Eldorado has been built in its place, with much of the old-style charm intact. Rooms tend to be small and cozy, with light carpets, floral patterns, and antique furnishings; many have balconies affording superb views of Okanagan Lake. The Boardwalk Restaurant has earned a fine reputation, serving fresh rack of lamb and seafood dishes. Ask for a seat on the waterfront patio. *500 Cook Rd., V1W 9L5, tel. 604/763–7500, fax 604/861–4779. 20 rooms. Facilities: restaurant, lounge, conference room, marina, Jacuzzi suite. Dress: casual but neat. AE, MC, V. Expensive.*

Dining and Lodging
★

Lake Okanagan Resort. This well-acclaimed Hotels and Resorts property is a popular, self-contained destination on the west side of Okanagan Lake. All rooms have either kitchens or kitchenettes and range in size from one-room suites in the main hotel to spacious three-room chalets situated around the 300 acres. The resort shows some signs of age, particularly in the worn floors; but functional, earthtone furnishings, wood-burning fireplaces, perfect views of the lake, and all the resort activities make this a good choice of accommodations. Lakeside Terrace rooms renovated in 1993 are the best choice. *2751 Westside Rd., V1Y 8B2; tel. 604/769–3511 or 800/223–0888, fax 604/769–6655. 150 rooms. Facilities: restaurant, café, poolside lounge, Jacuzzi and saunas, 3 pools, par-3 9-hole golf course, 7 tennis courts, stables, marina, scuba shop, pro shop, hiking/biking trails, nature and dinner cruises. AE, D, DC, MC, V. Very Expensive.*

Merritt
Dining and
Lodging
★

Corbett Lake Country Inn. The locals want to keep this one a secret, but not owner Peter McVey, a French-trained chef. His restaurant offers a different fixed menu every night; favorites include rack of lamb and chateaubriand. The six single cabins (with extra beds) and two duplexes are comfortable, but not plush, and there are also three rooms in the main lodge. Small pets are allowed. *Off Hwy. 5A, 11 km (6.8 mi) south of Merritt, Box 327, V0K 2B0, tel. 604/378–4334. 10 cabins, 3 rooms. Facilities: boat rentals, cross-country ski trails. Reservations required for restaurant. Dress: casual. No credit cards. Closed Mar.–Apr., Oct. 15–Dec. 23. Moderate.*

Penticton
Dining
★

Granny Bogner's. The decor in this mostly Continental restaurant is a bit contrived, with flowing lace curtains, Oriental rugs, wood chairs, cloth-covered tables, and waitresses adorned in long paisley skirts, conveying that this is a "homey" place. But the food is excellent and prepared meticulously to order. The poached halibut and roasted duck have contributed to the widely held belief that this is the best restaurant in the Okanagan. *302 Eckhardt Ave. W, tel. 604/493–2711. Reservations advised. Dress: casual. AE, MC, V. Closed lunch; Sun. and Mon.; Jan. Moderate–Expensive.*

Lodging

Coast Lakeside Resort. On the shore of Okanagan Lake, the inn is both a peaceful retreat and right in the center of the action. The waterfront offers relaxation, and the nearby Penticton Golf and Country Club invites a competitive round of golf. Vancouver businesspeople love this place because it provides comfort and convention facilities. The newly renovated rooms are bright and airy, and half of them have lake views. *21 Lakeshore Dr. W, V2A 7M5, tel. 604/493–8221 or 800/663–1144; fax 604/493–0607. 204 rooms. Facilities: 2 restaurants, lounge, beauty salon, 2 tennis courts, volleyball, windsurfing, sailing, waterskiing, indoor pool, health club, sauna, Jacuzzi, games room, shuffleboard, masseuse. AE, DC, MC, V. Very Expensive.*

★

Riordan House. When John and Donna Ortiz bought and restored the former Tiffin Tea House/Riordan Restaurant for their residence, they didn't expect to give guided tours to the newly spiffed-up 1921 house. But people seemed to like the place, built by a Prohibition rum-runner and furnished now with family antiques, so the Ortizes bowed to the inevitable and opened it as a bed-and-breakfast. One bedroom has a fireplace and one a sitting area; all look out on the surrounding hills. The Continental breakfast stars house-baked croissants, scones, muffins, and a selection of seasonal fruit; box lunches are packed on request (and Granny Bogner's is 60 paces away). Lake Okanagan is only a short walk, and you can drift on a rubber raft down the canal that connects it with Skaha Lake. *689 Winnipeg St., V2A 5N1, tel. 604/493–5997. 3 rooms share 3 baths. Facilities: airport pickup, shuttle to lake beach, robes and slippers, fresh flowers. MC, V. Inexpensive–Moderate.*

For bed-and-breakfast information contact **Okanagan Bed and Breakfast** (Box 5135, Kelowna V1Y 8T9, tel. 604/868–2700).

Silver Star
Mountain
Dining
★

Craigellachie Dining Room. The home-cooked meals in the dining room of the Putnam Station Hotel are filling rather than fancy. Soups and sandwiches are on the lunch menu, while old favorites like barbecue ribs, lasagne, pork chops, steaks, and pastas are offered in the evenings. The daily three-course special is generally a good deal. *Silver Star Mountain Resort, Box*

4, Silver Star Mountain, tel. 604/542–2459. Reservations accepted. Dress: casual. AE, MC, V. Moderate.

Dining and Lodging

★ **Vance Creek Hotel.** Looking more like the set of a spaghetti Western than a modern hotel, the Vance Creek enjoys a prime location in the heart of the *Gaslight*-era-themed village resort, atop Silver Star Mountain. Rooms are simple, with coordinated decor, long vanities in the entryway, and boxy bathrooms. Those on the first floor are popular with families because they are equipped with kitchenettes, bunk beds for the kids, and private entrances that open outside the hotel. Willow furniture and fireplaces add a touch more comfort to rooms in the annex completed in 1993. *Silver Star Mountain Resort, Box 3, Silver Star Mountain V0E 1G0, tel. 604/549–5191; fax 604/549–5177. 84 rooms. Facilities: 2 restaurants, lounge, bar, hot tubs, ski locker, meeting room, resort amenities including hiking/biking trails, indoor pool, horseback riding, bike and in-line skate rentals. Reservations accepted in restaurants. Dress: casual. Closed mid-Apr.–mid-May. AE, D, MC, V. Expensive.*

★ **Silver Lode Inn.** To complete the alpine experience on Silver Star Mountain, head to the Silver Lode Restaurant for raclette or fondue. Owners Max Schlaepfer and Trudi Amstutz, originally from Berne, Switzerland, serve hearty helpings of the real thing in the cheerful restaurant of their inn. No-frills rooms offer the basic comforts and are the most reasonably priced in the village. *Silver Star Mountain Resort, Box 5, Silver Star Mountain V0E 1G0, tel. 604/549–5105; fax 604/549–2163. Facilities: restaurant, bar, lounge, ski locker, hot tub, meeting room, resort amenities including hiking/biking trails, indoor pool, horseback riding, bike and in-line skate rentals. Reservations accepted in restaurant. Dress: casual. AE, MC, V. Moderate–Expensive.*

Vernon **Intermezzo.** This intimate Italian restaurant combines dim
Dining lighting, high-backed chairs, olive-green wall paneling, and a lounge with a fireplace. The effect is formal and old European, although the service is anything but stiff. Owner Jean DeLisle offers standard veal, fish, and pasta dishes, and an excellent selection of wines, as displayed in the wood cabinet of the main dining room. *3206 34th Ave., Box 22, Vernon V1T 6M1, tel. 604/542–3853. Reservations accepted. Dress: casual but neat. AE, MC, V. Inexpensive.*

Lodging **Village Green Hotel.** This hotel offers access to four golf courses and to the Silver Star Ski Resort, just 22 kilometers (14 miles) away. The bright, pleasant decor and reasonable prices make this hotel a good alternative to the other accommodations that line Highway 97. The rooms are spacious and the service is personal and friendly. *4801 27th St., V1T 4Z1, tel. 604/542–3321; fax 604/549–4252. 138 rooms. Facilities: restaurant, coffee shop, gift shop, lounge, night club, 4 tennis courts, volleyball, indoor and outdoor pools, sauna, Jacuzzi, shuttle to ski resort and golf courses. AE, D, DC, MC, V. Moderate.*

7 The Canadian Rockies

By Peter Oliver

*Peter Oliver is a
New York writer
whose articles
have appeared in*
Backpacker, The
New York Times,
Skiing, Summit,
*and many other
publications. He is
author of* The
Insider's Guide to
the Best Skiing in
New England.

Comparing mountains is a subjective and imprecise business. Yet few would argue that the 640-kilometer (400-mile) stretch of the Canadian Rockies easily ranks as one of the most extravagantly beautiful ranges on earth. With little standing between the mountains and the Alberta prairie, the Rockies etch on the horizon an abrupt and stony line of chaotic grandeur that can be seen from 100 kilometers (60 miles) away to the east. Behind the prairie, granite walls rise thousands of feet above evergreen forests and glacially carved basins.

The peak that best epitomizes the character of the Canadian Rockies is Mt. Robson, which, at 3,954 meters (12,931 feet), is the highest of them all. A colossus of tumbling glaciers and cliff walls, usually shrouded in storm clouds, Mt. Robson creates its own irascible climate zone: The rush of avalanches down its flanks has triggered wind blasts well over 320 kilometers (200 miles) an hour.

In this region, keeping mountain ranges straight can be tedious. The Columbia Mountains, a series of parallel ranges just west of the Rockies, are often lumped together with the Rockies (as in fact they are in this chapter). This makes logistical sense when visiting the region for at least two good reasons: first, because the Columbias are in close proximity to the Rockies, and second, because many recreational activities that are prohibited in the national parks of the Rockies (notably helicopter-assisted skiing and hiking) are allowed in the Columbias.

However, this is the sort of travel-guide gerrymandering that undoubtably gives geologists fits. In fact, geologically speaking, the actual Rockies rise along the Continental Divide and are, at about 60 million years old, relative youngsters as mountains go. The Columbias, by comparison, were first formed about 180 million years ago and consist of four sub-ranges: the Cariboos to the north and, farther south, the Purcells, Selkirks, and Monashees, from east to west, respectively.

Measured against the U.S. Rockies, the Rockies and Columbias of Canada are not exceptionally high; elevations generally average 600–900 meters (about 2,000–3,000 feet) lower than those in Colorado, for example. Still, the Rockies and Columbias *seem* higher. For one thing, they start at a much lower elevation. The Columbia River Valley (or "trench," as it is often called) separating the Rockies and Columbias is surprisingly low at only about 600 meters (2,000 feet) high on average. By comparison, valley elevations in the Colorado Rockies typically range between 2,100 and 2,800 meters (about 7,000–9,000 feet). In addition, the tree line—the approximate elevation above which trees generally can't grow—is lower. In the Canadian Rockies, the tree line is at about 2,000 meters (6,500 feet), but Colorado's tree line usually starts above 3,000 meters (9,750 feet).

While glaciers in the United States have all but disappeared (except for those in Alaska and the mountains of the Pacific Northwest), they are still a common sight in Canada. Glacier National Park in the Columbias, for example, has more than 400 glaciers, covering 10% of the park's territory. The pale glacial blue strikes a dramatic balance against the blue-gray granite, the deep green of fir, spruce, and larch forests, and the panchromatic sweep of wildflowers. The glacial melt also feeds high-mountain lakes with mineral-rich silt deposits that tint the waters emerald green and cobalt blue, colors that change with the moods of the weather and the seasons.

Recognizing early the exceptional natural beauty of the region, the Canadian government began shielding the area from human development and resource exploitation in the 1880s. In 1885, the government created a park preserve around the Cave and Basin Hot Springs in Banff. Two years later, Canada's first national park, Rocky Mountain Park (later Banff National Park), was officially established. Lands that would later become Yoho National Park and Glacier National Park in the Columbias were first set aside in 1886.

Today, approximately 25,000 square kilometers (roughly 10,000 square miles)—an area larger than the state of New Hampshire—are protected in seven national parks in the Rockies and the Columbias. Because they were protected early on, the parks of the Rockies—Waterton Lakes, Banff, Kootenay, Yoho, and Jasper—have remained relatively untouched by human development. The only significant clusters of human settlement are the town centers of Banff, Jasper, and Waterton Lakes, and the area around Lake Louise. Several thousand more square kilometers are also protected as wilderness areas and provincial parks, most notably Mt. Robson and Mt. Assiniboine provincial parks and Kananaskis Country.

Essential Information

Important Addresses and Numbers

Tourist Information
The three major sources of tourism information are **Alberta Tourism** (Main Level, City Centre, 10155 102 St., Edmonton, AB T5J 4L6, tel. 800/661–8888), **Tourism British Columbia** (Parliament Bldgs., Victoria, BC V8V 1X4, tel. 800/663–6000), and **Canadian Parks Service** (Information Services, Box 2989, Station M, Calgary, AB T2P 3H8, tel. 403/292–4401). Parks Canada information is also available at the **Parks Information Office** (Box 900, 224 Banff Ave., Banff, AB T0L 0C0, tel. 403/762–4256). Specify particular interests when requesting information; all the organizations have an extensive list of maps and publications. It's best to call the Information Office first, but if need be (e.g., for current weather conditions or camping availability), you can also contact individual offices of the four contiguous Rockies parks directly: **Banff** (tel. 403/762–1500), **Jasper** (tel. 403/852–6161), **Kootenay** (tel. 604/347–9615), or **Yoho** (tel. 604/343–6324). For local information in Banff, contact the **Banff-Lake Louise Chamber of Commerce** (335 Beaver St., Banff, AB T0L 0C0, tel. 403/762–3777); in Jasper, **Jasper Park Chamber of Commerce** (Box 98, Jasper, AB T0E 1E0, tel. 403/852–3858); in Kananaskis Country, **Kananaskis Country** (Suite 100, 1011 Glenmore Trail SW, Calgary, AB T2V 4R6, tel. 403/297–3362); in Waterton Lakes, **Waterton Lakes National Park** (Superintendent, Waterton Park, AB T0K 2M0, tel. 403/859–2224) or **Waterton Park Chamber of Commerce** (Box 55, Waterton Park, AB T0K 2M0, tel. 403/859–2203); in Revelstoke and Glacier Parks, **Mount Revelstoke and Glacier National Parks** (Park Superintendent, Box 350, Revelstoke, BC V0E 2S0, tel. 604/837–5155); and in the British Columbia

Rockies, the **Rocky Mountain Visitors Associati**
Kimberley, BC V1A 2Y5, tel. 604/427–3344).

Emergencies Throughout Alberta and British Columbia **911** is the nu
for **police** or **ambulance.** For any extended trip into the ba.
country, always register with the nearest park warden's office.

Arriving and Departing by Plane

Calgary is the most common gateway for travelers arriving by
plane. Those who plan to visit only Jasper and northern park
regions may prefer to use Edmonton as a gateway city. Both
cities have international airports served by several major carriers; the Calgary flight schedule is somewhat more extensive.

Airports and **Calgary International Airport** and **Edmonton International**
Airlines **Airport** serve the British Columbia Rockies region. (For airline
information, *see* Arriving and Departing by Plane in Chapter
8.)

Air Canada and **Canadian Air** have daily flights to and from
Cranbrook's airport, in southern British Columbia; most of
these flights connect with flights through Vancouver International Airport and the international airports in Calgary and
Edmonton.

Arriving and Departing by Car, Train, and Bus

By Car Route 1, the Trans-Canada Highway, is the principal east–west
route into the region. Banff is 128 kilometers (80 miles) west
of Calgary on Route 1 and 858 kilometers (515 miles) east of
Vancouver. The other major east–west routes are Route 16 to
the north, the main highway between Edmonton and Jasper,
and Route 3 to the south. The main routes from the south are
Route 89, which enters Canada east of Waterton Lakes National Park from Montana, and Route 93, also from Montana,
which provides access to the British Columbia Rockies.

By Train **Rocky Mountaineer Railtours** (tel. 800/665–7245) offers service connecting Vancouver, Kamloops, Banff, Jasper, and Calgary. **VIA Rail** (tel. 800/361–3677) trains stop in Jasper, with
connecting overnight runs to and from Toronto, Edmonton,
and Vancouver. Call for schedules.

By Bus **Greyhound/Trailways** (call local listing) provides regular service to Calgary, Edmonton, and Vancouver, with connecting
service to Jasper and Waterton Lakes. **Brewster Tours** (tel.
800/661–1152) offers service between the Calgary International Airport and Banff, Jasper, and Lake Louise.

Getting Around

A fee is charged to all vehicles entering the national parks. A
day pass is $4.25; a four-day pass, $9.50; and an annual pass,
for any stay longer than four days, $26.75. You are permitted
to leave and reenter the park for the duration of the pass without additional charge.

By Car Unless you plan to go, literally, off the beaten path (in Kananaskis Country or in the Columbias; vehicles aren't permitted off major roadways in the national parks), a special vehicle
(e.g., a four-wheel-drive jeep) is not necessary. Major roadways
are well maintained. Keep in mind, however, that snow arrives

n early fall and remains until late spring. When traveling between October and April, stay informed of local road conditions, especially if you're traveling over mountain passes or along the Icefields Parkway (Route 93). A few roads, such as Route 40 over Highwood Pass in Kananaskis Country, are closed during the winter.

Rental Cars Car-rental outlets are located at the Calgary and Edmonton airports, as well as in Banff, Jasper, and Cranbrook. Daily rentals for sightseeing are available but should be reserved well ahead of time, especially in summer.

Guided Tours

Orientation **Brewster Transportation and Tours** (Box 1140, Banff, AB T0L
Bus Tours 0C0, tel. in Banff, 403/762–6700; in Jasper, 403/852–3332; in Calgary, 403/221–8242; or 800/661–1152) offers half-day, full-day, and multiday sightseeing tours of the parks. Prices start at about $30 per person.

Tauck Tours (11 Wilton Rd., Westport, CT 06881, tel. 203/226–6911) and **Holland American Westours** (300 Elliot Ave. W, Seattle, WA 98119, tel. 206/281–3535) feature multiday bus tours through the region. Some Tauck Tours include heli-hiking options.

Boat Tours **Minnewanka Boat Tours** (Box 2189, Banff, AB T0L 0C0, tel. 403/762–3473) offers 1½-hour tours in summer ($20 adult, $10 children) on Lake Minnewanka, near Banff.

Maligne Lake Scenic Cruises (Box 280, 626 Connaught Dr., Jasper, AB T0E 1E0, tel. 403/852–3370) runs 1½-hour tours on Maligne Lake, near Jasper, from mid-May through September.

Scenic Boat Cruises (Box 126, Waterton, AB T0K 2M0, tel. 403/859–2362) offers half-day and full-day cruises of Waterton Lake, some with hiking options.

Auto Tours Audiocassette tapes for self-guided auto tours of the parks are produced by **Inc. Auto Tape Tours** and **Rocky Mountain Tape Tours.** Tapes can be rented or purchased at news or gift shops in Banff, Lake Louise, and Jasper.

Special-interest **Challenge Enterprises** (1300 Railway Ave., Box 2008, Canmore,
Seasonal Tours AB T0L 0M0, tel. 403/678–2628) has a variety pack of tour options, including fishing, rafting, and cycling trips in summer, as well as snowmobiling, ice fishing, and dogsledding tours in winter.

Kingmik Expeditions (Box 227, Lake Louise, AB T0L 1E0, tel. 604/344–7288) specializes in dogsledding tours, from half-day to five-day outings.

For hiking, mountaineering, or backcountry ski tours, **Banff Alpine Guides** (Box 1025, Banff, AB T0L 0C0, tel. 403/678-6091) organizes tours according to weather conditions. Bookings can be arranged for private groups. The **Canadian School of Mountaineering** (Box 723, Canmore, AB T0L 0M0, tel. 403/678–4134) offers tours and instruction for mountaineering (in summer and winter) and backcountry skiing. In the Jasper area, the **Jasper Climbing School and Mountaineering Service** (Box 452, Jasper, AB T0E 1E0, tel. 403/852–3964) has guided hiking and mountaineering trips, as well as ski tours in winter, with private guides available.

In Waterton Lakes National Park,
68, Waterton Park, AB T0K 2M0, tel. 40...
ing and hiking tours, focusing on regional flor...

Alberta Tourism's booklet, "Winter Vacationer's Guid...
listings and descriptions of more than 50 ski-tour operator...
that package trips to the region. Tours include downhill, heli-
skiing, cross-country, and backcountry packages. The booklet
is available from **Alberta Tourism** (*see* Essential Information,
above).

Bicycle Tours   Several operators offer guided on-road and off-road bicycle
tours. **Rocky Mountain Cycle Tours** (Box 1987, Canmore, AB
T0L 0M0, tel. 403/678–6770) features one- to seven-day tours,
both in the Banff area and in British Columbia.

Exploring the Canadian Rockies

Most people who come to the Canadian Rockies arrive from
the east, from Calgary, via Route 1. Because it is just more than
an hour's drive west of Calgary, and because of the abundant
lodging, dining, and shopping options, Banff is the logical first
stop for most visitors. Many, however, continue on to Lake Louise, a half hour's drive north of Banff.

From Banff, the most popular excursion is the scenic drive
north, along the Icefields Parkway (Route 93), to Jasper, 280
kilometers (180 miles) away. Excursions into Yoho and Kootenay parks are not as common.

A sensible and economical alternative to using Banff as a base
camp is to stay in Canmore, 40 kilometers (25 miles) east,
where generally less expensive lodging makes up for a rather
plain-Jane character. Canmore is an excellent stepping-off
point for those interested in exploring Kananaskis Country, the
mountain ranges that stretch south of Banff. With fewer restrictions than the national parks, Kananaskis Country is
popular with sportsmen—horseback riders, hunters, snowmobilers, and the like.

Another economical option to staying in Banff is to find accommodations in the British Columbia Rockies. Inexpensive
lodging is abundant in Radium Hot Springs, 128 kilometers (80
miles) southwest of Banff, at the southern edge of Kootenay
National Park. Also, consider staying in Golden, on Route 1, 80
kilometers (50 miles) west of Lake Louise. Although in character these towns fall somewhere between truck stops and resort towns, they are nevertheless good access points to the
Columbia ranges as well as the Rockies.

Waterton Lakes National Park, 354 kilometers (220 miles) to
the south, is a rare side trip from Banff, with much of the drive
along a relatively undistinguished route (though no drive in
this part of the world really lacks scenery). People who visit
Waterton Lakes generally make it their principal destination
or combine it with a vacation in Glacier National Park across
the U.S. border in Montana.

Tour 1: Banff and Lake Louise

*Numbers in the margin correspond to points of interest on the
Canadian Rockies and Banff maps.*

❶ **Banff** is a town of unlikely contrasts: Amid the bustle of commercialism, elk regularly graze on the town common; tour-bus
sightseers carrying souvenir-stuffed bags mix on Banff Avenue (the main drag) with rugged outdoorspeople, among them
some of the world's most accomplished mountaineers. For almost all who come to the Canadian Rockies, Banff is the central
depot in their Canadian Rockies travel. The reason is simple:
Except for Jasper, the crossroads hamlet of Lake Louise, and
tiny Field in Yoho, Banff is the only town in the four contiguous
parks.

Banff, by far the largest of the four towns, straddles a thin line
between mountain resort town and tourist trap. It is certainly
not a quaint little western outpost; except for the oft-photo-
graphed Banff Springs Hotel, its architecture is mostly modern, simple, and undistinguished. Because of the limitations
that park regulations have set on growth, Banff hasn't expanded in recent years but has instead compressed in on itself.
The result is a hub of hyperactivity, especially during the summer—a hub that seems all the more hectic in contrast to the
surrounding wilderness.

The two points of reference that Banff explorers use are Banff
Avenue and the Banff Springs Hotel. An amazing number of
shops and restaurants have been crammed together on the
❷ short stretch of **Banff Avenue** that composes the core of downtown. Clustered together in about a half-dozen indoor malls are
art galleries, clothing stores, photo stores, bookstores, and con-
fectioners whose fudge and cookie output makes Banff Avenue
a mine field for anyone with a sweet tooth. Items sold in the
galleries range from trinkets to kitsch to genuine art. Let the
buyer unable to distinguish the differences beware: Price does
not necessarily indicate real value. Except for a few stores in
Jasper and a few boutiques in the Chateau Lake Louise and
Samson Mall in Lake Louise, this is pretty much where shopping begins and ends in the national parks.

Heading south, Banff Avenue crosses the Bow River over a
❸ great stone bridge, ending in a T in front of the **Parks Administration Building.** (Note: The administration building is only
a reference point for exploring Banff. For park information
such as maps, park regulations, etc., the park information office is at *224 Banff Ave., tel. 403/762-4256. Open daily 8 AM–10
PM, mid-May–Sept.; 8–6 Oct.–mid- May.)*

④ A left turn (about 2 kilometers, or 1 mile) leads to the **Banff Springs Hotel** (*see* Lodging, *below*), a year-round three-ring circus. Built in 1888, the hotel is easily recognized by its castlelike exterior; inside the visitor can expect to get lost in the crazy-quilt network of restaurants, shops, salons, and ballrooms. Even renovators got confused; evidently, the hotel has a hidden room—one that was accidentally sealed off by an overzealous plasterer. It was left that way to add a chapter to the hotel lore.

South of the administration building, take Kootenay Avenue to Mountain Avenue. Follow Mountain Avenue for about 2 kilo-
⑤ meters (1 mile) to **Upper Hot Springs** (tel. 403/762–2056) for a
⑥ dip, or to the **Sulphur Mountain Gondola** for a vista. Views during the steep eight-minute ride to and from the summit are spectacular, but they are hardly private. The observation decks and short summit trails are well visited, especially in summer.

A right turn off Banff Avenue at the Parks Administration
⑦ Building leads to the **Cave and Basin Centennial Centre.** Once considered sacred by the Stoney Indians, the springs were discovered by prospectors in 1883; they became the birthplace of the park system when they were given national park protection in 1885. Two interpretive trails provide good insight into the geology and plant life of the region, with 1/2-hour and one-hour ranger-guided tours available.

The **Upper Hot Springs** and the **Cave and Basin Centre Pool** (Cave Ave., 2 km, or 1 1/4 mi, west of downtown Banff, tel. 403/762–4900) can be soothing, invigorating, or both. The Upper Hot Springs is more of a soak; Cave and Basin is more of a swim. Lockers, suits, and towels are available to rent at both. The Cave and Basin Centre is open July and August; the Upper Hot Springs is open year-round.

Several short excursions are possible from the town of Banff.
⑧ **Vermilion Lakes Drive,** just off the west Banff exit from Route 1, offers one of the best opportunities for wildlife sightings: elk, bighorn sheep, muskrat, and the occasional moose. A sure bet
⑨ for wildlife sightings is a trip to the **buffalo paddock,** near the east Banff exit from Route 1, where a small herd of buffalo is kept during the summer. Unfortunately, because buffalo can be dangerous if provoked, visitors to the paddock must stay in their cars.

⑩ Also on the eastern side of town, **Tunnel Mountain Drive** makes a scenic 4.8-kilometer (3-mile) loop. Two points of particular interest along the drive are the Hoodoos, fingerlike rock for-
⑪ mations caused by erosion, and the **Banff Centre** (St. Julien Rd., tel. 403/762–6300), *the* place in town and in the parks for performances ranging from poetry readings to rock concerts.

Most people traveling from Banff to Lake Louise take Route 1 for about 56 kilometers (35 miles) north along the Bow River. But if you aren't in a hurry, the two-lane Route 1A, running approximately parallel to Route 1, is the more scenic option.

At the Lake Louise junction, a right turn leads to the Lake Louise ski area, generally regarded as one of Canada's best
⑫ and home to a World Cup downhill race each spring. The **Lake Louise Gondola,** which carries skiers to the ski-area summit in winter, is open for sightseeing rides in summer. Hiking trails—as well as ski trails that can be hiked—lead from the summit. In nice weather, the sundeck of the Whitehorn Tea House, at

The Canadian Rockies

Edmonton

Morinville

2

WeHwy.Yellowhead

Weluskiwin

Red Deer

27

43

39

Drayton Valley

2

Olds

ALBERTA

11

Rocky Mountain House

Saskatchewan River

11

16

32

Edson

Bow Pass

15

Icefield Centre 16

93

YOHO NATIONAL PARK

Athabasca River

Miette Hot Springs

Pyramid and Patricia Lakes

Connaught Drive 18

Maligne Lake 21

BANFF NATIONAL

Icefields Pkwy.

PARK

Takakkaw Falls 11

23 Mt. Robson 22

Connaught Drive

Medicine Lake 17

COLUMBIA ICEFIELDS 93

Sunwapta Falls

THE COLUMBIAS

Jasper Tramway 19

Jasper 20

JASPER NATIONAL PARK

Athabasca Falls

Indian R.

WILLMORE WILDERNESS PARK

Grande Cache

40

16

Hinton

Canoe Reach

23

McBride

16

Valemount

5

WELLS GRAY PROVINCIAL PARK

Murtle Lake

Hobson Lake

the top of the gondola, is a good place to break for lunch. *Lake Louise Gondola, exit Rte. 1 at Lake Louise, tel. 403/522–3555. Admission: $8 adults ($5.50 one-way hikers), $4 children 5–12, children under 5 free. Open June–Sept.*

A left turn at the junction leads to what ostensibly is the center of Lake Louise: a crossroads, a train crossing, a few hotels, and a small shopping center just off Route 1. Almost all visitors zip through town barely noticing it on their way to **Chateau Lake Louise** (another 6 kilometers, or 3³/₄ miles), built in 1923, which overlooks the blue-green lake and the Victoria Glacier. The hotel's setting is as scenic as it is popular; camera shutters must certainly click thousands of times a day during the summer months. Canoe rentals are available at the boat house. The chateau is also a departure point for several short, moderately strenuous, well-traveled hiking routes. The most popular hike (about 3.5 kilometers, or 2¹/₄ miles) is to the small teahouse overlooking Lake Agnes. The tiny lake hangs on a mountain-surrounded shelf that opens to the east with a distant view of the Bow River valley.

Time Out   The **Lake Agnes teahouse** is a one-room café tucked onto a ledge overlooking the small lake and the waterfall that descends steeply from it. Fresh baked goods and a variety of teas are a welcome reward for the short hike, and the view from the porch is fabulous. The Lake Agnes hike can also be a good rainy-day outdoor activity for those with rain slickers and sturdy boots: The intimacy of the small teahouse is enhanced with inclement weather brooding outside and without the usual fair-weather crowds.

A longer hike (about 6 kilometers, or 3³/₄ miles) leads to a larger teahouse-restaurant on the Plain of the Six Glaciers, at the edge of the Victoria Glacier moraine. This is a popular trail's end for day hikers—a great place for picnicking or basking in the sun on a warm day—as well as a starting point for more ambitious climbers headed for the high glacial ridges.

The other popular place to visit is **Moraine Lake,** 11 kilometers (7 miles) from the heart of Lake Louise. In an area dubbed the "Valley of the Ten Peaks," the lake reflects in deep blue the granite peaks that rise abruptly around it. As beautiful as it is, don't expect Moraine Lake necessarily to offer an escape from the Lake Louise crowd; it is one of the two main stops that tour buses make in Lake Louise (Lake Louise itself being the other), as well as a popular departure point for hikers.

If you are seeking more solitude, several moderate hiking trails lead from the lake into some spectacular country. A popular overnight hike is the trek over Sentinel Pass and through Paradise Valley to Lake Louise. For great views, the short (3-kilometer, or 1⁷/₈-mile) but steep hike from Moraine Lake to Larch Valley is well worth the effort. Another escape option is to rent a canoe, available from the office of Moraine Lake Cabins. *Moraine Lake Cabin Office, Box 70, Lake Louise, AB T0L 1E0, tel. 403/522–3733. Open June 1–Sept. 30.*

Tour 2: North and West of Banff

Heading North   Just north of Lake Louise, Routes 1 and 93 diverge. Route 93, the **Icefields Parkway,** continues northward for more than 230 kilometers (143 miles) to Jasper. Route 1 bears west over Kicking Horse Pass—named, according to local lore, after an unpleasant encounter between a pack animal and a member of an exploratory expedition in the mid-1800s—into Yoho National Park and British Columbia (to continue in this direction, *see* "West of Banff," and Tour 4, The British Columbia Rockies, *below*).

If possible, pick a clear day to drive the Icefields Parkway. Basically, the *only* thing to do along the parkway is to take in the scenery, whether through a car or bus window or from a hiking trail. (Also, be sure to bring along an extra clothing layer or two. Because of the altitude and the abundant ice, a chill can remain in the air even on a nice day.) As you drive north, the more dramatic scenery will be on your left. The peaks demarcate the Continental Divide; many of the great rivers of western Canada spring from the glaciers and ice fields along the divide. (Ice fields are essentially giant frozen lakes, while glaciers are the frozen rivers that extend from them.) There are several scenic overlooks and short, well-marked hiking trails along the highway, providing not only breathtaking mountain views but also firsthand lessons in glacial dynamics. Only experienced hikers or climbers should venture far onto the glacier without a guide. Hidden crevasses and other hazards can make a simple jaunt treacherous.

⓯ The parkway begins a steady climb from the intersection of Routes 1 and 93 to **Bow Pass,** which, at 2,088 meters (6,850 feet), may be covered with snow as late as May and as early as September. On the north side of the pass is Peyto Lake; on the south side is Bow Lake, source of the Bow River that flows through Banff. Above Bow Lake hangs the edge of Crowfoot Glacier; to the south, across the lake, is the beginning of the Waputik Icefield. Around the lake are stubbly pines and underbrush—the tree line ends here, and high-alpine country begins.

Time Out From Bow Pass, the road gradually descends past Peyto Lake to **Saskatchewan River Crossing.** Between Lake Louise and Jasper, this is the only place from fall to spring where you can get food and refuel (during the summer, you can refuel at the Icefield Centre; *see below*). Stop for the gas, but you'll be wise to bring a picnic lunch; the cafeteria food is overpriced and unimpressive.

The road descends from the crossing into the North Saskatchewan River valley. Three river systems diverge here—the Saskatchewan, Howse, and Misaya rivers. From several overlooks you can see the three river valleys and the glaciers that reach from the giant ice fields ahead. The **Parker Ridge trail**—a 3-kilometer (1⅞-mile) loop north of the crossing—provides an excellent view of the Saskatchewan Glacier, where the river of the same name begins.

Shortly, the road begins to climb again, in places along steep hairpin turns, toward **Sunwapta Pass**—the juncture of Banff and Jasper national parks. Wildlife abounds in this area and is most visible in spring and autumn after a snowfall, when herds of bighorn sheep come to the road to lick up the salt used to melt snow and ice. Drive cautiously.

After Sunwapta Pass, **Athabasca Glacier,** an extension of the Columbia Icefield, appears on your left. The Columbia Icefield, covering 325 square kilometers (125 square miles), is the largest mass of ice in subarctic North America and is just one of a series of ice fields along the route. Well worthwhile is a trip onto the Athabasca Glacier, via buses (called snow-coaches) modified to drive on ice. Hikers can also walk onto the tongue of the glacier, but the going can be slow and chilly. *Bus tours: Brewster Tours, tel. 403/762–6700. Admission to buses May–mid-Oct.: $17.50 adults, $7 children, for 1¹/₂-hr tour. Walking tours: tel. 403/852–4242. $20 for 5-hr walk, $15 for 3-hr walk.*

⑯ Across the highway, on your right, is the **Icefield Centre,** where you can get food, gas, and even lodging in the summer. The center also provides interpretive exhibits, including a model of the entire ice field and an audiovisual presentation. Worth keeping in mind is that the summer midday rush (between 11 and 3) can be so intense that even the Icefield Centre's promotional materials suggest you choose another time of day to come. *125 km (75 mi) north of Lake Louise on Rte. 93, tel. 403/852–6161. Open Sept.–May, daily 9–5; June–Aug., daily 9–7.*

From Icefield Centre the highway descends gradually into Jasper National Park, leaving the glaciers, ice fields, and water-**⑰** falls behind. One point of interest along the way is **Athabasca Falls,** where the Athabasca River is squeezed through a narrow gorge. The site is especially dramatic in early summer, when the river is swollen by the snowmelt. At Athabasca Falls there is a juncture: Route 93 continues ahead, while Route 93A bears left toward Mt. Edith Cavell, perhaps the most imposing peak in the park. From here you can pick up trails leading to Tonquin Valley, *the* most popular hiking (as well as horse-packing and backcountry skiing) area in the park. Twenty-four kilometers (15 miles) later the highways converge. Nearby, Route 93 joins Route 16, also called the Yellowhead Highway, which reaches east 360 kilometers (225 miles) to Edmonton.

The town of Jasper is at the edge of a broad, open valley where the Athabasca and Miette rivers converge. The modest but attractive town first came into being in 1911–1912, with the arrival of the railroad. As you enter the town from the south onto **⑱ Connaught Drive,** the main drag, train tracks run parallel on the right.

On the left, stores, restaurants, and inexpensive motels line Connaught Drive. The shopping and dining scene in the town of Jasper is even more casual than in Banff; Jasper is used by most visitors as a stepping-off point for the vast, surrounding backcountry, not as a destination in itself.

Many people consider Jasper the preeminent backpacking area in North America. Multiday loops of more than 160 kilometers (100 miles) are possible on well-maintained trails. Backpacking and horse-packing trips in the northern half of the park offer legitimate wilderness seclusion, if not the dramatic glacial scenery of the park's southern half. However, day trips are much more common, especially around Mt. Edith Cavell, Pyramid Lake, Jasper Park Lodge, and Maligne Lake.

⑲ Attractions nearest to the town are the **Jasper Tramway,** 3 kilometers (1⁷/₈ miles) south of town off Route 93 on Whistlers Mountain Road. The tram rises 950 vertical meters (3,000 feet) on the steep flank of Whistlers Mountain, and you can take in stunning views from the summit of Mt. Robson (when clear) to the west and the Miette and Athabasca valleys, making the trip well worth it. *Tel. 403/852–3093. Admission: $7.50 adults, $3.75 children. Open mid-Apr.–mid-Oct.; call for times; hours vary throughout season.*

Time Out At the summit of Whistlers, have a leisurely dinner on the glass-enclosed terrace of the **Tramway Restaurant** (Continental cuisine, fully licensed). After a sunset meal, a short after-dinner hike, and glorious views, take the 11 PM (summer) tram back down to the bottom.

20 Another short, popular excursion·is to **Pyramid** and **Patricia lakes,** just 4 kilometers (2½ miles) from town. Different sorts of boats can be rented from Pyramid Lake Resort, including canoes, kayaks, catamarans, and motorized surfboards. *Pyramid Ave., tel. 403/852–4900. Open May–Oct., approximately 8 AM–10 PM. Boat rentals start at $10/hr per boat.*

A somewhat longer excursion will take you 30 kilometers (18 miles) to Maligne Lake, one of the largest glacier-fed lakes in the world. Follow Maligne Lake Road, which begins 3 kilometers (1⅞ miles) east of town, off Route 16. You'll pass Maligne Canyon, where the Maligne River cuts a deep, narrow gorge through limestone bedrock. It is an impressive sight, but the 4-kilometer (2½-mile) trail along the canyon can be crowded, so it's best saved for evening, when the crowds thin out. The other point of interest along this road is **Medicine Lake.** A complex, underground drainage system causes the lake to empty completely at times, leaving only a bed of glacial silt and residue.

21 **Maligne Lake,** 22 kilometers (14 miles) long, can be explored on a 1½-hour guided cruise or on a rented boat. Spirit Island, which earned its name because its beauty elevates the spirit of those who witness the sight, is a small outcropping in the middle of the lake and is the main destination. Several moderately long hikes (5 to 10 miles round-trip or 8 to 16 kilometers), some with brief, steep sections, lead to promontories offering panoramas of the lake and the surrounding mountain ranges. *Maligne Lake Tours, 626 Connaught Dr., tel. 403/852–3370. $26 adults, $13 children under 12. Open mid-May–Sept., daily 9–5, every hour on the hour.*

Eighty kilometers (50 miles) west of Jasper on Route 16 is towering **Mt. Robson.** First sighted by Hudson's Bay Company
22 explorers about 1820, this peak was not successfully scaled until 1913, despite numerous attempts. Certain routes on Robson are still considered by experienced mountaineers to be some of the world's most challenging. Pick as clear a day as possible to go; Mt. Robson's weather is notoriously bad even when the weather elsewhere is perfectly fine; it is a rare day that the summit is not encircled by clouds. A favorite backpacking trip on the mountain is the strenuous 18-kilometer (11-mile) hike to Berg Lake, through the wonderfully named Valley of a Thousand Falls. Berg Lake is no tranquil body of water; the grunt and splash of chunks of ice calving from Robson's glaciers into the lake are regular sounds in summer. The 5-kilometer (3-mile) hike to Kinney Lake, along the Berg Lake trail, is a good option for day hikers.

㉓ For a more relaxing side trip from Japser, spend a day at **Miette Hot Springs,** 58 kilometers (36 miles) from Jasper. Visitors come here to soak in naturally heated mineral waters originating from three springs that are some of the warmest waters in the Canadian Rockies. *Tel. 403/866–3750. $2 adults, $1.25 children; suit, locker, and towel rentals available. Open mid-May–early Sept., daily 8:30 AM–10:30 PM.*

Driving east from Jasper, you will notice scenery that's different from that to the west. As the Athabasca River widens along the flat floodplain, notice how the trees begin to thin out, a sign that you're moving into the drier climate of the prairie.

West of Banff Smaller and less renowned than Banff and Jasper national parks are the less-visited siblings: Kootenay and Yoho national parks. When the tourist population of Banff swells during the busy summer months, Kootenay and Yoho remain surprisingly quiet, although not for lack of natural beauty; the scenery in both parks can certainly match that of Banff and Jasper.

Kootenay National Park, named after the Kootenai Indians who settled in the area, is 16 kilometers (10 miles) northwest of Banff and is reached by bearing north on Route 1 and west **㉔** on Route 93. The highway climbs steeply to **Vermilion Pass,** where Banff and Kootenay parks meet. The atmosphere is eerie here. In 1968, a huge forest fire swept over thousands of acres, leaving only charred spars in its wake. Regeneration has begun, though; amidst the skeletons left by the fire, new growths have reached heights of 2–3 meters (6–10 feet).

Just beyond the Vermilion Pass summit is the trailhead for the Stanley Glacier trail, one of the fine choices for a day hike in the park. The trail climbs easily for 4 kilometers (2½ miles), through fire remnants and new growth, across rock debris and glacial moraine, ending in the giant amphitheater of the Stanley Glacier basin.

From the Stanley Glacier trailhead, Route 93 turns south, and on the right, the Rockwall, a high, rocky ridge that is the park's most predominant feature, can be seen. Among the popular **㉕** hiking destinations is **Floe Lake,** a 10-kilometer (6-mile) trek from the highway. The area surrounding the lake, a 1,000-meter-high (3,300-foot-high) dark limestone wall, characterizes the Kootenay terrain.

Along the 65-kilometer (40-mile) stretch from the intersection of Routes 1 and 93 to Radium Hot Springs (*see* Tour 4, *below*), the only service area is at Vermilion Crossing, the approximate halfway point. South of Vermilion Crossing, the mountains open up gradually, their flanks covered by thick stands of Douglas fir, as the Vermilion River joins with the wider Kootenay River. From there, the highway heads west, winding through the narrow limestone canyon cut by the Sinclair River before reaching the springs.

Farther north, along Route 1, **Yoho National Park** can be reached by continuing west on the highway at its intersection with the Icefields Parkway (Route 93), just north of Lake Louise. The park's name is an Indian word that translates, approximately, to "awesome." Indeed, the park is awesome, featuring some of the most outstanding scenery in the Canadian Rockies.

Yoho is divided by Route 1 into two parts—the northern half, which includes Emerald Lake and the Yoho River Valley, and the southern half, of which Lake O'Hara is the physical and spiritual epicenter.

The two main accesses to the northern half of Yoho are the Takakkaw Falls road and the Emerald Lake Lodge road. The **Takakkaw Falls,** 254 meters (833 feet) high, are spectacular, especially in early summer, when the water volume of the falls is increased by the runoff of melting snow and ice. (Also, the flow of the falls can increase during summer hot spells, which speed the melt of glacial ice.) But the falls are just a taste of what lies ahead for day hikers and backpackers. The Yoho River valley, leading toward the pyramid-capped Yoho glacier, is bound on one side by the peaks of the President Range and, on the other, by the distant Wapta Icefield.

Enthusiastic hikers can also reach points throughout the Yoho Valley from the vivid green **Emerald Lake** by taking well-marked trails. Otherwise, those who come to this corner of Yoho can take an easy stroll around the lake, rent a canoe, or have a cup of tea at the teahouse by the lodge. Emerald Lake is also a popular area for cross-country and backcountry skiers in winter.

Lake O'Hara, Yoho's other half, is widely regarded as one of *the* places for outdoor enthusiasts to go in the Canadian Rockies. For summer, Lake O'Hara Lodge (*see* Lodging, *below*) is booked months in advance. Although the 11-kilometer (6.8-mile), forest-lined fire road between Route 1 and the lake can be hiked, it makes more sense to ride the lodge-run bus even if you aren't staying at the lodge. (Call the lodge for times and space availability.) Save your legs for hiking any of several moderately strenuous trails that radiate from the lodge into a spectacular, high-alpine world of small lakes surrounded by escarpments of rock and permanent snowpack. Keep in mind, however, that the bus makes the Lake O'Hara area accessible to many other people, too. If you're looking for a true wilderness experience, other places (notably Kootenay) are better choices.

Also in Yoho, the **Burgess Shale site,** halfway between the Takakkaw Falls road and the Emerald Lake Lodge road, contains the fossilized remains of 120 marine species dating back 530 million years. Burgess Shale was designated a World Heritage Site in 1981; reservations for guided hikes through fossil sites can be made through the Yoho Park Information Centre (*Box 99, Field, BC V0A 1G0, tel. 604/343–6324*). The guided hikes are the only way to see the actual fossil sites, and they're popular, so reservations are recommended. The hikes are conducted July through mid-September, and the going is fairly strenuous; the round-trip distance is 20 kilometers (12 miles).

Three kilometers ($1^7/_8$ miles) west of the border between Alberta and British Columbia, you come to the observation deck for the **Spiral Tunnels,** train tunnels that make figure-eight loops on each side of Route 1. These were the engineering answer to the problem of getting trains up and down the steep grade of the Rockies' western slope. The tunnels wind in circles through the mountainside, allowing trains to climb and descend more gradually, as if on spiral stairs. Many trains use the tunnels, and the Great Canadian Railtour Company (tel. 800/665–7245) and CPR provide schedules so you can time your arrival to the roadside observation deck off Route 1 for when a train is passing through. Without a train, the tunnels simply look like holes in the mountainside; but when a train goes through, its engine can be seen coming from one tunnel, while its caboose can be seen entering the other, almost directly above the engine.

Tour 3: South of Banff

Canmore and Kananaskis Country **③②** Until Calgary was awarded the Olympics in 1988, the area immediately south of Banff—the town of **Canmore** and **Kananaskis Country**—was generally the stomping ground of local folks from Calgary and Banff. Canmore, outside the park boundary, offered affordable housing for people living in Banff; Kananaskis Country, just an hour's drive from Calgary and with fewer restrictions on horseback riding, snowmobiling, and hunting, was a popular weekend locale for folks from the city. Then came the Olympics. Olympics organizers originally planned to hold several events at existing facilities around Banff and Lake Louise. But when national-park officials nixed that idea, brand-new facilities were developed in and around Canmore and in Kananaskis Country. Several years later, the Olympics-inspired development continues to receive mixed reviews.

The **Canmore Nordic Centre** (*see* Sports and Outdoor Activities, *below*), built for Olympic Nordic skiing events, has been a hit–a state-of-the-art facility that is free to the public and lighted for evening skiing. *Box 1979, Canmore, AB T0L 0M0, tel. 403/658–2400. No trail fee; rentals available. Open dawn until 9:00 PM.*

Less successful has been the Nakiska ski area, half an hour away in Kananaskis Country. Not being in a natural snow belt and exposed to the occasional warming Chinook winds, Nakiska (also known as Mt. Allen) relies heavily on snowmaking and does not generally have the natural-snow coverage of the Banff area resorts. The result has been a ski resort regarded by many locals as a white elephant.

The last key component of the Olympic development effort was **Kananaskis Village** (*see* Lodging, *below*). While the modern village was certainly not everyone's architectural cup of tea, it did bring first-class lodging and dining (and golf) to Kananaskis Country. As a result, the 4,000-square-kilometer (1,600-square-mile) Kananaskis Country has become, since 1988, a legitimate alternative to more crowded Banff for resort-minded vacationers. *Kananaskis Country, Suite 100, 1011 Glenmore Trail SW, Calgary, AB T2V 4R6, tel. 403/297–3362.*

The character of post-Olympics Canmore is not radically different from its pre-1988 incarnation. The former coal-mining outpost remains a bedroom community for Banff workers, although now more park visitors also save money by staying in Canmore's less expensive lodgings. The attractive, boutique-lined Main Street and several good restaurants are indications that Canmore is no longer strictly a locals' town; it's become the regional center for the active outdoor life—with streets full of young, robust types who live for climbing, hiking, and mountain-biking in the summer, cross-country and alpine skiing in winter. Several outfitters, climbing schools, and guide services make their base in Canmore.

This does not, however, add up to a town of historic or scenic attractions. You can get a good meal here, or a place to bed down at a reasonable price, and you can zip around the tracks at the Nordic center. Generally, Canmore is a place to think of, as local people do, as a base camp for going into the parks or Kananaskis Country. The main highway through Kananaskis Country is Route 40 (closed in winter about 20 kilometers, or 12 miles, south of Kananaskis Village), also known as the **Kananaskis Trail.** The highway begins 23 kilometers (14 miles) east of Canmore, off Route 1, and climbs past Kananaskis Village and Nakiska, which appear on the right at about the 20-kilometer (12-mile) point. Rather than staying in the village, many visitors to the region stay at one of the several campgrounds, most of which can accommodate recreational vehicles.

The highway proceeds through **Peter Lougheed Provincial Park** (essentially a subsection of Kananaskis Country) and over Highwood Pass (2,208 meters, or 7,280 feet), the highest drivable pass in Canada. It then descends to join Route 541, east of Longview. Access to East Kananaskis Country, a popular area for horseback-riding trips, is via Route 66, which heads west from Priddis.

The climate in the mountains of Kananaskis Country is surprisingly different from that of the mountains in the neighboring parks. On the eastern slope of the Rockies, the Kananaskis mountains tend to get less precipitation, including snow. Closer to the prairie, the Kananaskis mountains are also exposed to more wind.

Kananaskis Country has little of the glacial spectacle of the parks; its scenery is simpler in some ways, with thick pine forests and granite mountain peaks. Regularly modulating temperatures cause frequent snow and rock slides. Anyone interested in the power of sliding snow or rock should take a short drive on Route 40 south of Kananaskis Village, to see where the steep mountainsides are raked with one slide path after another.

As a multipurpose area run by the Alberta provincial government, Kananaskis Country offers advantages over the parks, but some disadvantages as well. On the plus side, a greater variety of recreational activities can be experienced in Kananaskis Country than in the parks. For example, in its northeastern corner (take Route 68 east from Route 40), a large area has been set aside for motorcycles, all-terrain vehicles, and snowmobiles—all machinery that are anathema in the parks. East Kananaskis Country, where pine forests mix with stands of aspen, has been divvied up for use by licensed horse-pack outfitters. Also, the provincial government has made special efforts to accommodate disabled visitors. **William Watson Lodge,** near the Kananaskis Lakes, is a rarity: a lodge designed exclusively for disabled people and senior citizens. Access points have been built along Mt. Lorette Ponds north of Kananaskis Village to accommodate fishermen who use wheelchairs, and many hiking trails near the village have been cut wide and gentle enough for wheelchair travel. *William Watson Lodge located 30 km (18 mi) south of Kananaskis Village on Rte. 40; for information contact Kananaskis Country, Box 280, Cranmore, AB T0L 0M0, tel. 403/591-7227. Overnight and day-*

use facilities for senior citizens and disabled people. Office open weekdays 8:30–4:30; cabin reservations available year-round.

On the down side, wildlife does not flourish in Kananaskis Country as it does in the parks, primarily because hunting is permitted in season; animals are much more cautious about human interaction here than they are in protected areas.

Finally, Kananaskis Country is not all free-range land for recreational enthusiasts. Forestry, gas, and ranching operations may restrict backcountry travel in some areas.

Waterton Lakes National Park ㉝ Geologically, **Waterton Lakes National Park** is the meeting of two worlds—the flatlands of the prairie and the abrupt upthrust of the mountains. Chief Mountain, the squared-off peak on the eastern end of the stand of mountains seen as you drive from the north, juts up from the prairie, dominating the horizon from the north and east. In this juncture of worlds, the park squeezes into a relatively small arena (525 square kilometers, or 200 square miles) an unusual mix of wildlife, biota, and climate zones.

Take a drive up **Red Rock Canyon** (turning right before the town of Waterton), the bottom of which is covered with scrub pine and prairie grasses. Turn a few kilometers later at the center of Waterton onto the Akima Parkway. Follow this road to **Cameron Lake,** and you'll find a land of high basins and glacially carved cirques, filled in summer with hundreds of varieties of alpine wildflowers, including about 22 varieties of wild orchids.

The common denominator in the park is wind. Although the mountains and canyon walls provide protection in some areas, the wind blows powerfully and regularly from the prairie, often at speeds of more than 50 kilometers (30 miles) an hour. Trees along the lakeside bear the evidence, as they grow at about an 80-degree angle, rather than straight up.

Politically, too, Waterton represents a meeting of worlds. Although the park was officially established in 1895, it was joined in 1932 with Glacier National Park in Montana to form Waterton/Glacier International Peace Park—a symbol of friendship and peaceful coexistence between Canada and the United States. In fact, some services in the park, including the Prince of Wales Hotel—perhaps the park's most recognizable landmark—are under Glacier Park management in the United States.

Whether it is a pervading spirit of international peace or the long driving distance from Calgary (especially compared with the short Calgary–Banff drive), Waterton is a decidedly low-key place. Hiking, horseback riding, and boating are the main activities. The park offers numerous short hikes for day-trippers and some longer treks for backpackers. Boats can be rented at the townsite for Upper Waterton Lake or at Cameron Lake. For windsurfing enthusiasts, the winds that rake across Upper Waterton Lake make for an exciting ride. These prairie winds, squeezed through the narrow gap in the mountains in which the lake lies, come with such force and regularity that lakeside trees in the Waterton townsite grow at wind-deferring angles.

One of the most popular things to do in the park is to take a two-hour cruise on Upper Waterton Lake from the townsite south to **Goat Haunt,** where there are shelters, a ranger station, and a boat dock. From here, several short, easy hikes are possible before you return to Waterton; properly equipped overnighters can also camp out at Goat Haunt. (Because Goat Haunt is in the United States, travelers going to and from must clear Customs.) *Shoreline Cruise Co., tel. 403/859–2362. Cruises run mid-May–mid-Sept.; call for schedules.*

Whatever the day's activity, turning in early is the order of things in Waterton. Except for reading and conversation, nightlife is virtually nonexistent. Most of Waterton turns in early for the season, too—from early October until mid-May, the park has all but closed up shop.

Because of Waterton's proximity to the U.S. border and its bond with Glacier National Park, many visitors come to the park from the south. The common thing to do is to fly into Great Falls or Kalispell, Montana, and drive to Waterton. Those who choose instead to drive the 264 kilometers (158 miles) from Calgary (via Routes 2, 3, and 6) have a couple of interesting side trips worth considering—to **Crowsnest Pass** or **Head-Smashed-In Buffalo Jump** (*see* Off the Beaten Track, *below*).

Tour 4: The British Columbia Rockies

"British Columbia (B.C.) Rockies" is in part a misnomer. It is a term often used to designate an area of southeastern British Columbia abutting the western slope of the Rockies but including the Columbia Mountains, which technically (or geologically) are not a part of the Rockies.

If differentiating the Columbias from the Rockies seems confusing, at least their separation is made obvious by the broad, low valley of the Columbia River, known colloquially as the Columbia River trench. Not so easy is discerning between the discrete ranges of the Columbias themselves. Four separate ranges form the Columbias: To the north are the Cariboos, west of Jasper and Mt. Robson parks; reaching south like three long talons from the Cariboos are (west to east) the Monashees, the Selkirks, and the Purcells. Finally, perhaps the best-known mountains of all—the Bugaboos—are only a few dramatic peaks in the Purcells but are often thought of as encompassing the entire region.

In subtle and overt ways, the world of the British Columbia Rockies region is very different from that of the national parks. Perhaps the most obvious differences are the conspicuous lumber yards, mining pits, farms, and ranches in the Columbia River trench—signs of development throughout the British Columbia Rockies that are not present in the industry-shielded parklands to the east. This physical evidence attests to minimally successful attempts made to mine gold, silver-lead ore, and other metals. The significant difference between the two ranges, however, is age. More than 100 million years older than the Rockies, the Columbias show the signs of their years: The effects of erosion are more in evidence, along with the more dramatic effects of upthrust and glaciation. This is not to suggest that the Columbias lack drama or beauty. The pyramidal peaks of Glacier National Park and the Bugaboo and Howser spires, rising in the Purcells like slender granite fingers from glacial beds, are sights as striking as anything in the four contiguous parks.

As the first ranges to capture storms moving from the west across the plains of interior British Columbia, the Columbias get much more rain and snow than do the Rockies. Annual precipitation in many areas exceeds 152 centimeters (60 inches), and in the Monashees, the most westerly of subranges, annual snowfalls have exceeded 2,032 centimeters (800 inches).

Such precipitation has helped to create the large, deep glaciers that add to the high-alpine beauty of the Columbias. Lower down, a rain-forest climate has contributed to a lush life of ferns, grasses, flowers, and shrubbery not found in the Rockies to the east. In winter, the deep snows have made the Columbias a must port-of-call for aficionados of deep-powder and helicopter skiing.

34 Of course, such extreme conditions can be hazardous, too. **Rogers Pass,** the center of Canada's **Glacier National Park,** is a case in point. In the early 1900s, avalanches claimed the lives of hundreds of railway-construction workers and continued to be a threat during highway construction in the 1950s.

Today, the Rogers Pass war against avalanches is both active and passive. Heavy artillery—105mm howitzers—is used to shoot down snow buildups before they can become so severe as to threaten a major avalanche. (If traveling in the backcountry, even in summer, be alert to unexploded howitzer shells that pose a potential hazard.) On the passive side, train tunnels and long snow sheds along the highway shield travelers from major slide paths.

The park's history is well documented at the **Rogers Pass Centre**—worth a visit whether you're staying in Glacier or just passing through. Open year-round, the center displays geology and wildlife and offers 30-minute movies on subjects ranging from avalanches to bears. *Tel. 604/837–7500. Admission free. Open May–Sept., daily 7 AM–9 PM; Oct.–Apr., Mon.–Fri. 9–4.*

Not all of the British Columbia Rockies region is inundated by rain and snow. Storms tend to exhaust themselves in the Columbias—the reason the Columbia River trench stays relatively dry. The annual precipitation in Golden is only about 500 millimeters (20 inches), less than half of what it is in Revelstoke, 148 kilometers (80 miles) west at the foot of the Monashees and the western extreme of the region discussed in this section.

35 For the most part, the towns of the Columbia River trench are not beautiful, nor do they aspire to be. For example, **Golden**—a town best described as a service center—is the epitome of this unassuming character. Primarily a stopping-off point for anyone journeying elsewhere, Golden is a base for several river runners, outfitters, and guide services.

The 105 kilometers (63 miles) south from Golden to Radium Hot Springs, where Route 93 joins Route 95, across the rolling flood plain of the Columbia River, are relatively uneventful. To the right are the river and the Purcell Mountains; more immediately to the left are the Rockies, although the major peaks are hidden by the abrupt frontal ranges. Even though the landscape might not be as inspiring as in the parks, this is prime

RV country. Resorts catering to RVs—hard to find in the parks—abound here. These include hotels and motels that offer RV hookups in addition to regular accommodations (*see* Lodging, *below*). Climbers and hikers should look for unpaved roads out of the towns of Spillimacheen and Brisco that lead to

36 the **Bugaboo Recreation Area.**

The Bugaboos are especially popular among experienced rock climbers. Granite "spires" that rise from glaciers like giant rocket cones are both dramatic to look at and challenging to climb. This is wild country: Except for the Bugaboo Lodge—reserved mainly for heli-hiking and heli-skiing guests—and remote alpine huts, there are no facilities in this area.

For less adventurous tourists, follow the 90-kilometer (56-mile)

37 stretch of Route 93/95 from **Radium Hot Springs** toward Kimberley. The hot springs on Route 93, 2 kilometers (1¼ miles) northeast of the Routes 93 and 95 junction, are the town's longest-standing attraction, and the summer lifeblood for the numerous motels in the area. There is a large outdoor pool tucked beneath the walls of Sinclair Canyon. Lockers, towels, and suits are available to rent. *Jct. Rtes. 93 and 95, tel. 604/347–9615. Admission: Full day—$4 adults, $2.50 children 16 and under; half day—$2.50 adults, $1.25 children. Schedules vary with season; open 9 AM–11 PM mid-summer.*

However, sitting in the hot springs or hiking the short trails of Sinclair Canyon aren't the only things to do in this part of the world. Windermere and Columbia lakes—actually extrawide stretches of the Columbia River—are popular among boaters and boardsailers. Golf is becoming a growing attraction, with

38 several fine courses between Radium Hot Springs and **Fairmont Hot Springs.** And a right turn at the Invermere intersection leads to **Panorama** (*see* Lodging, *below*), the year-round resort known best for skiing in winter, and to the **Purcell Wilderness,** a large area devoted to backcountry hiking, camping, and fishing.

After traveling south for about 60 kilometers (36 miles), the road splits; Route 93/95 continues southeast to Fort Steele, and Route 95A leads to Kimberley. The two routes join again north of Cranbrook.

Fort Steele and Kimberley are historically significant because they were the home to many German and Swiss immigrants who arrived a century ago to work as miners and loggers. Southeastern British Columbia was not unlike the Tyrol region they had left, so it was easy to settle here. Later, a demand for experienced alpinists to guide and teach hikers, climbers, and skiers brought more settlers from the alpine countries, and Tyrolian influence is evident throughout southeastern British Columbia. Chalet-style buildings here are as common here as log cabin–style structures are in the national parks. Schnitzels and fondues appear on menus as often as burgers and fries.

39 **Fort Steele Heritage Town,** a reconstructed 19th-century mining outpost, is a step back to those silver-lead mining days. Its theater, milliner's, barbershop, and dry-goods store breathe authenticity, helping to preserve the 1890s life-style. Plan a half-day or more; there is enough here to hold the interest of children and adults alike. *Ft. Steele, 16 km (10 mi) northeast of Cranbrook on Rte. 93/95, tel. 604/426–6923. Admission for 2 con-*

*secutive days: $5 adults, $3 children 13–18 and senior cit izens,
$1 children 6–12, $10 families. Open mid-June–early Sept.; Old
West shows performed in the summer months. Although buildings are closed in winter, the grounds are open to visitors free of
charge, dawn to dusk, weather permitting.*

40 **Kimberley,** a cross between a quaint and a kitschy town, is rich
with Tyrolian character. The Platzl ("small plaza," in German),
a walking mall of shops and restaurants styled after a Bavarian
village, is crowned by what is reputed to be the world's largest
cuckoo clock. In the summer Kimberley plays its Bavarian
theme to the hilt: Merchants dress up in lederhosen and
dirndls, and promotional gimmicks abound.

Beyond Kimberley or Fort Steele, **Cranbrook** (28 kilometers,
or 18 miles), primarily a service center, has an airport and offers moderately priced gas, lodging, and food. Back at Golden,
Route 1 continues west through Glacier and Mt. Revelstoke
national parks. When the weather is clear, many of the glaciers
can be seen from the highway. However, to fully appreciate Glacier, one must take to the trail. From the Illecillewaet Campground, a few kilometers west of the Rogers Pass Centre (off
Route 1), several trails lead to good overlooks and glacier
tongues, offering good day-hiking opportunities. One of the
best, although fairly strenuous, is the Asulkan Valley trail. Its
13-kilometer (8-mile) round loop crosses brooks and moraine,
passes waterfalls, and yields views of the Asulkan Glacier and
three massifs, called the Ramparts, the Dome, and Mt. Jupiter.
A much easier hike is the 1.6-kilometer (1-mile) Loop Brook
trail (6 kilometers, or 3¹⁄₂ miles, west of the Rogers Pass Centre), with views of the glaciers of Mt. Bonney.

41 Conceived primarily as a day-use park, **Mt. Revelstoke National Park** covers just 260 square kilometers (100 square
miles). The park's principal attraction is the 26-kilometer
(15¹⁄₂-mile) Summit Road to the top of the mountain, at 1,938
meters (6,395 feet). The gravel road begins from Route 1, 2
kilometers (1¹⁄₄ miles) before the turnoff to the town of Revelstoke, and its last few kilometers may be closed off by melting
snows until well into July. There are several easy hikes to follow
from the summit parking lot, taking you past small lakes, views
of the Selkirk and Monashee ranges, and mountain meadows
full of wildflowers.

Shortly after the Summit Road turnoff is the junction with
Route 23, which leads north to Mica Dam. Four kilometers (2¹⁄₂
miles) along this road is **Revelstoke Dam,** a large hydroelectric
and flood-control project. A free, self-guided tour and a short
film provide information about the dam and water power. Lake
Revelstoke, a reservoir created by the dam on the Columbia
River, is a popular boating area in summer, primarily along its
southern reaches. *Visitor Centre, tel. 604/837–6515. Self-guided
tours free. Open Mar. 14–July 14 and mid-Sept.—mid-Oct.,
daily 9–5; June 15–mid-Sept., daily 8–8.*

From Revelstoke Dam, Route 23 continues another 145 kilometers (90 miles) north to Mica Dam, the juncture of Revelstoke and Kinbasket lakes. Those who venture along this route
are entering wild country—a world of wilderness canoeing, big
fish, abandoned mining camps, and bears.

42 The town of **Revelstoke,** a skiers' headquarters in winter, is
worth a brief side trip. In 1986, the town began to restore its

downtown district, creating an attractive, authentic turn-of-the-century renovation that today houses modern shops, restaurants, and businesses.

What to See and Do with Children

Fort Steele Heritage Town (*see* Tour 4, *above*).

Rogers Pass Centre, Glacier National Park (*see* Tour 4, *above*).

The **Jasper-Yellowhead Museum** in Jasper (400 Pyramid Lake Rd., tel. 403/852–3013) features historical exhibits showing what life in the area was like when prospectors, surveyors, settlers, and the like arrived more than a century ago. *Admission by donation. Open 10 AM–4:30 PM in summer; 1:30–4:30 in winter.*

Another museum well worth a visit is the **Frank Slide Interpretive Centre** (*see* Off the Beaten Track, *below*).

The **Railway Museum** (1 Van Horne St. N, Canmore, tel. 604/489–3918), housed in restored Canadian Pacific Railway cars, presents a good picture of rail travel in the 1920s.

If you're visiting the Invermere area June through August, one of the best museums is the **Windermere Valley Pioneer Museum** (622 3rd St., tel. 604/342–9769), depicting the life of 19th-century pioneers.

Off the Beaten Track

A possible detour on the Calgary–Waterton trip is to continue for 60 kilometers (36 miles) on Route 3, past the turnoff for Route 6 to Waterton, until you reach **Crowsnest Pass.** In the early 1900s, Crowsnest Pass developed as a coal-mining community and was touted as "the Pittsburgh of Canada." From the outset, however, the coal-mining industry in Crowsnest Pass was ill-fated. In April of 1903, some 90 million tons of rock from Turtle Mountain buried a portion of the town of Frank, killing about 70 people. Then, in 1914, a massive mine explosion killed 189 people, and a few years later, with the uncertainties of an impending war, the coal-mining industry all but collapsed. The story of the slide and the history of coal-mining in the region are well recorded at the **Frank Slide Interpretive Center** (Crowsnest Pass, tel. 403/562–7388).

Another possible Calgary-to-Waterton side trip is a visit to **Head-Smashed-In Buffalo Jump,** located 18 kilometers (11 miles) northwest of Ft. Macleod on Route 785 (off Route 2). It is considered one of the best-preserved examples of a site where Plains Indians herded buffalo to their death over a low cliff and later harvested the meat and fur from the carcasses. As an archaeological site, it is not especially inspiring; it is, simply, a ledge in the middle of the rolling prairie. However, the museum at the site provides not only a fascinating explanation of the buffalo jump tradition but also insight into the life and customs of the Plains Indians, particularly the Blackfoot. Guided walks and audiovisual exhibits are presented. *Tel. 403/553–2731. Admission: $5 adults, $2 children 7–17. Open summer, daily 9–8; Labor Day–May 15, daily 9–5.*

Shopping

When shopping in the Canadian Rockies, you'll find the best selection in Banff, although Canmore may offer better bargains. The **Banff Springs Hotel** and shops on **Banff Avenue** have the usual souvenirs, as well as native crafts, sporting gear, landscape paintings, woolens, and outdoor wear.

In general, expect to pay a resort premium for most goods; if you're on a budget, you'll probably find better bargains in Calgary for things like camping supplies and sporting goods. On the other hand, shopping is generally more convenient in Banff, with so many stores so close together, and for local and native crafts, it is certainly the place to shop.

Native Crafts One of the most authentic places to find authentic articles is the **Banff Indian Trading Post** (Birch and Cave Aves., tel. 403/762–2456).

Local Crafts Of the numerous galleries and shops along Banff Avenue, perhaps the best for crafts and other art items, principally by Canadian craftspeople, is **The Quest for Handcrafts** (105 Banff Ave., tel. 403/762–2722).

Several galleries in Banff, Canmore, and Jasper offer arts and crafts, including handmade jewelry and watercolor paintings. Among those in Banff (with the widest selection) worth checking out are the **Canadian House Gallery** (Caribou and Bean Sts., tel. 403/762–3757) and the **Banff Indian Trading Post** (Birch and Cave Aves., tel. 403/762–2456).

Sporting Goods For sporting gear, **Mountain Magic** (224 Bear St., Banff, tel. 403/762–2591) has four floors of hiking, climbing, skiing, running, and biking equipment, and a 30-foot indoor climbing wall for gear testing.

Monod's (tel. 403/762–4571), with stores in Banff (111 Banff Ave.) and at the Chateau Lake Louise, also offers a wide array of sports equipment as well as clothing.

Sports and Outdoor Activities

Biking Around Banff, the **Vermilion Lakes loop** and the more strenuous **loop over Tunnel Mountain** are popular half-day bike tours. For a longer ride, **Route 1A** between Banff and Lake Louise is a good choice. Those seeking a rugged workout can test lungs and legs on the steep switchbacks leading up to **Mt. Norquay** ski area.

Mountain biking has become increasingly popular in recent years, leading to a rare source of controversy in the Canadian Rockies. Park officials have reported problems resulting from breakdowns (e.g., flat tires, broken frames) in remote areas, occasionally requiring rescue. There have also been reported problems with mountain bikers unwittingly breaking scent lines between bear mothers and cubs. As the Parks Service puts it in its brochure, "Trail Bicycling Guide" (available from the information office in Banff): "Cyclists are susceptible to bear encounters because of the speed and generally silent passage of bikes." As a result, although mountain bikes provide good access to the backcountry, they are restricted to relatively few trails, primarily fire roads in the parks. Needless to say, such restrictions tend to irk mountain-bike enthusiasts. Check with the information office in Banff, the nearest park warden, or nearest bike store before heading off-road.

Bikes can be rented from **Park and Pedal Bike Shop** (229 Wolf St., tel. 403/762–3190) in Banff. Bikes can also be rented from **Freewheel Cycle** (off Miete St., between Patricia and Giekie Sts., tel. 403/852–3898) in Jasper; in Revelstoke try **Revelstoke Cycle Shop** (118 MacKenzie Ave., tel. 604/837–2648).

Guided bike tours, on-road and off-road, are also offered by several operators (*see* Guided Tours in Essential Information, *above*).

Camping There are more than 40 public campgrounds within the national parks, not including backcountry sites for backpackers and climbers. Most operate on a first-come, first-served basis, though a few allow reservations a few days in advance. The season generally runs from mid-May to October, although a few campgrounds are open year-round. Campground information is available from the **Canadian Parks Service** (Information Services, Box 2989, Station M, Calgary, AB T2P 3H8, tel. 403/859–2203) and from **Kananaskis Country** (Suite 100, 1011 Glenmore Trail SW, Calgary, AB T2V 4R6, tel. 403/297–3362).

Numerous privately run campgrounds, for which reservations usually can be made, offer sites outside park boundaries. Contact **Tourism British Columbia** for its "Super Camping" publication, which lists more than 25 campgrounds in the Canadian Rockies region, or contact the Canadian Parks Service or Alberta Tourism (*see* Important Addresses and Numbers in Essential Information, *above*).

Climbing Except for Waterton Lakes, where the rock is generally crumbly, the Canadian Rockies is one of the world's great climbing regions. Among the ascents considered to be classics are **Mt. Assiniboine,** the oft-dubbed "Matterhorn of the Rockies"; glacier-cloaked **Mt. Athabasca,** near Sunwapta Pass; **Mt. Sir Donald,** in Glacier National Park; the daunting **Mt. Robson;** and, in the Purcells, the spires of the **Bugaboos.** Climbing and mountaineering are year-round activities in the Canadian Rockies, although October and November—after the summer and before ice-falls are solid enough for winter climbing—are the least desirable months.

Climbing permits are required for activities within the parks and can be obtained at park warden offices. Except for very experienced mountaineers, guide and instruction services are essential for climbers in the Canadian Rockies.

The **Canadian School of Mountaineering** (629 10th St., Box 723, Canmore, AB T0L 0M0, tel. 403/678–4134) and **Banff Alpine Guides** (Box 1025, Banff, AB T0L 0C0, tel. 403/762–2791), catering to all ability levels, lead trips throughout the parks. Both organizations also conduct ski mountaineering tours in winter. Climbing gear can be rented at outdoor stores in Banff.

In the Jasper area, the **Jasper Climbing School and Mountaineering Service** (Box 452, Jasper, AB T0E 1E0, tel. 403/852–3964) offers guided trips as well as climbing instruction.

Climbers or backpackers interested in extended stays of more than three or four days might consider membership in the **Alpine Club of Canada** (Box 2040, 278 St. Barbara's Terrace, Canmore, AB T0L 0M0, tel. 403/678–3200). The club maintains several mountain huts in the parks and leads hikes and climbs of varying difficulty.

Fishing The principal game fish in the Canadian Rockies is trout—cutthroat and rainbow being the most common varieties. The best fishing tends to be in streams, rivers, and lakes in the valleys, rather than in waters from glacial sources. The **Bow River** and the **lakes of British Columbia** are considered to have some of the best fishing in the region.

Fishing licenses are required and can be purchased at information centers and sports shops throughout the region. A basic, six-day license for nonresident Canadians is $11 and $15 for non-Canadians; annual licenses are $19 and $27, respectively. For more information, contact the **Ministry of Environment & Parks** (Fish & Wildlife Branch, 780 Blanchard St., Victoria, BC V8V 1X4, tel. 604/387–4573). A British Columbia license is good only in British Columbia; an Alberta license is good only in Alberta.

Alberta Tourism and Tourism British Columbia (*see* Important Addresses and Numbers in Essential Information, *above*) can provide lists of outfitters and guides who offer half-day to week-long fly-in adventure services.

Golf The golf season is short, running from about mid-May through mid-October. Given the abundance of water in the region, golf courses are generally in excellent playing condition, with lush grasses and well-kept greens. If hole lengths seem long, keep in mind that at the elevation of Canadian Rockies courses (above 1,200 meters, or 4,000 feet), a golf ball tends to travel 10% farther than at sea level.

Canadian Rockies courses, situated on the relatively flat valley floors, are not difficult to walk for those so inclined; the mountains simply provide dramatic backdrops. All courses listed below offer full pro-shop services, including cart rentals. Most courses enforce a standard dress code, requiring shirts with collars and Bermuda-length shorts or long pants.

Greens fees range from $20 to $50 for 18 holes. Cart rentals range from $15 to $30.

Within the parks, the **Banff Springs Hotel** (tel. 403/762–2211, ext. 162) and the **Jasper Park Lodge** (tel. 403/852–3301) each have an 18-hole course. **Kananaskis Village** (tel. 403/591–7070) has two 18-hole courses.

The area between Golden and Kimberley in British Columbia is growing as a golfing hotbed: Golfers here can now choose from ten 18-hole courses and two nine-hole courses. Arrangements for golfing can be made through **Fairmont Hot Springs Resort** (tel. 604/345–6311 or 800/663–4979), with two courses on site; **Radium Hot Springs Resort** (tel. 604/347–9311), with one course on site; and **Panorama** (tel. 604/342–6941). All offer multicourse, multiday packages.

Hiking The four contiguous parks (Banff, Jasper, Kootenay, and Yoho) have 2,900 kilometers (1,750 miles) of hiking trails. In Waterton Lakes there are 183 kilometers (114 miles) of trails, with further access to more than 1,200 kilometers (750 miles) of trails in adjacent Glacier National Park in the United States. Kananaskis Country offers numerous hiking and backpacking opportunities (although water can be in short supply, especially in late summer and fall), while Revelstoke and Glacier parks in British Columbia are generally best for shorter day hikes.

The hiking season runs from mid-May to early November, depending on the latitude and elevation of the trail. Trails along the Icefields Parkway, where elevations are generally highest, tend to be passable only between June and September. The hiking season in Waterton Lakes Park, far to the south, tends to be longest. Though most trails are restricted to foot traffic, horses and mountain bikes are permitted in some areas. Check with the park warden for selected trails.

Backpackers are required to register with the nearest park warden for permits. This is principally for safety reasons—so that you can be tracked down in case of emergency—as well as for trail-usage records. There is generally no fee for the use of backcountry campsites, although there is a fee for reservations, which can be made by contacting the park superintendent up to three weeks in advance. The park warden's office can also supply trail and topographical maps and information on current trail status.

Anyone interested in hiking or backpacking should obtain one of several good books that describe various routes and route combinations. One of the best, *The Canadian Rockies Trail Guide,* by Brian Patton and Bart Robinson (Summerthought Ltd., $14.95), is available in most bookstores in Banff, Lake Louise, and Jasper.

Banff The trails of Banff tend to get the most traffic, especially in summer. Although there are several trails within and leading from Banff townsite, more interesting hikes tend to be north of town. The most popular day-hiking areas, both accessible and scenic, are around **Lake Louise** and **Moraine Lake.**

Jasper **Jasper,** with the most extensive trail network (nearly 1,000 kilometers, or 600 miles), is popular for hikers seeking to get deep into the wilderness for several days at a time. Be aware that, in an effort to minimize environmental impact, park officials in Jasper set quotas for some of the park's most popular backpacking routes. In the height of the summer season, be prepared to encounter filled quotas for areas such as the Skyline Trail and Tonquin Valley. About a third of each trail's quota is pre-booked by reservations, which can be made up to three weeks in advance by contacting the Jasper National Park Superintendent (*see* Important Addresses and Numbers, *above*). **Tonquin Valley,** near Mt. Edith Cavell, is considered one of Canada's classic backpacking areas. Its high mountain lakes, bounded by a series of steep, rocky peaks known as the Ramparts, receive many visitors in the height of summer. One drawback: Some trails in this area are open to horse-pack trips. Horses, however, are not permitted on the Skyline Trail, which wanders for 44 kilometers (28 miles), at or above the treeline, past some of the park's most spectacular scenery. Good day-hiking areas in Jasper are around **Maligne Lake** and **Mt. Edith Cavell.**

Kootenay The trail that best characterizes the hiking in Kootenay is the strenuous **Rockwall trail,** which runs along the series of steep rock facades that are the predominant feature of the park. **Floe Lake,** sitting at the base of a sheer, 1,000-meter (3,300-foot) wall, is a trail highlight. Several long day-hike spurs connect the trail with Route 93.

Yoho Yoho is divided into two parts: the popular hiking arena around **Lake O'Hara,** dotted with high-alpine lakes, and the less-traveled **Yoho River valley,** terminating at the Yoho Glacier. Access to the Lake O'Hara region is somewhat restricted by the long, rather uneventful fire road from Route 1. Most hikers and climbers take the Lake O'Hara Lodge shuttle bus (*see* Lodging, *below*). Entry into the Yoho River valley is more immediate, either from Takakkaw Falls or from Emerald Lake.

Heli-hiking Another way to experience high-alpine hiking is by heli-hiking, a summer offspring of heli-skiing. **Canadian Mountain Holidays** (CMH, Box 1660, Banff, AB T0L 0C0, tel. 403/762–7100), in conjunction with **Tauck Tours** (11 Wilton Rd., Westport, CT 06881, tel. 203/226–6911), offers heli-hiking tours for three to nine days, using CMH's relatively luxurious remote lodges in the Cariboo and Purcell ranges. While CMH has in recent years added more strenuous programs to its heli-hiking schedule, most programs feature relaxed hiking over fairly gentle terrain—a great opportunity for elderly or less physically able people to experience a high-alpine world.

Horseback Riding One of the most popular ways to experience the Canadian Rockies is on horseback. Horses are restricted from many trails within the national parks, but there are still some opportunities; among the most popular areas for pack trips within the parks is Tonquin Valley in Jasper. Restrictions are far fewer in Kananaskis Country, the provincial parks, and the British Columbia Rockies region.

Arrangements for hourly or daily rides, as well as riding instruction, can be made through the sports desks at the **Banff Springs Hotel, Chateau Lake Louise, Emerald Lake Lodge,** and **Jasper Park Lodge** (*see* Lodging, *below*). Other stables in the region include **Alpine Stables** (Box 53, Waterton Park, AB T0K 2M0, tel. 403/859–2462), **Boundary Stables** (Box 44, Kananaskis Village, AB T0L 2H0, tel. 403/591–7171), **Brewster Stables** (Box 2280, Banff, AB T0L 0C0, tel. 403/762–2832), and **Pyramid Riding Stables** (Box 787, Jasper, AB TOE 1EO, tel. 403/852–3562).

Alberta Tourism and Tourism British Columbia can provide listings of pack-trip outfitters and guest ranchers, which proliferate the fringes of the national parks. In British Columbia, further information is also available from the **Guide-Outfitters Association** (Box 759, 100 Mile House, BC V0K 2E0, tel. 604/395–2438).

Rafting Rafting opportunities range from gentle floats along the Bow River near Banff to rollicking white-water rides on the Kicking Horse River near Golden. Most trips are half-day or full-day. For those seeking white water at its frothiest, June is the best month, when rivers are still swollen with the snow melt but not dangerously so.

In the Banff area, **Rocky Mountain Raft Tours** (Box 1771, Banff, AB T0L 0C0, tel. 403/762–3632) features one- to three-hour trips on the Bow River and also offers canoe rentals. In the Jasper area, **Jasper Raft Tours** (Box 398, Jasper, AB TOE 1E0, tel. 403/852–3613) offers half-day float trips on the Athabasca. **Maligne River Adventures** (626 Connaught Dr., Jasper, AB T0E 1E0, tel. 403/852–3370) offers half-day white-water trips on the Maligne.

Alpine Rafting Company (Box 1409, Golden, BC V0A 1H0, tel. 604/344–5016) offers a variety of whitewater trips on the Kicking Horse and the Illecillewaet, between Glacier National Park and Revelstoke, including multiday trips combining rafting and horseback riding.

Skiing There are 11 lift-service ski areas in the region, five of which are within an hour's drive of Banff; daily lift tickets cost between $22 and $36. Cross-country opportunities are also plentiful, and many backcountry lodges are winterized and offer guide services for backcountry touring. Numerous tour operators—based both in the region and elsewhere—feature ski packages; Alberta Tourism or Tourism British Columbia can assist you in choosing a tour that best suits your interests, abilities, and budget.

Cross-Country **The Canmore Nordic Centre** (Box 1979, Canmore, AB T0L 0M0, tel. 403/678–2400) was the site of most 1988 Olympic Nordic events. With 56 kilometers (36 miles) of groomed trails, the center features the most extensive, groomed cross-country network in the region. Some trails are lit for night skiing, and, best of all, there is no trail fee. A 3-kilometer (1.8-mile), paved trail is open in summer for rollerskiing and in-line skating. Other groomed trails (and rental equipment) can be found near the **Banff Springs Hotel, Chateau Lake Louise, Jasper Park Lodge, Fairmont Hot Springs Resort,** and **Mt. Engadine Lodge** (*see* Lodging, *below*).

Lake O'Hara Lodge, Mt. Assiniboine Lodge, and **Skoki Lodge** (*see* Lodging, *below*) are among several lodges that offer guided backcountry ski touring. In Jasper, reservations for backcountry huts in Tonquin Valley can be made through **Tonquin Valley Ski Tours** (Box 520, Jasper, AB T0E 1E0, tel. 403/852–3909). The **Canadian School of Mountaineering** (Box 723, Canmore, AB T0L 0M0, tel. 403/678–4134) and **Banff Alpine Guides** (Box 1025, Banff, AB T0L 0C0, tel. 403/678–6091) also lead backcountry ski tours.

Downhill The three ski areas in the immediate Banff vicinity are **Lake Louise** (Box 5, Lake Louise, AB T0L 1E0, tel. 403/522–3555), **Mt. Norquay** (Box 1258, Banff, AB T0L 0C0, tel. 403/762–4421), and **Sunshine Village** (Box 1510, Banff, AB T0L 0C0, tel. 403/762–6500 or 800/661–1363). Lake Louise's terrain is large and varied; Mt. Norquay's is generally short and steep (although more intermediate terrain has been opened in the last couple of years); Sunshine Village's terrain is mostly intermediate and above the tree line.

Nakiska (Box 1988, Kananaskis Village, AB T0L 0M0, tel. 403/591–7777), about 45 minutes southeast of Banff, was the site of the 1988 Olympic alpine events and features wide-trail intermediate skiing. **Marmot Basin** (Box 1300, Jasper, AB T0E 1E0, tel. 403/852–3816), near Jasper, has a wide mix of terrain.

In the British Columbia Rockies, **Panorama** (Panorama, BC V0A 1T0, tel. 604/342–6941 or 800/663–2929) has the largest lift-serviced vertical rise (1,156 meters, or 3,800 feet) of any ski area in the region. **Fernie Snow Valley** (Box 788, Fernie, BC V0A 1M0, tel. 604/423–4655) and **Kimberley Ski Resort** (Box 40,

Kimberley, BC V1A 2Y5, tel. 604/427–4881) have vertical rises of more than 600 meters (2,000 feet). Sunshine Village, Nakiska, Panorama, Fernie Snow Valley, and Kimberley have on-mountain lodging and resort facilities.

Heli-skiing Heli-skiing has become increasingly popular in the region, and tours can be arranged through several operators on a daily or weekly basis. Heli-skiing was once considered an activity exclusively for experienced, well-conditioned skiers. But in recent years, heli-ski operators also have introduced programs for intermediate skiers with little or no powder-skiing experience. Daily tours start above $250 per person, and weekly packages (including meals and lodging but not airfare) begin at about $2,000.

The original, and by far the largest, heli-skiing operator in the region is **Canadian Mountain Holidays** (*see* Heli-hiking, *above*). Perhaps the best known of the CMH permit areas is the Bugaboos, a subrange of the Purcells, where the whole heli-skiing business started in the mid-'60s. The Bugaboos, however, is now just one of nine areas in which CMH operates, each with 1,500 to 3,000 square kilometers (580 to 1,160 square miles) of skiable terrain. Skiers are housed mostly in remote mountain lodges. CMH runs only weekly tours, and reservations should be made several months in advance. Other weekly operators include **Mike Wiegele Helicopter Skiing** (Box 249, Banff, AB T0L 0C0, tel. 403/762–5548 or 800/661–9170), which operates out of Blue River in British Columbia, and **Selkirk Tangiers Heli-Skiing** (Box 1409, Golden, BC V0A 1H0, tel. 604/344–5016). Selkirk Tangiers also offers daily tours. **R.K. Heli-Ski** (Box 695, Invermere, BC V0A 1K0, tel. 604/342–3889 or 800/661–6060), based at the Panorama ski area, offers daily tours as well as multiday packages.

Water Sports With an abundance of lakes and rivers in the region, watersport opportunities abound. However, the glacier-fed waters of the Canadian Rockies tend to be cold, even in midsummer. Whether you're waterskiing, board sailing, boating, or swimming, know the conditions and wear proper gear.

Boat and canoe rentals are available at **Lake Louise** and **Moraine Lake** in Banff National Park, at **Emerald Lake** and **Lake O'Hara** in Yoho, and at **Pyramid Lake** in Jasper. However, the main centers of boating activity within the four contiguous parks are Lake Minnewanka in Banff and Maligne Lake in Jasper. In Banff, **Minnewanka Boat Tours** (Box 2189, Banff, AB T0L 0C0, tel. 403/762–3473) offers boat and canoe rentals; **Monod Sports** (111 Banff Ave., tel. 403/762–4571) offers sailboard rental and instruction. Boat rentals on Maligne Lake are available at the boat house by the **Maligne Lake Chalet** and through **Maligne Lake Scenic Cruises** (Box 280, 626 Connaught Dr., Jasper, AB T0E 1E0, tel. 403/852–3370).

Spray Lakes reservoir and Kananaskis Lake are the main sites of boating activity in Kananaskis Country, and boat rentals are available through **Peregrin Sports** (Kananaskis Village, T0L 2H0, tel. 403/591–7453). Lake Invermere, in British Columbia, is popular among sailors, board sailors, and waterskiers and is warm enough for swimming in the midsummer months. For information and equipment rentals, contact the **Invermere Travel Information Centre** (Box 2605, Invermere on the Lake, BC V0A 1K0, tel. 604/342–6316). To the north, the long, dam-controlled Kinbasket and Revelstoke lakes give boaters, canoeists, and fishermen more of a wilderness experience. There are several boat ramps on the lakes but few services.

For sailors and board sailors who like strong winds, Waterton Lakes, with winds from the Alberta prairies often exceeding 50 kilometers (30 miles) per hour, is the place to be. The **Athabasca, Bow, Kicking Horse,** and **Maligne rivers** provide various levels of river-running challenges for canoeists and kayakers—from relatively still water to white water (*see* Rafting, *above*).

Dining and Lodging

Dining

Dining in the Canadian Rockies is, for the most part, a casual affair. Given the general mix of travelers to the region—families and active outdoorspeople—emphasis is on good food served in large quantities, at moderate prices. This is not the place for the traveler who expects haute service and cuisine; there is only a handful of top-caliber restaurants in the region. However, people who like fresh game and fish will not be disappointed. Trout, venison, elk, moose, quail, and other game are items that even modest dining establishments feature on their menus.

Highly recommended restaurants are indicated by a star ★.

Category	Cost*
Very Expensive	over $30
Expensive	$20–$30
Moderate	$10–$20
Inexpensive	under $10

per person, excluding drinks, service, and sales tax

Lodging

The hotels, inns, and lodges of the Canadian Rockies compose an eclectic list, ranging from rustic, backcountry lodges without electricity or running water to standard roadside motels to hotels of supreme luxury. With just a few exceptions, however, they share one common trait—room rates that are considerably higher in the summer than during the rest of the year. The week between Christmas and New Year's often commands a higher rate as well. For this reason, flexibility in travel planning can mean considerable savings—a room that goes for $100 a night on September 15 may well drop to $50 on September 16. Lodgings are categorized according to their off-peak rates. High-season rate increases, if any, are noted within each listing.

Highly recommended lodgings are indicated by a star ★.

Category	Cost*
Very Expensive	over $120
Expensive	$80–$120
Moderate	$50–$79
Inexpensive	under $50

*All prices are for a standard double room (or an equivalent, where not applicable), are in Canadian dollars, and do not include a 5% room tax in Alberta, an 8% room tax in British Columbia, and in some areas, a small municipal tax.

Banff
Dining
★

Le Beaujolais. Elegantly decorated in a neoclassical style, this restaurant is strikingly out of place in casual Banff. Tapestries on the wall give the restaurant a hint of baronial splendor, and the richness of the food is a suitable match. Traditional French preparations of beef, veal, and duck are featured menu items. The wine cellar is lavishly and imaginatively stocked. *212 Buffalo St. at Banff Ave., tel. 403/762–2712. Reservations required. Jacket and tie required. AE, MC, V. Dinner only. Very Expensive.*

Banff Springs Hotel. This hotel (*see* Lodging, *below*) houses 17 bars and lounges of varying formality and cuisine, from coffeehouses to a grand dining room. Samurai, a Japanese restaurant, may have the best food—its standards must be high enough to satisfy the hotel's large Japanese clientele. The best overall dining experience may be at the Waldhaus, where a Bavarian-style meal is often followed by a Bavarian-style singalong. The Grapes Wine Bar, which serves a light-fare menu, including salads, pâtés, and fondue, is tucked away in a small, quiet room on the mezzanine level. Big windows make for nice views here. The Alhambra, open in summer only, specializes in Spanish-style cuisine and flambé in a grottolike setting. In the Rob Roy Supper Club, waiters negotiate flambé carts around guests who come here to dance to live music. A hotel highlight in summer is the barbecue on the Red Terrace. The flavor of the traditional barbecue fare—steaks, corn on the cob, roast potatoes—seems greatly enhanced by the view of Rundle Mountain, the Bow River, and the hotel golf course. *Spray Ave., tel. 403/762–2211. Dining hours, dress codes, and reservation policies vary among restaurants. Dinner reservations in summer required at most restaurants. AE, DC, MC, V. Moderate–Very Expensive.*

Caboose. Situated in the railway depot, the Caboose is reminiscent of the bygone train era. Old train-engine, rail-car, and train-depot paraphernalia fills the dining room; dim lighting adds to the spirit of nostalgia. The Continental dishes, served with salad, are good but basic: simply prepared prime rib, crab legs, beef, and salmon steaks. *Elk and Lynx Sts., tel. 403/762–3622. Dinner only. Reservations advised. Dress: neat but casual. AE, MC, V. Expensive.*

Ticino. A stucco-and-wood-beam dining room is decorated with Swiss canton banners. The menu is great for variety lovers: It combines both Italian and Swiss entrées. For Swiss tastes, the schnitzels are among the choice items. Pasta and veal dishes are good choices for Italian palates. *205 Wolf St., tel. 403/762–*

3848. Reservations recommended. Dress: neat but casual. AE, MC, V. Expensive.

Buffalo Mountain Lodge. An exposed, rough-hewn post-and-beam interior gives the dining room a comfortable likeness to a converted barn. This is a woodcrafter's showcase, highlighted by the large polished wine cabinet that divides the dining and bar areas. The menu features fish, meat, and game dishes with sweet-tasting nouvelle sauces and is supplemented by hearty soups and fresh-baked breads. *Tunnel Mountain Rd., tel. 403/762–2400. Reservations advised. Dress: neat but casual. Open 7 AM–11 PM. AE, MC, V. Moderate–Expensive.*

★ **Giorgio's.** This is two restaurants in one: **La Pasta,** a casual spot, is located downstairs; **La Casa,** the more formal dining room, is upstairs. La Casa serves classic Italian fare with a romantic, dinner-under-the-eaves atmosphere. La Pasta is immensely popular with the local crowd, so you might have to wait a bit during busy hours for a table. The menu consists mainly of pizzas and pasta dishes, served in a dimly lit, tavernlike room. *219 Banff Ave., tel. 403/762–5116 (La Casa); 403/762–5114 (La Pasta). Dinner only. Reservations advised for La Casa. Dress for La Casa: neat but casual; La Pasta: casual. AE, MC, V. Moderate (La Pasta)–Expensive (La Casa).*

Balkan Restaurant. The bright blue-and-white decor, with tile trim, cane-back chairs, and plants, evokes the Mediterranean. The menu offers classic Greek dishes, such as moussaka and souvlakia, as well as creative ethnic mixes, such as Greek chow mein (rice and veggies with feta cheese). Lunchtime can attract a crowd. *120 Banff Ave., tel. 403/762–3454. Reservations accepted. Dress: casual. AE, DC, MC, V. Moderate.*

Melissa's Missteak. Behind an ersatz German-beerhaus facade is an ersatz log-cabin interior. Upstairs, the lounge is true roadside-America, with popcorn, video games, and TV monitors. The restaurant serves decent food at fair prices, three meals daily. Steaks are the predominant dinner-menu item, although deep-dish pizza is a house specialty. *218 Lynx St., tel. 403/762–5511. Reservations advised for dinner. Dress: casual. AE, MC, V. Moderate.*

★ **Barbary Coast.** This sports-theme restaurant with neo-California cuisine is a local favorite. The plant-filled, skylighted dining room is littered with paraphernalia from all manner of sport, from baseball to bobsledding. Pizzas with pesto sauce are a house favorite, along with oddities such as the Einstein Theory salad (chicken, bananas, sprouts, etc., in a curry dressing). Live rock and blues bands play in the bar after 9 PM on weekends. *119 Banff Ave., upstairs, tel. 403/762–4616. Reservations for parties of 6 or more only. Dress: casual. AE, MC, V. Inexpensive-Moderate.*

★ **Joe Btfsplk's Diner.** This place is fun, camp, or overbearing, depending on your tastes. It's a re-created '50s-style diner, with red vinyl banquettes, chrome-trimmed tables, and waitresses dressed in vintage '50s attire. The menu is taken straight from a true-Americana cookbook: meat loaf and hash for lunch or dinner, eggs and biscuits for breakfast. Fresh-baked cookies and muffins, available for take-out, are the culinary highlight. *221 Banff Ave., tel. 403/762–5529. No reservations. Dress: casual. AE, MC, V. Inexpensive.*

Lodging **Banff Springs Hotel.** Built in 1888, this castlelike hotel was the beginning of Banff's tourism boom. The massive, stone-walled hotel has a seemingly endless maze of hallways and stairwells, huge sitting areas, and banquet rooms, complemented by lots of dark wood furnishings and chandeliers. The complexity of the hotel's floor plan, however, can be disorienting, and the lobby is surprisingly small—contributing to traffic jams during checkout time. The 829 guest rooms come in all shapes and sizes, with such old-hotel characteristics as high ceilings, rattling windows, and layers of cream-color paint. Refurbished bathrooms are a plus. The hotel caters to tour groups and conventioneers—a $23 million convention center being the hotel's most recent major addition—making this ever-active lodge anything but a getaway mountain retreat. Rooms are not soundproof, and often the noises carry. *Spray Ave., Box 960, T0L 0C0, tel. 403/762–2211 or 800/268–9411. 760 rooms, 69 suites. Facilities: 17 restaurants and pubs, 24-hr room service, cable TV, shops, health club, indoor miniature golf, 5 tennis courts, riding stables, 27 holes of golf. Premium rates mid-May–mid-Oct. AE, DC, MC, V. Very Expensive.*

Banff Park Lodge. The high, slanted ceiling and dark-cedar paneling, in addition to the lean, modern, and unembellished style, exude a Scandinavian feeling. On a quiet street in downtown Banff, the lodge is within walking distance of shops and restaurants. The rooms are bright, with lots of beige and ecru. A few have large, in-room Jacuzzis, two giant steps from bedside. *222 Lynx St., Box 2200, T0L 0C0, tel. 403/762–4433 or 800/661–9266. 211 rooms, some with steam showers and Jacuzzis. Facilities: 2 restaurants, room service, whirlpool, sauna, indoor pool, shops, cable TV. Premium rates June–Sept. AE, DC, MC, V. Expensive.*

Banff Rocky Mountain Resort. Five kilometers (3 miles) east of Banff, this resort, with chalet-style buildings and numerous outdoor facilities, is the place for active people. Inside, rooms are bright, with white walls, wall-to-wall carpeting, and lots of blond-wood trim. Many rooms have fireplaces and kitchens with microwave ovens. *Banff Ave. and Tunnel Mountain Rd., Box 100, T0L 0C0, tel. 403/762–5531, 800/661–9563 or 800/667–3529. 170 studio, 1-bedroom, and 2-bedroom units. Facilities: cable TV, 2 tennis courts, squash courts, weight room, games room, indoor pool complex, video service on premises, shuttle-bus service to and from Banff. Approximate 35% to 50% rate increase mid-June–mid-Sept. and late-Dec.–early-Jan. AE, DC, MC, V. Expensive.*

★ **Buffalo Mountain Lodge.** Part of the Canadian Rocky Mountain Resorts group, along with Emerald Lake Lodge in Yoho and Deer Lodge in Lake Louise, this lodge is similar in ambience and style. The lobby area, with lots of polished pine and exposed rough-hewn beams, is dominated by a large stone hearth with a buffalo head over the mantel. There is a main lodge, with lobby and restaurant; a new hotel-condo cluster built in 1987; and an older group of chalet buildings. Newer rooms are dressed in pastel shades and have small fireplaces, wicker chairs, and pine cabinetry. Older chalet units are larger, with two bedrooms, and are similarly decorated. Although the lodge sits high atop the road, on the outskirts of Banff, few rooms have views. *Tunnel Mountain Rd., Box 1326, T0L 0C0, tel. 403/762–2400 or 800/661–1367. 85 units, including hotel rooms, and 2-bedroom condos. Facilities: cable TV, hot tub, steam room. Approximately 60% rate increase mid-June–mid-Sept. AE, MC, V. Expensive.*

★ **Storm Mountain Lodge.** This is one of the original Canadian Pacific Railway backcountry lodges, built in 1922. Not nearly as back-country today, it is on Route 93, just east of Vermilion Pass. The sitting area of the main, log cabin–style lodge is dominated by a large fireplace that is crowned by the head of a big-horn sheep. The dining area embodies the elegance of simplicity: straight-back wood chairs and white tablecloths on an enclosed porch with big glass windows overlooking the pass. Sleeping cabins, tucked in the woods, are smallish but cozy, made so by fireplaces, old lamps, and down comforters. *Rte. 93, 4.8 km (3 mi) west of Rte. 1 interchange. Box 670, T0L 0C0, tel. 403/762–4155. 12 cabins. Facilities: restaurant, lounge, hiking trails. Closed mid-Sept.–late-May. AE, MC, V. Moderate–Expensive.*

Castle Mountain Village. The Village, about halfway between Banff and Lake Louise, consists of three different chalet styles. The smallest—about 3½ by 4¼ meters (12 by 14 feet)—have kitchens, bathrooms, and sleeping areas with fireplaces. Although cramped and on the dark side, they are clean and quiet. Larger and newer pine-log chalets have two bedrooms and can sleep as many as six. For four people, the large chalets are a comfortable, economic choice. Request a cabin with a view of Castle Mountain. *Rte. 1A between Banff and Lake Louise, Box 1655, T0L 0C0, tel. 403/762–3868. 21 chalets. Facilities: satellite TV, convenience store, barbecue facilities. 35%–40% rate increases June–Oct. and Christmas week. Pets $10 extra. MC, V. Moderate.*

High Country Inn. There is nothing fancy here—just clean, simple, comfortable motel rooms. The units are slightly more spacious than those in the Red Carpet Inn next door, wood-veneer furnishings are a little newer, and cedar-covered walls give some rooms a touch of regional character. Ask for a room in the back, away from heavy traffic running along Banff Avenue. *419 Banff Ave., Box 700, T0L 0C0, tel. 403/762–2236 or 800/661–1244. 71 rooms. Facilities: restaurant, satellite TV, whirlpool, heated parking. Premium rates May–mid-Sept. AE, MC, V. Moderate.*

Red Carpet Inn. Under the same management as the High Country Inn next door, Red Carpet offers one of the few moderately priced lodging options in downtown Banff. Like its neighbor, this motel is basically no-frills; the lobby is modestly adorned with a desk, an office, and a postcard stand. Motel-style rooms are small, but by Banff standards, so are the prices, which are slightly below those of the High Country Inn. Rooms in the front, on Banff Avenue, get traffic noise. *425 Banff Ave., Box 1800, T0L 0C0, tel. 403/762–4184. 46 rooms. Facilities: satellite TV, indoor pool, whirlpool. Premium rates May–mid-Sept. AE, MC, V. Moderate.*

Canmore Dining

★ **Pepper Mill.** The small dining room is simply adorned with off-white walls, brown tablecloths, and cloth-covered hanging lamps. Reputed for its pepper steak, the restaurant offers well-prepared pasta dishes as well. In summer, meals are also served on a deck in front, alongside a quiet Canmore side street. *726 9th St., tel. 403/678–2292. Reservations advised. Dress: neat but casual. AE, MC, V. Dinner only. Moderate–Expensive.*

Faro's. Colorful drawings of Canmore hung against white walls and blond-wood tabletops lend to a bright, casual environment. The menu is eclectic, offering barbecued dishes, pizzas, and steaks, but such Greek entrées as souvlakia are the house specialties. *8th St. and 8th Ave., tel. 403/678–2234. Reservations recommended after 5 PM. Dress: casual. Open 11 AM–10 PM. AE, MC, V. Moderate.*

Lodging   **Bow Valley Motel.** Located in the center of Canmore, this two-story, few-frills motel is enhanced by the friendliness of its management and its proximity to town. For those who put a premium on being able to walk to dining and shopping, this is the place to stay. Recently refurbished rooms are clean and simply furnished, with bed, dresser, and a 20-inch TV, but who needs much more? Five rooms have kitchens. *610 8th St., Box 231, T0L 0M0, tel. 403/678–5085. 25 rooms. Facilities: cable TV. Premium rates June–Sept. AE, DC, MC, V. Moderate.*

Rocky Mountain Ski Lodge. In terms of facilities and prices, several motels in Canmore are pretty much interchangeable as lower-price alternatives to Banff accommodations. Of these, Rocky Mountain Ski Lodge (formerly the Skiland Motel) is a notch above the rest. Part of the reason is that it comes with several options, being really three separate motel properties rolled into one. The newer motel section is certainly more attractive than the somewhat older motel building. Slanting, exposed wood-and-beam ceilings give a chaletlike feel to otherwise simple motel rooms. Rooms in the older section have kitchenettes, but the decor is more '60s American than Swiss-chalet. Most recently, the lodge owners bought the neighboring Rocky Mountain Chalets, featuring condo-style accommodations. *Highway 1A, Box 696, Canmore, AB T0L 0N0, tel. 403/678–5445 or 800/655–6111. Facilities: 82 units, some with kitchens, kitchenettes, and/or fireplaces. Steam room, exercise room, playground, cable TV. Premium rates June–Sept. MC, V. Moderate.*

★   **Mt. Engadine Lodge.** Hiking and cross-country skiing trails begin out the back door of this backcountry-style lodge, where the mountains and lakes of Kananaskis Country are an immediate presence. The surroundings draw young and old, and most of the clientele come here to enjoy the outdoors. Wood is the lodge's main design feature, with cedar walls on the exterior and white-pine ceilings and furnishings inside. Rooms (dormitory-style as well as private) have a scrubbed simplicity to them, as do the common areas. Meals, served family-style, are included in the rate. The lodge operators are also backcountry guides, and hiking or skiing packages are available. *At Mt. Shark: turn off on Spray Trail, 38 km (22 mi) south of Canmore. Box 1679, Canmore T0L 0M0, tel. 403/678–4080. Lodging for 28 persons in dorm-style, shared, and private rooms, all with shared baths. Facilities: restaurant, sun deck. Winter rates slightly higher than in summer. MC, V. Inexpensive–Moderate.*

Cranbrook   **City Cafe.** If you find yourself stuck for lunch in the fast-food
Dining   world of Cranbrook, City Cafe will be a breath of fresh air. The flowered tablecloths, low ceilings, and pine banquettes give the small dining room a French-country-bistro air, especially in the morning, when breakfast is served. Sandwiches served on fresh, crusty French bread are tasty and very reasonably priced. *1015 Baker St., tel. 604/489–5413. Reservations advised. Dress: casual. MC, V. Inexpensive–Moderate.*

Fairmont Hot   **Fairmont Hot Springs Resort.** With an extensive selection of
Springs   activities from golf to heli-hiking, a vacation at this resort is
Lodging   like being at camp. In addition to the recreational facilities, Fairmont also has hot springs, a spa, and an airport. Rooms,

available in condo villas and the main lodge, are familiarly furnished with contemporary decor, and many are wood-paneled. The low-slung, bungalow-style architecture is attractive. Some rooms are equipped with kitchens and have balconies or patios. *Rte. 93/95, Box 10, Fairmont Hot Springs V0B 1L0, tel. 604/345–6311 or 800/663–4979. 140 lodge rooms and 194 villa units, some with kitchens, patios, and/or balconies. Also 265 RV sites. Facilities: 7 restaurants, lounge, snack bar; 2 golf courses, 10 tennis courts, heli-hiking, 4 pools, hot springs, spa, airport. Golf, ski, and spa packages. AE, MC, V. Expensive.*

Glacier National Park
Lodging

Glacier Park Lodge. This modern, two-floor motel at the top of Rogers Pass offers ambience in the familiar Best Western format: wood-veneer tables and chairs, maroon wall-to-wall carpeting, and undecorated walls. The steep-sloping A-frame roof is a design concession to the heavy winter snows. Since this is the only lodging within Glacier National Park boundaries, the location is the main attraction. Situated on Highway 1, the lodge accommodates long-distance travelers with its 24-hour service station, 24-hour coffee shop, and gift shop. *The Summit, Rogers Pass, BC V0E 2S0, tel. 604/837–2126 or 800/528–1234. 51 motel-style rooms. Facilities: restaurant, 24-hr coffee shop, outdoor hot tub, heated outdoor pool. AE, MC, V. Moderate.*

Golden
Lodging

Swiss Village. This is a combination motel and campground lodging, with a little more modern polish than some of its Golden neighbors. There is nothing special here, just basic motel rooms—bed, bathroom, TV—at a fair price. The RV sites have electrical setups and water. *Off Rte. 1, west end of Golden. Box 765, V0A 1H0, tel. 604/344–2276. 40 motel rooms, 10 RV sites. Facilities: satellite TV, whirlpool. AE, MC, V. Inexpensive.*

Invermere
Dining
★

Chalet Edelweis. This cute little chalet really looks as if it could have been plucked and transplanted from a hillock in the Swiss countryside. The interior is refreshingly simple—a few blond-wood tables, scrubbed white walls, and a small bar. The atmosphere inspires you to try the fondue, but schnitzels and fettuccine are also good. *934 7th Ave., tel. 604/342–3525. Reservations advised. Dress: casual. MC, V. Dinner only. Moderate–Expensive.*

Lodging
★

Delphine Lodge. This is the sort of place for those seeking an out-of-the-way cubbyhole. Originally built in 1899, this hotel has been restored and it now feels like a cozy bed-and-breakfast. Big, lace-curtained windows shed lots of light on a living/dining area that is distinguished by its polished, wide-board floors, huge stone hearth, and antique straight-back chairs and wicker rockers. Handcrafted pine furnishings and down comforters fill the smallish, pastel-shaded bedrooms. Full breakfast is served every morning. *Main St., 5 km (3 mi) from Invermere, Box 2797, V0A 1K0, tel. 604/342–6851. 6 rooms, 1 with private bath, 5 sharing 2 baths. V. Inexpensive.*

Jasper
Dining

Beauvert Room and **Moose Nook.** For fancy dining and a wide-ranging Continental menu, the Beauvert Room is the place to go around Jasper. The huge dining room, whose main decor is stone pillars and hard angles, conveys a big-hotel-style ambience. Moose Nook, more intimate but retaining a modernistic coolness, has an imaginative, game-oriented menu that includes pheasant, reindeer, and buffalo steaks, although the quality can be uneven. Both restaurants are open for breakfast. *Jasper Park Lodge, 4 km (2¹/2 mi) northeast of Jasper, off Rte.*

16, tel. 403/852–3301. Reservations required. Jacket advised for dinner. AE, MC, V. Very Expensive.

★ **Le Beauvallon.** This is often the restaurant of choice for Jasperites going out for a special meal. Upholstered chairs, blue tablecloths, and wood-trimmed crimson walls give the dining room an air of elegance. The menu has some seafood items, but meat dishes are the main feature, including lamb in pesto sauce and an elk, beef, and pork mélange. The giant Sunday-brunch buffet has epic feast potential for active outdoorspeople. Try Le Beauvallon for breakfast, too. *Chateau Jasper, 96 Giekie St., tel. 403/852–5644. Dinner reservations advised. Dress: neat but casual; jacket advised for dinner. AE,DC, MC, V. Expensive– Very Expensive.*

★ **L'Auberge.** French cuisine is offered in this small mountain-lodge retreat with panoramic views of the Athabasca River. Weather permitting, meals are served on the porch in front, but traffic noise from nearby Route 93 may make indoor dining preferable. The menu is creatively assembled from French classics; highlights are brie baked in puff pastry (appetizer) and veal with wild mushrooms (entrée). Though no lunch is served, breakfast begins at 8 AM. *Near Becker's Chalets, 5 mi south of Jasper on Rte. 93, tel. 403/852–3535. Reservations advised for dinner. Dress: casual. AE, MC, V. Closed lunch and mid-Oct.–Apr. Expensive.*

L & W. Plants adorning the sloping greenhouse roof bring life to this otherwise ordinary hotel coffee shop. The menu is all over the lot—pizzas, Greek dishes, barbecued ribs—with the common denominator being a salad bar. Dishes are adequately prepared, and the simplest—burgers and pizzas—are the best choices. Families come here for a decent meal at a reasonable price. Take-out and delivery service are available. *Hazel and Patricia Sts., tel. 403/852–4114. No reservations. Dress: casual. AE, MC, V. Moderate.*

The Palisades. A surprisingly rich Greek streak runs through Jasper, and this restaurant is a good place to get a feel for it. Bright-white walls, a greenhouse ceiling over part of the dining room, and numerous plants evoke a sunny Mediterranean mood. Moussaka and souvlakia, along with baklava for dessert, are the characteristic Greek items, although pizzas are available, too. *Cedar Ave., near Connaught Dr., tel. 403/852–5222. Dinner reservations accepted. Dress: casual. AE, MC, V. Moderate.*

Mountain Foods. This is a good place to pick up a morning cup of coffee or sandwiches for a picnic lunch. The café has a health-food store in the back and a deli counter up front. Though the emphasis is on health foods, you can still get an old-fashioned three-meat hero to eat in or take out. The tabbouleh salad is especially good. Browse through the store's book rack while waiting for your sandwich to be made. *606 Connaught St., tel. 403/852–4050. No reservations. Dress: casual. MC, V. Inexpensive.*

Lodging **Jasper Park Lodge.** Jasper's original resort, a lakeside compound northeast of town, hums with on-site recreational amenities, including guided activities. The main lodge, with a large window overlooking Beauvert Lake and the mountains, features polished-stone floors, carved totem-pole pillars, and high ceilings that convey a cool, open-warehouse atmosphere. The rooms vary: Some are in a modern, hotel-room style; others have an exposed-log, rustic character, with fireplaces; but most are arranged in one-story cottages, and all have brightly patterned down comforters covering the beds, plus a porch, patio, or balcony. Breakfast and dinner at the lodge's restaurants, the Beauvert Room and Moose Nook (*see* Dining, *above*), are included in most room rates. Unfortunately, the lodge has acquired a bad reputation for overbooking, forcing preregistered guests to stay in other accommodations. Confirm reservations often and just before your arrival date. *4 km (2¹/2 mi) northeast of Jasper, off Rte. 16, Box 40, T0E 1E0, tel. 403/852–3301; in the United States, 800/828–7747. 437 rooms. Facilities: 6 restaurants and lounges, satellite TV, golf course, 2 tennis courts, boating, bicycling, horseback riding, fishing. 40%–50% rate increase June–Sept. AE, DC, MC, V. Very Expensive.*

Chateau Jasper. Big wood beams cantilevered over the front door of this two-story inn suggest a Scandinavian interior, but rooms are of the American motel style with Colonial motif, most notable in the Colonial-style headboards. Burgundy carpets and low ceilings add coziness to largish rooms; some units have kitchen areas, though they are spare and in need of a facelift. The hotel's restaurant, Le Beauvallon, is excellent (*see* Dining, *above*). *96 Giekie St., T0E 1E0, St., tel. 403/852–5644. 119 rooms, 6 with kitchen. Facilities: satellite TV, heated indoor parking, indoor pool, whirlpool, roof-top sun deck. Premium rates June–Sept. AE, DC, MC, V. Expensive.*

Jasper Inn. A modern interpretation of chalet-style architecture, this inn has lots of oblique angles and hard edges, with sleek, low-slung furniture to match. This angular coolness is warmed by slanted cedar ceilings and red brick. During breakfast, the skylighted dining area can be as bright as the beach on a sunny day. Accommodations are arranged in a variety of ways, but living areas in condo-style units are particularly spacious. Most units have kitchenettes and fireplaces. In addition to the full-service restaurant, an Oriental restaurant with takeout service recently opened in the hotel. *Giekie St. and Bonhomme Ave., Box 879, T0E 1E0, tel. 403/852–4461. 141 rooms, including 14 suites. Facilities: satellite TV, two restaurants, indoor pool, sauna, whirlpool, steam bath. Approximately 40% rate increase June–Sept. Children under 12 stay free in parents' room. AE, DC, MC, V. Moderate–Expensive.*

Pyramid Lake Resort. Situated on the shores of active Pyramid Lake, this lodging is a great place for those who enjoy hiking, boating, horseback riding, and marvelous sunrises, or crosscountry skiing and ice skating in winter. The 16 units built in 1988 in two log-cabin chalets are preferable to the older bungalows that are closer to the lake but more run-down. All units have kitchenettes. The restaurant is fair, but Jasper, a few kilometers down the road, has many others to offer. *Pyramid Lake Rd., 5.6 km (4 mi) from Jasper. Box 388, T0E 1E0, tel. 403/852–4900. 42 units in 10 bungalows and 2 chalets. Facilities: satellite TV, beach with boat, canoe, and sailboard rentals; 16 units have whirlpools. MC, V. Moderate.*

★ **Alpine Village.** Located just south of town, this is one of Jasper's bargains. Logs in many cabins are left exposed on interior walls, adding to the warm, rustic feeling of this family-run operation. Furnishings are garage-sale eclectic, and frilly throw cushions abound. Most units, including 12 recently built logcabin chalets, have fireplaces and sun decks; two-bedroom cabins have full kitchens. There is a view of Mt. Edith Cavell in the distance, and Athabasca River is just out front, though you must cross a small road to get to it. *Rte. 93A, 1 km (²/₃ mi) south of Jasper. Box 610, T0E 1E0, tel. 403/852–3285. 42 units, including 1-room sleeping cabins and 2-bedroom cabins. 25%–35% rate increase mid-June–mid-Dec. DC, V. Closed mid-Oct.–Apr. Inexpensive–Moderate.*

Kananaskis Country Dining

L'Escapade. In the evening, the atmosphere in L'Escapade is tastefully elegant and romantic, with such fine details as white tablecloths, real silver, candlelight, and soft, live music. The menu is French-influenced and features such items as lamb Niçoise, duck breast, and lobster linguine. Together, the fare and ambience make this restaurant the most elegant in all the village. Breakfast is served. *Hotel Kananaskis, Kananaskis Village, Hwy. 40, tel. 403/591–7711. Reservations advised for dinner. Dress: neat but casual; jacket advised for dinner. AE, DC, MC, V. Very Expensive.*

Lodging

Kananaskis Village. This is the lodging village built for the 1988 Olympics. The full-service resort, sandwiched on a small plateau between the Nakiska ski area and two 18-hole golf courses, is tastefully designed and decorated. Accommodations are in three facilities—the Inn, the Lodge, and the Hotel. All surround an attractively landscaped, artificial pond that provides a nice lounging spot on a summer day. Of the three, the Inn is the most moderately priced, with log pillars and a redwood exterior inviting you into the motel-style rooms, some with private balconies (balconies facing west get the best sun), kitchenettes, or fireplaces. Larger and more lavish, some rooms in the Lodge and Hotel have rosewood furnishings, ceramic-base lamps, and rustic wood armoires to hide TV sets. The hotel throws in special amenities, such as bathrobes and hair dryers, and some rooms have fireplaces and Jacuzzis. Several restaurants, skewed toward high-end elegance, offer food ranging from sushi to haute cuisine. The Peaks dining room in the Lodge, with floor-to-ceiling windows casting light on a dark wood motif, may have the nicest atmosphere for those seeking a fancy meal. *Hwy. 40, 28 km (17 mi) south of Rte. 1. Kananaskis Village T0L 2H0. Inn: 96 rooms, tel. 403/591–7500. Lodge: 253 rooms and suites, tel. 403/591–7711 or 800/828–7447 for reservations. Hotel: 68 rooms and suites, tel. same as for lodge. Facilities: 5 restaurants, satellite TV, indoor pool, sauna, whirlpool, health club, ski area, two 18-hole golf courses, stables nearby, shops, post office, heated indoor parking for the Lodge and Hotel. Lodge and Hotel: AE, DC, MC, V; Inn: AE, MC, V. Expensive–Very Expensive.*

Kimberley Dining ★

Chef Bernard's Kitchen. Dining in this small, homey storefront restaurant on the Kimberley pedestrian mall is like dining in someone's pantry. The decor is alpine—with goat horns, cowbells, and photos adorning the walls. The menu is small but widely varied, including pastas and fondues. Breakfast is served in summer. *170 Spokane St., tel. 604/427–4820. Reservations advised. Dress: neat but casual. MC, V. Moderate–Expensive.*

Lodging

Inn of the Rockies. In keeping with downtown Kimberley's Bavarian theme, the hotel's exterior is very German, with exposed-wood beams and stucco, and tinted, blown-glass windows. (The hotel's former name, Rhinekastle, is still used by many Kimberley locals.) Large rooms have a small sitting area and are plainly furnished with dark brown wood–veneer furniture, including a bed, bureau, and TV. The restaurant serves good, reasonably priced food. Just a block from the Platzl, this is *the* hotel in Kimberley. *300 Wallinger Ave., V1A 1Z4, tel. 604/427–2266 or 800/661–7559. 41 hotel rooms. Facilities: restaurant, lounge, cable TV. AE, MC, V. Moderate.*

Lake Louise **Post Hotel.** Here is one of the true epicurean experiences in the
Dining Canadian Rockies. The restaurant receives numerous com-
★ mendations and awards, and with good reason. A low, exposed-beam ceiling and a stone hearth in the corner lend a warm, in-from-the-cold atmosphere; white tablecloths and fanned napkins provide an elegant touch. Traditional European cuisine that's combined with a lighter, California influence is the main fare—veal and venison are the house specialties. Homemade pastries and desserts cap off the meal; you can also order them for afternoon tea in the hotel lobby (*see* Lodging, *below*). Breakfast and lunch are also served. While the food is excellent, service can be stuffy. *200 Pipestone St., tel. 403/522–3989. Reservations advised. Jacket advised for dinner. AE, MC, V. Very Expensive.*

Chateau Lake Louise. Several restaurants and pubs in this hotel (*see* Lodging, *below*) present an array of options, from light snacking in the Glacier Saloon to night-on-the-town elegance in the Edelweiss Dining Room. Regardless of choice, dining inevitably defers to the view, brought into play by arced, 10-foot-high windows. The size of the Victoria Dining Room, with seating for more than 300, is nicely toned down by plush carpeting, upholstered chairs, and standing plants. The food and atmosphere are European hotel–style—croissants and jam for breakfast, Continental fare for lunch and dinner—with white cotton tablecloths and polished silver. For simpler, less expensive, coffee shop–style eating throughout the day, there is the Poppy Room. From early June to early October, afternoon tea in the Lakeside Lounge is a culinary highlight that usually includes fresh scones, pastries, or croissants—along with coffee and tea—served on high-tea silver. *Lake Louise Dr., tel. 403/522–3511, ext. 52. Dinner reservations required in summer for most restaurants. Dress: casual; jacket required for dinner in Edelweiss Dining Room. AE, DC, MC, V. Moderate (Poppy Room)–Very Expensive (Edelweiss and Victoria dining rooms).*

Laggan's Mountain Bakery and Deli. This six-table coffee shop is where the local work crews, mountain guides, and park wardens come for an early-morning muffin and a cup of coffee. Located in the Sampson Mall, Laggan's has excellent baked goods, especially the poppy-seed sweet breads. You might want to pick up a sandwich here for your drive north on the Icefields Parkway. *Samson Mall, off Rte. 1, tel. 403/522–2017. No reservations. Dress: casual. No credit cards. Inexpensive.*

Lodging **Chateau Lake Louise.** There's a good chance that no hotel—
★ anywhere—has a more dramatic view out its back door than this chateau. Terraces and lawns reach to the famous aquamarine lake, backed up by the Victoria Glacier. The impressive turn-of-the-century stone facade opens to a similarly grand interior, with lobby and sitting areas that convey a stadiumlike sense of spaciousness. A $60 million general renovation, completed in 1991, has been tastefully done. In the public areas, off-white walls, polished wood and brass, and burgundy carpeting blend well with the lake view, seen through large, horseshoe-shaped windows. Guest rooms feature bright, floral-pattern wallpaper and neo-Colonial furnishings; some

have terraces. In spite of all the space, though, the hotel can become very crowded with bus tours, hikers, day-trippers from Banff, and hotel guests. *Lake Louise, AB T0L 1E0, tel. 403/522–3511 or 800/828–7447. 515 rooms and suites. Facilities: 5 restaurants, indoor pool, canoeing, riding stables, steam room, exercise room, whirlpool, shops. AE, DC, MC, V. Very Expensive.*

★ **Post Hotel.** The location, next to the small shopping mall just off Highway 1, is rather ordinary, but the hotel makes up for it in other ways. A gold-colored wood dominates the decor, giving the hotel an atmosphere of muted elegance—a modern interpretation of the country-lodge concept. Rooms come in 15 different configurations, from standard doubles to units with sleeping lofts, kitchens, balconies, and fireplaces. The wood theme extends to the furniture, made of solid Canadian pine. Bathrooms are large, most equipped with whirlpool tubs. Two recently renovated, stream-side log cabins—each intended for two people—date back to the original Post Hotel, built in 1938, and evoke a mood of old-fashioned, in-the-mountains romance. The restaurant (*see* Dining, *above*) is regularly rated as one of the best in the Canadian Rockies. *Box 69, T0L 1E0, tel. 403/522–3989 or 800/661–1586. 93 units. Facilities: cable TV, indoor pool, steam bath, whirlpool. 25%–35% rate increase mid-May–mid-Sept. and Christmas week. AE, MC, V. Expensive.*

Lake Louise Inn. This five-building complex offers a variety of accommodations, from motel rooms to two-bedroom condo units. A three-story building, completed in early 1991, with 12 one-room suites and 24 motel-style rooms, adds to the wide array of lodging options here. Catch the morning sun in the recently renovated lobby, with its wood and stone-wall decor. For economy-minded travelers, the Pinery, a separate 56-room building, offers spare but comfortable accommodations. *210 Village Rd., Box 209, T0L 1E0, tel. 403/522–3791 or 800/661–9237. 222 rooms and condo units, many with balconies, fireplaces, and/or kitchenettes. Facilities: restaurant, pub, cable TV, indoor pool, sauna, whirlpool, exercise room, ski-area shuttle-bus service, multiday ski packages. AE, D, DC, MC, V. Moderate.*

Paradise Lodge & Bungalows. This lodge is only 2 kilometers (1¼ miles) down the access road from the lake, and this location and the moderate prices are what attract guests. Six small rooms share baths upstairs in the log-cabin main lodge. The bungalows, or log-sided cabins (some with kitchenettes), are more rustic from the outside than from the inside. As the lodge is set in a spruce and pine grove, rooms can be somewhat dark and feel cramped, but are well maintained. *Box 7, T0L 1E0, tel. 403/522–3595 (summer), 403/522–3987 (winter). 6 lodge rooms with shared bath, 21 one- and two-room cottages. Facilities: barbecue facilities, playground. Closed mid-Oct.–mid-May. MC, V. Moderate.*

Panorama Lodging

Panorama Resort. The resort, at the edge of the Purcell Wilderness, has a wide variety of accommodations and activities. The lodge at the base of the ski lifts is more casual and conveys a college-dorm atmosphere, with its long hallways and doors that look as though they've been kicked a few times with ski boots. Inside, rooms are large, with yellow walls and lots of mirrors. The other accommodations are in condo villas that look to be part of a mountainside suburb. Attractively decorated, the villa rooms follow a light-brown-and-beige color scheme, and many rooms have fireplaces, patios, or balconies. Originally conceived as a winter resort, Panorama has a fine ski area, but mountain biking and hiking trails, in addition to an outdoor pool and tennis courts make this a rich year-round destination, as well. *18 km (11 mi) west of Invermere. Box 7000, Panorama V0A 1T0, tel. 604/342–6941 or 800/663–2929. 355 lodge and condo units. Facilities: satellite TV, sauna, indoor and outdoor whirlpools, outdoor pool, tennis courts, skiing, heli-skiing. AE, MC, V. Expensive.*

Dining **Toby Creek Lodge.** The restaurant, part of a 1960s-era ski lodge, has cedar walls, lighting fixtures that look like upside-down buttercups, a slant-roof ceiling, and—in winter—a big roaring fire in the central fireplace. In the summer, the outside deck offers fresh air, though not much of a view. The menu is varied, offering salads, steaks, stir-fry, and chicken dishes. Toby Creek is also open for breakfast, too. *Panorama Resort, 18 km (11 mi) west of Invermere, tel. 604/342–6941. Dinner reservations advised during ski season. Dress: neat but casual. AE, MC, V. Expensive.*

Radium Hot **The Chalet.** In a town where ordinary, interchangeable motels
Springs abound, the Chalet is a cut above—figuratively and literally.
Lodging The hotel sits on a crest above town and has several rooms with expansive views of the Columbia River valley, though these units come at a premium. The decor is nothing special—lots of browns, navy blue, and wood veneer—but each room comes with a sitting area and minikitchen (microwave, refrigerator, sink), and many have balconies. This is a good, economical choice for a family with one or two small children. *Madsen Rd., Box 456, V0A 1M0, tel. 604/347–9305. 17 suites. Facilities: complimentary coffee, cable TV, sauna, exercise equipment, whirlpool, gameroom, gift shop. AE, DC, MC, V. Expensive.*

Radium Hot Springs Resort. Although the architecture and style of this resort are undistinguished, the recreational facilities and activities bring to life this otherwise basic Best Western property. Rooms, decorated with bright colors and modern furnishings, are simple but functional; some have kitchens and wet bars. Breakfast in the main dining room is a good way to start the day, as the morning sun shines brightly through the big windows. *Off Rte. 93, south of Radium Hot Springs. Box 310, V0A 1M0, tel. 604/347–9311 or 800/655–3585. 119 hotel and condo units. Facilities: indoor pool, hot tub, sauna, whirlpool, exercise room, 2 tennis courts, squash and racquetball court, golf, cross-country skiing, cable TV. Golf and ski packages available. 25% rate increase May–mid-Oct. and Christmas week. AE, MC, V. Moderate–Expensive.*

Revelstoke **One-Twelve.** Housed in the Regent Inn (*see* Lodging, *below*),
Dining this restaurant is the real star of the British Columbia Rockies,
★ where dinner is usually an ordinary affair. Lots of cedar, low ceilings, and an abundance of historic photos lend a warm atmosphere. Continental dishes, such as salmon, chicken Cordon Bleu, and beef brochette, are the basic fare, but the unrivaled king of the menu is the lamb broiled with rosemary and red wine. *Regent Inn, 112 1st St. E, tel. 604/837–2107. Reservations advised. Lunch and dinner. Dress: neat but casual. AE, DC, MC, V. Expensive.*

Lodging **Regent Inn.** This inn mixes many styles: colonial, with its brick-arcade facade; true Canadian, in its pine-trimmed lobby area and restaurant; and Scandinavian, in the angular, low-slung wood furnishings of the guest rooms. Rooms are on the large side but have no spectacular views. The hotel is located downtown, in a revitalized, two-block area of Revelstoke, and is near several boutiques and restaurants. The hotel's own restaurant, One-Twelve (*see* Dining, *above*), is among the best in the Rockies. *112 Victoria Rd., Box 450, V0E 2S0, tel. 604/837–2107. 43 rooms. Facilities: restaurant, club with live entertainment, cable TV, whirlpool, sauna, complimentary Continental breakfast. AE, MC, V. Moderate.*

Waterton Lakes
Lodging

Bayshore Inn. As the name suggests, the two-story inn is on the lakeside, and rooms with balconies take full advantage of the setting. Indeed, the setting is the thing; otherwise, the inn's common areas and motel-style rooms are rather ordinary, although some have balconies and kitchenettes. A distinctive touch is the heart-shaped tubs in the three honeymoon suites. When the usual Waterton wind is mellow, the lakeside patio is a great spot for light meals and drinks. *Main St., Box 38, Waterton Park, AB T0K 2M0, tel. 403/859–2211. 70 rooms, including 2-bedroom and honeymoon suites. Facilities: restaurant, coffee shop, satellite TV, gift shop. AE, MC, V. Closed Oct.–Apr. Moderate–Expensive.*

★ **Prince of Wales Hotel.** Situated between two lakes, this property has a breathtaking view of a mountain backdrop from one direction, and a lake-and-prairie setting from another. Eaves, balconies, and turrets fantastically adorn this hotel, and it's crowned by a high steeple. The baronial, dark-paneled interior evokes the feeling of a royal Scottish hunting lodge. Expect creaks and rattles at night—the old hotel (built in the 1920s) is exposed to rough winds. *Waterton townsite. Write to: Mail Station 5570, Phoenix, AZ 85078, tel. 602/248–6000. 81 rooms. Facilities: restaurant. Children under 12 stay free in parents' room. MC, V. Closed mid-Sept.–May. Moderate–Expensive.*

★ **Kilmorey Lodge.** The 60-year-old inn with a log-cabin facade sits at the edge of the Waterton Lakes townsite. Rooms are steeped in country-cottage atmosphere, with pine-wood walls, Indian rug wall hangings, sloped floors, and homespun antique furnishings. Some rooms have additional sleeping or sitting areas. There is a decent full restaurant that serves three meals a day. This is the only lodging in Waterton Lakes that's open year-round. *Box 100, Waterton Park, T0K 2M0, tel. 403/859–2334 or 800/661–8069. 25 rooms. Facilities: restaurant. AE, MC, V. Moderate.*

Yoho
Dining and Lodging
★

Emerald Lake Lodge. This is an enchanted place, set at the edge of a secluded, glacier-fed lake in Yoho National Park. It's a great spot for canoeing on the lake, hiking, and cross-country skiing through miles of trails in the park. A sitting area in the main lodge has overstuffed chairs and small tables and offers light meals served around a large stone hearth. Cottages surround the log-cabin main lodge. Guest rooms have fireplaces, and many have balconies with lake views. Soundproofing is the one amenity lacking—you can hear your neighbors. The dining room is a glass-enclosed terrace, with views of the lake through tall stands of evergreens. The furnishings are eclectic, some tables with upholstered chairs, some straight-backs, but all evoking an old-lodge atmosphere. Also eclectic is the menu, which mixes traditional Canadian and American fare—steaks, game, and fish—with nouvelle sauces like ginger-tangerine glaze. Excellent pastas and hamburgers are also available. For those who want a light meal in a more casual setting, salads, quiches, and baked cheeses are served around a giant stone hearth in the lounge area. The lodge also serves breakfast. *9.5 km (6 mi) north of Field, BC. Box 10, Field, BC V0A 1G0, tel. 604/343–6321 or 800/663–6336. 85 units in 2- and 4-room cottages. Facilities: restaurant, teahouse, bar, exercise room, game room, sauna, outdoor hot tub, boat rentals, stables. AE, MC, V. Expensive.*

Backcountry Lodges and Guest Ranches

Backcountry lodges have been an integral part of Canadian Rockies travel since the '20s. They vary considerably in terms of accommodations and accessibility: At the luxurious end are lodges with private rooms, private baths, full electricity, telephones, and restaurant-style dining; at the rugged extreme are lodges with bunk beds, kerosene lamps for evening light, and outhouses. A few are accessible by car in the summer, some can be reached only by hiking or by skiing in winter, and still others can be reached only by helicopter.

Surprisingly—given the difficulty of getting supplies to remote locations—meals served at most backcountry lodges tend to be excellent, no doubt improved by the fresh mountain air and appetites swelled by the active life of the backcountry. The lodges and ranches listed below are a sampling. Both Alberta Tourism and Tourism B.C. can provide more complete lodge and ranch listings as well as descriptions (*see* Important Addresses and Numbers in Essential Information, *above*).

Backcountry Lodges

Lake O'Hara Lodge. Secluded in the heart of one of the most scenic and popular hiking and climbing regions in the Canadian Rockies, this lodge is situated just west of Lake Louise. In summer, guests are ferried by a lodge-operated bus along an 11.25-kilometer (7-mile) fire road between Highway 1 and the grounds. In winter, guests must ski the distance. The lodge and lakeside cabins offer fairly luxurious backcountry living, including private rooms with baths and a restaurant that serves three meals a day (included in room rates). *Off Hwy. 1 in Yoho National Park. Box 55, Lake Louise, AB T0L 1E0, tel. 604/343–6418 or 403/762–2118 in the off-season. 23 units in lodge and cabins. Facilities: hiking, climbing, canoeing. Reservations for high season should be booked several months in advance. Closed May, Oct., Nov., Dec. MC, V. Moderate–Expensive.*

Mt. Assiniboine Lodge. Built by the Canadian Pacific Railroad in 1928, the handsome, log-sided main lodge appears to have changed little in more than 60 years. The lodge's setting is classically alpine—at the edge of mile-long Lake Magog, with the rocky pyramid of Mt. Assiniboine as a backdrop. Guests can hike in from Sunshine Village or hike (or ski) in from Spray Lakes Reservoir, the distance ranging between 20 and 30 kilometers (12 and 18 miles) depending on the route chosen. Many guests choose to fly in by helicopter from Canmore, saving their hiking legs for high-country jaunts from the lodge. Among the lodge's noteworthy amenities are large down comforters on the beds and hearty meals served family-style. The lodge has some electricity and running water, but guests should be prepared to use outhouses. *Box 1527, Canmore, AB T0L 0N0, tel. 403/678–2883. 6 rooms in main lodge, plus 6 cabins sleeping 2–4 people. Room rates include all meals and hiking (or skiing) guide service. Guided hiking in summer; guided backcountry skiing in winter. No credit cards. Moderate.*

Skoki Lodge. An 11-kilometer (6½-mile) hike or ski from the Lake Louise ski area, Skoki is the kind of backcountry lodge you must work to get to. The high-alpine scenery of Skoki Valley makes the travel well worthwhile, as does the small log-cabin lodge itself, built in 1930. The log walls, big stone fireplace, and mantel cluttered with old ski gear make Skoki seem the epitome of backcountry coziness. So, too, do the rooms upstairs in the main lodge, with beds tucked tightly under the wood eaves. Don't expect such luxuries as private baths, running water, or electricity, but meals are included in the rates. An afternoon tea, with freshly baked breads and sweets, is also served to lodge guests and day-trippers. *Box 5, Lake Louise, AB T0L 1E0, tel. 403/522–3555. Lodging in 22 guest rooms and cabins with wood-burning stoves and outdoor washrooms. Reservations must be made in advance. AE, MC, V. Inexpensive–Moderate.*

Guest Ranches   **Homeplace Ranch.** Just east of the Kananaskis Country foothills, the ranch is just as its name suggests: homey. It is secluded, several miles along gravel roads, surrounded by other working ranches. Bedrooms have tiny, private baths (unusual for ranch accommodations), and the small living/dining area is cluttered with books and magazines that provide good nightly reading, the principal evening activity. During the day, the activity is riding over the rolling land, aspen groves, and open meadows near the ranch. Also available are extended, multiday pack trips into Kananaskis Country. Meals, included in the guest rate, are served family-style, and such is the homey atmosphere that you might find yourself wanting to pitch in and help with the cooking or the dishes. *Off Rte. 2, 10 km (6 mi) west of Priddis. R.R. 1, Box 6, Priddis, AB T0L 1W0, tel. 403/931–3245. Lodging for 12 in private rooms in ranch house. Packages, including pack trips, available. Moderate–Expensive.*

Kananaskis Guest Ranch. Set near the Bow River at the edge of Kananaskis Country, a main lodge with restaurant and lounge is surrounded by cabins and larger "chalets." Cedar walls and, in some units, cedar-beamed ceilings give a rustic flavor to two otherwise plain, double-bed bedrooms. The Donut Tent—a log-and-wood-roofed "tent" with a large hole in the middle, where bonfires are built for family-style barbecues—is the ranch's claim to fame. In addition to the obligatory horseback riding, the ranch also offers jet-boat trips on the Bow River. *Ranch office on Ranch Rd., from the Seebe-Exshaw exit on Rte. 1 east of Canmore, General Delivery, Seebe AB T0L 1X0, tel. 403/673–3737. Lodging for 50 in cabins and chalets. Facilities: dining room, lounge, souvenir shop, whirlpool. AE, MC, V. Closed Nov.–Apr. Inexpensive–Moderate.*

The Arts and Nightlife

The Arts

Most of the cultural activity in the Canadian Rockies is in and around Banff. Unquestionably, the hub of cultural activity is the **Banff Centre** (St. Julien Rd., tel. 403/762–6300). Presenting a performing-arts grab bag throughout the year, with pop and classical music, theater, dance, and film, the center peaks in summer with the two-month Banff Festival of the Arts.

Galleries and Museums Housed in Banff Centre is the **Walter J. Philips Gallery,** which focuses principally on works by Canadian artists and artists at the Banff Centre School of Fine Arts. *Tel. 403/762–6253. Admission free. Open noon–5.*

Also in Banff, the **Whyte Museum** features art, photography, historical artifacts, and exhibits about life in the Canadian Rockies. *111 Bear St., tel. 403/762–2291. Admission: $2, children free. Open mid-May–mid-Oct., daily 10–6; off-season hours vary.*

The **Banff Park Museum** features wildlife displays, wildlife art, and a library on natural history. *93 Banff Ave., tel. 403/762–1558. Admission free. Open 10–6; Sept.–May, 1-5.*

The **Jasper-Yellowhead Museum** features exhibits on the history of the Jasper area. *400 Pyramid Lake Rd., Jasper, AB TOL 1E0, tel. 403/852–3013. Donations requested. Open Memorial Day through Labor Day 10–4:30; off-season, 1:30–4:30, closed Thurs.*

Performing Arts The **Jasper Activity Centre** (303 Pyramid Ave., tel. 403/852–3381) hosts local troupes presenting theater, music, and dance productions throughout the year.

The **Jasper Summer Theatre** (Giekie and Miette Sts., tel. 403/852–5325) performs shows from June through August, at the Anglican Church Hall.

At the **Wild Horse Theater** (Fort Steele, BC V0B 1N0, tel. 604/426–6923), in Fort Steele, college presentations are staged from late June to mid-September.

Music During the summer months, Bavarian bands in Kimberley strike up with oompah music on the Platzl, especially when festivals are in swing. The **Old Time Accordion Championships,** in early July, is a Kimberley musical highlight.

In late summer, the Royal Canadian Mounted Police perform their precision **Musical Ride at Fort Steele** (tel. 604/426–6923).

Nightlife

Like many activities in the Canadian Rockies, nightlife, too, is an outdoor event. In summer darkness doesn't fall until after 10 PM, so an after-dinner hike, sail, or even nine holes of golf is possible.

For cocktails and socializing, the big hotels—the **Banff Springs Hotel, Chateau Lake Louise, Jasper Park Lodge,** and the **Lodge at Kananaskis**—have lounges or dining rooms with entertainment and dancing (*see* Lodging, *above*).

In Banff, **Wild Bill's** (Banff Ave. and Caribou St., tel. 403/762–0333) is a cowboy bar with live music and the place for two-steppers to strut their stuff.

In Canmore, local folk kick back at **Sherwood House** (738 8th St., tel. 403/678–5211), which occasionally has live bands on weekends.

In Jasper, the **Athabasca Hotel's** nightclub (510 Patricia St., tel. 403/852–3386) features dancing to Top-40 music and live bands.

Also in Jasper, the **Astoria Hotel** (404 Connaught, tel. 403/852–3351) is known for a happy hour that can become crowded and raucous.

8 Manitoba Saskatchewan Alberta

By Theodore Fischer

Updated by Robin and Arlene Karpan

Between the wilds of western Ontario and the eastern slopes of the Rockies lie Canada's three prairie provinces: Manitoba, Saskatchewan, and Alberta. This is Canada's heartland: the principal source of such solid commodities as wheat, oil, and beef. These provinces are also the home of a rich stew of ethnic communities that make the area unexpectedly colorful and cosmopolitan.

The term "prairie provinces" is a bit of a misnomer, as most of this region (the northern half of Alberta and Saskatchewan, and the northern two-thirds of Manitoba) consists of sparsely populated expanses of lakes, rivers, and forests. Most of northern Saskatchewan and Manitoba belong to the Canadian Shield, with a foundation of Precambrian rock that is some of the oldest in the world. The fertile plains of the south are home to Canada's agricultural heartland, where wheat is still king, but other crops, as well as livestock, help boost the economy. The landscape is quite diverse, with farms and ranches interspersed with wide river valleys, lakes, rolling hills, badlands, and even dry hills of sand.

The Prairies' history is quite significant, dating back to 75 million years ago when dinosaurs roamed what was then semitropical swampland; 12,000 years ago the first human settlers crossed the Bering Strait from Asia. In the 17th century European fur traders began arriving, and in 1670 the British Crown granted the Hudson's Bay Company administrative and trading rights to "Rupert's Land," a vast territory whose waters drained into Hudson Bay. A hundred years later, the North West Company went into direct competition by building outposts throughout the area. From this fur-trading tradition arose the Métis—mostly French-speaking offspring of Indian women and European traders who followed the Roman Catholic religion but adhered to a traditional Indian life-style.

By 1873 the North West Mounted Police was established in Manitoba, just six years after the formation of the Canadian government. In 1874, the Mounties began their march west: Their first chores included resolving conflicts between the Indians and American whiskey traders and overseeing the orderly distribution of the free homesteads granted by the Dominion Lands Act of 1872. The Mounties played a role in the North West Rebellion—a revolt by Métis, who feared that the encroachment of western settlement would threaten their traditions and freedom. Although the Métis eventually succumbed, and their leader, Louis Riel, was hanged in 1885, Riel is now hailed as a martyr of the Métis and a statue of him stands on the grounds of Manitoba's Legislature Building.

Railroads arrived in the 1880s and with them a torrent of immigrants seeking free government land. An influx of farmers from the British Isles, Scandinavia, Holland, Germany, Eastern Europe, Russia, and especially Ukraine, plus persecuted religious groups, such as the Mennonites, Hutterites, Mormons, and Jews, transformed the prairies into a rich wheat-growing breadbasket and cultural mosaic that is still very much in evidence today. In 1947, a big oil strike transformed Edmonton and Calgary into gleaming metropolises full of "blue-eyed Arabs."

The people of the prairie provinces are relaxed, reserved, and irascibly independent. They maintain equal suspicion toward

"Ottawa" (big government) and "Toronto" (big media and big business). To visitors, the people of this region convey a combination of Western openness and Canadian-style courtesy: no fawning, but no rudeness. Visitors also find exceptional outdoor recreational facilities—a spectrum of historical attractions that focuses on Mounties, Métis, dinosaurs, and railroads; excellent accommodations and cuisine at reasonable (but not low) prices; and quiet, crowdless expanses of extraordinarily wide open spaces.

Essential Information

Important Addresses and Numbers

Tourist Information
Manitoba

Travel Manitoba (Dept. 2036, 7th floor, 155 Carlton St., Winnipeg, Man., R3C 3H8, tel. 204/945–3777 or 800/665–0040) distributes a free road map and several useful brochures. The office is open weekdays 8:30–4:30.

Manitoba Travel Information Centers are located just inside the Manitoba border along major routes. The centers are open mid-May through early September from 8 AM to 9 PM.

Saskatchewan

Tourism Saskatchewan (Saskatchewan Trade & Convention Centre, 1919 Saskatchewan Dr., Regina, Sask. S4P 3V7, tel. 800/667–7191) can provide you with brochures and maps of attractions, accommodations, and parks inside and outside the province. The main office is open weekdays 8–7, Saturday 10–4.

Information centers are located in cities throughout the province, and in the summer along major highways leading into the province.

Alberta

Alberta Tourism (Box 2500, Edmonton, Alberta, T5J 2Z4, tel. in Edmonton, 403/427–4321; in Alberta, 800/222–6501; in United States and Canada, 800/661–8888) distributes extremely comprehensive and useful free promotional literature. The office is open weekdays 9–4:30.

Arriving and Departing by Plane, Bus, and Train

By Plane

Air Canada has direct or connecting service from Boston, New York, Chicago, San Francisco, and Los Angeles to Winnipeg, Regina, Saskatoon, Calgary, and Edmonton. Commuter affiliates serve other U.S. and Canadian destinations. U.S. airlines serving the prairie provinces include **Northwest** to Winnipeg; **America West, American, Continental, Delta,** and **United** to Calgary; **American, Delta,** and **Northwest** to Edmonton.

By Bus

Greyhound (consult local directory) and local bus companies provide service from the United States, other parts of Canada, and throughout the prairie provinces.

By Train

There is no rail service between the United States and the prairie provinces.

Via Rail trains (from New York and Connecticut, tel. 800/361–3677; from the Atlantic seaboard, 800/561–3949; from the Midwest, 800/387–1144; from the western United States, 800/665–0200) connect eastern Canada and the west coast through Winnipeg–Saskatoon–Edmonton.

Getting Around

By Car   Two main east–west highways link the major cities of the prairie provinces. The Trans-Canada Highway (Route 1), mostly a four-lane divided freeway, runs through Winnipeg, Regina, and Calgary on its nationwide course. The two-lane Yellowhead Highway (Route 16) branches off the Trans-Canada Highway west of Winnipeg and heads northwest toward Saskatoon, Saskatchewan, and Edmonton, Alberta. Traveling north–south, four-lane divided freeways connect Saskatoon–Regina (Route 11) and Edmonton–Calgary (Route 2).

From the United States, interstate highways cross the Canadian border, and two-lane highways continue on to major prairie province cities. From Minneapolis, I–94 and then I–29 connect to Highway 75 at the Manitoba border south of Winnipeg. Driving distance between Minneapolis and Winnipeg is 691 kilometers (432 miles). A main route to Alberta is I–15 north of Helena, Montana, which connects to Highways 4, 3, and 2 to Calgary. Calgary is 690 kilometers (425 miles) from Helena; it's also 670 kilometers (419 miles) from Seattle, via the Trans-Canada Highway.

Winnipeg

With a population of just more than 600,000, Winnipeg ranks as Canada's seventh-largest city and the largest population center between Toronto and Calgary. Though geographically isolated, this provincial capital has become a center for both commerce and culture, boasting a symphony orchestra, ballet and opera companies, a lively theater scene, and a thriving community of local and native artists.

The first stop on the great Canadian land rush of the late-19th century, Winnipeg is still home to descendants of the original French and British settlers, and it has distinct neighborhoods of Ukrainians, Jews, Italians, Mennonites, Hungarians, Portuguese, Poles, and Chinese. Unlike the boom-and-bust towns farther west, Winnipeg has enjoyed steady growth, with a diversified economy based on manufacturing, banking, transportation, and agriculture. Winnipeg looks like the cosmopolitan centers of midwest America—Minneapolis, Milwaukee, Chicago—with a downtown area filled with cast-iron buildings and established neighborhoods of older homes along curving, tree-lined streets.

Originally, buffalo-hunting Plains Indians were the only inhabitants of the area that was franchised by the British Crown to the Hudson's Bay Company. That was until Pierre Gaultier de Varennes established in 1738 a North West Company fur-trading post at the junction of the Red and Assiniboine rivers. Lord Selkirk, a Scot, brought a permanent agricultural settlement in 1812; Winnipeg was incorporated as a city in 1873; and soon after, in 1886, the Canadian Pacific Railroad arrived, bringing a rush of European immigrants. Winnipeg boomed as a railroad hub, a center of the livestock and grain industries, and a principal market city of western Canada.

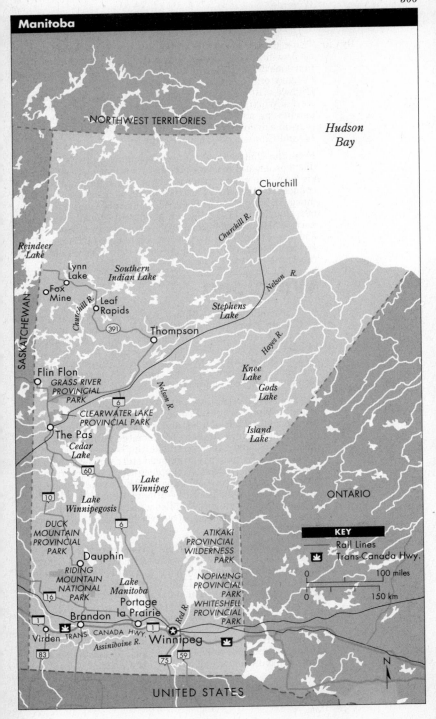

Manitoba

Important Addresses and Numbers

Tourist Information The **Government Tourist Reception Office** (Broadway and Osborne St., tel. 204/945–3777 or 800/665–0040), housed in the Manitoba Legislative Building, is open May–Labor Day, daily 8:30 AM–9 PM; Labor Day–April, weekdays 8:30–4:30. **Tourism Winnipeg** (375 York Ave., 2nd floor, tel. 204/943–1970) is open weekdays 8:30–4:30; and there's an airport location (tel. 800/665–0204) that's open 7:30 AM–10 PM.

Emergencies Dial 911 for **fire, police, ambulance,** or **poison control.**

Hospital Emergency rooms are located at the **Health Sciences Centre** (700 William Ave., tel. 204/787–3167 general emergency; tel. 204/787–2306 children's emergency), **Winnipeg Municipal Hospital** (1 Morley Ave., tel. 204/452–3411), and **Misericordia General Hospital** (99 Cornish Ave., tel. 204/788–8188).

Late-night Pharmacy **Metro Drugs** (905 Corydon Ave., tel. 204/453–8331) is open until 9 PM.

Arriving and Departing by Plane

Winnipeg International Airport is served by Northwest, Air Canada, Canadian Airlines International, and several commuter airlines. Because the airport is only about 8 kilometers (5 miles) away, taxi fare downtown runs about $10. Some airport-area hotels provide complimentary airport shuttles.

Getting Around

By Bus The **City of Winnipeg Transit System** (tel. 204/284–7190) operates an extensive network of buses throughout the city and metropolitan area. Adult fare is $1.20 exact change for adults, 60¢ for senior citizens and children; transfers are free.

Free **Downtown Area Shuttle** (DASH) buses loop downtown and around the warehouse area weekdays 11–3: Look for DASH bus stops along Broadway, Main Street, Graham Avenue, King Street, and elsewhere.

By Taxi Taxis—relatively expensive by U.S. standards—can be found outside downtown hotels or summoned by phone. Car services are **Unicity** (tel. 204/947–6611) and **Duffy's Taxi** (tel. 204/775–0101).

Guided Tours

Boat Tours Several lines ply the Red and Assiniboine rivers between May and mid-October. The ***Paddlewheel River Rouge*** (tel. 204/942–4500) offers a variety of cruises (dining, dinner-dance, evening), combining sailings with double-decker bus tours.

Train Tours The **Prairie Dog Central Steam Train** (tel. 204/832–5259) plies a 58-kilometer (36-mile) route from the CNR St. James Station (1661 Portage Ave.) to Grosse Isle on Sunday, June–September.

Walking Tours Walking tours of the turn-of-the-century **Exchange District** begin at the Manitoba Museum of Man & Nature (190 Rupert Ave., tel. 204/943–3139 or 204/956–2830) during July and August.

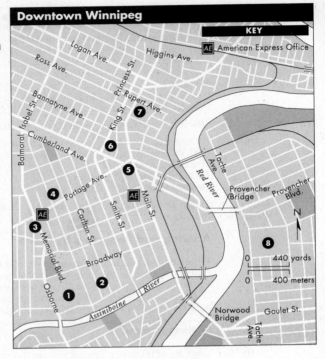

Exploring Downtown Winnipeg

*Numbers in the margin correspond to points of interest on the
Downtown Winnipeg map.*

It's somewhat difficult to get one's bearings in Winnipeg. The
downtown area is located just north of the junction of the Red
and Assiniboine rivers, and its streets interconnect at skewed
angles with the curving rivers, creating diagonal streets in all
directions. Much of downtown Winnipeg is linked by a network
of enclosed overhead pedestrian overpasses and underground
concourses. The intersection of Portage Avenue and Main
Street is the focal point of the city, with Portage Avenue (Hwy.
1) the principal artery heading west and Main Street (Hwy. 52)
heading north. South of Winnipeg, the main drag is Pembina
Highway (Hwy. 42). Streets in St. Boniface, east of the Red
River, are labeled in French—evidence of the community's ethnic heritage.

Begin at the southeast corner of downtown Winnipeg at the
tourist information center (*see* Important Addresses and Numbers, *above*), housed in the **Legislative Building.** The classic
Greek-style structure made of local Tyndall stone contains the
offices of Manitoba's premier and members of the cabinet, as
well as the chamber where the legislature meets. The 240-foot
dome supports Manitoba's symbol, Golden Boy—a gold-
sheathed statue with a sheaf of wheat under his left arm and
the torch of progress in his right hand. Along the grounds and
gardens surrounding the riverside stand statues that celebrate
Manitoba's ethnic diversity, including Scotland's Robert

Burns, Iceland's Jon Sigurdson, Ukrainian poet Taras Ahevchenko, and Métis leader and "Father of Manitoba" Louis Riel.

Walk east on Broadway and south on Carlton Street to **Dalnavert,** a Queen-Anne-Revival-style house built in 1895 for Sir Hugh John Macdonald, who became premier of Manitoba. Costumed guides escort visitors around the premises. *61 Carlton St., tel. 204/943–2835. Admission: $3.21 adults, $2.14 senior citizens, $1.50 students, $1 children 5–12. Open June–Aug., daily 10–6; Sept.–Dec., daily noon–5; Jan.–Feb., weekends noon–5; Mar.–May, daily noon–5.*

❸ Back at the Legislature, head north on Osborne Street past the stately The Bay store (the legacy of the Hudson's Bay Company) to the **Winnipeg Art Gallery.** The gallery, which owns the world's largest collection of Inuit sculpture and art, also houses contemporary Canadian art and sculpture. *300 Memorial Blvd., tel. 204/786–6641. Admission: $3 adults, $2 senior citizens and students, $5 families, children under 12 free; free Wed. Open mid-June–Labor Day, Thurs.–Tues. 10–5, Wed. 10–9; Sept.– early June, Tues. and Thurs.–Sun. 11–5, Wed. 11–9; closed Mon.*

❹ Turn east at the north end of the Winnipeg Art Gallery to Portage Avenue. The north side of Portage between Balmoral and Carlton streets is occupied by sprawling **Portage Place,** an indoor mall encompassing 150 stores (*see* Shopping, *below*).

Time Out   Winnipeg's oldest restaurant, the 1918 **Chocolate Shop** (268 Portage Ave., tel. 204/942–4855), serves generous sandwiches for lunch and more ambitious entrées at dinnertime. Teacups and tarot cards are read 1–9.

❺ Continue east on Portage Avenue to Main Street and what's reputed to be the windiest intersection in the world. Five floors above the breeze, visit **The Winnipeg Commodity Exchange** and observe the controlled chaos of wild men (and a few women) involved in the buying and selling of grains, cooking oils, gold, and silver. *360 Main St., tel. 204/949–0495. Open weekdays 9:30–1:20.*

❻ Below-ground is **Winnipeg Square,** an underground concourse with shops and fast-food stores. Emerge to street level on the north side of Portage Avenue and into the **Exchange District**— a concentration of renovated warehouses, banks, and insurance companies that were built during Winnipeg's turn-of-the-century boom period but now stand as a thriving nightlife spot. On Sunday, May–October, attention focuses on **Old Market Square Park** (King St. and Bannatyne Ave.), a new marketplace bursting with fresh produce, fish, crafts, and street performers.

❼ Continue north on Main Street to Rupert Avenue and **Centennial Centre,** site of a concert hall, the **Manitoba Museum of Man and Nature,** and the dazzling **Manitoba Planetarium.** Exhibits at the museum focus on prehistoric Manitoba, local wildlife, the native peoples of the region, and the exploration of Hudson Bay. Downstairs, the planetarium presents a variety of cosmic adventures in the multimedia **Star Theater;** 60 interactive multisensory exhibits in Touch the Universe explain laws of nature. *190 Rupert Ave., tel. 204/943–3139 (museum), tel. 204/943–3142 (planetarium). Admission: museum $3.50, plane-*

tarium $4, Touch the Universe $2.50, all three $7.50 adults; $2.50, $2.50, $2, $5.50 students; $2.50, $2.50, $2.75, $4.50 senior citizens and children 4–12. Open mid-May–early Sept., daily 10–6; Sept.–mid-May, Tues.–Thurs. 10–6, weekends noon–6, closed Mon.

St. Boniface, about 2.5 kilometers (1¹/₂ miles) away, can be reached by crossing the Provencher Bridge and turning right onto Avenue Tache. The largest French community in western Canada was founded as Fort Rouge in 1783 and became an important fur-trading outpost for the North West Company. Upon the arrival of Roman Catholic priests, the settlement was renamed St. Boniface. Remnants of a 1908 basilica that survived a 1968 fire can be seen outside the perimeter of the present **St. Boniface Cathedral** (av. de la Cathedral and av. Tache, tel. 204/233–7304), built in 1972. The grave of Louis Riel, the St. Boniface native son who led the Métis rebellion, is in the churchyard.

Housed in the oldest (1846) structure in Winnipeg and the largest oak log building in North America, the **St. Boniface Museum** tells the French and Métis side of Manitoba history. Artifacts include an altar crafted from papier-mâché, the first church bell in western Canada, and a host of innovative household gadgets. *494 av. Tache, tel. 204/237–4500. Admission free, but donations accepted. Open mid-May–Sept., daily 9–9; Sept.–mid-May, weekdays 9–5, weekends and holidays 10–5.*

You can see Canadian and foreign coins rolling off the presses at the **Royal Canadian Mint,** 6.4 kilometers (4 miles) southeast of downtown off Highway 1 or by Bus 50, available on the east side of Fort Street between Portage and Graham avenues on weekdays. Tours run 9–3. *520 Lagimodière Blvd. (at the Trans-Canada Hwy.), Winnipeg, R2J 3E7, tel. 204/257–3359. Admission: $2.*

Other Points of Interest

About 48 kilometers (30 miles) southeast of Winnipeg is the town of **Steinbach,** populated with nearly 10,000 descendants of Mennonites who fled religious persecution in late 19th-century Europe. Note the large number of automobile dealerships: Manitoban car buyers flock here because of the Mennonite reputation for making square deals.

In the **Mennonite Heritage Village,** a 40-acre museum, guides demonstrate blacksmithing, wheat grinding, and old-time housekeeping chores while conversing in the Mennonite Low German dialect. During the Pioneer Days festival in early August, everyone wears costumes and demonstrates homespun crafts. An authentic and extremely low-priced restaurant serves Mennonite specialties, such as borscht, pirogies, and *ukrenky* (cheese or potato torte). *Hwy. 12, 2 km (1¹/₄ mi) north of Steinbach, tel. 204/326–9661. Admission: $2 adults, $1 students and senior citizens, 75¢ children grades 1–6. Open May and Sept., Mon.–Sat. 10–5, Sun. noon–5; June–Aug., Mon.–Sat. 9–7, Sun. noon–7.*

Lower Fort Garry, built in 1830, is the oldest stone fort remaining from the Hudson's Bay Company fur-trading days. Nowadays, costumed employees describe daily tasks and recount thrilling journeys by York boat, the "boat that won the west."

Beaver, raccoon, fox, and wolf pelts hang in the fur loft as a reminder of the bygone days. *Hwy. 9, 32 km (20 mi) north of Winnipeg, tel. in Winnipeg, 204/983–6341; in Selkirk, 204/482–6483. Admission: $3.25 adults, $1.50 children 5–16. Grounds open year-round in daylight hours. Buildings open mid-May–Sept. 2, daily 10–6; Sept., weekends 10–6.*

Gimli, the largest Icelandic community outside the homeland, was once the center of the independent state of New Iceland. A giant Viking statue proclaims allegiance to the far-off island; the **Gimli Historical Museum,** on the Gimli harbor waterfront, preserves the ethnic heritage of early Ukrainian and Icelandic settlers and records the history of the Lake Winnipeg commercial fishing industry. *Hwy. 9, Gimli harbor area, tel. 204/642–5317. Admission: $1.25 adults, 75¢ children, $3 families, senior citizens free.*

City and Provincial Parks

Assiniboine Park, situated in Winnipeg along the river of the same name, encompasses 376 acres of cycling paths, picnic areas, playgrounds, a miniature railway, formal English and French gardens, a conservatory, and a cricket pitch. **Assiniboine Zoo,** also on the grounds, houses more than 1,200 species in reasonably natural settings. *Assiniboine Park and Zoo, tel. 204/986–6921. Admission to zoo: $3 adults, $2.75 senior citizens, $1.50 youths 13–17, $1 children 2–12, children under 2 free, $7.50 families. Open daily 10 AM–dusk.*

The Forks National Historic Site, at the junction of the Red and Assiniboine rivers, is where Winnipeg began 6,000 years ago. Today, the 56 acres host a playground, riverside promenade, small boat dock, amphitheater, and archaeological excavations. The promenade has recently been extended, and interpretive programs are available. *At the confluence of the Red and Assiniboine rivers, tel. 204/983–2007. Open Victoria Day–Labor Day, daily 9:30–6; Labor Day–Victoria Day, weekdays 8–4:30.*

Grand Beach Provincial Park is on the eastern shore of Lake Winnipeg, the seventh-largest lake in North America. On summer weekends, crowds flock here from Winnipeg for the white-powder sand, the grass-crowned 30-foot dunes, and a lagoon that makes bird-watchers' dreams come true. **Grand Marais** is the service area at the southern portal to the park. *Hwy. 12, 87 km (54 mi) northwest of Winnipeg, tel. 204/754–2212. Open May–Sept.*

Hecla Provincial Park, about a 2½-hour drive from Winnipeg, is a densely wooded archipelago named for the Icelandic volcano that drove the area's original settlers to Canada. The park is located on the central North American flyway, and 50,000 waterfowl summer here. **Moose Tower** is a good spot in the early morning and evening to view moose and other wildlife. The original 1880s Hecla Icelandic Fishing Village is restored near **Gull Harbour,** the tourist center of the park and site of the luxurious **Gull Harbour Resort** (tel. 204/475–2354), complete with a marina, hiking trails, and a devilishly difficult golf course. *Hecla Provincial Park, Hwy. 8, 175 km (109 mi) north of Winnipeg, tel. 204/378–2945. Open May–Sept.*

Spruce Woods Provincial Heritage Park encompasses, among rolling hills of spruce and basswood, the desertlike Spirit

Sands, a 16-square-kilometer (10-square-mile) tract of cactus-filled sand dunes. Walk the self-guided trail through the dunes, but keep your eyes peeled for lizards and snakes! Your final destination will be **Devil's Punch Bowl,** a dramatic pit dug out by an underground stream. You can also tour the park in a horse-drawn covered wagon. *Hwy. 5, 180 km (114 mi) west of Winnipeg, tel. 204/827–2458. Open May–Sept.*

Whiteshell Provincial Park, a 2,590-square-kilometer (1,550-square-mile) tract on the edge of the Canadian Shield, encompasses 200 lakes that offer some of the best northern pike, perch, walleye, and lake-trout fishing in western Canada. The **Falcon Lake** area has a shopping center, a golf course, tennis courts, a very good beach, a sailing club, and top-grade accommodations in the 34-room **Falcon Lake Resort & Club** (tel. 204/349–8400). **Beaver Creek** trail is a short walk to wilderness denizens like beaver and deer. Farther on, **West Hawk Lake** (or Crater Lake)—formed a few thousand years ago by a falling meteor—is 111 meters (365 feet) deep and full of feisty small-mouth bass. Scuba divers love it. *Whiteshell Provincial Park, Hwy. 1E, 143 km (89 mi) from Winnipeg, tel. 204/369–5232. Open daily 8 AM–11 PM.*

What to See and Do with Children

Assiniboine Park and Zoo (*see* City and Provincial Parks, *above*).

Fort Whyte Center for Environmental Education (1961 McCreary Rd., Winnipeg, tel. 204/989–8355) makes use of several cement quarries and the 200 acres of land around them to re-create the natural habitats of Manitoba's lakes and rivers. Self-guided nature trails and an interpretive center explain all.

Fun Mountain Water Slide Park (Rte. 1, east at Murdock Rd., Winnipeg, tel. 204/255–3910), located about 13 kilometers (8 miles) east of downtown, includes bumper boats, a mammoth hot tub, rides, and a playground.

Manitoba Children's Museum (109 Pacific Ave., Winnipeg, tel. 204/957–0005) is western Canada's first hands-on museum for children, and it shows them how to operate a grain elevator, put on a circus, understand their senses, and much more.

Manitoba Museum of Man and Nature/Planetarium (*see* Exploring Downtown Winnipeg, *above*).

Skinner's Wet n' Wild Waterslide Park (Hwy. 44, Lockport, tel. 204/757–2623) has four big slides, two kiddie slides, and many other damp attractions.

Shopping

Malls and Shopping Districts Downtown shopping is dominated by **Portage Place** (Portage Ave. between Balmoral and Carlton Sts.) and **Eaton Place** (bounded by Graham Ave., Hargrave St., St. Mary Ave., and Donald St.), two malls with numerous stores, fast-food joints, and movie theaters.

Across the Assiniboine River, the **Osborne Village** area (Osborne St. between River and Corydon Aves.) has 150 trendy boutiques and specialty shops, cafés, restaurants, and crafts shops.

Art and Crafts The **Crafts Guild of Manitoba** (183 Kennedy St., tel. 204/943–1190) features works by Manitoba carvers, weavers, and jewelers. **Northern Images** (#216 393 Portage Ave., tel. 204/942–5501; Airport Executive Centre, 1790 Wellington Ave., tel. 204/788–4806) markets the work of the Inuit and Dene members of the NWT Co-operative, which owns the stores. For more Indian art, check out the **Great Canadian Print Company** (75 Albert St., tel. 204/942–1002) or **The Upstairs Gallery** (266 Edmonton St., tel. 204/943–2734) for prints, drawings, wall hangings, and sculpture.

Sports

Participant Sports
Bicycling and Jogging Most public parks in Manitoba have marked biking and jogging paths. For routes, pick up maps from **Travel Manitoba** (*see* Important Addresses and Numbers in Essential Information, *above*).

Health and Fitness *Clubs* Drop-in rates and a full slate of classes and equipment are available at **Body Options** (1604 St. Mary's Rd., Winnipeg, tel. 204/255–6600) and **Bodyworks** (2 Donald St., Winnipeg, tel. 204/477–1691).

Spectator Sports
Football The **Winnipeg Blue Bombers** of the Canadian Football League play home games at the **Winnipeg Arena** (1430 Maroons Rd., Winnipeg, tel. 204/784–2583).

Hockey The **Winnipeg Jets** confront National Hockey League opposition between October and April at the **Winnipeg Arena** (1430 Maroons Rd., Winnipeg, tel. 204/982–5387).

Horse Racing **Assiniboia Downs** (3975 Portage Ave. at Perimeter Hwy. W, Winnipeg, tel. 204/885–3330) hosts Thoroughbred racing May–October.

Soccer The **Winnipeg Fury** of the Canadian Soccer League play a May–September schedule at **Winnipeg Soccer Complex** (1465 Maroons Rd., Winnipeg, tel. 204/475–3879).

Dining and Lodging

Dining Although places specializing in generous helpings of Canadian beef still dominate the scene, restaurants throughout the prairie provinces now tastily reflect the region's ethnic makeup and offer a wide variety of cuisine to fit every price range.

Highly recommended restaurants in each price category are indicated by a star ★.

Category	Cost*
Very Expensive	over $25
Expensive	$20–$25
Moderate	$15–$19
Inexpensive	under $15

three-course dinner, per person, excluding drinks, service, and taxes

Dining **Le Beaujolais.** This sophisticated, bright spot in the French St.
★ Boniface district presents waiters in black tie; a softly lit am-

bience with French blue, coral, and burgundy decor; fresh-cut flowers; and a menu that combines classic French with lighter nouvelle cuisine. Fresh salmon with herb vinaigrette is the recommended seafood; tournedos with green peppercorns, veal with Roquefort and leeks, and rack of lamb are other entrée suggestions. Save room for dessert. *131 Provencher Blvd., tel. 204/237–6306. Reservations advised. Jacket advised. AE, DC, MC, V. Very Expensive.*

Restaurant Dubrovnik. The setting is a romantic Victorian town house, with seating on an enclosed veranda overlooking the Assiniboine River. An extensive menu blends Continental specialties, such as rack of lamb, breast of duck, and pheasant, with southern Yugoslavian dishes. Two good dishes to try are the *gibanica* (feta cheese in phyllo pastry) and the *muckalica* (pork, lamb, chicken, and sausage casserole). A lengthy wine list is available. *390 Assiniboine Ave., tel. 204/944–0594. Reservations advised. Jacket required. AE, MC, V. Closed Sun. Very Expensive.*

Victor's. Located in the elegant Marlborough Inn (*see* Lodging, *below*), with its rich wood paneling and chandeliers, Victor's serves Continental cuisine for those who want a stylish, upscale evening. Joanna's Café, in the same hotel, is a more casual dining spot and one that's appropriate for before- or after-dinner drinks. In both restaurants, poppyseed cake is a must for dessert. *331 Smith St., tel. 204/947–2751. Reservations advised. AE, DC, MC, V. Closed Sun. Very Expensive.*

Amici. The sophisticated and posh downtown *ristorante* is the local avatar of *cucina nuova*, the Italian version of nouvelle cuisine. Clever pastas and such dishes as roast quail on radicchio and chicken stuffed with goat cheese are served in a second-floor dining room that's divided by partitions of frosted glass. Downstairs, the Bombolini Wine Bar serves many of the simpler dishes at lower prices. *326 Broadway, tel. 204/943–4997. Reservations advised. Jacket advised for Amici; casual for Bombolini. AE, DC, MC, V. Closed Sun. Expensive.*

★ **Bistro Dansk.** Wood tables, bright red chairs, and strains of classical music convey a cozy European air. Dinner entrée selections mingle Danish specialties like *frikadeller* (meat patties) and more-expected Continental dishes like roast chicken. A less expensive lunch menu features a vast variety of open-face sandwiches. *63 Sherbrook St., tel. 204/775–5662. Reservations advised. Dress: casual. DC, V. Closed Sun. Moderate.*

Mandarin. The Sargent Avenue Mandarin is a crowded, 12-table west-side place with unique and reasonably exotic northern Chinese dishes. Complete "Gourmet Delight Dinners" include soup, dumplings, entrées, and dessert. Wine is the only alcohol served. The River Mandarin, a spin-off, has a slightly different menu, a calmer pace, and a full liquor license. *Mandarin, 613 Sargent Ave., tel. 204/775–7819; River Mandarin, 252 River Ave., tel. 204/284–8963. Reservations advised. Dress: casual. V. Moderate.*

Picasso's. It may be named after a Spanish painter, but this is a Portuguese restaurant, featuring outstanding seafood. On the street level it's a bustling neighborhood café; upstairs there's a subdued atmosphere where white tablecloths, candlelight, and soft music prevail. Try the salmon or Arctic char; Portuguese favorites are paella, octopus stew, and steak Picasso. *615 Sargent Ave., tel. 204/775–2469. Reservations advised. Dress: casual. AE, DC, MC, V. Moderate.*

★ **d'8 Schtove.** The name is Mennonite for "the eating room," and, true to its name, the menu features heavyweight servings of soup, salads, and Mennonite concoctions, usually involving meat, potatoes, onions, and vegetables. Try the *klopz* (ground-beef-and-pork meatballs) or *wrenikje* (cottage-cheese pierogies). The new south-side location is bright and immaculately clean, and it looks spacious, although you may still have to wait for a table. Service is quick and friendly. *1842 Pembina Hwy., tel. 204/275–2294. No reservations. Dress: casual. AE, DC, MC, V. Inexpensive.*

Homer's. This good-time, downtown place, with a definite Mediterranean atmosphere, has been one of the city's favorite Greek restaurants for more than 15 years. Greek specialties include roast leg of lamb and moussaka, but Homer's is also famous for ribs, steak, seafood, pasta, and fresh hot bread. In the summer ask to be seated outside on the patio. *520 Ellice Ave., tel. 204/788–4858. Reservations advised. Dress: casual. AE, DC, MC, V. Inexpensive.*

Kelekis. This north-end shrine has purveyed legendary burgers, hot dogs, and fries for more than 60 years. Decor includes a photo montage of family history and autographed celebrities' photos. Breakfast is served daily. *1100 Main St., tel. 204/582–1786. No reservations. Dress: casual. No credit cards. Inexpensive.*

Lodging Highly recommended lodgings in each price category are indicated by a star ★.

Category	Cost*
Very Expensive	over $150
Expensive	$75–$150
Moderate	$50–$74
Inexpensive	under $50

*All prices are for a standard double room, excluding taxes.

Lodging **Birchwood Inn.** This bright and sumptuous modern property is located on the Trans-Canada Highway's western approach to Winnipeg, near the airport, race track, and shopping areas. Rooms are large, with modern earthtone furnishings. Executive suites, decorated in blue and green, are a bit fancier than standard units. The atrium is a lush setting for a pool and poolside lounge. *2520 Portage Ave., R3J 3T6, tel. 204/885–4478 or 800/665–0352. 210 rooms. Facilities: 2 restaurants, lounge, indoor pool, sauna, exercise room. AE, DC, MC, V. Expensive.*

Holiday Inn Crowne Plaza. Winnipeg's largest hotel, this Holiday Inn is 17 stories high and connects to the Convention Centre. Rooms, having recently undergone a major renovation, are decorated in pastels and have pleasant modern furnishings; some rooms overlook the skylighted pool. Ticker's lobby bar is a lively spot for a rendezvous. *350 St. Mary Ave., R3C 3J2, tel. 204/942–0551 or 800/465–4329. 406 rooms, including nonsmoking rooms. Facilities: 3 restaurants, lounge, cabaret, indoor and outdoor pools, sauna, whirlpool, exercise room. AE, MC, V. Expensive.*

★ **Place Louis Riel.** This luxury-class bargain is a converted apartment building that has 250 contemporary suites with living rooms, dining areas, and fully equipped kitchens. Though all rooms are up-to-date, the suites on the upper floors facing west are preferred because of their view of the Parliament Building. The supreme downtown location—adjacent to Eaton Place mall—is only one of the hotel's highlights. *190 Smith St., R3C 1J8, tel. 204/947–6961; in Canada, 800/665–0569. 250 suites. Facilities: restaurant/lounge, free parking. AE, DC, MC, V. Expensive.*

★ **Westin Hotel Winnipeg.** The top luxury hotel is located near Winnipeg's hub—Portage and Main streets—and is connected by the skywalk to office buildings and Portage Place Mall. The 21st-floor rooftop indoor pool makes a dramatic setting for a swim. Chimes offers a contemporary setting for light meals. Other restaurants include the elegant Velvet Glove Dining Room, and Café Express for quick meals at affordable prices. *2 Lombard Pl., R3B 0Y3, tel. 204/957–1350 or 800/228–3000. 350 rooms; nonsmoking rooms available. Facilities: 3 restaurants, lounge, indoor pool, sauna, whirlpool, fitness center. AE, DC, MC, V. Expensive.*

Winnipeg Relax Lodge. Positioned at the low end of the expensive range, this high-rise venture of Canada's oldest budget chain is in a strategically desirable location, next to the bus depot and adjacent to The Bay and Winnipeg Art Gallery. Rooms on the south side look out on the Legislative Building, and north-side rooms overlook the city. Guest rooms have subdued modern furnishings in either neutral or pastel colors. *360 Colony St., R3B 2P3, tel. 204/786–7011 or 800/661–9563. 157 rooms, including nonsmoking rooms. Facilities: restaurant, indoor pool, whirlpool. AE, DC, MC, V. Expensive.*

★ **Charter House.** Half the refurbished rooms in this five-story low-rise on the south side of downtown have balconies. Furnishings are contemporary motel style, and the atmosphere is quite friendly. The Rib Room is a popular, moderately priced place for dinner. *330 York Ave., R3C 0N9, tel. 204/942–0101; in Manitoba, 204/942–0101 or 800/782–0175. 90 rooms, some nonsmoking. Facilities: 2 restaurants, lounge, outdoor pool. AE, MC, V. Moderate.*

Gordon Downtowner Motor Hotel. There's nothing fancy here, but it's a good deal on the edge of downtown a block from the Portage Place mall. Most rooms are decorated in dusty rose with gray carpeting. Two-room suites, modernly furnished, are the best bargains. *330 Kennedy St., R3B 2M6, tel. 204/943–5581. 40 rooms. Facilities: restaurant, pub, free parking. AE, DC, MC, V. Moderate.*

Hotel Fort Garry. Built in 1913 and known far and wide as the Grand Castle, the old railroad hotel has been completely renovated and has resumed its role as one of Winnipeg's gathering places. Located on the south edge of downtown, near Union Station, the hotel and its hushed spacious lobby are furnished with inviting armchairs and original marble, brass, and crystal finishes. Large guest rooms still have classic dark-wood furnishings and floral wallpapers. *222 Broadway, R3C 0R3, tel. 204/942–8251 or 800/665–8088. 270 rooms. Facilities: 2 restaurants, lounge, cabaret. AE, DC, MC, V. Moderate.*

Journey's End. This is a reliable choice for a moderately priced south-side lodging. The rooms are an adequate size and are furnished in contemporary style, with rose or beige carpets and either dusty rose or earthtone accessories. There's no charge for local phone calls, and morning coffee is free. *3109 Pembina Hwy., R3T 4R6, tel. 204/269–7390 or 800/668–4200. 80 rooms. AE, MC, V. Moderate.*

Marlborough Inn. Inside this ornate old (1914) Gothic structure located in the Financial District are Joanna's Café and Victor's, with vaulted ceilings and a stained-glass window. The public areas were renovated in 1993, and guest rooms will receive a face-lift in 1994. The lounge provides an intimate setting for guests, with piped-in music. In the spacious lobby, with its marble floors, high ceilings, and wood paneling, there are soft comfortable couches and Chesterfields. *331 Smith St., R3B 2G9, tel. 204/942–6411, 204/942–2017, or 800/667–7666. 121 rooms. Facilities: 2 restaurants, lounge. AE, DC, MC, V. Moderate.*

Assiniboine Gordon Inn on the Park. This two-story hotel and motor inn is adjacent to a park on the west side, not far from the airport. Rooms are modern and large, albeit somewhat overwrought with masculine dark wood and bold designs. *1975 Portage Ave., R3J 0J9, tel. 204/888–4806. 48 rooms. Facilities: restaurant, lounge, disco. AE, MC, V. Inexpensive.*

The Arts and Nightlife

The Arts
Theater
One of Canada's most acclaimed regional theaters, the **Manitoba Theatre Centre,** produces serious plays from many sources on the 785-seat **Mainstage** (174 Market Ave., Winnipeg, tel. 204/942–6537) and more experimental work in the **MTC Warehouse Theatre** (140 Rupert Ave., Winnipeg, tel. 204/942–6537). The **Prairie Theatre Exchange** focuses on local playwrights in an attractive facility in the Portage Place mall (Portage Ave. and Carlton St., Winnipeg, tel. 204/942–5483).

Music and Dance
Winnipeg's principal venue for serious music, dance, and pop concerts is the magnificent 2,263-seat Centennial Concert Hall in the **Manitoba Centennial Centre** (555 Main St., Winnipeg, tel. 204/956–1360). From September to mid-May it is the home of the **Winnipeg Symphony Orchestra** (tel. 204/949–3999); the **Royal Winnipeg Ballet** (tel. 204/956–2792) performs there in October, December, March, and May; and the **Manitoba Opera** (tel. 204/942–7479) presents three operas a year—in November, February, and May. Throughout the year, pop concerts use the center.

The **Winnipeg Art Gallery** (300 Memorial Blvd., tel. 204/786–6641) features jazz, blues, chamber music, and contemporary groups. For contemporary dance and new music, check out **Le Rendez-Vous** (768 av. Tache, tel. 204/233–9214 or 204/237–7692) in St. Boniface. Other performance spaces include **Pantages Playhouse Theatre** (180 Market Ave. E, tel. 204/986–3003) and the **Winnipeg Convention Centre** (375 York Ave., tel. 204/956–1720).

Film
In Winnipeg, the best places to find imports, art films, oldies, and midnight cult classics are at **Cinémathèque** (100 Arthur St., Winnipeg, tel. 204/942–6795) and **Cinema 3** (585 Ellice Ave., Winnipeg, tel. 204/783–1097). The **WAG** (Winnipeg Art Gallery, 300 Memorial Blvd., Winnipeg, tel. 204/786–6641) also has a cinema series.

Nightlife
Bars and Clubs
Hy's Steak Loft (216 Kennedy St., Winnipeg, tel. 204/942–1000) is convenient for cocktails and has a late-evening piano bar. A

most convincingly British pub in the Exchange District is **The King's Head** (120 King St., Winnipeg, tel. 204/957–1479).

Casinos   Play blackjack, baccarat, la boule, and roulette at the **Crystal Casino** (7th floor, Hotel Fort Garry, 222 Broadway Ave., Winnipeg, tel. 204/957–2600) daily.

Comedy   **Rumors Comedy Club** (2025 Corydon Ave., Winnipeg, tel. 204/488–4520) or the **Comedy Oasis** (531 St. Mary's Rd., Winnipeg, tel. 204/231–1463), just for laughs.

Music   Country-and-western music fans flock to Winnipeg's **Golden Nugget** (1155 Main St., Winnipeg, tel. 204/589–6308) and the **Palomino Club** (1133 Portage Ave., Winnipeg, tel. 204/772–0454). The hardest-rocking places in town are the **Circuit** (611 rue Archibald, Winnipeg, tel. 204/231–2111), the **Spectrum** (176 Fort St., Winnipeg, tel. 204/943–6487), and the **Albert** (48 Albert St., Winnipeg, tel. 204/943–8750). A more sedate dance floor comes alive after 9 PM in **Windows Lounge** in the Sheraton Winnipeg (161 Donald St., Winnipeg, tel. 204/942–5300).

Regina

Regina was originally dubbed Pile O'Bones, in reference to the remnants left by years of buffalo hunting, but it was later renamed after the Latin title of former Queen Victoria, the reigning monarch in 1883. It was at this time, when the railroad arrived, that the city became the capital of the Northwest Territories, and the Mounties made it their headquarters. When the province of Saskatchewan was formed in 1905, Regina was chosen as its capital. At the beginning of the 20th century, immigrants from the British Isles, Eastern Europe, and the Far East rushed in to claim parcels of the river-fed prairie land for $1 per lot. Oil and potash were discovered in the 1950s and 1960s, and Regina became a major agricultural and industrial distribution center as well as the head office of the world's largest grain-handling cooperative.

The centerpiece of this city of 185,000 is Wascana Park, created by expanding meager Wascana Creek into the broad Wascana Lake and surrounding it with 2,000 acres of parkland. This unique multipurpose site contains the city's major museums, the Saskatchewan legislature, the University of Regina campus, and all the amenities of a big-city park and forest preserve.

Important Addresses and Numbers

Tourist Information   **Tourism Regina** (Box 3355, Regina, Sask. S4P 3H1, tel. 306/789–5099) has an information center on the Trans-Canada Highway (Rte. 1) on the eastern approach to the city and is open Victoria Day–Labor Day, 8–6; Labor Day–Victoria Day, weekdays 8:30–4:30. The **Tourism Saskatchewan** information center (Saskatchewan Dr. and Rose St., tel. 306/787–2300) is open weekdays 8–7, Saturday 10–4.

Emergencies   Dial 911 for emergency **fire, police,** or **ambulance service.**

Hospitals   Emergency rooms are located at **Regina General Hospital** (1140 14th Ave., tel. 306/359–4444), **Plains Health Centre** (4500 Wascana Pkwy., tel. 306/584–6211), and **Pasqua Hospital** (4101 Dewdney Ave., tel. 306/359–2222).

Saskatchewan

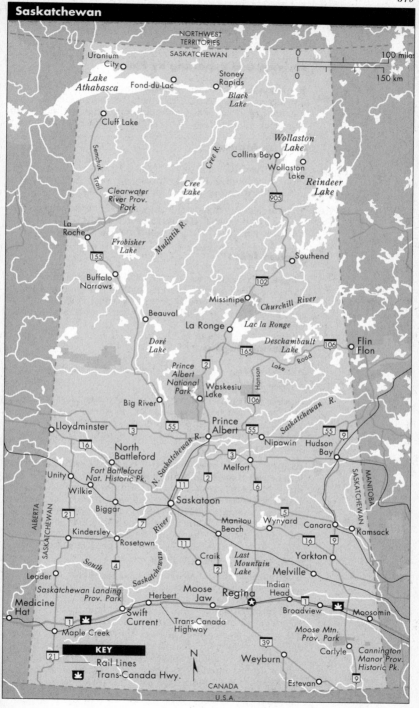

NORTHWEST
TERRITORIES
SASKATCHEWAN

Uranium
City

*Lake
Athabasca*

Fond-du-Lac

Stoney
Rapids

*Black
Lake*

Cluff Lake

*Semchuk
Trail*

Cree R.

Collins Bay

*Wollaston
Lake*

Wollaston
Lake

*Reindeer
Lake*

*Clearwater
River Prov.
Park*

*Cree
Lake*

905

La
Roche

*Frobisher
Lake*

Mudjatik R.

155

Southend

Buffalo
Narrows

102

Missinipe

Churchill River

Beauval

*Doré
Lake*

La Ronge

Lac la Ronge

*Deschambault
Lake*

106

Flin
Flon

165

Road

2

*Prince
Albert
National
Park*

Waskesiu
Lake

106

Hanson   Lake

Saskatchewan R.

Big River

55

Prince
Albert

55

Nipawin

Hudson
Bay

55

9

Lloydminster

3

N. Saskatchewan R.

16

North
Battleford

*Fort Battleford
Nat. Historic Pk.*

3

Melfort

6

Unity

2

Wilkie

11

Biggar

Saskatoon

River

5

21

7

Manitou
Beach

Wynyard

Canora

Kamsack

Kindersley

Rosetown

11

16

9

ALBERTA

SASKATCHEWAN

MANITOBA

SASKATCHEWAN

4

Craik

*Last
Mountain
Lake*

Yorkton

Leader

South

Saskatchewan

2

Melville

*Saskatchewan Landing
Prov. Park*

Herbert

Moose
Jaw

Regina

Indian
Head

1

Medicine
Hat

1

Swift
Current

*Trans-Canada
Highway*

Broadview

Moosomin

21

Maple Creek

KEY
Rail Lines
Trans-Canada Hwy.

*Moose Mtn.
Prov. Park*

39

Carlyle

*Cannington
Manor Prov.
Historic Pk.*

N

Weyburn

9

CANADA

Estevan

U.S.A.

Late-night **Bi-Rite Drugs** locations (Northgate Mall, tel. 306/777–8010;
Pharmacy Broad St. and 14th Ave., tel. 306/757–8100; Gordon Rd. and
Albert St., tel. 306/777–8040; and Victoria Square, tel. 306/777–
8060) are open until midnight.

Arriving and Departing by Plane

Regina Airport, located 8 kilometers (5 miles) southwest of
downtown, is served by Air Canada, Canadian Airlines International, and several Canadian commuter airlines. Cabs
charge about $7 for the 10- to 15-minute ride downtown.

Getting Around

By Bus **Regina Transit's** (tel. 306/777–7433) 19 bus routes serve the
metropolitan area daily except Sunday. The fare is $1.10 for
adults, 65¢ for students, 55¢ for children 5–14.

By Taxi Taxis are easy to find outside major hotels, or they can be summoned by phone. Call **Regina Cabs** (tel. 306/543–3333), **Capital
Cab** (tel. 306/781–7777), or **Co-op Taxis** (tel. 306/586–6555).

Guided Tours

Classic Carriage Service (tel. 306/543–9155) offers horse-drawn
carriage rides around the city during summer and horse-
drawn sleigh and hayrides around Wascana Park during winter. Both tours accommodate 15–20 people and $60–$75
per hour.

Exploring Regina

*Numbers in the margin correspond to points of interest on the
Regina map.*

Streets in Regina run north–south; avenues, east–west. The
most important north–south artery is Albert Street (Rte. 6);
Victoria Avenue is the main east–west thoroughfare. The
Trans-Canada Highway (Route 1) bypasses the city to the
south and east.

❶ Begin at the northwest corner of **Wascana Centre,** at the **Saskatchewan Museum of Natural History.** A time line traces local
history from prehistory through the dinosaur era to today. The
Earth Sciences Gallery depicts 2 billion years of Saskatchewan
geological history, while the **First Nations Gallery** highlights
aspects of native life and history. The museum is home to Canada's first animated dinosaur, "Megamunch." *College Ave. and
Albert St., tel. 306/787–2815. Admission free. Open May–Sept. 2,
daily 9–8:30; Sept. 3–Apr., daily 9–4:30.*

Continue south on Albert Street past **Speakers Corner** where,
as in London's Hyde Park, free speech is volubly expressed.
Turn left on Legislative Drive, to the quasi-Versailles-style
❷ **Legislative Building.** "The Ledge" was built in 1908–12, with
local Tyndall stone on the exterior and an interior composed of
34 types of marble from all over the world. As you tour the
Legislative Assembly Chamber, note the huge picture of Queen
Elizabeth—a reminder that Canada retains a technical allegiance to the monarchy. *Legislature Dr., tel. 306/787–5357.
Admission free. Open Victoria Day–Labor Day, daily 8–9; winter, daily 8–5. Free tours leave on the half hour.*

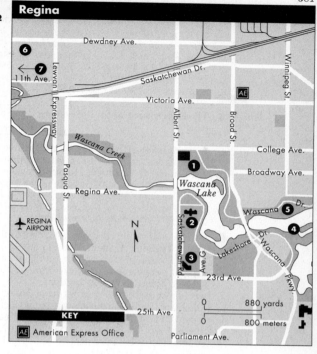

Regina

Dewdney Ave.

Saskatchewan Dr.

11th Ave.

Lewvan Expressway

Winnipeg St.

Victoria Ave.

Albert St.

Broad St.

AE

Wascana Creek

College Ave.

Broadway Ave.

Pasqua St.

Regina Ave.

Wascana Lake

Wascana Dr.

REGINA AIRPORT

N

Saskatchewan Rd.

Lakeshore Dr.

Wascana Pkwy.

Ave. G

23rd Ave.

25th Ave.

0   880 yards

0   800 meters

KEY

AE American Express Office

Parliament Ave.

3 Take Saskatchewan Road (west of the Legislature) south to the new location of the **MacKenzie Art Gallery,** which displays 19th- and 20th-century European art, and Canadian historical and contemporary works, with a special emphasis on western Canadian art. The popular Prairie Artists Series allows emerging Saskatchewan artists to display recent work. For three nights a week in August, a stage becomes the courtroom setting for "The Trial of Louis Riel." Riel led rebellions of the Métis against the new Canadian government in the 1870s and 1880s and was tried in Regina (and ultimately hanged) for treason. *3475 Albert St., tel. 306/522–4242. Admission free. Open Fri.– Tues. 11–6, Wed. and Thurs. 11–10.*

4 Continuing along Saskatchewan Road, turn north on Avenue G and then east on Lakeshore Drive to the **Wascana Waterfowl Park Display Ponds,** a boardwalk constructed over a marsh and accompanied by display panels that help identify the more than 60 breeds of migrating waterfowl found here. *Lakeshore Dr., tel. 306/522–3661. Admission free. Open year-round, daily 9–9; guided tours available (if there is a group) June–Sept. at 3.*

5 Return to Broad Street (Wascana Parkway), cross the bridge to Wascana Drive, and head toward Winnipeg Street and the new **Saskatchewan Science Centre,** now housed in the old Sask-Power powerhouse. Hands-on exhibits encourage visitors to build bubbles, juggle hot-air balloons, make voice prints, and take apart human bodies; demonstrations of biological, geological, and astronomical phenomena take place on the hour. Located in the complex is the **Kramer IMAX Theatre,** which screens breathtaking films several times daily on a five-story screen. *Winnipeg St. and Wascana Dr., tel. 306/352–5811. Admission: $5.50 adults, $3.50 senior citizens and students, children under 6 free. Open early May–early Sept., Mon.–Wed. 9–6; Thurs. and Fri. 9–9, weekends and holidays noon–9; Sept.–early May, Tues.–Fri. 9–4, weekends and holidays noon–6. Admission to IMAX: $6.50 adults, $4.50 senior citizens and youths 6–18, $3 children under 6. Screenings year-round, weekdays 10:45 and 3; weekends 1, 2, and 7.*

Time Out | **The Edgewater Café** at the Science Centre serves fine French cuisine.

A car or bike will be necessary to continue this tour. Return to Broad Street and take it north to Dewdney Avenue, then head **❻** west to the **Government House.** Between 1891 and 1945 this was the lavish home of Saskatchewan's lieutenant governors. *4607 Dewdney Ave., tel. 306/787–5726. Admission free. Open Oct.–Mar., Tues.–Fri. 1–4, Sun. 1–5; Apr.–Sept., Tues.–Sat. 1–4, Sun. 1–5. Closed Sat. July and Aug.*

❼ Continue west on 11th Avenue to the **Royal Canadian Mounted Police Training Academy,** the Mounties' only training center. Visitors can tour the grounds and nondenominational RCMP Chapel, a converted cookhouse originally built in 1883 and considered Regina's oldest building. Try to arrive about 12:45 weekdays for the stirring Sergeant Major's parade on Parade Square (in Drill Hall during winter and inclement weather). On the grounds is the **Centennial Museum,** featuring exhibits and mementos of the Mounties (originally the North West Mounted Police). The order's proud history is revealed by weaponry, uniforms, photos, and oddities, such as Sitting Bull's rifle case and tobacco pouch. *11th Ave. W, tel. 306/780–5838. Admission free. Open June–mid-Sept., daily 8 AM–6:45 PM; mid-Sept.–May, daily 10–4:45.*

Other Points of Interest

Cannington Manor Historic Park, just south of Moose Mountain Provincial Park (*see* National and Provincial Parks, *below*), preserves the 1880s life-styles of this experimental aristocratic Victorian settlement. Abandoned after 15 years, what remains to be seen are the original manor house, a church, shops, and a museum housed in the original schoolhouse. *Hwy. 603, 16 km (10 mi) northeast of Manor, tel. 306/787–9573. Donations accepted. Open late May–early Sept., daily 10–6.*

Moose Jaw, Saskatchewan's third-largest city (population 35,000), is a prosperous railroad and industrial center, renowned as a wide-open Roaring '20s haven for American gangsters. It is said that Al Capone visited here from Chicago, on the old Soo Line train. Today, Moose Jaw's most prominent citizen is Mac the Moose, an immense sculpture that greets travelers alongside the visitor information center (Rte. 1 east of Rte. 2, tel. 306/692–6414) on the Trans-Canada Highway.

A stop at the information center can direct you to other Moose Jaw attractions, including the **Moose Jaw Wild Animal Park** (7th Ave. SW, tel. 306/691–0111), with more than 50 North American species and exotic animals, in addition to the amusement park, surrounded by a log fortress. The **Western Development Museum** (50 Diefenbaker Dr., tel. 306/693–6556), which focuses on air, land, water, and rail transportation, presents the "Snowbirds Gallery" devoted to Canada's military flying team, the Snowbirds, who are stationed at the nearby Armed Forces base. **The Moose Jaw Art Museum** (Crescent Park, Athabasca St. and Langdon Crescent, tel. 306/692–3144), displays Indian art and small farm implements. While there, pick up *A Walking Tour of Downtown Moose Jaw* ($1.50), a guide to the city's notable and notorious landmarks. As you drive around Moose Jaw notice the giant historical murals that cover the exterior walls of many downtown buildings.

National and Provincial Parks

Grasslands National Park is located between Val Marie and Killdeer in southwestern Saskatchewan. The Frenchman River Valley, part of which is within the Grasslands, was the first portion of mixed grass prairie in North America to be set aside as a park, and is famous for strange land formations and badlands. Colonies of black-tailed prairie dogs are the most numerous of the many animal species found here. Interpretive and visitor services are limited at this time. Tent camping is permitted, and electrical hook-ups are provided; all sites cost $10 per night. *Box 150, Val Marie, Sask. S0N 2T0, tel. 306/298–2257. Park office open June–Aug., daily 8–6; Sept.–May, weekdays 8–4:30. Information center open late May–early Sept., daily 8–6.*

Moose Mountain Provincial Park is 401 square kilometers (155 square miles) of rolling poplar and birch forest that forms a natural refuge for moose and elk and a wide variety of birds. A 24-kilometer (15-mile) gravel road accesses moose and elk grazing areas (best times: early morning and early evening). The park supplements wildlife experiences with beaches, golf, tennis, and riding horses. There are 330 campsites available; 1/3 have electric hook-ups. The Kenosee Inn (Kenosee Village, S0C 2S0, tel. 306/577–2099) is a 30-room accommodation on the park grounds. *Hwys. 9 and 209, tel. 306/577–2131; 306/577–2144 for camping reservations. Admission: $6/day per car, senior citizen drivers free. Camping fees: $14 per night w/electricity; $12 w/o electricity. Open year-round.*

A 50-kilometer (31-mile) drive north on Highway 4, from Swift Current, will bring you to **Saskatchewan Landing Provincial Park** (tel. 306/375–2434). The 54-square-kilometer (21-square-mile) natural preserve is situated at the point where Indians and pioneers forded the South Saskatchewan River en route to northern Saskatchewan. Campsites, picnic facilities, and an interpretive center are on hand. *Hwy. 4, tel. 306/375–2434. Admission: $6/day per car, senior citizen drivers free. Camping fees: mid-Sept.–mid-May, $8 w/electricity, $7 w/o electricity; mid-May–mid-Sept., $14 w/electricity, $12 w/o electricity. Open year-round.*

What to See and Do with Children

RCMP Training Academy and **Centennial Museum** (*see* Exploring Regina, *above*).

Saskatchewan Museum of Natural History (*see* Exploring Regina, *above*).

Saskatchewan Science Centre (*see* Exploring Regina, *above*).

Tee Off Park. This is a family-fun complex with year-round indoor miniature golf and, between June and September, a walkthrough maze and kiddieland rides. *3310 Pasqua St., Regina, tel. 306/586–4585. Admission: $3 golf, $3 maze, $1.50–$3 for rides. Open weekdays 3–9, weekends 1–9.*

Maxwell's Amusements. Go-karts, miniature golf, bumper boats, and a games alley bring kids and adults by the hordes. *Hwy. 1 E, tel. 306/789–2585 or 306/569–8333. Admission: free, rides cost extra. Open June–Aug., daily 11–10. Reduced hours in Apr.–May and Sept.–Oct.*

Shopping

Malls **Cornwall Centre** (11th Ave. and Saskatchewan Dr.), located downtown, is an indoor mall with more than 100 shops, including Eaton's and Sears. Indoor passages connect to the **Galleria** (11th Ave. and Saskatchewan Dr.), an indoor mall with more than 50 stores. Other major malls include **Victoria Square Mall** (223 Victoria Ave. E), **Northgate Mall** (Albert St. N and 9th Ave. N), with more than 80 stores, and **Southland Mall** (Albert St. S and Gordon Rd.), which also has more than 80 stores.

Art and Antiques The **Strathdee Shoppes** (Dewdney Ave. and Cornwall St.) consist of arts, crafts, antiques, and specialty stores—plus a food court. The **Antique Mall** (1175 Rose St., tel. 306/525–9688) encompasses 28 antiques, art, and collectibles sellers. Also featuring arts and crafts are **Patchworks** (3026 13th Ave., tel. 306/522–0664), **Sarah's Corner** (1853 Hamilton St., tel. 306/565–2200), and **Affinity's Antiques** (1178 Albert St., tel. 306/757–4265).

Sports

Participant Sports **Wascana Place** (2900 Wascana Dr., Regina, tel. 306/522–3661)
Bicycling and provides maps of the many jogging, biking, and hiking trails in
Jogging **Wascana Park.** The Devonian Pathway—8 kilometers (about 5 miles) of paved trails that follow Wascana Creek and pass through six city parks—is a favorite of walkers, joggers, and cyclists. Rent bikes within Wascana Centre at the **Wascana Pool** (2211 College Ave., Regina, tel. 306/777–7921).

Health and The **Regina Sportplex & Lawson Aquatic Centre** (1717 Elphin-
Fitness Clubs stone St., Regina, tel. 306/777–7156 for fieldhouse; tel. 306/777–7323 for aquatic center) encompasses a pool and diving well, a 200-meter track, tennis and badminton courts, weight rooms, a sauna, a whirlpool, and drop-in aerobic and aquacize sessions.

Spectator Sports Check out this incredibly popular local sport at the **Curlodrome**
Curling (Exhibition Park, Lewvan Expwy. and 11th Ave., Regina, tel. 306/352–9809).

Football The **Saskatchewan Roughriders** (tel. 306/525–2181) of the Canadian Football League play their home games at Taylor Field.

Hockey The **Regina Pats** play other Western Hockey League (minor league) teams in the **Agridome** (Exhibition Park, Lewvan Expwy. and 11th Ave., Regina, tel. 306/522–5604).

Horse Racing **Queensbury Downs Raceway** (Exhibition Park, Lewvan Expwy. and 11th Ave., Regina, tel. 306/781–9310) hosts Thoroughbred or Standardbred racing in the summer and televised racing year-round.

Dining and Lodging

For price categories, *see* Winnipeg Dining and Lodging, *above*.

Dining **Mieka's.** Chef Mieka Wiens learned her craft at the Cordon
★ Bleu; her art-filled walls and sleek contemporary furniture certainly reflect outside influence. The menus of this downtown
café change with the season but always include imaginative
combinations of fresh seafood and meat, local produce, spices,
and liquors. There are also creative sandwiches, unusual salads, and a terrific cheesecake. *1810 Smith St., tel. 306/522–6700.
Reservations advised. Dress: casual. DC, MC, V. Closed Sun.
Expensive.*

Bartleby's. This good-time downtown "dining emporium and
gathering place" is a veritable museum of western memorabilia, musical instruments, and old-time carnival games. Victorian lampshades and heavy leather armchairs further convey
the whimsical tone. Karioke music at night adds a bit of fun.
The menu features big sandwiches and western beef, especially
prime rib. *1920 Broad St., tel. 306/565–0040. Reservations advised. Dress: casual. AE, DC, MC, V. Moderate.*

C.C. Lloyd's. Locals esteem the fine service and casual elegance
of the dining room in the downtown Chelton Inn. The decor
evokes the atmosphere of Manhattan circa 1930, and the menu
features international classics such as rack of lamb, chicken en
croûte dijonnaise, fillet of beef Madeira, shrimp Provençal, and
a variety of tasty steaks. *1907 11th Ave., tel. 306/569–4650. Reservations advised. Jacket advised. AE, MC, V. Moderate.*

Brewsters. The copper kettle and shiny fermentation tanks are
proudly prominent in Saskatchewan's first brew pub. This full
mash brewery has 11 in-house concoctions on tap, as well as a
large selection of imports and domestic beers, wine, and spirits.
The menu consists of pub snacks and a full-service menu. *Victoria East Plaza, 1832 Victoria Ave. E, tel. 306/761–1500. No reservations. Dress: casual. AE, MC, V. Inexpensive.*

Simply Delicious. Everything is homemade in this small country-style café. Specialties include cinnamon buns, fresh pies,
chicken noodle and vegetable soups, several salads, and specialty coffees. *826 Victoria Ave., tel. 306/352–4929. No reservations. Dress: casual. No credit cards. Inexpensive.*

Lodging **The Delta Regina.** This modern downtown property has a
★ dramatic multilevel, sun-filled lobby that's graced by abundant
foliage and a charming waterfall. A second-floor Oasis is the
perfect setting for water-theme pastimes such as a soothing
soak in the whirlpool or, for the children, a dip in either the
kiddie or standard pool. Rooms are airy and modernly furnished in light colors and dusty rose. *1818 Victoria Ave., S4P
0R1, tel. 306/569–1666 or 800/268–1133. 251 rooms. Facilities: 2
restaurants, lounge, pub, underground heated parking, indoor
pool, sauna, whirlpool, games room. AE, DC, MC, V. Expensive.*

Hotel Saskatchewan Radisson Plaza. The one-time railway
hotel built in 1927 was recently restored to its former grandeur
and is lovely. Rooms are decorated in an early 1930s style, with
lots of wood and lace curtains. Every afternoon in the Victoria
Room, high tea is served, and fine dining is offered every evening in the Cortlandt Hall Dining Room. For a light lunch or
evening cocktails visit the cozy and casually elegant Monarch
Lounge. *2125 Victoria Ave., S4P 0S3, tel. 306/522–7691 or
800/333–3333. 217 rooms including nonsmoking rooms. Facili-*

ties: *2 restaurants, lounge, indoor spa pool, steam room, health club. AE, DC, MC, V. Expensive.*

Ramada Renaissance. The tallest building in Saskatchewan, Regina's newest and most luxurious hotel rises 25 stories over the city and is attached to the Saskatchewan Trade & Convention Centre. Rooms are furnished in subtle pastels and have modern amenities. The pool has a three-story waterslide, and there's a Tourism Saskatchewan information center in the lobby. *1919 Saskatchewan Dr., S4P 4H2, tel. 306/525–5255 or 800/268–8998. 255 rooms, including nonsmoking rooms. Facilities: 2 restaurants, 1 lounge, indoor pool, waterslide, whirlpool. AE, DC, MC, V. Expensive.*

Regina Inn. A plant-filled lobby welcomes you into this modern downtown hotel, where all the guest rooms—decorated with blues, grays, and browns—have balconies overlooking either Broad or Victoria streets. On the ground floor is the Lauderdale Bar and Grill, the local hot spot. *1975 Broad St. at Victoria Ave., S4P 1Y2, tel. 306/525–6767 or 800/667–8162. 237 rooms. Facilities: 2 restaurants, lounge, nightclub, indoor parking, 2 outdoor hot tubs, weight room. AE, DC, MC, V. Expensive.*

Regina Travelodge. The hotel's convenient location, on Regina's main thoroughfare and close to downtown, is the biggest draw for its guests. The other feature is the well-known waterslide complex on the property. In the evenings the pub, the Blarney Stone, is a fun place to grab a beer or soda. *4177 Albert St., S4S 3R6, tel. 306/586–3443 or 800/255–3050. 200 rooms. Facilities: restaurant, pub, indoor pool and waterslide complex, hot tub. AE, DC, MC, V. Expensive.*

Chelton Inn. This property, situated in the heart of downtown, is one of Regina's biggest bargains. The inn is an older property, but its rooms have been modernized and are downright huge. Contemporary, light wood furnishings match the earthtones that are used in the dry goods and fabrics. Service is particularly friendly. The cuisine in C.C. Lloyd's (*see* Dining, *above*) is among the best in town. *1907 11th Ave., S4P 0J2, tel. 306/569–4600 or 800/667–9922. 56 rooms. Facilities: restaurant, coffee shop, lounge. AE, DC, MC, V. Moderate.*

★ **Landmark Inn.** This three-story property on the south side of town has large, modern rooms and a unique indoor-outdoor waterslide. Rooms, decorated in pastel greens and white, are light and airy and have modern furnishings. *4150 Albert St. (Hwy. 6), S4S 3R8, tel. 306/586–5363; in Saskatchewan, 800/667–9811; elsewhere in Canada, 800/667–8191. 188 rooms, including nonsmoking rooms. Facilities: restaurant, lounge, indoor pool, waterslide, sauna, whirlpool, games room. AE, DC, MC, V. Moderate.*

★ **Relax Inn South West.** This is a dependable accommodation, with average-size, well-furnished rooms, and Saskatchewan's largest private indoor pool. *4025 Albert St. (Hwy. 6), S4S 3R6, tel. 306/586–2663 or 800/667–3529. 105 rooms. Facilities: indoor pool. AE, DC, MC, V. Inexpensive.*

The Arts and Nightlife

The Arts On a theater-in-the-round stage inside the old Regina City
Theater Hall, the **Globe Theatre** (1801 Scarth St., Regina, tel. 306/525–9553) offers classics and contemporary Saskatchewan works from October to April. **Regina Little Theatre** (Regina Perform-

American Express offers Travelers Cheques built for two.

American Express® Cheques *for Two*. The first Travelers Cheques that allow either of you to use them because both of you have signed them. And only one of you needs to be present to purchase them.

Cheques *for Two* are accepted anywhere regular American Express Travelers Cheques are, which is just about everywhere. So stop by your bank, AAA* or any American Express Travel Service Office and ask for Cheques *for Two*.

Travelers Cheques

ing Arts Centre, 1077 Angus St., Regina, tel. 306/352–5535 or 306/543–7292) presents lighthearted original productions.

Music and Dance Two theaters in the **Saskatchewan Centre of the Arts** (Wascana Centre, 200 Lakeshore Dr., Regina, tel. 306/565–0404) are venues for the Regina Symphony, pop concerts, dance performances, and Broadway musicals and plays.

Nightlife **Caper's,** in the Ramada Renaissance (1919 Saskatchewan Dr.,
Bars and Clubs Regina, tel. 306/525–5255), is where local movers and shakers mingle with visitors from the convention center next door.

Music **W.H. Shooters** (2075 Broad St., Regina, tel. 306/525–3525) features Canadian and American country-and-western bands. **Delbert's** (1433 Hamilton St., tel. 306/757–ROCK) is known for high energy rock 'n' roll. **Longbranch Saloon** (1400 McIntyre St., tel. 306/525–8336) specializes in country and western music.

Excursion from Regina: Swift Current to Cypress Hills Provincial Park

West of Regina, the square townships and straight roads of the grain-belt prairie farms gradually give way to the arid rolling hills of the upland plains ranches.

The Trans-Canada Highway skirts the edge of the Missouri Coteau—glacial hills that divide the prairie from the dry western plain—on its way west to **Swift Current** (174 kilometers, or 108 miles). Swift Current (population 16,000), cultivates its western image during Frontier Days Regional Fair and Rodeo (*see* Festivals and Seasonal Events in Chapter 1). Further depicting Swift Current are the exhibits at the **Swift Current Museum,** where pioneer and Indian artifacts and exhibits of local natural history are displayed. *105 Chaplin St., tel. 306/778–2775. Admission free. Open July–Aug., daily 2–5, 7–9; June and Sept.–mid-Oct., weekends and Mon. 2–5, Tues.–Fri. 7–9; mid-Oct.–May, Sun. and Mon. 2–5.*

A recent addition to Swift Current is the **Canadian Country Music Hall of Fame** with its portraits, memorabilia, and artifacts of North American country music. An art gallery features artwork on nature and western themes. *1100 Fifth Ave. NE, tel. 306/773–7854. Admission: $4 adults, children under 13 free. Open summer: Mon., Thurs., Fri. 9–8; Tues., Wed. 9–5; weekends 11–8 and winter: daily 9–5.*

Along the next 128-kilometer (80-mile) stretch of the Trans-Canada Highway, the road skirts the southern edge of the **Great Sand Hills.** These desertlike remnants of a huge glacial lake now abound with such native wildlife as pronghorn antelope, mule deer, coyote, jackrabbit, and kangaroo rats. Heading south on Highway 21 will bring you into **Maple Creek,** a self-styled "old cow town," with a number of preserved Old West storefronts. Saskatchewan's oldest museum, the **Old Timer's Museum,** features pictures and artifacts of Mounties, early ranchers, and Indians. *218 Jasper St., tel. 306/662–2474. Admission: $2 adults, $1 senior citizens, 50¢ children. Open June–Aug., daily 9–5; Sept.–May, weekdays 1–4.*

Drive south on Highway 21 for another 27 kilometers (17 miles) to **Cypress Hills Provincial Park,** which is open year-round. Cypress Hills consists of two sections, a Centre Block and a West

Block, which are about 25 kilometers (16 miles) apart and separated by nonpark land. The larger West Block abuts the border with Alberta and is connected to Alberta's Cypress Hills Provincial Park (*see* Excursion from Calgary, *below*). Within the Centre Block, the Cypress Hills plateau, rising more than 4,000 feet above sea level, is covered with spruce, aspen, and lodgepole pines that were erroneously identified as cypress by early European explorers. From Lookout Point you have a 50-mile-range (80-kilometer-range) view of Maple Creek and the Great Sand Hills beyond. In addition to the wildlife and flora that abound in the park, there is Cypress Four Seasons Resort (*see* Lodging, *below*), complete with a golf course, tennis courts, campgrounds, riding stables, and a full complement of winter sports. Maps are available at the Administrative Building near the park entrance. *Cypress Hills Provincial Park, Hwy. 21, tel. 306/662–4411. Admission: $6/day per car; senior citizen drivers free. Open year-round.*

A rough gravel road connects the Cypress Hills Centre Block plateau with the West Block plateau. During wet weather, take Highway 21 north to Maple Creek and Highway 271 southwest to the West Block.

The two blocks share the same plant life, animal life, and scenic vistas, but the West Block also encompasses **Fort Walsh National Historic Park.** The original fort was built by the Mounties in 1875 to establish order between the "wolfers" (whiskey traders) and the Assiniboine Indians. Fort Walsh remained the center of local commerce until its abandonment in 1883. Today, free bus service is available between the **Visitor Reception Centre** and the reconstructed fort itself, Farwell's Trading Post, and a picnic area. No private vehicles are permitted beyond the parking area. *Ft. Walsh, Hwy. 271, 55 km (34 mi) southwest of Maple Creek, tel. 306/662–2645. Admission free. Open mid-May–mid-Oct., daily 9–5.*

Dining	For rates, *see* Winnipeg Dining and Lodging, *above.*
Cypress Hills	**Cypress Four Seasons Resort.** This resort is located within the Centre Block of Cypress Hills Provincial Park, and its restaurant is a bright and woodsy place with picture windows that overlook the forest. The standard Canadian fare is more successful than the Chinese dishes on the menu. *Box 1480, Maple Creek, tel. 306/662–4477. No reservations. Dress: casual. MC, V. Moderate.*
Swift Current	**Wong's Kitchen.** This longtime area favorite features fine Canadian food and an even better Oriental menu: Dry garlic ribs are the star attraction. Count on live entertainment nightly. *Hwy. 1, S. Service Rd., tel. 306/773–6244. Reservations advised. Dress: casual. AE, MC, V. Expensive.*
Lodging *Cypress Hills*	**Cypress Four Seasons Resort.** It's not part of the Four Seasons chain, but the rooms here are new, comfortable, modern, and right in the middle of a lodgepole pine forest. Either pastels or earthtones adorn the rooms, which are contemporary and have basic amenities. *Box 1480, Maple Creek, S0N 1N0, tel. 306/662–4477. 35 rooms; cabins and condos. Facilities: restaurant, lounge, indoor pool, whirlpool. MC, V. Moderate.*
Swift Current	**Horseshoe Lodge.** It's conveniently situated along the Trans-Canada Highway service road, yet the rooms still have fine views of the surrounding countryside. The cocktail lounge is a

popular meeting spot, and the restaurant features solid Canadian cooking. *Mobile Rte. 35 Hwy. 1E, S9H 3X6, tel. 306/773-4643. 49 rooms. Facilities: 2 restaurants, lounge, outdoor pool. AE, DC, MC, V. Inexpensive.*

Saskatoon

Saskatchewan's largest city is Saskatoon (population 185,000), nicknamed "City of Bridges" because seven spans cross the South Saskatchewan River that cuts the city in half diagonally. Saskatoon was founded in 1882 when a group of Ontario Methodists were granted 200,000 acres to form a temperance colony. Teetotaling Methodists controlled only half the land, however, and eventually the influence of the other "half" turned the town "wet." The coming of the railroad in 1890 made it the major regional transportation hub, but during the 20th century it became known for its three major resources: potash, oil, and wheat. Saskatoon today is the high-tech hub of Saskatchewan's agricultural industry and is also home to the University of Saskatchewan—a major presence in all aspects of local life.

Important Addresses and Numbers

Tourist Information The **Saskatoon Visitor & Convention Bureau** (310 Idylwyld Dr. N, Box 369, Saskatoon, Sask. S7K 3L3, tel. 306/242–1206) is open weekdays 8:30–5:00 year-round. In summer, information booths are set up at various points along the highway.

Emergencies Dial 911 for **police, fire, ambulance, poison,** and **emergency** services.

Hospitals Emergency rooms include **City Hospital** (Queen St. and 6th Ave. N, tel. 306/242–6681), **Royal University Hospital** (University Grounds, tel. 306/244–2323), and **St. Paul's Hospital** (1702 20th St. W, tel. 306/382–3220).

Late-night Pharmacy **Pinders Drug** stores (2410 22nd St. W, tel. 306/382–5005; 610 Taylor St. E, at Broadway Ave., tel. 306/343–1608) are open until midnight.

Arriving and Departing by Plane

Saskatoon Airport, 7 kilometers (4½ miles) northwest of downtown, is served by Canadian Airlines International, Air Canada, and Canadian commuter carriers. Taxis to the downtown area cost about $9.

Getting Around

By Bus **Saskatoon Transit** (tel. 306/975–3100) buses offer convenient service to points around the city. The fare is $1.10 for adults, 65¢ for students, 55¢ for children 5–12.

By Taxi Taxis are plentiful, especially outside downtown hotels, but they are fairly expensive. For service, call **United Yellow Cab** (tel. 306/652–2222), **Blueline Taxi** (tel. 306/653–3333), or **Saskatoon Radio Cab** (tel. 306/242–1221).

Guided Tours

W.W. Northcote River Cruises (tel. 306/665–1818; tours run June–Aug., daily 10–8) depart on the hour for 11-kilometer (7-mile) tours of the South Saskatchewan River.

Exploring Saskatoon

Numbers in the margin correspond to points of interest on the Saskatoon map.

Reasonably compact for a Western city, Saskatoon proper is easily accessible to drivers and cyclists. Idylwyld Drive divides the city into east and west; 22nd Street divides the city into north and south. The downtown area and the Spadina Crescent are located on the west side of the South Saskatchewan River.

❶ Begin exploring at **Meewasin Valley Centre,** a small museum that traces Saskatoon history back to temperance-colony days. Meewasin is Cree for "beautiful valley," and this is a fitting place to embark upon the **Meewasin Valley Trail,** a 17-kilometer (10-mile) biking and hiking trail along both banks of the beautiful South Saskatchewan River. *Meewasin Valley Centre, 402 3rd Ave. S, tel. 306/665–6888. Admission free. Open weekdays 9–5, weekends 10:30–5.*

Follow Spadina Crescent north along the river and past the
❷ **Delta Bessborough** (*see* Lodging, *below*), the most prominent old building in the Saskatoon skyline. A few blocks farther
❸ north is the **Ukrainian Museum of Canada,** which celebrates—through photos, costumes, textiles, and of course the famous *pysanky* (Easter eggs)—the rich history of the Ukrainian people who make up 10% of Saskatchewan's population. *910 Spadina Crescent E, tel. 306/244–3800. Admission: $2 adults, $1 senior citizens, 50¢ children. Open June–Aug., Mon.–Sat. 10–5 and Sun. 12–5; Sept.–May, weekdays and Sun. 1–4:30.*

From Spadina Crescent, head east over the river via the Uni-
❹ versity Bridge to the **University of Saskatchewan,** which occupies a 2,550-acre site overlooking the river. Turn left into the campus at Wiggins Avenue and look for the **Place Riel Campus Centre,** where University of Saskatchewan Tours (tel. 306/966–5788) guides visitors through the **Animal Science Farm, Natural Sciences Museum, Little Stone School House, Museum of Antiquities, Biology Museum, Gordon Snelgrove Gallery,** and other places on campus. A highlight is the **Right Hon. John G. Diefenbaker Centre** (tel. 306/966–8382; open weekdays 9:30–4:30 and weekends and holidays 12:30–5), a museum, art gallery, and working archives commemorating Canada's 13th prime minister. The center explores Diefenbaker's life and times. Two replica rooms represent the Privy Council Chamber and the prime minister's Ottawa office where he served in the late 1950s and early 1960s.

Exit the campus, head west on College Drive, and then pick up University Drive, lined with grand old homes. University Drive
❺ eventually becomes **Broadway Avenue,** the city's oldest business district and location of more than 150 shops, restaurants, and a cinema.

Broadway Avenue, **5**
Delta Bessborough, **2**
Meewasin Valley Centre, **1**
Saskatoon Prairieland Exhibition Grounds, **7**
Ukrainian Museum of Canada, **3**
University of Saskatchewan, **4**
Western Development Museum, **6**

Time Out   Unpretentious and entirely too small, **Calories** (721 Broadway Ave., tel. 306/665–7991) is a crowded but delicious place to stop for cheesecakes and pastries, ice cream, sandwiches, and superb coffee.

6 Take Broadway Avenue south to 8th Street; then head west to Lorne Avenue and south to the **Western Development Museum.** One of Saskatchewan's four such museums, the Saskatoon branch is called "1910 Boomtown" and re-creates early 20th-century life in the Canadian west. *2610 Lorne Ave. S, tel. 306/931–1910. Admission: $4 adults, $3.50 senior citizens, $1.50 children 5–12. Open summer, daily 9–5. Call for winter hours.*

7 The museum is part of the **Saskatoon Prairieland Exhibition Grounds** (tel. 306/931–7149), a vast plot that encompasses space for agricultural shows and rodeos and horse races.

To return to downtown Saskatoon, take the scenic route: Head north on Lorne Avenue, then west on Ruth Street to the river. Follow St. Henry Avenue, Taylor Street, Herman Avenue, and Saskatchewan Crescent past the fine old homes that overlook one of the prettier stretches of the South Saskatchewan River. Cross over the 19th Street Bridge.

Other Points of Interest

Wanuskewin Heritage Park, just a few kilometers north of Saskatoon, is a relatively new complex, which portrays 6,000 years of Northern Plains Indian culture. The Interpretive Centre has an archaeological laboratory, displays, films, and hands-on activities. Outside walking trails take you to archaeological sites, including a medicine wheel, tipi rings, bison kills and pounds, habitation sites, and stone cairns. *R.R. 4, Saskatoon, S7K 3J7, tel. 306/931–6767. Admission: $5 adults, $4.25 senior citizens, $2 children 5–12, $12 families. Open Victoria Day– Labor Day, daily 9–8; Labor Day–Victoria Day, daily 9–5.*

Park Batoche, 100 kilometers (60 miles) northeast of Saskatoon, is a large historic park and the center of Métis heritage. It was here that the Métis under Louis Riel fought and lost their last battle against the Canadian militia in 1885. The site includes a visitor center, displays, historic church and rectory, and walking trails taking you by many of the battle sites. Take Highway 11 north of Saskatoon and follow the signs to the park. *Tel. 306/423–6227. Admission to park free, to film $1.50. Open July–Aug., daily 10–6; Sept.–June, daily 9–5.*

Prince Albert, 141 kilometers (88 miles) north of Saskatoon, is Saskatchewan's fourth-largest city (population 34,000), the center of the lumber industry, and the self-proclaimed "Gateway to the North." It's a prosperous modern city straddling the North Saskatchewan River, and the most interesting attractions are downtown. Pick up a walking-tours pamphlet at the **Prince Albert Historical Museum,** housed in an old firehouse. *River St. and Central Ave., tel. 306/764–2992. Admission: $1 adults, 50¢ children. Open mid-May–Aug., Mon.–Sat. 10–6; Sun. 10–9.*

The **Western Development Museum** in North Battleford, 138 kilometers (86 miles) northwest of Saskatoon, presents a re-created 1920s farming village, complete with homes, offices, churches, and a Mountie post. The museum also exhibits vintage farming tools and provides demonstrations of agricultural skills used. *Hwys. 16 and 40, tel. 306/445–8033. Admission: $3.50 adults, $2.50 senior citizens, $1.50 children 5–12. Open May– Oct., daily 9–6.*

While in North Battleford, visit the **Allen Sapp Gallery,** which features the paintings of Cree Indian artist Allen Sapp. The gallery is rare in that it is devoted to the work of a living artist. *1901 100th St., tel. 306/445–7266. Admission free. Open Tues.– Thurs. 12–9*

For a refreshing, revitalizing 124-kilometer (77-mile) getaway from Saskatoon, take Routes 16 and 365 southeast, to **Manitou Beach.** Fifty years ago the town of Manitou Beach was a world-famous spa nicknamed the "Carlsbad of Canada." The mineral water in Little Manitou Lake is said to be three times saltier than the ocean and dense enough to make anyone float. Today, **Manitou Springs Mineral Spa** (open year-round) attracts vacationers as well as sufferers of arthritis, rheumatism, and skin disorders to the spa resort. *Hwy. 365, Manitou Beach, tel. 306/946–3949.*

National and Provincial Parks

Fort Battleford National Historic Park pays tribute to the role of mounted police in the development of the Canadian west. The fort was established in 1876 as the North West Mounted Police headquarters for the District of Saskatchewan. Costumed guides explain day-to-day life at the post, and an interpretive center has exhibits relating to the history of the

Mounted Police and life-styles of Indians and settlers. *Central Ave., tel. 306/937–2621. Admission free. Open May–mid-Oct., daily 9–6.*

Prince Albert National Park, 220 kilometers (137 miles) north of Saskatoon, encompasses nearly a million acres of wilderness and waterways and is divided into three landscapes: wide-open fescue grassland, rolling wooded parkland, and dense boreal forest.

In addition to hiking trails, the park has three major campgrounds, with more than 500 sites, plus rustic campgrounds and primitive sites in the backcountry. Pick up maps and information at the visitor center in **Waskesiu,** a townsite with restaurants, motels, and stores within the park.

The **Nature Centre,** located inside the visitor center, can help to orient you to the plant and animal life of the area. Hiking along the marked trails, you have a good chance of spotting moose, deer, bear, elk, and red fox. Canoes, rowboats, and powerboats can be rented from Waskesiu Lake Marina. Lodging in Waskesiu includes the Lakeview Hotel (Lakeview Dr., Box 26, S0J 2Y0, tel. 306/663–5311), a year-round accommodation. *Prince Albert National Park, off Hwy. 2, tel. 306/663–5322. Admission: $5/day per car; $10 for 4 days. Open year-round. Waskesiu Lake Visitor Center, Rtes. 263 and 264, tel. 306/663–5322. Open May–Sept., daily 8 AM–10 PM; Oct.–Apr., weekdays 8–4:30.*

What to See and Do with Children

Forestry Farm Park and Zoo (off Attridge Dr. in NE Saskatoon, tel. 306/975–3382) has more than 300 animals and spotlights such species native to Saskatchewan as deer, wolf, bear, coyote, and fox. The park encompasses barbecue areas, nature displays, cross-country ski trails, and sports fields.

Kinsmen Park (Spadina Crescent and 25th St., Saskatoon, tel. 306/975–3366) is a riverside amusement park and a children's play village.

Wanuskewin Heritage Park (*see* Exploring Saskatoon, *above*).

Western Development Museum (*see* Exploring Saskatoon, *above*).

Shopping

Malls and Shopping Districts
Midtown Plaza (22nd St. and 1st Ave., tel. 306/652–9366) and **Scotia Centre Mall** (123 2nd Ave., tel. 306/665–6120) are enclosed malls located downtown. The area around **Broadway Avenue,** between 8th and 12th streets east of the river, has 150 boutiques and services.

Specialty Stores
Trading Post Limited (226 2nd Ave. S, tel. 306/653–1769) carries an extensive and reasonably priced selection of Inuit and Indian crafts and Canadian foodstuffs—including Saskatoon berry products. Local crafts are also available at **Handmade House** (710 Broadway Ave., tel. 306/665–5542) and the **Homespun Craft Emporium** (212 3rd Ave. S, tel. 306/652–3585).

Sports

Participant Sports
Bicycling and
Jogging
The **Meewasin Valley Trail** (tel. 306/665–6888) is a gorgeous 15-kilometer (10-mile) biking and jogging trail along both banks of the South Saskatchewan River in Saskatoon.

Health and
Fitness Clubs
The **Riverraquet Athletic Club** (322 Saguenay Dr., Saskatoon, tel. 306/242–0010) has racquetball and squash courts, a weight room, aerobics classes, minigolf, and beach volleyball in summer. The **Saskatoon Field House** (University of Alberta, 2020 College Dr., Saskatoon, tel. 306/975–3354) has tennis courts, a weight room, a gymnastics area, an indoor track, a fitness dance area, and drop-in fitness classes.

Spectator Sports
Hockey
The **Saskatoon Blades** play Canadian Hockey League (minor league) matches at **Saskatchewan Place** (3515 Thatcher Ave., Saskatoon, tel. 306/938–7800).

Horse Racing
Marquis Downs Racetrack (Prairieland Exhibition Centre, enter on Ruth St., Saskatoon, tel. 306/242–6100) has Thoroughbred and harness racing early May–mid-October.

Dining and Lodging

For price categories, *see* Winnipeg Dining and Lodging, *above.*

Dining
R.J. Willoughby's. The lush, tropical, pink-and-green color scheme of the Holiday Inn's main dining room is enhanced by copious groves of bamboo and foliage. The menu features Continental preparations plus themed evenings with specialty buffets (prime rib on Wednesday, pasta on Friday, seafood on Sunday). The Sunday Brunch, which features an impressive array including custom-made omelettes and flambé fruit, is very popular. *Holiday Inn, 90 22nd St. E, tel. 306/665–7576. Reservations advised. Jacket advised. AE, DC, MC, V. Expensive.*
Lydia's. One of the best features of this Broadway Avenue restaurant is that it has a split personality. The front room of this old building is an unpretentious setting for Ukrainian and East European specialties such as *nalysnyky* (crêpes), *varenyky* (mashed potato and cheddar cheese wrapped in dough, boiled with butter, and served with sour cream), and smoked sausage. The flip side—the back room—is the oak and stained-glass white-tablecloth venue for such exotic concoctions as "A Night in Hungary" (pork Tokany), "Ascent to the Carpathians" (Dijon veal), and chicken Kiev. The wine list is short but affordable. *650 Broadway Ave., tel. 306/652–8595. Reservations advised. Dress: casual. MC, V. Moderate.*
St. Tropez Bistro. This sophisticated bistro is a short stroll from downtown hotels, and offers intimate French-bistro decor, with blue-and-pink florals, candle-lit tables, and imaginative preparations that change daily. Veal, fish, pasta, quiche, and outstanding homemade bread are often offered. A tasty specialty is the blackened chicken. For dessert, try the chocolate fondue. *243 3rd Ave. S, tel. 306/652–1250. Reservations advised. Dress: casual. AE, MC, V. Closed Sun. Moderate.*
Saskatoon Station Place. The station is newly built, but the railroad cars and decorative antiques are fascinatingly authentic. The newspaper-style menu headlines Canadian prime rib and steaks, seafood, and Greek specialties, such as Greek ribs and souvlakia. *221 Idylwyld Dr. N, tel. 306/244–7777. Reservations advised. Dress: casual. AE, MC, V. Moderate.*

★ **Adonis.** By day such Middle Eastern dishes as falafel, hummus, and donair are served cafeteria-style. At night, tablecloths and candles transform the room into a romantic setting for couscous, dolmades, steak Andalousia, and other Mediterranean delights. It's one of Saskatoon's few outdoor cafés and a great place for breakfast. *101 3rd Ave. S, tel. 306/652–9598. No reservations. Dress: casual. AE, MC, V. Inexpensive.*

Taunte Maria's. This is a Mennonite restaurant, which is to suggest a menu of hearty soups, huge farmer's sausages, cottage cheese varenyky potato salad, homemade bread, and noodles steeped in gravy. The decor, too, reflects the Mennonite tradition: simple, functional, and comfortable. *Try* to save room for Ho-Ho Cake (chocolate cake with cream filling and chocolate icing) or bread pudding with ice cream. Taunte Maria's is convenient to the airport. *51st St. and Faithfull Ave., tel. 306/931–3212. No reservations. Dress: casual. MC, V. Closed Sun. Inexpensive.*

Lodging **Delta Bessborough.** Saskatoon's grand old landmark, opened
★ in 1935, looks like a castle and dominates the skyline from its riverfront setting. The hotel has recently been restored and upgraded with modern amenities, but still retains the grand appearance. *601 Spadina Crescent E, S7K 3G8, tel. 306/244–5521 or 800/268–1133. 227 rooms, including nonsmoking rooms. Facilities: 2 restaurants, 2 lounges, indoor and outdoor pools, sauna, whirlpool. AE, DC, MC, V. Expensive.*

Ramada Renaissance. Saskatoon's newest luxury property has a prime riverfront location downtown, and 19 floors of classically styled, ample-size rooms. Units are large, and the peach, gray, and pastel colors make them bright and airy; for still more atmosphere, request a river view. The elaborate Waterworks Recreation Complex encompasses an indoor pool, whirlpool, sauna, and two three-story waterslides. *405 20th St. E, S7K 6X6, tel. 306/665–3322 or 800/228–9898. 295 rooms, including nonsmoking rooms. Facilities: 2 restaurants, lounge, indoor pool, sauna, whirlpool, waterslides. AE, DC, MC, V. Expensive.*

Sheraton Cavalier. Located downtown opposite Kiwanis Park, this eight-story property features unusually large mauve-and-blue rooms that face either the city or the river, and an elaborate water-sports complex. Benedict's Dining Room is the place for elegant dining, while Windows Café is more informal and offers a view of the river from every table. Lorenzo's Lounge is a piano bar featuring nightly music. The Barley Bin is a sophisticated but chummy pub. *612 Spadina Crescent E, S7K 3G9, tel. 306/652–6770 or 800/325–3535. 250 rooms, including nonsmoking rooms. Facilities: 2 restaurants, pub, 2 indoor pools, waterslides, sauna, whirlpool, games room. AE, DC, MC, V. Expensive.*

Travelodge. This sprawling property near the airport has themed its decor around the two flora-filled indoor pool complexes. Rooms come in a great variety of sizes and shapes; many have balconies overlooking the pool. The Aloha Gardens offers informal poolside dining; the Heritage Dining Room is the place for fine dining. *106 Circle Dr. W, S7L 4L6, tel. 306/242–8881 or 800/255–3050. 220 rooms, including nonsmoking rooms. Facilities: 2 restaurants, lounge, bar, 2 indoor pools, waterslides, sauna, whirlpools, games room. AE, DC, MC, V. Moderate.*

Colonial Square Motel. This pink-stucco, two-story motel opened in 1989 east of the river, along a fast-food strip. Rooms are furnished in pastel colors and have two queen-size beds or a double bed plus pullout sofa. Across the parking lot is the Venice Pizza House and Lounge. *1301 8th St. E, S7H 0S7, tel. 306/343–1676 or 800/667–3939. 80 rooms, including nonsmoking rooms. Facilities: restaurant, lounge. AE, MC, V. Inexpensive.*

★ **King George.** Situated in the center of downtown, opposite the transit mall, this older hotel is conveniently located, and will appeal to anyone who's looking for a bargain. The rooms are large and have been newly renovated. There's a dining room, coffee shop, karaoke lounge, and Szyd's nightclub with evening entertainment. *157 2nd Ave. N, S7K 2A9, tel. 306/244–6133 or 800/667–1234. 104 rooms. Facilities: 2 restaurants, 2 lounges, bowling alley. AE, MC, V. Inexpensive.*

The Arts and Nightlife

The Arts
Theater

Saskatoon's oldest professional theater, **25th Street Theatre Centre** (420 Duchess St., Saskatoon, tel. 306/664–2239), produces mostly works by Canadian playwrights, as well as **The Fringe on Broadway Theatre Festival** every summer. **Persephone Theatre** (2802 Rusholme Rd., Saskatoon, tel. 306/384–7727) presents six plays and musicals a year. **Gateway Players** (709 Cumberland St., Saskatoon, tel. 306/653–1200) presents five productions October–April. **Nightcap Productions** (tel. 306/653–2300) offers "Shakespeare on the Saskatchewan" in a riverside tent in July and August, as well as midnight improvisational comedy at the Broadway Theatre (715 Broadway Ave., Saskatoon, tel. 306/652–6556). Each summer Saskatoon is home to the popular **Saskatchewan Jazz Festival,** when jazz musicians from around the world put on over 125 performances throughout the city.

Music and Dance

The **Saskatoon Symphony** (tel. 306/665–6414) performs an October–April season at **Saskatoon Centennial Auditorium** (35 22nd St. E, Saskatoon, tel. 306/644–9777). When the symphony isn't in concert, the 2,003-seat auditorium hosts ballet, rock and pop concerts, comedians, musical comedies, and opera. The **Mendel Art Gallery** (950 Spadina Crescent E, Saskatoon, tel. 306/975–7610) has a regular concert program, and the **Saskatoon Jazz Society** performs in its permanent space, **The Bassment** (245 3rd Ave. S, Saskatoon, tel. 306/652–1421).

Nightlife
Bars and Clubs

One Up (410 22nd St. E, Saskatoon, tel. 306/244–0955) is a civilized rooftop place with great river views. Saskatoon's businesspeople interface with traveling executives at **Caper's Lounge** (405 20th St. E, Saskatoon, tel. 306/665–3322) in the Ramada Renaissance.

Literature Music

See top rock groups at **Bud's On Broadway** (817 Broadway Ave., Saskatoon, tel. 306/244–4155) and **Amigos** (632 10th St. E, Saskatoon, tel. 306/652–4912). The **Artful Dodger** (100–119 4th Ave. S, Saskatoon, tel. 306/653–2577) is a pub with live entertainment. Go out to **Texas T** (3331 8th St. E, Saskatoon, tel. 306/373–8080) for country sights and sounds around the city's largest dance floor.

Calgary

With the eastern face of the Rockies as its backdrop, Calgary's crisp concrete-and-steel skyline seems to rise from the plains as if by sheer force of will. In fact, all the elements in the great saga of the Canadian West—Mounties, Indians, railroads, cowboys, oil—have converged to create a city with a brand-new face and a surprisingly traditional soul.

Calgary, Gaelic for "preserved pasture at the harbor," was founded in 1875 at the junction of the Bow and Elbow rivers as a North West Mounted Police post. The Canadian Pacific Railroad arrived in 1883, and ranchers established major spreads on the plains surrounding the town. Incorporated as a city in 1885, Calgary grew quickly, and by 1911 its population had reached 43,000.

The major growth came with the oil boom in the 1960s and 1970s, when most Canadian oil companies established their head offices in the city. Today, Calgary is a city of more than 720,000 mostly easygoing and downright neighborly people. It is Canada's third-largest center for corporate head offices. Downtown is still evolving, but Calgary's planners have made life nice by connecting most of the buildings with Plus 15, a network of enclosed walkways 15 feet above street level.

Important Addresses and Numbers

Tourist Information The main **Calgary Convention & Visitors Bureau** (237 8th Ave. S.E. T2G 0K8, tel. 403/263–8510 or 800/661–1678) is open daily 8 AM–9 PM in summer, varying hours the rest of the year. There is also a walk-in Visitor Service Centre, May–August at the base of the Calgary Tower.

Emergencies Dial 911 for all emergencies; **police**, tel. 403/266–1234; **poison center**, tel. 403/670–1414.

Hospitals Emergency rooms are located at **General Hospital** (841 Centre Ave. E, tel. 403/268–9111), **Foothills Hospital** (1403 29th Ave. NW, tel. 403/670–1110), **Alberta Children's Hospital** (1820 Richmond Rd. SW, tel. 403/229–7211), and **Rocky View Hospital** (7007 14th St. SW, tel. 403/541–3000).

Late-night Pharmacy The **Super Drug Mart** (504 Elbow Dr. SW, tel. 403/228–3338) is open daily until midnight.

Arriving and Departing by Plane

Calgary International Airport is 20 minutes northeast of the city center. Along with Air Canada and Canadian Airlines International, Calgary is served by the U.S. carriers American, Delta, Horizon Airlines, and United. Taxis make the 20-minute trip for about $16.

Getting Around

By Car Although many attractions are located in the downtown area and can be reached on foot, a car is advisable for visiting outlying attractions. June–September visitors can obtain a three-day **Visitor Car Park** permit offering "hassle-free" parking at

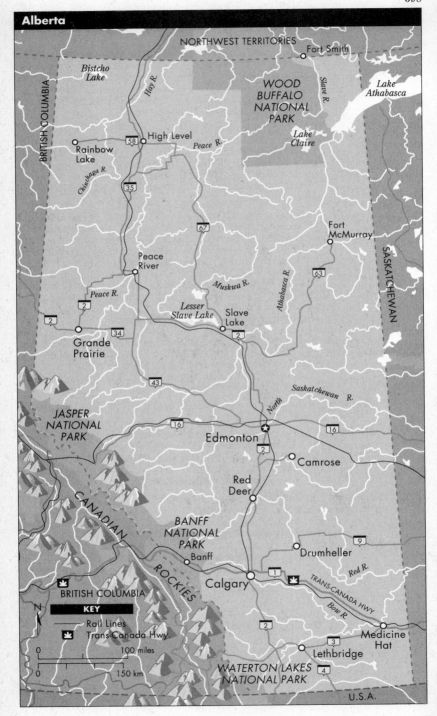

Alberta

NORTHWEST TERRITORIES

Fort Smith

Bistcho Lake

Hay R.

BRITISH COLUMBIA

WOOD BUFFALO NATIONAL PARK

Slave R.

Lake Athabasca

58 High Level

Rainbow Lake

Peace R.

Lake Claire

Chinchaga R.

35

67

Fort McMurray

Peace River

Peace R.

Muskwa R.

Athabasca R.

63

2

Lesser Slave Lake

Slave Lake

2

SASKATCHEWAN

34

Grande Prairie

43

Saskatchewan R.

North

16

JASPER NATIONAL PARK

16

Edmonton

2

Camrose

Red Deer

BANFF NATIONAL PARK

Drumheller

9

Banff

Red R.

CANADIAN

ROCKIES

Calgary

1

TRANS-CANADA HWY

BRITISH COLUMBIA

Bow R.

KEY

—— Rail Lines
Trans-Canada Hwy.

N

2

3

Medicine Hat

Lethbridge

4

0   100 miles
0   150 km

WATERTON LAKES NATIONAL PARK

U.S.A.

street-level city meters. The permit is free at the **Calgary Convention & Visitors Bureau** (*see above*).

By Bus/LRT Calgary Transit (206 7th Ave. SW, tel. 403/276–7801) operates a comprehensive bus system and light rail transit system (the **"C-Train"** or **"LRT"**) throughout the area. Fares are $1.50 for adults, 90¢ for children 6–14. Books of 10 children's tickets are $8.50; 10 adults' tickets $12. A CT Day Pass good for unlimited rides costs $4 adults, $2.50 children. The C-Train has lines running northwest (Brentwood), northeast (Whitehorn), and south (Anderson) from downtown.

By Taxi Taxis are fairly expensive, at $2.05 for the "drop" and about $1 for each additional mile. Major taxi services are **Checker** (tel. 403/299–9999), **Yellow Cab** (tel. 403/250–8311), **Prestige** (tel. 403/250–5911), **Red Top** (tel. 403/250–9222), and **Associated Cabs** (tel. 403/299–1111).

Guided Tours

Several companies offer tours of Calgary and environs, although none operate on regular schedules. Call the **Calgary Convention and Visitors Bureau** (tel. 800/661–1678) for up-to-date information.

Exploring Calgary

Numbers in the margin correspond to points of interest on the Downtown Calgary and Greater Calgary maps.

In the Calgary grid pattern, numbered streets run north–south in both directions from Centre Street, and numbered avenues run east–west in both directions from Centre Avenue.

❶ Begin your downtown walking tour at **Calgary Tower,** a 190-meter (626-foot), scepter-shape edifice that affords great views of the city's layout, the surrounding plains, and the face of the Rockies rising 80 kilometers (50 miles) west. A flame on top is lit for special occasions; the revolving **Panorama Dining Room** and **Sky's Rotisserie & Wine Bar** provide refreshment. *9th Ave. and Centre St. S, tel. 403/266–7171. Admission: $3.75 adults, $2.50 senior citizens and children 13–17, $1.75 children 6–12. Open weekdays and Sat. 7:30 AM–11:30 PM, Sun. 7:30 AM–10:30 PM.*

❷ Take the "plus 15 walkway" (it is 15 feet above street level) over 9th Avenue Southwest to **Glenbow Museum,** Calgary's premier showcase of both art and history. Along with traveling exhibits, the Glenbow has comprehensive displays devoted to Alberta's native (Indian and Inuit) inhabitants, early European settlers, and later-day pioneers. The mineralogy collection and cache of arms and armor are superb. *130 9th Ave. SE, tel. 403/264–8300; tel. 403/237–8988 for exhibit information. Admission: $3 adults, $2 students 13–17, $1 senior citizens. Sat. free. Open daily 10–6. Closed Mon.*

❸ Take the pedway over 1st Street Southeast to the **Calgary Centre for the Performing Arts** (tel. 403/294–7444), a complex of three theater spaces, a concert hall, and shopping area. The center was pieced together with the historic Calgary Public Building (1930) and the Burns Building (1913). Come at night for a performance (*see* The Arts and Nightlife, *below*), or take a one-hour walking tour at noon most weekdays.

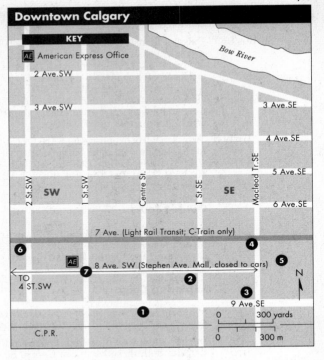

Downtown Calgary

KEY

AE American Express Office

4 Step outside into **Olympic Plaza** (7th Ave. SE and Macleod Trail SE), site of the Olympic medals presentation. Now, during lunchtime, it's a popular park space full of governmental brown-baggers; at night, there's a full slate of entertainment.

5 You're not likely to overlook the **Municipal Building** (8th Ave. SE and Macleod Trail), an angular mirror-walled structure that reflects city landmarks. One of the most stunning reflections is **City Hall,** a stately 1911 sandstone building that still houses the mayor's office and some city offices.

6 Seventh Avenue Southeast is closed to cars to make room for the C-Train, Calgary's light rail system. Hop on for a free ride (along 7th Avenue downtown only) to the center of the downtown shopping district. Literally, the top attraction of the area is **Devonian Gardens,** above Toronto Dominion Square. The 2¹/₂-acre enclosed roof garden has 20,000 mostly tropical plants, nearly a mile of lush walkways, a sculpture court, and playground. Accessed by a glass-enclosed elevator just inside the 8th Avenue door, the Devonian Gardens has a reflecting pool that turns into a skating rink in winter and a small stage for musical performances year-round. *Between 2nd and 3rd Sts., and 7th and 8th Aves. SW. Admission free. Open daily 9–9.*

7 Seventh Avenue Southeast, between Macleod Trail and 4th Street Southwest, is a pedestrian-only shopping area called **Stephen Avenue Mall.** Shops, nightclubs, and restaurants occupy the ground floors of Calgary's oldest structures, mostly sandstone buildings erected after an 1886 fire destroyed almost everything older.

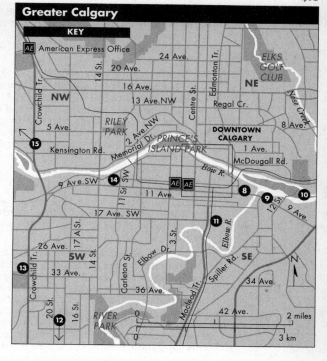

Greater Calgary

Time Out **The Prospector** (205 8th Ave. SW, tel. 403/263–4909) provides an excellent breakfast/lunch/supper with basic pork, lamb, chicken, seafood, steak, salads, hot sandwiches, and burgers at reasonable prices. Try the chocolate pecan pie. It's at street level on Stephen Avenue Mall and provides a good location for people-watching.

8 You'll need a car to continue from here. Head on to **Fort Calgary**, at the confluence of the Bow and Elbow rivers. Established in 1875 by the North West Mounted Police, the fort was to subdue local whiskey traders who raised havoc among the Indians. In the 40-acre park in the valley occupied by Fort Calgary, a line of stumps traces the outline of the original post, and an ultracontemporary interpretive center traces the history of area
9 Indians, Mounties, and white settlers. The **Deane House** (809 9th Ave. SE, tel. 403/269–7747), situated directly across the 9th Avenue Bridge, is the renovated 1906 post commander's house; it has free tours and a tearoom serving light meals. *Ft. Calgary Interpretive Centre, 750 9th Ave. SE, tel. 403/290–1875. Admission free. Open daily 9–5.*

10 Continue east on 9th Avenue, turn north on 12th Street, and cross the bridge to St. George's Island and the **Calgary Zoo**, with more than 1,400 animals, including 388 rare and endangered species, in plausibly natural settings. Polar bears and seals cavorting underwater are perennial crowd pleasers. The **Kinsmen's Children's Zoo,** part of the larger site, offers hands-on experiences with baby animals, and the adjacent Prehistoric

Park displays dinosaur replicas in a bygone natural habitat. *1300 Zoo Rd. NE, tel. 403/232–9372. Admission: $7.50 adults, $4.75 senior citizens, $3.75 children 2–15; $5 adults and senior citizens free on Tues. Open 9 AM, closing times seasonally adjusted.*

⑪ Head south and east to Olympic Way and **Stampede Park** (17th Ave. and 2nd St. SE, tel. 403/261–0101), the focus each July of the world-famous Calgary Exhibition and Stampede (*see* Festivals and Seasonal Events in Chapter 1). Throughout the year the Roundup Centre, Big Four Building, and Agriculture Building host trade shows; the Olympic Saddledome has concerts and Calgary Flames hockey games; and the Grandstand is the site of Thoroughbred and harness racing (*see* Sports, *below*). Visitors can wander the grounds, take free one-hour tours of the **Saddledome** (tel. 403/261–0400), and visit the free **Grain Academy** in Roundup Centre, an interesting little museum that proudly proclaims itself "Canada's only grain interpretive centre." *Grain Academy in Stampede Park, tel. 403/263–4594. Admission free. Open weekdays 10–4, Sat. noon–4.*

⑫ Follow Macleod Trail past a strip of fast-food outlets, motels, and shopping centers and go west on Heritage Drive to **Heritage Park,** where more than 100 authentic structures from all over western Canada have been collected in a parklike setting beside Glenmore Reservoir. The "neighborhoods," inhabited by costumed staff, range from an 1850s fur-trading post to a 1910-era town. Steam trains, horse-drawn buses, and paddlewheel steamers provide transportation, and North America's only antique amusement park re-creates bygone thrills. Theme snacks—sarsaparilla, beef jerky, fresh apple pie— abound. *1900 Heritage Dr. SW, tel. 403/259–1900. Admission: $6 adults, $5 senior citizens, $3 children 3–16. Open late-May– June, weekdays 10–4, weekends 10–6; July–Sept. 2, daily 10–6; Sept. 3–early Oct., weekends and holidays 10–5.*

⑬ East across Glenmore Reservoir, turn north on Crowchild Trail to reach the **Canadian Forces Currie Barracks** (4225 Crowchild Trail SW), site of two military museums in one building: **Lord Strathconas (Royal Canadian) Horse Museum** (tel. 403/242– 6610) features an extensive collection of medals and weapons; **Princess Patricia's Canadian Light Infantry** (tel. 403/240–7901) displays memorabilia of a distinguished old regiment (founded in 1914) that fought in both world wars and joined with the United Nations peacekeeping forces. Note: Both museums are free, but you may need to show identification to enter the military base. *Bldg. B6, Currie Barracks, 4225 Crowchild Trail SW. Admission free. Horse Museum open weekdays 9–4, weekends 10–4; Infantry Museum open Tues.–Fri. and Sun. 10–4.*

⑭ Continuing north on Crowchild Trail, turn east on 9th Avenue Southwest and then north again on 11th Street Southwest to the **Alberta Science Centre/Planetarium.** The Science Centre in the lower chamber has more than 35 hands-on exhibits of scientific marvels, such as holograms, frozen shadows, and laser beams; user-friendly demonstrations are given Friday– Sunday. Up in the planetarium, the 360-degree Star Chamber presents educational Star Shows with children's matinees on weekends, Laser Shows on Friday–Sunday nights. Imaginative combinations of special effects, magic tricks, and old-time show-biz make performances fascinating for all ages. *701 11th*

St. SW, tel. 403/221–3700. Admission: Science Centre, $2.25 adults and senior citizens, $1.75 children, free with Star Show ticket; Star Shows, $5.75 adults, $1.75 senior citizens and children; Laser Shows, $5. Open 10–9.

⑮ Follow Crowchild Trail north to 16th Avenue Northwest (Rte. 1) and then head west about 8 kilometers (5 miles) to **Canada Olympic Park,** site of the 1988 Winter Olympics and a year-round attraction. A one-hour bus tour goes over, under, around, and through the 70- and 90-meter ski jumps, bobsled, and luge tracks (in summer you have the option of walking down the slopes). In winter the slopes are open to the public (lessons available). Visitors can experience Olympic-size thrills on the one-minute Tourist Bobsleigh Ride ($100) and slightly briefer Tourist Luge Ride ($10); safety equipment is provided. Premises include a day lodge with a cafeteria, and the **Olympic Hall of Fame,** a collection of Olympic memorabilia and video displays. The highlight here is the scarifying four-man bobsled simulator. *Trans-Canada Hwy. W (Rte. 1) at Bowfort Rd. NW, tel. 403/286–2632. Admission: Bus or self-guided tour, $6.95 adults, $3.75 senior citizens, students, and children. Hall of Fame, $3.50 adults, $2.50 senior citizens, students, and children. Tour and Hall of Fame, $9.10 adults, $4.85 senior citizens, students, and children. Park open mid-June–Sept. 2, daily 7 AM–9 PM; Sept. 3–mid-June, daily 8 AM–9 PM; Hall of Fame open daily 10–5.*

What to See and Do with Children

Calaway Park (Rte. 1, 10 km, or 6 mi, west of Calgary, tel. 403/240–3822). Western Canada's largest outdoor amusement park also has live entertainment, mini-golf, driving range, maze, petting farm, food outlets, and shops. There's a new RV park and campground, which cost $19 per night for a full-service site; $16 per night for a bare site.

Calgary Zoo (*see* Exploring Calgary, *above*).

Canada Olympic Park (*see* Exploring Calgary, *above*).

Heritage Park (*see* Exploring Calgary, *above*).

Shopping

Malls and Shopping Districts Calgary's premier shopping areas are located in the center of the downtown area, and you can wander through various shopping centers connected by indoor walkways. Major complexes include **Bankers Hall,** with exclusive specialty shops, restaurants, and cinemas; **Scotia Centre,** with fashion, accessory, and other retail outlets; **Penny Lane Mall** in renovated, early 20th-century buildings; and **Toronto Dominion Centre,** which is home to the indoor park—Devonian Gardens—as well as more than 100 stores. For outdoor shopping, the six-block stretch of 8th Avenue Southwest, between 3rd Street Southwest and Macleod Trail Southeast, has been turned into the traffic-free Stephen Avenue Mall.

Specialty Stores **Uptown 17** is a trendy shopping district just outside the city center along 17th Avenue Southwest, and features several craft shops, antiques stores, boutiques, galleries, cafés, and coffee shops.

Sports

Participant Sports
Bicycling and Jogging

Calgary has about 200 kilometers (120 miles) of bicycling and jogging paths, most of which wind along rivers and through city parks. Maps are available at visitor centers (*see* Important Addresses and Numbers in Calgary, *above*) and bike shops. Rent bikes at **Sports Rent** (4424 16th Ave. NW, Calgary, tel. 403/292–0077).

Health and Fitness Clubs

Three **Leisure Centre** waterparks in Calgary have wave pools and waterslides, plus gymnasiums and training facilities; Southland and Family have racquetball and squash courts. *Village Square Leisure Centre, 2623 56th St. NE, tel. 403/280–9714; Family Leisure Centre, 11150 Bonaventure Dr. SE, tel. 403/278–7542; Southland Leisure Centre, 2000 Southland Dr. SW, tel. 403/251–3505. Rates and hours vary.*

Just south of downtown, the striking white-dome **Lindsay Park Sports Centre** (2225 Macleod Trail SW, Calgary, tel. 403/233–8619) encompasses a 50-meter natatorium, a 200-meter track, racquetball and squash courts, and a weight room.

Spectator Sports
Football

The **Calgary Stampeders** of the Canadian Football League play home games in **McMahon Stadium** (1817 Crowchild Tr. NW, tel. 403/289–0205) throughout the season, which runs July–November.

Hockey

The **Calgary Flames** play National Hockey League matches October–April at the **Olympic Saddledome** (17th Ave. and 2nd St. SE, Calgary, tel. 403/261–0475) in Stampede Park.

Horse Racing

There's racing year-round (except March) in **Stampede Park** (17th Ave. and 2nd St. SE, Calgary, tel. 403/261–0101). Thoroughbreds race April–May and September–November; trotters May–September and December–February. **Spruce Meadows** (just south and west of the Calgary city boundary, tel. 403/254–3200) is one of the world's finest show-jumping facilities, with major competitions held June–September.

Dining and Lodging

For price categories, *see* Winnipeg Dining and Lodging, *above*.

Dining
★

Owl's Nest Dining Room. Plush armchairs and dark-wood booths express the subdued confidence of a restaurant long proclaimed the best in town. Standards are maintained, and all dishes are served with impeccable Continental flair. Alberta beef entrées are still ample and tender; British Columbia salmon is memorably fresh; the wine list is still exhaustive. *Westin Hotel, 320 4th Ave. SW, tel. 403/266–1611. Reservations advised. Jacket advised. AE, DC, MC, V. Very Expensive.*

Cannery Row Restaurant. People dine at this cozy eatery housed in a former warehouse, whose decor consists of exposed piping, brick walls, hardwood floors, and high ceilings. Fresh creole and Cajun dishes make good use of the seafood that's flown in. The crowds are entertained here by live New Orleans–style jazz bands and special dining events that are organized sporadically throughout the year. *317 10th Ave. SW, tel. 403/269–8889. Reservations needed for lunch. Dress: casual. AE, DC, MC, V. Expensive.*

Hy's Steak House. This is where Calgary (and Edmonton, Winnipeg, Toronto, and elsewhere in Canada) goes for immense portions of charcoal-broiled steaks, fresh seafood, chicken, and a huge selection of wines. Wood paneling and earthy decor are evidence of the sedate Victorian ambience. *316 4th Ave. SW, tel. 403/263–2222. Reservations advised. Jacket advised. AE, DC, MC, V. Closed Sun. Expensive.*

Silver Dragon. A Chinatown institution for more than 20 years, the huge L-shape dining room is mellowed out by soft carpeting and delicate Chinese paintings. The menu includes standard beef, pork, and poultry dishes but shines on concoctions of rock cod, crab, abalone, cuttlefish, and other seafood. Dim sum lunch is featured daily. *106 3rd Ave. SE, tel. 403/264–5326. No reservations. Dress: casual. AE, DC, MC, V. Expensive.*

Salsas Grill & Bar. Surrounded by cacti and green and orange walls, diners feast on a mix of traditional Mexican fare and burgers and salads. This two-year-old restaurant is refreshingly bright and airy. *601 12th Ave. SW, tel. 403/294–1499. Reservations advised on weekends. Dress: casual. AE, MC, V. Moderate.*

★ **Buzzards Cafe.** This lively European-style downtown café serves 70 wines by the bottle or glass and the exclusive home brew, Buzzard Breath Ale. Wine-theme prints and posters adorning the walls remind you of the original attraction to this place. However, fine food selections include various species of eight-ounce Alberta beef Buzzard Burgers, pub grub, and low-priced entrées, such as teriyaki chicken and fettuccine Alfredo. In summer, dine out on the patio. Adjoining the café is Bottlescrew Bill's Old English Pub. *140 10th Ave. SW, tel. 403/264–6959. No reservations. Dress: casual. AE, DC, MC, V. Inexpensive.*

Green Street. This lively and unpretentious spot serves Italian and Cajun specialties in a three-level setting that's loaded with greenery inside and out. Adding to the atmosphere is an ever-changing exhibit of local artwork that adorns the walls. The menu, which changes monthly, includes many dishes named after famous artists, since Green Street attracts lots of local artists; one favorite: "Rembrandt's rack of lamb." The list of wines available by the glass is extensive, and the staff emphasizes matching food and wine. *815 7th Ave. SW, tel. 403/266–1551. Reservations advised. AE, DC, MC, V. Inexpensive.*

Lodging **Delta Bow Valley.** The bright, 24-story high rise occupies a relatively quiet street on the southern edge of downtown. Decent-size contemporary rooms, with rose-and-green furnishings, have good views on upper floors. For the brightest and most colorful units, request a room with a northern exposure. The sunny lobby—decorated in pink tones and with lush foliage—is an uplifting addition to an already lively setting. *209 4th Ave. SE, T2G 0C6, tel. 403/266–1980 or 800/268–1133. 400 rooms. Facilities: 2 restaurants, lounge, indoor pool, saunas, exercise room, nonsmoking floors. AE, DC, MC, V. Very Expensive.*

Sheraton Cavalier. This recently renovated northeast Calgary hotel features a lobby decorated with pale colors, lots of plants, and a large marble water fountain. It's furnished with comfortable couches and chairs seated around marble coffee tables. **Barlow's Lounge** hosts live entertainment from Thursday through Saturday. For sports fans, there's **Henry's Pub,** the hotel's sports bar with large TV screens. One other highlight is the **Oasis River Country,** on the second floor of the hotel, which has two 200-foot waterslides and a recreation and exercise area. *2620 32nd Ave. NE, T1Y 6B8, tel. 403/291–0107 or 800/325–3535. 307 rooms, including nonsmoking rooms. Facilities: restaurant, bar, indoor pool. AE, DC, MC, V. Very Expensive.*

Skyline Plaza Hotel. This is a business-class hotel with a convenient location in the heart of downtown, connected to the Calgary Convention Centre. Also surrounding the property are the Glenbow Museum and the Calgary Centre for Performing Arts, which provide executive and leisure guests nearby options for their spare time. The warm, inviting lobby works well with the clean pastel-and-maroon-toned rooms. *110 9th Ave., T2G 5A6, tel. 403/266–7331 or 800/661–7776. 387 rooms. Facilities: 2 restaurants, 2 lounges, indoor pool, sauna, fitness club, racquetball arrangements at nearby club, nonsmoking floors. AE, DC, MC, V. Very Expensive.*

Carriage House. This unique, locally owned property, located almost 10 kilometers (6 miles) south of City Centre, has a lobby with fish tanks, caged songbirds, and a waterfall. Room decor is comfortably mismatched. Nighttime entertainment options include a disco and rock club, country and rock saloon, and an English pub. Guests get discounts at nearby Family Leisure Centre (*see* Sports, *above*). *9030 Macleod Trail S, T2H 0M4, tel. in U.S. call collect, 403/253–1101; or 800/661–9566. 175 rooms, including nonsmoking rooms. Facilities: 2 restaurants, 3 lounges, outdoor heated pool, indoor whirlpool and sauna. AE, DC, MC, V. Expensive.*

★ **The Palliser.** The downtown area of every Canadian city has a grand old railroad hotel, and The Palliser is Calgary's. This landmark, built in 1914, was recently restored to its former grandeur. Guest rooms are tastefully appointed with classic furnishings, ornate moldings, and high ceilings. *133 9th Ave. SW, T2P 2M3, tel. 403/262–1234 or 800/268–9411. 406 rooms. Facilities: restaurant, bar, exercise room, nonsmoking floor. AE, DC, MC, V. Expensive.*

★ **Westin Hotel.** The luxury high rise in the midst of downtown connects to most other important structures via Calgary's Plus 15 pedway system. Rooms in the Tower Section, especially, are large and decorated with tasteful contemporary furniture and are dominated by pastel peach tones and neutrals. The rooftop pool is one of this lodging's unique attractions, in addition to the Owl's Nest restaurant (*see* Dining, *above*), one of the best dining spots in town. For lighter meals stop into the Lobby Court, which features Fitness Buffet breakfasts. *320 4th Ave. SW, T2P 2S6, tel. 403/266–1611 or 800/228–3000. 525 rooms, including nonsmoking rooms. Facilities: 2 restaurants, 2 lounges, indoor pool, fitness club, sauna. AE, DC, MC, V. Expensive.*

Prince Royal Inn. Calgary's bargain inn has quite a lot going for it within its 28 floors: downtown and convenient location, all-suite (studios, one, and two bedrooms) accommodations with fully equipped kitchens, free parking, free Continental breakfast, and a health club. Large rooms with kitchens make it a great deal for families. *618 5th Ave. SW, T2P 0M7, tel. 403/263–0520; in Canada, 800/661–1592. 300 suites. Facilities: restaurant, bar, health club with sauna, exercise equipment, convenience store, florist, dry cleaner, nonsmoking floors. AE, DC, MC, V. Moderate.*

Ramada Inn Airport. This convenient and comfortable property is located on the northeast side of town a few minutes from Calgary International Airport. Bright rooms are large, have

standard furnishings, and are tastefully decorated with a rose-
and-mauve scheme. *1250 McKinnon Dr. NE, T2E 7T7, tel.
403/230–1999 or 800/661–5095. 168 rooms, including nonsmoking rooms. Facilities: restaurant, bar, indoor pool, sauna, sun
deck. AE, DC, MC, V. Moderate.*

The Arts and Nightlife

Tickets for events at the Calgary Centre for the Performing
Arts, Jubilee Auditorium, and Olympic Saddledome are available at Ticketmaster outlets at Calgary Centre box office, The
Bay, Sears, or by telecharge (tel. 403/270–6700 or 403/266–
8888).

The Arts Calgary's showcase theater facility is the **Calgary Centre for**
Theater **the Performing Arts** (205 8th Ave. SE, Calgary, tel. 403/294–
7455), with three modern auditoriums in two contiguous historic buildings. Productions by resident Alberta Theatre
Projects (ATP) of principally Canadian playwrights are highly
recommended. More than 20 local companies use the stage of
the **Pumphouse Theatre** (2140 9th Ave. SW, Calgary, tel.
403/263–0079). The **University of Calgary Theatre** (Reeve Theatre, 2500 University Drive NW, Calgary, tel. 403/220–4900)
features classic and contemporary works.

Music and Dance **Calgary Philharmonic Orchestra** (tel. 403/294–7420) concerts,
chamber groups, and a broad spectrum of music and dance
shows are performed in the 1,755-seat **Jack Singer Concert
Hall** in the **Calgary Centre for the Performing Arts** (205 8th Ave.
SE, Calgary, tel. 403/294–7455). The larger **Jubilee Auditorium**
(1415 14th Ave. NW, Calgary, tel. 403/297–8000) hosts the Alberta Ballet company and a variety of classical music, opera,
dance, pop, and rock concerts. Concerts are also performed at
University of Calgary Theatres (2500 University Dr. NW, Calgary, tel. 403/220–4900).

Nightlife **Loose Moose** (2003 McKnight Blvd. NE, Calgary, tel. 403/291–
Bars and Clubs 5682) features competitive "Theatresports" and all sorts of fun
and games.

Casinos In Calgary, play blackjack, roulette, and wheel of fortune at
River Park Casino (1919 Macleod Trail S, Calgary, tel. 403/269–
6771), **Cash Casino Place** (4040B Blackfoot Trail SE, Calgary,
tel. 403/287–1635), **Tower Casino** in Tower Centre, and **Frontier Casino** in the Big Four Building in Stampede Park.

Comedy The Calgary outpost of **Yuk Yuk's** (Blackfoot Inn, 5940 Blackfoot Trail, Calgary, tel. 403/258–2028), Canada's comedy chain,
has name performers from Canada and the United States.
Jester's (239 10th Ave. SE, Calgary, tel. 403/269–6669) has comedians and Wednesday-night open mikes.

Music Calgary's **Sparky's Live** (1006 11th Ave. SW, Calgary, tel.
403/244–4888) presents a pleasing array of blues, rock, folk,
and big-band performers. The Casablanca-style **Cafe Calabash**
(107 10A St. NW, Calgary, tel. 403/270–2266) has live jazz every
night but Sunday. For Western sights and sounds, head for
Ranchman's (9615 Macleod Trail S, Calgary, tel. 403/253–1100)
or the **Longhorn Dance Hall** (9631 Macleod Trail S, Calgary,
tel. 403/258–0528). The **Rocking Horse Saloon** (24 7400
Macleod Trail S, Calgary, tel. 403/255–4646) also features country music every night but Sunday. **Orete's Restaurant and**

Lounge (739 2nd Ave. SW, tel. 403/266–1646) has dancing to smooth rock music in the evening.

Excursion from Calgary: Southern Alberta

Head east on the Trans-Canada Highway (Route 1) out of Calgary and enter the vast Canadian prairie of seemingly endless expanses of flat country in every direction. About 20 kilometers (12 miles) east of Calgary, turn north on Highway 9 and drive 120 kilometers (75 miles) to Drumheller, a coal-mining center for several years. The town is situated in the rugged valley of the Red Deer River, where millions of years of wind and water erosion exposed the "strike" that produced what amounts to present-day Drumheller's major industry: dinosaurs.

The barren lunar landscape of stark badlands and eerie rock cylinders (called hoodoos) may seem an ideal setting for the herds of dinosaurs that stalked the countryside 75 million years ago, but in fact, when the dinosaurs were here the area had a semitropical climate and verdant marshlands not unlike the Florida Everglades. You learn this and more geological and paleontological history of Alberta at the **Royal Tyrell Museum of Paleontology.** Participate in hands-on exhibits and meet the local hero, Albertosaurus, a smaller, fiercer version of Tyrannosaurus rex that was the first dino discovered around here. *Hwy. 838, 6 km (4 mi) west of Drumheller; tel. 403/823–7707; in Calgary, 403/294–1992. Admission: $5 adults; $2 children 7–17. Tues. free. Open mid-May–early Sept., daily 9–9; mid-Sept.– mid-May, Tues.–Sun. 10–5.*

Capitalizing on its rich paleontological past, Drumheller has a number of dinosaur-related businesses. **Reptile World** (Hwy. 9, tel. 403/823–TOAD) boasts a crowd-pleasing collection of poisonous snakes; the **Homestead Antique Museum** (Hwy. 838, tel. 403/823–2600) packs 4,000 Indian artifacts, medical instruments, period clothing, and other items of Canadiana into a roadside quonset hut; **Ollie's Rock & Fossil Shop** (off Hwy. 575, tel. 403/823–7625) depicts life-size dinosaurs in a badlands setting and sells a vast selection of fossils, bones, rocks, and petrified wood. No visit to Drumheller is complete without a family portrait beside the comic-book Tyrannosaurus rex guarding the Highway 9 bridge over the Red Deer River.

Continuing the dinosaur tour of Alberta requires a 142-kilometer (90-mile) drive south from Drumheller on Highway 56. Go east on the Trans-Canada Highway (Route 1), north at Brooks on Highway 873, east on Highway 544, and follow the signs to **Dinosaur Provincial Park**, a 15,000-acre park encompassing Canada's baddest badlands. Soft sedimentary rock was deposited by 72-million-year-old rivers and sculpted into starkly fascinating shapes by melting waters of the Ice Age that occurred a mere 14,000 years ago. Incessant wind, water, and frost erosion have exposed one of the world's most important collections of fossilized bones. Roads access some *in situ* fossil sites; two looped interpretive trails lead to more, with guided tours on weekends. During summer, 90-minute bus tours explore backcountry areas from which visitors are otherwise restricted. The cacti bloom from June through August. The **Royal Tyrell Museum of Paleontology Field Station** in the park offers a concise orientation to the prehistoric world. Note: Since concessions are limited, bring a lunch to eat in one of the picnic areas.

Hwy. 544, Patricia, 48 km (30 mi) northeast of Brooks, tel. 403/378–4587. Admission: $1.50. Tyrell Field Station open mid-May–early Sept., daily 9–9; Sept.–mid-May, Wed.–Sun. 10–5.

Medicine Hat lies about 95 kilometers (60 miles) southeast of Patricia on the Trans-Canada Highway. Roadside views consist of small well pumps and storage tanks amid endless expanses of "prairie wool," principally spear and blue grama grass. There is much local lore concerning the origin of the name Medicine Hat, but one legend tells of a battle waged between Cree and Blackfoot Indians; the Cree fought bravely until their medicine man deserted, losing his headdress in the South Saskatchewan River. The site's name, "Saamis," meaning "medicine man's hat," was later translated by white settlers into Medicine Hat.

Medicine Hat is a prosperous and scenic city built on high banks overlooking the South Saskatchewan River. Alberta's fifth-largest city's wealth derives from vast deposits of natural gas below, some of which gets piped up to fuel quaint gas lamps in the turn-of-the-century downtown area. Prosperity is similarly communicated by the striking glass-sided **Medicine Hat City Hall**. *1st St. SE and 6th Ave. SE, tel. 403/529–8100. Open weekdays 8:30–4:30. Guided group and self-guided tours available.*

But Medicine Hat's greatest achievement was turning the land alongside the South Saskatchewan River and Seven Persons Creek into parkland and environmental preserves interconnected by 15 kilometers (9⅓ miles) of walking, biking, and cross-country ski trails. Detailed trail maps are available at the **Tourist Information Centre** (8 Gehring Rd. SW, tel. 403/527–6422). Other Medicine Hat attractions include a half-mile of falling water at **Riverside Waterslide** (Hwy. 1 and Power House Rd., tel. 403/529–6218) and **Echo Dale Regional Park** (Holsom Rd. off Hwy. 3, tel. 403/529–6225), the riverside setting for swimming, boating, fishing, a 1900s farm, and an historic coal mine.

Head west out of Medicine Hat toward **Lethbridge** on Crowsnest Highway (Rte. 3). Lethbridge, Alberta's third-largest city, is an 1870s coal boomtown that is now the center of agriculture, oil, and gas. The main attraction, **Fort Whoop-Up,** part of the **Indian Battle Park,** is a reconstruction of a southern Alberta whiskey fort. Along with weapons, relics, and a 15-minute audiovisual historical presentation, Fort Whoop-Up has wagon-train tours of the river valley and other points of local historical interest. *Indian Battle Park, Whoop-Up Dr. and Oldman River, tel. 403/329–0444. Fort Whoop-Up admission free. Open late May–Labor Day, daily 10–8. Call for off-season hours.*

Henderson Lake Park, 3 kilometers (2 miles) east on the other side of downtown Lethbridge, is filled with lush trees, a golf course, baseball stadium, tennis courts, a swimming pool, and a 60-acre man-made lake. Alongside the lake, **Nikka Yuko Japanese Gardens** is a tranquil setting for manicured trees and shrubs, miniature pools and waterfalls, a teahouse, and pebble designs constructed in Japan and reassembled alongside Henderson Lake. *Henderson Lake Park, Mayor Magrath Dr. and S. Parkside Dr., tel. 403/320–3020; Gardens, tel. 403/328–3511. Admission: $2 adults, $1 senior citizens and students 12 and* *over. Open mid-May–mid-June, daily 9–5; mid-June–Aug., daily 9–8; Sept.–early Oct., daily 9–5.*

Travel west along Highway 3 for 50 kilometers (31 miles) to **Fort Macleod.** Southern Alberta's oldest settlement, the installation was founded by the Mounties in 1874 to maintain order among the farmers, Indians, whiskey vendors, and ranchers beginning to settle here. The wood-frame buildings (pre-1900) and the more recent sandstone-and-brick buildings have established this as Alberta's first historic area. For information about guided and self-guided tours, visit the information booth (tel. 403/553–2500) beside Fort Macleod Museum. An authentic reconstruction of the 1874 fort, **Fort Macleod Museum** grants almost equal exhibitory weight to settlers, Indians, old North West Mounted Police, and today's Royal Canadian Mounted Police. *25th St., tel. 403/553–4703. Admission: $3 adults, $2.50 senior citizens, $1 students 13–18, 50¢ children 6–12. Open May–June 14 and Sept. 3–Oct. 15, daily 9–5; June 15–Sept. 2, daily 9–7.*

Head-Smashed-In Buffalo Jump is about a 15-minute drive from Fort Macleod. Take Highway 3 west and follow signs. A large interpretive center is built into the side of a cliff and explains how Plains Indians herded buffalo over the edge to their death, so the natives could later harvest meat and fur from the carcasses. On the site are museum displays that describe the tradition and offer some insight into the life and customs of the Plains Indians, especially the Blackfoot. Also, walking trails are available, and tours are given by native guides. *On Hwy. 785, 16 km (9 mi) northeast of Fort Macleod; tel. 403/553–2731. Open year-round, Tues.–Sun. 9–8. Admission: $5 adults, $2 children 7–17. Free admission on Tues.*

Dining For rates, *see* Winnipeg Dining and Lodging, *above.*

Lethbridge **Cafe Martinique.** This locally renowned fine dining spot, located in the El Rancho Motor Hotel, specializes in aged steaks and chateaubriand made with tender Alberta beef. For something lighter in a more informal setting, try the El Rancho coffee shop, on the same property. Live music and dancing take place most nights. *526 Mayor Magrath Dr., tel. 403/327–5701. Reservations advised. Jacket advised. AE, DC, MC, V. Expensive.*

Sven Eriksen's Family Restaurant. The homey, colonial-style place features hearty and tasty versions of Canadian prairie standards like chicken and an especially good prime rib. "Family Restaurant" label notwithstanding, there's a full bar. *1715 Mayor Magrath Dr., tel. 403/328–7756. Reservations advised, especially on weekends. Dress: casual. AE, MC, V. Moderate.*

Lodging **Lethbridge Lodge Hotel.** This modern-day lodge has great
Lethbridge Oldman River views and a pleasant tropical indoor courtyard filled with exotic plants, a swimming pool, whirlpool, waterfall, and chairs for lounging. The hotel boasts two restaurants: At the more formal **Anton's** the waitstaff is dressed in tuxedos and reservations are needed. *320 Scenic Dr., T1J 4B4, tel. 800/661–1232 or 403/328–1123. 190 rooms, including nonsmoking rooms. Facilities: restaurant, lounge, indoor pool, whirlpool. AE, MC, V. Moderate.*

Parkside Inn. This comfortable nearly 40-year-old hotel is a good bargain, and is conveniently located across the street from a golf course and within walking distance of Henderson

Lake Park and the Japanese Gardens. Renovated in the last two years, the lobby is done in muted burgundies and blues, while rooms are styled in grays and rusts. The hotel's tavern has live country-and-western music on weekends and the lounge features video lottery machines. *1009 Mayor Magrath Dr., T1K 2P7, tel. 403/328–2366. 65 rooms, including nonsmoking rooms. Facilities: restaurant, lounge. AE, MC, V. Inexpensive.*

Medicine Hat   **Medicine Hat Lodge.** Although it's situated on the edge of town adjacent to a shopping mall, this hotel has several rooms with inward views of the indoor pool, whirlpool, and huge, curving waterslide. The Atrium Dining Room serves fine Continental meals. J.D.'s is a hotel country-and-western spot. *1051 Ross Glen Dr. SE, T1B 3T8, tel. 403/529–2222 or 800/661–8095. 190 rooms, including nonsmoking rooms. Facilities: 2 restaurants, 2 lounges, indoor pool, whirlpool, waterslide, steam room. AE, DC, MC, V. Moderate.*

Edmonton

Lucky Edmonton is a recidivist boomtown that never seems to go bust. The first boom arrived in 1795, when the North West Company and Hudson's Bay Company both established fur-trading posts in the area. Boom II came in 1897, when Edmonton became principal outfitter on the overland "All Canadian Route" to the Yukon goldfields; as a result, Edmonton was named capital when the province of Alberta was formed in 1905. The latest and greatest of booms began on February 13, 1947, when oil was discovered in Leduc, 40 kilometers (25 miles) to the southwest. More than 10,000 wells were eventually drilled within 100 kilometers (62 miles) of the city and with them fields of refineries and supply depots. By 1965 Edmonton had solidified its role as the "Oil Capital of Canada."

More interesting is how wisely Edmonton has spread the wealth to create a beautiful and livable city. Shunning the uncontrolled development of some other oil boomtowns, Edmonton turned its great natural resource, the North Saskatchewan River Valley, into a 27-kilometer (17-mile) greenbelt of parks and recreational facilities. With a population of 850,000, Edmonton is the largest northerly city in the Americas and the fifth-largest city in Canada. It is also Canada's largest city in land area—681 hectares (270 square miles). As the seat of the Alberta government and home to the University of Alberta, Edmonton has an unusually sophisticated atmosphere that has generated many fine restaurants and a thriving arts community. Its premier attraction, the West Edmonton Mall, is a year-round drawing card for shoppers and families, complete with facilities ranging from an amusement park to a shopping center and hotel, from a cinema complex to a water park.

Important Addresses and Numbers

Tourist   An **Edmonton Tourism Information Centre** (97th St. and Jas-
Information per Ave., tel. 403/496–8400 or 800/463–4667) is located downtown at the Edmonton Convention Centre. The office is open mid-May–September, daily 8:30–4:30; September–mid-May, weekdays 8:30–4:30. Other offices are open around Edmonton; for locations and times call the above number.

Emergencies	Dial 911 for **police, fire, ambulance,** and **poison center.**
Hospitals	Emergency rooms are located at the **Royal Alexandra Hospital** (10240 Kingsway Ave., tel. 403/477–4111) and **University of Alberta Hospitals** (8440 112th St., tel. 403/492–8822).
Dentists	For 24-hour dental care, contact **Denta Care** (472 Southgate Shopping Centre, 111th St. and 51st Ave., tel. 403/434–9566).
Late-night Pharmacy	**Mid-Niter Drugs** (11408 Jasper Ave., tel. 403/482–1171) is open until midnight.

Arriving and Departing by Plane

Edmonton has two airports, though most international flights and long-haul domestic flights use **Edmonton International Airport.** Short-haul flights, mainly to neighboring provinces, use **Edmonton Municipal Airport,** just north of downtown. Along with the major Canadian airlines (Air Canada, Canadian Airlines International), Edmonton is served by American, Delta, and Northwest.

Taxi rides from Edmonton International can be costly, but **The Grey Goose Airporter** (tel. 403/463–7520) provides frequent service between the airport and major downtown hotels. Fare is $11 one way, $18 round-trip. Grey Goose also provides service between Edmonton International and Edmonton Municipal Airport or West Edmonton Mall ($11 one way, $18 round-trip).

Getting Around

By Bus/LRT Edmonton Transit (tel. 403/421–INFO) operates a comprehensive system of buses throughout the area and a light rail transit (**LRT**) line from downtown to the northeast side of the city. The fare is $1.35 for adults, 80¢ for senior citizens and children 6–16; transfers are free. Adult fares are $1.60 during weekday rush hours. Buses operate from 5:30 AM to 2 AM. The LRT is free in the downtown area (between Churchill and Grandin stations) weekdays 9–3 and Saturday 9–6. The **Downtown Information Centre** above Central LRT Station (100A St. and Jasper Ave.) provides free information, timetables, and maps, weekdays 9–5.

By Taxi Taxis tend to be costly: $2 for the first 105 meters, and 10¢ for each additional 105 meters. Cabs may be hailed on the street, but phoning is recommended. Call **Alberta Co-op Taxi** (tel. 403/425–8310), **Checker** (tel. 403/455–2211), or **Yellow** (tel. 403/462–3456).

Guided Tours

From early May to early October three **Royal Tours** (tel. 403/488–9090) itineraries hit the high points of Edmonton. **Klondike Jet Boats** (tel. 403/486–0896) ply the North Saskatchewan River, May–October. **North Saskatchewan Riverboat Company** (tel. 403/424–2628) operates up to six cruises per day, May–October.

Exploring Downtown Edmonton

Numbers in the margin correspond to points of interest on the Downtown Edmonton map.

The Edmonton street system is a straight grid with numbered streets running north–south and numbered avenues running east–west. Meeting at the center are 100th Street and 100th Avenue; Edmontonians often use the last digit or two as shorthand for the complete number: the Inn on 7th is on 107th Street; the 9th Street Bistro can be found on 109th Street. Edmonton's "Main Drag" is Jasper Avenue, which runs east–west through the center of downtown.

The city's striking physical feature, where most recreational facilities are located, is the broad green valley of the North Saskatchewan River, running diagonally northeast–southwest through the city center. The downtown area lies just north of the river, between 95th and 109th streets.

① Start exploring downtown Edmonton from the top: at **Vista 33,** the 33rd floor of the **Alberta Government Telephone** (AGT) corporate headquarters. It's not the tallest building in town (that honor goes to ManuLife Place at 34 stories), but it's high enough for you to appreciate the North Saskatchewan River and to overlook 4,000 square kilometers (2,500 square miles) of (mostly flat) Alberta countryside. In addition to the view, Vista 33 includes the **Telecommunications Museum,** which traces the history of the telephone. *10020 100th St., tel. 403/493–3333. Admission: $1 adults and children, senior citizens and preschoolers free. Open weekdays, 10–4.*

Walk north on 100th Street and turn right on Jasper beside the Hotel Macdonald, a grand old railroad hotel that had been closed since 1983 for major renovations but reopened in mid-**②** 1991. Walk two blocks to the **Edmonton Convention Centre** (9797 Jasper Ave., tel. 403/421–9797), a most unconventional building filled with surprises. On street level the building houses the **Edmonton Tourism Information Centre** (*see* Important Addresses and Numbers, *above*), a repository of useful brochures and advice. It's all literally downhill from here, since the Centre has been built onto a slope with various terraced levels accessed by glass-enclosed escalators with great views of the North Saskatchewan River valley. On the Pedway Level check out the **Canadian Country Music Hall of Honor,** actually a wall filled with plaques memorializing good old boys like Hank Snow, Wilf Carter, and Orval "The Canadian Plowboy" Prophet.

Return to 99th Street and turn north to the **Civic Centre,** a six-block area that incorporates many of Edmonton's major **③** institutions; Civic Centre structures surround **Sir Winston Churchill Square.** The largest theater complex in Canada, the **Citadel Theatre** (*see* The Arts and Nightlife, *below*) houses five different venues (plus workshops and classrooms) and an indoor garden with waterfall. Across 99th Street the **Edmonton Public Library** (7 Sir Winston Churchill Sq., tel. 403/423–2331) augments books and art exhibits with a lively round of activities in the Children's Art Department.

As you cross 102nd Avenue, glance east at **Chinatown Gate,** a symbol of friendship between Edmonton and sister city Harbin, China; it spans the portal to Edmonton's meager Chinatown. A new city hall was recently constructed across the square from the **Edmonton Art Gallery,** site of more than 30 yearly exhibits of classical and contemporary art from Canada and the rest of the world. *2 Sir Winston Churchill Sq., tel.*

Downtown Edmonton

Alberta Government
Centre, **8**

Alberta Legislature
Building, **9**

The Bay, **7**

Eaton Centre, **5**

Edmonton Convention
Centre, **2**

Edmonton Centre, **4**

ManuLife Place
and City Centre
Building, **6**

Sir Winston Churchill
Square, **3**

Vista 33, **1**

403/422–6223. Admission: $3 adults, $1.50 senior citizens and youths, children 12 and under free. Open Mon.–Wed. 10:30–5, Thurs. and Fri. 10:30–8, weekends and holidays 11–5; free Thurs. after 4.

Directly west of Churchill Square begins a maze of multilevel shopping malls, department stores, cinemas, and office buildings—all climatically controlled and interconnected by a network of tunnels and second-floor pedways. Cross 100th Street **4 5** to enter **Edmonton Centre;** head west to **Eaton Centre,** with a miniature golf course in the middle of the mall; south of 102nd **6** Avenue are the shops of **ManuLife Place and City Centre Building;** and on 102nd Street you'll find the domain of one of Can- **7** ada's most powerful institutions, **The Bay,** contemporary retail descendant of the Hudson's Bay Company (*see* Shopping, *below*).

Time Out   For a change of scenery, exit briefly to **Boardwalk Market** (102nd Ave. and 103rd St., tel. 403/424–5570). The bright and airy renovated historic block encompasses an indoor-outdoor market with everything from Mongolian beef to steamed clams and pastries, all accompanied by a lively assemblage of street entertainers.

Emerging from The Bay on Jasper Avenue, enter the LRT station at 103rd or 104th Street for the ride to Grandin Station **8** and the seat of the Alberta government. The **Alberta Government Centre** (109th St. and 97th Ave.) encompasses several hectares of carefully manicured gardens and fountains highlighted by the Government Greenhouse (tel. 403/427–7445). **9** The **Alberta Legislature Building** is a stately 1912 Edwardian structure overlooking the river on the site of an early trading post. Frequent free tours of the building help to explain the intricacies of the Albertan and Canadian systems of government. *109th St. and 97th Ave., tel. 403/427–7362. Admission and tours free. Open May–Sept., weekdays 9–8:30, weekends 9–4:30.*

Other Points of Interest

The **Muttart Conservatory** is one of the most important botanical facilities in North America. Separate greenhouses each contain flora of a different climate: arid, tropical, temperate. A show pavilion features special seasonal floral displays. *9626 96A St., tel. 403/496–8755. Admission: $4 adults, $3 senior citizens and youths 13–18, $2 children. Open Sun.–Wed. 11–9, Thurs.–Sat. 11–6.*

The **Old Strathcona Historic Area** (the area surrounding 104th Street and 82nd Avenue) is a district of restored houses and shops built mainly when Strathcona Town amalgamated with Edmonton, in 1912. The low buildings and wide streets have a decidedly Old West air, and Old Strathcona is a good place to get out and wander. For a more determined exploration, pick up a walking tour map at the Old Strathcona Foundation. *8331 104th St., tel. 403/433–5866. Open weekdays 8:30–4:30.*

The **Provincial Museum of Alberta** hosts exhibits concerning paleontology, geological evolution, native crafts and life, and pioneer settlement. Displays of Canadian wildlife in near-natural settings are especially informative. *12845 102nd Ave., tel.*

403/453–9100. Admission: $3 adults, $1 children 7–17, $7 families. Open May–Sept., daily 9–8; rest of the year, Tues.–Sun. 9–5.

The **Edmonton Space and Science Centre** explores the heavens with a stunning variety of high-tech techniques. Standing exhibits and a fascinating science shop are always of interest, but the star attractions include laser-light concerts and IMAX films of an appropriately celestial nature. *11211 142nd St., tel. 403/451–7722. Admission: $5 adults, $3 children 4–12, $17 families; IMAX $7 adults, $4.50 children, $20 families. Combination tickets: $10.25 adults, $6.25 children, $29 families. Senior citizens 65 years and older get 50% off Tues. 10–6. Open June–Sept., Sun.–Thurs. 10–10; weekends 10–11; Oct.–May, Tues.–Thurs. 10–10; Sun. 10–10; closed Mon., Fri., Sat.*

Fort Edmonton Park is home to an authentic re-creation of several periods in Edmonton history. There is a fur press, blacksmith shop, saloon, and jail along 1885 Street; photo studios and a firehouse on 1905 Street; and relatively modern conveniences on 1920 Street. Horse wagon, streetcar, stagecoach, and pony rides are available; a farmers' market operates on summer Sundays. *Whitemud and Fox Drs., tel. 403/435–0755. Admission: $4.75 adults, $4.50 senior citizens and youths 13–17, $3 children 12 and under, $17.50 families. Open mid-May–June, weekdays 9:30–4, weekends 10–6; July–early Sept., daily 10–6; early Sept.–mid-Oct., Sun. and holidays 11–5; closed mid-Oct.–mid-May.*

West Edmonton Mall, acclaimed by the *Guinness Book of World Records* as the world's largest mall, is Edmonton's preeminent attraction. Its sheer magnitude and variety transform it from a mere shopping center to an indoor city with high-rent districts, blue-collar strips, and hidden byways waiting to be discovered. The credentials shout for themselves. There are 800 stores, including 11 major department stores, 19 movie theaters, and 110 places to eat, but the mall also contains an amusement park; an ice-skating rink; a replica of Columbus's ship the *Santa Maria;* an 18-hole miniature-golf course; the Deep Sea Adventure submarine ride and dolphin show; the five-acre World Waterpark water amusement park; a luxury hotel (*see* Lodging, *below*); auto dealerships; a playhouse; a bingo parlor; a chapel; and casino. If you don't feel like walking the Mall, rent an electric scooter or hitch a ride on a rickshaw. *8770 170th St., tel. 403/444–5200. Admission: Amusement Park, day pass $19.95 adults, $9 senior citizens, $15.95 children under 46 inches, $49.95 families of up to 4, individual ride tickets 95¢ with rides costing 1–7 tickets. World Waterpark, day pass $18.95 adults, $15.95 senior citizens, $7.95 children 3–10, $49.95 families of up to 5. Deep Sea Adventure, $11.50 adults, 6.50 senior citizens and children 3–10, $36.95 families. Open mid-June–early Sept., Mon.–Sat. 10–10, Sun. 11–7; early Sept.–mid-June, Mon.–Thurs. noon–7, Fri. and Sat. 10–9.*

What to See and Do with Children

Edmonton Space and Science Centre (*see* Other Points of Interest, *above*).

Fort Edmonton Park (*see* Other Points of Interest, *above*).

Old Strathcona Model and Toy Museum (8603 104th St., tel. 403/433–4512) features playthings from the past.

Valley Zoo (134th St. and Buena Vista Rd., tel. 403/496–6911) is a small but imaginative zoo in riverside Laurier Park that uses well-known storybook settings with exotic species.

William Hawrelak Park (off Groat Rd., just south of North Saskatchewan River, tel. 403/428–3559) invites children only—or adults in their company—to fish in this rainbow trout–stocked pond. Park includes paddleboats and adventure playground.

West Edmonton Mall (*see* Other Points of Interest, *above*).

Whitemud Drive Amusement Park (7411 51st Ave., tel. 403/465–1190) features go-carts, bumper-boats, miniature golf, and batting cages.

Wild Waters Waterslide Park (21515 103rd Ave., tel. 403/447–4476) offers lots of wet fun on the western edge of the city.

Shopping

Malls and Shopping Districts In the heart of **downtown,** between 100th and 103rd streets, is a complex of shopping centers (Eaton Centre, 120 stores; ManuLife Place, 65 stores; Edmonton Centre, 140 stores) and department stores (The Bay, Eaton's, Woodward's) connected by tunnels or second-level pedways. **West Edmonton Mall** (87th Ave. and 170th St.; *see* Other Points of Interest, *above*) has 800 retail establishments, including such department stores as Sears, The Bay, Eaton's, Woodward's, Zeller's, Ikea (furniture), and Canadian Tire. **Strathcona Square** (8150 105th St., tel. 403/424–6060) in the Old Strathcona Town (*see* Other Points of Interest, *above*) 1913-era post office has been converted into a cheerful market filled with restaurants and enticing boutiques. **High Street/124th Street** (along 124th and 125th streets between 102nd and 109th avenues) is an outdoor shopping area full of boutiques, bistros, bookstores, and galleries.

Sports

Participant Sports
Bicycling and Jogging The North Saskatchewan River valley is the longest stretch of urban parkland in Canada. For information about jogging and cycling trails call the **River Valley Outdoor Centre** (10125 97th Ave., Edmonton, tel. 403/428–3033).

Health and Fitness Clubs The **Kinsmen Sports Centre** (9100 Walterdale Rd., Edmonton, tel. 403/428–5350) and **Mill Woods Recreation Centre** (7207 28th Ave., Edmonton, tel. 403/428–2888) have swimming pools and a variety of facilities for the entire family.

Spectator Sports
Hockey The **Edmonton Oilers** play National Hockey League hockey October–April at the **Northlands Coliseum** (118th Ave. and 74th St., Edmonton, tel. 403/471–2191).

Horse Racing **Northlands Park** (112th Ave. and 74th St., Edmonton, tel. 403/471–7378) hosts harness racing from early March to mid-May and from mid-September through November. Thoroughbred racing occupies the summer months, mid-May through early September.

Dining and Lodging

For price categories, *see* Winnipeg Dining and Lodging, *above*.

Dining **La Boheme.** Resting on the historic east-side Gibbard Block is this fittingly splendid restaurant that presents classic French cuisine, prepared with invention and served with solicitous care. The setting features Edwardian pressed-tin ceilings and a French provincial fireplace surrounded by Voltaire chairs. Specialties include lamb sausages, pâté maison, and daily concoctions of fresh fish. *6427 112th Ave., tel. 403/474–5693. Reservations advised. Jacket advised. AE, MC, V. Very Expensive.*

★ **Unheardof Dining Lounge.** Hardly "unheard of" any longer, this is an extremely popular restaurant in an antiques-filled old house. The seven-course prix-fixe dinner changes weekly but is likely to feature game in autumn, poultry or beef the rest of the year. Dinners begin with a light pâté and are punctuated by surprising salads and refreshing sorbets. Desserts, especially the Danish cream-cheese cheesecake, are light and delicious. *9602 82nd Ave., tel. 403/432–0480. Reservations required. Jacket advised. AE, MC, V. Closed lunch Tues.–Sat. Very Expensive.*

Bistro Praha. Table lamps and paintings of Praha (Prague) street scenes make this European-style café feel as homey as Grandma's living room. Background music is classical, clientele mainly urban young professional. The menu features Eastern European favorites such as cabbage soup and Wiener schnitzel. A rich selection of desserts and a choice from 12 brands of tea make this place a perfect stop for snacks. *10168 100A St. at Jasper Ave., tel. 403/424–4218. No reservations. Dress: casual. AE, DC, MC, V. Expensive.*

La Spiga. Admirable Northern Italian cuisine is served in a flower-filled 1913 home that feels more like Montréal than the western plains. Menu highlights include rack of lamb with grappa, breast of chicken with fresh tomato, and various renditions of veal. Portions are large and accompanied by fettuccine; the wine list is long. *10122 125 St., at 102nd Ave., tel. 403/482–3100. Reservations advised. Jacket advised. AE, MC, V. Closed lunch and Sun. Expensive.*

Bourbon Street. This is actually an assemblage of moderately priced restaurants situated around a cul-de-sac on the main floor of West Edmonton Mall. "Exterior" decor features New Orleans street lamps and wrought-iron balconies. **Café Orleans** serves Cajun/Creole dishes such as jambalaya and oysters. **Sherlock Holmes** is an English pub with imported draft beer and dishes like Mrs. Hudson's Home Made Pies. **Albert's** has deli fare including the Montréal favorite, smoked meat. Other spots include **Zambelli's Pizza & Steak House, Pacific Fish Co.** (*see below*), and, for belly-up-to-the-bar drinking, the **Bourbon Street Saloon.** *West Edmonton Mall, 8770 170th St., Entrance 6. No reservations. Dress: casual. AE, MC, V. Moderate.*

Pacific Fish Company. Three locations satisfy landlocked Edmonton's appetite for fresh seafood with daily fly-ins. Order oysters Rockefeller and whiskey shrimp as appetizers, and anything charbroiled over mesquite turns out fine. Decor varies slightly, but count on the deck flooring, corrugated walls, and nets dangling overhead. *10020 101A Ave., tel. 403/422–0282; Argyll Plaza, 6258 99th St., tel. 403/437–7472; West Edmonton Mall, Bourbon St., Entrance 6, tel. 403/444–1905. Reservations advised. Dress: casual. AE, MC, V. Moderate.*

★ **Chianti Café.** This extremely popular spot occupies part of the main floor of Strathcona Square, a converted post office in the lively Old Strathcona District. A mostly young crowd gathers for square meals featuring tasty shellfish appetizers, more than 20 varieties of pasta, a couple dozen veal dishes, and a discriminating selection of desserts. Be prepared to wait for seating on weekend evenings. *10501 82nd Ave., tel. 403/439–9829. No reservations. Dress: casual. AE, DC, MC, V. Inexpensive.*

Mongolian Food Experience. The "experience" is selecting from a vast buffet of raw meat (lamb, beef, turkey), vegetables (mushrooms, scallions, sprouts, cabbage), and exotic sauces and then having the chef barbecue it for you. Non-"experience" dishes, such as Szechuan beef, lemon chicken, and moo shoo pork, are also available. Decor is bright and unpretentious. *10160 100A St., tel. 403/426–6806; 12520 102nd Ave., tel. 403/452–7138. Reservations advised. Dress: casual. AE, MC, V. Inexpensive.*

Vi's. In summer, this old house has outdoor seating on a deck overlooking the river; in winter, tables are warmed by a blazing fire. All year the menu emphasizes the basics: hearty soups, fresh salads, extravagant sandwiches, and desserts—with special mention for chocolate pecan pie. Try Vi's for Sunday brunch. *9712 111th St., tel. 403/482–6402. No reservations. Dress: casual. AE, MC, V. Inexpensive.*

Lodging **Edmonton Hilton.** Formerly the Four Seasons, and a Hilton
★ International property since 1988, this financial-district luxury high rise connects by second-level passageways to five major office buildings and two shopping centers. Rooms—all with bay windows and blue-and-gray color schemes—are decorated with sophistication and include marble tabletops, walnut furniture, and accents of brass. Mezzanine-level Patisserie serves a bargain Loonie Breakfast (coffee and muffin for a buck), and The Rose and Crown is an authentic English pub, perfect for throwing darts and drinking draft beers. *10235 101st St., T5J 3E9, tel. 403/428–7111 or 800/268–9275. 312 rooms. Facilities: 4 restaurants, 2 lounges, indoor pool, whirlpool, saunas, access to exercise room and squash and racquetball courts, nonsmoking floors. AE, DC, MC, V. Very Expensive.*

Cherrywood Inn. The renovated property on a quiet street a few blocks from downtown features a lobby and fair-size guest rooms with old-style flair: richly appointed cherry-wood furniture and a warm, cozy ambience. Some rooms have balconies, and almost all have MovieBars—a unit that includes TV, VCR, minibar, and snacks. A selection of videotapes is for rent in the lobby. Room rates include breakfast buffet. *10010 104th St., T5J 0Z1, tel. 403/423–2450. 138 rooms. Facilities: restaurant, lounge, indoor pool, sauna, exercise room, nonsmoking floors. AE, DC, MC, V. Expensive.*

★ **Edmonton House.** The building's cylindrical design creates oddly shaped but large and comfortable one- and two-bedroom, and executive suites. All units have balconies with views of the skyline or river valley, and kitchens are fully equipped (down to a toaster). A small mezzanine-level convenience store supplies basic essentials. Weekend and long-term rates are available. *10205 100th Ave., T5J 4B5, tel. 403/424–5555 or 800/661–6562. 293 suites. Facilities: restaurant, lounge, underground parking, complimentary shuttle service to West Edmonton Mall, indoor pool, sauna, fitness center, games room, nonsmoking floors. AE, DC, MC, V. Expensive.*

Fantasyland Hotel & Resort. This important component of massive West Edmonton Mall (*see* Other Points of Interest, *above*) has regular and theme rooms; the latter include Victorian coach rooms, where guests sleep in open carriages; Roman rooms, with classic round beds; truck rooms, where the bed is the back of a pickup; and Polynesian rooms, with catamaran beds and waterfalls. All theme rooms have Jacuzzis, and nontheme quarters are comfortable and tidy. *17700 87th Ave., T5T 4V4, tel. 403/444–3000 or 800/661–6454. 334 rooms, 125 theme rooms. Facilities: 2 restaurants, lounge, shopping mall with 800 shops, 5-acre water park, miniature golf course, indoor amusement park. AE, DC, MC, V. Expensive.*

Inn on 7th. Edmonton shorthand provides the name for this cheerful property on 107th Street. The foliage-filled lobby features Paul Bunyan–size easy chairs. A former Holiday Inn now run by the Courtyard Inn chain, this hotel caters to tourists, government employees, and Pacific Coast League baseball teams who play in nearby John Ducey Park. Rooms are comfortably modern; the location is convenient but not stressful. *10001 107th St., T5J 1J1, tel. 403/429–2861 or 800/661–7327. 180 rooms. Facilities: restaurant, lounge, deli, nonsmoking floors. AE, DC, MC, V. Expensive.*

Westin Hotel. The stunning, brown block structure in the heart of downtown has large, comfortable rooms that are tastefully decorated with attractive artwork. The atrium lobby, with a decorative mobile, trees, and plants, conveys comfort and luxury; beige-and-pastel rooms, in keeping with the hotel's outward appearance, are equally sophisticated, down to the Caswell and Massey toiletries. The experienced staff speaks a total of 29 languages. Some of the finest food in the downtown area can be found in The Carvery. *10135 100th St., T5J 0Z1, tel. 403/426–3636 or 800/228–3000. 420 rooms. Facilities: 2 restaurants, 2 lounges, indoor pool, sauna, whirlpool, nonsmoking floors. AE, DC, MC, V. Expensive.*

West Harvest Inn. This clean, modern three-story hotel catering to families is on the western edge of town and is only five minutes away from West Edmonton Mall. Rooms in the new wing are slightly larger and more expensive than those in the older wing, but all are comfortable. Grainfield's family restaurant is located on the premises; Xian Chinese restaurant is next door. *17803 Stony Plain Rd. (Rte. 16), T5S 1B4, tel. 403/484–8000 or 800/661–6993. 162 rooms. Facilities: restaurant, lounge. AE, MC, V. Moderate.*

Relax Inn. Canada's home-grown budget chain operates two clean and functional motels (plus the spiffier, moderately priced Relax Inn–Edmonton International Airport). Relax Inn–West is located on the edge of town, not far from West Edmonton Mall; Relax Inn–South is on the road to the airport. *18320 Stony Plain Rd., T5S 1A7, tel. 403/483–6031 or 800/661–9563, 227 rooms including nonsmoking rooms. 10320 45th Ave. S, T6H 5K3, tel. 403/436–9770, 222 rooms including nonsmoking rooms. Facilities: restaurant, lounge, indoor pool, whirlpool. AE, DC, MC, V. Inexpensive.*

YMCA of Edmonton. This Y is in an outstanding location: in the heart of downtown adjacent to Edmonton Centre shopping mall. Rooms are small and spare but carpeted and cheerfully furnished. Singles and couples are invited to stay for $25–$29 a night. All facilities are available to overnight guests. *10030 102A Ave., T5J 0G5, tel. 403/421–9622. 113 rooms, 30 with bath. Facilities: cafeteria, indoor pool, fitness center, weight room, running track, racquetball courts. MC, V. Inexpensive.*

The Arts and Nightlife

Tickets for events in Edmonton are available from Ticketmaster located in Edmonton Centre, Citadel Theatre box office, Champions in West Edmonton Mall, and Sears stores, or call 403/451–8000 to telecharge tickets to most events.

The Arts
Theater

Edmonton has 13 professional theater companies. The paramount facility is the glass-clad downtown **Citadel Theatre Complex** (99th St. and 101A Ave., Edmonton, tel. 403/425–1820), where four theaters mingle esoteric works and classics. **Northern Light Theater** (Kaasa Theatre, Jubilee Auditorium, 118th Ave. and 74th St., Edmonton, tel. 403/471–1586) takes chances that usually succeed.

Music and Dance

The **Edmonton Opera** (tel. 403/424–4040), **Edmonton Symphony Orchestra** (tel. 403/428–1414), and **Alberta Ballet Company** (tel. 403/428–6839) all perform in the **Northern Alberta Jubilee Auditorium** at the University of Alberta (87th Ave. and 114th St., Edmonton, tel. 403/427–9622).

Film

Edmonton's **Metro Cinema** (NFB Theatre, Canada Place, 9700 Jasper Ave., Edmonton, tel. 403/425–9212) presents classics, imports, and brave new films on weekend nights. The **Edmonton Film Society** screens an ambitious program at a theater in the **Provincial Museum of Alberta** (12845 102nd Ave., Edmonton, tel. 403/427–1730). The **Princess Theatre** (10337 Whyte Ave., Edmonton, tel. 403/433–5785), an old-time movie house in Old Strathcona district, presents revivals, experiments, and foreign films.

Nightlife
Bars and Clubs

The **Rose & Crown** English-style pub in the Edmonton Hilton (10235 101st St., Edmonton, tel. 403/428–7111) is a popular downtown gathering place with dart boards and a huge selection of beers. **Elephant & Castle Pubs** are pleasant watering holes in downtown Edmonton's Eaton Centre (tel. 403/424–4555) and the West Edmonton Mall (tel. 403/444–3555).

Casinos

Roulette, blackjack, and wheel of fortune action usually takes place in Edmonton between noon and midnight daily except Sunday at the **Casino ABS Downtown** (10161 112th St., Edmonton, tel. 403/428–6679), **Casino ABS South** (7055 Argyll Rd., Edmonton, tel. 403/466–0199), and the **Palace Casino** at the West Edmonton Mall (tel. 403/444–1246).

Comedy

Edmonton boasts two branches of **Yuk Yuk's** (7103 78th Ave., tel. 403/466–2131).

Music

The **Sidetrack Cafe** (10333 112th St., Edmonton, tel. 403/421–1326) features top-name entertainers, big-screen telecasts of sports events, Variety Night on Sunday, and the Monday-night Comedy Bowl. **Yardbird Suite** (10203 86th Ave., Edmonton, tel. 403/432–0428) is Edmonton's premier jazz showcase. **Club Malibu** (10310 85th Ave., Edmonton, tel. 403/432–7300) blasts out Top-40 hits in a converted armory. **Goose Loonies** (9933 Argyll Rd., Edmonton, tel. 403/438–5571) has two levels of lights, lasers, and loudness. **Cook County Saloon** (8010 103rd St., Edmonton, tel. 403/432–0177) has mellow honky-tonk ambience and country-and-western music.

9 Province of Ontario

David E. Scott

*David E. Scott is
author of the
best-selling* The
Ontario Getaway
Guidebook, A
Taste of Ontario
Country Inns,
Ontario Place
Names, *and*
Ontario for Free.

Ontario is an Iroquoian word variously interpreted as: beautiful lake, beautiful water, or rocks standing high beside the water (the last an apparent reference to Niagara Falls). Ontario is Canada's second-largest province—from east to west the traveler will cross 2,080 kilometers (1,300 miles) and one time zone. However, only 10 million people live in this vast area, and 90% of them are within a narrow strip just north of the U.S. border.

Ontario is Canada's most urbanized province; half of its population lives in four cities whose boundaries have spread to such an extent that they almost adjoin. Metropolitan Toronto has more than 2 million people. To the east, Oshawa has 125,000 people and heavily populated suburbs. South and west of Toronto are Hamilton with 450,000 people and St. Catharines with 125,000. Half of Ontario's population is British, but the province contains the largest settlement of Finns outside Finland, at Thunder Bay. Toronto has half a million Italians, the largest Chinese community in Canada, and the biggest Portuguese colony in North America.

The towns and cities of northern Ontario are strung along the railway lines that brought them into being. And the discovery of immense deposits of gold, silver, uranium, and other minerals by railway construction gangs sparked mining booms that established communities such as Sudbury, Cobalt, and Kirkland Lake, which continue to owe their existence to mining.

Ontario has the most varied landscape of any Canadian province. The most conspicuous topographical feature is the Niagara Escarpment, which runs from Niagara to Tobermory at the tip of the Bruce Peninsula in Lake Huron. The northern 90% of Ontario is covered by the Canadian Shield, worn-down mountain ranges of the world's oldest rock, reaching only 682 meters (2,183 feet) above sea level at their highest point. On James Bay January temperatures range from 14°C to 28°C (7°F to 15°F).

East of Hamilton toward Niagara Falls is a narrow strip along the south shore of Lake Ontario in a partial rain shadow of the Niagara Escarpment. The climate, moderated in winter by Lakes Ontario and Erie, allows the growing of tender fruits and grapes, making it Canada's largest wine-producing area.

You could spend a lifetime exploring this enormous province and still not see it all. But by using three cities—Ottawa, Sault Ste. Marie, and Toronto—as bases for one- and two-day excursions, you can see all the major sights and some special little corners that even many Ontarians don't know about.

Essential Information

Important Addresses and Numbers

**Tourist
Information
*Ontario***
Ontario has a wealth of excellent and free tourist information. From within Canada or the continental United States (except Yukon, Northwest Territories, and Alaska) dial 800/668–2746, 8–8 daily, mid-May–Labor Day, and 8–4:30 weekdays the rest of the year. Or write to the **Ministry of Tourism and Recreation** (77 Bloor St. W, Toronto, Ont. M7A 2R9). When requesting information, specify your areas of interest: antiquing, boating,

camping, fishing, dining, hiking, etc. There is literature available on the entire province. Free booklets on accommodations, camping, country inns, marinas, cruises, antiques markets, and more can all be obtained.

This same information is also available at Travel Information Centers at every major entry point by road and at dozens of Regional Travel Information Centers province-wide.

Hamilton   For information on Hamilton, contact the **Greater Hamilton, Regional Municipality of Hamilton–Wentworth** (1 James St. S, 3rd floor, Hamilton, Ont. L8P 4R5, tel. 416/546–4222 or 800/263–8590).

Kingston   Contact the **Kingston District Chamber of Commerce** (209 Wellington St., Kingston, Ont. K7K 2Y6, tel. 613/548–4453).

Kitchener   Contact the **Kitchener Chamber of Commerce** (Box 2367, 67 King St. E, Kitchener, Ont. N2H 6L4, tel. 519/742–4760).

Midland   Contact **Midland Chamber of Commerce** (Box 158, Midland, Ont. L4R 4K8, tel. 705/526–7884).

Niagara Falls   Contact **Niagara Falls, Canada Visitor and Convention Bureau** (4673 Ontario Ave., Niagara Falls, Ont. L2E 3R1, tel. 416/356–6061).

Ottawa   For information on Ottawa, contact **Ottawa Tourism and Convention Authority** (Ottawa–Carleton Centre, 2nd floor, 111 Lisgar St., Ottawa, Ont. K2P 2L7, tel. 613/237–5150 or 800/465–1867).

Peterborough   Contact **Greater Peterborough Chamber of Commerce** (135 George St. N, Peterborough, Ont. K9J 3G6, tel. 705/748–9771).

Sault Ste. Marie   Contact **Hospitality & Travel** (99 Foster Dr., 3rd floor, Sault Ste. Marie, Ont. P6A 5X6, tel. 705/759–5432).

Windsor   Contact **Convention and Visitors Bureau of Windsor, Essex County, and Pelee Island** (80 Chatham St. E, Windsor, Ont. N9A 2W1, tel. 519/255–6530).

Emergencies   Dial 911 for **police, fire,** or **ambulance** anywhere in Ontario. The main hospitals in Ottawa are **Ottawa General Hospital** (tel. 613/737–7777) and **Ottawa Civic Hospital** (tel. 613/761–4000). **Shoppers Drug Mart** (1460 Merivale Rd., tel. 613/224–7270) is open 24 hours a day. The main hospitals in Sault Ste. Marie are **General Hospital** (tel. 705/759–3333) and **Plummer Memorial Public Hospital** (tel. 705/759–3800). Also available for emergency service is **Group Health Centre** (240 McNabb St., tel. 705/759–1234). There are no 24-hour pharmacies in Sault Ste. Marie, but **Shoppers Drug Mart** (tel. 705/949–2143) in the Cambrian Mall is open seven days a week.

Arriving and Departing by Plane

Airports and   Toronto, the area's major city, is served by most major inter-
Airlines   national airlines. *See* Chapter 2 for details.

Ottawa International Airport (tel. 613/998–3151), 18 kilometers (12 miles) from downtown, is served by **Air Canada** (tel. 800/776–3000), **First Air** (tel. 800/468–8292), **City Express** (tel. 800/387–2664), **Air France** (tel. 800/237–2747), **Canadian Airlines** (tel. 800/426–7000), **KLM** (tel. 800/777–5553), **Lufthansa** (tel. 800/645–3880), **Intair** (tel. 613/233–6062), **USAir** (tel.

800/428–4322), and **Nation Air** (tel. 613/737–4202). Toll-free numbers apply only within the 613 area code.

Arriving and Departing by Car, Train, and Bus

By Car The **Macdonald–Cartier Freeway,** known as Highway 401, is Ontario's major highway link. It runs from Windsor in the southwest through Toronto, along the north shore of Lake Ontario, and along the north shore of the St. Lawrence River to the Québec border west of Montréal. The **Trans-Canada Highway** follows the west bank of the Ottawa River from Montréal to Ottawa and on to North Bay. From North Bay to Nipigon at the northern tip of Lake Superior, there are two Trans-Canada highways, and from just west of Thunder Bay to Kenora, near the Manitoba border, another two. For 24-hour road condition information anywhere in Ontario, call 416/235–1110 or 800/268–0637.

By Train Ontario is served by cross-Canada **Via Rail** (tel. 800/361–1235 outside Toronto, Kingston, London, Windsor, Hamilton; within those cities check local listings) service and connects with **Amtrak** (tel. 800/872–7245) service at Windsor (Detroit) and Fort Erie (Buffalo). Via Rail operates frequent trains on the Windsor–London–Toronto–Kingston–Montréal corridor and the Ottawa rail station at the southeastern end of town (200 Tremblay Rd., tel. 613/238–8289; in Canada, 800/361–5390).

By Bus **Voyageur Colonial Bus Lines** (265 Catherine St. tel. 613/238–5900) offers frequent service from Montréal and Toronto to Ottawa, including some express buses.

Getting Around

By Taxi Major cab companies such as **Blue Line** (tel. 613/238–1111) and **Diamond** (tel. 613/235–1821) operate in and around Ottawa.

By Bus **OC Transpo** serves the metropolitan region of Ottawa–Carleton on the Ontario side of the Ottawa River. It operates buses on city streets and on the Transitway, a system of bus-only roads. All bus routes in downtown Ottawa meet at the Rideau Centre (Rideau St. between Nicholas and Sussex and the Mackenzie King Bridge). From mid-June to September 2, from 9 AM to 6 PM, a Visipass is available on a loop route through Ottawa and Hull that passes 22 of the major tourist attractions in both cities. You can get on and off the loop as many times as you wish for $3 a day, per person (tel. 613/741–4390).

By Car A valid driver's license from any country is good in Ontario for up to three months. Ontario is a no-fault province, and minimum liability insurance is $200,000. If you're driving across the Ontario border, either bring the policy or the vehicle registration forms and a free Canadian Non-Resident Insurance Card from your insurance agent. If you're driving a borrowed car, also bring a letter of permission signed by the owner. Driving motorized vehicles (including boats, all-terrain vehicles, and motor bikes) while impaired by alcohol is taken seriously in Ontario and results in heavy fines or imprisonment, or both. You can be convicted for refusing to take a breathalyzer test. Radar warning devices are not permitted in Ontario even if they are turned off and are just in transit to other provinces. Police can seize them on the spot, and heavy fines may be imposed. Seat belts must be worn by adults and children weighing more than 18 kg (40 lb), if the car is designed with them; infants from birth to 9 kg (20 lb) must travel in a rear-facing child restraint system; children 9–18 kg (20–40 lb) must travel in a safety seat.

Both studded tires and window coatings that do not allow a clear view of the vehicle interior are forbidden in Ontario. Right turns on red lights are permitted unless otherwise noted.

Guided Tours

Ottawa City Tours The **Gray Line** (tel. 613/748–4426) operates frequent, two-hour, 50-kilometer (31-mile) orientation tours from mid-April through October. **Picadilly Bus Tours** (tel. 613/235–7674) has a regular schedule of 1¾-hour tours in double-decker London buses to Ottawa's major sites, May through mid-October.

Boat Tours **Paul's Boat Lines Limited** (office, tel. 613/225–6781; boat dock, tel. 613/235–8409) offers seven 75-minute cruises daily on the Rideau Canal and four 90-minute cruises daily on the Ottawa River from mid-May to mid-October. Canal boats dock across from the National Arts Centre; river cruise boats dock at the Bytown Museum at the foot of the Ottawa Locks on the Rideau Canal. **Ottawa Riverboat Company** (tel. 613/562–4888) operates two-hour sightseeing tours on the Ottawa River from May through October. The SS *Bytown Pumper* (tel. 613/737–6601) is a wood-burning steamboat that offers tours on the Rideau River from mid-May to mid-October. It has an 1897 engine in a 1903 hull. Cruises depart daily at 10, noon, 2, and 4 from Hog's Back Marina Park; dinner cruises are available (call ahead because the boat is sometimes chartered for the evening).

Niagara Falls City Tours **Double Deck Tours** (tel. 416/295–3051) touches all the bases in its 4½- to five-hour tours in double-decker English buses, which include most of the major sights of Niagara Falls. The tours operate daily from mid-May through October. The fare of $34.90 for adults and $18.40 for children 6–12 includes GST and admissions to Table Rock Scenic Tunnels, Maid of the Mist, and a trip in the Niagara Spanish Aero Car. A shorter tour does not stop at attractions to which admission is charged, and costs $16.50 for adults and $8.50 for children. The **Niagara Parks Commission** operates People Mover System, consisting of semiarticulated air-conditioned buses, on a loop route between its public parking lot above the falls at Rapids View Terminal (well signposted) and the Niagara Spanish Aero Car parking lot about 8 kilometers (5 miles) downriver. With a day's pass (available at any booth on the system: $3 adults, $1.50 children 6–12) you can get on and off as many times as you wish at the well-marked stops along the route.

Boat Tours **Maid of the Mist Steamboat Company Ltd.** (tel. 416/358–5781) operates small cruise boats that pass so near the American and Horseshoe Falls that passengers are outfitted with hooded rain slickers. The boats sail frequently between mid-May and the third week in October. *Admission: $8.65 adults, $5 children 6–12.*

Air Tours **Niagara Helicopters Ltd.** (tel. 416/357–5672) takes you over the Giant Whirlpool, up the Niagara Gorge, and past the American Falls and then banks around the curve of the Horseshoe Falls for a never-to-be-forgotten thrill—if you can keep your eyes open! *$65 per adult, $120 per two adults, $20 children 2–12 (cost includes GST). Open daily 9 AM to half-hour after sunset.*

Sault Ste. Marie City Tours **Hiawathaland Tours** (tel. 705/759–6200) operates three city tours by double-decker bus and three wilderness tours by mini-van to Wawa, Aubrey Falls, or St. Joseph's Island from June 15 to October 15. A 75-minute evening tour is also available.

Boat Tours **Lock Tours Canada** (tel. 705/253–9850) runs two-hour excursions through the 21-foot-high Soo Locks, the 16th and final lift for ships bound for Lake Superior from the St. Lawrence River. Tours aboard the 200-passenger MV *Chief Shingwauk* or 156-passenger MV *Bon Soo* leave from the Norgoma Dock just downriver from the Holiday Inn, May 15–October 15 and up to eight times daily July 1–Labor Day. *$14 adults, $7 children 5–12, $10.50, 13–18.*

Train Tours The **Agawa Canyon Train** or the **Snow Train** (tel. 705/254-4331)—the name varies with the seasons—runs from Sault Ste. Marie to Mile 114 in summer, and to Mile 120 in winter. Trains operate daily June 5–October 15 and on Saturday and Sunday only January–March. Trains leave Sault Ste. Marie at 8 AM in summer and 8:30 AM in winter and return at 5 PM. *$42.75 adults, $21.40 children.*

The **Choo-Choo Steam Train Company** runs a 75-minute excursion along the Gatineau River between Hull and Wakefield, in Quebec (*see* Guided Tours in Chapter 10).

Exploring Ontario

Highlights for First-time Visitors

Canada's best bird/butterfly-watching, Tour 4: Fort Erie-Windsor
Changing of the Guard in front of the Parliament Buildings, Tour 1: Ottawa
Fort Wellington, Tour 2: Ottawa–Kawartha Lakes
Hamilton's Castle, Tour 5: Niagara Falls–London
Mennonite country, Tour 5: Niagara Falls–London
Niagara's Horseshoe Falls, Tour 5: Niagara Falls–London
Old Fort Henry, Tour 2: Ottawa–Kawartha Lakes
Ontario's grand canyons, Tour 6: Sault Ste. Marie–Thunder Bay
Polar Bear Express to the Gateway to the Arctic, Tour 8: Moosonee and Moose Factory Island
Shaw Festival, Tour 5: Niagara Falls–London
Stratford's Shakespearean Festival, Tour 5: Niagara Falls–London
Upper Canada Village, Tour 2: Ottawa–Kawartha Lakes

Tour 1: Ottawa

Numbers in the margin correspond to points of interest on the Lower Ontario Province, Downtown Ottawa, and Greater Ottawa and Hull maps.

Canadians are taught in school that it was Queen Victoria's fault their capital is inconveniently situated off the main east–west corridor along the U.S. border. But the facts are that politicians of the day were no more capable of making an unpopular

Lower Ontario Province

Ottawa River

Sturgeon Falls

North Bay

Mattawa

17

Elliot Lake

Sudbury

Lake Nipissing

ALGONQUIN PROVINCIAL PARK

Espanola

Blind River

KILLARNEY PROV. PARK

Key Harbour

60

Little Current

69

32 Parry Sound

11

Huntsville

36 Dorset

S. Baymouth

Manitoulin I.

Georgian Bay

35 Bracebridge

34 Gravenhurst

Tobermory

6

Wiarton

Penetanguishene 30

31

Midland

Orillia

33

Lake Simcoe

Petroglyp Provinc Pa

Peterborough

26

11

12

Lake Huron

Owen Sound

Saugeen R.

Barrie

29

Port Hope

Port Elgin

Kincardine

Goderich

6

400

401

Goderich

Elora

Elmira

Ajax

Oshawa

Toronto

Niagara-on-the-Lake

St.

Catharines

65

Niaga Falls

49

St. Jacobs 69

Waterloo

Kitchener 68

Hamilton

66

Queen Elizabeth Way

Stratford

70

Brantford

67

Welland 39

37 Fort Erie

403

Jarvis

38 Port Colborne

London 71

41

St. Thomas

40 Port Dover

402

Sarnia

42 Port Stanley

401

Chatham

Lake St. Clair

Windsor

48

Southwestern Ontario Heritage Village

46 Leamington

45 Jack Miner's Bird Sanctuary

47 Amherstburg

43 Point Pelee National Park

44 Pelee Island

Lake Erie

Erie

decision than many who have followed them. They dithered
from 1841 to 1857 trying to decide among five possible sites,
including Québec City, Montréal, Cobourg, Kingston, and
Ottawa. In 1857 they passed the buck to Buckingham Palace,
and Queen Victoria got them off the hook.

She chose Ottawa for five reasons, all valid at the time: The site
was politically acceptable to both Canada east and Canada
west. It was also centrally located, reassuringly remote from
the hostile United States, and industrially prosperous. And it
had a naturally beautiful setting at the confluence of the
Ottawa and Rideau rivers.

Three decades earlier, when Colonel John By and his Royal
Engineers arrived to build a canal from Ottawa to Kingston,
there were only a few scattered settlers at what is now Ottawa.
The waterway was to ensure a protected supply route from
Montréal to the Great Lakes in the event of a repeat of the War
of 1812 against the Americans. Between 1826 and 1832 the
canal was hacked through 200 kilometers (125 miles) of swamp,
rock, and lakes whose different levels were overcome by locks.

By established his canal headquarters at what is now Ottawa,
and the population growth was immediate as men arrived with
their families, seeking employment on the biggest construction
project on the continent. The settlement, then called Bytown,
grew rapidly and fast became a rowdy, rough-and-tumble back-
woods town. The Ottawa River then was used for floating timber to Montréal—each spring lumberjacks tied their rafts of

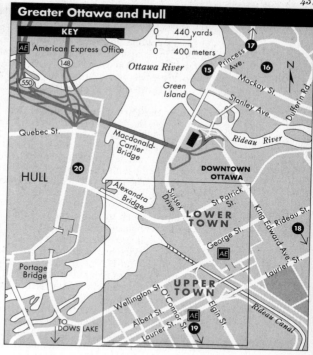

Greater Ottawa and Hull

KEY

AE American Express Office

0   440 yards
0   400 meters

Ottawa River

N

Princess Ave.

Mackay St.

Stanley Ave.

Dufferin Rd.

Green Island

Quebec St.

Macdonald-Cartier Bridge

Rideau River

HULL

20

Alexandra Bridge

DOWNTOWN OTTAWA

Sussex Drive

St Patrick St.

LOWER TOWN

George St.

King Edward Ave.

Rideau St.

18

Portage Bridge

AE

Laurier St.

UPPER TOWN

Wellington St.

O'Connor St.

Elgin St.

Rideau Canal

TO DOWS LAKE

Albert St.

Laurier St.

AE

19

timber to the shore and celebrated their release from isolated lumber camps in the taverns and brothels of Bytown.

By 1837, when its population had reached 2,400, Bytown was declared by the attorney general of Upper Canada to be a town. Government moved slowly even then, and it was not legally incorporated until 1850. Five years later, when the population had reached 10,000, Bytown became a city and was farsightedly given the name Ottawa, an Indian name meaning "a place for buying and selling."

Construction started on the Parliament Buildings in 1859. The buildings are magnificent, but their location in the mid-1850s earned Ottawa the nickname "Westminster in the Wilderness." More recently, perhaps because of their neo-Gothic towers and spires—or possibly because of legislation passed inside them— some refer to Parliament Hill as "Disneyland on the Rideau."

As early as 1899, federal politicians were concerned with more than just the grounds around the Parliament Buildings, known as "The Hill." A variety of commissions and committees and plans have become today's National Capital Commission (NCC). The NCC works with all municipalities within the 2,903-square-kilometer (1,800-square-mile) National Capital Region, which includes neighboring Hull and a big chunk of Québec, to coordinate development in the best interests of the region. The result is a profusion of beautiful parks, bicycle paths, jogging trails, and the world's longest skating rink, a 6-kilometer (4-mile) stretch of the Rideau Canal kept cleared and smooth and provided with heated huts, food concessions, and skate-sharpening and rental services.

Ottawa's population is only 308,000, but parking is at a premium. This is also a tricky city for the first-time visitor to negotiate by car: One wrong turn, it seems, and you're on one of five bridges across the Ottawa River to Hull. Therefore, much ❶ of your **Ottawa** sightseeing will be on foot.

❷ Begin at the **Parliament Buildings.** Like London's Buckingham Palace, these striking buildings will be passed by visitors moving around Ottawa whether they plan to visit them or not. What you see on The Hill is similar to what opened in 1867, but the only part not destroyed by fire in 1916 was the 1876 Library of Parliament behind the Centre Block and the northwest wing. There are three massive buildings on a promontory overlooking the Ottawa River, though none face it. The **Centre Block** is where the Senate and House of Commons, the two houses of Parliament, work to shape the laws of the land. The central **Peace Tower** houses a Memorial Chamber with an Altar of Sacrifice, which houses the names of 66,651 Canadians killed during active service in World War I and 44,895 Canadians who died in World War II. There is also a 53-bell carillon whose bells individually range from 10 pounds to 11 tons, and together weigh 60 tons. Concerts are performed by the **Dominion Carillonneur** (tel. 613/992–4793) daily from 12:30–12:45. North (toward the river) of the Centre Block and reached from it is the **Library of Parliament,** which escaped the fire of 1916 but was damaged in its own fire in 1952. A statue of a young Queen Victoria is the centerpiece of the many-sided chamber, whose walls are lined with books, many of them priceless, and carved wooden galleries restored from the 1952 fire. In front of, and to either side of, the Parliament Buildings are the **East Block** and **West Block.** The East Block has four historic rooms open to the public: the original Governor General's office restored to the period of Lord Dufferin, 1872–1878; the offices of Sir John A. Macdonald and Sir George-Étienne Cartier, Fathers of the Confederation in 1867; and the Privy Council Chamber. The West Block, originally designed to house the civil service, has been converted to offices for parliamentarians and is not open to the public. The Parliament Buildings are surrounded by 29 acres of lawns that contain statues of famous Canadians. *Tel. 613/992–4793. Open summer, daily 9–8:30; winter, daily 9– 4:30. Free 40-min. tours given in English or French. To avoid waiting in the busy summer period, visitors may make same- day reservations for tours at the white Infotent just east of the Centre Block.*

There's lots of room to stand and no charge for the colorful **Changing of the Guard ceremony** that takes place in front of the Peace Tower at 10 AM daily, June 22–August 25, weather permitting. The Ceremonial Guard brings together two of Canada's most historic regiments, the Canadian Grenadier Guards and the Governor General's Foot Guards.

Against the backdrop of the imposing Parliament Buildings, a half-hour **Sound and Light Show** highlights Canada's history. There's bleacher seating, and the shows are free. Shows are daily from early July through Labor Day, and four nights a week from early May through June and in September. In summer there are two shows daily, English first, followed by

French. Check dates and times with the Public Information Office (tel. 613/992–4793).

3 Turn right onto Wellington Street and walk past Bank Street to the **Bank of Canada,** inside which is the **Currency Museum.** The ancestors of the credit card are all here: bracelets made from elephant hair, cowrie shells, whale's teeth, and what is believed to be the world's largest coin. Here, too, of course, is the most complete collection of Canadian notes and coins. *245 Sparks St., tel. 613/782–8914. Admission free. Open May–Sept., Mon.–Sat. 10:30–5, Sun. 1–5; Sept.–May, Tues.–Sat. 10:30–5, Sun. 1–5.*

4 Turn right onto Kent Street to the **Supreme Court.** It was established in 1875, and in 1949 it became the ultimate court of appeal in the land. The nine judges sit only in Ottawa in three sessions each year in their stately art deco building. *Kent and Wellington Sts., tel. 613/995–5361. Free tours May–Aug., daily 9–5; Sept.–Apr., weekdays 9–5.*

5 At the end of Wellington Street is the **Garden of the Provinces,** which commemorates confederation with the emblems of Canada's 10 provinces and two territories. Across from the park is **6** the **National Archives of Canada** and the **National Library of Canada.** The archives, Canada's oldest cultural institution, contains more than 60 million manuscripts and government records, 1 million maps, and about 11 million photographs. The National Library collects, preserves, and promotes the published heritage of Canada and exhibits books, paintings, maps, and photographs. *395 Wellington St., tel. 613/995–5138 for archives; 613/992–9988 for library. Admission free. Open daily 9–9.*

7 Return toward Parliament Hill via **Sparks Street Pedestrian Mall,** where the automobile has been banished and browsers wander among fountains, rock gardens, sculptures, and outdoor cafés. **8** Emerging from the mall, you'll face **Confederation Square** and the **National War Memorial** honoring the 66,651 Canadian dead of World War I.

9 Adjacent to the square stands the **National Arts Centre,** a huge theater complex designed around the repetitive motif of the hexagon. The complex includes an opera hall, a theater, a studio theater, and a salon for readings and concerts. The center has its own orchestra, and touring companies offer more than 900 performances a year. Its canal-side café, **Le Cafe,** spills outside in warm weather and is popular for a meal or drink. *53 Elgin St., tel. 613/996–5051. Admission free. 30- to 40-min. tours depart from the main lobby May 1–Aug. 31, daily at noon, 1:30, and 3; Sept.–Apr., Tues., Thurs., and Sat. (Sun. to the end of Oct.).*

10 **11** **12** Ottawa's oldest building, now the **Bytown Museum,** houses a collection of 3,500 artifacts of Colonel By and Ottawa memorabilia at the **Rideau Locks** between The Hill and Ottawa's grand hotel, the **Château Laurier Hotel** (*see* Lodging, *below*). By built the stone building in 1826, and it was his commissariat for payroll monies and supplies during construction of the canal. *Tel. 613/234–4570. Admission: $2.25 adults, $1.10 students and senior citizens, 50¢ children, $5.50 families. Open mid-May–mid-Oct., Mon. and Wed.–Sat. 10–4, Sun. 2–5; Apr. 1–mid-May and mid-Oct.–Nov. 30, weekdays 10–4.*

Between the Château Laurier Hotel and the Rideau Canal is the **Museum of Contemporary Photography,** which opened in

1992. The museum has 158,000 images, shown in changing exhibitions. There's a 50-seat theater and a boutique. *1 Rideau Canal, tel. 613/990–8257. Admission: $2.50 adults, $1.25 senior citizens and students, under 12 free. Free Thurs. Open Thurs.–Tues. 11–6, Wed. 4–8.*

There has been a farmer's market here since 1840 with fresh produce, maple products, and flowers; surrounding the market stalls are permanent specialty food shops, some well over 100 years old. In **By Ward Market** there are cafés, restaurants, patios, boutiques, and bars, and the area hops day and night. ⓭

⓮ The **National Gallery of Canada,** a magnificent glass-towered temple to art, reflects the Parliament Buildings in its modern mirror-and-granite facade. The gallery contains the most comprehensive collection of Canadian art. Inside is the reconstructed Rideau Convent Chapel, a classic example of 19th-century French Canadian architecture with the only neo-Gothic fan-vaulted ceiling on the continent. The building has three restaurants and a large bookstore with publications on the arts. *380 Sussex Drive, tel. 613/990–1985. Admission: $5 adults, $3 senior citizens and students, under 16 free. Free Thurs.Closed Mon. and holidays in winter.*

It's best to continue the tour by car or bicycle as Sussex Drive skirts the Ottawa River above limestone bluffs. An address known to most Canadians, 24 Sussex Drive is the official **residence of the prime minister.** Don't try parking near the mansion; security is tight. The best way to view the mansion is by slowing down your car as you pass the gates, though all you'll get is a glimpse of a couple of roof gables and some expensive landscaping. ⓯

⓰ Government House, also known as **Rideau Hall,** has been the official residence of the governor general of Canada since 1865. Visiting heads of state, royalty, and the monarch stay here while on official business. The 1830 mansion has a ballroom, and there are a skating rink and a cricket pitch. Sentries of the Canadian Grenadier Guards and the Governor General's Foot Guards are posted outside the main gate of Rideau Hall from late June through August. Free walking tours of the grounds are conducted year-round, but days and times change frequently according to season. *1 Sussex Dr., tel. 613/993–0311.*

Follow Sussex Drive past Rideau Hall to the Rockcliffe Driveway and then signs that say 4 kilometers (2.5 miles) to the **National Aviation Museum** at Rockcliffe Airport. There are more than 100 aircraft in this collection, from a replica of the Silver Dart that made the first powered flight in Canada through World War I Sopwiths. *Tel. 613/993–2010 or 800/463–2038. Admission: $4.28 adults, $3.50 students and senior citizens, $1.50 children 6–15, under 6 free, $9 families. Free Thurs. Open May–Aug., Wed.–Fri. 9–8, Sat.–Tues. 9–6; Sept.–Apr., Tues.–Sun. 9–5, Thurs. 9–8. Closed Mon. except public holidays.* ⓱

⓲ Don't plan on scampering through the **National Museum of Science and Technology** collections in half an hour. There are static displays of printing presses, antique cars, steam locomotives, and agricultural machinery, and there are ever-changing exhibits, many of which are hands-on, or "minds-on." Take the St. Laurent Boulevard South exit from the Queensway. The entrance is 1.6 kilometers (1 mile) south off Lancaster Road. *1867 St. Laurent Blvd., tel. 613/991–3044. Admission: $4.28* *adults, $3.50 senior citizens and students, $1.50 children 6–15, $9 families. Free Thurs. 5–9. Open May–Aug., Wed.–Fri. 9–8, Sat.–Tues. 9–6; Sept.–Apr., Tues.–Sun. 9–5, Thurs. 9–9. Closed Mon. except holidays.*

⓳ **The Canadian Museum of Nature** collection used to be called the National Museum of Natural Sciences, and some of the collection has gone across the river to Hull to help fill galleries in the enormous Canadian Museum of Civilization (*see below*). But there's lots of interest left in this grand old building that was briefly the seat of government in 1916 after the Parliament Buildings burned. The dinosaur collection is fabulous, and so are the stuffed birds and animals in simulated habitats. *McLeod St. at Metcalfe, tel. 613/996–3102. Admission: $4 adults, $3 students and senior citizens, $2 children 6–16, $12 families. Free Thurs. Open May 1–Aug., Fri.–Wed. 9:30–5, Thurs. 9:30–8; Sept.–Apr., Fri.–Wed. 10–5, Thurs. 10–8.*

⓴ Although the **Canadian Museum of Civilization** is not in Ontario, it is definitely considered part of the Ottawa scene, literally, because visitors can see it on the other side of the Ottawa River from behind the Parliament Buildings on The Hill. This immense, modernistic building on the Québec shore of the Ottawa River features galleries, displays, films, lectures, theaters, and exhibitions chronicling thousands of years of Canadian history. In the Grand Hall, six native longhouses, towering totem poles, and life-size reconstructions of Canadian historic scenes help you travel through time. Special exhibitions throughout the year are offered for an additional admission fee at Cineplus, the first theater to project the larger-than-life Imax and Omnimax. *100 Laurier St., Hull, tel. 819/776–7002. Admission to the museum: $4.50 adults, $3 students and senior citizens, children 15 and under free, free Thurs. 5–8; Cineplus, tel. 819/776–7010. Prices change depending on the program, but are usually $7 adults, $5 students and senior citizens, and children. Open May–Sept., daily 9–5, Thurs. 9–8; Sept.–Apr., Tues.–Sun. Closed Christmas and New Year's Day.*

Tour 2: Heritage Highway

From Ottawa, Highway 31 runs southeast about 75 kilometers (46 miles) to scenic Highway 2 at Morrisburg. One of the province's major tourist attractions is 11 kilometers (7 miles) west by Highway 2 or Highway 401. Eight villages disappeared under rising waters when the St. Lawrence Seaway opened in 1959, but their best historic buildings were moved to a new **㉑** village called **Upper Canada Village,** a faithful re-creation of an Ontario community from the 1800s. The village occupies 66 acres of the 2,000-acre **Crysler's Farm Battlefield Memorial Park,** a site that figured prominently in the War of 1812. Newfangled gadgets such as radios, walkie-talkies, and tape players are banned in this throwback to the days of the United Empire Loyalists. The village has three mills, two farms, two churches, two hotels, and 25 other buildings. A leisurely tour takes three to four hours. There are more than 150 staff people on the site, all in early 1800s costume, to answer questions. The Village Store is open year-round and sells Canadian crafts and village-made bread, cheese, and flour. At Willard's Hotel, licensed for beer and wine, lunches, full-course meals, and teas are served. Two-day passes are available (at reduced rates). *Hwy. 2 E, tel. 613/543–3704. Admission: $9/$13.75 for two days* *adults, $6/$9 students, $5.25/$7.75 senior citizens, $3.75/$5.75 children 6–12. Open mid-May–mid-Oct., daily 9:30–5; in winter, open for special events only.*

Head west on Highway 2 about 40 kilometers (25 miles) to
22 **Prescott** and its second fort, Fort Wellington, built by the British in 1813 to protect goods and troops moving between Montréal and Upper Canada after the outbreak of the War of 1812. The fort was never attacked and was completed in 1814, the year the war ended. The Ottawa–Kingston Rideau Canal eliminated its need and it was abandoned. In 1837 rebellion broke out in Upper and Lower Canada, and the British built a new and stronger Fort Wellington on the site. The buildings are furnished in the 1846 period. *370 Vankoughnet St., tel. 613/925–2896. Admission free. Open mid-May–Aug., daily 10–6; Sept.-mid-Oct., daily 10–5; mid-Oct–mid-May by reservation only.*

Ontario's oldest barracks building is one block west of Fort Wellington at 356 East Street and open daily in July and August as a museum. Lunches and dinners at **Stockade Barracks and Hospital Museum** feature historical menus year-round. By prior arrangement, groups of 15–40 can have five- or six-course meals of 1812-style dishes served by mess waiters in military uniforms. *356 East St., tel. 613/925–4894. Admission: $2 adults, children under 12 free, families $5.*

23 **Kingston**'s imposing architecture has been impressing visitors since 1673, when LaSalle chose the location as the site for a meeting between Governor Frontenac and the Iroquois. Before the meeting, Frontenac built a stockaded fort to impress the Indians and thus tap into the fur trade. Thanks to misguided American strategy, Kingston survived the War of 1812 almost totally unscathed. Many of its beautiful limestone buildings remain in mint condition today. From 1841 to 1844, Kingston was the capital of the province of Canada; today the gorgeous, cut-limestone city hall building dominates the city's downtown core, facing a riverfront park. Tours are given weekdays in the summer, but visitors can wander through the lobby area any time of the year.

The city occupied a strategic site at the junction of the St. Lawrence River and Rideau Canal system, and four Martello towers still guard the harbor. The **Royal Military College of Canada** features a museum in Fort Frederick, the largest of the Martello towers. The museum contains the internationally renowned Douglas Arms Collection, which includes the small-arms collection of General Porfirio Díaz, president of Mexico from 1886 to 1912. *Off Hwy. 2 just east of Kingston, tel. 613/541–6663 or 613/541–6652. Admission free. Open last weekend in June–Labor Day, daily 10–5.*

The massive **Fort Henry** was built during the War of 1812 to repel a possible American invasion, which never came. Students in period military costume guide visitors through, hold parades, and re-create the pomp and pageantry of an era past. *Hwys. 2 and 15, tel. 613/542–7388. Admission: late May to Thanksgiving, $9 adults, $5 senior citizens, $5.85 students, $3.80 children 6–12; Thanksgiving to mid-May, $3.40 adults, $1.75 senior citizens, students, and children. Open daily 9–5.*

Locals nicknamed it Tea Caddy Castle, Molasses Hall, and Pekoe Pagoda, but Canada's first prime minister, Sir John A. Macdonald, who lived in the house for a year, called it **Bellevue** because of its view over the St. Lawrence River. Today the 1840 house is a National Historic Park site restored and furnished to the 1848 period when Macdonald lived there. *35 Centre St., tel. 613/545–8666. Admission free. Open May–Nov., daily 9–6; Dec.–Apr., daily 10–5.*

All you'd ever want to know about steam engines and their history—and then some—is available on display in the **Pump House Steam Museum** (23 Ontario St., tel. 613/546–4696), the restored Victorian-style 1849 municipal water-pumping station. All the exhibits run on steam (only between mid-May and Labor Day), and the collection is believed to be the largest in the world. Models range from miniatures to an 1897-model Toronto-built engine with a 9-ton flywheel. The **Marine Museum of the Great Lakes at Kingston** (55 Ontario St., tel. 613/542–2261), under the same management, features a rambling display area at the historic former Kingston Drydock that traces Great Lakes shipping since 1678. The 3,000-ton, 210-foot retired icebreaker, the *Alexander Henry,* is also on tour from mid-May to mid-October. Summer visitors can rent a stateroom and sleep aboard. Tickets are available for one, two, or all three of these attractions. *Admission: $3.25/$4.75/$6.25 adults, $2.25/$3.75/$5.25 senior citizens and children. Both museums open Apr.–Dec., daily 10–5; Jan.–Mar., weekdays 10–4.*

Kingston is the birthplace of organized hockey—the first league game was played in the city in 1885. So it seems fitting that the city is also home to the **International Hockey Hall of Fame,** the shrine to puck-chasing. *York and Alfred Sts., 1 block north of Princess St. (Hwy. 2), tel. 613/544–2355. Admission: $2.14 adults, $1.61 senior citizens and students, children under 12 free, $4.28 families. Open mid-June–mid-Sept., daily 10–5; weekends the rest of the year, or by appointment.*

Highway 2 or 401 will take you to **Belleville,** but consider Highway 33, which will take you past Kingston's Gothic penitentiary at Collins Bay to Picton in the island county of Prince Edward. A free, 10-minute ferry ride (service every 15 minutes in summer) lands you at Glenora on the island, and it's 9 kilometers (6 miles) to Picton, the county seat.

㉔ **Picton** is a serene town of 4,000 with fine old buildings and strong associations with Sir John A. Macdonald, Canada's first prime minister, who practiced law at the 1834 county courthouse that is still in use. Within the town is the **Macaulay Heritage Park,** which sits on about 15 acres of land and includes picnic facilities, the Macaulay House, and the County Museum. Tours of the park and town's attractions are available by prior arrangement and may include a visit to the jail, where a double gallows is kept handy (although it hasn't been used since 1884). *Tel. 613/476–3833. Admission to house: $2 adults, children free. House open weekdays 10–4:30.*

New Englanders wandering the island might find themselves wondering if they had ever left home—so similar are the scenery and the pages of history that brought both regions into being. The island was one of the earliest parts of Ontario to be settled after the American Revolution, and the Loyalist influence remained dominant for generations. The first of these settlers landed at Adolphustown Reach from Bateaux on June 16, 1784, and village locals nicknamed the landing area the Plymouth Rock of Ontario. The earliest burial ground in the district is located here, and the Loyalist church erected in 1822 is still used as a parish meeting hall.

About an hour west of Belleville, or 90 minutes from Picton, are the towns of **Cobourg** and **Port Hope,** both richly endowed with mansions originally built as summer homes by Americans. Again, the traveler has the choice of the four-lane Highway 401 or Highway 2, which is closer to the shore of Lake Ontario and wanders through the pretty communities of **Brighton, Colborne,** and **Grafton.** Cobourg is another community that expected to be chosen as the provincial capital. It was passed over, but not before the town just about bankrupted itself building the magnificent **Victoria Hall,** officially opened in 1860 by the young Prince of Wales, later King Edward VII. The hall was used for town council meetings, formal balls, and concerts on the second floor; a courtroom modeled after London's Old Bailey was located on the ground floor. Today's visitor can take a free tour of some of the 41 rooms in the building. *55 King St. W, tel. 416/372–5831. Admission free. Guided tours in summer or by prior arrangement.*

From Port Hope, take Highway 28 for about 40 kilometers (25 miles) into the Kawartha lakes region to reach the small city of **Peterborough,** home of Trent University and 68,000 people. High notes in Peterborough are the signature lift locks on the Trent-Severn Waterway, which are the world's highest, and Centennial Fountain in Little Lake, which at 250 feet is the highest jet fountain in Canada. The lift lock on the Trent Canal system was built in 1904. In less than 10 minutes it lifts boats, and the water they're floating in, 65 feet straight up. The lock and the Trent Canal operate mid-May–mid-October; slides and films at a visitor center explain their mechanism. *Hunter St. E, tel. 705/745–8389. Admission free. Open June–Sept., daily 9–6; Oct.–June daily 9–5 (call ahead).*

Southeast of Peterborough, around the town of **Keene,** are several attractions. **Serpent Mounds Provincial Park** is 13 kilometers (9 miles) southeast of Peterborough on the shores of Rice Lake. About 2,000 years ago a nomadic native tribe buried its dead in nine earth mounds, the largest of which is shaped like a 200-foot-long serpent. An interpretation center explains the site and displays artifacts. *Tel. 705/295–6879. Admission: $5 per vehicle. Open mid-May–Thanksgiving, daily.*

On the way to the park, about 3 kilometers (2 miles) north of the village of Keene is the well-signed **Lang Pioneer Village,** with its museum and 26 pioneer buildings. There are displays and demonstrations of pioneer arts and crafts in the summer. *Tel. 705/295–6694. Admission, including GST: $5.50 adults, $4.50 senior citizens and students, $2.75 children under 14, $12.50 families. Open mid-May–mid-Oct., weekdays 11–5, Sat. 1–5, Sun. 1–6; museum gallery open daily except Christmas, 1–5 PM.*

Canada's largest concentration of native rock carvings was found at the east end of Stoney Lake, outside the hamlet of Stonyridge, in 1954. The site, 50 kilometers (31 miles) northwest of Peterborough, is now within **Petroglyphs Provincial Park.** The well-preserved symbols and figures, which are carved on a flat expanse of white marble almost 70 feet wide, are encased in a protective building. The more than 900 carvings are believed to be of Algonkin spirit figures. *East of Hwy. 28 on Northey's Bay Rd., tel. 705/877–2552. Admission: $5 per vehicle. Open mid-May–Thanksgiving, daily.*

Tour 3: North of Toronto to the Lakes

㉙ Barrie, a city of 61,000 on the shores of Lake Simcoe, is about 75 kilometers (46 miles) north of Toronto on the four-lane Highway 400. A winter carnival attracts ice fishermen, dogsled racers, and ice motorcyclists. From late June through Labor Day, there's straw-hat theater in Gryphon Theatre at Georgian College and harness racing at Barrie Raceway.

㉚㉛ From just north of Barrie, take Highways 400 and 93 about 50 kilometers (30 miles) to the towns of **Penetanguishene** (known locally as Penetang) and **Midland** in a small corner of northern Simcoe County known as Huronia. This 30- by 60-kilometer (20- by 40-mile) area was the scene of some of the most grisly episodes in North American history. Each town sits on a snug, safe harbor at the foot of two bays that lead out to Georgian Bay.

Just 5 kilometers (3 miles) east of Midland on Highway 12, visitors can explore a complete reconstruction of **Sainte-Marie among the Hurons.** Jesuit missionaries built the Sainte-Marie mission at this spot in 1639. The Jesuits preached Christianity, and the Hurons—also called Wendat—taught the French settlers how to survive in the harsh climate. By 1648 the mission was home to one-fifth of the European population of New France. The villagers built Ontario's first hospital, farm, school, and social service center here and constructed a canal from the Wye River. A combination of disease and Iroquois attacks led to the mission's demise. Twenty-two structures, faithfully reproduced from a scientific excavation, including an Indian longhouse and wigwam, can now be toured. The canal is working again; staff in period costume saw timber, repair shoes, sew clothes, and grow vegetables. *Tel. 705/526–7838. Admission: $5.75 adults, $3.50 students, $3.25 senior citizens, children under 6 free. Open mid-May–Labor Day, daily and some weekends in winter (call ahead).*

On a hill overlooking Sainte-Marie is **Martyr's Shrine,** a twin-spired stone cathedral built in 1926 to honor the eight missionaries who died in Huronia (the name given to the area originally); in 1930 five of the priests were canonized by the Roman Catholic church. The grounds include a theater, souvenir shop, cafeteria, and picnic area. *Tel. 705/526–3788. Open daily Victoria Day through Thanksgiving weekend.*

The best artifacts from several hundred archaeological digs in the area are displayed at **Huronia Museum and Gallery of Historic Huronia** in Little Lake Park in Midland. Behind the museum and gallery building is **Huron Indian Village,** a full-scale replica of a 16th-century Huron Indian village. *Little Lake Park, tel. 705/526–2844. Admission to museum and village: $4.75 adults, $4.25 senior citizens, $3.50 students. Open Jan.–late May, weekdays 9–5; late May–Thanksgiving, Mon.–Sat. 9–5, Sun. 10–5.*

Cruises leave from the town docks of both Midland and Penetang to explore the 30,000 Island region of Georgian Bay from May to Thanksgiving. From Midland town dock the 215-passenger MS *Miss Midland* (tel. 705/526–0161 or 800/461–1767 in Ontario) offers one to four 2½-hour sightseeing cruises. From the Penetang town dock, the 200-passenger MS *Georgian Queen* (tel. 705/549–7795) takes passengers on three-hour tours of the islands, from late May through Thanksgiving. The cruises leave once daily at 2 PM.

From Penetang or Midland, it's 110 kilometers (68 miles) by Highways 12 and 69 to **Parry Sound.** Here Canada's largest, $3 million sightseeing cruise ship, the *Island Queen,* offers a more extensive three-hour cruise of Georgian Bay, one to two times daily, depending on season. There's free parking at the town dock. *9 Bay St., tel. 705/746–2311. Admission: $15 adults, $7.50 children. Operates June–Thanksgiving.*

From mid-July to mid-August, Festival of the Sound (tel. 705/746–2410) is held. Jazz, popular music, classical piano, and show tunes are performed in the auditorium of Parry Sound High School and aboard the *Island Queen* .

Orillia, about 35 kilometers (21 miles) north of Barrie on Highway 11 at the junction of Highway 12, will be recognized by readers of Canada's greatest humorist, Stephen Leacock, as Mariposa, the "little town" he described in *Sunshine Sketches of a Little Town.* The writer's former summer home is now a museum, the **Stephen Leacock Memorial Home.** In the Mariposa Room, characters from the book are matched with the Orillia residents who inspired them. *Off Hwy. 12B in the east end of Orillia (well signposted), tel. 705/326–9357. Admission: $3 adults, $1 high school students and senior citizens. Open mid-Apr.–mid-June and Labor Day–mid-Dec., daily 10–2 and by appointment; mid-June to Labor Day, daily 10–5. Closed Dec. 15–Apr. 15.*

North along Highway 11, rolling farmland suddenly changes to pine trees amid granite outcrops of the Canadian Shield. This region, called Muskoka, is the playground of folks who live in the highly urbanized areas in and on either side of Toronto. **Gravenhurst,** 39 kilometers (24 miles) north of Orillia, is a town of 9,000 and the birthplace of Canada's least-known hero—least known in Canada, that is. In China, Norman Bethune's name is as well known as Wayne Gretzky's is in Canada. Bethune is remembered for his heroic work in China as a field surgeon and medical educator. The **Bethune Memorial House,** an 1880-vintage frame home, has become a shrine of sorts to Chinese diplomats visiting North America. *235 John St., tel. 705/687–4261. Admission free. Open June–Labor Day, daily 10–6; the rest of the year 10–5. Closed on holidays in winter.*

The RMS *Segwun* (the initials stand for Royal Mail Ship) is the sole survivor of a fleet of steamships that once provided transportation through the Muskoka Lakes. The 128-foot boat, built in Scotland and assembled in Gravenhurst in 1887, carries 99 passengers on cruises from early June to early October. Cruises range from 90 minutes to two days in length (passengers dine aboard but sleep in one of Muskoka's grand resorts). Reservations are strongly recommended. *Muskoka Lakes Navigation and Hotel Company Limited, Box 68, Gravenhurst, Ont. P0C 1G0, tel. 705/687–6667.*

Just 11 kilometers (8 miles) north of Gravenhurst outside **Bracebridge** is **Santa's Village and Mister Rudolph's Funland.** After letting Santa know what they'd like to find under the

Christmas tree, youngsters can delight in the Kris Kringle Riverboat, the Candy Cane Express Train, minibikes, bumper boats, paddleboats, or pony rides, to name a few. Mister Rudolph's Funland is for children 12 and up and offers go-karts, batting cages, in-line skating, 18-hole mini-putt and an indoor activity center with video games. *Just west of Bracebridge, well signposted, tel. 705/645–2512. Admission: $13.98 adults, $8.13 senior citizens and children 2–4; unlimited rides all day. Open mid-June–Labor Day, daily 10–6. Mister Rudolph's Funland open late May–mid-June and Labor Day–Thanksgiving, weekends 10–10; mid-June–Labor Day, daily 10–10.*

㊱ **Dorset** is a pretty village on a narrows between two bays of the Lake of Bays, about 40 kilometers (25 miles) east of Huntsville by Highways 60 and 35. The village is home to **Robinson's General Store** (tel. 705/766–2415), which makes the modest claim "Voted Canada's Best Country Store." Voting was by the editors of *Canadian Living* magazine, but visitors are not likely to question the choice. With the exception of the World War II years, the store, established in 1921, has been open continuously and operated by a Robinson. You'll find everything here from moose-fur hats to stoves and pine furniture. You can circle back to Toronto on scenic Highway 35 or make Dorset a circle tour from Huntsville around the Lake of Bays.

Tour 4: Fort Erie and West to Windsor

㊲ **Fort Erie** is at the extreme southeast tip of the Niagara Peninsula, 155 kilometers (95 miles) south of Toronto and just across the International Peace Bridge over the Niagara River from Buffalo, New York. It's a drab, boom-or-bust town of fast-food chains, taverns, and gas stations whose profits rise or fall with the exchange rate between Canadian and U.S. dollars. The heavy American influx to the area is not without historic irony; the last American presence on Canadian soil took place here at the end of the War of 1812.

Old Fort Erie, situated at the south end of Fort Erie, has been reconstructed as it existed before it was destroyed at the end of the War of 1812. The Old Fort's colorful and bloody history reveals thousands of soldiers lost their lives within sight of the earthworks, drawbridges, and palisades. The fort itself was destroyed in 1779 and again in 1803 by spectacular storms that drove masses of ice ashore at the foot of Lake Erie. Visitors are conducted through the display rooms by guards in period uniforms of the British army. During summer the guards stand sentry duty, fire the cannon, and demonstrate drill and musket practice. *Tel. 416/871–0540. Admission: $3.50 adult, $3.15 senior citizens, $2 students, $9 family. Open daily mid-May–mid-Sept.*

The town's other major attraction, the **Fort Erie Race Track,** opened in 1897, but it is one of the most modern—and picturesque—tracks in North America. Glass-enclosed dining lounges overlook a one-mile dirt track and a seven-furlong turf course. Also in view are gardens, ponds, and waterways. *Tel. 416/871–3200.*

㊳ Lake Erie's **Port Colborne,** or "The Ports," is about 30 kilometers (20 miles) west of Fort Erie by Highway 3 (at the south end of the Welland Canal—*see* Tour 5, *below*). There's no admission charge to **Port Colborne Historical and Marine Museum,** a six-building complex where afternoon tea is served (at a price) from Arabella's Tea Room. *200 King St., tel. 416/834–7604. Admission free. Open May–Dec., daily noon–5.*

39 About 10 kilometers (6 miles) north of Port Colborne is the industrial city of **Welland.** For years the city was bypassed by the 14–16 million tourists who visit Niagara Falls annually, so in 1988 Welland initiated its Festival of Arts Murals. There now are 27 giant murals on downtown buildings; the longest is 130 feet, and the tallest is three stories high. Visitors can pick up a free mural tour map from **Welland Tourism** (32 E. Main St., tel. 416/735–8696) or from brochure racks at City Hall and in local restaurants and hotels. *Festival of Arts, 800 Niagara St. N, tel. 416/788–3000.*

40 From Welland, Highway 3 wanders west through rolling farm country occasionally slashed by a river emptying into Lake Erie. At **Jarvis,** 80 kilometers (50 miles) west, turn south on Highway 6 to **Port Dover,** home of the world's largest fleet of freshwater fishing boats. It's a pretty beach resort town where freshwater fish is served up steamy and golden at a number of restaurants.

Time Out The **Erie Beach Motor Hotel** (19 Walker St., tel. 519/583–1391) dining rooms have developed a following since the Schneider family opened the first one in 1946. For those not eager to dig into a platter of local perch or pickerel, steak or shrimp are on the menu, as well as a variety of draft beers by the glass or pitcher.

41 Take Highway 24 north to Simcoe to rejoin Highway 3 westbound. **St. Thomas'**s first buildings went up in 1810, over a decade and a half ahead of the first building in London, 28 kilometers (17 miles) north. For all its premature cosmopolitanism, its population has leveled at 29,000, while London's has hit the 300,000 mark. Note the **statue of Jumbo,** the Barnum and Bailey circus elephant, killed there in a freak railway accident in 1885. The monument is a 10%-larger-than-life-size statue of the largest elephant ever in captivity. Adjacent to the Jumbo monument is a railway caboose, summer office of the St. Thomas Chamber of Commerce, and a gift shop for Jumbo kitsch. *538 Talbot St., tel. 519/631–1981; monument, tel. 516/631–8188. Chamber office open year-round 8:30–5; monument office open May–Labor Day, daily 9–9.*

42 About 15 kilometers (10 miles) south of St. Thomas is the summer resort town of **Port Stanley,** with a fine brown sand beach and the boutiques, snack bars, and kitsch stands that survive on vacationers following the sun.

It isn't hauled by a steam engine anymore, but the London and Port Stanley Railroad (L&PS) still packs in travelers. The operation has proven so popular the little train now runs year-round and its trackage has been doubled. The railroad was built in 1856 between London and Port Stanley and intended as a main trade link between Canada and the United States. The trade didn't materialize, but the railroad survived on excursion traffic until 1957. Railroad buffs restored some passenger cars and repaired the line to Union, in 1992 extending it to St. Thomas. You can take a 45-minute excursion to Union year-round, or—from June through October—a two-hour round-trip to St. Thomas. *Port Stanley Railway Station, tel. 519/782–9993.*

Round-trip fares to Union: $5.50 adults, $4.75 senior citizens, $2.75 children under 12, all plus tax; to St. Thomas: $10 adults, $9 senior citizens, $5 children, tax included.

From Port Stanley/St. Thomas the fastest way to cover the 150 kilometers (95 miles) to the extreme southwest corner of Ontario is on Highway 401, but it's a flat, straight, and deadly dull trip. The two-lane Highway 3 is a better choice—it follows the shore of Lake Erie and passes through a number of towns and villages. In summer and fall, vegetable stands sprout like mushrooms along this route, offering fresh locally grown fruits and vegetables.

Point Pelee juts into Lake Erie, serving as a rest stop for migrating birds and butterflies. The southern tip of the point, **④③ Point Pelee National Park,** has the smallest dry land area of any Canadian national park, yet it manages to draw more than half a million visitors every year. There's no overnight camping, and there are a lot of other rules and regulations to observe because the park is home to a number of endangered species of plants and reptiles. Drive slowly to the visitor center, 5 kilometers (3 miles) inside the park, where there are exhibits, slide shows, and a keen, knowledgeable staff to answer questions. Seven hundred kinds of plants and 347 species of birds have been recorded here. A propane-powered, open-sided train operates from the center to the tip of Point Pelee, the southernmost part of the Canadian mainland. September in Pelee is the best time to see monarch butterflies resting before they head 3,350 kilometers (2,100 miles) south to winter in the Sierra Madre of Mexico. It is also among the best locations in North America for bird-watching, especially during spring and fall migrations. In September, groups of birders bedecked with camera lenses the size of rocket launchers and clanking with binoculars, tape recorders, video equipment, and even CB radios converge on the park and on the hotels, highways, motels, and restaurants of nearby Leamington, an otherwise quiet town of 14,000. *Tel. 519/322–2365. Admission: $5 per vehicle Apr.–Labor Day, free rest of the year. Open daily 10–6.*

④④ Pelee Island is a small, flat island, roughly 13 by 6 kilometers (8 by 4 miles), at the west end of Lake Erie, served spring through fall by ferry boats that link it with Kingsville and Leamington in Ontario and Sandusky in Ohio. In winter there are scheduled flights from Windsor. Ferries land at either West Dock or Scudder Dock, the main communities on the island. The permanent population is 270, but in summer that quadruples as vacationers, mostly from Ohio, cram into 200 private cottages. At the end of October and beginning of November, 700 hunters arrive to fill 18,000 pheasants with buckshot. The island has raised pheasants for hunters since 1932, a business that helps reduce taxes. There's usually someone to inform visitors about Pelee's biggest industry, the pheasant farm in the middle of the island, and explain why the chicks wear what look like sunglasses. (It's so they can't peck one anothers' eyes out.) Pelee Island is not the most southerly place in Canada— that honor belongs to neighboring Little Middle Island—but Pelee *is* south; it's on the same latitude as northern California and northern Spain.

From the community of **West Dock** you can see **Perry's Victory and International Peace Monument,** a 352-foot-high monument commemorating American commander Captain Oliver Hazard

Perry, who won control of Lake Erie at Put-in-Bay Island, Ohio, in 1813 by sailing straight into the British fleet while firing broadside, succinctly reporting: "We have met the enemy and they are ours."

From Leamington, take Highway 18 west to Kingsville and then follow Division Road north to Essex County Road 29. The **45** road to **Jack Miner's Bird Sanctuary** is well signposted. Jack Miner was an avid hunter who realized no species could survive both its natural enemies *and* man. In 1904 he dug ponds, planted trees, and introduced four Canada geese with clipped wings to the ponds. That number grew to the 50,000 that now winter here. From 1910 to 1940 Miner lectured on conservation and convinced kings and presidents of its need, thus earning him the Order of the British Empire in 1943. His former home is now a trust, open year-round except Sundays. No admission is charged and nothing is sold on the grounds. A two-story museum in the former stables has a wealth of Miner memorabilia, and at a pond beside the house you can feed far-from-shy geese and ducks with free feed. At 3 and 4 PM daily, including Sunday, the birds are flushed for "air shows," circling wildly overhead until they feel it's safe to land. The best times to view migrations are late March, October, and November. *On Essex County Rd. 29, 5 km (3 mi) north of Kingsville, tel. 519/733–4034. Admission free. Open year-round, daily. Museum closed Sun.*

The **John R. Park Homestead and Conservation Area,** 8 kilometers (5 miles) west of Kingsville, is a pioneer village anchored by one of Ontario's few examples of American Greek Revival architecture, an 1842 home. The 10 buildings include the house of John R. Park, a shed built with no nails, a smokehouse, icehouse, outhouse, blacksmith shop, sawmill, and livestock stable. *County Rd. 50 at Iler Rd., tel. 519/738–2029. Open July 1–Labor Day, daily 10–5; Oct.–mid-May, Mon.–Fri., and Sun. 10–4, when special events are held.*

46 The turn-of-the-century **Southwestern Ontario Heritage Village** has 20 historic buildings on 54 wooded acres. Volunteers in period dress show visitors how pioneers baked, operated weaving looms, and dipped candles. The **Transportation Museum of the Historic Vehicle Society of Ontario, Windsor Branch,** features a fine collection of travel artifacts, from snowshoes to buggies to vintage automobiles. The gem of the collection is the world's only 1893 Shamrock. This adorable two-seater was the second effort at a workable prototype built by the Mira Brothers. When this one didn't run properly, either, the brothers abandoned their brief career as auto manufacturers. *About halfway bet. Kingsville and Essex on County Rd. 23, tel. 519/776–6909. Open Apr.–Nov., Wed.–Sun. 11–5; July–Aug., daily 11–5.*

47 The riverside parks in the quiet town of **Amherstburg** are great places from which to watch the procession of Great Lakes shipping. **Navy Yard Park,** with flower beds ringed by old anchor chains, has benches overlooking Bois Blanc Island and the narrow main shipping channel.

Fort Malden was the British base in the War of 1812, when Detroit was captured, though its history goes back to 1727, when a Jesuit mission began occupying lands in the area. Now the fort is an 11-acre National Historic Park, which includes remains of the original earthworks, restored barracks, a military pensioner's cottage, two exhibit buildings, and picnic facilities. *Tel. 519/736–5416. Admission free. Open in winter, daily 10–5; June–Labor Day, daily 10–6.*

The **North American Black Historical Museum** tells of daring escapes by U.S. slaves and the Underground Railroad system many used to flee to Canada. Between 1800 and 1860, 30,000–50,000 slaves made the pilgrimage to Canada, the Promised Land, and many of those crossed the Detroit River at Amherstburg because it was the narrowest point. An 1848-vintage church and log cabin contain exhibits, artifacts, and biographies. *227 King St., tel. 519/736–5433. Admission free. Open Wed.–Fri. 10–5, weekends 1–5.*

48 **Windsor,** long an unattractive industrial city that hosted Ford, General Motors, and Chrysler manufacturing plants, has become an attractive place to visit. The riverfront has pretty parks, some with fountains and statues, all overlooking the spectacular Detroit skyline. The cities are linked by the Ambassador Bridge and the Windsor–Detroit Tunnel. If you're traveling by car, start your visit at the Convention and Visitors Bureau (80 Chatham Street East), where you can get a free date-stamped parking pass for use during your stay.

The **Art Gallery of Windsor** features changing displays of contemporary and historic Canadian and foreign art. *445 Riverside Dr. W, tel. 519/258–7111. Admission free. Open Tues., Wed., Sat., Sun. 11–5; Thurs., Fri. 11–9.*

The **Francois Baby House: Windsor's Community House** is a collection of area artifacts displayed in the 1812 house where the Battle of Windsor, the final incident in the Upper Canada Rebellion, was fought in 1838. *254 Pitt St., tel. 519/253–1812. Admission free. Open Tues.–Sat. 10–5, Sun. 2–5.*

Farmers, butchers, and bakers from southwestern Ontario sell their fresh produce at **Windsor City Market,** which rents space to more than 100 permanent vendors. *Chatham St. E. between MacDougall and Market Sts., tel. 519/255–6260. Open Wed.–Thurs. 7–4, Fri. 7–6, Sat. from 5 AM. Some stalls open Mon. and Tues.*

Willistead Manor is the former home of Edward Chandler Walker, second son of Hiram, who founded Walker's Distillery in 1858. The 15-acre estate is now a city park, and tours of the manor are available. Work on the mansion was completed in 1906, and no expense was spared building the 36-room spread designed in the 16th-century Tudor-Jacobean style of an English manor house. *Niagara St. at Kildare Rd., tel. 519/255–6545 or 519/255–6270. Admission: $2.75 adults, $2.25 senior citizens, $1.25 children. Open for tours Sept.–June, 1st and 3rd Sun. of each month, 1–4 (last tour at 3:30); July–Aug., Sun.–Wed., 1–4 (last tour at 3:30).*

Since 1959, Windsor and Detroit have combined their national birthday parties (Canada Day, July 1; and Independence Day, July 4) into a massive bash called **International Freedom Festival.** The two-week party includes nonstop entertainment with more than 100 special events on both sides of the river and a spectacular fireworks display, billed as the largest in North America. *Tel. 519/255–6530.*

Tour 5: Niagara and West to London

There is probably no natural attraction exploited as thoroughly as the falls at **Niagara.** You can go over the falls in a helicopter; get almost directly underneath them by boat; go around them on bridges; or go behind them in a tunnel. The first travel writer to visit Niagara Falls more than 300 years ago wrote, "The universe does not afford its parallel. The roar of them can be heard 15 leagues away" (a distance of 72 kilometers, or 45 miles). And explorer and missionary Father Louis Hennepin described their height as 600 feet—when in fact they are 176 feet high. When Europeans read Hennepin's 1678 accounts, they ranked Niagara among the Seven Wonders of the World. Despite Hennepin's gross exaggerations, few have ever been disappointed by a visit to the falls. About 12 million tourists visit each year. And daredevils have been drawn to the falls since 1828. Eight people have survived plunging over them in a variety of contraptions, and the list of those who perished in the attempt is a long one. Fines for performing illegal stunts on property owned by the Niagara Parks Commission (NPC) have been raised to $10,000, but the stunt-lovers keep on coming.

Numbers in the margin correspond to points of interest on the Niagara Falls map.

The NPC was formed in 1885 to preserve the area around the falls. Beginning with a small block of land, the NPC has gradually acquired most of the land fronting on the Canadian side of the Niagara River, from Niagara-on-the-Lake to Fort Erie. This 56-kilometer (35-mile) riverside drive is a 3,000-acre ribbon of parkland lined with parking areas, picnic tables, and barbecue pits, and the public is welcome to use the facilities at no charge. The NPC's **Greenhouse and Plant Conservatory** (tel. 416/356–4699), just south of the Horseshoe Falls, is open daily year-round.

Visitors are also welcome at the **NPC School of Horticulture** several miles north of (downriver from) the falls, on the Niagara Parkway. The school has been graduating professional gardeners since 1936, and students display their expertise with flowers and shrubbery.

From the school it's a short distance (downriver) to one of the world's largest **floral clocks.** Its 40-foot-wide "living" face is planted in a different design each year.

Heading back upriver, there are trails maintained by the NPC in the **Niagara Glen.** A **bicycle trail** that parallels the Niagara Parkway from Fort Erie to Niagara-on-the-Lake winds between beautiful homes on one side and the river, with its abundant bird life, on the other. There are free band concerts on summer Sundays at **Queenston Heights Park, Queen Victoria Park,** and **Old Fort Erie** (*see* Tour 4, *above*), as well as **Rainbow Bridge Carillon** recitals. And don't forget to catch the free colored illumination of the falls 365 nights a year.

The **Festival of Lights** runs from the end of November to the third week of February. It started in Niagara Falls, Ontario, in 1981, and now stretches the length of the Niagara Parkway between Fort Erie and Niagara-on-the-Lake. The city claims a lot of superlatives during this period: world's largest Christ-

Niagara Falls

KEY

AE American Express Office

mas tree (the Skylon Tower), world's largest gift (Your Host Motor Inn decorated to look like a giant gift-wrapped box), world's largest candle (the Minolta Tower), etc. The festival started with massive corporate displays, but the idea caught on with smaller businesses and private residents. There are now so many displays that tours are offered ranging from 2½ to 3½ hours.

54 *Maid of the Mist* boats have been operating since 1846, when they were wooden-hulled, coal-fired steamboats. Nowadays, passengers are issued hooded rain slickers for the 30-minute trip because the three modern boats get so close to both falls that the spray is heavy. *Boats leave from the foot of Clifton Hill, tel. 416/358–5781. Admission: $8.65 adults, $5 children 6–12. Open mid-May–late Oct., daily. Late June–Labor Day, boats leave as often as every 15 min. from 9:45 to 7:45; off-season, boats leave every 30 minutes weekdays from 9:45.*

55 At **Table Rock Scenic Tunnels** your admission ticket includes use of rubber boots and a hooded rain slicker. You walk to an observation plaza just under the lip of the falls, and from there a tunnel takes you almost to the middle of the falls and behind the wall of crashing water. *Tours begin at Table Rock House in Queen Victoria Park, tel. 416/354–1551. Admission: $5.25 adults, $4.75 senior citizens, $2.65 children 6–12. Open mid-June–Labor Day, 9–11; 9–5 the rest of the year. Closed Dec. 25.*

56 The **Niagara Spanish Aero Car,** a cable car that crosses the Whirlpool Basin in the Niagara Gorge, has been operating since 1918. This trip is not for the fainthearted; when you're swinging high above the roiling whirlpool, those cables seem awfully thin. **The Great Gorge Adventure** involves taking an elevator to the bottom of the Niagara Gorge where you can walk a boardwalk beside the roaring torrent of the Niagara River. There the gorge is forced between sheer cliffs as it enters the Giant Whirlpool. *On River Rd., 3 km (2 mi) north of the falls, tel. 416/354–5711. Aero Car Admission: $4.50 adults, $4.05 senior citizens, $2.25 children 6–12. Great Gorge Adventure Admission: $4.25 adults, $3.85 senior citizens, $2.15 children. Open June–Labor Day, 9–9; shorter hours through mid-Oct., weather permitting. The NPC sells an Explorer Passport for admission to Table Rock Scenic Tunnels, Spanish Aero Car, and the Great Gorge Adventure for a 10% savings: $12.60 adults, $6.35 children 6–12.*

57 **Marineland,** a theme park with marine shows, wildlife displays, and rides, is located 1.5 kilometers (1 mile) south of the falls. The daily marine show includes performing dolphins, harbor seals, and sea lions. Children can pet and feed a herd of 500 deer and get nose-to-nose with North American freshwater fish. Among the many rides is the world's largest steel roller coaster. Marineland is signposted from Niagara Parkway or reached from the Queen Elizabeth Way by exiting at McLeod Road (Exit 27). *7657 Portage Rd., tel. 416/356–9565 for recording or 416/356–8250. Admission: $17.95 adults, $14.95 children 4–9 and senior citizens. In winter rides are closed and prices drop more than 50%. Open mid-May–June, daily 10–5; June–Aug., daily 9–6; Sept., daily 10–5.*

58 The **Niagara Falls Museum** claims to be North America's oldest museum and is chockablock with everything from stuffed birds to an excellent display of Egyptian mummies. It houses the

Daredevil Hall of Fame and displays barrels and other contraptions in which people have gone over the falls. There are 26 galleries on four floors and 700,000 exhibits, so gauge your time accordingly—this museum is well worth two hours of browsing. *5651 River Rd., tel. 416/356–2151. Admission: $5.75 adults, $5 senior citizens, $3.75 students, $2.75 children 5–10. Open mid-June–Labor Day, daily 8:30–11; Labor Day–mid-June, daily 10–5.*

Three towers and a huge Ferris wheel offer **panoramic views** of the falls and surrounding area, as does Niagara Helicopters Ltd. (*see* Guided Tours, *above*). The view of the Horseshoe Falls
59 60 is best from the **Skylon Tower** or **Minolta Tower** (at the base of
61 which is a reptile display and aquarium), but the **Kodak Tower** at Maple Leaf Village has the best view over the American Falls, Niagara Gorge, and the rapids above the falls. You can also get a good look over all the falls from atop North America's largest Ferris wheel at **Maple Leaf Village Amusement Park.**

Skylon Tower, 520 feet above ground level, 5200 Robinson St. (directly above the Horseshoe Falls), tel. 416/356–2651. Admission: $5.95 adults, $4.95 senior citizens, $3.50 children 6–12, $16.95 families (2 adults, 2 children). For dining, elevator rate is $1.50 adults, $1 children and senior citizens. Open mid-June–Labor Day, daily 8–1; 10–9 rest of the year.

Minolta Tower, 325 feet above ground level, 6732 Oakes Dr., tel. 416/356–1501. Admission to tower only: $4.95 adult, $3.50 students 5–18 and senior citizens. Admission to tower and aquarium and reptile exhibit: $6.95 adults, $5.95 students and senior citizens. Open in summer, 9–midnight; in winter, 9–9.

Maple Leaf Village and Kodak Tower: The tower is 360 feet above ground level; the top of the Ferris wheel is 175 feet above ground level; 5685 Falls Ave., tel. 416/357–3090. Admission to the village is free. Admission to tower and daredevil exhibit: $5.50 adults, $3.50 senior citizens, $1.50 children under 12. Single ride on Ferris wheel: $3.30, children under 3 free. Open mid-May–mid-Oct., daily 10:30–4; summer, 10–6:30.

62 **Clifton Hill,** almost directly opposite the American falls, is probably the most touristy corner of Niagara Falls. Sometimes referred to as "Museum Alley," this area encompasses the Guinness World of Records Museum, Ripley's Believe It Or Not Museum, Louis Tussaud's Waxworks Museum, The Haunted House, The Funhouse, The House of Frankenstein and Super Star Recording (where you can record the musical number of your choice), Movieland Wax Museum, Criminals Hall of Fame Wax Museum, The Elvis Presley Museum, and the That's Incredible Museum.

63 **White Water Water Park** offers just about every means of getting wet there is, including Canada's biggest waterslide, two hot tubs, and a wave pool. If you arrive within the first hour of the day, you'll receive $1 off the admission price. *7430 Lundy's La., tel. 416/357–3380. Admission: $13.95 adults, $10.95 children, senior citizens free. Open June–Labor Day, daily 10–8.*

64 **Ride Niagara** is a relatively new attraction that opened in 1991. The ride is divided into three portions: a theater presentation, an elevator ride down to the tunnel, and the shuttle that's located near the falls and simulates plunging down the rapids in a barrel. The entire event takes about 20–25 minutes. *5755*

River Rd., tel. 416/374–7433. Admission: $7.95 adults, $6.95 youths 13–18 and senior citizens, $4.25 children 5–12, children 3–5 free. Not recommended for children under 3. Open year-round, daily. Hours vary so call ahead.

Some of the Niagara Peninsula's 13 **wineries** are on the Niagara Parkway between Niagara Falls and Niagara-on-the-Lake (*see below*), or on Highway 55 from the Queen Elizabeth Way. All offer tours, and the product may be sampled and bought. For exact times, call ahead: **Chateau des Charmes Wines Ltd.** (tel. 416/262–4219), **Hillebrand Estates Winery** (tel. 416/468–7123), **Iniskillin Wines** (tel. 416/468–3554), **Konzelmann Winery** (tel. 416/935–2866), **Reif Winery** (tel. 416/468–7738), and **Willow-bank Estate Wines** (tel. 416/468–4219).

Numbers in the margin correspond to points of interest on the Lower Ontario Province map.

65 The Victorian town of **Niagara-on-the-Lake,** 15 kilometers (10 miles) north of Niagara Falls (downriver), is one of Ontario's showplaces. Stately homes sit back from tree-shaded streets, well apart from their neighbors. Though most are at least a century old, their modern-day owners maintain their original charm by keeping rose trellises painted and brass door knockers gleaming. A dozen lovely inns here, some a century and a half old, make this a perfect getaway for Torontorians and tourists worn down by the neon of this village's southern neighbor. Any proposed new business is screened by the village council to ensure that no chrome, glass, or neon-girdled atrocity will mar the Victorian character. There's no room on these tiny roads for the invasion of motor homes, campers, and buses that occurs here each summer, so be prepared for long traffic snarls. The best way to experience the town at any time of year is to stroll.

Don't miss the **Niagara Apothecary,** a pharmacy museum on the main street, across from the 1848 courthouse, which replicates the pharmacy that first opened here in 1866. The serving counters are solid planks of walnut, and the crystal chandeliers are reproductions of original gasoliers. *5 Queen St., tel. 416/962–4861. Admission free. Open mid-May–Labor Day, daily noon–6.*

The **Niagara Historical Society Museum,** built in 1906, houses a collection of artifacts from native times through the arrival of the Loyalists and the War of 1812. *43 Castlereagh St., tel. 416/468–3912. Admission: $2 adults, $1 students, 50¢ children under 12. Open May–Oct., daily 10–5; Jan.–Feb., weekends only 1–5; Mar.–Apr. and Nov.–Dec., daily 1–5.*

The British **Fort George** was fully restored in 1939. Today soldiers in period dress perform drills and musical programs on the parade square. *Niagara Pkwy., tel. 416/468–4257. Admission: $2.75 adults, $1.25 youths 6–16, $7 families, children under 6 and senior citizens free. Open late May–June, daily 9:30–4:30; July–Labor Day, daily 10:30–5:30.*

The event that has really put Niagara-on-the-Lake on the map is the **Shaw Festival** (*see* The Arts and Nightlife, *below,* for details).

The **Niagara Peninsula** is Ontario's fruit basket. From mid-summer to late fall, fruit and vegetable stands proliferate along the highways and byways, and there are several farmers' markets along the Queen Elizabeth Way. One of the best displays of fruits and vegetables is on Lincoln County Road 55 between Niagara-on-the-Lake and the Queen Elizabeth Way, the route you'll take to Hamilton. **Harvest Barn Market**, marked by a red-and-white-striped awning, not only features regional fruits and vegetables but also tempts with a bakery offering sausage rolls, tiny loaves of bread, and fruit pies. You can test the market's wares at the picnic tables, where knowledgeable locals have lunch.

66 **Hamilton** is Canada's steel capital—the Dofasco and Stelco mills produce 60% of Canada's iron and steel. This isn't the sort of city where you'd expect to find 2,700 acres of gardens and exotic plants, a symphony orchestra, a modern and active theater, 45 parks, a 100-voice choir, and an opera. But they're all here in Ontario's second-largest city and Canada's third-busiest port.

The city's downtown is on a plain between the harbor and the base of "the mountain," a 250-foot-high section of the Niagara Escarpment. Downtown Hamilton is a potpourri of glass-walled high rises, century-old mansions, a convention center, coliseum, and shopping complex. Hamilton is also home to Canada's largest indoor farmers' market—176 stalls spread over more than 20,000 square feet—started in 1837. Its new home adjoins Jackson Square and the new Eaton Centre. *Tel. 416/546–2096. Open Tues., Thurs., and Sat. 7–6, Fri. 9–6.*

The 50-year-old **Royal Botanical Gardens** encompass five major gardens and 48 kilometers (30 miles) of trails that wind across marshes and ravines, past the world's largest collection of lilac, two acres of roses, and all manner of shrubs, trees, plants, hedges, and flowers. Two teahouses are open May 1– Thanksgiving. *Plains Rd. (Hwy. 2) in Burlington, accessible from the Queen Elizabeth Way and Hwys. 6 and 403, tel. 416/527–1158; in Ontario and Quebec, 800/668–9449. Admission: (summer) $4.25 adults, $3.25 senior citizens and children 5–12; (winter) no charge to grounds but $2 per visitor to the greenhouse. Main bldg. open daily 9–5; outdoor garden open daily 9:30–6. Closed Christmas.*

Sir Allan Napier MacNab, War of 1812 hero and Upper Canada's pre-Confederation prime minister, built a 35-room mansion called **Dundurn Castle** in 1832–35. It has been furnished to reflect the opulence in which MacNab lived at the height of his political career. *Dundurn Park at York Blvd., tel. 416/522– 5313. Open June–Labor Day, daily 11–4; rest of the year 1–4. Closed Christmas and New Year's Day.*

Flamboro Downs harness racing track, just west of Hamilton, has matinee and evening races year-round, though not on a daily basis. The clubhouse has two dining areas that overlook the track. *Hwy. 5., tel. 416/627–3561.*

67 **Brantford,** 40 kilometers (25 miles) west of Hamilton on Highway 403, is named after Joseph Brant, the Loyalist Mohawk chief who brought members of the Six Nations Confederacy into Canada after the American Revolution.

King George III showed gratitude to Chief Brant and his loyal Indian subjects by building the **Mohawk Church.** In 1904, by Royal assent, it was given the name His Majesty's Chapel of the Mohawks (now changed to Her Majesty's). It is the oldest

Protestant church in Ontario and the only one that may suggest Royal in its name. The simple, white-painted frame building has eight stained-glass windows depicting the colorful history of the Six Nations people. *291 Mohawk St., tel. 519/445–4528. Admission free. A guide is available. Open July–Aug., daily 10–6; the rest of the year, Wed.–Sat. 10–6, Sun. 1–5.*

Woodland Indian Cultural Educational Centre is a museum of sorts that aims to preserve and promote the culture and heritage of the native people of the First Nation. The modern building contains displays and exhibits showing early Woodland Indian culture. *184 Mohawk St., near the Mohawk Chapel, tel. 519/759–2650. Open weekdays 9–4:30, weekends 9–5.*

Although the city is the hometown of hockey star Wayne Gretzky, it is better known as "The Telephone City" because Alexander Graham Bell invented the device here and made the first long-distance call from his parents' home to nearby Paris in 1874. The **Bell Homestead** is now a National Historic Site. Next door is the house of the Reverend Thomas Henderson, a Baptist minister who left the church when he recognized the profit potential in telephones. His home was the first telephone office and now is a museum of telephone artifacts and displays. *94 Tutela Heights Rd., tel. 519/756–6220. Admission: $1 adults, children under 16 free. Guides available. Open mid-Mar.–Thanksgiving, Tues.–Sun. 10–5:45.*

About 27 kilometers (18 miles) north of Brantford by Highway 24 are the cities of **Kitchener** and **Waterloo,** which merge into each another and are usually referred to as K–W. The region was settled around 1800 by Swiss-German Mennonites from Pennsylvania. The German origins remain obvious: There's a huge glockenspiel downtown by Speakers' Corner, and each October since 1967 the city has hosted Oktoberfest. The event now draws more than 600,000 people who swarm to 21 festival halls where they dance, gorge on German-style food, listen to oom-pah bands, and drink with a fervor that seems driven by an irrational fear that all Canadian breweries are about to go on strike.

There are farmers' markets all over Ontario, but the **Kitchener Market** is particularly well known. It isn't the oldest or biggest, but it's been around since 1869 and since 1986 has been housed in spacious quarters at Market Square. The block-long complex is wrapped in green-tinted glass and contains 70 shops and snack bars and an Eaton's department store. *At Frederick and Duke Sts., tel. 519/741–2287. Open Sat. 5 AM–2 PM; mid-May–mid-Oct., Wed. 7 AM–2 PM.*

William Lyon Mackenzie King, who was prime minister of Canada for almost 22 of the years between 1821 and 1848, spent his teenage years in a rented 10-room house called Woodside, now **Woodside National Historic Park.** There's no particular imprint here of the bachelor prime minister whose diaries reveal his belief in mysticism, portents, and communications with the dead, but the house has been furnished to reflect the period of the King family occupancy. *528 Wellington St., tel. 519/742–5273. Admission free. Open daily 10–5. Closed Jan.–Apr.*

The **Seagram Museum** is a shrine to booze, and every exhibit in the enormous former barrel warehouses and new exhibition building relates to the product. Tour guides are available, and for those who develop a powerful thirst while browsing, there's a specialty liquor store that sells Seagram products and gift items. Lunch and dinner are available in a fine dining room on the premises. *57 Erb St. W, tel. 519/746–1673. Open Tues.–Fri. 11–8, Sat.–Sun. 11–5. Closed Mon.*

Doon Heritage Crossroads is a complete pioneer village just north of Highway 401, a few kilometers south and west of Kitchener. The village tranquilly recalls the life-style of a people who lived near the main highway of the early 1800s—the Huron Road. Visitors wander through tree-shaded roadways where neither automobiles nor the noises of the urban complex to the north intrude. Staff at the village wear period costumes, and some work at the old-time crafts. *Tel. 519/748–1914. Open May–Labor Day, weekdays 10–4:30; Labor Day–Dec., weekdays 1:30–4:30. Closed Jan.–Apr.*

69 The villages of **St. Jacobs** and **Elmira,** a few kilometers north of K–W, are in the heart of Mennonite and Hutterite country. These are peaceful people who live off the land, refuse to participate in wars, and have a strict moral code. They also resist modern conveniences, such as cars, electricity, and the internal combustion engine. The region is a shopper's paradise, with many stands selling all manner of fresh and preserved foods and gift items handcrafted by the Mennonites.

70 The city of **Stratford** is 46 kilometers (28 miles) west of Kitchener by Highways 7 and 8. It was named by homesick English settlers; all that the town would have had in common with England's Stratford was a river called Avon meandering through rolling countryside—and not even particularly similar countryside.

The **Stratford Festival** hosts music, opera, and drama annually for more than 400,000 people. (*See* The Arts and Nightlife, *below,* for details.)

71 To reach **London** from Stratford, take Highway 7 west and turn south on Highway 4 at Elginfield. This will bring you into the city's north end and past the entrance to the University of Western Ontario. London is a quiet, provincial city where old money rules the arts and development projects. Its nickname is The Forest City—it has more than 50,000 trees on city property and 1,500 acres of parks, including 1,000 acres along the Thames River. This low-key city has been called a microcosm of Canadian life; it is so "typically Canadian," it's often used as a test market for new products—if something will sell in London, it will probably sell anywhere in Canada.

The easiest way to get an overview of the town is to take a tour on a big, red, double-decker—what else?—London bus. They operate from City Hall, July 1 to Labor Day (at 10 and 2). From June through October you can get another view of London by cruising on the Thames River in a 60-passenger boat. Afternoon cruises (tel. 519/473–0363) depart every hour, June through August, from Storybook Gardens.

Because **Storybook Gardens** is owned and operated by the city's Public Utility Commission, this is one of the least expensive children's theme parks in the country. It's on the Thames River in the 281-acre Springbank Park. You'll see a castle, storybook characters, and a zoo with foreign and indigenous animals, including those from Old MacDonald's Farm. Children can slide down Jack and Jill's hill and the throat of Willie the

Whale. *696 Headley Dr., tel. 519/661–5770. Admission: $3 adults, $1 children. Open May–Labor Day, daily 10–8; Labor Day–Thanksgiving, weekends 10–6.*

London Regional Art and Historical Museum is as interesting from the outside as its exhibits are on the inside. The gallery is contained in six joined, glass-covered structures whose ends are the shape of croquet hoops. *At The Forks of the Thames, tel. 519/672–4580. Open year-round, Tues.–Sun. 10–5 and holidays.*

The **London Museum of Archaeology** houses more than 40,000 native artifacts and a gallery of artists' conceptions of the lives of the Neutral, or Attawandaron, natives who lived on the Lawson site some 500 years ago. Nearby is a reconstructed multi-family longhouse on its original site. *1600 Attawandaron Rd., south of Hwy. 22., tel. 519/473–1360. Admission: $3.50 adults, $2.75 students and senior citizens, $1.50 children, $8 families. Open year-round, daily 10–5.*

London's oldest building is also one of its most impressive. The wrecker's ball came awfully close to the **Old Courthouse Building,** and it got one wall of the former Middlesex County Gaol. But a citizens' group prevailed, and in 1981, after a $2.5 million face-lift, the Old Courthouse, modeled after Malahide Castle in England, reopened as the home of Middlesex County council. On weekday afternoons free tours are available. *Tel. 519/434–7321.*

On the grounds of **Labatt's Brewery** is a well-researched replica of the 1828 London Brewery, which became Labatt's Brewery in 1853. Samples are not offered. *150 Simcoe St., tel. 519/667–7308. Admission free. Open June–Labor Day, Mon.–Sat. 11–5.*

Tour 6: Sault Ste. Marie and West to Thunder Bay

Numbers in the margin correspond to points of interest on the Upper Ontario Province map.

72 **Sault Ste. Marie** has always been a natural meeting place and cultural melting pot. Long before Etienne Brule "discovered" the rapids in 1622, Ojibwa tribes gathered here. Whitefish, their staple food, could easily be caught year-round, and the rapids in the St. Marys River linking Lakes Huron and Superior were often the only open water for miles during the winter. When Father Jacques Marquette opened a mission in 1668, he named it Sainte Marie de Sault. Today everybody but tourists call it simply "The Sault," and the smaller city across the river in Michigan is called "The Soo." Different spelling, identical pronunciation.

The elegant **Ermatinger Stone House** was built by Montréal fur trader Charles Oakes Ermatinger in 1814 and is the oldest building in Canada west of Toronto. Ermatinger married Charlotte, a daughter of influential Indian chief Katawebeda, a move that didn't hurt his business. Today, costumed interpreters show visitors through the house and demonstrate cooking, baking, and crafts. *831 Queen St. E, tel. 705/759–5443. Admission: donation. Open Apr.–May, weekdays 10–5; June–Sept., daily 10–5; Oct.–Nov., daily 1–5.*

One of The Sault's most-touted sights is a boat tour through the **Soo Locks,** the 16th and final lift for ships bound for Lake

Upper Ontario Province

QUÉBEC

ONTARIO

MICHIGAN

Lake Superior

Lake Nipigon

Moosonee **81**

Moose Factory **82**

Otter Rapids

Ontario Northland Railway (Polar Bear Express)

Hearst

Kapuskasing

Smooth Rock Falls

Cochrane **83**

Kirkland Lake

66

101

144

101

560

129

Thunder Bay

Kakabeka Falls **76**

Ouimet Canyon **75**

77

527

Nipigon

17

White River **74**

Wawa **73**

Pukaskwa National Park

Lake Superior Prov. Park

17

Sault Ste. Marie **72**

St. Joseph Island **78**

17

Espanola

Manitoulin Island

Killarney Prov. Park

Sudbury **80**

6 **79**

Superior Route

Northern Route

North Bay

Algonquin Provincial Park

17

TO OTTAWA

KEY

Rail Lines

Trans-Canada Hwy.

N

0   100 miles

0   150 km

Superior from the St. Lawrence River, 600 feet lower and 3,200 kilometers (2,000 miles) downstream. Your cruise boat will be lifted only 21 feet through one of the four locks on the U.S. side, but if you haven't been through a lock before it's an interesting experience. Two-hour tours aboard the **MV** *Chief Shingwauk* or the **MV** *Bon Soo* leave the Norgoma Dock near the Holiday Inn mid-May to mid-October, and up to eight times daily July to Labor Day. *Tel. 705/253–9850.*

The Algoma Central Railway (129 Bay St., tel. 705/254–4331) not only operates main line track between The Sault and iron mines at Hearst and Michipicoten Harbor but also runs a lucrative sideline of tour trains to and from scenic Agawa Canyon, through which their main line passes. From spring through fall the **Agawa Canyon Train Tour** runs from The Sault to Mile 114 (182 kilometers). In winter, the **Snow Train** goes to Mile 120 (192 kilometers). In summer the train stops for two hours in **Agawa Canyon,** a deep valley 19 kilometers (12 miles) long with cliff walls up to 800 feet high through which the Agawa River flows. During the stopover, passengers can lunch in a park, hike to their choice of three waterfalls, or climb to a lookout 250 feet above the train. Tour trains run daily June 5 to mid-October and on Saturday and Sunday only, January through March. Trains depart at 8 AM in summer and 8:30 AM in winter and return at 5 PM. Dining car service is continuous 7 AM–3:45 PM.

Gas up in The Sault before you head north on Highway 17, **The Great North Road.** There is some spectacular scenery along this route. The highway climbs through high hills, and from the top of headlands there are vistas across wide bays in Lake Superior. At the crossings of the Batchawana, Montreal, Agawa, and Michipicoten rivers, south of **Wawa** there are picnic spots. It's 225 kilometers (131 miles) from The Sault to Wawa; the last 80 kilometers (50 miles) is through **Lake Superior Provincial Park.** If you're going to Thunder Bay, 690 kilometers (400 miles) northwest, plan to stop for gas at **Wawa** or **White River.**

㉓ **Wawa** is an Ojibwa word meaning "wild goose," and the 4,000 residents of Wawa have erected a massive goose monument at the entrance to town from Highway 17. Next door is the town's new log-cabin tourist information office.

㉔ **White River,** 90 kilometers (56 miles) north on Highway 17, is marked by a huge thermometer indicating 72 degrees below zero and a sign that advises: "White River—coldest place in Canada." Mayor Ollie Chapman says she'd love to see the thermometer torn down and have a large statue of Winnie-the-Pooh erected in its place to honor the black bear from White River immortalized in Christopher Robin children's stories by British author A. A. Milne. The town is trying to raise half a million dollars for it.

Continue west on the Trans-Canada Highway, around the top of Lake Superior. Just past the town of Hurkett, west of **㉕** Nipigon, watch for signs to **Ouimet Canyon.** This geological anomaly is a midget compared to Agawa Canyon but, because of the vantage point, it is more spectacular. At Ouimet, the visitor strolls a wide path and suddenly comes to the edge of the canyon. Viewing platforms extend over the edge so you can look straight down 329 feet. The far wall is only 492 feet away, and the chasm is only 2.4 kilometers (1.5 miles) long. Geologists believe the canyon could be a gigantic fault in the world's surface, or it could have been carved by a glacier. *The turnoff to Ouimet Park is 67 km (42 mi) northeast of Thunder Bay. Admission: free. Open mid-May–Thanksgiving, daily 9–5.*

76 Although they amalgamated into one city of 110,000 in 1970, there are still **Port Arthur** and **Fort William** sections of **Thunder Bay**. The city is the world's largest grain-handling center and Canada's second-largest port. It has an extraordinary ethnic mix, with 42 nationalities clearly represented, 110 churches, and the largest Finnish population outside Finland. The area has Ontario's best skiing and longest ski season, superb fishing and hunting, unlimited canoe and boating routes, and even mountain climbing. The city has an art gallery, hundreds of restaurants, nine shopping malls, and **Old Fort William** (tel. 807/577–8461), a reconstructed fur-trading fort with 42 historic buildings on a 125-acre site.

The double-decker cruise ship *Welcome* carries visitors on harbor tours and to and from Old Fort William. The harbor cruises get the visitor closer to the giant grain elevators, the ships servicing them, and the nearby islands. Visitors can take the *Welcome* to the fort and return on the cruise company's bus. In mid-summer there are three harbor tours daily, including an evening cruise. *467 Parkwood Dr., tel. 807/344–2512. Admission to harbor cruise: $12.50 adults, $11.50 senior citizens, $6.50 children 6–14, children under 6 free. Admission to Old Fort William cruise and return by bus: $15 adults, $14 senior citizens, $6.50 children 6–14, children under 6 free. Cruises run mid-May–early Oct.*

If legend is to be believed, wearing an amethyst will protect you from hangovers. Ontario's gemstone is an imperfect quartz, tinted violet or purple by the impurity of iron atoms mixing with the original liquid rock. There are five amethyst mines between Sleeping Giant Provincial Park and Ouimet Canyon, a distance of 50 kilometers (31 miles) along Highways 11 and 17 east of Thunder Bay. All are signposted from the highway, and each offers the opportunity to hand-pick some samples (you pay for them by the pound). If you don't want to drive to a mine, the stone is sold in jewelry stores, and several of the mines have shops in the city. **Thunder Bay Amethyst Mine Panorama** is closest to the city and claims to be North America's largest. Also, on the site is a gift shop and custom-jewelry store. Tours run four times daily at 11, 12:30, 3, and 5. Follow Loon Lake Road from Highways 11 and 17, east of Thunder Bay. *East Loon Rd., tel. 807/622–6908. Admission for tours: $1. Open mid-May–June and Sept.–mid-Oct., Mon.–Sat. 10–5; July–Aug., Mon.–Sat. 10–7. Closed Sun.*

77 **Kakabeka Falls** on the Kaministikwia River, 40 kilometers (25 miles) northwest of Thunder Bay, drop 154 feet over a limestone ledge into a deep gorge. The falls can be seen from either side and there are large, free parking lots.

Tour 7: East along Georgian Bay and South to Manitoulin Island

78 **St. Joseph Island** is a sparsely settled island about 24 by 30 kilometers (16 by 20 miles) in the mouth of the St. Mary's River, 40 kilometers (25 miles) southeast of The Sault and connected by causeway and bridge to the mainland. In spring the island is a scented riot of wild lilac, and you're likely to see moose and deer along the quiet side roads. In fur-trading days, Fort St. Joseph was a British fort at the southeast tip of the island that guarded the trade route from Montréal to the upper Great Lakes. Today's visitor can wander the rounded peninsula on which the fort and commercial buildings once stood and see the outlines and a few above-ground stone ruins of the 42 building sites that have been identified. Free walking tours and a free walking-tour booklet are available at the visitor center, which is located about 30 minutes from the bridge. Call ahead for directions. *Tel. 705/246-2664. Open late May–Thanksgiving, daily 10–5.*

East of St. Joseph Island and south of **Espanola,** along Route 6, the world's largest freshwater island sits at the top of Lake Huron plugging the mouth of Georgian Bay. **Manitoulin Island** is 160 kilometers (100 miles) long and varies in width from 3 to 64 kilometers (2 to 40 miles). The island is pretty and rugged, with granite outcrops, forests, meadows, rivers, and rolling countryside. Only 20% of the land is arable, and much of the rest is used for grazing sheep and cattle. Yachtsmen rate the waters around the islands among the best in the world, and hunters and fishermen have taken advantage of the island's riches for generations. Hikes and exploration could easily turn this "side trip" into a week-long stay. This is a place that for the most part has been unravaged by time. Archaeological digs on Manitoulin Island have produced traces of human habitation that are more than 30,000 years old, making them the oldest on the North American continent. There is no interim record of people living on the island until explorer Samuel de Champlain met some island residents in 1650.

Little Current–Howland Centennial Museum, about 18 kilometers (12 miles) south of **Little Current,** in the village of Sheguiandah on Highway 6, displays native and pioneer artifacts. *Tel. 705/368-2367. Admission: $1.50 adults, $1 senior citizens and students, 75¢ children 5–12. Open June–mid-Sept., daily 10–4:30 and Thanksgiving weekend.*

The extreme eastern end of the island is **Wikwemikong,** 484 square kilometers (300 square miles). One of Manitoulin's most colorful events is the Wikwemikong Pow Wow, held on Civic Holiday weekend. Dancers accompanied by drummers and singers compete for prizes while performing the steps of their ancestors.

Back on the mainland, about 60 kilometers (40 miles) east of Espanola, is the mining town of **Sudbury,** which used to bear the brunt of a lot of unkind jokes. After all, didn't the U.S. astronauts go there to train in the type of terrain they were likely to encounter on the moon? Today, the Greening of Sudbury, a student planting project, and other renovations have given this clean city of 90,000 a face-lift. New, imaginatively designed buildings, well-lighted streets, and a downtown anchored by a spiffy Civic Square Provincial Tower invite visitors. There are concerts in the park, art centers, and a cruise on Lake Ramsey, the largest freshwater lake inside city limits in North America.

Northern Ontario's biggest tourism magnet, **Science North,** opened in 1984. This hands-on science museum is housed in two snowflake-shaped buildings that cling to a rocky ledge of the shore of Lake Ramsey. Lie on a bed of nails, create a soapstone carving, or make your own hurricane or snowstorm. At every turn there are eager museum staff to answer questions and encourage participation in the dozens of laboratories. *100 Ramsey Lake Rd., tel. 705/522–3701. Admission: $7.50 adults, $5 children. Open May–Oct., daily 9–5; Nov.–Apr., daily 10–4.*

The Big Nickel, a 30-foot replica of the Canadian 1951 commemorative coin, has been synonymous with Sudbury for almost three decades. It is the largest coin in the world and stands on a barren hillside on the west side of the city, overlooking the smokestacks of the International Nickel Company (INCO). Near the Big Nickel is the entrance to **The Big Nickel Mine.** At 23 meters (73 feet), it is one of the shallowest mines in the area. Science North (*see above*) offers tours of the mine in summer. Visitors are given hard hats, coats, and boots and lowered into the mine shaft in a "cage" elevator. In the 400-meter-long (437-yard-long) drifts, or tunnels, miners demonstrate mining techniques. *At Hwy. 17 and Big Nickel Mine Rd., tel. 705/673–5659 or 705/522–3701. Tour runs May–June 25, daily 9–5; June 26–Labor Day, daily 9–7; Labor Day–Oct. 9, daily 9–5.*

The 2½-hour **Path of Discovery Tour** bus leaves from The Big Nickel and Science North several times daily. Visitors are taken to the spot where a railroad worker discovered copper and nickel ores 4 kilometers (2.5 miles) west of the townsite in 1884. The tour also goes to the edge of the Sudbury Basin, a massive indentation in the landscape created 2 billion years ago by a meteorite, a volcanic eruption, or a combination of the two. The event created an elliptical depression 59 kilometers (40 miles) long and 27 kilometers (18 miles) wide. The tour visits Sudbury's oldest mine, historic sites in Copper Cliff, and the smelter and super stack at INCO, the world's largest integrated nickel mining, smelting, and refining complex. *Tel. 705/673–5659 or 705/522–3701. Admission: $11 adults, $7 children and senior citizens, children under 5 free. Same hours as Science North, above.*

Tour 8: From Cochrane to Moosonee and Moose Factory Island

⑧① ⑧② **Moosonee** and **Moose Factory** are considered Ontario's gateway to the Arctic. Although you can fly to Moosonee (Air Creebac, tel. 705/264–9521, has service from Timmins), Ontario Northland's **Polar Bear Express** train is the more popular and the more nostalgia-inducing option. The Polar Bear makes a
⑧③ round-trip from **Cochrane,** 300 kilometers (200 miles) south, every day of the week except Friday, from late June to Labor Day. There's train service to Cochrane from Toronto or North Bay. The Polar Bear Express leaves Cochrane at 8:30 AM and arrives at Moosonee just before 1 PM. It departs Moosonee at 5:15 PM and returns to Cochrane by 9:20 PM. Meals, light lunches, and snacks are available in the restaurant-snack car.

Moose Factory Island, one of a number in the delta of the Moose River, is 8 kilometers (5 miles) long and just over a kilometer wide. It's a 20-minute boat ride from Moosonee. Passengers then transfer to a bus or van. The island was the site of the second Hudson's Bay Company trading post, established in 1672 on what was then called Hayes Island, 24 kilometers (16 miles) up the Moose River from James Bay. It was captured by the French in 1686 and renamed Fort St. Louis. Contrary to popular myth, the holes in the floor of **St. Thomas Anglican Church** are to let floodwater *out* and to ventilate the foundation. When the church was being built in 1864, the foundation floated a short distance in a spring flood, but the church itself has never floated anywhere. The altar cloths and lectern hangings are of moose hide decorated with beads.

The Hudson's Bay Post is a modern building, and the company now goes by the name of Northern Stores. Beside it is the 1850 **Hudson's Bay Staff House** in which are sold animal pelts, carvings, snowshoes, gloves, slippers, and beadwork.

Some guidebooks will tell you the **Blacksmith's Shop** in Centennial Park on Moose Factory Island is the oldest wooden building in Ontario. It isn't, but the stone forge inside it may be the oldest "structure" in the province. The original shop was built in the late 1600s but moved back from the riverbank in 1820. Because the forge stones had been transported a long distance, they were disassembled and rebuilt at the present location. In summer an apprentice smithy runs the forge and explains its operation.

Moosonee is Ontario's only tidal port and, even though it's almost 20 kilometers (14 miles) from James Bay, summer tides average 5 feet. The community came into existence only in 1903, when the Revillon Frères Trading Company of France established a post to compete with the Hudson's Bay Company. It wasn't until the Ontario Northland Railway arrived in 1932 that the region's population began to catch up to that of Moose Factory. The Moosonee visitor center (tel. 705/336–2480) is in a small, one-floor office building on First Street. Next door is a theater in which free videos on wildlife and natural and cultural history are shown. Opposite the dock on Revillon Road, a small, two-story frame house has displays and artifacts recalling the heyday of the area's fur trade. Farther down Revillon Road is the modern Ministry of Natural Resources Interpretive Centre, offering exhibits of regional wildlife and of the area's geological and geographical history. During tourist season there are stalls on Revillon Road where natives sell handcrafts ranging from moccasins and buckskin vests to trinkets, beadwork, and wood and stone carvings.

For more information about the area, or if you're interested in an overnight stay, contact **Ontario Northland** (65 Front St. W, Toronto, Ont. M5J 1E6, tel. 416/965–4268).

What to See and Do with Children

African Lion Safari, Rockton, near Hamilton. Lions, tigers, cheetahs, elephants, and zebras abound in this wildlife park. You can drive your own car or take an air-conditioned tram over a 9-kilometer (6-mile) safari trail. *Off Hwy. 8, south of Cambridge, tel. 519/623–2620. Admission: $13.50 adults, $11.50 senior citizens and youths 13–17, $9.50 children 3–12. Grounds open early Apr.–Oct., daily 9–6:30; tours run weekdays 10–4, weekends 10–5.*
Doon Heritage Crossroads, near Kitchener (*see* Tour 5).
Maple Leaf Village Amusement Park, Niagara Falls (*see* Tour 5).

Marineland, Niagara Falls (*see* Tour 5).
National Museum of Science and Technology, Ottawa (*see* Tour 1).
Old Fort William, Thunder Bay (*see* Tour 6).
Sainte-Marie among the Hurons, Midland (*see* Tour 3).
Santa's Village, Bracebridge (*see* Tour 3).
Science North (*see* Tour 7).
Storybook Gardens, London (*see* Tour 5).
Upper Canada Village, Morrisburg (*see* Tour 2).

Shopping

Native Crafts

Ottawa, Sault Ste. Marie, Midland, and Thunder Bay have museum shops and galleries that specialize in native and Inuit crafts. In Thunder Bay, **The North West Company Inc.** (413 Victoria Ave. E, tel. 807/623–2241) has Inuit soapstone carvings, fossilized ivory, and Hudson's Bay point blankets and coats.

Antiques

John Coles at the **Astrolabe Gallery** (90 Sparks St., tel. 613/234–2348) is a good source for 19th-century prints of Ottawa scenes or antique maps of North America. Some of the best antiques can be found at small shops in **Bayfield, Cobourg, Meaford, Peterborough, Shakespeare,** and **St. Jacobs.** Sunday flea markets in **Aberfoyle, Burlington, Grand Bend,** and **Hamilton** can be another good source of antiques.

Shopping Centers and Malls

Rideau Centre at Rideau and Sussex streets in Ottawa has more than 200 stores, including The Bay, Ogilvy's, and Eaton department stores.

In Hamilton, **Hess Village** is a small area crammed with interesting boutiques, cafés, and pubs.

Windsor draws shoppers from nearby Michigan seeking British imports of china and woolens.

In Paris, try **Halls's** on the main street for Irish linens.

Sports and Outdoor Activities

Bicycling

Ottawa has 114 kilometers (65 miles) of **bicycle paths.** On Sunday, **Queen Elizabeth Drive** and **Colonel By Drive** are closed to traffic until noon for cyclists. There are miles of bicycle trails in and around **Toronto,** but two of the best biking spots are **Hanlan's Point Island** and **Ward's Island** in Lake Ontario, just offshore from Toronto. In summer, ferries leave the foot of Bay Street every 15 minutes. The NPC operates 55 kilometers (30 miles) of **bicycle trails** along the Niagara River between Fort Erie and Niagara-on-the-Lake. The city of **Brantford** is protected by a flood-control dam on top of which is a bicycle trail that passes most of the city's many interesting tourist attractions. Two other popular bikes routes can be accessed from **Fergus,** 24 kilometers (15 miles) northwest of Guelph: One is a 32-kilometer (20-mile) tour around Lake Belwood, and the other is a 40-kilometer (25-mile) loop around Eramosa Township. There is little traffic on these scenic routes, and restaurants are few and far between, so it's advised that you take a picnic lunch along. Another scenic spot, **London's Springbank Park,** has miles of pretty bicycle trails.

Camping

There are 261 provincial parks in Ontario and hundreds of other parks that are privately owned and operated as businesses. The provincial parks are owned, maintained, and protected by the province, and they range in size from being only a few acres to massive areas of land such as Polar Bear Provincial Park, which, at 15,000 square kilometers (9,300 square miles), is just a tad smaller than 15,498-square-kilometer (9,609-square-mile) state of Vermont. Algonquin, created in 1893, is Ontario's oldest park, and at 4,764 square kilometers (2,954 square miles), it's only 495 square kilometers (307 square miles) smaller than the combined size of the states of Rhode Island and Delaware.

Most of the provincial parks offer a variety of services for campers, from electrical outlets and sturdy, covered picnic shelters to laundry facilities and camp stores for provisions. Additionally, many sponsor educational programs that teach children wilderness survival techniques and aim to offer a better understanding of nature.

In southern Ontario most provincial parks are in full operation from mid-May until Labor Day weekend; in northern Ontario provincial parks are generally open from early June until Labor Day weekend. Even when "closed," however, the parks never completely shut down and visitors are welcome in the off-season, though few facilities are maintained. Some parks may be gated to prevent vehicular entry, but all are accessible to pedestrians from sunrise to sunset. Expect vault privies to be open, fireplace grates should be available, and fees usually will be collected through self-serve registration. Winter camping, which is becoming a popular pastime, is allowed in some provincial parks, though most are unsupervised and facilities are limited. During the fall and winter months reservations are not required at most parks.

Peak season in Ontario's parks is June through August, and it is advised that you reserve a campsite, if reservations are accepted. It's possible to request space in advance by telephone (tel. 416/963–2992 or 800/ONTARIO for reservations and availability), mail, or in person, and sites can be guaranteed by using a Visa or MasterCard credit card. However, reservations are not always accepted or necessary: All provincial parks have some sites available on a first-come, first-served basis. In an effort to avoid overcrowding on canoe routes and hiking or backpacking trails in major canoeing parks such as Algonquin, Quetico, Killarney, and Frontenac parks, daily quotas have been established governing the number of people permitted in the parks. In these parks interior permits can be reserved ahead of time.

In the four above-mentioned parks and in Lake Superior Provincial Park, cans and bottles are banned throughout, and are permitted only in the organized car campground areas. For more detailed information on parks and campgrounds in Ontario, write to Ontario Ministry of Tourism (77 Bloor St. W, Toronto, Ont. M7A 2R9) for the free catalogue.

Dog Sledding

Dog-sledding excursions ranging from half-hour runs to overnights in wilderness outpost cabins are offered by outfitters at Shanty Bay (near Barrie), Temagami, Dorset, and Vermilion Bay. Two companies offer one- to four-day dog-sledding packages from downtown Toronto. **Harbourfront Canoe School** (283A Queen's Quay W, Toronto, Ont. M5V 1A2, tel. 416/861–1233) has a one-day dog-sled excursion to the edge of Algonquin Park for $176.55 per person, including taxes, instruction, trip, and lunch and supper. **Voyageur Quest** (129 Coldstream Ave., Toronto, Ont. M5N 1X7, tel. 416/322–3605) offers a four-day combination dog-sledding/snowshoeing/cross-country skiing package to Temagami at $275 per person including all equipment, accommodation, food, and instruction. **Burton Penner** (Box 151, Vermilion Bay, Ont. P0V 2V0, tel. 807/227–5593) of Vermilion Bay, 91 kilometers (57 miles) east of Kenora, offers guided dog sled tours into the wilderness, overnighting in an outpost cabin or heated-wall tent. Rates run from $300 per person for a one-night trip to $595 per person for a three-night trip, maximum of three people per trip, everything included.

Fishing

Ontario has about 250,000 lakes and 150,000 rivers that contain an inestimable number of species of fish. The favorite trophies of most anglers are salmon and trout but others lust after pike or muskie and still others swear that battling a frenzied black bass on light tackle is life's ultimate piscatorial challenge.

Licenses are required for fishing in Ontario and may be purchased from the Ministry of Natural Resources district offices and from most sporting goods stores, outfitters, and resorts. Seasons and catch limits change annually and some districts infringe closed seasons. Restrictions are published in *Summary of the Fishing Regulations,* free from the Ministry of Natural Resources (Public Information Centre, Macdonald Block, Room M1-73, 900 Bay St., Toronto, Ont. M7A 1W3, tel. 416/314–2000).

Fishing Lodges There are about 500 fishing resorts and lodges listed in the current catalogue of fishing packages issued by the Ontario Ministry of Tourism (77 Bloor St. W, Toronto, Ont. M7A 2R9) and available free. The establishments listed are not hotels that happen to be located near bodies of water that contain fish but are businesses designed to make sport fishing available to their guests. To that end, each property offers such things as boats, motors, guides, float planes, freezers, and all the other accoutrements of the modern fisherman.

When planning your vacation at a fishing lodge, you may be surprised by the rates: Horse racing may be the sport of kings, but modern-day sport fishing must run a close second in terms of the cost of equipment, apparel, and logistics. A good example is **Totem Lodge** (Sioux Narrows, off Lake of the Woods; Totem Lodge, Box 180, Sioux Narrows P0X 1N0, tel. 807/226–5275), 60 kilometers (37 miles) south of Kenora, with standards by which other lodges in the province may be gauged. Guests can stay in deluxe suites at the lodge or deluxe housekeeping cabins, all with air-conditioning, satellite TV, and wood-burning fireplaces. There's a store on the grounds for supplies and a dining room with no set meal hours. The lodge's fleet of fishing boats and motors is brand new each year and the boats are equipped with videographs, downriggers, depthfinders, live wells, and two-way VHF marine-band radios. Since not all fishermen want to stay on top of the stock market or office crises when the big ones are biting, cellular telephones in the boats are optional. Another option is to have your catch cleaned, packaged, and frozen, so you won't even have to touch it once it's been hooked. A six-night, five-day package at Totem Lodge starts at $1,195 per person, double occupancy, and includes three meals daily, fishing boat with gas and bait, fishing license, guide, and pickup and return to Kenora.

Ice Fishing During the winter most of Ontario's 250,000 lakes freeze, providing good fishing for hardy souls who want to drill a hole through the ice and drop down a baited hook and line. The best ice-fishing spots in Ontario are Mitchell's Bay off Lake St. Clair, Lake Simcoe, Lake Nipissing, and lakes between and around North Bay and Temagami. Licenses are required for any fishing in Ontario, and they may be purchased from the Ministry of Natural Resources district offices, and most sporting goods stores, tourist outfitters, and resorts. Seasons and catch limits change annually and there are closed seasons in some districts. Regulations are published in the above-mentioned *Summary of the Fishing Regulations.*

Hiking

Hiking trails are signposted along all Ontario highways, and usually there's parking, trail information, and comfort stations. A popular mini-hike in southern Ontario (part of the Grand Valley Trail) is the 5-kilometer (3-mile) pathway along the Elora Gorge between Fergus and Elora. Among the features are a whirlpool at Templin Gardens, a restored English garden, and a bridge across the gorge at Mirror Basin, where there are excellent views up and down the gorge. This hike should not be attempted in street shoes.

Other trails include the 680-kilometer (430-mile) **Bruce Trail,** which stretches along the limestone Niagara Escarpment from the orchards of the Niagara Peninsula to the cliffs and bluffs at Tobermory, at the end of the Bruce Peninsula. Contact the Bruce Trail Association (Box 857, Hamilton, Ont. L8N 3N9). Also, there's the **Grand Valley Trail,** running 128 kilometers (80 miles) between Elora and Brantford. Contact the Grand Valley Trail Association (Box 1233, Kitchener, Ont. N2G 4G8). The **Rideau Trail** runs 406 kilometers (241 miles) along the Rideau Canal from Kingston to Ottawa. Access points from the highway are marked with orange triangles. Contact Rideau Trail Association (Box 15, Kingston, K7L 4V6).

Ice Climbing

Only one Ontario company offers ice-climbing instruction and expeditions. **Alpamayo Exploration and Adventure Services Co.** (Box 2204, Thunder Bay, Ont. P7B 5E8, tel. 807/344–9636) has one-day trips or expeditions up to five days in length in the Thunder Bay area. One-day trips with one instructor per four participants costs $75 per person including all equipment, but no meals. Five-day ice-climbing trips for beginner, intermediate, or advanced climbers cost $900 per person. Deluxe accommodations in rustic cabins or motels are provided, but meals are not included.

Skiing

Cross-country   Nordic ski trails exist just about anywhere in the province where you'll find snow and accommodations for skiers. Around Toronto, try **Caledon Ski Club** (tel. 519/927–5221) in Caledon; **Glen Eden Ski Area** (tel. 416/878–5011) near Milton; and **Hockley Valley Resort** (tel. 519/942–0754) near Orangeville. **Horseshoe Valley** (tel. 705/835–2790) near Barrie also offers Nordic skiing.

In southern Ontario, the Huntsville area (215 kilometers, 134 miles) north of Toronto is usually the cross-country skier's best bet for an abundance of natural snow. The region is riddled with lakes and streams, stands of virgin birch and pine, and deer and smaller forest dwellers that live along the trail. Because the area is Toronto's summer playground, too, there is no shortage of year-round resorts from spectacular, self-contained communities such as the ultra-deluxe **Deerhurst Resort** (tel. 705/789–6411) to the rustic cottages of **Norseman Restaurant** at **Walker Lake Resort** (tel. 705/635–2473), which overlook deer-feeding stations on either side of the frozen lake.

Lodge-to-Lodge   From the town of Haliburton, 250 kilometers (156 miles) northeast of Toronto, three- and four-night guided lodge-to-lodge cross-country ski packages are available along the Haliburton Nordic Trail system. There are groups for skiers of all levels, and the trips cover 8–25 kilometers (5–16 miles) per day, depending on the group's abilities. Eight lodges participate in the program and skiers stay and dine at a different lodge each night; by the time skiers come off the trail, luggage will be in their rooms. Packages include all meals, trail passes, and a guide. Three-night packages cost $349 single, $319 per person, double occupancy; four-night packages are $419 single, $379 per person, double occupancy.

Downhill   Ontario has hundreds of alpine slopes, although most are under 200 meters (640 feet) in vertical drop. All major Ontario ski centers have high-tech snow-making equipment, which in average years has guaranteed good skiing from late November through early April. For a recorded snow report of most Ontario resorts call 416/314–0998.

The highest ski slopes are **Candy Mountain Resort** (tel. 807/475–5633) and **Loch Lomond** (tel. 807/475–7787), both just outside Thunder Bay and both with 235 meters (750 feet) of vertical. Lift tickets are interchangeable between Candy Mountain and Loch Lomond. Also close to Thunder Bay are **Big Thunder National Ski Centre** and **Mount Baldy Ski Area.**

Big Thunder has a vertical drop of 200 meters (650 feet) and a 5-kilometer (3-mile) lighted trail, and is served by a double chair and T-bar. Mount Baldy Ski Area is served by a double chair and T-bar and has a vertical drop of 195 meters (650 feet).

Blue Mountain (tel. 705/445–0231 or 416/869–3799 in Toronto), near Collingwood north of Toronto, is the most extensively developed and heavily trafficked mountain, with a vertical drop of 216 meters (720 feet). It has 31 pistes serviced by a high-speed quad lift, three triple chairs, eight double chairs, two pomas, and a rope tow. The acclaimed **Blue Mountain Inn** (tel. 705/445–0231) with 103 rooms, indoor swimming pool, fireplaces in some rooms and an assortment of restaurants and lounges, is at the base of the ski hills.

Near Barrie, 90 kilometers (56 miles) north of Toronto, is **Horseshoe Resort,** with 22 trails serviced by a quad and two triple and three double lifts. The vertical drop is only 94 meters (309 feet), but seven of the runs are rated for advanced skiers. The popular **Inn at Horseshoe** has 102 rooms and suites on the hill, as well as an indoor swimming pool, lounges, and fine dining. Many of the suites have whirlpools and wood-burning fireplaces.

Mount Madawaska ski area (tel. 613/756–2931), near Barry's Bay west of Ottawa, has a vertical drop of 120 meters (400 feet).

Snowmobiling

Ontario is crisscrossed by thousands of miles of snowmobile trails, most of which are kept groomed by enthusiastic members of dozens of snowmobile clubs. For many trails a permit must be purchased. Overnight guided excursions are available in Haliburton Highlands/Algonquin Park and out of Kenora. **C Mac Snow Tours** (R.R. 3 Walton, Ont. N0K 1Z0, tel. 519/887–6686) has five-night, four-day trips for $590–$690 per person, double occupancy. The all-inclusive excursions are in Haliburton Highlands/Algonquin Park. At Kenora, **Halley's Camps** has guided excursions on wilderness trails to outpost camps for three to six nights, starting at $595 per person. The expeditions are all-inclusive, including fishing tackle for ice fishing, cross-country skis, snowshoes, and a snowmobile with gas and oil. (Box 608, Kenora, Ont. P9N 3X6, tel. 807/224–6531 or 800/465–3325 in all provinces but B.C.)

Dining and Lodging

Dining

Highly recommended restaurants in each price category are indicated by a star ★.

Category	Cost*
Very Expensive	over $50
Expensive	$35–$50
Moderate	$15–$35
Inexpensive	under $15

per person, excluding drinks, service, 7% GST, 8% food tax, and 10% bar tax

Lodging

Reservations are strongly recommended anywhere in Ontario during summer months.

Generally you get what you pay for at Ontario hotels and motels, though rates are often double or more than those charged in the United States for comparable accommodation.

Bed-and-breakfast associations exist in most cities, but many of those rates exceed what you'd pay for a good hotel or motel room south of the border.

In Niagara Falls, the closer the hotel is to the falls, or the better the view is of them, the higher the rate.

Highly recommended lodgings in each price category are indicated by a star ★.

Category	Cost*
Very Expensive	over $100
Expensive	$75–$100
Moderate	$35–$75
Inexpensive	under $35

All prices are for a standard double room, excluding 10% service charge.

Alton
Dining and Lodging
★

The Millcroft Inn. Situated about 80 kilometers (50 miles) northwest of Toronto is this former 19th-century stone knitting mill, which has been converted to an exquisite full-service country inn beside the millpond. It is one of Canada's finest hostelries and a member of the Relais & Chateaux Association. The dining room is a stage for the Millcroft's executive chef, Fredy Stamm, who changes the menus monthly but with advance notice will prepare any guest's favorite dish. *John St., L0N 1A0, tel. 519/941–8111. 42 rooms and suites, some with fireplaces. Reservations advised for dining room. Dress: casual. AE, DC, MC, V. Very Expensive.*

Bracebridge
Dining and Lodging
★

Inn at the Falls. Recently redone by professional new owners, this Victorian inn and its annex of motel-style rooms command a magnificent view of the pretty Bracebridge Falls on the Muskoka River. The main dining room and pub-lounge offer food and live entertainment; there's an outdoor patio for dining and sipping as well. The innkeepers live up to their boast of "the best steak-and-kidney pie this side of the Atlantic." *17 Do* *minion St., Box 1139, P0B 1C0, tel. 705/645–2245. 17 rooms, 6 with fireplaces. Facilities: dining room, pub, dining patio, parlor, outdoor heated pool. Reservations advised for restaurant. Dress: casual. AE, MC, V. Expensive.*

Cambridge
Dining and Lodging
★

Langdon Hall. This magnificent colonial-revival-style mansion on 40 landscaped acres has grand public rooms and huge fireplaces. It was built in 1898 as a summer home for a great-grandson of John Jacob Astor and has been sensitively converted to a grand country hotel with 13 guest rooms in the original building and 28 in a modern annex. The chef, Nigel Didcock, has trained in a number of prestigious kitchens in France, and his menu offers variations on French and Continental dishes. *Take Exit 275 from Hwy. 401 west of Kitchener, travel south on Fountain St./Homer Watson Blvd., to Blair Rd. Go through the village of Blair to Langdon Rd. Turn at the first driveway on the left and follow the lane to Langdon Hall, RR3, N3H 4R8, tel. 519/740–2100. Facilities: meeting rooms, conservatory and drawing room, outdoor heated pool, sauna, whirlpool, exercise equipment, billiard room, card room, canoes (for the nearby Grand River), ballooning, tennis, croquet, 24-hour room service. Jacket recommended in dining room. AE, MC, V. Very Expensive.*

Cochrane
Dining and Lodging

If you plan to take the *Polar Bear Express* train, you'll probably need to stay over in Cochrane. There are seven motels in and around Cochrane, ranging in size from seven to 42 units. Only two have restaurant facilities, but all are geared to early wake-up calls for guests taking the *Polar Bear Express* and late check-ins for those returning from the excursion. The four largest are **Westway Motor Motel,** 21 First St., tel. 705/272–4285; **First Canada Inns,** 200 Railway St., tel. 705/272–3500; **Motel Cochrane,** R.R. 2, tel. 705/272–4253; and **Chimo Motel,** Box 2326, tel. 705/272–6555. The postal code for all four is P0L 1C0.

Elora
Dining and Lodging
★

Elora Mill. This is one of Canada's few remaining five-story gristmills, which has been converted to luxury accommodations and offers superb dining. There are 16 guest rooms in the 1859 mill building and 16 more rooms in four other historic stone buildings in the immediate vicinity of the mill. The inn is in the heart of a village with historic stone buildings that could have been lifted from England's Cotswolds or southern France. The cuisine is a mix of imaginative Canadian and European dishes. *77 Mill St. W, tel 519/846–5356. Reservations advised for dining room. Dress: casual. AE, MC, V. Expensive.*

Goderich
Dining
★

La Brassine. The kitchen in this large farm home–cum–country inn produces some of the finest French cuisine west of the Québec border. It's available only to those few who have booked ahead at least 24 hours for Wednesday–Saturday dinners or daily for residents of the five double guest rooms in the inn. Everything served is created in-house; the linen-covered tables are set with crystal and silver. *Off Hwy. 21, midway between Bayfield and Goderich; turn toward Lake Huron on Kitchigami Rd., RR2, N7A 3X8, tel. 519/524–6300. Dress: casual; no shorts or T-shirts. Cash or personal check preferred to major credit cards. Note: no license for beer, wine, or liquor. Moderate.*

Hamilton
Dining

Ancaster Old Mill. This historic mill is just outside Hamilton and worth the trip if only to sample the bread, baked daily with flour made at the mill on millstones installed in 1863. The dining rooms are light and bright and have hanging plants. Try to get a table overlooking the mill stream and a waterfall. *548 Old Dundas Rd., Ancaster, L9G 3J4 (from Hwy. 403 west of Hamilton take Mohawk Road W exit to Wilson St. in Ancaster. Turn right to Montgomery Dr., turn left and follow signs), tel. 416/648–1827. AE, DC, MC, V. Moderate.*

Dining and Lodging **The Royal Connaught Hotel.** The venerable Royal Connaught Hotel in the heart of downtown Hamilton was built in 1914 and is one of those grand old places complete with ballroom. The lobby and seventh floor have recently been renovated. The indoor swimming pool has one of Canada's longest waterslides. The Grill is the hotel's very popular dining room. Meat is broiled over an open fire of mesquite. There's a marble floor, and after you've eaten—or while you're waiting for your entrée to be flamed—you can dance in the gazebo. *112 King St. E, L8N 1A8, tel. 416/546–8111 or 800/263–8558; fax 416/546–8144. 207 rooms, 21 suites. Facilities: restaurant, lounge, comedy cabaret, sauna, whirlpool. Dress: casual. AE, MC, V. Expensive.*

Kingston **The Prince George Hotel** and the **Canoe Club Bar and Grill.**
Dining and Lodging Located just down the street from the city's magnificent town hall, this hotel, built in 1809, is also one of the city's historic showplaces. The Canoe Club (which gets its name from the 60-foot-long rowing scull built for Olympic rowers in 1950 and hanging from the ceiling) is a popular dining spot with an eclectic menu. And the hotel is a cozy charmer. Rooms are decorated in Victorian style and overlook a park and Lake Ontario. Continental breakfast is included with the room rate. *200 Ontario St., K7L 2Y9, tel. 613/549–5440. 22 rooms, 2 suites. AE, MC, V. Hotel: Moderate. Restaurant: Inexpensive.*

Kitchener **Valhalla Inn.** This modern hotel has a major sports complex in
Dining and Lodging its basement and is connected by a glassed-in skywalk to the Market Square shopping mall and Farmers' Market. Shatzi's, the main restaurant, seats 75 and the attached café accommodates about 40. All three meals are served in both dining areas, but for more formal, romantic occassions the main, candlelit room—decorated in earthtones—is more suitable. Continental fare dominates the menu. *105 King St. E, N2G 3W9, tel. 519/744–4141. 203 rooms. Facilities: dining room, lounge, restaurant, banquet room, fitness center with indoor pool, sauna, whirlpool, miniature golf. AE, MC, V. Expensive.*

Walper Terrace Hotel. This rejuvenated 1893 hotel sustains a Kitchener tradition started in 1820 by Phineas Varnum, who leased land from Joseph Schneider (of packing-house fame) to build what was then called the Varnum Inn. It now features at least one piece of period cherry-wood furniture in each of the guest rooms. The wooden-trim moldings, carved marble pillars, and the ornate brass banister of the main staircase have been preserved. The Terrace Cafe has an art deco floor, vaulted ceilings, marble pillars, stained glass windows, and a view of one of the city's major intersections. The setting is romantic, and meals are moderately priced. *1 King St. W, N2G 1A1, tel. 519/745–4321. 90 rooms, 12 suites. Facilities: restaurant, lounge, mini shopping mall, ballroom. AE, MC, V. Expensive.*

London **Marienbad and Chaucer's Pub.** Reasonably priced Czechoslo-
Dining vakian fare is served in surroundings that will remind you of your Eastern European vacation (if you had one). Great goulash, schnitzels, and sauerbraten are among the choices. *122*

Carling St., N6A 1H6, tel. 519/679–9940. Dress: casual. AE, MC, V. Moderate.

Michael's on the Thames. This popular lunch and dinner spot overlooking the Thames River offers flambéed dishes and has a maître d', Jack DiCarlo, who has become something of a local celebrity with his impromptu song-and-dance acts. The Canadian and Continental cuisine includes fresh seafood, chateaubriand, and flaming desserts and coffees. *1 York St. at the Thames River, N6A 1A1, tel. 519/672–0111. Reservations advised. Dress: casual. AE, MC, V. Moderate.*

Lodging **Idlewylde Inn.** Though an elevator was installed in this converted 1878 mansion, the architects succeeded in keeping many original features in the 25 luxurious guest rooms and suites and in the public rooms. Complimentary breakfast and snacks are included in the rate. *36 Grand Ave., N6C 1L1, tel. 519/433–2891. AE, DC, MC, V. Very Expensive.*

Sheraton Armouries Hotel. This 20-story silver-mirrored tower rises from the center of the 1905 London Armoury. The lobby is a greenhouse of vines, trees, plants, and fountains wrapped in marble and accented by rich woods and old yellow brick. The architects left as much of the original armory intact as possible. A set of steps through manicured jungle takes you to the indoor swimming pool, sauna, and whirlpool. Guest rooms are spacious and decorated in pastel shades. Suites vary in size and grandeur—for example, the Middlesex Suite has a grand piano. *325 Dundas St., N6B 1T9, tel. 519/679–6111 or 800/325–3535. 250 rooms and suites. Facilities: racquetball and squash courts, pool, sauna, whirlpool, entertainment, sushi restaurant, dining room. AE, MC, V. Expensive.*

London also has a strip of motels on Wellington Road north of Highway 401 and on Dundas Street East, out toward the airport.

Midland **The Highland Inn.** This is a completely self-contained year-round hotel/motel/resort, most of which is contained in an enormous atrium. Sunday brunches by the pool in the Garden Cafe are popular. There are four dining areas, honeymoon suites with heart-shaped tubs or sunken Jacuzzis, meeting rooms, a tanning room, exercise and weight rooms, and a full-time fitness director. *King St. and Hwy. 12, Box 515, L4R 4L3, tel. 705/526–9307; 800/461–4265 for reservations. 125 rooms and suites. AE, MC, V. Moderate.*
Dining and Lodging

Moosonee In Moosonee you can choose either the 30-room **Polar Bear Lodge** (tel. 705/336–2345) or the 21-room **Moosonee Lodge** (tel. 705/336–2351), both of which are on Revillon Street facing the Moose River. Rates are high for the caliber of accommodation, but if you want to stay, these are your choices. Both hotels serve meals, but alcohol is served only during the dinner hour, and then only to those dining at the hotel. The mailing address for both Moosonee hotels is: 65 Enterprise Rd., Rexdale, Ont. M9W 1C4.
Dining and Lodging

Niagara Falls **Capri Restaurant.** Soft chairs and a softly tinkling piano create an elegant mood here. The combination of good steak, seafood, and Italian dishes makes this one of the better Niagara dining spots. *5438 Ferry St., tel. 416/354–7519. Dress: casual. AE, MC, V. Moderate.*
Dining

Queenston Heights Restaurant. This is one of four restaurants operated by the NPC, which ensures good food at fair prices.

Queenston Heights Restaurant is a few kilometers north of (downriver from) the falls, and you can have a relaxed lunch or dinner overlooking a golf course or, if you're lucky, the Niagara Gorge. *Tel. 416/262–4274. Dress: casual. AE, DC, MC, V. Moderate.*

Skylon Tower's Revolving Dining Room and Summit Suite Restaurant. If you have just one night for dining at the falls, make a reservation at the Skylon Tower's Revolving Dining Room. It makes a full circle every hour, and the view of the illuminated falls at night—at any time of the year—is a sight long remembered. The Canadian and Continental cuisine is usually excellent. The Skylon's Summit Suite Restaurant serves buffet breakfasts, plus lunch and dinner, and it has dancing, but it doesn't revolve. *Skylon Tower, tel. 416/356–2651. Dress: casual. AE, DC, MC, V. Moderate.*

Lodging **Skyline Brock Hotel, Skyline Foxhead Hotel, Skyline Village Hotel.** The former Sheraton-Foxhead Hotel is now the 232-room Skyline Brock Hotel, the 395-room Skyline Foxhead Hotel, and the 208-room Skyline Village Hotel, and all are located at 5685 Falls Avenue. The most distinguishing characteristic of these hotels is the price. The Foxhead rates start lower than those at the other two but climb to as high as $209 for some rooms. Many guest room windows overlook the falls; some have particularly splendid views, and rates are based to some extent on the view. The hotels have bars, lounges, restaurants, coffee shops, dining rooms. *5685 Falls Ave., L2E 6W7, tel. (for all 3) 416/374–4444. AE, MC, V. Expensive.*

Michael's Inn. If you're on a first, second, third, or even fourth honeymoon, consider something fun and romantic. Michael's Inn has a number of theme rooms, all of which overlook the American falls and the gorge. Carry your mate across the threshold into deepest Africa, the Old South, or the Orient. The "Midnight at the Oasis" room has a Jacuzzi for two surrounded by mirrors, a 2-meter-high (6½-foot-high) stuffed tiger, palm-leaf wallpaper, and bamboo trees. *5599 River Rd., L2E 3H3, tel. 416/354–2727. 130 rooms. Facilities: indoor swimming pool with slide, sauna, whirlpool, gift shop, lounge, and The Embers dining room. AE, MC, V. Moderate.*

Niagara-on-the-Lake
Dining and Lodging
★

Prince of Wales. This hotel is a family affair. The Wiens family has been doling out its gracious hospitality since 1975, turning a 16-room inn into a 105-room hotel. The original section of the inn was built as Long's Hotel in 1864. The additions over the years now make the hotel a block long, but the changes (inside and out) have been so sensitively wrought that only an expert could guess where most of the changes were made. One obvious exception is the Patio Restaurant, where tables are under a canopy of hanging plants and behind glass walls overlooking the main street. Guest rooms are furnished in reproduction French provincial or traditional English furniture. Guests may dine in the Dining Room, the Queen's Royal Lounge, or the Greenhouse Patio Restaurant, particularly popular with the local lunch crowd. *6 Picton St., L0S 1J0, tel. 416/468–3246; within the 416 area code, 800/263–2452. 105 rooms and suites with bath, some with fireplaces. Facilities: 3 dining areas, lounge, indoor swimming pool, sauna, whirlpool, health club, tennis. AE, MC, V. Very Expensive.*

Oban Inn. This elegant, historic country inn is centrally located and has a view of Lake Ontario. The respected dining room offers standard treatments of beef, duck, lobster, and steak.

160 Front St., L0S 1J0, tel. 416/468–2165. 23 rooms, some with fireplaces. Facilities: dining room, lounge, lap pool, indoor pool, whirlpool, exercise room. AE, DC, MC, V. Expensive.

★ **Queen's Landing.** Also called the Inn at Niagara-on-the-Lake, this remarkable property is a welcome addition to an old town that has had no new places in a long while. The owner—who also runs the Pillar & Post—has obtained antique furnishings and installed fireplaces in 78 rooms and Jacuzzis in 44 rooms. Located at the mouth of the Niagara River, right across from historic Fort Niagara, the hotel has knockout views. And, unlike other century-old country inns of this lovely town, Queen's Landing has a superb indoor swimming pool, lap pool, and even a fully equipped exercise room. The dining room has recently won some acclaim. The views, too, make for a romantic night out. *Cnr. Melville and Bryon Sts., Box 1180, L0S 1J0, tel. 416/468–2195. 137 rooms. Facilities: dining room, lounge, lap pool, indoor pool, whirlpool, exercise facilities, baby-sitting service, 24-hour room service, tennis and golf nearby. AE, DC, MC, V. Expensive.*

Ottawa Flippers. As the name suggests, this is a seafood restaurant, **Dining** and the specialties change almost daily as different kinds of fresh fish and seafoods are available. Part of the decor in the old building on Bank Street is marine artifacts and model ships. *823 Bank St. on the 2nd floor, tel. 613/232–2703. Reservations recommended. Dress: casual. AE, MC, V. Expensive.*

Grenville's. This is one of Ottawa's finest dining establishments, located in an old house on Somerset Street between Banks and O'Connor. The cuisine is North American, and there's a nice touch for those having difficulty deciding which of the tempting appetizers or desserts they wish. The kitchen will put together a sampler of either course—a half order of each of your two choices. *315 Somerset St. W, tel. 613/235–0369. Reservations recommended. Dress: casual. AE, MC, V. Expensive.*

Chequers. In this three-story, Gothic-style 1868 country inn 25 kilometers (16 miles) southwest of Ottawa, the specialties are French and Spanish haute cuisine. The service is European and so is the decor. *5816 Hazeldean Rd., Stittsville K0A 3G0 (from the Queensway, take Terry Fox Dr. south to Hazeldean Rd.—old Hwy. 7), tel. 613/836–1665. Reservations required. Dress: casual. AE, MC, V. Moderate.*

Courtyard Restaurant. Fine French cuisine is served in this lovely, historic limestone building on a quiet cul-de-sac near By Ward Market, a five-minute stroll from the Parliament Buildings. The forerunner of today's elegant dining establishment was a log tavern built in 1827, likely inspired by construction of the nearby Rideau Canal. The humble log tavern was replaced by the limestone Ottawa Hotel a decade later. Extensive renovations created Courtyard Restaurant, and its cuisine and ambience established a dedicated following. *21 George St., tel. 519/565–2611. Reservations recommended. Dress: informal. AE, MC, V. Moderate.*

Lodging Château Laurier Hotel. Ottawa has all kinds of posh new hotels with great service and food, but this hotel is an institution. It's one of Canada's great railroad hotels, built in 1916. It now has 480 large, airy rooms; an indoor pool; a variety of dining rooms, lounges, and bars; and indoor parking. The Château, as it's known, is part of the Ottawa experience; it's also smack dab in the middle of the must-see list for Ottawa. *1 Rideau St., K1N 8S7, tel. 613/232–6411. AE, MC, V. Very Expensive.*

Minto Place Suite Hotel. One- and two-bedroom suites in this 31-story hotel, which overlooks the capitol and is within strolling distance of Sparks Street Mall, have full kitchen and laundry facilities. The hotel has a sauna, indoor pool, whirlpool, health spa, indoor parking, licensed lounge, and dining room. *433 Laurier Ave., W K1R 7Y1, tel. 613/232–2200. AE, MC, V. Expensive–Very Expensive.*

O'Connor House Bed and Breakfast. In the heart of downtown Ottawa, this former hotel has 34 guest rooms and family suites. Ice skates and bicycles are available to guests along with a lounge, 24-hour snacks, and a full breakfast. *172 O'Connor St., K2P 1T5, tel. 613/236–4221. AE, MC, V. Moderate.*

Peterborough
Dining and Lodging

Stel Red Oak Inn. This 181-room hotel has an indoor swimming pool, sauna, and whirlpool, and it's connected to the city's largest downtown indoor shopping complex. Guest rooms are comfortably furnished. Sir William's Dining Room offers Continental fare and lighter meals, and snacks are served at the Garden Cafe in the pool area. There is free underground parking. *100 Charlotte St., K9J 7L4, tel. 705/743–7272. AE, D, MC, V. Expensive.*

Picton
Dining and Lodging

Isaiah Tubbs Resort. A dozen kilometers west of Picton, this posh 58-room property has rooms and suites with fireplaces, indoor and outdoor swimming pools, saunas and whirlpool, 12 cottages, and 35 housekeeping cottages. There's fine dining in The Restaurant on the Knoll Overlooking the Sandbanks at West Lake. (That's the correct name of the restaurant and that's what it overlooks!) *RR 1, K0K 2T0, tel. 613/393–2090 or 800/267–0525. AE, MC, V. Moderate.*

Lodging

Merrill Inn. This beautiful 1870 home is a short stroll from the heart of downtown Picton. It has been converted to a cozy 15-room inn by the same folks who created Idlewyld Inn at London (*see above*). The refrigerator is stocked with soft drinks and the sideboard with croissants, muffins, tea, and coffee 24 hours a day, but no meals are served. *343 Main St. E, K0K 2T0, tel. 613/476–7451. MC, V. Expensive.*

Port Stanley
Dining and Lodging
★

Kettle Creek Inn. This small, elegant, full-service country inn features fine food and a friendly pub ambience. Two new suites with balconies, fireplaces, and whirlpools and five new rooms with baths were installed in the original inn in 1992, and in 1990 eight rooms, three suites, and full facilities for small business meetings were added in a cleverly designed annex. Some of the new rooms have whirlpool baths and gas fireplaces. There are other nice touches, such as old-fashioned pedestal sinks, interesting local artwork, and views from all the rooms and suites of a landscaped courtyard and gazebo. Continental breakfast is included in room rates. The three dining rooms in the original inn offer daily specials, including fresh Lake Erie fish just brought ashore by the local fishing fleet. Fresh Ontario lamb and pork tenderloin are also featured. *Main St., N0L 2A0, tel. 519/782–3388, fax 519/782–4747. 10 rooms, 5 suites. AE, D, DC, MC, V. Moderate–Expensive.*

Rossport
Dining and Lodging

Rossport Inn. The hamlet of Rossport on a harbor off Lake Superior is about as close as you can get to an outport on the Great Lakes. The inn was built in 1884 as a railroad hotel and now has six small guest rooms sharing two bathrooms. This is one of the nicest country inns in the province. It's cozy and down-home—the nightlife consists of swapping lies with the innkeepers and other guests about fish that got away. Breakfast is included in the room rate. The dining room's home-style cooking of locally caught fish, as well as of steak, chicken, pork chops, and lobster is irresistible. *On Rossport Loop, 1/2 mile from Trans-Canada Hwy., Bowman St., P0T 2R0, tel. 807/824–3213. MC, V. Closed Nov.–May. Moderate.*

St. Jacobs
Dining and Lodging
Benjamins. This is a lovely re-creation of the original 1852 Farmer's Inn. Nine guest rooms on the second floor are furnished in antiques, and every bed is covered with a locally made Mennonite quilt. The licensed restaurant has pine ceiling beams, an open-hearth fireplace, lots of greenery, and imaginative French cuisine. *17 King St., N0B 2N0, tel. 519/664–3731. AE, MC, V. Expensive.*

Sault Ste. Marie
Dining and Lodging
Quality Inn Bayfront. If you're planning to take the Agawa Canyon Snow Train, try to get a room at this popular hotel. The 110 rooms (including 18 suites) are clean and modern with many creature comforts, including a sauna and in-house movies. Most important—because the train leaves at 8 AM and you should be at the station by 7:30 AM at the latest—the hotel is directly across the street from the Algoma Central Railroad station. That means you can enjoy a room-service or dining-room breakfast, stroll across the street, and leave your car parked at the hotel. When you return at night, the hotel's swimming pool and dining room await you. Blossoms Bistro in the hotel offers good prices, friendly service . . . and edible floral garnishes! The dining area is bright and airy with lots of brass and greenery, and reservations are suggested. *180 Bay St., P6A 6S2, tel. 705/945–9264. 82 rooms, 18 suites. Facilities: indoor pool, sauna, whirlpool, exercise room. AE, MC, V. Expensive.*

Stratford
Dining and Lodging
The Queen's Inn at Stratford. In this beautifully restored 1853 hotel, guests can enjoy traditional Canadian food in the dining room while listening to tinkling music from a baby grand piano. Light fare is served in one half of the divided room, and there are also a popular pub-lounge and two function rooms. *161 Ontario St., N5A 3H3, tel. 519/271–1400, fax 519/271–7373. 30 rooms with bath. Facilities: restaurant, lounge. AE, MC, V. Expensive.*
Woods Villa Bed and Breakfast. Owner Ken Vinen has restored this elegant 1875 home of a wealthy magistrate to its original grandeur, and some of the five rooms have fireplaces. Vinen uses the public rooms to display an astonishing collection of vintage juke boxes, music boxes, and player pianos he has restored to mint condition. If he doesn't have the old favorite you want to hear, he'll sit down at one of the pianos and pound it out for you. In summer, breakfast is served on an outside patio beside an enormous, ceramic-tiled swimming pool. Woods Villa does not accept children or pets; the latter might ruffle the feathers of Vinen's three pet macaws. *62 John St. N, Stratford, N5A 6K7, tel. 519/271–4576. 5 rooms. Major credit cards accepted, but cash preferred. Moderate.*

Windsor
Dining
Brigantino's. This popular establishment is outstanding for home-style Italian cooking and melt-in-your-mouth pasta. *851 Erie St. E, tel. 519/254–7041. Reservations advised. Dress: casual. AE, D, DC, MC, V. Moderate.*
The Old Fish Market. A wonderful ambience is created here with hanging plants and brass railings and lots of lovely woodwork. The menu lives up to the name and is heavy on seafoods.

It has a deserved reputation of excellence. *156 Chatham St. W, tel. 519/253–7417. Weekend reservations advised. Dress: casual. AE, DC, MC, V. Moderate.*

Lodging **Hilton International Windsor.** Each of the 293 guest rooms in this 22-story, downtown riverbank hotel has a view of Detroit's impressive skyline and the shipping activity on the world's busiest inland waterway. The Park Terrace Restaurant and Lounge offers a wide menu and spectacular river view. In the River Runner Bar and Grill, there's music and dancing. *277 Riverside Dr. W, N9A 5K4, tel. 519/973–5555. Facilities: indoor pool, sauna, whirlpool, meeting facilities, room service. AE, MC, V. Very Expensive.*

The Arts and Nightlife

Hamilton Opera Hamilton holds performances in the Great Hall of Hamilton Place September through April (Summers Lane, opposite the Art Gallery of Hamilton, tel. 416/527–7627).

The Shaw Festival A stage-struck Toronto lawyer's dream in 1961 now has an impressive track record and a world-class reputation. Brian Doherty started the festival in 1961 with a few Shaw plays produced on weekends in the old town courthouse. The performances were well received, and the company drew continuing support, mainly from Toronto. Government kicked in most of the $3 million needed to build the 863-seat Shaw Festival Theatre, which opened in 1973. Shaw Festival is the only theater group in the world specializing in the works of George Bernard Shaw and his contemporaries. The festival starts at the end of April and runs through mid-November. *Tel. 416/468–2172.*

The Stratford Festival It all started in 1953, in a massive tent, with Sir Alec Guiness playing Richard III. The next year, musical programs were added to augment Shakespeare's plays. The venture was a huge success, and the 1957 season opened in a permanent home with 2,262 seats, none of which is more than 65 feet from the stage. The 1901-vintage, 1,107-seat Avon Theatre became a partner in the festival in 1967, and The Third Stage, seating 410, opened in 1971. Stratford Festival now starts in late April and runs into November. *For information: Stratford and Area Visitors and Convention Bureau, 38 Albert St., Stratford, Ont. N5A 3K3, tel. 519/271–5361; box office, tel. 519/273–1600.*

Nightlife The brochure says **Lulu's Roadhouse** has a "warm, casual atmosphere" but doesn't try to suggest it's "cozy" or "intimate." This unique play spot, located in a former K-Mart store just south of Kitchener, is Canada's largest bar. It can seat 2,000 customers at 450 tables and on bar stools, and there's room for another 1,000 standing along the longest and second-longest bars in the world. (The world's longest bar is 333 feet; the second-longest is 310 feet.) Since Lulu's opened in 1984, it's been packing 'em in to watch performances by big-name rock-and-roll entertainers. *4263 King St. E (Hwy. 8), tel. 519/653–8333 or 800/265–6782. Cover charge varies with entertainment. Open Thurs.–Sat. 4:30 PM–1 AM, sometimes Wed. for special concerts. Jeans not permitted.*

10 Province of Québec

By Dorothy Guinan

Dorothy Guinan is a political researcher for the Montréal Gazette and is a freelance writer.

Among the provinces of Canada, Québec is set apart by its strong French heritage, a matter not only of language but of customs, religion, and political structure. Québec covers a vast area—almost one-sixth of Canada's total—although the upper three-quarters is only sparsely inhabited. Most of the population lives in the southern cities, especially Montréal (*see* Chapter 3) and Québec City (*see* Chapter 4). Outside the cities, however, you'll find serenity and natural beauty in the province's innumerable lakes, streams, and rivers; in its farmlands and villages; in its great mountains and deep forests; and in its rugged coastline along the Gulf of St. Lawrence. Though the winters are long, there are plenty of winter sports to while away the cold months, especially in the Laurentians, with its many ski resorts.

Québec's recent threats to secede from the Canadian union are part of a long-standing tradition of independence. The first European to arrive in Québec was French explorer Jacques Cartier, in 1534; another Frenchman, Samuel de Champlain, arrived in 1603, determined to build French settlements in the region, and Jesuit missionaries followed in due course. Louis XIV of France proclaimed Canada a crown colony in 1663, and the land was allotted to French aristocrats in large grants called *seigneuries*. As tenants, known as *habitants*, settled upon farms in Québec, the Roman Catholic church took on an importance that went beyond religion. Priests and nuns also acted as doctors, educators, and overseers of business arrangements between the habitants and between French-speaking fur traders and English-speaking merchants. An important doctrine of the church in Québec was *survivance*, the survival of the French people and their culture. Couples were told to have large families, and they did—families of 10 or 12 children were the norm.

Although the British won control of Canada in the French and Indian War, in 1763, Parliament passed the Quebec Act in 1774, which ensured the continuation of French law in Québec and left provincial authority in the hands of the Roman Catholic church. In general, the law preserved the traditional Québecois way of life. Tensions between Québec and English-speaking Canada accelerated throughout the 20th century, however, and in 1974 the province defiantly proclaimed French its national language. In 1990 a three-year attempt by the Canadian government to add Québec's signature to the Canadian Constitution failed. Québec had been willing to sign provided that it received special status to promote its French language and culture. However, two of the 10 provinces would not agree to Québec's request. The incident became known as Meech Lake. In 1992 the Canadian government came up with a new plan that would have vastly changed the 125-year-old Constitution by recognizing Québec as a distinct society and giving more powers to the provincial governments. On October 26, in a nationwide referendum, Québec and five other provinces rejected the offer, and today the problem remains unresolved.

Being able to speak French can make your visit to the province more pleasant—many locals do not speak English. If you don't speak French, arm yourself with a phrase book or at least a knowledge of some basic phrases. It's also worth your while to sample the hearty traditional Québecois cuisine, for this is a province where food is taken seriously.

Lower Québec

James Bay

Kesagami Lake

Harricana R.

⑩109

Matagami

⑪113

Lake Mistassini

Albanel Lake

⑩167

Lake Abitibi

La Sarre

⑩109

QUEBEC

Parent Lake

Gouin Reservoir

Mistassi

⑩111

Amos

⑩101

Noranda

⑩117

Malartic
Val-d'Or

Louvicourt

⑩113

Saint-Félicien

Lake St-Jean

Chambord

⑩169

New Liskeard

⑩101

Kipawa Lake

La Vérendrye Prov. Park

⑩155

Lau Pre

La Tuque

⑪11

⑩117

Manouane

Mauricie Nat. Park

Qué

Mattawa

⑪17

Ottawa R.

Algonquin Prov. Park

Pembroke

⑩60 ⑩62

Mont-Laurier

Mont-Tremblant Prov. Park

St-Zénon

St-Donat

Trois-Rivières

⑩40 ⑩132

⑩20

Victo

⑪11

⑩60

⑩105

⑩309

St-Jovite

Ste-Agathe-des-Monts

Sorel

Richmond

⑩17

Gatineau Nat. Park

Hawkesbury

⑩158

Laval

Montréal

⑩10

Sherbrooke

OTTAWA

Hull

⑩17

Dorion

⑩29

Ottawa

⑩31

⑩15 ⑩133

⑩55

⑩28

⑩62 ⑩41

⑩7

Cornwall

CANADA

Rideau

⑩401

Massena

U.S.

⑩91

Lake Simcoe

Ogdensburg

St. Regis R.

VERMONT

⑦7

⑩401

Lake Ontario

NEW YORK

⑧87

Lake Champlain

N
HAMP

Niagara Falls

Buffalo

Rochester

⑩90

⑨90

⑨90

Genesee R.

⑩15

⑨81

Hudson R.

⑩91

MASSACHUSET

NEWFOUNDLAND

Manouane
Lake

Labrador
City

Gagnon

Rivière-
aux-Graines

Havre-
St-Pierre

Sept-Iles

Baie-
Ste-Clair

Anticosti
Island

389

Pipmuacan
Reservoir

Port-Cartier

138

Godbout

St. Lawrence
River

Baie-Comeau

Anse-
Pleureuse

Rivière-au-Renard

Forestville

Matane

Gaspése
Prov. Park

Gaspé

Forillon
Nat. Park

Les
Escoumins

Mont-
Joli

132

Cascapedia R.

Bonaventure R.

Percé

Chicoutimi

Saguenay R.

Rimouski

Amqui

132

New
Richmond

Chandler

aie

132

Trois-Pistoles

Campbellton

Dalhousie

Baie des Chaleurs

Gulf of
St. Lawrence

381

Saint-
Siméon

Rivière-
du-Loup

185

Cabano

11

11

s

k

138

20

Edmundston

17

8

Montmagny

Grand Falls

NEW
BRUNSWICK

Chatham

11

Prince Edward
Island

Île d'Orléans

Saint John R.

2

8

Northumberland Strait

hetford
ines

108

173

Houlton

St. John   R.

Fredericton

Cape
Tormentine

2

Lac
Mégantic

Moosehead
Lake

95

7

Saint
John

Fundy
Nat. Park

2

urn

Westfield

102

ok

MAINE

St. George

Bay of Fundy

NOVA
SCOTIA

Halifax

Kennebec R.

Campobello
Island

1

10

95

Grand
Manan

Rossignol

103

Bar
Harbour

Yarmouth

N

Portland

95

ATLANTIC OCEAN

KEY
— Rail Lines
🚢 Ferry
🍁 Trans-Canada Hwy.

0   50 miles

0   75 km

Essential Information

Important Addresses and Numbers

Tourist
Information
Québec

Tourism Québec (C.P. 20000, Québec City G1K 7X2, tel. 514/873–2015, toll-free from the Montréal area; from Québec, Canada, or the United States, 800/363–7777) can provide information on provincial tourist bureaus throughout the province.

The Laurentians

The major tourist office is the **Maison du Tourisme des Laurentides** at Saint-Jérôme, just off the Autoroute des Laurentides 15 at exit 39. *14142 rue de Lachapelle, RR 1, St-Jérôme J7Z 5T4, tel. 514/436–8532. Open mid-June–Aug., daily 8:30–8; Sept.–mid-June, daily 9–5.*

You can also get information in person at **Infotouriste** (1001 Square Dorchester, Montréal). Year-round regional tourist offices are located in the towns of Labelle, Mont Laurier, Mont Tremblant, Saint-Antoine, Saint-Eustache, Saint-Faustin, Saint-Sauveur-des-Monts, Saint-Jovite, Sainte-Adèle, and Sainte-Agathe-des-Monts. Seasonal tourist offices (mid-June–Labor Day) are also located in Bois Briand, Grenville, Lachute, L'Annociation, Sainte-Marguerite-du-Lac-Masson, Notre-Dame-du-Laus, Piedmont, Saint-Adolphe-Howard, and Val David. For information about ski conditions, tel. 514/522–2754.

L'Estrie

In Montréal, information about l'Estrie is available at **Infotouriste** (*see above*). Year-round regional provincial tourist offices are located in the towns of Bromont, Danville, Granby, Magog, Sherbrooke, and Sutton. Seasonal tourist offices (June–Labor Day) are also located in Ayer's Cliff, Coaticook, Knowlton, La Patrie, Lac-Mégantic, Lennoxville, Masonville, North Hatley, and Pike River. Seasonal bureaus' schedules are irregular, so contact the **Association Touristique de l'Estrie** (25 Brocage, Sherbrooke, J1L 2J4, tel. 819/565–5469) before visiting. The association also provides lodging information.

Arriving and Departing by Plane

Most airline arrivals will be into either of Montréal's airports (Mirabel or Dorval) or Québec City's airport (*see* Chapters 3 and 4).

Arriving and Departing by Car, Train, and Bus

By Car

The major highways are Autoroute des Laurentides 15, a six-lane highway from Montréal to the Laurentians; Autoroute 10 East from Montréal to l'Estrie; U.S. 91 from New England, which becomes Autoroute 55 as it crosses the border to l'Estrie; and Highway 138, which runs from Montréal along the north shore of the St. Lawrence River.

By Train

Regular **Via Rail** passenger service connects all the provinces with Montréal and Québec City and offers limited service to the Gaspé Peninsula.

By Bus

Most major bus lines in the province connect with **Voyageur** (tel. 514/842–2281).

Getting Around

Québec Province
By Car The province has fine roads, along which drivers insist on speeding. Free road maps are available at any of the numerous seasonal or permanent Québec Tourist Offices (call 800/363–7777 for the nearest location). Major entry points are Ottawa/Hull, U.S. 87 from New York State south of Montréal, U.S. 91 from Vermont into l'Estrie area, and the Trans-Canada Highway just west of Montréal.

By Bus Most bus traffic to the outer reaches of the province begins at the bus terminal in downtown Québec City (225 boul. Charest E, tel. 418/524–4692).

The Laurentians
By Car Autoroute des Laurentides 15, a six-lane highway, and the slower but more scenic secondary road, Route 117, lead to this resort country. Try to avoid traveling to and from the region on Friday evenings or Sunday afternoons, as you're likely to sit for hours in bumper-to-bumper traffic.

By Bus Frequent bus service is available from the Terminus Voyageur (505 boul. de Maisonneuve E, tel. 514/842–2281) in downtown Montréal. **Limocar Laurentides'** service (tel. 514/435–8899) departs regularly for L'Annociation, Mont Laurier, Sainte-Adèle, Sainte-Agathe-des-Monts, and Saint-Jovite, among other stops en route. Limocar also has a service to the Basses Laurentides (Lower Laurentians) region, departing from the Laval bus terminal at the Métro Henri-Bourassa stop in north Montréal, stopping in many towns, and ending in Saint-Jérôme.

L'Estrie
By Car Take Autoroute 10 East from Montréal or from New England on U.S. 91, which becomes Autoroute 55 as it crosses the border at Rock Island.

By Bus Buses depart daily from the Terminus Voyageur in Montréal (505 boul. de Maisonneuve E, tel. 514/842–2281), to Granby, Lac-Mégantic, Magog, Sherbrooke, and Thetford Mines.

Guided Tours

Special-interest
Nature tours The **Montréal Zoological Society** (2055 rue Peel, Montréal H3A 1V4, tel. 514/845–8317) is a nature-oriented group that offers lectures, field trips, and weekend excursions. Tours include hiking and bird-watching in national parks throughout Québec, Canada, and the northern United States.

Whale watching **Croisières Navimex Canada, Inc.** (25 Pl. Marché Champlain, Suite 400, Québec City G1K 4H2, tel. 418/692–4643), offers three-hour whale-watching cruises ($34 for adults, $17 children under 14) and 4½-hour dinner cruises on the Saguenay Fjord ($45 for adults, $22.50 children under 14). Cruises depart from Baie-Ste-Catherine, Tadoussac, and Rivière du Loup.

Graduate-student marine biologists from the **Montréal Zoological Society** (*see above*) accompany whale-watching excursions in the St. Lawrence estuary, a habitat for many whale species, including the endangered beluga.

River Excursions **Croisières Navimex Canada, Inc.** (*see above*) also offers a 10-hour boat trip along the St. Lawrence River between Québec and Montréal for about $100. The package includes two meals, a few hours of free time at the port-of-call (Québec or Montréal, depending on the city of departure), and return bus transportation the same evening. The trip is not recommended for children under 12.

Train Tours   The **Choo-Choo Steam Train Company** (tel. 819/778–7246) operates a 4½-hour scenic excursion along the Gatineau River from Hull to Wakefield and back, daily or on weekends, depending on season. There's room for 600 passengers—70 per car—and the train makes a two-hour stopover in Wakefield, where there's a museum, a gristmill, and a crafts shop. Fares range from $20 (weekdays) to $22 (weekends) for adults, $10.50 for children under 12, 10% discount for senior citizens.

Exploring Québec

There are two major attractions beyond the city limits of Montréal: l'Estrie (formerly the Eastern Townships), where city folk retreat in summer, and Les Laurentides (the Laurentians), where they escape in winter. Les Laurentides are characterized by thousands of miles of unspoiled wilderness and world-famous ski resorts, while l'Estrie has rolling hills and farmland. As major vacation areas in both winter and summer, they offer outdoor activities on ski slopes and lakes and in their provincial parks. The two other regions worth exploring are Charlevoix, often called the Switzerland of Québec because of its landscape, and the knobby Gaspé Peninsula, where the St. Lawrence River meets the Gulf of St. Lawrence.

Highlights for First-time Visitors

Basilica of Ste-Anne-de-Beaupré, Sainte-Anne-de-Beaupré, Tour 3: Charlevoix
Bonaventure Island and its gannet colony, off Percé, Tour 4: The Gaspé Peninsula
Cross-country skiing in Les Laurentides, Tour 1: Les Laurentides
Jardin Zoologique de Granby, Granby, Tour 2: L'Estrie
"Sugaring off" at a sugar shack in Les Laurentides, Dining
Théâtre Lac Brome, Knowlton, Tour 2: L'Estrie
Whale watching in the St. Lawrence Seaway, Guided Tours and Tour 3: Charlevoix

Tour 1: Les Laurentides

Avid skiers might call Montréal a bedroom community for the Laurentians; just 56 kilometers (35 miles) to the north, they are home to some of North America's best-known ski resorts. The Laurentian range is ancient, dating to the Precambrian era (more than 600 million years ago). These rocky hills are relatively low, worn down by glacial activity, but they include eminently skiable hills, with a few peaks above 2,500 feet. World-famous Mont Tremblant, at 3,150 feet, is the tallest.

The **P'tit Train du Nord** made it possible to easily transport settlers and cargo to the Upper Laurentians. It also opened them up to skiing by the turn of the century. Before long, trainloads of skiers replaced settlers and cargo as the railway's major trade. The Upper Laurentians soon became known worldwide as the number-one ski center in North America—a position that they still hold today. Initially a winter weekend getaway for Montréalers who stayed at boardinghouses and fledgling resorts while skiing its hills, the Upper Laurentians began attracting an international clientele, especially with the advent of the Canadian National Railway's special skiers' train, begun in 1928. (Its competitor, the Canadian Pacific Railway, jumped on the bandwagon soon after, doubling the number of train runs bringing skiers to the area.)

Soon, points north of Saint-Jérôme began to develop as resort areas: Saint-Sauveur-des-Monts, Saint-Jovite, Sainte-Agathe-des-Monts, Mont Tremblant, and points in between became major ski centers. The Upper Laurentians also began to grow as a winter haven for prominent Montréalers, who traveled as far north as Sainte-Agathe-des-Monts to establish private family ski lodges. A number of these properties continue to be preserved in their rustic turn-of-the-century wilderness settings.

Accessible only by train until the 1930s, when the highway was built, these were used primarily as winter ski lodges. But once the road opened up, cottages became year-round family retreats. Today, there is an uneasy alliance between the longtime cottagers and resort-driven entrepreneurs. Both recognize the other's historic role in developing the Upper Laurentians, but neither espouses the other's cause. At the moment, commercial development seems to be winning out. A number of large hotels have added indoor pools and spa facilities, and efficient highways have brought the country closer to the city—45 minutes to Saint-Saveur, 1½–2 hours to Mont Tremblant. Montréalers can drive up to enjoy the fall foliage or engage in spring skiing and still get home before dark. The only slow periods are early October, when there is not much to do, and June, when there is plenty to do but the area is beset by blackflies.

Les Basses Laurentides The Laurentians are actually divided into two major regions—les Basses Laurentides (the Lower Laurentians) and les Hautes Laurentides (the Upper Laurentians). But don't be fooled by the designations; they don't signify great driving distances.

The Lower Laurentians start almost immediately outside Montréal. Considered the birthplace of the Laurentians, this area is rich in historic and architectural landmarks. Beginning in the mid-17th century, the governors of New France, as Québec was then called, gave large concessions of land to its administrators, priests, and top-ranking military, who became known as *seigneurs*. In the Lower Laurentians, towns like Terrebonne, Saint-Eustache, Lac-des-Deux-Montagnes, and Oka are home to the manors, mills, churches, and public buildings these seigneurs had built for themselves and their *habitants*— the inhabitants of these quasi-feudal villages.

Numbers in the margin correspond to points of interest on the Laurentians map.

❶ Two of the most famous seigneuries are within an hour of Montréal: **La Seigneurie de Terrebonne**, on l'Île-des-Moulins, is about 20 minutes from Montréal; La Seigneurie du Lac-des-Deux-Montagnes, in St-Scholastique, is 40 minutes from Montréal. You reach Terrebonne by taking boulevard Pie-IX in Montréal to the bridge of the same name. From the bridge take Highway 25 North. Exit at Terrebonne to Highway 440.

Governor Frontenac gave the land to Sieur André Daulier in 1673. Terrebonne was maintained by a succession of seigneurs

The Laurentians

Reservoir Taureau

Lac Anicet

Lac du Diable

Lac Forbes

Parc du Mont Tremblant

131

14 **Parc Mont Tremblant**

Saint-Donat

Lac Archambault

Rivière Jamet

Lac Tremblant

Mont Tremblant

Lac Ouareau

117

Gray Rocks

Mont-Tremblant-Village

329

125

Saint-Jovite

Sainte-Agathe-des-Monts

Hôtel la Sapinière

Lac des Îles

13

12

Estérel **11**

Sainte-Marguerite-du-Lac-Masson

10

Val David

Sainte-Adolphe d'Howard

Sainte-Adèle **8** **9**

Mont-Rolland

335

7

Morin Heights

6

Saint-Sauveur-des-Monts

Saint-Jérôme

5

Laurentides

327

La Seigneurie de Terrebonne

1

640

158

15

La Seigneurie du Lac-des-Deux-Montagnes

2

148

Ste.-Scholastique

Mirabel

117

25

Saint-Eustache

4

MONTRÉAL

Oka Calvary

3

Oka

TRANS-CANADA HWY.

40

ONTARIO
QUÉBEC

20

138

15

0   20 miles

0   30 km

N

until 1832, when Joseph Masson, the first French Canadian millionaire, bought it. He and his family were the last seigneurs de Terrebonne; their reign ended in 1883.

Today, Terrebonne offers visitors a bona fide glimpse of the past. Now run by the Corporation de l'Île-des-Moulins rather than a French aristocrat, the seigneurie's mansions, manors, and buildings have all been restored. Take a walk through Terrebonne's historical center and then stop at the **Centre d'Interprétation Historique de Terrebonne Museum.** It features three exhibits: the Seigneurial Regime; the water, saw, flour, and wool mills of the region that gave the island its name; and the beginning of the Industrial Revolution in Terrebonne. The Île-des-Moulins art gallery hosts exhibitions of works by local artists, and a theater presents plays in French as well as musical matinees and outdoor summer shows. Most activities are free. *Corner boul. des Braves and rue St-Pierre, tel. 514/471–0619. Admission free. Open mid-May–June, Tues.–Sun. 10–5; July–Aug., Tues.–Sun. 10–8.*

❷ **La Seigneurie du Lac-des-Deux-Montagnes** was allotted to the Sulpician priests in 1717. Already appointed the seigneurs of the entire island of Montréal, the priests used this as the base from which to establish an Amerindian mission. To reach this mission, take Highway 13 or 15 North out of Montréal to Highway 640 West. Exit from Highway 640 West at Highway 148. Take this road into the town of Saint-Scholastique. A highlight of the seigneurie is the Sulpicians' seignorial manor on rue Belle-Rivière, erected between 1802 and 1808 in the village of Saint-Scholastique. The manor was used as part of the set for the late Claude Jutra's acclaimed film, *Kamouraska,* based on the novel by Québec's prize-winning author Anne Hébert.

❸ To promote piety among the Amerindians, the Sulpicians erected the **Oka Calvary (Stations of the Cross)** between 1740 and 1742. Three of the seven chapels are still maintained, and every September 14 since 1870, Québecois pilgrims have congregated here from across the province to participate in the half-hour ceremony that proceeds on foot to the Calvary's summit. A sense of the divine is inspired as much by the magnificent view of Lac-des-Deux-Montagnes as by religious fervor.

In 1887, the Sulpicians gave about 865 acres of their property located near the Oka Calvary to the Trappist monks, who had arrived in New France in 1880 from the Bellefontaine Abbey in France. Within 10 years they had built their monastery, the **Abbaye Cistercienne d'Oka,** and they transformed this land into one of the most beautiful domains in Québec. The abbey is one of the oldest in North America. Famous for creating Oka cheese, the Trappists established the Oka School of Agriculture, which operated until 1960. Today, the monastery is a noted prayer retreat. Tour the miller's modest home, where the Trappists stayed when they first arrived here, and visit the gardens and the chapel. *1600 chemin d'Oka, tel. 514/479–8361. Admission free. Chapel open daily 8–8; gardens and boutique open weekdays 9:30–11:30 and 1–4:30, Sat. 9–4.*

Close by is the **Ferme Avicole d'Oka,** one of Québec's largest poultry farms, also developed by the Trappists. Tours of the breeding grounds for exotic pheasant, partridge, and guinea-hen fowl, as well as for the ordinary variety, are given, and there is a slide show of the transition from farm to table—an interesting encounter for city children. Fresh eggs and fowl can be bought on site. *1525 chemin d'Oka, tel. 514/479–8394. Store open weekdays 9–noon and 1–5, Sat. 9–5, Sun. 1–5.*

Kanestake, a Mohawk Indian reserve near Oka, made the headlines during the summer of 1990 when a 78-day armed standoff between Mohawk Warriors (the reserve's self-proclaimed peacekeeping force) and Canadian and provincial authorities took place. The Mohawks of Kanestake opposed the expansion of the Oka golf course, claiming the land was stolen from them 273 years before. When the standoff ended, the golf course was not expanded.

❹ Nearby **Saint-Eustache** is another must for history buffs. One of the most important and tragic scenes in Canadian history took place here: the 1837 Rebellion. Since the British conquest of 1760, French Canadians had been confined to preexisting territories while the new townships were allotted exclusively to the English. Adding to this insult was the government's decision to tax all imported products from England, which made them prohibitively expensive. The result? In 1834, the French Canadian Patriot party defeated the British party locally. Lower Canada, as it was then known, became a hotbed of tension between the French and English, with French resistance to the British government reaching an all-time high. Rumors of rebellion were rife, and in December 1837, some 2,000 English soldiers led by General Colborne were sent in to put down the "army" of North Shore patriots by surrounding the village of Saint-Eustache. Jean-Olivier Chénier and his 200 patriots took refuge in the local church, which Colborne's cannons bombed and set afire. Chénier and 80 of his comrades were killed during the battle, and more than 100 of the town's houses and buildings erected during the seignorial regime were looted and burned down by Colborne's soldiers. Even today, traces of the bullets fired by the English army cannons are visible on the facade of Saint-Eustache's church at 123 rue St-Louis. Most of the town's period buildings are open to the public. Note especially **Manoir Globenski** and **Moulin Légaré,** the only water mill still in operation in Canada. For a guided tour or for a free brochure that gives a good walking-tour guide, visit the town's Arts and Cultural Services Center (235 rue St-Eustache, tel. 514/472–4440, ext. 433). Tours are offered from April until December.

Time Out   Before heading north, stop at **Pâtisserie Grande-Côte** (367A chemin de la Grande-Côte, tel. 514/473–7307) to sample the wares of St-Eustache's most famous bakery and pastry shop.

Les Hautes   Rivaling Saint-Eustache in Québec's historic folklore is **Saint-**
Laurentides   **Jérôme,** founded in 1830. Today a thriving economic center and
❺   cultural hub off Route 117, it first gained prominence in 1868 when Curé Antoine Labelle became pastor of this parish on the shores of Rivière du Nord. Curé Labelle devoted himself to opening up northern Québec to French Canadians. Between 1868 and 1890, he founded 20 parish towns—an impressive achievement given the harsh conditions of this vast wilderness. But his most important legacy was the famous P'tit Train du Nord railway line, which he persuaded the government to build in order to open Saint-Jérôme to travel and trade.

Follow Saint-Jérôme's **promenade,** a 4-kilometer-long (2½-mile) boardwalk alongside the Rivière du Nord from rue de Martigny bridge to rue St-Joseph bridge for a walk through the town's history. Descriptive plaques en route highlight episodes of the Battle of 1837. The **Centre d'Exposition du Vieux-Palais** housed in St-Jérôme's old courthouse has temporary exhibits of contemporary art, featuring mostly Québec artists. A music hall next door sometimes hosts concerts. *185 rue du Palais, tel. 514/ 432–7171. Admission free. Open Tues.–Fri. noon–5, Sun. 1–5.*

Saint-Jérôme's **Parc Régional de la Rivière-du-Nord** (1051 boul. International, tel. 514/431–1676) was created as a nature retreat. Paths throughout the park lead to the spectacular Wilson Falls (*chutes,* in French). Rain or shine, the Pavillon Marie-Victorin is open daily, with summer weekend displays and workshops devoted to nature, culture, and history.

The resort vacation area truly begins at Saint-Sauveur-des-Monts (Exit 60) and extends as far north as Mont Tremblant, where it turns into a wilderness of lakes and forests best visited with an outfitter. Laurentian guides planning fishing and hunting trips are concentrated around Saint-Donat near Parc Mont Tremblant.

To the first-time visitor, the hills and resorts around Saint-Sauveur, Sainte-Marguerite Station, Morin Heights, Val Morin, and Val David, up to Sainte-Agathe, form a pleasant hodgepodge of villages, hotels, and inns that seem to blend one into another.

❻ Saint-Sauveur-des-Monts, exit 60 off the Autoroute, is the focal point for area resorts. It has gone from a 1970s sleepy Laurentian village of 4,000 residents that didn't even have a traffic light to a thriving year-round town attracting some 30,000 cottagers and visitors on weekends. Its main street, rue Principale, once dotted with quaint French restaurants, now boasts *brochetteries* and sushi bars, and the narrow strip is so choked in summertime by cars and tourists that it has earned the sobriquet "Crescent Street of the North," borrowing its name from the well-known, action-filled street in Montréal. Residents here once won the battle against a McDonald's opening. Now the parking lots of major franchise fast-food eateries are always packed. Despite all this development, Saint-Sauveur has managed to maintain some of its charming, rural character.

The gleaming white spires of **Saint-Sauveur Church** still dominate rue Principale, but **Saint Francis of the Birds** has not been so lucky. Built in 1951 with support from Montréal's Molson family, this sturdy, rustic log church with its fine stained-glass-window portraits of the Laurentian countryside no longer offers the worshiper or visitor a secluded and peaceful spiritual retreat. Where only a few years ago its immediate neighbors were modest chalets dotting the forest, today the empty, bankrupt Delta Hotel complex sits in the church's backyard. However, classical concerts can still be heard in the church every second Saturday evening during September and October (tel. 514/227–2423).

But for those who like their vacations—winter or summer—lively and activity-filled, Saint-Sauveur is *the* place where the action rolls nonstop. In winter, skiing is the main thing. (Mont-Saint-Sauveur, Mont Avila, Mont Gabriel, and Mont Olympia all offer special season passes and programs, and some ski-center passes can be used at more than one center in the region.) From Mont-Saint-Sauveur to Mont Tremblant, the area's ski centers (most situated in or near Saint-Sauveur, Sainte-Adèle, Sainte-Agathe, and Saint-Jovite) offer night skiing. All have ski instructors—many are members of the Canadian Ski Patrol Association.

Just outside Saint-Sauveur, the $7 million Mont Saint-Sauveur **Water Park** and tourist center (exit 58 or 60) will keep children occupied with slides, wave pools, snack bars, and more. The "Children's Island" is the park's latest attraction, with calm, shallow wading ponds designed for youngsters 1 to 6 years old. The man-made "Colorado" rafting river attracts the older, braver crowd. The nine-minute ride follows the natural contours of steep hills and requires about 12,000 gallons of water to be pumped per minute. *350 rue Saint-Denis, Saint-Sauveur-des-Monts, tel. 514/871–0101 or 800/363–2426. Open mid-June–Aug., daily 10–7. Admission: full day—$22 adults, $16 children 3 and over; half day (after 3 PM)—$18 adults, $14 children 3 and over; evening (after 5 PM)—$14 adults, $11 children 3 and over.*

❼ Nearby in **Morin Heights,** there's a new spin on an old sport at **Ski Morin Heights** (exit 60, Autoroute 15 N, tel. 514/227–2020 or 800/661–3535), where snowboarding is the latest craze. Likened to surfing a big wave, riding a skateboard down a hill, or windsurfing on a white-capped lake, snowboarding demands similar skills and dexterity, not to mention the fearlessness of the lionhearted. Nonetheless, the sport is carefully supervised by Ski Morin Heights' instructors. Although it doesn't have overnight accommodations, Ski Morin Heights boasts a 44,000-square-foot chalet with a full range of hospitality services and sports-related facilities, eateries, après-ski activities, pubs, a health club, and a day-care center. There's also a large nursery on-site and special ski-lesson programs for children ages 2 and up.

The town's architecture and population reflect its English settlers' origins. Most residents are English-speaking. Morin Heights has escaped the overdevelopment of Saint-Sauveur but still offers the visitor a good range of restaurants, bookstores, boutiques, and crafts shops to explore. During the summer months, windsurfing, swimming, and canoeing on the area's two lakes are popular pastimes. The most recent addition is **Théâtre Morin Heights** (tel. 514/226–5863), whose "professional amateur" productions are presented at Ski Morin Heights during the summer months. Popular musicals, lighthearted comedies, mysteries, and children's plays are in the repertoire. A dinner-show package costs about $25 per person. Reservations are a must.

In the summer, holiday goers head for the region's golf courses (two of the more pleasant are 18-hole links at Sainte-Adèle and Mont Gabriel), campgrounds at Val David, Lacs Claude and Lafontaine, and beaches; in the fall and winter, they come for the foliage as well as alpine and Nordic skiing.

❽ The busy town of **Sainte-Adèle** is full of gift and Québec-crafts shops, boutiques, and restaurants. It also has an active nightlife, including a few discos.

Just as much of a rave with adults as with children are the **Super Splash** waterslides. *1791 boul. Ste-Adèle, tel. 514/229–*

2909. 2 giant slides for adults, 3 for children. Admission: $17 adults, $12 children under 12, $42 families. Open June–Aug., daily 10–7.

A couple of miles north on Highway 117, the reconstructed **Village de Seraphin's** 20 small homes, grand country house, general store, and church recall the settlers who came to Sainte-Adèle in the 1840s. This award-winning historic town also features a train tour through the woods. *Tel. 514/229–4777. Admission: $9 adults, $7 children 12–17, $5.50 children 5–11. Open mid-May–late June and early Sept.–mid-Oct., weekends 10–5, weekdays reservations only; late June–early Sept., daily 10–5.*

9 In **Mont Rolland, Station Touristique de Mont Gabriel** offers superb skiing, primarily for intermediate and advanced skiers. The on-site lodge, **Auberge Mont Gabriel** (*see* Lodging, *below*), has week-long and weekend packages. *Autoroute 15, exit 64, Mont Rolland J0R 1G0, tel. 514/229–3547.*

10 Neighboring community **Sainte-Marguerite-du-Lac-Masson** celebrated its 125th anniversary in 1990. The town's Service des Loisirs (tel. 514/228–2545) is the place to call for details about events, as well as cruises and skating on Lac-Masson.

11 The permanent population of the town of **Estérel** is a mere 80 souls. But visitors to **Ville d'Estérel,** a 135-room resort at Autoroute 69, near Sainte-Marguerite Station, swell that number into the thousands. Founded in 1959 on the shores of Lac Dupuis, this 5,000-acre domain was bought by Fridolin Simard from Baron Louis Empain. Named Estérel by the baron because it evoked memories of his native village in Provence, Ville d'Estérel soon became a household word for holiday vacationers in search of a first-class resort area. (For more details, *see* Lodging, *below*.)

12 Children know **Val David** for its **Santa Claus Village.** This is Santa Claus's summer residence, where children can sit upon Santa's knee and speak to him. (He's bilingual, too: French and English.) On the grounds is a petting zoo, with goats, sheep, horses, and colorful birds. Bumper boats and games are run here, as well. *987 rue Morin, Val David, tel. 819/322–2146. Admission: $7 adults, $5.50 children 2–12. Open late May–early June, weekends 10–6; early June–late Aug., daily 10–6.*

Val David is a rendezvous for mountain climbers, ice scalers, dogsledders, hikers, and summer or winter campers. For equipment rentals and other information, contact the Maison du Tourisme des Laurentides (tel. 514/436–8532).

Val David is also a haven for artists, many of whose studios are open to the public. Most of their work is for sale. The **Atelier Bernard Chaudron, Inc.** (2449 chemin de l'Île, tel. 819/322–3944), sells hand-shaped and hammered lead-free pewter objets d'art.

13 About 96 kilometers (60 miles) from Montréal, overlooking Lac des Sables, is **Sainte-Agathe-des-Monts,** the largest commercial center for ski communities farther north. This lively resort area attracts campers to its spacious **Camping Ste-Agathe** (Rte. 329, 50 rue St. Joseph, Sainte-Agathe-des-Monts J8C 1M9, tel. 819/ 324–0482), bathers to its municipal beach, and sailors to its lake cruises on the *Alouette* (tel. 819/326–3656) touring launch. Sailing is the favorite summer sport, especially during the "24 Heures de la Voile," a weekend sailing competition (tel. 819/326–0457) that takes place each year in June.

Scuba diving is also popular here. The **Service Ambulance Gilles Thibault Inc.** (124 rue Principale, tel. 819/326–4464) will refill air tanks and provide information about equipment rentals.

Perhaps the best way to view the scenery of the Upper Laurentians is to mountain climb. The **Fédération Québécoise de la Montagne** (4545 rue Pierre-de-Coubertin, C.P. 1000, Succursale M, Montréal H1V 3R2, tel. 514/252–3004) can give you information about this sport, as can the region's tourist offices.

About 1 kilometer (½ mile) north of Sainte-Agathe-des-Monts is the **Village du Mont-Castor,** an attractive re-creation of a turn-of-the-century Québecois village; more than 100 new homes have been built here in the traditional fashion of full-length logs set *pièce sur pièce* (one upon the other).

Farther north lie two of Québec's best-known ski resorts—Gray Rocks and Mont Tremblant Resort (*see* Lodging, *below*). Mont Tremblant is also car-racing country. Racing champion Jackie Stewart has called Mont Tremblant "the most beautiful racetrack in the world." The **Formula 2000 "Jim Russell Championships"** of the Canadian Car Championships (tel. 819/425–2739) take place here on weekends in June, July, August, and September.

The mountain and the hundreds of square miles of wilderness beyond it constitute **Parc Mont Tremblant.** Created in 1894, this was once the home of the Algonquin Indians, who called this area Manitonga Soutana, meaning "mountain of the spirits." Today it is a vast wildlife sanctuary of more than 500 lakes and rivers protecting some 230 species of birds and animals, including moose, deer, bear, and beaver. In the winter, its trails are used by cross-country skiers, snowshoers, and snowmobile enthusiasts. Moose hunting is allowed in season, and camping and canoeing are the main summer activities.

Tour 2: L'Estrie

Numbers in the margin correspond to points of interest on the L'Estrie (Eastern Townships) and Montérégie map.

L'Estrie (also known as the Eastern Townships) refers to the area in the southeast corner of the province of Québec, bordering Vermont and New York State. Its northern Appalachian hills, rolling down to placid lakeshores, were first home to the Abenaki natives, long before "summer people" built their cottages and horse paddocks here. The Abenaki are gone, but the names they gave to the region's recreational lakes remain—Memphremagog, Massawippi, Mégantic.

L'Estrie was initially populated by United Empire Loyalists fleeing the American War of Independence and, later, the newly created United States of America, to continue living under the English king in British North America. It's not surprising that l'Estrie is reminiscent of New England with its covered bridges, village greens, white church steeples, and country inns. The Loyalists were followed, around 1820, by the first wave of Irish immigrants—ironically, Catholics fleeing their country's union with Protestant England. Some 20 years later the potato famine sent more Irish pioneers to the townships.

The area became more Gallic after 1850, as French Canadians moved in to work on the railroad and in the lumber industry, and later to mine asbestos at Thetford. Around the turn of the century, English families from Montréal and Americans from the border states discovered the region and began summering at cottages along the lakes. During the Prohibition era, the area attracted even more cottagers from the United States. Lac Massawippi became a favorite summer resort of wealthy families whose homes have since been converted into gracious inns, including the Manoir Hovey and the Hatley Inn.

Today the summer communities fill up with equal parts French and English visitors, though the year-round residents are primarily French. Nevertheless, the locals are proud of both their Loyalist heritage and Québec roots. They boast of "Loyalist tours" and Victorian gingerbread homes and in the next breath direct visitors to the snowmobile museum in Valcourt, where, in 1937, native son Joseph-Armand Bombardier built the first *moto-neige* (snowmobile) in his garage. (Bombardier's inventions were the basis of one of Canada's biggest industries, supplying New York City and Mexico City with subway cars and other rolling stock.)

Over the past two decades, l'Estrie has developed from a series of quiet farm communities and wood-frame summer homes to a thriving all-season resort area. In winter, skiers flock to eight downhill centers and some 20 cross-country trails. By early spring, the sugar huts are busy with the new maple syrup. L'Estrie's southerly location makes this the balmiest corner of Québec, notable for its spring skiing. In summer, boating, swimming, sailing, golfing, and bike riding take over. And every fall the inns are booked solid with "leaf peepers" eager to take in the brilliant foliage.

⑮ Granby, about 80 kilometers (50 miles) from Montréal, is considered to be the gateway to l'Estrie. This town is best known for its zoo, the **Jardin Zoologique de Granby.** It houses some 800 animals from 225 species. Two rare snow leopards on loan from Chicago's Lincoln Park Zoo and New York's Bronx Zoo have won the zoo recognition from the International Union for the Conservation of Nature. The complex includes amusement park rides and souvenir shops as well as a playground and picnic area. *347 rue Bourget, tel. 514/372–9113. Admission: $15 adults, $13 senior citizens, $8 children 5–17, $4 children 1–4. Open June–early Sept., daily 9–5.*

Granby is also gaining repute as the townships' gastronomic capital. Each October, the month-long Festival Gastronomique attracts more than 10,000 *gastronomes* who use the festival's "gastronomic passport" to sample the cuisines at several dining rooms. To reserve a passport, contact: Festival Gastronomique de Granby et Région, 650 rue Principle, Granby J2G 8L4. *Tel. 514/378–7272.*

The **Yamaska** recreation center on the outskirts of town features sailboarding, swimming, and picnicking all summer, and cross-country skiing and snowshoeing in winter.

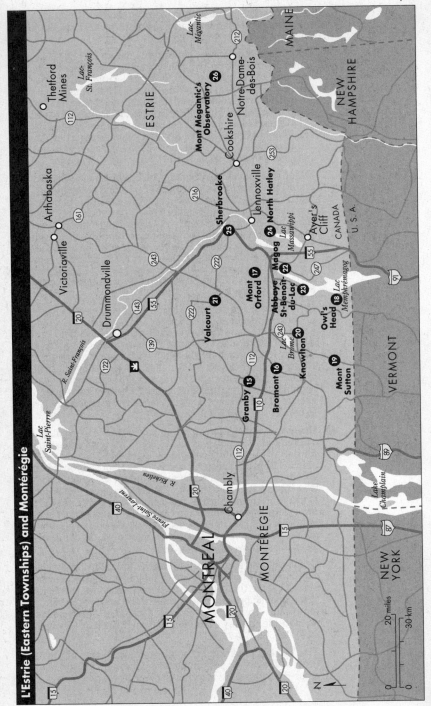

L'Estrie (Eastern Townships) and Montérégie

In the past two decades, l'Estrie has developed into a scenic and increasingly popular ski center. Although it is still less crowded and commercialized than the Laurentians, it boasts ski hills on four mountains that dwarf anything the Laurentians have to offer, with the exception of lofty Mont Tremblant. And, compared with those in Vermont, ski-pass rates are still a bargain.

⑯ **Bromont,** closest to Montréal, is as lively at night as during the day. It offers the only night skiing in l'Estrie and a slope-side disco, **Le Débarque,** where the action continues into the night ⑰ après-ski. **Mont Orford,** located at the center of a provincial park, offers plenty of challenges for alpine and cross-country ⑱ skiers, from novices to veterans. **Owl's Head** has become a mecca for skiers looking for fewer crowds on the hills. It also boasts a 4-kilometer (2.4-mile) intermediate run, the longest in l'Estrie. Aside from superb skiing, Owl's Head offers tremendous scenery. From the trails you can see nearby Vermont and Lac Memphrémagog. (You might even see the lake's legendary sea dragon, said to have been sighted some 90 times since ⑲ 1816.) As it has for decades, **Mont Sutton** attracts the same diehard crowd of mostly Anglophone skiers from Québec. It's also one of the area's largest resorts, with trails that plunge and wander through pine, maple, and birch trees slope-side. **Sutton** itself is a well-established community with crafts shops, cozy eateries, and bars (La Paimpolaise is a favorite among skiers).

Bromont and Orford are *stations touristiques* (tourist centers), meaning that they offer a wide range of activities in all seasons—boating, camping, golf, horseback riding, swimming, tennis, water parks, trail biking, canoeing, fishing, hiking, cross-country and downhill skiing, and snowshoeing. A waterslide park (tel. 514/534–2200)—take exit 78 off Autoroute 10—and a large flea market (weekends from May to mid-November) offer pleasant additions to horseback riding. The same exit will bring you to Bromont's factory outlet shopping malls (50 rue Gaspé). There are about 30 shops that carry Canadian, American, and European designer goods at discount prices.

⑳ Along the shore of Lac Brome is the village of **Knowlton,** a pleasant place to shop for antiques and gifts. In summer check to see what's playing at Knowlton's popular **Théâtre Lac Brome** (*see* The Arts, *below*). In winter many Montréalers come here to ski at **Glen Mountain** (off Route 243, tel. 514/243–6142).

㉑ **Valcourt** is the birthplace of the inventor of the snowmobile, so it follows that this is a world center for the sport, with more than 1,500 kilometers (1,000-plus miles) of paths cutting through the woods and meadows. The **Musée Joseph-Armand Bombardier** displays this innovator's many inventions year-round. *1001 av. Joseph-Armand Bombardier, tel. 514/532–5300. Admission: $5 adults, $3 students and senior citizens, children under 5 free, $13 families.* Open late June–Aug., daily 10–5:30; Sept.–late June, Tues.–Sun. 10–5.

South of Mont Orford at the northern tip of Lac Memphrémagog, a large body of water reaching into northern Vermont, lies ㉒ the bustling resort town of **Magog,** which celebrated its centenary in 1988. A once sleepy village, the town has grown into a four-season resort destination. Two sandy beaches, great bed-and-breakfasts, hotels and restaurants, boating, ferry rides, bird-watching, sailboarding, aerobics, horseback riding, and snowmobiling are just some of the activities offered.

Stroll along Magog's **rue Principale** for a look at boutiques, art galleries, and crafts shops with local artisans' work. Other shops are spread throughout the town's downtown, where the streets are lined with century-old homes and churches, some of which have been converted into storefronts, galleries, and theaters.

Magog is lively after dark, with a variety of bars, cafés, bistros, and great restaurants to suit every taste and pocketbook. **La Lanterne** (tel. 819/843–7205) is a popular hangout. The more sedentary may find **La Source's** (tel. 819/843–0319) array of cheeses, pâtés, and Swiss chocolates irresistible.

㉓ Near Magog is the **Abbaye St-Benoît-du-Lac.** To reach St-Benoît from Magog, take the road to Austin and then follow the signs for the side road to the abbey. This abbey's slender bell tower juts up above the trees like a fairy-tale castle. Built on a wooded peninsula in 1912 by the Benedictines, the abbey is home to some 60 monks, who sell apples and apple cider from their orchards as well as distinctive cheeses: Ermite, St-Benoît, and ricotta. Gregorian masses are held daily. Check for those open to the public (tel. 819/843–4080). The abbey is also known as a favorite retreat for some of Québec's best-known politicians; they abandon the thrust-and-cut of their secular concerns for spiritual rejuvenation.

㉔ One of the pastimes of **North Hatley** crosses language barriers easily. The town on the tip of Lac Massawippi is home to **The Pilsen,** Québec's earliest microbrewery. Although the beer is no longer brewed on-site, the Pilsen (tel. 819/842–2971) still serves Massawippi pale ale on tap. For those who ask, proprietor Gilles Peloquin will arrange a visit to the famous brewery, now located in nearby Lennoxville. The pub also has great food, loads of atmosphere, and a convivial crowd year-round. The avant-garde **Piggery** theater is based in North Hatley (*see* the Arts, *below*).

㉕ The region's unofficial capital and largest city is **Sherbrooke,** named in 1818 for Canadian Governor General Sir John Coape Sherbrooke. Founded by Loyalists in the 1790s, and located along the St-François River, it boasts a number of art galleries, the **Musée des Beaux-Arts de Sherbrooke** (174 rue Palais, tel. 819/821–2115; admission: $2 adults, $1 students and senior citizens; open Tues.–Sun. 1–5), and the historic **Domaine Howard,** headquarters of the township's historic society, which conducts city tours from late June through August. For reservations, telephone the Sherbrooke Tourist Information Center (48 rue Dépôt, tel. 819/564–8331).

㉖ For a more cosmic experience, continue from Sherbrooke along Route 212 to **Mont Mégantic's Observatory.** Both amateur stargazers and serious astronomers are drawn to this site, located in a beautifully wild and mountainous part of l'Estrie. The observatory is at the summit of l'Estrie's second-highest mountain (3,601 feet), whose northern face records annual snowfalls rivaling any in North America. The observatory is a joint venture by l'Université de Montréal and l'Université Laval. Its powerful telescope allows resident scientists to observe celestial bodies 10 million times smaller than the human eye can detect. There's a welcome center on the mountain's base, where amateur stargazers can get information about the evening celestial sweep sessions, Thursday through Saturday. *Notre-Dame-des-Bois, tel. 819/888–2822. Open late June–Labor Day, daily 10–5.*

Tour 3: Charlevoix

Numbers in the margin correspond to points of interest on the Charlevoix map.

Stretching along the St. Lawrence River's north shore east of Québec City from Sainte-Anne-de-Beaupré to the Saguenay River, Charlevoix embraces mountains rising from the sea and a succession of valleys, plateaus, and cliffs cut by waterfalls, brooks, and streams. The roads wind into villages of picturesque houses and huge tin-roof churches.

New France's first historian, the Jesuit priest François-Xavier de Charlevoix, gave his name to the region. Charlevoix (Sharlevwah) was first explored by Jacques Cartier, who landed in 1535, although the first colonists didn't arrive until well into the 17th century. They developed a thriving shipbuilding industry, specializing in the sturdy schooner they called a *goelette*, which they used to haul everything from logs to lobsters up and down the coast in the days before rail and paved roads. Shipbuilding has been a vital part of the provincial economy until recent times, though wrecked and forgotten goelettes are visible from many beaches in the region.

㉗ Charlevoix begins about 33 kilometers (20 miles) east of Québec City, in the tiny town of **Sainte-Anne-de-Beaupré** (named for Québec's patron saint). Each year more than a million pilgrims visit the region's most famous religious site, the **Basilica of Sainte-Anne-de-Beaupré** (*see* Chapter 4), which is dedicated to the mother of the Virgin Mary.

㉘ Only 8 kilometers (5 miles) beyond the pilgrimage center is the **Cap Tourmente Wildlife Reserve,** where more than 100,000 greater snow geese gather every October and May. Other parts of the region offer whale-watching cruises, and you can often spot whales, seals, and dolphins, on occasion, from ferries and on land, so nature-lovers are encouraged to bring their binoculars. *St-Joachim G0A 3X0, tel. 418/827–3776.*

In fact, the region is a haven for anyone who enjoys being active in the outdoors, including hikers, joggers, cyclists, and, in particular, skiers. Charlevoix has three main ski areas, with excellent facilities for both the downhill and cross-country skier. **㉙ ㉚** **Parc du Mont-Sainte-Anne** (*see* Chapter 4), outside Québec City, is on the World Cup downhill ski circuit; **Mont Grand Fonds** (1000 chemin des Loisirs, La Malbaie, tel. 418/665–4405) has 14 slopes and 141 kilometers (87 miles) of cross-country **㉛** trails; and **Le Massif** (1350 rue Principale, C.P. 68, Petite Rivière St. François, tel. 418/632–5879) is a three-peak ski resort that boasts the province's highest vertical drop (762 meters, or 2,500 feet).

㉜ **Baie-St-Paul,** Charlevoix's earliest settlement after Beaupré, is popular with hang-gliding fans and artists. You will find artisans working in old habitant houses. Here, the high hills circle a wide plain holding the village beside the sea. Many of Québec's greatest landscapists portray the area, and their

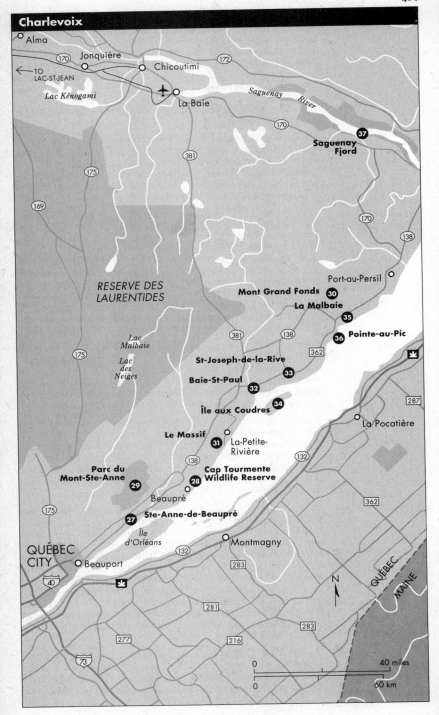

Charlevoix

Alma

Jonquière

Chicoutimi

170

172

← TO LAC-ST-JEAN

Lac Kénogami

La Baie

Saguenay River

170

Saguenay Fjord 37

381

175

169

170

138

RESERVE DES LAURENTIDES

Port-au-Persil

Mont Grand Fonds 30

La Malbaie 35

381

138

Pointe-au-Pic 36

362

175

Lac Malbaie

Lac des Neiges

St-Joseph-de-la-Rive 33

Baie-St-Paul 32

34

287

Île aux Coudres

La Pocatière

Le Massif 31

La-Petite-Rivière

132

138

Cap Tourmente Wildlife Reserve 28

362

Parc du Mont-Ste-Anne 29

Beaupré

175

27 **Ste-Anne-de-Beaupré**

Île d'Orléans

Montmagny

QUÉBEC CITY

Beauport

132

283

40

281

QUÉBEC

MAINE

277

216

283

73

0   40 miles

0   60 km

work is on display year-round at the **Centre d'Art Baie-St-Paul** (4 boul. Faford, tel. 418/435–3681). Recently the center has garnered a reputation in North America as a major regional arts center promoting the area's own talent, as well as providing those just starting out with wider exposure while they study their crafts. At town-center, **Auberge la Maison Otis,** an 1858 stone house, has been converted into what many consider the area's finest inn-restaurant (*see* Lodging, *below*).

From Baie-St-Paul, you can take the open, scenic coastal drive (Rte. 362) or the faster Route 138 to **Pointe-au-Pic, La Malbaie,** and **Cap-à-l'Aigle.** This section of Route 362 has memorable views of rolling hills—green, white, or ablaze with fiery hues, depending on the season—meeting the broad expanse of the "sea" as the locals like to call the St. Lawrence estuary.

㉝ A secondary road leads sharply down into **St-Joseph-de-la-Rive,** with its line of old houses hugging the mountain base on the narrow shore road. The town is host to peaceful inns and inviting restaurants, such as l'Auberge sous les Pins, which means "inn under the pines." Nearby Papeterie St-Gilles produces unusual handcrafted stationery, using a 17th-century process. The small **Charlevoix Musée** commemorates the days of the St. Lawrence goelettes. From St-Joseph you can catch

㉞ a ferry to **Île aux Coudres,** an island where Jacques Cartier's men gathered *les coudres* (hazelnuts) in 1535. Since then, the island has produced many a goelette, and former captains now run several small inns. Larger inns feature folk-dance evenings. Many visitors like to bike around the 16-kilometer (10-mile) island taking in inns, windmills, and old schooners, as well as boutiques selling paintings and local handcrafts, such as household linen.

Continuing on Route 362, you will come to one of the most elegant and historically interesting resorts in the entire province.

㉟ **La Malbaie** was known as Murray Bay in an earlier era when wealthy Anglophones summered here and in the neighboring villages of Pointe-au-Pic and Cap-à-l'Aigle. The regional museum—**Musée de Charlevoix**—traces its history as a vacation spot in a series of exhibits and is developing an excellent collection of local paintings and folk art. *1 rue du Havre, Pointe-au-Pic, tel. 418/665–4411.*

Once called the "summer White House," this area became popular with both American and Canadian politicians in the late 1800s when Ottawa Liberals and Washington Republicans partied decorously through the summer with members of the Québec judiciary. William Howard Taft built the first of three

㊱ summer residences in **Pointe-au-Pic** in 1894, when he was the American civil governor of the Philippines. He became the 27th president of the United States in 1908, and later chief justice of the Supreme Court. Locals still fondly remember the Tafts and the parties they threw in their elegant summer homes.

Now many Taft-era homes serve as handsome inns, guaranteeing an old-fashioned coddling, with extras such as breakfast in bed, gourmet meals, whirlpools, and free shuttles to the ski areas in winter. Many serve lunch and dinner to nonresidents, so you can tour the area going from one gourmet's delight to the next. The cuisine, as elsewhere in Québec, is genuine French, rather than a hybrid invented for North Americans.

The road, the views, and the villages continue all the way up to Baie-Ste-Catherine, which shares the view up the magnificent **Saguenay Fjord** with the small town of **Tadoussac.** Jacques Cartier made a stop at this point in 1535, and it became an important meeting site for fur traders in the French Territory until the mid-19th century. Whale-watching excursions and cruises of the fjord now depart from Tadoussac, as well as from Chicoutimi, farther up the deep fjord. As the Saguenay River flows from Lake St-Jean south toward the St. Lawrence, it has a dual character: Between Alma and Chicoutimi, the once rapidly flowing river has been turned into hydroelectric power; in its lower section, it becomes wider and deeper and flows by steep mountains and cliffs, en route to the St. Lawrence. The white beluga whale breeds in the lower portion of the Saguenay in summer, and in the confluence of the fjord and the seaway are many marine species, which attract other whales, such as pilot, finback, humpback, and blues.

Sadly, the beluga is an endangered species, and the estimated 400 left, along with 27 species of mammals and birds and 17 species of fish, are being threatened by pollution from the St. Lawrence River. This has inspired a $100 million project funded by both the federal and provincial governments. An 800-square-kilometer (496-square-mile) marine park at the confluence of the Saguenay and St. Lawrence rivers has been created to protect its fragile ecosystem in hope of reversing some of the damage already done. Full-day and half-day cruises from Chicoutimi operate daily June–September (tel. 418/543–7630); other trips leave from Hotel Tadoussac (tel. 418/235–4421) from May through mid-October.

Tour 4: The Gaspé Peninsula

Numbers in the margin correspond to points of interest on the Gaspé Peninsula map.

Jutting into the stormy Gulf of St. Lawrence like the battered prow of a ship, the Gaspé Peninsula remains an isolated region of unsurpassed wild beauty, an area where the land ends. Sheer cliffs tower above broad beaches, and tiny coastal fishing communities cling to the shoreline. Inland rise the Chic-Choc Mountains, eastern Canada's highest, the realm of woodland caribou, black bear, and moose. Townspeople in some Gaspé areas speak mainly English, though *Gaspésiens* speak slightly Acadian-accented French.

Jacques Cartier landed on the Gaspé in 1534, but it wasn't until the early 1800s that the first settlers arrived. Today, the area still seems unspoiled and timeless, a blessing for travelers dipping and soaring along the spectacular coastal highways or venturing on river-valley roads to the interior. Geographically, the peninsula is among the oldest lands on earth. A vast, mainly uninhabited forest covers the hilly hinterland. Local tourist officials can be helpful in locating outfitters and guides to fish and hunt large and small game. The Gaspé's four major parks—**Port Daniel, Forillon, Causapscal,** and **Gaspé Park**—cover a total of 2,292 square kilometers (885 square miles).

Take the Trans-Canada Highway northeast along the southern shore of the St. Lawrence River to just south of Rivière-du-Loup, where you pick up the 270-kilometer (150-mile) Route 132, which hugs the dramatic coastline. At Ste-Flavie, follow the southern leg of Route 132. Windsurfers and sailors enjoy the breezes around the Gaspé; there are windsurfing marathons in **Baie des Chaleurs** (at Carleton) each summer.

The Gaspé was on Jacques Cartier's itinerary—he first stepped ashore in North America in the town of Gaspé—but Vikings, Basques, and Portuguese fisherfolk had come long before. The area's history is told in countless towns en route. Acadians, displaced by the British from New Brunswick in 1755, **㊳ ㊴** settled **Bonaventure; Paspébiac** still has a gunpowder shed built in the 1770s to help defend the peninsula from Ameri**㊵** can ships; and United Empire Loyalists settled **New Carlisle** in 1784.

㊶ The largest colony of gannets in the world summers on the Gaspé's **Bonaventure Island,** off Percé. The most famous sight in the region is the huge fossil-embedded rock off the town of **㊷** **Percé** that the sea "pierced" thousands of years ago.

㊸ The region boasts Québec's longest ski season and highest peaks. For instance, **Sainte-Anne-des-Monts,** on the north shore of the peninsula, offers the only heli-skiing east of the Rockies, with deep powder, open bowl, and glade skiing clear into June on peaks that rise to 2,700 feet. Other centers operate from mid-November through May.

What to See and Do with Children

Jardin Zoologique de Granby, Tour 2: L'Estrie

Mont Saint-Sauveur Water Park, Tour 1: Les Laurentides

Santa Claus Village, Tour 1: Les Laurentides

Shopping

When in the Laurentians, consider strolling along Saint-Sauveur-des-Monts' rue Principale amid shops, fashion boutiques, and outdoor café terraces decorated with bright awnings and flowers. Housed in a former bank, **La Voute Boutique** (239B rue Principale, tel. 514/227–4144) carries such international labels as Byblos and an up-to-the-minute all-season selection of coordinates in cotton, knits, suede, and leather, plus sequined dresses, sweaters, pants, jackets, and suits from France, Italy, and Spain. If you are hungry, have a bite at **Jardin des Oliviers** (239 rue Principale, tel. 514/227–2110), a popular, moderately priced French restaurant in the middle of town.

Saint-Sauveur-des-Monts is also home to **Les Factoreries Saint-Sauveur** (100 rue Guindon, Exit 60 from Hwy. 15, tel. 514/227–1074), a new factory outlet mall with 11 boutiques. Canadian, American, and European manufacturers sell a variety of goods at reduced prices, from designer clothing to exclusive household items.

Magog's rue Principale, in l'Estrie, is another interesting place to browse. The street is dotted with boutiques, art galleries, and crafts shops with local artisan's work. **Amandine** (499 rue Principale O, tel. 819/847–1346) is a lovely gift shop with unusual dishes, stemware, luxury bath items, and Belgian chocolates. When you want a rest, drop by **La Source** (420 rue Principale O, tel. 819/843–0319) for an array of cheeses, pâtés,

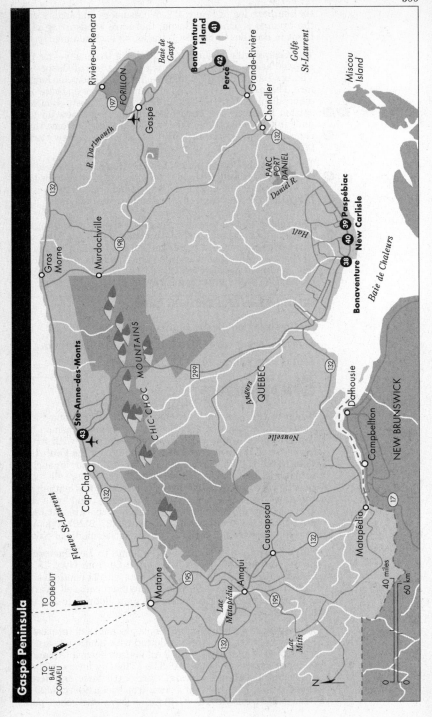

Gaspé Peninsula

TO BAIE COMAEU

TO GODBOUT

Fleuve St-Laurent

Matane

195

Amqui

Lac Matapédia

195

132

Lac Mitis

Cap-Chat

132

Ste-Anne-des-Monts **43**

CHIC-CHOC MOUNTAINS

299

Causapscal

132

QUEBEC

Angers

Nouvelle

Matapédia

17

Campbellton

NEW BRUNSWICK

Dalhousie

132

Baie de Chaleurs

Bonaventure **38**

40 New Carlisle

39 Paspébiac

Hall

Daniel R.

PARC PORT DANIEL

132

Chandler

132

Grande-Rivière

42 Percé

41 Bonaventure Island

Baie de Gaspé

Gaspé

FORILLON

197

Rivière-au-Renard

R. Dartmouth

132

Murdochville

198

Gros Morne

Golfe St-Laurent

Miscou Island

N

0 40 miles

0 60 km

and Swiss chocolates. Other shops are spread throughout the town's downtown, where the streets are lined with century-old homes and churches, some of which have been converted into storefronts, galleries, and theaters.

Factory outlet shopping is gaining popularity in l'Estrie also— especially in Bromont, where **Les Versants de Bromont** (50 rue Gaspé, Exit 78 from Hwy. 10, tel. 819/843–8300) houses 27 boutiques. Shoppers can save between 30% and 70% on items carrying national and international labels such as Liz Claiborne, Vuarnet, and Oneida.

Sports and Fitness

Bicycling   **Estrie à Bicyclette** (C.P. 772, Sherbrooke, J1H 5K7, tel. 819/346–6795) sells a cycling guide of l'Estrie for less than $10, and can be found at most bicycle rental shops. **Base de Plein Air Davignon** (319 chemin Gale, Bromont, tel. 514/534–2277 or 800/363–8952) rents bicycles, and the **Sutton Tourist Association** (20 Place Sutton, C.P. 418, Sutton J0E 2K0, tel. 514/538–2646) has a list of places to rent bicycles throughout the region.

Deltaplaning   If white-water rafting isn't adventure enough, there is always deltaplaning, in which man and machine become one. The **Vélidelta Free-Flying School** (C.P. 631, Mont Rolland J0R 1G0, tel. 514/229–6887) offers lessons on free-flying, flight simulation, and the more advanced tricks of the trade you'll need to earn the required deltaplane pilot's license, including flight maneuvers, speed, and turns. Equipment is provided. You can choose a half-day initiation lesson, one-day flying lesson, or four-day course.

Fishing   There are more than 60 outfitters (a.k.a. innkeepers) in the northern Laurentians area, where provincial parks and game sanctuaries abound. Pike, walleye, and lake and speckled trout are plentiful just a three-hour drive north of Montréal. Outfitters provide the dedicated angler with accommodations and every service wildlife and wilderness enthusiasts could possibly require. Open year-round in most cases, their lodging facilities range from the most luxurious first-class resort to the log-camp type "back of beyond." As well as supplying trained guides, all offer services and equipment to allow neophytes or experts the best possible fishing in addition to boating, swimming, river rafting, windsurfing, ice fishing, cross-country skiing, hiking, or just relaxing amid the splendor of this still spectacularly unspoiled region.

Outfitters recommended by the Laurentian tourist association include **Pourvoirie des 100 Lacs Nords** (tel. 514/444–4441), run by Claude Lavigne; **Club de Chasse et Pêche du Lac Beauregard** (tel. 819/425–7722) in Saint-Jovite; and **Pourvoirie Boismenu** (tel. 819/597–2619) at Lac-du-Cerf, run by Adrien Boismenu. Before setting off into the wilds, consult the Fédération des Pourvoyeurs du Québec (Québec Outfitters Federation, 2485 boul. Hamel, Québec G1P 2H9, tel. 418/527–5191) or ask for its list of outfitters available through tourist offices.

Don't forget: Fishing requires a permit, available from the regional offices of the Ministère du Loisir, de la Chasse et de la Pêche (6255 13ième av., Montréal H1X 3E6, tel. 514/374–2417), or inquire at any Laurentians sporting-goods store displaying an "authorized agent" sticker.

Golf Club de Golf Chantecler Sainte-Adèle is an 18-hole golf course in the Laurentians. *Exit 67, 2520 chemin du Golf, Ste-Adèle, tel. 514/229–3742.*

Les Rochers Bleus is an 18-hole golf course in Sutton, located in Estrie. Reservations must be made in advance. *550 Rte. 139, Sutton, tel. 514/538–2324.*

When in the Charlevoix region, you may want to try the 18-hole course in Pointe-au-Pic, **Club de Golf de Manoir Richelieu.** *181 ave. Richelieu, Pointe-au-Pic, tel. 418/665–3703 or 800/463–2613.*

Horseback Riding As the former Olympic equestrian site, **Bromont** is horse country, and every year in late June and early July it holds a riding festival (tel. 514/534–3255).

Mountain Mountain climbing is one of the best ways to view the scenery
Climbing of the Upper Laurentians. For information, contact the **Fédération Québéçoise de la Montagne.** *4545 rue Pierre-de-Coubertin, C.P. 1000, Succ. M, Montréal H1V 3R2, tel. 514/ 252–3004.*

River Rafting The Rivière Rouge in the Laurentians rates as one of the best in North America, according to expert river rafters, so it's not surprising that this river has spawned a miniboom in the sport. Just an hour's drive north of Montréal, the Rouge cuts across the rugged Laurentians through rapids, canyons, and alongside beaches. From April through October, the adventurous can experience what traversing the region must have meant in the days of the voyageurs and *coureurs du bois,* though today's trip, by comparison, is much safer and more comfortable.

Four companies specializing in white-water rafting are on-site at the trip's departure point near Calumet. (Take Rte. 148 past Calumet; turn onto chemin de la Rivière Rouge until you see the signs for the access road to each rafter's headquarters.) **Aventures en Eau Vive** (tel. 819/242–6084), **Nouveau Monde** (tel. 819/242–7238), **Propulsion** (tel. 514/953–3300), and **W-3 Rafting** (tel. 514/334–0889) all offer four- to five-hour rafting trips. All provide transportation to and from the river site, as well as guides, helmets, life jackets, and, at the end of the trip, a much-anticipated meal. Most have facilities on-site or nearby for dining, drinking, camping, bathing, swimming, hiking, and horseback riding.

Skiing With the longest vertical drop (2,131 feet) in eastern Canada,
Les Laurentides **Mont Tremblant** (tel. 819/425–8711) offers a wide range of ski trails. Beginners favor the 5-kilometer (3-mile) Nansen trail; intermediate skiers head for the steeply sloped Flying Mile and Beauchemin runs. Experts choose the challenging Duncan and Expo runs on the mountain's north side. The Vancouver-based developers who bought the resort in 1991 promised to invest $47 million over five years in order to turn Mont Tremblant into a world-class ski and four-season resort. The speedy Duncan Express, a quadruple chair lift, is only a beginning.

Ski Mont Gabriel (tel. 514/229–3547) in Mont Rolland has 16 downhill trails primarily for intermediate and advanced skiers. The most popular runs are the Tamarack and the O'Connell trails for advanced skiers and Obergurgl for intermediates.

For something different, try **Ski Morin Heights** (*see* Tour 1, Les Laurentides, *above*), where snowboarding is the latest craze.

L'Estrie In l'Estrie the larger downhill slopes include **Mont Bromé** (tel. 514/534–2200) in Bromont (site of the 1986 World Cup) with 23 trails, **Mont Orford** (tel. 819/843–6548) with 39, **Owl's Head** (tel. 514/292–3342) with 26, and **Mont Sutton** (tel. 514/538–2339), where you pay to ski by the hour, with 53. The steepest drop, one of 853 meters (2,800 feet), is at Orford. All four resorts feature interchangeable lift tickets so skiers can test out all the major runs in the area. Call Ski East, tel. 819/820–2020.

With more than 20 cross-country sites, l'Estrie is a peaceful getaway. Trails at Bromont crisscross the site of the 1976 Olympic equestrian center. Three inns—Le Manoir Hovey, Auberge Hatley, and the Ripplecove Inn (*see* Dining and Lodging, *below*)—offer the **Skiwippi,** a week-long package of cross-country treks from one inn to another. The network covers some 32 kilometers (20 miles) of l'Estrie.

Snowmobile **Point de Vue Canada** offers snowmobilers tours in the Laurentians, in Charlevoix, and as far north as the James Bay region. The group also has such adventure packages as "Winter Passion," a five-night, six-day tour featuring ice fishing, water rafting, skiing, and trapping, accompanied by Montagnais Indians. Another tour, "The Magic of the Nunavik Arctic," is a week-long adventure in Québec's Grand Nord, where participants spend one night in an igloo, travel on dogsleds, and ice fish. *1227 av. St-Hubert, Suite 200, Montréal H2L 3Y8, tel. 514/843–8161.*

Dining

Whether you enjoy a croissant and espresso at a sidewalk café or order *poutine* (a streetwise mix of homemade french fries—*frites*—from a fast-food emporium), you won't soon forget your meals in Québec. There is no such thing as simply "eating out" in the province, as restaurants are an integral slice of Québec life.

Outside of Montréal and Québec City, you can find both good value and classic cuisine. Cooking in the province tends to be hearty, with such fare as cassoulet, *tourtières* (meat pies), onion soup, and apple pie heading up menus. In the Laurentians, chefs at some of the finer inns have attracted international followings. Local blueberries and maple syrup find their way into a surprising number of dishes.

Early reservations are essential. Monday or Tuesday is not too soon to book weekend tables at the best provincial restaurants. If you have any doubt about acceptable dress at a restaurant, call ahead. Jacket and tie are still the rule at many first-rate restaurants, even in summer.

Granby and its environs is one of Québec's foremost regions for traditional Québecois cuisine, here called *la fine cuisine estrienne.* Specialties include mixed-game meat pies like *cipaille* and sweet, salty dishes like ham and maple syrup. Actually, maple syrup—on everything and in all its forms—is a mainstay of Québecois dishes. L'Estrie is one of Québec's main maple-sugaring regions.

In addition to maple sugar, cloves, nutmeg, cinnamon, and pepper—the same spices used by the first settlers—have never gone out of fashion here, and local restaurants make good use of them in their distinctive dishes. The full country experience of l'Estrie includes warm hospitality at lodges and inns in the area as well.

Highly recommended restaurants in each price category are indicated by a star ★.

Category	Cost*
Very Expensive	over $35
Expensive	$25–$35
Moderate	$15–$25
Inexpensive	under $15

per person, excluding drinks, service, 7% federal tax, and 4% provincial tax

Les Laurentides

Ste-Adèle **La Clef des Champs.** This family-owned hillside restaurant, well known for its gourmet French cuisine, is a charming alternative to even the most superbly prepared hotel fare. The restaurant, hidden among trees and facing a mountain, offers elegant dishes in a cozy, romantic atmosphere. Try the *noisette d'agneau en feuilleté* (lamb in pastry) or fresh poached salmon in red wine sauce. Top off your meal with the *gâteau aux deux chocolats* (a two-chocolate cake). *875 chemin Ste-Marguerite, tel. 514/229–2857. Reservations advised. Dress: casual. AE, DC, MC, V. Closed 2 weeks after Easter and Mon. Oct.–May, except on holidays. Very Expensive.*

★ **L'Eau à la Bouche.** A consistent award winner in gastronomic circles, the restaurant has received top awards among the Laurentians region's auberge/restaurants for its superb marriage of nouvelle cuisine and traditional Québec dishes. L'Eau à la Bouche is also distinguished as one of the area's most expensive restaurants. However, the care and inventiveness of chef-proprietor Anne Desjardins, who opened the Bavarian-style property a decade ago with her husband, Pierre Audette, is extraordinary. Such dishes as goat cheese tart, saddle of rabbit with onions, *baluchon* of lobster and scallops, roast partridge stuffed with oyster mushrooms and cream sauce, *pavé* of dark chocolate with English cream, and *cachette* of rhubarb and strawberries leave dinner guests clamoring for more. *3041 boul. Ste-Adèle, Rte. 117, tel. 514/229–2991. Reservations required. Dress: casual but neat. AE, MC, V. Very Expensive.*

Ste-Agathe **Chatel Vienna.** Run by Eberhards Rado and his wife, who is
★ also the chef, this moderately priced Austrian restaurant offers Viennese and other Continental dishes served up in a lakeside setting. You may want to try the prize-winning home-smoked trout, served with an herb and spice butter, and garden fresh vegetables. Also offered are a variety of schnitzels (veal dishes), a sauerkraut plate, and venison. Meals are accompanied by hot spiced wine, Czech pilsner beer, or dry Austrian and other international white wines. A Sunday buffet brunch

with about 30 dishes is served from 11:30 until 2 for about $17.95. *6 rue Ste-Lucie, tel. 819/326–1485. Reservations advised. Dress: casual. MC, V. Moderate–Expensive.*

Chez Girard. This restaurant serves up moderately priced, excellent French cuisine in an auberge on the shores of Lac des Sables. The airy dining room has windows facing the lake and pastel colors that create a soft, romantic atmosphere. Some of the house specialties include *saumon au champagne* (salmon with champagne), lamb with cream of garlic sauce, caribou, *feuilleté d'escargots et de pleurotes* (escargots and mushroom pastry). A Sunday brunch is offered for $16.95. *18 rue Principale O, tel. 819/326–0922. Reservations advised. Dress: casual. AE, MC, V. Moderate–Expensive.*

St-Sauveur-des-Monts **Auberge Saint-Denis.** This classic Québec inn has earned the title "Relais Gourmand" for its fine French cuisine. Specializing in game, the artfully presented dishes are served in one of three dining rooms with a huge stone fireplace, and pastel colors creating a warm atmosphere. Try the *arrivage de gibier*, an assortment of wild game served with an exotic fruit sauce. *61 St-Denis, tel. 514/227–4602. Reservations advised for dinner. Dress: casual but neat. AE, DC, MC, V. Expensive.*

l'Estrie

Ayer's Cliff **The Ripplecove Inn.** This inn vies with the Hatley and Hovey inns (*see* Lodging, *below*) for best in the region. Its accommodations and service are consistently excellent, and Ripplecove's dining room is an award winner. Its English-pub style dining offers a combination of classical and French cuisine with such dishes as *mousseline de rouget et truite* (mullet and trout mousse served with lobster and dill sauce) followed by *rable de lapereau* (stuffed rabbit with paprika sauce), topped off with a sublime dessert such as *nougat glacé au coulis framboise* (nougat with raspberry sauce). *700 chemin Ripplecove, C.P. 246, tel. 819/838–4296. Reservations advised on weekends. Dress: casual. AE, MC, V. Expensive.*

Magog **Auberge de l'Étoile.** This popular restaurant serves three meals a day in casual surroundings. Its somber interior, decorated in dark colors, is brightened by the windows facing Lac Memphé-Magog. House specialties include wild game and Swiss fondue. *1150 rue Principale O, tel. 819/843–6521. Reservations advised. Dress: casual. AE, DC, MC, V. Moderate.*

Notre-Dame-des-Bois **Aux Berges de l'Aurore.** This tiny bed-and-breakfast is situated at the foot of Mont Mégantic, and although the view is spectacular, the draw here is the inn's cuisine. The award-winning restaurant features a five-course meal with ingredients supplied from the inn's huge fruit, vegetable, and herb garden, as well as wild game from the surrounding area: boar, fish, hare, and quail. It has been attractively furnished by its owners, Michel Martin and Daniel Pepin, and is closed from early January until mid-April. *51 chemin de l'Observatoire, tel. 819/888–2715. Reservations advised. Dress: casual. MC, V. Expensive.*

Sherbrooke **Restaurant au P'tit Sabot.** This restaurant recently won an award for the best local-style eatery in the region. Among the many provincial dishes are wild boar, quail, and bison. *1410 rue King O, tel. 819/563–0262. Reservations advised. Dress: casual. AE, MC, V. Moderate.*

Charlevoix

Baie-St-Paul **Auberge la Maison Otis.** Québec-oriented French cuisine is how chef Bernard Paten describes his cuisine. The restaurant is a 150-year-old Norman-style house, elegantly decorated in pink pastel, centered on a huge stone fireplace. This four-star restaurant's menu continually changes, always adapting to the region and the season. *Ballotine de faisan* (pheasant), stuffed with quail and served in a venison sauce, is an example of the chef's creativity. Finish your meal with either an assortment of cheese or one of many delicious desserts. *23 rue St-Jean-Baptiste, tel. 418/435–2255. Reservations advised. Dress: casual but neat. MC, V. Expensive.*

Mouton Noir. This restaurant offers French cuisine amid flowers on the terrace in the summer or in a cozy rustic setting in the winter. You'll always find a varied menu, with pasta, fish, and meat, for a very reasonable price. The restaurant comes highly recommended from the locals. *43 rue Ste-Anne, tel. 418/435–3075. Reservations accepted. Dress: casual. AE, DC, MC, V. Closed Nov. Moderate.*

La Malbaie **Auberge sur la Côte.** Fine French cuisine is served here in a rustic setting. The simple, white tablecloths complement the natural wood and stone walls. A house specialty is *agneau de Charlevoix*, lamb seasoned with lemon and thyme, served with fresh vegetables. Lunch is served in summer only, but the dining room is open in the evening year-round. *205 chemin des Falaises, tel. 418/665–3972. Reservations advised. Dress: casual. AE, MC, V. Expensive.*

Pointe-au-Pic **Auberge des 3 Canards.** This inn has made a name for itself in the region, not only for its accommodations but also for its award-winning restaurant. Nouvelle cuisine, with a varied menu including game, fish, and meat is elegantly presented in a rustic setting. The warmth of the natural wood contrasts with the pale and deep blue touches throughout. *49 côte Bellevue, tel. 418/665–3761. Reservations advised. Dress: casual. AE, MC, V. Very Expensive.*

Gaspé Peninsula

Gaspé **La Belle Hélène.** This restaurant evokes a feeling of warmth, with natural wood surroundings and large windows facing the bay filled with busy fishing boats. The menu specializes in regional cuisine, namely seafood and game. In the summer, the restaurant features *crêpes bretonnes*, thin pancakes with a variety of fillings and toppings. *135A rue de la Reine, tel. 418/368–1455. Reservations in summer advised. Dress: casual. MC, V. Moderate.*

La Brise-Bise Bistro. This chic bistro-bar, overlooking the Gaspé Bay, offers deluxe fast food, such as sauerkraut and sausages, a variety of imported beer, and live entertainment. *2 côte Carter, tel. 418/368–1456. Reservations accepted. Dress: casual. MC, V. Inexpensive.*

Pabos Mills **La Sieur de Pabos.** This rustic restaurant overlooking Pabos Bay, just outside of Chandler, specializes in seafood and boasts the best in the province. The chef suggests *crêpe de la signeurie*, a seafood crepe with a delicately seasoned white sauce. *325 Rte. 132, tel. 418/689–2281. Reservations accepted. AE, MC, V. Inexpensive.*

Sugar Huts

Every March the combination of sunny days and cold nights causes the sap to run in the maple trees. Sugar huts (*cabanes à sucre*) go into operation boiling the sap collected from the trees in buckets (now, at some places, complicated tubing and vats do the job). The many commercial shacks scattered over the area host "sugaring offs" and tours of the operation, including the tapping of maple trees, the boiling vats, and *tire sur la neige*, when hot syrup is poured over cold snow to give it a taffy consistency just right for "pulling" and eating. A number of cabanes offer hearty meals of ham, baked beans, and pancakes, all drowned in maple syrup. It's best to call before visiting these cabanes: **Erablière Patoine,** 1105 chemin Beauvoir, in Fleurimont, near Sherbrooke, tel. 819/563–7455, and **Bolduc** in Cookshire, 525 chemin Lower, tel. 819/875–3022.

Lodging

Weary travelers have a full spectrum of accommodation options in Québec: from large resort hotels in the Laurentians and Relais et Châteaux properties in l'Estrie to shared dormitory space in rustic youth hostels near the heart of Gaspé. For information on camping in the province's private trailer parks and campgrounds, write for the free publication "Québec Camping," available from Tourisme Québec, Box 20,000, Québec City, G1K 7X2, tel. 418/643–2280. Inquiries about camping in Québec's three national parks should be directed to Parks Canada, Information Services, 3 Buade St., Box 6060, Haute Ville, Québec City, G1R 4V7, tel. 418/648–4177. **Agricotours** (4545 av. Pierre de Couberten, C.P. 1000, Succursale M, Montréal H1V 3R2, tel. 514/252–3138), the Québec farm-vacation association, can provide lists of guest farms in the province.

Highly recommended lodgings in each price category are indicated by a star ★.

Category	Cost*
Very Expensive	over $125
Expensive	$90–$125
Moderate	$50–$90
Inexpensive	under $50

Prices are for a standard double room, excluding 10% service charge, 7% federal tax, and 4% provincial tax, unless Modified American Plan (MAP) is indicated. MAP charges apply to each guest and include all meals, service charges, and taxes.

Charlevoix

Baie-St-Paul **Auberge la Maison Otis.** Situated in the center of the village,
★ this inn offers calm and romantic accommodations in three buildings, including an old stone house. Chef Bernard Paten specializes in nouvelle "Québec" cuisine—nouvelle cuisine with

a regional twist—and summer lunches are served amid flowers on an outdoor terrace. Some of the 30 country-style rooms have whirlpools, fireplaces, and antique furnishings; all are air-conditioned and have private bath, TV, and radio. Skiing and ice-skating are nearby. *23 rue St-Jean-Baptiste, G0A 1B0, tel. 418/435–2255. 30 rooms, 3 suites. Facilities: restaurant, piano bar, lounge, indoor pool, health center, and sauna. MAP optional. MC, V. Expensive–Very Expensive.*

Cap-à-l'Aigle **Auberge la Pinsonnière.** The Pinsonnière is a member of the ★ French association of fine country hotels, the Relais & Châteaux. Some even classify this small inn as a resort. Rooms offer a commanding view of Murray Bay on the St. Lawrence River. An atmosphere of country luxury prevails. Each room is decorated differently, some featuring fireplaces, whirlpools, and king-size four-poster beds. The weary traveler may relax in one of the three lounges within the auberge. *124 rue St-Raphael, G0T 1B0, tel. 418/665–4431. 22 rooms, 6 suites. Facilities: 2 restaurants, tennis court, indoor pool, sauna, private beach, and horseback riding. MAP. AE, MC, V. Very Expensive.*

Île aux Coudres **Hôtel Cap-aux-Pièrres.** This hotel, located on Coudres Island ★ in the St. Lawrence River, provides top-notch accommodations in both a traditionally Canadian main building and a motel section (open summer only). About a third of the rooms afford river views, and all have color TV and telephones. The restaurant serves a mix of Québec standards and nouvelle cuisine, and entertainment includes folk dancing on Saturday evenings in the summer. *246 rue Principale, La Baleine, G0A 2A0, tel. 418/438–2711 or 800/ 463–5250. 98 rooms. Facilities: restaurant, bar, indoor and outdoor heated pools. MAP. AE, DC, MC, V. Moderate–Expensive.*

Pointe-au-Pic **Hôtel Manoir Richelieu.** The Manoir Richelieu, an imposing castle nestled amid trees on a cliff overlooking the St. Lawrence River, has been offering first-class accommodations to vacationers for centuries, literally. It was founded in 1776 as a haven for wealthy travelers. Although still rich in elegance and charm, the resort has adapted to the needs of today's visitor and is now an affordable vacation spot. Guests can swim in the hotel's indoor and outdoor swimming pools and enjoy horseback riding, golf, and cross-country and downhill skiing. Whale-watching and snowmobile packages are available. *181 rue Richelieu, G0T 1M0, tel. 418/665–3703 or 800/463–2613. 391 rooms. Facilities: restaurant, indoor and outdoor pools, golf course, cross-country skiing, tennis, sauna, snowmobiling. AE, DC, MC, V. Very Expensive.*

St-Irenée **Les Studios du Domaine.** This unique retreat, located at the foot of the Charlevoix Mountains facing the St. Lawrence River, is an artists' colony in the summer but is open to tourists during the winter season. Studio apartments, each with one bedroom, bathroom, and living area with fully equipped kitchenette, are available for a rather reasonable price. Although its workshops and studios make this a great setting for artists, it's also a good base for sports lovers: Golf and cross-country and downhill skiing are all nearby. *398 chemin les Bains, G0T 1V0, tel. 418/452–3535. 30 apartments. Facilities: 5 artists' workshops. MC, V. Open Sept.–May. Inexpensive–Moderate.*

Gaspé Peninsula

Matane **Auberge des Gouverneurs.** This seaside motor inn, built in 1975, is well equipped with recreational facilities and offers many rooms with an ocean view. The rooms are not fancy, but all are comfortable, with whirlpool baths. Located near the dock of the ferry for Baie Comeau, it's a good choice for visitors who have come to ski or fish. All rooms have telephone and color TV. *250 av. du Phare E, G4W 3N4, tel. 418/566–2651. 72 rooms, 2 suites. Facilities: restaurant, lounge, outdoor pool, tennis court, sauna, exercise room, parking. AE, DC, MC, V. Moderate.*

Percé **La Normandie Hotel/Motel.** All but four rooms of this decade-old split-level motel face the ocean, with views of Percé Rock and Bonaventure Island. The location in the center of town puts shops and restaurants within walking distance. Lower floors were recently renovated, decorated in fresh pastel colors. Third-floor rooms are more spacious. *Rte. 132, C.P. 129, G0C 2L0, tel. 418/782–2112 or 800/463–0820. 45 rooms. Facilities: restaurant, lounge, exercise room, sauna, beach and municipal pool nearby. AE, DC, MC, V. Open May–Oct. Expensive.*

La Bonaventure-sur-Mer Hotel. Though the decor is motel-standard, the waterfront location with views of Percé Rock and Bonaventure Island makes this a pleasant property. The older section is a big hotel building; some motel units offer kitchenettes. *Rte. 132, C.P. 339, G0C 2L0, tel. 418/782–2166. 90 rooms. Facilities: dining room, solarium, private beach, water sports, parking. AE, MC, V. Open June–Oct. Moderate–Expensive.*

La Côte Surprise Motor Hotel. Most of the rooms of this recently renovated motel have views of Percé Rock and the village. Decor is the same motel-standard style in motel and second-floor hotel units, but the private balconies and terraces are a plus. *Rte. 132, C.P. 339, tel. 418/782–2166. 36 rooms. Facilities: dining rooms, snack bar, lounge, parking. AE, MC, V. Open June–Oct. Moderate.*

Les Laurentides

Coeur du Québec **L'Auberge du Lac Saint-Pierre.** This modern small hotel on the ★ lake near Trois Rivières, halfway between Montréal and Québec City, was built in 1988 and has quickly gained the highest ratings for cuisine and accommodations. The luxurious rooms are done in soothing pastel blues, peach, and rose, with television, telephones, and many whirlpool baths. The views to the lake from the dining room, the conservatory, and many of the guest rooms add to the tranquillity, but the food is, on the other hand, exciting. It's an ideal stop on a tour of southern Québec. *1911 rue Notre-Dame (Rte. 138), Box 10, Pointe-du-Lac G0X 1Z0, tel. 819/377–5971, fax 819/377–5579. 30 rooms. Facilities: restaurant, heated outdoor pool, tennis court, meeting rooms for 40 and 15, business equipment rentals. MAP optional. AE, MC, V. Expensive.*

Estérel **Hôtel d'Estérel.** If this all-inclusive resort were in the Caribbean, it would probably be run by Club Med, given the nonstop activities. The hotel features a private 18-hole golf course, beach, marina, downhill-skiing facilities, 87 kilometers of cross-country ski trails, outdoor skating rink, and sports complex. Comfortable rooms offer a view of either the lake or the beautiful flower gardens. *39 boul. Fridolin Simard, J0T 1E0,* *tel. 514/228–2571 or 800/363–3623. 135 rooms. Facilities: restaurant, disco, indoor pool, tennis courts, and gym. MAP optional. AE, DC, MC, V. Very Expensive.*

Mont Rolland **Auberge Mont Gabriel.** This resort is worth a stay—overnight or for longer. Relax in one of the spacious, modern rooms with a view of the valley or be close to nature in one of the cozy log cabins with fireplaces to keep you warm. This deluxe resort, located on a 1,200-acre estate, offers superb dining. Tennis, golf, and ski-week and -weekend packages are available. *Autoroute 15, Exit 64, J0R 1G0, tel. 514/229–3547. 120 rooms, 10 suites. Facilities: restaurant, 18-hole golf course, indoor and outdoor pools, tennis court. MAP optional. AE, MC, V. Expensive.*

Mont Tremblant **Station Mont Tremblant Lodge.** Only 90 minutes from Mont-
★ réal, on 14-kilometer-long (9-mile-long) Lac Tremblant, this is the northernmost resort that is easily accessible in the Upper Laurentians. Accommodations include modern condo units with kitchenettes, a rustic lodge, and individual cabins. The partying is lively in the winter, with lots of après-ski bars in the hotel and the immediate area. In the summer, guests swim, windsurf, and sail. *3005 chemin Principale, J0T 1Z0, tel. 819/425–8711 or 800/461–8711. Facilities: restaurant, bar, disco, golf course, tennis courts, horseback riding, private beach. MAP. AE, MC, V. Very Expensive.*

Club Tremblant Canadian Pacific. Across the lake from Mont Tremblant Lodge, this hotel and condominium complex uses the mountain for its skiing. Built as a private retreat in the 1930s by a wealthy American, the original large log-cabin lodge is furnished in colonial style, with wooden staircases and huge stone fireplaces. The rustic but comfortable main lodge has excellent facilities and a dining room with four-star gourmet cuisine. Both the main lodge and the deluxe condominium complex (fireplaces, private balconies, kitchenettes, and split-level design de rigueur), built just up the hill from the lodge, offer magnificent views of Mont Tremblant and its ski hills. At this hotel bordering Lac Tremblant, summer activities include swimming, fishing, boating, and tennis. There is a golf course nearby. *av. Cuttle, J0T 1Z0, tel. 819/425–2731. 150 rooms. Facilities: restaurant, indoor pool, exercise room. MAP optional. AE, MC, V. Expensive–Very Expensive.*

Auberge Villa Bellevue. This equally venerable and less expensive alternative to Gray Rocks (*see below*) is on Lac Ouimet, and has been run by the Dubois family for more than three generations. Supporting its reputation as a family resort, the inn invites children under 18 who share a room with their parents to stay free and pay only for meals during the summer. In winter, weekend packages include transportation to nearby Mont Tremblant. The hotel has a list of local baby-sitters, and offers a full program of children's activities. Accommodations range from hotel rooms to chalets and condominiums. In summer, tennis lessons for adults and children are available. Sailing, windsurfing, waterskiing, and lounging about on the outdoor lakeside terrace are other possible pastimes at Villa Bellevue. The indoor swimming pool and fitness center offer nonskiers plenty of physical activity during the winter without having to step outdoors. *845 rue Principale, J0T 1Z0, tel. 819/425–2734 or 800/567–6763. 98 rooms, 14 suites. Facilities: restaurant, indoor pool, gym, tennis courts, private beach, marina. MAP optional. AE, DC, MC, V. Expensive.*

Auberge du Coq de Montagne. This auberge, situated on Lac Moore, has earned a favorable reputation for its owners, Nino and Kay Faragalli. Moderately priced, this cozy family-run inn is touted for its friendly service, great hospitality, and modern accommodations. Kudos have also been garnered for the great Italian cuisine served up nightly, which also draws a local crowd: Making reservations is a must. Year-round facilities and activities on-site or close by include canoeing, kayaking, sailboarding, fishing, badminton, tennis, horseback riding, skating, and skiing. *2151 chemin Principale, C.P. 208, Lac Moore, J0T 1Z0, tel. 819/425–3380. 16 rooms. Facilities: restaurant, exercise room, sauna, private beach. MC, V. Moderate.*

Morin Heights **The Auberge Swiss Inn.** Located within 4 kilometers (3 miles) from Ski Morin Heights, this moderately priced inn is a well-situated bargain. The authentic Swiss-style chalet exudes coziness, from the wood paneling and fireplace lounge to the individually decorated rooms. *796 Rte. St-Adolphe J0R 1H0, tel. 514/226–2009. 10 rooms. Facilities: restaurant, canoeing, cross-country skiing, lounge. MC, V. Moderate.*

Ste-Adèle **Le Chantecler.** This Montréaler favorite on Lac Rond is nestled at the base of a mountain with 22 downhill ski runs. Skiing is the obvious draw—trails begin almost at the hotel entrance. (It's the official training site of the National Alpine Ski Teams.) The condominium units, hotel rooms, and chalets all have a rustic appeal, furnished with Canadian pine. Summer activities include tennis, golf, and boating. An indoor pool and spa, as well as a beach, make swimming a year-round possibility. *1474 chemin Chantecler, C.P. 1048, J0R 1L0, tel. 514/229–3555; elsewhere in Québec, 800/363–2420. 300 rooms, 20 suites. Facilities: restaurant, indoor pool, spa, private beach, golf course. MAP optional. AE, DC, MC, V. Very Expensive.*

L'Eau à la Bouche. This 25-room auberge has received commendations for superb service, luxurious appointments, and first-class status as an intimately scaled resort, perfect for weekend getaways or business retreats. Its restaurant is a draw in itself (*see* Dining, *above*). The auberge faces Le Chantecler's ski slopes, so skiing is literally at the door. Tennis, sailing, horseback riding, and a golf course are nearby. Package rates are available. Some suites with fireplaces. *3003 boul. Ste-Adèle, J0R 1L0, tel. 514/229–2991. 25 rooms. Facilities: restaurant, outdoor pool, flower garden terrace, wine cellar, facilities for the disabled. MAP optional. AE, MC, V. Expensive–Very Expensive.*

Auberge aux Croissants. Situated at the foot of the Laurentian Mountains, this inn is only a five-minute drive from Mont-Saint-Sauveur. Although most rooms have no TV or telephone, such conveniences are found in one of the two cozy lounges, and an impressive brunch is included with the price of the room. *750 chemin Ste-Marguerite, J0R 1L0, tel. 514/229–3838. 13 rooms with private bath. MC, V. Moderate–Expensive.*

Ste-Agathe **Auberge du Lac des Sables.** A favorite with couples, this inn offers a quiet, relaxed atmosphere in a country setting with a magnificent view of Lac des Sables. Enjoy the view from your balcony or from the dining room. All rooms have contemporary decor, with queen-size beds and color TVs. A complimentary breakfast is served. *230 St-Venant, J8C 3A3, tel. 819/ 326–3994. 19 rooms. Facilities: dining room, whirlpool. AE, MC, V. Expensive.*

Ste-Jovite **Gray Rocks.** This oldest ski resort in the Laurentians was founded by the Wheeler family more than three generations ago. Gray Rocks has its own private mountain ribboned by 20 ski runs; it presents a sprawling wood hotel with modern chalets and condominium units that overlook Lac Ouimet. The winter ski weeks and weekends, including cross-country, are good value for the money, as are the summer tennis packages. Gray Rocks also runs the more intimate Auberge le Château with 36 rooms farther along Route 327 North. *Rte. 327 N, J0T 2H0, tel. 819/425–2771 or 800/567–6767. 306 rooms, 13 with shared bath. Facilities: restaurant, 22 clay tennis courts, tennis school, riding stables, marina, La Spa fitness center with hot tubs, indoor swimming pool, children's activity programs, private airstrip and seaplane anchorage. MAP optional. Ski packages available. AE, MC, V. Moderate–Very Expensive.*

Val David **Hôtel La Sapinière.** Comfortable accommodations are offered in this homey, dark-brown frame hotel with its bright country flowers. However, the property is best known for its fine dining room and wine cellar. *1244 chemin de la Sapinière, J0T 2N0, tel. 819/322–2020 or 800/567–6635. 70 rooms. MAP. AE, DC, MC, V. Very Expensive.*

L'Estrie

Bromont **Le Château Bromont Resort Spa.** This European-style resort spa offers massages, algotherapy, electropuncture, algae wraps, facials, and aroma therapy. The Atrium houses an indoor pool, hot tubs, and a sauna, and there are also outdoor hot tubs, squash, racquetball, and badminton courts. After your workout, head for the château's dining room, Les Quatres Canards, where "cuisine sauvage" is created by chef Daniel Guay. (There is also a special spa menu offered.) Its L'Equestre Bar, named for Bromont's equestrian interests, features a cocktail hour and live entertainment. *90 rue Stanstead, J0E 1L0, tel. 514/534–3433. 147 rooms. Facilities: restaurant, bar, spa, indoor pool, sauna. MAP optional. AE, DC, MC, V. Expensive–Very Expensive.*

Eastman **Centre de Santé Eastman.** This four-season resort offers respite to the bone-weary and bruised skier. The 20 country-style rooms are located in three separate houses: the rustic Maison Canadienne, the country-style Volet Bleu, and the modern Pavillon Kaufman. Holistic spa treatments include massage (Swedish and shiatsu) and gentle body conditioning and stretch workouts. There's also horseback riding and cross-country skiing. Top off an already healthy day with fine vegetarian cuisine offered in the dining room. *895 chemin Diligence, J0E 1P0, tel. 514/297–3009. 20 rooms. Facilities: dining room. MAP. AE, MC, V. Expensive–Very Expensive.*

Lennoxville **Bishop's University**. If you are on a budget, this is a great place to stay. The prices can't be beat, and the location near Sherbrooke is good for touring. The university's grounds are lovely, with a river cutting through the campus and its golf course. Much of the architecture is reminiscent of stately New England campuses. Visit the university's 135-year-old chapel, and also look for the butternut tree, an endangered species in l'Estrie. Reservations for summer guests are accepted as early as September, so it's a good idea to book in advance. *Rue College, J1M 1Z7, tel. 819/822–9651. 515 beds. Facilities: sports com-*

plex with Olympic-size indoor pool, outdoor tennis courts. V.
Open mid-May–Aug. Inexpensive.

Magog **Club Azur.** This is a Club Med–type condo facility that is perfect
for family ski trips. Each unit has a fireplace and fully equipped
kitchenette so you can warm up with some hot cocoa after a full
day of skiing. In the summer, the beach is a convenient two-
minute walk away, and tennis courts and indoor and outdoor
pools are on the grounds. The club occasionally organizes activities for children and has a list of local baby-sitters on hand
for hotel guests. During the month of July and the two weeks
surrounding Christmas, units are rented on a two-day basis
only. *81 Desjardins, R.R. 4, J1X 5X8, tel. 819/847–2131 or*
800/567–3535. 140 units. Facilities: restaurant, bistro, sauna,
tennis courts, recreation complex. AE, MC, V. Expensive–Very
Expensive.

O'Berge du Village. Half of this condo complex is on a time-
share basis, and the other condos are run like a hotel. Rustic
Canadian pine furniture and fireplaces are scattered throughout. The condos, accommodating from two to eight people, all
have both a balcony facing the lake and a fully equipped kitchenette. However, if you don't feel like cooking, you can try the
bistro. For those with something more elaborate in mind, enjoy
dinner in the formal dining room. *261 rue Merry S, J1X 3L2,*
tel. 819/843–6566 or 800/567–6073. 117 rooms. Facilities: restau-
rant, bistro, wine bar, indoor and outdoor pools, gym, marina,
aquatic sports, day-care service, daily activities in the summer.
AE, MC, V. Moderate–Expensive.

North Hatley **Auberge Hatley.** Gourmet cuisine is the main attraction at this
country inn, whose dining room was once named the top res-
taurant in Québec in the annual Ordre du Mérite de la Restau-
ration awards. After eating one of chef Alain Labrie's fine
meals, guests sleep it off in one of the 25 charmingly decorated
rooms in this 1903 country manor, a member of Relais &
Châteaux. *325 Virgin Hill, C.P. 330, J0B 2C0, tel. 819/842–2451.*
25 rooms, some with Jacuzzi and fireplace. Facilities: restau-
rant. MAP. MC, V. Closed last 2 wks in Nov. Very Expensive.

★ **Manoir Hovey.** Overlooking the perfectly pristine Lac Massawippi, this retreat has the ambience of a private estate, while
offering the activities of a resort—boating, water skiing, mountain biking, cross-country skiing, tennis, and more. Built in
1900 as a summer home for Henry Atkinson, then owner of
Georgia Power in Atlanta, Hovey Manor resembles George
Washington's home at Mount Vernon, Virginia. Each wallpa-
pered room has personality, with a mix of antiques and newer
wood furniture, richly printed fabrics, and lace trimmings. A
stay here is like a visit to a very wealthy aunt's home. Many
rooms have working fireplaces and private balconies. The dining room serves exquisite Continental and French cuisine; the
changing dinner menu might include warm roulades of Swiss
chard with spring lamb, preserved apricots, and roasted hazelnuts; swordfish with a sabayon of leeks and pink peppercorns
au gratin; or grilled tenderloin of beef marinated with juniper
berries and a sauce of tarragon and horseradish. Dinner,
breakfast, and most sports facilities are included in room rates.
C.P. 60, J0B 2C0, tel. 819/842–2421; fax 819/842–2248. 35 rooms
and 4-bedroom cottage. Facilities: dining room, library, bar,
heated outdoor pool, tennis courts, beach, water sports, moun-
tain bikes, ice fishing, ski trails. MAP. AE, DC, MC, V. Very Ex-
pensive.

Orford **Auberge Estrimont.** An exclusive complex in cedar combining hotel rooms, condos, and larger chalets, Auberge Estrimont is close to ski hills, riding stables, and golf courses. Every room, whether in the hotel or in an adjoining condo unit, has a fireplace and a private balcony. *44 av. de l'Auberge, C.P. 98, Orford-Magog, J1X 3W7, tel. 819/843–1616 or 800/567–7320. 76 rooms, 7 suites. Facilities: restaurant, bar, indoor and outdoor pools, tennis, squash, raquetball courts, exercise room, sauna, Jacuzzi, cross-country ski trails. AE, DC, MC, V. Expensive.*

Sutton **Auberge la Paimpolaise.** This auberge is located right on Mont Sutton, 50 feet from the ski trails. Although it offers nothing fancy, its location is hard to beat. Rooms are simple, comfortable, and clean, with a woodsy appeal. All-inclusive weekend ski packages are available. A complimentary breakfast is always served. *615 rue Maple, J0E 2K0, tel. 514/538–3213. 29 rooms. MAP optional. AE, MC, V. Moderate—Expensive.*

Auberge Schweizer. No matter what the season, this lodge is the perfect place to relax. It has its own farm, and guests feast on home-cooked meals with vegetables straight from the garden. Nearby is a pond for swimming, as well as some hiking trails; ski trails are nearby. In addition to the standard accommodations, the auberge has a two-bedroom chalet, each bedroom with private bath and powder room; and a three-bedroom chalet with one bath and a playroom. All the chalets have kitchens as well as washers and dryers. *357 chemin Schweizer, J0E 2K0, tel. 514/ 538–2129. 11 rooms, 2 chalets with fireplace. V. Inexpensive—Moderate.*

Montérégiê

St-Marc-sur-Richelieu **Hostellerie Les Trois Tilleuls.** This romantic little place, a Relais et Châteaux member on a quiet country road, is a lovely spot to hole up in and investigate the surrounding Montérégiê region, or to return to after a hard day exploring the big city (Montréal is 20 minutes away). The rooms are modern, conveniently arranged, and well equipped (with hair dryers and magnifying mirrors), and each has a balcony or terrace facing the lovely Rivière Richelieu just outside. Packages are available for summer theatergoers and cross-country skiers, among others. Montréalers come to savor the cuisine of chef Roger Robin—and in the hopes of taking home one of his recipes. *290 Richelieu, Saint-Marc-sur-Richelieu, Que. J0L 2E0, tel. 514/584–2231, fax 514/584–3146. 24 rooms with bath, 1 suite. Facilities: restaurant, bar, indoor pool, 2 tennis courts, boating, 6 meeting rooms. AE, DC, MC, V. Expensive–Very Expensive.*

★

The Arts and Nightlife

The Arts

Lac Brome **Théâtre Lac Brome** (tel. 514/243–0361) is an English-language theater company that presents staged productions of classic Broadway and West End hits. The 175-seat, air-conditioned theater is located behind Knowlton's popular pub of the same name.

Lac Massawippi **L'Association du Festival du Lac Massawippi** presents an annual antiques and folk-arts show (tel. 819/842–2637) each July. The association also sponsors concerts, exhibitions, and poetry readings at various venues throughout the town from late April until the end of June.

Lennoxville Lennoxville's **Centennial Theatre** at Bishop's University (tel. 819/822–9692) presents a roster of international, Canadian, and Québecois jazz, classical, and rock concerts, as well as dance, mime, and children's theater. Jazz greats Gary Burton, Carla Bley, and Larry Coryell have appeared here, as have classical artists like the Amsterdam Guitar Trio and the Allegri String Quartet.

Magog **Théâtre le Vieux Clocher** (64 rue Merry N, tel. 819/847–0470) presents pop and rock concerts, and occasionally French plays.

North Hatley **The Piggery,** housed in a former pig barn in North Hatley on the shores of Lac Massawippi, reigns supreme in l'Estrie cultural life. The venue is renowned for its risk taking, often presenting new plays by Canadian playwrights and even experimenting with bilingual productions. *Box 390, North Hatley J0B 2C0, tel. 819/842–2432 or 819/842–2431. Reservations required. Season runs June–Aug.*

Orford Orford's regional park is the site of an annual arts festival highlighting classical music, pops, and chamber orchestra concerts. Since 1951, thousands of students have come to the **Orford Arts Center** to study and perform classical music in the summer. Canada's internationally celebrated Orford String Quartet originated here. Lately, Festival Orford has expanded to include jazz and folk music. *Orford Arts Center, Box 280, Magog J1X 3W8, tel. 819/843–3981; in Canada from May to Aug., 800/567–6155.*

Sutton Sutton is also home to the visual and performing arts. **Arts Sutton** (7 rue Academy, tel. 514/538–2563) is a long-established mecca for the visual arts.

Nightlife

The Laurentians and l'Estrie are your best bets when looking for nightlife in Québec's outlying regions. Après-ski bars, bistros, and cafés are spread throughout the Laurentians. In Piedmont, **La Nuit Blanche** (762 rue Principale, tel. 514/227–5419) is a popular dancing spot. If live music is what you want, head to **Bourbon Street** (2045 Rte. 117, tel. 514/229–2905) in Mont Rolland. **Les Vieilles Portes** (185 rue Principale, tel. 514/227–2662) in Saint-Sauveur is a popular pub where you can relax, order your favorite beer, and if you are hungry, have a bite to eat.

If you are looking for action in l'Estrie, visit Magog, a village that comes to life after dark. **La Lanterne** (70 rue du Lac, tel. 819/843–7205) is a popular restaurant-bar that often hosts theme nights. For information, tune in to the local radio station. **La Grosse Pomme** (276 rue Principale O, tel. 819/843–9365) is also a popular place. This multilevel complex considers itself a cinema-bar, with huge video screens, dance floors, and restaurant service. An outdoor summer terrace has live entertainment. **The Auberge Orford** (20 rue Merry S, tel. 819/843–9361) is another outdoor summer terrace that doesn't stop. Here you can enjoy live entertainment nightly.

11 Nova Scotia

By Silver Donald
Cameron

Novelist, playwright, and sailor, Silver Donald Cameron is one of Canada's most versatile authors. His recent books Wind, Whales and Whisky: A Cape Breton Voyage *and* Sniffing the Coast: An Acadian Voyage *record cruises in Nova Scotia and Prince Edward Island with his wife and son in* Silversark, *a 27-foot cruising sailboat, which they built themselves.*

"Infinite riches in a little room," said Elizabethan playwright Christopher Marlowe. Was he speaking of Nova Scotia, Canada's second-smallest province that packs an impossible variety of cultures and landscapes into a mass that's half the size of Ohio?

Nova Scotia's landscapes echo every region of Canada. Mountain clefts in Cape Breton Island could pass for crannies in British Columbia. Stretches of the Tantramar Marshes are as board-flat as the prairies. The glaciated interior, spruce-swathed and peppered with lakes, looks just like the Canadian Shield in northern Manitoba. The apple blossoms in the Annapolis Valley are as glorious as those in Niagara, and parts of Halifax could masquerade as downtown Toronto. A massive Catholic church in a tiny French village recalls Québec. The warm salt water and long sandy beaches of Prince Edward Island are also found on the mainland side of Northumberland Strait, and the brick-red mudflats of the Bay of Fundy echo their counterparts in New Brunswick. Neil's Harbour looks just like a Newfoundland outport—and sounds like one, too, since many of its people are Newfoundlanders by origin.

As with the land, so with the people. The Micmac Indians have been here for 10,000 years. The French came to the Annapolis Basin in 1605. In the 1750s, the English settled cockneys and Irish in Halifax and "Foreign Protestants"—chiefly Germans—in Lunenburg. By then Yankees from New England were putting down roots in Liverpool, Cape Sable Island, and the Annapolis Valley. In the 1780s they were joined by thousands of "Loyalists"—many of them black—displaced by the American Revolution. Soon after, the Scots poured into northern Nova Scotia and Cape Breton, evicted from the Highlands by their landlords' preference for sheep. The last wave of immigrants, in the 1890s, became steelworkers and coal miners in Cape Breton. They came from Wales, the West Indies, Poland, the Ukraine, and the Middle East. They're all Nova Scotians, and they're all still here, eating their own foods, worshipping in their own churches, speaking in their rich, full-flavored voices.

Infinite riches: Gaelic street signs in Pugwash and Mabou. French masses in Cheticamp and Point de l'Eglise. Black gospel choirs in Halifax and Micmac handcrafts in Eskasoni. Onion-dome churches in Sydney, sauerkraut in Lunenburg, and Yankee Puritanism in Clark's Harbour.

This is a little buried nation, compact and distinctive, with a capital city the same size as Marlowe's London. Before Canada was formed in 1867, Nova Scotians were prosperous shipwrights and merchants, trading with the world. Who created Cunard Lines? A Haligonian, Samuel Cunard. Those spacious days brought democracy to the British colonies, left Victorian mansions in all the salty little ports that dot the coastline, and created a uniquely Nova Scotian outlook: worldly, approachable, sturdily independent.

"Infinite riches in a little room." Kit Marlowe would love it here.

Essential Information

Important Addresses and Numbers

Tourist Information The **Nova Scotia Department of Tourism and Culture** (Box 456, Halifax, NS B3J 2R5, tel. 902/424–5000) publishes a range of literature, including an exhaustive annual travel guide to sights, accommodations, and transportation.

Halifax The **Nova Scotia Tourism Information Centre** (Old Red Store at Historic Properties, tel. 902/424–4247), and **Tourism Halifax** (City Hall, Duke and Barrington Sts., tel. 902/421–8736) are open mid-June–Labor Day, daily 9–6, and sometimes later; Labor Day–mid-June, weekdays 9–4:30.

Emergencies Dial "0" for operator in emergencies; check the front of the local phone book for specific medical services.

Hospital **Victoria General** (tel. 902/428–2110) is Halifax's major hospital.

Arriving and Departing

By Plane The **Halifax International Airport** is 40 kilometers (25 miles) northeast of downtown Halifax. **Sidney Airport** is 13 kilometers (8 miles) east of Sidney.

Air Canada (tel. 902/429–7111 or 800/776–3000) provides regular, daily service to Halifax and Sydney, Nova Scotia, from New York, Boston, Toronto, Montréal, and St. John's, Newfoundland. **Canadian Airlines International** (tel. 800/527–8499) has service to Halifax via Toronto and Montréal. **Air Nova** (tel. 902/429–7111 or 800/776–3000) and **Air Atlantic** (tel. 800/426–7000 or 800/665–1177 in Canada) provide regional service to both airports with flights to Toronto, Montréal, and Boston.

Between Airport and City Center Airport bus service to most of Halifax's downtown hotels costs $18 round-trip, $11 one-way. Normal taxi fare is $33 each way, but if you book in advance with **Aero Cab** (tel. 902/445–3393) the fare is $24.60 cash, slightly more by credit card (MC or V). The trip takes 30–40 minutes.

By Car The Trans-Canada Highway reaches Nova Scotia through New Brunswick. Entering the province at Amherst, it becomes Highway 104. To reach Halifax, pick up Highway 102 at Truro. To reach Cape Breton, continue on Highway 104.

Highways throughout Nova Scotia, numbered from 100 to 199, are all-weather, limited-access roads, with 100 kilometers-per-hour (62.5 miles-per-hour) speed limits. The last two digits usually match the number of an older trunk highway along the same route, numbered from 1 to 99. Thus, Highway 102, between Halifax and Truro, matches the older Route 2, between the same towns. Roads numbered from 200 to 399 are secondary roads that usually link villages. Unless otherwise posted, the speed limit is 80 kilometers per hour (50 miles per hour) except on the 100-series highways.

Most highways in the province lead to Halifax-Dartmouth. Highways 3/103, 7, 2/102, and 1/101 terminate in the twin cities.

Rental Cars Halifax is the most convenient place from which to begin your driving tour of the province. The following list details city and airport venues of rental-car agencies: **Avis** (5600 Sackville St., tel. 902/423–6303; airport, tel. 902/873–3523); **Budget** (1558 Hollis St., tel. 902/421–1242; airport, tel. 902/873–3509); **Hertz** (Halifax Sheraton, tel. 902/421–1763; airport, tel. 902/873–3700); **Thrifty** (6930 Lady Hammond, tel. 902/422–4455; airport, tel. 902/873–3527); **Tilden** (1130 Hollis St., tel. 902/422–4433; airport, tel. 902/873–3505).

By Ferry Three car ferries connect Nova Scotia with Maine and New Brunswick. **Marine Atlantic** (tel. 800/341–7981) sails from Bar Harbor, Maine, and **Prince of Fundy Cruises** (tel. 800/341–7540) from Portland; both arrive in Yarmouth. From Saint John, New Brunswick, to Digby, Nova Scotia, ferry service is provided by **Marine Atlantic** (tel. 800/565–9470 in New Brunswick).

Marine Atlantic also operates ferries between New Brunswick and Prince Edward Island, and between Cape Breton and Newfoundland. In Nova Scotia, call 902/794–5700; in Newfoundland, 709/772–7701.

Between May and December, **Northumberland Ferries** (tel. 902/485–6580; in Nova Scotia, 800/565–0201) operate between Caribou, Nova Scotia, and Wood Islands, Prince Edward Island.

By Train **Via Rail** (tel. 800/561–3949) provides service from Montréal to Halifax via Moncton and Saint John, in New Brunswick; and Amherst and Truro, in Nova Scotia.

Amtrak (tel. 800/USA–RAIL) from New York City makes connections in Montréal.

By Bus **Greyhound** (800/231–2222) from New York, and **Voyageur Inc.** (tel. 613/238–5900) from Montréal, connect with **Scotia Motor Tours** or **SMT** (tel. 506/458–6000) through New Brunswick, which links (rather inconveniently) with **Acadian Lines Limited** (tel. 902/454–8279), which provides inter-urban services within Nova Scotia.

Getting Around

Halifax Walking and biking are excellent ways to get around and see the city, especially on weekdays when parking in the downtown area can be a problem. A pleasant alternative, however, is to take one of the rickshaws, available downtown during summer.

By Taxi Rates begin at about $2.40 and increase based on mileage and time. A crosstown trip should cost $4–$5, depending on traffic. Hailing a taxi can be difficult, but there are taxi stands at major hotels and shopping malls. Most Haligonians simply phone for a taxi service. Call **Aero Cab** (tel. 902/445–3393).

By Bus The **Metropolitan Transit Commission** (tel. 902/421–6600) bus system covers the entire Halifax-Dartmouth area. The base fare is $1.15 adults, 65¢ children 5–15; exact change only.

By Ferry The **Dartmouth Ferry Commission** (tel. 902/464–2336) runs two-passenger ferries from the George Street terminal in Halifax to the Portland Street and Woodbine terminals in Dartmouth, from 6 AM to midnight on an hourly and half-hourly schedule. The fare for a single crossing is 65¢, which is well worth it considering you get an up-close view of both waterfronts.

Elsewhere in Nova Scotia You will need a car to explore the province beyond Halifax. For rental car information, *see* Rental Cars in Arriving and Departing by Car, *above*.

As you explore Nova Scotia, be on the lookout for the 10 designated "Scenic Trails" that appear throughout the province and are easily identified by roadside signs with icons that correspond with trail names. These routes, as well as tourist literature (maps and the provincial *Tour Guide*) that has been published in accordance with this scheme, have been developed by the Nova Scotia Department of Tourism and Culture.

Guided Tours

Boat Tours **Halifax Water Tours** (tel. 902/420–1015) operates an excellent two-hour, narrated cruise of Halifax Harbor and the Northwest Arm, from mid-June through October. Tours depart from Privateer's Wharf up to four times a day in mid-season, and cost $13.50 for adults, $12.50 for senior citizens, $10 for youths 13–18, $8 children 5–12, $29.50 families.

Bluenose II (tel. 902/422–2678 or 902/424–5000) is an exact replica of Nova Scotia's 143-foot fishing schooner *Bluenose*, the ship that was the undefeated champion in international schooner racing for nearly 20 years and is featured on the Canadian dime. *Bluenose II* departs from Privateer's Wharf three times daily on a two-hour harbor sail in summer. Fares are $14 for adults, $7 for senior citizens and children, but are subject to change.

Bus Tours Both **Gray Line Sightseeing** (tel. 902/454–8279) and **Cabana Tours** (tel. 902/423–6066) run coach tours through Halifax-Dartmouth and Peggy's Cove. **Halifax Double Decker Tours** (tel. 902/420–1155) offers two-hour tours on double-decker buses that leave daily from Historic Properties. You can also charter a bus from the **Metropolitan Transit Commission** (tel. 902/421–6600) for a narrated tour.

Exploring Nova Scotia

Highlights for First-time Visitors

Cape Breton Highlands National Park, Tour 4: Cape Breton Island

Fortress Louisbourg National Historic Park, Tour 4: Cape Breton Island

Halifax Citadel National Historic Park, Tour 1: Halifax and Dartmouth

Historic Annapolis Royal, Tour 2: The South Shore and Annapolis Valley

Historic Properties and *Bluenose II*, Tour 1: Halifax and Dartmouth

Lunenburg's Nautical Heritage, Tour 2: The South Shore and Annapolis Valley

Pictou's Scottish Heritage, Tour 3: Northern Nova Scotia

Sherbrooke Village, Tour 3: Northern Nova Scotia

Tour 1: Halifax and Dartmouth

Numbers in the margin correspond to points of interest on the Nova Scotia and Halifax maps.

① Salty and urbane, learned and plain-spoken, **Halifax** is large enough to have the trappings of a capital city—symphonies and scandals, smart hotels and carnivorous consultants, spicy gossip and first-class air service—and yet small enough to retain the warmth and convenience of a small town. In their hearts, Haligonians know there is no better place to live.

They may be right, too.

② Begin your walking tour at **Purdy's Wharf**—twin office towers shaped like milk cartons with feet, standing right in the harbor. Much of downtown Halifax is connected by overhead pedways, making it convenient for executives in Purdy's Wharf to shop, lunch, meet with bankers and brokers, and greet out-of-town guests without venturing outdoors. Take the pedway to the Sheraton, built low to match the historic ironstone buildings next door. If the weather is fine, try the Sheraton's outdoor bar, right on the water, and admire the schooner *Bluenose II* (*see* Guided Tours, *above*) and the ketch *White Heather,* moored alongside and awaiting charter parties.

③ Next door are the warehouses of **Historic Properties,** dating from the early 19th century when trade and war made Halifax prosperous. They were built by such raffish characters as Enos Collins, who did business in the Collins Bank building. A privateer, smuggler, and shipper whose vessels defied Napoleon's blockade to bring American supplies to the Duke of Wellington, Collins was also a prime mover into the Halifax Banking Company, which evolved into the Royal Bank of Canada, the country's largest bank. Look up and to the right: There's the Royal Bank's office tower, three blocks away. When Collins died in 1871, at 99, he was said to be the richest man in Canada. The buildings have been taken over by quality shops and restaurants, boisterous pubs, and chic offices.

④ Walk along the water behind the modern Law Courts to the **Dartmouth ferry terminal,** jammed with commuters during the rush hour. Beyond lies the Cable Wharf, so named because it was once home to the ships that laid the undersea telegraph and telephone cables to Europe. There's a fishmarket here and a floating restaurant.

⑤ Pass the offices of the federal Department of Fisheries (other government offices are in the Central Guaranty Trust tower, across the street) and you'll arrive at the **Maritime Museum of the Atlantic,** housed in a restored chandlery and warehouse. The exhibits include an assortment of small boats once used around the coast, as well as displays describing Nova Scotia's proud heritage of sail—when the province, on its own, was one of the world's foremost shipbuilding and trading nations. *1675 Lower Water St., tel. 902/424-7490 or 902/424-7491. Admission free. Open year-round but times vary so call ahead.*

The wharves outside the museum are favorite berths for visiting transatlantic yachts and sail-training ships; at any time you may find South American and European square-riggers, classic yachts, and even Viking longships. The hydrographic

NEW BRUNSWICK

PRINCE

Borden

Cape Tormenti

Northumberlan

Pugwash

Amherst

Oxford

Trans-Canada

39

Ta

Joggins **41**

40 **Springhill**

Balm

Chignecto Game Sanctuary

Deber

Parrsboro

42

2

Great Village

104

Advocate Harbour

Cape Split

Cape Blomidon

Cobequid Bay

Minas Basin

Maitland

St.

St. John

Bay of Fundy

Minas Channel

358

Wolfville

Kentville

Hantsport

Shub

29

30

Evangeline Trail

1

Windsor

31

Uniacke House

32

Berwick

Kingston

Three Mile Plains

101

Minas Channel

Annapolis Royal

101

Middleton

Upper Sackville

Lower Sackville

28

Bridgetown

Middle Sackville

33 **Bedford**

Port Royal

12

103

St. Margarets Bay

Dartmo

Digby

Bear River

Mahone Bay

Chester

Peggy's Cove

Easte

Digby Neck

KEJIMKUJIK NATIONAL PARK

Herring Cove

Ho

Tiverton

Westport

Trail

Bridgewater

21

20

19

Big and Little Tancook Islands

26 **Point de l'Eglise**

1

Brier Island

Evangeline

101

TOBEATIC WILDLIFE MANAGEMENT AREA

Lake Rossignol

3

La Have

Lunenburg

ATLAI

TO BAR HARBOR (MAINE)

1

Milton

22

Brooklyn

103

Liverpool

TO PORTLAND (MAINE)

25 **Yarmouth**

3

Shelburne **23**

103

Lockeport

Woods Harbour

24 **Barrington**

Iles de la Madeleine

Gulf of St. Lawrence

Aspy Bay

CAPE BRETON HIGHLANDS
NATIONAL PARK

Chéticamp 47   **Ingonish** 48   *Cape
Smoky*

C A P E   B R E T O N

TO PORT-AUX-BASQUES
(NEWFOUNDLAND)

TO ARGENTIA
(NEWFOUNDLAND)

**Margaree
Harbour** 46   **Bird Islands** 49   **Sydney
Englishtown** 50   Mines   *Glace
Bay*

St. Ann's   162   **Sydney**

ARD ISLAND

*Gulf of
St. Lawrence*   **Inverness** 45   **Baddeck** 51   125   Westmount   53   Mira Road

Mabou 44   52   **Estmere**   54

**Port
Hood** 43   *Trans-Canada Hwy.*   *Bras d'Or
Lake*   **Fortress of
Louisbourg
Nat'l Historic
Park**

trait   Wood Islands   *Cape
George*   Creignish   **Dundee**
Ballantynes
Cove   *St. George's
Bay*   105   **Port** 56   55   **St. Peter's**

Malignant
Cove   (245)   (337)   104

gouche   Knoydart   New   **Antigonish**   Hawkesbury   *Isle Madame*

37   Glasgow   36   Auld Cove   57   **Arichat**

Pictou   *Trans-Canada Hwy.*   Mulgrave

38   104   Westville   Thorburn   104   Canso
Causeway   Canso

Hill   Stellarton

cke   LISCOMB
GAME
SANCTUARY   Guysborough

adie   **Sherbrooke**

35

7

Sheet Harbour

4   Tangier

**Musquodoboit
Harbour**

ssage

N

C OCEAN

KEY

🚗 Ferry

🏕 Trans-Canada Hwy.

0 ————————— 50 miles

0 ————————— 75 km

steamer *Acadia* is moored here permanently, after a long life of charting the coasts of Labrador and the Arctic.

At the next wharf, in summer, is Canada's naval memorial, HMCS *Sackville,* the sole survivor of a fleet of doughty little corvettes (highly maneuverable warships) that escorted convoys of ships from Halifax to England during World War II. An interpretation center (open mid-June–Sept., Mon.–Sat. 10–5, Sun. 1–5), adjacent to the ship, explains that the convoys assembled in Bedford Basin, Halifax's vast inner harbor, where the first ships were launched in the early morning and others would follow in a steady stream all day long. The last ones would still be steaming out late at night.

Time Out Between the Maritime Museum and Cornwallis Place (the modern office building just to the south) is an open square and playground at the bottom of Sackville Street. The square is a favorite lunchtime promenade for Halifax office workers, and a setting for concerts associated with the Atlantic Jazz Festival. This is a perfect people-watching or picnic spot. Coffee shops and restaurants are within a few blocks, mostly back the way we came.

6 Just south of the square is the **tugboat terminal,** which is about to become world famous: Andrew Cochran Associates—a local film company—recently produced an animated television series called *Theodore Tugboat,* based on the ships' fictional adventures.

❼ Leave the tugboats and walk up to Water Street and enter the **Brewery Market,** a sprawling ironstone complex that was once Keith's Brewery (named for its Alexander Keith, a 19th-century brewer) but now houses boutiques, offices, restaurants, and a Farmers' Market. This area is a favored haunt of knowledgeable Haligonians on Saturday mornings.

Take the elevator at the office-end of the complex, and emerge on Hollis Street. Turn left, past several elegant Victorian townhouses—notably Keith Hall (1475 Hollis St.)—once the executive offices of the brewery. Turn right on Bishop Street and walk up to Barrington Street, Halifax's main downtown thoroughfare. Ahead of you is the **Technical University of Nova Scotia,** one of six Halifax universities; it offers degrees in engineering, architecture, and similar fields.

❽ Turn right on Barrington. The stone mansion on your right is **Government House,** the official residence of Nova Scotia's Lieutenant-Governor, built in 1799 for Sir John Wentworth, the Loyalist governor of New Hampshire and his racy wife, Fanny. Thomas Raddall's novel *The Governor's Lady* tells their story. Across the street is **The Old Burying Ground,** the city's first cemetery, dating from 1749. One of its residents is General Robert Ross, leader of the attack on Baltimore in 1814 that inspired the anthem *The Star-Spangled Banner.* Its Sebastopol Monument honors two Halifax heroes of the Crimean War (1853–1856).

Beyond Government House is **St. Matthew's Church** (1859), and **Maritime Centre,** a towering office block above a shopping mall. Turn left on Spring Garden Road and go past the Catholic cathedral church to **St. Mary's Basilica** (1833), with the tallest polished-granite spire in the world.

Time Out In the summer, the front lawn of the public library is crowded with people listening to street singers and snacking on french fries bought from **Bud the Spud,** a chip-wagon parked at the curb. Surrounding the lawn are plenty of opportunities for a more substantial take-out lunch.

❾ From the library walk west on Spring Garden Road to the South Park Street entrance of the **Halifax Public Gardens,** where the statues of Robbie Burns and Sir Walter Scott face one another from across Spring Garden Road. The gardens were first laid out in 1753, but the present design was created in 1889 by Richard Power, who had been gardener to the Duke of Devonshire. Power's descendants cared for the gardens until the 1960s. Gravel paths wind among ponds, trees, and flower beds, revealing an astonishing variety of plants from all over the world. The centerpiece is a filigreed bandstand erected in 1887 for Queen Victoria's Golden Jubilee.

❿ The **Nova Scotia Museum of Natural History,** on the South Commons, holds collections of human and natural-history artifacts and administers them to the smaller provincial museums throughout Nova Scotia. The museum is best known for its exhibits and events honoring tiny frogs known as "spring peepers." A huge fiberglass frog is mounted on the corner of the building, beginning in May and lasting until the real creatures fall silent in the autumn. *1747 Summer St., tel. 902/424–7353. Admission: $2.25 adults, 50¢ children 5–16. Open*

mid–May–Oct., Mon., Tues., Thurs.–Sun. 9:30–5:30 and Wed.
9:30–8; Nov.–early May, Tues., Thurs.–Sun. 9:30–5, Wed. 9:30–8.

Between the Commons and the compact downtown rises the
11 green bulk of **Citadel Hill,** topped by its star-shaped fort. The
Citadel was the heart of the city's fortifications, and was linked
to smaller forts and gun emplacements on the harbor islands
and on the bluffs above the entrance. It is now a National Historic Site, with kilted soldiers drilling in front of the **Army Museum,** once the barracks. Every day at noon a cannon is fired;
some local businesspeople in the towers below time their nego-
tiations so the cannon's blast will throw their associates off-
stride. *Citadel Hill, tel. 902/426–5080. Admission:*
mid–June–Labor Day, $2 adults, $1 children, senior citizens
free. Open July–Labor Day, daily 9–6; Labor Day–mid–June,
daily 10–5.

Most of the city's secondary fortifications have been turned
into public parks. **Point Pleasant Park,** a favorite recreation
spot, encompasses 186 wooded acres, veined with walking
trails and seafront paths. The park was leased from the military by the city for 999 years, at a shilling a year. Its major
military installation is a massive round Martello tower dating
from the late 18th century. Point Pleasant is about 12 blocks
down South Park Street from Spring Garden Road.

The handsome four-sided **Town Clock** on Citadel Hill was given
to Halifax by Prince Edward, Duke of Kent, military commander from 1794 to 1800. The prince was enamored of round buildings, of which two survive: **St. George's Church,** downtown at
Brunswick and Cornwallis streets, and **Julie's Music Room,** on
a knoll beside the Bedford Highway. "Julie" was the prince's
French mistress, with whom he lived for more than 20 years
before being summoned to marry a princess and produce an
heir to the British throne. He did his duty, and the result was
Queen Victoria.

Pause over the view from the Citadel, and take in the details:
the spiky downtown crowded between the hilltop and the harbor; the wooded islands at the harbor's mouth; and the naval
dockyard under the Angus L. MacDonald Bridge, the nearer
of the two bridges connecting Halifax with its sister city of
Dartmouth.

From the Citadel, walk down Sackville Street toward the har-
12 bor. On your right is the **Royal Artillery Park,** with its little-
known but excellent military library. The School Board building at Sackville and Brunswick streets is the old Halifax Academy, attended by author Hugh MacLennan.

Farther down Sackville, where it meets Argyle Street, is the
13 **Neptune Theatre,** Canada's first professional repertory
theater, which offers full summer and winter seasons. Argyle
Street is the center of the Halifax dining and nightlife scene
and a lively place on a Saturday night. A block north of the
theater is the **Carleton Hotel,** built of cut stone from the original Fortress of Louisbourg. The hotel, which dates from 1760,
was once the home of Richard Bulkeley, one of Halifax's founders, and it later served as a Court of Admiralty.

14 Turn left on Barrington Street. A block north is **St. Paul's
Church** (1749), Canada's oldest Protestant church, Britain's
first overseas cathedral, and the burial site of many colonial

notables. Inside, on the north end, a piece of metal is embedded in the wall. It is a fragment of the *Mont Blanc,* one of the two ships whose collision caused the Halifax Explosion of December 1917, the greatest manmade explosion prior to Hiroshima. The blast flattened a square mile of the North End and left 2,000 dead, another 2,000 seriously injured, and 6,000 homeless.

⑮ Leaving St. Paul's, you will find yourself on the **Grand Parade,** facing City Hall. Musicians perform here at noon on fine summer days. From here, look uphill: The tall, stylish brick building is the **World Trade and Convention Centre** and is attached to the 10,000-seat **Halifax Metro Centre**—the site of hockey games, rock concerts, and political conventions. Farther to the right are the office towers above **Scotia Square,** the leading downtown shopping mall.

⑯ Walk downhill a block, and you'll see **Province House,** "a gem of Georgian architecture," according to Charles Dickens. The provincial legislature still meets in this lovely sandstone building, erected in 1819. *Hollis St., tel. 902/424–5982. Admission free. Open weekdays 9–6, Sat. 9–4.*

Across Hollis, on Cheapside—a pedestrian-way directly opposite Province House—is the **Art Gallery of Nova Scotia,** which
⑰ features work by Canadian and international artists. The gallery, housed in a renovated four-story building, displays extensive collections of maritime, Canadian, and folk art, and hosts contemporary traveling exhibitions from around the world. *1741 Hollis St. at Cheapside, tel. 902/424–7542. Admission: $2.50 adults, $1.25 students and senior citizens, children under 12 free, $5.50 families. Open June–Oct., Tues, Wed., Fri., Sat. 10–5:30, Thurs. 10–9, Sun. noon–5:30; Sept.–May, Tues–Fri. 10–5, Sat.–Sun. noon–5.*

Return to Province House, turn left, and go one block back to Historic Properties, where this tour began. In addition to owning the warehouses near Purdy's Wharf, Historic Properties also owns the 19th-century buildings between Granville, Duke, and Lower Water streets, at Duke. The upper floors of most of these buildings are used by the **Nova Scotia College of Art and Design** (NSCAD)—the first degree-granting arts university in Canada and a formidable influence in the world of art.

Go up the hill a block to Granville Street, past NSCAD's unobtrusive main entrance and turn right at the Split Crow pub, into the one-block **pedestrian mall** with its iron park benches, outdoor cafés, and chic shops. Near the end of the block is the
⑱ **Anna Leonowens Gallery,** which belongs to NSCAD, and often shows the most challenging exhibits in Halifax. The gallery is named for the College's founder, a remarkable Victorian woman who served the King of Siam as governess and wrote a book about the experience; Rodgers and Hammerstein eventually turned it into the Broadway production of *The King and I,* starring Yul Brynner and Deborah Kerr. *1891 Granville St., tel. 902/422–7381. Admission free. Open Tues.–Fri. 11–5, Sat. noon–4.*

Turn right when you leave the gallery. At the end of the block, look toward the harbor: Just across the street is the Sheraton, *Bluenose II,* and Privateer's Warehouse. Welcome back to the beginning of the tour. From here, the tour continues on to two areas: the Northwest Arm and Dartmouth. To continue the tour it will be necessary to travel by car.

"The Arm" is Halifax's recreational secondary harbor, with a popular park, many elegant waterfront homes, and two yacht clubs. From Historic Properties, follow either Duke Street or Cogswell Street (both converge at the Commons) to Quinpool Road, a busy shopping street. Quinpool takes you to a traffic circle called the Armdale Rotary, which heads the Northwest Arm. Take the exit for Purcell's Cove Road (Rte. 253), which winds along the Arm to the pretty village of **Purcell's Cove,** and passes the Armdale Yacht Club, Flemming Park, the Royal Nova Scotia Yacht Squadron, and the historic cliff-top fortifications of York Redoubt, before ending at the tiny fishing harbor of **Herring Cove.** There is no similar shorefront drive on the Halifax side of the Arm, though several Halifax streets terminate at the Arm's shores.

Dartmouth is Nova Scotia's second city, but it has always been overshadowed by the capital. It was first settled by Quaker whalers from Nantucket, and boasts Canada's largest Coast Guard base and Nova Scotia's most successful industrial park, at Burnside. The 23 lakes within Dartmouth's boundaries provided the Micmacs with a canoe route to the province's interior and to the Bay of Fundy. A 19th-century canal system connected the lakes for a brief time, but today there are only ruins, which have been partially restored as heritage sites.

Halifax-Dartmouth has North America's third-largest concentration of marine scientists, mostly due to the **Bedford Institute of Oceanography,** off Windmill Road just under the A. Murray Mackay Bridge. The institute also has a substantial fleet of specialized ships and submersibles. Visitors can take self-guided walking tours of the facility, or guided tours by reservation; call ahead. *Challenger Dr., tel. 902/426–4093. Admission free. Open weekdays 9–4.*

Tour 2: The South Shore and Annapolis Valley

Mainland Nova Scotia is a long, narrow peninsula; no point in the province is more than 56 kilometers (35 miles) from salt water. The South Shore is on the Atlantic side, the Annapolis Valley on the Fundy side, and though they are less than an hour apart by car, the two destinations seem like different worlds.

The South Shore is rocky coast, island-dotted bays, fishing villages, and shipyards; the Valley is lumber, farms, vineyards, and orchards. The South Shore is German, French, and Yankee; the Valley is stoutly British. The South Shore is Lutheran, Catholic, and Puritan and boasts a Catholic university; the Valley university is Baptist. The sea is everywhere on the South Shore; in the Valley the sea is blocked from view by a ridge of mountains.

Highway 103, Route 3, and various secondary roads form the province's designated **Lighthouse Route,** which leads from Halifax down the South Shore. It touches the heads of several big bays and small harbors, revealing an ever-changing panorama of shoreline, inlet, and island. Charming little towns are spaced out every 50 kilometers (30 miles) or thereabouts. This tour mostly focuses on the towns along the route, but you should follow the side roads whenever the inclination strikes; the South Shore rewards slow, relaxed exploration.

Leave Halifax on Route 3 or 103—or 333, the scenic road around the shore. **St. Margaret's Bay,** just minutes from Halifax, has always been a favorite summer haunt for Haligonians and is rapidly becoming an outer suburb.

Peggy's Cove, on Route 333, stands at the mouth of the bay facing the open Atlantic. The cove, with its houses huddled around the narrow slit in the boulders, is probably the most-photographed village in Canada. It also has the only Canadian post office located in a lighthouse (open April–November). Be careful exploring the bald, rocky shore. Incautious visitors have been swept to their deaths by the towering surf that sometimes breaks here.

Chester, with just over 1,100 people, is the first stop on Lunenburg County's Mahone Bay. The bay has literally hundreds of islands and, according to local claims, there is one for every day of the year. In summer Chester swells with its well-established population of U.S. visitors and Haligonians and with the sailing and yachting community. In mid-August the town celebrates **Chester Race Week,** the largest regatta in Atlantic Canada.

⑲ A passenger-only ferry runs from the dock in Chester to **Big and Little Tancook Islands,** 8 kilometers (5 miles) out in the bay. The boat runs four times daily Monday–Thursday; six times daily Friday; and twice daily on weekend days, and costs $1 for the 45-minute trip. Reflecting its part-German heritage, Big Tancook claims to make the best sauerkraut in Nova Scotia.

Take Route 12 inland from Chester to the **Ross Farm** at New Ross. The restored 19th-century farm-cum-museum illustrates the evolution of agriculture from 1600 to 1925. *Rte. 12, New Ross, tel. 902/689–2210. Admission: $2.25 adults, 50¢ children 5–16, $5.50 families. Open June–mid-Oct., daily 9:30–5:30.*

The town of **Mahone Bay** presents a dramatic face to visitors: Three tall wooden churches—of different denominations—stand side by side, their images reflected in the harbor water. Once a shipbuilding community, Mahone Bay is now a crafts center and also home to the **Wooden Boat Festival,** held during the first week of August, when the works of some of Lunenburg County's top wooden-boat builders are displayed.

⑳ **Lunenburg,** about 9½ kilometers (6 miles) away, is a feast of ornate German architecture, wooden boats, steel draggers (a fishing boat that operates a trawl), historic inns, and good restaurants. In the center of town is a national historic district, and the fantastic old school on the hilltop is the finest remaining example of Second Empire architecture, an ornate style that began in France.

Lunenburg also boasts being homeport to *Bluenose* and *Bluenose II* (*see* Guided Tours, *above*), the great racing schooner and its replica. Both were built at the Smith and Rhuland yard here, as was the replica of HMS *Bounty,* used in the film *Mutiny on the Bounty.*

The **Fisheries Museum of the Atlantic,** part of the Nova Scotia Museum complex, is housed in a renovated waterfront building and includes a traditional fishing schooner, the *Theresa E. Con-*

nor; and a steel-hulled stern trawler, *Cape Sable;* as well as an aquarium; dory shop; and a wide range of displays. *Bluenose Dr., tel. 902/634– 4794. Admission: $2.25 adults, 50¢ children 5–16, $5.50 families. Open daily June–mid-Oct. 9:30–5:30.*

Before leaving Lunenburg, you may want to visit the **Houston North Gallery,** which represents both trained and self-taught Nova Scotian artists and Inuit (Eskimo) soapstone carvers and printmakers. The gallery, in a large converted house, overlooks the harbor and is near the Fisheries Museum. *110 Montague St., tel. 902/634–8869. Open Feb.–Dec., Mon.–Sat. 10–6 and Sun. 1–6.*

❷❶ **Bridgewater,** located at the head of navigation on the La Have River, is the main market town of the South Shore. Another of those towns whose focus was shipping and shipbuilding, Bridgewater, with its more than 7,000 residents, is now sustained by the large Michelin Tire plant nearby.

Just west of Bridgewater, on Route 325, is the **Wile Carding Mill,** which was built in 1860 and retains its original machinery. The mill itself was once powered by an overshot waterwheel. *242 Victoria Rd., tel. 902/543–8233. Admission free. Open June– Sept., Mon.–Sat. 9:30–5:30, Sun. 1–5:30.*

Farther down the La Have River, at La Have on Route 331, is **Fort Point Museum,** a former lighthouse-keeper's house that's open daily in the summer.

❷❷ The Lighthouse Route winds on to **Liverpool,** on the estuary of the Mersey River. This community, settled around 1760 by New Englanders, is a fishing and paper-milling town and also serves as a convenient base for the 381-square-kilometer (147-square-mile) **Kejimkujik National Park,** an inland wilderness reached in about 45 minutes via Route 8. The Mersey is the oldest documented canoe route on the continent; it drains Lake Rossignol, Nova Scotia's largest freshwater lake. The interior of the province here is almost entirely unsettled and is ideally explored by canoe. There is also good trout and salmon fishing. For outfitters, go into the town of Greenfield, on Route 210, off Route 8.

During the American Revolution and the War of 1812, Liverpool was a privateering center; later, it became an important shipping and trading port. In the center of town is the **Simeon Perkins House** (109 Main St., tel. 902/354–4058; open June– mid-Oct., Mon.–Sat. 9:30–5:30, Sun. 1–5:30), built in 1766, which was the former home of a prominent early settler who kept an extensive and revealing diary. The house is now part of the Queens County Museum.

The Perkins diary was used extensively by Thomas Raddall, whose internationally successful novels and stories are sometimes set in and around Liverpool. *His Majesty's Yankees* (1944) is a vivid account of a local family's deeply divided loyalties during the American Revolution, when many Nova Scotians sympathized with the rebels, not the Crown. Raddall still lives in Liverpool.

❷❸ The high noon of **Shelburne** occurred right after the Revolution, when 16,000 Loyalists briefly made it one of the largest communities in North America. Today it is a fishing and shipbuilding town situated on a superb harbor at the mouth of the

Roseway River. Many of its homes date back to the Loyalists, including the **Ross-Thomson House** (9 Charlotte La., tel. 902/875–3141; open June–mid-Oct., daily 9:30–5:30), which is now a provincial museum. Also in Shelburne, and worth a stop is the **Dory Shop** (Dock St.; open mid-June–mid-Sept., daily 9:30–5:30), a provincial museum property that was officially opened in 1983 by Prince Charles and Princess Diana. Dories are flat-bottom boats with flaring sides and a sharp bow, well-suited to North Atlantic waters. Until last year, 97 year-old Sidney Mahaney built dories at the shop twice weekly. Although he may not be up to building more dories in 1994, he will still occasionally be welcoming visitors interested in his trade.

South of Shelburne, from Barrington to Digby, is the most prosperous fishing region in the province. With a noticeably milder climate than the rest of Nova Scotia and easy access to the rich fishing grounds of George's Bank, fishermen can work almost all year to bring in a rich harvest of lobster, scallops, and groundfish.

㉔ **Barrington,** with only 349 residents, was the home of Captain Benjamin Doane, whose book *Following the Sea* is a fine, lucid account of 19th-century whaling and trading. Visit the **Barrington Woolen Mill,** built in 1884 and now a provincial museum, with the original machinery intact and exhibits on weaving wool into bolts of twills and flannels, blankets and suitings. *2368 Rte. 3, tel. 902/637–2185. Admission free. Open mid-June–Sept., Mon.–Sat. 9:30–5:30, Sun. 1:30–5:30.*

Now turn off for **Cape Sable Island,** Nova Scotia's southernmost extremity. Like Barrington, Cape Sable Island is a Yankee community, as common family names attest; everyone seems to be named "Smith" or "Nickerson." Interestingly, there is a bewildering variety of small evangelical churches, which presumably reflects the Puritan enthusiasm for irreconcilable disagreements over fine points of doctrine. The largest community on Cape Sable is **Clark's Harbour** (locally pronounced "Cla'k's Ha'bah," sounding more like a town in Massachusetts), named for Michael Swim, an early settler who could read and write. He was thus described as a clerk or, to the British, a "clark."

The famous Cape Islander fishing boat was developed here. By now you have seen hundreds of examples of them: Sitting high on the water, with its pilothouse forward and its high, flaring bow and low stern, the Cape Islander is Nova Scotia's standard inshore fishing boat. Boatbuilding (in fiberglass as well as wood) is still a thriving occupation along these shores. Successful fishermen buy new boats and sell the older ones to less-favored regions such as the Eastern Shore and Cape Breton, and many boats eventually turn up as spacious, inexpensive pleasure craft.

Upon reaching **Pubnico** you enter the Acadian milieu; from here to Digby the communities are mostly French-speaking. Favorite local fare includes fricot, a stew made mostly of vegetables but sometimes has rabbit meat; and rappie pie, made of meat or poultry with potatoes from which much of the starch has been removed.

You'll no doubt notice that there are no fewer than seven Pubnicos: Lower West Pubnico, Middle West Pubnico, and West

Pubnico, all on the west shore of Pubnico Harbour; three East Pubnicos on the eastern shore; and just plain Pubnico, at the top of the harbor. These towns were founded by Phillipe Muis D'Entremont, and they once constituted the only barony in French Acadia. He was a prodigious progenitor: To this day, many of the people in the Pubnicos are D'Entremonts, and most of the rest are D'Eons or Amiraults.

You'll also notice the Acadian flag, tricolored with a gold star representing *stella maris,* the star of the sea. The star guides the Acadians during troubled times, which have been frequent. In 1755, after residing for a century and a half in Nova Scotia, chiefly in the Annapolis Valley, the Acadians were expelled by the British—an event that inspired Longfellow's famous *Evangeline.* Some eluded capture and others slowly crept back, and many settled in New Brunswick and along this shore of Nova Scotia.

㉕ The next stop en route is **Yarmouth,** the largest town in southern Nova Scotia, the biggest port west of Halifax, and the point of entry for travelers arriving by ferry from Maine. Its population is relatively big, as well, with 8,500 people. The ferries are a major reason for Yarmouth's prosperity, as they pull in much revenue by providing quick, inexpensive access for merchants and consumers going to the Boston market for fish, pulpwood, boxes and barrels, knitwear, Irish moss, Christmas trees, and berries.

In the 19th century Yarmouth was an even bigger shipbuilding center than most, and its location put the port on all the early steamship routes. The award-winning **Yarmouth County Museum,** housed in a late-19th-century church, does a fine job of unraveling the region's history with its displays of period furniture, costumes, tools, and toys, as well as a significant collection of ship models and paintings. *22 Collins St., tel. 902/742–5539. Admission: $1 adults, 50¢ students, 25¢ children under 14, $2.50 families. Open June–mid-Oct., Mon.–Sat. 9–5, Sun. 1–5; mid-Oct.–May, Tues.–Sat. 2–5.*

Yarmouth has another museum that's surprisingly interesting: The **Firefighters Museum of Nova Scotia,** located one block from the waterfront, presents the evolution of fire fighting through its displays of equipment from the leather bucket to the chemical spray. *451 Main St., tel. 902/742–5525. Admission: $1 per person, $2 families. Open June, Mon.–Sat. 9–5; July–Aug., Mon.–Sat. 9–9, Sun. 10–5; Sept., Mon.–Sat. 9–5; Oct.–May, Mon.–Fri. 10–noon and 2–4.*

The Lighthouse Route ends here, and the **Evangeline Trail** begins, winding along the shore of St. Mary's Bay, through a succession of Acadian villages collectively known as the French Shore. The villages blend seamlessly into one another for about 32 kilometers (nearly 20 miles), each one, it seems, with its own wharf, fish plant, and enormous Catholic church. Hence, this part of Route 1 is sometimes called "the longest main street in the world."

Along this shore and through Nova Scotia as far east as Truro are nondescript shops called Frenchy's. "Frenchy" refers to Ed Theriault of Meteghan, who hit upon the idea of importing quality used clothing in bulk from Boston and selling it at flat-rate bargain prices. Normally it costs as much to dry-clean the clothes as it does to buy them. Today, even well-heeled Nova Scotians root through the tables at Frenchy's.

26 **Point de l'Eglise** (Church Point), past Meteghan River, is the site of **Université Ste-Anne,** the only French-language institution among Nova Scotia's 17 degree-granting colleges and universities. Founded in 1891, this small university is a focus of Acadian studies and culture in the province.

St. Mary's Church (1905) at Point de l'Eglise is the tallest and largest wooden church in North America, at 58 meters (190 feet) long and 56 meters (185 feet) high. The steeple requires 40 tons of rock ballast to keep it steady in the ocean winds. **St. Bernard,** just a few miles farther and marking the end of the French Shore, has an equally impressive granite gothic church, which seats 1,000 people. Built entirely by local people, beginning in 1910, this monument took 40 years to complete.

The other side of St. Mary's Bay is known as Digby Neck. To explore it, drive on to Digby and follow Route 217. Digby Neck is actually a long basalt peninsula extended seaward by two **27** narrow islands, Long Island and **Brier Island.** On the far side is the mouth of the Bay of Fundy; ferries going between the islands have to crab sideways against the ferocious Fundy tidal streams that course back and forth through the narrow gaps. The ferries operate hourly, 24 hours a day, and cost $1 for cars, but are free to pedestrians. One of the boats is called *Joshua Slocum* and the other is *Spray;* the former is named for Westport's most famous native, and the latter for the 11-meter (36-foot) oyster sloop, which he rebuilt and in which he became the first man to single-handedly circumnavigate the world, in 1894–96. At the southern tip of Brier Island is a cairn commemorating the voyage.

An important stop on the Atlantic Flyway, Brier Island is an excellent spot for bird-watching; because the surrounding waters are rich in plankton they attract a variety of whales, including fins, humpbacks, minkes, and right whales, as well as harbor porpoises. Whale-watching tours are available through several companies, including **Pirate's Cove Whale Cruises** (Rte. 217, Tiverton, Long Island, tel. 902/839–2242), which operates June–October and costs $33 for adults, $16.50 for children 6–14.

Digby is the terminus of the ferry service from Saint John, New Brunswick, and an important fishing port with several good restaurants and a major resort, The Pines. The town is particularly famous for its scallops and for smoked herring known as "Digby Chicks." Digby is located on the almost-landlocked Annapolis Basin, into which the Annapolis River flows after its long course through the valley that bears its name.

Swing inland to **Bear River,** a jewel of a village with a large arts-and-crafts community and many gift stores; or follow the shore of the Basin to the **Upper Clements Park,** a theme park that celebrates Nova Scotia's crafts and heritage and has a variety of rides and attractions, including a waterslide, carousel, and roller coaster. *Box 99, Clementsport, tel. 902/532–7557 or 800/565–PARK in Atlantic provinces. Admission free, but visitors pay for rides. Open June, Sat.–Sun. 10–7; July–Aug., daily 10–7; Sept., Sat.–Sun. 10–7.*

28 At the head of the Annapolis Basin is **Annapolis Royal,** the oldest European settlement in Canada, founded in 1605. Samuel de Champlain called it Port Royal and established his settlement 8 kilometers (5 miles) down the opposite side of the Basin; the settlement has been reconstructed and is now **Port Royal National Historic Site.** *Tel. 902/532–2898. Admission free. Open mid-May–mid-Oct., daily 9–6; closed rest of year.*

Fort Anne National Historic Site was fortified in 1643; the present structures are the remains of the fourth fort erected here and garrisoned by the British as late as 1854. The officers' quarters are now a museum, with exhibits on the site's history. *On the waterfront, tel. 902/532–2397. Admission free. Open mid-May–mid-Oct., daily 9–6; mid-Oct.–mid-May, weekdays 9–6.*

Annapolis Royal was Nova Scotia's first capital and first military base. Local businesses (or the tourist information center, located in the Annapolis Royal Tidal Power Building; *see below*) can provide *Footprints with Footnotes,* a self-guided walking tour of the town; guided tours leave from the lighthouse on St. George Street, daily at 10 AM and 2:30.

Don't miss the **Annapolis Royal Historic Gardens,** 10 acres of magnificent themed gardens connected to the wildlife sanctuary, maintained by Ducks Unlimited. *441 St. George St., tel. 902/532–7018. Admission: $3.50 adults, $3 children and senior citizens, $9.75 families. Open mid-May–mid-Oct., 8–dusk.*

Located just ¼ mile from Annapolis Royal, on the causeway that crosses the Annapolis River to the Granville Ferry is the **Annapolis Royal Tidal Power Project.** Designed to test the feasibility of generating electricity from tidal energy, this pilot project is the only saltwater generating station in existence. The interpretation center explains the process. *Tel. 902/532–5454. Admission free. Open mid-May–mid-June, daily 9–5:30; mid-June–Aug., daily 9–8; Sept.–mid-Oct. 9–5:30.*

The **Annapolis Valley** runs northeast like a huge trench, flat on the bottom, sheltered on both sides by the long ridges of the North and South Mountains. Occasional roads over the South Mountain lead to the South Shore; short roads over the North Mountain lead to the Fundy shore. The rich soil of the valley bottom supports dairy herds, hay, grain, root vegetables, tobacco, grapes, plums, strawberries, peaches, pears, cherries, and apples, apples, apples. The best time to visit? Apple blossom season: late May and early June.

Like the South Shore, the Valley is punctuated with pleasant small towns, each with a generous supply of extravagant Victorian homes and churches. (Annapolis Royal is particularly well supplied with imposing mansions, particularly along the upper end of St. George Street.) For most visitors, the Valley towns go by like charming milestones, among them: Bridgetown, Lawrencetown, Aylesford, Greenwood, Berwick. Each has its distinctions: the Gallery at Saratoga in **Bridgetown** features the paintings of Kenneth Tolmie, whose works reveal Valley scenes and hang in many leading galleries, including the National Gallery of Canada; **Lawrencetown** is the site of the Nova Scotia College of Geographical Sciences, which offers internationally recognized training in cartography, surveying, and various applications of high-technology to geography. **Aylesford** has a farm zoo; **Greenwood** is the home of Canada's antisubmarine aircraft squadrons; **Berwick** is the birthplace

(1885) of Alfred Fuller, the original Fuller Brush man. Most of the Valley towns have small museums. But the major impression of the region is one of tranquillity: lush farmland and a settled agricultural society.

Kentville, New Minas, Greenwich, and Wolfville run into one another almost like the towns of the French Shore; their more-than-12,000 residents form the Valley's largest urban cluster.

㉙ At **Kentville, Agriculture Canada** (tel. 902/678–1093) maintains an important research station on horticulture and poultry; the grounds are beautiful, and free guided tours can be arranged from June through August, weekdays 8–4:30.

㉚ **Wolfville,** a bucolic college town, is the seat of Acadia University. The school's **Beveridge Art Centre** (Acadia University, Highland Ave., tel. 902/542–2201; open Sept.–May, Tues.–Fri. 11–5, weekends 1–4; June-Aug., daily 12–5) includes several works by Alex Colville, the internationally celebrated magical realist painter who lives on Wolfville's main thoroughfare and has served as Acadia's Chancellor.

At Greenwich, take Route 358 to Cape Blomidon via Port Williams and Canning for a spectacular view of the Valley and the Bay of Fundy from **The Lookoff.** Cape Blomidon itself rises 231 meters (760 feet) from the Bay. Continue to **Scots Bay,** where rock shelves contain ribbons of amethyst, jasper, and carnelian. A popular hiking trail leads from the end of Route 358 to the dramatic cliffs of Cape Split.

Beyond Wolfville is **Grand Pré,** once a major Acadian site, where a small stone church, at the Grand Pré National Historic Site (open mid-May–mid-Oct., daily 9–6), commemorates Longfellow's heroine Evangeline, and houses an exhibit on the 1755 deportation of the Acadians from the Valley. While here, visit **Grand Pré Vineyards** (tel. 902/542–1470), an estate winery with 150 acres of grapes under cultivation. Free tours can be arranged, and the estate has a wine salesroom and crafts shop.

㉛ **Windsor,** the last of the Valley towns, was settled in 1703 as an Acadian community, and **Fort Edward** (no tel.; open mid-June–Labor Day, daily 10–6)—one of the assembly points for the expulsion of the Acadians—still stands as the only remaining colonial blockhouse in Nova Scotia. Flora MacDonald, the Scottish heroine who helped Bonnie Prince Charlie escape to France, spent the winter of 1779 in Windsor while her husband was posted at the fort.

Windsor is also the home of Judge Thomas Chandler Haliburton—lawyer, politician, historian, and humorist. His best-known work, *The Clockmaker,* which is still in print, pillories Nova Scotian follies from the viewpoint of a Yankee clockmaker. **Haliburton's Home** (Clifton Ave., tel. 902/798–2915; open mid-May–mid-Oct., Mon.–Sat. 9:30–5:30, Sun. 1–5:30), set on a manicured 25-acre estate, now belongs to the Nova Scotia Museum.

The tide's average rise and fall at Windsor is over 40 feet, and you can see the tidal bore (the leading edge of the incoming tide) rushing up the Meander River and sometimes reaching a height of 3 feet. The local tourist office (902/798–2690) can tell you estimated tide times.

Continuing along the Evangeline Trail, Halifax is only about 45 minutes away, but one site 30 miles (18 miles) from Windsor deserves attention: **Uniacke House,** built about 1815 for Richard John Uniacke. During the American Revolution Uniacke, who was fighting on the rebel side, was captured in Cumberland County, just across the Bay of Fundy. The young Irishman was released through some hazy politics and came to Nova Scotia seeking his fortune. He eventually found it as Attorney-General and Advocate-General to the Admiralty Court, where his fees in one three-year period during the War of 1812 amounted to the stupendous sum of £50,000. Some of that money went into Uniacke House, a superb example of colonial architecture, situated on spacious grounds near a lake. The house, which is now part of the Nova Scotia Museum, is preserved in its original condition with many authentic furnishings. *758 Windsor Hwy., tel. 902/866–2560. Admission free. Open mid-May–mid-Oct., Mon.–Sat., 9:30–5:30, Sun. 1–5:30.*

Highway 101 cuts across the peninsula through gypsum hills to **Bedford,** at the head of Bedford Basin. Once a toney summer resort, Bedford is now a favored suburb of Halifax. Follow the Bedford Highway to Halifax, noting **Julie's Music Room** (*see* Tour 1) as you pass through Prince's Lodge. If you take Windsor Street downtown, you will be following the 18th-century route between Windsor and Halifax—a proper conclusion to a memorable tour.

Tour 3: Northern Nova Scotia

This tour takes in parts of three of the official Scenic Trails, including **Marine Drive, The Sunrise Trail,** and **The Glooscap Trail.** Any one leg of the route could be done comfortably as an overnight trip from Halifax; for the whole tour, allow three or four days.

Pick up Route 7 at Dartmouth. The Eastern Shore—the Atlantic coast east of Halifax-Dartmouth—is perhaps the most scenic and unspoiled stretch of coastline in mainland Nova Scotia. Because it is unspoiled, of course, the Eastern Shore's facilities are relatively few and simple. The road winds along a deeply indented, glaciated coastline of rocky waters interspersed with pocket beaches, long narrow fjords, and fishing villages. Take the time to prowl the side roads and discover your own favorite rock pools and islets—there are plenty to find.

Musquodoboit Harbour, with about 930 residents, is a substantial village at the mouth of the Musquodoboit River, not far east of Dartmouth. The river itself offers good trout and salmon fishing, and the village touches on two slender and lovely harbors. One of the Eastern Shore's best beaches, **Martinique Beach,** is about 12 kilometers (8 miles) south of the village, and other fine beaches are at Clam Bay and Clam Harbour, several kilometers (a few miles) east of Martinique.

The pretty villages slip by: Jeddore, Salmon River, Lake Charlotte. An increasingly important part of their economies is aquaculture: Nearby, in **Ship Harbour,** the provincial Department of Fisheries has developed an aquaculture **Demonstration Centre** (Rte. 7, tel. 902/845–2991; admission free; open May–Sept., weekdays 9–3), with a small interpretive center on the hatchery, open to the public. As you travel a bit farther, take note of the strings of white buoys in Ship Harbour, marking North America's largest cultivated mussel farm.

This part of the shore experienced a small gold rush during the first part of this century, complete with a 1936 mine disaster, during which the first live, on-the-spot radio newscasts were made throughout Canada and the world. A small local museum at **Moose River Gold Mines,** about 30 kilometers (19 miles) north of Tangier, commemorates the period. *Rte. 224, tel. 902/384–2630. Admission free. Open late-June–Labor Day, Tues.–Sat. 10–5, Sun. 1–6.*

Time Out   Don't fail to stop in Tangier for some delicious smoked salmon, eel or mackerel from **Willy Krauch's Danish Smokehouse** (Rte. 7, tel. 902/772–2188; open Apr.–Christmas, daily 8–7; Christmas–Apr., daily 8–5).

Sheet Harbour is the major service center for the Eastern Shore, with a bank, hospital, accommodations, and campgrounds. Like Musquodoboit, this town straddles two harbors, from one of which is shipped pulpwood to Europe.

The road winds on through a string of uniquely named villages: Necum Teuch, Ecum Secum, Marie Joseph, Spanish Ship Bay. The latter was named for a ghostly galleon, which is said to enter the harbor in flames every seven years. Just beyond, at Liscomb Mills, is Liscomb Lodge, a full-service resort with a very respectable restaurant.

35   The next major center is **Sherbrooke,** which has fewer than 400 residents, but is the Shore's leading tourist center. The St. Mary's River, which flows through the hamlet, is one of Nova Scotia's best salmon rivers, and much of the village itself has been rebuilt by the Nova Scotia Museum to its late 19th-century character, with a blacksmith shop, water-powered sawmill, horse-drawn wagons, tearooms, and stores. Twenty-five buildings have been restored on their original sites for the living history village. *Tel. 902/522–2400. Admission: $2.25 adults, 50¢ children under 16. Open June–mid-Oct., daily 9:30–5:30.*

From Sherbrooke you'll have to decide in which direction you wish to continue. Marine Drive continues down the shore through wild, harsh, lovely country rarely visited by tourists. To see Nova Scotia unbuttoned, as it were, follow the Drive down to **Canso,** pick up the Trans-Canada Highway via Guysborough, and talk to people at every stop. You will find few tourist attractions, although Canso itself has a stirring history and a National Historic Site; in this part of the province you'll come closer to traditional Nova Scotian ways of life than you will anywhere else.

The alternative is to stay on Route 7, which turns inland up the St. Mary's River through spruce woods and rolling farmland to Antigonish, an hour's drive away. The drive takes you from the Atlantic to the Northumberland Strait, part of the Gulf of St. Lawrence: from cold water and rocky shores to warm water and broad sandy beaches. If water sports are your thing, this is your shore: there are miles of wonderful beaches all along Northumberland Strait.

36   **Antigonish** is the home of **St. Francis Xavier University,** a center for Gaelic studies and for the co-operative movement. Its

Coady International Institute offers training to co-op and credit union workers from foreign countries. It's also a cathedral town with a population of about 5,200.

Follow Route 337, the Sunrise Trail, for a glorious drive along St. George's Bay with its many good swimming beaches, before the road abruptly climbs 1,000 feet up and over to **Cape George.**

Time Out   There's a little take-out shop on the wharf at **Ballantyne's Cove,** a tiny artificial harbor near the tip of Cape George, that is said to have the best fish-and-chips in Nova Scotia. Grab an order and enjoy the views.

After following the Cape, high above the sea, the road runs along Northumberland Strait through lonely farmlands and tiny villages such as Arisaig and Lismore. If, after hearing those names, you have any doubt about the Scottish origin of the people, they will be laid to rest by a stone cairn in Lismore that commemorates Bonnie Prince Charlie's Highland rebels, slaughtered by the English at Culloden in 1746.

Much of the rest of the road runs inland, but the turnoff to Merigomish leads into a maze of inlets, beaches, and islands that are well worth exploring. Either way you go, you'll eventually emerge at Highway 104, the Trans-Canada. Turn right a kilometer and a half (a mile) later, and follow the shore road to **Melmerby Beach**—a favorite local spot—and continue on to New Glasgow by a circuitous shoreside road. Alternatively, stay on the Trans-Canada to reach New Glasgow a few kilometers (2 miles) away.

New Glasgow is one of five industrial towns on the three rivers that flow into Pictou Harbour. Combined, the five towns have a population of nearly 30,000, making this one of the largest urban centers in the province. New Glasgow is a steel-fabricating and manufacturing center; **Trenton** manufactures railway cars; **Westville** and **Stellarton** are coal-mining towns.

�37 For the visitor, however, the most interesting town by far is **Pictou,** somewhat sullied by a papermill across the harbor, but nevertheless one of the most engaging communities in Nova Scotia. Lining its streets are typically Scottish-style stone cottage homes and public buildings, and there's a good selection of very attractive small hotels and restaurants. Using the main highway system, Pictou can be reached in about two hours from Halifax.

To Pictou Harbour in 1773 came the *Hector*—the nearest thing to a Canadian *Mayflower*—inaugurating the torrent of Scottish immigration that permanently altered the character of the province and the nation. A replica of the *Hector* is under construction at the *Hector Heritage Quay* (tel. 902/485–8028).

Under the inspired leadership of men such as the pioneering educator Thomas McCulloch, Pictou quickly became a center of commerce, education, theological disputation, and radical politics. **McCulloch House,** a restored 1806 building with displays of McCulloh's scientific collection and personal items such as furniture, is preserved as part of the Nova Scotia Museum. *Old Haliburton Rd., tel. 902/485–4563. Admission free. Open June–mid-Oct., Mon.–Sat. 9:30–5:30, Sun. 11:30–5:30; mid-Oct.–May, weekdays 9–5.*

Leave Pictou on Route 6, the Sunrise Trail. The road runs beside an apparently endless string of beaches, with many summer homes plunked in the adjoining fields. **River John** is a good meal stop, especially May, June, and July, when the community prepares lobster suppers; or in August, when chicken barbecues are on the menu.

38 At Brule, take Route 326, then turn right on Route 256 to reach the water-powered gristmill at **Balmoral Mills** (1860), the oldest operating mill in Nova Scotia, and one of five that once operated on this stream. It is now a museum with milling demonstrations, and the grounds include a picnic park. *Tel. 902/657–3016. Admission free. Open June–mid-Oct., Mon.–Sat. 9:30–5:30, Sun. 1–5:30; demonstrations 10–12.*

Follow Route 256 to Route 311 and turn right to rejoin the Sunrise Trail. **Tatamagouche,** a market center for farmers and fishermen, is beautifully situated on a ridge overlooking a small estuarine harbor. Beyond Tatamagouche, turn right to Malagash to find **Jost Vineyards** (tel. 902/257–2636 or 800/565–4567 in Canada), one of three farm wineries in the province. Jost produces a surprisingly wide range of very acceptable wines, and offers tours at 3 PM daily, during mid-June through September.

39 The road continues through the small community of Wallace, on another small harbor, to **Pugwash.** This was the home of Cleveland industrialist Cyrus Eaton, at whose estate numerous Thinkers' Conferences brought together leading intellectual figures from the West and the Soviet Union during the 1950s and 1960s. Pugwash is still Scottish terrain, as attest the Gaelic street signs. The town is also the home of **Seagull Pewter** (Durham St., tel. 902/243–2516) a husband-and-wife crafts operation that has grown into a $25-million business by exporting pewter vessels, picture frames, and other artifacts worldwide. The showroom fronts on the main highway.

From Pugwash a half-hour drive will take you to Amherst, through rolling hills and along the edge of Amherst Marsh, part of the Tantramar Marsh. The Tantramar covers most of the Isthmus of Chignecto, the narrow neck of land that joins Nova Scotia to the rest of North America, and it is said to be the largest marsh in the world. If you have not yet had your fill of sandy beaches, however, an attractive alternative route leads through Northport, Lorneville, and Tidnish Dock.

Amherst stands on one of the glacial ridges that borders the Tantramar Marsh. Like New Glasgow, Truro, Oxford, and several other towns along what is now the Canadian National main line, Amherst was once a thriving manufacturing center for many products, including pianos and furnaces. During World War II, Amherst's aerospace factories (which still survive, but on a much smaller scale) built hundreds of Anson bombers; they flew off to war from a now-vanished airport. The town is historically significant for another reason: In 1917, en route from New York to Russia, the Communist leader Leon Trotsky was confined here for a month in a prisoner-of-war camp.

From Amherst, a two-hour drive via Highways 104 and 102 will return you directly to Halifax. However, the Glooscap Trail from Amherst through Parrsboro to Truro is much more interesting and takes only about an hour longer. Relatively few tourists travel the latter route, which provides some of the most striking scenery in Nova Scotia.

If you opt for the Glooscap Trail, there are several roads that connect Amherst and Parrsboro. Route 2 leads through the coal-mining town of **Springhill**, the site of the famous mine disaster immortalized in the folk song "The Ballad of Springhill" by Peggy Seeger and Ewen McColl, and hometown of singer Anne Murray, whose career is celebrated in the **Anne Murray Centre** (Main St., tel. 902/597-8614; open May–Oct., daily 9–5). Routes 2 and 302 offer the most direct passage to Parrsboro, running through tall hills and farmland to join Route 2 at Southampton.

An alternative—and better—option is to take the Glooscap Trail, which branches off via Route 242 to **Joggins,** where coal age fossils are embedded in 150-foot sandstone cliffs. Visit the **Joggins Fossil Centre,** where you can learn about the region's geological and archaeological history. Also, guided tours of the fossil cliffs are available, but departure times depend on the tides. *30 Main St., tel. 902/251–2727. Admisson to center: $3.50 adults, $3 senior citizens, $2 children 5–18. Admission for tours: $10 adults, $8 senior citizens, $4 children 5–18. Open June–Sept., daily 9–6:30.*

From Joggins, the Glooscap Trail runs along the shore of Chignecto Bay through Shulie and Sand River to Apple River. You are now on the Bay of Fundy, the third coastline of this tour, where stupendous volumes of water rushing into a narrow shelving bay create the world's highest tides, which sometimes reach heights of 50 feet. **Advocate Harbour** was named by Champlain for his friend Marc Lescarbot, who was a lawyer or "avocat." Built on flat shore land with a tall ridge behind it and a broad harbor in front of it, Advocate is eerily beautiful. The road continues past the spectacular lighthouse at **Cape d'Or,** a piece of land that juts out and divides the waters of the main Bay of Fundy from the narrow enclosure of the Minas Basin. As the tides change, fierce riptides create spectacular waves and overfalls. The view from the ridge down to the lighthouse is superb; the view from the lighthouse itself is almost equally magnificent, but the road down is rather primitive and should only be attempted in four-wheel drives.

Route 209 continues through the 19th-century shipbuilding communities of **Spencer's Island** and **Port Greville.** A cairn at Spencer's Island commemorates the construction of the famous *Mary Celeste,* which was found in 1872, sailing in the mid-Atlantic without a crew. She had been abandoned at sea with the table still set for dinner—a story that is one of the enduring mysteries of the sea.

Parrsboro, a center for rockhounds and fossil hunters, is the main town on this shore, and hosts the annual **Rockhound Roundup,** held every August. Among the exhibits and festivities are geological displays, concerts, and other special events. To sustain geologists' interests year-round will be the **Fundy Geological Museum** (Two Island Rd.; tel. 902/254–3814 open summer, daily 9–7; winter weekdays 9–5), scheduled to open in August 1993. The spacious museum will house exhibits on geology, from the days of the dinosaurs to present. Parrsboro is an appropriate setting for the new museum since it's not far from the site where the world's smallest dinosaur fossil was found; these tiny fossils will also be displayed at the new venue. Also, a favorite pastime of the town's visitors is to hunt for amethysts and agates that constantly wash out of the nearby cliffs.

Fossils are Parrsboro's claim to fame, but this harbor town was also a major shipping and shipbuilding port, and its history is described at the **Ottawa House Museum-by-the-Sea.** Ottawa House, which occupies a striking location overlooking the Bay of Fundy, was the summer home of Sir Charles Tupper, a former Premier of Nova Scotia who was briefly Prime Minister of Canada. *Whitehall Rd., tel. 902/254–2376. Admission: $1. Open July–early Sept., daily 10–8.*

From Parrsboro, Route 2 runs along the shore of the Minas Basin to Truro; almost 5 kilometers (about 3 miles) from Parrsboro is the 125-foot-high **Hidden Falls** (tel. 902/254–2505; admission free; open mid-May–Nov.), on private property but open to the public. The adjoining gift shop is a jumble of antique furniture, books, crockery, and bric-a-brac that warrants a visit.

Among the most beautiful scenic areas along Route 2 is **Five Islands,** which, according to Micmac legend, was created when the god Glooscap threw handfuls of sod at Beaver. A provincial park on the shore of Minas Bay includes a campground, a beach, hiking trails, and some interpretation of the region's unusual geology.

Route 2 rejoins the Trans-Canada (Highway 104) at **Glenholme.** From here it is a 75-minute drive to Halifax.

Tour 4: Cape Breton Island

Allow three or four days for this meandering tour that begins by entering the cape via the Canso Causeway on Highway 104; turn left at the rotary, and take Route 19, the Ceilidh Trail. The road winds along the mountainside, with fine views across St. George's Bay to Cape George. This western shoreline of Cape Breton faces the Gulf of St. Lawrence, and is famous for its sandy beaches and warm salt water.

If Halifax is the heart of Nova Scotia, Cape Breton is its soul, complete with soul music: flying fiddles, boisterous rock, velvet ballads. Cape Breton musicians—weaned on Scottish jigs and reels—are among Canada's finest, and you can hear them all over the island, all summer long, at dozens of local festivals and concerts (*see* Festivals and Seasonal Events in Chapter 1).

43 **Port Hood** is the first stop on this tour because of its particularly good beaches and because it's a pleasant excursion: **Port Hood Island,** whose 17 traditional homes are now used primarily as a summer retreat by urban refugees. The island has scenic hills, rock formations on the shore, sandy beaches, and is surrounded by warm water. It's accessible only by an informal ferry operated by Bertie Smith (tel. 902/787-2515), the island's last year-round resident.

44 On the way from Port Hood to **Mabou,** the land lies low until Mabou Harbour, where it rises abruptly to the tall hills of the Mabou Highlands. Mabou itself has been called "the prettiest village in Canada," and it is also perhaps the most Scottish, with its Gaelic signs and a deep tradition of Scottish music and dancing. This is the hometown of innumerable great fiddlers such as John Allan Cameron, and the Rankin Family; stop at a local gift shop and pick up some tapes to play as you drive down the long fjord of Mabou Harbour to **Mabou Mines.** The mines is a place so hauntingly exquisite that you expect to meet the *sidhe*, the Scottish fairies, capering on the hillsides. Within these hills is some of the finest hiking in the province, and above the land fly bald eagles, plentiful in this region. Inquire locally or at the tourist office on Margaree Forks for information about trails.

The Ceilidh Trail winds on through green wooded glens and hidden farms to **Glenora Distillers** in **Glenville,** North America's only distillers of single-malt whisky. The distillery is built around a courtyard bisected by MacLellan's Brook, and includes a bar, a restaurant, and a small inn. *Rte. 19, tel. 902/258-2662. Tours: $2. Open June–Oct., daily 11–4.*

45 The road continues through **Inverness,** a fishing port and former coal-mining town with many services, and on to **Broad Cove,** the site of one of the most venerable Cape Breton Scottish concerts, held annually in late July. The road forks at **Dunvegan,** the home of Alastair MacLeod, whose powerful short stories pierce deeply into the life of these Scottish communities. Look for his collections *The Lost Salt Gift of Blood* or *As Birds Bring Forth the Sun* for a better understanding of the region.

Take Route 219 at Dunvegan, following the coast through **Chimney Corner** and **Whale Cove.** One of the beaches near Chimney Corner has "sonorous sands": When you step on the sand or drag a foot through it, it squeaks and moans. The
46 Ceilidh Trail joins the Cabot Trail at **Margaree Harbour** at the mouth of the Margaree River, a famous salmon-fishing stream and a favorite canoe route. Stop at the schooner *Marion Elizabeth,* now the Schooner Village restaurant and free museum, with many small shops and a good selection of books about Cape Breton. On the grounds is writer Farley Mowat's schooner *Happy Adventure,* featured in his book *The Boat That Wouldn't Float.*

The Margaree River is a cultural dividing line: South of the river the settlements are Scottish, up the river they are largely Irish, and north of the river they are Acadian French. The Cabot Trail crosses the river and runs along the shore through Belle Cote and **Cap Le Moine.** Don't miss Joe Delaney's whimsical scarecrow farm and gift shop at Cap Le Moine (Cabot Trail, tel. 902/235–2108). Most of the harbors on this bold, straight coast are the estuaries of small rivers, with treacherous sandbars at their mouths. Stop at **Friar's Head** and look over the cliff: The tiny cleft in the rocks below was long used as a fishing harbor.

47 **Cheticamp,** an Acadian community, is the best harbor and the largest settlement on the shore. With its tall silver steeple towering over the village, it stands exposed on a wide lip of flat land below a range of bald green hills, behind which lies the high plateau of the Cape Breton Highlands. Cheticamp is famous for its hooked rugs, available at many local gift shops, and for whale cruises, which depart in June, once daily; July and August, three times daily from the government wharf. **Whale Cruisers Ltd.** (tel. 902/224–3376) is one of the reliable charter companies in the area. Cruises cost $25 for adults, $10 for children 6–12.

At the outskirts of Cheticamp begins **Cape Breton Highlands National Park,** a 597-square-kilometer (370-square-mile) wilderness of wooded valleys, plateau barrens, and steep cliffs that stretches across the northern peninsula of Cape Breton from the Gulf Shore to the Atlantic. The highway through the park is magnificent, as it rises to the tops of the coastal mountains and descends through tight switchbacks to the sea. For wildlife watchers there's much to see, including moose, eagle, deer, bear, fox, and bobcat. *Tel. in summer 902/285–2535, in winter 902/285–2270. Admission June–Sept.: $5 per vehicle per day, $10 for 4-day pass, $20 for annual pass. Admission free in winter. No charge for vehicles passing through on Cabot Trail. Camping fees: $11 for tent camping, $17 for full hookup.*

Pleasant Bay is a tiny village in a cleft of the mountains, where the Grande Anse River reaches the sea. A spur road creeps along the cliffs to Red River, beyond which is **Gampo Abbey**— the only Tibetan Buddhist monastery in America—situated on a broad flat bench of land high above the sea. The main road climbs North Mountain, past the trail to **Lone Shieling,** a recreation of a Scottish crofter's cottage. The cottage, about a 20-minute scenic walk from the highway, includes displays about the region's history and flora. Its name is taken from the anonymous "Canadian Boat Song," which expresses yearnings for the emigrants' lost Scottish home:

From the lone sheiling on the misty island
Mountains divide us, and the waste of seas;
But still the blood is strong, the heart is Highland
And we in dreams behold the Hebrides.

The most northerly tip of the island is not part of the National Park; turn off to discover **Bay St. Lawrence** and **Meat Cove,** set in an amphitheatre of bare green hills, and looking northward to the killer island of **St. Paul's,** site of more than 60 charted shipwrecks. Whale-watching cruises are available June through August, three times daily, through **Whale Watch Bay St. Lawrence** (tel. 902/383– 2981); the cost is $22 for adults, $11 for children 6–12.

The main road reenters the park near **Cabot's Landing,** the long sandy beach in Aspy Bay where Cape Breton folks believe that John Cabot made his landfall in 1497; this theory, however, is vigorously denied in Newfoundland. Dingwall, in the center of the bay, is an archetypal fishing village; so are White Point, New Haven, and Neil's Harbour.

48 **Ingonish,** one of the leading holiday destinations on the island, is actually several villages on two bays, divided by a long narrow peninsula called Middle Head. Each bay has a sandy beach, and Middle Head includes the provincially owned **Keltic Lodge,** a first-class hotel and resort complex. The hamlet offers a wide range of activities, among them, downhill and cross-country skiing, golfing, swimming, and hiking. Stop at **Lynn's Craft Shop and Art Gallery** (on Hwy., tel. 902/285–2735), which offers the work of noted local artist Christopher Gorey and others.

The road serpentines up Cape Smokey and along the face of the mountains, offering spectacular views from high above the sea. **Wreck Cove** is the headquarters of *Cape Breton's Maga-*

zine, an award-winning oral-history publication whose home-spun appearance belies its essential sophistication. Look for it on newsstands throughout the island.

(49) Notice the small islands on the far side of the mouth of St. Ann's Bay: These are the **Bird Islands,** breeding grounds for Atlantic puffins, black guillemots, razor-billed auks, and cormorants. Landing on the islands is forbidden, but boat tours are available from **Bird Islands Boat Tour** (tel. 902/674-2384) in Big Bras d'Or. The road descends at last to the flatlands around the mouth of the bay.

(50) If you'd like to extend your drive, take the short ferry ride (runs 24 hours and costs 50¢) to **Englishtown,** home of the celebrated Cape Breton Giant, Angus MacAskill. A museum holds the remains of a 7'9" man. *Tel. 902/929–2875. Admission: $1 adults, 50¢ children. Open May–Oct., 9–6.*

This alternative route around the head of the bay brings you to **St. Ann's,** home of North America's only **Gaelic College** (tel. 902/295– 3441), with the Great Hall of the Clans and a Scottish gift shop. The college offers courses in Gaelic language and literature, Scottish music, and dancing, weaving, and other Scottish arts. In the first week of August Gaelic College hosts the **Gaelic Mod,** a week-long festival of games, theater, and music.

(51) Turn right on Highway 105 for **Baddeck,** the most highly developed tourist center in Cape Breton, with more than 1,000 motel beds, a golf course, many fine gift shops, and numerous restaurants. Baddeck is the main town on the **Bras d'Or Lakes,** a vast, warm, almost-landlocked inlet of the sea, which occupies the entire center of Cape Breton. The coastline of the Lakes is more than 967 kilometers (600 miles) long, and yachtspeople sail from all over the world to cruise their serene, unspoiled coves and islands. Four of the largest communities along the shore are Micmac Indian reserves.

Baddeck's attractions include the **Centre Bras d'Or Festival of the Arts,** which offers live music and drama every evening during the summer, and the annual regatta of the Bras d'Or Yacht Club, held in the first week of August. Sailing tours and charters are available locally, as are bus tours along the Cabot Trail. A free ferry (passengers only) shuttles between the government wharf and the sandy beach, by the lighthouse at Kidston Island.

The **Alexander Graham Bell National Historic Site** commemorates the great inventor who spent his summers here and is buried on the mountaintop above his mansion, still owned by his family and visible from the town. The site contains displays and detailed records of Bell's research into an astonishing range of subjects. *Chebucto Rd., tel. 902/295–2069. Admission free. Open July–Sept, daily 9–9, Oct.–June, daily 9–5.*

(52) Continue along the lake shore through several Indian villages to **Little Narrows,** then take the ferry (runs 24 hours and costs 25¢) to the Washabuck Peninsula. Take Route 223 to **Estmere** and **Iona,** site of the **Nova Scotia Highland Village,** set high on a mountainside, with a spectacular view of two major Bras d'Or Lakes and the narrow Barra Strait, which joins them. The village's 10 historic buildings were assembled from all over Cape Breton to depict Highland Scots' way of life from their origins in the Hebrides to the present day. Among the participants at this living-history museum are a smith in the blacksmith shop and a clerk in the store. *Rte. 233, tel. 902/725–2272. Admission: $3 adults, $2.50 senior citizens, $1 students, $6 families. Open mid-June–mid-Sept., Mon.–Sat. 9–5, Sun. 11–6.*

A ferry carries you from Iona to Grand Narrows, and a few kilometers (about 2 miles) from the ferry, bear right toward Eskasoni and East Bay. (If you miss this turn, don't worry: you'll have just as scenic a drive along St. Andrews Channel.) The East Bay route runs through the Micmac village of **Eskasoni,** the largest native community in the province. This is one of the friendliest villages in the province, with a fascinating cultural heritage: Find an excuse to stop and talk, perhaps at a gift shop or a general store.

53 Farther on, East Bay becomes a prosperous outer suburb of **Sydney,** the heart of Nova Scotia's second-largest urban cluster. "Industrial Cape Breton" encompasses villages, unorganized districts, and half-a-dozen towns—most of which sprang up around the coal mines, which fed the steel plant at Sydney. These are warmhearted, interesting communities with a diverse ethnic population, including Ukraines, Welsh, Polish, Lebanese, West Indians, Italians; most residents descended from the miners and steelworkers who arrived a century ago when the area was booming. Sydney is also the only significantly industrialized district in Atlantic Canada, and it has suffered serious environmental damage.

Industrial Cape Breton has the island's only real airport, its only university, and a lively entertainment scene that specializes in Cape Breton music. The **University College of Cape Breton** offers many facilities for the public, such as a theater, art gallery, the Cape Breton Archives, and the Beaton Institute of Cape Breton Studies. The campus is located on the Sydney-Glace Bay Highway, not far from the airport.

Sydney is also a popular departure point: Fast ferries leave from **North Sydney** for Newfoundland, and scheduled air service to Newfoundland and the French islands of St. Pierre and Miquelon departs from Sydney Airport.

54 Situated about 30 minutes from Sydney, on Route 22, is **Fortress of Louisbourg National Historic Park,** the most remarkable site in Cape Breton. Louisbourg tends to be chilly, so pack a warm sweater or windbreaker. After the French were forced out of mainland Nova Scotia in 1713, they established their headquarters here, in a walled and fortified town on a low point of land at the mouth of Louisbourg Harbour.

The fortress was twice captured by the British and once returned; after the second siege, in 1758, it was razed to the ground. Its capture essentially ended the French Empire in America. During the past 30 years, a quarter of the original town has been rebuilt on its foundation, just as it was in 1744, before the first siege. Costumed actors re-create the lives and activities of the original inhabitants; you can watch a military drill, see nails and lace being made, and eat food prepared from 18th-century recipes in the town's two inns. Plan on spending at least half a day. Tours available. *Tel. 902/733–2280. Admission: $6.25 adults, $3.25 children 5–16, senior citizens free, $16 families. Open June and Sept., daily 9:30–5; July–Aug., daily 9–6.*

While in Louisbourg, consider stopping at the railway museum at the **Sidney and Louisburg Historical Society,** or the **Atlantic Statiquarium,** a marine museum devoted largely to underwater treasure. *Railway Museum: 7336 Main St., tel. 902/733–2720. Admission free. Open June–Sept., weekdays 9–5, July–Aug., daily 9–7. Statiquarium: 7523 Main St., tel. 902/733–2220. Admission: $2.50 adults, $1 children 5–16, $5 families. Open June–Sept., daily 10–8.*

To return, you must retrace your tracks, via Route 22, Highway 125, and Route 4 to East Bay; continue down the east side of the Bras d'Or Lakes.

Time Out   On your return route, you'll come to **Big Pond,** home of singer/songwriter Rita MacNeil, who operates a tearoom here. Stop for tea and oatcakes, and pick up one of her tapes. *Rte. 4. Open June, daily 10–6; July–Aug., daily 10–8; Sept.–Oct., daily 10–6.*

Route 4 continues along the lake, sometimes close to the shore and sometimes high in the hills. The **Chapel Island Reserve** is the site of a major Micmac spiritual and cultural celebration, which draws 5,000 visitors every year during the last weekend in July. The event combines native and Roman Catholic ceremonies, and non-natives are welcome.

From St. Peter's to Port Hawkesbury the population is largely ⑤ Acadian French. At **St. Peter's** the Atlantic Ocean is connected with the Bras d'Or Lakes by the century-old St. Peter's Canal, still heavily used by pleasure craft and fishing vessels. The town is a service center for the surrounding region, and offers such amenities as a marina, hotels, restaurants, and a liquor store. From St. Peter's, Route 247 leads through the Acadian villages of Grand Greve and L'Ardoise to a fine beach at Point Michaud.

The road onward along the Bras d'Or Lakes leads through pretty Acadian villages along the twisting channel of St. Peter's Inlet, with many coves and islands, and then along the main ⑤ body of the lake to **Dundee,** a large resort with a spectacular hilltop golf course overlooking the island-studded waters of West Bay. The alternative route, equally engaging, leads along the Atlantic coast, through coves and islands past River Tillard and River Bourgeois to Louisdale.

Turn off on Route 320 for Isle Madame, a 27-square-kilometer (17- square-mile) island named for Madame de Maintenon, second wife of Louis XIV. Route 320 leads through the villages of Poulamon and D'Escousse, and overlooks the protected waterway of Lennox Passage, with its spangle of islands. Route 206 meanders through the low hills to a maze of land and water at West Arichat. Together, the two routes encircle the island, meeting at Arichat, the principal town of **Isle Madame.**

⑤ **Arichat** was once the seat of the local Catholic diocese; **Notre Dame de l'Assumption church,** built in 1838, still retains the grandeur of its former cathedral status. The bishop's palace, the only one in Cape Breton, is now a law office. The two cannons overlooking the harbor were installed after the town was sacked by John Paul Jones, founder of the U.S. Navy, during the American Revolution. When Jones returns, Arichat will be prepared. The town was an important shipbuilding and trading center during the 19th century, and some fine old houses from that period still remain, along with the 18th-century **LeNoir Forge** (902/226–9364; open May–Sept., weekdays 9–5, Sat. 10–3).

A dead-end road leads to the Acadian villages of Petit de Grat, Sampson's Cove, and **Little Anse;** with its rocky red bluffs, cobble shores, tiny harbor, and brightly painted houses, the latter is particularly attractive to artists and photographers.

From Louisdale, Route 104 speeds through the woods and crosses the Inhabitants River to **Port Hawkesbury,** a new industrial center around the deep-water port created when, in 1955, the Canso Causeway blocked the once-fierce currents from the Gulf of St. Lawrence. Port Hawkesbury has a paper mill, an electrical generating station, a gypsum wallboard plant, and an oil-transshipment depot. It also has all the usual services, including a number of motels.

Eight kilometers (5 miles) farther on is **Port Hastings,** at the Cape Breton end of the Canso Causeway. Many visitors find this presents them with the greatest decision they've had to face in Cape Breton thus far: When the time comes to leave, should they stay? The choice is yours. You don't have to cross the Causeway. If you do, Halifax is a three-hour drive away.

Shopping

You may claim a refund of Nova Scotia's 10% sales tax (nonrefundable on accommodations, meals, and alcohol) paid on goods you transport home. Refund claims must be filed within 90 days of leaving Nova Scotia and must be in excess of $15. (Refunds of the national Goods and Services Tax must be applied for separately; *see* Shopping in Chapter 1). For refund forms and information, contact the **Provincial Tax Commission** (Tax Refund Unit, Box 755, Halifax, NS B3J 2V4, tel. 902/424–5946 or 1/424–6708 in Nova Scotia).

Halifax The Spring Garden Road area has two new, stylish shopping malls, with shops selling everything from designer clothing to fresh pasta. **Jennifers of Nova Scotia** (5635 Spring Garden Rd., tel. 902/425–3119) sells locally made jewelry, pottery, wool sweaters, and soaps. You can also find fine crafts in Historic Properties and the Barrington Inn complex, near the waterfront, at such shops as **Pewter House** (1875 Granville St., tel. 902/423–8843) and the **Stornoway** (1873 Granville St., tel. 902/422–9507). The **Plaid Place** (1903 Barrington Pl., tel. 902/429–6872) has a dazzling array of tartans and Highland accessories. The **Wool Sweater Outlet** (1870 Hollis St., tel. 902/422–9209) offers wool and cotton sweaters at good prices.

Elsewhere in Nova Shopping malls in Nova Scotia are similar to those in other
Scotia parts of Canada or in the United States. The two largest malls
Shopping Malls are the **MicMac Mall** in Dartmouth, off the A. Murray Mackay Bridge; and the **Halifax Shopping Centre** on Mumford Road. On Route 4 in Sydney you'll find the **Mayflower Mall** on the way to Glace Bay.

Specialty Shops Antiques, gifts, and crafts are especially popular in Cape Breton, but shops selling these items appear in numbers throughout the province. You'll find everything from blacksmithing in East Dover and silversmithing in Waverley to leaded glass ornaments in Purcells Cove, hooked rugs in Cheticamp, woolens in Yarmouth, wooden toys in Middletown, pewter in Wolfville, pottery in Arichat, and apple dolls in Halifax. A good shoppers' guide is the *Buyers Guide to Art and Crafts in Nova Scotia*, from the Department of Tourism and Culture (*see* Important Addresses and Numbers in Essential Information, *above*).

Sports and the Outdoors

The Department of Tourism and Culture (*see* Important Addresses and Numbers in Essential Information, *above*) publishes *Nova Scotia Outdoors*, a comprehensive guide to aviation, diving, kayaking, river rafting, rockhounding, windsurfing, skiing, and many others. They also publish a Sportsman's Calendar and *Master Guides*, a full catalog of outfitters.

Biking *Bicycle Tours in Nova Scotia* (US$21.95, C$24.95) is published by **Bicycle Nova Scotia** (5516 Spring Garden Rd., Box 3010, Halifax B3J 3G6, tel. 902/425–5450). The organization also conducts a variety of excursions around the province. **Backroads** (1516 5th St., Suite Q333, Berkeley, CA 94710, tel. 510/527–1555 or 800/245–3874) offers five- and six-day bike trips on the Evangeline Trail.

Bird-watching Nova Scotia is located on the Atlantic "flyway" and is an important staging point for migrating species. An excellent, beautifully illustrated book, *Birds of Nova Scotia*, by Robie Tufts, is a must on every ornithologist's reading list. One of the highest concentrations of bald eagles in North America—about 250 nesting pairs—is located in Cape Breton, along the Bras d'Or Lake region or in Cape Breton Highlands National Park. July and August are the best eagle-watching times. MacNabs Island, in Halifax harbor, has a large osprey population. The Bird Islands, off the coast of Cape Breton, are home to a variety of sea birds, including the rare Atlantic puffin.

Canoeing Nova Scotia is seamed with small rivers and lakes, by which the Micmac Indians roamed both Cape Breton and the peninsula. Especially good canoe routes are within Kejimkujik National Park (*see* National Parks, *below*). The publication *Canoe Routes of Nova Scotia* and a variety of route maps are available from the Nova Scotia Government Bookstore (Box 637, 1 Government Pl., Halifax B3J 2T3, tel. 902/424–7580).

Fishing Nova Scotia has more than 9,000 lakes and 100 brooks; practically all lakes and streams are open to visitors. The catch includes Atlantic salmon (June–September), brook and sea trout, bass, rainbow trout, and shad. You can get a nonresident fishing license from any Department of Natural Resources office in the province and at most sporting-goods stores.

Golf Nova Scotia and Cape Breton have 38 golf courses, as well as driving ranges and miniature golf courses. The 9-hole course at Parrsboro and the 18-hole links at Dundee offer spectacular views of the Minas Basin and Bras d'Or Lake, respectively. One of Canada's finest courses is at The Pines Resort Hotel, in Digby (*see* Lodging, *below*), offering 18 challenging holes amid a pine forest.

Hiking The province has a wide variety of trails along the rugged coastline and inland through forest glades, which enable you to experience otherwise inaccessible scenery, wildlife, and vegetation. Maps of Nova Scotia trails are available through the **Canadian Hostelling Association** (5516 Spring Garden Rd., Box 3010, Halifax B3J 3G6, tel. 902/425–5450).

Windsurfing Wind and water conditions are often excellent for windsurfing, the fastest-growing aquatic summer sport in Nova Scotia. Lessons and equipment rentals are available from retail outlets throughout the province.

Beaches

The province is one big seashore. The warmest beaches are found on the Northumberland Strait shore and include Heather Beach, Caribou, and Melmerby, all in provincial parks. The west coast of Cape Breton and the Bras d'Or Lakes also offer fine beaches and warm salt water.

National Parks

Nova Scotia has two national parks: **Cape Breton Highlands National Park** (*see* Tour 4, *above*), through which the Cabot Trail runs; and **Kejimkujik National Park** (*see* Tour 2, *above*), in the interior of the western part of the province. Essentially a wilderness area with many lakes, Kejimkujik offers well-marked canoe routes into the interior, with primitive campsites. Nature trails are marked for hikers, boat rentals are available, and there's freshwater swimming. One precaution: Check for ticks after hiking in the deep woods. *To Kejimkujik: Take Hwy. 8 from Liverpool or Annapolis Royal, Box 36, Maitland Bridge, B0T 1N0, tel. 902/682–2770. Park fee: $4 per vehicle per day, $9 for 4-day pass, $25 for annual pass. Camping fee: $8.50–$13 per day.*

Dining and Lodging

Dining

Many of Halifax's restaurants are set in refurbished historic homes or other restored quarters. The menus almost always center on seafood, including Malpeque oysters, Fundy lobster, and Digby scallops. Unless otherwise noted, dress is casual; only in expensive restaurants is a jacket required.

Along the main highways, your best bet for a meal will be at truck stops, particularly the **Irving Big Stops.** Expect nothing fancy, just generous helpings of plain, solid food at reasonable prices.

Highly recommended restaurants in each price category are indicated by a star ★.

Category	Cost*
Very Expensive	over $50
Expensive	$35–$50

Moderate	$15–$35
Inexpensive	under $15

*per person, excluding drinks, service, 7% GST, and 10% sales tax on meals more than $3.

Lodging

Nova Scotia has a superb computerized system called **Check In** (tel. 800/565–0000; in Halifax-Dartmouth, 902/425–5781; in the continental U.S., 800/341–6096; in Maine, 800/492–0643), which provides information and makes reservations with more than 700 hotels, motels, inns, campgrounds, and car-rental agencies. Check In also represents most properties in Prince Edward Island and some in New Brunswick.

Several hotel and motel chains operate in Nova Scotia. **Best Western** (tel. 800/528–1234) and **Wandlyn Inns** (in eastern Canada, tel. 800/561–0000; in the U.S., 800/561–0006) are midrange chains, quite suitable for families. **Journey's End** (tel. 800/668–4200) is a chain of new budget hotels with clean and pleasant rooms, but no facilities.

In addition to the reliable chains, Halifax-Dartmouth has a number of excellent hotels, and reservations are necessary year-round, and can be made by calling **Check In** (*see above*). Expect to pay considerably more in the capital district than elsewhere. Those on a budget might try a hostel, country inn, or bed-and-breakfast.

Highly recommended lodgings in each price category are indicated by a star ★.

Category	Cost*
Very Expensive	over $80
Expensive	$65–$80
Moderate	$45–$65
Inexpensive	under $40

*All prices are for a standard double room, excluding 10% service charge.

Halifax-Dartmouth

Dining
★ **Clipper Cay.** This restaurant gets the prize for the best location in the city: It overlooks Privateer's Wharf and the entire harbor. Request a table with a window view and choose the smoked salmon from the menu. In summer the downstairs eatery, **The Cay Side,** serves seafood lunches outside on the wharf. *1869 Upper Water St., tel. 902/432–6818. Reservations advised. AE, DC, MC, V. Expensive.*
Ryan Duffy's. Steaks are the specialty at this spot, in the Spring Garden Place shopping mall, where you can select your own cut by the ounce; other options include an array of seafood and lamb. Upstairs, corner window seats allow you to watch the world walk by from inside this brass and wood-paneled dining room. The green-and-burgundy color scheme adds to Ryan

Duffy's old-time atmosphere. *5640 Spring Garden Rd., tel. 902/421–1116. Reservations advised for dining room. AE, MC, V. Moderate–Expensive.*

Daily Catch. Don't be fooled by appearances: This small, non-descript neighborhood restaurant in a working-class section of town serves fabulous food. The menu, scribbled on a black-board on the wall, features Italian seafood. Try the lobster Fra Diavolo—lobster, squid, mussels, shrimp, clams, and scallops served over linguini, in a cast-iron skillet. *2590 Agricola St., tel. 902/429–2223. Reservations advised. AE, MC, V. Moderate.*

Da Maurizio. This popular northern Italian restaurant, in the Brewery Center, and the adjoining wine bar, **Baccus,** are under the same management. Chef-owner Maurizio serves pastas with olive oil; ravioli stuffed with duck or rabbit; grilled fish and meats; and the only risotto in town. The brewery's enormously high ceilings—15 and 20 feet—and its stone-and-brick walls are warmed by fresh flowers, gleaming silver and linen, and a Venetian carnival theme, with paintings and masks adorning the walls. There's a wide wine selection by the bottle and by the glass, and food is served in the wine bar, too. *1496 Lower Water St., tel. 902/423–0859. Reservations recommended. Closed Sat. lunch and Sun. AE, MC, V. Moderate.*

★ **Old Man Morias.** Authentic Greek specialties at this turn-of-the-century Halifax townhouse include lamb on a spit and moussaka. Greek music, tapestries, and archways set the mood for a traditionally Greek evening, and full-flavored dishes enrich the spirit. Sample the fried squid and Greek fried cheese appetizers. *1150 Barrington St., tel. 902/422–7960. Reservations advised. Closed Sun. AE, DC, MC, V. Moderate.*

Scanway. Scandinavian dishes are the specialty of this bright, pretty restaurant, decorated with pine wood and orange-and-yellow drapes. Try the *sjokreps* (Danish scampi with garlic and parsley butter). The dessert menu alone makes Scanway worth a visit: homemade ice cream, King Olav's cake (chocolate truffle torte), marzipan cake filled with fresh fruit. *1569 Dresden Row, tel. 902/422–3733. Reservations advised. AE, MC, V. Moderate.*

Privateer's Warehouse. Inside this building are three restaurants, all sharing the early 18th-century stone walls and hewn beams, and serving food in descending order of elegance. **Bradley's Upper Deck,** a comfortably elegant place with great views of the harbor, specializes in regional Nova Scotian cooking, with fresh ingredients and lots of seafood. The **Middle Deck** has a bistro-style, casual atmosphere and serves pan-fried haddock and barbecued ribs, among other items, until 10 PM and snacks until midnight; on Thursday, Friday, and Saturday maritime folk music fills the air. The **Lower Deck** is a boisterous pub with long trestle tables, a patio, beer mugs for thumping, and lots of hand-holding and singing of traditional maritime, Irish, and Scottish songs; fish and chips and other pub food is served. *Historic Properties, tel. 902/422–1289. Reservations advised for Upper Deck. Upper Deck closed Sat. lunch and Sun.; Middle and Lower Decks closed Sun. AE, DC, MC, V. Moderate–Inexpensive.*

Satisfaction Feast. This small, vegetarian restaurant and bakery is informal, friendly, and usually packed at lunchtime. The food is simple and wholesome, with a truly homemade flavor. Try the fresh whole wheat bread and one of the daily curries.

No smoking permitted. *1581 Grafton St., tel. 902/422–3540. MC, V. Inexpensive.*

Lodging **Cambridge Suites.** You can get "a suite for the price of a room" is this hotel's motto . . . and a good one it is. Choose among three suite sizes, but all have sitting room and kitchenette. What makes this lodging even more desirable is its convenient location near the Citadel and the Spring Garden Road shopping district, and it's only a short walk from downtown. Complimentary Continental breakfast is served. *1583 Brunswick St., B3J 3P5, tel. 902/420–0555 or 800/565–1263 in Canada. 200 mini-suites and one-bedrooms. Facilities: whirlpool, sauna, rooftop sundeck, exercise room. AE, MC, V. Very Expensive.*

Chateau Halifax. This first-class Canadian Pacific hotel offers large, pretty rooms in a perfect location, near Scotia Square and Historic Properties. There's a good dining room and an upbeat bar with live entertainment. *1990 Barrington St., B3J 1P2, tel. 902/425–6700. 279 rooms, 21 suites. Facilities: restaurant, coffee shop, lounge, pool, sauna. AE, DC, MC, V. Very Expensive.*

Citadel Inn. Situated at the base of Citadel Hill, this business-oriented hotel is still within walking distance of the action. Rooms with a harbor view are recommended, though they will cost more than those without. Free parking is an asset in car-clogged Halifax. *1960 Brunswick St., B3J 2G7, tel. 902/422–1391. 261 rooms, 6 suites. Facilities: restaurant, indoor pool, fitness center, sauna, whirlpool, and exercise room. AE, DC, MC, V. Very Expensive.*

Delta Barrington. This traditional-style hotel was built in 1979 using the original facade of an entire city block. It has a prime downtown location, and the rooms are spacious. All-weather walkways connect the hotel to Scotia Square shops. *1875 Barrington St., B3J 3L6, tel. 902/429– 7410. 200 rooms, 1 suite. Facilities: restaurant, lounge, piano bar, sauna, whirlpool, and pool. AE, DC, MC, V. Very Expensive.*

The Halifax Hilton. This wonderful, spacious old hotel, formerly the Nova Scotian, was recently bought by Hilton International and totally renovated. It's down by the harbor near the end of Lower Water Street. There's ample parking, a tennis court, and a roof terrace where you can sit in the evening and look out over the city. This Hilton is a popular site for meetings and conventions, with its 13 conference rooms and lavish breakfast buffet. *1181 Hollis St., B3H 2P6, tel. 902/423–7231 or 800/445–8667; fax 902/422–9465. 307 rooms. Facilities: 2 restaurants, indoor pool, sauna, ballroom, tennis court, roof terrace. AE, D, DC, MC, V. Very Expensive.*

Halliburton House Inn. A registered heritage property, this hotel is an elegant renovation of several 19th-century townhouses. All units are furnished with period antiques, lending a homey ambience to the inn. Continental breakfast is included in the room rate. *5184 Morris St., B3J 1B3, tel. 902/420–0658. 30 rooms, jr. suites and suites. Facilities: private garden courtyard, conference rooms. AE, DC, MC, V. Very Expensive.*

Holiday Inn Halifax Centre. This first-class property overlooks Halifax Commons, and is 1 kilometer (½ mile) west of Scotia Square, and features standard Holiday Inn decor with modern amenities. *1980 Robie St., B3H 3G5, tel. 902/423–1161. 228 rooms, 3 suites. Facilities: restaurant, piano bar, pool, sauna, whirlpool, gift shop, free parking. AE, DC, MC, V. Very Expensive.*

Prince George Hotel. The Prince George is a luxurious and understated business-oriented hotel. The contemporary mahogany furnishings include a writing desk. The building is conveniently connected by underground tunnel to the World Trade and Convention Center. *1725 Market St., B3J 3N9, tel. 902/425–1986 or 800/565–1567 in Canada. 208 rooms, 3 suites. Facilities: restaurant, café, 2 lounges, pub, pool, whirlpool, fitness center, concierge, children's playroom, roof deck and gardens. AE, DC, MC, V. Very Expensive.*

Sheraton Halifax. The convenient location, in Historic Properties, contributes to the elegance of this waterfront hotel. Other assets include the hotel's indoor pool with a summer sun deck and spa facilities. There's also docking space for yachts. In summer you can sit on an outdoor terrace at the **Café Maritime** restaurant and eat lobster while you watch the ships go by. *1919 Upper Water St., B3J 3J5, tel. 902/421–1700 or 800/325–3535. 332 rooms, 24 suites. Facilities: restaurant, 24-hr. room service, concierge, shops, meeting facilities, boat slips, skywalk to shopping and office complexes. AE, DC, MC, V. Very Expensive.*

Ramada Renaissance. Located in Dartmouth's Burnside Industrial Park, this new luxury hotel is aimed squarely at the business traveler, with modern amenities. *240 Brownlow Ave., B3B 1X6, tel. 902/468–8888 or 800/268–8998. 178 rooms, suites available. Facilities: restaurant, lounge, bar, 24-hr. room service, pool, whirlpool, sauna, exercise room, gift shop, meeting and banquet facilities. AE, DC, MC, V. Very Expensive.*

Waken'n Eggs B&B. Situated across the Common from the Citadel is this Victorian, built as two homes side-by-side, but is now a single house. The comfortable, eclectic furnishings include antiques and folk art and the helpful service makes this a hospitable B&B. *2114 Windsor St., B3K 5B4, tel. 902/422–4737. 3 rooms with 1 private, 1 shared bath. No credit cards. Moderate.*

Mainland Nova Scotia

Annapolis Royal
Lodging

Wandlyn Royal Anne Motel. Offering clean rooms at reasonable rates is this modern, no-frills motel that was renovated and enlarged several years ago. Enjoy the pleasant quiet country setting by taking a walk on the motel's 20 acres of land. *Box 628, B0S 1A0, tel. 902/532–2323. 30 rooms. Facilities: whirlpool, sauna, conference room. AE, DC, MC, V. Moderate.*

The Moorings B&B. This tall, beautiful home overlooking Annapolis Basin was formerly the home of author H. R. Percy and comes complete with fireplace, tin ceilings, and antiques and contemporary art. *Box 118, Granville Ferry B0S 1K0, tel. 902/532–2146. 3 rooms, 2 w/half-baths, 2 shared full baths. V. Inexpensive.*

Antigonish
Dining

Lobster Treat Restaurant. Once a two-room schoolhouse, this property has since been converted into a cozily decorated brick, pine, and stained-glass restaurant. Located on the Trans-Canada Highway, it's convenient for travelers following the Sunrise Trail. The menu features fresh seafood and vegetables year-round, as well as bread and pies baked on the premises. Because of a relaxed atmosphere and a varied menu, including a separate list for the children, families like to frequent this restaurant. *241 Post Rd., tel. 902/863–5465. Reservations advised in summer. AE, DC, MC, V. Closed Jan. Moderate.*

Chester
Dining

The Galley. Decked out in nautical bric-a-brac and providing a spectacular view of the ocean, this restaurant offers a pleasant, relaxed atmosphere. The menu features seafood: Smoked salmon and mussel dishes are the local favorites, but save room for the homemade blueberry pie. *Hwy. 3, on the Marina, tel. 902/275–4700. Reservations advised. AE, MC, V. Closed mid-Dec.–mid-Mar. Inexpensive.*

Debert **Shady Maple Inn B&B.** Here's a unique property: a working
Lodging dairy farm where you can breakfast on fresh eggs, the farm's own maple syrup, jams, and jellies. Enjoy the smoke-free rooms and sun-dried linen, and take a dip in the pool. One of the three rooms is a deluxe suite with a water bed. *R.R. 1, B0M 1G0, tel. 902/662–3565. MC, V. Moderate–Expensive.*

Digby **The Pines Resort Hotel.** Complete with fireplaces, sitting
Dining and Lodging rooms, a colossal dining room, and a view of Digby Harbor, this elegant property offers myriad amenities. Seafood with a French touch is served daily in the restaurant, and there is live entertainment in the lounge nightly. *Box 70, Shore Rd., B0V 1A0, tel. 902/245–2511. 90 rooms in main lodge, 60 in cottages. Facilities: restaurant, lounge, tennis, outdoor pool, golf. AE, DC, MC, V. Closed mid-Oct.–May. Expensive.*

Lorneville **Amherst Shore Country Inn.** Located 32 kilometers (20 miles)
Dining and Lodging from Amherst on Route 366 is this superb inn with four rooms
★ in-house and a rustic seaside cottage with fireplace. The comfortable decor includes quilts and antiques. Four new units, featuring Jacuzzi baths, efficiencies, and canopy beds will be added in early 1994. Incredibly well-prepared four-course dinners are served at one daily seating, at 7:30 PM (reservations required). *R.R. 2, Amherst, B4H 3X9, tel. 902/661–4800. 5 rooms. Facilities: restaurant. AE, DC, MC, V. Open May–Oct. Expensive.*

Lunenburg **Bluenose Lodge.** This 130-year-old mansion has nine large bed-
Lodging rooms and offers a full complimentary breakfast featuring treats such as freshly baked muffins, stewed rhubarb, and quiche. The bedrooms and sitting areas are furnished with distinctive antiques. The lodge also arranges deep sea fishing, biking, and whale watching excursions. *Box 339, 10 Falkland St., B0J 2C0, tel. 902/634–8851. 9 rooms. MC, V. Closed Nov.–Apr. Moderate–Expensive.*

Boscawen Inn. Antiques and fireplaces decorate this elegant century-old mansion, located in the center of town. The inn has views of this historic town's harbor. An annex, with four suites, is scheduled to open in 1994. *150 Cumberland St., Box 1343, B0J 2C0, tel. 902/634–3325. 17 rooms. AE, MC, V. Closed New Year's–Easter. Moderate–Expensive.*

Pictou **The Walker Inn.** A hospitable and energetic Swiss couple run
Lodging this downtown inn in their brick Georgian-style townhouse, built in 1865. Every room is different, the dining room is fully licensed, and there's a new library-conference room where guests have an opportunity to meet each other. A Continental breakfast buffet is included in room rate. *34 Coleraine St., Box 629, B0K 1H0, tel. 902/485–1433. 10 rooms with bath. Facilities: restaurant, meeting room. AE, MC, V. Moderate.*

Salmon River **Salmon River House.** About 35 minutes east of Dartmouth,
Lodging where Route 7 crosses the Salmon River, is this unpretentious white-frame inn, situated on 30 acres and offering glorious views. The home has a licensed dining room, sun room, wheelchair-accessible guest room, and one room with a water bed and whirlpool bath. *R.R. 2, head of Jeddore, B0J 1P0, tel.*

902/889–3353 or 800/341–6096. *6 rooms with bath or shower. Facilities: dining room, canoe and boat rentals, fishing arranged. MC, V. Moderate–Expensive.*

Wolfville
Dining and Lodging

Blomidon Inn. Rooms at this elegant 19th-century sea-captain's mansion, restored in 1981, are uniquely decorated in authentic colonial and Victorian fashion. The inn is located on 2½ acres of terraced land shaded by century-old elms, chestnuts, and maples. The dining room serves local cuisine cooked in traditional style, using fresh seasonal produce. Complimentary tea is served every day at 4 PM. *127 Main St., B0P 1X0, tel. 902/542–2291. 27 rooms. Facilities: dining room, conference room, tennis court. MC, V. Closed Dec. 24–26. Expensive.*

Yarmouth
Dining and Lodging

Manor Inn. With superior rooms and good food in pleasant surroundings, this colonial mansion on Highway 1 is a nice find. There are three settings to choose from: a lakeside cottage, the main estate, or the more secluded side wing. Steak and lobster are the specialties in the dining room; reservations are required. *Box 56, Hebron, B0W 1X0, tel. 902/742–2487. 54 rooms. Facilities: 2 dining rooms, 2 bars, whirlpool, heated pool, tennis court, fireplaces. AE, DC, MC, V. Moderate.*

Cape Breton Island

Baddeck
Lodging

Inverary Inn Resort. These pleasant accommodations, in a 100-year-old inn, cottages, motel units, and duplex cabins are all situated within a waterfront complex on the island's scenic central drive. The property offers boating and swimming and close proximity to the village, but the resort remains tranquil. Families will appreciate the on-site children's playground, and most guests appreciate the wharfside restaurant. The main lodge with its paneled walls, stone fireplace, and polished horse brasses, has a strong Scottish flavor. *Box 190, B0E 1B0, tel. 902/295–2674. 137 rooms. Facilities: restaurant, chapel, indoor and outdoor pools, fitness and games room, tennis, sauna. AE, MC, V. Very Expensive.*

Iona
Lodging and Dining

Highland Heights Inn. The rural surroundings, the Scottish homestyle cooking served near the dining room's huge stone fireplace, and the unspoiled view of the lake substitute nicely for the Scottish Highlands. The inn is located on a hillside beside the Nova Scotia Highland Village, overlooking the village of Iona, where some residents still speak the Gaelic language of their ancestors. Enjoy the salmon (or any fish in season), fresh-baked oat cakes, and homemade desserts. *Box 19, Iona, tel. 902/725–2360. 26 rooms. Facilities: dining room. AE, MC, V. Closed mid-Oct.–mid-May. Moderate.*

Margaree Valley
Lodging

Normaway Inn. This secluded, 1920s inn is nestled in the hills of the river valley, on 250 acres. Many of the cabins have wood-burning stoves. Take advantage of the recreation barn and the nightly traditional entertainment, including square dancing. The inn is known for its gourmet country food, all of which is prepared on the premises. The owners will organize salmon-fishing trips for interested guests. *Box 326, B0E 2C0, tel. 902/248–2987. 9 rooms, 17 cabins. Facilities: restaurant, tennis, bicycles. AE, MC, V. Closed Oct. 16–mid-June. Moderate.*

Northeast Margaree
Lodging

Heart of Hart's Tourist Farm. This 100-year-old rural farmhouse on the Cabot Trail is within walking distance of the village. The theme is "very country," with wood stove, antiques, and old-fashioned deep tubs in two of the bathrooms. Hot homemade oatmeal and Red River cereal are a favorite part of the full breakfast that is included in the room rate. Salmon and trout-fishing trips can be arranged. *On Cabot Trail, B0E 2H0, tel. 902/248–2765. 5 rooms. No credit cards. Open May–Oct. Inexpensive.*

Sydney **Joe's Warehouse.** For excellent food in the heart of town, stop
Dining here, where the specialties include local seafood and prime rib. The porridge rolls and homemade scones also win rave reviews. In summer, when the patio is open, the restaurant seats 200 people. Dress is casual and the atmosphere fun. After dinner head downstairs for live music and dancing at Smooth Herman's. *424 Charlotte St., tel. 902/539–6686. AE, DC, MC, V. Moderate.*

Lodging **Delta Sydney.** This new hotel is located on the harbor, beside the yacht club and close to the center of town. The attractively decorated guest rooms have all the amenities, and each has a view of the harbor. The intimate dining room specializes in seafood and Continental cuisine. *300 Esplanade, B1P 6J4, tel. in Canada, 902/562–7500 or 800/268–1133; in U.S., 800/887–1133; 152 rooms. Facilities: restaurant, lounge, indoor pool, sauna, fitness center. AE, DC, MC, V. Expensive.*

The Arts and Nightlife

The Arts

Theater Canada's oldest professional repertory theater, the **Neptune Theatre** (5216 Sackville St., Halifax, tel. 902/429–7300), presents a full season each summer and winter of performances from classics to contemporary Canadian drama. The **Mulgrave Road Co-Op Theatre** (tel. 902/533–2092) is a small but active professional company performing all over the Maritime Provinces, producing original plays based on local history. **Mermaid Theatre** (tel. 902/798–5841), based in Windsor, travels the world with original children's plays that make extensive use of masks and puppets.

The **Atlantic Fringe Festival** presents 40 shows in eight venues during the first week of September. Dinner theaters in Halifax include the **Historic Feast Company** (tel. 902/420–1840), which presents shows set in the 19th century at Historic Properties Thursday, Friday, and Saturday evenings; and the **Grafton Street Dinner Theatre** (1741 Grafton St., tel. 902/425–1961), where shows run Wednesday through Saturday.

Parrsboro's professional **Ship's Company Theatre** (tel. 902/254–2003) offers a summer season of plays based on historical events of the region, performed aboard the MV *Kipawo*, a former Minas Basin ferry. The **Chester Summer Theatre** (tel. 902/275–2933) operates throughout the summer. Among the best of Nova Scotia's thriving amateur companies are the **Kipawa Show Boat Company** (tel. 902/542–3500), which performs in Wolfville on summer weekends, and **Theatre Antigonish** (tel. 902/867–3954), which performs at St. Francis Xavier University in Antigonish.

Many other towns have theaters that present touring shows and occasional local productions, notably Chester, Liverpool,

Yarmouth, Annapolis Royal, Middle Musquodoboit, Pictou, and Sydney. Glace Bay's opulent old opera house, the **Savoy Theatre,** is the home of the summer-long Festival on the Bay.

Music   Live concerts and musical presentations are held in Halifax at the **Metro Centre** (Brunswick and Duke Sts., tel. 902/451–1202) and the **Rebecca Cohn Auditorium** (6101 University Ave., tel. 902/494–2646). **Symphony Nova Scotia** normally appears at "the Cohn."

Scotia Festival of Music (tel. 902/429–9469) presents internationally recognized classical musicians in concerts and master classes each May and June at various locations in Halifax. **Musique Royale** hosts an August series of superb Renaissance and baroque concerts in historic buildings around the province. The **Atlantic Jazz Festival** takes place in Halifax in mid-July.

Talented musicians abound in Nova Scotia, ranging from traditional fiddlers to folk singers and rock bands. They appear in clubs, concerts, dances and a constant stream of open-air festivals. Names to watch for include The Rankin Family, The Barra MacNeills, the Minglewood Band, Sam Moon, Rita MacNeil, David MacIsaac, Scott Macmillan, and John Allan Cameron, as well as traditional fiddlers such as Buddy MacMaster, Ashley MacIsaac, Sandy MacIntyre, Lee Cremo, Jerry Holland, and Natalie MacMaster. An annual **Nova Scotia Bluegrass** and **Oldtime Music Festival** is held in Ardoise the last weekend in July; the **Lunenburg Folk Harbour Festival,** devoted to acoustic instruments and authentic folk music, takes place in early August; many leading fiddlers appear at Cape Breton's **Big Cove Concert** in mid-July.

Film

Halifax has a dynamic and growing film industry, which presents current work during the **Atlantic Film Festival,** held in Halifax the third week in September. The festival also showcases feature films, TV movies, and documentaries made elsewhere in the Atlantic Provinces. **Wormwood's Dog** and **Monkey Cinema** (2015 Gottingen St., tel. 902/422–3700) shows Canadian, foreign-language, and experimental films. Its associated video store, Critic's Choice, specializes in hard-to-find films on videotape.

Nightlife

The multilevel entertainment center in Historic Properties, **Privateer's Warehouse** (tel. 902/422–1289), is a popular nighttime hangout. At the ground-level Lower Deck tavern you can quaff a beer to Celtic music or enjoy jazz riffs at the Middle Deck on the second floor. There is a cover for both decks, and they are packed on weekends, so get there early.

Other popular Halifax night spots include **Cheers** (1743 Grafton St., tel. 902/421–1655), with bands and entertainment nightly, and **O'Carroll's** (1860 Upper Water St., tel. 902/423–4405), a restaurant, oyster bar, and lounge where you can hear live Irish music nightly.

The **Flamingo Café and Lounge** (1505 Barrington St., tel. 902/420–1051) features a wide variety of live entertainment, including open-mike night on Mondays.

12 Prince Edward Island

Prince Edward Island seems too good to be true, with its crisply painted farmhouses, manicured green fields rolling down to sandy beaches, the warmest ocean water north of Florida, lobster boats in trim little harbors, a vest-pocket capital city packed with architectural heritage.

When you experience PEI, you'll understand instantly that it was no accident that Lucy Maud Montgomery's novel of youth and innocence, *Anne of Green Gables*, was framed against this land. What may have been unexpected, however, was how the story burst on the world in 1908 and is still selling untold thousands of copies every year. After potatoes and lobsters, Anne is the island's most important product, particularly since the advent of the internationally aired television series *Anne of Green Gables* and its successor, *The Road to Avonlea*.

Anne is everywhere on the island: At the Confederation Centre of the Arts in Charlottetown you can peruse Montgomery's original handwritten manuscript; even on cars throughout the province you'll see the freckled redhead, as the government recently stamped her face on the province's license plates. But Anne's fame stretches beyond PEI and Cavendish—fondly referred to as Anne country. She attracts international attention, especially from the Japanese, with whom she is hugely popular.

Those visitors who have come because of Anne usually leave having fallen in love with her island. Outside of the tourist mecca of Cavendish, the island seems like an oasis of peace in a world of turmoil. Here you'll find fishing ports, crossroads villages, small family farms. You can choose full-service resorts and gourmet restaurants, or you can sample the lobster suppers, farm vacations, deep-sea fishing cruises, and bed-and-breakfasts, where you can experience for the first time what life is like on a working farm or fishing harbor.

Visitors often tour the island in a loop: They take the ferry from New Brunswick to Charlottetown, see Anne country and then PEI National Park, and depart by ferry to Nova Scotia. This is a good strategy; but, to more deeply experience the island's character, stray to the wooded hills of the east—to compact, bustling Montague, straddling its river; or to the estuarine maze of Murray Harbour. Or go west to the Acadian parishes of Egmont Bay and Tignish and the silver fox country around Summerside. Even if you're in a rush, it won't take long to get off the beaten path: In most places you can cross the island, north to south, in half an hour or so.

PEI is ringed by beaches, and few of them are heavily used. Ask a dozen islanders to recommend their favorites. Bothwell Beach, near Souris, says one—miles of singing sands, utterly deserted. Drop your clothes on the way in and pick them up on the way out. West Point, says a second—life guards, restaurant nearby, showers at the provincial park. Greenwich, near St. Peter's Bay, another suggests—a half-hour walk through magnificent wandering dunes brings you to an endless empty beach.

When you're back in Charlottetown see the musical "Anne of Green Gables." Have dinner first, though—there's a great little place two blocks from the theater. Let's go.

Essential Information

Important Addresses and Numbers

Tourist Information — For prices and information before your trip, contact the **Prince Edward Island Department of Tourism and Parks,** Visitor Service Division (Box 940, Charlottetown, PEI C1A 7M5, tel. 902/368–5555 or 800/463–4PEI). The department publishes an excellent annual "Visitor's Guide," and maintains eight Visitor Information Centres (VICs) on the island. The main VIC, open year-round, is in Charlottetown (Oak Tree Pl., University Ave., tel. 902/368–4444), and is open mid-May–October, daily; November—mid-May, weekdays.

Emergencies — **Police** and **fire,** dial 0.

Hospitals — **Queen Elizabeth Hospital,** Charlottetown, tel. 902/566–6200.

Arriving and Departing by Plane

Charlottetown Airport is 5 kilometers (3 miles) north of town. **Air Canada** (tel. 800/776–3000) and **Canadian Airlines International** (902/892–4581) offer daily service to major cities in eastern Canada and the United States.

Arriving and Departing by Ferry

Two car-ferry services serve Prince Edward Island. **Marine Atlantic** (tel. 902/794–5700 or 902/855–2030) sails between Cape Tormentine, New Brunswick, and Borden, year-round, crossing daily between 6:30 AM and 1 AM. The crossing takes about 45 minutes and costs $17.50 per car round-trip and $6.75 per adult. The second service, **Northumberland Ferries** (tel. 902/566–3838; in the Maritimes, 800/565–0201), sails between Caribou, Nova Scotia, and Wood Islands, from May to mid-December. The crossing takes about 75 minutes, and the round-trip costs $25.75 per automobile and $7.90 per person (reduced price for senior citizens and children). No fares are collected inbound; you pay only on leaving the island. Neither service takes reservations.

Getting Around

By Car — There are more than 3,700 kilometers (2,294 miles) of paved road in the province, including the three scenic coastal drives called Lady Slipper Drive, Blue Heron Drive, and Kings Byway.

Guided Tours

The island offers about 20 sightseeing tours, including double-decker bus tours, cycling tours, harbor cruises, and walking tours. Most tour companies are located in Charlottetown and offer excursions around the city and to the beaches.

Exploring Prince Edward Island

The tours here divide Prince Edward Island into central Queens County, Kings County in the east, and Prince County at the western end of the island. Tour 1 is primarily a walking tour, while tours 2, 3, and 4 follow the major scenic highways—Blue Heron Drive, Kings Byway, and Lady Slipper Drive. There are plenty of chances to get out of the car, go fishing, hit the beach, collect wildflowers, or just watch the sea roll in.

Highlights for First-time Visitors

Anne of Green Gables farmhouse, Tour 2: Blue Heron Drive
North Cape, Tour 4: Lady Slipper Drive
Orwell Corner Pioneer Village, Tour 3: Kings Byway
Province House, Tour 1: Charlottetown
Seascapes and July's wild lupins near Souris, Tour 3: Kings Byway

Tour 1: Charlottetown

Sheltered on an arm of the Northumberland Strait, Prince Edward Island's only city is named for the stylish consort of King George III. Charlottetown, the largest community on the island, is a small city (population 15,800) with generous, gingerbread-clad Victorian houses and tree-shaded squares. It is often called "the Cradle of Confederation," a reference to the 1864 conference held here that led to the union of Nova Scotia, New Brunswick, Ontario, and Québec in 1867.

Charlottetown's main activities center on government, tourism, and private commerce. While new suburbs were springing up around it, the core of Charlottetown remained unchanged and the waterfront was restored to recapture the flavor of earlier eras. Today the waterfront includes the Prince Edward Hotel and Convention Centre, several informal restaurants, and handcraft and retail shops. You can easily explore the downtown by foot in a couple of hours. Irene Rogers's *Charlottetown: The Life in Its Buildings* gives much detail about the architecture and history of downtown Charlottetown.

Numbers in the margin correspond to points of interest on the Prince Edward Island and Charlottetown maps.

❶ ❷ **Charlottetown's** historic redbrick core is the setting for the modern concrete **Confederation Centre of the Arts,** opened in 1964 as a tribute to the Fathers of Confederation. The Confederation Centre houses a 1,100-seat theater, an art gallery, a library, a children's theater, a memorial hall, and a gift shop with an assortment of Canadian crafts. From June to September the center's **Charlottetown Festival** offers excellent professional theater, including the annual musical adaptation of *Anne of Green Gables. Queen St., bet. Grafton and Richmond Sts., tel. 902/628–1864; box office 902/566–1267. Open July–Sept., daily 9–8; Oct.–June, Mon.–Sat. 9–6, Sun. 2–5.*

❸ Next door, on Richmond Street, is the Georgian-style **Province House,** the meeting place of the provincial legislature. The

Prince Edward Island

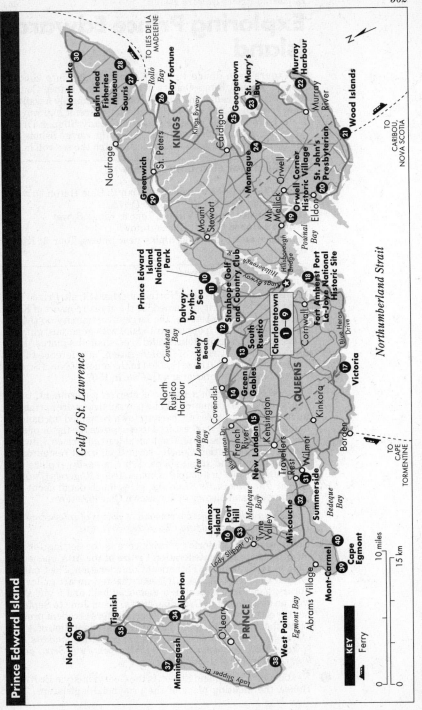

Gulf of St. Lawrence

Northumberland Strait

TO ILES DE LA MADELEINE

TO CARIBOU, NOVA SCOTIA

TO CAPE TORMENTINE

KINGS

QUEENS

PRINCE

North Lake 30
Basin Head Fisheries Museum
Souris 27
28
26 Bay Fortune
Naufrage
Greenwich
St. Peters
29
Mount Stewart

Bay Fortune
Kings Byway
Cardigan
25 Georgetown
23 St. Mary's Bay
22 Murray Harbour
Murray River
21 Wood Islands
24 Montague
19 Orwell Corner Historic Village
20 St. John's Presbyterian
Eldon
Mt. Mellick
Orwell
Pownal Bay

Prince Edward Island National Park
Dalvay-by-the-Sea
10
11 Stanhope Golf and Country Club
12
Coveheadt Bay
Brackley Beach
13 South Rustico
Charlottetown 1–9
18 Port La-Joye National Historic Site
Fort Amherst
Cornwall
Blue Heron Drive
17 Victoria
Hillsborough Bridge
Kings Byway

North Rustico Harbour
Green Gables 14
Cavendish
New London Bay
15 New London
French River
Blue Heron Dr.
Kensington
Travellers Rest
Wilmot
Kinkora
Borden

31 Summerside
32
Miscouche
Bedeque Bay
Malpeque Bay
Lennox Island 16
Port Hill
33
Tyne Valley
Lady Slipper Dr.
40 Cape Egmont
39 Mont-Carmel
Abrams Village
Egmont Bay

North Cape 36
35 Tignish
34 Alberton
O'Leary
37 Miminegash
38 West Point
Lady Slipper Dr.

KEY
Ferry

0   10 miles
0   15 km

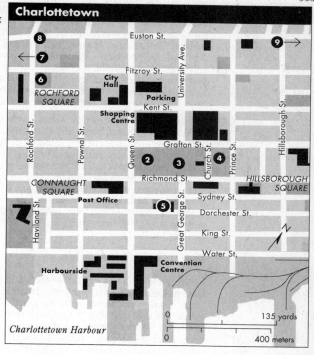

Charlottetown

three-story sandstone building, completed in 1847, contains the Confederation Chamber, where representatives of the 19th-century provinces met to discuss creating a union. The room, restored to its 1864 condition, and the legislative chamber are open to the public. Displays and a slide presentation portray the historic meeting. *Richmond St., tel. 902/566–7626. Admission free. Open July and Aug.–Labor Day, daily 9–8; June and Labor Day–mid-Oct., daily 9–5; mid-Oct.–May, weekdays 9–5. Note: When the legislature is in session, certain rooms are closed to the public.*

4 Two churches near Province House are noteworthy. **St. Paul's Anglican Church** (east of Province House) was erected in 1747, **5** making it the oldest Protestant church on the island. **St. Dunstan's Basilica,** south of Province House on Great George Street, is the seat of the Roman Catholic diocese on the island. Known for its twin Gothic spires and fine Italian carvings, it is one of Canada's largest churches.

Time Out   The **Gainsford** (104 Water St., tel. 903/368–3840), located in a Victorian home near the waterfront, is a cozy spot for a light lunch, a late-afternoon tea, or a full meal. *MC, V.*

6 A few blocks northeast of Province House, on Rochford Square, is **St. Peter's Cathedral.** All Saints Chapel contains murals by Robert Harris, the famous Canadian portrait painter. The chapel was designed in 1888 by his brother W. C. "Willy" Harris, the most celebrated of the island's architects, and the designer of many historic homes and buildings.

7 At the southern tip of the city is the beautiful 40-acre **Victoria Park,** overlooking the Charlottetown Harbour. Next to the park, on a hill between groves of white birches, is the white colonial Government House, built in 1835 as the official residence of the province's lieutenant-governors. Near the park entrance, **Beaconsfield,** a gracious Harris-designed Victorian mansion, contains the offices of the PEI Museum and Heritage Foundation and a bookstore with publications about the island. *Park open year-round, daily sunrise–sunset.*

9 At the eastern end of the city is the **Charlottetown Driving Park** on Kensington Road, home of a sport that is dear to the hearts of islanders—harness racing. Standardbred horses are raised on farms throughout the island, and harness racing on the ice and on country tracks has been popular for generations. In fact, there are more horses per capita on the island than in any other province of Canada. *Kensington Rd., tel. 902/892–6823. Admission: $2 adults, 50¢ children. Races are held year-round twice a week Jan.–May; three nights a week in June, July, and most of Aug.; and twice daily (except Sun.) during Old Home Week in mid-Aug.*

Tour 2: Blue Heron Drive

Circling the island's center segment and roughly outlining Queens County, Blue Heron Drive is 190 kilometers (114 miles) long. It takes its name from the great blue heron, a stately water bird that migrates to Prince Edward Island every spring to nest in the shallow bays and marshes. You are likely to see several herons along the route. The highway marker is a white square with a blue border and a blue heron in the center.

From Charlottetown, Blue Heron Drive follows Route 15 north to the north shore, then winds along Route 6 through the north-shore fishing villages, the spectacular white sand beaches of Prince Edward Island National Park and Cabot Provincial Park, through the Anne of Green Gables country, and finally along the south shore with its red sandstone seascapes and historic sites. This drive circles some of the island's most beautiful landscapes and best beaches, but its north shore, around picturesque Cavendish and the Green Gables farmhouse, is also cluttered with tourist traps. If you're looking for unspoiled beauty, you'll have to look beyond the fried chicken joints, the tacky gift shops, King Tut's Tomb, and Ripley's Believe It Or Not, and try to keep in your mind's eye the island's simpler days.

10 **Prince Edward Island National Park** stretches for about 40 kilometers (25 miles) along the north shore of the island on the Gulf of St. Lawrence. Follow the shore road for views of the beaches and bluffs—especially Orby Head, with red sandstone cliffs up to 30 meters (33 yards) high. At Brackley Beach, you can see sand dunes 18 meters (19½ yards) high. The park has several hiking trails; the longest, about 8 kilometers (5 miles), starts near the Cavendish Campground. Among more than 200 species of birds are the northern phalarope, Swainson's thrush, and the protected piping plover. The park **Visitor Centre** in Cavendish provides a slide presentation and exhibit. The 56-acre campground has toilets, showers, electrical hookups, and a laundromat. *24 km (15 mi) north of Charlottetown, tel.*

902/672–6350. Park open daily; Visitor Centre open June–Oct., daily 9–8.

⓫ At the eastern end of the park is **Dalvay-by-the-Sea,** built in the 1890s as a summer home by an oil magnate. The park now operates the hotel as a resort lodge (*see* Lodging, *below*).

Time Out The dining room of **Dalvay-by-the-Sea** (tel. 902/672–2048) specializes in fresh seafood and homegrown vegetables, and is known for a traditional dessert called blueberry grunt.

⓬ A few kilometers west of Dalvay, off Route 6, along beautiful Covehead Bay, is the **Stanhope Golf and Country Club.** The course is among the island's longest, most challenging, and most scenic.

⓭ Moving west, you pass Brackley Beach and then come to **South Rustico,** on Route 243. Rustico is an Acadian French district, one of several on the Island. South Rustico sits on a peninsula on Rustico Bay, with a collection of Victorian houses gathered around a dainty church. One of Canada's first cooperative banks—a precursor of the credit-union movement—was founded here; it is now a National Historic Site and museum.

⓮ Continue along the shore road and follow the signs to **Green Gables,** the green-and-white farmhouse that is the setting for Lucy Maud Montgomery's first and most famous novel, *Anne of Green Gables.* The book was published in 1908, and it became one of the most popular children's books ever written. It's about a young orphan girl adopted by a strict but kindly brother and sister who live on a Prince Edward Island farm. The story has so caught the imagination of readers that thousands from around the world visit Green Gables every summer. The house, once owned by Montgomery's cousins, is organized to reflect the story. *Near Cavendish, in Prince Edward Island National Park, tel. 902/673–6350. Open mid-May–late June, daily 9–5, late June–Aug., daily 9–7; Sept.–Oct., daily 9–5.*

⓯ In **New London,** east of Cavendish on Route 6, is the modest white house where Lucy Maud Montgomery was born in 1874. Among memorabilia on display are the author's wedding dress and personal scrapbooks. *In New London, on Rte. 6, tel. 902/886–2596. Admission: $1 adults, 50¢ children. Open June and early Sept.–mid-Sept., daily 9–5; July–Aug., daily 9–7; mid-Sept.–mid-Oct., daily 9–5.*

⓰ The Blue Heron Drive follows the coastline south to the other side of the island through rolling farmland by the shores of Malpeque Bay, almost into Summerside. Across Malpeque Bay is **Lennox Island,** the largest Micmac Indian reserve in the province. The head of Malpeque Bay almost meets Bedeque Bay, nearly cutting the island in two. At Carleton, Blue Heron Drive intersects with Route 1, the main highway between Charlottetown and Borden and the terminus for the New Brunswick ferries.

⓱ Paralleling the coast, the drive continues past a fine Harris church at Crapaud to **Victoria,** a picturesque fishing village with antiques, art galleries, handcraft shops, and live summer theater in the historic **Victoria Playhouse** (tel. 902/658–2025 for ticket information and reservations).

⑱ The drive winds on through Argyle Shore to **Fort Amherst Port-La-Joye National Historic Site,** at the mouth of Charlottetown Harbour. This pretty spot, with its lighthouses, is the location of the first settlement on the island, established in 1720 during French rule. You can picnic on the site while watching boats and cruise ships sail into the harbor. *32 km (20 mi) south of Charlottetown on Rte. 19 at Rocky Point, tel. 902/675–2220. Open June–Labor Day, daily 10–6.*

Tour 3: Kings Byway

The Kings Byway follows the coastline of Kings County for 375 kilometers (225 miles) on the eastern end of the island. The route passes woodlots, patchwork-quilt farms, fishing villages, and historic sites in this green and tranquil section of the province. Starting at Charlottetown, take Route 1 east and follow Kings Byway counter-clockwise.

⑲ **The Orwell Corner Historic Village** re-creates a 19th-century rural settlement in the form of a living farm museum. Farming is done by methods used by Scottish settlers in the 19th century, including the use of handsome draft horses. The village contains a beautifully restored store and post office, school, church, farmhouse, and barns. Musical evenings (ceilidhs) in the village feature traditional Scottish music by local musicians. *Tel. 902/651–2013. Admission: $3 adults, children under 12 free. Open late June–Labor Day, daily 9–5; mid-May–late June and Labor Day–late Oct., weekdays 10–3.*

⑳ One of the island's most historic churches, **St. John's Presbyterian,** in Belfast, is just off Route 1 on Route 207. This pretty white church, on a hill against a backdrop of trees, was built by settlers from the Isle of Skye who were brought to the island in 1803 by Lord Selkirk.

㉑ Route 1 passes **Wood Islands,** the terminus for the Northumberland Ferries service to Nova Scotia, which operates while Northumberland Strait is free of ice, generally from May **㉒** through December. The island-dotted waters of **Murray Harbour** drain five rivers, and empty through the narrow gut between Poverty Beach and Beach Point. This favorite refuge for island yachtsmen supports a large fishing fleet.

Time Out **Brehaut's Restaurant** (tel. 902/962–3141) in Murray Harbour village, right by the fishermen's wharf, has a take-out and café downstairs and a pleasant dining room upstairs. Tasty, wholesome food in a rustic ambience, with very pleasant service, is what you'll get here.

The eastern coastline is dotted with fishing villages and long uncrowded beaches. Seal-watching and bird-watching boat **㉓** tours are available at Murray River and Montague; **St. Mary's Bay,** inside Panmure Island, offers excellent windsurfing behind a long protective beach. Three rivers enter into Cardigan **㉔** Bay. Seductive **Montague,** on the Montague River, is the busi- **㉕** ness hub of eastern PEI, while **Georgetown,** on a point between the Cardigan and Brudenell rivers, is a shipbuilding town with **㉖** a lively summer theater. **Bay Fortune,** a little-known scenic spot, has been a secret refuge of well-heeled Americans for two generations.

In early summer, you can see whole fields of blue, white, pink, and purple wild lupins sloping down to red cliffs and blue sea. The view from the hill overlooking the town of **Souris,** on the northeastern coast, is especially lovely. At Souris, a car-ferry links PEI with the Québec-owned Magdalen Islands. The Souris area is noted for its fine traditional musicians. An outdoor Scottish concert at Rollo Bay in July, featuring fiddling and step-dancing, attracts thousands every year.

Time Out The **Uptown Restaurant** (tel. 902/687–4123), on the main street in Souris, is a Chinese restaurant with a difference. Ask about the silver aliwana fish—a Chinese species—in an aquarium on the wall, and try the "bumbleberry" pie.

North of Souris, the **Basin Head Fisheries Museum** is located on a bluff overlooking the Atlantic Ocean. Displays include a boat shed, an aquarium, a smokehouse, a fish-box factory, and fishermen's sheds. On the grounds is a fine beach. *Box 248, Souris, tel. 902/357–2966. Admission: $3 adults, children under 12 free. Open mid-June–Labor Day, daily 9–5; Labor Day–Sept., weekdays 9–5.*

Walk over the cast-iron bridge by the museum. The exquisite, silvery beach stretches northeast for miles, backed by high, grassy dunes. Scuff your feet in the sand: it will squeak, squawk and purr at you. These are known locally as the "singing sands," a phenomenon found in only a few favored locations worldwide.

For even more extensive dune scenery, follow Route 2 to St. Peter's Bay, and Route 313 to **Greenwich.** The road ends among sandhills, but from here you can take a half-hour walk through beige dunes to reach the superb beach. These dunes are moving, gradually burying the nearby woods; here and there the bleached skeletons of trees thrust up through the sand like wooden ghosts. Along the eastern and northern coasts of the island you can charter deep-sea fishing boats that will outfit you for angling the world-record bluefin tuna that thrive in these waters. An especially good spot is **North Lake,** several kilometers (a few miles) from Basin Head.

Tour 4: Lady Slipper Drive

This drive—named for the delicate lady slipper orchid, the province's official flower—winds along the coast of the narrow indented western end of the island through very old and very small villages, which still adhere to a traditional way of life. Many of these hamlets are inhabited by Acadians, descendants of the original French settlers. The area is known for its oysters and Irish moss, but most famously for its potato farms: The province is a major exporter of seed potatoes worldwide, and half the crop is grown here.

From Charlottetown, take Route 2 to **Summerside,** the second-largest community on the island. A self-guided walking tour of Summerside, arranged by the Summerside Tourism Office, is a pleasant excursion through the leafy streets, with their spacious houses. Some of these homes are known as "fox houses"; silver foxes were first bred in captivity in western PEI, and for several decades Summerside was the headquarters of a virtual gold rush based on fox ranching. For more history and walking-tour brochures, stop in at the **International Fox Museum and Hall of Fame.** *286 Fitzroy St., tel. 902/436–2400 or 902/436–1589. Admission free; $1 donation accepted. Open May–Sept., Mon.–Sat. 9–6.*

The eight-day **Summerside Lobster Carnival,** held every July, includes livestock exhibitions, harness racing, fiddling contests, and lobster suppers. In early August, **Grand Prix hydroplane races** take place in the harbor. The boats are powered by 1,500-horse power engines and attain speeds of 150 miles (240 kilometers) per hour.

Take Route 1A from Summerside to St. Eleanors, then turn west on Route 2 to the **Acadian Museum of Prince Edward Island,** on your way to **Miscouche.** The museum's artifacts predate the 19th century and include household and farm implements. *Rte. 2, 23 Main Dr. E, tel. 902/436–6237. Admission: $2 adults, $1 children 6–17. Open early Sept.–mid-June, weekdays 9:30–4; mid-June–early Sept., weekdays 9:30–4, Sun. 1–5.*

Relatively few visitors travel west of Summerside, which is unfortunate for them and fortunate for you. Route 2 travels straight as an arrow through the drab plain of the Miscouche Swamp. Avoid this route by following the Lady Slipper signs from Miscouche to **Port Hill,** about 35 kilometers (22 miles) north and west of Summerside. The **Green Park Shipbuilding Museum and Historic House** was originally the home of shipbuilder James Yeo, Jr. This 19th-century mansion, restored and open to visitors, is topped by a cupola, from which Yeo observed his nearby shipyard through a spyglass. The modern museum building on the site details the history of the shipbuilder's craft. *Rte. 12, Port Hill, tel. 902/831–2206. Admission: $2.50 adults, children under 12 free. Open mid-June–Labor Day, daily 9–5.*

Lady Slipper Drive continues around Foxley Bay and Cascumpec Bay to **Alberton,** where Jacques Cartier made his first landing on the island. Oulton Island, just offshore, was the first place foxes were bred successfully in captivity and claims to be the world's first fur ranch.

Follow the shore north to **Tignish,** another Acadian community. Everything in Tignish seems to be co-operative, including the supermarket, insurance company, fishplant, service station, and credit union. The imposing **parish church of St. Simon and St. Jude Parish House** (315 School St. tel. 902/882–2049), across from Dalton Square, has a superb Tracker pipe organ, one of the finest such instruments in eastern Canada, and is often used for recitals by world-renowned musicians.

The **Dalton Centre,** on Church Street, was built by the first fox-breeder, Sir Charles Dalton, a Tignish native; it now includes a museum. *Church St., tel. 902/882–2488. Admission: $1.50 adults, 75¢ children. Open mid-June–Aug., Sun.–Fri. 10–5.*

Drive on to **North Cape,** where the island fades to a narrow north-pointing arrow of land with an imposing lighthouse. The curious structures nearby are wind turbines at the **Atlantic Wind Test Site,** set up on this breezy promontory to evaluate the feasibility of electrical generation by wind power. *Tel. 902/882–2746. Admission free. Open July–late Aug., daily 10–8.*

Time Out **Wind & Reef** (tel. 902/882–3535) is a full-service seasonal restaurant that offers superb views from its location near the North Cape lighthouse. Not surprisingly, the specialty is seafood, but note that meals can get pricey here.

From the cape, Lady Slipper Drive turns almost due south along the island's western shore. You may have seen draft horses around North Cape: Those were "moss horses," used in harvesting a versatile and valuable sea plant known as Irish moss. At **Miminegash,** visit the **Irish Moss Interpretive Centre,** and find out how much Irish moss was in your last ice-cream cone. *On Rte. 152 off Rte. 2, tel. 902/882–2920. Admission free. Open late June–Aug., weekdays 9–5.*

At the southern tip of the western shore is **West Point,** with a tiny man-made fishing harbor, provincial campsite, supervised beach, and what one recent visitor called an "insanely friendly" community. Above all, there is the **West Point Lighthouse,** 115 years old and the tallest on the island. When the lighthouse was automated, the community took over the building and converted it into a miniature inn and museum, with a gift shop and an excellent, moderately priced restaurant attached. *Rte. 14, tel. 902/859–3605. Admission: $1.65 adults, $1.40 senior citizens, 85¢ children. Open mid-May–mid-Oct., daily 8–9:30.*

Lady Slipper Drive meanders back to Summerside through Région Evangeline, the main Acadian district of the island. At **Cape Egmont,** stop for a look at the **Bottle Houses,** two tiny houses and a chapel built by a retired carpenter entirely out of glass bottles mortared together like bricks. In **Mont-Carmel,** an adjoining community, is a magnificent brick church overlooking Northumberland Strait, and an **Acadian Pioneer Village** with a church, school, blacksmith shop, store and dwellings. *Rte. 11, tel. 902/854–2227. Admission to village: $2 adults, 75¢ students, children 50¢. Open mid-June–mid-Sept, daily 8–9.*

Shopping

Prince Edward Islanders have been making beautiful homemade items since colonial days, when crafts were necessities of life. Island craftspeople excel at quilting, rug-hooking, weaving, knitting, and pottery, to name a few of the crafts. Full information on outlets and types of crafts is provided by the **PEI Crafts Council** (156 Richmond St., Charlottetown, PEI C1A 1H9, tel. 902/892–5152). There are more than 100 crafts outlets throughout the island.

The **Island Craft Shop** has a wide selection of weaving, pottery, woodwork and other items. *156 Richmond St., Charlottetown. Open July–Aug., Mon.–Sat. 9–8, Sun. 11–4; Sept.–June, Mon.–Sat. 10–5:30.*

The **Wood Islands Handcraft Co-op Association Ltd.,** in southeastern Kings County, sells a large number of knitted and crocheted items and other crafts. *Murray River, Kings County, tel. 902/962–3539. Open daily 9–5; July–Aug., 9–6.*

Along Lady Slipper Drive look for hand-turned bird's-eye maple products at the **Leavitts' Wood Craft** in Alberton. *Alberton, tel. 902/853–2504. Open Mon.–Sat. 8–5.*

Shoreline Sweaters, sometimes known as Tyne Valley Studios, in Tyne Valley, is where Lesley Dubey sells handmade sweaters and local crafts. *Lady Slipper Dr., Tyne Valley, tel. 902/831–2950. Open mid-May–Sept., daily 9:30–5:30.*

You can buy fresh, canned, or frozen lobster and other seafood at numerous processing plants and retail stores throughout the island. Some, such as **Crabby's Seafood** in Wood Islands, will pack for travel. *Wood Islands, next to ferry, tel. 902/962–3228. Open daily 7–7.*

Sports and Outdoor Activities

Bicycling Prince Edward Island is popular with bike-touring companies for its moderately hilly and always stunning scenery. Most of the island offers level areas, especially east of Charlottetown to Montague and along the north shore. However, the shoulderless, narrow roads and summer's car traffic can be dismal for cyclists. An 8.7-kilometer (5.4-mile) path near Cavendish campground loops around marsh, woodland, and farmland. Cycling trips are organized throughout the province, and the Department of Tourism and Parks can recommend tour operators (*see* Important Addresses and Numbers in Essential Information, *above*). Also, bicycles can be rented in Charlottetown and Cavendish.

Fishing PEI offers some of the best brook-trout fishing in eastern Canada, as well as excellent deep-sea fishing off the island's northeast coast. Charter boats leave from the fishing ports of Cove Head, North Lake, and North Rustico, daily in summer for very elusive tuna and rich mackerel fishing, and there are more than 20 boat charters to choose from.

Clam digging is possible in many less-populated coastal areas around the island.

Golf Golf isn't a popular pastime of islanders, but it is with tourists. **Stanhope Golf Course** (*see* Tour 2) is one of the more challenging courses on the island. In the western end, **Mill River Provincial Golf Course** (tel. 902/859–2238) in Mill River Provincial Park, 57 kilometers (35 miles) west of Summerside, is among the most scenic and challenging courses in eastern Canada. **Brudenell River Provincial Golf Course** (tel. 902652–2332) at the east end of the island has hosted four national championships and three CPGAs. The latter two courses are within major resort complexes.

Dining

On Prince Edward Island, plain, wholesome, home-cooked fare is a matter of course. The service is friendly—though a little pokey at times—and the setting is informal everywhere but in a few restaurants in Charlottetown. Seafood is generally good anywhere on the island, with top honors being given to lobster and any dish using local produce. Unless noted, there is no need to wear a jacket and tie.

Look for lobster suppers, offered both commercially and by church and civic groups. These meals feature lobster, rolls, salad, and mountains of sweet, home-baked goodies, and are usually presented at New London, New Glasgow, St. Ann's Church in Hope River, and Fisherman's Wharf in North Rustico. Check the local papers or the bulletin boards at local grocery stores.

Highly recommended restaurants in each price category are indicated by a star ★.

Category	Cost*
Very Expensive	over $35
Expensive	$25–$35
Moderate	$15–$24
Inexpensive	under $15

per person, excluding drinks, service, 10% sales tax, and 7% GST.

Brackley Beach
Very Expensive
★

Shaw's Hotel and Cottages. This family-oriented hotel dating from the 1860s offers fine home cooking in an elegant, country setting. Lobster is served twice weekly, and the grand Sunday-night buffets draw people from near and far to sample fresh salmon, seafood casserole, home-baked breads, and a variety of popular desserts, such as cheesecake and fresh berries in season. Lunch is not served. *Rte. 15, tel. 902/672–2022. Reservations advised. AE, MC, V. Closed Oct.–May.*

Cavendish
Inexpensive

Fiddles 'n Vittles. Lively, friendly, and decorated in rustic marine, with fishnets hanging in the dining room, the restaurant is true to its theme: House specialties are fresh and fried seafood. *Bay Vista Motor Inn, R.R.1, Breadalbane, tel. 902/963–3003. AE, DC, MC, V. Closed mid-Sept.–mid-June.*

Charlottetown
Moderate–Expensive
★

Claddagh Room Restaurant. You'll find some of the best seafood in Charlottetown here. The "Galway Bay Delight," one of the Irish owner's specialties, is a savory combination of fresh scallops and shrimp sautéed with onions and mushrooms, flambéed in Irish Mist, and doused with fresh cream. A pub upstairs features live Irish entertainment every night in summer and on weekends in winter. *131 Sydney St., tel. 902/892–9661. AE, DC, MC, V.*

★ **The Griffin Room.** This cozy dining room of the Dundee Arms Motel and Inn has a working fireplace and is filled with antiques, copper, and brass. The French Continental cuisine prepared here uses no artificial preservatives or additives, only fresh natural ingredients. Fresh seafood is served year-round, and salmon, scallops, and crab are available all winter. Specialties include rack of lamb, chateaubriand, and poached or grilled fillet of salmon in a light lime-dill sauce. *Dundee Arms Motel and Inn, 200 Pownal St., tel. 902/892–2496. MC, V.*

Moderate

Off Broadway. Popular with Charlottetown's young professional set is this attractive, cozy spot located near the Confederation Centre of the Arts. It began modestly as a crêpe-and-soup joint, and indeed, you can still make a meal of the lobster or chicken crêpe and the spinach or Caesar salad that's served with it. But the restaurant also has a fairly inventive menu of Continental entrées such as the hearty mussel chowder, fillets, and salmon. The old-fashioned private booths won't reveal your indiscretions—including your penchant for one of the many desserts. *125 Sydney St., tel. 902/566–4620. AE, MC, V.*

Inexpensive **Captain Scott's.** The fish-and-chips served at this spot in the Confederation Court Mall rival any found in England. *Cor. of Grafton and Queen Sts., tel. 902/628–1674. No credit cards. Closed Sun.*

Cornwall **Bonnie Brae.** What you'll find here is a welcoming and comfort-
Expensive able modern restaurant that offers well-prepared fresh sea-food and steaks, as well as Swiss specialties created by the Swiss owner-chef. Summer's nightly all-you-can-eat lobster buffet is guaranteed to satisfy any appetite, but leave room for desserts such as Black Forest cake and raspberry cheesecake. *Trans-Canada Hwy., tel. 902/566–2241. AE, DC, MC, V.*

Grand Tracadie **Dalvay-by-the-Sea.** Choose a table by the stone fireplace or dine
Very Expensive with a lake view on the enclosed terrace. The menu at this ele-gant Victorian dining room includes island lobster, curried scal-lops, poached halibut, peppercorn steak, and filet mignon—all served with fresh vegetables. Desserts are baked on the pre-mises by the restaurant's pastry chef; blueberry grunt, a sweet dumpling with blueberry sauce, is the Dalvay's own traditional specialty dessert. *Rte. 6, near Dalvay Beach, tel. 902/672–2048. Reservations advised. AE, MC, V.*

★ **Shady Lady Restaurant.** This restaurant is located in a log house built by the chef-owners—twin sisters—who financed the project by working as cooks in the Yukon. It's a warm and charming place decorated in Victorian style, and each table set-ting is different, with linens and fine china collected by the own-ers. The cuisine is basically French, with an emphasis on steaks and seafood. All desserts are made on the premises, including the unforgettable Hawaiian tropical fruit-almond cake, made with fruit soaked in brandy for 30 days. *Rte. 6, tel. 902/ 672–2003. MC, V. Open daily mid-May–Oct., weekends the rest of the year.*

Lodging

Prince Edward Island offers a variety of accommodations at a variety of prices, from full-service resorts and luxury hotels to moderately priced motels, cottages, and lodges, to farms that take guests. Lodgings on the north coast in summer should be booked early, especially if you're planning a long stay.

Highly recommended lodgings in each price category are indi-cated by a star ★.

Category	Cost*
Very Expensive	over $75
Expensive	$55–$75
Moderate	$40–$54
Inexpensive	under $40

*All prices are for a standard double room, excluding 10% provincial sales tax and 7% GST.

Brackley Beach
Very Expensive
★

Shaw's Hotel and Cottages. Each room is unique in this 1860s hotel, with antique furnishings, floral-print wallpapers, and hardwood floors. Half the cottages have fireplaces. This country elegance doesn't come cheap, as Shaw's is one of the most expensive hotels on the island. Guests can choose to include in their room rate a home-cooked breakfast and dinner in the Shaw's dining room (*see* Dining, *above*). *Rte. 15, C0A 2H0, tel. 902/672–2022. 40 units, including 18 cottages and 2 suites. Facilities: cocktail bar, sailboats, windsurfing, beach nearby. AE, MC, V. Closed late-Sept.–May.*

Cavendish
Expensive

Bay Vista Inn. This clean, friendly motel caters to families. Parents can sit on the outdoor deck and admire the New London Bay panorama while keeping an eye on their children in the motel's large playground. Almost all of the rooms have views of the bay. Fiddles 'n Vittles (*see* Dining, *above*) is a great place to eat with the family. *R.R.1, Breadalbane, C0A 1E0; in winter, R.R.1, North Wiltshire, C0A 1Y0, tel. 902/963–2225. 30 units, including 2 motel efficiencies. Facilities: restaurant, outdoor heated pool, playground, boating, deep-sea fishing, golf nearby. AE, MC, V. Closed late Sept.–mid-June.*

Charlottetown
Very Expensive

Best Western MacLauchlan's Motel. This is one of the many good motels in the Best Western chain. Two convenient apartment suites have a bedroom, living room, kitchen, and bathroom. *238 Grafton St., C1A 1L5, tel. 902/892–2461. 149 units, including 2 suites. Facilities: dining room, lounge, indoor pool, sauna, Jacuzzi, laundry facilities. AE, DC, MC, V.*

★

The Charlottetown. This classic five-story, redbrick hotel with white pillars and a circular driveway is just two blocks from the center of Charlottetown. The rooms and public areas offer the latest amenities but retain the hotel's old-fashioned flavor, with well-detailed, antique-reproduction furnishings. *Kent and Pownal Sts., Box 159, C1A 7K4, tel. 902/894–7371. 109 rooms, including 2 suites. Facilities: dining room, lounge with entertainment, indoor pool, sauna, whirlpool, parking. AE, DC, MC, V.*

Dundee Arms Motel and Inn. Depending on your mood, you can choose to stay in either a 1960s motel or a 1904 inn. The motel is simple, modern, and neat; the inn is homey and furnished with brass and antiques. The Griffin Room (*see* Dining, *above*), the inn's dining room, serves fine French cuisine. Continental breakfast is included in motel and inn rates. *200 Pownal St., C1A 3W8, tel. 902/892–2496. 18 rooms, including 2 suites. Facilities: restaurant, pub. MC, V.*

★

Prince Edward Hotel and Convention Centre. Two-thirds of the rooms in this 10-story hotel overlook the developed Charlottetown waterfront. A member of the Canadian Pacific chain of hotels and resorts, the Prince Edward has all the comforts and luxuries of its first-rate counterparts—from Jacuzzis in some suites to a grand ballroom and conference center. Guest rooms are modern and decorated in warm pastels. The lobby is a bright, open, two-story atrium completed with a waterfall above the front desk. *18 Queen St., Box 2170, C1A 8B9, tel. 902/566–2222 or 800/828–7447. 211 rooms, including 33 suites. Facilities: 3 restaurants, lounge with nightly entertainment, heated indoor pool, whirlpool, sauna, Nautilus equipment. AE, DC, MC, V.*

Moderate

Duchess of Kent Inn. This turreted Victorian bed-and-breakfast is packed with antiques, even in the bedrooms. It's within walking distance of Charlottetown's major sites, including the

Confederation Centre. *218 Kent St., C1A 1P2, tel. 902/566–5826.*
8 rooms share 5 baths. Facilities: guest kitchen, bicycle storage.
MC, V. Closed Dec.–May.

Inexpensive **Court Bed and Breakfast.** In a residential area 2 kilometers (1.2
miles) from downtown, this two-story bed-and-breakfast with
a welcoming red door offers large, simple, comfortable rooms
and a full, hearty breakfast, including ham, eggs, bacon, muffins, and fresh fruits in season. *68 Hutchinson Ct., C1A 8H7, tel.*
902/894–5871. 2 rooms with shared bath. No credit cards. Closed
early Sept.–Apr.

Sherwood Motel. This is a small, clean, family-oriented motel
about 5 kilometers (3.1 mi) north of downtown Charlottetown
on Route. 15. The friendly owners offer help in reserving tickets for events and planning day trips. Don't be daunted by the
Sherwood's proximity to the airport—the motel sees very little
traffic. *R.R.1, Winsloe C0A 2H0, tel. 902/892–2622. 30 rooms*
with bath; pets permitted. Facilities: kitchenettes (22 rooms),
cable TV. MC, V.

Cornwall **Blue Heron Hideaways.** The MacAndrews, the owners, are a
Very Expensive film producer and a journalist who run these executive-style
cottages, a luxury beach-house, and a honeymoon cottage located just a few minutes from downtown. The safe, private
beach offers access to sand dunes and much wildlife and it's a
great place for windsurfing. An outboard motorboat and gas
barbecues are available for guest use. Weekly rentals only
early June through mid-October. *R.R.2, Blooming Point, C0A*
1H0, tel. 902/566–2427. One 2-bedroom cottage, 2 3-bedroom cot-
tages, 1 waterfront cottage with bunkhouse. No credit cards.

Grand Tracadie **Dalvay-by-the-Sea.** Just within the borders of the Prince Ed-
Very Expensive ward Island National Park is this Victorian house, built in 1896
★ as a private summer home. Now a popular inn and restaurant,
Dalvay-by-the-Sea offers elegant but homey rooms furnished
with original antiques and reproductions. Guests can sip drinks
or tea on the porch while admiring the inn's gardens, Dalvay
Lake, or the nearby beach. Breakfasts and dinners in the dining room, included in the room rates, are exceptional (*see* Dining, *above*). *Rte. 6, near Dalvay Beach. Box 8, York, C0A 1P0, tel.*
902/672–2048, or 902/672–2546 in winter. 31 rooms in main
house and 2 cottages. Facilities: restaurant, lounge, 2 tennis
courts, driving range, canoes, rowboats, windsurfing. AE, MC,
V. Closed mid-Sept.–mid-June.

Montague **Lobster Shanty North.** Roses growing outside the windows of
Moderate its weathered-wood facade, and old fishnets draped around the
barn-board walls of the dining room, contribute to the truly
charming style of this motel. All rooms have picture windows
and open onto a deck that overlooks the Montague River.
Main St., Box 158, C0A 1R0, tel. 902/838–2463. 11 rooms. Fa-
cilities: restaurant, lounge, golf, clam-digging, swimming
nearby. AE, MC, V.

O'Leary **Rodd's Mill River Resort and Conference Centre.** With activi-
Very Expensive ties ranging from night skiing and tobogganing to golfing, this
is truly an all-season resort. Ask about family-package weekends, offered year-round. *Box 399, C0B 1V0, tel. 902/859–3555*
or 800/565–RODD. 90 rooms including 3 suites. Facilities: din-
ing room, 2 bars, 2 heated indoor pools, golf course, pro shop,
tennis court, 2 squash courts, fitness center with whirlpool and
sauna, games room, gift shop, canoeing, windsurfing, bike rent-

al, ice-skating rink, toboggan run, cross-country skiing. AE, MC, V. Closed Nov.–early Dec., Apr.

Summerside **Quality Inn Garden of the Gulf.** Close to downtown Summer-
Moderate– side, this clean motel is a convenient place to stay. The nine-hole
Expensive golf course on the property slopes to Bedeque Bay. *618 Water
St. E, C1N 2V5, tel. 902/436–2295. 83 rooms, including 6 suites.
Facilities: restaurant, coffee shop, lounge, heated outdoor pool,
9-hole golf course. AE, DC, MC, V.*

Moderate **Glade Motor Inn and Cottages.** Conveniently located 10
minutes from the Borden Ferry Terminal, this property has
comfortable if generic motel rooms as well as one- and two-bedroom cottages and one four-bedroom "house" that can accommodate up to eight people. What's different about the place is
that it is set on a 300-acre farm, with horseback riding and
nature trails. Kids get free rides in the corral. *Box 1387, C1N
4K2, tel. 902/436–5564. 33 units. Facilities: restaurant, lounge,
heated outdoor pool, horseback riding, nature trails. AE, MC, V.
Closed late-Sept.–mid-June.*

West Point **West Point Lighthouse.** This unique property is still a function-
Expensive ing lighthouse (though automated), situated within a provincial
park. Nearby are nature trails and opportunities to clam-dig,
fish, and bike. Within the lighthouse is a museum and licensed
dining room and patio; outside is the beach. Two rooms have a
whirlpool tub. Complimentary breakfast is served on your first
morning. *R.R.2, O'Leary, C0B 1V0, tel. 902/859–3605. 9 rooms.
MC, V. Open mid-May–late Sept. 27.*

The Arts

The highlights of the island's theater season are the productions of the **Charlottetown Festival,** which take place from June
through October at the Confederation Centre of the Arts.

Special art exhibitions are offered in the Confederation Centre
Gallery, one of Canada's premier museums. The permanent
collection features the country's largest assemblage of paintings by Robert Harris (1848–1919), Canada's foremost portrait
artist. For information and tickets to the festival, contact the
Confederation Centre of the Arts (Box 848, Charlottetown, PEI
C1A 7L9, tel. 902/628–1864; box office, 902/566–1267).

The **King's Playhouse** (tel. 902/652–2053) in Georgetown, 50
kilometers (30 miles) east of Charlottetown, offers varied entertainment from June through early September. The **Victoria
Playhouse** (tel. 902/658–2025) in Victoria, a half-hour's drive
west of Charlottetown, features professional repertory
theater.

Concerts and musical festivals abound on the island, especially
in summer. Live traditional Celtic music, with fiddling and
step-dancing, can be heard almost any day of the week. Best
bets: the outdoor fiddle festival at Rollo Bay in late July (tel.
902/368–5555); Monday night ceilidhs at the **Benevolent Irish
Hall** (tel. 902/892–2367) in Charlottetown; and the Sunday concerts of classical, sacred, and traditional music at **St. Mary's
Church** (tel. 902/836–3733) in Indian River, between Charlottetown and Summerside.

13 New Brunswick

By Colleen
Whitney
Thompson

Updated by Ana
Watts

New Brunswick is where the great Canadian forest, sliced by sweeping river valleys and modern highways, meets the sea. It's an old place in New World terms, and the remains of a turbulent past are still in evidence in some of its quiet nooks. Near Moncton, for instance, bees gather nectar and wild strawberries perfume the air of the grassy slopes of Fort Beausejour, where, in 1755, one of the last battles for possession of Acadia took place—the English finally overcoming the French. The dual heritage of New Brunswick (35% of its population is Acadian French) provides added spice. If you decide to stay in both Acadian and Loyalist regions, a trip to New Brunswick can seem like two vacations in one.

More than half the province is surrounded by coastline—the rest nestles into Québec and Maine, creating slightly schizophrenic attitudes in border towns. The dramatic Bay of Fundy, which has the highest tides in the world, sweeps up the coast of Maine, around the enchanting Fundy Isles at the southern tip of New Brunswick and on up the province's rough and intriguing south coast. To the north and east, the gentle, warm Gulf Stream washes quiet beaches.

New Brunswick is still largely unsettled—85 percent of the province is forested lands. Inhabitants have chosen the easily accessible area around rivers, ocean, and lakes, leaving most of the interior to the pulp companies. For years this Cinderella province has been virtually ignored by tourists who whiz through to better-known Atlantic destinations. New Brunswick's residents can't seem to decide whether this makes them unhappy or not. Money is important in the economically depressed maritime area, where younger generations have traditionally left home for higher-paying jobs in Ontario and "The West." But no one wishes to lose the special characteristics of this still unspoiled province by the sea.

This attitude is a blessing in disguise to motorists who leave major highways to explore 2,240 kilometers (1,400 miles) of spectacular seacoast, pure inland streams, pretty towns, and historical cities. The custom of hospitality is so much a part of New Brunswick nature that tourists are perceived more as welcome visitors than paying guests. Even cities often retain a bit of naiveté. It makes for a charming vacation, but don't be deceived by ingenuous attitudes. Most residents are products of excellent school and university systems, generally travel widely, live in modern cities, and are well versed in world affairs.

Essential Information

Important Addresses and Numbers

Tourist
Information

Department of Economic Development and Tourism (Box 6000, Fredericton E3B 5H1, tel. 506/453–2170 or 800/561–0123) can provide information on the seven provincial tourist bureaus. Also helpful are information services of the cities of: **Bathurst** (tel. 506/548–0400), **Campbellton** (tel. 506/753–7767), **Fredericton** (tel. 506/452–9500), **Moncton** (tel. 506/853–3333), and **Saint John** (tel. 506/658–2990).

Emergencies

Dial 911 for medical emergencies and police in New Brunswick cities and their surrounding areas. For other areas find emergency numbers inside the front cover of the local telephone directory.

Hospitals **Dr. Everett Chalmers Hospital** (Priestman St., Fredericton, tel. 506/452–5400); **Moncton City Hospital** (135 MacBeath Ave., Moncton, tel. 506/857–5111); **Dr. Georges Dumont Hospital** (330 Archibald St., Moncton, tel. 506/858–3232); **Saint John Regional Hospital** (Tucker Park Rd., Saint John, tel. 506/648–6000); **Chaleur Regional Hospital** (1750 Sunset Dr., Bathurst, tel. 506/548–8961); **Campbellton Regional Hospital** (189 Lilly Lake Rd., Campbellton, tel. 506/789–5000); **Edmundston Regional Hospital** (275 Hébert Blvd., tel. 507/739–2200); **Hôtel Dieu** (53 Lobban Ave., Chatham, tel. 506/773–4401).

Arriving and Departing by Plane

Canadian Airlines International through **Air Atlantic** (tel. 800/665–1177) operates in Saint John, Fredericton, Moncton, Charlo, and Chatham and serves the Atlantic provinces, Montréal, Ottawa, and Boston. **Air Canada** and its regional carrier **Air Nova** (tel. 800/776–3000) serve the Atlantic provinces, Montréal, Toronto, and Boston.

Arriving and Departing

By Car Ferry There are car ferries from Prince Edward Island and Nova Scotia. **Marine Atlantic** (tel. 902/794–7203) has a car-and-passenger ferry from Digby, Nova Scotia, which takes 2½ hours. For reservations in the United States (except Maine), call 800/341–7981; in Maine, tel. 800/432–7344.

By Train **Via Rail** offers passenger services three times a week from Moncton to Montréal and Halifax. The southern route connects Montréal with Halifax by way of Fredericton Junction, Saint John, and Moncton. The northern route goes through Campbellton and on to Moncton and Halifax. Bus connections are available to Prince Edward Island and Newfoundland.

By Bus **SMT** (tel. 506/859–5100) within the province connects with most major bus lines.

Getting Around

By Car New Brunswick has an excellent highway system with numerous facilities. The only map you'll need is the free one given out at the tourist information centers listed above. Major entry points are at St. Stephen, Houlton, Edmundston, and Cape Tormentine from Prince Edward Island, and Aulac from Nova Scotia.

Guided Tours

Boat Tours Harbor tours are offered in Saint John by **Partridge Island Tours** (tel. 506/693–2598) and **DMK Marine Tours** (tel. 506/635–5100).

City Tours **Heritage Tour Guide Service** (856 George St., Fredericton, tel. 506/459–5950) provides step-on guides for bus tours of Fredericton.

The **Calithumpians** theater company offers guides dressed in 18th-century costumes for free historical walks from City Hall (Queen St., tel. 506/457–1975).

In Saint John free guided walking tours begin in Market Square at Barbours General Store. For information call the Saint John Tourist and Convention Center (tel. 506/658–2990).

Special-interest More than 240 species of seabirds nest on Grand Manan Island, and the island is a paradise for painters, nature photographers, and hikers, not to mention whale-watchers. Any of these activities can be arranged by calling **Tourism New Brunswick** at 800/561–0123. **Covered Bridge Bicycle Tours** (Box 693, Dept. K, Main Post Office, Saint John E2L 4B3, tel. 506/849–9028) offers bike tours. **East Coast Expeditions** (Box 6713, Station A, Saint John, E2L 4S2, tel. 506/658–1906) offers guided hiking in the Fundy area.

Exploring New Brunswick

Our exploration of New Brunswick is broken down into four areas: a tour of the city of Fredericton, a tour of the Saint John Valley ending at the city of Saint John, a tour of the Fundy Coast, and a jog north to the sunny Acadian Peninsula.

Highlights for First-time Visitors

Acadian Village, Grand Anse, Tour 4: Moncton and the Acadian Peninsula
Beaverbrook Art Gallery, Tour 1: Fredericton
Campobello Island, Tour 3: The Fundy Coast
Fundy National Park, Tour 3: The Fundy Coast
Kings Landing, Prince William, Tour 1: Fredericton
Kouchibouguac National Park, Acadian Peninsula, Tour 4: The Acadian Peninsula
Market Square and Market Slip, Saint John, Tour 2: Saint John River Valley
Moncton's Tidal Bore and Magnetic Hill, Tour 4: Moncton and the Acadian Peninsula

Tour 1: Fredericton

Numbers in the margin correspond to points of interest on the New Brunswick and Fredericton maps.

The small inland city of **Fredericton** spreads itself on a broad point of land jutting into the Saint John River. Its predecessor, the early French settlement of Ste-Anne's Point, was established in 1642, during the reign of the French governor, Villebon, who made his headquarters at the junction of the Nashwaak and the Saint John rivers. Settled by Loyalists and named for Frederick, second son of George III, the city serves as the seat of government for New Brunswick's 728,500 residents. From the first town plan, the wealthy and scholarly Loyalists set out to create a gracious and beautiful place, and thus even before the establishment of the University of New Brunswick, in 1785, the town served as a center for "liberal arts and sciences."

New Brunswick

Gulf of
St. Lawrence

PRINCE
EDWARD

Gaspé
Peninsula

QUÉBEC

Baie

Des

Chaleurs

Miscou
Island

Lameque
Shippagan

Caraquet
35 Acadian
Historical
Village
36
Youghall
Beach

Tracadie

Neguac

Allardville

Pointe
Verte

Bathurst

11

8

Pointe
Escuminac

34 Kouchibouguac
National Park

St. Louis de Kent
Richibucto
Rexton
11

Bass
River

Buctouche

Cocagne

116

Dalhousie

Campbellton

Glenlivet

White Brook

17

St-Quentin

MT. CARLETON
PROV. PK.

Grand River

St. Leonard

8 Grand
Falls

2

Edmundston

7

New Denmark

Plaster Rock

Red Rapids

Limestone

Perth-Andover

105

Bath

Juniper

Florenceville

Doaktown

108

107

Boiestown

Lake

Wayerton

Newcastle

Renous

Blackville

Rogersville

Chatham

Colette

Miramichi
Bay

CANADA
USA

MAINE

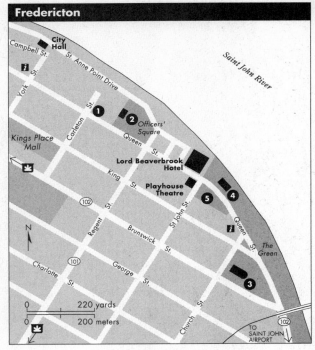

Fredericton's streets are shaded by leafy plumes of ancient
elms. Downtown Queen Street runs parallel with the river, and
its blocks enclose historic sites and attractions. Most major
sites are within walking distance.

● The **Military Compound** (including Officer's Quarters, parade
grounds, Guard House, and Soldiers' Barracks) extends two
blocks along Queen Street. The buildings have been restored
and are partly open to the public. Redcoats stand guard and
act as guides; in summer a changing-of-the-guard ceremony
takes place at 11 and 7. *Queen St. at Carleton St., tel. 506/453–
3747. Admission free. Open June 15–Labor Day, Sat.–Thurs.
10–5, Fri. 10–9. Closed Labor Day–June 14.*

Within the Military Compound, on the corner of Queen and
Carleton streets, stands the John Thurston Clark Building—
an outstanding example of Second Empire architecture. On the
main floor is the **National Exhibition Centre.** You'll have fun
with the scintillating displays of works by local and regional
artists and artisans. Upstairs you'll find the Sports Hall of
Fame, which celebrates the surprising array of locals who have
made sports history, most notably, Ron Turcotte, who won
horse racing's Triple Crown on the immortal Secretariat. The
Hall of Fame's collection of original charcoal portraits of honored members is the largest of its kind in Canada. *503 Queen
St., tel. 506/453–3747. Admission free. Both attractions open
May 1–Labor Day, Sat.–Thurs. 10–5, Fri. 10–9; after Labor
Day–Apr. 30, Tues.–Fri. noon–4:30, Sat. 10–5, Sun. 1–5.*

2 Officer's Quarters houses the **York-Sunbury Museum,** a living picture of the community from the time when only natives inhabited the area, through the pioneer days, to the immediate past. It also contains the shellacked remains of one of Fredericton's legends, the puzzling Coleman Frog. This giant frog, allegedly discovered in nearby Killarney Lake by late hotelier Fred Coleman, supposedly weighed 42 pounds soaking wet at the time of its death (by a dynamite charge set by unorthodox fishermen). Coleman had the frog stuffed and displayed it for years in the lobby of his hotel. Take a look and judge for yourself—the frog just keeps on smiling. *Officer's Sq., Queen St., tel. 506/455–6041. Admission: $1 adults, 50¢ senior citizens and students, $2.50 families. Open May 1–Labor Day, Mon.–Sat. 10–6 (July and Aug., Tues. and Thurs. 10–9 and Sun. noon–6); Labor Day–mid-Oct., weekdays 9–5, Sat. noon–4; mid-Oct.–Apr., Mon., Wed., Fri. 11–3 or by appointment.*

Just a block or so east along the same street, at the intersection where Queen Street becomes Waterloo Row, you'll come to the **3** **Christ Church Cathedral,** one of Fredericton's prides. Completed in 1853, the gray stone building is an excellent example of decorated Gothic architecture and the first new cathedral foundation built on British soil since the Norman Conquest. Inside you'll see a clock known as "Big Ben's little brother," the test-run for London's famous timepiece, designed by Lord Grimthorpe.

The late Lord Beaverbrook, former New Brunswick resident and multimillionaire British peer and newspaper magnate, showered gifts upon his native province. Near the cathedral **4** you'll find the **Beaverbrook Art Gallery,** displaying works by many of New Brunswick's noted artists. Salvador Dali's gigantic canvas *Santiago el Grande* is worth more than a passing glance. There are also canvases by Reynolds, Turner, Hogarth, Gainsborough, the Canadian Group of Seven, and even Andy Warhol. The gallery has the largest collection in any institution of the works of Cornelius Krieghoff, famed Canadian landscape painter of the early 1800s. *703 Queen St., tel. 506/458–8545. Admission: $3 adults, $2 senior citizens, $1 students. Open July–Aug., Sun. and Mon. noon–8, Tues. and Wed. 10–8, Thurs.–Sat. 10–5; in fall and winter, Tues.–Sat. 10–5, Sun.–Mon. noon–5.*

Beside the gallery sits **The Playhouse** (686 Queen St., tel. 506/458–8344), a gift of the Beaverbrook and Dunn Foundation to the city and province. It is the home of the professional **Theatre New Brunswick,** whose major season runs from September through May.

5 Directly across the street from the gallery is the 1880 **Provincial Legislature.** In its library, past the freestanding spiral staircase, is a rare copy of the Domesday Book, the Western world's first census, commissioned by William the Conqueror in 1085. You must ask to see the piece, however. Also to be found here is a four-volume 1834 set of the priceless king-size Audubon bird books, more than 3 feet high, containing 435 hand-colored pictures. *Queen St., tel. 506/453–2527. Admission free. Legislature tours: mid-June–Labor Day, daily 9–9; early Sept.–mid-June, weekdays 9–4. Library open 8:15–4:30 in summer, 8:15–5 Sept.–June.*

Continue east on Waterloo Row (Rte. 102), turn south at University Avenue to the **University of New Brunswick** campus. Be prepared to climb—the buildings are scattered over a fairly steep hill. The college was established in 1785—ancient by Canadian standards—and was originally called the College of New Brunswick, and later Kings College. Its Old Arts Building is the oldest university structure still in use in the country.

Tour 2: The Saint John River Valley to Saint John

To understand New Brunswick's background and history, visit
❻ Kings Landing Historical Settlement, located about 30 kilometers (23 miles) west of Fredericton on the Trans-Canada Highway. This reconstructed village—more than 60 buildings, including homes, inn, forge, store, church, school, working farms, and sawmill—illustrates life in the central Saint John River valley between 1790 and 1900. Winding country lanes, creaking wagons, old houses, and freshly baked bread pull you back a century or more. The costumed staff is friendly and informative. The Tap Room of Kings Head Inn is a congenial spot to try a draft of cold beer or a mug of frosty cider; the restaurant upstairs serves tasty, old-fashioned traveler's fare. After a hearty meal of King George III's roast beef or Mrs. Long's chicken vegetable pie, drop by the General Store. It's the heart of the community and the genial storekeeper makes everyone feel welcome. *Box 522, Fredericton, tel. 506/363–5090. Admission: $7.50 adults, $5 senior citizens, $4 students, children under 6 free, $15 families. Other discounts and group rates available. Open June–mid-Oct., daily 10–6.*

The Saint John River forms 120 kilometers (75 miles) of the border with Maine and rolls down to Saint John, New Brunswick's largest, and Canada's oldest, city. Gentle hills of rich farmland and the blue sweep of the water make this a pretty drive. The Trans-Canada Highway (Highway 2) follows the banks of the river for most of its winding, 403-kilometer (250-mile) course.

At the northern end of the valley, near the border with Québec, you will find yourself in the mythical Republic of Madawaska. In the early 1800s the narrow wedge of land was coveted by Québec on one side and New Brunswick on the other; the United States claimed it as well. Seeking to retain it for New Brunswick, Governor Sir Thomas Carleton found it easy to settle with Québec. He rolled dice all night with the governor of British North America at Québec, who happened to be his brother. Sir Thomas won at dawn—by one point. Settling with the Americans was more difficult. The border had always been disputed, and even the lumbermen engaged in combat. Finally, in 1842, the British flag was hoisted over Madawaska county. One old-timer, tired of being asked to which country he belonged, replied, "I am a citizen of the Republic of Madawaska." So began the republic, which exists today with its own flag (an independent eagle on a field of white) and a coat of arms.

❼ Edmundston, the unofficial capital of Madawaska, has always depended on the wealth of the deep forest around it. Even today, Edmundston looks to the Fraser Company pulp mills as the major source of employment. It was in these woods that the legend of Paul Bunyan was born. Tales spread to Maine and even to the West Coast. The Foire Brayonne festival, held annually during the last week of July, is proud to claim the title of the biggest festival outside of Québec's Winter Carnival. It is certainly one of the most lively and vibrant cultural events in New Brunswick, offering prestigious concerts by acclaimed artists as well as local musicians and entertainers who enliven the Arts & Crafts Square. In winter the whole province enjoys skiing on the slopes of Mt. Farlagne.

8 About 50 kilometers (30 miles) downriver, at **Grand Falls,** the Saint John throws itself over a high cliff, squeezes through a narrow rocky gorge, and emerges as a wider river. The result is a magnificent cascade, whose force has worn strange round wells in the rocky bed—some as much as 16 feet in circumference and 30 feet deep. Take the Gorge Walk ($2 adults, $1 children, $5 families) where you'll see the holes and the magnificent stream up close. According to Indian legend, a young maiden named Malabeam led her Iroquois captors to their deaths over the foaming cataract rather than guide them to her village. Local history is depicted at the **Grand Falls Historical Museum.** *209 Sheriff St., no phone. Admission free. Open July–Aug., Mon.–Sat. 9–5, Sun. 2–5; Sept.–June, by appointment.*

Although Grand Falls is largely French-speaking, English becomes more prevalent as you move down the Saint John River valley. Stop in **Florenceville** for a look at the small but reputable Andrew and Laura McCain Gallery, which has launched the career of many a New Brunswick artist.

The Trans-Canada Highway is intriguingly scenic, but if you're looking for less crowded highways and typical small communities, cross the river to Route 105 at Hartland, via the **longest covered bridge** in the world—1,282 feet in length.

If you prefer, stay on the Trans-Canada Highway until you reach the quiet hamlet of **Woodstock** (population 4,911). The town was named for a novel by Sir Walter Scott, and is most lively during its Old Home Week celebrations, in July. The **Old Courthouse** (built in 1833)—once a coaching stop, a social hall, a political meeting place, and the seat of justice for the area— has been carefully restored.

Time Out | Between Woodstock and Meductic, look for good German food at **Heino's Restaurant,** in the John Gyles Motel (junction Route 2 and Trans-Canada Highway).

9 Within the **Mactaquac Provincial Park** is Mactaquac pond, whose existence is attributed to the building of the hydroelectric dam, which has caused the upper Saint John River to flood as far up as Woodstock. Although there are several privately owned campgrounds in the area, cars line up sometimes all night to claim an empty site in the morning. *Hwy. 105 and Mactaquac Dam, tel. 506/363–3011. 300 campsites, supervised recreation, 2 beaches, 2 marinas, 18-hole golf course, and lodge with dining room. Admission: $3.50 per vehicle summer, free in offseason. Open May 15–Sept. 2, 24 hrs; early Sept.–Nov., 8–6; Dec.– mid-May, 8–11.*

From Fredericton to Saint John you have a choice of two routes. Route 7 cuts away from the river to run straight south for its fast 109 kilometers (68 miles). Route 102 leads along the Saint John River through engaging communities. You make your decision at **Oromocto,** the site of the Canadian Armed Forces Base, **Camp Gagetown** (not to be confused with the pretty town of Gagetown farther down river), the largest military base in Canada (Prince Charles completed his helicopter training here). An interesting military museum within the base is open to the public. *Tel. 506/422–2630. Admission free. Open June–Aug., weekdays 9–5, weekends 12–5; Sept.–May, weekdays 9–4, closed weekends.*

⑩ **Gagetown,** one of New Brunswick's pleasant historic communities, bustles with artisans' studios and the summer sailors who tie up at the marina. The gingerbread-trimmed **Tilley House** takes you back to Canada's beginnings. Once the home of Sir Leonard Tilley, one of the Fathers of Confederation, it is now home of the Queens County Museum. *Front St., tel. 506/488–2966. Admission: $1 adults, 25¢ students. Open June–Sept. 15, daily 10–5.*

From Gagetown you can ferry to Jemseg and continue to **Grand Lake Provincial Park** (tel. 506/385–2919), which offers freshwater swimming off sandy beaches. At Evandale you can ferry to Belleisle Bay and the beautiful **Kingston Peninsula,** with its mossy Loyalist graveyards and pretty churches.

As you travel south you'll begin to get a feeling for how old New ⑪ Brunswick really is, and nowhere more so than in **Saint John.** It was the first incorporated city in Canada and has that weather–beaten quality common to so many antique seaport communities. Although sometimes termed a blue-collar town because so many of its residents work for Irving Oil, its genteel Loyalist heritage lingers; you sense it in its grand old buildings, the ladies' teas at the old Union Club, and the beautifully restored downtown harbor district.

The city has spawned many of the province's major artists— Jack Humphrey, Millar Brittain, Fred Ross—along with such Hollywood notables as Louis B. Mayer, Donald Sutherland, and Walter Pidgeon. There's also a large Irish population that emerges in a jubilant Irish Festival every March. In July costumed residents re-enact the landing of the Loyalists during Saint John's Loyalist Days.

In 1604 two Frenchmen, Samuel de Champlain and Sieur de Monts, landed here on St. John the Baptist Day to trade with the natives. Nearly two centuries later, in May of 1785, 3,000 Loyalists escaping from the Revolutionary War poured off a ship to found a city amid the rocks and forests. From those beginnings Saint John has emerged as a thriving industrial port.

Up until a few years ago the buildings around Saint John's waterfront huddled together in forlorn dilapidation, their facades crumbling and blurred by a century of grime. A recent surge of civic pride sparked a major renovation project that reclaimed old warehouses as part of an enchanting waterfront development.

Numbers in the margin correspond to points of interest on the Downtown Saint John and Greater Saint John maps.

You can easily explore Saint John's town center and harbor ⑫ area on foot. Get your bearings on **King Street,** the town's old main street, whose sidewalks are paved with red brick and lit

13 with old-fashioned lamps. King Street connects **Market Slip** on the waterfront with King Square at the center of town.

14 At Market Slip, where the Loyalists landed in 1783, and the adjoining **Market Square** you can while away a morning among the shops, historic displays, and cafés (some with outdoor dining in summer). Market Slip is the site of **Barbour's General Store** (tel. 506/658–2939), a fully stocked 19th-century shop redolent of the past: Inside, the scents of tobacco, pickles, smoked fish, and peppermint sticks mingle with the tangy, unforgettable aroma of dulse, the edible seaweed. Beside the store is a 19th-century red schoolhouse, now a tourist information center. Skywalks and underground passages lead from Market Square to City Hall, the new Delta Hotel, and Brunswick Square, an adjoining shopping mall.

15 Stroll up King Street to Germain Street, turn left, and walk up to the block-long **Old City Market**, built in 1876, which offers a variety of temptations, including red fresh-cooked lobster, great cheeses, dulse, and other inexpensive snacking along with much friendly chatter.

16 The imposing **Old Loyalist House**, built in 1810 by Daniel David Merritt, a wealthy Loyalist merchant, is distinguished by its authentic period furniture and eight fireplaces. *120 Union St., tel. 506/652–3590. Admission: $2 adults, 25¢ children. Open Mon.–Sat. 10–5, Sun. 2–5, or by appointment.*

17 **18** Follow Union Street away from the harbor to Sydney Street and turn right to visit the **Old Loyalist Burial Grounds.** At one corner, in adjacent **King Square,** you'll find a strange mass of metal on the ground. It is actually a great lump of melted stock from a neighboring hardware store that was demolished in Saint John's Great Fire of 1877, in which 115 buildings were destroyed.

19 At the corner of King and Sydney streets is the **Old Courthouse.** Its spiral staircase, built of tons of unsupported stone, ascends seemingly by miracle for three stories.

20 Walk around the south side of King Square to visit **Trinity Church** (115 Charlotte St., tel. 506/693–8558), which dates from 1877, when it was rebuilt after the great fire. Inside, over the west door, note the coat of arms—a symbol of the monarchy—rescued from the council chamber of the colony at Massachusetts Bay. The coat of arms was deemed a worthy refugee and given a place of honor in the church.

21 If you have a car, drive north from downtown on Prince William Street to Main Street; in a park on your right you'll find **Fort Howe** (Rockland Road and Magazine Street). The reconstructed fortress sits atop a cliff overlooking the harbor and affords fine views from its walls. It is believed to be near the site of Fort LaTour, a French stronghold resolutely defended by Madame La Tour from her absent husband's fur-trading rival. Finally surrendering on the condition that the lives of her men would be spared, the unfortunate woman was betrayed and forced to watch them all put to death. She died shortly after, of a broken heart it is said—a romantic fate befitting her former profession as star of the Paris stage.

22 Main Street soon crosses Douglas Avenue; turn left to reach two of the city's most notable attractions. First is the **New**

Brunswick Museum, the first museum to be built in Canada, and still recognized as one of the best of its size. Behind its neoclassical facade, supported by Corinthian columns, are exhibits reflecting the history, culture, and spirit of New Brunswick. It displays its own fine arts, natural science, marine history, and immense collection of historical artifacts. Also, many traveling exhibits of universal historic and cultural scope are presented here. *277 Douglas Ave., tel. 506/658–1842. Admission: $2 adults, 50¢ students, senior citizens and children under 6 free, families $4. Group tours can be arranged. Open daily 10–5. Closed only on Good Friday and Christmas Day.*

㉓ Continue west on Douglas Avenue to reach the **Reversing Falls Rapids,** touted by all tourist brochures as a sight no one should miss. Actually, you *should* see it, though less for its beauty than its interest: It's a series of rapids and whirlpools at which, twice a day, the strong Fundy Tides attempt to push the river water back upstream. When the tide ebbs, the river once again pours over the rock ledges and the rapids appear to reverse themselves. A pulp mill on the bank is less scenic, and the stench it occasionally sends out is one of the less-than-charming parts of a visit. To learn more about the phenomenon, see the excellent free film shown in the tourist information center on the site.

㉔ **Cherry Brook Zoo,** at the very northern tip of Rockwood Park, houses Siberian tigers, wildebeest, and other exotic species. *Tel. 506/634–1440. Open daily 10–dusk. $3.25 adults, $2.25 senior citizens and students, $1.40 pre-schoolers, children under 2 free. Tour rates available.*

Greater Saint John

Cross the river on Bridge Road to **West Saint John.** Make a
right on Lancaster Avenue and proceed to Charlotte Street,
where you can't miss the **Carleton Martello Tower.** Like Fort
Howe, this is a great place to survey the harbor. The tower was
built in 1810 as a precaution against American attack. Costumed guides point out 8-foot-thick walls and pose for photographs. *Charlotte Ext. W, tel. 506/636–4011. Admission free.
Open June 1–mid-Oct., daily 9–5.*

Tour 3: The Fundy Coast

*Numbers in the margin correspond to points of interest on the
New Brunswick map.*

Bordering the chilly and powerful tidal Bay of Fundy is some
of New Brunswick's loveliest coastline. A tour of the region will
take you from the border town of St. Stephen, through tiny
fishing villages and past rocky coves, to Fundy National Park,
where the world's most extreme tides rise and fall twice daily.
St. Stephen, on the Maine border, is a mecca for chocoholics,
who converge on the small town during the Chocolate Festival
held the first week in August. Choctails and chocolate pud-
dings, cakes, and complete meals should come as no surprise
when you realize that it was here that the chocolate bar was
invented. Sample Ganong's famed hand-dipped chocolates at
the factory store, **The Ganong Chocolatier.** *73 Milltown Blvd.,
tel. 506/465–5611. Open July–Aug., weekdays 9–8, Sat. 9–5, Sun.
noon–5; Sept.–Dec., daily 9–5; Jan.–mid-May, Mon.–Sat. 9–5.
Closed Dec. 25, Jan. 1.*

A small side trip along Ledge Road will take you to **Crocker Hill Studios,** on the banks of the St. Croix River. Walk down the garden path to the artist's studio with its paintings and carved decoys. It is surrounded by a fragrant, tranquil herb garden. Relax in one of the comfortable garden benches and watch the golfers across the river in the state of Maine. *Tel. 506/466–4251. Admission: $3 adults. Open June–Sept., daily 10–5; Oct.–June by appointment.*

27 Take Route 127 off Route 1 to **St. Andrews-by-the-Sea,** one of North America's prettiest and least-spoiled resort towns. Long the summer place of the affluent (mansions ring the town), St. Andrews retains its year-round population of fishermen, and little has changed in the past two centuries. Of the town's 550 buildings 280 were erected before 1880; 14 have survived from the 1700s. Some Loyalists brought their homes with them piece by piece from Castine, Maine, across the bay, when the war didn't go their way.

Pick up a walking-tour map at the tourist information center on Water Street and follow it through the pleasant streets. Particular gems are the **Court House** and **Greenock Church.** The church owes its existence to a remark someone made at an 1822 dinner party about the "poor" Presbyterians not having a church of their own. Captain Christopher Scott, who took exception to the slur, spared no expense on the building, which is decorated with a carving of a green oak tree in honor of Scott's birthplace, Greenock, Scotland. Also along Water Street are numerous antiques shops and artists' studios. The porch of the **Shiretown Inn** (218 Water St., tel. 506/529–8877) is a perfect place for a snack and a view.

The **Ross Memorial Museum** features a fine antiques collection. *188 Montague St., tel. 506/529–3906. Admission free. Open late May–early Oct., Mon.–Sat. 10–4:30, Sun. (July–Sept.) 1:30–4:30.*

A drive up Joe's Point Road takes you to the **Huntsman Aquarium and Museum,** which houses marine life and displays. *Brandy Cove Rd., tel. 506/529–8895. Admission: $4 adults, $3.50 senior citizens, $2.75 children under 18, children under 4 free; families $10.70. Open May–June, daily 10–4:30; July–Aug., daily 10–6; Sept.–mid-Oct., daily 10–4:30. Closed mid-Oct–Apr.*

Back on Route 1 is **St. George,** a pretty town with some excellent bed-and-breakfasts, one of the oldest Protestant graveyards in Canada, and a fish ladder running up the side of a dam.

The Fundy Isles—Grand Manan, Deer Island, and Campobello—are havens of peace that have lured harried mainlanders for generations. **Grand Manan Island,** largest of the three, **28** is also farthest away (about two hours by car-ferry from Black's Harbour); you might see spouting whales, sunning seals, or a rare puffin on the way. Circular herring weirs dot the coastal water, and fish sheds and smokehouses lie beside long wharfs that reach out to bobbing fishing boats. Place names are romantic—Swallowtail, Southern Head, Seven Days Work, and Dark Harbour. It's easy to get around—only about 32 kilometers (20 miles) of road lead from the lighthouse at Southern Head to the one at Northern Head. A living encyclopedia of birds, Grand Manan attracted John James Audubon in 1831. The puffin is the island's symbol. Whale-watching expeditions can be booked at the Marathon Hotel and the Compass Rose, and scuba diving to old wrecks is popular.

㉙ Connected to Lubec, Maine, by an international bridge, **Campobello Island** may be approached from the other side by toll ferry from Deer Island. Neatly manicured, preening itself in the bay, Campobello Island has always had a special appeal to the wealthy and the famous. It was here that the Roosevelt family spent their summers. The home of Franklin Delano Roosevelt, former president of the United States, is now maintained as a lovely museum in his honor. Located in the center of Roosevelt International Park, a joint project of the Canadian and American governments, **President Roosevelt's home** was the setting for the movie *Sunrise at Campobello. Roosevelt Park Rd., tel. 506/752–2922. Admission free. House open late May-mid-Oct., daily 10–6; grounds open year-round.*

The island's **Herring Cove Provincial Park** has camping facilities and a nine-hole golf course.

㉚ An easy, 20-minute, free ferry ride from Letete near St. George brings you to the relaxing **Deer Island.** You'll enjoy exploring the fishing wharves such as those at **Chocolate Cove.** The world's largest lobster pound is at **Northern Harbour,** and you can walk through a small nature park at **Deer Point** while waiting for the toll ferry to nearby Campobello. If you listen carefully, you may be able to hear the sighing and snorting of "the Old Sow," the second largest whirlpool in the world. If you can't hear it, you'll be able to see it, just a few feet off-shore. Exploring the island takes only a few hours; it's 12 kilometers (7½ miles) long, varying in width from almost 5 kilometers (3 miles) to a few hundred feet at some points.

After returning from the Fundy Isles to the mainland, proceed east along coastal Route 1. If you have the time, dip down to the peaceful, hidden fishing villages of **Maces Bay, Dipper,** and **Chance Harbour,** all much the same as they have been for centuries. At Dipper Harbour, you can rent sea kayaks and canoes, arrange for whale watching and deep-sea fishing (Eastern Outdoors Marine, tel. 506/634–1530), or buy a lobster roll to munch on while strolling the long sun-warmed wharf.

㉛ Drive east through Saint John along a scenic stretch of Route 1 to Route 114, which angles south to the 129-square-kilometer (80-square-mile) **Fundy National Park.** Stand on a sandstone ledge above a dark-sand beach and watch the bay's phenomenal tide rise or fall. *Box 40, Alma E0A 1B0, tel. 506/887–2000. Admission: $5 per car in summer; free rest of the year.*

Alma is the small seaside town that services the national park. Here you'll find great lobster and the local specialty, sticky buns. Past Alma, the coast road to Moncton winds by covered bridges and along rocky coasts, past photogenic spots such as the wild driftwood-cluttered beach at **Cape Enragé** and **Hopewell Cape,** home of the famous giant flowerpots, rock formations carved by the Fundy Tides.

Tour 4: Moncton and the Acadian Peninsula

㉜ A friendly town, often called the Gateway to Acadia because of its mix of English and French and its proximity to the Acadian shore, **Moncton** has a pretty downtown where wisely placed malls do a booming business.

This city has long touted two natural attractions, the Tidal Bore and the Magnetic Hill. You may be disappointed if you've read too much tourist hype. In days gone by, before the harbor mouth filled with silt, the **Tidal Bore** was indeed an incredible sight, a high wall of water that surged in through the narrow opening of the river to fill red-mud banks to the brim. It still moves up the river, and the moving wave is worth waiting for, but it's nowhere near as lofty as it used to be, except sometimes in the spring when the tides are very high. Bore Park on Main Street is the best vantage point; viewing times are posted there.

❸❸ **Magnetic Hill,** north of town just off the Trans-Canada Highway, creates a bizarre optical illusion. If you park your car in neutral at the designated spot, you'll seem to be coasting up hill without power. An excellent family water-theme park, **Magic Mountain,** is adjacent to the hill. *On Magnetic Hill, tel. 506/857–9283. Admission: $17.25 adults/$10.50 afternoon; $11.75 children under 12 and senior citizens/$9.50 afternoon; $53.25 for a family of 4 for a full day. Open mid-June–July and mid-Aug.–Labor Day, daily 10–6; July–mid-Aug. 10–8.*

Among Moncton's notable man-made attractions is the **Acadian Museum,** at the University of Moncton, whose remarkable collection of artifacts reflects 300 years of Acadian life in New Brunswick. *Clement Cormier Bldg., University of Moncton, tel. 506/858–4088. Admission free. Open June–Sept., weekdays 10–5, weekends 1–5; Oct.–May, Tues.–Fri. 1–4:30, weekends 1–4. Closed Mon., holidays.*

Turn northeast along the coast from Moncton to the salty shores of unique Acadian communities such as **Shediac, Cocagne, Buctouche,** and **Rexton,** where you'll find long warm sand dunes, lobster feeds, lighthouses, weathered wharves, and sea-stained churches. The friendliness of the Acadians makes this trip a joy, and the white, dune-edged beaches of
❸❹ **Kouchibouguac National Park** are among the finest on the continent. *Kent County, tel. 506/876–2443. Admission: $5 per vehicle, senior citizen $4. Day and annual passes available. Open year-round.*

Route 11 continues north to the Miramichi River and the fabled **Miramichi region** of lumberjacks, fishermen, and "come all ye's." Celebrated for its salmon rivers and the ebullient nature of its residents (Scottish, English, Irish, and a smattering of French and Indian), this is a land of stories, folklore, and lumber kings. Pleasant towns and villages of sturdy wood homes dot the banks of Miramichi Bay at **Chatham** and **Newcastle** (where the politician and British media mogul Lord Beaverbrook grew up and is buried). At **Doaktown** (south of Newcastle on Route 8), the **Miramichi Salmon Museum** (tel. 506/365–7787) provides a look at the endangered Atlantic salmon and at life in noted fishing camps along the rivers.

The **Woodmen's Museum** of Boiestown (in the exact center of the province), with artifacts that date from the 1700s to the present, is housed in what looks like two giant logs set on more than 60 acres of land. The museum portrays a lumberman's life through its displays, but its tranquil grounds are excuse enough to visit. Picnic facilities and camping sites are also available. *Rte 8, Boiestown, tel. 506/369–7214. Admission: $5 adults,*

$4 senior citizens, $2 children, $12 families. Open June–mid-Sept., daily 10–5:30.

35 Return to Newcastle and swing north and east on Route 11 to **Caraquet,** on the Acadian Peninsula. The town is perched along the Baie des Chaleurs, with Québec's Gaspé Peninsula beckoning across the inlet.

36 The *pièce de résistance* of the Acadian Peninsula is, without doubt, the **Acadian Historical Village,** 10 kilometers (6 miles) west of Caraquet on Route 11, near Grand Anse. As Kings Landing depicts the early English settlement, this village recreates an early Acadian community between 1780 and 1890. Summer days are wonderfully peaceful. A chapel bell tolls, ducks waddle and quack under a footbridge, wagons creak, and the smell of hearty cooking wafts from cottage doors. Costumed staff act as guides, and a restaurant serves old-Acadian dishes. *Tel. 506/727–3467. Admission: $7.50 adults, $4.25 children under 18, $15 families. Open June–Aug., daily 10–6; Sept., daily 10–5.*

Shopping

New Brunswick is famous for its crafts, and the *Directory of New Brunswick Craftsmen & Craft Shops* provides comprehensive listings of potters, weavers, glassblowers, jewelers, and carvers throughout the province. Get a copy from Tourism New Brunswick (Box 6000, Fredericton, E3B 5H1, tel. 800/561–0123).

Fredericton Mammoth crafts markets are held occasionally in town and every Labor Day weekend in Mactaquac Park. **Aitkens Pewter** (81 Regent St.) offers beautiful pewter hollowware, goblets, belt buckles, and jewelry. **Shades of Light Studio and Gift Shop** (28 Regent St.) features stained glass and other local crafts. **Mulhouse Country Classics,** about 2 kilometers (1 mile) from downtown in Lower St. Marys across the river on the north side, is a gem for crafts and handmade furniture.

Excellent men's shoes can be bought at **Hartt's Shoe Factory** (York St.); **The Linen Closet** (King St.) sells laces, exquisite bedding, and Victorian nightgowns.

Gagetown **Flo Grieg's** on Front Street carries superior pottery. **Claremont House B&B,** on Tilley Road, displays unusual batik items and copper engravings. **Loomcrofters,** just off Main Street, is a good choice for handwoven items.

Moncton Five spacious malls and numerous pockets of shops in downtown Moncton make it one of the best places to shop in New Brunswick. Among the crafts to look for are the yarn portraits of La Sagouine, "the old sage" of Buctouche. The sayings of the old Acadian woman as she does her daily chores were made famous in Antonine Maillet's novel *La Sagouine.*

St-Andrews-by-the-Sea This "veddy British" town has many places to buy English and New Brunswick woolens, English bone china, and marvelous wool yarn, among them **The Sea Captain's Loft** (Water St.) and **Cottage Craft** (Town Sq.). Antiques and rare and out-of-print books are sold at the **Pansy Patch** (Carleton St.), a stunning old home across from the Algonquin Hotel. On Water Street, the main shopping strip, head to **Tom Smith's Studio** (Water St.) for highly regarded oriental Raku pottery.

Saint John The little antiques stores and crafts shops sprinkled around the downtown area provide the best shopping in Saint John. **Prince William Street** has interesting browsing in antiques shops and crafts boutiques; **House of Tara** (72 Prince William St.) is wonderful for fine Irish linens and woolens. Airy **Brunswick Square** and **Market Square** in the new harborfront have many top-quality boutiques. **Old City Market,** between Charlotte and Germain streets, bustles six days a week and always stocks delicious local specialties, such as maple syrup and lobster.

St. Leonard A visit to the studio and store of the **Madawaska Weavers** (Main St.), whose handwoven items are known the world over, is a must. Handsome skirts, stoles, and ties are some of the items on sale.

Sports and Fitness

Bicycling Byroads, lanes, and rolling secondary highways run through small towns, along the ocean, and into the forest. Set out on your own; or try a guided adventure with a specialist tour operator such as **Covered Bridge Bicycle Tours** (Dept. F, Box 693, Main Post Office, Saint John, E2L 4B3, tel. 506/849–9028). Bed-and-breakfasts frequently have bicycles for hire and the Department of Economic Development and Tourism has listings and free cycling maps (*See* Important Addresses and Numbers in Essential Information, *above*). Information on competitive cycling and races is available from **Velo New Brunswick** (457 Chartersville Rd., Dieppe, NB, E1A 5H1).

Fishing Dotted with freshwater lakes, crisscrossed with fish-laden rivers, and bordered by 1,129 kilometers (700 miles) of seacoast, this province is one of Canada's natural treasures. Sportspeople are drawn by the excellent bass fishing and the world-famous salmon rivers such as the Miramichi, the Restigouche, and the Nashwaak. Commercial fishermen often take visitors line fishing for ground fish. An annual freshwater fishing license for out-of-province visitors costs $25 for three days; $50 for seven days; $100 for the season (plus GST). For more information, call New Brunswick Fish and Wildlife (tel. 506/453–2440).

Golf There are 36 excellent golf courses in New Brunswick—many, such as the **Algonquin Golf Club** (tel. 506/529–3062) in St. Andrews and the **Gowan Brae Golf and Country Club** (tel. 506/546–2707) in Bathurst, with sparkling views of the sea. The **Fundy National Park Golf Club** (tel. 506/887–2970) at Alma is nestled near cliffs overlooking the restless Bay of Fundy; deer grazing on the course are one of its hazards. Greens fees run about $20–$25, $15 for some nine-hole courses; and visitors are generally welcome. For a list of golf courses, ask for the free "New Brunswick Travel Guide" from the Department of Economic Development and Tourism (Box 6000, Fredericton, E3B 5H1).

Hiking Rocky coastline and inland highland trails offer hiking opportunities for both experienced and casual trekkers. **East Coast Expeditions** (Box 6713, Station A, Saint John, E2L 4S2, tel. 506/658–1906) and **Miramichi Four Seasons Outfitters** (Box

705, RR 2, Newcastle, E1V 3L9, tel. 506/622–0089) offer guided hiking tours. For trail information, call Eric Hadley, of **New Brunswick Trails Club,** at the Department of Natural Resources and Energy (tel. 506/453–2883).

Skiing
Cross-country
A perfect province for cross-country skiing, New Brunswick offers groomed trails at provincial and national parks such as Mactaquac Provincial Park near Fredericton, Fundy National Park in Alma, and Kouchibouguac National Park between Moncton and Bathurst. Many communities and small hotels offer groomed trails, but it's also possible to set off on your own in almost every section of the province.

Downhill
New Brunswick downhill ski areas usually operate from mid-December through April. They include **Crabbe Mountain Winter Park** (tel. 506/463–8311) in Lower Hainesville (near Fredericton); **Sugarloaf Provincial Park** (tel. 506/789–2366) in Campbellton, northern New Brunswick; **Mont Farlagne** (tel. 506/735–8401) in St. Jacques, near Edmundston; **Poley Mountain Ski Area** (tel. 506/433–3230) in Sussex; and **Silverwood Winter Park** (tel. 506/450–3380) in Fredericton.

Tennis
Courts are available in most city and town parks. Most are free. Many resorts and hotels have courts.

Water Sports
Canoeing and Kayaking
Kayaking along the coasts of Fundy and Chaleur has become very popular. A list of canoe and kayak liveries is available from Department of Economic Development and Tourism (Box 6000, Fredericton, E3B 5H1). For canoes, try **A to Z Rentals** (128 Prospect St., tel. 506/452–9758) in Fredericton and in St. John (535 Rothesay, tel. 506/633–1919). Outfitters such as **Fundy Marine** (Brunswick Square, Saint John, tel. 506/634–1530) offer single and double kayaks, lessons, and tours.

Sailing
Sailboats can be chartered in many areas including **Fundy Yacht Sales and Charter** (Dipper Harbour, Rte. 2, Lepreau, E0G 2H0, tel. 506/659–2769). Information on charters is available from **The New Brunswick Sailing Association** (Box 4005, Station B, Saint John, E2M 5E6).

Rowing
Shells can be rented at the **Kennebecasis Club** (tel. 506/849–9910) in Rothesay, and at the **Aquatic Center** (tel. 506/458–5513) in Fredericton.

Whale watching
One New Brunswick experience that is difficult to forget is the sighting of a huge humpback, right whale, finback, or minke. Whale-watching tours are available from a number of operators such as **Ocean Search** (Marathon Inn, North Head, Grand Manan, tel. 506/662–8488) and **West Isles World** (Lambertville, Deer Island, tel. 506/747–2946). **Cline Marine Tours** (tel. 506/529–2287) in St. Andrews and Deer Island offers whale-watching, as well as scenic, tours. **Chaleur Phantom** (tel. 506/684–4722) in Dalhousie combines scenic tours to observe marine life in the calmer waters around the islands with deep-sea fishing excursions.

Dining and Lodging

Dining

Although there are not a lot of choices for fine dining in New Brunswick, a few good restaurants exist, and families will find plenty of quality food in many outlets. A number of gourmet restaurants have popped up in Saint John in recent years—so there is hope that the dining scene will improve throughout the province.

In the spring, once the ice has left streams and rivers, a provincial delicacy–the fiddlehead fern–is picked from the shores. Eaten as a vegetable (boiled, drenched with lemon, butter, salt, and pepper), fiddleheads have something of an artichoke taste and go well with spring's bony fish, shad, and gaspereaux. Silver salmon, once a spring staple when set nets were allowed, is still available but quite costly. Most salmon served in restaurants is farm reared. Lobster, a favorite maritime dish, is available in most restaurants, but is not always cheap. The custom of the residents is to buy it fresh from the fishermen or shore outlets and devour it in huge quantities. Because of the cool waters, shellfish is especially tasty. Look for oysters, scallops, clams, crab, and mussels. And be sure to try the purple seaweed called dulse that the residents eat like potato chips. To be truly authentic, accompany any New Brunswick–style feast with hearty Moosehead beer, brewed in Saint John and one of the province's well-known exports.

Dress is casual everywhere except at the Expensive and Very Expensive listings, and, unless noted, no reservations are needed.

Highly recommended restaurants in each price category are indicated by a star ★.

Category	Cost*
Very Expensive	over $40
Expensive	$20–$40
Moderate	$10–$19
Inexpensive	under $10

per person, excluding drinks, service, and 11% sales tax

Lodging

New Brunswick has a number of officially designated Heritage Inns—historically significant establishments built in the last century. Many have antique china and furnishings or other charming touches, and their accommodations run the gamut from elegant to homey.

Hotels and motels in and around Saint John and Fredericton are adequate and friendly. Accommodations in Saint John are at a premium in summer, so reserve ahead to ensure a place to stay.

Highly recommended lodgings in each price category are indicated by a star ★.

Category	Cost*
Expensive	over $60
Moderate	$45–$60
Inexpensive	under $40

*All prices are for a standard double room, excluding 10% service charge.

Campbellton
Dining and Lodging
★

Aylesford Inn. Truly a find, this friendly inn housed in a Victorian mansion near the Québec border and Sugarloaf Provincial Park has guest rooms handsomely furnished with Eastlake and Canadian-pine antiques. Large gardens and verandas offer views of the Restigouche River. Excellent dinners are served to guests (quail and frogs' legs are featured entrées), and full breakfasts are included in the room rate. Nonguests are welcome for afternoon tea. *8 MacMillan Ave., E3N 1E9, tel. 506/759–7672. 7 rooms, 1 with bath. Facilities: dining room, croquet. AE, MC, V. Moderate.*

Campobello Island
Lodging
★

Owen House. Mellow with history, this 200-year-old home was built by Admiral Owen, who fancied himself ruler of the island. Its gracious old rooms have hosted such luminaries as actress Greer Garson, who stayed here (in a room with a fireplace in the bathroom) when filming *Sunrise at Campobello.* Breakfasts are wonderful—pancakes come topped with local berries. *Welshpool, E0G 3H0, tel. 506/752–2977. 9 rooms. V. Moderate.*

Island Club Lodge. Originally a vacation home built by the Adams family (friends of the Roosevelts) around the turn of the century, these three attractive log buildings set on a bluff overlooking the Bay of Fundy have been converted into a modern guest lodge. The 12 available rooms occupy two of the cabins; the third houses the dining room, which specializes in simple but well-prepared local seafood. *Box 16, Welshpool, E0G 3H0, tel. 506/752–2487. 12 rooms. Facilities: restaurant. MC, V. Moderate.*

Caraquet
Dining and Lodging

Hotel Paulin. The word *quaint* really fits this property. There are pretty rooms, a bathroom down the hall, and an excellent small dining room specializing in fresh fish cooked perfectly. *143 Blvd. St. Pierre, tel. 506/727–9981. 10 rooms with shared bath. Facilities: restaurant. MC, V. Inexpensive.*

Deer Island
Dining and Lodging

45th Parallel Motel and Restaurant. Deer Island has only one motel, and it's clean and comfortable. A full breakfast is complimentary, and everything from lobster to pizza is available at the informal restaurant. Pets are welcome. *Fairhaven, E0G 1R0, tel. 506/747–2231. 10 rooms, 3 with kitchenette. Facilities: restaurant. AE, MC, V. Moderate.*

West Isles World B&B. This white frame house overlooks the cove and offers three snug rooms with an informal country feel; the big upstairs bedroom has a water view. The owners will arrange whale-watching cruises for you. A full breakfast is included in the room rate, and other meals are served on request. *Lord's Cove, E0G 2J0, tel. 506/747–2946. 3 rooms, 1 with bath. No credit cards. Moderate.*

Fredericton
Dining

Luna Steakhouse. Specialties include huge Caesar salad, garlic bread, escargots, brochettes, and Italian food. In fine weather you can dine on an outdoor terrace. *168 Dundonald St., tel. 506/455–4020. AE, DC, MC, V. Moderate.*

Bar B Q Barn. Special children's menus and barbecued ribs and chicken are the standards; the blackboard lists plenty of other daily dinner specials, such as salmon, scallops, and chili. This is a popular, attractive spot, great for winding down, and the bar serves fine martinis. *540 Queen St., tel. 506/455–2742. AE, MC, V. Inexpensive–Moderate.*

Pink Pearl. This restaurant features tasty Cantonese food, with exceptional wontons and weekend buffets. *343 Queen St., tel. 506/450–8997. MC, V. Inexpensive.*

Lodging

Howard Johnson Motor Lodge. This HoJo's, located on the north side of the river and at the north end of the Princess Margaret Bridge, has a terrace bar in a pleasant interior courtyard overlooked by balconies from many of the rooms. Guestroom decor is standard for the chain. *Trans-Canada Highway, Box 1414, E3B 5E3, tel. 506/472–0480. 116 rooms. Facilities: restaurant, bar, indoor pool, fitness center, indoor tennis courts. AE, DC, MC, V. Expensive.*

Lord Beaverbrook Hotel. A central location is this modern, seven-story hotel's main attraction, although 1991 renovations spruced things up a bit. Some rooms have Jacuzzis or minibars. The food in the main dining room is forgettable. There is a lively bar downstairs. *659 Queen St., E3B 5A6, tel. 506/455–3371. 163 rooms. Facilities: 1 restaurant, bar, indoor pool, nonsmoking rooms. AE, D, DC, MC, V. Moderate–Expensive.*

Sheraton Inn Fredericton. Brand-new and within walking distance of downtown, this big hotel offers modern rooms with sunset views over the river. *225 Woodstock Rd. Fredericton, E3B 2H8, tel. 506/457–7000. 223 rooms, all with minibars. Facilities: restaurant with outdoor terrace, bar, indoor and outdoor pools. AE, DC, MC, V. Expensive.*

Auberge Wandlyn Inn. Just off the Trans-Canada Highway, this hotel is away from the downtown area but close to three shopping malls, many restaurants, and theaters. The guest rooms are no-frills, but the family-oriented dining room is pretty, and there's a cozy bar. *58 Prospect St. W, Box 214, E3B 4Y9, tel. 506/452–8937. 116 rooms. Facilities: restaurant, bar, indoor and outdoor pools, sauna, hot tub. AE, DC, MC, V. Moderate.*

Carriage House Bed and Breakfast. This heritage mansion has lovely bedrooms. Homemade breakfast is served in the solarium. *230 University Ave., E3B 4H7, tel. 506/452–9924. 7 rooms, 3 with bath. MC, V. Moderate.*

Happy Apple Acres Bed and Breakfast. This B&B offers friendly atmosphere in a country setting. A full breakfast is included in the room rate, and the cooking is excellent. *Highway 105 (4.3 km/7 mi north of Fredericton), R.R. 4, Fredericton, E3B 4X5, tel. 506/458–1819. 3 rooms with bath, whirlpool and sauna. MC, V. Moderate.*

Grand Manan Island
Lodging

Compass Rose. Lovely guest rooms are available in the two old houses that have been combined into this small inn. It's conveniently near the ferry landing, and whale-watching tours can be arranged. Breakfast is included in the room rate. *North Head, E0G 3K0, tel. 506/662–8570. V. Moderate.*

The Marathon Inn. Perched on a hill overlooking the harbor, this gracious mansion built by a sea captain offers guest rooms furnished with antiques. The active bar is noisy, so book a room farthest from the fray. Whale- and bird-watching cruises can be arranged for those wishing to explore. *Box 129, North Head, E0G 2M0, tel. 506/662–8488. 28 rooms, 15 with bath. Facilities: restaurant, bar, pool, tennis. MC, V. Moderate–Expensive.*

Ludlow
Lodging

Pond's Chalet Resort. You'll get a traditional fishing-camp experience here, in a lodge and chalets set among trees overlooking a salmon river. *Ludlow (near Boiestown), E0C 1N0, tel. 506/369–2612. 10 rooms in lodge, 8 camps. Facilities: dining room. AE, DC, MC, V. Moderate.*

Moncton
Dining
★

Cy's Seafood Restaurant. This favorite for seafood, decorated in dark wood and brass, has been serving generous portions for decades. Though renowned for its seafood casserole, the restaurant also offers reliable scallop, shrimp, and lobster dishes. You can see the Tidal Bore from the windows. *170 Main St., tel. 506/857–0032. AE, DC, MC, V. Moderate.*

Fisherman's Paradise. In spite of the enormous dining area, which seats more than 350 people, this restaurant serves memorable à la carte seafood dishes in an atmosphere of candlelight and wood furnishings. The children's menu and down-home specials such as lobster-bake make this a good spot for families. *375 Dieppe Blvd., tel. 506/859–4388. AE, DC, MC, V. Moderate.*

Lodging
★

Hotel Beausejour. Moncton's finest hotel is decorated in Acadian style. The downtown location is convenient. Besides the standard guest rooms, there are some luxury suites. Staff in 18th-century costume lend a pleasant ambience to the main dining room, L'Auberge; the other restaurant is more formal. *750 Main St., tel. 506/854–4344. 317 rooms. Facilities: 2 restaurants, bar, outdoor pool, access to health club. AE, MC, V. Expensive.*

The Crystal Palace. Moncton's newest hotel is unique: There are theme rooms (want to be Ali Baba for a night?) and, for families, an indoor pool and a miniature wonderland of rides, midway stalls, and coin games. Champlain Mall is across the street. *499 Paul St., tel. 506/858–8584. 115 rooms. Facilities: restaurant, indoor pool. AE, DC, MC, V. Moderate–Expensive.*

Newcastle
Lodging

Wharf Inn. Here in Miramichi country, the staff is friendly and the restaurant serves excellent salmon dinners. This low-rise modern building has two wings; guest rooms in the executive wing have extra amenities. *Jane St., tel. 506/622–0302. 70 rooms. Facilities: restaurant, patio lounge, indoor pool. AE, MC, V. Moderate–Expensive.*

Sackville
Lodging
★

Marshlands Inn. In this white clapboard inn, a welcoming double living room with fireplace sets the informal, country atmosphere. Bedrooms are furnished with sleigh beds or four-posters, but they also have modern touches such as air-conditioning and in-room telephones. *Box 1440, E0A 3C0, tel. 506/536–0170. 21 rooms, 14 with bath. Facilities: restaurant. AE, DC, MC, V. Moderate–Expensive.*

St. Andrews
Lodging

Algonquin Hotel. The wraparound veranda of this grand old hotel overlooks wide lawns. Bellmen wear kilts. The dining room is noted for its buffets, and meals can be pleasant here if the staff is in the mood. *Rte. 127, E0G 2X0, tel. 506/529–8823. 243 rooms. Facilities: 3 restaurants (dining room, coffee shop, and veranda), 2 bars, pool, 2 golf courses, tennis. AE, MC, V. Closed winter. Expensive.*

L'Europe. You may be amused by the cheerful decor in this intimate restaurant, in particular the whimsical objets d'art reflecting the tastes of the German owners. The food is European—some French, Swiss, German dishes, and so on, with particular attention given to seafood. All meals are served with delicious homemade Black Forest bread and pâté. *48 King St., E0G 2X0, tel. 506/529–3818. Reservations advised. Open Mother's Day–Sept. Dinner, 6–midnight; closed Mon. V. Expensive.*

★ **Pansy Patch B & B.** Across the street from the Algonquin Hotel is this Norman-style farmhouse, built in 1912, distinguished by a turret and steep roofs. The guest rooms are appointed with antiques and have views of the water. The owners also operate an antiques shop and bookshop on the property. Full breakfast is included in the room rate. *59 Carleton St., E0G 2X0, tel. 506/529–3834. 4 rooms with shared bath. AE, MC, V. Closed mid-Oct.–mid-May. Expensive.*

St. George
Lodging

Granite Town Hotel. Although this hotel was just built in 1991, it nevertheless has an old-country-inn feeling to it. The decor is subtle, with pine and washed-birch woodwork prominent. Light blues and pinks dominate in the rooms. A restaurant is in the works that should be open for the 1994 season. The scenery is pleasant: one side of the building overlooking an apple orchard, the other just atop the bank of the Maguadavic River. A Continental breakfast is served but is not included in the room rate. *15 Main St., E0G 2Y0, tel. 506/755–6415. 32 rooms, 2 with Jacuzzi. AE, D, DC, MC, V. Moderate–Expensive.*

Saint John
Dining
★

La Belle Vie. At one of the province's best restaurants, you'll dine in the drawing rooms of a lovely Second Empire–style mansion, where 19th-century examples of trompe l'oeil adorn the ceilings and fine art graces the walls. The cooking is traditional French; try the lobster bisque. *325 Lancaster Ave., tel. 506/635–1155. Reservations advised. AE, DC, MC, V. Expensive.*

Turn of the Tide. Overlooking the harbor, this large hotel dining room is decorated with antiques. Although the dining is pleasant at all times, the best meal of the week is the Sunday buffet, with a long table full of dishes from the exotic to the tried-and-true. Fill your own crepes for dessert. *Hilton Hotel, Market Sq., tel. 506/693–8484. Reservations advised. AE, DC, MC, V. No lunch Sat. Expensive.*

Mexicali Rosa's. For a franchise, this restaurant has a lot of character. The decor is essentially Santa Fe–style with adobe arches and so forth. The specialty is "Cali-Mex" food, which is heavy on sauces, as opposed to "Tex-Mex," which concentrates more on meats. Guests waiting to be seated can order one of the fine margaritas in the large lounge. The fried chimichangas are with good reason the most popular dish. *88 Prince William St., tel. 506/652–5252. AE, DC, MC, V. Moderate.*

Grannan's. Seafood is featured in this nautically decorated restaurant, and the desserts here are memorable. Dining spills over onto the sidewalk in summer, and there are three lively bars connected to the restaurant. *Market Sq., tel. 506/634–1555. AE, DC, MC, V. No lunch Sun. Inexpensive–Moderate.*

Incredible Edibles. Here you can enjoy down-to-earth food—biscuits, garlic-laden hummus, salads, pastas, and desserts—in cozy rooms or, in summer, on the outdoor terrace. The menu has recently been expanded to include beef, chicken, and crab dishes. You'll get a good cup of coffee here, too. *42 Princess St.,* *tel. 506/633–7554. AE, DC, MC, V. Closed Sun. Inexpensive–Moderate.*

Reggie's. This popular spot near Brunswick Square begins serving breakfast at 6 AM. Later in the day specialties include chowders, bagel burgers, and lobster rolls. The restaurant closes at 6 or 7 PM, so come early if you want dinner. *26 Germain St., tel. 506/657–6270. MC, V. Inexpensive.*

Lodging **Saint John Hilton.** Part of the Market Square complex, the smallest Hilton in the world is furnished in Loyalist decor; guest rooms overlook the harbor or the town. Mellow antiques furnish corners of the dining room and the medieval-style Great Hall, which hosts banquets. Adjoining the 12-story property are shops, restaurants, bars, and a library. *1 Market Sq., E2L 4Z6, tel. 506/693–8484 or 800/361–6140. 197 rooms. Facilities: restaurant, bar, pool. AE, DC, MC, V. Expensive.*

★ **Shadow Lawn Country Inn.** This charming village inn is located in an affluent suburb with tree-lined streets and palatial houses, 10 minutes from Saint John. Tennis, golf, horseback riding, and a yacht club are nearby. The inn has eight old-fashioned bedrooms, some with fireplaces. Besides being open during breakfast (for guests, but not included in the room rate) and Sunday brunch served at 11, the dining room is open to the public for a set-menu dinner by reservation only; specialties include beef Wellington and seafood brioches. Pre-dinner sherry is served in the mahogany-paneled bar. *Box 41, Rothesay Rd., E0G 2W0, tel. 506/847–7539. 8 rooms with bath. DC, MC, V. Moderate–Expensive.*

Shediac
Dining and Lodging **Chez Françoise.** This lovely old mansion with a wraparound veranda has been decorated in Victorian style, with hardwood
★ floors and antiques; an annex across the street contains several guest rooms as well. Front rooms have water views. The dining room, open to the public for lunch and dinner, serves excellent traditional French cuisine with an emphasis on seafood. *93 Main St., tel. 506/532–4233. 10 rooms in main house, 6 with bath; 10 rooms in annex, 4 with bath. Facilities: restaurant. AE, MC, V. Closed Jan. 1–Easter. Inexpensive–Moderate.*

The Arts and Nightlife

The Arts

Theatre New Brunswick performs in the Playhouse in Fredericton (686 Queen St., tel. 506/458–8344) and tours the province. Top musical groups, noted professional singers, and other performers usually appear at the **Aitken Center** on the University of New Brunswick campus, at **Colosseum** in Moncton, and at the **Hilton Trade Center** in Saint John.

Beaverbrook Art Gallery in Fredericton is the province's major gallery, but art exhibitions are also held at the **Aitken Bicentennial Exhibition Center** (ABEC) in Saint John, at **Moncton City Hall,** and at the University of Moncton's **Acadian Museum.**

Nightlife

Fredericton The **Cosmopolitan Club** (King St.) sometimes presents great jazz and also has a back room where a younger crowd hangs out. The **Chestnut Inn,** on York Street, has dining and live country or folk music. Jazz and blues bands occasionally play at **Rye's Deli** (415 King St.), which also features hot-wings and popular Montréal smoked-meat sandwiches.

Saint John Taverns and lounges, usually with music of some kind, provide a lively nightlife. For quiet conversation with a "Play it again, Sam" background, try the **Brigantine,** in the Hilton.

14 Newfoundland and Labrador

By Margaret M.
Kearney
Updated by Peter
Gard

Peter Gard
is a freelance writer
and food critic
and author of
Trails of the Avalon.
He has lived and
traveled throughout
Newfoundland
for 17
years.

Newfoundland was the first place explorers John Cabot (1497) and Gaspar Corte-Real (1500) touched down in the New World. Exactly where they went no one knows, for neither survived a second voyage. But while he was here, Cabot reported that he saw fish in the water so thick you could dip your line in anywhere and catch what you wanted. Within a decade of the explorers' discovery, St. John's had become a crowded harbor. Fishing boats from France, England, Spain, and Portugal vied for a chance to catch Newfoundland's lucrative cod, which was to subsequently shape the province's history and geography.

At one time there were 700 hard-working settlements or "outports" dotting Newfoundland's coast, each devoted to catching, salting, and drying the world's most prolific and useful fish. Today, only about 600 of these settlements survive. Newfoundland's most famous resource has become so scarce that a fishing moratorium was declared in 1992. While the province waits for the cod to return, some 20,000 fishers and processors are going to school instead of going fishing. Still, the waters are busy with boats fishing for lobster, mackerel, herring, caplin, turbot, scallops, shrimp—and cod, too, on the west and south coasts of the island. Don't be shy to walk down to the wharf and find out what's being landed.

Newfoundland and Labrador became part of Canada in 1949. For almost 400 year previous, however, the government had survived perfectly well on its own, until the Great Depression forced its economy to go belly-up. After 40-some years of Confederation with Canada, the economy of the province has improved considerably, but the people are still of independent mind: Newfoundlanders regard themselves as North America's first separatists and have maintained a unique language and life-style and their own customs.

Visitors to Newfoundland find themselves straddling the centuries. Old accents and customs are common in small towns and outports, yet the major cities of St. John's on the east coast and Corner Brook on the west coast are very much part of the 20th century. Regardless of where you visit—an isolated outport or lively Water Street—you're sure to interact with some of the warmest, wittiest people in North America. Strangers have always been welcome in Newfoundland, since the days when locals brought visitors in from out of the cold, warmed them by the fire, and charmingly interrogated them for news of events outside the province.

Before you can shoot the breeze, though, you'll have to acclimate yourself to the language: It's English all right, but provincial dialects are strong and vary from place to place. Newfoundland is one of two provinces in Canada with its own dictionary; Prince Edward Island is the other, but its book has only 873 entries. *The Newfoundland Dictionary* has more than 5,000 words, mostly having to do with fishery, weather, and scenery. To get started, you can practice with the name of the province—it's *New'fun'l'nd*, with the accent on the "land." However, only "livyers" ever get the pronunciation exactly right.

Depending on the time of year you visit, your experiences will be dramatically different. In spring icebergs float down from the north, and fin, pilot, minke, and humpback whales hunt for food along the coast. Their preferred cuisine? Caplin, a small, smeltlike fish that moves in schools and spawns on Newfoundland's many pebble beaches. During the summer, temperate days turn Newfoundland's stark cliffs, bogs, and meadows into a riot of wildflowers and greenery; and the sea is dotted with boats and buoys marking traps and nets. Fall is a favored season: The weather is usually fine; cliffs and meadows are loaded with berries; and the woods are alive with moose, elk, partridges, and rabbits, to name just a few residents. In the winter, the forest trails hum with the sound of snowmobiles and ATVs hauling wood home or taking the fishermen to their favorite lodges and lakes.

The tourist season runs from June through September, when the province is awash with festivals, fairs, concerts, plays, and crafts shows. A popular vacation plan for locals is to go gravel-pit camping: It's the tradition of parking a trailer in a handy place near a brook or pond and setting up camp. There's usually no view, but free campsites and sociable company make up for most inconveniences. Not only is camping—in a bare site or one with amenities—an inexpensive way for the family to vacation together, but it's a good way to take advantage of Newfoundland's pollution-free environment: Nice days are just that, with bright, intense sunshine, free of smog or haze. The temperature in late June through early September hovers between 75 and 85 degrees, and gently cools off in the evening, providing a good night's sleep.

Essential Information

Important Addresses and Numbers

Tourist Information The Department of Tourism and Culture (Box 8730, St. John's, NF A1B 4K2, tel. 709/729–2830) distributes brochures and maps from its offices in the Confederation Building, West Block, St. John's. The province also maintains a tourism information line (tel. 800/563–6353), which operates year-round, 24 hours a day.

From June until Labor Day, a network of **Visitor Information Centers,** open 9–9, dots the province. These centers carry up-to-date information on events, accommodations, shopping, and crafts stores in their area. There are in-season visitor information booths at the airports in Gander and St. John's. The city of St. John's operates a complete information center in a restored railway carriage next to the harbor.

Emergencies Dial 911 for medical emergencies and police.

Hospitals **St. Clare's Mercy Hospital** (154 La Marchant Rd., tel. 709/778–3111), **Grace Hospital** (241 La Marchant Rd., tel. 709/778–6222), and **General Hospital** (300 Prince Philip Dr., tel. 709/737–6300) in St. John's; **George B. Cross Hospital** (tel. 709/466–3411) in Clarenville; **James Paton** (tel. 709/651–2500) in Gander; **Western Memorial** (tel. 709/637–5000) in Corner Brook; **Charles S. Curtis Memorial Hospital** (tel. 709/454–3333) in St. Anthony; and **Captain William Jackman** (410 Booth Ave., tel. 709/944–2632) in Labrador City.

Arriving and Departing by Plane, Car Ferry, and Train

By Plane The major airport for the province for connections from all major North American and European destinations is **St. John's. Canadian Airlines International** (tel. 800/426–7000 from the U.S., 800/665–1177 in Canada) and **Air Canada** (tel. 800/776–3000 in the U.S., 709/726–7880 in Canada) fly into Newfoundland. **Air Nova** (tel. 800/776–3000 from the U.S., 800/563–5151 from Newfoundland), **Provincial Airlines** (tel. 709/576–1666), **Labrador Airways** (tel. 709/896–8113 from the U.S., 800/563–3042 in Newfoundland), and **Air Atlantic** (tel. 800/563–8359 from the U.S., 709/576–0274 in Newfoundland) are regional connectors. Airports in Newfoundland are at Stephenville, Deer Lake, St. Anthony, Gander, and St. John's; airports in Labrador are located in Happy Valley–Goose Bay, Wabush, and Churchill Falls.

By Car Ferry **Marine Atlantic** operates a car ferry from North Sydney, Nova Scotia, to Port-aux-Basques, Newfoundland (crossing time is six hours); and, from June through October, from North Sydney to Argentia, twice a week (crossing time 12–14 hours). In all cases, reservations are required. Contact **Marine Atlantic** (Box 250, North Sydney, NS B2A 3M3, tel. 902/794–5700 or 709/772–7701, fax 902/564–3439; hearing-impaired 902/794–8109 or call TDD operator and request collect call). For information about getting to Labrador, *see* Tour 6, *below.*

By Train Rail service (tel. 514/871–1331) is provided between Sept Isles, Québec, and Labrador City by Iron Ore Canada's Québec North Shore and Labrador Railways. For more information about this train, *see* Exploring, Tour 6, *below.* There is no train on the island.

Getting around Newfoundland

By Bus **CN Roadcruiser** (tel. 709/737–5912) runs a trans-island bus service. Buses leave at 8 AM from St. John's and Port-aux-Basques. Small buses known as outport taxis connect the major centers with surrounding communities.

By Car Newfoundland has an excellent highway system, and all but a handful of secondary roads are paved. The province's roads are generally uncrowded, adding to the pleasure of driving. Traveling time along the Trans-Canada Highway from Port-aux-Basques to St. John's is about 13 hours, with time out for a meal in either Gander or Grand Falls. The trip from Corner Brook to St. Anthony at the northernmost tip of the island is about five hours. The trip from St. John's to Grand Bank on the southern tip of the Burin Peninsula takes about four hours.

In winter some highways may close during and after severe snowstorms. For winter road conditions on the west coast and in Labrador, call the **Department of Works, Services, and Transportation** (in Deer Lake, tel. 709/635–2162; in Grand Falls and Central Newfoundland, tel. 709/292–4300; in Clarenville, tel. 709/466–7953; in St. John's, tel. 709/729–2391).

Getting around Labrador

See Tour 6 in Exploring Newfoundland and Labrador, *below.*

Guided Tours

Boat Tours   The number of boat tours has increased in recent years. South of St. John's, in Bay Bulls, **O'Brien's Bird Island Boat Tours** (tel. 709/753–4850 or 709/334–2355) and **Gatherall's Sanctuary Boat Charters** (tel. 709/334–2887) offer a popular two-hour excursion featuring whale watching, cod jigging, and a visit to the impressive Witless Bay Islands bird sanctuary. Both companies offer a hotel pickup service. **Great Island Tours** (tel. 800/563–2355) begins farther south in Cape Broyle and includes the abandoned outport of La Manche in its tour.

On the Trinity–Bonavista Peninsula, **Ocean Contact Limited** (tel. 709/464–3269) is an established specialist in whale watching and whale research. **Ocean Watch Tours** (tel. 709/677–2327) operates near Terra Nova National Park in Burnside and features park-approved field guides and an attractive ecological program. **Island Rendezvous** (tel. 709/747–7253) offers two days of boating and an overnight stay on Woody Island, Placentia Bay. **Island View Boat Tours** (tel. 709/535–2258) promises a mussel and lobster boil-up on the beach and a chance to visit abandoned settlements and Indian sites in the Lewisporte area. **Twillingate Island Boat Tours** (tel. 709/884–2242) specializes in iceberg photography in the iceberg-rich waters around Twillingate.

On the west coast, 2,000-foot-high cliffs and spectacular landlocked fjords are the main attraction. **Bontours** (tel. 709/458–2730) runs the best-known of these trips—up Western Brook Pond in Gros Morne National Park. **Tableland Boat Tours** (tel. 709/451–2101) runs tours up Trout River Pond near the southern boundary of the park. **Seal Island Boat Tours** (tel. 709/898–2525) explores St. Paul's Inlet, an area of the park rich in seals, terns, and other marine and shore life.

Bus Tours   **McCarthy's Party** (tel. 709/781–2244) in St. John's offers guided bus tours across Newfoundland (May through October) in addition to a variety of convention and charter services. **Fleetline Motorcoach Tours** (tel. 709/722–2608) in Holyrood and **K.P. Motorcoach Tours** (tel. 709/632–5808) in Corner Brook also offer island-wide tours. Local tours are available for Port-aux-Basques, the Codroy Valley, Corner Brook, the Bay of Islands, Gros Morne National Park, the Great Northern Peninsula, and St. John's.

Adventure Tours   Adventure touring in Newfoundland and Labrador is experiencing a period of rapid growth. Local adventure tour operators offer sea-kayaking, ocean-diving, canoeing, wildlife viewing, mountain biking, white-water rafting, heli-hiking, and interpretive walks in the summer. In winter, snowmobiling, heli-skiing, and caribou- and seal-watching expeditions are popular. Before choosing an operator it's advisable to contact the Department of Tourism and Culture just to make sure you're calling a reputable outfit. **Eastern Edge Outfitters** (tel. 709/368–9720 or 709/782–1465) offers east coast sea-kayaking tours, as well as white-water rafting expeditions down Newfoundland's Main River. **Gros Morne Adventure Guides** (tel. 709/458–2722 or 709/686–2241) offers sea-kayaking up the fjords and land-locked ponds of Gros Morne National Park, as well as a variety of hikes and adventures in the area. **Tuckamore Lodge** (tel. 709/865–6361) in Main Brook uses its luxurious lodge on the Great Northern Peninsula as a base for viewing caribou, seabird colonies, and other wildlife. **Labrador Scenic Ltd.** (tel 709/497–8326) in North West River organizes tours through central and northern Labrador with an emphasis on wildlife and Labrador's spectacular coast.

Exploring Newfoundland and Labrador

Tours in this chapter divide the province into the island of Newfoundland, beginning with St. John's and the Avalon Peninsula, and move west. Labrador is considered as a whole, with suggested driving and train excursions.

Highlights for First-Time Visitors

Cape St. Mary's Ecological Reserve, Tour 1: St. John's and the Avalon Peninsula

Cape Spear National Historic Site, Tour 1: St. John's and the Avalon Peninsula

Discovery Trail on the Bonavista Peninsula, Tour 2: Clarenville and the Bonavista and Burin Peninsulas

Gros Morne National Park, Tour 4: Deer Lake and the Great Northern Peninsula to St. Anthony

L'Anse aux Meadows National Historic Park, Tour 4: Deer Lake and the Great Northern Peninsula to St. Anthony

Red Bay, Tour 6: Labrador

St. John's Heritage District, Tour 1: St. John's and the Avalon Peninsula

Signal Hill National Historic Park, Tour 1: St. John's and the Avalon Peninsula

Viking Trail, Tour 4: Deer Lake and the Great Northern Peninsula to St. Anthony

Tour 1: St. John's and the Avalon Peninsula

Numbers in the margin correspond to points of interest on the Newfoundland and Labrador map.

When Sir Humphrey Gilbert sailed into St. John's to establish British colonial rule for Queen Elizabeth in 1583, he found Spanish, French, and Portuguese fishermen actively working the harbor. As early as 1627, the merchants of Water Street, then known as the "Lower Path," were doing a thriving business buying fish, selling goods, and supplying booze to soldiers and sailors. Still today the city encircles the snug, punchbowl harbor that helped establish its reputation.

St. John's
❶ True early birds can begin their tour of the area at daybreak by filling up a thermos of coffee, getting some muffins, and driving on Route 11 to **Cape Spear,** so they can be among the first to watch the sun come up over North America. The "chit chit" of song birds in the dim light of dawn and the whooshing and blowing of whales feeding directly below the cliffs make an unforgettable beginning to a day. **Cape Spear Lighthouse** (tel. 709/722–5367), Newfoundland's oldest such beacon, has been lovingly restored to its original form and furnishings and is open to visitors mid-June–Labor Day.

2 Those who are less ambitious may wish to begin exploring **St. John's** a little later in the day, when the Tourist Chalet on the waterfront is open. This is an old converted railway caboose, staffed from May through October. *Harbor Drive, tel. 709/576–8514. Open 9–7 daily, May–Oct.*

Whichever way you look—left or right—you'll see the always-fascinating array of ships that tie up along **Harbour Drive.** Walk the harborfront, a favorite route in St. John's, to **The Battery,** a tiny, still-active fishing village perched precariously on the steep cliffs between hill and harbor. A well-maintained 5-kilometer (3-mile) walking path leads along the cliff edge, through the narrows, and zigzags through **Signal Hill National Historic Park.** Alternatively, you can drive on the road that also leads to the park.

In spite of its height, Signal Hill was difficult to defend: Throughout the 1600s and 1700s it changed hands with every attacking French, English, and Dutch force. A wooden palisade encircles the summit of the hill, indicating the boundaries of the old fortifications. En route to the hill is the **Park Interpretation Centre** (tel. 709/772–5367), with exhibits describing St. John's history.

Gibbet Hill, the rocky knob immediately to the west of the Interpretation Centre, was at one time used by local "authorities" as a place to hang miscreants. These dangling unfortunates were meant to send the message to anyone entering the harbor that misconduct would not be tolerated by the ruling fishing admiral. From the top of the hill it's a 500-foot drop to the narrow harbor entrance below.

Cabot Tower, at the summit of Signal Hill, was constructed in 1897 to commemorate the 400th anniversary of Cabot's discovery of Newfoundland. In 1901, in the shadow of the tower, Guglielmo Marconi received the first transatlantic wireless message from Cornwall, England—the opening salvo in a communication revolution that would change the world. The tower is open to the public and contains a display on communications history. *Tel. 709/772–5367. Admission free. Open year-round 8:30–4:30, 8:30–8 mid June–Labor Day; weekend guides in the summer.*

If you are driving, come down from Signal Hill, make a right turn at Quidi Vidi Road, and continue to the right, down Forest Road, to **Quidi Vidi Village,** an authentic fishing community whose history goes back to the beginning of St. John's. If you are walking, paths lead from the summit and the Interpretation Centre to the village. **Quidi Vidi Battery,** near the entrance to the village harbor, is a small, reconstructed 1762 redoubt, staffed by costumed interpreters who will tell you about the hard, unromantic life lived by a soldier of the empire. *Quidi Vidi Village, tel. 709/729–2460 or 709/729–2977. Admission free. Open 10–5:30 daily July–early Sept., winter by appointment.*

Quidi Vidi Lake, to the west of the village, is encircled by a leisurely path, popular with walkers and joggers, and is the site of the **St. John's Annual Regatta**—the oldest continuing sporting event in North America, it first took place in 1826. Weather permitting, the regatta begins on the first Wednesday in August: If you're in town you shouldn't miss it.

Newfoundland and Labrador

QUEBEC

Red Bay **55**

L'Anse **National**

Cooks
Har. **47**

Pinware

L'Anse Amour
L'Anse au Clair **54**
Blanc Sablon **53**

Strait of Belle Isle

Raleigh

48
St.
Anthony

Flowers Cove

Hare Bay

Brig Bay St. Barbe

St. Julien's

Groais I.

Bartletts Har.

Roddickton

Bell I.

Port au Choix

Hawke Bay

Bellburns

430

Harbour Deep

Portland Creek

The Arches Provincial Park **46**

Fleur de Lys

Cow Head

Baie Verte

La Scie

St. Pauls

Jackson Arm

430

Rocky Harbour **45**
Woody Point **43**
Trout River **44**

Cormack **42**

Sandy
Lake

Rattling
Brook

410

Nippers
Har. *Notre Dame*
Springdale *Bay*

Twillin

1

Cox
Cove

41
**Deer
Lake**

Millertown
Junction

South
Brook

1

Bay
of Islands

York Harbour

Voys Beach
Corner Brook **49**

Humbermouth

Badger

Windsor

37 **Grand
Falls**

Botw

Black Duck
Brook

Lewis Hills

50

*Grand
Lake*

Buchans

370

Mainland *Port Au
Port
Peninsula*

**Point au Mal
Prov. Park**

Red
Indian
Lake

360

51
Stephenville

St. Teresa

Mountains

Jeffery's

*Meelpaeg
Lake*

*Round
Lake*

Cape
Anguille

N. Branch

Range

St. Albans

Long

Hardy Cove

Terr

1

360

**Port-
aux-Basques**

52

Rose
Blanche

Burgeo

Harbour
Breton

Marystown
*Burin
Peninsu*
Salt
Pond

**Grand
Bank**

30

Gr. Miquelon I. **Fortune**

31

34

**Miquelon
(France)** **33**

220

St. Lo

Lit. Miquelon I.

**St. Pierre
(France)** **32** St. Pierre

Gulf of St. Lawrence

Long
Range
Mountains

White Bay

TO GOOSE BAY
(Labrador)

TO NORTH SYDNEY
(Nova Scotia)

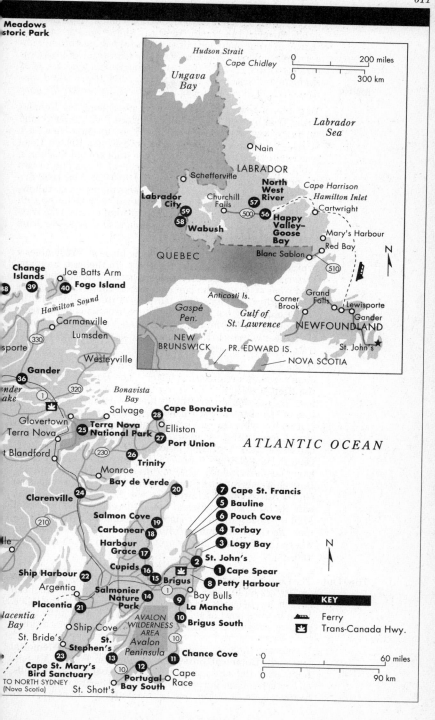

Meadows
storic Park

Hudson Strait
Cape Chidley

Ungava Bay

Labrador Sea

Nain

Schefferville

LABRADOR

North West River

Cape Harrison
Hamilton Inlet

Labrador City
Churchill Falls
57
Cartwright
59
56
58 Wabush
500
Happy Valley-Goose Bay
Mary's Harbour
Red Bay

QUEBEC
Blanc Sablon
510

N

Change Islands
Joe Batts Arm
40 Fogo Island
38 **39**
Anticosti Is.
Corner Brook
Grand Falls
Lewisporte
Hamilton Sound
Gaspé Pen.
Gulf of St. Lawrence
Gander
Carmanville
Lumsden
NEWFOUNDLAND
sporte
330
Wesleyville
NEW BRUNSWICK
PR. EDWARD IS.
St. John's
nder
ake
36
Gander
320
NOVA SCOTIA

Bonavista Bay
Salvage
28 Cape Bonavista
Glovertown
Terra Nova
25 Terra Nova National Park
Elliston
27 Port Union
t Blandford
230
26 Trinity
Monroe
Bay de Verde

ATLANTIC OCEAN

Clarenville
24
210
Salmon Cove
19
Carbonear
18
Harbour Grace
17
Cupids
16
15 Brigus
1
Ship Harbour
22
Argentia
Salmonier Nature Park
14
Placentia
21
lacentia Bay
Ship Cove
St. Stephen's
23
13
AVALON WILDERNESS AREA
Avalon Peninsula
10
St. Bride's
Cape St. Mary's Bird Sanctuary
TO NORTH SYDNEY
(Nova Scotia)
St. Shott's
12 Portugal Bay South
20
7 Cape St. Francis
5 Bauline
6 Pouch Cove
4 Torbay
3 Logy Bay
2 St. John's
1 Cape Spear
8 Petty Harbour
Bay Bulls
9 La Manche
10 Brigus South
11 Chance Cove
Cape Race

0   200 miles
0   300 km

0   60 miles
0   90 km

KEY
Ferry
Trans-Canada Hwy.

From the lake follow the **Rennies River Trail** (4 miles) that cuts through the city along a wooded stream and ends at the only public fluvarium in North America, where you can observe spawning trout and char in their natural habitat through underwater windows. *Newfoundland Freshwater Resource Center, Pippy Park, tel. 709/754–3474. Admission: $2.75 adults, $2.25 students and senior citizens, $1.50 children. Open 9–5 June–Aug., 10–4:30 Mon.–Wed.–Sat., 12–4:30 Sun. the rest of the year.*

To get back downtown, retrace your steps along the Rennies River Trail by foot, or drive down Prince Phillip's Drive and turn right onto Portugal Cove Road. This runs into New Cove Road—follow this and turn right onto King's Bridge Road which intersects with Water St. As you walk around St. John's, you'll notice the diversity of architectural styles due to two major fires: one in 1846 and another in 1892. The 1892 fire stopped where George and Water streets intersect, at **Yellowbelly Corner.** This junction was so-named because in the 19th century it was a gathering spot for Irish immigrants from Wexford who wore yellow sashes to distinguish themselves from their Waterford rivals.

Look west on Water Street, where the block still resembles a typical Irish market town of the 1840s. To the east, however, Victorian-style architecture predominates, with curved mansard roofs typical of the popular Second Empire style. After the 1892 fire the city's elite moved to **Circular Road,** in the center of the city, out of reach of future fires, and built a string of impressive and highly ornamented Victorian mansions, which bear witness to the sizable fortunes made in the old days from the humble cod.

While you're downtown, take a look at the churches of St. John's, rich in architectural history. The **Basilica of St. John the Baptist** (Military Road, tel. 709/754–2170), with a commanding position above Military Road, overlooks the older section of the city and the harbor. The land was granted to the church by young Queen Victoria, and the edifice was built with stones from both Ireland and Newfoundland. From here you can also see the **Anglican Cathedral of St. John the Baptist** (22 Church Hill, tel. 709/726–5677) on Church Hill, one of the finest examples of Gothic Revival architecture in North America. Both churches conduct summer tours. Nearby is the imposing **Gower Street United Church** (Grower St., tel. 709/753–7286), with its redbrick facade and green turrets. At the bottom of Military Road, adjacent to Hotel Newfoundland, is the **St. Thomas Old Garrison Church** (Military Road, tel. 709/576–6632), where the English soldiers used to worship in the early and mid-1800s.

Time Out   The **Commissariat House** (Kings Bridge Rd., tel. 709/729–2460 or 709/729–6730), just around the corner from the Anglican church, has been restored to the way it appeared in the 1830s. Drop in for a bowl of soup or beans, and chat with the interpreters, dressed in period costume, who will show you around.

If you have time, set aside an afternoon to visit the **Memorial University Botanical Gardens,** located at Oxen Pond on Mt. Scio Road. This 100-acre nature reserve has five attractive trails, an English cottage garden, Newfoundland heritage plants, and heather beds. It is also one of two butterfly farms in North

America and home to nesting ospreys. *Oxen Pond, Mt. Scio Rd., Pippy Park, tel. 709/737–8590. Admission free. Open Wed.–Sun. 10–5:30 May–Nov.*

Another beautiful spot in St. John's is **Bowring Park,** on Waterford Bridge Road. The expansive Victorian park was donated to the city by the wealthy Bowring family in 1911, and resembles the famous inner city parks of London, England, after which it was modeled. Dotting the grounds are artfully designed nooks and crannies, ponds, ducks to feed, and rustic bridges; there's also a statue of Peter Pan.

The Avalon Peninsula Several half-day, full-day, and two-day excursions are possible from St. John's, and in each direction a different personality of the region unfolds. On the southern half of the peninsula are small Irish hamlets separated by large tracts of wilderness. The northern half is more densely populated and still reflects its Dorset and Devon, England, origins. Here, homes are perched on narrow spits of land or tucked into the lee of cliffs.

Coast North of St. John's You can take a leisurely ½-day trip to explore the scenic coastline north of St. John's. Take Route 30 (Logy Bay Road) to Marine Drive, which winds along the coastline, passing

❸ through **Logy Bay** and its remarkable cliffs. Along the way is **Ocean Sciences Centre,** with its outdoor seal tank where you can watch the animals frolic. The seals look happy for good reason: They're participating in experiments to determine their year-round feeding habits. *Marine Lab Road, tel. 709/737–3706. Admission $2.50 adults, $1.50 children and senior citizens, under 6 free. Tours every ½-hour late June–early Sept., 10–5.*

❹ Follow Route 30 to **Torbay** and turn west onto Route 21 to
❺ **Bauline,** an unspoiled fishing village that overlooks Conception
❻ Bay. Continue on Route 21 to **Pouch Cove,** one of the province's oldest communities, where the adventurous should follow the
❼ unpaved road that leads to **Cape St. Francis.** On the way to the cape, there's a short coastal walk. A local legend centers around the wreck of the *Waterwitch,* which capsized in 1875 in the water at the northern edge of Pouch Cove. Alfred Moores rescued 11 people from the floundering vessel by lowering himself by rope down the cliff. A sign marks the site along the coastal walk, but you can't see the wreck.

Leave Pouch Cove on Route 20 and head straight back, or connect to Route 30, which loops around toward Logy Bay, on your return to St. John's. For one more scenic pleasure en route, take in some views at the village of **Flat Rock,** on Route 20 just past Pouch Cove.

Coast South of St. John's You can travel part of the peninsula's coast for a one- or two-day excursion, depending on how much time you have. Quaint coastal towns line the road, and the natural sites are beautiful and well-interpreted.

Just south of St. John's pick up Route 10 and follow it along the southern coast toward Trepassey. Locals call this trip "going up the shore," even though it looks like you're traveling down on a map. The wildness of this coast is usually what's most striking to visitors, and La Manche and Chance Cove—both now-abandoned communities turned provincial parks—attest to the bounty of natural resources of the region.

❽ Although a visit to many of the hamlets along the way will fill any void for prettiness, a few favorites are exceptional. **Petty**

⑨ ⑩ **Harbour, La Manche,** and **Brigus South,** have especially attractive settings and strong traditional flavors.

⑪ ⑫ In springtime, between **Chance Cove** and **Portugal Cove South,** in a stretch of land about 36 miles along, hundreds of caribou gather near the road with their calves on the wide barrens. Although the graceful animals are there during other times of the year, their numbers are few and it's difficult to spot them because they blend in so well with the scenery.

⑬ Route 10 loops around the peninusla and becomes Route 90, just past **St. Stephens.**

At the intersection of Routes 90 and 91, in Salmonier, you need to decide whether to continue north toward Salmonier Nature Park and on to Conception Bay, or to head west then south to Route 100 to Cape St. Mary's Ecological Reserve (*see* Route 100: The Cape Shore, *below*). Both options take about three hours.

⑭ If you've decided to go north, travel to **Salmonier Nature Park,** 9 miles along, where visitors can see many of the animal species that are indigenous to the province. The park is a 1214 hectare wilderness reserve area and has an enclosed 40.5 hectare exhibit that allows up-close viewing. *Salmonier Line, Rte. 90, tel. 709/729–6974 or 709/229–7888. Admission free. Admission 50¢ adults, 25¢ children, senior citizens free. Open early June–Labor Day, Thurs.–Mon., noon–7.*

Farther along Route 90 the road passes through the scenic Hawkes Hills, before meeting up with the Trans-Canada Highway (Route 1). Turn off at the Holyrood Junction (Route 62)
⑮ and follow Route 70, which parallels **Conception Bay,** to **Brigus.** Meander through this beautifully restored village with winding lanes, a tea house, and a museum set in a stone barn, where you can pick up a walking-tour brochure. *Ye Olde Stone Barn Museum, 4 Magistrate's Hill, tel. 709/528–3298. Admission $1 adults, 50¢ children, open noon–5 daily June–Sept.*

Brigus was the home of many sealing captains, including Captain Bob Bartlett, who in 1909 guided Commodore Perry to within 161 kilometers (100 miles) of the North Pole. Perry abandoned Bartlett before going on the last leg so he could claim full honors for himself. The move backfired, however, for without Bartlett's testimony Perry couldn't prove that he actually made the journey.

⑯ Continue on Route 70 to **Cupids,** the site of the first permanent colony in Newfoundland, which was founded in 1610 by the Bristol merchant John Guy.

Just beyond Brigus Route 70 passes by Clarke's Beach, where you should turn right and follow Route 72 along a narrow sliver of land to **Port de Grave** and **Hibbs Cove.** The **Port de Grave Fishermen's Museum, Porter House, and Old School House Community Museum** is actually located in Hibbs Cove. Here you can learn about Newfoundland fisherman lifestyles from the 1600s until the present. *Hibbs Cove, off Rte. 72, tel. 709/786–3912 or 709/786–3900. Admission: $1 adults, 50¢ students. Open 1–5 daily mid–late June, 10–noon and 1–5 Mon.–Sat., Sun. 1–5 July–Labor Day.*

(17) About 10 miles farther on Route 70 is **Harbour Grace,** which once was the headquarters of Peter Easton, a 17th-century pirate. Beginning in 1919, Harbour Grace was the departure point for many attempts to fly the Atlantic. Amelia Earhart left Harbour Grace in 1932 to become the first woman to fly solo across the Atlantic. Several handsome stone churches and buildings remain as evidence of the town's former pride.

(18) Continue along Route 70 to **Carbonear,** another town with a fascinating history. In 1696 it was burned to the ground by the French, but the inhabitants retreated to a small fortified island in the harbor and successfully defended it against capture. Carbonear Island has been designated a National Historic Site to mark its colorful military past.

(19) Farther along Route 70 is picturesque **Salmon Cove,** a sheltered bay with a grassy picnic area. The road is narrow and partly unpaved, but you'll be rewarded with the finest views of Conception Bay, especially as you drive up and over Blow Me **(20)** Down Head. If you plan to travel on to **Bay de Verde,** at the northern tip of the peninsula, and down the other side of the peninsula on Route 80 along Trinity Bay, consider turning in for the night at one of the several hotels or bed-and-breakfasts (*see* Lodging, *below*) in the Harbour Grace–Carbonear area. Otherwise turn around and follow the same route back.

Route 100: The Cape Shore If you opted for the Cape Shore route, from Salmonier west on Route 91 and south on Route 100, you're headed to Avalon's Cape St. Mary's Ecological Reserve.

(21) **Placentia,** at the end of Route 91, was the French capital of Newfoundland in the 1600s. Trust the French to select a beautiful place for a capital! **Castle Hill National Historic Park,** just north of town, is located on what remains of the French fortifications. The visitor's center has a "life at Plaisance" exhibit that shows the life and hardships endured by early English and French settlers. *Off Route 100, tel. 709/227–2401. Admission free. Open 8:30–8 June–Labor Day, 8:30–4:30 rest of year.*

(22) A worthwhile and nearby diversion from Placentia is **Ship Harbour,** an isolated, edge-of-the-world place that has the curious distinction of being the home of the free world. Off Route 102, amidst the splendor of Placentia Bay, an unpaved road leads to a monument marking the historic Atlantic Charter. It was on a ship in these waters where, in 1941, Roosevelt and Churchill signed the charter and formally announced the "Four Freedoms," which still shape the politics of the world's most successful democracies: freedom of speech, freedom of worship, freedom from want, and freedom from fear.

To continue on the Cape Shore tour, double back to Route 100 **(23)** and travel 24 miles to the **Cape St. Mary's Ecological Reserve** (tel. 709/729–2424), where about 5,000 pairs of gannets nest on Bird Rock, and as many again on the nearby cliffs. Additionally, there are thousands of kittiwakes and murres, especially during the nesting season, which is usually between June and August. An interpretation center is on the grounds and on-site nature guides are available during the summer. While walking out to the sanctuary, you'll experience some of the most dramatic coastal scenery in Newfoundland—that's if you hit it lucky and encounter a rare clear day on the cape. Fog is far more usual. Fortunately, the birds are close-at-hand, so you'll see and hear them no matter what the weather.

Tour 2: Clarenville and the Bonavista and Burin Peninsulas

㉔ **Clarenville** is about two hours from St. John's via the Trans-Canada Highway (Route 1) and is the departure point for two different excursions: the Discovery Trail and Terra Nova National Park. If you're interested in rugged terrain, golf, fishing, and camping, head 15 miles west along the Trans-Canada **㉕** Highway to **Terra Nova National Park,** on the exposed coastline that adjoins Bonavista Bay. If you are a golfer, you can play on one of the most beautiful courses in Canada, and the only one where a licensed salmon river cuts through the course. Call 709/543–2525, 800/461–0808 in Canada for a reservation. Fees run between $24 and $30 per person, 18 holes, depending on the season. The park also offers attractive campsites, whale-watching tours, and nature walks. *Tel. 709/533–2801 or 709/533–2358, fax 709/533–2706. Open year-round. Vehicle permit required in summer: $5 per day per vehicle, $10 for 4-day pass, $20 for seasonal pass.*

If history and quaint towns interest you, begin the tour in Clarenville, the starting point for Route 230—the **"Discovery Trail."** The route goes as far as the town of Bonavista, one of John Cabot's reputed landing spots in 1497. On your way visit **㉖** the historic village of **Trinity,** known as one of the jewels of Newfoundland. The village's picturesque views, winding lanes, and snug houses are the main attraction, and several homes have been turned into museums and inns. In the 1700s Trinity competed with St. John's as a center of culture and wealth. Its more contemporary claim to fame, however, is that its intricate harbor was a favorite anchorage for the British navy, and it was here that the smallpox vaccine was introduced to North America, by a local rector.

㉗ **Port Union,** just north of Trinity on Route 230, was built as a model fishing community a century ago by the pioneer unionist Sir William Coaker. **The Port Union Museum** (contact Linda Clarke, tel. 709/464–3315) in the old railway station follows his career.

㉘ Still farther north along Route 230 is **Cape Bonavista,** a popular destination because of its association with Cabot's landing. The lighthouse on the point has been restored to the 1870 period. While here, visit the Mockbeggar Property to learn about the life of a well-to-do outport merchant in the years immediately before Confederation. *Off Route 230, tel. 709/729–2460 or 709/468–7300. Admission free. Open 10–5:30 late June–early Sept; by appointment in winter.*

Burin Peninsula The journey down to the Burin Peninsula is a three- to four-hour drive from the intersection of Route 230 and Route 1 through the sometimes incredible landscapes along Route 210. The peninsula's history is tied to the rich fishing grounds of the Grand Banks, which established this area as a center for European fishery as early as the 1500s. By the early 1900s, one of the world's largest fishing fleets was based on the Burin Peninsula. Today its inhabitants still operate the fishery in the modern trawlers that harvest the Grand Banks.

㉙ **Marystown** is the largest town on the peninsula and is its major commercial center. The town's name was changed from Mortier to Marystown by a priest during World War I, and to keep the faith a 15-foot statue of the Virgin Mary watches the town and harbor. West from here the road meets with Route 220 and **30** passes through **Grand Bank,** an unusually attractive community with a fascinating fishing history. This town is famous in the area as one of the most beautiful communities on the Atlantic Seaboard. For details about the town's past visit the **Southern Newfoundland Seamen's Museum,** housed in a sail-shaped building that was the Yugoslavian Pavilion in Expo '67. *Marine Dr., tel. 709/832–1484. Admission free. Open 9–12, 1–5 Mon.–Fri., 2–5 weekends, closed holidays.*

31 Just south of Grand Bank is **Fortune,** where you can catch the ferry to France's only colony in North America—the islands of **32 33** **St. Pierre** and **Miquelon.** These islands are the place to go if you have a hankering for a French lunch or a bottle of perfume. Shopping and eating are both popular pastimes, and if you plan to stay overnight, consider the Hotel Robert. The ferry ride takes about two hours, and tourists should carry proof of citizenship. People from outside the U.S. and Canada will have to show valid visas and passports. Two passenger ferry companies provide service: **Lloyd G. Lake Ltd.** (tel. 709/832–2006) leaves Fortune daily at 2:15 PM from mid-June to late Sept. Crossing takes 55 minutes. The ferry leaves St. Pierre at 1:00 PM daily, and the round trip costs $47.95; children under 16 are free. **SPM Tours** (tel. 709/832–0429) leaves Fortune daily at 1:15 PM and leaves St. Pierre at 11 AM daily. Season and fares same as above.

34 Back on Route 220, you may wish to stop at **St. Lawrence,** where in 1942 one of the worst disasters befell the U.S. Navy. It was here that warships *Pollux* and *Truxton* went aground during a February storm. Two hundred sailors perished, but the people of the area heroically pulled another 182 over the cliffs to safety. In gratitude the U.S. Navy built a hospital for the community. In the summer of 1992, some survivors of the disaster returned to renew their friendships with the people of St. Lawrence and to unveil the "Echoes of Valour" monument on the cliff overlooking the spot where the ship sank.

Following Route 220 will take you around the peninsula to the **35** old town of **Burin,** a community amidst intricate cliffs and coves. This was an ideal setting for pirates and privateers who used to lure ships into the rocky, dead-end areas in order to escape. Captain Cook was among those who watched for smugglers from "Cook's Lookout" on a hill that still bears his name. Also in Burin is the Heritage House museum (tel. 709/891–2217, admission free, open 9–5 Mon., Tues., 9–9 Wed.–Sun.), considered one of the best community museums in Newfoundland, which gives you a sense of what life was like in past eras.

Tour 3: Gander, Grand Falls–Windsor, and Notre Dame Bay

The interior of Newfoundland is unpopulated beyond the main roads, with the towns of Gander and Grand Falls–Windsor the **36** focal points for the region. **Gander,** a busy center with 12,000 people, is the site of the Gander International Airport. During World War II it was chosen by the Canadian and U.S. Air Forces as a major strategic air base because of its favorable weather and secure location. After the war, the airport became an international hub, and young islanders would hang around to see the stars come and go, among them Zsa Zsa Gabor and Tyrone Power. Now, like all modern airports, it's tightly secured. Gander has many hotels and still makes a good base for your travels. The **Aviation Exhibition** in the airport's Domestic Passenger's Lounge (tel. 709/729–2460; open daily), traces Newfoundland's role in the history of air travel.

③⑦ **Grand Falls,** 50 minutes west of Gander along the Trans-Canada Highway (Route 1), was a paper-milling town founded by Lord Northcliffe in the early 1900s to supply newsprint for his growing newspaper empire. Within Grand Falls is the **Mary March Regional Museum,** which depicts the lives of the Beothuk Indians before they fell victim to disease and competition from early settlers. The museum is named for 23-year-old Demasduit (also named Mary March, for the month in which she was captured), one of the last Beothuks, who was captured in 1819 during a brutal encounter that resulted in the death of her husband and child. *St. Catherine St., off Rte. 1, tel. 709/489–9331. Admission free. Open weekdays 9–4:45, weekends and holidays, 10–5:45.*

Using either Route 330 from Gander via the Trans-Canada Highway (Route 1) or Route 340 from Grand Falls, wander north through wooded countryside and small villages to **③⑧** **Twillingate.** The inhabitants of this charming old fishing village make their living from the sea and have been doing so for nearly two centuries. Every year on the last weekend in July, the town hosts the **Fish, Fun and Folk Festival,** where all different kinds of fish are cooked every kind of way. Twillingate is also one of the best places on the island to see icebergs, and is known to the locals as "Iceberg Alley." These majestic and dangerous mountains of ice are awe inspiring to see while they're grounded in early summer.

③⑨ ④⓪ You might also be interested in taking a ferry ride to either **Change Islands** or **Fogo Island.** Branch off Route 340 to Route 335 which takes you through scenic coastal communities on the way to the ferry to either of the islands, located in Farewell. These islands give one the impression of a place frozen in time. Clapboard homes are precariously perched on rocks or built on small lots surrounded by vegetable gardens. As you walk the roads, watch out for moose and herds of wild Newfoundland ponies who spend their summers grazing and enjoying the warm breeze off the ocean.

Tour 4: Deer Lake and the Great Northern Peninsula to St. Anthony

④① **Deer Lake** was once just another small town on the Trans-Canada Highway, but the opening of Gros Morne National Park in the early '70s and a first-class paved highway passing right through to St. Anthony changed all that. Today, with an airport and car rentals available, Deer Lake is a good starting point for a fly-drive vacation.

Head north out of Deer Lake on Route 430 to Route 422 to **Sir Richard Squires Memorial Park.** This drive will take you **④②** through **Cormack,** which is one of the best farming regions in the island. The park remains natural and unspoiled, and it contains one of the most interesting salmon fishing areas in Newfoundland.

Return to Route 430, and in a short while you'll be on the **Viking Trail** leading into **Gros Morne National Park** (tel. 709/458–2059). Because of its geological uniqueness and immense splendor, this park has been named a UNESCO World Heritage Site. Among the more breathtaking visions are the expanses of wild orchids in springtime. There is an excellent **Interpretation Centre** (tel. 709/458–2066), which has displays and videos about the park. Camping and hiking are popular recreations in the park, and boat tours are available. It takes at least two days to see Gros Morne properly.

Scenic **Bonne Bay,** a deep, mountainous fjord, divides the park in two. You can either drive around the perimeter of the fjord on Route 430 going north, or make a ferry-crossing near its mouth from Route 431.

43 In the south of the park is **Woody Point,** a charming community of old houses and imported Lombardy poplars. Until it was bypassed by the railway, the community was the commercial capital of the West Coast. Rising behind Woody Point are the **Tablelands,** a unique rock massif that was once an ancient seabed. Its rocks are toxic to most plant life, and Ice Age conditions linger in the form of persistent snow and moving rock glaciers.

44 Follow Route 431 to scenic **Trout River Pond** and the once-isolated and still unusual community of **Trout River.** The **Green Gardens Trail,** a four- to five-hour hike, is along the way and it's one you'll remember for your lifetime, but be prepared to do a bit of climbing on your return journey. The trail passes through the Tablelands barrens and descends sharply down to a fairy tale coastline of eroded cliffs, sea stacks, and lush green meadows.

45 On the northern side of the park, situated along coastal Route 430, is **Rocky Harbour,** with a wide range of services and a luxurious indoor public pool—the perfect thing to soothe tired limbs after a strenuous day. The most popular attraction on the northern portion of Gros Morne is the boat tour up **Western Brook Pond,** which is reached by a leisurely 45-minute walk from the main highway through an interesting mix of bog and woods. Cliffs rise 2,000 feet on both sides of the gorge and high waterfalls tumble over ancient rocks. If you have strong legs and are in good shape, another decent attraction is the 10-mile hike up **Gros Morne Mountain,** at 2,644 feet the second-highest peak in Newfoundland. Weather permitting, your labor will be rewarded by a unique arctic landscape and spectacular views. The park's coast in the north offers visitors an unusual mix of sand beaches, rock pools, and trails through tangled dwarf forests known locally as "tuckamore." Sunsets, seen from Lobster Point Lighthouse, are spectacular. Keep an eye out for whales and visit the lighthouse museum, devoted to the human history of the area.

46 Just a short distance north of the park, on Route 430, is **The Arches Provincial Park,** a geological curiosity where the pounding sea has cut a succession of caves through a bed of dolomite.

Continuing north, parallel to the Gulf of St. Lawrence, you'll find yourself refreshingly close to the ocean and the wave-tossed beaches: Stop to breathe the fresh sea air and listen to the breakers. The Long Range Mountains to your right reminded Jacques Cartier, who saw them in 1534, of the long, rectangular-shaped farm buildings of his home village in France. Small villages are interspersed with rivers where salmon and trout get to be "liar-size." The remains of the Maritime Archaic Indians and Dorset Eskimos have been found in abundance along this coast, and there's an interesting Interpretation Centre (tel. 709/623–2601) at Port aux Choix.

47 Proceed about 130 miles on Route 430, then turn onto Route 436 to **L'Anse aux Meadows National Historic Site.** This UNESCO World Heritage Site was discovered in 1960 by a Norwegian team, Helge and Anne Stine Ingstad. Most believe the remains of the long sod houses here were built around 1000 as the site of Norseman Lief Erikson's colony in the New World. The Canadian Parks Service has established a marvelous **Interpretation Centre** (tel. 709/623–2601) and has meticulously reconstructed some of the sod huts. With fires burning inside and sheepskins about, one does get a sense of centuries past. *Rte. 436, tel. 709/623–2601 or 709/623–2608. Admission free. Visitor center open mid-June–Labor Day, daily 9–8.*

48 Return to Route 430 and about 10 miles from the junction with 430 is **St. Anthony,** a beautiful town settled around a natural harbor, at the tip of the Great Northern Peninsula. Take a trip out to the lighthouse—you may see an iceberg or two floating by.

Here is also the home of the **Grenfell Mission.** The huge hospital attests to the work done by Sir Wilfred Grenfell, a British medical missionary, who established nursing stations and cooperatives and provided medical services to the scattered villages of northern Newfoundland and the south coast of Labrador in the early 1900s. The main foyer of the hospital has a decorative tile mural that's worth a visit. **Grenfell House,** the home of Sir Wilfred and Lady Grenfell, has been restored to period condition and can also be visited. *On the west side of St. Anthony on a hill overlooking the harbor, adjacent to Charles S. Curtis Memorial Hospital, tel. 709/454–3333. Admission: $2 adults, $1 students and senior citizens, children under 5 free. Open daily 10–8 mid-May–mid-Oct., by appointment in winter.*

Don't leave without visiting the **Grenfell Handcraft** store (tel. 709/454–3576). Importing craftspeople to train the villagers to become self-sufficient in a harsh environment was one of Grenfell's aims. A windproof cloth that villagers turned into well-made parkas came to be known as Grenfell cloth. Beautiful clothes fashioned out of Grenfell cloth have quality and style not found anywhere else and they are available for sale here. Return to Deer Lake along Route 430.

Tour 5: Corner Brook and the West Coast

49 **Corner Brook** is Newfoundland's second-largest city and the hub of the west coast of the island. Mountains fringe three sides of the city and there are beautiful views of the harbor and the Bay of Islands. Corner Brook is also home to one of the largest paper mills in the world. Every July the city hosts the **Hangashore Folk Festival,** where you can go to hear some great traditional Canadian and Newfoundland music.

If you plan to explore the west coast, Corner Brook is a convenient hub and point of departure. It is only three hours from the Port aux Basques ferry and is an attractive and active city.

The town enjoys more clearly defined seasons than most of the rest of the island, and in summer there are many pretty gardens to view and enjoy. **The Marble Mountain Ski Resort** (tel. 709/639–8531 on the slopes or 709/634–2160 for the development office), just north of the city, has the highest slopes and snowfall in Eastern North America and is growing rapidly as a ski center.

The north and south shores of the **Bay of Islands** have fine paved roads—Route 440 on the north shore and Route 450 on the south—and both offer a pleasant and scenic half-day drive. On both roads, farming and fishing communities exist side by side. Take a camera with you—the scenery is breathtaking, with farms, mountains, and beautiful pockets of brilliant wildflowers.

On another day, drive farther west on the Trans-Canada Highway and turn off at Route 460. Spend some time on the **Point au Mal Provincial Park** stopping at **Stephenville**, home of the old Harmon Air Force Base and now home to the annual Stephenville Arts Festival (mid-July to early August). The peninsula itself was largely settled by the French who brought their way of life and language to this small corner of Newfoundland.

As you move farther down the Trans-Canada Highway toward **Port aux Basques,** Routes 404, 405, 406, and 407 will bring you into the small Scottish communities of the **Codroy Valley.** Nestled in the valley are some of the finest salmon rivers and most productive farms in the province, all of this against the backdrop of the Long Range Mountains and the Lewis Hills, from which gales strong enough to stop traffic hurl off the plateau and down to the coast.

Tour 6: Labrador

Isolated from the rest of the continent, Labrador has remained one of the world's truly wild places, and yet its two main centers of Labrador City–Wabush and Happy Valley–Goose Bay offer all the amenities available in larger, urban centers. Labrador is steeped in history, a place where the past invades the present and life evolves as it did many years ago, a composite of natural phenomena, wilderness adventure, history, and culture.

Labrador's vast landscape—294,330 square kilometers (113,204 square miles) of land and 8,000 kilometers (5,000 miles) of coastline—is home to a small but richly diverse population with a history that in some cases stretches back thousands of years; in other cases, the mining towns of Labrador West for example, the history goes back less than four decades.

Getting There From the island of Newfoundland, you can fly to Labrador via St. John's, Gander, Deer Lake, or Stephenville. Route 500 was opened in 1992 linking Labrador City with Happy Valley–Goose Bay via Churchill Falls. If you plan on doing any extensive driving in any part of Labrador, you should contact the Department of Tourism and Culture (tel. 709/729–2830 or 800/563–6353) for advice on the best routes and road conditions.

To explore the south coast of Labrador, catch the ferry at St. Barbe on Route 430 in Newfoundland to Blanc Sablon, Québec. From here you can drive to Red Bay along Route 510. Conditions on this 439-kilometer (300-mile) unpaved wilderness road are best between June and October.

In summer, you can travel by car ferry through **Marine Atlantic** (in Lewisporte, Newfoundland, tel. 709/535–6876; in Happy Valley–Goose Bay, Labrador, 709/896–0041; or in the United States, 800/341–7981). The ship travels from Lewisporte in Newfoundland to Cartwright, on the coast of Labrador, and then through the Hamilton inlet to Happy Valley–Goose Bay. Room is limited and reservations can be made only from within the province.

The Straits The trip from Blanc Sablon to Red Bay on Route 510 will take you through the small fishing communities of L'Anse au Clair, **53** Forteau, and L'Anse au Loup. In **L'Anse au Clair,** you can walk the "Doctor's Path," where long ago Dr. Marcoux searched out herbs and medicinal plants in the days when hospitals and nursing stations were few and far between. Anglers can try their luck for trout and salmon on the scenic Forteau and Pinware rivers. The Straits were a rich hunting-and-gathering ground for the continent's earliest peoples.

The elaborate Maritime Archaic Indian burial site discovered **54** near **L'Anse Amour,** about 12 miles from L'Anse au Clair, is 9,000 years old. A plaque marks the site. The L'Anse Amour lighthouse was constructed in 1857 and is the second-tallest lighthouse in Canada. During the month of August, the annual **Labrador Bakeapple Festival** in **Forteau** draws people from miles around for music, feasting, and celebration. The **Labrador Straits Museum** (Route 510, between Forteau and l'Anse-au-Loup, tel. 709/927–5659. Admission $1.50. Open daily during the summer.) provides an interesting glimpse into the history and life-style of the area.

You must drive to the very end of Route 510 to visit the area's **55** main attraction: **Red Bay,** the site of a 16th-century Basque whaling station and the province's newest UNESCO World Heritage Site. Basque whalers began harpooning migrating whales from flimsy boats in frigid waters a few years after Cabot's discovery of the coast in 1497. Between 1550 and 1600 Red Bay was the world's whaling capital. A new visitor center (tel. 709/920–2197, open 8–8 Mon.–Sat., noon–8 Sun., mid-June–early Oct.) interprets the Basque heritage through film and artifact. Between June and October, a boat will take you on a short journey over to the actual site of excavations on Saddle Island.

Coastal Labrador You can tour coastal Labrador aboard Marine Atlantic's car ferry (*see* Arriving and Departing, *above*) from Lewisporte, Newfoundland, which also carries of all types of food and goods for people living along the coast. The trip takes 33 hours one-way, and two regularly scheduled return trips are made weekly. A second ferry travels from Happy Valley–Goose Bay to Nain, Labrador's northernmost settlement. This trip takes two weeks to complete. As both ferries are supply boats, you'll stop at a number of summer fishing stations and coastal communities.

56 **Happy Valley–Goose Bay** is the chief service center for coastal Labrador. The town was founded in the 1940s as a top-secret air base used to ferry fleets of North American–manufactured aircraft to Europe. It is still used as a low-level flying training base by the British, Dutch, and German air forces.

57 **North West River** is a pleasant, half-hour drive to the east on Route 520, and on the way you'll pass the **Snow Goose Mountain Ski Club** (tel. 709/896–5923). North West River was founded as a Hudson's Bay trading post and is the former Labrador headquarters of the International Grenfell Association. It retains its frontier charm. Nearby **Sheshatshit** is the home of the Montagnais Innu, natives of Labrador. The spirit in which the Innu (Naskapi-Montagnais) people inhabited the interior for centuries can still be felt the moment you step outside the region's modern mining communities.

Labrador West   Labrador West's subarctic landscape is challenging and unforgettable. The area offers some of the world's best angling and wilderness adventure opportunities.

The best way to see this area is by taking the **Québec North Shore and Labrador Railway** (tel. 709/944–8205), which leaves Sept Isles, Québec, twice weekly. The 10-hour trip takes you through 419 kilometers (260 miles) of virgin forest, spectacular waterfalls, and majestic mountains. The refurbished vintage dome car is ideal for an expanded view of this breathtaking panorama. The train, though, is more than a pleasure ride—it carries iron ore from Wabush and Labrador City (site of the largest open-pit mining operation in the world) to various distribution points in Québec.

58 **59**   The modern towns of **Wabush** and **Labrador City** have all the amenities of larger, urban centers, including accommodations, sports and recreational facilities, good shopping, live theater, and some of the finest hospitality you will find anywhere. Nearby are the **Smokey Mountain Alpine Skiing Center** (open mid-November–early May, tel. 709/944–3505) and the **Menihek Nordic Ski Club** (tel. 709/944–6339 or 709/944–2154), with trails and slopes for both beginners and advanced skiers.

Shopping

The main centers of Newfoundland and Labrador—St. John's, Clarenville, Gander, Grand Falls, Corner Brook, Labrador West—all have modern shopping centers. However, the smaller communities often offer interesting crafts and native wares. Wander about—each town and village has its own country store and crafts store or general store. There are even some stores where packages are still being wrapped in brown paper and tied with twine.

NONIA (Newfoundland Outport Nurses Industrial Association), at 286 Water Street in St. John's, was started in 1923 to give Newfoundland women an opportunity to earn extra money. Throughout history, the women of Newfoundland had earned a reputation for turning homespun wool into exquisite clothing. In 1923 Jubilee Guilds supplied these outport women with wool of all kinds and colors, and in this shop on Water Street, even today, you can buy their well-made knitware. Other fine crafts stores in St. John's are the Salt Box, The Cod Jigger, the Devon House Craft Gallery, and the Newfoundland Weavery. For antiques, Murray's Antiques and Livyers are well worth a visit.

At St. Anthony, on the northern tip of Newfoundland, browse in the Grenfell Handcraft Store (*see* Exploring, *above*).

Most bookstores have a prominent section devoted to local history, fiction, and memoirs. **Word Play** (221 Duckworth St., tel. 709/726–9193 or 800/563–9100) also carries a wide selection of newspapers, magazines, and books of general interest to travelers. **Fred's Records** (198 Duckworth St., tel. 709/753–9191) has the best selection of local tapes and CDs, as well as other music.

Sports and Fitness

Many provincial and all national parks in Newfoundland have hiking and nature trails. The west coast offers opportunities for mountain climbing in the summer and skiing in the winter. There are also ski resorts near Clarenville, Labrador City, and Happy Valley–Goose Bay, and groomed cross-country ski trail systems in St. John's, Clarenville, Terra Nova National Park, Gros Morne National Park, Labrador City, and Happy Valley–Goose Bay, among other places.

Coastal and woods trails radiate from most small communities. However, you can never be sure how far the trail will go unless you ask a local. Be careful: Landmarks are few, the weather is changeable, and it is surprisingly easy to get lost. Many small communities now also have formal walking trails.

Newfoundland has 105 salmon rivers and trout streams. Angling in these unpolluted waters is a fisherman's dream. Seasonal and regulatory information can be obtained from the **Department of Tourism and Culture** (tel. 800/729–2830).

Dining and Lodging

Dining

John Cabot and Sir Humphrey Gilbert raved about "waters teeming with fish." Today Newfoundland's fish are still some of the best in the world and one of the best dining bargains you will find anywhere. In Newfoundland, if you ask for "fish," you will always get cod. In season you will be treated to local delicacies such as panfried, baked, or poached cod, cod tongues, salt cod, fish and brewis (cod of course!). Fresh lobster, halibut, scallops, mussels, and Atlantic salmon are also good choices in season.

Two other foods you shouldn't leave without trying are partridgeberries and bakeapples. Partridgeberries are a small, lush-tasting relative of the cranberry and locally they are used for just about everything—pies, jams, cakes, pancakes, and even as a sauce for turkey and game. Bakeapples in the wild are a low-growing berry that looks like a yellow raspberry—you'll see them ripening in bogs in August throughout Newfoundland and Labrador. Enterprising youngsters sell them by the side of the road in jars. If the ones you buy are hard, wait a few days and they'll ripen into a rich-tasting jam. They're popular on ice cream or spread on fresh homemade bread. In Scandinavia they're known as "cloudberries" and are made into a liqueur.

You may also hear Newfoundlanders talk about the herb they call summer savory. Newfoundlanders are so partial to this peppery herb that they slip it into most stuffings and stews. Growers in the province ship the product all over the world, and Newfoundlanders visiting relatives living outside the province are usually asked to "bring the savory."

Only the large urban centers across the province, especially St. John's and Corner Brook, have gourmet restaurants. Fish is a safe dish to order just about everywhere—even in the lowliest take-out. You'll be agreeably surprised by the quality of the meals along the Trans-Canada Highway: Restaurants in the Irving Gas Station chain, for example, offer thick homemade soups with dumplings, and Sunday dinners that draw in local customers for miles around. Don't be shy about trying some of the excellent meals offered in the province's expanding network of "hospitality homes," where home cooking goes hand in hand with the warm welcome for which Newfoundlanders are famous.

Dress is casual everywhere except at the Very Expensive listings.

Highly recommended restaurants and lodging in each price category are indicated by a star ★.

Category	Cost*
Very Expensive	over $50
Expensive	$35–$50
Moderate	$20–$35
Inexpensive	under $20

*per person, excluding drinks, service, and 12% sales tax

Lodging

Newfoundland and Labrador offer lodgings that range from modestly priced "hospitality homes" to luxury accommodations. In between, visitors can choose from affordable, basic lodging and mid-priced hotels. In remote areas, visitors should be prepared to find very basic lodgings. However, the lack of urban amenities is usually made up for by the home-cooked meals and the great hospitality that you'll encounter. Life is definitely more relaxed here: If you're expected at a "hospitality home" and you're running late, your host or hostess will leave your room key with a welcome note in the mailbox!

Highly recommended lodgings in each price category are indicated by a star ★.

Category	Cost
Expensive	over $100
Moderate	$60–$90
Inexpensive	under $50

Clarenville
Dining and Lodging

Holiday Inn. There are no surprises at this chain member. Rooms are standard Holiday Inn fare. The daily buffet is plentiful and well worth the drive. *Box 967, Clarenville, A0E 1J0, tel. 709/466–7911, fax 709/466–3854. 64 rooms. AE, MC, V. Moderate.*

Corner Brook
Dining and Lodging
★

The Glynmill Inn. This charming inn has the feel of old England. The inn was once the staff house for the visiting top brass of the mill. Rooms are cozy and the dining room serves basic and well-prepared Newfoundland seafood, soups, and specialty desserts made with Newfoundland partridgeberries. There's also a popular steak house in the basement. *Cobb La., Box 550, Corner Brook, A2H 6E6, tel. 709/634–5106, fax 709/634–5106. 90 rooms. AE, MC, V. Moderate.*

Holiday Inn. Again, there's nothing extraordinary here, aside from the convenience of being located right in town. The rooms were completely remodeled in 1991, so there are none of the '70s-style oranges and browns. The restaurant is average but has good seasonal fish dishes. *48 West St., Corner Brook A2H 2Z2, tel. 709/634–5381. 103 rooms. Facilities: lounge, restaurant, cable TV, minibars in some rooms, heated swimming pool. Pets allowed. AE, D, DC, MC, V. Moderate.*

Journey's End Motel. This is a comfortable, modern motel (built in 1988) with an attractive interior (the dominating colors are dusty rose and blue) and beautiful views of either the city or the Bay of Islands. *Box 1142, Corner Brook A2H 6T2 (on Rte. 1), tel. 709/639–1980. 81 rooms with color TV, pets allowed. AE, MC, DC, V. Moderate.*

★ **Mamateek Inn.** Rooms are more modern than at the Glynmill Inn. The dining room, which serves good Newfoundland home-cooked food, is known for its exquisite view looking out over the whole city. Sunsets, seen from the restaurant are remarkable. *Rte. 1, Box 787, Corner Brook, A2H 6G7, tel. 709/639–8901, fax 709/639–7567. 55 rooms. AE, MC, V. Moderate.*

Deer Lake
Dining and Lodging

Deer Lake Motel. The guest rooms here are clean and comfortable, and the food in the café is basic, home-cooked fare. You'll find the seafood dishes exceptionally well prepared. *Box 820, Deer Lake, A0K 2E0, tel. 709/635–2108, fax 709/635–3842. 54 rooms, 2 suites. AE, MC, V. Moderate.*

Gander
Dining and Lodging
★

Albatross Motel. This newly renovated motel has a deserved reputation as an attractive place to stop off for a meal. Try the cod au gratin—you won't find it this good anywhere else. Rooms are basic and clean. *Box 450, Gander, A1V 1W8, tel. 709/256–3956, fax 709/651–2692. 107 rooms, 4 suites. AE, MC, V. Moderate.*

Grand Falls
Dining and Lodging

Mount Peyton Hotel. The rooms aren't soundproof here, but they are clean and comfortable. And the excellent Newfoundland menu makes this a great place to break your journey across the island. *214 Lincoln Rd., Grand Falls, A2A 1P8, tel. 709/489–2251. 150 rooms. AE, MC, V. Moderate.*

L'Anse aux Meadows
Lodging

Valhalla Lodge Bed & Breakfast. Located adjacent to the Viking site at L'Anse aux Meadows, this is the only game in town, but that doesn't make it any less comfortable and inviting. Note the interesting fossils in the rock fireplace in the dining room. Hot breakfasts are available, and extra meals can be had on request. *Gunner's Cove, Griquet A0K 2X0, tel. 709/623–2018 (summer), 709/896–5476 (winter). 6 rooms. V. Inexpensive.*

Port aux Basques
Dining and Lodging

St. Christopher's Hotel. This clean, comfortable hotel is a new addition in Port aux Basque that offers quiet, air-conditioned rooms and good food. Caribou Rd., Box 2049, Port aux Basques, A0M 1C0, tel. 709/695–7034, fax 709/695–9841. 58 rooms. Facilities: banquet room, restaurant (reservations not necessary, dress casual), conference room, satellite TV. AE, MC, V. Moderate.

St. John's
Dining
★

The Cellar. This restaurant situated in a historic building on the waterfront gets rave reviews for its innovative Continental cuisine featuring the best local ingredients. Menu selections include blackened fish dishes and tiramisu for dessert. *Baird's Cove, between Harbour and Water Sts., St. John's, tel. 709/579–8900. Reservations advised. No jeans or sweatshirts. AE, MC, V. Expensive.*

★ **Stone House.** Situated in one of St. John's most historic buildings—an old restored 19th-century stone cottage—this dining room features imported game and Newfoundland specialties. *8 Kennas Hill, St. John's, tel. 709/753–2380. Reservations advised. Dress: casual. AE, MC, V. Expensive.*

Dining and Lodging
★

Hotel Newfoundland. This hotel replaces an old hotel that stood on this site for many years. St. John's residents gather here for many special occasions, and it's noted for its Sunday and evening buffets, its charming rooms that overlook St. John's harbor, its atrium, and the fine cuisine of the Cabot Club. *Box 5637, St. John's A1C 5W8, tel. 709/726–4980, fax 709/726–2025. 288 rooms, 14 suites. AE, MC, V. Expensive.*

★ **Radisson Plaza Hotel.** In this new convention hotel in downtown St. John's, rooms overlook the harbor and the city. It offers two dining rooms: Brazil Square, noted for its breakfast and noon buffets; and Newman's, a secluded dining room serving elaborately presented international dishes and Newfoundland cuisine. *120 New Gower St., St. John's A1C 1J3, tel. 709/739–6404. 276 rooms, 9 suites. AE, MC, V. Expensive.*

Journey's End Motel. This is the newest member of this hotel chain and it overlooks St. John's harbor. Like other Journey's Ends, it offers clean, comfortable rooms at a reasonable price. The hotel's restaurant, Rumplestiltskins, has a splendid view and an unpretentious, attractive menu. *Hill O'Chips, St. John's A1C 6B1, tel. 709/754–7788. 164 rooms. AE, MC, V. Moderate.*

Lodging
★

Compton House Bed & Breakfast. Housed in a charming, restored historic St. John's residence in the west end of the city, this inn is professionally run and beautifully decorated. Twelve-foot ceilings and wide halls give the place a majestic feeling, and rooms done in pastels and chintzes add an air of coziness. The location, within easy walking distance of downtown St. John's, is ideal. *26 Waterford Bridge Rd., St. John's A1E 1C6, tel. 709/739–5789. 4 rooms, 2 suites. AE, MC, V. Moderate.*

★ **Prescott House Bed & Breakfast.** Local art decorates the walls of this house, which has received a Heritage Award. It's the city's most popular bed-and-breakfast, made even better by a modernization that tastefully blended the new and the old. Located downtown, it's central to shopping and attractions. *17–19 Military Rd., St. John's A1C 2C3, tel. 709/753–6036. 10 rooms, 2 suites. MC, V. Moderate.*

The Arts and Nightlife

It has been a long-standing claim (since at least the 1700s) that St. John's has more bars per mile than any other city in North America. Each establishment has its own personality. Irish music, in particular, can be heard at Erin's Pub, Water Street, and the Blarney Stone on George Street. A mix of traditional folk songs and Irish music can be had at Bridgett's, Cookstown Road, St. John's.

George Street, in downtown St. John's, is a street of pubs and restaurants that has been beautifully restored. Open-air concerts can be heard there during the annual George Street Festival and on many other occasions.

Newfoundlanders love a party, and from the cities to the smallest towns they celebrate their history and unique culture throughout a summer of festivals and events. The **Newfoundland and Labrador Folk Arts Festival,** held in St. John's in early August, is the province's best-known traditional music festival. Local folk music festivals occur in every part of the province during the summer. You'll also encounter a host of community celebrations, community dinners, and church teas.

The province has an unusually active arts community, as well. Most major towns have an arts and culture center, which offers live theater presentations, ballet, and concerts by local, national, and international artists. The **Resource Centre for the Arts** (LSPU Hall), on Victoria Street (tel. 709/753-4531), is one of the country's oldest and most innovative experimental theaters. Like the arts and culture centers, it has a busy fall and winter season but is generally inactive during the summer. The **Stephenville Festival** (tel. 709/643-4982) is held throughout July and into August in Stephenville, an hour's drive south of Corner Brook. The festival is the province's major annual summer theatrical event and features a well-produced mix of light musicals and serious drama.

St. John's has a dozen commercial and public art galleries, nearly all of which feature local artists. Newfoundland's unique landscape, portrayed realistically or more experimentally, is a favorite subject. The province's largest public gallery, the **Memorial University Art Gallery** (tel. 709/737-8209) is located in the St. John's Arts and Culture Centre. The **Emma Butler Gallery** (tel. 709/739-7111) on George Street and **Christina Parker Fine Art** (tel. 709/753-0580) on Plank Road, in St. John's, offer the best selection of local fine art for sale. Several galleries specialize in reasonably priced work aimed at the visitor market.

15 Wilderness Canada

By Peter Oliver
and Mac Mackay

Almost without exception, the first topic that comes up in conversation about Canada's northern territories is the enormous amount of space they encompass. The Northwest Territories and Yukon Territory combine for roughly 4 million square kilometers (close to 1.5 million square miles). That's about half the size of the continental United States, and nearly three times the size of Alaska. That's a lot of land.

But what is really noteworthy about the far north is the extraordinary absence of humanity. The total population of Yukon and the Northwest Territories is about 85,000. Put in perspective, that's about half the population of, say, Montgomery, Alabama. More people squeeze into the Rose Bowl (102,083 seats) each year for the New Year's football game than live in the far north.

Furthermore, not very many people come here to visit. Tourism in the Northwest Territories has surged in recent years, but the 25,000 or so tourist visits each year are still only about the equivalent of a typical summer day's business at Arizona's Grand Canyon National Park.

So what makes the far north so uninviting? A few of the obvious answers: It's cold, and winters are long and dark (mid-winter daylight is a short interlude between periods of darkness in northerly communities). With few roads (and few of those roads paved), it's hard to get to—and hard to get around—most places once you've arrived. On top of this, due to the proximity of the magnetic north pole, even a reliable compass can go radically screwy, making it really difficult to get your bearings.

Economic possibilities are minimal, and dreariness is a way of life in winter. Suicide rates far exceed Canada's national average. The great stone sub-surface of the Canadian Shield, swooping down around Hudson's Bay, makes much of the land useless for serious cultivation, and even if it were arable, the shortness of any growing season makes most crop cultivation a ridiculous proposition. Here and there a few companies are scratching around for natural resources: some timber, some oil, some precious metals . . . not much. When the chosen professions of many people include bush-plane pilot, muskrat trapper, and soapstone sculptor, you're talking about a region in which it will be some time before citadels of thriving commerce will be built.

The next question, then, is: What's good about the place? That answer, too, should be obvious: absence of humanity. Except for the sparsely scattered communities where populations typically don't top 500, this is true, unpopulated wilderness, and there is certainly something appealing about that.

Wild animals apparently regard this as a very good deal. Elk herds numbering in the tens of thousands migrate through the tundra north. Grizzly bears fish the mountain streams and rivers of Yukon. The largest free-range herd of buffalo hang out in Wood Buffalo National Park, also favored by the exceedingly rare whooping crane. Foxes, Dall sheep, and migratory and predatory birds are common. While the Arctic North isn't exactly swarming with such rare beasts as musk oxen and polar bears, nonhuman mammals far outnumber humans. Other mammals who inhabit the region include seals, walruses, narwhals, and whales. Fish—trout, grayling, pike, Arctic char—are enormous by southerly continental standards; after all, how many fish can 25,000 tourists, a few commercial fishermen, and a few grizzlies and polar bears catch in a year?

A visitor ought to be moved by the intense, inherent beauty of the landscape: the St. Elias Mountains of the Yukon, featuring Mt. Logan, at 19,850 feet, the highest peak in Canada; the thundering waterfalls (Wilberforce and Virginia Falls) of undammed rivers; icebergs as large as apartment buildings; the resolute persistence of tundral wildflowers blooming when the severity of the land and climate would seem to make blooming an exercise in hopelessness.

If for some mysterious reason, however, the landscape fails to leave an indelible impression, the vast emptiness commands respect. Consider this activity in spatial awareness: Pull over on the Dempster Highway as it crosses the Arctic Circle, and face east. Could human vision bend around the curve of the globe, your line of sight would be unobstructed by any roads or human settlements for roughly 2,420 kilometers (1,500 miles) before settling on the tiny community of Repulse Bay. Animals come to the far north for the very reason that it is still profoundly wild, and that's the main reason why people come to visit, too.

The other reason to travel here, ironically, is for the people. The history of white settlement in the far north is fairly sparse. Explorers and surveyors (Henry Hudson, Martin Frobisher) began exploring about 400 years ago, and the Hudson's Bay Company sought profits from trapping and fur trading after being given title to much of the land in 1670. In 1896, gold was discovered in the Klondike River in the Yukon, spurring a mad rush of prospectors. In large part, however, the land has been left to native peoples (almost native, anyway, their ancient ancestors having first emigrated from Asia perhaps 30,000 years ago), primarily the Inuit and the Dene. Many of these people still go about their business as did their forefathers, as hunters, trappers, and fishermen. Even if modern luxuries such as electricity, and social curses such as alcohol abuse, have had some reforming influences on traditional ways, a native authenticity that has all but vanished elsewhere on the continent continues in the far north.

A visit to the far north does not happen without commitment and preparation. For one thing, one must commit money; experiencing the wilderness in relative comfort does not come cheaply. Lodging under $100 a day is the exception (unless you camp), and what you get at that price is unlikely to be fancy digs. Getting from one place to the next by plane—a not uncommon means of transport, given the roadlessness—can put a serious dent in a vacation budget. Guides and outfitters might seem expensive, too, and indeed they can be. But when you consider that most have only two or three summer months in which to cover the expenses of a year's worth of living, the cost starts to seem reasonable.

Visitors must also be willing to abide unfamiliar local customs, as well as possible discomforts and inconveniences. A few examples: In communities with recent histories of alcoholism (not uncommon in the far north), finding a beer can be tough. Mosquitoes rule the summer months, and anyone without a good insect repellent is in for big trouble. Having to pack an insulated parka and longjohns in August might strike you as weird, but having warm clothing is essential. Although summertime temperatures (in the south) occasionally reach into the 80s (F), they are just as likely to drop below freezing, especially in the north. Also incovenient will be the gravel roads, which can wreak havoc on cars that aren't armored. Screens over headlights are recommended to protect against flying debris.

But justifying a visit to this sometimes unforgiving part of the world is the lure of that incredible landscape, the abundant wildlife, the vast empty spaces—the "call of the wild," as Jack London, who spent a good deal of time in Yukon, dubbed it. This region can be daunting, frightening, and even dangerous, but for those few visitors who do prepare themselves and make the commitment, it can be nothing short of exhilarating.

Essential Information

Important Addresses and Numbers

Tourist Information Northwest Territories For free maps, guides, and brochures, contact **TravelArctic** (Box 1320, Yellowknife, X1A 2L9, tel. 403/873–7200 or 800/661–0788). For more detailed information, regional tourism offices may be more helpful.

For the Arctic coastal region, including such destinations as Bathurst Inlet and Cambridge Bay, contact **Arctic Coast Tourism Association** (Box 91, Cambridge Bay, X0E 0C0, tel. 403/983–2224). For Baffin and Ellesmere Island, contact **Baffin Tourism Association** (Box 820, Iqaluit, X0A 0H0, tel. 819/979–6551). For the southwestern territory, contact **Big River Tourism Association** (Box 185, Hay River, X0E 0R0, tel. 403/874–2422). For the far northwest, contact **Delta-Beaufort Tourism Association** (Box 2759, Inuvik, X0E 0T0, tel. 403/979–4321). For Keewatin, on the west coast of Hudson Bay, contact **Travel Keewatin** (Dept. EG, Box 328, Rankin Inlet, X0C 0G0, tel. 819/645–2618). For Yellowknife, the central region, and the north shore of Great Slave Lake, contact **Northern Frontier Visitors' Association** (Box 1107, Yellowknife, X1A 2N8, tel. 403/873–3131). For the western region and Great Bear Lake, contact **Sahtu Tourism Association** (Box 115, Norman Wells, X0E 0V0, tel. 403/587–2054).

Yukon **Tourism Yukon** (Box 2703, Whitehorse, Y1A 2C6, tel. 403/667–5340) is the central source of information for the entire territory. For additional information on the Whitehorse region, contact **Whitehorse Visitor Reception Centre** (102–302 Steele St., Whitehorse, Y1A 2C5, tel. 403/667–2915). For more information on Dawson City and the surrounding region, contact **Klondike Visitors Association** (Box 389, Dawson City, Y0B 1G0, tel. 403/993–5575).

Emergencies For emergency services in either Yukon or the Northwest Territories, dial 0 for the operator and explain the nature of the emergency. You will then be connected with the police, ambulance, fire department, or medical help, as needed.

It is a good idea when traveling in the far north—especially in remote wilderness areas (very likely) and especially if unescorted by a trained guide or outfitter—to pass along to someone at home a detailed itinerary, to facilitate emergency aid or rescue, if necessary.

Hospitals and Clinics Limited medical services, with staff on call 24 hours a day, are available at the nursing station in every community. If necessary, air ambulance service is available to the nearest full-service hospital. In the Northwest Territories, hospitals are located in **Fort Smith** (Fort Smith Health Centre, tel. 403/872–2713), **Hay River** (H.H. Williams Memorial Hospital, tel. 403/874–6512), **Inuvik** (Inuvik General Hospital, tel. 403/979–2955), **Iqaluit** (Baffin Regional Hospital, tel. 819/979–5231), **Pine Point** (H.H. Williams Memorial Hospital, tel. 403/393–2281), and **Yellowknife** (Stanton Yellowknife Hospital, tel. 403/920–4111). In Yukon, hospitals are located in **Dawson City** (Dawson Medical Clinic, tel. 403/993–5744), **Watson Lake** (Watson Lake Cottage Hospital, tel. 403/536–2541), and **Whitehorse** (Whitehorse General Hospital, tel. 403/667–8700, as well as other clinics).

Pharmacies Pharmacies are located in the major settlements of Yukon and the Northwest Territories, though late-night service is generally unavailable; after hours, contact the nearest hospital or nursing station (see Hospitals and Clinics above). If you have a pre-existing medical condition requiring special medication, be sure you are well supplied; getting unusual prescriptions filled can be difficult to impossible, depending on where you are.

Arriving and Departing by Plane

Airports and Airlines **Whitehorse International Airport** is the major airport for Yukon and is located in downtown Whitehorse. **Yellowknife Airport**, the main facility for the Northwest Territories, is 5 kilometers (3 miles) northeast of the center of Yellowknife. Many smaller, more remote communities—notably Cambridge Bay, Inuvik, and Iqaluit—also have regular, if infrequent, passenger service, with flights (depending on the community and airline) from Calgary, Edmonton, Montréal, Ottawa, Winnipeg, and Vancouver.

The major air carriers with connecting service from the United States to points in the Northwest Territories and Yukon are **Air Canada** and **Canadian Airlines**. Air Canada's service in the Northwest Territories and Yukon is provided in conjunction with its affiliates, **Air BC** and **NWT Air**. Air Canada's toll-free number for most of the United States is 800/776–3000; in Michigan and most of New York (except New York City), 800/387–2710; in Idaho and Washington, 800/663–8868. In Yukon, Air Canada's number is 800/663–9100; the numbers for NWT Air are 800/661–0789 and 403/920–2500.

The number for Canadian Airlines in the Unites States is 800/426–7000; in Yellowknife and the western Northwest Territories, 800/661–1505; in the eastern region, 800/665–1177; in Rankin Inlet, 800/665–1430. **First Air** (tel. 613/839–3340 or 800/267–1247) also offers extensive service into the Northwest Territories from Montréal and Ottawa.

Arriving and Departing by Car, Train, or Bus

By Car It hardly bears saying that getting to Yukon or the Northwest Territories by car calls for a good deal of driving. The best route into the region is the Alaska Highway (Rte. 97 in British Columbia), accessible from Edmonton via Routes 43, 34, and 2 and from Vancouver via Route 1. After Fort Nelson, Routes 7, 1, and 3 lead to Yellowknife; the Alaska Highway (Rte. 1 in Yukon) continues on to Whitehorse. The good news is that with so few roads in the region, it's difficult to make a wrong turn. The bad news is the amount of driving required to get from one point to another. For example, the distance from Vancouver to Whitehorse is more than 2,400 kilometers (1,500 miles). With relatively little lodging along the way, you might want to embark on the trip in a camper or recreational vehicle. **Ambassador Motorhome & Recreational Services Ltd.** (Mile 912, Alaska Hwy., Whitehorse, YT Y1A 3S9, tel. 403/667–4130) offers one-way rental options between British Columbia and Yukon.

By Train There is no rail service into Yukon or the Northwest Territories.

By Bus **Greyhound Lines of Canada Ltd.** (10234 103rd St., Edmonton, AB T5J 0Y9, tel. 403/421–4211) provides service from Edmonton to Hay River, Northwest Territories. Greyhound also has service from Edmonton or Vancouver to Whitehorse in Yukon.

Getting Around

By Car Regardless of horror stories you might have heard, road travel in the Yukon and Northwest Territories improves each year. The Alaska, Klondike, Dempster, and Mackenzie highways are hard-packed gravel roads with ever-increasing paved sections.

That said, you need to take a few precautions. Be sure to have a reliable vehicle with good suspension. With the exception of the Dempster, there are few stretches of road in excess of 160 kilometers (100 miles) without services, but even that's a pretty long distance. A full tank of gas, a good spare tire and jack, and extra parts (air filter, fan belt, fluids) are essential before setting out. Gravel can be nasty on cars, which is why cars in these parts sport plastic headlight protectors and even windshield shields. You'll be wise to follow suit.

Winter driving requires extra precautionary measures. Many a far-north resident can tell you a story about overnighting on the road and having to wait out fierce weather. So take along emergency survival gear, including ax, shovel, plenty of matches, kindling (paper or wood) to start a fire, sleeping bag, rugged outerwear, and food. Also, a properly winterized car, with light engine oil and transmission fluid, a block heater, recently installed anti-freeze, and tire chains, is much less likely to experience an annoying and possibly dangerous breakdown.

One other thing to think about: In the Northwest Territories, there are river crossings without real bridges. In summer, you ride a free ferry and in winter you cross via snow bridge. But there may be periods in between, when the snow isn't firm enough for a bridge but hasn't melted enough for the ferry, making the road simply impassable. For daily ferry reports in summer: Highways 1 and 3, tel. 403/873–7799 or 800/661–0751; for the Dempster Highway, tel. 403/873–0158 or 800/661–0752. For winter road conditions: Highways 1 through 7, tel. 403/873–0157 or 800/662–0750; for the Dempster Highway, tel. 403/873–0158 or 800/661–0752.

In Whitehorse and Yellowknife, major car-rental agencies are located at the airport, and in most cases they offer cars, trucks, and four-wheel drive vehicles. Touring by camper or motorhome is a popular way to see this part of the world, and you might consider springing for the extra rental cost.

In Whitehorse, **Budget** (tel. 403/667–6200 or 800/627–0700) and **Thrifty** (tel. 403/667–7936 or 800/FOR–CARS) have rental locations at the airport. For campers or motorhomes, contact **Ambassador Motorhome & Recreational Services Ltd.** (Mile 912, Alaska Hwy., Whitehorse, YT Y1A 3S9, tel. 403/667–4130) or **Klondike Recreational Rentals Ltd.** (108 Industrial Rd., Box 5156, Whitehorse, YT Y1A 4S3, tel. 403/668–2200). **Avis** (tel. 403/873–5648 or 800/331–1212) rents at the airport.

By Bus If you've arrived in Hay River via Greyhound bus, **Frontier Coachlines** (Box 1860, Yellowknife, NWT X1A 2P4, tel. 403/873–4892) has connecting service to Yellowknife. For connecting service from Hay River to Pine Point, Fort Resolution, or Fort Smith, contact **North of 60 Bus Lines** (Box 748, Fort Smith, NWT X0E 0P0, tel. 403/872–2467). **Greyhound Lines of Canada** (tel. 403/667–2223) offers service between Whitehorse and Vancouver, Edmonton, and other Canadian cities. In Whitehorse, **Norline Coaches** (2191 2nd Ave., Whitehorse, YT Y1A 4B4, tel. 403/668–3355) has service to and from Dawson City. **Alaskon Express** (208G Steele St., Whitehorse, YT Y1A 2C4, tel. 403/668–3225) provides service northwest on the Alaska Highway to Anchorage and Fairbanks, Alaska, and south on the Klondike Highway to Skagway, Alaska. From mid-May through September, **Dempster Highway Bus Service** (Box 960, Dawson City, YT Y0B 1G0, tel. 403/993–5175) offers twice-weekly trips between Dawson City and Inuvik.

By Plane Once outside Yukon or the southwest quadrant of the Northwest Territories, flying is essentially the only way to get around in wilderness Canada. **Canadian North** and **NWT Air** (*see* Arriving and Departing by Plane, *above*) are among the airlines with the most extensive regularly scheduled service within the region. **Alkan Air** (tel. 403/668–2107 or 800/661–0432) and **First Air** (tel. 613/839–3340 or 800/267–1247) also offer extensive service within the region. Chartering flights is a common practice, with dozens of charter companies offering service. Among the most reliable covering the widest territory are Alkan Air and NWT Air, as well as **Ptarmigan Airways** (tel. 403/873–4461) and **Spur Aviation** (tel. 403/873–3626). For a complete list of air charter services, contact Tourism Yukon or TravelArctic (*see* Important Addresses and Numbers, *above*).

Guided Tours Several tour operators offer general-interest tours, specialty tours, and tours combining sightseeing with such special interests as hiking, dog-sledding, and wildlife watching. Those tour operators included here offer the widest range of touring opportunities in the far north. For a complete list of tour operators, contact **Tourism Yukon** or **TravelArctic** (*see* Important Addresses and Numbers, *above*). For additional special-interest tours, also see Sports and Outdoor Activities, below. In most cases, multiday package prices include transportation from major Canadian cities: Whitehorse and Yellowknife as well as Edmonton, Montréal, Ottawa, and Vancouver.

Orientation **Canada North Expeditions** (Box 2435, Yellowknife, NWT X1A 2P8, tel. 403/920–2196) features tours of Yellowknife and surroundings, as well as tours of the Arctic North. **Canadian Motor Coach Travel Ltd.** (Greyhound Terminal, Main Floor,

10324–103 St., Edmonton, AB T5J 0Y9, tel. 403/448–1188 and reverse charges) features 10- and 11-day bus tours from Edmonton through the Northwest Territories' southwest, as well as to Inuvik in the Arctic North. **Polar Adventures Inc.** (Box 75218, White Rock, BC V4A 9N4, tel. 604/535–2424) features small group tours within the Arctic Circle, including trips to the North Pole.

Special Interest **Adventure Canada** (1159 W. Broadway Ave., Vancouver, BC V6H 1G1, tel. 604/736–7447 or 800/387–1483) features a variety of trips in the Arctic North, from cultural itineraries and Inuit villages to golf at the North Pole. **Arctic Tour Company** (Box 2021, Inuvik, NWT X0E 0T0, tel. 403/979–4100) specializes in wildlife-viewing tours, including whale watching in the Arctic region. **Blackfeather Wilderness Adventures** (1341 Wellington St. W, Ottawa, ON K1Y 3B8, tel. 613/722–9717) runs active adventures such as backpacking, canoeing, cross-country ski touring, and mountain-biking. **Mountain Travel/Sobek** (6420 Fairmount Ave., El Cerrito, CA 94530, tel. 510/527–8100 or 800/227–2384) offers sea-kayaking adventures in the Arctic, as well as whitewater rafting trips in Yukon and Alaska. **Sierra Club Outings** (730 Polk St., San Francisco, CA 94109, tel. 415/923–5522) specializes in hiking and wildlife excursions and leads trips to Baffin and Ellesmere islands. Also, for other special-interest tours, *see* Sports and Outdoor Activities, *below.*

Exploring Wilderness Canada

The sheer size of Canada's far north imposes the necessity of making choices when visiting. To try visiting, say, Baffin Island and Kluane National Park on the same trip would be like trying to tour New England and the Rocky Mountains on the same vacation. The choices fall roughly into three categories: visiting the main cities (Dawson City, Whitehorse, Yellowknife); excursions from the cities; and adventures in the Arctic North. The cities are probably the least interesting part of this package. While there are points of historical and cultural interest in each—enough to hold your attention for a couple of days—it makes little sense to come this far and not venture beyond the city limits.

Keep in mind that June through August are the primary months for visiting the Arctic North. In summer there's an abundance of daylight; even in the south, darkness may not come until after 11 PM, and it may barely come at all in the north. Much before and after the summer months the northern climate can get unfriendly and most outfitters and tour operators close up shop. In the south, however, you shouldn't rule out spring, fall, and even winter as possible times to visit. For example, a dog-sledding or cross-country skiing trip in March are options well worth considering.

Highlights for First-time Visitors

Bison and whooping cranes in Wood Buffalo National Park, Tour 5: Excursions from Yellowknife
Kaskawulsh Glacier in Kluane, Tour 2: Excursions from Whitehorse

Midnight Dome at Dawson City, Tour 3: Dawson City
Signpost Forest at Watson Lake, What to See and Do with Children
S.S. Klondike National Historic Site, Tour 1: Whitehorse
Virginia Falls in Nahanni National Park, Tour 5: Excursions from Yellowknife

Tour 1: Whitehorse

Whitehorse began as an encampment beside the White Horse Rapids of the Yukon River. Prospectors heading north in search of gold in 1898 were forced to portage their boats past the rapids, making this a logical place to take a break in their travels. From these roots, a city of more than 20,000 residents grew, mainly as a center of transportation and communication, and as the seat of the territorial government.

Two possibilities are logical starting points for a city tour. The first is the **Whitehorse Visitor Reception Centre,** one block north of Main Street. This is a good place to pick up information on local lodgings, restaurants, shops, attractions, and events. *302 Steele St., tel. 403/667–2915. Open mid-May–mid-Sept., daily 8–8.*

The other possible starting point is the **Yukon Historical and Museums Association.** The association leads daily city tours in July and August and also sells, for a nominal fee, maps and booklets for self-guided tours. *3126 3rd Ave., tel. 403/667–4704. Open July–Aug., daily 9:30–4 (although hours may vary). Admission free.*

From either starting point, your next stop should be the **Mac-Bridge Museum,** at 1st Avenue and Wood Street. Museum exhibits feature profiles of native cultures and the history of Yukon settlement, from early exploration through fur trading, the gold rush, and later development, including the construction of the Alaska Highway. *1st Ave. and Wood St., tel. 403/667–2709. Admission: $3.25 adults, $2.25 senior citizens, 50¢ children 6–12, $7.50 families. Open mid-May–Sept., daily 12–4; Oct.–mid-May, Sun. 1–4.*

Back on 1st Avenue, turn right on Main Street. On your left is the **WP&YR railroad station,** the transportation hub of downtown Whitehorse until the line shut down in 1982.

Time Out   For a quick refresher, visit **The Pot Belly** (106–102 Main St.), a street-level restaurant serving breakfast, sandwiches, salads, and rich desserts.

From The Pot Belly, head south on 2nd Avenue to the Yukon Territorial Government complex, just past Hanson Street. A couple of places are worth visiting in this area. In the Whitehorse Public Library, the **Territorial Art Gallery** features exhibits by local artists, as well as touring shows from other parts of Canada. *2nd Ave., tel. 403/667–5239. Admission free. Open weekdays 10–9, Sat. 10–6, Sun. 1–9.*

In the foyer of the main territorial government building is more art: The **Yukon Permanent Art Collection** features depictions of northern landscapes and cultures and emphasizes Yukon art. *Tel. 403/667–5239. Admission free. Open weekdays 8:30–5.*

ARCTIC OCEAN

Beaufort
Sea

Prince
Patrick
Island

Ne
Po

Melville
Island

Bath
Isla

Banks
Island

Viscount Melville
Sound

REINDEER
GRAZING RESERVE

Fort
McPherson

Inuvik

Arctic Red River

Amundsen Gulf

Victoria
Island

Pr
of V
Isl

McClintock Channel

PEEL
RIVER
PRESERVE

TREE LINE
(Approximate
northern
limit of trees)

Cambridge
Bay

Coppermine

Queen Maud
Gulf

Norman Wells

Fort Norman

Great Bear
Lake

Fort
Franklin

Bathurst Inlet

Mackenzie River

DISTRICT OF MACKENZIE

Garry
Lake

THELON GAME
SANCTUARY

River

Thelon

DI

K

Nahanni
National
Park

Fort Simpson

Yellowknife

Nahanni Butte

Fort Liard

Great Slave
Lake

Dubawnt Lake

Hay River

BRITISH
COLUMBIA

Wood Buffalo
National
Park

Fort Smith

Peace River

Lake
Athabasca

Uranium
City

Lake
Nueltin

The Yukon

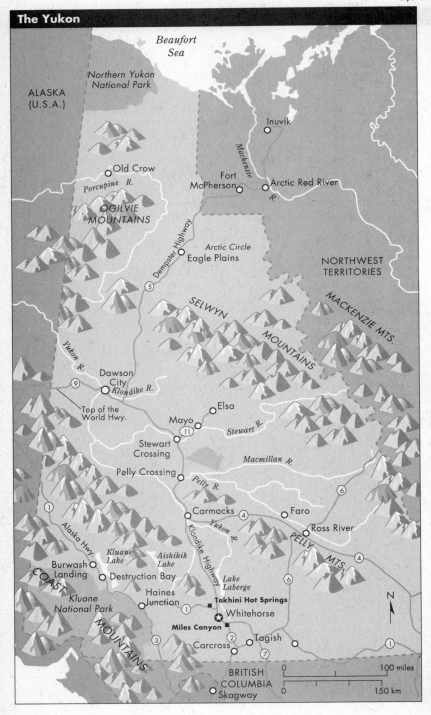

Beaufort
Sea

ALASKA
(U.S.A.)

Northern Yukon
National Park

Inuvik

Old Crow

Porcupine R.

OGILVIE
MOUNTAINS

Mackenzie R.

Fort
McPherson

Arctic Red River

NORTHWEST
TERRITORIES

Dempster Highway

Arctic Circle

Eagle Plains

5

Yukon R.

SELWYN

MOUNTAINS

MACKENZIE MTS.

Dawson
City

9

Klondike R.

Top of the
World Hwy.

Elsa

Mayo

11

Stewart R.

Stewart
Crossing

Pelly Crossing

Macmillan R.

Pelly R.

6

Carmacks

4

Faro

Ross River

1

Yukon R.

Alaska Hwy.

Kluane
Lake

Aishihik
Lake

Klondike Highway

PELLY

MTS.

4

Burwash
Landing

COAST

Destruction Bay

Kluane
National Park

Haines
Junction

Lake
Laberge

6

Takhini Hot Springs

1

MOUNTAINS

Miles Canyon

Whitehorse

3

Carcross

2

Tagish

N

7

1

BRITISH
COLUMBIA

Skagway

0   100 miles

0   150 km

From the government buildings you'll see in the distance the **S.S.** *Klondike* National Historic Site, just past Rotary Park on the other side of 2nd Avenue. The 71.6-meter (235-foot) stern-wheeler was built in 1929, sank in 1936, and was rebuilt in 1937. It was the largest boat running the Yukon River between Whitehorse and Dawson City in the days when the river was the main transportation link between the two cities. It is now drydocked, and has been restored to its 1930s glory. *Tel. 403/667–4511. Admission free. Daily tours, mid-May–mid-Sept.*

You can complete your central-city tour with a visit to the **Old Log Church Museum** at 3rd Avenue and Elliott Street. The church was built in 1900 and services continued to be held inside until 1960. Exhibits reveal the history of Yukon with special emphasis on the role of the Christian church in the north. *3rd Ave. and Elliott St., tel. 403/668–2555. Admission: $2 adults, $1 children 6–12, $5 families. Open June–Aug., Mon.–Sat. 9–8, Sun. noon–4.*

Other Points of Interest Before you leave Whitehorse, there are a few other attractions that are worth a peek. The **Yukon Transportation Museum,** located at the Whitehorse Airport, includes modes of transportation as diverse as snowshoes and planes, dog-sleds and cars. On display here, and highlighting the collection, is the *Queen of the Yukon,* the first commercial plane to serve the territory, in 1927. *Whitehorse Airport, tel. 403/668–4792. Admission free. Open June, Wed.–Sun. 10–6; July–Aug., daily 10–6.*

You might also be interested in watching fish fly at the **Whitehorse Rapids Dam and Fish Ladder,** located at the end of Nisultin Drive in the suburb of Riverdale. The ladder is a way for spawning Chinook salmon to bypass the dam in their annual migration. *Admission free. Open mid-July–mid-Sept., daily 8 AM–10 PM.*

Tour 2: Excursions from Whitehorse

If you're in a camper or motorhome, the trip from Whitehorse northwest along the Alaska Highway is certainly one of North America's great scenic road trips. It is a trip, of course, also possible in a car, as some lodging and campgrounds can be found along the way. But there is something to be said about having your lodging travel with you in remote country such as this, and there is also something nice about having lodging more solid than a tent when there are grizzlies and other pesky animals roaming around.

About 161 kilometers (100 miles) southwest of Whitehorse is **Haines Junction,** the main gateway to **Kluane National Park** (tel. 403/634–2251). Kluane is both beautiful and frustrating—beautiful in that it is a land of deep forests and valleys reaching up to glaciated St. Elias Mountains, the highest in Canada; frustrating in that much of the park is inaccessible to all but experienced backcountry travelers and mountaineers. Most visitors must be satisfied to get only a taste of Kluane's dazzling ruggedness.

The **Visitor Reception Centre** in Haines Junction is well worth a visit as an introduction to the park's geology, flora, and fauna. This area is, for example, the most earthquake-prone in Canada, with an average of 1,000 tremors (many of them barely perceptible) recorded each year. Kluane's mountains are also the youngest in North America, still in their formative stages. Among displays at the center is a seismograph, monitoring activity in the region. Dall sheep, grizzly bears, and mountain goats are among the prominent species that make the park their home.

A few short hiking trails, ranging from 2 to 8 kilometers (3/4–5 miles), lead into the park from the Haines–Alaska Highway. These trails provide a good introduction to the park's lowlands and front ranges, but they present little of the park's glacial spectacle. For that, the two-day excursion (27 kilometers or 16 miles; tent camping required) to the **Kaskawulsh Glacier** is about as close as backpackers can get. A flight by chartered plane offers a better view of the St. Elias Mountains; ask at the visitor center for a recommended charter service. If you are resolved to spend time in Kluane's rugged backcountry, sign on with an outfitter or guide service (*see* Sports and Outdoor Activities, *below*). *Kluane National Park, Haines Jct., YT Y0B 1L0, tel. 403/634–2251.*

Tour 3: Dawson City

Dawson City sprang up at the end of the 19th century, during the days of the gold rush, with its population at one point swelling to 30,000. That gave it the claim at that time of being the largest settlement west of Chicago and north of San Francisco. When the gold dwindled, so did the population: Today there are about 1,700 residents. Many of the original buildings have been restored, although many ramshackle structures remain, too, as reminders of Dawson City's one-time boomtown status. In recent years, attractions have been created in an effort to draw more visitors to the Klondike region.

Start your tour at the **Palace Grand Theatre,** which was showtime central during the gold rush days, staging everything from operas to wild west shows. It was restored in the 1960s by the Canadian government, and today it is the home of the **Gaslight Follies,** a Klondike-style variety show performed with song, dance, and colorful costumes. *Klondike Visitors Assn., tel. 403/993–5575. Admission: $13 adults, $5.50 children under 12. Shows June–mid-Sept., Wed.–Mon. 8 PM.*

On 8th Avenue, within a block from one another, are former **residences of Jack London** and **Robert Service,** the two writers most associated with the Yukon Territory and history. London's most famous work is *Call of the Wild,* and Service has been dubbed "the bard of the Klondike." The poetry and prose of these writers romanticized the beauty and isolation of the region. In addition to personal memorabilia, regular readings of the writers' works are recited at each home. *Jack London Interpretive Center, 8th Ave. and 1st St., tel. 403/993–5575. Admission free. Open June–mid-Sept., daily 10–noon and 1–6. Robert W. Service Cabin, 8th Ave. and Hanson St., tel. 403/993–5462. Admission free. Open July–Aug., daily readings 10–3.*

Back on 5th Avenue at Church Street is the **Dawson City Museum,** housed in the former Territorial Administration Building. The museum chronicles the history of the gold rush and native history of the region. A theater shows movies (historic silent films) on local history. The Klondike research center also provides assistance to historical and genealogical researchers. *5th Ave. past Missions St., tel. 403/993–5291. Admission: $3.50* *adults, $2.50 senior citizens and students, children under 6 free. Open June–early Sept., daily 10–6, May and Sept., Tues., Thurs., and Sat. 1–4.*

Head from here to the docks on Front Street, where you can see the **SS Keno,** one of the last sternwheelers to travel the Yukon and Stewart rivers. More than 200 riverboats worked the Yukon waterways until the mid-1950s. If you want to get a flavor of that river travel, the **Yukon Queen,** also docked along Front Street, makes the 173-kilometer (108-mile) trip west down the Yukon River to Eagle, Alaska, in seven hours. *Front St., tel. 403/993–5599 or 403/993–5482; 800/544–2206 to book as part of a 5- or 11-day package tour. Fares: $80 adult one-way, $40 children one-way, $124 adult round-trip, $62.50 children round-trip. Open June–Sept.*

For a shorter excursion, board the **Yukon Lou** for a 1½-hour cruise downriver to Pleasure Island, 5 kilometers (3 miles) away, and enjoy a salmon barbecue. *Box 859, Dawson City, YT Y0B 1G0, tel. 403/993–5482. Reservations required. Fares: $28 adults, $14 children. Open June–Aug., daily at 1.*

Finally, one of the real highlights of Dawson City is the **Midnight Dome.** The summit of the dome offers a panoramic view of the Klondike and Yukon River valleys, Dawson City, and the Ogilvie Mountains. The best time to go is at night when the sun is low, especially on the night of June 21, when the sun barely sets beyond the Ogilvie Mountains before immediately beginning its ascent again. Midnight Dome can be reached by driving up King Street; **Gold Street Tours** (on Front St. near Queen St., tel. 403/993–5175) also runs nightly, 1½-hour tours to the summit during the summer.

Tour 4: Yellowknife

The first settlement was established at Yellowknife in 1934, after the discovery of gold. By 1936, the small settlement had turned into a boomtown of hastily constructed homes and businesses that quickly took on a ramshackle look when the gold frenzy passed. Thereafter came Yellowknife's reincarnation as the hub of government, transportation, and communication for the Northwest Territories. In its second life, the city has seen its year-round population grow to about 15,000. This two-part history has created a two-part city: the "Old Town" surrounded by a modern—if small—metropolis.

Start your tour with a walk through **Old Town,** where shacks crowded onto bare-rock underpinnings during the gold rush days of the 1930s. Perched upon one of these rocks is the **Bush Pilot's Memorial,** which honors the daring pilots who helped open the north, as well as today's pilots who continue the tradition and remain a vital part of the Northwest Territories' limited transportation network. A quick climb to the top of the memorial provides a good panorama of Yellowknife and the surrounding area.

Time Out   While in Old Town, make sure to visit the **Wildcat Cafe,** a squat log building rebuilt to match the original 1930s version. The atmosphere evokes the rough-edged spirit of early Yellowknife, as does the menu, which features such far-north specials as caribou, Arctic char, and musk-ox.

The **Prince of Wales Northern Heritage Center,** on the shore of Frame Lake, is just a few minutes from downtown. It houses extensive displays of northern artifacts, including Inuit carvings, as well as dioramas of northern wildlife. Among the curiosities of the collection are large, moosehide boats and a piece of *Cosmos 954,* the Soviet satellite that crashed 480 kilometers (298 miles) east of Yellowknife in 1978. *On Frame Lake opposite City Hall, tel. 403/873–7551. Admission free. Open June–Aug., daily 10:30–5; Sept.–May, Tues.–Fri. 10–5.*

A good way to get a feel for the native history of Yellowknife and for the settlement's history is to take a cruise on the 33-foot **MV Naocha.** The two-hour tour leaves from Latham Island and explores the waterfront, the oldest gold mine in the region, and Dettah—a native settlement across Yellowknife Bay from the city. A four-hour cruise includes a northern-style barbecue of trout and whitefish. *Sail North, Box 2497, Yellowknife, NWT X1A 2P8, tel. 403/873–8019.*

Tour 5: Excursions from Yellowknife

For these excursions, Yellowknife is used as a reference point to get you oriented. In some cases, however, Yellowknife may not be your best starting point, especially if you're coming into the region by car or camper. For example, Hay River and Fort Smith are probably better departure points for visits to Wood Buffalo National Park; likewise, it's more logical to start from Fort Simpson or Watson Lake when heading to Nahanni National Park. Keep in mind however, that road access in both parks is limited (limited as in nonexistent in Nahanni), and that the most convenient way to visit the parks may be to hire a guide service that flies out of Yellowknife.

The waters and shores of **Great Slave Lake** offer obvious opportunities for excursions from Yellowknife. By car you can travel 120 kilometers (72 miles) northwest to the hybrid community of **Rae-Edzo,** the largest Dene community in the Northwest Territories and one with an interesting history. Fort Rae was originally established in 1852, while Edzo was developed more than 100 years later as a planned Dene community. The idea was that Edzo would gradually replace Fort Rae—but that never happened.

By boat the possibilities for exploring the lake are numerous. **Sail North** (*see* Tour 4, *above*) is one of several Yellowknife outfitters that charters boats, with or without crew, for fishing or simply cruising around the lake. Longer trips that combine a schooner crossing of the lake with rafting on the Great Slave River are organized by **Subarctic Wilderness Adventures** (Box 685, Fort Smith, NWT X0E 0P0, tel. 403/872–2126) and begin at Fort Smith and end in Yellowknife.

Several small lodges, encampments, and communities line the shores of the lake, as well as smaller lakes nearby, and are accessible essentially only by small plane. Fishing is the predominant recreational activity, although some lodges and camps also offer tours led by naturalists and photographers. Accommodations can range from full-service lodges to tents; how much you want to spend and how much you want to rough-it is up to you. A list of lodges is available from **TravelArctic** (*see* Important Addresses and Numbers, *above*).

The communities of **Snowdrift** and **Reliance,** both along the eastern arm of the lake, are among the choice fly-in destinations, with cliff-and-clear-water scenery inspiring enough to situate Reliance at the center of a proposed new national park.

To the southwest of Yellowknife is **Nahanni National Park,** where the South Nahanni River, the Flat River, and their tributaries dramatically cut through the Mackenzie Mountains. Perhaps the most impressive feature in the park is **Virginia Falls,** over 125 meters (410 feet) high and about 200 meters (656 feet) wide—essentially a thunderous wall of whitewater. The falls is the dividing line for the river: Above the falls the river is gentle and meandering; below the falls are several rapids and steep, narrow canyons. The only way to get into the park (other than paddling in by boat via one of the true wilderness rivers that feeds into the park from the northwest) is by chartered plane from Fort Simpson or Watson Lake. Planes can carry canoes and other equipment if you make arrangements ahead of time, but probably your best bet for visiting the park is to sign on with one of the several guide services that lead trips down the river (*see* Sports and Outdoor Activities, *below*). *Superintendent, Nahanni National Park, Bag 300, Fort Simpson, NWT X0E 0N0, tel. 403/695–3151.*

Due south of Yellowknife—across Great Slave Lake and straddling the Alberta/Northwest Territory border—is **Wood Buffalo National Park.** Measuring 283 kilometers (176 miles) north to south, and about 160 kilometers (100 miles) east to west, it is the largest national park in Canada. The larger portion of the park is in Alberta, although the main entry point for the park, as well as home to the park's administrative headquarters, is Fort Smith in the Northwest Territories. The reason for the park's existence is that it's principally a wildlife preserve. In fact, parts of the park (primarily in the south and west) are essentially inaccessible to visitors. Much of the land is covered by bogs, swamps, and meandering streams and rivers, and a vast subterranean water system has caused numerous sinkholes and cave formations in places. This environment is considered absolutely wonderful by mosquitoes in midsummer, and for that reason, visiting the park in spring, fall, or even winter, when the bugs aren't quite so fierce, is probably a good idea.

Although originally created in 1922 as a preserve for the eponymous buffalo, the park is also a summer home and nesting ground for numerous bird species, including bald eagles, peregrine falcons, and the exceedingly rare whooping crane. The short-form way to visit the park is to drive to **Pine Lake,** 65 kilometers (40 miles) south of Fort Simpson (which is technically in Alberta). There is a campground here, as well as interpretive presentations, naturalist programs, and hiking trails. For extended visits into the park's outback, consider one of several outfitters that lead trips using various means of transportation: foot, canoe, skis, and dog-sled. **TravelArctic** (*see* Important Addresses and Numbers, *above*) and the park superintendent can provide a list of such outfitters. *Superintendent, Wood Buffalo National Park, Box 750, Fort Smith, NWT X0E 0P0, tel. 403/872–2349.*

Tour 6: The Arctic North

It probably goes without saying that one doesn't "tour" the Arctic North in the usual sense of the word. Rather, the concept is more expeditionary: Choose a community such as Bathurst Inlet, Iqaluit, or Pangnirtung as a base camp from which to make day or extended side trips. Keep in mind, too, that the travel season is limited: July and August are not only the best months to visit, they are just about the only months. A few outfitters and guides start up earlier in the spring, but the pickings are limited, and this is not a part of the world most people would feel comfortable wandering through without the services of someone who really knows the lay of the land.

Several small communities lie on the shores of the many bays and inlets just north and south of the Arctic Circle, but let's focus on three, from west to east: Inuvik, Bathurst Inlet, and Iqaluit.

Inuvik is the point from which visitors explore the delta of the MacKenzie River as it flows into the Beaufort Sea. Of the four communities mentioned in this tour, it is the only one that can be reached by auto; the Dempster Highway, the most northerly route in North America, terminates in Inuvik. It is a drive for which you need to bring extra everything, including gas, car parts, food, and luck. From Dawson City northeast to Inuvik it's about 800 kilometers (500 miles), with almost no services along the way.

Once you arrive, don't be surprised by the sudden appearance of commercial activity after miles of open tundra. Oil deposits in this region spurred a boomlet of enterprise during the energy crisis of the '70s. Of course, capped oil wells aren't the reason to come to Inuvik. Wildlife viewing is.

Inuvik is surrounded by **Northern Yukon National Park** (also known as the Reindeer Grazing Preserve). Caribou, grizzly bear, Dall sheep, and Arctic fox inhabit this 10,000-square-kilometer (3,861-square-mile) preserve, accessible only by aircraft. You can charter a small plane for park fly-overs; park landings require prior approval from the park office. *Northern Yukon National Park, Inuvik, NWT X0E 0T0, tel. 403/979–3248.*

The Delta area is the summer home for large flocks of migrating geese and water birds; off-shore are beluga and bowhead whales. Guided trips by air to Banks Islands may yield sightings—if you're very lucky—of musk oxen or polar bears. Keep in mind, however, that wildlife watching is a hit-or-miss proposition, with more misses than hits. Be prepared to enjoy the eerie beauty of the landscape; if you happen to spot a polar bear, consider it a grand bonus. *The most complete tour operator and outfitter in the area is Arctic Tour Company, Box 2021, Inuvik, NWT X0E 0T0, tel. 403/979–2054. Air-assisted tours range from one-day helicopter fly-overs of the delta area to 5-day excursions to Banks Island. Arctic Tour also offers Mackenzie River cruises and whale-watching trips. The season runs June–August.*

Bathurst Inlet Lodge is really the only place to stay if you head to Bathurst Inlet. The lodge is 97 kilometers (60 miles) from the nearest settlement, and is accessible (as you might imagine) by plane. Despite its remoteness, however, the lodge offers good accommodations and food, and is a veritable hub of activities in summer. *Bathurst Inlet Lodge, Box 820, Yellowknife, NWT X1A 2N6, tel. 403/873–2595. Open mid-June–Aug. Costs start at $2,600 for a one-week stay, including transportation from Yellowknife.*

When you plan your Arctic North explorations, remember that what you see depends in large part on your mode of transportation: foot, plane, or boat. Day trips farther afield by plane may yield musk-ox and even polar-bear sightings, while day hikes could turn up caribou and foxes. In almost any case, you're likely to see a wide variety of birds, notably peregrine falcons, who spend their summers here. For canoers and kayakers, there is the Hudson River, a relatively easygoing stream until it arrives at the spectacular **Wilberforce Falls.**

Iqaluit might not in itself be considered a real destination, but it's the gateway to the Baffin region, which includes Ellesmere Island in the far north. Iqaluit is the sort of place where people meet up with their outfitter or guide, and then travel on. Two of the most popular places people do travel to are **Auyuittuq National Park** on Baffin and Ellesmere islands. Auyuittuq (pronounced eye-you-ee-took) is a land where summer meets perpetual winter—where ice melts away in places for a few months, but where the rest of the land is consumed by mountains, ice, and glaciers (some as long as 25 kilometers, 15 miles). About a third of the park is covered by the Penny Ice Cap, 3,543 square kilometers (2,200 square miles) of solid ice, from which all those glaciers flow.

The activity in the park is hiking the 98-kilometer (60-mile) **Pangnirtung Pass** trail, from Cumberland Sound to Davis Strait. This, however, is definitely not a trip for anyone disinclined to rough it: Your own tent is your accommodation, and you shouldn't attempt this without a knowledgeable guide (*see* Sports and Outdoor Activities, *below*). But with such features as 5,500-foot Thor, reportedly the highest continuous rock wall in the world, the so-called "Arctic Yosemite" has its rewards. *Auyuittuq National Park, Pangnirtung, NWT X0A 0R0 tel. 819/473–8828. The only accommodations in the area are at the 17-room Auyuittuq Lodge in Pangnirtung (Auyuittuq Lodge, Pangnirtung, NWT X0A 0R0, tel. 819/473–8955). Rates with meals are about $200 a night.*

What to See and Do with Children

Many of the adventurous activities in the far north are probably too strenuous for small children, not to mention too strenuous for many adults. If you do plan to bring small children on excursions into the wilderness, be sure to tell your outfitter or tour operator how old the children are. Perhaps the best type of trip for children is a river float (as opposed to whitewater rafting); the **Great Slave River** and the **South Nahanni River** in Nahanni National Park have long, gentle stretches.

About 35 kilometers (22 miles) south of Whitehorse on the Klondike Highway are **The Museum of Yukon Natural History** and **Frontierland Theme Park.** The museum features dioramas with mounted Yukon wildlife. Organized like the Yukon in miniature, the park includes an igloo, a trapper's cabin with tools of the trade, a mine shaft, and animals such as ducks, chickens, geese, sheep, and a stuffed saber-toothed tiger. Also, visitors have an opportunity to try their luck at a traditional Yukon activity—panning for gold. *Tel. 403/667–1055. Museum or park admission: $3 adults, $2 children under 12, $10 families; admission to both: $6 adults, $4 children under 12, $20 families. Open mid-May–mid-Sept., daily 8:30–6.*

Ten kilometers (6 miles) north of Whitehorse on the Klondike Highway is **Takhini Hot Springs.** In addition to swimming in the spring-warmed water (suits and towels available for rental), people picnic, visit the duck pond, and take guided horseback rides. *Tel. 403/633-2706. Open July–Aug., daily 7 AM–10 PM.*

A challenge for both adults and children is to find the name of your hometown at **Signpost Forest,** in Watson Lake. In 1942, a homesick U.S. soldier, who was working on the construction of the Alaska Highway, erected the first sign with the name of his hometown and its distance away, and he pointed it in the proper direction. Since then, more than 10,000 signs have been added to Signpost Forest.

Shopping

The idea of coming to the far north to go shopping seems almost silly. If you do, however, there are a few shopping guidelines to follow. First, beyond the cities of Whitehorse and Yellowknife, many basic goods such as food and clothing may be hard to come by, particularly if you have a special purchase in mind. If you're planning an extended trip into the territorial wilderness, it's a good idea to stock up on necessary supplies in Whitehorse or Yellowknife.

Native arts and crafts, from soapstone carvings to handstitched parkas, produce the most compelling reason to open your wallet in the far north. Quality, price, and availability vary considerably. Hotel gift shops and crafts stores in the cities offer everything from true art to trinkets. Before you buy, compare quality and price in a few shops. You may find you can get better craftsmanship at a better price from artists in outlying communities, although you'll probably have to pay cash. Carnivals and festivals held in outlying communities in June–August offer excellent opportunities to buy native art or local crafts. Finally, gold items, from well-crafted jewelry to pill vials filled with gold dust, are popular souvenirs rooted in the history of the region.

Dawson City **Maximilian's Gold Rush Emporium** (Front and Queen Sts., tel. 403/993–5486) has a good selection of books, gifts, and souvenirs. You can also have your picture taken with "Max" the stuffed moose. **The Raven's Nook** (2nd Ave. at Queen St., tel. 403/993–5530) has an interesting collection of gold-nugget jewelry.

Whitehorse **Murdoch's Gem Shop** (207 Main St., tel. 403/667–7403) is Yukon's largest manufacturer of gold-nugget jewelry. There are also Murdoch's outlets in Dawson City, Faro, and Watson Lake. **Yukon Native Products** (4230 4th Ave., tel. 403/668–5955; Front St., Dawson, tel. 403/993–5115) exclusively distributes the original, fur-trimmed Yukon parka, handmade by native craftspeople. **Indian Craft Shop** (504 Main St., tel. 403/667–7216) is a good source for mukluks, moccasins, and gold-nugget jewelry. **Yukon Gallery** (2093 2nd Ave., tel. 403/667–2391) carries native carvings, moosehair tuftings, and other souvenir items.

Yellowknife **Yellowknife Trading Post** (4 Lessard Dr., tel. 403/873–3020) carries Inuit and Dene arts and crafts, caribou tuftings, soapstone carvings, and Dene beading. Moosehair tuftings and other crafts are available from **Treeline Trappings** (50th Ave. and 52nd St., tel. 403/920–2854).

Sports and Outdoor Activities

A guide or outfitter is not required if you plan to engage in any of the numerous outdoor activities possible in Canada's far north. For the most part, however, you're inviting difficulties and possibly disaster by not hiring a guide, as the potential hazards of this wilderness are many. For one thing, encounters with grizzlies are not uncommon. First-aid skills in dealing with illness or injury are essential; emergency evacuation by helicopter or other means is usually unavailable. With few marked trails, getting lost is easy, while getting found after getting lost is not. In short, unless you are very experienced and confident with your backcountry abilities, go with a guide.

Bicycling

In a world with few roads, bicycling might seem an inappropriate activity. However, one excellent mountain-bike option is the **Canol Trail**, which runs 372 kilometers (224 miles) from Norman Wells in the Northwest Territories to Whitehorse. Originally a service road for an oil pipeline, the trail was built by the U.S. government during World War II. When the war ended, the pipeline was abandoned, but the road remained. The cycling can be rugged, including stream crossings, rough roads, and grizzly bears. The tent you bring with you is your accommodation, although there is **Oldsquaw Lodge** (Bag Service 2711, Whitehorse, YT Y1A 4K8, tel. 403/668–6732; open late June–mid-Sept.), the one accommodation along the way, and a good place to stop for a few days so you can take day hikes and view wildlife. *Blackfeather Wilderness Adventures (1341 Wellington St. W., Ottawa, ON K1Y 3B8, tel. 613/722–9717) leads 11-day mountain-biking trips along the Canol Trail. Cost: $2,350, including transportation from Whitehorse.*

Camping

Territorial, or public, campgrounds are found along all roads in the north, and most are open from the spring thaw until the fall freeze, although the exact dates vary from year to year. Most have drinking water (although you should boil or filter water before drinking it), fireplaces, and outdoor privies. The few territorial campgrounds in the Northwest Territories are free; there are also privately owned campgrounds that charge a fee. Yukon Territory campsites along the Alaska and Klondike highways charge $5 per night.

Cross-country Skiing

Although there are no downhill ski areas in the region, opportunities for backcountry ski touring abound. February through April is the best time in the south for skiing; April and May are prime skiing months in the Arctic North. Accommodations for extended tours range from lodges to tents. Among the more interesting possibilities, **Yukon Mountain and River Expeditions** (*see* Hiking, *below*) leads extended ski tours in Kluane National Park during April and May. **Canoe Arctic** (Box 130, Fort Smith, NWT X0E 0P0, tel. 403/872–2308) leads six-day trips in southern Northwest Territories in late March, with nights spent in wood-heated tents and days skiing among caribou herds (wildlife obliging).

Dog-Sledding

In a world where snow and ice can be a year-round phenomenon, dog-sledding is more than a sport: It remains for many residents, as it has for centuries, a legitimate means of transportation. In the Arctic North, on Baffin and Ellesmere islands, dog-sledding excursions from **Arctic Odysseys** are possible into late spring. Further south, dog-sledding is among the better ways to experience wilderness Canada in winter. From February until April, **Subarctic Wilderness Travel** leads three- to five-day trips in the Northwest Territories' southwest, with accommodations in cabins, guest homes, and teepees. You can drive your sled and even earn a dog-team driver's license, should you require such a thing. *Arctic Odysseys (3430 Evergreen Point Rd., Box 37E, Medina, WA 98039, tel. 206/455–1960) leads dog-sled excursions on Baffin Island Apr.–May. Cost: approximately $2,800, including transportation from Ottawa; cost varies depending on length of the trip and group size. Subarctic Wilderness Travel Ltd. (Box 685, Fort Smith, NWT X0E 0P0, tel. 403/872–2467) leads 3- to 5-day trips, Feb.–Apr. Cost: ranges between $1,300 and $2,000, including transportation from Yellowknife.*

Fishing

Fishing in wilderness Canada is a way of life, a means of sustenance for a good many native residents. What sustains the native people of the north is also what attracts sport fishermen: fish in large quantities, and of considerable proportions. Farther south on the continent, a five- to eight-pound trout might be considered a trophy fish; in the lakes and streams of the far north, it would be considered the norm. Arctic char, grayling, lake trout, pike, and whitefish are among the most popular catches in the region.

Numerous outfitters throughout the region can guide fishermen on day trips or short excursions; your best bet is to check with regional tourist offices (*see* Important Addresses and Numbers, *above*) for outfitter recommendations. For extended fishing trips, numerous fly-in lodges operate in the far north, with the high season generally running from June through August. (Ice fishing, incidentally, is also popular at other times of the year.) Some lakes and streams are accessible by road in Yukon and the southern Northwest Territories, but "road," when talking of anything beyond the main highways, can be a euphemistic term. If you plan to do much road-accessed fishing, you'll need a four-wheel-drive vehicle.

What can you expect on this kind of fishing trip? A couple of recommended examples are described here, to give you an idea of your options. For more complete listings of fly-in fishing services, contact territorial or regional tourist authorities.

Blachford Lake Lodge (Box 1568, Yellowknife, NWT X1A 2P2, tel. 403/873–3303) is a year-round lodge 100 kilometers (60 miles) east of Yellowknife. Guests stay in cabins and, except for larger groups, must bring their own food. While fishing (including ice fishing in winter) is a main activity at the lodge, it isn't the only activity; sightseeing and wildlife viewing by plane, as well as snowshoeing, cross-country skiing, and snowmobiling in winter, can be arranged. The lodge is a good choice for fishermen traveling with non-fishermen.

Meni Dene Lodge (General Delivery, Lac La Martre, NWT X0E 1P0, tel. 403/573–3161) is a very fishing-intensive experience with a little native culture mixed in, courtesy Dene guides who run the show. The lodge is located in Clum-Eh Island in the middle of Lac La Martre, northwest of Yellowknife. A single, main lodge provides accommodations for 16, with meals provided. The fishing here comes with a guarantee: Fishermen are assured of catching a 20-pound lake fish, pike and trout being the principal prey.

Peacock's Yukon Camps Ltd. (Dept. FS, 77 Alsek Rd., Whitehorse, YT Y1A 3K5, tel. 403/667–2846) provides access to eight fly-in lakes in the southern Yukon for unguided fishing. Boats are supplied and are required to pass such obstacles as beaver dams; navigation can be rugged. Accommodations are in housekeeping cabins, and supplies (whatever you need, including beer) are flown in. A 35-pound lake trout and 45-pound pike have been caught on record.

Hiking

While the landscape can be spectacular, the going can be rugged. Marked trails are relatively few, and often the only trails to follow are those beaten down by wild animals such as bears, sheep, goats, and caribou. Hikers must be prepared to deal with everything from deep-stream crossings to glacial crevasses, from deep brush to tundra, to permanent snowpack. Nevertheless, under the guidance of an experienced outfitter, some of the most unusual and exhilarating hikes are possible in this region.

In summer, the **Sierra Club** (730 Polk St., San Francisco, CA 94109, tel. 415/923–5522) leads a 120-kilometer (75-mile) backpacking trip from Tanquery Ford to Lake Hazen (the most northerly lake in the world), on Ellesmere Island. The trip reaches above 80 degrees north latitude, and obviously there is a good deal of travel through snow and ice, even in summer. Ice plateaus and glaciers are the major land features; with luck you'll spot musk oxen, seals, and whales.

The most striking feature of Kluane National Park is the St. Elias Mountain range, topped by Mt. Logan, the highest peak in Canada. Most of this high-alpine country, however, is extremely difficult to get to, much less get around in. A few trails lead into the park from the Alaska Highway near Haines Junction; among the best is the 25-kilometer (16-mile) Auriol Trail, which can be hiked in a day or two. Along with panoramic mountain views, expect to see Dall sheep and wildflowers, as well as—possibly—a grizzly.

A more rugged hike is the 27-kilometer (17-mile) walk to the Kaskawulsh Glacier and the beginning of Kluane's rugged mountain interior. If you want to venture farther, you'll need the help of an experienced guide service. **Yukon Mountain and River Expeditions** (Box 5405, Whitehorse, YT Y1A 4Z2, tel. 403/668–2513) leads extended (10-day to two-week) hiking trips in Kluane, July–August, as well as cross-country skiing trips, April–May.

Hunting

In both the Northwest Territories and Yukon, hunters are required to contract the services of a licensed outfitter to hunt big game such as caribou, moose, and bear. Each outfitter is assigned a specific area by the territorial government; your choice is determined more by *where* you want to do your hunting, not necessarily with which outfitter. The season runs approximately July–early October, depending on the region and the game you're after. **Tourism Yukon** and **TravelArctic** (*see* Important Addresses and Numbers, *above,* for both) can provide listings of licensed hunting outfitters. For more information about hunting licenses and regulations, contact: in the Northwest Territories, **Department of Renewable Resources** (Government of NWT, Box 1320, Yellowknife, NWT X1A 2L9, tel. 403/920–8716); in Yukon, **Fish and Wildlife Branch** (Government of Yukon, Box 2703, Whitehorse, YT Y1A 2C6, tel. 403/667–5221).

Water Sports

Certainly one of the best ways to experience the far north is by water, from whitewater rafting in Yukon to sea kayaking in the Arctic region. Virtually the only way to visit Nahanni National Park in the Northwest Territories is by canoe, kayak, or raft.

Among whitewater rafters, the Alsek and Tatshenshini Rivers, from Kluane National Park in Yukon through British Columbia, and emptying in Glacier Bay, Alaska, are considered classic trips. Each river runs for about 194 kilometers (120 miles) past spectacular mountain scenery, with trips ranging from 10 to 12 days in length. The Alsek is considered the much tougher of the two rivers, with one stretch—called Turnback Canyon—so dangerous that the only way around it is by helicopter portage.

Among companies offering trips on the Tatshenshini is **Sierra Club Outings** (730 Polk St., San Francisco, CA 94109, tel. 415/923–5522), its 10-day trip costing $1,895 (not including airfare to Whitehorse). **OARS** (Box 67, Angels Camp, CA 95222, tel. 209/736–4677) leads 12-day trips on the Alsek for $1,995. July and August are the principal river-running months.

Nahanni River Adventures (Box 8368, Station F, Edmonton, AB T6H 4W6, tel. 403/439–1316) leads both rafting and canoeing trips in Nahanni National Park. Trips vary from six days to three weeks for a full 400-kilometer (240-mile) run through the park.

Wildlife viewing is perhaps the pre-eminent reason to visit the Arctic region, and one of the best ways to do so is by sea kayak. **Mountain Travel/Sobek** (6420 Fairmount Ave., El Cerrito, CA 94530, tel. 510/227–2384 or 800/527–8100) leads a trip that combines two days of hiking on Ellesmere Island with a week of sea kayaking (weather permitting) to the Arctic Circle community of Resolute. Along the sea-kayaking route, you're likely to spot seals, walruses, white whales, Arctic birds, and narwhals; the Devon Island coast is reported to be the summer grounds for 85% of the North American narwhal population.

If you prefer setting off on your own, **Kanoe People** (Box 5152, Whitehorse, YT Y1A 4S3, tel. 403/668–4899) rents canoes and other boats and has a selection of guidebooks for waters in Yukon Territory. Kanoe people also organizes guided trips in the Whitehorse region.

Wildlife Watching

It is the ironic combination of rarity and abundance that makes Canada's wilderness an extraordinary land for those who appreciate seeing wildlife in a truly wild environment. Sightings of polar bears and musk oxen on the islands of the Arctic North may be rare, but where else in the world would you go if you wanted to try to catch a glimpse of these extraordinary creatures? On the other hand, herds of caribou may number in the hundreds of thousands during the late-spring migration period. And numerous bird species choose the far north—especially along the coasts of bays and inlets of the Arctic Ocean—as their summer habitat. Here again, though, rarity comes into play: Among the sightings prized by bird-watchers are peregrine falcons in the far north and whooping cranes (of which there are only about 100 in existence) that spend summers in Wood Buffalo National Park, in the south.

Several companies offer naturalist-led outings in the far north, reached by plane, boat, or foot. Many outfitters set a goal to see specific creatures such as whales, musk oxen, or certain birds.

Arctic Tour Company (Box 2021, Inuvik, NWT X0E 0T0, tel. 403/979–4100) offers year-round wildlife-watching trips in the Arctic North. Trips are led by Inuit guides informed about the culture and history of the area, as well as about wildlife. Among the company's more popular trips are whale-watching cruises and flights to Banks Island for four-day land trips to view musk oxen.

Canadian Holidays (191 The West Mall, 6th fl., Etobicoke, ON M9C 5K8, tel. 416/620–9267) organizes tours to see caribou herds and wolves on the northern tundra, and tours by dog-sled or snowmobile in the Arctic North to view walruses and polar bears. Bring along your fishing tackle; opportunities to fish for trout, grayling, and pike are included in some tours.

Western Arctic Nature Tours (Box 1530, Inuvik, NWT X0E 0T0, tel. 403/979–3400) links up with local guides and outfitters for wildlife-viewing tours in the northwestern Arctic region. Several tours emphasize the study of the wildflower bloom of the barren lands, as well as wildlife sightings. Depending on the tour, travel may be by boat, foot, or skis.

Dining and Lodging

Dining

Dining in the far north might fall short of grand epicurean standards, but it can be distinctive, making use of the foods most abundant here. This means that in some places it might be easier to find a caribou steak than a fresh salad. And once outside the main cities, you can expect your choices to be extremely limited; the dining room of the lodge where you are staying may well be your *only* choice. Even though the north isn't necessarily a gastronomic paradise, the restaurants listed here can still produce a good, hearty meal.

Highly recommended restaurants are indicated by a star ★.

Category	Cost*
Very Expensive	over $20
Expensive	$15–$20
Moderate	$10–$15
Inexpensive	under $10

per person, excluding drinks, service, and 7% GST

Lodging

Accommodations in the far north might not include some of the amenities (in-room TVs, private baths, etc.) and luxuries you might expect in a full-service hotel elsewhere in Canada. Furthermore, lodging prices are generally higher than you may find elsewhere, for a couple of reasons. In many communities, a lodge or hotel may be the only show in town, so if you don't like the price, you don't have much choice. Also, with the tourism season so short, lodging proprietors must try to make ends meet on only two or three months of serious vacation business. That said, however, accommodations listed here are generally comfortable and clean and, overall, proprietors are friendly and knowledgeable about things to do in the region. One thing to keep in mind: Prices can fall off sharply—as much as 70%—during the off-season (months other than July and August). Also keep in mind, however, that many places are closed from fall through spring.

Highly recommended lodgings in each price category are indicated by a star ★.

Category	Cost*
Very Expensive	over $150
Expensive	$120–$150

| Moderate | $90–$120 |
| Inexpensive | under $90 |

All prices are for a standard double room (or an equivalent, where not applicable), excluding gratuities and 7% GST.

Northwest Territories

Fort Smith
Lodging

Pelican Rapids Inn. This modern motel is conveniently located in the heart of Fort Smith. A restaurant and laundromat are across the street. *152 McDougal Rd., Box 52, Fort Smith, NWT X0E 0P0, tel. 403/872–2789. 50 rooms with private bath, including 6 kitchenettes. Facilities: telephones, TV. AE, MC, V. Open year-round. Inexpensive.*

Hay River
Lodging

Ptarmigan Inn. By Northwest Territories standards this hotel offers an unusual number of amenities on-site or nearby. Guests have access to a fitness center and swimming pool across the street, and there are tennis courts nearby. Rooms are modern, and the dining room and bar have been recently renovated. Given all that you get here, this is a good value. *17 Capital Crescent, Box 1000, NWT X0E 0R0, tel. 403/874–6781. 41 units, with private baths. Facilities: TV, telephones, laundry, hair salon, bank, gift shop, women's apparel shop. AE, MC, V. Open year-round. Moderate.*

Migrator Motel. This quiet motel just north of town caters to families, offers senior-citizen discount rates, and is one of the few in the area that allows pets. Built in 1973, the motel has modern and clean rooms, and two restaurants are within a half-block walking distance. *807 Mackenzie Dr., Box 1847, X0E 0R0, tel. 403/874–6792. 24 units with private bath, including 6 kitchenettes. Facilities: TV, telephones. AE, MC, V. Open year-round. Inexpensive.*

Inuvik
Dining and Lodging

Finto Motor Inn. A quiet atmosphere within a five-minute walk from the center of town is the drawing card at this hotel, located at the Marine Bypass and Mackenzie Road junction. Rooms are clean, bright, and tastefully decorated. The Peppermill restaurant features caribou and char in addition to more familiar menu items. *Box 1925, NWT X0E 0T0, tel. 403/979–2647. 52 rooms with private bath, 6 with shower only, 1 suite. Facilities: telephones, TV, laundry, room service. MC, V. Closed Christmas–New Year's Day. Expensive.*

Iqaluit
Dining and Lodging

Discovery Lodge Hotel. This is one of the cleaner, more cheerful hotels in town, and the installation of skylights in the lobby area a few years ago did much to lift the ambience. An oddity here is that some rooms have trapezoidal beds, wider at the top than the bottom. The Granite Dining Room features caribou brochettes and poached char, and each table is a slab of granite. *Box 387, Iqaluit, NWT X0A 0H0, tel. 819/979–4433. 38 rooms with private bath, 1 suite. Facilities: TV, telephones, laundry, airport shuttle. AE, DC, MC, V. Closed Christmas–New Year's Day. Very Expensive.*

Frobisher Inn. Major renovations three years ago thoroughly modernized this hotel, whose front rooms offer the best views of Iqaluit and Frobisher Bay. All rooms feature queen-size beds (some extra-long) and sofas. *Box 610, Iqaluit, NWT X0A 0H0, tel. 819/979–2222. 50 rooms with private bath. Facilities: TV,* *telephones, laundry, access to a neighboring indoor pool. AE, MC, V. Open year-round. Expensive.*

Yellowknife **Factor's Club.** The dining room of this restaurant, located in
Dining the Explorer Hotel (see below), overlooks Back Bay—a picturesque view in summer or winter. The Continental cuisine is
complimented by northern dishes that feature caribou, Arctic
char, and marinated musk ox that's reputed to be the best of
its kind in the north. A fireplace warms diners on cool evenings.
*49th St. and 48th Ave., tel. 403/873–3531. Reservations advised.
Jacket and tie suggested. AE, MC, V. Closed Sun. Expensive.*
The Red Apple. Traditional, American-style home cooking in a
friendly atmosphere is what you'll find at this restaurant located in the Discovery Inn. *4701 Franklin Ave., tel. 403/873–
2324. Reservations suggested. Dress: casual. AE, MC, V.
Moderate.*

Lodging **Explorer Hotel.** This modern and well-equipped eight-story
hotel is generally rated as the best hotel in Yellowknife, which
means it's probably the best hotel in the Northwest Territories.
Guest rooms on the east side have the favored views. Factor's
Club (see above), the hotel's restaurant, is good, and the Polaris
Lounge features live entertainment. *49th St. and 48th Ave.,
Postal 7000, NWT X1A 2R3, tel. 403/873–3531. 125 rooms with
private bath, including 2 suites. Facilities: TV, telephones,
café, lounges, dining room, gift shop, courtesy airport van,
air-conditioning, room service. AE, MC, V. Open year-round.
Very Expensive.*
Yellowknife Inn. Competing with the Explorer as Yellowknife's
other major hotel, the Yellowknife Inn also offers fine accommodations and facilities. Located next to the NWT Legislative
Assembly, this is a popular home-away-from-home for government officials and businesspeople. The hotel has set aside one
floor for nonsmokers. *Box 490, NWT X1A 2N4, tel. 403/873–2601
or 403/873–2600 (reverse charges). 150 rooms with private bath,
including 4 suites. Facilities: TV, telephones, café, lounge, dining room, tavern, gift shop, free airport bus. Very Expensive.*
Igloo Inn. Nothing special here—just basic, modern, and moderately priced accommodations, and most rooms are equipped
with kitchenettes. There are good views of Back Bay on one
side and Yellowknife's Old Town on the other. *4115 Franklin
Ave., Box 596, NWT X1A 2N4, tel. 403/873–8511. 44 rooms with
private bath, including 33 with kitchenettes. Facilities: TV, telephones, restaurant. AE, MC, V. Open year-round. Moderate.*

Yukon Territory

Dawson City **Downtown Hotel.** Located at 2nd Avenue and Queen Street,
Dining and Lodging this hotel lives up to its name: It's just a block from Dawson's
major entertainment venues such as Diamond Tooth Gertie's
and the Palace Grand Theatre. The Jack London Grill provides
a good meal at a good price. You can also take in a little local
color in the nearby Sourdough Saloon. *Box 780, YT Y0B 1G0,
tel. 403/993–5346 or 800/661–0514. 60 units with private bath,
including 2 suites. Facilities: TV, telephones, airport limousine, Jacuzzi. AE, DC, MC, V. Open year-round. Moderate.*
Eldorado Hotel. The draws at this 25-year-old hotel are the
Bonanza Dining Room and Sluice Box lounge. Rooms are spacious and casually appointed, and the central lobby is decorated
in turn-of-the-century style. *3rd Ave. and Princess St., Box 338,
YT Y0B 1G0, tel. 403/993–5451; in Alaska, 800/764–3536. 54 units*

with private bath, including 6 with kitchenettes and 4 suites. Facilities: TV, telephones, dining room, lounge, coin laundry, free airport shuttle service, room service in summer. AE, DC, MC, V. Open year-round. Moderate.

★ **Westmark Inn.** In the last four years, this hotel has grown from a 90-room to a 131-room establishment. Belinda's Café features a bright courtyard deck and salmon barbecues. The legendary Keno Lounge takes the spotlight, however, because it's home of the famous (in Dawson City, that is) Sour Toe Cocktail, for which the traditional recipe substitutes a severed human toe for the more appetizing olive. *5th Ave. and Harper St., Box 420, YT Y0B 1G0, tel. 403/993–5542; in Canada, 800/999–2570; in the U.S., 800/544–0970. 131 rooms with private bath, including 4 suites. Facilities: TV, telephones on request, dining room, lounge, gift shop, room service, access for the disabled. AE, D, DC, MC, V. Open mid-May–mid-Sept. Moderate.*

Haines Junction
Lodging

Kluane Park Inn. This well-kept inn, located along the Alaska Highway just before the Haines Highway cutoff, is a convenient, inexpensive stepping-off point for visiting the park. Sandwiches are served in the lounge. *Box 5400, YT Y0B 1L0, tel. 403/634–2261. 16 rooms with private bath, 2 rooms with showers, 2 rooms with kitchenettes. Facilities: satellite TV. AE, DC, MC, V. Open year-round. Inexpensive.*

Watson Lake
Dining and Lodging
★

Belvedere Hotel. This is the first hotel you come to upon arriving in Watson Lake from the south. There's a lounge and coffee shop within the property. *Box 228, YT Y0A 1C0, tel. 403/536–7712. 48 units with private bath. Facilities: TV, telephones in 21 rooms, Jacuzzi in one room, access for the disabled. AE, DC, MC, V. Open year-round. Moderate.*

Gateway Motor Inn. Three years ago this inn underwent extensive renovation and enlargement of the lobby and restaurant. The location is across the Alaska Highway from the post office. *Box 560, YT Y0A 1C0, tel. 403/536–7781. 53 units with private bath, including 1 suite and 3 kitchenettes. Facilities: TV, telephones. AE, MC, V. Open year-round. Moderate.*

Watson Lake Hotel. This hotel, located on the western edge of Watson Lake, provides basic services and clean, neat guest rooms at a reasonable price. The dining room is licensed, and there's a café and lounge. *Box 370, YT Y0A 1C0, tel. 403/536–7781. 48 units with private bath, including 1 suite and 3 kitchenettes. Facilities: TV, telephones, café, lounge, dining room, sauna, laundry. AE, DC, MC, V. Open year-round. Inexpensive.*

Whitehorse
Dining

Panda's. In the heart of downtown, Panda's provides a nostalgic Klondike setting for its French cuisine. It's a romantic spot—a good choice for that special night out. It's also one of the few places in wilderness Canada where you'll find escargot perfectly prepared. *212 Main St., tel. 403/667–2632. Reservations advised. Jacket and tie suggested. AE, MC, V. Dinner only. Closed January. Expensive.*

★ **Arizona Charlie's.** This Santa Fe–style restaurant is named after the legendary Arizona Charlie Meadows who toured with the Wild West Show and Buffalo Bill Cody. He was a roper, rifleman, and rider who opened the Palace Grand Theatre in Dawson City. The mixed menu features Mexican entrées, prime rib, a large selection of seafood, and 12 different appetizers—from buffalo wings and nachos to escargot. *2288 2nd Ave., tel. 403/668–4747. Reservations advised. Dress: casual. AE, D, MC, V. Open year-round. Moderate–Expensive.*

Talisman Cafe. The atmosphere of this relaxed café on Main Street tends to be busy, but the homemade food is good and reasonably priced. Among the house specialties is a Cajun seafood jambalaya. *2112 Main St., tel. 403/667–2736. Dress: casual. No reservations. No credit cards. Open year-round. Inexpensive.*

Lodging **Westmark Klondike Inn.** At the edge of downtown and at the bottom of Two-Mile Hill is this full-service accommodation with good nightlife. Arizona Charlie's (*see above*), the hotel's restaurant, and Trapper, the inn's nightclub, are both active spots. The inn offers many services, making this a good choice for travelers who want all their needs taken care of at one location. *228 2nd Ave., YT Y1A 1C8, tel. 403/668–4747 or 800/999–2570. 98 units with private bath, including 3 suites. Facilities: TV, telelphones, laundry, hair salon, gift shop, sauna, dining room, coffee shop, lounge, cabaret, access for the disabled, nonsmoking rooms. AE, DC, MC, V. Open year-round. Expensive.*

★ **Westmark Whitehorse Hotel.** This is Whitehorse's premier hotel, located downtown on Wood Street and 2nd Avenue. It has more facilities than most hotels in these parts, and the Frantic Follies (*see* Arts and Nightlife, *below*) liven things up during summer nights. This is as good as lodging gets in the Yukon. *Wood St. and 2nd Ave., Box 4250, YT Y1A 3T3, tel. 403/668–4700, 800/478–1111, or 800/999–2570. 181 units with private bath, including 5 suites. Facilities: TV, telephones, gift shop, barber shop, beauty salon, art gallery, travel agency, lounge, restaurant, access for the disabled. AE, DC, MC, V. Open year-round. Expensive.*

Yukon Inn. Nothing fancy here, just clean rooms at a fair price. The kitchenettes are a welcome feature for travelers on a budget. *4220 4th Ave., YT Y1A 3T3, tel. 403/667–2527 or 800/661–0454. 97 units with private bath, including 2 suites and 25 with kitchenettes. Facilities: TV, telephones, Jacuzzi, gift shop, hair salon, café, dining room. AE, MC, V. Open year-round. Moderate.*

The Arts and Nightlife

The Arts

Theater, music, and cabaret-style entertainment are very much a part of northern life, at least in the major civilization centers. Don't expect much entertainment once beyond the city, although during the summer, native groups often stage traditional shows for visitors, and native arts and crafts are one of the compelling cultural reasons to visit the far north. Keep alert for special presentations and exhibitions.

In Dawson City, **Gaslight Follies** at the Palace Grand Theatre (*see* Tour 3 in Exploring, *above*) performs vaudeville and melodrama. The **Dawson City Music Festival** (DCMF Association, Box 456, Dawson City, YT Y0B 1G0, tel. 403/993–5584), featuring a variety of folk musicians from around the north, is held each July.

In Whitehorse, plays and musical events are staged throughout the year at **Guild Hall** (tel. 403/633–5351) in the Porter Creek subdivision. The **Frostbite Music Society** (tel. 403/668–

4291) presents a summer concert series. For more information, call the **ArtsLine** (tel. 403/667–ARTS).

At the Westmark Whitehorse Hotel, the **Frantic Follies Vaudeville Show** (2nd Ave. and Wood St., tel. 403/668–3161) is the big show in town, a combination of cancan dance numbers and comedy skits. *Admission: $16.35 adults, $8.20 children under 12. Nightly performances late May–mid-Sept.*

The other Whitehorse show worth checking out is **El Dorado!**, at the **Gold Rush Inn** (411 Main St., tel. 403/668–6472). It is a musical revue featuring tales of the Yukon.

In Yellowknife, **Folk on the Rocks** (SENT, Box 326, Yellowknife, NWT X1A 2N3, tel. 403/873–4923) takes place each July. The two-day, open-air concert features native artists as well as other folk musicians from all over the north, Canada, and the United States. During the summer, the **Northern Arts and Cultural Centre** (Box 1025, Yellowknife, NWT X1A 2N7, tel. 403/837–3840) schedules a number of productions.

Nightlife

Perhaps the best show in town is the celestial phenomenon of the Northern Lights—a.k.a., the Aurora Borealis—caused by the combined influence of charged air particles, solar energy, and magnetic forces of the North Pole. No small amount of mysticism is associated with the Lights, to the point where some people insist that you can actually hear them.

Although you can find a few lively nodes of nightlife in the cities, it is probably fair to say that active nightlife is not one of the chief reasons to visit the far north. At least not "active" in the normal sense of the word; with daylight lasting 20 hours or more in the height of summer, it's possible to go hiking, boating, and fishing late into the night.

For a more familiar type of nightlife, **Diamond Tooth Gertie's** in Dawson City brings together various forms of traditional Yukon entertainment, including gambling, dancing, and a floor show. *4th Ave. at Queen St., tel. 403/993–5575. Admission: $4.50. Open mid-June–early Sept., Mon.–Sat. 8 PM–2 AM. Four shows nightly.*

Other popular night spots in Dawson City are **Midnight Sun** (3rd Ave. at Queen St., tel. 403/993–5463), with a crowded dance floor and live music three nights a week. Or you can drop by the **Keno Lounge** at the Westmark Inn (*see* Lodging, *above*) for a Sour Toe cocktail.

Hotel bars in the major cities are often the best places for active socializing and live music. In Whitehorse, lively (sometimes raucous) bar scenes can usually be found at the **Taku Hotel** (4109 4th Ave., tel. 403/668–4545) or the **98** (100 Wood St., tel. 403/667–2641). In Yellowknife, the **Polaris Lounge** in the Explorer Hotel and **Mackenzie Lounge** in the Yellowknife Inn (for both *see* Lodging, *above*) are popular night spots. For rock-and-roll music, pool, and darts, check out **RJ's Bar** in the Discovery Inn (4701 Franklin Ave., tel. 403/873–2789).

Index

WHEREVER YOU TRAVEL, _H_ELP IS NEVER FAR AWAY.

From planning your trip to providing travel assistance
along the way, American Express® Travel Service
Offices* are always there to help.

Alberta

BANFF
_403-762-3207_

CALGARY
_403-261-5982_

EDMONTON
_403-421-0608_

British Columbia

PRINCE GEORGE
_604-564-7000_

PRINCE RUPERT
_604-627-1266_

VANCOUVER
_604-669-2813_
_604-687-7686_

VICTORIA
_604-385-8731_

Manitoba

WINNIPEG
_204-949-9349_
_204-786-5671_

Northwest Territories

YELLOWKNIFE
_403-873-2121_

Nova Scotia

HALIFAX
_902-423-3900_

Ontario

OTTAWA
_613-563-0231_

THUNDER BAY
_807-623-7473_

TORONTO
_416-868-1044_
_416-967-3411_
_416-963-6060_

Quebec

MONTREAL
_514-284-3300_

QUEBEC CITY
_418-627-2580_

INTRODUCING

Fodor's
WORLDVIEW
TRAVEL UPDATE

AT LAST, YOUR OWN PERSONALIZED
LIST OF WHAT'S GOING ON IN THE
CITIES YOU'RE VISITING.

KEYED TO THE DAYS WHEN YOU'RE
THERE, CUSTOMIZED FOR YOUR
INTERESTS, AND SENT TO YOU
BEFORE YOU LEAVE HOME.

EXCLUSIVE FOR PURCHASERS OF
FODOR'S GUIDES...

Introducing a revolutionary way to get customized, time-sensitive travel information just before your trip.

Now you can obtain detailed information about what's going on in each city you'll be visiting <u>before</u> you leave home—up-to-the-minute, objective information about the events and activities that interest you most.

This is a special offer for purchasers of Fodor's guides – a customized Travel Update to fit your specific interests and your itinerary.

Travel Updates contain the kind of time-sensitive insider information you can get only from local contacts – or from city magazines and newspapers once you arrive. But now you can have the same information before you leave for your trip.

The choice is yours: current art exhibits, theater, music festivals and special concerts, sporting events, antiques and flower shows, shopping, fitness, and more.

The information comes from hundreds of correspondents and thousands of sources worldwide. Updated continuously, it's like having your own personal concierge or friend in the city.

You specify the cities and when you'll be there. We'll do the rest — personalizing the information for you the way no guidebook can.

It's the perfect extension to your Fodor's guide and the best way to make the most of your valuable travel time.

Your Itinerary:
Customized report available for 160 destinations

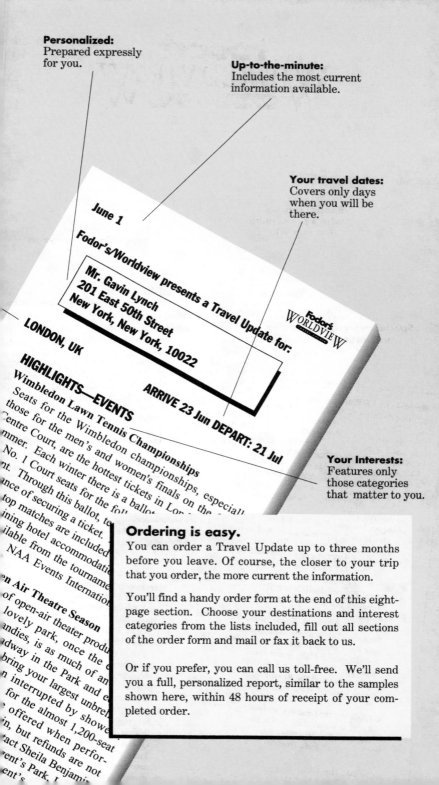

Personalized:
Prepared expressly for you.

Up-to-the-minute:
Includes the most current information available.

Your travel dates:
Covers only days when you will be there.

June 1

Fodor's/Worldview presents a Travel Update for:

Mr. Gavin Lynch
201 East 50th Street
New York, New York, 10022

Fodor's
WORLDVIEW

LONDON, UK

ARRIVE 23 Jun DEPART: 21 Jul

Your Interests:
Features only those categories that matter to you.

HIGHLIGHTS—EVENTS

Wimbledon Lawn Tennis Championships

Seats for the Wimbledon championships, especiall
those for the men's and women's finals on the
Centre Court, are the hottest tickets in Lon
mmer. Each winter there is a ballo
No. 1 Court seats for the fol
nt. Through this ballot, t
nce of securing a ticket.
top matches are included
ining hotel accommodatio
ilable from the tournam
NAA Events Internatio

n Air Theatre Season

of open-air theater produ
lovely park, once the e
andies, is as much of an
adway in the Park and e
bring your largest unbre
n interrupted by showe
for the almost 1,200-seat
offered when perfor-
n, but refunds are not
act Sheila Benjami
ent's Park, I

Ordering is easy.

You can order a Travel Update up to three months before you leave. Of course, the closer to your trip that you order, the more current the information.

You'll find a handy order form at the end of this eight-page section. Choose your destinations and interest categories from the lists included, fill out all sections of the order form and mail or fax it back to us.

Or if you prefer, you can call us toll-free. We'll send you a full, personalized report, similar to the samples shown here, within 48 hours of receipt of your completed order.

**Special concerts—
who's performing
what and where**

**One-of-a-kind,
one-time-only events**

**Special interest,
in-depth listings**

Children — Events

Angel Canal Festival

The festivities include a children's funfai
entertainers, a boat rally and displays on th
water. Regent's Canal. Islington. N1. Tub
Angel. Tel: 267 9100. 11:30am-5:30pm. 7/04

Blackheath Summer Kite Festival

Stunt kite displays with parachuting tedd
bears and trade stands. Free admission. SE3
BR: Blackheath. 10am. 6/27.

Megabugs

Children will delight in this infestation o
giant robotic insects, including a praying
mantic 60 times life size. Mon-Sat 10am-
6pm; Sun 11am-6pm. Admission 4.50
pounds. Natural History Museum, Cromwel
Road. SW7. Tube: South Kensington. Tel
938 9123. Ends 10/01.

Childminders

This establishment employs only women,
providing nurses and qualified nannies to

Music — Jazz & Blues

Tito Puente's Golden Men of Latin Jazz

The father of mambo and Cuban rumba king
comes to town. Royal Festival Hall. South Bank.
SE1. Tube: Waterloo. Tel: 928 8800. 8pm. 7/15.

Georgie Fame and The New York Band

Riding a popular tide with his latest album, the
smoky-voiced Fame and his keyboard are on a
tour yet again. The Grand. Clapham Junction.
SW11. BR: Clapham Junction. Tel: 738 9000.
7:30pm. 7/07.

Jacques Loussier Play Bach Trio

The French jazz classicist and colleagues.
Kenwood Lakeside. Hampstead Lane.
Kenwood. NW3. Tube: Golders Green, then bus
210. Tel: 413 1443. 7pm. 7/10.

Tony Bennett and Ronnie Scott

Royal Festival Hall. South Bank. SE1. Tube:
Waterloo. Tel: 928 8800. 8pm. 7/11.

Santana

Royal Festival Hall. South Bank. SE1. Tube:
Waterloo. Tel: 928 8800. 8pm. 7/12.

Count Basie Orchestra and Nancy Wilson Trio

Royal Festival Hall. South Bank. SE1. Tube
Waterloo. Tel: 928 8800. 8pm. 7/14.

King Pleasure and the Biscuit Boys

Royal Festival Hall. South Bank. SE1. Tube
Waterloo. Tel: 928 8800. 6:30 and 9pm. 7/16.

Al Green and the London Community Gospel Choir

Royal Festival Hall. South Bank. SE1. Tube
Waterloo. Tel: 928 8800. 8pm. 7/13.

BB King and Linda Hopkins

Mother of the blues and successor to Bessi
Smith, Hopkins meets up with "Blues Boy
Royal Festival Hall. South Bank. SE

Music — Classical

Marylebone Sinfonia

Kenneth Gowen conducts music by P
and Rossini. Queen Elizabeth Hall.
Bank. SE1. Tube: Waterloo. Tel: 928
7:45pm. 7/16.

London Philharmonic

Franz Welser-Moest and George Ben
conduct selections by Alexander G
Messiaen, and some of Benjamin's ow
positions. Queen Elizabeth Hall. South
SE1. Tube: Waterloo. Tel: 928 8800. 8

London Pro Arte Orchestra and Forest

Murray Stewart conducts selecti
Rossini, Haydn and Jonathan Willcock
Queen Elizabeth Hall. South Ban
Tube: Waterloo. Tel: 928 8800. 7:45p

Kensington Symphony Orchestra

Russell Keable conducts Dvorak's

Here's what you get . . .

Detailed information about what's going on — precisely when you'll be there.

Show openings during your visit

Reviews by local critics

Exhibitions & Shows—Antique & Flower

Westminster Antiques Fair
Over 50 stands with pre-1830 furniture and other Victorian and earlier items. Thu-Fri 11am-8pm; Sat-Sun 11am-6pm. Admission 4 pounds, children free. Old Royal Horticultural Hall. Vincent Square. SW1. Tel: 0444/48 25 14. 6-24 thru 6/27.

Royal Horticultural Society Flower Show
The show includes displays of carnations, summer fruit and vegetables. Tue 11am-7pm; Wed 10am-5pm. Admission Tue 4 pounds, Wed 2 pounds. Royal Horticultural Halls. Greycoat Street and Vincent Square. SW1. Tube: Victoria. 7/20 thru 7/21.

ampton Court Palace International Flower Show
Major international garden and flower show aking place in conjunction with the British

Theater — Musical

Sunset Boulevard
In June, the four Andrew Lloyd Webber musicals which dominated London's stages in the 1980s (Cats, Starlight Express, Phantom of the Opera and Aspects of Love) are joined by the composer's latest work, a show rumored to have his best music to date. The 1950 Billy Wilder film about a helpless young writer who is drawn into the world of a possessive, aging silent screen star offers rich opportunities for Webber's evolving style. Soaring, aching melodies, lush technical effects and psychological thrills are all expected. Patti Lupone stars. Mon-Sat at 8pm; matinee Thu-Sat at 3pm. In-person sales only at the box office; credit card bookings, Tel: 344 0055. Admission 15-32.50 pounds. Adelphi Theatre. The Strand. WC2. Tube: Charing Cross. Tel: 836 7611. Starts: 6/21

Leonardo A Portrait of Love
A new musical about the great Renaissance arti and inventor comes in for a London premier tested by a brief run at Oxford's Old Fire Stati autumn. The work explores the relations Vinci and the woman

Alberquerque • Atlanta • Atlantic City • N
Baltimore • Boston • Chicago • Cincinnati
Cleveland • Dallas/Ft.Worth • Denver • De
• Houston • Kansas City • Las Vegas • Los
Angeles • Memphis • Miami • Milwaukee •
New Orleans • New York City • Orlando •
Springs • Philadelphia • Phoenix • Pittsburg
Portland • Salt Lake • Phoenix • Pittsburg
• San Franc • San Antonio • San Di
Oslo • Wash • Seattle • St. Louis • Tamp
Hawaii • Kauai • Maui • Abacos • Bimini
Ex • Honolulu • Island
Ber • County side • Nashville • Islar
Antigua & B • Hamilton • Jar

Spectator Sports — Other Sports

Greyhound Racing: Wembley Stadium
This dog track offers good views of greyhound racing held on Mon, Wed and Fri. No credit cards. Stadium Way. Wembley. HA9. Tube: Wembley Park. Tel: 902 8833.

Benson & Hedges Cricket Cup Final
Lord's Cricket Ground. St. John's Wood Road. NW8. Tube: St. John's Wood. Tel: 289 1611. 11am. 7/10.

Business-Fax & Overnight Mail

Post Office, Trafalgar Square Branch
Offers a network of fax services, the Intelpost system, throughout the country and abroad. Mon-Sat 8am-8pm, Sun 9am-5pm. William IV Street. WC2. Tube: Charing Cross. Tel: 930

Fodor's WORLDVIEW TRAVEL UPDATE

Gorda • Barbados • Dominica • Forto
ucia • St. Vincent • Trinidad &Tobago
ymans • Puerto Plata • Santo Doming
Aruba • Bonaire • Curacao • St. Mac
ec City • Montreal • Ottawa • Toron
Vancouver • Guadeloupe • Martiniqu
helemy • St. Martin • Kingston • Ixta
o Bay • Negril • Ocho Rios • Ponce
n • Grand Turk • Providenciales •
St. John • St. Thomas • Acapulco • S
& Isla Mujeres • Cozumel • Guadal
• Los Cabos • Manzanillo • Mazatl
City • Monterrey • Oaxaca • Puerto
do • Puerto Vallarta • Veracruz • Ix
am • Athens • Darta •

Interest Categories

For <u>your</u> personalized Travel Update, choose the categories you're most interested in from this list. Every Travel Update automatically provides you with *Event Highlights* – the best of what's happening during the dates of your trip.

1.	**Business Services**	Fax & Overnight Mail, Computer Rentals, Photocopying, Secretarial , Messenger, Translation Services

Dining

2.	**All Day Dining**	Breakfast & Brunch, Cafes & Tea Rooms, Late-Night Dining
3.	**Local Cuisine**	In Every Price Range—from Budget Restaurants to the Special Splurge
4.	**European Cuisine**	Continental, French, Italian
5.	**Asian Cuisine**	Chinese, Far Eastern, Japanese, Indian
6.	**Americas Cuisine**	American, Mexican & Latin
7.	**Nightlife**	Bars, Dance Clubs, Comedy Clubs, Pubs & Beer Halls
8.	**Entertainment**	Theater—Drama, Musicals, Dance, Ticket Agencies
9.	**Music**	Classical, Traditional & Ethnic, Jazz & Blues, Pop, Rock
10.	**Children's Activities**	Events, Attractions
11.	**Tours**	Local Tours, Day Trips, Overnight Excursions, Cruises
12.	**Exhibitions, Festivals & Shows**	Antiques & Flower, History & Cultural, Art Exhibitions, Fairs & Craft Shows, Music & Art Festivals
13.	**Shopping**	Districts & Malls, Markets, Regional Specialities
14.	**Fitness**	Bicycling, Health Clubs, Hiking, Jogging
15.	**Recreational Sports**	Boating/Sailing, Fishing, Ice Skating, Skiing, Snorkeling/Scuba, Swimming
16.	**Spectator Sports**	Auto Racing, Baseball, Basketball, Football, Horse Racing, Ice Hockey, Soccer

Please note that interest category content will vary by season, destination, and length of stay.

Destinations

The Fodor's/Worldview Travel Update covers more than 160 destinations worldwide. Choose the destinations that match your itinerary from this list. (Choose bulleted destinations only.)

United States (Mainland)
- Albuquerque
- Atlanta
- Atlantic City
- Baltimore
- Boston
- Chicago
- Cincinnati
- Cleveland
- Dallas/Ft. Worth
- Denver
- Detroit
- Houston
- Kansas City
- Las Vegas
- Los Angeles
- Memphis
- Miami
- Milwaukee
- Minneapolis/ St. Paul
- New Orleans
- New York City
- Orlando
- Palm Springs
- Philadelphia
- Phoenix
- Pittsburgh
- Portland
- St. Louis
- Salt Lake City
- San Antonio
- San Diego
- San Francisco
- Seattle
- Tampa
- Washington, DC

Alaska
- Alaskan Destinations

Hawaii
- Honolulu
- Island of Hawaii
- Kauai
- Maui

Canada
- Quebec City
- Montreal
- Ottawa
- Toronto
- Vancouver

Bahamas
- Abacos
- Eleuthera/ Harbour Island
- Exumas
- Freeport
- Nassau & Paradise Island

Bermuda
- Bermuda Countryside
- Hamilton

British Leeward Islands
- Anguilla
- Antigua & Barbuda
- Montserrat
- St. Kitts & Nevis

British Virgin Islands
- Tortola & Virgin Gorda

British Windward Islands
- Barbados
- Dominica
- Grenada
- St. Lucia
- St. Vincent
- Trinidad & Tobago

Cayman Islands
- The Caymans

Dominican Republic
- Puerto Plata
- Santo Domingo

Dutch Leeward Islands
- Aruba
- Bonaire
- Curacao

Dutch Windward Island
- St. Maarten/ St. Martin

French West Indies
- Guadeloupe
- Martinique
- St. Barthelemy

Jamaica
- Kingston
- Montego Bay
- Negril
- Ocho Rios

Puerto Rico
- Ponce
- San Juan

Turks & Caicos
- Grand Turk
- Providenciales

U.S. Virgin Islands
- St. Croix
- St. John
- St. Thomas

Mexico
- Acapulco
- Cancun & Isla Mujeres
- Cozumel
- Guadalajara
- Ixtapa & Zihuatanejo
- Los Cabos
- Manzanillo
- Mazatlan
- Mexico City
- Monterrey
- Oaxaca
- Puerto Escondido
- Puerto Vallarta
- Veracruz

Europe
- Amsterdam
- Athens
- Barcelona
- Berlin
- Brussels
- Budapest
- Copenhagen
- Dublin
- Edinburgh
- Florence
- Frankfurt
- French Riviera
- Geneva
- Glasgow
- Interlaken
- Istanbul
- Lausanne
- Lisbon
- London
- Madrid
- Milan
- Moscow
- Munich
- Oslo
- Paris
- Prague
- Provence
- Rome
- Salzburg
- St. Petersburg
- Stockholm
- Venice
- Vienna
- Zurich

Pacific Rim Australia & New Zealand
- Auckland
- Melbourne
- Sydney

China
- Beijing
- Guangzhou
- Shanghai

Japan
- Kyoto
- Nagoya
- Osaka
- Tokyo
- Yokohama

Other
- Bangkok
- Hong Kong & Macau
- Manila
- Seoul
- Singapore
- Taipei

Fodor's WORLDVIEW Order Form

THIS TRAVEL UPDATE IS FOR (Please print):

Name

Address

City   State   ZIP

Country   Tel # ( ) -

Title of this Fodor's guide:

Store and location where guide was purchased:

INDICATE YOUR DESTINATIONS/DATES: Write in below the destinations you want to order. Then fill in your arrival and departure dates for each destination.

		Month	Day		Month	Day
(Sample)	LONDON	From: 6	21	To: 6	30
1		From: /		To: /	
2		From: /		To: /	
3		From: /		To: /	

You can order up to three destinations per Travel Update. Only destinations listed on the previous page are applicable. Maximum amount of time covered by a Travel Update cannot exceed 30 days.

CHOOSE YOUR INTERESTS: Select up to eight categories from the list of interest categories shown on the previous page and circle the numbers below:

1   2   3   4   5   6   7   8   9   10   11   12   13   14   15   16

CHOOSE HOW YOU WANT YOUR TRAVEL UPDATE DELIVERED (Check one):

❑ Please mail my Travel Update to the address above **OR**

❑ Fax it to me at **Fax #** ( ) -

DELIVERY CHARGE (Check one)

	Within U.S. & Canada	Outside U.S. & Canada
First Class Mail	❑ $2.50	❑ $5.00
Fax	❑ $5.00	❑ $10.00
Priority Delivery	❑ $15.00	❑ $27.00

All orders will be sent within 48 hours of receipt of a completed order form.

ADD UP YOUR ORDER HERE. *SPECIAL OFFER FOR FODOR'S PURCHASERS ONLY!*

	Suggested Retail Price	Your Price	This Order
First destination ordered	$13.95	$ 7.95	$ 7.95
Second destination (if applicable)	$ 9.95	$ 4.95	+
Third destination (if applicable)	$ 9.95	$ 4.95	+
Plus delivery charge from above			+
		TOTAL:	$

METHOD OF PAYMENT (Check one): ❑ AmEx   ❑ MC   ❑ Visa   ❑ Discover
❑ Personal Check   ❑ Money Order

Make check or money order payable to: Fodor's Worldview Travel Update

Credit Card #   **Expiration Date:**

Authorized Signature

SEND THIS COMPLETED FORM TO:
Fodor's Worldview Travel Update, 114 Sansome Street, Suite 700, San Francisco, CA 94104

OR CALL OR FAX US 24-HOURS A DAY
Telephone **1-800-799-9609** • Fax **1-800-799-9619** (From within the U.S. & Canada)
(Outside the U.S. & Canada: Telephone 415-616-9988 • Fax 415-616-9989)

(Please have this guide in front of you when you call so we can verify purchase.)

Offer valid until 12/31/94.